MODERN EQUITY

AUSTRALIA
LBC Information Services
Sydney

CANADA and USA
Carswell
Toronto

NEW ZEALAND
Brooker's
Auckland

SINGAPORE and MALAYSIA
Sweet & Maxwell Asia
and Kuala Lumpur

HANBURY & MARTIN

MODERN EQUITY

SIXTEENTH EDITION

BY

JILL E. MARTIN, LL.D. (Lond.)

Professor of Law, Kings College, London

Barrister, Lincoln's Inn

London
Sweet & Maxwell Ltd
2001

First Edition	1935	Fourth Impression	1974
Second Edition	1937	Fifth Impression	1975
Third Edition	1943	Tenth Edition	1976
Fourth Edition	1946	Second Impression	1979
Fifth Edition	1949	Eleventh Edition	1981
Sixth Edition	1952	Twelfth Edition	1985
Seventh Edition	1957	Thirteenth Edition	1989
Eighth Edition	1962	Second Impression	1990
Ninth Edition	1969	Fourteenth Edition	1993
Second Impression	1971	Fifteenth Edition	1997
Third Impression	1973	Sixteenth Edition	2001

Published by
Sweet & Maxwell Limited of
100 Avenue Road, London NW3 3PF
Computerset by Interactive Sciences Ltd, Gloucester
Printed in England by
Clays Ltd, St. Ives plc.

*A CIP catalogue record
for this book is available
from the British Library*

ISBN 0 421 71680 0

*No natural forests were destroyed
to make this product, only farmed timber
was used and re-planted.*

PREFACE

The last four years have certainly been eventful for those involved in the law of equity and trusts, culminating in the long-awaited Trustee Act 2000, which came into operation on February 1, 2001. The Act, based on the work of the Law Commission and the Trust Law Committee, is particularly significant in the context of investment, delegation and remuneration. It also updates the "prudent man of business" test, governing the standard of conduct of trustees, by the introduction of the statutory duty of care. Other statutory developments include the Trustee Delegation Act 1999, on delegation by individual trustees by way of power of attorney, and the Contracts (Rights of Third Parties) Act 1999, which has particular relevance to the topic of covenants to settle. The effect of the Human Rights Act 1998 on equitable remedies has already been seen in the cases of *Douglas v. Hello! Ltd* and *Venables v. Newsgroup Newspapers*, concerning injunctions to protect confidential information and privacy. The Act may influence charity law but is otherwise of little application to wills and trusts, although we must await caselaw developments.

Perhaps the most notable Law Commission paper in the trusts area over the last four years was Consultation Paper No. 154: *Illegal Transactions: The Effect of Illegality on Contracts and Trusts*. The paper on the property rights of cohabitants is still awaited. Further mention should also be made of the work of the Trust Law Committee. In addition to collaboration with the Law Commission on the topics now found in the Trustee Act 2000, the Committee has produced papers on the rights of third party creditors and on the question of capital and income (the apportionment rules and the problems arising from company demergers).

Turning to caselaw developments, the most significant decisions of the House of Lords have been *Att.-Gen. v. Blake*, dealing with confidentiality, the measure of damages under Lord Cairns' Act, the availability of the equitable remedy of account of profits to contract claims, and injunctions in the public law area; *Kleinwort Benson Ltd v. Lincoln City Council* on the recovery of payments made by mistake of law (not a case on equity and trusts but nevertheless highly significant to various topics discussed in this book); *Foskett v. McKeown* on tracing, where their Lordships found no opportunity to recast the rules on tracing at common law and in equity but rather supported traditional principles; and *Co-operative Insurance Society Ltd v. Argyll Stores (Holdings) Ltd*, denying the remedy of specific performance for breach of "keep open" covenants in leases. The most notable decision of their Lordships sitting as the Privy Council was *Air Jamaica Ltd v. Charlton*, on resulting trusts in the context of a pension fund surplus.

Important decisions of the Court of Appeal since the last edition include *Birmingham Midshires Mortgage Services Ltd v. Sabherwal* on estoppel as a proprietary interest and as an overreachable interest; *Bank of Credit and Commerce International (Overseas) Ltd v. Akindele*, imposing the "unconscionable" test for personal liability for receipt of trust property (and doubting the strict liability theory); *Armitage v. Nurse* on the construction of trustee exemption clauses; and *Gillett v. Holt* on proprietary estoppel in the context of promises to leave property by will. Decisions on the *O'Brien* cases (on the setting aside of mortgages on the grounds of undue influence or misrepresentation) have been too numerous to mention here, save for *Royal Bank of Scotland v. Etridge (No. 2)*, where the Court of Appeal laid down guidelines. Other cases of interest include *Dunbar v. Plant* on the forfeiture rule; *Southwood v. Att.-Gen.* on the doctrine that political trusts cannot be charitable; and *Swindle v. Harrison*, clarifying the application of *Target Holdings v. Redferns* to the question of compensation for breach of fiduciary duty.

Mention should also be made of the influential monographs which have been published since the last edition and which have informed the discussion in the relevant contexts: Smith, *The Law of Tracing* and Chambers, *Resulting Trusts*.

The structure of this edition is unchanged, save that the chapter on the Equitable Doctrines of Conversion, Election, Satisfaction and Performance has gone to make way for the new developments. The terminology of the Civil Procedure Rules 1998 has been adopted throughout the book, and, for simplicity, the term "claimant" has been used instead of "plaintiff" whether or not the case under discussion predated the 1998 Rules.

As always, thanks are due to the editorial staff of Sweet & Maxwell for their assistance. This edition is intended to state the law as at January 1, 2001, as updated wherever possible during the processing of the proofs.

Jill Martin
King's College, London
March 1, 2001

CONTENTS

PART I

INTRODUCTION

PART II

TRUSTS AND POWERS

PART III

TRUSTEES

PART IV

MISCELLANEOUS EQUITABLE REMEDIES AND DOCTRINES

TABLE OF ABBREVIATIONS

Books

Annual Report	*Annual Report of the Charity Commissioners.*
A.S.C.L.	*Annual Survey of Commonwealth Law.*
Cheshire	Cheshire and Burn, *The Modern Law of Real Property* (16th ed., 2000).
Goff and Jones	Goff and Jones, *The Law of Restitution* (5th ed., 1998).
Harris	Harris, *Variation of Trusts.*
Hayton and Marshall	Hayton and Marshall, Commentary and Cases on the Law of Trusts and Equitable Remedies (10th ed., 1996).
Heydon, Gummow & Austin	Heydon, Gummow & Austin, *Cases and Materials on Equity & Trusts* (4th ed., 1993).
Holdsworth *H.E.L.*	Holdsworth, *History of English Law.*
Maitland	*Maitland's Equity* (2nd ed., 1936).
M. & W.	Megarry and Wade, *The Law of Real Property* (6th ed., 2000).
Meagher, Gummow & Lehane	Meagher, Gummow & Lehane, *Equity: Doctrines & Remedies* (3rd ed., 1992).
Morris and Leach	Morris and Leach, *The Rule Against Perpetuities* (2nd ed., 1962).
Oakley	Oakley, *Constructive Trusts* (3rd ed., 1997).
Parker and Mellows	Parker and Mellows, *The Modern Law of Trusts* (7th ed., 1998).
Pettit	Pettit, *Equity and the Law of Trusts* (8th ed., 1997).
Picarda	Picarda, *The Law and Practice Relating to Charities* (3rd ed., 1999).

Preston and Newsom	Preston and Newsom, *Limitation of Actions* (3rd ed., 1953).
Scott	Scott, *Trusts* (4th ed., 1987).
Snell	Snell, *Principles of Equity* (30th ed., 2000).
Spry	Spry, *Equitable Remedies* (5th ed., 1997).
Tudor	*Tudor on Charities* (8th ed., 1995).
Underhill and Hayton	Underhill and Hayton, *Law Relating to Trusts and Trustees* (15th ed., 1995).

Journals

All E.R. Rev.	All England Law Reports Annual Review.
B.T.R.	British Tax Review.
C.F.L.Q.	Child and Family Law Quarterly.
C.L.J.	Cambridge Law Journal.
C.B.R.	Canadian Bar Review.
Col. L.R.	Columbia Law Review.
Conv.	Conveyancer and Property Lawyer.
C.L.P.	Current Legal Problems.
E.G.	Estates Gazette.
Fam. Law.	Family Law.
H.L.R.	Harvard Law Review.
I.C.L.Q.	International and Comparative Law Quarterly.
J.B.L.	Journal of Business Law.
J.L.H.	Journal of Legal History.
K.C.L.J.	King's College Law Journal.
L.M.C.L.Q.	Lloyd's Maritime and Commercial Law Quarterly.
L.Q.R.	Law Quarterly Review.
L.S.	Legal Studies.
L.S.Gaz.	Law Society's Gazette.
M.L.R.	Modern Law Review.
N.L.J.	New Law Journal.
R.L.R.	Restitution Law Review.
S.J.	Solicitors' Journal.
U.W.A.L.R.	University of Western Australia Law Review.

Acts of Parliament

A.E.A	Administration of Estates Act.
F.A.	Finance Act.
I.C.T.A.	Income and Corporation Taxes Act.
I.H.T.A.	Inheritance Tax Act.
L.C.A.	Land Charges Act.
L.P.A.	Law of Property Act.
L.P.(A).A.	Law of Property (Amendment) Act.
S.L.A.	Settled Land Act.
T.A.	Trustee Act.
T.C.G.A.	Taxation of Chargeable Gains Act.
T.L.A.T.A.	Trusts of Land and Appointment of Trustees Act.
V.T.A.	Variation of Trusts Act.

General

B.S.	Building Society.
Comm.	Commissioners.
C.P.R.	Civil Procedure Rules
I.R.C.	Inland Revenue Commissioners.
S.	Section.
S.E.	Settled Estates.
S.T.	Settlement Trusts.
W.T.	Will Trusts.

TABLE OF CASES

TABLE OF STATUTES

Full text references appear in bold

TREATIES AND CONVENTIONS

FOREIGN LEGISLATION

PART I

INTRODUCTION

CHAPTER 1

HISTORY AND PRINCIPLES

1. GENERAL

EQUITY is a word with many meanings. In a wide sense, it means that which is fair and just, moral and ethical; but its legal meaning is much narrower. Equity is the branch of the law which, before the Judicature Act of 1873 came into force, was applied and administered by the Court of Chancery.[1] It is not synonymous with justice in a broad sense. A litigant asserting some equitable right or remedy must show that his claim has "an ancestry founded in history and in the practice and precedents of the court administering equity jurisdiction. It is not sufficient that because we may think that the 'justice' of the present case requires it, we should invent such a jurisdiction for the first time."[2]

---

[1] This is "but a poor thing to call a definition"; Maitland, p. 1.
[2] *Re Diplock* [1948] Ch. 465 at 481, 482. See also Jessel M.R. in *Re National Funds Assurance Co.* (1878) 10 Ch.D. 118 at 128: "This court is not, as I have often said, a Court of Conscience, but a Court of Law."

3

Developed systems of law have often been assisted by the introduction of a discretionary power to do justice in particular cases where the strict rules of law cause hardship.[3] Rules formulated to deal with particular situations may subsequently work unfairly as society develops. Equity is the body of rules which evolved to mitigate the severity of the rules of the common law. Its origin was the exercise by the Chancellor of the residual discretionary power of the King to do justice among his subjects in circumstances in which, for one reason or another, justice could not be obtained in a common law court.

Principles of justice and conscience are the basis of equity jurisdiction, but it must not be thought that the contrast between law and equity is one between a system of strict rules and one of broad discretion.[4] Equity has no monopoly of the pursuit of justice. As Harman L.J. has said, equitable principles are "rather too often bandied about in common law courts as though the Chancellor still had only the length of his own foot to measure when coming to a conclusion. Since the time of Lord Eldon, the system of equity for good or evil has been a very precise one, and equitable jurisdiction is exercised only on well-known principles."[5] In similar vein Lord Radcliffe, speaking of common lawyers, said that equity lawyers were "both surprised and discomfited by the plenitude of jurisdiction and the imprecision of rules that are attributed to 'equity' by their more enthusiastic colleagues."[6] Just as the common law has escaped from its early formalism, so over the years equity has established strict rules for the application of its principles. Indeed, at one stage the rules became so fixed that a *"rigor aequitatis"*[7] developed; equity itself displayed the very defect which it was designed to remedy. We will see that today some aspects of equity are strict and technical, while others leave considerable discretion to the court.

The field of equity is delineated by a series of historical events, and not by a pre-conceived theory; an outline of these events will be given in the next section. We will then see that, until the Judicature Act 1873, the Court of Chancery had almost exclusive equity jurisdiction[8]; rules of equity were not enforced in the common law courts. If a defendant to a common law action had an equitable defence to it, he had to go to Chancery to obtain an injunction to stay the proceedings in the common law court and then start a new action

---

[3] The Praetor performed such a function in Roman Law: Buckland and McNair, *Roman Law and Common Law* (2nd ed.), pp. 1–6.

[4] See generally (1997) 113 L.Q.R. 601 (A. Duggan).

[5] *Campbell Discount Co. Ltd v. Bridge* [1961] 1 Q.B. 445 at 459.

[6] *Bridge v. Campbell Discount Co. Ltd* [1962] A.C. 600 at 626.

[7] Allen's *Law in the Making* (7th ed.), p. 417.

[8] For the equity jurisdiction of the Court of Exchequer, see Radcliffe and Cross, *English Legal System* (6th ed.), p. 171. The Common Law Procedure Act 1854 had given common law courts a limited power to issue injunctions.

in Chancery to establish his equitable rights. This complicated system led to a number of difficulties, as we shall see. The Judicature Acts of 1873 and 1875 created the Supreme Court of Judicature, all of whose branches exercise common law and equity jurisdiction. The division between law and equity is less marked, therefore, than it was prior to those Acts, but it is still necessary for various reasons to know whether a rule has its origins in law or in equity.[9]

2. HISTORICAL OUTLINE

The long history of the Court of Chancery is a fascinating story, the details of which must be sought elsewhere[10]; it is not possible here to do more than mention, in broad outline, those aspects which are essential to the understanding of modern equity.

A. The Medieval Chancellor

In the medieval period the Chancellor was the most important person in the country next to the King himself: Maitland described him as "the king's prime minister,"[11] "the king's secretary of state for all departments."[12] One very important function of the Chancery was to issue the royal writs which began an action at law.[13] By varying existing writs or inventing new ones, the Chancellor could have some influence on the development of the law; a limited influence, however, for the decision to issue a writ (now called a claim form in the Civil Procedure Rules 1998) did not create a new form of action. The litigant could not proceed without it; but the common law court could still decide that the writ disclosed no claim recognised by the law.

B. Petitions to the Chancellor[14]

A claimant could only sue at common law if his complaint came within the scope of an existing writ. In the thirteenth century the available writs covered very narrow ground. Even if the claim came

---

[9] *post*, pp. 20 *et seq.*
[10] Maitland Lectures I–IV; Holdsworth; *H.E.L.* i, Chap. 5; iv, pp. 407–480; v, pp. 215–338; vi, pp. 518–551, 640–671; ix, pp. 335–408; xii, pp. 178–330; xiii, pp. 574–668; xvi, pp. 5–135; Plucknett, *Concise History of the Common Law* (5th ed.), Part V; Milsom, *Historical Foundations of the Common Law* (2nd ed.), Chaps. 4, 9; Jones, *The Elizabethan Court of Chancery*; (1965) 81 L.Q.R. 562; (1966) 82 L.Q.R. 215 (J. Barton); Keeton and Sheridan's *Equity* (3rd ed.), Chap. 2.
[11] Maitland, p. 3.
[12] *ibid*, p. 2.
[13] See Maitland, *Forms of Action at Common Law.*
[14] Holdsworth, *H.E.L.* i, pp. 402 *et seq.*; Milsom, pp. 82 *et seq.*

within the scope of an existing writ, it may have been that for some reason, such as the power and influence of the defendant, his opponent could not get justice before a common law court. The King in his Council still retained wide discretionary power to do justice among his subjects, and the claimant could petition to the King and Council praying for a remedy.

Petitions were addressed to the Chancellor in situations in which a petitioner complained that his case was beyond the ordinary mechanism, and he sought another way. Milsom points out that, in its origins, this would not be regarded as an application of a separate and superior body of rules to those applied by the common law courts. "Not only was there no equity as a nascent body of rules different from those of the common law. There was no common law, no body of substantive rules from which equity could be different."[15] If the mechanism appeared to work unfairly, as where juries were misled, corrupted or intimidated, the petitioner would seek another way. The Chancery "was the head office of the organisation, and it was here that application was made when the ordinary mechanisms appeared to be incapable of working. The approach to the chancellor has no more mysterious origin than that."[16]

Later the petition was used to obtain relief in cases where the common law was inflexible and incapable of providing a remedy. The common law developed into a comprehensive system, but a litigant could only sue at common law if his complaint came within the scope of an existing writ. By the sixteenth century local jurisdictions, where many matters not covered by common law writs had been dealt with, played a much smaller part. The common law was taking on the aspect of a substantive as well as a comprehensive system, and the application to Chancery was ceasing to look like a request for the same justice, withheld below by some mechanical fault. There seemed to be two parallel systems, and the relationship between them had to be explained in theory and worked out in practice.

C. The Chancellor's Discretion

Maitland points out that in the thirteenth and fourteenth centuries the Chancellor probably did not regard himself as administering a new body of law.[17] He was trying to give relief in hard cases, and the medieval Chancellor was peculiarly well fitted for this work. He was usually an ecclesiastic, generally a bishop, and learned in the civil

[15] Milsom, p. 84.
[16] *ibid.*
[17] Maitland, p. 5.

and canon law.[18] The Chancellor would give or withhold relief, not according to any precedent, but according to the effect produced upon his own individual sense of right and wrong by the merits of the particular case before him. No wonder that Seldon could say that "Equity is a roguish thing. For law we have a measure . . . equity is according to the conscience of him that is Chancellor, and as that is longer or narrower, so is equity. 'Tis all one as if they should make the standard for the measure a Chancellor's foot."[19]

D. Attendance of the Defendant

In exercising this jurisdiction, the Chancellor was faced with the problem of ensuring the attendance of the defendant without the issue of a royal writ. "The Chancellor, having considered the petition or bill as it is called, orders the (defendant) to come before him and answer the complaint. The writ whereby he does this is called a *subpoena*—because it orders the man to appear upon pain of forfeiting a sum of money—*e.g. subpoena centum librarum.*"[20] The examination was made under oath; it did not need to be restricted to specific questions raised in the complaint; and issues of fact as well as issues of law were decided by the Chancellor.

E. Enforcement

A further question was that of enforcement. If the petition was successful, the Chancellor's conclusion would usually be different from that which the common law court would have reached; otherwise the matter would have been litigated at common law. If the Chancellor found that Blackacre was owned by A, but that, in conscience, it should be beneficially owned by B, he could order A to convey the land to B, or to hold the legal estate for the exclusive benefit of B. The Chancellor did not and could not in these circumstances hold that B was the owner. A's right at law was undoubted, and the Chancellor could not change the law. What the Chancellor did was to issue an order to A either to convey the land to B, or to refrain from action interfering with B's right. The Chancellor's jurisdiction was against the person; *in personam*,[21] and directed to the conscience of the individual in question. The Chancellor had the power to back up his orders with the threat of imprisonment for those in contempt. Although there was, theoretically, no interference

---

[18] There were some lay Chancellors at this period; see Trevelyan, *England in the Age of Wycliffe* (1899).

[19] *Table Talk of John Selden* (ed. Pollock, 1927), p. 43; quoted Holdsworth, *H.E.L.* i, pp. 467–468.

[20] Maitland, p. 5.

[21] *post*, p. 7.

with common law property rights, there was in substance an interference with common law jurisdiction. This was the subject of dispute later on.[22]

F. The Use[23]

"If we were asked what is the greatest and most distinctive
achievement performed by Englishmen in the field of jurisprudence
I cannot think that we should have any better answer to give than
this, namely the development from century to century of the trust
idea."[24] Such was the view of Maitland. A more recent statement is
that "Trust law is the finest legal concept we have given to a civi-
lised world."[25] Let us now examine the origins of that concept.

In medieval times, the Chancellor's jurisdiction was vague and
undefined; as wide as the subject-matter of the petitions which invoked it. The basis of intervention was that it was necessary on
grounds of conscience. His authority was unquestioned in cases of
fraud and breach of confidence. As stated above, the most significant
and far-reaching sphere of his jurisdiction was the enforcement of
the use of land.

If land was given to A on A's undertaking to hold the land to the
use and benefit of B, it was unconscionable for A to keep it for his
own benefit. B however had no legal claim or title to the land. The
conveyance to A gave him whatever legal estate was conveyed, and,
at common law, A could exercise all the rights which that estate
gave him.

Land might be given to A to the use of B for various reasons. If
B were going on a crusade, then there had to be someone to perform
and receive the feudal services. If B were a community of Franciscan friars which, because of the rule of poverty, was incapable of
holding property, it was necessary for someone to hold the land for
its benefit.[26] Perhaps, however, B was trying to escape from his
creditors; or feared that a conviction for felony would result in the
loss of his lands.[27] For various reasons it may have been advisable
or necessary to put the legal title to B's land in A. If B conveyed to
A subject to an undertaking to hold to the use of B, B would have
no protection at common law beyond that given in the fourteenth
century to covenants under seal; and if a third party conveyed the

---

[22] *post*, p. 11.
[23] Holdsworth, *H.E.L.* iv, pp. 407–480; Ames, *Lectures on Legal History*, pp. 233–247;
Plucknett, *Concise History of the Common Law*, p. 575; Milsom, Chap. 9; (1965) 81 L.Q.R.
562; (1966) 82 L.Q.R. 215 (J. Barton); (1997) 56 C.L.J. 175 (N. Jones).
[24] *Selected Essays*, p. 129.
[25] (1995) 9 *Trust Law International* 33 (J. Quarrell).
[26] Maitland, p. 25; Holdsworth, *H.E.L.* iv, p. 415; Milsom, pp. 203 *et seq.*
[27] *Davies v. Otty (No. 2)* (1865) 35 Beav. 208.

land to A to hold to the use of B, no relationship recognised by the common law existed between A and B.

The Chancellor interfered to compel A to hold the land for the exclusive use and benefit of B. The Chancellor could not say that B was the owner; A was. But all the beneficial interest in the land could be given to B by compelling A to keep the legal title only, and to give all the benefit of the land to B. This is what happened when the use was enforced. And, although the jurisdiction against A was a jurisdiction *in personam*, the Chancellor would enforce B's rights, not only against A, but against other persons who took the land from A.[28] It was not long before it was said that A was the owner at law, B the owner in equity. In the terminology of the time, A was the feoffee to uses, B the *cestui que use*. The use was the forerunner, as we will see, of the trust.

Gradually the Chancellors established the circumstances in which uses would be enforced. They had to decide also what equitable estates they would recognise; for example, if land were conveyed to A to the use of B for life and then to the use of C, should this be enforced? Broadly, the answer was that, in accordance with the maxim that equity follows the law, the estates and interests which could be created in equity corresponded with those which existed at law.

G. The Advantages of the Use

The employment of the use made it possible to avoid some of the feudal incidents. Under feudal law, the lord was entitled to a payment when an heir succeeded to feudal land, and to other valuable rights arising when the land was held by an under-age heir, and the right of escheat where there was no heir.[29] These burdens could be avoided if the land was vested in a number of feoffees to uses. They were unlikely to die together or without heirs. Those who died could be replaced, and the feoffees would never be children. Thus, the use, to feudal land owners, had something of the appeal of tax planning techniques at the present day. It was possible also, in spite of the rule that freehold land could not be devised, to create effective dispositions of equitable interests on death by vesting the land in feoffees and declaring the uses on which the land was to be held after the settlor's death. Further, uses made possible the creation of new types of interests in land which were not possible at common law.[30] For a time also, until prevented by statute, land held to uses could be

---

[28] Except a bona fide purchaser of a legal estate for value without notice, *post*, p. 32; Maitland, pp. 113–115.

[29] Cheshire and Burn, pp. 17 *et seq.*

[30] *e.g.* springing and shifting interests; Cheshire and Burn, p. 71.

enjoyed by religious houses in defiance of the Statutes of Mort-main,[31] or be placed beyond the reach of creditors.

H. The Statute of Uses 1535

Henry VIII found that his purse was being emptied by the avoid-ance of feudal incidents which the system of uses made possible. To small tenants who had no tenants of their own, the system of uses was entirely beneficial. To large landowners, it was beneficial in so far as they were tenants, and harmful in so far as they were lords. To the King, it was entirely harmful, because he was lord of all and tenant of none. The first part of Henry VIII's reign had been ex-pensive, and he was determined to restore the revenues of the Crown by attacking uses. The Statute of Uses of 1535 was intended to reduce greatly the scope of the use. After a grandiloquent preamble it provided, according to Maitland's summary of the first clause[32]: "where any person or persons shall be seised of any lands or other hereditaments to the use, confidence, or trust of any other person or persons, in every such case such person and persons that shall have any such use, confidence or trust in fee simple, fee tail, for term of life or for years or otherwise shall stand and be seised deemed and adjudged in lawful seisin estate and possession of and in the same lands and hereditaments in such like estates as they had or shall have in the use." In other words, the feoffees to uses were to disappear. The *cestui que use* was to have the legal estate.

The Statute did not however suppress all uses.[33] It only applied where the feoffee was *seised* to the use of another. If the feoffee held only a lease, he would not be seised, and the Statute would not apply. Again it did not apply to situations where the feoffees had active duties to perform. The feoffees were then necessary partici-pants, and the Chancellor held that a duty to sell the land, or to collect the rents and profits of the land and pay them to X, was a sufficiently active duty to exclude the Statute.[34]

I. A Use upon a Use. The Trust

It was possible, after the Statute, to create equitable interests in land by imposing a use upon a leasehold, or by requiring the legal owners of freehold land to collect the rents and profits and to pay them over to the beneficiaries. Such uses were not executed; nor

---

[31] Which forbade the conveyance of land to religious houses without permission of the Crown. Milsom, p. 204.

[32] Maitland, p. 35.

[33] Holdsworth, *H.E.L.* iv, pp. 467–473.

[34] Maitland, pp. 38–41; M & W., p. 1167.

were they invalid.[35] Passive uses of freehold land were, however, executed by the Statute, so that the beneficiary held the legal estate. What would happen if a second use were imposed? If land were limited to A to the use of B to the use of C, is it possible to argue that the first use will be executed, and that B will hold the legal estate to the use of C? Such a solution was reached by about 1700[36]; the second use is called a trust. A shorter form, which became settled practice, was to omit A, and to make the disposition "unto and to the use of B in trust for C."

The story of this development is confused and uncertain.[37] Most accounts start with the proposition that through the sixteenth century, the second use was repugnant to the first, and void.[38] When the turning-point came is unsettled, but it is clear that after the Restoration in 1660, a number of factors combined to facilitate the recognition of passive trusts of freeholds. The abolition of military tenures[39] and the consequent freedom to devise all freehold land,[40] the reduction in the value of money which followed the development of the New World, and the changes in the constitutional and financial structure of the country in the seventeenth century, all helped to make the collection of feudal dues a minor factor in the royal revenues. The Civil War determined once and for all that the Government was to be financed by Parliamentary vote. There was now no reason of policy why passive trusts of freeholds should not be enforced as were active trusts and trusts of leaseholds. The enforcement of the second use as a trust was so similar to that of the enforcement of the use against a feoffee to uses centuries before that Lord Hardwicke was able to say, in 1738, in a remark of greater dramatic power than legal or mathematical accuracy: " . . . by this means a statute made upon great consideration, introduced in a solemn and pompous manner, by this strict construction, has had no other effect than to add at most, three words to a conveyance."[41]

J. The Struggle over Injunctions

The story of the use and of the trust has taken us away from the chronological sequence. For it was at the close of the sixteenth century that the quarrel over the power of the Chancery to issue injunctions came to a head. The use of the injunction had the effect

---

[35] Simpson, *Introduction to the History of Land Law* (2nd ed.), p. 195.

[36] Simpson, *loc. cit.*, p. 203.

[37] Milsom, p. 208 suggests that the origin is in a situation in which a settlor wishes to settle upon himself with remainders over; (1977) 93 L.Q.R. 33 (J. Baker).

[38] Maitland, p. 42; Ames, *Lectures on Legal History*, pp. 243–247; Holdsworth, *H.E.L.* iv, pp. 471–473; *Jane Tyrell's Case* (1557) Dyer 155a.

[39] Tenures Abolition Act 1660.

[40] Previously only two-thirds of land held by knight service could be devised.

[41] *Hopkins v. Hopkins* (1739) 1 Atk. 581 at 591; see Holdsworth, *H.E.L.* iv, pp. 449 *et seq.*

of rendering the common law inoperative. That the clash did not come earlier was due partly to the statesmanlike qualities of men like More; and no doubt also to the reluctance to challenge the powers of royal officers in Tudor times. Chief Justice Coke was not willing to see the common law treated in this way, and in a number of cases decided that imprisonment for disobedience to injunctions issued by Chancery was unlawful.[42] In one case it was said that "if any court of equity doth inter-meddle with any matters properly triable at the common law, or which concern freehold, they are to be prohibited."[43] Lord Chancellor Ellesmere, equally determined, claimed that he was in no sense interfering with the common law; he was merely acting *in personam*, directing the individual that, on equitable grounds, he must not proceed to sue at law or enforce a judgment already obtained at law.

James I stepped in and referred the matter to Bacon, then Attorney-General, and others learned in the law. Acting on their recommendations, and no doubt in accordance with his own political views and interests, he decided in favour of the Chancery.[44] The victory did not remain long unchallenged. The success of the Parliament and of the common lawyers in the political struggles of the seventeenth century provided further impetus for the attack on the Chancery. As late as 1690, following the Revolution, a Bill was introduced in the House of Commons to restrain the interference by Chancery in any suit for which the proper remedy was at common law.[45] The Bill was not passed, and from that time the Chancellor's jurisdiction was not seriously challenged. Thereafter, law and equity worked together, as parts of a consistent whole; and this enabled Maitland to say that Equity had come, not to destroy the law, but to fulfil it.[46]

K. The Transformation of Equity into the Modern System[47]

From the beginning of the Chancellorship of Lord Nottingham in 1673 and to the end of that of Lord Eldon in 1827, equity was transformed from a jurisdiction based upon the personal interference of the Chancellor into a system of established rules and principles. We have seen that the early Chancellors were ecclesiastics. Lawyers and others were sometimes appointed during the Tudor and Stuart

---

[42] *Heath v. Rydley* (1614) Cro.Jac. 335; *Bromage v. Genning* (1617) 1 Rolle 368; *Throckmorton v. Finch* (1598) Third Institute 124 at 25.

[43] *i.e.* liable to be subject to the writ of Prohibition; *Heath v. Rydley* (1614) Cro.Jac. 335.

[44] *Reports of Cases in Chancery*, App. 1, p. 49; 21 E.R. 588.

[45] Holdsworth, *H.E.L.* i, pp. 463–465.

[46] *Equity*, p. 19.

[47] Pollock, *Essays in Legal History*, p. 286.

periods. The retirement of Lord Shaftesbury[48] in 1672 was the last occasion on which a non-lawyer held the Great Seal. This factor influenced the development of the system into one based on rules and precedents rather than on individual conscience. The first reported Chancery cases are dated 1557[49] and these cases are treated as authorities and followed.[50]

Lord Nottingham did much to weld together and consolidate the whole system. To him we owe the doctrine that there can be no "clog on the equity of redemption,"[51] a classification of trusts,[52] and the modern rule against perpetuities.[53] Throughout the eighteenth century, equity, in a period of legislative stagnation, became the great force that moulded the progress of the law right up to the beginning of the nineteenth century. In this period the modern law of trusts developed and was shaped to meet entirely new conditions of social life; equity took in hand the administration of the estates of deceased persons, on which depended the doctrines of election,[54] satisfaction,[55] ademption,[56] marshalling of assets,[57] and performance,[58] and in many cases it is possible to point to the Chancellor who first applied them.[59] In this period there were many great Chancellors, culminating in Lord Eldon (1801–06, 1807–27), one of the greatest equity lawyers. His decisions were thorough, painstaking, learned and clear. As Holdsworth said: "He had a thorough grasp of existing rules and principles; but he looked as anxiously into all the facts and circumstances of each case . . . as if there were no such rules and as if, therefore, he was under the necessity of determining each case as one of first impression."[60] The judgments were masterly. But it is hardly surprising that the business of the court was scandalously in arrears. The pattern and principles of equity were now established. "Nothing would inflict on me greater pain in quitting this place," he said, "than the recollection that I had done

---

[48] A member of the Cabal of Charles II; he had been educated as a lawyer, but never practised; Holdsworth, *H.E.L.* i, p. 411; vi, pp. 525–526.

[49] "Choyce Cases in Chancery"; Holdsworth, *H.E.L.* v. pp. 274–278; Jones, *The Elizabethan Court of Chancery*, p. 3.

[50] In the preface to Nelson's reports, at pp. 2–3, the author said that "Equity became artificial Reason, and hath ever since such a mixture of law in it, that it woud be much easier now for a Lawyer to preach, than for a Prelate to be a Judge of that Court"; Holdsworth, *H.E.L.* vi, p. 669.

[51] *Howard v. Harris* (1681) 1 Vern. 33.

[52] *Cook v. Fountain* (1676) 3 Swan. 585.

[53] *Duke of Norfolk's Case* (1683) 2 Swan. 454.

[54] *Snell*, Chap. 32.

[55] *ibid.*, Chap. 34.

[56] *ibid.*, p. 407.

[57] *ibid.*, p. 377.

[58] *ibid.*, Chap. 33.

[59] *Re Hallet's Estate* (1880) 13 Ch.D. 696 at 710.

[60] Holdsworth, *H.E.L.* i, p. 468.

anything to justify the reproach that the equity of this court varies like the Chancellor's foot."[61]

L. The Nineteenth Century and the Judicature Acts 1873 and 1875

The nineteenth century was a period of great development of the equitable jurisdiction, based upon the principles established by the end of Lord Eldon's tenure. The enormous industrial, international and imperial expansion of Britain in this period necessitated developments in equity to deal with a host of new problems. The accumulation of business fortunes required rules for the administration of companies and partnerships; and the change in emphasis from landed wealth to stocks and shares necessitated the development of new concepts of property settlements.

Clearly the old organisation of the Chancery Court, overloaded in Lord Eldon's time, could not hope to deal with the mass of business. "Remember this," said Maitland to his students at the turn of the twentieth century, "that until 1813 there were only two judges in the Court of Chancery. There was the Lord Chancellor, and there was the Master of the Rolls, and it was but by degrees that the latter had become an independent judge; for a long time he appears merely as the Chancellor's assistant. In 1813 a Vice-Chancellor was appointed. In 1841 two more Vice-Chancellors. In 1851 two Lords Justices of Appeal in Chancery. When the Court was abolished in 1875, it had seven judges. Cases in the first instance were taken before the Master of the Rolls, or one of the three Vice-Chancellors, and there was an Appeal Court constituted by the Chancellor and the two Lords Justices; but the Chancellor could sit as a judge of first instance if he pleased and sometimes did so."[62] At least however, the judges could deal with their work without the fear of opposition from the common law. The two courts had now become, "not rivals but partners in the work of administering justice."[63] The time had come for the fusion of these jurisdictions into a single Supreme Court.

Some limited steps were taken towards this fusion in the middle of the nineteenth century. The Common Law Procedure Act 1854 gave to the common law courts a certain power to give equitable remedies, and the Chancery Amendment Act 1858, commonly known as Lord Cairns' Act, gave to the Court of Chancery power to award damages in addition to, or in substitution for, an injunction or

---

[61] Holdsworth, *H.E.L.* i, pp. 468–469; *Gee v. Pritchard* (1818) 2 Swan. 402 at 414.
[62] Maitland, p. 14. There are now 17 judges, headed by the Vice-Chancellor, allocated to the Chancery Division.
[63] Holdsworth, *H.E.L.* v. p. 668.

an order for specific performance.[64] The major change however came with the Judicature Acts 1873 and 1875. These Acts abolished the old separate Courts of Queen's Bench, Exchequer, Common Pleas, Chancery, Probate, the Divorce Court, and the Court of Admiralty; it created the Supreme Court of Judicature with a High Court divided into Divisions known as the Queen's Bench Division, Chancery Division, and the Probate, Divorce and Admiralty Division. The latter was re-named the Family Division in 1970.[65] Its Admiralty jurisdiction was assigned to the Queen's Bench Division, and Probate business, other than non-contentious and common form probate business, to the Chancery Division. Each Division exercises both legal and equitable jurisdiction.[66] Thus any issue can be adjudicated in any Division; and any point of law or equity can be raised and determined in any Division; but, for the sake of administrative convenience, cases are allocated to the Divisions according to their general subject-matter.[67] Thus the court "is now not a Court of Law or a Court of Equity, it is a Court of complete jurisdiction."[68]

It was foreseen that a court which applied the rules both of common law and of equity would face a conflict where the common law rules would produce one result, and equity another. Section 25 of the Supreme Court of Judicature Act 1873 therefore provided for the solution of many problems in which those rules would conflict.[69] Subsection 11 contained a general residual clause:

> "Generally, in all matters not hereinbefore particularly mentioned in which there is any conflict or variance between the rules of equity and the rules of common law with reference to the same matter, the rules of equity shall prevail."

The effect of the Judicature Act is best shown by the leading case of *Walsh v. Lonsdale*.[70]

The landlord agreed in writing to grant to the tenant a lease of a mill for seven years. The agreement provided that the rent was

---

[64] *post*, pp. 747, 801.

[65] Administration of Justice Act 1970, s.1.

[66] Judicature Act 1873, s.24; Judicature Act 1925, ss.36–44; Supreme Court Act 1981, s.49.

[67] See Supreme Court Act 1981, Sched. 1, *post*, p. 40.

[68] *Pugh v. Heath* (1882) 7 App.Cas. 235 at 237, *per* Lord Cairns. Thus the three-fold division of the content of equity into the exclusive, concurrent and auxiliary jurisdictions lost importance after the Judicature Acts; Snell, pp. 12–13.

[69] Now Supreme Court Act 1981, s.49. Examples are found in s.25(1) of the Act of 1873, dealing with the order of priority of payment of debts of a person dying insolvent; and the refusal of common law but not of equity to recognise the assignment of debts and choses in action (s.25(6)). These matters are now dealt with by A.E.A. 1925, s.34(1) and L.P.A. 1925, s.136 respectively. See *Job v. Job* (1877) 6 Ch.D. 562; *Lowe v. Dixon* (1885) 16 Q.B.D. 455; *Berry v. Berry* [1929] 2 K.B. 316. See also L.P.A. 1925, s.41.

[70] (1882) 21 Ch.D. 9; *Warmington v. Miller* [1973] Q.B. 877; *Tottenham Hotspur Football and Athletic Co. Ltd v. Princegrove Publishers Ltd* [1974] 1 W.L.R. 113; (1974) 90 L.Q.R. 149 (M. Albery); (1987) 7 O.J.LS. 60 (S. Gardner).

payable in advance if demanded. No grant by deed of the lease—as required for a lease exceeding three years *at law*—was ever made.

The tenant entered and paid rent quarterly, not in advance. He became in arrears and the landlord demanded a year's rent in advance. It was not paid, and the landlord distrained. The tenant brought this action for illegal distress.[71]

The action failed. The distress would have been illegal at law, because no seven-year lease had been granted, and the yearly legal tenancy which arose because of the entering into possession and payment of rent did not include the provision for payment of rent in advance.[72] In equity, however, the agreement for the lease was as good as a lease. The tenant was liable to pay a year's rent in advance and the distress was lawful.

It will be seen that the effect of the Act is procedural only.[73] The rights of the parties, whether dependent on the rules of law or of equity, were under the Act determined at a single trial. But the same result would ultimately have been reached if the case had arisen before 1875; the procedure only would have differed. The claim, being one for damages for illegal distress, would have been brought at common law. To the tenant's argument that he held only on a lease from year to year, of which the covenant to pay rent a year in advance was not a term, the landlord would have had no reply in a court of law. The claim to specific performance of the agreement to take a lease was one that could only have been made in equity. The landlord would have had to obtain an injunction to stop the tenant's action at law, and then to obtain specific performance of the agreement; and then to have returned to the common law court with the lease duly created by deed in conformity with the decree of Chancery. The landlord would then have had a good defence in the common law court. The effect of the Judicature Acts was to enable the court to treat as done that which ought to be done, and to allow the landlord to use his equitable defence (based on his right to specific performance) to the common law claim. The principle that equity treats as done that which ought to be done was not new. The significance of the case is the recognition of that principle in a case involving a legal claim. The principle is not limited to agreements for leases, but is applicable to all cases where there is a specifically enforceable contract by a legal owner to convey or create a legal

---

[71] A landlord may distrain (*i.e.* issue a distress) upon a tenant who is in arrear, and in doing so may take and sell sufficient goods of the tenant (with exceptions) as are necessary to pay the arrears; M. & W., p. 891.

[72] A yearly tenancy which arises in these circumstances includes only such terms of any agreement as are consistent with a yearly tenancy. An agreement to pay a year's rent in advance is not consistent with a yearly tenancy; M. & W., p. 774.

[73] See (1966) 4 Alberta L.R. 134 (J. Coté).

estate, such as a contract to sell, to grant a lease or a mortgage. The principle has been applied "once removed"; as where A agreed to sell Blackacre to B who had agreed to grant a lease to C. C was treated as the lessee in equity of the land.[74] C would not become a lessee at law until the legal lease had been properly granted.

Whether developments in the century following the Judicature Acts have had the effect of fusing not only the jurisdictions but law and equity themselves is a disputed question which can best be considered after looking into the nature of equitable rights.

3. THE NATURE OF EQUITABLE RIGHTS

There has for many years been a learned and unsettled controversy on the question of the nature of equitable rights; and particularly of the nature of the interest of a beneficiary under a trust. In its simplest form, one view emphasises the fact that a beneficiary's remedy, historically and practically, is in the form of an action against the trustee; a right *in personam*. On the other hand, equitable interests under trusts are equitable proprietary interests, corresponding to legal estates, and the beneficiary can properly be regarded as the owner of the beneficial interest; and ownership is a right *in rem*. The controversy attracted many great scholars; with Langdell, Ames, Maitland and Holland on one side, and Austin, Salmond, Pomeroy and Scott on the other.[75]

Much of this controversy centred upon whether the beneficiary's right was a right *in personam* or a right *in rem*. This was because Austin, following the classifications of Roman law, laid down that rights must be of one type or the other. But, for the discussion to become meaningful, it is necessary to know what these terms mean. They mean different things in different contexts. It seems that the proper meaning of a right *in rem* in the present context is "a right enforceable against the world with respect to a particular thing."[76] It is assumed throughout that a legal owner does have rights *in rem*. Rights, that is, against all the world with respect to property. How, then, does a beneficiary under a trust measure up to this test?

The basis of equitable jurisdiction, historically and presently, is that, in accordance with the maxim, equity acts *in personam*, equitable rights grew up where the Chancellor was willing to intervene. The use has its origin in the insistence of the Chancellor that the feoffees to uses should administer the property for the

---

[74] *Industrial Properties (Barton Hill) Ltd v. Associated Electrical Industries Ltd* [1977] Q.B. 580; (1977) 40 M.L.R. 718 (P. Jackson).

[75] (1967) 45 C.B.R. at 221 (D. Waters); (1917) 17 Col.L.R. 269 (A. Scott); (1917) 17 Col.L.R. 467 (H. Stone); (1962) 40 C.B.R. at 270 (E. Mockler).

[76] (1962) 40 C.B.R. at 279.

benefit of the *cestui que use*. Similarly with the trust. "Equity did
not say that the *cestui que trust* was the owner of the land, it said that
the trustee was the owner of the land, but added that he was bound
to hold the land for the benefit of the *cestui que trust*."[77] This raised
the question of the effect of the sale of the land by the trustee. The
answer was that the beneficiary's interest was effective against
everyone except a bona fide purchaser for valuable consideration
without notice, actual or constructive, of the equitable interest.

Indeed equity could not have done differently. Its remedies of
specific performance and injunction were orders *in personam*. They
ordered the defendant to do something or to refrain from doing
something; and behind them was the threat that a recalcitrant defendant would be put in prison for contempt.

There is no space here to run through every aspect of equity
jurisdiction to establish the point that equity acts *in personam*. One
practical application of this proposition is the fact that a court of
equity will exercise jurisdiction to order specific performance of a
contract for the sale of land abroad,[78] or to administer assets abroad
if the executors are in England.[79] Where a father bought a flat in
France in his son's name and sought a declaration that the son was
a trustee and an order to vest the property in the father, his action
was classified as *in personam* for the purposes of the 1968 Brussels
Convention, so that the son's claim that only the French courts had
jurisdiction failed.[80] In *Re Hayward*,[81] on the other hand, the claim
by the trustee in bankruptcy of a deceased legal and beneficial
co-owner of a villa in Spain to his share of the property was held to
be *in rem*, so that the Spanish court had exclusive jurisdiction under
the Convention. It has been noted that the fact that English law has
been incapable of determining conclusively whether trust interests
are *in rem* or *in personam* "is a deficiency only exacerbated when
the concepts are carried into private international law".[82]

This debate does not prevent us from treating a beneficiary under
a trust as having equitable ownership. A beneficiary's interest behind a trust has long been treated as having the basic characteristics
of a proprietary interest in that it can be bought, sold, mortgaged,
and devised or bequeathed. Even though, historically, the protection
of the beneficiary was based on the Chancellor's willingness to

---

[77] Maitland, p. 17.
[78] *Penn v. Lord Baltimore* (1750) 1 Ves.Sen. 444; *Richard West and Partners (Inverness) Ltd
v. Dick* [1969] Ch. 424; *post* p. 716.
[79] *Ewing v. Orr-Ewing (No. 1)* (1883) 9 App.Cas. 34.
[80] *Webb v. Webb* [1994] Q.B. 696; (1994) 110 L.Q.R. 526 (A. Briggs); (1994) 53 C.L.J. 462
(P. Rogerson); (1994) 8 *Trust Law International* 99 (P. Birks); All E.R. Rev. 1994 p. 81 (J.
Collier); [1996] Conv. 125 (C. MacMillan). See also *Pollard v. Ashurst, The Times*,
November 29, 2000.
[81] [1997] Ch. 45.
[82] [1998] Conv. 145 at 150 (J. Stevens).

proceed *in personam* against the trustee, that protection has ended up by creating rights in the nature of ownership.[83] To argue that a beneficiary's rights are proprietary is not to say that legal rights are the same as equitable, or that equitable ownership is the same as legal. Rather, it is to accept the basic peculiarity of ownership under the English law of trusts. The trustee is the owner at law; and the beneficiary is the owner in equity.

In relation to some claims affecting the trust property, the trustee is able to sue and not the beneficiary. Thus, the trustee sues for rent,[84] or for possession; and, with personalty, the trustee, not the beneficiary, sues for conversion of the trust property.[85] The beneficiary's right is to compel the trustee to take action; though he may, in some cases, take action himself on behalf of the trust, joining the trustee as defendant.[86] This right may sometimes be inadequate; as where the trustee has sold the property to a bona fide purchaser of the legal estate for value without notice, who will defeat the equitable ownership of the beneficiary.[87] Does this require us to say that his rights are personal against the trustee, and are not properly regarded as proprietary? This was the deciding test for the supporters of the theory that equitable rights must be regarded as being *in personam*. But it shows the inadequacy of the test which is being applied as a means of distinguishing equitable ownership from legal ownership; which is accepted as being a right *in rem*. For legal rights of ownership are not good against all the world. There are many ways in which the legal owner of a chattel or chose in action may be involuntarily deprived of legal ownership.[88] The situation of the bona fide purchaser is not determinative of the question whether the beneficiary's interest is proprietary; or whether his rights are *in rem* or *in personam*. It demonstrates simply that legal and equitable ownership may have different effects.

From a practical point of view, it can be said that where the problem involves the working of the trust machinery, so that the beneficiary asserts his rights by an action against the trustees to enforce their duties, the old theory that equity acts *in personam* is

---

[83] *Sinclair v. Brougham* [1914] A.C. 398 at 444; (1954) 70 L.Q.R. 326 at 331 (Lord Evershed M.R.); *Tinsley v. Milligan* [1994] 1 A.C. 340 at 371.

[84] *Schalit v. Nadler Ltd* [1933] 2 K.B. 79.

[85] *MCC Proceeds Inc. v. Lehman Brothers International (Europe)* [1998] 4 All E.R. 675. The beneficiary can sue if he has a right to immediate possession; *Healey v. Healey* [1915] 1 K.B. 938. See (1996) 55 C.L.J. 36 (A. Tettenborn).

[86] See *Les Affréteurs Réunis Société Anonyme v. Leopold Walford (London) Ltd* [1919] A.C. 801; *Parker-Tweedale v. Dunbar Bank plc.* [1991] Ch. 12; *Bradstock Trustee Services Ltd v. Nabarro Nathanson (a firm)* [1995] 1 W.L.R. 1405.

[87] The beneficiary will have a personal right against the trustee for compensation and may be able to trace the proceeds; *post*, Chap. 23.

[88] Sale of Goods Act 1979, ss. 21, 24; Factors Act 1889, ss.2, 8, 9; Consumer Credit Act 1974, Sched. 4, para. 22.

wholly acceptable.[89] But, in other cases, usually tax cases,[90] the theoretical view is overtaken by a pragmatic approach; and the result determined by the language of the statute and a number of policy questions relating to the purposes of the particular statute. This is an area where Austin's theoretical analysis is the least helpful. Perhaps the better view is that the beneficiary's interest is *sui generis*.[91]

4. THE RELATIONSHIP BETWEEN LAW AND EQUITY: FUSION

The Judicature Act clearly "fused" the administration of law and equity by the creation of the High Court of Judicature exercising both law and equity and gave supremacy to equity in cases of conflict. A disputed question is whether that Act, or the subsequent development of law and equity, should be regarded as having effected the fusion of law and equity themselves.

The orthodox view is that only the jurisdictions have been fused. The changes made by the Judicature Act gave rise to no new cause of action, remedy, or defence, which was not available before. In a famous "fluvial" metaphor, Ashburner said "the two streams of jurisdiction, though they run in the same channel; run side by side, and do not mingle their waters."[92] Thus, legal rights remain legal rights, and equitable rights remain equitable rights, though administered in the same court. Other bills which were introduced prior to the Judicature Act would indeed have fused law and equity; but they failed, and the Judicature Act was a more cautious measure.[93]

There are, however, statements by great judges to the effect that law and equity are fused. Sir George Jessel said, as early as 1881; "there are not two estates as there were formerly, one estate in common law by reason of the payment of rent from year to year, and an estate in equity under the agreement. There is only one court, and equity rules prevail in it."[94] Subsequently Lord Diplock[95] discussed Ashburner's metaphor, and declared:

[89] (1967) 45 C.B.R. at 280 (D. Waters).

[90] See *Baker v. Archer-Shee* [1927] A.C. 844.

[91] Pettit, p. 77.

[92] *Principles of Equity* (2nd ed.), p. 18. See also (1954) 70 L.Q.R. 326 (Lord Evershed M.R.); (1961) 24 M.L.R. 116 (V. Delaney); (1977) 6 A.A.L.R. 119 (T. Watkin).

[93] (1977) 93 L.Q.R. 529 at 530 (P. Baker); (1870) 14 S.J. 548.

[94] *Walsh v. Lonsdale* (1882) 21 Ch.D. 14. He had previously expressed the orthodox view of the effect of the Act, in *Salt v. Cooper* (1880) 16 Ch.D. 544 at 549.

[95] *United Scientific Holdings Ltd v. Burnley Borough Council* [1978] A.C. 904 at 925. All the members of the House indicated their general acceptance of the principle of fusion. Lord Diplock is described as "the most forceful exponent of the fusion fallacy," in Heydon, Gummow and Austin, *Cases and Materials on Equity and Trusts* (4th ed.), p. 27. See also *Chief Constable of Kent v. V.* [1983] Q.B. 34 at 41.

"By 1977, this metaphor has in my view become most mischievous and deceptive. The innate conservatism of English lawyers may have made them slow to recognise that by the Supreme Court of Judicature Act 1873, the two systems of substantive and adjectival law formerly administered by courts of law and Courts of Chancery (as well as those administered by Courts of Admiralty, Probate and Matrimonial Causes), were fused."

In some jurisdictions in recent years, contrary to Lord Diplock's view, the distinction between law and equity "has achieved renewed prominence", as the courts have reasserted the old conscience-based jurisdiction of equity, with its different techniques, policies and doctrines.[96]

Others have expressed views to the effect that we ought to be addressing our minds to the *combined effect* of the systems of law and equity, and that to keep the systems always distinct is pedantic, and an impediment to the natural development of the law.[97]

It is important, in this discussion, to be clear as to what is meant by the claim that law and equity are fused. If it means that there is now no distinction or difference between legal rights and remedies and equitable rights and remedies, it cannot be supported.[98] It is still clear that legal ownership is different from equitable ownership; all the provisions of the legislation of 1925, dealing with unregistered land, are based on that assumption.[99] Again, the law of trusts assumes a distinction between legal and equitable rights. The equitable nature of the duties of a mortgagee has recently been emphasised,[1] although Sir Richard Scott V.-C. has said: "I do not, for my part, think that it matters one jot whether the duty is expressed as a common law duty or as a duty in equity. The result is the same."[2] Further, as discussed below,[3] it is still basically true to say that an equitable claim will provide only an equitable remedy.

---

[96] (1997) 113 L.Q.R. 601 at 601–602 (A. Duggan). The author goes on, however, to "debunk the myth" of the "new equity rhetoric".

[97] See (1948) J.S.P.T.L. 180 (Lord Evershed); (1952) C.L.P. 1 (Lord Denning); *The Court of Appeal in England*, p. 13 (Lord Evershed); (1961) 24 M.L.R. 116 (V. Delaney); Lord Denning, *Landmarks in the Law*, p. 86 ("the fusion is complete").

[98] (1977) 93 L.Q.R. 529 at 532 (P. Baker).

[99] The distinction between legal and equitable ownership is of little significance in registered land. But that is due to the classification of interests for the purposes of the system, and is unconnected with any question of fusion.

[1] *China and South Sea Bank Ltd v. Tan Soon Gin* [1990] 1 A.C. 536; *Parker-Tweedale v. Dunbar Bank plc* [1991] Ch. 12, criticising *Cuckmere Brick Co. Ltd v. Mutual Finance Ltd* [1971] Ch. 949 (common law damages and duty of care in tort imported); *Downsview Nominees Ltd v. First City Corporation Ltd* [1993] A.C. 295; *AIB Finance Ltd v. Debtors* [1998] 2 All E.R. 929; *Yorkshire Bank plc v. Hall* 1 All E.R. 879.

[2] *Medforth v. Blake* [2000] Ch. 86 at 102; [1999] Conv. 434 (A. Kenny); (2000) 59 C.L.J. 31 (L. Sealy); (2000) 63 M.L.R. 413 (S. Frisby).

[3] *post*, p. 24.

An equitable claim is required for the newly revived writ[4] *ne exeat regno.*[5] The common law and equitable rules for tracing property are different, as explained in Chapter 23; likewise the rules concerning payment of interest,[6] rescission of a contract for mistake,[7] and the transmission of the burden of a restrictive covenant.[8] Although common law damages and compensation in equity share the requirement of causation, they differ on remoteness and foreseeability.[9] The illustrations could be multiplied.

Nor is it true, at the other extreme, to say that rights exercisable in the High Court today are the same as those existing in 1875; nor that the application of equitable doctrines in the court has not had the effect of refining and developing the common law rules.[10] Both legal and equitable rules have developed since 1873; and the development of legal rules has sometimes been influenced by established equitable doctrine, with the effect that a situation which would at one time have been treated differently at law and in equity is now treated in the same manner. If that is what is meant by fusion, there is evidence of it, as shown below. It is a healthy and welcome development; and there are other situations which might be candidates for future inclusion.

In *Boyer v. Warbey,*[11] the question arose whether covenants in a lease bound assignees, not only where the lease was by deed, but also where the lease was a valid written lease (not exceeding three years). The Court of Appeal held that, whatever the position before 1875, this was not an area where distinctions based on formalities were now acceptable, and that the covenant should bind. It was further suggested that the same result would follow if there was merely a contract for a lease which was enforceable in equity. Whether it was law or equity that regarded the lease as effective, the rule as to the running of covenants should be the same. In a limited sense this is "fusion" in that the reasons why a particular lease is effective are ignored in favour of a uniform consequential rule.

---

[4] Now called a claim form in the Civil Procedure Rules 1998.

[5] See *Felton v. Callis* [1969] 1 Q.B. 200; *Allied Arab Bank Ltd v. Hajjar* [1988] Q.B. 787.

[6] *Mathew v. T.M. Sutton Ltd* [1994] 1 W.L.R. 1455; *Westdeutsche Landesbank Girozentrale v. Islington London Borough Council* [1996] A.C. 669; *Clef Aquitaine SARL v. Laporte Materials (Barrow) Ltd* [2000] 3 W.L.R. 1760.

[7] See *Clarion Ltd v. National Provident Institution* [2000] 1 W.L.R. 1888 at 1898.

[8] See *Rhone v. Stephens* [1994] 2 A.C. 310, especially at 321.

[9] *Target Holdings Ltd v. Redferns (a firm)* [1996] 1 A.C. 421 at 438, *post,* p. 652, approving the views of McLachlin J. in *Canson Enterprises Ltd v. Boughton* (1991) 85 D.L.R. (4th) 129.

[10] (1977) 93 L.Q.R. 536 (P. Baker); (1994) 110 L.Q.R. 238 and (1997–98) 8 K.C.L.J. 1 (Sir Anthony Mason); [1994] Conv. 13 (J. Martin); (1995) 9 *Trust Law International* 35 at 37 (Sir Peter Millett).

[11] [1953] 1 Q.B. 234, especially at 245–247, *per* Denning and Romer L.JJ. See also *Australian Blue Metal Ltd v. Hughes* [1963] A.C. 74 at 101–102.

In *Tinsley v. Milligan*[12] the question was whether an equitable interest could be asserted in spite of an element of illegality in its acquisition. Lord Browne-Wilkinson explained that legal and equitable interests had different incidents for historical reasons, but that "fusion" resulted in the adoption of a single rule as to the circumstances in which the court would enforce interests acquired under an illegal transaction. Thus the rule is the same whether the claim is to a legal or equitable title, and can be fully stated without reference to its origins. In *Napier and Ettrick (Lord) v. Hunter*[13] the nature of an insurer's subrogation right was in issue. Lord Goff examined the origins of subrogation at law and in equity and concluded that "No doubt our task nowadays is to see the two strands of authority, at law and in equity, moulded into a coherent whole."[14] Similarly, it has been held that set-off, whether legal or equitable, can be raised as a defence whether the relief sought by the claimant is legal or equitable.[15] In the context of limitation periods, it has been held that there is no distinction between an action for fraud at common law and an action in equity for deliberate and dishonest breach of fiduciary duty based on the same facts, which is the equitable counterpart of the common law claim[16]: "It would have been a blot on our jurisprudence if those self-same facts gave rise to a time bar in the common law courts but none in the court of equity".[17]

Much of the modern development of the law of estoppel, especially promissory estoppel and proprietary estoppel, has been achieved without enquiring whether the doctrines are doctrines of equity, or of law or of both. The doctrine of promissory estoppel works negatively; to give protection to the party who relied on the promise, but not to give a new cause of action.[18] But proprietary estoppel operates positively[19] and is capable of creating new rights. Such rights are recognised in equity only, and, in unregistered land, cannot bind a bona fide purchaser of a legal estate for value without notice. Proprietary estoppel must be regarded as a development in equity. Other estoppels can be regarded as being based on common law or equity.[20]

---

[12] [1994] 1 A.C. 340 at 371, 375, 376.

[13] [1993] A.C. 713.

[14] *ibid.* at 743.

[15] *B.I.C.C. plc v. Burndy Corp.* [1985] Ch. 232; (1985) 101 L.Q.R. 145; *Eller v. Grovecrest Investments Ltd* [1995] Q.B. 272.

[16] *Coulthard v. Disco Mix Club Ltd* [2000] 1 W.L.R. 707.

[17] *ibid.* at 730. See also *Cia de Seguros Imperio v. Heath (REBX) Ltd* [2000] 1 W.L.R. 112.

[18] *Combe v. Combe* [1951] 2 K.B. 215, *post*, p. 893.

[19] *post*, p. 893.

[20] These distinctions are no longer drawn in Australia; *post*, p. 890. See, however, *First National Bank plc v. Thompson* [1996] Ch. 231, emphasising the common law origin of certain types of estoppel.

One indication of fusion is a situation where the legal remedy of damages may be given for breach of an equitable right. The converse, an equitable remedy for breach of a legal right, such as an injunction to restrain a tort, or specific performance of a contract, is explicable as the exercise of equity's concurrent jurisdiction and is not an example of fusion. However, the House of Lords went further in *Att.-Gen. v. Blake*,[21] holding that the equitable remedy of account of profits (which is traditionally associated with some fiduciary relationship) could be awarded in exceptional cases for breach of contract. This remedy, like injunctions and specific performance, could be awarded at the court's discretion where the remedy of damages, based on loss, would be inadequate. Although no direct authority could be found, it was considered a modest step which did not contradict any recognised principle on the grant or withholding of the remedy of account. As Lord Nicholls observed, remedies are the law's response to a wrong. The different remedial responses of the common law and equity arose as "an accident of history".[22]

Prior to the Judicature Act, Lord Cairns' Act authorised, in certain circumstances, courts of common law to grant specific performance or an injunction instead of damages, and courts of equity to award damages. As will be seen, this Act, although overtaken by the Judicature Act, still has scope for operation.[23] Generally, however, the breach of an equitable right will provide an equitable remedy only. Thus, a breach of a restrictive covenant by a non-contracting party is remedied by an injunction, not damages; innocent misrepresentation, apart from the Misrepresentation Act 1967, by rescission and not damages; and breach of trust[24] or other fiduciary duty by various equitable remedies. The stages has not yet been reached at which it is immaterial whether a breach is of a legal or equitable duty. This situation was approached in *Seager v. Copydex Ltd*,[25] where the defendants had used a technical idea communicated to them in confidence by the claimant in marketing a carpet grip. Equity's remedies in such cases are an injunction and an account of profits. But the circumstances of this case suggested that the most just solution was an assessment of damages. Can an action for common law damages lie, however, for a breach of confidence, which is

---

[21] *Att.-Gen. v. Blake* [2000] 3 W.L.R. 625.

[22] *ibid.* at 634.

[23] *post*, p. 747.

[24] See *Metall und Rohstoff A.G. v. Donaldson Lufkin & Jenrette Inc.* [1990] 1 Q.B. 391 at 473 (common law damages not available).

[25] [1967] 1 W.L.R. 923, and *(No. 2)* [1969] 1 W.L.R. 809. Heydon, Gummow and Austin, *Cases and Materials on Equity and Trusts* (4th ed.), pp. 13 *et seq.*, treat this case as an example of "fusion fallacies," *i.e* cases where the results are explicable by the application of neither law nor equity, and could only result from a legislative change in substantive principles which is not found in the Judicature Act.

protected only in equity? The Court of Appeal held that the appropriate remedy must be granted; fictions of implied contracts or notional injunctions were not now necessary[26]; damages were thus ordered to be assessed.

Lord Goff has more recently said that damages are available for breach of confidence, despite the equitable nature of the wrong, "through a beneficent interpretation of the Chancery Amendment Act 1858 (Lord Cairns' Act)".[27] Commonwealth courts have gone further, regarding it as now settled that damages may be awarded for breach of confidence[28] or other fiduciary duty[29]: "equity and common law are now mingled or merged . . . a full range of remedies should be available as appropriate, no matter whether they originated in common law, equity or statute".[30] But the compensation in such cases has been classified not as common law damages, but as "equitable compensation".[31]

In *Swindle v. Harrison*[32] Hobhouse L.J. confirmed that common law damages were not available for breach of fiduciary duty. Evans L.J. explained that it was still necessary to take account of the distinction between common law and equity even after the Judicature Act reforms: "The reason is, of course, that the origins of both common law and equitable rules are always relevant to their scope, although we should endeavour now to identify the underlying common principles".[33] The issue in *MCC Proceeds Inc. v. Lehman Brothers International (Europe)*[34] was whether an equitable owner could sue for conversion. It was held that such an owner, who has no title at common law, could not bring such an action. That rule had not been altered by the Judicature Act, which was intended to achieve procedural improvements in the administration of law and equity and not to transform equitable interests into legal titles. Conversion was a common law action, and the common law recognised

---

[26] *i.e.* to enable damages to be granted in lieu under Lord Cairns' Act, *post*, p. 747. See *Seager v. Copydex Ltd, supra*, at 931–932. *cf. Nicrotherm Electrical Co. Ltd v. Percy* [1956] R.P.C. 272. See also *Fraser v. Thames Television Ltd* [1984] Q.B. 44, where damages were awarded for breach of confidence without any argument on this point; *Stephens v. Avery* [1988] Ch. 449; *Dowson & Mason Ltd v. Potter* [1986] 1 W.L.R. 1419. In employment cases, of course, use of confidential information may be a breach of contract sounding in damages.

[27] *Att.-Gen. v. Guardian Newspapers Ltd (No. 2)* [1990] 1 A.C. 109 at 286. See (1994) 14 L.S. 313 (D. Capper).

[28] *Catt v. Marac Australia Ltd* (1986) 9 N.S.W.L.R. 639; *Lac Minerals Ltd v. International Corona Resources Ltd* (1989) 61 D.L.R. (4th) 14; (1990) 106 L.Q.R. 207 (G. Hammond).

[29] *Day v. Mead* [1987] 2 N.Z.L.R. 443; (1989) 105 L.Q.R. 32 (M. McGregor Vennell); *New Zealand Land Development Co. Ltd v. Porter* [1992] 2 N.Z.L.R. 462.

[30] *Aquaculture Corporation v. New Zealand Green Mussel Co. Ltd* [1990] 3 N.Z.L.R. 299 at 301; (1991) 107 L.Q.R. 209 (J. Beatson).

[31] *Day v. Mead, supra.* See further (1998) 114 L.Q.R. 214 at 225 (Sir Peter Millett).

[32] [1997] 4 All E.R. 705 at 726.

[33] *ibid.* at 714.

[34] [1998] 4 All E.R. 675; [1998] 6 R.L.R. 150 (K. Barker).

only the title of the trustee: "It is of the character of legal remedies that they derive from legal rights. That is one reason why they are not discretionary and may impose strict liabilities upon innocent parties. Equitable rights are of a different character and are recognised by the grant of equitable remedies which too have a different character".[35] Thus it was impermissible to combine a strict legal remedy with a mere equitable right.

On the New Zealand approach, exemplary damages[36] or damages for mental distress[37] could be awarded for breach of equitable duties, and equitable compensation reduced for contributory negligence.[38] English courts have rejected the defence in cases of deceit and dishonest assistance in a breach of trust, unless the claimant has been "the author of his own misfortune".[39] As contributory negligence is not a defence at common law to intentional torts, it has been said that equity should be no less rigorous. Thus if the breach involves conscious disloyalty, the defendant is disabled from asserting that the claimant contributed to the loss by his own want of care, although there may come a point where the loss is too remote.[40] Whether a wider view on the applicability of contributory negligence or the availability of heads of damage such as mental distress is acceptable depends on whether the policy of the common law on which such concepts are based is the same policy as that on which equitable compensation is founded. This, it is submitted, is not necessarily so.[41] We should heed the warning of Stevenson J.: "I greatly fear that talk of fusing law and equity only results in confusing and confounding the law."[42]

Sufficient examples have been given to show that law and equity are not fused. What can be said is that a century of fused jurisdiction has seen the two systems working more closely together; each changing and developing and improving from contact with the other; and each willing to accept new ideas and developments, regardless of their origin. They are coming closer together. But they are not yet fused.

---

[35] [1998] 4 All E.R. 675 at 701.

[36] Differing views were expressed in the *Aquaculture* case, *supra*. See (1995) 69 A.L.J. 773 (P. McDermott); *X v. Att.-Gen.* [1997] 2 N.Z.L.R. 623.

[37] Accepted by Cooke P. in *Mouat v. Clark Boyce* [1992] 2 N.Z.L.R. 559 (not discussed on appeal at [1994] 1 A.C. 428).

[38] Also accepted by Cooke P. in *Mouat, supra*, and in (1995) 9 *Trust Law International* 35 at 38 (Sir Peter Millett). Differing views were expressed in *Canson Enterprises Ltd v. Boughton* (1991) 85 D.L.R. (4th) 129.

[39] *Corporacion Nacional del Cobre de Chile v. Sogemin Metals Ltd* [1997] 1 W.L.R. 1396.

[40] *Nationawide Building Society v. Various Solicitors (No. 3), The Times*, March 1, 1999. It was noted that the topic was highly contentious and academic opinion sharply divided.

[41] [1994] Conv. 13 at 21–22 (J. Martin); *cf. per* Cooke P. in *Mouat v. Clark Boyce, supra*, at 569. Differing views were expressed in *Canson Enterprises Ltd v. Boughton, supra*.

[42] *Canson Enterprises Ltd v. Boughton, supra*, at 165.

5. THE MAXIMS OF EQUITY

The maxims of equity embody the general principles which evolved in the Court of Chancery. They are not rules which must be rigorously applied in every case, but are more in the nature of general guidelines illustrating the way in which equitable jurisdiction is exercised. A few examples of their operation must suffice,[43] but they should be borne in mind when considering the various rules and doctrines of equity.

i. Equity will not suffer a wrong to be without a remedy. The principle behind this maxim is that equity will intervene to protect a right which, perhaps because of some technical defect, is not enforceable at law. It is not sufficient that the defendant may be guilty of some moral wrong: the claimant's right must be suitable for enforcement by the court. The classic example is the enforcement of trusts. The beneficiary had no remedy at common law if the trustee claimed the property for himself, as the trustee was the legal owner, but he could enforce his rights in equity. The maxim is also reflected in the area of equitable remedies, which may be granted where the defendant's wrong is one not recognised by the common law. In the field of injunctions, for example, the claimant may obtain a *quia timet* injunction to restrain a threatened wrong although he has no cause of action at law until the wrong is committed.[44]

ii. Equity follows the law. Clearly equity may not depart from statute law, nor does it refuse to follow common-law rules save in exceptional circumstances.[45] Thus equitable interests in land correspond with the legal estates and interests.[46] Similarly, the writ[47] *ne exeat regno*, applicable to equitable debts, will not be granted unless the conditions of the Debtors Act 1869, allowing arrest in the case of a legal debt, are satisfied.[48] Nor will equity depart from the common law rule that a third party cannot be made to perform a contract.[49]

iii. He who seeks equity must do equity. A claimant who seeks equitable relief must be prepared to act fairly towards the defendant. The operation of this principle can be seen where equity, in allowing rescission of a contract for mistake, puts the claimant on terms

[43] For a more detailed survey, see Snell, Chap. 3.
[44] *post*, p. 794.
[45] For the conflicts between the rules of law and equity, see *ante*, p. 15.
[46] Equity, however, recognised certain future interests which were not recognised at law. See Cheshire and Burn, p. 71.
[47] Now called a claim form in the Civil Procedure Rules 1998.
[48] *Felton v. Callis* [1969] 1 Q.B. 200.
[49] *Rhone v. Stephens* [1994] 2 A.C. 310 (positive covenant relating to land).

which appear to the court to be just and equitable.[50] A person seeking an injunction will not succeed if he is unable or unwilling to carry out his own future obligations.[51] This maxim is also the foundation of the doctrine of election.[52]

iv. He who comes to equity must come with clean hands.[53] This principle is closely related to the last one, save that the latter looks to the claimant's future conduct, while the "clean hands" principle looks to his previous conduct. Thus equity will not grant relief against forfeiture for breach of covenant where the breach in question was flagrant.[54] Examples abound in the field of equitable remedies: a tenant cannot get specific performance of a contract for a lease if he is already in breach of his obligations[55]; nor could a purchaser if he had taken advantage of the illiteracy of the vendor who was not separately advised[56]; so also in the case of injunctions,[57] but equitable relief will only be debarred on this ground if the claimant's blameworthy conduct has some connection with the relief sought. The court is not concerned with the claimant's general conduct. Thus in *Argyll (Duchess) v. Argyll (Duke)*,[58] the fact that the wife's adultery had led to the divorce proceedings was no ground for refusing her an injunction to restrain her husband from publishing confidential material. Nor will unclean hands debar a claim which does not involve reliance on one's own misconduct.[59] If both parties have "unclean hands," the court should consider only those of the applicant, and need not balance the misconduct of one against that of the other.[60]

v. Where the equities are equal the law prevails.

vi. Where the equities are equal the first in time prevails. These two related maxims, dealing with the priorities of competing interests, may be dealt with together. They provide the foundation for the doctrine of notice.[61] Thus a prior equitable interest in land

---

[50] See the terms imposed in *Solle v. Butcher* [1950] 1 K.B. 671 and *Grist v. Bailey* [1967] Ch. 532, *post*, p. 846. See also *Cheese v. Thomas* [1994] 1 W.L.R. 129 (undue influence).
[51] See *Chappell v. Times Newspapers Ltd* [1975] 1 W.L.R. 482, where employees failed to get an injunction to restrain their dismissal where they refused to undertake not to become involved in strikes.
[52] *Snell*, Chap. 32.
[53] [1990] Conv. 416 (P. Pettit).
[54] See *Shiloh Spinners Ltd v. Harding* [1973] A.C. 691.
[55] *Coatsworth v. Johnson* (1886) 54 L.T. 520.
[56] *Mountford v. Scott* [1975] Ch. 258.
[57] See *Hubbard v. Vosper* [1972] 2 Q.B. 84.
[58] [1967] Ch. 302.
[59] *Tinsley v. Milligan* [1994] 1 A.C. 340; *post*, p. 260.
[60] *Sang Lee Investment Co. Ltd v. Wing Kwai Investment Co. Ltd, The Times*, April 14, 1983.
[61] *post*, p. 34.

can only be defeated by a bona fide purchaser of a legal estate without notice. If the purchaser is bona fide and without notice, then the equities are equal and his legal estate prevails. If he took with notice the position is otherwise, as the equities are not equal. If he does not acquire a legal estate then the first in time, *i.e.* the prior equitable interest, prevails, as equitable interests rank in order of creation. The two maxims have lost some of their importance since the introduction in 1925 of the system of registration of certain interests in land and by the introduction of registered title.[62]

vii. Equity imputes an intention to fulfil an obligation. Where a person is obliged to do some act, and does some other act which could be regarded as a performance of it, then it will be so regarded in equity. This is the basis of the doctrines of performance and satisfaction.[63] For example, if a debtor leaves a legacy to his creditor (of an amount at least as great as the debt), this is presumed to be a repayment of the debt so that, unless the presumption is rebutted, the creditor cannot take the legacy and sue to recover the debt.

viii. Equity regards as done that which ought to be done. Where there is a specifically enforceable obligation equity regards the parties as already in the position which they would be in after performance of the obligation. Therefore in equity a specifically enforceable contract for a lease creates an equitable lease. This is the doctrine of *Walsh v. Lonsdale.*[64] Similarly, a specifically enforceable contract for the sale of land transfers the equitable interest to the purchaser, the vendor holding the legal title on constructive trust until completion.[65] The maxim is also the basis of the doctrine of conversion,[66] and the rule in *Howe v. Dartmouth,*[67] concerning the duty to sell unauthorised investments. The maxim has recently been invoked by the Privy Council and House of Lords. In *Att.-Gen. for Hong Kong v. Reid*[68] the issue was whether a fiduciary who took a bribe became constructive trustee of it or was merely personally accountable. Because he was under a duty to hand over the bribe to his principal, it was held that the property belonged to the principal in equity. The difficulty in this is that an obligation to pay money is

---

[62] *post*, p. 37.
[63] *Snell*, Chap. 34.
[64] (1882) 21 Ch.D. 9, *ante* p. 15. A contract relating to land must be in writing; Law of Property (Miscellaneous Provisions) Act 1989.
[65] *post*, p. 326. See also *Davis v. Richards & Wallington Industries Ltd* [1990] 1 W.L.R. 1511 (obligation to execute pension trust deed).
[66] *Snell*, Chap. 30.
[67] (1802) 7 Ves. 137, *post*, Chap. 19.
[68] [1994] 1 A.C. 324 (P.C.); *post*, p. 625.

not normally specifically enforceable.[69] Similarly, in *Napier and Ettrick (Lord) v. Hunter*[70] it was considered that the duty of an insured person to hand over any damages from the wrongdoer to the insurer was specifically enforceable, so that the insurer had immediate proprietary rights in the form of a lien over the money.

ix. Equity is equality. Where two or more persons are entitled to an interest in the same property, then the principle of equity is equal division, if there is no good reason for any other basis for division.[71] Equity, therefore, dislikes the joint tenancy where, by the doctrine of survivorship, the last survivor takes all. This may be contrasted with the tenancy in common, where the interest of each party devolves upon his personal representative on his death. In the absence of an express declaration to the effect that the equitable interest is held jointly, equity presumes a tenancy in common in certain cases where at law the parties are joint tenants: for example, where the purchase money has been provided in unequal shares, equity presumes a tenancy in common in shares proportionate to the contributions. Even where the equitable interest is held jointly, equity leans in favour of severance, meaning that equity is ready to regard an act or dealing as an act of severance, whereby the equitable interest is converted to a tenancy in common, thus excluding the possibility of survivorship.[72]

x. Equity looks to the intent rather than the form. This principle does not mean that formalities may be ignored in equity, but rather that equity looks at the substance rather than the form. Thus equity will regard a transaction as a mortgage even though it is not so described, if in substance it appears that the property was transferred by way of security. Similarly a trust may be created although the word "trust" has not been used.[73] A covenant will be regarded as a restrictive covenant if negative in substance even if it is worded in a positive form.[74] Although a party to a covenant can enforce the contract at law even though no consideration has been given, equity regards such a party as a volunteer and will not order specific performance in his favour.[75]

---

[69] [1994] 2 R.L.R. 57 (D. Crilley); (1994) 53 C.L.J. 31 (A. Oakley); (1994) 110 L.Q.R. 178 (P. Watts); All E.R.Rev. 1994 pp. 252 (P. Clarke) and 365 (W. Swadling); (1995) 54 C.L.J. 60 (S. Gardner); (1995) 58 M.L.R. 87 (T. Allen).

[70] [1993] A.C. 713.

[71] For a recent example, see *Rowe v. Prance* [1999] 2 F.L.R. 787 (yacht).

[72] See *Burgess v. Rawnsley* [1975] Ch. 429.

[73] *post*, p. 95.

[74] *Tulk v. Moxhay* (1848) 18 L.J.Ch. 83 (covenant "to keep uncovered by buildings" held negative).

[75] *Cannon v. Hartley* [1949] Ch. 213.

xi. Delay defeats equities. Equity aids the vigilant and not the indolent. This is the foundation of the doctrine of laches, whereby a party who has delayed cannot obtain equitable relief. This doctrine is superseded where the Limitation Act 1980 deals with the matter.[76] For example, actions against trustees for breach of trust must, by section 21, be brought within six years, and delay short of this will not bar relief. Where, however, the claimant has a legal right, for example, upon a contract, delay may prevent the grant of an equitable remedy such as specific performance even though the legal right is not statute-barred.[77] Interlocutory injunctions must always be sought promptly, but it seems that delay may not prevent the grant of a final injunction where the cause of action is not statute-barred.[78]

The doctrine of laches continues to apply to those equitable claims which are outside the Limitation Act 1980, for example a claim to set aside a purchase of trust property by a trustee.[79] Similarly, claims to rescission and rectification may be barred by delay.[80]

xii. Equity acts *in personam*. Equity has jurisdiction over the defendant personally. The personal nature of the jurisdiction is illustrated by the fact that failure to comply with an order, such as specific performance or an injunction, is a contempt of court punishable by imprisonment. Provided that the defendant is within the jurisdiction (or can be served outside it), it is no objection that the property which is the subject-matter of the dispute is outside it. Thus in the leading case of *Penn v. Lord Baltimore*,[81] specific performance was ordered of an agreement relating to land boundaries in Pennsylvania and Maryland, the defendant being in this country.

6. EQUITABLE REMEDIES

At common law, the normal form of relief is an award of damages, to which a claimant who has proved his case is entitled as of right. One of the greatest contributions of equity has been to supplement the limited range of legal remedies by introducing wide range of

---

[76] Either expressly or by analogy; *post*, p. 674.
[77] *post*, p. 741. See Limitation Act 1980, s.36(1).
[78] *Fullwood v. Fullwood* (1878) 9 Ch.D. 176; *H. P. Bulmer Ltd & Showerings Ltd v. J. Bollinger S.A.* [1977] 2 C.M.L.R. 625, *post*, p. 797.
[79] *post*, p. 674.
[80] *post*, pp. 865, 873.
[81] (1750) 1 Ves.Sen. 444, *post* p. 716; *Hamlin v. Hamlin* [1986] Fam. 11; *Webb v. Webb* [1994] Q.B. 696; *ante*, p. 18. See also Civil Jurisdiction and Judgments Act 1982, s.30(1).

equitable remedies,[82] which can be awarded both to enforce rights which are exclusively equitable and those which are legal. Their common features are that they are discretionary, their availability depends upon the inadequacy of common law remedies (which, in the case of exclusively equitable rights, will not be available at all) and they are governed by the doctrine that equity acts *in personam*.

The most significant of these remedies are specific performance, whereby the court orders a party to a contract to perform his contractual obligations, and an injunction, whereby the court orders a person to do, or, more commonly, to refrain from doing, some particular act. These, plus the remedies of rescission and rectification of contracts, will be examined in Part IV. Other equitable remedies include delivery up and cancellation of documents,[83] account[84] and receivers.[85] Mention might also be made of certain procedural remedies, equitable in origin, which have now been incorporated into the general rules of litigation. Examples include disclosure of documents[86] and suits for the perpetuation of testimony.[87] Equity's jurisdiction to award compound interest is not, however, regarded as an equitable remedy in the sense of being exercisable in aid of common law remedies.[88]

The ancient prerogative writ *ne exeat regno*,[89] later adapted by equity, has recently enjoyed something of a revival. It prevents the defendant from leaving the jurisdiction before final judgment, its purpose being to coerce him to give security for an equitable debt, on pain of arrest. The stringent conditions for its grant were laid down in *Felton v. Callis*,[90] but more recent cases have tended to relax them,[91] perhaps unjustifiably.[92] The conditions may also be sidestepped by the grant of an interlocutory injunction against leaving the jurisdiction.[93]

---

[82] See generally Meagher, Gummow and Lehane, *Equity—Doctrines and Remedies*; Heydon, Gummow and Austin, *Cases and Materials on Equity and Trusts*; Spry, *Equitable Remedies*, Chap. 1.

[83] Snell, Chap. 42.

[84] Snell, Chap. 44. See *Att.-Gen. v. Blake* [2000] 3 W.L.R. 625.

[85] Snell, Chap. 46.

[86] C.P.R. r. 31; Snell, p. 28.

[87] C.P.R. r. 34.8; Pettit, pp. 672–673.

[88] *Westdeutsche Landesbank Girozentrale v. Islington London Borough Council* [1996] A.C. 669 (Lords Goff and Woolf dissenting).

[89] For its history, see *Allied Arab Bank Ltd v. Hajjar* [1988] Q.B. 787.

[90] [1969] 1 Q.B. 200.

[91] *Lipkin Gorman v. Cass, The Times*, May 29, 1985; *Al Nahkel for Contracting and Trading Ltd v. Lowe* [1986] Q.B. 235; cf. *Allied Arab Bank Ltd v. Hajjar, supra*. See also *Thaha v. Thaha* (1987) 17 Fam.Law 234; *Re Jeffrey S. Levitt Ltd* [1992] Ch. 457.

[92] See (1986) 45 C.L.J. 189 (C. Harpum); (1987) 103 L.Q.R. 246 (L. Anderson); (1988) 47 C.L.J. 364 (N. Andrews); (1990) 20 U.W.A.L.R. 143 at 160 (J. Martin); *B. v. B. (injunction: jurisdiction)* [1998] 1 W.L.R. 329.

[93] *post*, p. 769.

The remedy of the declaration had some connection with equity in origin,[94] but the jurisdiction to grant it is now governed wholly by statute.[95] Finally, although not remedies in the traditional sense, the constructive trust and the doctrine of tracing are sometimes so described. These will be examined elsewhere.[96]

The differing character of equitable remedies must be appreciated. First, it is obvious that factors such as fraud, misrepresentation and mistake are relevant to the exercise of a discretionary jurisdiction to issue injunctions and orders of specific performance. Here, the question is ordinarily one of the manner in which an already existing legal or equitable right is enforced.[97] The right itself is not affected. Thus if equity refuses to order specific performance of a contract due to a defendant's mistake, the claimant's right to sue for damages still subsists[98]: it is merely that a supplementary method of enforcement is denied. But secondly, other equitable remedies are larger in their effect; if equity rescinds a deed or a contract, a right to sue on that contract or deed ceases to be available at law. Equity will exercise this jurisdiction on grounds on which law takes no similar action, for instance, in cases of constructive fraud or wholly innocent misrepresentations, so that the equitable remedy affects the substance of a claimant's rights, and not merely the manner of their enforcement. This is also true when the equitable remedy of rectification is called into operation, a remedy by which a term of a document is varied so as to make it accord with the parties' real intentions. Thirdly, it should be noted that an equitable remedy may fulfil a task intermediate between the situations so far considered, the task of enabling a claimant to take full advantage of a right at common law. A claimant may, for instance, have a right at common law to rescind a contract for fraud, but may be at common law unable to exercise that right[99] because a precise *restitutio in integrum* is not possible. Equity has a wider discretion to rescind in such a case by devising a fair, if not a precise, return of the parties to something approaching their original positions.[1]

As we shall see, it is in the field of remedies that equity displays perhaps the greatest inventiveness and capacity for development, providing relief in new situations as they arise.[2]

[94] See de Smith, Woolf and Jowell, *Judicial Review of Administrative Action*, (5th ed.), pp. 642–644.
[95] *Tito v. Waddell (No. 2)* [1977] Ch. 106 at 259 (Megarry V.-C). See also *Chapman v. Michaelson* [1909] 1 Ch. 238.
[96] *post*, pp. 301, 675.
[97] *post*, pp. 738, 796.
[98] *Wood v. Scarth* (1855) 2 K. & J. 33 (in equity); (1858) 1 F. & F. 293 (at law); *Webster v. Cecil* (1861) 30 Beav. 62; *Johnson v. Agnew* [1980] A.C. 367, *post*, p. 719.
[99] And would be confined to an action for damages.
[1] *Spence v. Crawford* [1939] 3 All E.R. 271; a decision showing that equity may be more willing to do so in cases of actual fraud than in others.
[2] See particularly search orders and freezing injunctions, *post*, pp. 831, 837.

7. The Bona Fide Purchaser of the Legal Estate for Value Without Notice

As we have seen, the use was enforceable against the feoffee to uses because the feoffee's conscience was bound by the undertaking which he had given to hold the property to the use and benefit of the *cestui que use*. Similarly with a trustee and beneficiary. So long as the same person remained trustee, this theory works quite simply. But if the legal estate passes from him to another person, how is the conscience of the transferee affected? The question is then one of determining, as a matter of policy, whether this new holder of the legal estates is to be bound by the trust.[3] Any way in which the equitable ownership of a beneficiary is destroyed is of course a serious weakening of the position of the beneficiary; and equity strives always to protect him.[4]

Thus, a trust is binding on a person to whom the trustee gave the property[5]; or a mere occupier[6] or adverse possessor,[7] and also on a purchaser who bought it if he knew or could by reasonable inquiries have found out about the existence of the trust.[8] In short, the trust is binding on everyone coming to the land except the bona fide purchaser of a legal estate for value without notice actual, constructive or imputed.[9]

The doctrine applies to land and personalty. As far as land is concerned, its importance has diminished now that the system of registration of title applies throughout England and Wales. Under this system the doctrine of notice has no application.[10] But much unregistered land remains, because there is no duty to register the title until a transaction after the area has become one of compulsory registration of title.[11] Even with unregistered land, the doctrine of notice was largely replaced, as will be seen, by the Land Charges Act 1925 (now the Act of 1972). In the account which follows, it should thus be borne in mind that in the case of registered land, the traditional doctrine applies only to transactions occurring before the

---

[3] Maitland, pp. 111 *et seq.* See also [1997] Conv. 431 (J. Howell).

[4] *ibid.* at 220.

[5] *Re Diplock* [1948] Ch. 465, at 544–545.

[6] *Mander v. Falcke* [1891] 2 Ch. 554.

[7] *Re Nisbet and Pott's Contract* [1906] 1 Ch. 386; affirming [1905] 1 Ch. 391.

[8] *Pilcher v. Rawlins* (1872) L.R. 7 Ch.App. 250.

[9] Such a purchaser can pass his good title to a purchaser with notice under the rule in *Wilkes v. Spooner* [1911] 2 K.B. 473.

[10] Minor interests protected on the register and overriding interests (L.R.A. 1925, s.70(1)) are binding on a purchaser of registered land, regardless of notice, and whether legal or equitable.

[11] L.R.A. 1925, s.123. The occasions for registration have been increased; Land Registration Act 1997 (mortgages, gifts and assents on death included).

title was registered, although some aspects of the doctrine have wider application.[12]

A. Purchaser for Value

The purchaser must have given consideration in money, or money's worth,[13] or the consideration of marriage.[14] Otherwise he is a donee, and bound by the trust regardless of notice. A purchaser includes a mortgagee[15] or lessee.

B. Legal Estate

This doctrine is based on the maxim that when the equities are equal the law prevails. In the case of a purchase of a legal estate for value without notice, the equities are equal between the purchaser and the beneficiaries; the purchaser's legal estate is allowed to prevail.

The position is different where the purchaser is a purchaser of an *equitable* interest only. The competition then is between two equitable interests; and the rule here is that the first in time prevails.[16] By way of exception, a purchaser of an equitable interest can defeat prior "mere equities", such as rights to rectification or to set aside a conveyance.[17] It seems that a bona fide purchaser of an equitable interest in the land for value without notice will take free of mere equities,[18] and, *a fortiori*, a purchaser of a legal estate.[19]

C. Notice

i. Meaning of Notice. Apart from legislation[20] a purchaser is taken to have notice of an equitable interest unless he can show that "he took all reasonable care and made inquiries, and that, having taken that care and made inquiry, he received no notice of the trust which affected the property".[21] He must show that he had no notice actual, constructive or imputed.

---

[12] *post*, p. 39.

[13] *Thorndike v. Hunt* (1859) 3 De G. & J. 563. Nominal consideration does not suffice; *Nurdin & Peacock plc v. D. B. Ramsden & Co. Ltd* [1999] 1 E.G.L.R. 119.

[14] *i.e.* a future marriage. An ante-nuptial settlement is deemed to be made for value in respect of the spouses and the issue of the marriage, *post*, p. 130.

[15] *Kingsnorth Finance Co. v. Tizard* [1986] 1 W.L.R. 783; see L.P.A. 1925, s.205(xxi).

[16] *Phillips v. Phillips* (1862) 4 De G. F. & J. 208 at 218; *Re Morgan* (1881) 18 Ch.D. 93; *McCarthy and Stone Ltd v. Hodge & Co.* [1971] 1 W.L.R. 1547.

[17] *Shiloh Spinners Ltd v. Harding* [1973] A.C. at 721. See, however, *Collings v. Lee, The Times*, October 26, 2000 (where transaction procured by fraudulent misrepresentation transferor retains full equitable interest and not a "mere equity" to set aside).

[18] *National Provincial Bank Ltd v. Ainsworth* [1965] A.C. 1175 at 1238; *Phillips v. Phillips, supra.*

[19] *Smith v. Jones* [1954] 1 W.L.R. 1089.

[20] Especiallly L.C.A. 1972, *post*, p. 37.

[21] *per* Fry J. in *Re Morgan* (1881) 18 Ch.D. 93 at 102.

Actual notice is the simple case where the purchaser subjectively knew of the equitable interest. Constructive notice exists where knowledge of the equitable interest would have come to him if he had made all such inquiries as a prudent purchaser would have made. Imputed notice covers actual or constructive notice to his agent who was acting as such in the transaction in question.[22]

ii. Duty to Make Inquiries. The inquiries which should be made will depend on the type of property in question. A purchaser, however, should always inspect the premises, and has notice of the interest of a person in occupation of the property.[23]

(a) *Land.* With the unregistered title system, a vendor satisfied a purchaser of his ownership of the land by producing title deeds which traced the history of the ownership of the land. The title had to start with a good root of title[24] at least 15 years old.[25] A prudent purchaser would examine that document and every one subsequent to it; he would normally be held to have constructive notice of every equitable interest which appeared on the title,[26] but not of those disclosed by earlier deeds with which he was not concerned. If he agreed to accept a title which began later than the statutory period of 15 years, he did so at his own risk, and would be bound by equitable interests disclosed by documents which were within the statutory period but prior to the agreed date.[27] There was an exception where there were in fact deeds which disclosed an equitable interest, but the vendor was able to produce an apparently perfect title after suppressing some of them.[28]

A person intending to enter into a lease is not entitled to examine the title of the lessor (the freeholder),[29] and does not have constructive notice of equitable interests which he would have discovered if he had examined it.[30] The lessee is however bound by land charges which are registered under the Land Charges Act.[31]

(b) *Personalty.* The doctrine of notice in the strict conveyancing sense does not apply to personalty, because there is no duty on the

---

[22] L.P.A. 1925, s.199.

[23] *Barnhart v. Greenshields* (1853) 9 Moo.P.C. 18; *Hunt v. Luck* [1902] 1 Ch. 428; *Kingsnorth Finance Co. Ltd v. Tizard* [1986] 1 W.L.R. 783; *cf. Bristol and West Building Society v. Henning* [1985] 1 W.L.R. 778.

[24] *i.e.* "a document which describes the land sufficiently to identify it, which shows a disposition of the whole legal and equitable interest contracted to be sold, and which contains nothing to throw any doubt on the title"; M. & W., p. 692.

[25] L.P.A. 1969, s.23.

[26] *Carter v. Carter* (1857) 3 K. & J. 617.

[27] *Re Nisbet and Pott's Contract* [1906] 1 Ch. 386; affirming [1905] 1 Ch. 391.

[28] *Pilcher v. Rawlins* (1872) L.R. 7 Ch.App. 259.

[29] L.P.A. 1925, s.44(3).

[30] *ibid.*

[31] *White v. Bijou Mansions* [1937] Ch. 610 at 619.

purchaser to examine the seller's title; and usually there are no documents of title.[32] A purchaser of shares is not required to inquire about beneficial ownership, nor may notice of any trust affecting the shares be entered on the company's register of shareholders. However, where some equitable interest or charge is disclosed to a purchaser of personalty or presents itself to his notice, he will be bound by it if it is not satisfied out of the purchase money.[33] The doctrine of constructive notice applies even to commercial dealings with personalty, where the facts known to the purchaser make it imperative to seek an explanation, without which it is obvious that the transaction is probably improper.[34]

iii. Registration. The Land Charges Act 1925 introduced a system of registration of various interests in unregistered land.[35] Local land charges are dealt with in the Local Land Charges Act 1975. Most of the registrable interests are equitable, but a legal mortgage where the mortgagee does not take possession of the title deeds is included,[36] and one is a statutory creation.[37] Registration is deemed to be actual notice to all persons so long as the registration remains in force[38] whereas failure to register makes the charge void against a purchaser.[39]

It will be seen that this enactment has vitally affected the old doctrine of notice. A purchaser is deemed to have notice of a charge if it is registered. If the charge is not registered, it has been held that he takes free even if he actually knows about it,[40] or if the interest in question is that of a person who is in actual occupation of the land,[41] and the House of Lords has held that the court cannot enquire into the good faith of the purchaser, nor into the adequacy of the consideration paid by him.[42]

---

[32] See Factors Act 1889, s.1(4). The registration book of a car is not a document of title: *Joblin v. Watkins and Roseveare (Motors) Ltd* [1949] 1 All E.R. 47.

[33] *Nelson v. Larholt* [1948] 1 K.B. 339.

[34] *Macmillan Inc. v. Bishopsgate Investment Trust plc (No. 3)* [1995] 1 W.L.R. 978 at 1014 (shares); affirmed [1996] 1 W.L.R. 387. See also the sequel, *MCC Proceeds Inc. v. Lehman Brothers International (Europe)* [1998] 4 All E.R. 675; *ante*, p. 25.

[35] L.C.A. 1972 does not apply to registered land; but all the interests contained in it can be protected by notice or caution under L.R.A. 1925.

[36] L.C.A. 1972, s.2(4) Class C(i).

[37] Class F. See Family Law Act 1996, re-enacting Matrimonial Homes Act 1983.

[38] L.P.A. 1925, s.198(1).

[39] L.C.A. 1972, s.4; L.P.A. 1925, s.199(1)(i).

[40] *Hollington Brothers v. Rhodes* [1951] 2 All E.R. 578n.

[41] *Smith v. Jones* [1954] 1 W.L.R. 1089; *Lloyd's Bank plc v. Carrick* [1996] 4 All E.R. 630.

[42] *Midland Bank Trust Co. Ltd v. Green* [1981] A.C. 513; (1981) 97 L.Q.R. 518 (B. Green); (1981) 40 C.L.J. 213 (C. Harpum); [1981] Conv. 361 (H. Johnson); (son, holding unregisterd option to purchase valuable land granted by father, not protected when father sold to mother for £500).

D. Overreaching

More important for our present purposes than the Land Charges
Act 1972 are the equitable interests enjoyed by beneficial owners
under trusts of land. Under the Law of Property Act 1925, s.1(1), the
only legal estates which can exist in land after 1925 are the fee
simple absolute in possession and the term of years absolute. Thus,
in every case in which the beneficial ownership of land is split into
successive interests (other than leases), the interests are equitable.

The 1925 legislation provided that all successive beneficial interests in land must be held either behind a trust for sale or under a
strict settlement under the Settled Land Act 1925. Under Part I of
the Trusts of Land and Appointment of Trustees Act 1996, this dual
system is replaced by the single system of the "trust of land".
Although existing strict settlements are unaffected,[43] no new ones
may be created. The 1996 Act applies to other trusts of land, whenever created. The "trust of land" now embraces situations (primarily
co-ownership and intestacy) where statutory trusts for sale were
imposed before the 1996 Act, expressly created trusts for sale, and
bare trusts of land (where the land is held for an adult beneficiary
absolutely entitled).[44] The legal estate is vested in trustees, who
have a power of sale. When the land is sold by the trustees (or by the
tenant for life of an existing strict settlement, in whom the legal
estate is vested), the purchaser takes free from the beneficial interests, which are transferred to the proceeds of sale.[45] Thus the beneficiaries have interests in the proceeds which are equivalent to those
which they had in the land. This is so whether the title is registered
or unregistered.

This process of transfer of beneficial interests from the land to the
purchase money is called "overreaching." Provided that any capital
money which is payable is paid to at least two trustees, the purchaser
takes free of the beneficial interests even if he knew of them. There
is no room for the application of the doctrine that occupation by the
beneficiaries gives constructive notice to the purchaser.[46] Nor, in
unregistered land, is there any machinery for the registration of such
interests. It has been held that overreaching applies also to interests
arising under the doctrine of proprietary estoppel.[47]

Where, however, the purchase money is paid to a sole trustee (for
example, a husband who is sole legal owner of a house in which his

---

[43] Save that no land held on charitable trusts may be settled land; s.2(5).
[44] s.1(1), (2).
[45] L.P.A. 1925, s.2(1), as amended by the 1996 Act.
[46] *City of London Building Society v. Flegg* [1988] A.C. 54. Overreaching can occur even if
no capital money is payable at the time of the conveyance; *State Bank of India v. Sood*
[1997] Ch. 276 (mortgage to secure existing and future debts); [1997] Conv. 134 (M.
Thompson); (1997) 56 C.L.J. 494 (M. Oldham); [1998] Conv. 168 at 182 (G. Ferris and G.
Battersby).
[47] *Birmingham Midshires Mortgage Services Ltd v. Sabherwal* (2000) 80 P. & C.R. 256.

wife has a share in equity), the doctrine of overreaching cannot apply. In such a case the doctrine of notice remains applicable in unregistered land, so that occupation by the wife is likely to give constructive notice to a purchaser or mortgagee.[48] In the case of an acquisition mortgage, however, where the legal owner could not have bought the property without the mortgage loan, it has been held that a person claiming an equitable interest has no rights against the mortgagee but only against the legal owner, even if in occupation.[49]

The doctrine of notice in its conveyancing sense therefore applies only in the cases of equitable interests in unregistered land which are neither registrable nor overreachable, such as a restrictive covenant entered into before 1926 and a few other examples.[50] The cases seem "to show that there may well be rights, of an equitable character outside the provisions as to registration and which are incapable of being overreached."[51]

It is important to appreciate, however, that the doctrine of notice still operates in the context of beneficial interests under a trust of unregistered land where the doctrine of overreaching cannot apply because there is only one trustee.[52] Although such interests cannot be registered, a wife's statutory right to occupy the matrimonial home is registrable.[53] This, however, has no effect on the enforceability of any equitable interest she may have.

E. Other Applications of the Doctrine of Notice

We have seen that the traditional doctrine is now restricted in its application. The doctrine in its wider form, however, remains significant. As discussed above, it can apply even to commercial dealings with personalty.[54] The defence of purchaser without notice operates in the context of personal claims arising from the receipt of trust property transferred in breach of trust and of proprietary tracing claims, as will be explained in Chapters 12 and 23 respectively.

The House of Lords applied the doctrine in its wider sense in *Barclays Bank plc v. O'Brien*,[55] where the question was whether a

---

[48] *Kingsnorth Finance Co. Ltd v. Tizard* [1986] 1 W.L.R. 783; *cf. Bristol and West Building Society v. Henning* [1985] 1 W.L.R. 778; *Abbey National Building Society v. Cann* [1991] 1 A.C. 56; *Equity & Law Home Loans Ltd v. Prestidge* [1992] 1 W.L.R. 137. (Equitable owner who acquiesced in or impliedly authorised mortgage by legal owner deemed to intend to cede priority to mortgagee).

[49] *Abbey National Building Society v. Cann, supra.*

[50] *Poster v. Slough Estates Ltd* [1968] 1 W.L.R. 1518 (right to enter to remove fixtures); *Shiloh Spinners Ltd v. Harding* [1973] A.C. 691 (equitable right of entry).

[51] *per* Lord Wilberforce in *Shiloh Spinners v. Harding* [1973] A.C. 691 at 721.

[52] *ante*, p. 38.

[53] Land Charges Act 1972, s.2(7) (Class F).

[54] *ante*, p. 37.

[55] [1994] 1 A.C. 180; *post*, p. 859.

wife could set aside a mortgage or guarantee entered into with the bank as a result of her husband's misrepresentation or undue influence. This was not the traditional doctrine because there was only one transaction. The issue was not whether the bank could take free of a prior interest but whether enforcement of the transaction by the bank would be taking advantage of the husband's equitable fraud.[56] The solution lay in the doctrine of constructive notice, whether the land had a registered or unregistered title. This was "not the same 'doctrine of notice' so beloved of property lawyers and now largely replaced by registration of title."[57] Thus the doctrine has a role to play beyond the confines of unregistered land. Indeed, it "lies at the heart of equity."[58]

8. THE SUBJECT-MATTER OF EQUITY

In this Introduction, it has only been possible to mention certain heads of equitable jurisdiction as they became relevant, and it may be helpful to the understanding of equity to list the subjects which should properly be included within it. No list can be exhaustive. Certain matters however are assigned to the Chancery Division by the Supreme Court Act 1981.[59] They are:

> The sale, exchange or partition of land, or the raising of charges on land;
>
> The redemption or foreclosure of mortgages[60];
>
> The execution of trusts;
>
> The administration of the estates of deceased persons;
>
> Bankruptcy;
>
> The dissolution of partnerships or the taking of partnership or other accounts;
>
> The rectification, setting aside or cancellation of deeds or other instruments in writing;
>
> Probate business, other than non-contentious or common form business;

---

[56] (1995) 15 L.S. 35 (G. Battersby).

[57] [1994] Conv. 421 at 423 (M. Dixon and C. Harpum). See also All E.R. Rev. 1993 p. 367 (W. Swadling); [1994] Conv. 140 (M. Thompson); (1994) 144 N.L.J. 765 (P. O'Hagan); [1995] Conv. 250 (P. Sparkes); (1995) 54 C.L.J. 280 (A. Lawson) and 536 (J. Mee); [1996] Conv. 34 (J. Howell).

[58] *Barclays Bank plc v. O'Brien, supra,* at 195 (Lord Browne-Wilkinson).

[59] s.61 and Sched. 1.

[60] See also R.S.C. Ord. 88, r. 2 (C.P.R. 1998, Sched. 1).

Patents, trade marks, registered designs or copyright;

The appointment of a guardian of a child's estate[61];

All causes and matters involving the exercise of the High Court's jurisdiction under the enactments relating to companies.

All divisions of the High Court, however, exercise co-ordinate jurisdiction. Where a matter arises which has not been assigned to one division, it should go to whichever division is the more appropriate and convenient; in many cases the claimant's counsel will be able to choose. If the action is brought in the wrong division, it may be retained or transferred at the discretion of the judge.[62]

9. THE TRUST IN MODERN LAW[63]

Trusts are primarily about money and the preservation of wealth. The idea of the trust developed as a means for providing for the family. Although the trust still plays a significant role in establishing ownership of property on family breakdown,[64] it "can no longer be doubted that equity has moved out of the family home and the settled estate and into the market-place".[65] A major area of activity is in the holding of the property of charities and other non-profit making bodies. A modern and significant role has emerged for the trust in the constitution of pension funds,[66] although such trusts differ from traditional trusts in so far as there is a contractual relationship of employment and the beneficiaries have given consideration.[67] Unit trusts and investment trusts[68] are designed to spread investment risks. Thus the trust continues to be a form of property-holding of ever-increasing importance because of its adaptability and convenience in effecting complicated forms of settlement. Indeed, "as the principles of equity permeate the complications of modern life, the nature and variety of trusts ever grow."[69]

---

[61] This work was transferred from the Chancery Division to the Family Division by the Adminsitration of Justice Act 1970. Now see Supreme Court Act 1981, Sched. 1, para. 3.

[62] Supreme Court Act 1981, ss.61(6), 65.

[63] See (1990) 106 L.Q.R. 87 (D. Hayton); (1994) 110 L.Q.R. 238 (Sir Anthony Mason); (1996) 10 *Trust Law International* 38 (W. Goodhart).

[64] *post*, Chap. 11.

[65] (1995) 9 *Trust Law International* 35 at 36 (Sir Peter Millett); (1997–98) 8 K.C.L.J. 1 at 4 *et seq.* (Sir Anthony Mason).

[66] *post*. Chap. 16.

[67] *post*, p. 475.

[68] *post*, p. 534. For other commercial uses of trusts, see *Modern International Developments in Trust Law* (ed. D. Hayton), Chap. 8.

[69] *Re a Solicitor* [1952] Ch. 328 at 332, *per* Roxburgh J.

If a settlor wishes to give property to his wife for life and after her death to various other members of the family, it would be possible to arrange a system of law by which it could be done without using a trust. Indeed, the early common law did so, in an elementary form. Roman law did so[70]; as do those countries which have followed modernised systems of Roman law.[71]

In England, full use has been made of the convenience of the system whereby the legal estate is in the trustees and the equitable or beneficial ownership is kept separate. We have seen that this is insisted upon for the creation of successive or concurrent interests in land under the 1925 legislation.[72] The legal title can be kept clear of beneficial interests; the land can be sold free of them to a purchaser, who can overreach them. Thus a most elaborate system of beneficial interests can be created without complicating the title to the land.

The same advantages exist with personalty. Most modern settlements deal wholly or partly with personalty in the form of investments. No system of legal future interests in personalty ever developed; for settlements of personalty did not arise until the system of trusts was well advanced. In this sphere also, it is most convenient to separate legal and equitable ownership; by doing so, the trustees can buy and sell shares without the purchaser being concerned with the beneficial interests.[73] The beneficial interests attach to whatever is held by the trustees for the time being.

Those are the simple cases. Settlors may wish to create other forms of settlement.[74] With a gift for charitable purposes, for example, there is no beneficial owner; such a gift is effected by a special form of trust.[75] A settlor may wish to protect a beneficiary from his own extravagance by making it impossible for creditors to proceed against his limited interest; this is done by protective trust.[76] The settlor may wish to allow his trustees to determine from time to time how the capital and income shall be distributed among the beneficiaries; this is done by a discretionary trust.[77] He may wish to provide for someone, such as his lover, by will without identifying

---

[70] Buckland and McNair: *Roman Law and Common Law* (2nd ed.), pp. 173 *et seq.*

[71] See (1980) *Journal of Legal History*, p. 6 (B. Beinart); (1974) 48 Tulane L.Rev. 917 (J. Merryman).

[72] *ante*, p. 38. Similarly a trust is necessary where there is incapacity to hold a legal estate in land, as in the case of a child.

[73] No notice of any trust can be entered on the register of shareholders (Companies Act 1985, s.360).

[74] It should not be forgotten that the trust may also be created unintentionally. See Resulting and Constructive Trusts, *post*, Chaps. 10, 12.

[75] *Post*, Chap. 15. Also a gift for a non-human object, such as the maintenance of an animal or a tombstone; *post*, pp. 368 *et seq.*

[76] *post*, Chap. 7.

[77] *post*, Chap. 8.

her in that document; this is done by a secret trust.[78] Each sort of trust will be considered in its proper place. It will in each case be seen that the desired result could have been effected without the existence of a trust; but that the trust is a very satisfactory and convenient way of effecting it; and that this has become the only way in which it can now be effected in English law. In some cases, however, the trust has not afforded a solution, for example, in the case of gifts for abstract non-charitable purposes.[79] Theoretical difficulties have also been encountered with the property of unincorporated associations.[80] Finally, it should never be forgotten that there is one factor which dominates all others in the context of the creation of trusts in modern law: taxation. Although the law of equity and trusts can be understood without it, it will be appreciated that the popular forms of trust in recent years have been those which reduce to a minimum the liability to tax. The Chancery lawyer's job is to be able to advise on these matters and to create the most appropriate trusts to meet the wishes of the settlor.

10. THE CREATIVITY OF EQUITY

One question which has arisen is whether the category of equitable interests is closed, or whether new ones might be created.[81] One clear example is the restrictive covenant, which, since Lord Eldon's day, has evolved from a contractual right to an equitable interest enforceable against the covenantor's successors in title. Another possibility is the contractual licence, although the matter awaits clarification in the House of Lords.[82] One view is that the modern machinery for law reform should be relied upon in preference to judicial creativity.[83]

Bagnall J., in a case concerning matrimonial property, warned against unwarranted extensions of equitable jurisdiction in the following words:

---

[78] *post*, Chap. 5. A modern variation is the "blind trust". A politician may receive funding of which the source is not revealed, or may place his assets with trustees to be administered on the basis that he is not informed of investments made. By these means his political decisions are seen to be uninfluenced by personal interests. See further (1998) 3 *Amicus Curiae* 22 (P. Matthews).

[79] *post*, Chap. 14.

[80] *post*, p. 373.

[81] Eveleigh L.J. in *Pennine Raceway Ltd v. Kirklees Metropolitan Council* [1983] Q.B. 382 at 392, said, "There has been a considerable development in the law in relation to equitable interests and I do not think that it is right to regard the category as closed." But at 397, Stephenson L.J. preferred to express no view.

[82] *post*, p. 884. See *Ashburn Anstalt v. Arnold* [1989] Ch. 1.

[83] As in the case of the matrimonial homes legislation (now Family Law Act 1996), replacing Lord Denning's "deserted wife's equity."

"In any individual case the application of these propositions may produce a result which appears unfair. So be it; in my view that is not an injustice. I am convinced that in determining rights, particularly property rights, the only justice that can be obtained by mortals, who are fallible and are not omniscient, is justice according to law; the justice which flows from the application of sure and settled principles to proved or admitted facts. So in the field of equity, the length of the Chancellor's foot has been measured or is capable of measurement. This does not mean that equity is past childbearing; simply that its progeny must be legitimate—by precedent out of principle. It is well that this should be so; otherwise no lawyer could safely advise on his client's title and every quarrel would lead to a law suit."[84]

Throughout this book it will be seen that the principles of equity have constantly developed and found new fields of application.[85] The reader, when examining these developments, might consider whether the words of Bagnall J. have been heeded. A few examples must suffice here.

Many new developments have been seen in the field of injunctions, notably the evolution of search orders and freezing injunctions, designed respectively to prevent removal or destruction of evidence and to prevent the assets of the defendant from being dissipated.[86] Equity's excursions into the criminal law, however, have been restricted.[87]

The constructive trust has also proved to be a fertile field, assisting in the enforcement of contractual licences against third parties[88]; and allowing unprotected minor interests to be enforced against purchasers of registered land.[89] Constructive and resulting trusts have operated to give security to unsecured creditors[90]; and to determine the ownership of matrimonial and "quasi-matrimonial" property.[91] Here we have seen the "new model constructive trust," a term first used by Lord Denning M.R. in the case concerning the claim of a cohabitant to a share in the home, where he said, "Equity is not past the age of childbearing. One of her latest progeny is a

---

[84] *Cowcher v. Cowcher* [1972] 1 W.L.R. 425 at 430.

[85] In some fields, however, the role of equity has declined. The entitlement to the funds on dissolution of an unincorporated association, for example, is today treated as more a matter of contract than of trusts. See *post*, p. 247.

[86] *post*, pp. 831–842.

[87] *R.C.A. Corp. v. Pollard* [1983] Ch. 135; *post*, p. 765.

[88] *Ashburn Anstalt v. Arnold, supra; post*, p. 886.

[89] *Peffer v. Rigg* [1977] 1 W.L.R. 285; *Lyus v. Prowsa Ltd* [1982] 1 W.L.R. 1044, *post*, p. 336.

[90] *Barclays Bank Ltd v. Quistclose Investments Ltd* [1970] A.C. 567, *post*, p. 52. See also *Re Kayford* [1975] 1 W.L.R. 279.

[91] *post*, Chap. 11.

constructive trust of a new model. Lord Diplock brought it into the world[92] and we have nourished it".[93]

Other areas where equity's creativity has shown itself in modern times include proprietary estoppel,[94] the rescission of contracts on the ground of mistake,[95] and the restriction of the rights of a mortgagee.[96] This brief survey indicates the dynamism of equity. The developments discussed above, and others, will be examined in the relevant parts of the book.

11. THE RECOGNITION OF TRUSTS ACT 1987[97]

The trust is an English concept which has spread to common law, but not civil law, jurisdictions.[98] The 1984 Hague Convention on the Law applicable to Trusts and their Recognition establishes common principles between states on the law governing trusts and provides guidelines for their recognition. The United Kingdom, by means of the Recognition of Trusts Act 1987, has ratified the Convention.

The ratification does not have the effect of changing the substantive law of trusts of the United Kingdom, nor of importing trusts into civil law jurisdictions. The Convention seeks to establish uniform conflict of laws principles and to assist civil law states to deal with trust issues arising within their jurisdiction. Recognition implies, for example, that the trustee may sue and be sued in his capacity as trustee, and that the trust property is a separate fund and is not part of the trustee's estate.[99] A trust is to be governed by the law chosen by the settlor, expressly or by implication. In the absence of any such choice, the trust is to be governed by the law with which it is most closely connected.[1] The applicable law governs the validity and construction of the trust, and its effects and administration.[2]

---

[92] In *Gissing v. Gissing* [1971] A.C. 886.

[93] *Eves v. Eves* [1975] 1 W.L.R. 1338 at 1341; *cf. Allen v. Snyder* [1977] 2 N.S.W.L.R. 685 at 701: "the legitimacy of the new model is at least suspect; at best it is a mutant from which further breeding should be discouraged." It seems that the "new model" is in decline; *post*, p. 332.

[94] *post*, p. 893.

[95] *Solle v. Butcher* [1950] 1 K.B. 671; *post*, p. 846.

[96] *Quennell v. Maltby* [1979] 1 W.L.R. 318 (right to possession must be exercised bona fide and to protect security).

[97] (1987) 36 I.C.L.Q. 260 (D. Hayton); Underhill, Chap. 23; (1998) 4 *Trusts & Trustees* 15 (M. Lupoi); *Modern International Developments in Trust Law* (ed. D. Hayton), Chaps. 2, 3.

[98] A Bill drafted by the French Ministry of Justice sought to introduce "La Fiducie", a device similar to the trust, into French law, but it was not enacted. See [1992] Conv. 407 (H. Dyson).

[99] Article 11, as set out in the Schedule to the 1987 Act.

[1] Articles 6 and 7.

[2] Article 8.

CHAPTER 2

NATURE AND CLASSIFICATION OF TRUSTS

1. DISTINCTIONS

MANY attempts have been made to define a trust, but none of them has been wholly successful.[1] It is more useful to describe than to define a trust, and then to distinguish it from related but distinguishable concepts.

A trust is a relationship recognised by equity which arises where property is vested in (a person or) persons called the trustees, which those trustees are obliged to hold for the benefit of other persons called *cestuis que trust*[2] or beneficiaries. The interests of the beneficiaries will usually be laid down in the instrument creating the

---

[1] Co.Litt. 272b; Underhill and Hayton (15th ed.), p. 3; used in *Re Marshall's W.T.* [1945] Ch. 217 at 219 and in *Green v. Russell* [1959] 2 Q.B. 226 at 241; Snell, p. 109; *Halsbury's Laws of England* (4th ed.), Vol. 48, p. 272; (1955) 71 L.Q.R. 39 (A. Scott).

[2] This is the correct plural; (1910) 26 L.Q.R. 196 (C. Sweet).

trust, but may be implied or imposed by law.[3] The beneficiary's interest is proprietary[4] in the sense that it can be sold, given away or disposed of by will; but it will cease to exist if the legal estate in the property comes into the hands of a bona fide purchaser for value without notice of the beneficial interest.[5] The subject-matter of the trust must be some form of property. Commonly, it is legal ownership of land or of invested funds; but it may be of any sort of property—land, money, chattels, equitable interests,[6] choses in action,[7] etc. There may also be trusts for charitable purposes; such trusts are enforced at the suit of the Attorney-General.[8] There is much doubt and uncertainty as to the status and validity of trusts for non-charitable purposes—as a trust for the building of a monument[9] or for the maintenance of the testator's horses, dogs, and cats.[10]

A trust must be distinguished from certain other legal phenomena which resemble the trust, but which must be kept separate from it. The point of such distinguishing is threefold: first, to compare the different legal consequences of a trust and the related concept; secondly, to identify the circumstances in which the one concept must exist to the exclusion of the other; and thirdly, to identify the circumstances in which a trust may co-exist with the related concept, as may be the case, for example, with certain contracts and debts.

A. Bailment

Bailment is a relationship recognised by the common law, and arises where a chattel owned by A is, with A's permission, in the possession of B.[11] The rights of the parties may or may not be governed by a contract. A is entitled to a certain standard of care by B in his stewardship of A's chattel. But this is very different from a trust. For there is no transfer of ownership from A to B; B's duties are dependent on the rules of common law and not upon equity; and these duties are entirely different from, and minimal in character as compared with, those which would exist if B held the property as trustee for A. A trustee of shares is the legal owner of the shares and

---

[3] *post*, pp. 69, 70.

[4] *ante*, p. 17. Discretionary trusts and trusts for persons for particular purposes need separate consideration: *post*, Chaps. 8 and 14.

[5] *ante*, p. 34.

[6] For example, where a beneficiary under a settlement makes a settlement of his beneficial interest.

[7] For example, a trust of the benefit of a covenant, or of a debt, or of a bank balance.

[8] See *post*, Chap. 15.

[9] *Mussett v. Bingle* [1876] W.N. 170; *Re Endacott* [1960] Ch. 232; *post*, p. 368.

[10] *Pettingall v. Pettingall* (1842) 11 L.J.Ch. 176; *Re Dean* (1889) 41 Ch.D. 552; *post*, p. 369.

[11] Bridge, *Personal Property Law*, pp. 23–30; *Aluminium Industrie Vaassen B.V. v. Romalpa Aluminium Ltd* [1976] 1 W.L.R. 676, *post*, p. 704; *Re Goldcorp Exchange Ltd* [1995] 1 A.C. 74 at 97.

the certificates, and not a mere bailee of the latter.[12] A bailor, A, could lose his legal ownership only through one of the ways in which legal owners may be deprived.[13] But if the property was held by B on trust for A, A's equitable title could be defeated by the transfer of the legal title in the property to a bona fide purchaser for value without notice of the trust.[14]

B. Agency

The relationship of principal and agent, which is normally contractual, is governed by rules of common law and equity, while the relationship of trustee and beneficiary, which is rarely contractual, is exclusively equitable. The function of an agent is to represent the principal in dealings with third parties, while a trustee does not bring the beneficiaries into any relationship with third parties. There are, however, many similarities.[15] The relationship of trustee and beneficiary is fiduciary; that of principal and agent is normally fiduciary, but not inevitably so.[16] Both trustees and agents must act personally and not delegate their duties[17]; neither may make unauthorised profits from their office.[18]

A significant distinction arises from the fact that the relationship of principal and agent is primarily debtor/creditor, while a trust is proprietary: the trust property vests in the trustee and the beneficiaries are the equitable owners. The crucial point here is that a proprietary right (so long as the property or its proceeds can be identified) is not affected by the defendant's insolvency, whereas a personal claim will abate with the claims of other creditors if the defendant cannot pay in full.

An agent does not necessarily hold any property for the principal. Even if he does, he may merely have possession rather than title. The principal will have proprietary rights against the agent only if the agent has acquired title to property for the benefit of the principal. "That proposition is clear enough in the abstract, but it is often extremely difficult to gauge, especially where the subject matter is money . . . (i) whether the agent has acquired title or mere possession, and (ii) if he has acquired title, whether there is an intention to

---

[12] *MCC Proceeds Inc v. Lehman Bros International (Europe)* [1998] 4 All E.R. 675 (beneficiary could not sue third party for conversion of certificates).

[13] *e.g.* through estoppel, or the operation of the Factors Act 1899, ss.2, 8, 9; Sale of Goods Act 1979, ss.21, 24, or the Consumer Credit Act 1974, Sched. 4, para. 22.

[14] *ante*, pp. 34 *et seq.* See *MCC Proceeds Inc v. Lehman Bros International (Europe)* [1998] 4 All E.R. 675, *supra*.

[15] See Fridman's *Law of Agency* (7th ed.), pp. 23–27.

[16] *post*, p. 613.

[17] *post*, p. 576.

[18] *post*, Chap. 21.

create a trust or to allow the agent to take an absolute title subject to a merely personal monetary obligation."[19]

The above discussion relates to assets lawfully received by the agent on behalf of the principal. Where property is received in breach of fiduciary duty, as in the case of a bribe, it is now settled that the agent holds the property on trust for the principal.[20] The consequence is that the principal's remedy does not depend on the agent's solvency, and the principal will be entitled to any increase in value of the property.

C. Contract

Trust and contract are quite different concepts. A contract is a common law personal obligation resulting from agreement between the parties. A trust is an equitable proprietary relation which can arise independently of agreement. However, there are various situations in which the distinction may be difficult to draw, or where the facts may give rise to both[21]; contracts and trusts are not mutually exclusive.[22]

i. Settlements and Covenants to Settle. Property which is vested in the trustees of a settlement is held upon the trusts of the settlement, and the beneficiaries are the owners in equity of their interests under the settlement. But if the property has not yet been conveyed to the trustees, and is merely subject to a covenant to settle, then until recently the beneficiaries could only enforce the covenant if they had given consideration or were parties to the deed.[23] This area is now subject to the development mentioned below.

ii. Third Party Rights under a Contract. There has been much discussion of the question whether the inability of a third party to sue upon a contract can be overcome by finding that one of the parties to the contract contracted as trustee for him. This is not really a question of distinguishing a trust from a contract. The question is whether there is a trust of the benefit of the contract. The answer to

---

[19] Heydon, Gummow and Austin, *Cases and Materials on Equity and Trusts* (4th ed.), p. 467.

[20] *Att.-Gen. for Hong Kong v. Reid* [1994] 1 A.C. 324; *post*, p. 625.

[21] As, for example, in the case of a constructive trust arising out of a specifically enforceable contract for sale, *post*, p. 326; or possibly in the case of a contractual licence, discussed below. Consideration does not negative a trust; *Carreras Rothmans Ltd v. Freeman Mathews Treasure Ltd* [1985] Ch. 207.

[22] *Baird v. Baird* [1990] 2 A.C. 548 at 560; *Imperial Group Pension Trust Ltd v. Imperial Tobacco Ltd* [1991] 1 W.L.R. 589 at 597. These employee pension fund cases are an important illustration of the co-existence of contractual and trust relationships.

[23] *post*, Chap. 4.

that question depends on whether there is an intention to create a trust of the benefit of the contract; this question is discussed elsewhere.[24] The question is of less significance now that third parties may enforce contracts for their benefit in certain circumstances under the Contracts (Rights of Third Parties) Act 1999.

iii. Unincorporated Associations. An unincorporated association is not a legal entity. Where there is a gift to an unincorporated association, there have been doubts as to whether the property is held on trust for the purposes of the association, or whether it belongs absolutely to the members, to be dealt with according to their contract.[25] On the dissolution of such an association the ownership of its funds has sometimes been determined by applying trust principles, but today the matter is more commonly treated as one of contract.[26]

iv. Contractual Licences. A contractual licence, normally involving the occupation of land, is created by agreement of the parties, applying the normal principles of the law of contract. There is authority,[27] however, especially in the context of enforceability against third parties, that a contractual licence may give rise to a constructive trust, thus giving the licensee an equitable interest in the land in addition to his contractual rights. The development of this theory is discussed elsewhere.[28]

D. Debt

A debt may or may not be contractual. Whether the obligation is contractual or not, the duty of the debtor is to pay money to the creditor; that of a trustee is to hold the trust property on trust for the beneficiary. The debtor's obligation is personal. The trust is proprietary. We have seen that the distinction becomes crucial on insolvency. Further, a trustee must invest the trust funds, and the beneficiaries are entitled to the income. With a debtor, or a stakeholder, this is a matter of agreement, express or implied.[29]

On the other hand, it may be to a person's own advantage to be a trustee rather than a person subject to a personal obligation. If money is borrowed and then stolen from the borrower, it must still

---

[24] *post*, p. 135.
[25] *post*, p. 373.
[26] *post*, p. 247.
[27] See *Ashburn Anstalt v. Arnold* [1989] Ch. 1.
[28] *post*, p. 886.
[29] *Potters v. Loppert* [1973] Ch. 399 (estate agent held entitled to retain interest earned by deposit held as stakeholder). See now Estate Agents Act 1979, s.13.

be repaid; but a trustee may not be liable for a loss which is not due to his own lack of care.[30]

A debt may, of course, be the subject-matter of a trust,[31] but the question here considered is whether the making of a loan can create a trust in favour of the lender, either initially or at some later stage. Sometimes a form of words is construed as creating both forms of obligation.[32] There is no reason why, in certain circumstances, a debt and a trust cannot co-exist; a loan to be held by the borrower on trust is repayable in debt if the purpose for which the money was lent is carried out, and may be held in trust for the lender if performance is impossible or is for some other reason not carried out. In *Barclays Bank Ltd v. Quistclose Investments Ltd*[33]:

> Rolls Razor Ltd, very much indebted to Barclays Bank, was in need of £209,719 to pay dividends which had been declared on its shares. This sum was borrowed from Quistclose under an arrangement whereby the loan was to be used only for that purpose. The money was paid into a separate account at Barclays bank, the Bank having notice of the nature of the arrangement.
>
> Before the dividend was paid, Rolls Razor went into liquidation. The question was whether the money in the account was owned beneficially by Rolls Razor in which case Barclays Bank claimed to set it off against the overdraft,[34] or whether Rolls Razor had received the money as trustee and still held it on trust for Quistclose.
>
> The House of Lords unanimously decided that the money had been received upon trust to apply it for the payment of dividends; that purpose having failed, the money was held on trust for Quistclose. The fact that the transaction was a loan, recoverable by an action at law, did not exclude the implication of a trust. The legal and equitable rights and remedies could co-exist. The Bank, having notice of the trust, could not retain the money against Quistclose.

The principle is that "equity fastens on the conscience of the person who receives from another property transferred for a specific purpose only and not therefore for the recipient's own purposes, so that such person will not be permitted to treat the property as his

---

[30] *Morley v. Morley* (1678) 2 Ch.Cas. 2.

[31] For an unusual example, see *Barclays Bank plc v. Willowbrook International Ltd* [1987] 1 F.T.L.R. 386, C.A., holding that where A charges to B a debt owed to A by C, any money paid by C to A is held by A on constructive trust for B.

[32] *Welby v. Rockcliffe* (1830) 1 Russ. & M. 571; *Wright v. Wilkin* (1862) 2 B. & S. 232 at 260.

[33] [1970] A.C. 567; (1980) 43 M.L.R. 489 (W. Goodhart and G. Jones). For other circumstances where an unsecured creditor can acquire a proprietary interest, see *Swiss Bank Corporation v. Lloyds Bank Ltd* [1982] A.C. 584.

[34] See Insolvency Act 1986, s.323.

own or to use it for other than the stated purpose."[35] The principle applies also where only part of the money lent is used for the specific purpose: the part not so applied is held on trust for the lender.[36]

The court in *Re Kayford Ltd (In Liquidation)*[37] went one step further, holding that circumstances apparently giving rise to a debt in fact created a trust which did not co-exist with the debt but excluded it. In that case, customers of a mail-order company paid in advance when ordering goods. The company, being in financial difficulties, decided to protect its customers in the event of its insolvency by opening a separate bank account, called "Customers' Trust Deposit Account," into which the purchase money was paid. In liquidation proceedings it was held that the money was held on trust for the customers and did not form part of the assets of the company. The customer could create a trust by using appropriate words or, as here, the company could do it by taking suitable steps on or before receiving the money, thus transforming the obligations from debt to trust. The customers never became creditors, so no question of a fraudulent preference[38] of creditors could arise.[39] No trust arose, however, where members of a financially troubled club deposited "rescue funds" in a separate account, for use when the club's future was known.[40] *Re Kayford Ltd* was distinguished on the ground that in the present case the circumstances in which the money could be used were not defined. Thus the terms of the intended trust were uncertain and the money was part of the club's assets and therefore available to its creditors.

---

[35] *Carreras Rothmans Ltd v. Freeman Mathews Treasure Ltd* [1985] Ch. 207 at p. 222. See generally (1985) 101 L.Q.R. 269 (P. Millett); *cf.* Chambers, *Resulting Trusts*, Chap. 3. It seems that the parties must have had a common intention to create the primary trust; see (1991) 107 L.Q.R. 608 (C. Rickett).

[36] *Re EVTR Ltd* [1987] B.C.L.C. 647 (loan for buying equipment, part of which was never delivered and money refunded to debtor by vendor). See also *Twinsectra Ltd v. Yardley* [1999] Lloyd's Rep. Bank. 438; [2000] Conv. 351 (S. Baughen); [2000] L.M.C.L.Q. 459 (A. Tettenborn); *R. v. Common Professional Examination Board, ex p. Mealing-McCleod, The Times*, May 2, 2000.

[37] [1975] 1 W.L.R. 279; distinguished in *Re Multi Guarantee Co. Ltd* [1987] B.C.L.C. 257, where a separate account was designated but no trust of the money was established because the company contemplated having further resort to the money. The decision is criticised at (1988) 85 L.S.Gaz. No. 36, at 14 (I. Hardcastle).

[38] The preference rules are now found in Insolvency Act 1986, s.239.

[39] *cf.* (1980) 43 M.L.R. 489 at 494 *et seq.* (W. Goodhart and G. Jones). The point that the customers never became creditors seems unconvincing. For this to be so, the trust must already have existed when the company received the money. In *Re Chelsea Cloisters* (1981) 41 P. & C.R. 98, tenants' deposits against damage were paid into a separate bank account, any balance to be credited to them at the end of the lease. The Court of Appeal held that a trust had been created, but doubted (on the authority of *Potters v. Loppert* [1973] Ch. 399, *supra*, n. 29), whether it had arisen at the outset. (See now Landlord and Tenant Act 1987, s.42). See also Heydon, Gummow and Austin, *Cases and Materials on Equity and Trusts* (4th ed.), p. 475, suggesting that *Re Kayford Ltd* and the *Quistclose* case "provide startling opportunities for well-advised lenders to obtain protection against the prospect of the borrower's insolvency."

[40] *Re Challoner Club Ltd (in liquidation), The Times*, November 4, 1997.

Re Kayford Ltd was not referred to in *Customs and Excise Commissioners v. Richmond Theatre Management Ltd*,[41] where a different, and somewhat surprising, result was reached in the context not of insolvency but of liability to value added tax. The theatre sold tickets in advance on terms which expressly imposed a trust on the money for the purchasers until the performance took place. Dyson J. held that no trust was created because the terms also provided that the theatre was "not accountable for interest or otherwise in respect of the use of the ticket money after its receipt." It was considered that the effect of this clause was that the purchasers accepted the risk of insolvency and that it would be inequitable to put them in a better position than unsecured creditors in that event. There was no reference to *R. v. Clowes (No. 2)*[42] where, in the context of theft, the Court of Appeal said that the requirement to keep money separately normally indicates a trust, and the absence of such a requirement normally negatives it *if there were no other indicators of a trust*; the fact that the transaction contemplates the mingling of money is not necessarily fatal to a trust. There the terms of an investment brochure were held to establish that investors' money was received on trust for them, to the exclusion of a debtor/creditor relationship.

In the context of informal family transactions, it may be difficult to determine whether a payment was intended to create a debt or not. Thus in *Hussey v. Palmer*,[43] where the plaintiff paid £607 for an extension to her son-in-law's house, Cairns L.J. held that it was a loan, Lord Denning M.R. held that it was not, and Phillimore L.J. thought that it "might be" a loan. The decision of the majority was that the payment gave rise to a resulting (or constructive) trust on the basis that it would be inequitable for the son-in-law to deny that she had an interest in the house.[44] If the payment was neither a gift nor a loan, this conclusion is not surprising, but Phillimore L.J. held that a resulting trust could arise even if it was a loan.[45] There is much force in the dissenting judgment of Cairns L.J., holding that a resulting trust of money paid by way of a loan could not arise. The question arose again in *Re Sharpe*,[46] where an aunt lent money to her nephew towards the purchase of a house on the understanding that she could live with him for the rest of her life. On the nephew's bankruptcy, the aunt claimed an interest in the house. Although her

[41] [1995] S.T.C. 257; criticised [1995] B.T.R. 332 (P. Matthews).
[42] [1994] 2 All E.R. 316. See also *Re Lewis's of Leicester Ltd* [1995] 1 B.C.L.C. 428.
[43] [1972] 1 W.L.R. 1286.
[44] *post*, p. 332.
[45] This would not be within the principle of *Barclays Bank Ltd v. Quistclose Investments Ltd*, *supra*, as the money *was* applied to the purpose for which it was paid. The trust was apparently of a proportionate share of the house.
[46] [1980] 1 W.L.R. 219. See also *Spence v. Brown* (1988) 18 Fam.Law. 291; *Risch v. McFee* (1991) 61 P. & C.R. 42.

claim succeeded on other grounds,[47] the argument that the loan gave rise to a resulting trust was rejected, *Hussey v. Palmer* being distinguished as a case on "very special" facts.

E. Conditions and Charges

It is sometimes difficult to determine whether a gift of property is subject to a trust or whether it is conditional upon, or charged with, the duty of making certain payments. Thus a bequest to X "but he is to pay £50 to Y" could give rise to several possible constructions, each of them having different consequences.[48]

The bequest could be construed as a gift to X upon trust to pay Y £50.[49] In that situation, Y would immediately become entitled in equity to the £50, provided that the property bequeathed was of sufficient value; a trustee is not required to produce money of his own to make up deficiencies in the trust property.[50] If there is a surplus, a trustee is not, on principle, entitled to obtain any benefit from the trust and the surplus will usually be held upon a resulting trust.[51] But a possible construction is that, even if there was a trust of the £50, X was intended to take the surplus beneficially, the trust being applicable only to the £50.[52]

The bequest might also be construed as a gift to X conditional upon his performing the obligation. In that situation, Y obtains no interest in the £50; X has the choice of keeping the property and paying £50 or of declining both.[53] It could also be construed so as to impose a charge on the property. Here again, X will only be obliged to make the payment if he receives the property. His obligation will be limited to the value of the property,[54] and he will be entitled to retain any surplus.[55] Y will have an equitable right by virtue of the charge,[56] but this right is a different one from that of a beneficiary under a trust.[57]

---

[47] *post*, p. 887.

[48] (1952) 11 C.L.J. 240 (T. Thomas).

[49] *Re Frame* [1939] Ch. 700 (devise to housekeeper "on condition that she adopt my daughter Alma and also gives to my daughters Jessie and May the sum of £5 each, and a like sum to my son Alexander."); *cf. Re Brace* [1954] 1 W.L.R. 955.

[50] *Re Cowley* (1885) 53 L.T. 494.

[51] *King v. Denison* (1813) 1 V. & B. 260 at 272; *Re West* [1900] 1 Ch. 84; *Re Rees' W.T.* [1950] Ch. 204; *post*, p. 162.

[52] *Re Foord* [1922] 2 Ch. 519 ("To my sister, Margaret Juliet, absolutely on trust to pay my wife per annum" £300); distinguished in *Re Osoba* [1979] 1 W.L.R. 247.

[53] *Att.-Gen. v. The Cordwainers Co.* (1833) 3 Myl. & K. 534.

[54] *Re Cowley* (1885) 53 L.T. 494.

[55] *Re Oliver* (1890) 62 L.T. 533.

[56] *Parker v. Judkin* [1931] 1 Ch. 475.

[57] See, however, *Barclays Bank plc v. Willowbrook International Ltd* [1987] 1 F.T.L.R. 386, C.A., holding that where a debt due to a company was charged by the company to the bank, the company held the money paid to it by the debtor on constructive trust for the bank.

The House of Lords has held that equity will protect the right of an insurer to be subrogated to the insured person's rights against the wrongdoer by imposing an equitable lien or charge, although not a trust, in favour of the insurer on the damages payable by the wrong-doer.[58] The imposition of a trust would be onerous, commercially undesirable and unnecessary to the protection of the insurer.

F. Interest under a Will or Intestacy

The relationship between a personal representative and a legatee or devisee bears many similarities to that of trustee and beneficiary. The origins of the relationship, however, are quite distinct, the former originating in the Ecclesiastical Court and the latter in Chancery and their basic function is different. The trustee's duty is to manage the trust so long as it continues. The personal representative's duty is to liquidate the estate and distribute the assets; either to individual beneficiaries, or, if a trust is established by the will, to the trustees. Commonly, the executors and the trustees are the same persons, and, as we shall see,[59] in the case of personalty the transfer to themselves is notional; in the case of land an assent is required. Although the two relationships often coalesce or overlap, there are important distinctions between them.

i. Whether a Personal Representative is a Trustee. The definition of trustee in the Trustee Act 1925 includes a personal representative[60] where the context so admits; and the Act, except where otherwise expressly provided, applies to executorships and administratorships.[61] A personal representative is sometimes treated in Administration of Estates Act 1925 as a trustee.[62] A personal representative is under fiduciary duties which are very similar to those of a trustee. There are, however, a number of ways in which a personal representative has been held not to be a trustee:

(a) *Different Periods of Limitation Apply.* Generally, an action for the recovery of trust property or for a breach of trust must be brought against a trustee within six years.[63] An action against a personal representative in respect of a claim to personal estate must be brought within 12 years, and an action for the recovery of arrears of interest on legacies within six years.[64]

---

[58] *Napier and Ettrick (Lord) v. Hunter* [1993] A.C. 713.
[59] *post*, p. 57.
[60] s.68(17); A.E.A. 1925, s.33; *contra*, I.C.T.A. 1988, s.686(6).
[61] s.69.
[62] A.E.A. 1925, ss.33, 46, 49; Intestates' Estates Act 1952.
[63] Limitation Act 1980, s.21(3); for exceptions, see s.21(1) and (2).
[64] *ibid.*, s.22.

(b) *Power of Disposition of Personalty.* The power of personal representatives to dispose of pure personalty is *several*; that of trustees is *joint*.[65] This means that one of several executors can pass title to a chattel; but in a sale by trustees, all must combine. It thus becomes important to ascertain when a personal representative becomes a trustee. Where, of course, a will appoints certain persons as executors and other persons as trustees, the executors, on the completion of the administration, must assent to the vesting of the property subject to the trust in the trustees. In the case of personalty the assent may be oral, or even implied,[66] in the case of a legal estate in land however an assent must be in writing, and it becomes an essential document of title in the case of unregistered land.[67]

When however, the executors are appointed trustees also, or where no provision is made for the appointment of trustees in a will which provides for property to be held in trust after the completion of administration, the question arises of the way in which, and of the time at which, the executors become trustees. The principle is that the transition from executors to trustees occurs automatically after completion of the administration, but as far as powers of disposition of property are concerned, there must also have been a sufficient assent by the executors in their own favour as trustees.

In *Attenborough v. Solomon*,[68] the House of Lords held that a pledge of silver plate by one of two executors, which was made 13 years after the completion of the administration of the estate, passed no title to the pledgee. The executors had long since become trustees; an assent in their own favour could be inferred from their conduct; and trustees must act jointly.

A similar view was taken in the cases allowing a personal representative to act as a trustee in the exercise of the statutory power of appointing new trustees.[69]

There is no distinction with regard to the power of disposition of land, the power being joint in both cases.[70] Formerly one of two or

---

[65] *Jacomb v. Harwood* (1751) 2 Ves.Sen. 265; *Attenborough v. Solomon* [1913] A.C. 76. The Law Reform Committee on Powers and Duties of Trustees (23rd Report, Cmnd. 8733 (1982)) recommended that the power should be joint in the case of personal representatives also.

[66] *Attenborough v. Solomon* [1913] A.C. 76. See [1990] Conv. 257 (C. Stebbings).

[67] "An assent to the vesting of a legal estate shall be in writing, signed by the personal representative, and shall name the person in whose favour it is given and shall operate to vest in that person the legal estate to which it relates; and an assent not in writing or not in favour of a named person shall not be effectual to pass a legal estate." A.E.A. 1925, s.36(4). This does not apply to the vesting of an equitable interest in land; *Re Edwards's W.T.* [1982] Ch. 30.

[68] [1913] A.C. 76.

[69] *Re Ponder* [1921] 2 Ch. 59; *Re Cockburn* [1957] Ch. 438. See also [1984] Conv. 423 (C. Stebbings).

[70] A.E.A. 1925, s.2(2).

more personal representatives could enter into a contract to sell land, but this is no longer possible.[71] Where there is only a single personal representative, he may give a receipt for capital money arising on the sale,[72] while at least two trustees or a trust corporation are required in the case of a conveyance by a tenant for life or trustees of land.[73] It is necessary for all personal representatives who are registered shareholders of a company to execute any transfer of the shares.[74]

(c) *Tenure of Office.* Formerly a personal representative held his office for life (unless the grant was for a limited period) and could not retire. Now, however, the court may discharge an executor or administrator and appoint a substitute.[75] A trustee, on the other hand, may retire without a court order.[76] Subject to the above, a personal representative's duties terminate with the completion of the administration of the estate, but his liabilities are limited only by effluxion of time. Thus solicitors who were sureties of an administrator and who handed over the residue of the estate to the administrator (who then absconded) were held liable on their bond.[77]

(d) *Duty to Estate: Duty to Beneficiaries.* Executors and trustees are both subject to fiduciary duties. A trustee's duty is to the beneficiaries, and he must "hold the balance evenly between the beneficiaries to whom the property belongs."[78] With an unadministered estate, no legatee, devisee or next of kin, has, as will be seen[79] beneficial ownership of the assets. The executor's duty is to the estate as a whole.[80] In *Re Hayes' Will Trusts,*[81] a testator appointed four persons, including his son, executors and trustees of his will, and gave power to "my trustees ... to sell ... to any person ... including my son despite his being a trustee and in his case at the value placed upon the same for purposes of estate duty." In agreeing the estate duty valuation of the farm, it was held that the executors were not obliged to consider the implications of the fact that a low

---

[71] Law of Property (Miscellaneous Provisions) Act 1994, s.16.

[72] L.P.A. 1925, s.27(2).

[73] T.A. 1925, s.14; *post,* p. 573.

[74] Companies Act 1985, s.183(3). For electronic transfer, see *post,* p. 121.

[75] Administration of Justice Act 1985, s.50.

[76] T.A. 1925, ss.36, 39; *post,* p. 521.

[77] *Harvell v. Foster* [1954] 2 Q.B. 367.

[78] *Re Hayes' W.T.* [1971] 1 W.L.R. 758 at 764.

[79] *post,* p. 59.

[80] *Re Charteris* [1917] 2 Ch. 379, where a postponement of sale of some assets acted to the disadvantage of the life tenant, although it was in the interest of the estate.

[81] [1971] 1 W.L.R. 758; (1971) 36 Conv.(N.S.) 136 (J. Mummery).

valuation benefited the son, a high one benefited the other beneficiaries. They negotiated in the usual way with the District Valuer
and agreed as low a valuation for tax purposes as they could obtain.
This was the usual correct procedure, and they were right to sell to
the son at that price.

(e) *Vesting of a Legal Estate.* A further question arises, however,
with a legal estate in land. Where trustees under an existing trust
make an appointment of a new trustee under a statutory power given
to them by Trustee Act 1925, s.36,[82] the legal estate in the trust
property vests in the new trustee under section 40.[83] Although personal representatives cannot appoint successors to their offices, they
may, after they have become trustees following the completion of
the administration of the estate,[84] appoint additional or successor
trustees. But in *Re King's Will Trusts*,[85] Pennycuick J. held that
Trustee Act 1925, s.40 did not apply to an appointment of a new
trustee by the surviving executor and trustee of a will, who had not
previously assented in writing to the vesting of the legal estate in
himself in his capacity as trustee. We have seen that an assent in
writing is necessary for the vesting of a legal estate in land, and that
it constitutes an essential document of title.[86] The executor could
have assented to the vesting of the legal estate in himself and the
new trustee after the appointment; or he could have assented, before
the appointment, to the vesting in himself as trustee; in which case
s.40 would have applied.

This decision has been criticised,[87] and it may have upset a number of unregistered titles which have relied on the practice established by earlier cases, but it is consistent with the principle of the
1925 legislation that every dealing with a legal estate in land should
be supported by a document of title. An assent to the vesting of an
equitable interest in land need not, however, be in writing, and may
be inferred from conduct.[88]

ii. The Nature of the Interest of a Legatee or Devisee. A lega-
tee or devisee does not, on the testator's death, become equitable
owner of any part of the estate. The executor takes full title to the

---

[82] *post*, p. 511.
[83] Registration is necessary in the case of registered land.
[84] *supra*, n. 69. See also Parry and Clark, *The Law of Succession* (10th ed.), pp. 489–493.
[85] [1964] Ch. 542; Mellows, *The Law of Succession* (5th ed.), pp. 326–327.
[86] *ante*, p. 57.
[87] (1964) 28 Conv.(N.S.) 298 (J. Garner); (1964) 80 L.Q.R. 328 (R. Walker); (1976) 29 C.L.P.
60 (E. Ryder). But see Law Com. No. 184 (1989), para. 1.6., suggesting that *Re King's Will
Trusts* is now accepted in practice and causes no problems.
[88] *Re Edwards's W.T.* [1982] Ch. 30. But see [1982] Conv. 4 (P. Smith) for the view that only
an executor, and not an administrator, can make such an implied assent.

testator's property, not merely a bare legal estate.[89] He is, by virtue of his office, subjected to various fiduciary duties, which can be enforced against him by persons interested; and these duties are inconsistent with his holding the property on trust for the legatee or devisee.[90] The equitable ownership is "in suspense."[91]

The fiduciary duties of the personal representatives are "to preserve the assets, to deal properly with them, and to apply them in a due course of administration for the benefit of those interested according to that course, creditors, the death duty authorities, legatees of various sorts, and the residuary beneficiaries. They might just as well have been termed 'duties in respect of the assets' as trusts. What equity did *not* do was to recognise or create for residuary legatees a beneficial interest in the assets in the executor's hand during the course of administration."[92] It may be, as with an insolvent estate, that nothing is left which can be applied for the beneficiaries. Even if the estate is solvent, the devisee or legatee is not the owner in equity of any asset in the estate. He has a chose in action, a right to compel the administration of the estate. In *Commissioner of Stamp Duties (Queensland) v. Livingston*,[93] the question was whether succession duty was payable under a Queensland statute which applied to property situated in Queensland. A widow died domiciled in New South Wales, and was residuary legatee under her husband's will. The estate, which was not administered at the date of the widow's death, contained land in Queensland. The Privy Council held that succession duty was not payable on that property. The widow was not the owner of it. She was the owner of a chose in action, and that was situated in New South Wales, the state of her domicile. In *Eastbourne Mutual Building Society v. Hastings Corporation*,[94] a husband occupied a house on his wife's intestacy. He was unable to claim compensation for the value of the house on compulsory purchase, because the estate was not administered, and he had no interest in the house. Similarly, in *Lall v. Lall*,[95] a widow wished to defend an action for possession of the matrimonial home,

---

[89] *Commissioner of Stamp Duties (Queensland) v. Livingston* [1965] A.C. 694 at 707, 708, 712. But, for the purposes of inheritance tax, a person who would become entitled to a residuary estate (or part thereof) on the completion of the administration is treated as having become entitled at the death of the deceased. Inheritance Tax Act 1984, s.91.

[90] *Sudeley (Lord) v. Att.-Gen.* [1897] A.C. 11; *Barnardo's (Dr.) Homes v. Income Tax Special Commissioners* [1920] 1 K.B. 468 at 479; [1921] 2 A.C. 1; *Corbett v. Commissioners of Inland Revenue* [1938] 1 K.B. 567 at 575–577; *Passant v. Jackson (Inspector of Taxes)* [1986] S.T.C. 164; see also *Skinner v. Att.-Gen.* [1940] A.C. 350. For a full discussion of Commonwealth cases, see (1967) 45 C.B.R. 219 (D. Waters).

[91] *J. Sainsbury plc v. O'Connor (Inspector of Taxes)* [1991] S.T.C. 318 at 326.

[92] *per* Lord Radcliffe [1965] A.C. 694 at 707; *Re Hayes' Will Trusts* [1971] 1 W.L.R. 758.

[93] [1965] A.C. 694. See also *Crowden v. Aldridge* [1993] 1 W.L.R. 433; [1994] Conv. 446 (J. Ross Martyn); *Marshall (Inspector of Taxes) v. Kerr* [1995] 1 A.C. 148.

[94] [1965] 1 W.L.R. 861.

[95] [1965] 1 W.L.R. 1249; (1965) 23 C.L.J. 144 (S. Bailey).

which had been owned by her deceased husband. No grant of administration of his estate had yet been made, and so she had no *locus standi* to defend the action. In *Re K. (deceased)*[96] residuary beneficiaries under an unadministered estate had not acquired an "interest in property" within section 2(7) of the Forfeiture Act 1982 so as to preclude the court from giving relief under the Act from the forfeiture rule in favour of an applicant who had killed the testator. On the other hand, in *Re Leigh's Will Trust*,[97] a bequest by a widow of "all the shares which I hold and any other interest or assets which I may have" in a particular company was held to be wide enough to include a claim to her husband's unadministered estate which contained such shares; and her claim passed under her will. Following on from this, a beneficiary of an unadministered estate who has taken possession of the land is a person "entitled to a beneficial interest in the land or in the proceeds of sale" within the Limitation Act 1980[98] (with the result that he cannot acquire title against the other beneficiaries).[99] Similarly, where a person entitled under an unadministered estate is bankrupt, the chose in action and its fruits are property of the bankrupt capable of passing to his trustee in bankruptcy.[1]

While it is settled that a residuary legatee or devisee or an intestate successor has no equitable interest in any particular assets of an unadministered estate, the position of a specific legatee or devisee is less clear. While there is some authority that such a legatee or devisee does have an equitable interest in the property in question as from the testator's death,[2] some statements in the *Livingston* case cast doubt on this.[3] The view of the Law Commission is that a specific legatee or devisee has no equitable interest during the period of administration.[4] After all, the assets in question may need to be used for the discharge of debts even if the estate is solvent.

A devisee or legatee may be said to become the equitable owner of specific property once property has been allocated by the executor for the purpose.[5] In the case of a residuary gift or a claim on intestacy, the allocation cannot occur until the residuary accounts

---

[96] [1986] Ch. 180; *post*, p. 331.

[97] [1970] Ch. 277; (1970) 86 L.Q.R. 20 (P.V.B.).

[98] Sched. 1, para. 9.

[99] *Earnshaw v. Hartley* [2000] Ch. 155.

[1] *Official Receiver in Bankruptcy v. Schultz* (1990) 170 C.L.R. 306 (High Court of Australia); [1992] Conv. 92 (J. Maxton).

[2] See *Re Neeld* [1962] Ch. 643 at 688.

[3] [1965] A.C. 694 at 707, 708. See also *Official Receiver in Bankruptcy v. Schultz, supra*, at 312.

[4] Law Com. No. 188 (1989), para. 2.16; *cf.* Snell, p. 384. Pending administration a specific devisee may make a valid contract to sell the land, which becomes specifically enforceable when his interest becomes proprietary; *Wu Koon Tai v. Wu Yau Loi* [1997] A.C. 179.

[5] *Phillipo v. Munnings* (1837) 2 Myl. & Cr. 309.

are prepared.[6] That is the time at which the executors are turning into trustees. The interest of the person entitled then becomes that of a beneficiary under a trust.

G. Powers[7]

i. Trusts Imperative; Powers Discretionary. The distinction between trusts and powers is fundamental. Trusts are imperative; powers are discretionary. Trustees must perform the duties connected with their trusts. A donee of a power may exercise it, or not, at his choice. If the donee of a power created by will predeceases the testator then the power lapses, but it is otherwise in the case of a trust, which does not fail for lack of a trustee.[8]

Trustees are under a duty to hold the trust property for the beneficiaries in accordance with the terms of the trust. The beneficiaries under a trust are the owners in equity of the trust property. Objects of a power own nothing, unless and until the donee of the power makes an appointment in their favour.[9] They merely have a hope that the power will be exercised in their favour. Until the power is exercised, equitable ownership in such a case is in those who will take in default of an appointment, their interest being subject to defeasance on its exercise. Thus, if a testator by his will leaves property to his widow for life and after her death to his children in equal shares, the widow and the children obtain vested interests in the property. Compare this with a gift to the widow for life and after her death as she shall appoint among the children, and, in default of appointment, to charity. Then the children obtain nothing unless and until an appointment is made in their favour.

Whether a trust or a power has been created is dependent upon the construction of the language of the instrument. A properly drafted instrument will leave no room for doubt.

The distinction is however complicated by the fact that a trust may give to the trustees considerable discretion. A trustee may be given a discretion to select beneficiaries from a specified class, or to determine the proportions in which specified beneficiaries are to take. This is the basis of a discretionary trust. Under such a trust no member of a class of the discretionary beneficiaries has an interest in a specific part of the trust property until the discretion of the

---

[6] *Re Claremont* [1923] 2 K.B. 718.

[7] Thomas, *Powers*; Halsbury's *Laws of England* (4th ed.), Vol. 36, p. 529; (1957) 35 C.B.R. 1060 (O. Marshall); (1953) 69 L.Q.R. 334 (D. Gordon); (1949) 13 Conv.(N.S.) 20 (J. Fleming); (1954) 18 Conv.(N.S.) 565 (F. Crane); (1971) C.L.J. 68 (J. Hopkins); (1971) 87 L.Q.R. 31 (J. Harris). For views on the changing nature of trusts and powers, see [1970] A.S.C.L. 187 (J. Davies); (1974) 37 M.L.R. 643 (Y. Grbich). *Post*, Chap. 6.

[8] *Brown v. Higgs* (1803) 8 Ves. 561.

[9] *Vestey v. I.R.C.* [1980] A.C. 1148.

trustees has been exercised in his favour. The beneficiaries as a whole, however, are the owners of the trust property. If all are adult and under no disability, they may combine together to terminate the trust and demand a distribution of the property.[10] The trustees throughout are under an obligation to perform the trust; that is to say, in the context of a discretionary trust, to exercise their discretion; and so to make a selection after proper consideration. "If the trustees fail to exercise their discretion, the court can compel them to exercise the trust."[11] Thus a beneficiary under a discretionary trust cannot demand payment. He has, however, the right to demand that the trustees exercise their discretion in accordance with the trust. What happens if the trustees refuse to do so is one of the matters discussed in *McPhail v. Doulton*.[12] The court could replace obstructive trustees with willing ones; and, if no suitable trustees would act, the court ultimately would need to make a selection. The point is that a discretionary trust puts the trustees under an obligation. Their duty is to make a selection. This is very different from a mere power to appoint; for in that case there is no duty to make a selection. It has been held, however, that the court has similar powers of intervention in the case of a fiduciary power where there is nobody to exercise it.[13]

Although the donee of a mere power of appointment is not obliged to exercise it, he does have certain duties. Thus he must consider periodically whether to exercise it, consider the range of objects, and the appropriateness of individual appointments. If he does decide to exercise the power, he must do so in a responsible manner according to its purpose and, of course, refrain from making any appointment which is not within the terms of the power.[14] This is the case where the power is given to a trustee as such; the duties described above are necessary to the performance of his fiduciary role. Where, however, the donee of the power is not a fiduciary, he is not subjected to these fiduciary duties, although he must, of course, keep within the terms of the power.

But it is difficult in borderline cases to draw a dividing line between discretionary trusts and powers,[15] and between fiduciary

---

[10] *Re Smith* [1928] Ch. 915; *Re Nelson* (1918) Ch. 926; *Vestey v. I.R.C. (Nos. 1 and 2)* [1980] A.C. 1148.

[11] *per* Lord Guest in *McPhail v. Doulton* [1971] A.C. 424 at 444; *Re Locker's S.T.* [1977] 1 W.L.R. 1323.

[12] [1971] A.C. 424; *post*, p. 104.

[13] *Mettoy Pension Trustees Ltd v. Evans* [1990] 1 W.L.R. 1587; *post*, p. 176.

[14] *Re Hay's S.T.* [1982] 1 W.L.R. 202; [1982] Conv. 432 (A. Grubb); *Turner v. Turner* [1984] Ch. 100.

[15] *Re Leek* [1969] 1 Ch. 563; *Re Gulbenkian's Settlements* [1970] A.C. 508 at 525, *per* Lord Upjohn. *McPhail v. Doulton, supra*, at 448; *Vestey v. I.R.C., supra*. See also, in the context of charity, *Re Cohen* [1973] 1 W.L.R. 415.

and personal powers. The decision turns on the proper construction of the language of the instrument.[16]

The matter is made more difficult by reason of the fact that a discretionary trust may be "exhaustive" or "non-exhaustive." An exhaustive discretionary trust is one where the trustees' duty to exercise their discretion can only be satisfied by making a distribution. A non-exhaustive discretionary trust, on the other hand, is one where the settlor has given the trustees power to decide not to distribute all of the income, for example, by giving them power to accumulate it for a certain period.[17] It must be admitted that the identification of the precise duty in the case of a non-exhaustive discretionary trust is a difficult task. The distinction from a power of appointment is a fine one, and the matter will be further discussed in Chapter 8. For present purposes the position may be summarised as follows: whereas the donee of a fiduciary power of appointment need only consider exercising the power, the trustee of a discretionary trust must actually exercise it, although in the case of a non-exhaustive discretionary trust this duty may be satisfied by deciding to accumulate rather than to distribute.

ii. Terminology. Nor is the matter helped by the terminology. Discretionary trusts have been referred to as a "power in the nature of a trust", or "a power coupled with a duty", or even as a "trust power". Terminology of this type adds to confusion. The situation is that if the limitation, on its proper construction, is held to impose a duty, then the limitation creates a trust—though one in which the trustees have a power of selection.

iii. Significance of the Distinction. The question may be material in a number of circumstances.

(a) *Whether the Class Takes if the Discretion is not Exercised.* If there is a gift in favour of such members of a class as X shall select, and X fails to make a selection, will the gift take effect in favour of the class, or will it fail? If the power is construed as a mere power, the non-exercise of the power will cause it to fail,[18] and the property will then pass on default of appointment, or go on resulting trust for the grantor. But if the gift is construed as a gift to the class subject to X's power of selection, the trust in favour of the class will take effect.

---

[16] *Re Scarisbrick's W.T.* [1951] Ch. 622 at 635, *per* Lord Evershed M.R.; *Mettoy Pension Trustees Ltd v. Evans* [1990] 1 W.L.R. 1507.

[17] This led some commentators to take the view that there is no longer any analytical distinction between trusts and powers. See [1970] A.S.C.L. 187 (J. Davies); (1974) 37 M.L.R. 643 (Y. Grbich); (1976) 54 C.B.R. 229 (M. Cullity).

[18] Subject to *Mettoy Pension Trustees Ltd v. Evans* [1990] 1 W.L.R. 1587; *post*, p. 176.

In *Burrough v. Philcox*[19] a testator provided that the survivor of his children should have power, by will, "to dispose of all my real and personal estates amongst my nephews and nieces, or their children, either all to one of them or to as many of them as my surviving child shall think proper." No appointments were made and the members of the class were held to take equally as a trust had been created. On the other hand in *Re Weekes' Settlement*,[20] a testatrix gave her husband a life interest and a power "to dispose of all such property by will amongst our children." He died intestate. There was held to be no trust, and so the children took nothing. In neither case was there a gift over in default.

The question is whether, on the proper construction of the limitation, it is possible to show an intention to benefit the objects in the event of no appointment being made.[21] It has been said that the courts are more inclined to such a construction when the objects are small in number, such as children under a marriage settlement.[22] But in *McPhail v. Doulton*[23] a deed was held to create a trust which provided that the trustees "shall apply the net income in making at their absolute discretion" grants to employees, past and present, and their dependants. The principle to be applied was laid down by Lord Cottenham in *Burrough v. Philcox*.[24] "When there appears a general intention in favour of a class, and a particular intention in favour of individuals of a class to be selected by another person, and the particular intention fails, from that selection not being made, the Court will carry into effect the general intention in favour of the class." The presence of a gift over in default of appointment destroys any such implication; the gift over shows that the settlor is providing for a situation where the donee does not appoint to the class; and this is inconsistent with a trust in favour of the class.[25] But there is no hard and fast rule that a trust is intended if there is no gift over.[26]

Where the court finds that there is a trust, the question arises of the share which each of the beneficiaries will take. In the nineteenth

---

[19] (1840) 5 Myl. & Cr. 72. Such a trust, it is submitted, should be regarded as a fixed trust subject to defeasance by exercise of the power of selection, and thus unaffected by *McPhail v. Doulton, infra.* See *post*, p. 114.

[20] [1897] 1 Ch. 289.

[21] *Harding v. Glyn* (1739) 1 Atk. 469; *Re Llewellyn's Settlement* [1921] 2 Ch. 281; *Re Arnold* [1947] Ch. 131.

[22] *Re Perowne* [1951] Ch. 785 at 790.

[23] [1971] A.C. 424.

[24] (1840) 5 Myl. & Cr. 72 at 92.

[25] This is so even if the gift over is void; *Re Sprague* (1880) 43 L.T. 236. But it would not be so because of a residuary gift, or a gift over in default of there being any objects of the power; *Re Leek* [1969] 1 Ch. 563.

[26] *Re Weekes* [1879] 1 Ch. 289; *Re Combe* [1925] Ch. 210; *Re Perowne* [1951] Ch. 785; *McPhail v. Doulton* [1971] A.C. 424.

century cases, where the question usually arose in the context of division among a family group, the rule of equal division was applied, on the principle that equality was equity.[27] Such a solution would be particularly inappropriate in the context of modern trusts in favour of employees of companies and their dependants. In *McPhail v. Doulton*,[28] the House of Lords, as we have seen, was more courageous, and accepted the obligation, where necessary, of itself making a decision on division.

(b) *The Test of Certainty*. With both trusts and powers, it is necessary for the beneficiaries, or the objects, to be defined with sufficient certainty to enable the trustees or the donees to exercise their functions, and for the court to supervise them. Before the decision of the House of Lords in *McPhail v. Doulton*,[29] it was necessary to draw a distinction between the requirement of certainty in the case of trusts (fixed and discretionary) and that required for mere powers. *McPhail v. Doulton*, however, decided that the test was the same for discretionary trusts and mere powers. The test came from *Re Gulbenkian's Settlements*,[30] a case on a power, and is whether "it can be said with certainty that any given individual is or is not a member of the class."[31] This test will be discussed in detail in Chapter 3. But it may be said here that the assimilation of the test of certainty for discretionary trusts and mere powers has greatly reduced the practical significance of the distinction between them. Prior to *McPhail v. Doulton*,[32] most of the litigation on the distinction between discretionary trusts and mere powers concerned the question whether a limitation had to comply only with the above test; or whether it was void for failure to comply with a stricter test which had earlier been applicable to all trusts.[33] That test was whether the description of the beneficiaries enabled the trustee to draw up a full list of the beneficiaries. That test still remains applicable to "fixed" as opposed to discretionary trusts; that is to say trusts which give a specific share to each beneficiary. Unless the court could make a complete list of all the beneficiaries, it would be impossible to make a division, or to supervise the trustees if they failed to distribute.

(c) *Terminating the Trust*. Where all the beneficiaries of a discretionary trust are adult and under no disability they may determine

---

[27] This will still be the result if such was the settlor's intention; *post*, p. 114.

[28] [1971] A.C. 424. Equal division would not be possible in any event if the total membership of the class was not known. As will be seen, the certainty test propounded in *McPhail v. Doulton* does not require all the objects to be ascertained.

[29] *supra*.

[30] [1970] A.C. 508.

[31] *per* Lord Wilberforce in *McPhail v. Doulton, ante*, at 456; *Re Baden's Deed Trusts (No. 2)* [1973] Ch. 9, *post*, p. 104.

[32] [1971] A.C. 424.

[33] *I.R.C. v. Broadway Cottages Trust Ltd* [1955] Ch. 20.

the trust and require the trust property to be shared out.[34] On the other hand, objects of a power can never claim any proprietary interest in the property until the power has been exercised in their favour.

2. Classification of Trusts[35]

Trusts have been variously classified and subdivided. The categories are not exclusive; some trusts could appear in more than one category. The basic division is between private trusts, and public or charitable trusts. Charitable trusts, which are dealt with in Chapter 15, are trusts for certain purposes which are so beneficial to the community that the Attorney-General undertakes responsibility for their enforcement. They are accorded special privileges in terms of non-liability to tax, and in terms of perpetual duration. Private trusts, on the other hand, are trusts for persons, the beneficiaries; and the beneficiaries can enforce the trust. It may also be noted here that there are a few anomalous cases in which trusts for non-charitable purposes, usually for the building of monuments or the upkeep of particular animals, have been upheld. Such trusts are usually called non-charitable purpose trusts, or trusts of imperfect obligation. The latter name indicates one of their main anomalies; who will enforce such a trust? These trusts are dealt with in Chapter 14.

Private trusts are divided into express, constructive and resulting trusts[36]; and express trusts may be divided into executed and executory, and into completely constituted and incompletely constituted trusts. Sometimes implied trusts are included as a further category of private trusts.[37] This classification serves little purpose, and the examples commonly given might preferably be regarded as express, resulting or constructive trusts, as the case may be. Trusts have often been established although express words to that effect have not been used,[38] yet such trusts are "express" because the settlors intended to create them. Trusts based on the presumed intention of the settlor as, for example, in the case of a voluntary conveyance, are sometimes described as implied trusts, but will here be treated as resulting trusts. Mutual wills are also sometimes described as implied trusts,[39] but will here be treated as constructive trusts. The term may be used

---

[34] *Re Smith* [1928] 1 Ch. 915.

[35] See (1999) 18 N.Z.U.L.R. 305 (C. Rickett).

[36] Chambers, *Resulting Trusts*, p. 5, prefers a classification distinguishing trusts generated by consent or by responses to wrongs, unjust enrichment or other events.

[37] Such a classification at times appears in statutes, for example, L.P.A. 1925 s.53(2).

[38] See *Paul v. Constance* [1977] 1 W.L.R. 527, and the cases discussed under the heading "Certainty of Intention," *post*, p. 94.

[39] Snell, p. 220.

as meaning any private trust which is not express, but the matter is purely one of terminology.

A. Express Trusts

An express trust is one intentionally declared by the creator of the trust, who is known a the settlor, or, if the trust is created by will, the testator. A trust is created by a manifestation of an intention to create a trust; though certain formalities, as will be seen, are required in the case of lifetime trusts of land and of all testamentary trusts.

Two subdivisions of express trusts should be mentioned.

(i) Executed and Executory. An executed trust is one in which the testator or settlor has marked out in appropriate technical expressions what interests are to be taken by all the beneficiaries. On the other hand, in an executory trust, the execution of some further instrument is required, in order to define the beneficial interests with precision. The property is immediately subject to a valid trust, but it remains executory until the further instrument is duly executed.

The practical significance of the distinction is that while the language of executed trusts is governed by strict rules of construction, executory trusts are construed more liberally. Where, in the case of an executed trust, the settlor has made use of technical expressions, as to the interpretation of which the law has laid down rules, equity will follow the law and give effect to such interpretation.[40] In the case of an executory trust, however, equity will attach less importance to the use or omission of technical words, but will seek to discover the settlor's true intention, and order the preparation of a final deed which gives effect to such intention. It is necessary, however, for the court to be able to ascertain, from the language of the instrument, the trusts which are intended to be imposed on the property.[41]

Executory trusts appeared most commonly in marriage articles, which often provided that certain property belonging to one of the parties should be settled upon them and their issue, and in wills. They are rarely met at the present day; due no doubt to the fact that many modern trusts have tax-saving implications, and it is necessary, for such purposes, to be precise and specific in drafting the trust.

A pension fund trust provides a more modern example. In *Davis v. Richards & Wallington Industries Ltd*[42] the question arose as to

---

[40] *Re Bostock's Settlement* [1921] 2 Ch. 469; see also L.P.A. 1925, s.60(1); *cf. Re Arden* [1935] Ch. 326.

[41] *Re Flavel's Will Trusts* [1966] 1 W.L.R. 445 at 447 ("for formation of a superannuation and bonus fund for the employees").

[42] [1990] 1 W.L.R. 1511; disapproved on another point in *Air Jamaica Ltd v. Charlton* [1999] 1 W.L.R. 1399.

entitlement to surplus funds. A pension scheme had been established by an interim trust deed, which provided for the execution of a definitive trust deed. This deed was later executed, and contained rules as to the entitlement to any surplus, but there was doubt as to its validity. In fact the definitive deed was upheld, but if it had not been, the court would have held the interim deed to be a valid executory trust. This could have been executed by a court order bringing into effect rules corresponding to those in the definitive deed, thereby resolving the issue as to the surplus.

(ii) Completely and Incompletely Constituted Trusts. There cannot be a trust unless the trust is completely constituted. This heading is therefore irrational; it is dealing, not with two different types of trust, but with a rule for distinguishing what is a trust from something that is void. Nevertheless, it is convenient to make the point here, and to deal in more detail with the matter below.[43]

A trust is only valid if the title to the property is in the trustee and if the trusts have been validly declared. A declaration that A holds on trust for B is ineffective if the property is not vested in A. The trust becomes constituted and valid when the property is vested in A. The form of transfer to A depends on the nature of the property —land, chattel, money, shares in a company, copyrights, patents, debts or other choses in action—and the appropriate method must of course be used.[44] In the case of a trust of land there must also be written evidence of the declaration of trust.[45] The settlor may of course declare himself trustee, and there is then an automatic constitution, because title was in the settlor throughout. Testamentary trusts are always completely constituted; for the executors, if not the trustees themselves, are under a duty to transfer the trust property to the nominated trustees.

Although no trust is created unless the trust is completely constituted, there are situations where intended beneficiaries under an incompletely constituted trust may compel the transfer of the property to the trustees. In general, they can do so if they have given consideration, but not if they are volunteers, for there is yet no trust and "equity will not assist a volunteer."[46]

B. Resulting Trusts[47]

A resulting trust exists where property has been conveyed to another, but the beneficial interest returns, or "results" to the transferor. This may happen in various situations; the simplest one is

[43] *post*, Chap. 4.
[44] *post*, pp. 121 *et seq.*
[45] L.P.A. 1925, s.53; *post*, p. 80.
[46] *post*, Chap. 4.
[47] *post*, Chap. 10.

where the property is conveyed to trustees upon certain trusts which fail or which do not exhaust the whole beneficial interest. The part undisposed of results to the settlor. For example, if there is a gift on trust for A for life and then on trust for X if X attains the age of 21, but X dies under 21 in A's lifetime, the property will result on A's death to the settlor.

Such a resulting trust has been described as "automatic,"[48] meaning that it arises by operation of law, without depending on the intention of the settlor. The better view, however, is that the so-called "automatic" resulting trust gives effect to the settlor's presumed intention.[49]

Another category, clearly based on the presumed intention of the settlor, is the "presumed" resulting trust in favour of the transferor where property is conveyed to a volunteer. The presumption is rebuttable by evidence of an intention to make a gift or, where the volunteer is the transferor's wife or child, by the presumption of advancement.[50] The modern analysis is that both kinds of resulting trust depend on the intention of the transferor. Such a trust arises in circumstances where the transferor did not intend the transferee to take beneficially.[51]

C. Constructive Trusts[52]

While express trusts arise from the act of the parties, constructive trusts arise by operation of law.[53] Equity says that in certain circumstances the legal owner of property must hold it on trust for others. The absence of the need for formalities in such circumstances is obvious. There is, however, much dispute and uncertainty as to the occasions on which constructive trusts arise, and also as to their nature.

The term has indeed been used in different senses. It can cover the duty of a trustee who has obtained benefits by fraud; the obligation of a transferee from an express trustee, unless he proves he was a bona fide purchaser for value without notice, to hold the transferred property on the trusts previously applicable; the obligation of a trustee who has made a profit, however innocently, through his office, to hold such profit for the benefit of his beneficiaries[54]; the position of a stranger to the trust who has dishonestly assisted in a

---

[48] *per* Megarry J. in *Re Vandervell's Trust (No. 2)* [1974] Ch. 269 at 291.

[49] *Westdeutsche Landesbank Girozentrale v. Islington London Borough Council* [1996] A.C. 669 at 708.

[50] *post*, p. 256.

[51] See Chambers, *Resulting Trusts*.

[52] *post*, Chap. 12. Waters, *The Constructive Trust*; Oakley, *Constructive Trusts* (3rd ed.).

[53] *cf.* (1999) 18 N.Z.U.L.R. 305 (C. Rickett) taking the view that all trusts are founded on intention.

[54] *Keech v. Sandford* (1726) Sel.Cas.t. King 61; *Boardman v. Phipps* [1967] 2 A.C. 46.

breach of trust[55]; the relationship of vendor and purchaser between the contract and the execution of the conveyance[56]; and other relationships, such as licensees, and claimants to a matrimonial home, where the introduction of a constructive trust was considered to be necessary to enable the court to reach a just solution.[57] A controversial question is whether the "remedial" constructive trust, favoured in some commonwealth jurisdictions, is available to prevent unjust enrichment whenever the personal remedy is inadequate.

Lord Denning M.R. pioneered a constructive trust "of a new model,"[58] to be imposed "whenever justice and good conscience required it . . . " as an equitable remedy "by which the court can enable an aggrieved party to obtain restitution."[59] The implications of these developments will be discussed in Chapter 12.

D. Bare Trusts

A distinction is sometimes made between bare or simple trusts, on the one hand, and "special" trusts on the other. There is said to be a bare trust when the trustee holds trust property in trust for an adult beneficiary absolutely. In such a situation the beneficiary may call for a conveyance of the legal estate at any time, and the trustee must comply.[60] In the meantime the trustee has no duties to perform and must deal with the trust property in accordance with the instructions of the beneficiary.[61]

It is said that all other trusts are "special" trusts. The description however, is not generally used except as a mode of contrast with a bare or simple trust.

A bare trust may arise at the outset, as where an absolute owner puts shares or other property into the name of trustees[62] or some other third party[63] to hold for himself. This may arise in a commercial context, as where a solicitor holds money for a client.[64] A trust which was not originally a bare trust may become one when an adult beneficiary becomes absolutely entitled, as on the death of A in a

---

[55] *post*, p. 306.

[56] *post*, p. 326.

[57] *Binions v. Evans* [1972] Ch. 359 (licensee); *Eves v. Eves* [1975] 1 W.L.R. 1338 (cohabitant); *Re Densham* [1975] 1 W.L.R. 1519 (wife). See *post*, p. 332.

[58] *Eves v. Eves* [1975] 1 W.L.R. 1338.

[59] *Hussey v. Palmer* [1972] 1 W.L.R. 1286 at 1289.

[60] As, indeed, could a multiplicity of beneficiaries, all adult and under no disability; *Saunders v. Vautier* (1841) 4 Beav. 115; *post*, p. 630.

[61] *Re Cunningham and Fray* [1891] 2 Ch. 567; Pettit, pp. 67–68; (1992) 1 J.I.P. 3 (D. Hayton).

[62] *Grey v. I.R.C.* [1960] A.C. 1.

[63] *Hardoon v. Belilios* [1901] A.C. 119; *Ingram v. I.R.C.* [2000] 1 A.C. 293.

[64] *Target Holdings Ltd v. Redferns (a firm)* [1996] 1 A.C. 421; *post*, p. 652.

trust for A for life, remainder to B. A bare trust need not be express, but can take the form of a resulting or constructive trust, as where the settlor fails to declare the beneficial interests[65] or did not intend any beneficial interest to pass to the fraudulent transferee.[66]

A bare trustee into whose name an absolute owner transfers property is sometimes called a nominee.[67] This must be distinguished from the situation where the trustees vest securities in a nominee in order to facilitate share dealings. Such a person is in effect an agent of the trustees.[68]

E. Trusts in the Higher Sense and Trusts in the Lower Sense

The word "trust" is used in various contexts which have no relationship to the legal meaning of the term.[69] The Crown may entrust ministers or officials with property, perhaps providing that they shall hold it "in trust" for the benefit of some person or body of persons. While such a situation is capable of creating a trust in the legal or "lower" sense, " 'trust" is not a term of art in public law and when used in relation to matters which lie within the field of public law, the words 'in trust' may do no more than indicate the existence of a duty owed to the Crown by the officer of state as servant of the Crown, to deal with the property for the benefit of the subject for whom it is expressed to be held in trust, such duty being enforced administratively or by disciplinary sanctions and not otherwise; *Kinlock v. Secretary of State for India.*[70]"[71] Similarly, where it is alleged that the Crown is trustee for members of the public. In *Tito v. Waddell*[72] phosphate had been mined on Ocean Island by a British company until 1920, when the mining rights were acquired by the governments of the United Kingdom, Australia and New Zealand. The Ocean Islanders claimed, *inter alia*, that the Crown stood in a fiduciary position to them and was liable for various breaches of trust. The claim failed. Although the relevant documents and Mining Ordinances used the word "trust", their wording was, as a

---

[65] *Vandervell v. I.R.C.* [1967] 2 A.C. 291.
[66] *Hodgson v. Marks* [1971] Ch. 892.
[67] See *Ingram v. I.R.C.*, *supra* (land conveyed by owner to solicitor as nominee as a step in a tax avoidance scheme).
[68] *post*, p. 000 (delegation of powers). See also custodian trustees; *post*, p. 580.
[69] See [1996] Conv. 186 (R. Bartlett), discussing National Health Service Trusts.
[70] (1882) 7 App.Cas. 619.
[71] *per* Lord Diplock in *Town Investments Ltd v. Department of the Environment* [1978] A.C. 359 at 382. But the Crown can be a trustee in the "lower sense"; *Civilian War Claimants Association Ltd. v. R.* [1932] A.C. 14; *Lonhro Exports Ltd v. Export Credits Guarantee Department* [1999] Ch. 158.
[72] (*No. 2*) [1977] Ch. 106.

matter of construction, consonant with the creation of a governmental obligation, for the breach of which the court was powerless
to give relief. This governmental obligation, or "trust in the higher
sense", was not a true trust in the conventional sense. It created no
fiduciary obligation, and was not justiciable in the courts.

PART II

TRUSTS AND POWERS

CHAPTER 3

REQUIREMENTS OF A TRUST

1. CAPACITY TO CREATE A TRUST

CAPACITY to create a trust is, generally speaking, co-extensive with the ability to hold and dispose of a legal or equitable interest in property, but there are two special situations to consider.

A. Children

A settlement made by a child is voidable; he may repudiate it before or within a reasonable time after attaining the age of 18.[1]

---

[1] *Edwards v. Carter* [1893] A.C. 360.

A child may not hold a legal estate in land.[2] If a child becomes entitled to a freehold or leasehold, the land is held in trust for him.[3]

B. Mentally Incapacitated Persons

Mental incapacity may affect the ability of a person to make a will, or a gift or to create a trust. In the case of a lifetime gift, it seems that the test varies according to the size of the gift and its relationship to the sum of the assets owned by the donor. In *Re Beaney*[4] a mother who was suffering from senile dementia made a gift of her house, the only substantial asset of her estate, to one daughter, Valerie, who had stayed at home to look after her mother for many years; but this had the effect of virtually disinheriting the other two (married) children. The position was summarised as follows[5]:

"The degree or extent of understanding required in respect of any instrument is relative to the particular transaction which it is to effect. In the case of a will the degree required is always high. In the case of a contract, a deed made for consideration or a gift *inter vivos*, whether by deed or otherwise, the degree required varies with the circumstances of the transaction. Thus, at one extreme, if the subject-matter and value of a gift are trivial in relation to the donor's other assets a low degree of understanding will suffice. But, at the other, if its effect is to dispose of the donor's only assets of value and thus for practical purposes to pre-empt the devolution of his estate under his will or on his intestacy, then the degree of understanding required is as high as that required for a will, and the donor must understand the claims of all potential donees and the extent of the property to be disposed of."

It was held that Mrs Beaney's gift to Valerie was void, because she was not capable of understanding the conflicting claims of her other children. These problems can be avoided if steps are taken to place the affairs of the donor under the control of the Court of Protection.

Under the Mental Health Act 1983 the Court of Protection has wide powers of dealing with the property and affairs of a person

---

[2] L.P.A. 1925, s.1(6).

[3] Trusts of Land and Appointment of Trustees Act 1996, Sched. 1, para. 1.

[4] [1978] 1 W.L.R. 770; [1978] Conv. 387 (F. Crane). See also *Simpson v. Simpson* [1992] 1 F.L.R. 601 (life-time gift which upset the balance of the will held void for want of mental capacity. Transferee of bank deposits held them on resulting trust).

[5] At 774.

who the judge finds to be incapable, by reason of mental disorder, of managing and administering his property and affairs.[6]

The guiding principle for the court is the consideration of what the patient would be likely to do if he were not subject to the disability. Thus, in *Re T.B.*,[7] the court approved the creation of a revocable trust in favour of the patient's illegitimate child; the property would otherwise have passed on intestacy to remoter relatives. If the matter had arisen after 1969, the court could have authorised the making of a will for the patient. Since that date,[8] the court has had power to make a will for an adult mental patient, if the judge has reason to believe that the patient lacks testamentary capacity. The judge must make such a will as the actual, and not a hypothetical patient, acting reasonably, would have been likely to make if restored to full mental capacity, memory and foresight, taking into account the beliefs, affections and antipathies he had (provided they were not "beyond reason") before losing testamentary capacity.[9] If the patient has never had capacity, the court will assume that he would have been a normal, decent person who would have acted in accordance with contemporary standards of morality.[10]

Applications to the court for the approval of schemes affecting the patient's property have commonly been brought in circumstances in which it was desirable in the interests of the family to reduce the tax liability of a rich patient. The applicant must show that the scheme is for the benefit of the patient.[11] It is sufficient that it is the sort of settlement which the patient would be likely to make in favour of other members of the family if he had been subject to no mental abnormality.[12]

2. FORMALITIES[13]

A. Lifetime

i. Creation. The basic rule is that a settlor may create a trust by manifesting an intention to create it. No formalities are required for the creation of a lifetime trust of personalty.[14] Evidence in writing is

---

[6] M.H.A. 1983, s.95. A settlement may be ordered under s.96(1)(*d*).

[7] [1967] Ch. 247. See also *Re S (Gifts by Mental Patient)* [1997] 1 F.L.R. 96.

[8] A.J.A. 1969, adding the provisions now found in M.H.A. 1983, ss.96(1)(*e*) and 97; (1970) 34 Conv.(N.S.) 150 (D. Hart and M. Reed). See *Re Davey* [1981] 1 W.L.R. 164.

[9] *Re D. (J.)* [1982] Ch. 237.

[10] *Re C (a patient)* [1991] 3 All E.R. 866.

[11] See *Re Ryan* [1911] W.N. 56.

[12] See *Re C.W.M.* [1951] 2 K.B. 714; *Re C.* [1960] 1 W.L.R. 92; *Re C.E.F.D.* [1963] 1 W.L.R. 329. For the variation of existing trusts, see Chap. 22.

[13] A Law Commission review is proposed; Law Com. No. 239, para. 5.20.

[14] *M'Fadden v. Jenkyns* (1842) 1 Ph. 153; *Paul v. Constance* [1977] 1 W.L.R. 521; *Re Kayford* [1975] 1 W.L.R. 279.

required for the creation of a trust of land, and all testamentary trusts must be in writing, signed by the testator and attested by two witnesses as required by the Wills Act 1837, s.9.[15]

It is necessary, however, to observe literally every word of the basic rule. The intention must be to *create a trust*; a general intention to benefit someone will not suffice.[16] The words or acts of the settlor must be sufficient to establish an intention that either another person (or persons), or the settlor himself, shall be trustee of property for the beneficiary. In practice lifetime trusts are created in writing and usually by deed. Such trusts usually have as one of their objects the saving of tax, and this can only be achieved where there is clear documentary proof of the date and terms of the trust.

With regard to trusts of land, the Law of Property Act 1925, s.53(1)(*b*), provides:

> "A declaration of trust respecting any land or any interest therein must be manifested and proved by some writing signed by some person who is able to declare such trust or by his will."[17]

The writing is required as evidence of intention; the declaration need not itself be in writing. Failure to comply with the requirements of s.53(1)(*b*) renders the trust unenforceable, and not void.[18] The signature will normally be that of the settlor, although there is authority that the transferee of the land may sign.[19]

These requirements apply to express trusts only, and not to resulting, implied or constructive trusts,[20] although, as will be seen from the case-law discussed below, dispositions of interests arising under such trusts are subject to the formality requirements.

ii. The Instrument of Fraud Principle. The question which next arises concerns the effect, if any, of an oral declaration of a trust of land. What should be done if a transferee procures a conveyance of land to him on the strength of a oral agreement to hold on trust for the transferor or a third party, and then seeks to shelter behind the statute?

Equity, where possible, will not permit a statute to be a cloak for fraud. The question is whether equity can, by acting *in personam*

---

[15] *post*, p. 93.
[16] *Jones v. Lock* (1865) L.R. 1 Ch.App. 25; *post*, p. 126; *Paul v. Constance* [1977] 1 W.L.R. 521.
[17] Replacing Statute of Frauds 1677, s.7.
[18] *Gardner v. Rowe* (1828) 5 Russ. 258.
[19] *ibid.*
[20] L.P.A. 1925, s.53(2). They do not apply to trusts arising from co-ownership; *Roy v. Roy* [1996] 1 F.L.R. 541.

against the fraudulent party, prevent the fraud without disregarding the statute.

In *Rochefoucauld v. Boustead*,[21] the claimant was the mortgagor of the Delmar Estates in Ceylon. They were sold by the mortgagee to the defendant, who had orally agreed to hold the estates on trust for the mortgagor subject to the repayment to the defendant of the purchase price, and expenses. The defendant sold the land at a profit, but did not account to the mortgagor. The defendant became bankrupt.

The mortgagor obtained an order for an account. The Court of Appeal refused to allow the Statute of Frauds to prevent the proof of fraud; and " . . . it is a fraud on the part of a person to whom land is conveyed as a trustee, and who knows it was so conveyed, to deny the trust and claim the land himself. Consequently, notwithstanding the statute, it is competent for a person claiming land conveyed to another to prove by parol evidence that it was so conveyed upon trust for the claimant, and that the grantee, knowing the facts, is denying the trust and relying upon the form of conveyance and the statute, in order to keep the land himself."[22]

The principle of this decision is that in the case of fraud oral evidence is admissible to establish the trust in spite of the statute. On this basis trust is express,[23] although modern cases have tended to treat trusts established in this way as constructive.[24]

Where the conveyance is by A to B on an oral trust for A, the effect of this doctrine is clearly that B holds on trust for A. The more difficult case is where the conveyance is by A to B on an oral trust for C. Should the beneficial interest be enjoyed by C, or held on resulting trust for A? The latter is all that is necessary to prevent B's unjust enrichment; to give the benefit to C looks like a disregard of the statute. It is a question of balancing the policy of the formality requirement against the injustice which may be caused by relying on the formality rule. If the trust is properly to be classified as express, it is easier to say that C should benefit, especially as the effect of

---

[21] [1897] 1 Ch. 196. See also *Davies v. Otty (No. 2)* (1865) 35 Beav. 208; *McCormick v. Grogan* (1869) L.R. 4 H.L. 82; *Bannister v. Bannister* [1948] 2 All E.R. 133; *Hodgson v. Marks* [1971] Ch. 892; *Binions v. Evans* [1972] Ch. 359; *Lyus v. Prowsa Ltd* [1982] 1 W.L.R. 1044; *Du Boulay v. Raggett* (1989) 58 P. & C.R. 12.

[22] *per* Lindley L.J. at p. 206.

[23] So held in *Rochefoucauld v. Boustead, supra*, but specifically in the context of the Limitation Act 1874.

[24] *Bannister v. Bannister, supra*; *Binions v. Evans, supra*; *Re Densham* [1975] 1 W.L.R. 1519; *Neale v. Willis* (1968) 19 P. & C.R. 839; *Ashburn Anstalt v. Arnold* [1989] Ch. 1. See further Elias, *Explaining Constructive Trusts*, pp. 106–113.

section 53(1)(*b*) is that the trust is not void but merely unenforceable. There are authorities tending to support C's claim,[25] and some commentators favour this view.[26] More compelling is the view that B should hold on trust for A.[27] To go further leaves section 53(1)(*b*) applying only where A orally declares himself trustee. The fraud doctrine cannot be invoked here, and it has been held that the beneficiary cannot assert a constructive trust and thereby avoid section 53(1)(*b*) unless he has acted to his detriment in reliance on the declaration.[28]

A similar question arises where a prospective legatee or devisee agrees with the testator to hold the property on trust for C. Here the doctrine of secret trusts allows C to benefit in spite of the requirements of the Wills Act 1837. Here the resulting trust solution is less appropriate because it is too late for the testator to make other provision for C. This is discussed in Chapter 5.

iii. Disposition.[29] A disposition of an equitable interest is required to be in writing; otherwise, the disposition is void. Section 53(1)(*c*) provides[30]:

> "A disposition of an equitable interest or trust subsisting at the time of the disposition must be in writing signed by the person disposing of the same, or by his agent thereunto lawfully authorised in writing or by will."

"The subsection . . . " said Lord Wilberforce,[31] "is certainly not easy to apply to the various transactions in equitable interests which now occur." Such transactions include attempts to avoid stamp duty on share transfers, and the practice of putting shareholdings in nominees. A question which has recently arisen is whether and how far the subsection applies to securities held in trust which are traded

---

[25] *Taylor v. Salmon* (1838) 4 Myl. & Cr. 134; *Binions v. Evans, supra; Neale v. Willis, supra; Lyus v. Prowsa Ltd, supra. Rochefoucauld v. Boustead* itself should not be regarded as such a case because effectively A arranged with B that B would buy from the mortgagee and hold on trust for A.

[26] (1915) 28 H.L.R. 237 at 366 (G. Costigan); (1984) 43 C.L.J. 306 and [1988] Conv. 267 (T. Youdan). See also Elias, *Explaining Constructive Trusts*, pp. 103 *et seq.* (supporting C's claim in the context of a wider view that formality rules should be abolished).

[27] [1987] Conv. 246 (J. Feltham). But as the oral declaration is not void, B may convey to C unless A has revoked his authority to do so.

[28] *Midland Bank Ltd v. Dobson* [1986] 1 F.L.R. 171; *cf. Re Densham* [1975] 1 W.L.R. 1519.

[29] (1966) 24 C.L.J. 19 (G. Jones); (1967) 31 Conv.(N.S.) 175 (S. Spencer); [1975] Ottawa L.R. 483 and [1979] Conv. 17 (G. Battersby); (1978) 94 L.Q.R. 170 (D. Sugarman and F. Webb).

[30] Re-enacting Statute of Frauds 1677, s.9, with some alterations, the most significant one being that s.9 applied to "all grants and assignments of any trust or confidence" while s.53(1)(*c*) applies to a "disposition of an equitable interest."

[31] In *Vandervell v. I.R.C.* [1967] 2 A.C. 291 at 329.

electronically.[32] Modern litigation has established some fine, and not always logical, distinctions.

Of course, it might be said that the equitable interest is disposed of whenever an absolute owner declares himself trustee of the property. Such a view would, however, make section 53(1)(*b*) meaningless. The word "subsisting" in section 53(1)(*c*) indicates that the subsection only applies where the equitable interest has already been separated from the legal estate.

(a) *Assignment of Equitable Interest.* The simple case is where a beneficiary under a trust assigns his interest to another. This is a disposition of an equitable interest, and is void unless in writing. This is so, whether the beneficial interest is a limited interest, such as a life interest, or an absolute interest which is held on a bare trust by a nominee. The subsection applies to equitable interests in both land and personalty.[33] The disposition must actually be in writing, and not merely evidenced in writing,[34] but a number of connected documents can provide the necessary writing.[35]

(b) *Direction to Trustees to Hold on Trust for Another.* Where a beneficiary directs the trustee to hold his interest upon other trusts, there is a disposition of the beneficiary's interest. This is the basis of *Grey v. I.R.C.*,[36] which was concerned with an attempt by the settlor to save stamp duty on shares being put into the settlement. At that time *ad valorem* stamp duty (*i.e.* varying with the value of the interest transferred) was payable on deeds of gift, although this is no longer the position.[37] Where stamp duty is payable, it is payable upon instruments whereby property is transferred, and not upon transactions.[38]

In *Grey v. I.R.C.*,[39] the settlor made six settlements of nominal sums in favour of his grandchildren. Later, he transferred shares of substantial value to the trustees, as his nominees, on trust for himself. That transfer attracted only nominal stamp duty. Then he orally instructed the trustees to hold that property upon the trusts of the six settlements. Finally, the trustees executed documents

---

[32] The issue has been examined by the Trust Law Committee on the basis of a paper by Joanna Benjamin. Further statutory disapplication of the subsection is expected, along the lines of Stock Transfer Act 1982, s.1(2) (gilts) and Uncertificated Securities Regulations 1995 (S.I. 1995 No. 3272) (CREST).

[33] See (1984) 47 M.L.R. 385 at 388 (B. Green), discussing L.P.A. 1925, s.205(1)(x).

[34] *cf.* L.P.A. 1925, s.53(1)(*b*). See further n. 40, *infra*.

[35] *Re Danish Bacon Co. Staff Pension Fund Trusts* [1971] 1 W.L.R. 248 at 255.

[36] [1960] A.C. 1; (1960) C.L.J. 31 (J. Thornley); [1979] Conv. 17 (G. Battersby); (1984) 47 M.L.R. 385 (B. Green). See also *Crowden v. Aldridge* [1993] 1 W.L.R. 433.

[37] F.A. 1985, s.82.

[38] *I.R.C. v. Angus* (1889) 23 Q.B.D. 579; *Oughtred v. I.R.C.* [1960] A.C. 206 at 227.

[39] *supra*.

confirming that they held the shares upon the trusts of the settlements. The settlor, though not expressed to be a party, executed the documents.

It was accepted that the trusts were validly declared. The question was whether they were declared by the settlor's oral declaration, in which case the subsequent documents were truly confirmatory, and passed no beneficial interest; or whether, as the Revenue argued, the documents effected a disposition of an existing equitable interest within section 53(1)(c), in which case they were subject to *ad valorem* duty.[40]

In argument, Pennycuick Q.C. posed the question thus[41]: "If X holds property in trust for A as absolute owner and A then directs X to hold the property on the settlement trusts for the benefit of B, C, and D, and X accepts the trust, is that direction a 'disposition' of a subsisting equitable interest within the meaning of section 53?" The House of Lords answered affirmatively. While the trustees held the shares as nominees for the settlor, the settlor owned the entire beneficial interest. When the trustees held them upon the trusts of the settlements, the beneficial interest passed from the settlor to the beneficiaries under the settlements. That, according to the natural meaning of the word, was a disposition. *Ad valorem* stamp duty was payable on the documents.

It seems that the settlor's objectives would have been achieved if he had orally declared himself trustee of the shares for the beneficiaries while still the legal owner; following the declaration with a confirmatory document; and retiring, when he wished, in favour of other trustees.

It appears that section 53(1)(c) is satisfied if the equitable owner writes to the trustee in terms which refer to prior oral instructions to hold on new trusts, even though the writing does not include the particulars of the new trusts.[42]

(c) *Conveyance of Legal Estate by Trustee.* The subsection does not apply where the trustee or nominee conveys the legal estate to a third party with the consent or at the direction of a beneficiary absolutely entitled. In that situation, "prima facie a transfer of the legal estate carries with it the absolute beneficial interest in the property transferred."[43]

---

[40] It was conceded that the documents should be regarded as dispositive in the event of the oral directions being held ineffective. See (1984) 47 M.L.R. 385 at 391 (B. Green).

[41] [1960] A.C. 1 at 4.

[42] *Re Tyler* [1967] 1 W.L.R. 1269. *Grey v. I.R.C., supra,* was cited in argument but not referred to in the judgment.

[43] *per* Diplock L.J. [1966] Ch. 261 at 287.

In *Vandervell v. I.R.C.*,[44] Vandervell wished to give sufficient
money to the Royal College of Surgeons to found a Chair of
Pharmacology. He decided to do so by arranging for the transfer
to the College of shares in Vandervell Products Ltd., subject to an
option exercisable by Vandervell Trustees Ltd., a company which
acted as trustee for various Vandervell family trusts, to repurchase
the shares for £5,000. The shares were held by the National
Provincial Bank Ltd as nominee for Vandervell.

The Bank transferred the shares to the College subject to
the option. Dividends amounting to £250,000 were declared
on the shares and paid to the College, and the income in the hands
of the College, being a charity, was not subject to income tax.
But the Revenue claimed surtax from Vandervell on the ground
that he had not completely divested himself of the beneficial
interest in the property.[45] The Revenue succeeded on the ground
that there had been no declaration of the trusts on which the
option was held by Vandervell Trustees Ltd, and accordingly they
held it on a resulting trust for Vandervell. This aspect of the case
is considered in Chapter 10 below.

A second argument of the Revenue was that, since the Bank had
held the shares on trust for Vandervell, the transfer by the Bank to
the College transferred only the bare legal estate; and the equitable
interest could not leave Vandervell except by a disposition in writing
signed by him. If A holds property on trust for B, and A transfers the
legal title to X, a volunteer, the ordinary rule would suggest that X
took subject to B's beneficial interest; that the beneficial interest, in
short, did not pass on the transfer of the legal title by A. Certainly
this would be the case if the transfer was in breach of trust, or was
only the appointment of a new trustee. On the other hand, there
could be no argument in favour of the application of the section in
the case of a transfer by an absolute owner, at law and in equity[46];
and the House of Lords held that the section was similarly not
applicable in the case of a transfer by a trustee on the directions of
a beneficial owner of the whole interest. Lord Upjohn explained the
object of the section as being to prevent hidden oral transactions
relating to equitable interests. "But when the beneficial owner owns
the whole beneficial estate and is in a position to give directions to
his bare trustee with regard to the legal as well as the equitable estate
there can be no possible ground for invoking the section where the

[44] [1967] 2 A.C. 291; (1966) 24 C.L.J. 19 (G. Jones); (1967) 31 Conv.(N.S.) 175 (S. Spencer); (1967) 30 M.L.R. 461 (N. Strauss); (1975) 38 M.L.R. 557 (J. Harris).
[45] The current legislation is I.C.T.A. 1988, ss.684, 685.
[46] Such a transfer would include the equitable interest unless there is evidence that such was not intended, or where the presumption of resulting trust applies; *post*, p. 254.

beneficial owner wants to deal with the legal estate as well as the equitable estate."[47]

Presumably, however, the subsection would apply if the beneficial owner were to direct that the legal title should be transferred to X, who should hold on trust for Y. In such a case the equitable interest, although passing at the same time as the legal title, would remain separated from it.[48]

(d) *Declaration of Trust with Consent of Beneficial Owner.* That decision did not exhaust the subtleties of the section in its application to Mr Vandervell's affairs. Faced with the surtax claim in 1961 in respect of the dividends paid to the Royal College of Surgeons, he instructed Vandervell Trustees Ltd to exercise the option. They did so, in the same year, using £5,000 from the Vandervell children's settlement for the purpose, manifesting an intention with Vandervell's consent that the shares which they thereby acquired should be held on the trusts of the children's settlement, and so informing the Revenue. In 1965, Vandervell executed a deed formally assigning to Vandervell Trustees Ltd any right or interest he might still have in the option or the shares.

The Revenue assessed Vandervell to surtax in respect of the years 1961–65. Up to 1961, there was a resulting trust in his favour of the option. He had not, until 1965, they argued, disposed of that beneficial interest in writing, and therefore he must still have it; though now in the shares into which the option had been converted.

The executors of Vandervell's estate stepped in before the Revenue's claim was litigated, and claimed from Vandervell Trustees Ltd the dividends paid during 1961–65.[49] They applied to join the Revenue as second defendants, but Vandervell Trustees Ltd successfully objected.[50] The executors' claim to the dividends succeeded before Megarry J. on the ground that the resulting trust which applied to the option applied also to the shares, and there had been no valid declaration of trust in favour of the children's settlement. This was reversed by the Court of Appeal, holding that the trustee company held the dividends on the trusts of the children's settlement. Four reasons were given[51]: first, that the trustees used funds of the children's settlement to exercise the option; secondly, that the trustees

---

[47] [1967] 2 A.C. 291 at 311.

[48] But compare the position in *Re Vandervell's Trusts (No. 2), infra,* where the subsection did not apply to a transaction whereby the legal title passed to the trustees and the equitable interest to the children's settlement, having previously been united in the Royal College of Surgeons. On the latter point it is distinguishable from the example in the text, and is in fact the converse of *Vandervell v. I.R.C.*

[49] *Re Vandervell's Trust (No. 2)* [1974] Ch. 269; (1975) 38 M.L.R. 557 (J. Harris).

[50] *Vandervell Trustees Ltd v. White* [1971] A.C. 912.

[51] Lord Denning also considered that Vandervell, having arranged for the exercise of the option and the payment of dividends to the children's settlement, was estopped from claiming any interest; [1974] Ch. 269 at 321.

and Vandervell showed an intention that the shares should be held on the trusts of that settlement; thirdly, that there had been a perfect gift of the dividends to the children's settlement; and fourthly, that the resulting trust attached to the option and not to the shares, and the trust of the option came to an end with the exercise of the option. Neither the extinction of the trust of the option nor the creation of the new trust of the shares, nor the two, viewed as a whole, amounted to a disposition by Vandervell of an interest within section 53(1)(*c*).

The subsection did not apply where a trustee, with the consent of the beneficiary, declared new trusts of what could be regarded as new property.

The decision of the Court of Appeal leaves many problems in its wake. Essential to the decision was the finding of a valid declaration of trust in favour of the children's settlement, but the three things relied on as constituting the declaration are unconvincing.[52] Surely an element of intention is necessary in the declaration of a trust, yet none of the parties had such an intention, but merely acted on the assumption that the children's settlement was entitled. It is difficult to accept the proposition that the use of the money from the settlement resulted in the acquisition of the beneficial ownership of the shares. Is not the owner of an option entitled to the fruits of it? The fact that it was exercised with X's money gives rights to X, but not equitable ownership.[53] Equally doubtful is the point that there was a "perfect gift" of the dividends to the children's settlement. A valid gift requires a donative intention and capacity to give. Here the dividends were paid to the children's settlement not with a donative intention but on the assumption that the children were already entitled to them.[54]

Other criticisms can be directed at the proposition that Vandervell had no interest in the shares but only in the option, so that when the option terminated (upon its exercise) there was no question of any interest in the shares passing from him to the children's settlement. Underlying the entire decision is the supposition that, if the children's claim failed, there would be a resulting trust of the shares to Vandervell. How could this be if he had no interest in them? Indeed, the House of Lords, in *Vandervell v. I.R.C.*,[55] had held that he had. He was liable to surtax on the dividends because his beneficial ownership of the option meant that he retained some interest in the

---

[52] *post*, p. 128.
[53] *ibid*.
[54] See, however *Milroy v. Lord* (1862) 4 De G.F. & J. 264 at 277 (dividends irrecoverable although gift of shares invalid).
[55] [1967] 2 A.C. 291.

shares.[56] Certainly this was not the entire beneficial interest, but it cannot be said that he had no interest in the shares.

Even assuming a valid declaration of trust for the children, it would have to occur no later than the exercise of the option in order to avoid a resulting trust to Vandervell, whereby any subsequent declaration would be a disposition of his interest.[57] Yet two of the three acts relied on as constituting the declaration occurred after the exercise of the option. Finally, how did the equitable interest in the shares pass from the college to the children's settlement without satisfying the subsection?[58] As the college was at that time also the legal owner, presumably section 53(1)(*c*) did not apply.[59]

(e) *Declaration by Equitable Owner of Himself as Trustee.* A further aspect of the matter which has not yet been worked out is the situation in which the beneficiary declares himself trustee of his equitable interest for another. On the one hand, it can be argued that this is, on its face, a declaration of trust, and not a disposition. It is a sub-trust, the subject-matter not being identical to that of the original trust.[60] On the other hand, it was said in *Grainge v. Wilberforce*[61] that "where A was trustee for B, who was trustee for C, A holds in trust for C, and must convey as C directed." Thus, B "disappears from the picture,"[62] and C becomes the beneficiary. This looks like a disposition. It may be otherwise where B retains active duties, as where he declares a trust of his interest for such of a class as he shall select.[63]

(f) *Specifically Enforceable Oral Contracts for Sale. Oughtred v. I.R.C.,*[64] like *Grey,* concerned an attempt to avoid stamp duty on a share transfer.

---

[56] See I.C.T.A. 1988, ss.684, 685.

[57] As in *Grey v. I.R.C.* [1960] A.C. 1, *supra.*

[58] See (1975) 38 M.L.R. 557 (J. Harris).

[59] On the basis that there was no "subsisting" separate equitable interest. Compare the reasoning of *Vandervell v. I.R.C., supra.* It might also be argued that the exercise of the option gave rise to a contract, which gave rise to a constructive trust, as in the *Oughtred* argument. Thus the equitable interest passed from the college, by virtue of s.53(2), without the need for a written disposition. But this would not solve the problem of where it went to. Presumably it would go to the beneficial owner of the option unless he had disposed of his interest elsewhere, which was the very issue.

[60] Compare the reasoning of *Re Vandervell's Trusts (No. 2), supra.*

[61] (1889) 5 T.L.R. 436 at 437; *post,* p. 120; see also *Re Tout & Finch* [1954] 1 W.L.R. 178; *D.H.N. Food Distributors Ltd v. Tower Hamlets L.B.C.* [1976] 1 W.L.R. 852; (1977) 93 L.Q.R. 171 (D. Sugarman and F. Webb); *Corin v. Patton* (1990) A.L.J.R. 256 at 272.

[62] *per* Upjohn J. in *Grey v. I.R.C.* [1958] Ch. 375 at 382.

[63] *Re Lashmar* [1891] 1 Ch. 258 at 268; see (1958) 74 L.Q.R. 180 (P.V.B.); (1984) 37 M.L.R. 385 at 396 (B. Green). This principle is confirmed in Law Com No. 260, *Trustees' Powers and Duties* (1999), p. 61, discussing the position where trustees vest the legal title to assets such as securities in a nominee. It is considered that the trustees would not "drop out of the picture" on losing legal title, because only limited functions would be delegated to the nominee.

[64] [1960] A.C. 206.

Mrs Oughtred was the owner of 72,700 shares in a company and was also tenant for life under a settlement which contained 100,000 preferences shares and 100,000 ordinary shares. Her son, Peter, was entitled in remainder. In order to reduce the estate duty which would be payable on Mrs Oughtred's death, an oral agreement was made in 1956 under which Peter would surrender his remainder interest in the settled shares in consideration for the transfer to him of his mother's 72,700 shares.

A deed was executed by Mrs Oughtred and Peter which recited that the settled shares were then held in trust for Mrs Oughtred absolutely. The trustees then transferred the shares to Mrs Oughtred; and she transferred the 72,700 shares to Peter. The question was whether *ad valorem* stamp duty was payable on the transfers. The document selected for the purpose of the claim was the transfer of the shares from the trustees to Mrs Oughtred.

The question depended on whether or not Mrs Oughtred was owner in equity of the shares before the legal transfer. Provided a contract is specifically enforceable, a constructive trust is said to arise as soon as the contract is entered into, whereby the equitable interest passes to the purchaser by virtue of his right to specific performance.[65] Contracts for the sale of land are normally specifically enforceable, provided they are in writing, as required by section 2 of the Law of Property (Miscellaneous Provisions) Act 1989. Contracts for the sale of personalty are specifically enforceable only if the remedy of damages would be inadequate. Thus contracts to sell shares in a public company are not normally specifically enforceable, but the position is otherwise in the case of shares in a private company, which are not available for purchase on the market. Mrs Oughtred was accordingly able to claim that the equitable interest had passed to her by virtue of her right to specific performance of the contract; or, putting the same point another way, that Peter, after the agreement, held his interest as constructive trustee for her (constructive trusts being exempted from the writing requirement by section 53(2)). The later document would then be only a transfer of the bare legal estate.

The House of Lords, however, by three to two, held to the contrary. For the majority, Lord Jenkins, with whose speech Lord Keith expressed entire agreement, accepted that Mrs Oughtred's interest, after the agreement, was similar to that of a purchaser of land between contract and conveyance. The purchaser's interest "is no doubt a proprietary interest of a sort, which arises, so to speak, in anticipation of the execution of the transfer for which the purchaser is entitled to call. But its existence has never (so far as I know) been

---

[65] *post*, p. 326.

held to prevent a subsequent transfer, in performance of the contract, of the property contracted to be sold from constituting for stamp duty purposes a transfer on sale of the property in question."[66] So here, the transfer of the legal estate was an instrument attracting duty.

Lord Radcliffe, dissenting, took the view that Mrs Oughtred became equitable owner of the reversionary interest in the settled shares by virtue of the specifically enforceable agreement to exchange. She became the absolute owner in equity. "There was . . . no equity to the shares that could be asserted against her, and it was open to her, if she so wished, to let the matter rest without calling for a written assignment, from her son. . . . It follows that, in my view, this transfer cannot be treated as a conveyance of the son's equitable reversion at all."[67] This argument is compelling, and it points out a number of questions relating to the nature of the interest which Mrs Oughtred held before the legal transfer from the trustees; the majority speeches leave these questions unanswered. It has always been held that stamp duty is payable on a conveyance of land, even though the beneficial interest in the property passed on the signing of the contract; similarly with a purchase of shares. This factor may have influenced the court's approach to the application of section 53. *Oughtred* may thus be viewed as a policy decision.

Later decisions in varying contexts have tended to support the view that an equitable interest can pass under a contract without formality, although the point is rarely fully argued. In *Re Holt's Settlement*,[68] concerning the Variation of Trusts Act 1958, Megarry J., relying on the minority judgments in *Oughtred*, accepted the proposition that where there is a specifically enforceable agreement, the beneficial interest passes to the purchaser under a constructive trust without writing. Similarly in *D.H.N. Food Distributors Ltd v. Tower Hamlets London Borough Council*,[69] concerning compulsory purchase, the Court of Appeal assumed that an equitable interest in land could pass without writing where the transaction was contractual.[70] In *Chinn v. Collins*,[71] concerning a capital gains tax avoidance scheme, Lord Wilberforce said that

---

[66] [1960] A.C. 206, at 240. See also *Henty and Constable (Brewers) Ltd v. I.R.C.* [1961] 1 W.L.R. 1504, at 1510. *Oughtred* was applied in *Parinv (Hatfield) Ltd v. I.R.C.* [1998] S.T.C. 305 (*sub nom. Bishop Square Ltd v. I.R.C.* (1999) 78 P. & C.R. 169), involving an unsuccessful attempt to avoid stamp duty by executing a declaration of trust for the purchaser prior to the transfer ("The appeal is as hopeless as any that I have heard").

[67] [1960] A.C. 206 at 228.

[68] [1969] 1 Ch. 100, at 116.

[69] [1976] 1 W.L.R. 852, at 865, 867.

[70] This argument is no longer tenable in the case of land because the contract must be in writing; Law of Property (Miscellaneous Provisions) Act 1989, s.2. See *United Bank of Kuwait plc v. Sahib* [1997] Ch. 107.

[71] [1981] A.C. 533, at 548.

"The legal title to the shares was at all times vested in a nominee . . . and dealings related to the equitable interest in these required no formality. As soon as there was an agreement for their sale accompanied or followed by payment of the price, the equitable title passed at once to the purchaser . . . and all that was needed to perfect his title was notice to the trustees or the nominee . . . "

The shares were in a public company, but Lord Wilberforce did not appear to consider a specifically enforceable contract to be essential to this proposition which, it should be noted, led to the establishment of capital gains tax liability. Neither *Oughtred* nor even section 53 itself was cited. Tax liability was not involved in *Neville v. Wilson*,[72] where nominees held shares in U Ltd on trust for J Ltd, a family company. The shareholders of J Ltd agreed informally to liquidate the company and to divide its equitable interest in the U Ltd shares amongst themselves in proportion to their existing shareholdings. The question was whether section 53(1)(*c*) invalidated this agreement (in which case the equitable interest would have passed to the Crown when J Ltd was struck off the register). The Court of Appeal held that each shareholder's agreement gave rise to an implied or constructive trust so that section 53(2)[73] applied. Thus the agreement was effective to vest the equitable interest in the shareholders without writing. The analysis of Lord Radcliffe in his dissent in *Oughtred v. I.R.C.*[74] that a specifically enforceable agreement to assign passed the equitable interest to the assignee was correct. It was noted that Lords Jenkins and Keith had left the point open and that Lord Denning (with whom Lord Cohen appeared to agree) had rejected the application of section 53(2) without giving reasons.

It is probable that section 53(2) was intended to embrace the kind of constructive trust which is imposed to prevent fraud,[75] and did not envisage the anomalous constructive trust arising on a specifically enforceable contract for sale. The latter is in any event only a qualified trust (under which the vendor retains valuable rights until the conveyance).[76] In favour of the *Oughtred* decision it might also be said that in the case of a contract there is a transfer of the

---

[72] [1997] Ch. 144; (1996) 55 C.L.J. 436 (R. Nolan); [1996] Conv. 368 (M. Thompson); (1997) 113 L.Q.R. (P. Milne); *cf. United Bank of Kuwait plc v. Sahib* [1997] Ch. 107, where Chadwick J. held that a contract to assign an equitable interest by way of mortgage required writing to satisfy s.53(1)(*c*) and doubted whether s.53(2) could apply. The point was not argued on appeal.

[73] "This section does not effect the creation or operation of resulting, implied or constructive trusts."

[74] [1960] A.C.206.

[75] As in *Bannister v. Bannister* [1948] 2 All E.R. 133; *Hodgson v. Marks* [1971] Ch. 892. See also *Midland Bank Ltd v. Dobson* [1986] 1 F.L.R. 171, *post*, p. 273.

[76] *post*, p. 327.

equitable interest from the vendor to the purchaser, whereas in the case of resulting trusts and constructive trusts imposed to prevent fraud, contemplated by section 53(2), there is no *passing* of the equitable interest, which remains throughout in the true beneficial owner.[77] It seems that the acceptance of the argument that a contract can shift the equitable interest without formality under the con- structive trust principle depends very much on the context, and that it is more likely to be accepted in the tax context where this would result in liability.

(g) *Variation of Trusts Act 1958*. We shall see in Chapter 22 that the Variation of Trusts Act 1958 gave power to the court to approve, on behalf of categories of persons unable to make the decision for themselves, variations of the existing beneficial interests under trusts where it is for the benefit of the beneficiaries to do so. Many variations had been approved by the courts when suddenly, in *Re Holt's Settlement*,[78] Megarry J. asked whether it was not necessary for the disposition of each existing beneficial interest to be in writ- ing under section 53. Megarry J. was able to satisfy himself that writing was not necessary, and the threat of invalidity to most of the variations previously approved was removed. The details of the matter are best postponed until the Act is explained.[79]

(h) *Right of Nomination under Staff Pension Fund*. The rules of the pension fund of the *Danish Bacon Co. Ltd* provided that employ- ees could nominate a person to receive moneys due in the case of death in service. Such a nomination might arguably be regarded as a lifetime disposition of an equitable interest under the pension fund trust; or as a testamentary disposition in that it took effect only in the event of the employee's death. In *Re Danish Bacon Co. Staff Pen- sion Fund Trusts*,[80] Megarry J. held that it was not a testamentary disposition. He very much doubted "whether the nomination falls within section 53(1)(c)"[81]; but held that, even if it did, the necessary writing was supplied by two connecting documents.

(i) *Disclaimer; Surrender*. In *Re Paradise Motor Co. Ltd*,[82] a stepfather made a gift of shares to his stepson. The transfer, though technically defective, was sufficient to make the stepson equitable

---

[77] Although Lord Browne-Wilkinson in *Westdeutsche Landesbank Girozentrale v. Islington London Borough Council* [1996] A.C. 669 at 705–706 suggests otherwise; *post*, p. 239.
[78] [1969] 1 Ch. 590.
[79] *post*, p. 637.
[80] [1971] 1 W.L.R. 248. Followed by the Privy Council in *Baird v. Baird* [1990] 2 A.C. 548 (application of Wills Act depends on each scheme); [1990] Conv. 458 (G. Kodilinye); *Gold v. Hill* [1999] 1 F.L.R. 54 (nomination did not dispose of any equitable interest).
[81] [1971] 1 W.L.R. 248 at 256.
[82] [1968] 1 W.L.R. 1125.

owner of the shares. The stepson knew nothing of the transfer. When he became aware of the circumstances, he stated in unmistakable language that he wished to make no claim to the shares. But when the company was in liquidation, he changed his mind and claimed his share of the proceeds. On the question whether there could be a disclaimer of an equitable interest without compliance with section 53, it was held that "a disclaimer operates by way of avoidance and not by way of disposition."[83] The disclaimer was effective and the claim failed.

However, the position seems otherwise as far as tax matters are concerned,[84] where it has been found necessary to make express provision that a disclaimer shall not be treated as a disposition for inheritance tax purposes.[85]

A surrender, on the other hand, appears to be a "disposition".[86] The House of Lords in *Newlon Housing Trust v. Alsulaimen*[87] considered that the surrender of a lease would be a "disposition" within section 37 of the Matrimonial Causes Act 1973, adding that the ordinary meaning of the term was an act by which someone ceased to be the owner of property at law or in equity and that, in some contexts, this might include a case where the property ceased to exist.

B. By Will

Additional formalities are required for the creation of a testamentary trust. Wills Act 1837, s.9, as amended by Administration of Justice Act 1982, s.17, provides:

"No will shall be valid unless:

(a) it is in writing, and signed by the testator, or by some other person in his presence and by his direction; and
(b) it appears that the testator intended by his signature to give effect to the will; and
(c) the signature is made or acknowledged by the testator in the presence of two or more witnesses present at the same time; and
(d) each witness either—

  (i) attests and signs the will; or

---

[83] *Re Paradise Motor Co. Ltd, supra*, at 1143; *Dewar v. Dewar* [1975] 1 W.L.R. 1532; *Allied Dunbar Assurance plc v. Fowle* [1994] 1 E.G.L.R. 122; *Lohia v. Lohia* [2001] W.T.L.R. 101. But see L.P.A. 1925, s.205(1)(ii).
[84] *Re Stratton's Disclaimer* [1958] Ch. 42 (estate duty).
[85] Inheritance Tax Act 1984, s.17.
[86] *cf.* [1960] B.T.R. 20 (J. Monroe).
[87] [1999] 1 A.C. 313.

(ii) acknowledges his signature,

> in the presence of the testator (but not necessarily in the presence of any other witness),

but no form of attestation shall be necessary."

No attempt will be made here to deal with the details of this enactment. The question of the validity of trusts taking effect on a testator's death which fail to comply with these provisions—the so-called "secret trusts"—will be discussed in Chapter 5.

3. CERTAINTY

A private express trust cannot be created unless the three certainties[88] are present; certainty of intention; certainty of subject matter; and certainty of beneficiaries. Each of these heads will be considered below. Different considerations apply to each; yet they are inter-related. "Uncertainty in the subject of the gift has a reflex action upon the previous words, and shows doubt upon the intention of the testator, and seems to show that he could not possibly have intended his words of confidence, hope, or whatever they may be—his appeal to the conscience of the first taker—to be imperative words."[89]

Similar, but distinct, questions about certainty may arise in relation to a conditional gift; whether a condition precedent to taking,[90] or a condition of defeasance.[91] Further, the requirement of certainty of beneficiaries operates differently with discretionary as opposed to fixed trusts, and with trusts for purposes as opposed to trusts for people. A trust for a non-charitable purpose is normally invalid; but where such a trust has been upheld, the court has insisted that the purpose be described with sufficient certainty.[92] With charitable trusts, there is no need to specify in any way which charity is to be benefited; but the language of the gift must clearly establish that the gift is applicable for charitable purposes only.[93]

A. Certainty of Intention

We have already seen that a trustee is under an obligation, but that the obligation may be inferred from the nature of the gift, considered

---

[88] See Lord Langdale in *Knight v. Knight* (1840) 3 Beav. 148 at 173. Extrinsic evidence is not generally admissible to aid the construction of a trust deed; *Rabin v. Gerson Berger Association Ltd* [1986] 1 W.L.R. 526.

[89] *Mussourie Bank v. Raynor* (1882) 7 App.Cas. 321 at 331.

[90] *Re Allen* [1953] Ch. 810; *Re Barlow's W.T.* [1979] 1 W.L.R. 278.

[91] *Clayton v. Ramsden* [1943] A.C. 320; *Blathwayt v. Lord Cawley* [1976] A.C. 397.

[92] *Re Astor's S.T.* [1952] Ch. 534; *post*, p. 372.

[93] *post*, p. 395.

as a whole.[94] Technical words are not required. The question is whether, on the proper construction of the words used, the settlor or testator has shown an intention to create a trust. A trust may be created without using the word "trust," and, conversely, the use of the word "trust" does not conclusively indicate the existence of a trust.[95] A "precatory" expression of hope or desire, or suggestion or request, is not sufficient. The words in each case must be examined to see whether the intention was to impose a trust upon the donee.

The Court of Chancery at one time leaned in favour of construing expressions of desire as intended to create a binding trust.[96] This was because an executor who had administered an estate was entitled to keep for himself any surplus which was undisposed of by the will, and the court was ready to find that he took as trustee in order to prevent this. This approach then spread beyond executors. In 1830, however, the Executors Act provided that undisposed-of residue should be held on trust for the next-of-kin; and from about the middle of the nineteenth century, a stricter construction was placed upon these "precatory words". Where, however, an express trust is construed from precatory words, it is, of course, just as much a trust as any other.[97]

The older cases are therefore unhelpful as guides to construction. *Lambe v. Eames*[98] is usually regarded as the case which marks the "turning of the tide". There the testator gave his estate to his widow "to be at her disposal in any way she may think best, for the benefit of herself and her family." By her will she gave part of the estate outside the family; it was held that she had been absolutely entitled to the property and that the gift was valid. Similarly in *Re Adams and the Kensington Vestry*,[99] where a testator gave his estate "unto and to the absolute use of my dear wife, Harriet . . . in full confidence that she will do what is right as to the disposal thereof between my children, either in her lifetime or by will after her decease." The Court of Appeal held that she took absolutely.

But a trust will be found from precatory words if on a proper construction of the language such was the intention of the testator.

---

[94] *ante*, p. 62. In the context of charity, see *Re Cohen* [1973] 1 W.L.R. 415.

[95] *Tito v. Waddell (No. 2)* [1977] Ch. 106, *ante*, p. 72; *Customs and Excise Commissioners v. Richmond Theatre Management Ltd* [1995] S.T.C. 257, *ante*, p. 54.

[96] See, however, *Cook v. Fountain* (1676) 3 Swan. 585.

[97] In *Re Williams* [1897] 2 Ch. 12 at 27 Rigby L.J. protested against the use of the term "precatory trust," calling it a "misleading nickname."

[98] (1871) L.R. 6 Ch. 597. See also *Re Hamilton* [1895] 2 Ch. 370 at 374.

[99] (1884) 27 Ch.D. 394; *Mussourie Bank v. Raynor* (1882) 7 App.Cas. 321 ("feeling confident that she will act justly to our children in distributing the same"); *Re Diggles* (1888) 39 Ch.D. 253 ("it is my desire that she allows . . . an annuity of £25); *Re Johnson* [1939] 2 All E.R. 458 ("I request that my mother will on her death leave the property or what remains of it . . . to my four sisters").

In *Comiskey v. Bowring-Hanbury*,[1] a testator gave to his wife "the whole of my real and personal estate . . . in full confidence that . . . at her death she will devise it to such one or more of my nieces as she may think fit and in default of any disposition by her thereof by her will . . . I hereby direct that all my estate and property acquired by her under this my will shall at her death be equally divided among the surviving said nieces." A majority of the House of Lords held that the testator intended to make a gift to his wife, with a gift over of the whole property at her death to such of her nieces as should survive her, shared according to the wife's will, and otherwise equally.

Where a form of words has once been held to create a trust, the testator's intention may be held to be such as to reach the same result, at any rate where the words have been used as a precedent, even though the words used, when subjected to the stricter modern construction, might be expected to produce a different result.[2]

Where the words used are held not to create a trust, the donee of the property takes beneficially.[3] This must be distinguished from the situation where there is certainty of intention to create a trust, but uncertainty as to the objects or the shares they are to take. In such cases, as we shall see, there is a resulting trust.

The question of certainty of intention may also arise where there is no document to construe. The question then is whether the acts or words of the parties indicate an intention to create a trust; as where a man tells his cohabitant that she can share his bank account[4]; or where a mail order company puts money sent by customers into a separate bank account.[5] This aspect of the problem will be discussed in Chapter 4, where the requirements of the declaration of trust are examined.[6]

Finally, the intention to create a trust must be genuine, and not a sham, as where the "settlor" did not intend the trust to be acted upon, but entered into it for some ulterior motive, such as deceiving

---

[1] [1905] A.C. 84.

[2] *Re Steele's W.T.* [1948] Ch. 603; following *Shelley v. Shelley* (1868) L.R. 6 Eq. 540; (1968) 32 Conv.(N.S.) 361 (P. Langan).

[3] *Lassence v. Tierney* (1849) 1 Mac. & Cr. 551; *Hancock v. Watson* [1902] A.C. 14; *Watson v. Holland* [1985] 1 All E.R. 290; *cf. Re Pugh's W.T.* [1967] 1 W.L.R. 1261.

[4] *Paul v. Constance* [1977] 1 W.L.R. 527. See also *Re Vandervell's Trusts (No. 2)* [1974] Ch. 269; *Swain v. The Law Society* [1983] 1 A.C. 598.

[5] *Re Kayford Ltd (in Liquidation)* [1975] 1 W.L.R. 279, *ante*, p. 53; *cf. Re Challoner Club (in Liquidation)*, *The Times*, November 4, 1997 (no trust where members' money paid into separate account as terms of intended trust uncertain). See also *R. v. Clowes (No. 2)* [1994] 2 All E.R. 316 (terms of investment brochures indicated a trust); *Re Lewis's of Leicester Ltd* [1995] 1 B.C.L.C. 428 (company created trust by paying takings of concessionaires into separate account, although its commission had not been deducted from the payments, thus the company was also a beneficiary).

[6] *post*, p. 125.

creditors or the Inland Revenue. In *Midland Bank plc v. Wyatt*[7] a declaration of trust was executed by a husband and wife in 1987 (when the husband was contemplating a new business) whereby the family home, their only real asset, was apparently settled on the wife and daughters. The document was kept in a safe and the couple continued to act as absolute owners of the property, in particular by mortgaging it. The husband's business failed and the bank obtained a charging order against the house. The husband then revealed the trust document. This was held to be a sham. The inference was that the husband had "kept it up his sleeve for a rainy day" in order to defeat future creditors and had not otherwise intended it to have any effect. This principle does not require a finding of fraud, and can apply if the transaction is the result of merely mistaken advice.

B. Certainty of Subject-Matter

The subject-matter may be an interest in land; it may be chattels or money; it may be a chose in action, such as a covenant[8] or a debt owed to the settlor. Whatever form it takes, it must be specified with reasonable certainty. Testamentary gifts have failed where they concerned "the bulk of my estate,"[9] or "such parts of my estate as she shall not have sold,"[10] or "anything that is left,[11] or "the remaining part of what is left"[12] or "all my other houses"[13] *i.e.* those remaining after a choice had been made by another beneficiary who died before choosing. Similarly a direction that the testator's widow was to get "such minimal part of [the] estate as she might be entitled to under English law for maintenance purposes" was void for uncertainty, as no such entitlement could be identified.[14] These cases should be contrasted with one where the subject-matter of the gift is to be determined in the discretion of a trustee. In *Re Golay's Will Trusts*,[15] a gift directing the executors to allow a beneficiary to "enjoy one of my flats during her lifetime and to receive a reasonable income from my other properties" was upheld. The executors could select the flat. The words "reasonable income" were not intended to allow the trustees to make a subjective decision: but they provided a sufficient objective determinant to enable the court, if

---

[7] [1995] 1 F.L.R. 696; *post*, p. 355; (1994) 8 *Trust Law International* 68 (J. Mowbray); (1998) 4 *Trusts & Trustees* 11 (P. Matthews). See also *Re Pfrimmer Estate* (1936) 2 D.L.R. 460; *Rahman v. Chase Bank (C.I.) Trust Co. Ltd* [1991] J.L.R. 103 (Jersey).

[8] *Fletcher v. Fletcher* (1844) 4 Hare 67; *post*, p. 135. See also *Swift v. Dairywise Farms Ltd* [2000] 1 W.L.R. 1177 (trust of milk quota).

[9] *Palmer v. Simmonds* (1854) 2 Drew. 221. See also Choithram (T.) *International S.A. v. Pagarani* [2000] 1 W.L.R. 1 (left open whether trust of "all my wealth" void for uncertainty).

[10] *Re Jones* [1898] 1 Ch. 438.

[11] *In the Estate of Last* [1958] P. 137.

[12] *Sprange v. Barnard* (1789) 2 Bro.C.C. 585.

[13] *Boyce v. Boyce* (1849) 16 Sim. 476.

[14] *Anthony v. Donges* [1998] 2 F.L.R. 775.

[15] [1965] 1 W.L.R. 969.

necessary, to quantify the amount. The problem, however, is that no
objective determination of words such as "reasonable" can be made
unless the context is known. In *Re Golay's Will Trusts*[16] it was
assumed that the criterion was the beneficiary's previous standard of
living. The word "reasonable" in isolation has little meaning. If a
testator were to give "a reasonable legacy" to X, then no doubt the
gift would fail, unless it was clear that the amount was to be fixed
by the executors.

Where the subject-matter of the trust is uncertain, then no trust is
created. There is nothing to form the subject-matter of a resulting
trust. If the purported trust has been attached to an absolute gift, then
the absolute gift takes effect. It may be, however, that the property
itself is certain, but the beneficial shares are not. Unless the trustees
have a discretion to determine the amounts, then the trust will fail,
and the property will be held on a resulting trust for the settlor. This
was the case in *Boyce v. Boyce*,[17] where the determination was to be
made by a beneficiary who died before choosing. Sometimes the
problem will be solved by the principle that equity is equality,[18] or
by the court determining what is the proper division according to the
circumstances.[19]

Certainty of subject matter has been in issue recently not only in
relation to express trusts but also in the commercial context of the
sale of goods. Where purchasers have paid for goods but have not
taken delivery prior to the seller's insolvency, they may seek to gain
priority over general creditors by claiming a trust of the goods in
their favour. Where the goods have not been segregated but form
part of a bulk, these claims failed (prior to a legislative reform
mentioned below) on the ground that there cannot be a trust of
unidentified chattels. Thus in *Re London Wine Co.*[20] the buyers of
wine stored in a warehouse and not segregated from the general
stock of similar wine could not establish a trust. It was otherwise
where the wine had been segregated for a group of customers (even
though not appropriated to each individual customer), as in *Re Sta-
pylton Fletcher Ltd*,[21] although the judge warned that the court
"must be very cautious in devising equitable interests and remedies
which erode the statutory scheme for distribution on insolvency. It
cannot do it because of some perceived injustice arising as a consequence only of the insolvency."[22] In that case the legal title had

---

[16] *supra.*
[17] (1849) 6 Sim. 476.
[18] *Burrough v. Philcox* (1840) 5 Myl. & Cr. 72; (1967) 31 Conv.(N.S.) 117 (A. Hawkins).
[19] *McPhail v. Doulton* [1971] A.C. 424 (selection of beneficiaries); *post*, p. 104.
[20] (1986) Palmer's Company Cases 121.
[21] [1994] 1 W.L.R. 1181 (tenancy in common); considered "eminently sensible and fair" in
  (1995) 48 C.L.P. 117 at 131 (A. Clarke).
[22] *ibid.* at 1203 (Paul Baker Q.C.)

passed to the customers and there was no need to consider the trust argument.

The leading authority is *Re Goldcorp Exchange Ltd*,[23] where purchasers of bullion, who had paid but had not taken delivery, asserted proprietary rights on the insolvency of the company. Save for a group of customers whose bullion had been segregated, these claims were rejected by the Privy Council. Legal title had not passed, nor was there any trust, as there was no identifiable property to which any trust could attach. Thus the customers were unsecured creditors.

Although no doubt some chattels can be regarded as identical to other chattels of the same description, the rationale of the rule that there cannot be a trust of chattels which have not been segregated from a mass of similar chattels is that they are not necessarily identical.[24] Even bottles of wine of the same label may not be identical; some may be "corked" and undrinkable. Now, however, the Sale of Goods (Amendment) Act 1995[25] provides that purchasers who have paid for unascertained goods forming part of an identified bulk (where the goods are interchangeable) acquire property rights as tenants in common of the bulk, subject to any contrary agreement. Thus they will prevail over general creditors in an insolvency. This provision will not, of course, apply to the creation of express trusts of chattels.

The chattels rule does not apply to money, shares and other choses in action because, in the nature of things, there is no difference between one pound and another pound, or one share and another share of the same class in the same company.[26] Difficult problems do, however, arise.

In *Hunter v. Moss*[27] the settlor owned 950 shares in M Co., which had an issued share capital of 1,000. He orally declared a trust of five per cent of the share capital, *i.e.* 50 shares. The Court of Appeal upheld the trust. Provided the shares were of the same class and in the same company, there was no need to segregate 50 shares before declaring the trust. *Re London Wine Co.*[28] was distinguished as involving chattels. Cases upholding bequests[29] of

---

[23] [1995] 1 A.C. 74; (1994) 53 C.L.J. 443 (L. Sealy); *post*, p. 690.

[24] *cf.* All E.R. Rev. 1994 250 (P. Clarke), doubting the distinction in an age of mass-produced goods.

[25] Amending the Sale of Goods Act 1979.

[26] Although they are distinguishable by serial number. See Smith, *The Law of Tracing*, p. 224.

[27] [1994] 1 W.L.R. 452; [1996] Conv. 223 (J. Martin). The position is otherwise in Australia; see *Re Harvard Securities Ltd (in Liquidation)* [1997] 2 B.C.L.C. 369; *post*, p. 101.

[28] *supra*.

[29] *Re Cheadle* [1900] 2 Ch. 620; *Re Clifford* [1912] 1 Ch. 29. These are considered distinguishable in (1994) 53 C.L.J. 448 (M. Ockelton).

part of a larger shareholding showed that the chattels rule did not apply to choses in action. Thus a declaration of trust of part of a larger shareholding or £50 out of a designated bank account with a larger balance would be valid. In fact the settlor had subsequently sold the shares to B Co. in exchange for shares in B Co. and cash, and the judgment was for five per cent of the consideration.

The decision has been criticised, but before considering the criticisms it is necessary to examine a different situation, where a settlor attempts to create a trust of money but (unlike in the bank account example above) does not designate the source of the money. In *MacJordan Construction Ltd v. Brookmount Erostin Ltd*[30] a building contract provided that the employer would retain three per cent of the contract price as trustee for the builder (pending confirmation that the work was satisfactory). The retention fund was never set up. On the employer's insolvency the builder claimed entitlement to the retention money in priority to a bank which had a floating charge over all the assets. This claim failed because no identifiable assets had been impressed with a trust for the builder. There was merely a contractual right, which did not "carry with it any equitable interest of a security character in the assets for the time being of the employer."[31] This is clearly correct, being in effect no different from an attempt by X to declare himself trustee of £100 for Y without identifying the source of the money. Thus in *Hemmens v. Wilson Browne (a firm)*[32] a document purporting to give A the right to call on B for payment of £110,000 at any time did not create a trust (or any other right) because there was no identifiable fund to form its subject matter. Likewise there is no trust of money paid into an overdrawn account, as there is no identifiable subject-matter.[33]

Of course, there is no difficulty in a trust of a co-owned share, but that solution was rejected in *Hunter v. Moss*[34]: the claimant did not have a tenancy in common interest in the whole but was equitable owner of 50 shares. Criticisms of *Hunter v. Moss* point to the difficulties which could arise on subsequent dealings with the shareholding or bank account of which an unsegregated part is subject to a trust. Before any such dealings, the beneficiary could call for a transfer of the money or shares. But what would happen if, after declaring a trust of 50 out of 950 shares, the settlor then sold 50

---

[30] [1992] B.C.L.C. 350.

[31] *MacJordan Construction Ltd v. Brookmount Erostin Ltd* [1992] B.C.L.C. 350.

[32] [1995] Ch. 223 (a professional negligence action).

[33] *Fortex Group Ltd v. MacIntosh* [1998] 3 N.Z.L.R. 171.

[34] [1994] 1 W.L.R. 452. Co-ownership is preferred in (1994–95) 5 K.C.L.J. 139 (P. Oliver). It is also the legislative solution for goods; Sale of Goods (Amendment) Act 1995, *supra*.

shares and invested the proceeds (disastrously or profitably)? Whose 50 shares were they? There seems no reason why the tracing rules relating to mixed assets should not apply.[35] Those rules normally deal with trust property which has subsequently become mixed with other property, but there seems no reason why they should be so confined. In any event, it could be said that a settlor who declares a trust of part of his shareholding or bank balance becomes under a duty to segregate the trust assets from his own. Tracing will not work, on the other hand, in a case like *MacJordan*[36] because there is no identifiable mixed fund; the employer there had only one bank account in credit at the insolvency but had never assumed an obligation to set up the retention fund out of that account.[37] It may be that the tracing rules will not always work in a case like *Hunter v. Moss*,[38] but inability to trace need not mean that there was no valid trust in the first place.

It has been said that the approval of *MacJordan*[39] by the Privy Council in *Re Goldcorp Exchange Ltd*[40] shows by inference that *Hunter v. Moss* is incorrect.[41] This would be so only if *Hunter* and *MacJordan* were indistinguishable, but the discussion above sought to establish that *Hunter* may be distinguished on the basis that the larger asset from which the trust was carved was identified. It is submitted that the *Hunter v. Moss* solution is fair, sensible and workable.[42] Unlike the other cases, it did not involve a claim by unsecured creditors to gain priority in insolvency. It is an example of the court's policy of preventing a clearly intended trust from failing for uncertainty.[43]

The academic criticisms of *Hunter v. Moss* were noted with some sympathy by the High Court in the context of an insolvency in *Re Harvard Securities Ltd (in Liquidation)*,[44] but the decision was regarded as binding and not effectively overruled by *Re Goldcorp*. It was noted that, after the latter decision, the House of Lords had refused the defendant in *Hunter* leave to appeal.[45]

---

[35] *post*, p. 688.

[36] *supra.*

[37] To claim a charge over the general assets would go beyond even the unorthodox dicta in *Space Investments Ltd v. Canadian Imperial Bank of Commerce Trust Co. (Bahamas)* [1986] 1 W.L.R. 1072; *post*, p. 689.

[38] See criticisms in All E.R. Rev. 1994 p. 250 (P. Clarke).

[39] *supra.*

[40] [1995] 1 A.C. 74; *supra.*

[41] (1994) 110 L.Q.R. 335 (D. Hayton); (1995) 9 *Trust Law International* 43 at 45 (P. Birks).

[42] See (1995) 48 C.L.P. 117 (A. Clarke).

[43] See *Re Golay's W.T.* [1965] 1 W.L.R. 969; *ante*, p. 97; *Re Tepper's W.T.* [1987] Ch. 358; *post*, p. 108.

[44] [1997] 2 B.C.L.C. 369; (1998–9) 9 K.C.L.J. 112 (T. Villiers).

[45] [1994] 1 W.L.R. 614.

Before leaving the question of certainty of subject-matter, it might be said that uncertainty as to the precise scope of property subjected to a secret trust,[46] a trust arising under mutual wills,[47] or a constructive trust of a family home,[48] has not proved fatal to its validity. Insistence on strict rules in these contexts could facilitate fraud or unjust enrichment.

C. Certainty of Objects: The Beneficiaries[49]

"It is clear law that a trust (other than a charitable trust) must be for ascertainable beneficiaries."[50] In the case of future interests, the beneficiaries must be ascertainable within the period of perpetuity.[51] The test to be applied to determine certainty of objects depends upon the nature of the trust. With a "fixed" trust, it is, and always has been, that a trust is void unless it is possible to ascertain every beneficiary. With a discretionary trust, the House of Lords decided in *McPhail v. Doulton*[52] that the test was: can it be said with certainty that any individual is or is not a member of the class?[53] That is the same test as was established for certainty of objects of a mere power in *Re Gulbenkian's Settlements*.[54] This assimilation of the tests for powers and discretionary trusts destroys what used to be one of the most important reasons for distinguishing between trusts and powers.[55]

i. Fixed Trusts. A fixed trust is one in which the share or interest of the beneficiaries is specified in the instrument. The beneficiary is the owner of the equitable interest allocated to him. This situation is contrasted with a discretionary trust; where the trustees hold the trust property on trust for such member or members of a class of beneficiaries as they shall in their absolute discretion determine. In that situation, no beneficiary owns any part of the trust fund unless

---

[46] *Ottaway v. Norman* [1972] Ch. 698, *post*, p. 157.
[47] *Re Cleaver* [1981] 1 W.L.R. 939, *post*, p. 324.
[48] *Gissing v. Gissing* [1971] A.C. 886 at 909; *Stokes v. Anderson* [1991] 1 F.L.R. 391; *post*, p. 283. Likewise remedial constructive trusts, where they are recognised; *Fortex Group Ltd v. MacIntosh* [1998] 3 N.Z.L.R. 171.
[49] (1971) 24 C.L.P. 133 (H. Cohen); (1971) 87 L.Q.R. 31 (J. Harris); (1971) 29 C.L.J. 68 (J. Hopkins); (1973) 5 N.Z.U.L.R. 348; (1974) 37 M.L.R. 643 (Y. Grbich); (1973) 7 V.U.W.L.R. 258 (L. McKay); (1975) 4 Anglo-American L.R. 442 (S. Fradley); (1982) 98 L.Q.R. 551 (C. Emery); Law Com. No. 58 para. 63. For the position in Australia, see (2000) 22 Sydney Law Review 93 (P. Creighton).
[50] *per* Lord Denning in *Re Vandervell's Trusts (No. 2)* [1974] Ch. 269 at 319; *Re Wood* [1949] Ch. 498.
[51] *Re Flavel's W.T.* [1969] 1 W.L.R. 444 at 446–447.
[52] [1971] A.C. 424.
[53] *per* Lord Wilberforce [1971] A.C. 424 at 454, 456.
[54] [1970] A.C. 508; *post*, p. 104.
[55] *Re Gestetner Settlement* [1953] Ch. 672.

and until the trustees have exercised their discretion in his favour.[56]

Commonly, but not necessarily, there is a fixed trust where there are successive interests in favour of individual beneficiaries; such as a trust for A for life and then for B absolutely. Where there is a gift for a class, it is necessary in the case of a fixed trust to lay down what share each beneficiary is to take; a discretionary trust will provide for the trustees to exercise a discretion in the selection of a beneficiary. The requirement of certainty in discretionary trusts is considered in (ii) below. The point here is that if trust property is to be divided among a class of beneficiaries in equal (or in any other fixed) shares, the trust cannot, in the nature of things, be administered unless the number and identify of beneficiaries are known. Some of the language in *McPhail v. Doulton*[57] might suggest the decision applied to all trusts. But it concerned a discretionary trust and the cases which it examines are cases of discretionary trusts.[58] Although the rule of certainty should be the minimum necessary to make the trust workable, a stricter rule is needed for fixed trusts. How could the trustee or the court administer a trust for "my employees, ex-employees and their relatives and dependants in equal shares"?[59]

To summarise the position, what is required of a fixed trust is that the description of beneficiaries should involve neither conceptual nor evidential uncertainty.[60] But the court will strive to uphold the trust and a common-sense approach will be taken.[61] Furthermore, provided the identity of the beneficiaries is known, it is no objection that their whereabouts or continued existence is not discoverable, as their shares can be paid into court.[62] The requirement is that a list will be able to be drawn, which is on balance of probabilities complete, as to the maximum number of shares, at the time for distribution.

ii. Discretionary Trusts. The rule of certainty should be no stricter than is necessary to permit trustees to perform their duties. We have seen that, where the trust property is to be divided into specific shares, it is necessary for the trustees to know exactly how many beneficiaries there are. Until 1971, the same rule applied to

---

[56] *post*, p. 209.

[57] [1971] A.C. 424.

[58] *Re Ogden* [1933] Ch. 678; *I.R.C. v. Broadway Cottages Trust* [1955] Ch. 678.

[59] *McPhail v. Doulton, supra.* See [1984] Conv. 22 (P. Matthews), suggesting that complete ascertainment is not necessary in the case of fixed trusts. This is doubted at [1984] Conv. 304 (J. Martin) and 307 (D. Hayton).

[60] *post*, p. 106.

[61] See *Gold v. Hill* [1999] 1 F.L.R. 54 (oral direction to recipient to "look after Carol and the kids" sufficiently certain although it could be interpreted in various ways).

[62] (1982) 98 L.Q.R. 551 (C. Emery); *cf.* [1984] Conv. 22 (P. Matthews).

discretionary trusts[63] (sometimes confusingly called "trust powers"[64]). If the trustees should fail or refuse to carry out their duty to
select the beneficiaries and distribute, the court must be able to do
so; and, it was argued, the court would necessarily distribute equally
on the basis that equality is equity and, for that purpose, the beneficiaries must be identifiable.[65] The fallacy of this argument was
shown in *McPhail v. Doulton.*[66]

> Bertram Baden executed a deed establishing a fund to provide
> benefits for the staff of a company and their relatives and de-
> pendants.
>   Clause 9(*a*) provided as follows: "The trustees shall apply the
> net income of the fund in making at their absolute discretion
> grants to or for the benefit of any of the officers and employees or
> ex-officers or ex-employees of the company or to any relatives or
> dependants of any such persons in such amounts at such times and
> on such conditions (if any) as they think fit."
>   The trustees were not obliged to exhaust the income of any
> year. Capital could be realised for the purpose of making grants if
> the income was insufficient.

The deed created a discretionary trust not a mere power. It was
not possible to make a list of all the members of the class of beneficiaries. The House of Lords, however, held that the test for certainty in discretionary trusts was that applied to fiduciary powers in
Re Gulbenkian's Settlements.[67] "Can it be said with certainty that
any given individual is or is not a member of the class?"[68] The case
was referred to the Chancery Division to determine whether the test
was satisfied. The Court of Appeal held that it was.[69]
    In reaching a decision on the question of the test to be applied, it
was necessary to deal with two main arguments in favour of the
stricter test. First, that a trustee's duty to distribute could only be
performed if he was able to consider every possible claimant; and
secondly, that the court could only execute the trust, on failure of the
trustees to do so, by equal division of the fund. If these arguments
could be answered, there was much to be said for assimilating the
test with that for powers; for, although the distinction between trust
and power is, in some contexts, basic to a lawyer, it is often difficult

---

[63] *I.R.C. v. Broadway Cottages Trust* [1955] Ch. 678.
[64] For a possible distinction between these two terms, see *post*, p. 114.
[65] [1971] A.C. 424 at 442, *per* Lord Hodson.
[66] *supra*; (1970) 34 Conv.(N.S.) 287 (F. Crane). One result of the decision is to confirm that a
trust may be valid although it is impossible to state who is entitled to the equitable interest.
See [1982] Conv. 118 (A. Everton).
[67] [1970] A.C. 508.
[68] *per* Lord Wilberforce [1971] A.C. 424 at 454, 456.
[69] [1973] Ch. 9; *post*, p. 106.

to ascertain which exists in any particular case. Thus a relaxation of the test was needed to save many trusts from failure.

A trustee's duty to distribute requires a consideration of the claims of possible recipients. "If [a trustee] has to distribute the whole of a fund's income, he must necessarily make a wider and more systematic survey than if his duty is expressed in terms of a power to make grants"[70]; and later, "a wider and more comprehensive range of inquiry is called for in the case of a trust power than in the case of a power."[71] But the difference is only one of degree; there is no need for a trustee of a discretionary trust to "require the preparation of a complete list of names."[72] The difference does not justify a stricter rule for certainty in discretionary trusts.

The main question is whether the court can execute the trust upon the failure of the trustees to do so. This is primarily a theoretical problem. In the reported cases there have been no examples of trustees refusing to execute a discretionary trust; if a trustee did so, he could be removed and replaced. Secondly, "it does not follow that execution is impossible unless there can be equal division."[73] There are a number of cases, prior to 1801,[74] in which the court exercised a discretion in relation to distribution, deciding in accordance with guidance given by the circumstances of the case.[75] In many of these situations equal division would have been inappropriate. As indeed it would be in modern forms of discretionary trusts for the benefit of employees and their dependants. It would have been paradoxical if the trust in *McPhail v. Doulton*[76] had failed because of the court's inability to divide equally; for equal division would have been a nonsensical solution. Thus, the court, if called upon to execute a discretionary trust, will do so in the manner best calculated to give effect to the testator's intentions. "It may do so by appointing new trustees, or by authorising or directing representative persons of the classes of beneficiaries to prepare a scheme of distribution, or even, should the proper basis for distribution appear, by itself directing the trustees so to distribute."[77] In cases where the trustees have failed to exercise their discretion within a reasonable time, the court may direct them to do so, provided there is no

---

[70] [1971] A.C. 424 at 449, 457; (1971) 87 L.Q.R. 31 at 61–62.

[71] [1973] Ch. 9 at 27.

[72] [1971] A.C. 424 at 449.

[73] *ibid.* at 451.

[74] *Kemp v. Kemp* (1801) 5 Ves.Jr. 849.

[75] *Mosely v. Mosely* (1673) Fin. 53; *Clarke v. Turner* (1694) Free Ch. 198; *Warburton v. Warburton* (1702) 4 Bro.P.C. 1; *Richardson v. Chapman* (1760) 7 Bro.P.C. 318.

[76] [1971] A.C. 424.

[77] *ibid.* at 457, *per* Lord Wilberforce. See also *Mettoy Pension Trustees Ltd v. Evans* [1990] 1 W.L.R. 1587, holding that the court has similar powers of intervention in the case of fiduciary powers.

evidence of bias or obstinacy.[78] There is no need therefore to require a stricter rule for discretionary trusts than that accepted in *Gulbenkian*[79] as applicable to powers.

It is thought that this less stringent test will also apply to purpose trusts upheld on the principle of *Re Denley's Trust Deed*[80] as being for the benefit of ascertainable individuals. It has been held that the strict test does not apply to *Quistclose* purpose trusts.[81]

iii. Conceptual Uncertainty[82] and Evidential Difficulties. In *Re Baden's Deed Trusts (No. 2)*, Brightman J.,[83] and then the Court of Appeal,[84] had to apply the test laid down by the House of Lords, and consider in particular whether the words "dependants" and "relatives" were too uncertain. In applying the test "it is essential to bear in mind the difference between conceptual uncertainty and evidential difficulties."[85] The test is concerned with the former; "the court is never defeated by evidential uncertainty."[86] The illustration given of a conceptual question is that of the contrasting cases "someone under a moral obligation", which is conceptually uncertain and "first cousins", which is conceptually certain.[87] It would be possible in the latter case, but not in the former, to say with certainty "that any given individual is or is not a member of the class."[88] It is no objection that it may be difficult to establish whether or not any given person satisfies the description, so long as the description is conceptually clear.[89] In each case the precise words must of course be examined to see whether the test is satisfied. Once the class is determined as being conceptually certain the question of inclusion is an issue of fact. "Relatives" and "dependants" were both sufficiently certain.

---

[78] *Re Locker's Settlement* [1977] 1 W.L.R. 1323; (1978) 94 L.Q.R. 177. The distribution must be in favour of those who were objects at the time the discretion should have been exercised. It is otherwise in the case of a mere power, where the default gift will operate if the power is not exercised within the proper time limits.

[79] [1970] A.C. 508.

[80] [1969] 1 Ch. 373, *post*, p. 363. See *R. v. District Auditor, ex p. West Yorkshire Metropolitan County Council* (1986) 26 R.V.R. 24, holding that "administrative unworkability" (*infra*) was fatal to a *Re Denley* type of purpose trust.

[81] *ante*, p. 52; *Twinsectra Ltd v. Yardley* [1999] Lloyd's Rep. Bank. 438.

[82] Sometimes called linguistic or semantic uncertainty.

[83] [1972] Ch. 607.

[84] [1973] Ch. 9; (1973) 36 Conv.(N.S.) 351 (D. Hayton).

[85] *per* Sachs L.J. [1973] Ch. 9 at 19; see also, *per* Lord Wilberforce [1971] A.C. 424 at 457.

[86] *ibid.* at 20; in *Re Tuck's S.T.* [1978] Ch. 49 at 59, Lord Denning M.R. in the context of a condition precedent, confessed that he found "the dichotomy most unfortunate."

[87] *ibid.*

[88] *ante*, p. 104.

[89] This is discussed further below. Such evidential difficulties would, however, invalidate a fixed trust; *ante*, p. 102.

Provided the class is certain in the above sense, it does not matter that the whereabouts or continued existence of an object is not known.[90]

iv. Problems with the Test. The test is not without its difficulties, theoretical and practical.

(a) *What is Conceptually Certain?* Different minds may take different views on the question of whether a particular description is conceptually certain or not. Indeed, the illustrations referred to in the previous paragraph, which were selected to make the point, are not wholly persuasive. The problem is that few descriptions of the kind likely to be encountered in trusts and powers are so clear as to admit of no borderline cases. Most fall between those which are indisputably certain, for example "Nobel prize winners", and those which are conceptually unclear, for example "friends." To insist on complete certainty would be to defeat most gifts. Dispositions ought if possible to be upheld and "should not be held void on a per-adventure."[91] Words such as "relatives" may cause difficulties[92] but trustees can be expected to act sensibly and not to select a remote kinsman.[93] The best solution, it is submitted, is to regard such words as conceptually certain, leaving it to the claimant to establish his case, as discussed below. Words such as "friends", on the other hand, must fall on the wrong side of the line. Although "old friends" was upheld in *Re Gibbard*,[94] this was the result of applying a test which has not survived later decisions,[95] namely that it was sufficient that there was some person who could be shown to be within the class. Browne-Wilkinson J., in *Re Barlow's Will Trusts*,[96] attempted to clarify who a "friend" was. But that was in the context of a gift subject to a condition precedent, which, as we shall see,[97] is governed by a less strict test.

Conceptual uncertainty may in some cases be cured by a provision that the opinion of a third party (the trustees or another person) is to settle the matter. The provision is more likely to be upheld where the settlor (or testator) leaves the definition of a term to the

---

[90] *Re Gulbenkian's Settlement Trusts* [1970] A.C. 508; (1982) 98 L.Q.R. 551 (C. Emery). This point is more significant in the case of fixed trusts.
[91] *Re Hay's Settlement Trusts* [1982] 1 W.L.R. 202 at 212.
[92] *infra.*
[93] *Re Baden's Deed Trusts (No. 2)* [1973] Ch. 9.
[94] [1967] 1 W.L.R. 42. See also *Re Byron's Settlement* [1891] 3 Ch. 474 (bare power).
[95] See *Gulbenkian's Settlement Trusts (No. 1)* [1970] A.C. 508.
[96] [1979] 1 W.L.R. 278. It was said that a trust or power in favour of "friends" would probably fail. See also *Re Byron's Settlement* [1891] 3 Ch. 474.
[97] *post*, p. 114.

third party as opposed to leaving it to the third party to determine the meaning the settlor himself intended it to have. In the former case the settlor in effect adopts the meaning ascribed by the third party.[98] In *Re Coxen*[99] it was held that the testator could validly make the trustees' opinion the criterion provided he had sufficiently defined the state of affairs on which they were to form their opinion. The question whether the testator's wife had "ceased permanently to reside" at a property passed this test, whereas in *Re Jones*[1] the question whether X should at any time have a "social or other relationship" with Y in the "uncontrolled opinion" of the trustees was insufficiently defined to enable the trustees to come to a proper decision. A gift to persons "having a moral claim" on the donor would be conceptually uncertain, but a gift to "such persons as the company may consider to have a moral claim" on the donor would satisfy the test.[2] Similarly, any uncertainty in the requirement of being of the Jewish faith and married to an "approved wife" could be cured by a provision that disputes were to be decided by a chief rabbi.[3] The settlor or testator cannot, however, purport to oust the jurisdiction of the court by giving the trustees conclusive power to construe the words used.[4] Such a clause will be void as contrary to public policy. Assuming the power to resolve an uncertainty has been validly given to trustees, the court may intervene if it is exercised in bad faith and possibly on other grounds.[5]

(b) *Proof of Inclusion and Exclusion; Proving Negatives.* Read strictly, the test means that it must be possible to show either that any person is within the class or that he is not within it. But, how could you show that a person is, for example, not your relative? Sachs L.J.[6] said that the claimant needs to show that he is within the class; if he cannot do that, he is not within it. His Lordship was here referring to evidential uncertainty. Clearly conceptual uncertainty

---

[98] Thomas, *Powers*, pp. 133–138.

[99] [1948] Ch. 747 at 761–762 (condition subsequent).

[1] [1953] Ch. 125 (condition subsequent).

[2] *Re Leek* [1969] 1 Ch. 563; *cf. Re Wright's W.T.* (1981) 78 L.S.Gaz. 841 (Gift to trustees "for such people and institutions as they think have helped me or my late husband" uncertain. There was an appeal on the issue of severance; *post*, p. 113). See also *Re Coates* [1955] Ch. 495 (for any friends the testator's wife might feel he had forgotten). In the case of a discretionary trust, difficulties might arise if the court is called upon to execute it.

[3] *Re Tuck's Settlement Trusts* [1978] Ch. 49 (in fact the condition was held certain). For a contrary view, see Underhill and Hayton (15th ed.), p. 71. See also *Re Tepper's Will Trusts* [1987] Ch. 358, holding that the meaning of "Jewish faith" could be elucidated by extrinsic evidence of the faith as practised by the testator; All E.R. Rev. 1987, at 159 (P. Clarke) and 260 (C. Sherrin); (1999) 19 L.S. 339 (D. Cooper and D. Herman). *cf.* A.J.A. 1982, s.21.

[4] *Re Wynn* [1952] Ch. 271; *Re Raven* [1915] 1 Ch. 673.

[5] *post*, p. 528.

[6] [1973] Ch. 9; and see (1973) 32 C.L.J. 36 (J. Hopkins).

cannot be cured by casting the onus of proof on to the claimant, because the matter would not be susceptible of proof.[7] Megaw L.J. said that the test was satisfied[8] "if, as regards at least a substantial number of objects, it can be said with certainty that they fall within the trust; even though, as regards a substantial number of other persons . . . the answer would have to be, not 'they are outside the trust,' but 'it is not proven whether they are in or out.' " His Lordship suggested that to require proof that every person was or was not within the class would return to the old rule requiring the making of a list. This seems doubtful. To be in a position to accept or reject the claim of any given person does not require ascertainment of the whole class. The "substantial number" test might be thought to be a return to the *Gibbard*[9] test which was rejected in *Gulbenkian*.[10] This is not so, as the *Gibbard*[11] test allowed a degree of conceptual uncertainty, while the statement of Megaw L.J. quoted above concerns evidential uncertainty. It is submitted that the majority view is to be preferred to the somewhat stricter test laid down by Stamp L.J., which seems to require that the trustees be in a position to say affirmatively whether any given person is within or outside the class. His Lordship considered that the validity or invalidity of a discretionary trust depended on[12] "whether you can say of any individual—and the accent must be on that word 'any' for it is not simply the individual whose claim you are considering who is spoken of—[that he] 'is or is not a member of the class,' for only thus can you make a survey of the range of objects or possible beneficiaries." If Stamp L.J. had not been able to construe "relatives" as meaning "next-of-kin" or "nearest blood relations" he would have held the trust void for uncertainty.[13]

(c) *Width of the Class; Administrative Unworkability.*[14] Lord Wilberforce in *McPhail v. Doulton*[15] indicated that there might be a

---

[7] *cf. Re Barlow's Will Trusts* [1979] 1 W.L.R. 278, *post*, p. 115.

[8] [1973] Ch. 9 at 24.

[9] [1967] 1 W.L.R. 42.

[10] [1970] A.C. 508.

[11] *supra.*

[12] [1973] Ch. 9 at 28.

[13] The view of the majority was that it meant "descendants from a common ancestor." It has long been established that "relatives" should be confined to next of kin only if this is necessary to save the gift, *e.g.* where the "list test" applies. See *Re Shield's W.T.* [1974] 2 W.L.R. 885; *Re Barlow's W.T.* [1979] 1 W.L.R. 278; *Re Poulton's W.T.* [1987] 1 W.L.R. 795.

[14] See (1991) 107 L.Q.R. 214 at 218 (S. Gardner): "it is not easy to see just what difficulty it is aimed at pre-empting."

[15] [1971] A.C. 424; criticised on this point in (1974) 38 Conv.(N.S.) 269 (L. McKay); (1974) 37 M.L.R. 643 (Y. Grbich).

difference in one situation between the test to be applied to discretionary trusts and that for mere powers. A description of beneficiaries which might comply with the certainty test laid down might be "so hopelessly wide as not to form 'anything like a class,' so that the trust is administratively unworkable,"[16] and he hesitatingly gave as an example a class consisting of "all the residents of Greater London." This was said in the context of a discretionary trust. The question has arisen whether this concept applies also to mere powers. Buckley L.J. assumed *obiter* that it did in *Blausten v. I.R.C.*[17] This was doubted in *Re Manisty's Settlement,*[18] where Templeman J. held that a mere power could not be invalid on the ground of width of numbers, preferring the view that its validity should depend on whether or not it was capricious. This point is discussed below. *Manisty* was preferred to *Blausten* by Megarry V.-C. in *Re Hay's Settlement Trusts.*[19] A mere power, whether or not fiduciary, was not invalid on the ground of the size of the class. Mere numbers could not prevent the trustee from considering whether to exercise the power nor from performing his other duties,[20] nor prevent the court from controlling him. But it was suggested that a discretionary trust in favour of the same wide class[21] as the mere power would have been void as administratively unworkable, as the duties of a discretionary trustee were more stringent, and the objects of a discretionary trust had rights of enforcement which objects of a mere power lacked. A similar view was taken in *R. v. District Auditor, ex p. West Yorkshire Metropolitan County Council,*[22] where a local authority, purporting to act under statutory powers, resolved to set up a trust "for the benefit of any or all or some of the inhabitants of the County of West Yorkshire."[23] There were 2,500,000 potential beneficiaries. The court was prepared to assume that "inhabitant" was sufficiently certain, but held the trust void for administrative unworkability as the class was far too large, applying Lord Wilberforce's dictum in *McPhail v. Doulton.*[24] *Re Manisty's Settlement*[25] was distinguished as concerning a power, where the function of the

---

[16] *McPhail v. Doultou* [1971] A.C. 424 at 427.

[17] [1972] Ch. 256. The power was upheld because the trustees' power to include any other person as an object was subject to the settlor's consent. The settlor had, therefore, put "metes and bounds" on the otherwise unrestricted class.

[18] [1974] Ch. 17. In *Re Beatty's W.T.* [1990] 1 W.L.R. 1503, [1991] Conv. 138 (J. Martin), a fiduciary power given to trustees in favour of "such person or persons as they think fit" was upheld without mention of the concept of administrative unworkability.

[19] [1982] 1 W.L.R. 202.

[20] *i.e.* to make no unauthorised appointment; to consider the range of objects; to consider the appropriateness of any individual appointment.

[21] Any person except the settlor, settlor's spouse or trustees.

[22] (1986) 26 R.V.R. 24 (Q.B.D.); (1986) 45 C.L.J. 391 (C. Harpum).

[23] The details of the trust, which was not charitable, are given in Chap. 14, *post*, p. 364.

[24] *supra*.

[25] *supra*.

court was more restricted. The weight of authority, therefore, supports the view that "administrative unworkability" can invalidate discretionary trusts but not mere powers.[26]

(d) *Capriciousness.* There is no general principle of English law that a capricious disposition is invalid. Wigram V.-C. in *Bird v. Luckie*[27] said, "No man is bound to make a will in such a manner as to deserve approbation from the prudent, the wise, or the good. A testator is permitted to be capricious and improvident, and moreover is at liberty to conceal the circumstances and the motives by which he has been actuated in his dispositions."

But while a capricious legacy may be valid, the position may be otherwise in a discretionary trust or power. Unlike an outright gift, discretionary trusts and powers involve fiduciary obligations, the performance of which may be rendered impossible if their terms are capricious. In upholding a power of great width in *Re Manisty's Settlement*[28] Templeman J. held that the terms of the power need not provide guidance to the trustees; an absolute discretion did not preclude a sensible consideration of whether and how to exercise the power. The example of a class comprising "residents of Greater London" would be capricious and void, not on the basis of numbers, but on the ground that the terms of the power negatived any sensible intention on the settlor's part and any sensible consideration by the trustees. The objects must either be unlimited, in which case the trustees can perform their obligations sensibly, or limited to a "sensible" class. The disposition would be void if membership of the class of objects was accidental and irrelevant to any purpose or to any method of limiting or selecting beneficiaries.[29]

Is "capriciousness" the same notion as "administrative unworkability?"[30] The latter, as we have seen, has been held inapplicable to mere powers, while the former has been held applicable to both mere powers and discretionary trusts.[31] In *R. v. District Auditor, ex p. West Yorkshire Metropolitan County Council*[32] a trust for the

---

[26] *cf.* [1982] Conv. 432 at 434 (A. Grubb); (1982) 98 L.Q.R. 551 (C. Emery); [1990] Conv. 24 (I. Hardcastle), taking the view that it applies also to powers, and Riddall, *The Law of Trusts* (5th ed.), p. 33, taking the view that it applies also to fixed trusts. It has been suggested that one result of *Mettoy Pension Trustees Ltd v. Evans* [1990] 1 W.L.R. 1587, which adapts discretionary trust remedies to fiduciary powers, may be to make the concept of administrative unworkability appicable to powers; (1991) 107 L.Q.R. 214 (S. Gardner).

[27] (1850) 8 Hare 301. See also *Re James's Will Trusts* [1962] Ch. 226.

[28] [1974] Ch. 17.

[29] *ibid.* at 26. See [1982] Conv. 432 at 435 (A. Grubb) explaining that the "appointment criteria", necessary to avoid invalidity on the ground of capriciousness, need not be apparent from the power itself.

[30] See (1982) 98 L.Q.R. 551 (C. Emery) for the view that they are the same.

[31] See *Re Manisty's Settlement, supra; Re Hay's Settlement Trusts* [1982] 1 W.L.R. 202.

[32] (1986) 26 R.V.R. 24; (1986) 45 C.L.J. 391 (C. Harpum); *ante*, p. 110.

benefit of 2,500,000 inhabitants of West Yorkshire was held void for administrative unworkability (as being too large a class) even though it was not capricious because the local authority (the settlor) had every reason to wish to benefit the inhabitants in the ways specified. Thus it appears that the two concepts are distinct, although the same example may give rise to invalidity on both grounds. Capriciousness has no necessary connection with width of numbers, which is the characteristic of administrative unworkability.

It might also be mentioned that the capricious exercise of a fiduciary power or trust, as where objects are chosen by height or complexion, will be invalid even though the power or trust is valid.[33]

(e) *Duty to Survey the Field.* Clearly the trustees of a discretionary trust are not obliged to consider every object, as the trust may be valid although the identity of all the objects is not known. But as we have seen, Lord Wilberforce in *McPhail v. Doulton*[34] considered that the trustees ought to make such a survey of the range of objects as would enable them to carry out their fiduciary duty, and that a wider or more comprehensive range of enquiry was called for in the case of discretionary trusts than in the case of powers. In the case of a wide-ranging discretionary trust, where the number of objects may run to hundreds of thousands, the trustees' duty is to assess in a businesslike way "the size of the problem."[35] Megarry V.-C. in *Re Hay's Settlement Trusts*,[36] said:

> "The trustee must not simply proceed to exercise the power in favour of such of the objects as happen to be at hand or claim his attention. He must first consider what persons or classes of persons are objects of the power... there is no need to compile a complete list of the objects, or even to make an accurate assessment of the number of them: what is needed is an appreciation of the width of the field, and thus whether a selection is to be made merely from a dozen or, instead, from thousands or millions. ...
> Only when the trustee has applied his mind to the 'size of the problem' should he then consider in individual cases whether, in relation to other possible claimants, a particular grant is appropriate. In doing this, no doubt he should not prefer the undeserving to the deserving; but he is not required to make an exact calculation whether, as between deserving claimants, A is more deserving than B."

This was the duty which had emerged from cases concerning discretionary trusts, but "plainly the requirements for a mere power

---

[33] *Re Manisty's Settlement, supra; Re Hay's Settlement Trusts, supra.*
[34] [1971] A.C. 424; criticised in (1974) 37 M.L.R. 643 (Y. Grbich).
[35] *Re Baden's Deed Trusts (No. 2)* [1973] Ch. 9 at 20 (*per* Sachs L.J.)
[36] [1982] 1 W.L.R. 202 at 209–210.

cannot be more stringent than those for a discretionary trust."[37] The duties of a trustee of a discretionary trust are more stringent than those of the donee of a fiduciary power because of the obligation to distribute. The precise scope of the less onerous duty to survey in the case of a power awaits clarification.[38]

(f) *Many Certain Categories; One Uncertain.* Further difficulties could arise with a definition of a class of beneficiaries which contained a long series of categories which complied with the *McPhail v. Doulton* test, but to which there was added one category which did not. What, for example, would the court say to a trust in the same language as that in *McPhail v. Doulton* but to which there was added "any other person to whom I may be under a moral obligation and any of my old friends"? . . . which is, let it be assumed, conceptually uncertain. The same problem could arise in a case of power.

In this situation, the class as the whole does not satisfy the test. It would however be unfortunate to declare the whole trust void because of the final addition. After all, the trust is workable as it is. Such a trust, however, may be held void unless it is possible to excise the offending phrase by severance: this suggestion has sometimes been made,[39] but the severance principle has yet to be established. Thus in *Re Wright's Will Trusts*,[40] where the class consisted of identifiable named charities and other bodies which could not be identified, the Court of Appeal refused to give effect to the gift in favour of the named charities only.

v. Effect of Certainty Tests on Rights of Objects. When, prior to *McPhail v. Doulton*,[41] complete ascertainment of objects was required in the case of a discretionary trust, it was thought that each object had a right to be considered, and to share in the fund if the trustees failed in their duty to exercise their discretion. Clearly this is no longer accurate, now that the trust may be valid without the necessity of ascertaining the full membership of the class. The question of equal division in default of exercise has already been dealt

---

[37] [1982] 1 W.L.R. 202 at 209–210. This may be contrasted with the view of Harman J. in *Re Gestetner* [1953] Ch. 672 at 688: " . . . there is no obligation on the trustees to do more than consider from time to time the merits of such persons of the specified class as are known to them. . . . " See also Templeman J. in *Re Manisty's Settlement* [1974] Ch. 14 at 25.

[38] See [1982] Conv. 432 at 437 (A. Grubb), suggesting that the duty is merely to consider those who press claims and present themselves for inspection; there is no need to "go forth and search out worthy candidates." Presumably this duty arises only if the donee has decided to exercise the power.

[39] *per* Sachs L.J. in *Re Leek* [1969] 1 Ch. 563 at 586 (assuming, however, that legislation would be required); and in the case of a power (Winn L.J.) in *Re Gulbenkian's Settlements* [1968] Ch. 126 at 138 (C.A.). *cf.* decisions on trusts which are not exclusively charitable; *post*, p. 442.

[40] (1999) 13 *Trust Law International* 48 (decided 1982); *ante*, p. 108.

[41] [1971] A.C. 424.

with.[42] Any right to be considered must be confined to the situation where the claim is brought to the attention of the trustees. The right of the object is simply to require that the trustees perform their obligation to allocate the fund after surveying the range of objects, as described above.[43] If the unknown or unascertainable object is not considered by the trustees, at any rate he is no worse off than he would have been prior to *McPhail v. Doulton*,[44] when the possibility of his existence would have caused the discretionary trust to fail.

vi. Trust-Powers in the Old Sense; Trusts with a Power of Selection. If, as a matter of construction, it can be inferred that the settlor's intention was that the entire class should take if the trustee failed to make a selection, then no doubt equal division is still appropriate, in which case the "complete ascertainment" test must still be satisfied. This is more likely to be the case in a family trust, where the objects are not large in number, as in *Burrough v. Philcox*.[45] It may be that the minority and the majority in *McPhail v. Doulton*[46] were talking at cross-purposes, the former having in mind the more old-fashioned trust-power as described above, while the latter analysed the modern discretionary trust in favour of a large class, where the settlor could not have contemplated equal division.[47]

vii. Gifts Subject to a Condition Precedent. A less strict test applies where there is a gift subject to a condition precedent as opposed to a discretionary trust or power. A degree of conceptual uncertainty does not invalidate such a gift.[48] The test, as laid down in *Re Allen*,[49] is that the gift is valid if it is possible to say that one or more persons qualify, even though there may be difficulty as to others. This test may also apply to personal (non-fiduciary) powers.[50]

---

[42] *ante*, p. 104.

[43] See generally *Re Hay's Settlement Trusts, supra; Turner v. Turner* [1984] Ch. 100; *Murphy v. Murphy* [1999] 1 W.L.R. 282 (undesirable for trustees to be "badgered" with claims by many beneficiaries).

[44] *supra*.

[45] (1840) 5 Myl. & Cr. 72; *ante*, p. 65.

[46] *supra*.

[47] See (1974) 37 M.L.R. 643 (Y. Grbich); (1982) 98 L.Q.R. 551 (C. Emery). For the proper meaning of "trust power", see [1984] Conv. 227 (R. Bartlett and C. Stebbings).

[48] A stricter test applies to a condition subsequent. The distinction, though criticised by Lord Denning M.R. in *Re Tuck's Settlement Trusts* [1978] Ch. 49, was acknowledged by the House of Lords in *Blaithwayt v. Lord Cawley* [1976] A.C. 397 at 425; *post*, p. 342. See also *Re Tepper's Will Trusts* [1987] Ch. 358; *Ellis v. Chief Adjudication Officer* [1998] 1 F.L.R. 184.

[49] [1953] Ch. 810.

[50] (1982) 98 L.Q.R. 551 (C. Emery); *Re Byron's Settlement* [1891] 3 Ch. 474.

This test fell to be considered by Browne-Wilkinson J. in *Re Barlow's Will Trust*,[51] where the testatrix left a valuable collection of paintings, directing her executor to sell those not specifically bequeathed, subject to a proviso that "any friends of mine who may wish to do so" be allowed to purchase any of them at a price below the market value. This disposition was held sufficiently certain. Total ascertainment of the testatrix's friends was not required. A "friend" was a person who had a relationship of long standing with the testatrix, which was a social as opposed to a business or professional relationship; and who had met her frequently when circumstances permitted.[52] The effect of the gift was to confer on her friends a series of options to purchase. There was no legal necessity to inform them of their rights, although this would be desirable. The claimant must prove "by any reasonable test" that he qualified.[53] In case of doubt, the executors could apply to the court for directions. The justification for this less strict test was that in the case of individual gifts, unlike trusts and powers, uncertainty as to some beneficiaries did not affect the quantum of the gift in respect of those who clearly qualified. To uphold the gift in the case of the latter gave effect, at least in part, to the donor's intention.[54]

Although the "condition precedent" test is now settled, this decision illustrates the difficulties inherent in it. The trustees could be in real difficulty in giving effect to such a disposition. The solution that trustees could apply to court in cases of doubt is unsatisfactory. How can the court be in any better position than the trustees to pronounce on the question whether X is a "friend" of Y?

---

[51] [1979] 1 W.L.R. 278; criticised [1980] Conv. 263 (L. McKay). (1982) 98 L.Q.R. 551 (C. Emery). See also Underhill and Hayton (15th ed.), pp. 80–82.

[52] [1979] 1 W.L.R. 278 at 282.

[53] *cf. Re Baden's Deed Trusts (No. 2)* [1973] Ch. 9, where the onus of proof on the claimant concerns evidential, and not conceptual, uncertainty.

[54] This has not been regarded as sufficient to justify a less strict test in the case of trusts and powers.

CHAPTER 4

CONSTITUTION OF TRUSTS
EQUITY WILL NOT ASSIST A VOLUNTEER

1. THE GENERAL PROBLEM

A. Requirements of Conveyance and Declaration

We have seen that the interest of the beneficiary under a trust is a proprietary interest. The legal title is in the trustee; the equitable and beneficial title is in the beneficiary. The trust may be of any form of property—land, chattels, money, choses in action—and for any interest known to the law, whether legal or equitable, in posses-sion, remainder[1] or reversion. An intention to create a trust is, as we have seen, one of the requirements for the creation of an express trust,[2] but it is not sufficient in itself. To declare that A is to hold

---

[1] *Re Ralli's W.T.* [1964] Ch. 288.
[2] *ante*, p. 94.

Blackacre on trust for B does not create a trust unless Blackacre is conveyed to A. Similarly, a conveyance to A does not create a trust of Blackacre for B unless the trust is properly declared. In short, it is necessary both to declare the trust *and* to convey the property to the trustee. The principle is that "Although equity will not aid a volunteer, it will not strive officiously to defeat a gift".[2a]

Many difficulties have been caused by failure to observe these basic propositions. Even where they are observed, complications can arise, and a number of questions are left open. Is it necessary that the conveyance and the declaration be contemporaneous? If X conveys Blackacre to A to hold upon trust for B, a trust is created in favour of B; also if X conveys to A upon trust and later declares the trusts.[3] If X conveys Blackacre to A, he cannot then tell A to hold on trust for B, because after the conveyance A became the absolute owner. May the declaration precede the conveyance? May X create a trust for B by declaring that A is to hold on trust for B; and later convey Blackacre to A? This question raises a number of difficulties as we will see; they will be discussed in this chapter and also in Chapter 5.

B. Methods of Benefiting an Intended Donee

If X is the owner at law and in equity, he can make B the beneficial owner in any one of three ways:

i. Outright Transfer. He can transfer legal and equitable ownership to B. In the case of land, this transaction is called a conveyance. With a chattel, it is called a sale or gift; with a chose in action, it is called an assignment; with shares it is usually called a transfer. Whatever type of transaction, X, by following the correct procedure appropriate to the type of property, can transfer his absolute interest, legal and equitable, to B. Obviously if X does not follow the correct procedure, he will not transfer the legal or beneficial interest to B. This self-evident proposition is stated here because arguments have unsuccessfully been raised that an unsuccessful transfer to B might be construed as a declaration of trust for B. It is not.[4]

ii. Transfer to Trustee. X may transfer the property to A to hold on trust for B. Provided that the legal title is correctly transferred to A, according to the type of property concerned, A will become legal owner; and provided that an intention to create a trust in favour of

---

[2a] *Choithram (T.) International S.A. v. Pagarani* [2001] 1 W.L.R. 1 at 11, *per* Lord Browne-Wilkinson.
[3] *Re Tyler* [1967] 1 W.L.R. 1269; *Grey v. I.R.C.* [1960] A.C. 1; *ante*, p. 83.
[4] *post*, pp. 125 *et seq.*

B is sufficiently manifested, B will become equitable and beneficial owner. A holds on trust for B.

iii. Declaration of Self as Trustee.
X may declare that he holds the property on trust for B. In this situation all that is necessary is a declaration of trust in favour of B. There is no problem of the legal estate being vested in the trustee. It was, and remains, in X, who is the trustee, holding on trust for B. These three situations should be borne in mind in the discussion which follows.

C. Contracts to Convey or to Create a Trust

Situations (ii) and (iii) above concern the creation of trusts in the strict sense. B in each case will obtain an equitable proprietary interest. In such a situation, it is immaterial whether B gave consideration or not. A gift confers title just as effectively as a sale.

If, however, the transaction in question had been *in*effective to transfer the legal title from X to B in situation (i), what is B's position? If B gave no consideration there is nothing more that he can do; the gift fails, just as it would fail if a Christmas present were promised and not given. Equity will not assist a volunteer. If B gave consideration, the position is different. B could either sue X for damages for breach of contract, or, in appropriate circumstances, obtain specific performance of the contract.[5] If, in situation (ii), B gave consideration for any contract by X to convey to A on trust for B, or—more realistically, for this question usually arises in connection with marriage settlements—if B is treated as being within the marriage consideration,[6] B can compel A to take proceedings against X, either to obtain the property or damages for breach, and to hold the property or the damages on the trusts declared. Thus, B, not being a volunteer, is entitled to enforce the contract; and, in accordance with the principle that equity considers as done that which ought to be done, may be treated as entitled in equity to the property which was the subject of the contract.[7] Even if B is a volunteer, he may now enforce the contract between X and A in his own right in certain circumstances under the Contracts (Rights of Third Parties) Act 1999.[8]

D. Beneficial Owner under a Trust

Reference should also be made here to the way in which an equitable owner (the legal title being in trustees) may create interests in favour of other persons out of his equitable interest.

[5] *post*, Chap. 24.
[6] *post*, pp. 130 *et seq.*
[7] See *Pullan v. Koe* [1913] 1 Ch. 9; *post*, p. 130.
[8] *post*, p. 129.

In *Timpson's Executors v. Yerbury*,[9] Romer L.J. said: "Now the equitable interest in property in the hands of a trustee can be disposed of by the person entitled to it in favour of a third party in any one of four . . . ways. The person entitled to it (1) can assign it to the third party directly; (2) can direct the trustees to hold the property in trust for the third party (see *per* Sargant J. in *Re Chrimes*[10]); (3) can contract for valuable consideration to assign the equitable interest to him; or (4) can declare himself to be a trustee for him of such interest." Category (2), as Lord Evershed pointed out in *Grey v. I.R.C.*[11] "appears . . . to have been regarded as distinct from both an assignment, on the one hand, and a declaration of trust of the interest in the beneficial owner's hands, on the other."

We know however that such a direction is a "disposition" within Law of Property Act 1925, s.53, according to the wide construction put upon that word by the House of Lords,[12] and required therefore to be in writing. If the beneficial owner authorises the trustees to transfer the legal estate to donees, then the beneficial interest passes to the donees without express mention.[13]

It should also be noted that category (4) creates what is usually called a sub-trust; a situation in which A holds property on trust for B, and B declares himself to be trustee of his interest for C. Unless B has specific duties to perform, he is a bare trustee and apparently drops out, the original trustee A holding on trust for C.[14]

2. TRANSFER OF THE PROPERTY TO TRUSTEES UPON TRUST

A. Legal Interests

The classic statement of the law relating to the requirement of a transfer of the property to trustees is that of Turner L.J. in *Milroy v. Lord*[15]:

"I take the law of this Court to be well settled, that, in order to render a voluntary settlement valid and effectual, the settlor must have done everything which, according to the nature of the property comprised in the settlement, was necessary to be done in order to transfer the property and render the settlement binding upon him. He may, of course, do this by actually transferring the property to the persons for whom he intends to provide, and the

---

[9] [1936] 1 K.B. 645 at 664.
[10] [1917] 1 Ch. 30.
[11] [1958] Ch. 690 at 709 (C.A.).
[12] *Grey v. I.R.C.* [1960] A.C. 1; *ante*, p. 83.
[13] *Vandervell v. I.R.C.* [1967] 2 A.C. 291; *ante*, p. 85.
[14] *Grainge v. Wilberforce* (1889) 5 T.L.R. 436; *ante*, p. 88.
[15] (1862) 4 De G.F. & J. 264 at 274–275. For the position where the trustee disclaims, see *Mallott v. Wilson* [1903] 2 Ch. 494; [1981] Conv. 141 (P. Matthews).

provision will then be effectual, and it will be equally effectual if he transfers the property to a trustee for the purposes of the settlement, or declares that he himself holds it in trust for those purposes; and if the property be personal, the trust may, as I apprehend, be declared either in writing or by parol; but, in order to render the settlement binding, one or other of these modes must, as I understand the law of this court, be resorted to, for there is no equity in this court to perfect an imperfect gift. The cases, I think, go further to this extent, that if the settlement is intended to be effectuated by one of the modes to which I have referred, the Court will not give effect to it by applying another of those modes. If it is intended to take effect by transfer, the court will not hold the intended transfer to operate as a declaration of trust, for then every imperfect instrument would be made effectual by being converted into a perfect trust."

The transfer to the trustees must accord with the rules applicable to the property concerned. Legal estates in land must be transferred by deed,[16] equitable interests[17] and copyright[18] by writing, chattels by deed of gift[19] or by an intention to give coupled with a delivery of possession,[20] a bill of exchange by endorsement,[21] and shares by the appropriate form of transfer followed by registration.[22] Since July 1996 it has been possible to transfer shares in most quoted companies electronically, thereby avoiding the need for transfer forms and share certificates, but this does not detract from the principle that legal title passes only on registration.[23]

In *Milroy v. Lord*,[24] a settlor executed a voluntary deed purporting to transfer shares in the Bank of Louisiana to Samuel Lord to be held on trust for the claimant. The shares, however, could only

---

[16] L.P.A. 1925, s.52(1). Registration of freeholds and long leases is necessary under the registered title system; L.R.A. 1925. See *Mascall v. Mascall* (1985) 49 P. & C.R. 119, *post*, p. 125.

[17] L.P.A. 1925, s.53(1).

[18] Copyright Designs and Patents Act 1988, s.90(3).

[19] Thus it has been held that a trust of a painting was validly constituted without physical delivery to the trustees (one of whom was in Ireland) on the ground that the formal declaration of trust transferred the property in the painting to the trustees, each of whom had a copy of the document and agreed to act; *Jaffa v. Taylor Gallery Ltd*, *The Times*, March 21, 1990.

[20] *Ryall v. Rolls* (1750) 1 Ves.Sen. 348; *Kilpin v. Raltey* [1892] 1 Q.B. 582; *Re Cole* [1964] Ch. 175; *Thomas v. Times Book Co. Ltd* [1966] 1 W.L.R. 911; (1953) 12 C.L.J. 355 (J. Thornely); (1964) 27 M.L.R. 357 (A. Diamond).

[21] Bills of Exchange Act 1882, s.31; see, however, Cheques Act 1957, ss.1, 2.

[22] See Companies Act 1985, ss.182, 183; Stock Transfer Act 1963, s.1.

[23] This is the CREST system. It is not compulsory for companies or investors to use it. It is designed for speedy and economic transfer, and will eventually achieve immediate ownership on payment. See (1996) 146 N.L.J. 964 (R. Pinner). Gilts were taken into CREST in 2000.

[24] (1862) 4 De G.F. & J. 264.

be transferred by the appropriate transfer form followed by registration of the name of the transferee in the books of the Bank.
Lord held a power of attorney to act on behalf of the settlor, and
it would have enabled him to take all necessary further steps to
obtain registration. But this was not done. The Court of Appeal in
Chancery held that there was no trust, although the intention
clearly was to benefit the intended beneficiary.

On the other hand, once the property has been vested in the
trustees, and the trusts declared, the trust is constituted, and the
settlor is unable to reclaim the property, even though the beneficiaries may be volunteers.[25] It has been held that the trust may be
constituted where the property is vested in the trustees, even though
it reached them in a capacity distinct from their office as trustees of
the trust in question.

In *Re Ralli's Will Trusts*,[26] a testator left his residuary estate on
trust for his widow for life and then for his two daughters Irene
and Helen. Helen's marriage settlement included a covenant to
settle existing and after-acquired property in favour of (in the
events which happened) volunteers. Helen predeceased her
mother and so never transferred her remainder interest pursuant to
her covenant. The claimant was the trustee both of the testator's
will and also of Helen's marriage settlement. Buckley J. had to
decide on what trusts the residue was held. He concluded, as one
ground for his decision, that the vesting of the property in the
trustee was sufficient to constitute the trusts of the remainder
interest even though the property came to him in his other capacity as trustee of the will. "The circumstance that the [claimant]
holds the fund because he was appointed a trustee of the will is
irrelevant. He is at law the owner of the fund, and the means by
which he became so have no effect upon the quality of his legal
ownership."[27]

This may be contrasted with *Re Brooks' Settlement Trusts*,[28]
where a settlor made a voluntary settlement under which he purported to assign after-acquired property to the trustee, Lloyds Bank.
Subsequently a power of appointment under another settlement of
which Lloyds Bank was also trustee was exercised in the settlor's

---

[25] *Paul v. Paul* (1882) 20 Ch.D. 742; *Jefferys v. Jefferys* (1841) Cr. & Ph. 138; *Re Ellenborough* [1903] 1 Ch. 697 (the assets received under her sister's will); *Re Bowden* [1936] Ch. 71; similarly for voluntary covenants to settle: *Re Adlard* [1954] Ch. 29. For the current position with regard to the enforcement of the covenant, see Contracts (Rights of Third Parties) Act 1999, *post,* p. 129.

[26] [1964] Ch. 288.

[27] *ibid.* at 301.

[28] [1939] 1 Ch. 993, not cited in *Re Ralli's W.T.*

favour. It was held that the settlor was entitled to be paid the appointed sum by the Bank because the assignment of a mere expectancy was ineffective. Thus the beneficiaries had no claim.

B. Equitable Interests

The same general principle applies where the settlor's interest is equitable. A correct transfer of the equitable interest to a trustee upon properly declared trusts is necessary to create a trust of that equitable interest. A disposition of an equitable interest must, as has been seen, be in writing.[29] In *Kekewich v. Manning*,[30] shares were held on trust for A for life and then for B. B assigned his equitable interest in remainder to trustees to hold on certain trusts, and this was held to create a trust of the equitable interest in remainder.

C. Act of Third Party Required to Perfect Title

Difficulties can arise where the act of a third party is necessary to perfect the transfer of legal title. The problem commonly involves shares, the legal title to which is transferable by the execution of the form of transfer required by the company's articles, followed by registration in the share register of the company.[31] If the transaction is for consideration, the purchaser becomes equitable owner of the shares from the date of the execution of the document of transfer, and is entitled to dividends declared after that date.[32] The position is the same where shares are transferred electronically.[33] The purchaser becomes equitable owner on generation of the instruction to the registrar and legal owner on registration.

The transfer of shares in a private company is restricted, and the Articles usually provide that the directors may refuse to register the transfer. A difficult situation arises where a settlor makes a voluntary settlement of such shares, executing a transfer which purports to transfer the shares to trustees to be held on the trusts of the settlement. The expectation is that the registration of the transfer will follow and the trust become constituted. The directors however may refuse to register the transfer. In that case, under the strict rule of *Milroy v. Lord*,[34] the trust will be incompletely constituted and a nullity. The validity of the trust would be dependent upon the uncontrollable discretion of the directors. Even if they do register it, the date on which this happens may be crucial in determining whether

---

[29] L.P.A., s.53(1)(c); *ante*, p. 82.
[30] (1851) 1 De G.M. & G. 176; *Gilbert v. Overton* (1864) 22 H. & M. 110.
[31] See Companies Act 1985, ss.182, 183. Stock Transfer Act 1963, s.1.
[32] *Black v. Homersham* (1878) 4 Ex.D. 24; *Re Wimbush* [1940] Ch. 92.
[33] *ante*, p. 121.
[34] (1862) 4 De. G.F. & J. 264. There, however, the correct transfer form was not used.

the transfer is liable to inheritance tax at the full death rate applicable to gifts made within three years of death or at the lower rates for gifts made three to seven years before death.[35]

In *Re Rose*,[36] a settlor by voluntary deed transferred shares in a private company to trustees to be held on certain trusts. The directors, who had power to refuse to register transfers, registered this transfer some two months later. The settlor died at a time at which the shares would be treated as part of his estate for tax purposes if the date of the transfer were the date of registration; but would not be so treated if the date was the date of the deed. The Court of Appeal held that the relevant date was that of the deed; for the settlor had at that time done everything possible to divest himself of the property. All that was needed in addition was the formal act of registration by the third party.

Evershed M.R. went so far as to say that after the execution of the transfer, the settlor held the shares as trustee for the beneficiaries.[37] He did not however give any convincing answer to the Crown's argument that, consistently with *Milroy v. Lord*,[38] the transfer was either a valid transfer at law; or a declaration of trust; or it was ineffective. The settlor clearly did not intend to declare himself a trustee,[39] and would have been surprised to have been told that, if the directors had refused to register, he was unable to withdraw from the transfer because he was a trustee; or that he was required to exercise the voting powers conferred by the shares in the interests of the beneficiaries.[40] *Re Rose* thus creates a number of theoretical difficulties,[41] although one rationalisation may be that it is possible for legal and equitable title to be separated without all the incidents of trusteeship.[42] It is submitted, however, that it is an eminently sensible decision in a context in which the liability to tax may be

---

[35] I.H.T.A. 1984, s.7; *post*, p. 225.

[36] [1952] Ch. 499; *Re Fry* [1946] Ch. 312; *Re Rose* [1949] Ch. 78; *Re Paradise Motor Co. Ltd* [1968] 1 W.L.R. 1125; *Vandervell v. I.R.C.* [1967] 2 A.C. 291 at 330.

[37] "If a man executes a document transferring all his equitable interest, say, in shares, that document, operating, and intended to operate, as a transfer, will give rise to and take effect as a trust; for the assignor will then be a trustee of the legal estate in the shares for the person in whose favour he has made an assignment of his beneficial interest." [1952] Ch. 499 at p. 510. See Oakley, *Constructive Trusts* (3rd ed.), p. 318, suggesting that a constructive trust arises in these circumstances.

[38] (1862) 4 De G.F. & J. 264.

[39] See *Jones v. Lock* (1865) L.R. 1 Ch.App. 25.

[40] *Butt v. Kelsen* [1952] Ch. 197; *cf. Re George Whichelow Ltd* [1954] 1 W.L.R. 5.

[41] (1976) 40 Conv.(N.S.) 139 (L. McKay), criticising the reasoning. *Re Rose* was described in *Rowlandson v. National Westminster Bank Ltd* [1978] 1 W.L.R. 798 at 802 as a "gloss" on the principle of perfect gifts.

[42] (1998) 57 C.L.J. 46 (S. Lowrie and P. Todd), relying on *Westdeutsche Landesbank Girozentrale v. Islington London Borough Council* [1996] A.C. 669 at 706–707.

affected by the date on which the transfer is treated as being effective. *Re Rose* can be contrasted with *Re Fry*,[43] where the donor was domiciled abroad, and had not, at the critical time, done everything that was needed of him, as he had not obtained Treasury consent to the transfer.

The *Re Rose* principle was applied to a transfer of registered land in *Mascall v. Mascall*,[44] where a father executed a transfer of a house to his son, a volunteer, and handed over the land certificate. After the transfer had been sent to the Inland Revenue for stamping, and returned, the father (having fallen out with the son), sought a declaration that the transfer was ineffective. The son had not yet sent the documents to the Land Registry in order to become registered proprietor and had, therefore, not acquired legal title.[45] It was held that the gift was complete. The father had done all that he could, as the application to the Land Registry could be made by the son, from whom the father had no right to recover the transfer and land certificate. In the case of the assignment of a lease which has not been completed by registration, the *Re Rose* principle would apply as between assignor and assignee, but has been held not to affect the legal position as between the assignor and the landlord.[46] Thus the assignor retained the right to exercise an option to terminate conferred by the lease. The issue was not the ownership of the equitable interest, which would be resolved by *Re Rose*, but the location of the legal estate, from which derived the legal rights and duties of the landlord and tenant.

3. DECLARATION OF SELF AS TRUSTEE

There is no difficulty if a settlor wishes to declare himself trustee of some or all of his property. All that is needed is a manifestation of an intention to declare a trust; and, if the property is land, evidence in writing of such intent. The settlor "need not use the words, 'I declare myself a trustee,' but he must do something which is equivalent to it, and use expressions which have that meaning; for, however anxious the Court may be to carry out a man's intention, it is

---

[43] [1946] Ch. 312 (he had applied for consent, but further information might have been required); *Re Transatlantic Life Assurance Co. Ltd* [1980] 1 W.L.R. 79; Keeton & Sheridan's *Equity* (3rd ed.), p. 246.

[44] (1985) 49 P. & C.R. 119. *cf. Corin v. Patton* (1990) 169 C.L.R. 540 (gift incomplete where transferor had not requested mortgagee to produce land certificate, without which transferee could not be registered).

[45] L.R.A. 1925, s.19.

[46] *Brown & Root Technology Ltd v. Sun Alliance and London Assurance Co. Ltd* (1997) 75 P. & C.R. 223.

not at liberty to construe words otherwise than according to their proper meaning."[47] It is necessary to show, not only an intention to benefit someone; but an intention to be trustee for that person. "Men often mean to give things to their kinsfolk, they do not often mean to constitute themselves trustees. An imperfect gift is no declaration of trust."[48] Where the settlor is to be one of the co-trustees, the trust is constituted by his declaration of trust of property vested in him, even though the property has not yet been vested in the co-trustees. He must give effect to the trust by transferring the property into the names of all the trustees.[48a]

The issues which arise in this section are quite different from those discussed in section 2. There, the question was whether the property was vested in the trustee. Here, there is no such problem; if there is a trust the settlor is trustee (or may be one of co-trustees, as mentioned above). The question here is whether a trust has properly been declared. The problems usually arise in cases where the settlor's intention was to make a gift to a donee but the gift failed, and the question is whether the intent to benefit the donee can be construed as a declaration of trust in his favour.

The rule is that equity will not construe a void gift as a declaration of trust. What is needed is a manifestation of an intention to declare a trust.

In *Jones v. Lock*,[49] a father, being chided for failing to bring a present from Birmingham for his baby son, produced a £900 cheque payable to himself, saying: "Look you here, I give this to baby; it is for himself." He gave it to the child, who was about to tear it up, and the father took it away and put it in a safe. The father died and the cheque was found among his effects.

The question was whether the child was entitled to the cheque or whether it formed part of the father's estate. It would belong to the father unless he gave it to the child, or declared himself trustee of it. Clearly, he had not given it to the child, because a gift of a non-bearer cheque requires endorsement.[50] Had he declared himself trustee? No. He intended to give it to the child. There was no evidence that he intended to declare himself trustee of it, and to burden himself with a trustee's duties, including that of investing it in trustee securities and being personally liable for failure to do

---

[47] *Richards v. Delbridge* (1874) L.R. 18 Eq. 11 at 14, *per* Jessel M.R.
[48] Maitland, p. 72.
[48a] *Choithram (T.) International S.A. v. Pagarani* [2001] 1 W.L.R. 1 (P.C.).
[49] (1865) L.R. 1 Ch.App. 25. See also *Pappadakis v. Pappadakis, The Times,* January 19, 2000 (invalid assignment failing to identify assignee who would hold on trust could not operate as declaration of trust).
[50] Under the Cheques Act 1992, s.1, cheques are no longer transferable if they are crossed and the words "account payee" appear.

so. There was no such intention here; nor was there an effective gift. The child took nothing.

Similarly, in *Richards v. Delbridge*,[51] a grandfather who was entitled to leasehold premises endorsed on the lease a memorandum as follows: "This deed and all thereto belonging I give to [my grandson] from this time forth, with all the stock-in-trade." He delivered the document to the grandson's mother, and then died, making no mention of the property in his will. Jessel M.R. held that no interest passed; not at law, because the endorsement was ineffective to assign a lease; and not in equity, for the words were inappropriate for the declaration of a trust.

These cases may be contrasted with the situation where the legal owner has not attempted to transfer the property to the third party, but has shown that he considers himself to hold the property as trustee for the third party. Whether or not, in any case, the evidence is sufficient will depend on the facts; it has been held that the intent can be implied from conduct where the evidence is clear.[52]

So in *Paul v. Constance*[53] the conduct of the parties was sufficient to establish an intention to declare a trust. Mr Constance was separated from his wife, and lived with the claimant, Mrs Paul. He received, as damages for an injury suffered at work, a cheque for £950 and he and Mrs Paul decided to put it into a deposit account at Lloyds Bank. The account was opened in the name of Mr Constance only; because he and Mrs Paul felt an embarrassment in opening a joint account in different names. Mr Constance indicated on many occasions that the money was as much Mrs Paul's as his. On his death, the widow claimed the money in the account as part of her husband's estate. The question was whether the account was owned beneficially by Mr Constance, or whether, on the particular facts, he had shown an intention to hold the property as trustee for Mrs Paul, or as trustee for the two of them in equal shares. The Court of Appeal found that the evidence was sufficient to support an intention in Mr Constance to declare himself a trustee; although it was not easy to pinpoint a specific

---

[51] (1874) L.R. 18 Eq. 11.

[52] *New, Prance and Garrard's Trustee v. Hunting* [1897] 2 Q.B. 19. See also *Re Kayford Ltd* [1975] 1 W.L.R. 279; *Re Chelsea Cloisters Ltd* (1981) 41 P. & C.R. 98; *ante*, p. 53.

[53] [1977] 1 W.L.R. 54; convincingly criticised in Heydon, Gummow and Austin, *Cases and Materials on Equity and Trusts* (4th ed.), p. 142: "The law of express trusts normally requires an intention to benefit the *cestui que trust* specifically by way of trust—a mere intention to benefit him in some way is insufficient." See also *Choithram (T.) International S.A. v. Pagarani* [2001] 1 W.L.R. 1, where words indicating an outright gift were construed in the context as words of a gift to be held on the trusts of a settlement created by the donor.

moment of declaration.[54] Mrs Paul was thus able to recover half of the proceeds of the account.

This decision was applied in *Rowe v. Prance*,[55] where the defendant, a wealthy man who was conducting an extra-marital relationship with the claimant, Mrs Rowe, acquired an ocean-going boat which was registered in his sole name. After the relationship broke down, Mrs Rowe succeeded in her claim to a half share. The defendant had repeatedly referred to the boat as "our boat", had assured Mrs Rowe that her interest in the boat was her security, and had felt bound to give an explanation (although absurd[56]) as to why he alone could be registered as owner. As no formalities were required in the case of personalty, the trust had been sufficiently declared. On the other hand, where a house in the joint names of a mother and father was transferred, pursuant to a consent order, to the mother "for the benefit of the child", no trust was created for the child, who had since fallen out with her mother and left home.[57]

A lenient view of the requirements of a declaration of trust was taken by the Court of Appeal in *Re Vandervell's Trusts (No. 2)*.[58] An option to purchase certain shares was held by trustees on a resulting trust for Vandervell. The trustees exercised the option, using money from Vandervell's children's settlement. It was held that the shares were henceforth held on trust for the children's settlement. There was no declaration of trust by Vandervell, but such a declaration could be inferred from certain acts of the trustees[59]: first, the use of the money from the children's settlement; secondly, the subsequent payment of the dividends to that settlement; and thirdly, the trustees' notification to the Revenue that they now held the shares on trust for that settlement. The inadequacy of these three acts as establishing a declaration of trust lies in the fact that the second and third merely indicate what the trustees thought the position to be, while the first ignores Vandervell's beneficial ownership of the option. This has already been examined.[60]

It will be noted that it is not necessary that the beneficiary should be aware of the declaration of trust.[61] The beneficiary becomes equitable owner just as he would become legal owner if the property had been conveyed to him.

---

[54] This could cause problems. See Heydon, Gummow and Austin, *op. cit.*, at p. 142.

[55] [1999] 2 F.L.R. 787.

[56] He stated that the claimant could not be registered as she did not possess a master's certificate.

[57] *Re B (Child: Property Transfer)* [1999] 2 F.L.R. 418.

[58] [1974] Ch. 269.

[59] Trustees cannot normally declare a trust, but here it was accepted that the option was held on such trusts as might thereafter be declared by Vandervell or the trustees.

[60] *ante*, p. 87.

[61] *Middleton v. Pollock* (1876) 2 Ch.D. 104; *Standing v. Bowring* (1885) 31 Ch.D. 282.

4. COVENANTS TO SETTLE

If a settlor has neither conveyed the property to trustees nor declared himself a trustee, no trust is created. If he has covenanted by deed to settle the property, the crucial question is whether or not the intended beneficiary can compel him to carry out the covenant and settle it.

A. Contracts (Rights of Third Parties) Act 1999

Until recently the general rule was that a third party could not enforce a contract purporting to benefit him. The position is now changed by the Contracts (Rights of Third Parties) Act 1999. Section 1 of the Act, which does not affect any right or remedy of a third party that exists apart from the Act,[62] provides that a third party may in his own right enforce a term of the contract if the contract expressly provides that he may, or if the term purports to confer a benefit on him, unless on a proper construction of the contract it appears that the parties did not intend the term to be enforceable by the third party. The section further provides that the third party must be expressly identified by name, as a member of a class, or as answering a particular description, but need not be in existence when the contract is entered into. Thus a third party could now enforce a covenant to convey property to trustees for his benefit.

Clearly section 1 enables a third party who falls within it to enforce the contract by an action for damages. So far as specific performance is concerned, section 1(5) provides that "there shall be available to the third party any remedy that would have been available to him in an action for breach of contract if he had been a party to the contract (and the rules relating to damages, injunctions, specific performance and other relief shall apply accordingly)." This might be interpreted as meaning that the third party may obtain specific performance if the subject-matter is such that the remedy of damages would be inadequate.[63] On the other hand, it is established that a volunteer may not obtain specific performance.[64] In *Cannon v. Hartley*[65] a volunteer beneficiary who was a party to a deed was

---

[62] Contracts (Rights of Third Parties) Act 1999, s.7. The Act implements Law Com. No. 242 (1996).

[63] Consider the Explanatory Notes to s.1, to the effect that subsection (5) "makes it clear that the courts may award all the remedies which are available to a person bringing a claim for breach of contract to a third party seeking to enforce his rights under subsection (1). The normal rules of law applicable to those remedies . . . apply to the third party's claim."

[64] *post*, p. 726.

[65] [1949] Ch. 213; *post*, p. 131.

able to sue upon it for damages, but would not have been able to obtain specific performance. It is difficult to see why a third party, who has not given consideration, should be in a better position under the 1999 Act.

Section 10 of the 1999 Act provides that the Act does not apply to contracts entered into before the end of the period of six months beginning with the day on which it was passed,[66] save in the case of a contract entered into during that six month period which expressly provides for the application of the Act.

The law relating to covenants to settle which were entered into prior to the 1999 Act will be considered in the remainder of this part and in part 5 of this Chapter.

B. Covenants to Settle prior to the Contracts (Rights of Third Parties) Act 1999

A beneficiary who has given consideration can enforce the covenant by obtaining specific performance; one who has not given consideration cannot do so. Equity will not assist a volunteer.

For this purpose, "consideration" has a wider meaning than at common law, in that equity also treats as having given consideration, in the case of a covenant in a marriage settlement, the husband and wife and issue of the marriage.[67] They are said to be "within the marriage consideration."[68] It seems, however, that illegitimate children,[69] children by a former marriage, and children to whom one of the parties stands *in loco parentis*, cannot be included unless their interests are so closely intertwined with those of the natural issue of the marriage that the latter may be said to take only on terms which admit the former to a participation with them.[70]

In *Pullan v. Koe*,[71] a marriage settlement of 1859 settled property on the husband and wife and prospective children, and also contained a covenant by the wife to settle on the same trusts any property she later acquired of the value of £100 and upwards. In

---

[66] November 11, 1999.

[67] *Att.-Gen. v. Jacobs-Smith* [1895] 2 Q.B. 341. "Issue" includes remoter issue; *MacDonald v. Scott* [1893] A.C. 642.

[68] This is so whether the settlement is made on the marriage, or made before but in consideration of the marriage, or a post-nuptial settlement in pursuance of an ante-nuptial agreement.

[69] This principle seems unaffected by the Family Law Reform Act 1987, which in general equates the rights of children of married and unmarried parents.

[70] See *Att.-Gen. v. Jacobs-Smith* [1895] 2 Q.B. 341; *Rennell v. I.R.C.* [1962] Ch. 329 at 341, affd. [1964] A.C. 173; *Re Cook's S.T.* [1965] Ch. 902 at 914.

[71] [1913] 1 Ch. 9. See (1979) 32 C.L.P. 1 at 4–5 (C. Rickett).

1879 the wife received £285, part of which was used for her own purposes and part invested in bearer bonds, which remained at the bank in the husband's name until his death in 1909. The question was whether the trustees could then take steps to obtain the bonds from his executors and hold them on the trusts of the settlement.

Swinfen-Eady J. held that it was the duty of the trustees to enforce the covenant on behalf of those who were within the marriage consideration. Indeed, the beneficiaries could have taken action themselves if the trustees had refused to do so. Here, however, the common law action on the covenant was barred by the lapse of time; but the court held that the £285 was impressed with the trust at the moment the wife received it, and that the trust could be enforced against the bonds.

Such a covenant would not however be enforceable in favour of next-of-kin, for they are volunteers.[72] Thus, if there had been no children of the marriage, the next-of-kin, or other persons entitled in default of children, would not have been able to enforce the covenant.

Where the covenant is enforced by persons within the marriage consideration, the court may order the covenantor to settle the property in accordance with the covenant[73]; or, as in *Pullan v. Koe*,[74] declare that the property is subject to the trusts of the settlement. However where one of the intended beneficiaries is a party[75] to the covenant, even though a volunteer, there is no reason why an action on the covenant for damages should not be brought, although the equitable remedy of specific performance would not lie.

In *Cannon v. Hartley*,[76] a settlement upon a separation, to which the spouses and a daughter were parties, provided that the father should pay to the daughter any sum exceeding £1,000 which he might inherit from his parents. Having inherited, he failed to make the payment. The daughter was a volunteer. She

---

[72] *Re D'Angibau* (1880) 15 Ch.D. 228; *Re Plumptre's Marriage Settlement* [1901] 1 Ch. 609; *Re Cook's S.T.* [1965] Ch. 902. Nor will it be enforceable on this principle if, although for consideration, the covenant is not specifically enforceable, as in the case of a covenant to pay money; *Stone v. Stone* (1869) 5 Ch.App. 74.

[73] This may have the effect of benefiting volunteers, as in *Davenport v. Bishopp* (1843) 2 Y. & C.C.C. 451 (life interest to husband, remainder to volunteers).

[74] [1913] 1 Ch. 9, *supra*.

[75] For the meaning of which, see *Beswick v. Beswick* [1968] A.C. 58 at 102.

[76] [1949] Ch. 213. See generally (1988) 8 L.S. 172 (M. Macnair), suggesting that there is some historical support for allowing specific performance of covenants in favour of volunteers.

could however sue upon her father's covenant, and recover damages for breach of covenant at common law.

5. ACTION FOR DAMAGES BY THE TRUSTEES. TRUSTS OF CHOSES IN ACTION

There is no difficulty in enforcing a completely constituted trust of a chose in action.[77] Where a contractual right is held by A on trust for B, A may sue and obtain damages or specific performance on behalf of B[78]; or B may obtain such relief on his own account if A refuses to act, joining A as a co-defendant in the action.[79]

The question is whether this principle can assist a volunteer in the case of a covenant to settle existing or after-acquired property.[80] Such a volunteer may now be able to enforce the covenant directly under the Contracts (Rights of Third Parties) Act 1999.[81] The remainder of this section deals with the position where the covenant was entered into prior to that Act and is unaffected by it. In the case of such a covenant by a spouse to settle after-acquired property in favour of the children of the marriage, and in default in favour of the next-of-kin, we have seen that the next-of-kin, being volunteers, are unable to sue on the covenant.[82] Could not the trustees sue, recover damages, and hold them on trust for the next-of-kin?[83] Or could not the next-of-kin argue that there is already a completely constituted trust of the benefit of the covenant, a trust of a chose in action for which they are the beneficiaries, and thus entitled to enforce?[84]

The courts have given volunteers no comfort in this respect. In *Re Pryce*,[85] Eve J. held that the trustees should not be compelled to pursue whatever remedy they may have at law on the covenant, and in *Re Kay's Settlement*,[86] Simonds J. decided that they should be instructed not to do so. In *Re Cook's Settlement Trusts*,[87] Buckley J.

---

[77] *post*, p. 135.

[78] *Lloyd's v. Harper* (1880) 16 Ch.D. 290.

[79] *Les Affréteurs Réunis Société Anonyme v. Leopold Walford Ltd* [1919] A.C. 801; *Parker-Tweedale v. Dunbar Bank plc* [1991] Ch. 12. This exception to the privity rule is less important after the Contracts (Rights of Third Parties) Act 1999.

[80] *i.e.* property which might come subsequently to the settlor. It was common in a marriage settlement for the spouses to covenant to add to the settlement any property which they subsequently might acquire.

[81] *ante*, p. 129.

[82] *ante*, p. 131.

[83] (1960) 76 L.Q.R. 100 (D. Elliott).

[84] (1962) 78 L.Q.R. 228 (J. Hornby); (1969) 85 L.Q.R. 213 (W. Lee); (1975) 91 L.Q.R. 236 (J. Barton); (1976) 92 L.Q.R. 427 (R. Meagher and J. Lehane); (1979) 32 C.L.P. 1 and (1981) 34 C.L.P. 189 (C. Rickett).

[85] [1917] 1 Ch. 234.

[86] [1939] Ch. 329.

[87] [1965] Ch. 902; (1965) 24 C.L.J. 46 (G. Jones); (1966) 29 M.L.R. 397 (D. Matheson); (1966) 8 Malaya L.R. 153 (M. Scott); [1967] A.S.C.L. 387 *et seq.* (J. Davies).

distinguished *Fletcher v. Fletcher*,[88] *Williamson v. Codrington*[89] and *Re Cavendish-Browne's Settlement Trusts*,[90] and refused to allow volunteers to enforce a covenant even though another person had given consideration. These however are all decisions of courts of first instance, and the matter should be analysed more closely.

A. Action by the Trustees

There are certain difficulties which lie in the way of the proposition that the trustees, as parties to the covenant, can sue to recover damages with a view to holding the money received on trust for the (volunteer) beneficiaries. One question is whether the trustee would recover substantial damages in an action at law on the covenant. If he can recover only nominal damages, the action will be of no help to the beneficiary.[91]

The general rule is that the claimant may recover in an action for breach of contract damages sufficient to compensate him for his loss. Damages suffered by third parties are not recoverable by the claimant unless, as explained below, the claimant contracted as trustee for the third parties. An attempt by the Court of Appeal in *Jackson v. Horizon Holidays Ltd.*[92] to permit the claimant to recover damages in respect of the loss suffered by third parties has been firmly disapproved by the House of Lords.[93]

The real question, however, is this: what does the common law regard as the claimant's own loss? In the context of a voluntary covenant to settle, it has been said that "for breach of a covenant to pay a certain sum the measure of damages (if that is the appropriate expression) is the certain sum; and for breach of a covenant to transfer property worth a certain sum, it is the value of the property".[94] There is no doubt that this is the usual rule, as shown by the cases where the volunteer beneficiary is a party to the covenant.[95] Applying this rule, substantial damages should be recoverable at law

---

[88] (1844) 4 Hare 67.

[89] (1750) 1 Ves.Sen. 511.

[90] [1916] W.N. 341.

[91] See (1950) 3 C.L.P. 30 at p. 43 (O. Marshall).

[92] [1975] 1 W.L.R. 1468.

[93] *Woodar Investment Developments Ltd v. Wimpey Construction (U.K.) Ltd* [1980] 1 W.L.R. 277. See also *Beswick v. Beswick* [1968] A.C. 58; *post*, p. 137; *Darlington Borough Council v. Wiltshier Northern Ltd* [1995] 1 W.L.R. 68; *Panatown Ltd v. Alfred McAlpine Construction Ltd* [2000] 4 All E.R. 97.

[94] (1960) 76 L.Q.R. 100 at 112 (D. Elliott); (1975) 91 L.Q.R. 236 at 238 (J. Barton); [1988] Conv. 19 at 21 (D. Goddard). See also [1982] Conv. 280 at 281 (M. Friend), agreeing that substantial damages are available on the basis of debt in the case of a voluntary covenant to pay money, but suggesting that this is less clear in the case of specific property other than money.

[95] *Cannon v. Hartley* [1949] Ch. 213; *Synge v. Synge* [1894] 1 Q.B. 466.

by B where A covenants to pay a certain sum (or to transfer Blackacre) to B to be held on trust for C. It is no answer at common law
to say that B suffers no loss by the breach of such a covenant. At law
the position is no different from that of a trustee of a completely
constituted trust, who may recover substantial damages for the
breach of any contract he may make as trustee even though he
personally suffers no loss. There is, however, little direct authority
in the context of an incompletely constituted trust. Of the cases
usually quoted on this question, *Re Cavendish-Browne's Settlement
Trusts*[96] is most clearly in point.

> The covenantor was absolutely entitled under two wills to a
> share of real estate in Canada, which he entered into a voluntary
> covenant to settle. The trustees sued for damages and were
> awarded a sum equivalent to the value of the property which
> would have come into their hands if the covenant had been per-
> formed, and this money was to be held on the trusts of the set-
> tlement.

This, then, supports the view that a covenantee may recover substantial damages at law for breach of a covenant to pay money or to
transfer specific property, although he has suffered no loss personally. But even if this be correct, it may not follow that the same view
would prevail in the context of cases like *Re Pryce*[97] and *Re Kay's
Settlement*.[98] The covenant in those cases was not to pay a sum of
money or to transfer specific property, but to transfer after-acquired
property to the covenantee.[99]

Even though substantial damages may be available at law in an
action by the trustee-covenantee, this would not be the end of the
difficulties, for it may be argued that any such damages would be
held on a resulting trust for the covenantor (settlor) and not for the
volunteer beneficiaries.[1] The argument (as yet untested) is that, in
the absence of any completely constituted trust of either the property
or the benefit of the covenant (discussed below), the volunteers

---

[96] [1916] W.N. 341; (1916) 61 S.J. 27; *cf. Perspectives of Law* (ed. R. Pound), p. 243; (1969)
85 L.Q.R. 213 at 219. The decision was prior to the cases holding that a trustee cannot sue;
ante, p. 132. See, however, (1979) 32 C.L.P. 1 (C. Rickett), suggesting that the decision was
based on the "trust of the promise" theory (discussed below).

[97] [1917] 1 Ch. 234.

[98] [1939] Ch. 329. In this case and in *Re Pryce, supra*, it was assumed that the trustees, if they
sued at law, would recover substantial damages. See also *Coulls v. Bagot's Trustee* (1967)
40 A.L.J.R. 471; *Cannon v. Hartley* [1949] Ch. 213.

[99] See, however, [1988] Conv. 19 at 21 (D. Goddard), suggesting that *Re Cavendish-Browne's
S.T.* did involve after-acquired property. The testators from whom the property in question
derived had died, but their estates were unadministered at the date of the covenant.

[1] See Underhill and Hayton, *Law of Trusts and Trustees* (15th ed.), p. 156. *cf. Re Cavendish-
Browne's S.T., supra.*

would have no claim. The trustee-covenantee, it need hardly be added, could not keep the money himself.

B. Trust of the Benefit of the Covenant

If there is a completely constituted trust of the benefit of the covenant, there is no difficulty, as has been seen,[2] in enforcing it, either by the trustees on behalf of the beneficiaries, or by the beneficiaries themselves. It was said, however, in *Re Cook's Settlement Trusts*,[3] that a covenant to settle future property cannot be the subject-matter of a trust, because it does not "create a debt enforceable at law . . . that is to say, a property right."[4] It is submitted that this restriction is not supportable.[5] Of course, future property itself, or unascertained property, or a mere (a hope of acquisition), cannot be the subject-matter of a trust.[6] But a covenant to pay a sum to be ascertained in the future is just as good a chose in action as a covenant to pay a specified sum, and it creates legal property of value. The subject-matter of the trust *res* is the benefit of the covenant, the chose in action; not the property which will be obtained by its performance.[7] There is no difficulty in a trust of a bank account, which is a chose in action, its value varying with the state of the account from day to day; nor in a trust of an insurance policy under which the obligation is to pay an undetermined sum on a future event which may not happen. The decision in *Re Cook's Settlement Trusts*[8] is justifiable, however, on the basis that there was no manifestation of an intention to create a trust of the benefit of the covenant.

On the assumption that there is no difficulty in the concept of a trust of the benefit of a covenant, there is nevertheless considerable difficulty in any particular case in deciding whether or not there was an intention to create one.[9] The critical case is *Fletcher v. Fletcher*,[10] a decision which presents certain difficulties.

---

[2] *ante*, p. 132.

[3] [1965] Ch. 902.

[4] [1965] Ch. 902 at 913; (1976) 92 L.Q.R. 427 (R. Meagher and J. Lehane).

[5] (1965) 24 C.L.J. 46 at 49 (G. Jones); *cf.* (1969) 85 L.Q.R. 213 at 223 (W. Lee). See also (1979) 32 C.L.P. 1 and (1981) 34 C.L.P. 189 (C. Rickett); (1982) 98 L.Q.R. 17 (J. Feltham); [1982] Conv. 280 (M. Friend); [1982] Conv. 352 (S. Smith).

[6] *post*, p. 140; *Williams v. C.I.R.* [1965] N.Z.L.R. 395.

[7] *Williamson v. Codrington* (1750) 1 Ves.Sen. 511; *Fletcher v. Fletcher* (1844) 4 Hare 67; *Lloyd's v. Harper* (1880) 16 Ch.D. 290; *Re Cavendish-Browne's S.T.* [1916] W.N. 341; (1975) 91 L.Q.R. 236 at 238 (J. Barton); (1976) 92 L.Q.R. at 428.

[8] [1965] Ch. 902.

[9] *Vandepitte v. Preferred Accident Insurance Corp. of New York* [1933] A.C. 70; *Re Schebsman* [1944] Ch. 83; *Green v. Russell* [1959] 2 Q.B. 266; *Scruttons Ltd v. Midland Silicones Ltd* [1962] A.C. 446; *Beswick v. Beswick* [1968] A.C. 58; *Swain v. Law Society* [1983] 1 A.C. 598.

[10] (1844) 4 Hare 67.

Ellis Fletcher entered into a voluntary covenant with trustees to pay to them £60,000 to be held on trust, in the events which happened, for his illegitimate son Jacob. The trustees did not wish to accept the trust or to receive the money unless they were required to do so. Vice-Chancellor Wigram held that Jacob was able to claim the money, saying that equity would either allow Jacob to use the name of the trustee to sue at law, or to recover in his own name in a court of equity.

Wigram V.-C. was of course fully aware of the rule forbidding aid being given to a volunteer, and this argument was pressed upon him:

"According to the authorities, I cannot, I admit, do anything to perfect the liability of the author of the trust, if it is not already perfect. This covenant, however, is already perfect. The covenantor is liable at law, and the Court is not called upon to do any act to perfect it. One question made in argument has been whether there can be a trust of a covenant the benefit of which shall belong to a third party; but I cannot think that there is any difficulty in that. ... The proposition, therefore, that in no case can there be a trust of a covenant is too large, and the real question is whether the relation of trustee and *cestui que trust* is established in the present case."[11]

There was, then, a trust of the benefit of the covenant, and the beneficiary could enforce it. The trustees were, analytically, in the same position as Lloyd's in *Lloyd's v. Harper.*[12] It was there decided that Lloyd's had contracted with Harper (who guaranteed the debts of his son as a Lloyd's underwriter) as trustee for the persons insured, and that, therefore, Lloyd's could sue, on behalf of the persons insured, and recover the damages which they, the beneficiaries, had suffered on the son's bankruptcy. The crucial question in these cases is whether or not there has been a manifestation of an intention to declare a trust of a chose in action, and this is a matter in which the courts have not, over the years, maintained a consistent approach. There are some difficulties in holding that there was a trust of the chose in action on the facts of *Fletcher v. Fletcher.*[13] In the first place, positive evidence of intention is lacking. Ellis Fletcher, the covenantor, covenanted that he would pay the £60,000 to trustees "to be held on the following trusts." There is clearly a trust which will affect the money once it is received by the trustee, but no

---

[11] (1844) 4 Hare 67 at 74. The position will be otherwise if the covenant is statute-barred. *cf. Pullan v. Koe* [1913] 1 Ch. 9; *ante*, p. 130, where the beneficiaries' interest, owing to the presence of consideration, was not merely in the covenant but in the property itself.
[12] (1880) 16 Ch.D. 290.
[13] (1844) 4 Hare 67.

evidence of an intention by either party to create a trust of a chose in action. It cannot be assumed from the fact that the property itself is to be subjected to a trust that an immediate trust of the benefit of the covenant was also intended.[14]

Another question is whether the relevant intention is that of the covenantor (settlor) or the covenantee (trustee). Certainly there was no intention to create a trust of the chose in action on the part of the trustees, if that is the requirement, in *Fletcher v. Fletcher*[15]: they did not know about the arrangement, and wished to decline the trust upon hearing of it. A trust of tangible property is declared by the owner of the property, whether he declares himself trustee or transfers it to another on trust. As a general rule, a trust of a debt is declared by the creditor. Thus in *Paul v. Constance*[16] the question whether a trust of a bank account had been created was determined by examining the intention of the account-holder (creditor), Mr Constance. It is submitted, however, that a distinction must be drawn between covenants supported by valuable consideration and those which are not. Where there is consideration, the relevant intention to create a trust of the chose in action is that of the covenantee.[17] This will usually be proved by showing that the latter covenanted as trustee for the persons nominated by the covenantor. Where, on the other hand, the covenant is voluntary, as in *Fletcher v. Fletcher*,[18] the better view is that "the promisor is the creator of the trust, and if he manifests an intention that the promisee's rights under the promise shall be held in trust, the promisee immediately becomes trustee of his rights under the promise".[19]

C. Specific Performance at the Suit of the Contracting Party

Beswick v. Beswick[20] suggests the possibility of another approach to this problem. If the administratrix of old Mr Beswick could in that case obtain specific performance against young Mr Beswick and compel him to perform his promise to make payments to the widow

---

[14] *cf.* (1982) 98 L.Q.R. 17 (J. Feltham), suggesting that such an assumption should be made, in order to avoid the absurdity that voluntary covenants to settle are otherwise unenforceable.

[15] (1844) 4 Hare 67.

[16] [1977] 1 W.L.R. 54; *ante*, p. 127.

[17] See the insurance cases: *Vandepitte v. Preferred Accident Insurance Corp. of New York* [1933] A.C. 70; *Swain v. The Law Society* [1983] 1 A.C. 598. The question in these cases is whether the policy-holder intended to hold the company's obligation on trust. See (1982) 98 L.Q.R. 17 (J. Feltham); [1998] Conv. 88 (J. Jaconelli).

[18] *supra.*

[19] *The Restatement of Trusts* (2nd ed.), para. 26. See also (1979) 32 C.L.P. 1 at 13 (C. Rickett); Heydon, Gummow and Austin, *Cases and Materials on Equity and Trusts* (4th ed.), p. 606. Difficulties could arise in cases such as *Re Cook's S.T.* [1965] Ch. 902, where the covenant is made with persons of whom some, but not all, have given consideration.

[20] [1968] A.C. 58; *post*, pp. 752 *et seq.*; [1967] A.S.C.L. 387 *et seq.* (J. Davies); (1988) 8 L.S. 14 (N. Andrews).

Beswick (a volunteer), can it not be argued that the trustee-cove-
nantees should be able to obtain specific performance of the promise
to settle after-acquired property in favour of volunteers? At least in
Beswick v. Beswick the House of Lords saw no objection to a solution which permitted the widow to obtain by this indirect method
what she could not obtain directly.[21] Simonds J. in *Re Kay's Settlement*[22] had taken the opposite view.

It is submitted however that the principle of *Beswick v. Beswick*[23]
does not apply to the case of voluntary covenants. In that case, old
Mr Beswick gave consideration for the promise of young Mr Beswick and had a right of action for damages against him. When the
loss was shown to be nil, and the damages therefore nominal, specific performance became available instead. That remedy is available where the legal remedy of damages is inadequate.[24] Where
valuable consideration has been given, the remedy of nominal damages is inadequate, although there is no loss to the contracting party,
because the result is the unjust enrichment of the defendant. In the
case of a voluntary covenant to pay to trustees the situation (assuming that damages would be nominal[25]) is different. There is no unjust
enrichment of the covenantor; nominal damages are therefore adequate. Specific performance in any event is not available to a volunteer, and most trustees are volunteers.[26] Furthermore, the availability
of specific performance in *Beswick v. Beswick*[27] was not hampered
by the principle that trustees are not allowed to sue,[28] because the
claimant there was not a trustee.[29]

We have seen that it made no difference in *Re Cook's Settlement
Trusts*[30] that one of the parties had given consideration.

> In *Re Cook's Settlement Trusts*, property including a Re-
> mbrandt was settled on H for life, remainder to his son, F. Under
> the terms of a resettlement the property became F's absolutely
> and he covenanted to pay to the trustees the proceeds of sale of
> the Rembrandt (and other pictures) if sold in H's lifetime, to be
> held on trust for F's children (volunteers). F gave the Rembrandt
> to his wife, who wished to sell it. Buckley J. held that the trustees
> could not enforce the covenant if the Rembrandt were sold.

[21] *per* Lord Pearce [1968] A.C. 58 at 89.
[22] [1939] Ch. 329 at 342.
[23] [1968] A.C. 58.
[24] *post*, p. 716.
[25] Which may not be correct; *ante*, p. 132.
[26] Nominal consideration is not sufficient in equity. See (1966) 8 Malaya L.R. 153 at 158 (M. Scott).
[27] [1968] A.C. 58.
[28] *ante*, p. 132.
[29] She was a personal representative, but the position was exactly the same as if Mr Beswick senior had been in a position to bring the action himself. There was no trust.
[30] [1965] Ch. 902; *ante*, p. 132.

The decision preceded *Beswick v. Beswick*,[31] in which it was apparently not cited. A similarity between the two cases appears on close analysis. H entered into a contract for consideration with F, one of the terms of which was that F would confer a benefit on X. If H had sued F, could he succeed, as in *Beswick v. Beswick*, by saying that the damages awardable for the breach were inadequate, and that specific performance of the covenant to pay should be decreed in favour of X? The covenant was not in terms to pay to the volunteers, but to the trustees, who would hold the money in trust for them; but this seems immaterial. It is H who, on this reasoning, could sue (although he would not be obliged to) and not the trustees; but the action should not be dependent upon H's physical survival, for his estate, on the reasoning of *Beswick*, should be able to do so.[32]

It was suggested in *Coulls v. Bagot's Trustee*,[33] where the contract was not in the form of a covenant, that where the promise is made jointly to H (who gave the consideration) *and* to X (who gave none), *both of whom* are parties to the contract or covenant, X can sue by joining H (irrespective of H's wishes) although X personally has provided no consideration. Enforcement would then be on the basis of contract.[34]

It is doubtful whether *Coulls* or *Beswick* will enable trustees to enforce voluntary covenants to settle. But in the case of a covenant with a third party in a marriage settlement to settle after-acquired property, that person, or his estate after his death, having provided consideration, and being a party to the transaction, may, on the authority of *Beswick v. Beswick*[35] be able to obtain specific performance for the benefit of the volunteers.

That line of reasoning is wholly separate from the question of the enforcement of a covenant in the *Fletcher v. Fletcher* type of situation.[36] There, no consideration was given. The covenant was voluntary. It would be enforceable by, or on behalf of the beneficiaries if, and only if, there was found to be a trust of the chose in action. That brings us back to the most basic question of all in relation to the creation of trusts: whether the settlor has manifested an intention to create a trust.

---

[31] [1968] A.C. 58.

[32] *cf.* (1979) 32 C.L.P. 1 at 14 (C. Rickett).

[33] (1967) 40 A.L.J.R. 471 at 477 (Barwick C.J.); [1967] A.S.C.L. at 395 (J. Davies); (1978) 37 C.L.J. 301 (B. Coote). Compare the facts of *Cannon v. Hartley* [1949] Ch. 213, *ante*, p. 131, where another party to the covenant had given consideration.

[34] The promisee is the entity (H+X). This entity has provided consideration, it being irrelevant whether it was actually furnished by H or X. So viewed, this complies with the normal contract rules. Judgment would be for (H+X). See (1989) 48 C.L.J. 243 (P. Kincaid).

[35] [1968] A.C. 58.

[36] (1844) 4 Hare 67.

The question whether such an intention can be found has been the subject of much litigation since the privity rule was established by *Tweddle v. Atkinson*,[37] and it is well known, both that the courts have been inconsistent in their decisions, and that, since *Walford's* case,[38] they have been more reluctant to find such an intention. It was very different in Jacob Fletcher's day which predated *Milroy v. Lord*,[39] *Jones v. Lock*[40] and *Tweddle v. Atkinson*.[41] There is little doubt that a modern court would fail to find the necessary intention on the facts of *Fletcher v. Fletcher*.

All this is of reduced importance now that the Contracts (Rights of Third Parties) Act 1999[42] permits third parties in certain cases to enforce contracts in their own right. The old learning, however, will remain relevant for some years to come in relation to covenants entered into before the Act.

6. TRUSTS OF FUTURE PROPERTY

A contract for consideration to convey future property to trustees upon trust is valid[43] and, in most cases, specifically enforceable.[44] A voluntary covenant to convey future property to trustees is actionable at law by a beneficiary who is a party to the covenant.[45] If the beneficiary is not a party he may now have rights of enforcement under the Contracts (Rights of Third Parties) Act 1999. A purported assignment of an expectancy[46] cannot be a conveyance because there is nothing to convey. Nor can there be a valid declaration of trust of property not yet existing.[47] If consideration is given for a purported conveyance, it will be construed as a contract to assign

---

[37] (1861) 3 B. & S. 393.
[38] *Les Affréteurs Réunis Société Anonyme v. Leopold Walford (London) Ltd* [1919] A.C. 801. See *Swain v. The Law Society* [1983] 1 A.C. 598 (the Law Society did not contract as trustee by using words "on behalf of all solicitors" in insurance contract). Outside the contract area, however, an intention to create a trust has been upheld without strong evidence; see *Paul v. Constance* [1977] 1 W.L.R. 54, *ante*, p. 127.
[39] (1862) 4 De G.F. & J. 264.
[40] (1865) L.R. 1 Ch.App. 25.
[41] *supra*.
[42] *ante*, p. 129. The ambiguous drafting of s.1(5) in relation to the availability of specific performance to the third party has been noted.
[43] *Re Lind* [1915] 2 Ch. 345; *Re Gillott's Settlements* [1934] Ch. 97; *Re Haynes' W.T.* [1949] Ch. 5.
[44] *Pullan v. Koe* [1913] 1 Ch. 9.
[45] *Cannon v. Hartley* [1949] Ch. 213; *ante*, p. 131.
[46] *Williams v. C.I.R.* [1965] N.Z.L.R. 345; ("the first £500 of the net income which shall accrue to the assignor . . . from the Trust."). An assignment of the assignor's life interest under the trust would, of course, have been valid.
[47] *cf. Re Ralli's W.T.* [1964] Ch. 288 (valid declaration of trust of remainder interest, which is not future property). See also *Simpson v. Simpson* [1992] 1 F.L.R. 601 (share of proceeds of sale of cottage which was not yet sold).

and enforceable as such.[48] But if it is made gratuitously it is a nullity.[49]

In *Re Ellenborough*,[50] the sister of Lord Ellenborough purported to convey by voluntary settlement the property which she would receive under her brother's will. On his death she declined to transfer the property to the trustees, and Buckley J. held that the trustees could not compel her to do so.

A further question is whether such a gratuitous covenant, assignment or declaration in respect of future property can subsequently be treated as an effective declaration of trust if the property does later vest in the trustee. The situation can arise if the property, on materialising, is transferred to trustees without a further declaration of the trusts, or where the property vests in the settlor after he has declared the trusts on which he is to hold it.

We have seen that, prior to the Contracts (Rights of Third Parties) Act 1999, a covenant in a marriage settlement to settle after-acquired property is not enforceable at the suit of the next-of-kin because they are volunteers[51]; and that a deed purporting to convey future property upon trust is ineffective.[52] But if, in either of these cases, the property found its way into the hands of the trustees, it would presumably be held upon the trusts declared in the relevant documents.[53] If the settlor, in either case, conveyed the property to the trustees, that action could be construed as a further declaration of the trusts; but if the property reached the trustees by another route, being conveyed perhaps by the executors of the testator from whom the property came,[54] or coming into the hands of the trustee in a different capacity,[55] the possibility of finding that there was a further declaration of trust is less strong. There appear to be three possible solutions to such a case: that the trustees take beneficially, that they hold on trust for the settlor, or that they hold on the trusts declared in the previous document. The first is obviously untenable. The second involves the proposition that the settlor could claim

---

[48] *Re Burton's Settlement* [1955] Ch. 82. See also *Don King Productions Inc v. Warren* [2000] Ch. 291 (agreement for value to assign non-assignable contracts took effect as declaration of trust of benefit of contracts). For criticisms, see [1999] L.M.C.L.Q. 353 (A. Tettenborn).

[49] *Meek v. Kettlewell* (1842) 1 Hare 464; *Re Brooks' S.T.* [1939] Ch. 993; *Williams v. C.I.R.* [1965] N.Z.L.R. 345.

[50] [1903] 1 Ch. 697; *cf. Re Bowden* [1936] Ch. 71; *Re Adlard* [1954] Ch. 29.

[51] *Re D'Angibau* (1880) 15 Ch.D. 228; *Re Plumptre's Settlement* [1910] 1 Ch. 609.

[52] *Re Ellenborough* [1903] 1 Ch. 697; *Re Brooks' S.T.* [1939] Ch. 993.

[53] *Re Ellenborough, supra.* Miss Emily Towry Law had already handed over to the trustees the property which she received under her sister's will; and no attempt was made to recover it; *Re Adlard* [1954] Ch. 29; *Re Ralli's W.T.* [1964] Ch. 228.

[54] *Re Adlard* [1954] Ch. 29.

[55] *Re Ralli's W.T.* [1964] Ch. 288.

back in equity property which he had covenanted or purported to settle.[56] The third avoids the necessity of making the ultimate destination of the property depend upon the route by which it reached the trustees; it is consistent with the expressed intention of the parties and appears to be the most satisfactory solution.[57]

Where the property comes to the settlor himself, it is possible for the court to hold that a previous declaration of trust,[58] followed by the vesting of the property in him, constitutes the trust. It is clear that a previous declaration is not of itself sufficient[59]; subsequent confirmation of a previous declaration is sufficient.[60] In less obvious cases it is no doubt a question of construction to determine whether or not the settlor is to be taken to have made a subsequent declaration or to have affirmed a previous one. If he made the declaration every day, the last declaration being made the moment before he received the property, this would no doubt be sufficient. But in the absence of authority, it is unsafe to predict to what extent an argument on these lines might be acceptable. What is clear in these cases is that the beneficiaries must show that the trust was properly declared and properly constituted. There appears to be nothing intrinsically wrong in holding that the declaration of a trust may precede its constitution, as in the secret trusts cases.[61]

7. Exceptions to the Rule that Equity will not Assist a Volunteer

A. The Rule in Strong v. Bird[62]

Where an incomplete gift is made during the donor's lifetime, and the donor appointed the donee as executor,[63] or, in the case of an intestacy, the donee is appointed administrator,[64] the vesting of the property in the donee in his capacity as executor or administrator may be treated as the completion of the gift, overriding the claims of the beneficiaries under the will or intestacy. Similarly with the

---

[56] Dicta in *Re Ralli's W.T.* [1964] Ch. 288, indicate that this could be regarded as unconscionable. *cf. Re Brooks' S.T.* [1939] Ch. 993.

[57] So held in *Re Ralli's W.T., supra,* discussed *ante,* p. 122.

[58] As opposed to a mere covenant to settle or purported assignment; *Re Ellenborough, supra.*

[59] *Brennan v. Morphett* (1908) 6 C.L.R. 22; *Permanent Trustee Co. v. Scales* (1930) 30 S.R. (N.S.W.) 391 at 393; *Williams v. C.I.R.* [1965] N.Z.L.R. 345.

[60] *Re Northcliffe* [1925] Ch. 651.

[61] Chap. 5.

[62] See [1982] Conv. 14 (G. Kodilinye).

[63] (1874) L.R. 18 Eq. 315. It is sufficient if he is appointed one of the executors; *Re Stewart* [1908] 2 Ch. 251.

[64] *Re James* [1935] Ch. 449; *Re Gonin* [1979] Ch. 16 (where, however, doubts were expressed by Walton J.); (1977) 93 L.Q.R. 485. In *Strong v. Bird* itself, the rule was said only to apply to an executor.

release of a debt owed to the donor. At common law the appointment of the debtor as executor released the debt. In equity such a debtor had to account to the estate unless the testator intended in his lifetime to release the debt, such intention continuing until death.

In *Strong v. Bird*,[65] B borrowed £1,100 from A, his stepmother, who lived in his house, paying £212 10s. a quarter for board, and it was agreed that the debt should be paid off by a deduction of £100 from each quarter's payment. Deductions of this amount were made for two quarters; but on the third quarter-day and thereafter, A paid the full amount. Thus on her death, some four years later, £900 remained owing. B was appointed her sole executor, and proved the will. Later A's next-of-kin claimed for the balance of the debt. It was held that the appointment of B as executor released the debt.

It is necessary to show that the donor intended to make an immediate lifetime gift[66] (or to release a debt, as the case may be), and also that he had a continuing intention until the date of his death. Thus, an intention to make a testamentary gift is not sufficient.[67] The intention must relate to a specific item of property. It is not sufficient that there was a vague desire to provide something for the donee. In *Re Gonin*[68] a mother wished to leave her house to her daughter, who had given up a career to look after her parents, but thought for some reason that she could not do so because the daughter was illegitimate. Instead, she wrote a cheque for £33,000 in the daughter's favour, which was found after her death. (The cheque could not be cashed, as the death terminated the bank's mandate to pay it.) The daughter became administratrix, but failed in her claim to the house. There was no evidence of a continuing intention that the daughter should have an immediate gift of the house. The drawing of the cheque, as a substitute, pointed the other way. Nor will the rule apply if the testator, subsequently to the act on which the executor relies as establishing the intention to give a chattel, acted inconsistently with that intention by giving or lending the chattel to someone else,[69] nor if the testator, having once had an intention to give, forgot the gift, and treated the property as his own.[70]

[65] (1874) L.R. 18 Eq. 315; *Re James* [1935] Ch. 449 (a gift of realty).
[66] *cf. Re Ralli's W.T.* [1964] Ch. 288, *ante*, p. 122 (covenant to settle in the future). See also *Simpson v. Simpson* [1992] 1 F.L.R. 601 (future gift of proceeds of sale of cottage which was not yet sold).
[67] *Re Stewart* [1908] 2 Ch. 251; *Re Innes* [1910] Ch. 188.
[68] [1979] Ch. 16; (1977) 93 L.Q.R. 488.
[69] *Re Freeland* [1952] Ch. 110.
[70] *Re Wale* [1956] 1 W.L.R. 1346.

B. Donatio Mortis Causa[71]

i. The Principle. A *donatio mortis causa* is a lifetime gift which
is conditional upon, and which takes effect upon, death. It must be
distinguished on the one hand from a normal lifetime gift, under
which title passes immediately to the transferee; and, on the other
hand, from a testamentary gift which takes effect under the provisions of a will.[72] It may therefore be regarded as an exception either
to the rules governing lifetime gifts, or to the rules governing testamentary gifts. In the present context, we are concerned with the
former aspect. But the assistance of equity will not be required by
the donee in all cases. Where the subject-matter is a chattel which
has been delivered to the donee, the donee's title is complete on the
donor's death, no further act being necessary. In the case of a chose
in action or land, on the other hand, the donee's title is not complete
on the donor's death as the legal title vests in the donor's personal
representatives. The donee can seek the assistance of equity to compel the personal representatives to do whatever is necessary to perfect the donee's title.[73] It is in this latter situation that the doctrine
of *donatio mortis causa* can be seen as an exception to the rule that
equity will not assist a volunteer to perfect an imperfect gift.

The three essentials for a valid *donatio mortis causa* were laid
down by Lord Russell C.J. in *Cain v. Moon*.[74]

(a) The gift must have been in contemplation, though not necessarily in the expectation, of death[75];

(b) the subject-matter of the gift must have been delivered to the
donee[76];

(c) the gift must have been made under such circumstances as to
show that the property is to revert to the donor if he should recover.[77]

ii. Contemplation of Death. The donor must have been contemplating death more particularly than by merely reflecting that we
must all die some day. Commonly, *donationes mortis causa* are
made in reference to a particular illness, but the principle applies
equally to other causes such as a hazardous journey,[78] or possibly

---

[71] See Borkowski, *Deathbed Gifts—The Law of Donatio Mortis Causa*.
[72] For the distinction between a *donatio mortis causa* and a legacy, see Snell, p. 432. As to
availability to meet deceased donor's debts, see [1978] Conv. 130 (S. Warnock-Smith).
[73] *Duffield v. Elwes* (1827) 1 Bli.(N.S.) 497; *Re Lillingston* [1952] 2 All E.R. 184.
[74] [1896] 2 Q.B. 283; *Re Craven's Estate* [1937] Ch. 423 at 426; *Delgoffe v. Fader* [1939] Ch.
922. The requirements should be stringent as claims are often made without independent
evidence; *Wilson v. Paniani* [1996] 3 N.Z.L.R. 378.
[75] *Wilkes v. Allington* [1931] 2 Ch. 104.
[76] *Cain v. Moon* [1896] 2 Q.B. 283.
[77] *Re Lillingston* [1952] 2 All E.R. 184.
[78] cf. *Thompson v. Mechan* [1958] O.R. 357: the ordinary risks of air travel do not suffice.

even to the contemplation of active service in war.[79] If death occurs, the *donatio* may still be valid even though it comes from a cause different from that contemplated.

In *Wilkes v. Allington*[80] the donor was suffering from an incurable disease, and made a gift in the knowledge that he had not long to live; as things turned out, he had an even shorter time than he imagined, for he died two months later of pneumonia. It was held that the gift remained valid.

iii. Delivery of Subject-matter. A *donatio mortis causa* will not be valid without a delivery of the property to the donee[81] with the intention of parting with the "dominion" over it. It will not suffice if the property is handed over merely for safe custody.[82]

(a) *Chattels*. The donor must hand over either the chattel itself or the means of getting control over it such as, for example, a key to the box or place where the subject-matter is located.[83] In the case of a car, it is not necessary that the log book be handed over.[84]

(b) *Choses in Action*. The position is more difficult if the title to the chose in action does not pass by mere delivery of any document. The donor must hand over such documents as constitute "the essential indicia or evidence of title, possession or production of which entitles the possessor to the money or property purported to be given".[85] Thus the delivery of a bank deposit pass-book,[86] a Post Office Savings Bank-book,[87] national savings certificates[88] or a cheque or promissory note payable to the donor[89] have been held to create a *donatio mortis causa* of the chose in action represented by the document in question, so that, on the death of the donor, the

---

[79] *Agnew v. Belfast Banking Co.* [1896] 2 I.R. 204 at 221.

[80] [1931] 2 Ch. 104. A valid *donatio mortis causa* cannot be made in contemplation of suicide; *Re Dudman* [1925] 1 Ch. 553. This is probably not affected by the Suicide Act 1961, whereby suicide is no longer a crime.

[81] *Ward v. Turner* (1752) 2 Ves.Sen. 431.

[82] *Hawkins v. Blewitt* (1798) 2 Esp. 663.

[83] *Re Lillingston* [1952] 2 All E.R. 184; *Re Cole* [1964] Ch. 175. It may not suffice if the donor retains a duplicate key; *Re Craven's Estate* [1937] Ch. 423, at 428. *cf. Woodard v. Woodard* [1995] 3 All E.R. 980 (possible retention of second set of car keys by donor who was too ill to use them held insignificant).

[84] *Woodard v. Woodard, supra*; [1992] Conv. 53 (J. Martin).

[85] *Birch v. Treasury Solicitor* [1951] Ch. 298 at 311. *cf. Re Weston* [1902] 1 Ch. 680; *Delgoffe v. Fader* [1939] Ch. 922.

[86] *Birch v. Treasury Solicitor* [1951] Ch. 298.

[87] *Re Weston* [1902] 1 Ch. 608. It is otherwise if withdrawals may be made without producing the book; *Delgoffe v. Fader* [1939] Ch. 922.

[88] *Darlow v. Sparks* [1938] 2 All E.R. 235.

[89] Even though unendorsed and therefore not transferable by delivery. See *Re Mead* (1880) 15 Ch.D. 651; *Wilson v. Paniani* [1996] 3 N.Z.L.R. 378 (where the claim failed because there was no delivery).

donee can compel the personal representatives to perfect his legal title.

(c) *Land.* It had long been considered that land could not be the subject-matter of a *donatio mortis causa.* Although there was no English authority directly in point, Lord Eldon had doubted the possibility.[90] The reason may have been the supposed difficulty of parting with the "dominion" over land. The matter was reviewed by the Court of Appeal in *Sen v. Headley.*[91]

> The claimant and the deceased, who was separated from his wife, had lived together for ten years until 1964, after which they remained on close terms. When the deceased was terminally ill in hospital he said to the claimant "The house is yours, Margaret. You have the keys. They are in your bag. The deeds are in the steel box." The claimant had always had a set of keys to the house. After the deceased died (intestate), she found the box in a cupboard, used the key (which the deceased had slipped into her bag) and took possession of the deeds.

The claimant's entitlement to the house was upheld. The title deeds were essential indicia of title to the house (which had an unregistered title[92]), and had been constructively delivered to her. As in the case of a chose in action, parting with dominion over the essential indicia of title sufficed. The donor's continuing theoretical ability to deal with the property, and his retention of keys to the house to which he knew he would not return, did not amount to a retention of dominion. Every *donatio mortis causa*, whether or not of land, circumvented the Wills Act. The additional statutory formalities for lifetime transfers of land provided no greater obstacle than the Wills Act, as the trust on the donor's death was implied or constructive. The exception to the formality rule now contained in section 53(2) of the Law of Property Act 1925 was not as well developed in Lord Eldon's day as now. The policy of the law that formalities were required for the transfer of land should be upheld, but it should be acknowledged that that policy had been substantially modified by the developments in estoppel and constructive trusts.[93] The doctrine of *donatio mortis causa* was anomalous, but to except land from it would be a further anomaly.

---

[90] *Duffield v. Elwes* (1827) 1 Bli.(N.S.) 497 (where a *donatio mortis causa* of a mortgage of land was upheld).

[91] [1991] Ch. 425; [1991] Conv. 307 (M. Halliwell); (1991) 50 C.L.J. 404 (J. Thornely); All E.R. Rev. 1991, at 207 (P. Clarke); (1991) 1 Carib.L.R. 100 (G. Kodilinye); (1993) 109 L.Q.R. 19 (P. Baker); (1994) 144 N.L.J. 48 (M. Pawlowski).

[92] The result would be the same if the land certificate of registered land had been delivered.

[93] See generally (1995) 15 L.S. 356 (M. Howard and J. Hill).

iv. The Intention of the Donor. The donor's intention must be to make a gift which is conditional upon death, and revocable upon recovery by the donor. Thus, there is no *donatio mortis causa* if the intention is to make an immediate unconditional gift, even though the gift may fail,[94] nor where the intention is to make a future gift.[95] The conditional nature of the gift need not be expressed, but may be implied from the circumstances.[96]

v. Revocation. In addition to automatic revocation upon the donor's recovery,[97] the donor may revoke expressly, or by recovering dominion over the subject-matter,[98] but he cannot revoke by will, the reason being that the donee's title is complete before the will takes effect.[99] It might be added that the gift fails if the donee predeceases the donor.[1]

vi. Exceptions. It has been held that a *donatio mortis causa* cannot be made of the donor's own cheque[2] or promissory note.[3] The former is merely a revocable mandate to the bank,[4] while a gift of the latter is merely a gratuitous promise, thus they are not the "property" of the donor at all. It may be otherwise if the cheque is actually paid in the donor's lifetime, or before the bank has been informed of his death, or if it has been negotiated for value.[5]

There is some authority that stocks and shares cannot form the subject-matter of a *donatio mortis causa*. It was held in *Ward v. Turner*[6] that South Sea annuities could not be the subject-matter of such a gift. The decision may have been based on the inadequacy of the transfer on the facts, but it has been applied in cases concerning railway stock[7] and building society shares.[8] On the other hand, it has been held that shares in a public company can be the subject-matter of a *donatio mortis causa*.[9] This exception is, therefore, a doubtful one.

---

[94] *Edwards v. Jones* (1836) 1 My. & Cr. 226.
[95] *Solicitor to the Treasury v. Lewis* [1900] 2 Ch. 812.
[96] *Re Lillingston* [1952] 2 All E.R. 184.
[97] *Staniland v. Willott* (1852) 3 Mac. & G. 664.
[98] *Bunn v. Markham* (1816) 7 Taunt. 224.
[99] *Jones v. Selby* (1710) Prec.Ch. 300 at 303.
[1] *Tate v. Hilbert* (1793) 2 Ves. 111 at 120.
[2] *Re Beaumont* [1902] 1 Ch. 886.
[3] *Re Leaper* [1916] 1 Ch. 579.
[4] Only a holder for value can sue.
[5] *Tate v. Hilbert* (1793) 2 Ves. 111.
[6] (1752) 2 Ves.Sen. 431.
[7] *Moore v. Moore* (1874) L.R. 18 Eq. 474.
[8] *Re Weston* [1902] 1 Ch. 680.
[9] *Staniland v. Willott* (1852) 3 Mac. & G. 664.

C. Statutory Exception; Conveyance to Child

For the sake of completeness, the position concerning a conveyance to a child is mentioned, although the exception arises from statute and not from the rules of equity.

A conveyance (whether it is for value or not) which purports to convey a legal estate to a child[10] operates as a declaration that the land is held in trust for the child.[11]

D. Proprietary Estoppel

It has long been settled that promissory estoppel works as a shield and not as a sword.[12] In other words, where one person has been led to act upon the statement of another, he can prevent that other person from acting inconsistently with his statement.

There is another doctrine of long standing, which received its modern formulation in the dissenting speech of Lord Kingsdown in *Ramsden v. Dyson*,[13] and a more precise formulation by Fry J. in *Willmott v. Barber*,[14] and which can have the effect of creating a proprietary interest in a volunteer although there was no valid gift or trust in his favour. The doctrine is based on acquiescence and has in modern times acquired the name of Proprietary Estoppel.

Most of the modern applications of this doctrine have been in the context of licences to occupy land, and the matter will be fully discussed in Chapter 27. It will there be seen that, in applying the doctrine, the court exercises a wide discretion in reaching a solution which is appropriate to the facts of a particular case. Solutions will be seen to vary from finding, in some cases, that a volunteer has acquired a proprietary interest; in others that a mere licence is appropriate, with many variations in between.

---

[10] Who is incapable of holding a legal estate; L.P.A. 1925, s.1(6).

[11] Trusts of Land and Appointment of Trustees Act 1996, Sched. 1, para. 1 (replacing earlier legislation).

[12] *Combe v. Combe* [1951] 2 K.B. 215; (1952) 15 M.L.R. 1 (Denning L.J.)

[13] (1866) L.R. 1 H.L. 129 at 170.

[14] (1880) 15 Ch.D. 96 at p. 105. See now *Taylors Fashions Ltd v. Liverpool Victoria Trustees Co. Ltd* [1982] Q.B. 133, where a broader approach is formulated.

CHAPTER 5

TESTAMENTARY GIFTS NOT COMPLYING WITH THE WILLS ACT 1837, SECRET TRUSTS

1. GENERAL[1]

WE have seen that certain formalities are necessary for the creation of *inter vivos* trusts of land and for testamentary dispositions. A trust of land must be evidenced in writing,[2] and all testamentary dispositions must be in writing and signed by the testator, in the presence of two or more attesting witnesses present at the same time.[3] We now have to consider the effect of intended dispositions which fail to comply with the necessary formalities.

The problem over the enforcement of secret trusts is the fact that the terms of the trusts are not expressed in a form which complies with the Wills Act; though, in cases in which the testator's intention is clear and there is no possibility of doubt or fraud, there is a real compulsion to enforce the secret trust. The question is whether the enforcement of the secret trust infringes the Wills Act; or whether there is recognised doctrine which allows secret trusts to be enforced in spite of the Wills Act. What should be done, for example, where a legatee or devisee persuades the testator to make a will in his favour in reliance on an oral promise to hold on trust for a third

---

[1] (1947) 12 Conv.(N.S.) 28 (J. Fleming); (1951) 67 L.Q.R. 314 (L. Sheridan); (1963) 27 Conv.(N.S.) 92 (J. Andrews); (1972) 36 Conv.(N.S.) 113 (R. Burgess); (1999) 115 L.Q.R. 631 (P. Critchley); [2000] Conv. 420 (D. Kincaid).

[2] L.P.A. 1925, s.53(1)(*b*); *ante* p. 80.

[3] Wills Act 1837, s.9; *ante*, p. 93.

party? Or an intestate successor similarly persuades the intending testator not to make a will at all?

We saw in Chapter 3 that there is an established principle that equity will not allow a statute to be used as an instrument of fraud. It was there suggested, in the context of formalities for the creation of a lifetime trust, that the better solution was to require the trustee to hold on resulting trust for the settlor where land had been conveyed to the trustee pursuant to an oral declaration of trust for a third party.[4] In the case of wills, it is more complicated; for the solution of a resulting trust for the settlor is less satisfactory; in the case of a living settlor he can think again; with a will he is dead, and a resulting trust for the residuary estate is often what the testator most wished to avoid.

There may be many reasons why a testator wishes to be secret about his testamentary dispositions. In many of the older cases, the reason was that he wished to make a gift to support an illegitimate child and its mother. To include the gift in the will would give unwanted publicity; either among members of the family when its provisions are disclosed, or to any person who makes official application to examine the will. At the present day, the usual reason is that the testator cannot make up his mind upon all the details of the disposition of his estate.[5] By using a secret trust, he is able to escape from the policy of the Wills Act, and to retain for himself a power to make future gifts which do not comply with the Act. There seems to be no good reason why he should be able to do so. It is also common to make a lifetime settlement and then, by will, to add further property to the settlement. The details of the disposition do not in that case appear in the will; but this is not a proper case of a secret trust, but of incorporating the other document into the will by reference.

To create a secret trust the testator will usually arrange to leave a legacy to a trusted friend (often his solicitor) who undertakes to hold it upon certain trusts; or the will may give it to him "to be held upon such trusts as I have declared to him." The question in the former case is whether the friend could keep the legacy for himself; if not, and clearly in the latter case he cannot, who can claim it: the intended beneficiaries, or the estate?

Different considerations apply to these two situations, as will be seen. The former case is known as a fully secret trust; the latter a half- or semi-secret trust. Before attempting to answer these questions in the context of secret trusts, it is necessary to mention other ways in which a trust or gift may be created by will although the will

---

[4] *ante*, p. 82.

[5] This has been described as an abuse of the doctrine, as secrecy is irrelevant; [1981] Conv. 335 (T. Watkin). See *Re Snowden* [1979] Ch. 528.

does not spell out the precise terms. First, the details may be supplied by extrinsic evidence, the admissibility of which is governed by the principles relating to the construction of wills. Thus if the testator creates a trust in favour of "my grandchildren" or "my partners" their identity can be established by extrinsic evidence. The trust is an ordinary testamentary trust, not a secret trust. What the testator cannot do is to make a gift in favour of persons named in an unattested document, unless that document is incorporated into the will. This leads us to the second way of creating a trust, the details of which do not appear in the will itself. This is the doctrine of incorporation by reference, which bears superficial similarity to the doctrine of half secret trusts, but which must be distinguished from it.

2. INCORPORATION BY REFERENCE

" . . . if a testator, in a testamentary paper duly executed, refers to an existing unattested testamentary paper, the instrument so referred to becomes part of his will; in other words it is incorporated into it; but it is clear that, in order that the informal document should be incorporated in the validly executed document, the latter must refer to the former as a written instrument then existing—that is at the time of execution—in such terms that it may be ascertained."[6] It is not sufficient that the document was in existence; it must be *referred to as an existing document.* Where the doctrine of incorporation applies, the incorporated document is admitted to probate, and the advantage of secrecy is lost. We will see that this doctrine appears to be in the minds of some judges when they are dealing with cases of secret trusts, and that the rules applicable to this doctrine have sometimes been applied to secret trust cases.[7]

It is common practice to make a bequest to trustees of an existing settlement to be held by them upon the trusts of that settlement. There is no difficulty in doing so if the existing settlement is incorporated by reference in the will.

However, the requirement that only an existing document may be incorporated causes difficulty where a settlement is amended after the date of the will. In *Re Jones*,[8] a testamentary gift which attempted to include future alterations of the settlement was held void even though no alterations were made. The testator was there

---

[6] *per* Gorell-Barnes J. in *In bonis Smart* [1902] P. 238 at 240. For an unusual example, see *Re Berger (decd.)* [1990] Ch. 118.

[7] For differing views as to whether this doctrine is the basis of half secret trusts, see [1979] Conv. 360 (P. Matthews); [1980] Conv. 341 (D. Hodge); [1981] Conv. 335 (T. Watkin); (1999) 115 L.Q.R. 631 (P. Critchley).

[8] [1942] Ch. 328.

attempting to reserve for himself a power to dispose of his property by future unattested document.[9] Is this so whenever there is a testamentary addition to a settlement which includes a power of revocation or amendment? A strict application of the rules of incorporation by reference would suggest that it is; but the courts have been willing, where possible, to find a construction which will allow the testamentary gift to be upheld.[10]

In *Re Schintz's Will Trusts*,[11] a settlor made a settlement in which he expressly reserved a power to amend or to revoke. His will provided that the residuary estate should be held on the trusts of the settlement and those which might be created by future deeds executed under the power of amendment or revocation "or as near thereto as the situation will admit." No new trusts were declared. Wynn-Parry J. upheld the gift, finding, as a matter of construction, that the words referring to the future deeds were "otiose and . . . really no more than descriptive of the terms of the settlement."[12] *Re Jones*[13] was distinguished on that ground.

It is not common for a settlor to reserve a power of revocation and amendment, for tax reasons. But the point is important because it is common to include in settlements a provision for the trustees to have power to amend the trusts, or to appoint upon new trusts, or to terminate the settlement; and it is necessary to know the effect of these factors upon a testamentary addition to the settlement.

If the settlement has not been changed at the date of the testator's death, the question is whether the testamentary addition is valid or not. Where the settlement has been altered, there are three possible solutions; first, that the testamentary addition is void; secondly, that it takes effect upon the settlement in its original form; thirdly, that it takes effect upon the settlement as amended. The testator's intention would in most cases be the third choice. He will know of the amendment of the trust made before his death, and which may have been made for tax or for family reasons. But clearly the doctrine of incorporation by reference is incapable of incorporating an amendment made after the date of the will. We have seen that the courts can sometimes escape the necessity of holding the gift void. But the second solution is not satisfactory on any argument.

The third solution could be achieved by legislation, such as the Uniform Testamentary Additions to Trusts Act 1960 in the United

---

[9] The gift was to the trustees of the settlement "or any substitution therefor or modification thereof or addition thereto which I may hereafter execute."

[10] *Re Edwards'* W.T. [1948] Ch. 440.

[11] [1951] Ch. 870.

[12] *ibid.* at 877.

[13] [1942] Ch. 328.

States, which enables the testamentary gift to be held on the trusts of the settlement in accordance with any amendments made to those trusts prior to the testator's death. In England the matter must be resolved by applying the doctrine of incorporation by reference, with all its limitations.[14]

3. FULLY SECRET TRUSTS

A. Informal Disclosure of the Existence and the Terms of the Trust

Where an absolute gift has taken effect in favour of the donee, it is too late to impose a trust. This is so whether the disposition is a lifetime transfer or a gift by will, which takes effect on the testator's death. Thus in *Wallgrave v. Tebbs*[15] no secret trust was established where the testator's instructions were not communicated to the legatees, who took absolutely on the face of the will, but were found among his papers after his death. Where, however, a testator makes a gift by will to a legatee in reliance upon the legatee's express or implied[16] undertaking to hold the property upon certain trusts, or to dispose of it in a certain way by his will,[17] it would not be satisfactory to permit the legatee to take advantage of the requirement of testamentary formality and to keep the property for himself.[18] The doctrine applies also where the deceased failed to revoke an existing gift,[19] or revoked a codicil so as to revive a previous testamentary gift,[20] or where an intestate, in reliance on the undertaking of those entitled on intestacy, failed to make a will.[21] "It is altogether immaterial whether the promise is made before or after the execution of the will, that being a revocable instrument."[22]

If the legatee or intestate successor is not allowed to take the property beneficially, the next question is whether the oral trust

---

[14] For other possibilities, see *Re Playfair* [1951] Ch. 4.

[15] (1855) 2 K. & J. 313; *McCormick v. Grogan* (1869) L.R. 4 H.L. 82; *Re Boyes* (1884) 26 Ch.D. 531; *Re Hawkesley's Settlement* [1934] Ch. 384.

[16] "Acquiescence either by words of consent or by silence": *per* Wood V.-C. in *Moss v. Cooper* (1861) 1 J. & H. 352 at 366. The communication may be by the testator or by his agent.

[17] *Re Gardner* [1920] 2 Ch. 523; *Re Young* [1951] Ch. 344; *Ottaway v. Norman* [1972] Ch. 698.

[18] *Drakeford v. Wilks* (1747) 3 Atk. 539; *Stickland v. Aldridge* (1804) 9 Ves.Jr. 516; *Wallgrave v. Tebbs* (1855) 2 K. & J. 313 at 320. For the position where the trustee revokes his acceptance during the testator's lifetime, see Hayton and Marshall, *Cases and Commentary on the Law of Trusts and Equitable Remedies* (10th ed.), pp. 106–107.

[19] *Chamberlaine v. Chamberlaine* (1678) Free. Ch. 34; *Moss v. Cooper, supra*.

[20] *Tharp v. Tharp* [1916] 1 Ch. 142; [1916] 2 Ch. 205.

[21] *Stickland v. Aldridge, supra*, at 519; (1948) 12 Conv.(N.S.) 28 (J. Fleming).

[22] *per* Wood V.-C. in *Moss v. Cooper* (1861) 1 J. & H. 352 at 367.

should be enforced, or whether the legatee or intestate successor should hold on resulting trust for the estate. The rule in these cases is that the secret trust is enforced in favour of the beneficiary.[23]

This result is justifiable if it is correct to say, as explained below,[24] that a secret trust is enforced because the testator validly declared a trust during his lifetime, and the trust became constituted by the vesting of the property on his death in the trustee. That, as will be seen below, is the modern theoretical explanation of the enforcement of secret trusts. That is not, however, the reason which has been relied on historically to enforce fully secret trusts. Without that theory, the courts were in real difficulty in that the Wills Act laid down the requirements for the creation of a testamentary trust, and those requirements were not met. If, therefore, the trusts were enforced, was not the Wills Act being disregarded? Or, as they said, did the courts not "give the go-by" to it?[25] The courts searched for a justification in not observing the terms of the Wills Act, and found it in the doctrine of fraud: it would be fraudulent if the legatee were to take beneficially in the circumstances. The fraud theory was laid down in the clearest terms by Lord Hatherley L.C. and Lord Westbury in *McCormick v. Grogan*,[26] although the House of Lords held in that case that the testator had not intended to impose an obligation on Grogan, the sole executor, and that, therefore, no trust existed on the facts of the case. To base the court's intervention on the ground of fraud could well be a sufficient justification for not applying the Wills Act; but the next step was not so obvious; it would be wrong for the legatee to keep the property, but it was difficult to see how the prevention of fraud would justify the projection forward of the beneficial interest to the beneficiary. As we will see, this matter became all the more clear when the courts were dealing with the question of half-secret trusts, where the testator requires the legatee to take the property as trustee, without saying in the will who the beneficiaries are. In that situation, there was no possibility of the legatee being fraudulent, in the sense of enriching himself, because he was expressed to take as trustee. In *Blackwell v. Blackwell*,[27] the leading case on half-secret trusts, the enforcement of the half-secret trust was justified by saying that the intention of the testator was clear, and that it was communicated to and acquiesced in by the legatee. As explained above, the modern view is to justify the enforcement of secret trusts upon the theory that a life-

---

[23] *Thynn v. Thynn* (1684) 1 Vern. 296.
[24] *post*, p. 164.
[25] *Re Pitt-Rivers* [1902] 1 Ch. 403 at 407; *Blackwell v. Blackwell* [1929] A.C. 318 at 337.
[26] (1869) L.R. 4 H.L. 82.
[27] [1929] A.C. 318.

time trust has been declared and that it is constituted by the testamentary gift to the legatee. There are, as will be seen, some theoretical difficulties in this view also.[28]

B. Proof

Related to the question whether the doctrine is based upon fraud is the question of the standard of proof required to establish a secret trust. A high standard of proof is required to prove fraud, and there are dicta in many cases indicating that a secret trust can only be proved where there is "clear evidence,"[29] and suggesting that the standard is the same as that required to support the rectification of a written instrument.[30] In *Re Snowden*,[31] however, Megarry V.-C. disregarded the historical connection of the doctrine of secret trusts and the requirement of fraud; and laid down that the standard required to prove communication and acceptance is the ordinary civil standard of proof required to establish an ordinary trust.[32] The evidence may, of course, establish an intention to create a trust, and its acceptance by the legatee, without establishing who the beneficiaries were. The legatee would then hold on resulting trust.[33] If questions of fraud or other special factors arose, the standard required would rise. The onus is on the person contending that the trust exists.[34]

C. Disclosure to the Legatee of the Existence of the Trust but not its Terms

If the testator discloses to the legatee the fact that he is to hold the legacy on trust, but does not disclose the terms of the trust before his death, the legatee will hold on resulting trust for the estate.[35] The intended trust, not being declared before the death, cannot be enforced. The imposition of the resulting trust will prevent the unjust enrichment of the legatee.

---

[28] *post*, p. 165.

[29] See *McCormick v. Grogan* (1869) L.R. 4 H.L. 82 at 87, *per* Lord Westbury; *Ottaway v. Norman* [1972] Ch. 698 at 699.

[30] *Fowler v. Fowler* (1859) 4 De G. & J. 250 at 264; *Crane v. Hegeman-Harris Co. Inc.* [1939] 4 All E.R. 68 at 71; *Joscelyne v. Nissen* [1970] 2 Q.B. 86 at 98; *Ottaway v. Norman*, *supra*.

[31] [1979] Ch. 528; (1979) 38 C.L.J. 260 (C. Rickett); (1991) 107 L.Q.R. 194 (B. Robertson).

[32] *ibid.* at 537.

[33] *Re Boyes* (1884) 26 Ch.D. 531.

[34] *Jones v. Badley* (1868) L.R. 3 Ch.App. 362.

[35] Similarly if the terms, although disclosed, are unlawful or uncertain. See *Re Pugh's W.T.* [1967] 1 W.L.R. 1262; *Brown v. Pourau* [1995] 1 N.Z.L.R. 352; *Gold v. Hill* [1999] 1 F.L.R. 54 ("Look after Carol and the kids" sufficiently certain).

In *Re Boyes*,[36] a legacy was given to the testator's solicitor, who had undertaken to hold the property according to directions which he would receive by letter. The letter was found only after the death. The solicitor accepted that he held as trustee, and wished to carry out the trust. Kay J. held that there was a resulting trust in favour of the next-of-kin; and explained the rule by saying: "The essence of all these decisions is that the devisee or legatee accepts a particular trust which thereupon becomes binding upon him, and which it would be a fraud in him not to carry into effect.[37]

This situation is similar to that of half-secret trusts in that the legatee takes as a trustee. But there is an important difference. In *Re Boyes*,[38] the gift was absolute on its face; the trust could have been enforced if the terms had been declared before death.[39] Where the existence of a trust is disclosed on the face of the will, the communication, as we shall see, must be prior to or contemporaneous with the execution of the will.[40]

D. Methods of Communication

We have seen that the trust must be communicated before the testator's death. The communication may be made orally or in writing; and it appears that, just as "a ship which sails under sealed orders, is sailing under orders though the exact terms are not ascertained by the captain till later,"[41] a testator may, during his lifetime, give to the legatee a sealed envelope which is not to be opened until the testator's death. This is sufficient provided the legatee knows that it contains details of the trust.

E. Additions to the Secret Trust

A testator must communicate not only the trust and the terms, but also the identity of the property to be held on trust.

In *Re Colin Cooper*,[42] the testator left £5,000 to two persons as trustees, and informally communicated to them the terms of the trust. By a later codicil he purported to increase the sum to be devoted to the secret trust to £10,000, they "knowing my wishes

---

[36] (1884) 26 Ch.D. 531; *Re Hawkesley's Settlement* [1934] Ch. 384.
[37] *ibid.* at 536.
[38] (1884) 26 Ch.D. 531.
[39] *Re Gardner* [1920] 2 Ch. 523.
[40] *post*, p. 160.
[41] *per* Lord Wright in *Re Keen* [1937] Ch. 236 at 242; *Re Boyes, supra*, at 536.
[42] [1939] Ch. 811; criticised in [2000] Conv. 420 at 428–430 (D. Kincaid).

regarding that sum." This addition was not communicated to the trustees. It was held that the first instalment could be devoted to the secret trusts; but the later instalment went on a resulting trust.[43]

F. Undertaking to Leave by Will

A secret trust may impose an obligation not only to hold on trust for a beneficiary on the testator's death; but also an obligation to make provision for an intended beneficiary after the legatee's death.

> In *Re Gardner (No. 1)*,[44] a wife left her estate to her husband for life, and there was an agreement that the property should be divided among certain beneficiaries on his death. The husband died intestate, and the Court of Appeal decided that he held the property, after his life interest, on trust for the beneficiaries.
> *Ottaway v. Norman*[45] took the matter a stage further. The testator agreed with his housekeeper that she should have a bungalow after his death, and she agreed to leave it to the testator's son by her will. The testator left the bungalow (plus its contents and some money) to her absolutely. She first made a will in favour of the testator's son; but she then changed that will, and left the bungalow to the defendant. Brightman J. held that the son was entitled to the bungalow and its contents, although not to the money.

The enforcement of a secret trust in this situation creates a number of problems concerning the status of the trust during the housekeeper's lifetime, and the theoretical basis on which secret trusts are enforced. This question is discussed in section 6 below, but some of the questions arising from *Ottaway v. Norman*[46] are more conveniently considered in Chapter 12.

G. Tenants in Common and Joint Tenants

Where a testamentary gift is made to two or more persons as tenants in common, and secret trusts are communicated to some but not all of the tenants in common, those to whom the communication

---

[43] Had it been a fully secret trust, the legatees would have been beneficially entitled to the addition.
[44] [1920] 2 Ch. 523; *Re Young* [1951] Ch. 344; *post*, p. 165.
[45] [1972] Ch. 698; (1972) 36 Conv.(N.S.) 129 (D. Hayton).
[46] *supra*.

was made are bound, the others taking beneficially.[47] To hold otherwise would enable one beneficiary to deprive the rest of their benefits by setting up a secret trust."[48]

But where a gift is made to them as joint tenants, a distinction is
made between the case where the trust is communicated before the
making of the will, and where the communication is between the
will and the death. In the former case, all joint tenants are bound.[49]
In the latter, only those who have accepted the trust are bound by
it,[50] "the reason being that the gift is not tainted with any fraud in
procuring the execution of the will."[51]

Farwell J. was dissatisfied with his own explanation. He confessed that he was "unable to see any difference between a gift made
on the faith of an antecedent promise and a gift left unrevoked on the
faith of a subsequent promise."[52] It has been suggested that gifts
upon secret trusts to joint tenants and tenants in common should be
decided on the principle of *Huguenin v. Baseley*,[53] that "no man may
profit by the fraud of another."[54] Thus "if A induces B to make or
leave unrevoked a will leaving property to A and C,"[55] whether as
joint tenants or tenants in common, C will be bound "if the testator
would not have made any gift to C unless A had promised. . . . If the
testator would still have left property to C even if A had not promised, C is not bound. . . . Whether A and C are joint tenants or
tenants in common, and whether A's promise was before or after the
making of the will are matters of evidence that may help to determine whether or not there was such an inducement, but of themselves both matters are inconclusive."[56] The argument is persuasive;
but the cases say otherwise. The wrong turning was taken in
Rowbotham v. Dunnett.[57]

The principles discussed above have emerged from cases concerning fully secret trusts. Of course, in the case of half-secret trusts
there could be no question of the legatees taking beneficially. The
issue would be whether a valid half-secret trust could be created by
communication to fewer than the whole number of trustees. It seems
that the principles applicable to fully secret trusts would be applied
by analogy, bearing in mind that half-secret trustees will invariably
be joint tenants, and that communication after the will is ineffective

[47] *Tee v. Ferri* (1856) 2 K. & J. 357.
[48] *Re Stead* [1900] 1 Ch. 237 at 241.
[49] *Russell v. Jackson* (1852) 10 Hare 204; *Jones v. Badley* (1868) L.R. 3 Ch.App. 362; *Re Gardom* [1914] 1 Ch. 662; *Re Young* [1951] Ch. 344.
[50] *Burney v. MacDonald* (1845) 15 Sim. 6; *Moss v. Cooper* (1861) 1 J. & H. 352.
[51] *per* Farwell J. in *Re Stead* [1900] 1 Ch. 237 at 241.
[52] *ibid.*
[53] (1807) 14 Ves. 273.
[54] (1972) 88 L.Q.R. 225 at 226 (B. Perrins).
[55] *per* Farwell J. in *Re Stead* [1900] 1 Ch. 237 at 241.
[56] (1972) 88 L.Q.R. 225 at 226 (B. Perrins).
[57] (1878) 8 Ch.D. 430.

in the case of half-secret trusts, as explained below. Hence communication to one of the trustees prior to the making of the will is effective.[58]

4. HALF-SECRET TRUSTS

Where the will gives property to a legatee *upon trust*, without, however, saying what the intended trusts are, the question of the enforcement of a secret trust communicated to the legatee has been treated very differently from the case where the property was given to the legatee *absolutely* in the will. The courts have found it more difficult to enforce a secret trust in the former case—where the legatee takes expressly as trustee—than in the latter case. It is difficult to see any sense, however, in a rule which allows a secret trust to be enforced if the trust is nowhere mentioned in the will; but holds it void if the testamentary gift discloses the fact that the legatee takes as trustee. If it is right that secret trusts are express trusts operating wholly outside the scope of the Wills Act, it is difficult to see why the two situations should not be treated alike.

But there is a historical explanation. We saw that the nineteenth century judges said that secret trusts were enforced to prevent fraud[59]; to prevent the legatee taking for himself what he had promised the testator to hold upon trust. The element of fraud, however, was not present in the case of the gift to a legatee as trustee. As he took in a fiduciary capacity, he could in no circumstances take the property for himself. There was no possibility of fraud, and no justification, so the argument ran, for not applying the Wills Act. And it was at one time held that the mention of the existence of a trust did prevent the operation of the doctrine of secret trusts.[60] The validity of half-secret trusts was not finally established until the House of Lords decision in *Blackwell v. Blackwell*[61] in 1929.

The testator by a codicil gave a legacy of £12,000 to legatees upon trust to apply the income "for the purposes indicated by me to them." The trust had been accepted prior to the execution of the codicil. The House of Lords enforced the trust. They were assisted by *Re Fleetwood*[62] and *Re Huxtable*[63] where it was held

[58] See *Re Gardom* [1914] 1 Ch. 662.
[59] *Ante*, p. 154.
[60] *Moss v. Cooper* (1861) 1 J. & H. 352 at 367; *Le Page v. Gardom* (1915) 84 L.J.Ch. 749 at 752; (1937) 53 L.Q.R. 501 (W. Holdsworth).
[61] [1929] A.C. 318. If the words in the will are insufficient to impose a trust, any secret trust will be fully secret; *Jankowski v. Petek Estate* (1995) 131 D.L.R. (4th) 717 (gift to executor "to deal with as he may in his discretion decide upon").
[62] (1880) 15 Ch.D. 594.
[63] [1902] 2 Ch. 793.

that the secret trust doctrine applied although the gift was in terms a gift upon trust, and where therefore there was no question of fraud in the legatee. Lord Sumner concluded that "it is communication of the purpose to the legatee, coupled with acquiescence or promise on his part, that removes the matter from the provision of the Wills Act and brings it within the law of trusts, as applied in this instance to trustees, who happen also to be legatees."[64] The effect of the bequest "remains to be decided by the law as laid down by the Courts before and since the [Wills] Act, and does not depend on the Act itself."[65] Thus the trust operated outside the Act and could be enforced without proof of fraud.

In *Blackwell v. Blackwell*[66] the trusts were communicated before the will and were stated to have been so communicated. Will the same rule apply where the trusts are or may be declared in the future? On the one hand, there is logically no difference between declarations of trusts before and after the will; for the will is ambulatory and of no effect until the death.[67] The distinction is not made, as we have seen, with fully secret trusts.[68] If the trust operates independently of the Wills Act, the date of the will should be immaterial. On the other hand, it is more difficult to *assume* acquiescence where the communication is after the will; in the absence of proof of express agreement, the fact of non-revocation may be the only basis on which to presume acquiescence. More importantly, "a testator cannot reserve to himself a power of making future unwitnessed dispositions by merely naming a trustee and leaving the purposes of the trust to be supplied afterwards. . . . "[69] To allow that to be done by half-secret trust would be to give a wider rule for secret trusts (which might be oral) than that which as we have seen is applied in the case of incorporation of documents by reference.[70] It would be surprising if the law of wills permitted this; but, if the proper explanation of the enforcement of secret trusts is that they operate outside the will and independently of the Wills Act, then the rules relating to incorporation by reference are, as has been pointed out, quite irrelevant.[71] And what Lord Sumner feared can always be achieved by a fully secret trust.

With half-secret trusts however the distinction appears to be made.

---

[64] [1929] A.C. 318 at 339–340; *Ottaway v. Norman* [1972] Ch. 698 at 711.

[65] *ibid.* at 339.

[66] [1929] A.C. 318.

[67] (1937) 53 L.Q.R. 501 (W. Holdsworth).

[68] *ante*, p. 153; *Re Gardner* [1920] 2 Ch. 523.

[69] *per* Lord Sumner in *Blackwell v. Blackwell* [1929] A.C. 318 at 339.

[70] *In bonis Smart* [1902] P. 238; [1979] Conv. 360 (P. Matthews).

[71] (1937) 53 L.Q.R. 501 (W. Holdsworth); *Moss v. Cooper* (1861) 1 J. & K. 352 at 367.

In *Re Keen*[72] the testator gave a sum of money to trustees "to be held upon trust and disposed of by them among such person, persons or charities as may be notified by me to them or either of them during my lifetime. . . . " Previously, one of the trustees had been given a sealed envelope containing the name of the beneficiary of the intended trust. In deciding in favour of the residuary legatees, the Court of Appeal held that the handing over of the sealed envelope was a communication of the trust, but that this, being *prior* to the date of the will,[73] was inconsistent with the terms of the will which provided for "a future definition . . . of the trust subsequent to the date of the will," while "the sealed letter relied on as notifying the trust was communicated . . . before the date of the will."[74]

The trust would, however, have failed independently of the question of inconsistency. The disposition contained a power to declare trusts in the future. This was void, for it "would involve a power to change a testamentary disposition by an unexecuted codicil and would violate section 9 of the Wills Act."[75]

The criticisms of this rule have been discussed. The contrary rule exists in Ireland,[76] New South Wales[77] and in most of the American jurisdictions.[78] The matter is still open to the House of Lords; it may be that the true ratio of *Re Keen*[79] is the narrow point of inconsistency; but it was followed in *Re Bateman's Will Trusts*,[80] where, it seems, the rule was not challenged. The present position is unsatisfactory; there is no sense in a rule which (in the case of communication between the will and the death) enforces a trust in a bequest "to X" but disregards the trust in a bequest "to X upon trust."[81]

Other views are that the distinction is justified because wills creating half-secret trusts are invariably drawn up by solicitors, and so stricter rules are appropriate[82]; or that consistency should be achieved by requiring the communication to be before the will even

---

[72] [1937] Ch. 236; *Johnson v. Ball* (1851) 5 De G. & Sm. 85; (1972) 23 N.I.L.Q. 263 (R. Burgess).

[73] *Re Huxtable* [1902] 2 Ch. 793.

[74] *Re Keen, supra*, at 248; *Re Rees' W.T.* [1950] Ch. 204.

[75] *Re Keen, supra*, at 247; *Johnson v. Ball* (1851) 5 De G. & Sm. 85; *Re Hetley* [1902] 2 Ch. 866.

[76] *Riordan v. Banon* (1876) 10 Ir.R.Eq. 469; *contra Balfe v. Halfpenny* [1904] 1 Ir.R. 486; *Re Browne* [1944] Ir.R. 90; (1951) 67 L.Q.R. 413 (L. Sheridan); [1992] Conv. 202 (J. Mee); (1991) 5 *Trust Law International* 69 (P. Coughlan).

[77] *Ledgerwood v. Perpetual Trustee Co. Ltd* (1997) 41 N.S.W.L.R. 532, following *Re Browne, supra*.

[78] *Restatement of Trusts*, § 55, comment (c), (h).

[79] [1937] Ch. 236.

[80] [1970] 1 W.L.R. 1463.

[81] But see [1985] Conv. 248 (B. Perrins), supporting the communication rules as being based on the extrinsic evidence rule.

[82] [1995] Conv. 366 (D. Wilde).

in the case of a fully secret trust. If the trusteeship was accepted after the will, the legatee would hold on trust for the residuary legatee or next-of-kin. This would have the advantage of preventing reliance on the doctrine of secret trusts by testators who are merely in-decisive[83] and thus not within the rationale of the doctrine.[84]

We have seen that the doubts concerning the effectiveness of a communication after the will in the case of a half-secret trust derive from the testamentary formality rules. These rules do not apply to the analogous situation of a trust of a life policy nomination. In *Gold v. Hill*[85] the insured nominated X and referred to him (erroneously) as executor on the nomination form. Later he informed X of the nomination and asked him to use the proceeds to "look after" his common law wife and children and to make sure that his widow got nothing. It was held that a trust analogous to a half-secret trust was validly created even though the communication was after the nomination.

5. CAN THE SECRET TRUSTEE TAKE A BENEFIT?

The legatee may claim that the testator intended him to take some benefit from the gift, perhaps, for example, a specific sum, or possibly any surplus after performing the trust. Two separate questions arise here; first, was this the testator's intention? Secondly, how far is evidence of such an intention admissible in favour of the trustee?

To consider first the question of intention, it is necessary to construe the language of the will to determine whether the testator's intention was to make the legatee a trustee of the whole of the property given, or to make a beneficial gift to him subject to his performing certain obligations.[86] In the former case, any surplus left after carrying out the trusts is held upon resulting trusts[87]; in the latter, the legatee may keep it.[88] There is thus no difficulty in a case where the will itself makes it clear that the trust does not extend to the whole of the legacy, but the will may be silent on the matter, and

---

[83] As in *Re Snowden* [1979] Ch. 528.

[84] [1981] Conv. 335 (T. Watkin). See also the discussion of how the suggested reform would operate in the case of a person who refrains from making a will in reliance upon the acceptance of a trust by the next-of-kin.

[85] [1999] 1 F.L.R. 54. It was doubted in *Kasperbauer v. Griffith* (November 21, 1997, un-reported) whether a secret trust or any trust could be made of a pension scheme death benefit, as it was not owned by the testator: at most he could require it to be paid to his estate rather than to his widow under the rules of the pension scheme.

[86] *ante*, p. 55. This construction is more likely where the legatee is a relative for whom the testator may be supposed to have been intending to provide. See *Irvine v. Sullivan* (1869) L.R. 8 Eq. 673 (fiancée).

[87] *ante*, p. 55.

[88] *ante*, p. 55; *Irvine v. Sullivan* (1869) L.R. 8 Eq. 673.

the only evidence extrinsic. This leads us to the second question, namely whether the trustee may be permitted to prove his claim to benefit by relying on documentary or even oral evidence.

The difficulty, whether the trust be fully or half-secret, is the danger of fraud by the secret trustee. A further problem in the case of a half-secret trust is that the evidence would contradict the terms of the will, which impose a trust on the entire legacy.[89]

In *Re Rees' W.T.*[90] the testator by will appointed a friend and his solicitor (thereinafter called his trustees) to be executors and trustees. He left the whole estate "unto my trustees absolutely they well knowing my wishes concerning the same."

The testator had told the trustees that he wished them to make certain payments and to retain any surplus for themselves. A substantial surplus remained. It was held that the trustees were not entitled to the surplus, which passed as on intestacy. The will, on its true construction, imposed a trust on the whole, and evidence was not admissible to show that the trustees were to take a benefit. It was not without significance that the trustee was the testator's solicitor. As Evershed M.R. said, "In the general public interest it seems to me desirable that, if a testator wishes his property to go to his solicitor and the solicitor prepares the will, that intention on the part of the testator should appear plainly in the will and should not be arrived at by the more oblique method of what is sometimes called a secret trust."[91]

In *Re Tyler*,[92] however, there are suggestions that evidence is admissible as to all the terms of a trust, including any in favour of the trustee himself, although such evidence will not lightly be admitted. Pennycuick J. found difficulty in the reasoning of *Re Rees*. But evidence contained in the (now deceased) trustee's own written memorandum did not suffice.[93]

Finally, we have seen that if a secret trust fails for non-compliance with the communication rules, or for uncertainty, the secret trustee holds on trust for the residuary legatee or next-of-kin. He could not claim the legacy for himself if the trust was half-secret,

---

[89] We have seen, in the context of communication, that evidence inconsistent with the will is not admissible; *Re Keen* [1937] Ch. 236, *ante*, p. 161.

[90] [1950] Ch. 204. See also *Re Pugh's W.T.* [1967] 1 W.L.R. 1262, suggesting that it is easier to infer an intention that a sole trustee should take beneficially than that two or more trustees should do so.

[91] [1950] Ch. 204 at 211.

[92] [1967] 1 W.L.R. 1269 (concerning a lifetime trust). See also *Ottaway v. Norman* [1972] Ch. 698, *ante*, p. 157, where the secret trustee took a benefit in the form of a life interest. This was clearly the testator's intention and the point was not discussed. In any event, the interest had already been enjoyed.

[93] Although generally such a memorandum is *admissible* under the Civil Evidence Act 1995 to prove the terms of the trust.

or, although fully secret, if he had accepted trusteeship. A question might arise to whether the secret trustee could take the property if he himself was the residuary legatee or next-of-kin. There is no reason in principle why he should not, as he would be claiming in a different capacity, but the court might intervene if he disclaimed the legacy in order to benefit.[94]

6. THEORETICAL BASIS OF SECRET TRUSTS

A. Lifetime Trust Outside the Will

The formal requirements for a will, contained in the Wills Act 1837, are based upon a sound policy. It is important to avoid doubt, fraud and uncertainty in connection with testamentary dispositions; and it is essential to rely upon written formalities as there is no other way of ascertaining the intention of the testator. If secret trusts, which effectively create dispositions of property on death, are to be allowed, it is important to justify the failure to apply the provisions of the Wills Act. In terms of policy, it is easy to favour an exception in cases in which the intention of the testator is clear, and is opposed only by the formalities which were set up in the hope of establishing it. But further justification is needed. The Wills Act is a statute, and not merely an expression of policy. The question is whether some theory can be found to justify the enforcement of secret trusts.

We have seen that the early cases were explained on the ground of fraud[95]; the fear that the legatee would otherwise keep the property for himself. There is substantial authority for a refusal to allow a statute to be used as an instrument of fraud, but the fraud theory appears not to justify the enforcement of half-secret trusts, because the legatee, being named as a trustee, cannot claim. On the other hand, it may be said that a secret trustee who relies on the Wills Act to defeat the testator's expectation commits a fraud against the testator and the secret beneficiary even in the absence of personal benefit, and recent authority on mutual wills has confirmed that fraud can be perpetrated without gain.[96] On this view the fraud theory can explain both kinds of secret trust. What is clear, however, is that it is not sufficient to say as did Lord Sumner in *Blackwell v.*

---

[94] See *Blackwell v. Blackwell* [1929] A.C. 318 at 341. Disclaimer might in any event not cause a half-secret trust to fail, by reliance on the maxim that a trust does not fail for want of a trustee; but it has been said that a fully secret trust will fail if the trustee disclaims; *Re Maddock* [1902] 2 Ch. 220 at 231; *cf. Blackwell v. Blackwell, supra*; Oakley, *Constructive Trusts* (3rd ed.), p. 252. See also [2000] Conv. 420 at 440 (D. Kincaid).

[95] *ante*, p. 154; doubted in Oakley, *Constructive Trusts* (3rd ed.), pp. 252–253.

[96] *Re Dale (deceased)* [1994] Ch. 31; (1995) 58 M.L.R. 95 (A. Brierley); *post*, p. 323. See generally [1980] Conv. 341 (D. Hodge), supporting the fraud theory as the basis of half secret trusts. This is doubted in Oakley, *loc. cit.*, p. 248.

Blackwell[97] that secret trusts are based upon the essential elements of intention, communication and acquiescence, for this assumes a new basis for the enforcement of testamentary dispositions which is wholly inconsistent with the Wills Act, and suggests that a testator could "contract out of" the Wills Act, and create testamentary dispositions by a different method. The modern view is that secret trusts can be enforced because they are not trusts created by will; but are trusts arising outside and independently of the will[98]; that they arise by reason of the personal obligation accepted by the legatee.[99]

In *Re Young*,[1] the testator made a bequest to his wife with a direction that on her death she should leave the property for the purposes which he had communicated to her. One of the purposes was that she would leave a legacy of £2,000 to the chauffeur. The chauffeur had witnessed the will. A witness may not normally take a legacy, and the question was whether he had thereby forfeited his interest.[2] Danckwerts J. held that he had not; the trust in his favour was not a trust contained in the will but one created separately and imposed upon the legatee.[3]

It is one thing to say that the trust operates outside the will, but it is another to say just how and when the trust takes effect. If some of the propositions discussed in Chapter 4[4] are sound, the most natural way for this to occur is to treat the communication to the trustee as the declaration of trust, and the vesting of the property in the trustee

---

[97] [1929] A.C. 318 at 340.

[98] *per* Lord Westbury in *Cullen v. Att.-Gen. for Northern Ireland* (1866) L.R. 1 H.L. 190 at 198; *per* Lord Sumner in *Blackwell v. Blackwell* [1929] A.C. 318 at 340; Oakley, *Constructive Trusts* (3rd ed.), p. 253. The theory is rejected in (1999) 115 L.Q.R. 631 (P. Critchley).

[99] "I think the solution is to be found by bearing in mind that what is enforced is not a trust imposed by the will, but one arising from the acceptance by the legatee of a trust communicated to him by the testator, on the faith of which acceptance the will was made or left revoked, as the case might be": *per* Lord Warrington of Clyffe in *Blackwell v. Blackwell* [1929] A.C. 318 at 342. For New Zealand views, see *Brown v. Pourau* [1995] 1 N.Z.L.R. 352.

[1] [1951] Ch. 344; *Cullen v. Att.-Gen. for Northern Ireland* (1866) L.R. 1 H.L. 190.

[2] Wills Act 1837, s.15. *cf. Re Fleetwood* (1880) 15 Ch.D. 594; *O'Brien v. Condon* [1905] Ir.R. 51. If it is the secret trustee who attests there should be no difficulty if it is a half-secret trust, as he takes no beneficial interest on the face of the will. If it is fully secret, the position is less clear. For the view that it would fail, see Oakley, *Constructive Trusts* (3rd ed.), p. 250.

[3] To the contrary is *Re Maddock* [1902] 2 Ch. 220, where the property subject to a fully secret trust was treated as being subject to a specific bequest for the purpose of the payment of debts out of the estate. No doubt the legacy would be treated as part of the estate for tax purposes and for the purposes of the Inheritance (Provision for Family and Dependants) Act 1975, rather than as property disposed of prior to the death.

[4] *ante*, pp. 117 *et seq.*

by the will as the constitution of the trust. If this is so, it is a lifetime declaration, and the Wills Act has no effect upon it; the only statutory formalities that are relevant are Law of Property Act 1925, s.53(1)(*b*),[5] which requires that declarations of trusts of land should be evidenced in writing; but this would not affect the rule requiring a fraudulent trustee in a fully secret trust of land to hold on a constructive trust.[6] There would be no awkward distinction between declarations prior to and subsequent to the will in half-secret trusts[7]; the sole question would be whether or not a trust was declared of the property before the death, and whether that trust became properly constituted by the vesting of the property in the trustee.

We have seen that the usual rule in the case of property coming to a person who had previously declared himself trustee of it was that the trust did not become constituted without a further manifestation of intention.[8] It was submitted that where a third person accepted an instruction to hold the property on certain trusts and the settlor subsequently transferred the property to him without further declaration, the trust would be constituted. It should make no difference whether the property passed to the trustee by a conveyance or by a will.[9] It will probably fail however if the trustee predeceases the testator, at any rate in the case of a fully secret trust.[10] Assuming its terms were known, it may be that a half-secret trust could be saved by the maxim "a trust does not fail for want of a trustee."[11]

Ottaway v. Norman[12] raises a further complication. There the secret trust was upheld as to the bungalow (and its contents). Assuming that it is correct to say that the testator made a lifetime declaration that the bungalow was to be held on trust for his son after the housekeeper's death, and that the trust was constituted by the vesting of the property in the housekeeper as trustee, then the trust of the bungalow arose on the testator's death, the housekeeper's interest effectively being a life interest. But the son also claimed entitlement to so much of the money left to the housekeeper as

[5] *ante*, p. 80. *Re Baillie* (1886) 2 T.L.R. 660 at 661; but there was no writing in *Ottaway v. Norman* [1972] Ch. 698; *infra*.

[6] L.P.A. 1925, s.53(2). As to whether he should hold on trust for the secret beneficiaries, see *post*, p. 168.

[7] *Re Keen* [1937] Ch. 236; *ante*, p. 161.

[8] *ante*, p. 142.

[9] As with the property received by Miss Towry Law from her sister and conveyed to the trustees: *Re Ellenborough* [1903] 1 Ch. 697; *Re Adlard* [1954] Ch. 29; *Re Ralli's W.T.* [1964] Ch. 288.

[10] *Re Maddock* [1902] 2 Ch. 220 at 251; Oakley, *Constructive Trusts* (3rd ed.), p. 250; *cf.* [2000] Conv. 420 at 439 (D. Kincaid).

[11] Unless the particular trustee is regarded as essential to the trust. For the view that a half secret trust would also fail, see [1995] Conv. 366 at 373 (D. Wilde); *cf.* Oakley, *Constructive Trusts* (3rd ed.), p. 250. The question of disclaimer by the secret trustee has already been considered; *ante*, p. 164.

[12] [1972] Ch. 698; (1972) 36 Conv.(N.S.) 129 (D. Hayton); (1972) 36 Conv.(N.S.) at 115 (R. Burgess); [1971] A.S.C.L. 375 at 384 (J. Hackney).

remained at her death. This claim failed. The testator had not intended to impose an obligation on the housekeeper as to *all* her money, nor had he intended to impose an obligation as to the money derived from his will, because this would be unworkable unless this money was to be kept separately, which was not envisaged. But Brightman J. was content to assume, without deciding, that if property was given on the understanding that the primary donee would dispose of such assets, if any, as he may still have at his death in favour of a secondary donee, there would be a valid trust, "in suspense"[13] during the lifetime of the primary donee but attaching to the estate of the primary donee on the latter's death. This would be a "floating trust,"[14] such as was recognised by the High Court of Australia in *Birmingham v. Renfrew*[15] but which can hardly be said to be a recognised legal concept. The situation during the primary donee's lifetime would be similar to that existing during the lifetime of the survivor of makers of mutual wills. But the origin of the trust is of course quite different. In the former case it is based upon the declaration of the trust, followed by communication and acquiescence and the vesting of the property in the trustee; in the case of mutual wills, it is based on the contract between the parties followed by the death of the first testator in reliance upon non-revocation by the survivor. Once the trust has attached, however, the problems are similar, and will be discussed in Chapter 12.

Until the property has so vested, there is no completely constituted trust; the declaration can have no effect, and cannot create property rights. The will can be revoked or altered, or the property may be disposed of during the testator's lifetime. The testator can revoke his instructions to the secret trustee at any time,[16] and if he acts as if he had forgotten the declaration or assumed it to be no longer existent, no doubt it will be treated as having expired. No rational theory, it is suggested, can be found which will justify the remarkable decision in *Re Gardner (No. 2)*.[17] We have seen that a wife left her estate to her husband for life,[18] and that after his death it was to be held on secret trust for five named beneficiaries. One of the beneficiaries predeceased the wife. The representatives of the deceased beneficiary successfully claimed the share.

---

[13] [1972] Ch. 698 at 713.

[14] (1972) 36 Conv.(N.S.) at 132 (D. Hayton).

[15] (1937) 57 C.L.R. 666. Applied in *Re Cleaver* [1981] 1 W.L.R. 939.

[16] But any substituted instructions given after the will is executed will be invalid in the case of a half secret trust.

[17] [1923] 2 Ch. 230. See Oakley, *Constructive Trusts* (3rd ed.), p. 251, suggesting that there is no clear rule against a non-testamentary trust for a dead person. This is doubtful, as such a beneficiary has no legal personality, unless it is clear that his estate is intended to take.

[18] *Re Gardner (No. 1)* [1920] 2 Ch. 523; *ante*, p. 157.

A gift by will normally lapses if the donee predeceases the testator,[19] and the estate of the donee can only claim if the donee acquired some interest in the property before he died. No such interest could exist in this case; and the theory which suggests that a secret trust can be treated as a lifetime declaration of trust does not suggest that any interest is obtained by any beneficiary prior to the constitution of the trust by vesting of the legal estate in the trustee.

B. Express or Constructive Trust

Closely connected with the theoretical basis of secret trusts is the question whether a secret trust is properly categorised as an express or constructive trust.[20] The question is not merely academic, for, as we have seen,[21] constructive trusts of land are excepted from the requirement of written evidence. Is an oral secret trust of land valid?

An express trust is one declared by the settlor; a constructive trust is one imposed by the law.[22] The analysis of secret trusts as being declarations outside the will categorises them as express trusts, whether they are fully or half secret. In the case of a half secret trust the will itself expressly declares a trust. While this element is absent with a fully secret trust, such a trust may claim to be express on the basis of the testator's express declaration to the secret trustee. There is authority that a half-secret trust of land is not enforceable without written evidence.[23] In *Ottaway v. Norman*,[24] however, a fully secret trust of land was upheld without written evidence, but the point was not discussed.

Fully secret trusts however have, as it were, another string to their bow. They were enforced long before secret trusts were thought of as taking effect outside the will. We have seen that they have been said on high authority to be enforceable on the ground of fraud,[25] and they can claim also to be constructive trusts.[26] It is submitted that fully secret trusts can be enforced under either head.

---

[19] A special exception is made in the case of children of the testator who predecease him, leaving issue: Wills Act 1837, s.33. Such a gift takes effect in favour of the issue.

[20] One view is that the attempt to classify as express or constructive is misguided because the secret trust doctrine is concerned with the procedural question of admitting evidence of a trust and not with the nature of the trust itself; [1985] Conv. 248, at 253 (B. Perrins).

[21] *ante*, p. 80.

[22] *post*, p. 297.

[23] *Re Baillie* (1886) 2 T.L.R. 660 at 661.

[24] [1972] Ch. 698. See also *Strickland v. Aldridge* (1804) 9 Ves.Jr. 516; *Brown v. Pourau* [1995] 1 N.Z.L.R. 352; [1996] Conv. 302 (C. Rickett). Similarly with lifetime transfers; *Rochefoucauld v. Boustead* [1897] 1 Ch. 196.

[25] *McCormick v. Grogan* (1869) L.R. 4 H.L. 82; *ante*, p. 154.

[26] This is assumed *obiter* in *Re Cleaver* [1981] 1 W.L.R. 939 at 947.

If it becomes established that even a fully secret trust is express, it does not follow that the secret trustee would take beneficially if the trust fails for lack of compliance with the formality requirements. The result in such a case would be that, having accepted trusteeship, he would hold on trust for the residuary beneficiary or next-of-kin.[27]

C. Conclusion

Ultimately, the enforcement of secret trusts is a matter of policy relating to testamentary dispositions. The rules of the Wills Act 1837 are intended to achieve a reasonable degree of certainty in respect of testamentary dispositions. Secret trusts have, in effect, created a wide gap in the law relating to testamentary formalities. It is possible to take the view that secret trusts should not be enforced beyond preventing the unjust enrichment of the fraudulent legatee; or, on the other hand, to hold that the testator's intention should be upheld in every case. This is really a matter for the legislature, and it is submitted that it would be more satisfactory to review the whole matter and to incorporate into the statutory scheme as much of the secret trust doctrine as it is desired to retain.

[27] [1985] Conv. 248 (B. Perrins); (1986) 36 N.I.L.Q. 358 (M. Thompson). Another view is that both fully and half-secret trusts are constructive, as both are imposed to prevent fraud on the testator, which may occur without any benefit to the secret trustee; [1980] Conv. 341 (D. Hodge). *cf.* (1951) 67 L.Q.R. 413 (L. Sheridan); Oakley, *Constructive Trusts* (3rd ed.), p. 258.

POWERS

1. POWERS[1] AND TRUSTS

A POWER is an authorisation to do certain things which affect property to which the appointor is not solely entitled, and in which he may have no beneficial interest at all. A person may hold a power in a personal or an official capacity, a distinction relevant to the question whether he has fiduciary obligations. The source of the power may be express grant or a statute. Thus trustees have by statute powers of investment, sale, and so on. They may also be given other powers by the terms of the trust instrument, such as a power of appointment which enables those holding the power to effect the disposal of the settlor's property by "appointing" it to other people. It is with "powers" in the latter sense that this chapter is concerned.

---

[1] See *Farwell on Powers*; Thomas, *Powers*; Halsbury (4th ed.), Vol. 36, p. 529; Keeton & Sheridan's *Equity* (3rd ed.), Chap. 9.

It has been seen that there are important points of distinction between powers and trusts.[2] Essentially a trust is imperative and a power discretionary. The dividing line is not always clear; for many trusts contain discretionary elements; and many powers are given to trustees who are governed by fiduciary duties in the exercise of their powers.

The practical importance of the distinction lies in the extent of the obligations imposed on a trustee as compared with the donee of a power, for example, the question how far he is obliged to consider the claims of possible recipients,[3] also the extent of the rights of objects of a trust as compared with a mere power, including the question of entitlement to the property in default of exercise and the question whether the beneficiaries, all being adult and under no disability, can terminate the trust and either divide the trust property[4] or alienate it.[5]

Whether a particular disposition creates a mere power or a discretionary trust is a question of construction. This has already been discussed.[6]

2. BARE POWERS AND FIDUCIARY POWERS

A distinction must also be made between a bare power (sometimes called a personal power) and a power to which some fiduciary obligation is attached, such as a power given to trustees of property exercisable in relation to that property. Several manifestations of this distinction will be explained in connection with powers of appointment. Of general application however is the rule that a bare power given to an individual can only be exercised by him,[7] and a bare power given to two or more by name cannot (subject to any contrary intent in the instrument creating it) be executed by the survivor.[8] But a power given to trustees is prima facie given to them by virtue of their office, and may be exercised by the survivor,[9] or by their successors in office,[10] and powers given to two or more trustees jointly may be exercised by the survivor or survivors of

---

[2] *ante*, pp. 62 *et seq.*

[3] *McPhail v. Doulton* [1971] A.C. 424; *esp.* at 456; *ante*, p. 112.

[4] *Saunders v. Vautier* (1841) 4 Beav. 115; *Re Brockbank* [1948] Ch. 206; *ante*, p. 66, *post*, p. 629.

[5] *Re Smith* [1928] Ch. 915; *Re Nelson* (1918) [1928] Ch. 920 n.

[6] *ante*, p. 65.

[7] *Re Harding* [1923] 1 Ch. 182; *Re Lysaght* [1966] Ch. 191.

[8] Thomas, *Powers*, p. 26; Halsbury (4th ed.), Vol. 36, § 861; *Re Beesly's W.T.* [1966] Ch. 223 (contrary intention).

[9] *Re Bacon* [1907] 1 Ch. 475; *Bersel Manufacturing Co. Ltd v. Berry* [1968] 2 All E.R. 552; T.A. 1925, s.18(1).

[10] *Re Smith* [1904] 1 Ch. 139; *Re De Sommery* [1912] 2 Ch. 622.

them, or by the personal representatives of the last of them, pending the appointment of new trustees.[11]

3. POWERS OF APPOINTMENT

A power of appointment is one given (by the donor of the power) to the donee of the power (the appointor) to appoint property to some person (the appointee). Such powers are useful in that they make it possible for the donee of the power to take into consideration circumstances existing at the date of the appointment which the settlor or testator could not have foreseen. Thus, a husband may give his estate to his widow for her life, and after her death to their children. He may leave his widow to decide upon the shares which each child is to receive by giving to her a power to appoint among the children in such shares as she shall in her absolute discretion select, with a gift in default of appointment to the children in equal shares. Powers feature in trusts of all sorts, and modern trusts commonly give various powers of appointment to the trustees in addition to imposing the obligation to hold the property upon trust. In such situations the property is owned by the beneficiaries who are entitled in default of appointment, subject to defeasance upon the exercise of the power.[12]

A. General, Special and Intermediate (or Hybrid) Powers

A gift to A for life with remainder to whomsoever he shall appoint is a general power; A may appoint to himself and become absolute owner. A general power is in most cases equivalent to ownership.[13] If, however, in the illustration given above, the power were exercisable only by will, it would still be a general power even though A would then be unable to appoint to himself. A special power is one in which the choice of appointees is restricted by the terms of the power: for example a power to appoint in favour of one's own children, or of the employees of a company and their families and dependants.[14] The power is special even though the appointor is himself a member of the restricted group.[15] A power which does not fit neatly into these categories is one where the donee is given power to appoint to anyone except certain people or

---

[11] T.A. 1925, s.18, and see *ibid.* s.36(7); *Re Wills' Trust Deeds* [1964] Ch. 219, *post*, p. 188.

[12] *Re Brooks' S.T.* [1939] Ch. 993 at 997; Thomas, *Powers*, p. 21.

[13] See, for example, Inheritance Tax Act 1984, s.5(2); Inheritance (Provision for Family and Dependants) Act 1975, s.25(1).

[14] *Re Gestetner* [1953] Ch. 672; *Re Sayer* [1957] Ch. 423.

[15] *Re Penrose* [1933] Ch. 793. See, however, Perpetuities and Accumulations Act 1964, s.7.

groups of people, for instance himself,[16] or all persons except the settlor and his wife,[17] or to all persons living at the death of the donee[18]; such powers are called intermediate or hybrid powers,[19] and they may be treated as general powers for some purposes, and special for others.[20] Intermediate powers are classified as special powers for the purpose of the Wills Act 1837, s.27,[21] and for the purposes of the rule against perpetuities.[22]

A power may be exercisable in the donee's lifetime, or by will, or by either method. A power which is exercisable by will only is called a testamentary power; and may be general or special.

B. The Requirement of Certainty; Wide Powers; Capricious Powers

These matters have been dealt with in Chapter 3, where the requirements of trusts and powers are compared.[23]

C. Duties of Donee of Power; Rights of Objects

A donee of a power is not, as such, under any fiduciary duties. In the example given above of the power given to the wife to determine the shares in which the children shall receive the property from their father's estate, the widow is under no obligation to exercise the power or even to consider its exercise, although if she does exercise it, then she owes a duty to the default beneficiaries to keep within the terms of the power.[24] This is a bare, or personal, power of appointment. This must be contrasted with a fiduciary power held by a trustee by virtue of his office, which in turn must be distinguished from the obligation of a trustee of a discretionary trust.

A discretionary trust is a trust in which the property is held by the trustees on trust, not for named beneficiaries in fixed proportions,

---

[16] *Re Park* [1932] 1 Ch. 580; *Re Byron's Settlement* [1891] 3 Ch. 475 (except "her husband or any friend or relative of his.") *Re Abraham's W.T.* [1969] 1 Ch. 463 at 474; *Re Lawrence's W.T.* [1972] Ch. 418 (except his "wife's relatives").

[17] To avoid aggregation of the income of the trust with that of the settlor; I.C.T.A. 1988, ss.673, 683. Also to avoid "reservation of benefit" under the inheritance tax system.

[18] *Re Jones* [1945] Ch. 105.

[19] *Re Lawrence's W.T.* [1972] Ch. 418; *Re Manisty's Settlement* [1974] Ch. 17; *Re Hay's S.T.* [1982] 1 W.L.R. 202; *Re Beatty's W.T.* [1990] 1 W.L.R. 1503.

[20] "This division (*i.e.* of powers into general and special) is neither precise nor exhaustive, for these are some powers which may be general for some purposes and not for others." (Halsbury (4th ed.), Vol. 36, § 805.)

[21] *post*, p. 178.

[22] P.A.A. 1964, s.7; *Re Earl of Coventry's Indentures* [1974] Ch. 77. For the significance of the distinction in the contect of perpetuity, see Maudsley, *The Modern Law of Perpetuities*, pp. 60–64, 162–166.

[23] See also Chap. 2, p. 66.

[24] *Re Hay's S.T.* [1982] 1 W.L.R. 202; *Mettoy Pension Trustees Ltd v. Evans* [1990] 1 W.L.R. 1587.

but on trust for such members of a class of beneficiaries as the trustees shall in their absolute discretion select. That situation has many points of similarity with a power of appointment held by trustees to appoint among a group of objects. The distinction however remains that a trust is obligatory, a power permissive. In many aspects the distinction is theoretical only. We have seen that the test for certainty of objects has been assimilated, but clear distinctions remain in the area of the rights and duties of the parties.

Although a power is discretionary and permissive, a trustee who is the donee of a power must act in accordance with his fiduciary duty. The duties in the case of a fiduciary power arise, as it were, not from the power, but those inherent in the office of trustee. Thus, a trustee may not disregard a power, or forget about it, or release it. His fiduciary duty requires him to give consideration to the exercise of the power, and particularly to any application made to him by an object of the power requesting an exercise in his favour.[25] "Trustees of a power must consider from time to time whether and how to exercise the power."[26] "A settlor or testator who entrusts a power to his trustees must be relying on them in their fiduciary capacity so they cannot simply push aside the power and refuse to consider whether it ought in their judgment to be exercised."[27]

The duties of the donee of a fiduciary power were analysed by Megarry V.-C. in *Re Hay's Settlement Trusts*.[28] He must make no unauthorised appointment; he must consider periodically whether to exercise the power; he must consider the range of objects[29]; and he must consider the appropriateness of individual appointments. These duties, which were not intended to be exhaustive,[30] were further explained as follows: the donee, if he exercises the power, must do so "in a responsible manner according to its purpose. It is not enough for him to refrain from acting capriciously; he must do more. He must 'make such survey of the range of objects or possible beneficiaries' as will enable him to carry out his fiduciary duties."[31] He must not simply exercise the power in favour of those objects who happen to be at hand or to claim his attention. He must first consider who the objects are. He need not compile a list or assess the number: ". . . what is needed is an appreciation of the width of the field, and thus whether a selection is to be made merely from a dozen or, instead, from thousands or millions. . . . Only when the

---

[25] *Re Gestetner* [1953] Ch. 672 at 688; *Re Manisty's Settlement* [1974] Ch. 17 at 25.

[26] [1974] Ch. 17 at 22, *per* Templeman J.; *Re Gestetner (supra)*; *Re Abraham's W.T.* [1969] 1 Ch. 463 at 474; *Re Gulbenkian's Settlements* [1970] A.C. 508 at 518; *McPhail v. Doulton* [1972] A.C. 424 at 456; *Mettoy Pension Trustees Ltd v. Evans* [1990] 1 W.L.R. 1587.

[27] *Re Gulbenkian's Settlements, supra*, at 518.

[28] [1982] 1 W.L.R. 202.

[29] Further discussed in Chap. 3.

[30] For the duty not to delegate, and to appoint in good faith, see *post*, pp. 180, 182.

[31] [1982] 1 W.L.R. 202 at 209, quoting from *McPhail v. Doulton* [1971] A.C. 424 at 449.

trustee has applied his mind to 'the size of the problem' should he then consider in individual cases whether, in relation to other possible claimants, a particular grant is appropriate. In doing this, no doubt he should not prefer the undeserving to the deserving; but he is not required to make an exact calculation whether, as between deserving claimants, A is more deserving than B."[32]

The question arises of what the court will do if the trustees fail in their duty to consider the exercise of the power. "Normally the trustee is not bound to exercise it, and the court will not compel him to do so. That, however, does not mean that he can simply fold his hands and ignore it, for normally he must from time to time consider whether or not to exercise the power, and the court may direct him to do this."[33] A recalcitrant trustee may be removed. Where the power has been exercised, the court "will intervene if the trustees exceed their power, and possibly if they are proved to have exercised it capriciously."[34] The court will also intervene if the trustees have failed in any other respect to discharge the duties described above. Thus, in *Turner v. Turner*,[35] the exercise of a power of appointment was invalid when the trustees, who were not professional trustees, failed to appreciate their powers and duties and left all the decision-making to the settlor (who was not a trustee). They executed documents of appointment at his behest without reading them, and without understanding that they had a discretion. The settlor "held the reins", and the trustees acted as a "rubber-stamp." This was a breach of their duty to consider the exercise of the power and the appropriateness of the appointments made. There was no effective exercise at all, and the appointments accordingly were null and void, save to the extent that one appointment concerned land and was effective to transfer the legal title, which was held on trust by the appointee for the trustees of the settlement.

A further question is whether the court may intervene in a more positive way than merely removing a trustee or setting aside an appointment made in breach of duty. It was held in *Mettoy Pension Trustees Ltd v. Evans*[36] that where the court was called upon to intervene (because of breach of duty or where there was nobody left to exercise a fiduciary power),[37] it could adopt any of the methods

---

[32] *Re Hay's Settlement Trusts* [1982] 1 W.L.R. 202 at 210.

[33] *ibid.* at p. 209.

[34] [1971] A.C. 424 at 456, *per* Lord Wilberforce.

[35] [1984] Ch. 100. See also *Re Hastings-Bass* [1975] Ch. 25.

[36] [1990] 1 W.L.R. 1587; (1991) 107 L.Q.R. 214 (S. Gardner); [1991] Conv. 364 (J. Martin); K.C.L.J. 2 (1991–92), p. 127 (R. Ellison); (1994) 8 *Trust Law International* 35 at 36 (Vinelott J.)

[37] See now Pensions Act 1995, s.25(2) (fiduciary powers exercisable by independent trustee of pension fund on employer's insolvency); *post*, p. 480.

suggested by Lord Wilberforce in *McPhail v. Doulton*[38] in the context of discretionary trusts. Thus it could appoint new trustees, authorise the beneficiaries to prepare a scheme of distribution, or itself order a distribution.[39]

Whatever the form of the court's intervention, it is based upon the breach by the trustee of his fiduciary duty, and not upon any property right or entitlement among the objects of the power to compel a payment to them. The right of an object is not to compel an exercise of the power, in his own favour or at all, but merely to insist that the trustees consider the exercise of the power, to restrain any invalid exercise of the power, and, of course, to retain any property duly appointed to him.[40]

D. Power to Apply for Purposes

There seems to be no reason why a power should not permit the application of money for specific purposes, as opposed to being paid to persons. The purposes must be sufficiently certain to enable a court to determine whether any particular application is within the terms of the power or not. Such a power may be useful as a means of permitting the application of money to non-charitable purposes; a trust for non-charitable purposes lacks a means of enforcement and is void. That is a problem which is not faced by a power. The matter is discussed in Chapter 14.

4. EXERCISE OF POWERS OF APPOINTMENT

A. General Rule

i. Lifetime. No technical words are required for the exercise of a power. All that is required is an intention on the part of the donee that the fund shall pass to some one who is an object of the power.[41] If the appointment relates to land, it must comply with Law of Property Act 1925, s.53(1)(b), and be evidenced in writing, signed by the donee of the power; an appointment of personalty may be made orally.[42] The terms of the power may require certain further

---

[38] [1972] A.C. 424, *ante* p. 105.
[39] Reliance was placed on *Klug v. Klug* [1918] 2 Ch. 67, *post*, p. 527, which was not cited in *Re Manisty's Settlement* [1974] Ch. 17, where the appointment of new trustees is said to be the only remedy. The *Mettoy* approach was followed in *Thrells Ltd v. Lomas* [1993] 1 W.L.R. 456 and *Re William Makin & Sons Ltd* [1993] O.P.L.R 171 (pension trust cases).
[40] *Vestey v. I.R.C. (No. 2)* [1979] Ch. 198 (Walton J.); affirmed [1980] A.C. 1148.
[41] *Re Ackerley* [1913] 1 Ch. 510; *Re Lawrence's W.T.* [1972] Ch. 418; Thomas, *Powers*, pp. 236–237.
[42] Halsbury (4th ed.), Vol. 36, para. 864.

formalities[43] for its exercise, or specific reference to the power or to the property subject to it,[44] and such requirements must be strictly complied with. Thus, if a power is to be executed by deed, it cannot be validly exercised by will,[45] and a power to be executed by will cannot be validly exercised by any instrument to take effect in the lifetime of the donee of the power.[46]

ii. By Will. Wills Act 1837, section 27, provides, in relation to both realty and personalty, and subject to a contrary intention, that, where a testator has a "power to appoint in any manner he may think proper," a general devise[47] or bequest shall operate as an execution of the power. This clearly excludes special powers, and also intermediate or hybrid powers, which in any way restrict the donee's freedom of choice.[48] The section applies even though the will was executed before the power was created.[49]

Any power to which the section does not apply is only exercised by will if "there is an indication of intention to exercise the power," a sufficient indication being "either a reference to the power or a sufficient reference to the property subject to the power."[50] Whether or not this is so in any particular case is often a question of great difficulty.[51]

B. Excessive Execution[52]

The donee has only the power which is given to him by the instrument. Thus he may not exercise it in favour of non-objects; nor in breach of the perpetuity rule; nor impose unauthorised conditions.[53] Any such purported exercise will be void. Difficult questions can arise when an appointment is partly good and partly bad, as where there is an appointment of a sum greater than that authorised; or where some of the appointees are objects and some are not. The rule is that the court will sever the good from the bad where possible: ". . . if there is a complete execution of the power with

---

[43] *Hawkins v. Kemp* (1803) 3 East 410; subject to L.P.A. 1925, s.159, *post*, p. 180.

[44] *Re Lane* [1908] 2 Ch. 581; *Re Priestley's W.T.* [1971] Ch. 562, 858; *Re Lawrence's W.T.* [1972] Ch. 418; (1971) 121 N.L.J. 41, 597, 808 (C. Sherrin).

[45] *Lord Darlington v. Pulteney* (1797) 3 Ves.Jr. 384; *Re Phillips* (1889) 41 Ch.D. 417 at 419; Thomas, *Powers*, p. 222.

[46] *Reid v. Shergold* (1805) 10 Ves.Jr. 370; *Re Evered* [1910] 2 Ch. 147 at 156.

[47] *e.g.* a devise which refers generally to realty and not specifically to separate pieces; *e.g.* "all my realty."

[48] *Re Ackerley* [1913] 1 Ch. 510; *Re Byron's Settlement* [1893] 3 Ch. 474 (death of excluded persons would make the power general).

[49] *Boyes v. Cook* (1880) 14 Ch.D. 53.

[50] *Re Ackerley, supra*, at 513; *Re Priestley's W.T.* [1971] Ch. 858.

[51] *Re Ackerley, supra*; *Re Priestley's W.T.* [1971] Ch. 562, 858; *Re Lawrence's W.T.* [1972] Ch. 418; (1971) 121 N.L.J. 41, 597, 808 (C. Sherrin).

[52] See Halsbury (4th ed.), Vol. 36, para. 951; Thomas, *Powers*, Chap. 8.

[53] See *Re Hay's S.T.* [1982] 1 W.L.R. 202, *post*, p. 181.

the addition of something improper, the execution is good and the excess bad, whereas if there is no complete execution, or if the boundaries between the excess and the execution are not distinguishable, the whole appointment fails. In order to be valid, the appointment must be distinct and absolute."[54] It is believed that this rule will apply where the exercise of a power makes an appointment and contains a release; if the release is invalid, the rest of the appointment may stand.[55]

C. Defective Execution

The donee of a power should exercise it in accordance with the provisions of the instrument creating it. Thus the necessary formalities should be observed, and the required consents obtained. Failure to comply will usually render the exercise void, but there is a jurisdiction in equity and under statute to validate certain cases of defective execution.

i. In Equity. Where the donee "shows an intention to execute the power in discharge of some moral or natural obligations"[56] equity will act upon the conscience of those entitled in default to compel them to make good the defect in the execution. Relief may be obtained in favour of purchasers for value, creditors, charities, and persons to whom the donee is under a natural or moral obligation to provide.[57]

The essential features of the intended execution must be proved; these are the intention to dispose of the property to the persons to be benefited and the amount of the benefit. Also, the defects must not go to the essence of the power.[58] There will not normally be relief against the non-execution of a power,[59] except perhaps in the case of fraud by the person entitled in default.[60] The doctrine, which is falling into disuse, applies to defects in the form of the execution of the power, but not to the situation where the trustees have purported to exercise the power after it has expired.[60a]

The jurisdiction applies to the execution of express powers generally, but not to defective execution of statutory powers; for "it is difficult to see how the court can give validity to any such act if done

---

[54] Halsbury, (4th ed.), Vol. 36, para. 951; *Re Holland* [1914] 2 Ch. 595; see also Halsbury, paras. 952–955, for illustrations. The rule applies also where part of the appointment is void under the doctrine of "fraud on a power," *post*, p. 182.

[55] *post*, p. 188.

[56] Thomas, *Powers*, p. 495; *Chapman v. Gibson* (1791) 3 Bro.C.C. 229 at 230.

[57] Halsbury, (4th ed.), Vol. 36, para. 957.

[58] *Garth v. Townsend* (1869) L.R. 7 Eq. 220; *Kennard v. Kennard* (1872) L.R. 8 Ch.App. 227; Thomas, *Powers*, pp. 496–507.

[59] *Tollet v. Tollet* (1728) 2 P.Wms. 489 at 490; *Holmes v. Coghill* (1806) 12 Ves.Jr. 206. *cf. Mettoy Pension Trustees v. Evans* [1990] 1 W.L.R. 1587; *ante*, p. 176.

[60] *Bath and Montague's Case* (1693) 3 Ch.Cas. 84 at pp. 108, 122; *Vane v. Fletcher* (1717) 1 P.Wms. 352 at 355.

[60a] *Breadner v. Granville-Grossman* [2000] 4 All E.R. 705.

otherwise than in accordance with the statutory requirements; to give relief in such a case would be to legislate afresh."[61]

ii. By Statute.

(a) *Lifetime Appointment.* Law of Property Act 1925, s.159, provides that the execution of a deed of appointment will be valid if executed in the presence of and attested by two or more witnesses, even though it does not comply with additional formalities stipulated in the instrument. This provision does not however dispense with any necessary consents, nor does it apply to any acts required to be performed which have no relation to the mode of executing and attesting the document. Nor does it require a power to be exercised by deed where another method of exercise complies with the terms of the power.

(b) *Appointment by Will.* Similarly, an appointment by will is valid as regards execution and attestation if the provisions of the Wills Acts relating to the formalities of wills are complied with.[62]

D. Contract to Exercise

A valid contract to exercise a general power, if capable of specific performance, operates as a valid exercise of the power in equity; but there can never be specific performance of a contract to exercise a testamentary power, and the only remedy for breach is an action for damages against the estate.[63] A contract to exercise a special testamentary power is not enforceable[64]; but a release, in appropriate circumstances,[65] can be effective, as can a contract not to exercise the power[66]; the property will then go in default of appointment.

5. DELEGATION OF POWERS

In general, a person to whom a discretion has been given, whether personally or by virtue of his being in a fiduciary relationship, may not delegate his discretion to others. *Delegatus non potest delegare.*[67] A donee may delegate the performance of merely ministerial

---

[61] *Farwell on Powers*, p. 394. This is criticised in Thomas, *Powers*, pp. 500–501, where it is suggested that relief might be given if the defective execution was procured by fraud, accident or mistake, or where the statutory provision was ambiguous.

[62] Wills Act 1837, s.10; Wills Act 1963, s.2; *Taylor v. Meads* (1865) 4 De G.J. & S. 597 at 601.

[63] *Re Parkin* [1892] 3 Ch. 510; *post*, p. 734.

[64] *Re Bradshaw* [1902] 1 Ch. 436; *Re Cooke* [1922] 1 Ch. 292.

[65] *post*, p. 186.

[66] *Re Evered* [1910] 2 Ch. 147.

[67] *post*, p. 576.

acts[68]; and the donee of a general power equivalent to absolute ownership may appoint to a class in such proportions as another shall select.[69] But many powers involve a personal discretion and this prevents delegation.[70] There is no objection however to a testator or settlor giving a power of appointment to a trustee.[71] Such a power given by a testator is not to be impugned as a delegation of testamentary disposition. In *Re Beatty's Will Trusts*[72] the testatrix gave her personal estate and £1.5 million to trustees to allocate "to or among such person or persons as they think fit." Hoffmann J. upheld the power, rejecting the supposed "anti-delegation" rule: there was no doubt as to the validity of testamentary powers, whether special, general or intermediate.

In the absence of express provision in the instrument creating a special power, the donee may not appoint on discretionary trust.[73] This question arose in *Re Hay's Settlement Trusts*.[74]

Trustees had a power to appoint to "such persons or purposes" as they should in their discretion select, except the settlor, her husband, or the trustees. Prior to the appointment, the income was to be applied, at the trustees' discretion, for the settlor's nephews and nieces, or for charity. The trustees exercised the power of appointment by appointing the property to themselves on a discretionary trust for similar purposes. Prior to the distribution, the income was to be applied to any person or charity. Megarry V.-C. held that the exercise of the power was void, so that the property vested in the persons entitled in default of appointment (the period during which the power was exercisable having expired). The appointment did not designate the persons appointed, as the settlement required. It merely provided a mechanism whereby the appointees might be ascertained. The power was to appoint persons, and not to nominate persons to make an appointment. Intermediate powers were subject to the rule against unauthorised delegation, and it was immaterial that the donees of the power were the same persons as the trustees of the discretionary trust.

---

[68] *Re Hetling and Merton's Contract* [1893] 3 Ch. 269; Farwell, pp. 503–504.

[69] Thomas, *Powers*, p. 392; *White v. Wilson* (1852) 1 Drew. 298 at 304; *Re Trifftt's Settlement* [1958] Ch. 852 (explained in *Re Hay's S.T.* [1982] 1 W.L.R. 202 as showing that the rule does not apply to bare powers).

[70] *De Bussche v. Alt* (1878) 8 Ch.D. 286; *Re Morris' Settlement* [1951] 2 All E.R. 528; *Re Hunter's W.T.* [1963] Ch. 372; (1954) 23 Conv.(N.S.) 27, 423 (D. Waters).

[71] *Houston v. Burns* [1918] A.C. 337; *Att.-Gen. v. National Provincial Bank* [1924] A.C. 262; *Re Manisty's Settlement* [1974] Ch. 17 at 26; *Re Park* [1932] 1 Ch. 580; *Re Abraham's W.T.* [1969] 1 Ch. 463 at 475.

[72] [1990] 1 W.L.R. 1503; (1991) 107 L.Q.R. 211 (J. Davies); [1991] Conv. 138 (J. Martin).

[73] *Re Morris' Settlement* [1951] 2 All E.R. 528.

[74] [1982] 1 W.L.R. 202.

If the donee appoints on protective trusts,[75] the determinable life interests will be valid, but the discretionary trusts due to take effect on forfeiture of the life interest are void and the trusts in default take effect.[76] There is no objection, however, to the inclusion in an appointment of a power of advancement.[77] Generally, where it is desired that the donee should be able to make an appointment which itself includes a power of appointment or involves any other delegation of discretion, express provision should be made in the instrument creating the power.

6. Fraud on a Power

An appointor, in the typical case of a special power of appointment with a gift over in default, is under no duty to exercise the power; but if he chooses to exercise the power, he must exercise it honestly.[78] Unless he is a fiduciary,[79] he need not weigh the merits of the possible beneficiaries; he may appoint all the available assets to any one beneficiary, who may indeed be himself.[80] But he must exercise it within the limits imposed by the donor or testator who created it.[81] If, of course, he expressly exceeds those limits the exercise of the power will be void unless it can be cut down by severing the invalid excess.[82] But the doctrine of fraudulent exercise of a power goes further than this, for it extends to the intent with which a power is exercised. The theory is that, in the case of a special power, the property is vested in those entitled in default of its exercise subject to its being divested by a proper exercise of the power,[83] and that an exercise of the power for any "sinister object" is not proper, is a fraud on those entitled in default, and void.[84] It should be appreciated that the term "fraud" is used here in a special sense: "The equitable doctrine of 'fraud on a power' has little, if anything, to do with fraud".[85] It signifies "in more modern parlance an improper use of the power for a collateral purpose".[86]

---

[75] *post*, Chap. 7.

[76] *Re Boulton's S.T.* [1928] Ch. 703; *Re Morris' Settlement, supra; Re Hunter* [1963] Ch. 372.

[77] *Re May's Settlement* [1926] Ch. 136; *Re Mewburn's Settlement* [1934] Ch. 112; *Re Morris' Settlement* [1951] 2 All E.R. 528; *Re Wills' W.T.* [1959] Ch. 1; *Pilkington v. I.R.C.* [1964] A.C. 612; *post*, p. 597.

[78] *Cloutte v. Storey* [1911] 1 Ch. 18.

[79] In which case, see *Re Hay's S.T.* [1982] 1 W.L.R. 202, *ante*, p. 175.

[80] *Re Penrose* [1933] Ch. 793.

[81] (1977) 3 Monash L.R. 210 (Y. Grbich), describing the doctrine of fraud on a power as an "*ultra vires* appointments" doctrine.

[82] *Churchill v. Churchill* (1867) L.R. 5 Eq. 44; *Re Oliphant* (1917) 86 L.J.Ch. 452.

[83] *Re Brook's S.T.* [1939] Ch. 993.

[84] *Vatcher v. Paull* [1915] A.C. 372. *cf. Re Greaves* [1954] Ch. 434 at 446.

[85] *Medforth v. Blake* [2000] Ch. 86 at 103.

[86] *Hillsdown Holdings plc v. Pensions Ombudsman* [1997] 1 All E.R. 862 at 883.

A. Prior Agreement

The first type of case in which an apparently valid exercise of a power will be void for what in this context is termed fraud[87] is where the appointment is made as the result of a prior agreement with the appointee as to what he will do with the proceeds. Such an exercise of a power will be wholly void save when the appointor is the person entitled in default, or where the person entitled in default is a party to it.[88]

B. Benefit to Appointor

A second type of case is where the power is exercised so as to benefit the appointor. The benefit is usually financial in character, as where an appointment is made to an ailing child by its father, who will benefit on the child's death,[89] but it is not restricted to financial benefit.[90] For the exercise of the power to be void, there must be more than a hope of benefit. Thus an appointment to a healthy child by a father will be valid.[91] For fraud to operate, the appointment must have been made with intent to benefit the appointor. An appointment is sometimes made, however, which in fact benefits the appointor, but which is clearly intended to, and does, benefit the appointees; this is true of many an appointment that forms part of the variation of a trust, for the tax savings achieved will often be a benefit to the appointor. Thus in *Re Merton*,[92] Wynn-Parry J. decided that there was no inflexible rule that forced him to declare such an exercise of a power to be void. The intent that renders an appointment void is a matter "of fact or of inference rather than of law,"[93] and must be ascertained as a single fact after consideration of all the relevant evidence.[94] In the context of variation of trusts however, modern cases have shown a reluctance to apply this benevolent view.[95]

Pension trusts provide further scope for the application of the doctrine, as in *Hillsdown Holdings plc v. Pensions Ombudsman*.[96] In that case the pension scheme had a substantial actuarial surplus. Its rules did not permit payment of surplus to the employer, but did

---

[87] *supra.* See the classification in Thomas, *Powers*, p. 460, and also Sheridan, *Fraud in Equity*, pp. 116 *et seq.*

[88] See generally *Vatcher v. Paull* [1915] A.C. 372.

[89] *Lord Hichinbroke v. Seymour* (1789) 1 Bro.C.C. 395; *Lady Wellesley v. Earl Mornington* (1855) 2 K. & J. 143.

[90] *Cochrane v. Cochrane* [1922] 2 Ch. 230.

[91] *Henty v. Wrey* (1882) 21 Ch.D. 332.

[92] [1953] 1 W.L.R. 1096 at 1100; *Re Robertson's W.T.* [1960] 1 W.L.R. 1050.

[93] *Re Holland* [1914] 2 Ch. 595 at 601, *per* Sargant J.

[94] *Re Crawshay* [1948] Ch. 123.

[95] *Re Wallace's Settlements* [1968] 1 W.L.R. 711; *Re Brook's Settlement* [1968] 1 W.L.R. 1661; *post*, p. 643, [1968] B.T.R. 199 (J.G.M.); (1969) 32 M.L.R. 317 (S. Cretney).

[96] [1997] 1 All E.R. 862.

permit the transfer of funds to another scheme provided the transfer did not seriously prejudice the members. The trustees transferred the entire fund to another pension scheme, of which the rules could be amended to permit the payment of surplus to the employer. This was done pursuant to an agreement with the employer whereby the benefit to the members would be increased and the surplus (over £11 million) paid to the employer. Although the trustees acted under legal advice and considered the arrangement to be beneficial to the members, it was a breach of trust in the nature of a fraud on a power. The power to transfer the funds had been exercised improperly for the collateral purpose of paying the surplus to the employer.

C. Non-objects

An appointment is sometimes drafted so that the intent appears to be to benefit objects of the power, but the real intent is to benefit non-objects. It will then be void, even though the appointee was in no sense a party, and might not even have known of the appointment or its intent.[97] Thus, in *Re Dick*[98]:

A widow had a power to appoint amongst her brothers and sisters and their issue, but she wished to provide for a family who were looking after her. She had inadequate free capital to do so. She appointed by will to her favourite sister, but coupling the appointment with a request "without imposing any trust or legal obligation" that the sister should provide an annuity for the family concerned. The Court of Appeal held that the absence of obligation on the appointee was not crucial; but rather that the whole intent in making the appointment was to secure a benefit to non-objects by subjecting the appointee to "strong moral suasion to benefit a non-object, which suasion the [appointee] would in the appointor's opinion, be unable to resist."[99] This intent was enough to constitute the exercise of the power as fraudulent.

Difficulties arise from this rule as to real intent, for it is not easy to distinguish cases such as *Re Dick* from cases where there was a real intent to benefit the appointee but coupled with a hope that the

---

[97] *Re Nicholson's Settlement* [1939] Ch. 11. This case decided that the doctrine as to the real intent behind an appointment did not apply to a power exercisable only in favour of one person and so exercised. But see the criticism in Sheridan, *Fraud in Equity*, p. 122 and Keeton & Sheridan's *Equity* (3rd ed.), p. 297.

[98] [1953] Ch. 343; *Re Kirwan* (1884) 25 Ch.D. 373 *cf. Re Marsden's Trusts* (1859) 4 Drew. 594.

[99] The matter was put in this way by Cohen L.J. in *Re Crawshay* [1948] Ch. 123 at 135, a case which contained the additional vitiating factor of a covenant by the appointee assigning to non-objects any benefits received by the exercise of the power; (1948) 64 L.Q.R. 221 (H. Hanbury).

appointee would benefit a non-object, which cases are of course not within the doctrine of fraud on a power. But the intent in many cases is simply dual—genuinely to benefit the appointee but also to subject him to strong moral persuasion as to part of the benefit appointed. It may therefore be relevant in *Re Dick*[1] that a substantial proportion of the sum appointed would have been absorbed by the annuity and that a great deal of planning and discussion had gone into the making of the appointment coupled with the expression of the request in formal memoranda. For the danger inherent in extending the doctrine too far is that, if the appointment is void, the appointee loses all benefit unless the appointor is alive to reappoint,[2] a loss to the appointee which is not justified if intent to benefit him was a substantial element in the exercise of the power.

D. Excessive Exercise; Severance

If there is a genuine intent to benefit the appointee, something expressly superadded so as to benefit a non-object can be severed, leaving the appointment valid.[3] But severance will not occur in the absence of such a genuine intent.[4] Again if, in a will by which he exercises a power, a testator makes a gift of *his own* property conditional on the appointee resettling the *appointed* property, this is a valid condition on his own gift and the exercise of the power also is valid, provided there was a genuine intent to benefit the appointee.[5] This would be difficult to reconcile with strict emphasis on the intent with which a power was exercised as being "entire and single."[6]

E. Releases

The doctrine of fraud on a power does not apply to releases, for releases simply benefit those entitled in default. It is irrelevant that the appointor, in releasing his power, is intended to benefit thereby, as he has no duty in respect of the disappointed objects.[7] Nor does

---

[1] *supra.*

[2] There can be no severance in these cases as there is nothing to sever. But *Re Chadwick's Trusts* [1939] 1 All E.R. 850 shows that a fresh appointment is valid if free from the element that vitiated a prior one.

[3] *Re Kerr's W.T.* (1878) 4 Ch.D. 600; *Re Holland* [1914] 2 Ch. 595; followed in *Re Burton's Settlements* [1955] Ch. 82.

[4] *Re Cohen* [1911] 1 Ch. 37. Severance will not of course occur when there has been a prior agreement with the appointee.

[5] *Re Burton's Settlements* [1955] Ch. 82.

[6] In *Re Simpson* [1952] Ch. 412, Vaisey J. had held that *Re Crawshay* and *Re Dick* impelled him to take this strict view on facts analogous to those in *Re Burton's Settlements* in which case, however, Upjohn J. rightly refused to follow the lead.

[7] *Re Somes* [1896] 1 Ch. 250. Releases may be an important element in the variation of a trust; *Re Ball's Settlement Trusts* [1968] 1 W.L.R. 899, *post*, p. 642.

the doctrine apply to the revocation of the exercise of a power.[8] An appointment may only be revoked where such right of revocation has been reserved. Where such right exists, it seems that the appointor is under no duty to the appointees. It has even been said that, in revoking, he may stipulate for a benefit, but it would be strange if, by first exercising a power and then revoking it, an appointor could obtain a benefit rightly denied him on an appointment, and it is significant that, in the leading case,[9] the revocation was followed by a release.[10]

F. Position of Third Parties

The position of a bona fide purchaser, for instance a mortgagee, of an interest appointed to his vendor in such a manner as to amount to a fraud on the power is complicated. Those entitled in default of appointment who can challenge the exercise of the power as fraudulent have an interest in the property appointed which in principle prevails over the interest of its bona fide purchasers for value,[11] because no legal title passes under the ordinary power of appointment. The Law of Property Act 1925, s.157, protects such purchasers, but only if the vendor-appointee was at least 25 years of age at the time of sale, and only to the extent to which he was presumptively entitled in default of appointment. Apart from this curious and limited protection, a fraudulent appointment is void even against a bona fide purchaser.

7. RELEASE OF POWERS

A. Why Release?

As a power is discretionary, it may be asked why it becomes advantageous to release it as opposed merely to not exercising it. This may be for various reasons; for example, to create indefeasible interests in those entitled in default,[12] to make a gift charitable by releasing a power to appoint to anyone else,[13] to avoid the "reservation of benefit" rules under the inheritance tax system by excluding

---

[8] *Re Greaves* [1954] Ch. 434.
[9] *ibid.*
[10] *cf.* Evershed M.R. in *Re Greaves, supra,* at 448.
[11] *Cloutte v. Storey* [1911] 1 Ch. 18. See also *Turner v. Turner* [1984] Ch. 100, *ante,* p. 176, on the effect of appointments made in breach of the duty to consider; and *Re Hay's S.T.* [1982] 1 W.L.R. 202, *ante,* p. 181, on the effect of an appointment in breach of the duty not to delegate.
[12] *Re Mills* [1930] 1 Ch. 654; *Mettoy Pension Trustees Ltd v. Evans* [1990] 1 W.L.R. 1587 (where default beneficiary insolvent).
[13] *Re Wills* [1964] Ch. 219.

the settlor from the class of objects,[14] and especially to avoid the effect of Income and Corporation Taxes Act 1988, ss.671–675. They provide for the income of a settlement to be treated as that of the settlor where, for example, the settlor or his wife may benefit from the exercise of a power of appointment. Until 1958, it had been common to include the wife of the settlor as a member of the discretionary class; and it thus became important to exclude her.[15] This was usually done by exercising the trustees' power to appoint on new trusts which were identical with the old ones except that the wife was omitted. This is in effect a partial release of the earlier power, and is treated as such.[16] As we will see, many of the releases which have been made in this way are of doubtful validity.

B. How to Effect a Release

Trustees may in effect surrender their trusts and powers by paying the money into court under the Trustee Act 1925, s.63[17]; or they may apply to the court for an administration order; or they may ask the court for directions as to the way in which they should act on questions arising in the administration of the trust. Usually, however, the court will not give general directions concerning the exercise of discretionary powers in the future.[18]

They may also effect a release of a power, in appropriate circumstances, by executing a deed of release, or by a contract not to exercise the power.[19] A power may also be extinguished by implication by any dealing with the property by the donee which is inconsistent with its further exercise[20]; or by obtaining the approval of the court to an arrangement which is so inconsistent. There is much uncertainty concerning the validity of releases in some circumstances, and it is important that express provision should be made in the instrument creating the power which expressly authorises the donees of the power to release it.[21]

---

[14] *post*, p. 227.

[15] F.A. 1958, s.22, now I.C.T.A. 1988, s.674; *Blausten v. I.R.C.* [1972] Ch. 256; (1972) 36 Conv.(N.S.) 127 (D. Hayton).

[16] *Re Wills, supra; Muir v. I.R.C.* [1966] 1 W.L.R. 251 and 1269; *Blausten v. I.R.C. (supra)*.

[17] *post*, p. 550; this is now rare; (1968) 84 L.Q.R. 67 (A. Hawkins). See also *Thrells Ltd v. Lomas* [1993] 1 W.L.R. 456 (exercise of fiduciary power properly surrendered to court to avoid conflict of duties).

[18] *Re Allen-Meyrick's W.T.* [1966] 1 W.L.R. 499; (1967) 31 Conv.(N.S.) 117 (A. Hawkins); *post*, p. 550.

[19] L.P.A. 1925, ss.155, 160.

[20] *Re Christie-Miller's Settlement* [1961] 1 W.L.R. 462; *Re Wills* [1964] Ch. 219; *Muir v. I.R.C.* [1966] 1 W.L.R. 251, 1269; *Re Courtauld's Settlement* [1965] 2 All E.R. 544; *Blausten v. I.R.C.* [1972] Ch. 256; (1968) 84 L.Q.R. 92–93 (A. Hawkins).

[21] *Muir v. I.R.C.* [1966] 1 W.L.R. 1269; *Blausten v. I.R.C., supra.*

C. Validity of Release

It is not possible to lay down with confidence what are the circumstances in which, in the absence of express provision, a release will be valid. The Law of Property Act 1925, s.155, provides that: "A person to whom any power, whether coupled with an interest or not, is given may by deed release or contract not to exercise, the power."[22]

The question arose whether this provision applied to a situation where the donees of the power were trustees who held the power in a fiduciary capacity. Admittedly they cannot be compelled to exercise it; but can they be allowed to release it? The courts answered this question in the negative[23]; the problem is how to determine which are the cases to which the statute does not apply.

i. Trusts. The first category is that discussed above where the situation is not really a power but a discretionary trust. Here the trustees are under a duty to appoint; if they fail to do so, the court will declare the property to be held on trust for the possible appointees.[24] There is no question of release here.

ii. Fiduciary Powers. Where a power is conferred upon a person by virtue of his office, he may not release it. "*In the absence of words in the trust deed authorising [him] so to do.*"[25] Here there may be a gift over in default, either to the class of appointees or to a different class. This is a power proper, and not a trust. But the power is one given to the trustees to be exercised in a fiduciary capacity. They cannot discard it; they are, as has been seen,[26] under a duty to consider from time to time whether and how to exercise the power. This is so whether it is given to them as trustees, or whether it is given to persons by name if on the true view of the facts, they were selected as donee of the power because they were trustees.[27] Conversely, persons selected as individuals may be described as trustees. In *Re Wills' Trust Deeds*[28] a power of appointment in respect of property which was the subject of a *settlement* was given to the trustees of the settlor's *will*; this was not given by virtue of their office. Modern pension fund cases provide illustrations of the rules as to the release of powers. In *Re Courage Group's Pension*

---

[22] Replacing earlier legislation.

[23] *Re Eyre* (1883) 49 L.T. 259; *Saul v. Pattinson* (1886) 55 L.J.Ch. 831.

[24] Equal division is not necessary in the case of the modern discretionary trust; *ante*, p. 105.

[25] *Muir v. I.R.C.* [1966] 1 W.L.R. 1269 at 1283, *per* Harman L.J.; the italics are original; *Blausten v. I.R.C.* [1972] Ch. 256.

[26] *ante*, p. 175.

[27] *Hall v. May* (1857) 3 K. & J. 585; *Re Cookes' Contract* (1877) 4 Ch.D. 454.

[28] [1964] Ch. 219. (The actual decision probably does not survive that of the Court of Appeal in *Muir v. I.R.C.* [1966] 1 W.L.R. 1269).

Schemes[29] fiduciary powers were vested in a committee set up to manage a pension scheme. It was held that even if existing members of the committee could release, fetter, or agree not to exercise their powers (which was not decided),[30] they could not deprive their successors of the right to exercise their powers. In *Mettoy Pension Trustees Ltd v. Evans*[31] there was a power in favour of the pension fund beneficiaries, with the employer company taking in default. On the company's insolvency, the liquidator sought to release the power in the interests of the creditors. This could not be done because the power was fiduciary. The liquidator could not exercise the power because of a conflict of duties,[32] and so the court could intervene to protect the objects.[33]

iii. Bare Powers. Where the power is given to a person in his private capacity, the donee is prima facie able to release it,[34] even if the release operates in favour of the donee, as where a father releases a power so that the shares of his sons (who are entitled in default) become absolute, and that of a deceased son passes to the donee.[35] A release, or a covenant not to exercise it, (which will be equivalent to a release)[36] may be effective if it refers only to part of the property,[37] or if it relates only to one or more of several objects.[38]

iv. Variation of Trusts Act 1958. Section 1 of the Variation of Trusts Act 1958 makes no express reference to powers. Many powers are vested in trustees, as in the case of discretionary or protective trusts; and a variation of such powers will no doubt be covered by the provisions of the Act. It appears that an arrangement under the Act which recites the release of a power,[39] or one which is inconsistent with the future exercise of the power,[40] will effectively release it.

---

[29] [1987] 1 W.L.R. 495.
[30] See (1993) 7 *Trust Law International* 69 (H. Arthur).
[31] [1990] 1 W.L.R. 1587. See also *British Coal Corp. v. British Coal Staff Superannuation Scheme Trustees Ltd* [1995] 1 All E.R. 912.
[32] See now Pensions Act 1995, s.25(2).
[33] *ante,* p. 176.
[34] This is Buckley J.'s fifth category in *Re Wills' Trust Deeds* [1964] Ch. 219.
[35] *Re Radcliffe* [1892] 1 Ch. 227; an appointment in favour of the estate of the deceased son would have been a fraud on the power.
[36] *per* Buckley L.J. in *Re Evered* [1910] 2 Ch. 147 at 161.
[37] *Re Evered, supra.*
[38] *Re Brown's Settlement* [1939] Ch. 944; Thomas, *Powers,* p. 614.
[39] *Re Christie-Miller's S.T.* [1961] 1 W.L.R. 462.
[40] *Re Courtauld's Settlement* [1965] 2 All E.R. 544; *Re Ball's S.T.* [1968] 1 W.L.R. 899.

CHAPTER 7

PROTECTIVE TRUSTS

1. THE GENERAL PROBLEM

A DEBTOR'S property is in principle available for the satisfaction of
his creditors and, if he becomes bankrupt, it will pass to his trustee
in bankruptcy; but it is possible, by making use of a protective trust,
to obtain a measure of protection against such an event.

In the development of protective trusts the courts have been torn
between two conflicting pressures. On the one hand, nobody should
have the power of defeating his creditors by putting his property
beyond their grasp; on the other, a settlor should be able to create a
trust in any form, so long as it is not unlawful; and there is much to
be said for allowing some means of protecting a person's dependants from the ill-effects of his extravagance. The technique of protective trusts involves the giving of a determinable life interest with
a gift over upon the happening of certain events. Originally, the gift
over was usually in favour of other members of the family[1]; but the
modern practice is to provide for a gift over to trustees to hold on
discretionary trusts in favour of a class which includes the life tenant
and members of his family; and this pattern is provided for by the
Trustee Act 1925, s.33.[2] In most American jurisdictions, it is possible to make an equitable life interest inalienable whether voluntarily
or involuntarily. This is known as a "spendthrift trust",[3] and is
justified on the ground that the settlor, in creating the trust, should

[1] *e.g. Re Detmold* (1889) 40 Ch.D. 585.
[2] *post*, p. 194.
[3] Griswold, *Spendthrift Trusts* (2nd ed.).

191

be allowed to create such equitable interests as he wishes. This has never been allowed in England,[4] but, as will be seen, the technique of the protective trust as at least an equivalent protection. Protective trust clauses are commonly used today in occupational pension schemes, to prevent alienation of pension rights.[5] A similar result was achieved in *Re Scientific Pension Plan Trusts*,[6] where a forfeiture clause operating on the bankruptcy of a member prevented the benefits passing to the trustee in bankruptcy. Instead they passed to the pension scheme trustees, who had power to apply them for the benefit of the member's dependants.

2. Determinable and Conditional Interests

A distinction is made in law between an interest subject to a condition subsequent and a determinable interest.[7] The former exists where there is a gift of an absolute interest which is then cut down by the application of a condition; such as a gift to X absolutely, but if he should change his nationality, then over to Y. A determinable interest exists where something less than an absolute interest is given in the first place; as a gift to X until he changes (or so long as he retains) his nationality. The distinction is subtle[8]; it depends entirely upon the language of the gift; but it is a distinction that has importance in several contexts. The relevance in the present context is twofold: first, that a condition against alienation is void[9]; secondly, that a condition subsequent, being one which effects a forfeiture of an existing interest, is strictly construed[10]; if the condition is held void, the interest becomes absolute.[11] The determining event, however, in the case of a determinable interest is less strictly construed; and if it should be held invalid, the whole interest fails.[12]

---

[4] But from the early 19th century until 1935 it was possible to create a trust for the separate use of a married woman to impose a restraint upon the anticipation or alienation. See Law Reform (Married Women and Tortfeasors) Act 1935 and Married Women (Restraint upon Anticipation) Act 1949.

[5] *post*, p. 489.

[6] [1999] Ch. 53. See now Welfare Reform and Pensions Act 1999, s.14(3).

[7] *Brandon v. Robinson* (1811) 18 Ves.Jr. 429 at 433 (Lord Eldon); M. & W., pp. 65 *et seq.*; Cheshire and Burn, pp. 364 *et seq.* The clue to the existence of a determinable limitation is the use of words such as "until," "so long as," "whilst," as distinct from phraseology such as "but if" and "when, if ever."

[8] "Little short of disgraceful to our jurisprudence," *per* Porter M.R. in *Re King's Trusts* (1892) 29 L.R.Ir. 401 at 410; "The distinction is not a particularly attractive one, being based on form rather than substance", *per* Rattee J. in *Re Scientific Investment Pension Plan Trusts* [1999] Ch. 53 at 59.

[9] Co.Litt. 223a; *Re Brown* [1954] Ch. 39.

[10] *Clavering v. Ellison* (1859) 7 H.L.Cas. 707; *Sifton v. Sifton* [1938] A.C. 656.

[11] Co.Litt. 206a, b; *Re Greenwood* [1903] 1 Ch. 749.

[12] *Re Moore* (1888) 39 Ch.D. 116. (Gift of a weekly sum to T's sister "whilst . . . living apart from her husband" construed as a gift determinable upon returning to her husband, and held void); *Re Tuck's S.T.* [1978] Ch. 49.

Thus it is clear that a *condition* so drafted as to terminate an interest upon alienation[13] or bankruptcy[14] is void and the prior interest is absolute. But an interest *determinable* on alienation or bankruptcy is valid.[15] The basis of protective trusts is therefore a determinable life interest.

3. SELF-PROTECTION

A settlor cannot make a settlement which will protect himself against his own bankruptcy.[16]

In *Re Burroughs-Fowler*,[17] the settlor, by ante-nuptial settlement, settled property upon trust to pay the income to himself for life or until one of certain events should occur, including his bankruptcy, after which event the income was to be paid to his wife. The settlor was adjudicated bankrupt during the wife's lifetime. It was held that the life interest vested indefeasibly in his trustee in bankruptcy, who could validly dispose of it.

A settlor may however protect himself against other forms of alienation, voluntary or involuntary. And if the limitation, as is usual, provides for the termination of his interest upon any one of such events *or* upon his bankruptcy, the gift over, as we have seen, is void in the event of bankruptcy, but valid in all other cases.[18] If the gift over has taken effect upon, for example, an attempt to charge the life interest, the subsequent bankruptcy of the settlor has no effect upon it.

In *Re Detmold*,[19] a marriage settlement of the settlor's own property provided for the payment of the income to the settlor for life or "till he shall become bankrupt or shall . . . suffer something whereby the same . . . would . . . by operation of law . . . become . . . payable to some other person . . . " and, after such

---

[13] *Brandon v. Robinson* (1811) 18 Ves.Jr. 429; *Re Dugdale* (1888) 38 Ch.D. 176; *Re Brown* [1954] Ch. 39; (1943) 59 L.Q.R. 343 (Glanville Williams).

[14] *Younghusband v. Gisborne* (1846) 15 L.J.Ch. 355; *Re Sanderson's Trust* (1857) 3 K. & J. 497; *Re Scientific Investment Pension Plan Trusts, supra.*

[15] *post*, p. 194; see also the earlier authorities relied on by Turner V.-C. in *Rochford v. Hackman*, (1852) 9 Hare 475.

[16] *Mackintosh v. Pogose* [1895] 1 Ch. 505; *Re Wombwell* (1921) 125 L.T. 437; this rule is preserved by T.A. 1925, s.33(3). Nor may he settle his property on a third party to prejudice his own creditors; *post*, pp. 352 *et seq.*

[17] [1916] 2 Ch. 251; *Official Assignee v. NZI Life Superannuation Nominees Ltd* [1995] 1 N.Z.L.R. 684.

[18] *Re Detmold* (1889) 40 Ch.D. 585; *Re Brewer's Settlement* [1896] 2 Ch. 503; *Re Johnson* [1904] 1 K.B. 134.

[19] (1889) 40 Ch.D. 585.

determination, on trust to pay the income to his wife. In July 1888, an order was made appointing a judgment creditor to be receiver of the income; and in September 1888 the settlor was adjudicated bankrupt. It was held that the forfeiture took place upon the involuntary alienation of the income by process of law. The wife then became entitled to the income, and she did not lose the right on the subsequent bankruptcy.

4. Protected Life Interests in Persons Other than the Settlor

Though a person cannot make a settlement of his own property upon himself until bankruptcy, and then over, yet a trust created by A to pay the income to B until B dies or becomes bankrupt alienates or charges his life interest and then over to C is good in the event of the occurrence of any of those events, including B's bankruptcy.[20] The essence of the device of protected life interests[21] is that, on the occurrence of a determining event, such as alienation or bankruptcy, the interest of the life tenant determines, and the trustees then hold the property on discretionary trusts for the benefit of the life tenant and his family.

Some early attempts to reach this result failed, owing to the absence of any clear gift over of the income.[22] Eventually, however, discretionary trusts became accepted,[23] and in modern times quite independently of protective trusts.

The court may exercise its jurisdiction to vary trusts so as to convert a beneficial interest into a protected life interest where it is feared that the beneficiary cannot manage his affairs in a responsible manner.[24]

5. Trustee Act 1925, s.33

Before 1926 it was necessary to set out expressly the terms of the trusts; and a settlor may still do so if he wishes.[25] In relation,

---

[20] *Re Ashby* [1892] 1 Q.B. 872; *Re Scientific Investment Pension Plan Trusts* [1999] Ch. 53.

[21] (1957) 21 Conv.(N.S.) 110 (L. Sheridan).

[22] The point is discussed in *Rochford v. Hackman* (1852) 9 Hare 475.

[23] And may take effect where the forfeiture precedes the settlement; as where the bankruptcy began before the testator died: *Metcalfe v. Metcalfe* [1891] 3 Ch. 1. See also *Re Forder* [1927] 2 Ch. 291; *Re Walker* [1939] Ch. 974.

[24] *Hambro v. Duke of Marlborough* [1994] Ch. 158; *post*, p. 635 (unsuitability of Marquess of Blandford to manage Blenheim). See also *Re Abram (deceased)* [1996] 2 F.L.R. 379 (protected life interest ordered under Inheritance (Provision for Family and Dependants) Act 1975, where any capital sum would have gone to applicant's creditors).

[25] *Re Shaw's Settlement* [1951] Ch. 833; *Re Rees (decd.)* [1954] Ch. 202; *Re Munro's S.T.* [1963] 1 W.L.R. 145.

however, to trusts coming into operation after 1925, Trustee Act 1925, s.33, "provides a shorthand arrangement whereby a settlor may establish a trust without setting forth in detail all the terms upon which the property is to be held."[26] The section applies although the statutory formula "on protective trusts" may not be used, so long as the intention is clear.[27] The section then applies subject to any modification contained in the instrument creating the trust.[28]

Section 33(1) provides:

"Where any income, including an annuity or other periodical income payment, is directed to be held on protective trusts for the benefit of any person (in this section called 'the principal beneficiary') for the period of his life or for any less period, then, during that period (in this section called the 'trust period') the said income shall, without prejudice to any prior interest, be held on the following trusts, namely:—

(i) Upon trust for the principal beneficiary during the trust period or until he . . . does or attempts to do or suffers any act or thing, or until any event happens, other than an advance under any statutory or express power, whereby, if the said income were payable during the trust period to the principal beneficiary absolutely during that period, he would be deprived of the right to receive the same or any part thereof,[29] in any of which cases . . . this trust of the said income shall fail or determine;

(iii) [and during the remainder of the trust period] . . . upon trust for the application thereof for the maintenance or support, or otherwise for the benefit, of all or any one or more exclusively of the other or others of the following persons[30] (that is to say)—

    (*a*) the principal beneficiary and his or her wife or husband, if any, and his or her children or more remote issue, if any; or

    (*b*) if there is no wife or husband or issue of the principal beneficiary in existence, the principal beneficiary and the persons who would, if he were actually dead, be entitled to the trust property or the income thereof or the annuity fund, if any, or arrears of the annuity, as the case may be;

---

[26] Griswold, *Spendthrift Trusts*, p. 375.
[27] *Re Wittke* [1944] Ch. 166 ("under protective trusts for the benefit of my sister").
[28] T.A. 1925, s.33(2).
[29] See *Re Smith's Will Trusts* (1981) 131 N.L.J. 292.
[30] Relationships are to be construed in accordance with s.1 of the Family Law Reform Act 1987 (*i.e.* without regard to legitimacy); F.L.R.A. 1987, Sched. 2, para. 2.

as the trustees in their absolute discretion, without being liable to account for the exercise of such discretion, think
fit."

6. Forfeiture of the Life Tenant's Interest

It is necessary in each case to decide whether or not the event which
has occurred is sufficient to determine the interest of the life tenant,
and thus to bring the discretionary trusts into operation.[31] The question usually arises under trusts governed by the Trustee Act 1925,
s.33. Where the question arises in respect of an express protective
trust, the question will depend on the construction of the particular
trust under consideration.[32] The principles applicable will however
be the same.

It will be appreciated that a forfeiture is not in the bankruptcy
cases a disaster. The forfeiture deprives the life tenant of his life
interest, which would otherwise have become available to his creditors. The effect of the forfeiture is to allow the protective provisions
to come into effect, and to keep the principal beneficiary's interest
from his trustee in bankruptcy.[33]

A. Determining Events

If the principal beneficiary alienates his interest,[34] or goes bankrupt, a forfeiture obviously occurs. In other circumstances, it is often
difficult to draw a clear dividing line between those which will and
those which will not effect a forfeiture. The matter is best explained
by illustrations. The first three are cases of express protective trusts
in which the instrument provided that the life interest should be
determinable upon the happening of some event whereby some or
all of the income became payable to another person.

In *Re Balfour's Settlement Trusts*,[35] the trustees had, at the life
tenant's request, and in breach of trust, advanced parts of the
capital to him. They then asserted their right to retain the income
of the fund in order to make good the breach. Subsequently, the
life tenant became bankrupt. Farwell J. held that the life tenant's
interest had determined because the trustees became entitled to

---

[31] *Re Brewer's Settlement* [1896] 2 Ch. 503.

[32] *ibid.* at 507; *Re Dennis' S.T.* [1942] Ch. 283 at 286; *Re Hall* [1944] Ch. 46.

[33] See *Re Scientific Investment Pension Plan Trusts* [1999] Ch. 53.

[34] *Gibbon v. Mitchell* [1990] 1 W.L.R. 1304, *post*, p. 872 (surrender of protected life interest
to remaindermen for tax purposes caused forfeiture, but deed set aside for mistake).

[35] [1938] Ch. 928; *Re Gordon* [1978] Ch. 145.

the income.[36] The life interest was thus saved from the bankruptcy.

In *Re Baring's Settlement Trusts*,[37] a sequestration order was made against the property of a mother who failed to obey a court order to return her children to the jurisdiction. Morton J. held that the order effected a forfeiture, although the mother's loss of income was only temporary.

In *Re Dennis' Settlement Trusts*,[38] the settlor's son was entitled to a protective life interest under a family settlement. A rearrangement took place on his attaining the age of 21, and provided that for the next six years the trustees should pay to him only part of the income and should accumulate the rest for him. The rearrangement caused a forfeiture.

In *Re Gourju's Will Trusts*,[39] the protective trust was one governed by the Trustee Act 1925, s.33. The life tenant ceased to be entitled to receive the income of the trust because she lived in Nice, which became enemy occupied country during the Second World War. This caused a forfeiture. The Custodian of Enemy Property had no claim; nor could the trustees treat the tenant for life is still entitled, and retain income for her until the end of the war. The discretionary trusts came into effect, and the income was payable to one or more members of the class of beneficiaries.

On the other hand, residence in enemy occupied territory did not cause a forfeiture in *Re Hall*,[40] where forfeiture was to take place if the annuitant should "do or suffer any act" whereby the annuity should be payable elsewhere. The annuity could no longer be paid to the annuitant; but this was not due to anything that she had done or permitted; the Custodian of Enemy Property was entitled. Nor was there a forfeiture where a life tenant under a protective trust (terminable if the income became "payable to ... some other person") assigned his interest to the trustees of his marriage settlement (of which he was tenant for life), authorised the trustees to charge their expenses to the fund and appointed them his attorneys to receive the income.[41] Again there was no forfeiture where the life tenant was of unsound mind and a receiver was appointed.[42]

---

[36] Distinguishing *Re Brewer's Settlement* [1896] 2 Ch. 503, where bankruptcy took place before the trustees exercised their right.

[37] [1940] Ch. 737.

[38] [1942] Ch. 283.

[39] [1943] Ch. 24; *Re Wittke* [1944] Ch. 166; *Re Allen-Meyrick's Will Trusts* [1966] 1 W.L.R. 499. See also Trading with the Enemy (Custodian) (No. 2) Order, 1945 (S.R. & O. 1945 No. 887) providing that vesting in the Custodian should not take place if it would cause a forfeiture.

[40] [1944] Ch. 46; *Re Harris* [1945] Ch. 316; *Re Pozot's S.T.* [1952] Ch. 427.

[41] *Re Tancred's Settlement* [1903] 1 Ch. 715. Similarly an assignment of income already accrued; *Re Greenwood* [1901] 1 Ch. 887.

[42] *Re Oppenheimer's W.T.* [1950] Ch. 633; *Re Marshall* [1920] 1 Ch. 284.

Nor does the fact that a receiver's fees become payable out of the estate of such a person effect a forfeiture.[43] An authority to pay to creditors the dividends due from a company for a period of time during which the company declared no dividend did not cause a forfeiture.[44]

B. Order of the Court under Trustee Act 1925, s.57[45]

The court may make an order under Trustee Act 1925, s.57, which may affect the operation of a trust. If an order is made authorising the trustees to raise money to pay the debts of a life tenant under a protective trust, there is no forfeiture; for the power must be treated as if it had been "inserted in the trust instrument as an over-riding power."[46] If the order provides that the life tenant effects an insurance policy to secure a like amount of money at his death, and that the trustees shall pay the premiums out of the income if the life tenant fails to do so, there is no forfeiture so long as the life tenant makes the payments; but if the life tenant fails to pay and they become payable by the trustees from the income, there would be a forfeiture.[47]

C. Order of the Court under Matrimonial Causes Acts 1859–1973

It is not clear whether a forfeiture is effected when a court order is made which alters a protected life interest under a marriage settlement.[48] In *Re Richardson's Will Trusts*,[49] the court ordered that the principal beneficiary should charge his interest with an annual payment of £50 in favour of his divorced wife. The charge was held to create a forfeiture. On the other hand, in *General Accident Fire and Life Assurance Corporation Ltd v. I.R.C.*[50] an order diverting part of the income from the life tenant in favour of a former wife was held not to effect a forfeiture.

These cases are distinguishable on a narrow ground of construction of section 33.[51] But the broader ground of the decision, that this

---

[43] *Re Westby's Settlement* [1950] Ch. 296; Mental Health Act 1983, s.106(6).

[44] *Re Longman* [1955] 1 W.L.R. 197.

[45] *post*, p. 634.

[46] *Re Mair* [1935] Ch. 562 at 565, *per* Farwell J.

[47] *Re Salting* [1932] 2 Ch. 57 at 65.

[48] Which the court has power to do under Matrimonial Causes Act 1973, s.24(1).

[49] [1958] Ch. 504, illustrating the advantage of establishing a series of protective trusts, "one set until the beneficiary is twenty-five, another from twenty-five to thirty-five, a third from thirty-five to forty-five, and another for the rest of his life." A forfeiture of, or a charge upon, the principal beneficiary's interest in one of the trusts would not affect his interest in subsequent trusts. He would get a fresh start. (1958) 74 L.Q.R. 182 (R.E.M.).

[50] [1963] 1 W.L.R. 1207.

[51] *ibid*. See Donovan L.J. at 1217 and Russell L.J. at 1221; (1963) 27 Conv.(N.S.) 517 (F. Crane).

situation has no relevance to the real purpose of protective trusts, would seem to apply to the charge in *Re Richardson's Will Trusts*[52] as much as to the diversion of part of the income in the *General Accident* case.[53] It is submitted that the principle of the *General Accident* case is sound. As Donovan L.J. said[54]: " . . . the section is intended as a protection to spendthrift or improvident or weak life tenants. But it can give . . . no protection against the effect of a court order such as was made here. Furthermore, if such an order involves a forfeiture much injustice could be done." Perhaps the problem can be rationalised with the cases on section 57 by saying with Russell L.J., who made clear, however, that he did not rest his decision on this approach: "the settlement throughout was potentially subject in all its trusts to such an order as was made."[55] *Re Richardson's Will Trusts*[56] was not mentioned; but an earlier case on the Matrimonial Causes Act 1859 in favour of forfeiture, *Re Carew*,[57] was overruled. It is tempting to say that *Re Richardson's Will Trusts* is wrong; but it should be noted that in that case, as in *Re Carew*, the decision in favour of forfeiture forwarded the broad policy of section 33; for the forfeiture in those cases allowed the discretionary trusts to operate when otherwise the trustee in bankruptcy would have claimed the interest.

7. ADVANCEMENTS

Section 33(1) expressly exempts, as a cause of forfeiture, an advancement under any statutory[58] or express power. Thus the fact that the life tenant no longer receives the income of the part of the capital which has been advanced does not effect a forfeiture.[59] It appears that the same rule applies in the case of an express protective trust.[60] *Re Stimpson*[61] is to the contrary, but is regarded as of doubtful authority.

---

[52] [1958] Ch. 504.
[53] [1963] 1 W.L.R. 1207.
[54] *ibid. per* Donovan L.J. at 1218.
[55] *ibid.* at 1222.
[56] [1958] Ch. 504.
[57] (1910) 103 L.T. 658.
[58] T.A. 1925, s.32; *post*, p. 594.
[59] See however *General Accident, etc. v. I.R.C.* [1963] 1 W.L.R. 1207 which suggests that an advancement does not effect a forfeiture and that the proviso to s.33 is *ex abundanti cautela*.
[60] *Re Hodgson* [1913] 1 Ch. 34; *Re Shaw's Settlement* [1951] Ch. 833; *Re Rees (decd.)* [1954] Ch. 202.
[61] [1931] 2 Ch. 77.

8. EFFECT OF FORFEITURE

When a forfeiture has taken place, the life interest of the principal beneficiary is terminated, and the trusts in section 33(1)(ii), or those expressly contained in the instrument, as the case may be, come into play.[62] The termination is not, however, an occasion of charge to inheritance tax.[63] Under section 33 there are discretionary trusts in favour of the principal beneficiary and other persons, depending on whether or not a spouse or issue of the principal beneficiary is in existence. The trustees may apply the income for the remainder of the trust period for any member of the discretionary class. The principal beneficiary is not entitled to any income; but the trustees may, if they wish, pay it to him. They must pay the income to one or more of the members.[64] If the trustees decide to pay some income to the principal beneficiary, they face the problem that the money may be claimed by the trustee in bankruptcy as the assignee of his "interest" under the discretionary trust,[65] or perhaps only the surplus above that needed for his "mere support."[66] They may, however, in their absolute discretion, apply the money for his use and benefit.[67] Thus, "if the trustees were to pay an hotel-keeper to give him a dinner he would get nothing but the right to eat a dinner, and that is not property which could pass by assignment or bankruptcy."[68] It is safer to pay the money to third persons in satisfaction of services provided for the bankrupt.

[62] See also the forfeiture clause in *Re Scientific Investment Pension Plan Trusts* [1999] Ch. 53 (interest passed to pension scheme trustees with power to apply to member's dependants).

[63] Inheritance Tax Act 1984, s.88; *post*, p. 235.

[64] *Re Gourju's W.T.* [1943] Ch. 24.

[65] *Re Coleman* (1888) 39 Ch.D. 443; *Re Bullock* (1891) 64 L.T. 736 at 738.

[66] *Re Ashby* [1892] 1 Q.B. 872 at 877.

[67] *Re Bullock (supra); Re Coleman (supra); Re Smith* [1928] Ch. 915 at 919; *Public Trustees v. Ferguson* [1947] N.Z.L.R. 746.

[68] *Re Coleman, supra*, at 451.

CHAPTER 8

DISCRETIONARY TRUSTS

1. GENERAL

IT has been seen that discretionary trusts were used as a means of dealing with the income of a protective trust after the interest of the principal beneficiary had determined. Other advantages which discretionary trusts could offer came to be appreciated, especially in the context of estate duty saving, and they developed into one of the principal tools of estate and tax planners. Estate duty was replaced by capital transfer tax (now inheritance tax) in the Finance Act 1975. An explanation of the current tax position will be delayed until the next chapter, so that the fiscal situation of different types of trusts may be considered together. It will then be seen that discretionary trusts suffered substantially upon the introduction of capital transfer tax, and became at a disadvantage in relation to other trusts.[1] The disadvantage has been increased now that the discretionary trust is the only form of trust to be initially chargeable to inheritance tax upon its lifetime creation. Outright gifts and non-discretionary trusts are generally potentially exempt (*i.e.* chargeable only if the transferor dies within seven years).[2] The importance of discretionary trusts has been reduced, but they need to be examined because they retain many advantages outside the fiscal field; also because they raise a number of interesting and important theoretical questions in the law of trusts.

2. Uses of Discretionary Trusts

There are various reasons why a settlor may prefer to establish discretionary trusts rather than fixed trusts. As previously indicated, the most important reason used to be the saving of estate duty, and this will be referred to in Chapter 9. The emphasis is now on the other advantages.

A. To Protect the Beneficiary Against Creditors

If one member of a class of beneficiaries under a discretionary trust goes bankrupt, the trustee in bankruptcy is not entitled to claim any part of the fund.[3] The trustee in bankruptcy is however entitled to goods and money paid over by the trustees to the beneficiary in the exercise of their discretion[4]; or perhaps only to the amount in excess of that needed for the maintenance of the beneficiary.[5] The trustee in bankruptcy is however excluded if the trustees make the maintenance payments to third parties, such as a hotel keeper[6] or tradesman.[7]

---

[1] Although the rules applicable to discretionary trusts were substantially amended and rationalised by the Finance Act 1982. It should be added that the rates of inheritance tax under F.A. 1988 are not high, the maximum being 40 per cent on death and 20 per cent for chargeable lifetime transactions.

[2] See F.A. 1986, s.101, introducing the potentially exempt transfer for lifetime gifts other than trusts, and Finance (No. 2) Act 1987, s.96, extending this to non-discretionary trusts.

[3] *Re Ashby* [1892] 1 Q.B. 872 at p. 877; *Re Bullock* (1891) 64 L.T. 736. If the bankrupt is the sole member of the discretionary class, the interest passes to the trustee in bankruptcy: *Green v. Spicer* (1830) 1 Russ. & M. 395. See also *Re Trafford's Settlement* [1985] Ch. 32, *post.* p. 210.

[4] *Re Coleman* (1888) 39 Ch.D. 443.

[5] *Re Ashby, supra,* at 877; *Page v. Way* (1840) 3 Beav. 20, *ante,* p. 200.

[6] *Re Coleman, supra,* at 451; *ante,* p. 200.

[7] *Godden v. Crowhurst* (1842) 10 Sim. 642 at 656.

We have already seen that discretionary trusts are employed under protective trusts as a means whereby a protected life tenant may continue to receive some benefit from settled funds after his bankruptcy.[8] Indeed, this was their earliest use.

B. To Continue to Exercise Control over Young or Improvident Beneficiaries

Many take the view that it is unwise to put large sums of money at the disposal of beneficiaries if they are young or extravagant. This is due not only to the fear of the loss of family capital in case of insolvency; but also because a rich young beneficiary may be encouraged to develop habits of idleness and extravagance, and waste the inheritance; older beneficiaries may already have done so. While the discretionary trust is in operation, each member of the class of beneficiaries is entitled only to the money which the trustees see fit to allocate to him in the exercise of their discretion. The settlor may, whether or not he is a trustee, be able to influence the selection so as to exercise some element of control over the beneficiaries.[9]

C. To React to Changes in Circumstances

The trustees can exercise their discretion in relation to distribution of income and capital according to the circumstances existing at the time. When the trust is set up, there is no way of knowing how the beneficiaries will fare in the future; which of them will be most in need; which will be deserving, which spendthrift, which inebriate; which will marry millionaires, and which missionaries. The trustees can take all these factors into consideration in making their decisions; and will be much influenced by the wishes of the settlor. In making these decisions, they will also take tax factors into consideration; it is more economical to give income to those with smaller incomes; and capital given to rich beneficiaries may bear inheritance tax not only on the distribution but also when disposed of by them. Decisions by trustees which favour one beneficiary over another may of course give rise to criticism and resentment by disappointed beneficiaries.[10] All these factors need to be taken into consideration.

---

[8] *ante*, pp. 191 *et seq.*

[9] But if he influences the trustees to such an extent that they fail to exercise their discretion independently, the appointment will be void; *Turner v. Turner* [1984] Ch. 100, *post*, p. 215.

[10] The trustees need not disclose the reasons for their decisions; *Re Beloved Wilkes's Charity* (1851) 3 Mac. & G. 440, *post*, p. 524.

3. Usual Form of Discretionary Trusts

A. Trustees' Discretion

The essential feature of a discretionary trust is that the property is conveyed to trustees to be held by them on trust to apply the income or the capital or both for the benefit of the members of a class of beneficiaries in such proportions as the trustees shall, in their absolute discretion, think fit. Most discretionary trusts are concerned with distribution of income; the distribution of capital is commonly effected under a power to appoint. It used to be common to include a wider class of beneficiaries as objects of the power of appointment, and a narrower, more specific class of beneficiaries of the discretionary trusts.[11] But, since *McPhail v. Doulton*,[12] the test of certainty of beneficiaries of a discretionary trust has been assimilated to that of objects of a mere power, and the wider class can now be employed for both purposes. During the period of the trust, no individual beneficiary is entitled to any share of the property, income or capital; he receives what the trustees see fit to give him and no more.

B. The Trust Period

Provision will be made for the discretionary trust to continue for the trust period; which can be any desired period which is not in excess of the perpetuity period. Discretionary trusts provide a special situation for the application of the perpetuity rule. Since no individual beneficiary has any interest under the trust, property only vests in a beneficiary upon the exercise of the trustees' discretion in his favour; and such a vesting is void unless it takes place within the perpetuity period.[13] A discretionary trust can only exist, therefore, for the duration of the perpetuity period.

A discretionary trust will therefore be designed to terminate before the end of the period. This is normally done by postulating the "trust period" at the conclusion of which the discretionary trust will terminate, and providing for a gift over on fixed trusts which will themselves vest within the perpetuity period. Since 1964, a period of years not exceeding 80 years may be specified.[14]

C. Power to Accumulate

In many cases the income beneficiaries will not need the trust income each year, and it may be that, because the beneficiaries'

---

[11] *Re Gestetner* [1953] Ch. 672.

[12] [1971] A.C. 424; *ante*, p. 104.

[13] *Re Coleman* [1936] Ch. 521.

[14] P.A.A. 1964, s.1. A period of 125 years is proposed in Law Com. No. 251, *The Rules Against Perpetuities and Excessive Accumulations* (1998).

income tax rates are higher than those of the trust, the tax payable will be higher if the income is paid out than it would be if it were retained in the trust.[15] The trustees are commonly given a power to accumulate. Without such a power, they will be obliged to distribute the income[16]; not to any particular beneficiary, but among the beneficiaries. It was noted above[17] that such a power makes the distinction between exhaustive and non-exhaustive discretionary trusts. The trust is non-exhaustive as to the income if the income is not required to be distributed each year; and non-exhaustive as to the capital if the trustees are not obliged to distribute all the capital during the currency of the trust.

There are, however, statutory restrictions upon powers of accumulation. The permitted periods are (by the Law of Property Act 1925, s.164 as amended by the Perpetuities and Accumulations Act 1964, s.13)[18]:

(a) the life of the grantor or settlor; or

(b) a term of 21 years from the death of the grantor, settlor or testator; or

(c) the duration of the minority or respective minorities of any person or persons living or *en ventre sa mère* at the death of the grantor, settlor or testator; or

(d) the duration of the minority or respective minorities only of any person or persons who under the limitations of the instrument directing the accumulations would, for the time being, if of full age be entitled to the income directed to be accumulated; or

(e) a term of 21 years from the date of the making of the disposition; or

(f) the duration of the minority or respective minorities of any person or persons in being at that date.

The settlor may select whichever period he wishes. If he selects a period which is in excess of those permitted, the accumulation will be invalid only as to the excess. The court will select whichever period is the most appropriate to the settlor's intent.[19] At the conclusion of the period of accumulation, the income must be distributed. The Law Commission has proposed the abolition of the rule against

---

[15] Even though the rate applicable to trusts (34 per cent) is payable on the trust income: I.C.T.A. 1988, s.686. Discretionary trusts now have their own Schedule F rates on dividends; *post*, p. 220.

[16] *Re Gourju's W.T.* [1943] Ch. 24; *Re Locker's S.T.* [1977] 1 W.L.R. 1323; subject to T.A. 1925, s.31, *post*, p. 586.

[17] *ante*, p. 64.

[18] The section does not apply to a corporate settlor: *Re Dodwell & Co. Ltd's Trust Deed* [1979] Ch. 301; [1979] Conv. 319 (J.T.F.).

[19] Maudsley, *The Modern Law of Perpetuities*, p. 208; Morris & Leach, p. 272.

excessive accumulations (although not retrospectively) on the ground that it no longer fulfils any policy objective not otherwise met by the law, is too complex, and produces anomalous results.[20]

D. Power to Add to, or to Exclude from, the Class of Beneficiaries

The trustees may be given a power to add new members to the class of beneficiaries, or to exclude existing members.[21] The power to exclude members became important when Finance Act 1958[22] provided that a settlor should be liable to income tax upon the income of a settlement if the settlor or the spouse of the settlor might benefit from the income or property of the settlement. Many settlements in existence at that date included the spouse of the settlor as a member of the class of beneficiaries, and the Act provided that the settlor should not be so liable if, amongst other conditions, the power to make the payments was not exercisable after April 9, 1959. Similar situations may arise in the future. A difficulty could arise if the trustees decided to exclude a member of the class for no good reason. Arbitrary exclusion will be inconsistent with the trustees' fiduciary duties.[23] It might also be construed as an improper release of a power held in a fiduciary capacity.[24] Yet it is difficult to see how the excluded member could establish loss; because, as a member of a class of beneficiaries under a discretionary trust, he was not entitled to any interest under the trust, and would be deprived of nothing except the hope or expectation of favourable consideration by the trustees.

It may be useful also to give power to the trustees to add new members to the class. Care has to be taken to ensure that the trustees cannot include persons, such as the settlor or his spouse, whose inclusion would have damaging tax consequences.[25] The power to add new members to the class is usually done by defining a class of excepted persons, and giving to the trustees a power to include in the class of beneficiaries any person who was not a member of the excepted class. Such a provision was upheld in *Re Manisty's Settlement*,[26] concerning a power of appointment; the settlor's mother,

[20] Law Com. No. 251, *The Rules Against Perpetuities and Excessive Accumulations* (1998), para. 10.15. The proposals do not apply to charitable trusts.

[21] *Re Manisty's Settlement* [1974] Ch. 17; *Blausten v. I.R.C.* [1972] 1 Ch. 256.

[22] s.22; now I.C.T.A. 1988, s.674; *Watson v. Holland* [1985] 1 All E.R. 290. See also s.674A, added by F.A. 1989, s.109.

[23] *post*, pp. 212 *et seq.*

[24] *ante*, p. 188.

[25] Inclusion of the settlor (but probably not the settlor's spouse) would, for example, attract the "reservation of benefit" rules of inheritance tax; *post*, p. 227.

[26] [1974] Ch. 17; the power was described as an "intermediate" power; *ante*, p. 173: *Re Park* [1932] 1 Ch. 580; *Re Abraham's W.T.* [1969] 1 Ch. 463. See also *Re Hay's S.T.* [1982] 1 W.L.R. 202.

and any person who should become his widow, were added to the class of beneficiaries. The validity of trusts and powers in favour of very large classes was discussed in Chapter 3.

E. Power to Appoint Upon New Trusts

It is common to give to trustees power to appoint on further trusts, including discretionary and protective trusts, and also in favour of trustees of a foreign settlement[27] and to give them full power of delegation. This makes possible a resettlement on new trusts at the end of the accumulation period, or at any time at which it becomes advantageous for fiscal or other reasons, to do so. Such an appointment must keep within the perpetuity period as measured from the date of the original settlement,[28] and it may not provide for accumulation for any period beyond that which was available to the original settlor.[29] The periods of perpetuity and of accumulation will only start again if appointments are made to a beneficiary who resettles; but such a course would result in a double transfer of the capital, which may have damaging inheritance tax consequences.

F. Miscellaneous Administrative Provisions

Trustees of every trust need to be given the powers necessary to enable them to perform their duties. Obvious powers which they need are the power to sell, to invest, to apply income for the maintenance of child beneficiaries, to make advancements, to make payments to, and accept receipts from, guardians of children, etc. It was at one time necessary to include all such powers in the settlement. But now the basic necessary powers are given to trustees by the Trustee Acts 1925 and 2000, discussed in detail below.[30] The statutory powers can be added to, or restricted, by the terms of the trust instrument. It is usual, in the case of a discretionary trust, to give to the trustees the widest and most extensive powers. They may also be given a power to amend the trust. In terms of bulk, these administrative provisions will form the greater part of the trust instrument.

4. THE SELECTION OF TRUSTEES

The selection of the right trustees is important in the case of any trust; but particularly so in the case of a discretionary trust, where

---

[27] *post*, p. 520.

[28] *Pilkington v. I.R.C.* [1964] A.C. 612.

[29] Because the appointors cannot be given powers in excess of those available to the settlor.

[30] *post*, Chap. 20.

the trustees are given such extensive discretionary powers. The technical aspects of the matter are postponed to Chapter 17; but it may be useful here to anticipate some of that discussion. The settlor, in confiding such broad discretion, will wish to select individuals whose judgment and co-operation he respects. He can select his most trusted friends, but they may have no expertise in investment, accounting or law or taxes.[31] He may thus favour the inclusion of some professionals; who should do the job more efficiently; but they will need to be paid for their work. In a case of executorships or trusts generally, it is common to appoint a corporate trustee, usually the Executor and Trustee Company of a bank, but there may be reluctance to appoint a corporate trustee in a case of a discretionary trust, because it may be felt that the trust officer will not be in as good a position as a personal friend to exercise the broad discretions contained in a discretionary trust. It is common to select a mixture of professionals and non-professionals; and there is no legal reason why a corporation and an individual should not be trustees.

As the disposition of the property is dependent upon the discretion of the trustees, the settlor may wish to be appointed trustee in order to be able to participate in decisions on distribution. Such an appointment has, in the past, been considered unadvisable because it might be possible for him to obtain a benefit under the settlement, and, under the estate duty system, this would have had the effect of treating the trust property as being part of the settlor's estate for estate duty purposes.[32] Under the system of inheritance tax the old estate duty concept of "reservation of benefit" has been reintroduced.[33] In the context of the discretionary trust, this means that the property is treated as remaining part of the settlor's estate if he is within the class of objects.[34] If the settlor is merely a trustee it is unlikely that the "reservation of benefit" rules will apply, but it will be otherwise if he can in fact derive benefit from his trusteeship, for example by way of remuneration. In view of these uncertainties, the appointment of the settlor as trustee is best avoided.

Even if he is not a trustee, it is possible for the settlor to exert some influence upon the trustees in the way in which they exercise their discretion.[35] However, if the settlor effectively dictates the distribution of the property in such a way that the trustees exercise no independent discretion, any appointments so made will be void.[36]

---

[31] For an illustration of the dangers of appointing such persons without the inclusion of professionals, see *Turner v. Turner* [1984] Ch. 100, *post*, p. 215.

[32] *Oakes v. Stamp Duty Commissioner for N.S.W.* [1954] A.C. 51.

[33] F.A. 1986, s.102 and Sched. 20.

[34] See (1986) 83 L.S.Gaz. 3728.

[35] For example, by a "letter of wishes".

[36] *Turner v. Turner, supra.*

5. The Nature of the Interest of the Beneficiaries under a Discretionary Trust

The nature of the interest of beneficiaries under a discretionary trust raises some important theoretical and practical questions. The discussion will tie in with some of the points made earlier in the distinction between trusts and powers.[37] In that context, the present discussion will justify the recognition of the basic difference between trusts and powers as being one of obligation or discretion. But it will be clear that the "duty" concept in the case of discretionary trusts is a very different duty from that recognised in the case of fixed trusts.[38]

A. Exhaustive and Non-exhaustive Discretionary Trusts

If the trustees are required to distribute the whole of the income, the discretionary trust is exhaustive. Where, as in the case of most modern discretionary trusts, the trustees may apply the income for some purposes other than distribution among the beneficiaries, as where there is a power to accumulate income not so applied, there is a non-exhaustive discretionary trust. The rights of the beneficiaries are more complex in the case of a non-exhaustive discretionary trust. For the income beneficiaries cannot argue that they are, as a group, *entitled* to the income. The income may be accumulated in whole or in part and added to the capital.

B. The Nature of the Interest of the Beneficiaries

i. Individual Beneficiaries. In the case of a fixed trust, we saw that the beneficiary's interest is regarded as proprietary. He is the owner of an equitable interest under the trust. This is not so in the case of a beneficiary under a discretionary trust. He is dependent upon the exercise by the trustees of their power of selection in his favour.[39] This point was crucial to the success of discretionary trusts in the estate duty days; because estate duty was payable when property "passed" on a death,[40] as on the death of a life tenant.[41] A discretionary beneficiary could not be said to be entitled to any quantifiable share. He therefore owned no part of the property and

---

[37] *ante*, p. 62.
[38] (1976) 54 C.B.R. 229 (M. Cullity); [1970] A.S.C.L. 187 (J. Davies); (1974) 37 M.L.R. 643 (Y. Grbich).
[39] He can renounce his position as class member; *Re Gulbenkian's Settlement (No. 2)* [1970] Ch. 408.
[40] F.A. 1894, s.2.
[41] *Earl Cowley v. I.R.C.* [1899] A.C. 198.

no property passed on his death. The position is similar under the inheritance tax system. As we will see, the death of a discretionary beneficiary is not an event upon which the trust fund is taxable. Inheritance tax is, however, payable on a payment to a beneficiary and on certain other occasions.[42]

A sole member of a class of discretionary beneficiaries cannot claim entitlement to the income so long as there is a possibility that another member could come into existence.[43] The trust fund may be regarded as financial resources of a sole beneficiary for the purpose of an order for financial provision (in favour of or against the beneficiary) under section 25 of the Matrimonial Causes Act 1973, provided the order would not put improper pressure on the trustees in the exercise of their discretion.[44]

ii. The Class. Whether or not the class of beneficiaries is properly regarded as the owner is a different matter. We have seen that a sole beneficiary of a discretionary trust and the beneficiaries entitled upon the determination of the trust on his death, may, if all are adult and under no disability, call for the capital to be paid over to them, or may validly assign to a third party who will become the beneficiary.[45]

Cases on estate duty have indicated that a class of beneficiaries may not hold a proprietary interest which "passes" for estate duty purposes. "Two or more persons," said Lord Reid, "cannot have a single right unless they hold it jointly or in common. But clearly objects of a discretionary trust do not have that: they have individual rights, they are in competition with each other and what the trustees give to one is his alone." This was said in *Gartside v. I.R.C.*[46] which was a case of a non-exhaustive discretionary trust, but in *Re Weir's Settlement*[47] and *Sainsbury v. I.R.C.*[48] the same analysis was applied to exhaustive discretionary trusts. Lord Reid's rejection of the "group or class" interest concept "seems equally applicable, whether the trust is exhaustive or not exhaustive."[49] The question has ceased to be of significance in relation to estate duty, but is relevant to determine where the beneficial interest is in a discretionary trust; and whether the class of beneficiaries, all being adult

---

[42] *post*, Chap. 9.
[43] *Re Trafford's Settlement* [1985] Ch. 32 (capital transfer tax). See also *Figg v. Clarke (Inspector of Taxes)* [1997] 1 W.L.R. 603 (capital gains tax).
[44] *Browne v. Browne* [1989] 1 F.L.R. 291 (order against wife who was sole beneficiary); *J. v. J. (C. Intervening) (Minors: Financial Provision)* [1989] Fam. 29 (maintenance of two children, the only beneficiaries, who would become absolutely entitled at majority).
[45] *Green v. Spicer* (1830) 1 Russ. & My. 395; *Re Smith* [1928] Ch. 915.
[46] [1968] A.C. 553 at 605–606.
[47] [1969] 1 Ch. 657, reversed on a different point [1971] Ch. 145.
[48] [1970] Ch. 712.
[49] [1970] Ch. 712 at 724, *per* Ungoed-Thomas J.

and under no disability, is able to call for a transfer of the legal title and to terminate the trust. It is submitted that the beneficial ownership should be in all those persons in whose favour the discretion may be exercised, including the beneficiaries of an accumulation provision under a non-exhaustive trust; and that, on the principle of *Re Smith*,[50] they should be able to terminate the trust in appropriate circumstances, if all adult and under no disability.[51]

C. Powers and Duties

It may be useful at this stage to recapitulate some of the points, discussed above,[52] in connection with the nature of rights, duties and discretions in the context of trusts and powers. It will be seen that the basic distinction between trusts and powers continues to be that between obligations and discretions; but it is important to be able to identify what the trustees' duty is in the case of a discretionary trust. There are various contexts in which the question of the distinction between trusts and powers arises.

i. Fixed Trust. At one end of the spectrum is the case of trustees of a fixed trust. This is clearly an obligation upon the trustees. Having once accepted the trusteeship, they have no choice of whether or not to perform the trust. They are obliged to do so; they can be required by the court to perform, and are personally liable for breach. Some of the trustees' duties will require the exercise of a discretion in their performance. Thus, trustees are under a duty to invest;[53] but, they will of course exercise a discretion in the selection of investments. The trustees' duty may be seen as a correlative of the beneficiaries' rights. The position is wholly different from that at the other end of the spectrum; that of the donee of a power held in a non-fiduciary capacity. As will be seen, the question whether to exercise such a power is wholly a matter of the donee's discretion.

ii. Trust with a Power of Selection. We have seen that there are cases in which the trustees hold property upon trust for a specified group of persons, subject to a power to select the shares and proportions in which those persons shall take. Thus in *Burrough v. Philcox*[54] the disposition was "among my nephews and nieces, or their

---

[50] [1928] Ch. 915; *supra*; *Saunders v. Vautier* (1841) 4 Beav. 115, affirmed Cr. & Ph. 240. But see Pettit, p. 71, suggesting that the beneficial interest is in suspense until the discretion is exercised.

[51] This will not be possible unless all members are ascertainable, which may not be the case since *McPhail v. Doulton* [1971] A.C. 424.

[52] *ante*, p. 62.

[53] *post*, p. 532.

[54] (1840) 5 My. & Cr. 72.

children, either all to one or to as many of them as my surviving child shall think proper." We saw that, in the absence of an appointment being made, the nieces and nephews took in equal shares. The nieces and nephews thus held a vested interest under the trust, subject to divestment upon an appointment being made. Their situation is exactly the same as it would have been if the testamentary provisions had given to a donee a power to appoint, and in default of appointment to my nephews and nieces in equal shares. Those entitled in default are treated as owners in equity subject to divestment on the exercise of the power.[55] The trust in their favour is a fixed trust.[56] The division into equal shares makes it necessary to identify each member, and to know how many there are. This case is the same as that of a fixed trust; but the beneficiaries' interests are subject to defeasance. The trustee's duty to the beneficiaries is clear. It is a question of construction whether the instrument creates such a trust or creates a discretionary trust, discussed below.

iii. Discretionary Trusts: Exhaustive and Non-exhaustive. A discretionary trust may require the trustees to distribute all the income; or it may give to the trustees a power to accumulate for a period allowed by law. Similarly, it may require the trustees to dispose of the capital during the trust period, or it may provide for a gift over of the assets of the trust at the end of the trust period. Whether the trust is exhaustive or non-exhaustive, an individual beneficiary is not regarded as having any proprietary interest in the trust property.[57] If the trust is exhaustive, there is authority to say the class as a whole, if adult and under no disability, can terminate the trust.[58]

This raises the question: what is the trustee's duty? Clearly, it is different from the case of a fixed trust. Where are the beneficiary's correlative rights? This situation does not fit neatly into the right-duty correlation. The beneficiary has no proprietary rights. Is it correct to describe the situation as a trust; which, by definition, involves a duty? The answer, it is submitted, is: yes; this is a trust, and it involves a duty, although different from that in the case of a fixed trust.

The duty here is to exercise the discretion. In the case of an exhaustive discretionary trust, a selection must be made; whereas if the discretionary trust is non-exhaustive, the discretion may be exercised by deciding to accumulate. As Harris argued[59] persuasively,

---

[55] *Re Brooks' S.T.* [1939] Ch. 993 at 997.
[56] And thus not affected by the decision in *McPhail v. Doulton* [1971] A.C. 424, *ante*, p. 104. See (1982) 98 L.Q.R. 551 (C. Emery).
[57] *ante*, p. 209.
[58] *Re Smith* [1928] Ch. 915; *Re Nelson* [1928] Ch. 920n.; *ante*, p. 211.
[59] (1971) 87 L.Q.R. 231.

"the discretionary trust in fact depends on a rule-concept of duty, with no such necessity for correlative rights." Herein is the trustee's duty in a discretionary trust; and here is the point of distinction between a discretionary trust and a mere power. Each member of the class of beneficiaries under a discretionary trust has standing to sue in order to have the trustees' duty performed. Not that such a beneficiary will necessarily benefit by the performance of the trustees' duty; as it is a duty, not to pay to that beneficiary, but to exercise their discretion as described above.

In *Re Locker's Settlement*,[60] the terms of an exhaustive discretionary trust required the trustees to pay, divide and apply the income for charitable purposes or among the class of beneficiaries as the trustees "shall in their absolute discretion determine." Because of subsequent expressions of wishes by the settlor, the trustees failed to make distributions of income from 1965 to 1968. The question arose in 1975 what should be done with that income, and particularly whether the trustees' discretion had expired.

Goulding J. held that the discretion still continued, and that the trustees should apply their discretion in the distribution of the money among those who were members of the class of beneficiaries in the relevant years. In discussing the question of the trustees' duty and the court's power to enforce the exercise of the discretion, he said,[61] "it is common ground that it was the duty of the trustees to distribute the trust income within a reasonable time. ... A court of equity, where the trustees have failed to discharge their duty of prompt discretionary distribution of income, is concerned to make them, as owners of the trust assets at law, dispose of them in accordance with the requirements of conscience. ... " If the trustees refuse to perform their duty, the court can itself execute the trust—"by appointing new trustees, or by authorising or directing representative persons of the classes of beneficiaries to prepare a scheme for distribution, or even, should the proper basis for distribution appear, by itself directing the trustees so to distribute."[62] The trustees in *Locker*,[63] as is usual in these cases,[64] were ready and willing to perform, and did so.

The point is that the trustees under these circumstances are under a duty to distribute. That is an obligation which is subject to enforcement by the court in one of the ways stated. *Locker*[65] was a case of

[60] [1977] 1 W.L.R. 1323; *Re Gourju's W.T.* [1943] Ch. 241; *McPhail v. Doulton* [1971] A.C. 424.

[61] [1977] 1 W.L.R. 1323 at 1325.

[62] *ibid.* at 1325, quoting Lord Wilberforce in *McPhail v. Doulton* [1971] A.C. 424 at 457.

[63] *supra.*

[64] As pointed out by Lord Wilberforce at 449.

[65] *supra.*

an exhaustive discretionary trust; though the individuals in the class of beneficiaries were not, as a class, entitled to the whole of the income, because the trustees could make payments to charity. The duty and obligation of the trustees, however, is the same in the case of a non-exhaustive discretionary trust as in *McPhail v. Doulton*[66] itself. The difference is that in a non-exhaustive trust the duty to exercise the discretion can be satisfied by deciding to accumulate.

iv. Powers Held as Trustee. Fiduciary Powers.[67]

The situation is quite different where the trustees, as one of the terms of the trust instrument, are given a power of appointment. Here there is no duty to exercise; and the court will not order the trustee to exercise the discretion. Typical is *Re Allen Meyrick's Trust*[68] where:

> A will gave property to trustees to hold "upon trust that they may apply the income thereof in their absolute discretion for the maintenance of my said husband and subject to the exercise of their discretion on trust for my two godchildren ... in equal shares absolutely." Various difficulties arose. The husband was an undischarged bankrupt. Some of the money was applied in paying the rent and certain debts. The trustees could not agree on the disposal of other income, and attempted to surrender their discretion to the court.

The court refused to accept, and was willing only to hear applications for directions in particular circumstances as they arose. Nor were the trustees ordered to exercise their discretion. The trust here was in favour of the godchildren, subject to the overriding power. If the trustees could not reach unanimity as to the exercise of the power, the godchildren became entitled.

This is not, of course, to say that the trustees in this situation are not subject to duties in relation to the exercise of the power. They hold the power in a fiduciary capacity, and are subject to the highest fiduciary duties in the way in which they make their decision. They must do more than refrain from acting capriciously. Their duty is to consider periodically whether to exercise the power, and to consider the range of objects in such manner as will enable them to carry out their fiduciary duties. If they decide to exercise the power they must, of course, keep within its terms; they must exercise it in a responsible manner according to its purpose and consider the appropriateness of individual appointments.[69] The court will intervene if they

---

[66] *supra.*

[67] See Chap. 6.

[68] [1966] 1 W.L.R. 499.

[69] *Re Hay's S.T.* [1982] 1 W.L.R. 202; [1982] Conv. 432 (A. Grubb). These duties, which were laid down in *McPhail v. Doulton* [1971] A.C. 424, *Re Gestetner* [1953] Ch. 672, and *Re Gulbenkian's S.T.* [1970] A.C. 508, are not necessarily exhaustive.

exceed their powers or act capriciously.[70] Furthermore, they must not release the power, nor delegate it without authority.[71] They must appreciate that the discretion is theirs and not that of the settlor. If they merely obey the settlor's instructions without any independent consideration, they will be in breach of the duties described above, and any appointment made in such circumstances will be void.[72] These duties stem from the fact that the power is fiduciary; not from any duty to exercise the power. If they decide not to do so, the court will not interfere. It has been held, however, that the court must step in where a fiduciary power is left with no-one to exercise it.[73] In such a case the court can adopt any of the methods indicated by Lord Wilberforce in *McPhail v Doulton*[74] in the context of discretionary trusts, *i.e.* it may appoint new trustees, direct the beneficiaries to prepare a scheme of distribution, or itself direct a distribution.[75]

v. Powers Held in a Non-fiduciary Capacity. As is seen in Chapter 6, no duty is imposed upon a donee who holds a power in a non-fiduciary capacity. If a grandparent leaves property on trust for his grandchildren, and gives his son a power to appoint in favour of charity, the son is under no duty to appoint or even to consider the rival claims of charity or the grandchildren. He is, of course, if he makes an appointment, required to keep within the terms of the power, and to avoid exercising the power for an improper purpose.

vi. The Rule of Certainty in Ascertaining Beneficiaries or Objects. Reference should be made to Chapter 3, where this aspect of discretionary trusts is fully discussed.

vii. Discretionary Trusts Since 1974. Because of the change in tax policy, discretionary trusts of this type became unpopular in tax planning circles. Such trusts created after March 1974 suffer higher rates of tax than those existing before the capital transfer tax legislation came into operation.[76] Since the introduction of inheritance tax,

---

[70] *McPhail v. Doulton* [1971] A.C. 424 at 456–457.

[71] *Re Hay's S.T., supra.*

[72] *Turner v. Turner* [1984] Ch. 100.

[73] *Mettoy Pension Trustees Ltd v. Evans* [1990] 1 W.L.R. 1587 (fiduciary powers of company directors ceased on appointment of liquidator, but could not be exercised by liquidator or receiver because of conflict of duties); (1991) 107 L.Q.R. 214 (S. Gardner); [1991] Conv. 364 (J. Martin).

[74] *supra.*

[75] *Mettoy Pension Trustees Ltd v. Evans, supra. Re Manisty's Settlement* [1974] Ch. 17, suggested that the only remedy was the appointment of new trustees, but *Klug v. Klug* [1918] 2 Ch. 67, *post*, p. 527, was not there cited.

[76] Relief was given on distributions before April 1983 from pre-1974 discretionary trusts; F.A. 1975, Sched. 5, para. 15; F.A. (No. 2) 1979, s.23(1)(*b*).

we have seen that discretionary trusts have suffered further by reason of their exclusion from the "potentially exempt transfer" regime.[77] The lifetime creation of such trusts is, therefore, taxable even if the settlor survives a further seven years. For this reason few discretionary trusts of substantial size (other than "offshore" trusts) are likely to be created under the present tax system,[78] although more modest discretionary trusts falling within the settlor's inheritance tax "nil rate band"[79] may still be attractive.

[77] *ante*, p. 225.

[78] Unless they are within the class of discretionary trusts which are given preferential treatment, *e.g.* accumulation and maintenance trusts, *post*, p. 233.

[79] *post*, p. 233. The reduction of the maximum lifetime rate to 20 per cent by F.A. 1988 alleviates the position to some extent.

CHAPTER 9

TAXATION AND TRUSTS[1]

1. ESTATE AND TAX PLANNING

THE most significant factor in the lifetime creation of trusts has been the avoidance of taxation. A wealthy person may benefit the family by making gifts to them, and then leave property to them by will. But tax legislation imposes higher rates on larger accumulations of property, and this wealthy person will seek ways of conferring benefits on the family and at the same time reducing tax liability. The tax payable by 10 people on incomes of £5,000 each is less in total than that payable by one person with an income of £50,000. Similarly, tax on capital is at its highest in large concentrations. More details of the income, and especially of the capital tax system, will be given below. The point here is that a wealthy person can best preserve the family fortune by sharing out, and that this has commonly been done by creating lifetime trusts. This tax planning of an estate is one of the most important and sophisticated functions of trust lawyers.

Until comparatively recently the courts in determining the effectiveness of any scheme of tax avoidance applied the principle laid down by Lord Tomlin in *I.R.C. v. Duke of Westminster*[2]: "every man is entitled if he can to order his affairs so that the tax attaching

---

[1] See Thomas, *Taxation and Trusts*; Shipwright, *Trusts and U.K. Taxation* (2nd ed.); Maudsley and Burn, *Trusts and Trustees*; *Cases and Materials* (5th ed.), Part 3; Mellows, *Taxation for Executors and Trustees* (3rd ed.); Foster, *Inheritance Tax*; Whiteman, *Capital Gains Tax* (4th ed.); Whiteman, *Income Tax* (3rd ed.).

[2] [1936] A.C. 1. The principle is confirmed in H.C.Deb., Vol. 226, col. 765 (1993).

under the appropriate Acts is less than it otherwise would be."[3] But starting in *W. T. Ramsay v. I.R.C.*,[4] the House of Lords began to elaborate a new and much more restrictive principle to apply in dealing with questions of the effectiveness of complex tax avoidance schemes. Where there occurs a pre-ordained series of transactions (or a single composite transaction) designed to reduce tax payable by a particular taxpayer the court is free to disregard any of those transactions if they are inserted for no good commercial purposes other than the reduction of tax. The transactions will be treated as a single composite whole and taxed accordingly. This principle is "founded on a broad purposive interpretation, giving effect to the intention of Parliament".[5] It applies to the creation and manipulation of trusts as well as to commercial and corporate dealings.[6]

As the circumstances of each individual differ, so each situation needs individual treatment. The estate- or tax-planner, with the assistance of accountants and other specialists, will present to the client various possible solutions, indicating the tax implications of each. The client must then decide how much to give away immediately and irrevocably, and to whom; and how much to keep; and, in days of inflation, many people will hesitate before making gifts, and thereby running the risk of leaving themselves short of capital in their old age. What is kept will be disposed of by will, and a testamentary trust may be created. Those whose fortunes are insufficient to create tax problems will not be concerned with lifetime tax planning; but may, again, create testamentary trusts on their deaths.

2. THE TAX STRUCTURE

To explain how best to minimise liability to tax, it is essential to explain the tax system in detail. There is no room to do that here, and only a few highlights can be given. It is in any case dangerous, in a book of this nature, to include too much detail; for each annual Budget may be expected to make some changes in the rates; and, if there is a change of Government, the policy behind the tax system

---

[3] [1936] A.C. 1 at 19. But these observations "have ceased to be canonical as to the consequence of a tax avoidance scheme"; *I.R.C. v. McGuckian* [1997] 1 W.L.R. 991 at 1000.

[4] [1982] A.C. 300. See also *I.R.C. v. Burmah Oil Co. Ltd* (1981) 54 T.C. 200; *Furness v. Dawson* [1984] A.C. 474; *Craven (Inspector of Taxes) v. White* [1989] A.C. 398 (where the House of Lords refused to extend this principle); *Ensign Tankers (Leasing) Ltd v. Stokes* [1992] 1 A.C. 655; *Moodie v. I.R.C.* [1993] 1 W.L.R. 266; *I.R.C. v. McGuckian* [1997] 1 W.L.R. 991; *Macniven (H.M. Inspector of Taxes) v. Westmoreland Investments Ltd* [2001] 2 W.L.R. 377.

[5] *I.R.C. v. McGuckian, supra*, at 1000.

[6] *I.R.C. v. Fitzwilliam* [1993] 1 W.L.R. 1189 (but *Ramsay* principle did not apply on facts, Lord Templeman dissenting); [1994] Conv. 67 (J. Kirkbride).

also changes. Tax policy is often dictated more by political philosophy than by the search for a system which is rational and just.

The greatest revenue raiser is income tax. The net receipts from capital taxes have been disappointingly small.[7] A Government in need of money has therefore an interest in keeping income tax rates high; though the logic of the matter would seem to be that you should pay lower taxes on the money that you work for, than on inheritances. There was a substantial argument to the effect that income tax rates, reaching up to 83 per cent,[8] resulted in the stifling of initiative and enterprise. The Conservative Government in 1979[9] heeded that argument and reduced the top rate to 60 per cent, and it has since been reduced to 40 per cent.[10] More recently, reductions have been made to the basic and starting rates rather than the top rate. The tax system has hitherto been regarded not only as a revenue raiser, but also as a means of promoting the social, economic and political philosophy of the Government.

A. Income Tax

Tax is chargeable upon an individual's taxable income[11] at the rates laid down annually in the Finance Act. Currently the first £1,520 of taxable income (savings and earned) is subject to the starting rate of 10 per cent. The basic rate of 22 per cent is then payable on taxable earned income above £1,520 and up to £28,400, with a rate of 20 per cent payable on savings income. Thereafter the rate is 40 per cent for savings and earned income.[12] A special rate of 10 per cent, or 32.5 per cent in the case of higher-rate taxpayers, is payable on UK dividends. There are a number of allowances and reliefs to which individuals are entitled.

We are concerned, however, with the taxation of trusts. Trustees are not individuals for income tax purposes. Trusts as such therefore enjoy no personal allowances. Nor does the starting rate of 10 per cent apply.[13] The income of a trust is chargeable at the basic rate, and the trustees are assessable.[14] In a wider range of circumstances

---

[7] In 1997/98 income tax raised 65.43 per cent of direct taxation, capital gains tax 1.2 per cent and inheritance tax 1.4 per cent; Whitehouse, *Revenue Law, Principles and Practice* (17th ed.). Customs and Excise duties raised over half of all tax revenue.

[8] On incomes over £21,000 in 1979.

[9] F. (No. 2) A. 1979, s.5.

[10] F.A. 1988, s.24(1).

[11] I.C.T.A. 1988, s.835; and means income calculated in accordance with Scheds. A–F, I.C.T.A. 1988, ss.15–20. Schedules B and C have been abolished.

[12] F.A. 2000, ss.31, 32.

[13] F.A. 1992, s.9(2).

[14] There is no specific statutory provision. The higher rates do not apply to trustees because they are not "individuals"; I.C.T.A. 1988, s.1(2). See Maudsley and Burn, *Trusts and Trustees: Cases and Materials* (5th ed.), p. 553; (1991) 5 *Trust Law International*, 143 (M. Jacobs).

the income arising under a trust may be treated as the settlor's income.[15] The trustees need take no action in respect of dividend income from most stock exchange investments which is paid net of the Schedule F ordinary rate payable on UK dividends (currently 10 per cent). The beneficiary who is entitled to the income is responsible for the payment of any Schedule F upper rate tax (currently 32.5 per cent) which may be due; and it is often convenient to arrange for the dividends to be paid direct to him. The trustees will, however, need to deduct and account for income tax which is due on any income of the trust which has been received without deduction of tax, such as income from land or profits if they carry on a trade, and also for the rate applicable to trusts (currently 34 per cent) which becomes due in the case of the income of a trust where there is no person currently entitled to the income.[16]

With such a trust, the income may either be paid out or, if the trust contains such a power, it may be accumulated. If it is accumulated, there is no liability beyond the rate applicable to trusts (34 per cent). Where the income is paid to or for the benefit of a beneficiary, the ultimate tax liability is dependent upon the beneficiary's tax situation.[17] He is treated as having received the value of the payment grossed up to reflect the rate applicable to trusts.[18] If the beneficiary's taxable income is in excess of £32,785, he will be liable to make up the difference between the tax already paid (34 per cent) and the tax due at his marginal rate (40 per cent). On the other hand, if his other income does not exhaust his allowances and reliefs and the various rates below 34 per cent, he may claim a repayment of an appropriate amount on producing to the Revenue the trustees' certificate of deduction of tax. It will thus be seen that income tax may be saved if the trustees have a discretion as to the distribution of income, and use it to make payments to those on low incomes whose tax rate is lower than the trust's. Thus, £66 of trust income after tax at 34 per cent, if paid to a beneficiary whose taxable income, including the payment, is £35,000, will bear another £6 in tax; but if paid to a child with no income, the child would get a rebate of £34.[19] There is, of course, no choice where the beneficiaries are entitled to

---

[15] I.C.T.A. 1988, Part XV. See *Watson v. Holland* [1985] 1 All E.R. 290. These provisions are intended to prevent and penalise tax avoidance.

[16] I.C.T.A. 1988, s.686, as amended. The Schedule F trust rate on dividends is 25 per cent. This includes income of a disretionary trust or an accumulation and maintenance trust; *post*, p. 231. The tax is charged on the whole income of the trust, after deducting expenses properly chargeable to income under the general law; *Carver v. Duncan (Inspector of Taxes)* [1985] A.C. 1082.

[17] But where the payment is in favour of the unmarried child under 18 of the settlor, the income is treated as that of the settlor: I.C.T.A. 1988, s.663 (similarly where the income is retained in a bare trust for the settlor's child; F.A. 1999, s.64); *post*, p. 234.

[18] I.C.T.A. 1988, s.687, as amended.

[19] The child is entitled to the personal allowance of £4,385; I.C.T.A. 1988, s.257. It is no longer possible to obtain a rebate in respect of the 10 per cent dividend rate.

the income or a specified share. Moreover none of the above consequences apply if the sum as received by the beneficiary is capital in his hands, for example where it is paid pursuant to a power of appointment restricted to capital or out of accumulated income.[20]

B. Capital Gains Tax

Capital gains tax was introduced by the Finance Act 1965, and originally imposed at a rate of 30 per cent upon the gains accruing upon the disposal of an asset. The Finance Act 1988 wrought significant changes in the tax. The position is now governed by the consolidating Taxation of Chargeable Gains Act 1992. The tax on individuals is charged at income tax rates on savings (20 and 40 per cent).[21] In many cases the gain accruing on a disposal of an asset is computed as though the disposer's acquisition cost had been the market value of the asset on March 31, 1982.[22] Thus gains attributable to a period of ownership prior to the 1982 date escape tax.[23] Capital gains tax is payable upon a sale, exchange or gift.[24] The tax is not payable on death, though the deceased's property is deemed to be acquired by his personal representatives on his death at a consideration equal to its then market value.[25] This generally involves a "tax-free uplift" in the notional acquisition cost of the assets in question, since their market value at death is usually greater than the acquisition cost enjoyed by the deceased. When the personal representatives pass the assets to the legatee[26] no disposal is deemed to occur and the legatee acquires the assets with an acquisition cost equal to that of the personal representatives. Finally, capital gains tax is payable where disposals are deemed to occur, as where a capital sum is derived from an asset.[27]

There are many exemptions from liability to capital gains tax, the most important being an annual exemption of gains of £7,200 for individuals and £3,600 for a trust,[28] the taxpayer's main or only residence,[29] a chattel worth less than £6,000[30] and dated gilt-edged

---

[20] I.C.T.A. 1988, s.687(1). See also *Stevenson (Inspector of Taxes) v. Wishart* [1987] 1 W.L.R. 1204.

[21] T.C.G.A. 1992, s.4, as amended. The income tax starting rate of 10 per cent applies to capital gains tax only where that rate band has not been fully used for income tax; F.A. 2000, s.37. The rate for trusts is 34 per cent; T.C.G.A. 1992, s.4 (IAA).

[22] *ibid.* s.35. The date is that of the introduction of indexation allowance.

[23] This is not so in all cases; s.35(3).

[24] Relief on gifts was withdrawn (with exceptions) by F.A. 1989, s.124.

[25] T.C.G.A. 1992, s.62.

[26] *ibid.* Defined in s.64(2) to include "any person taking under a testamentary disposition or on an intestacy or partial intestacy, whether he takes beneficially or as trustee . . . "

[27] *ibid.* ss.22–24. See also *Zim Properties v. Proctor* [1985] S.T.C. 90.

[28] *ibid.* s.3, Sched. 1; Capital Gains Tax (Annual Exempt Amount) Order 2000 (S.I. 2000 No. 808). The exemptions are index-linked.

[29] *ibid.* s.222.

[30] *ibid.* s.262.

securities.[31] From April 1998 taper relief replaced the indexation allowance.[32]

The settlor will be liable to capital gains tax on making the settlement since this is a disposal even where the settlor declares himself trustee.[33] Under the settlement, the trustees will be affected in two quite different ways.[34] First, in relation to the disposition of assets of the trust. On a disposal, the trustees are liable to tax on gains, as individuals would be.[35] Currently the rate of tax is 34 per cent.[36] This situation normally arises where trustees switch investments in the ordinary course of administration of the trust. There is no liability, however, on the trustees of a trust where the majority of the trustees are resident abroad, and the administration of the trust is carried on abroad; liability is imposed on resident beneficiaries in relation to their interests under the trust. In certain circumstances gains of a non-resident trust may be attributed to beneficiaries for the purposes of liability.[37]

Secondly, there are certain occasions on which a disposal is deemed to have been made. Disposals are deemed to be made on various occasions, but the only one in this context on which tax is chargeable is that on which a person becomes absolutely entitled against the trustee[38] as, for example, where the beneficiary becomes absolutely entitled upon fulfilling a condition, such as majority, or where an advancement is made to a beneficiary. As originally enacted, tax was chargeable on the death of a life tenant, but that was changed by the Finance Act 1971[39] to bring the settlement provisions in line with the death rule for free estates.

C. Inheritance Tax

Inheritance tax is a modified version of its predecessor, capital transfer tax. Estate duty was replaced by capital transfer tax by the Finance Act 1975,[40] with effect from March 26, 1974. This was part

---

[31] T.C.G.A. 1992, s.115.

[32] *ibid.* ss.2A, 53 (IA).

[33] *ibid.* s.70. See also s.77.

[34] See generally (1991) 88/17 L.S.Gaz. 24 (M. Hutton); (1991) 5 *Trust Law International* 143 (M. Jacobs) and 152 (J. Brown).

[35] Unless the gains are chargeable on the settlor because he has an interest in the settlement; T.C.G.A. 1992, s.77.

[36] *ante*, p. 221, n. 21.

[37] T.C.G.A. 1992, s.87.

[38] *ibid.* s.71. See *Jenkins (Inspector of Taxes) v. Brown* [1989] 1 W.L.R. 1163; *Swires (Inspector of Taxes) v. Renton* [1991] S.T.C. 490; *Figg v. Clarke (Inspector of Taxes)* [1997] 1 W.L.R. 603 (beneficiaries not absolutely entitled if birth of further class member possible, however unlikely). A deemed disposal, whether or not tax is charged, has the effect of establishing the acquisition value in the hands of the recipient.

[39] See now T.C.G.A. 1992, s.72.

[40] The provisions are now consolidated by the Inheritance Tax Act 1984, hereafter referred to as I.H.T.A. 1984.

of a complete reorganisation of the structure of the taxation of capital, which was extended to lifetime gifts. A wealth tax, in the form of an annual tax on ownership of assets, was planned in 1974, but was never introduced. The application of capital transfer tax to lifetime gifts was largely removed by the Finance Act 1986, in which the tax was renamed as inheritance tax.

i. Estate Duty. Before March 26, 1974, estate duty was the only tax on private capital. It was a death tax only, and payable upon property passing on a death.[41] It could therefore be avoided by disposing of property before death; save that transfers made within seven years before death were subject to the tax.[42]

The disposal would often be by the lifetime creation of a trust. The settlor would wish to avoid estate duty, not only on his death, but also upon the deaths of the beneficiaries. It was held that estate duty was payable upon the whole capital of a trust upon the death of a life tenant, or of the holder of some other limited interest.[43] The members of a class of beneficiaries of a discretionary trust owned no interest, however, in the fund[44]; they had no more than a hope that the trustees' discretion would be exercised in their favour. It was possible, therefore, to avoid liability to estate duty, until 1969, on the death of the settlor and of any of the beneficiaries by creating a discretionary trust at least seven years before the death of the settlor.[45] No wonder that the tax was called a "voluntary tax." The Finance Act 1969 imposed a charge upon the death of any beneficiary who had received payments of income in the past seven years.[46] The charge was on a portion of the capital equivalent to the share of the income received by the deceased during the "relevant" period. This system had little time to work, and would not in any case have been very effective because the trustees of a discretionary trust could pay the income to those whom they judged least likely to die in the near future; and so long as the income was thus disposed of, there was no objection to making capital payments to the old and sick beneficiaries.[47]

ii. Capital Transfer Tax. In a White Paper on Capital Transfer Tax[48] and a Green Paper on Wealth Tax,[49] the Labour Government in 1974 announced its intention of imposing both taxes. The policy

---

[41] F.A. 1894, ss.1, 2.
[42] F.A. 1968, s.35.
[43] *Cowley (Earl) v. I.R.C.* [1899] A.C. 198.
[44] Eventually so decided in *Gartside v. I.R.C.* [1968] A.C. 553; *ante*, p. 210.
[45] See *Pearson v. I.R.C.* [1980] Ch. 1, *per* Templeman L.J. at 25.
[46] ss.36, 37.
[47] See F.A. 1969, s.37(3)(*b*).
[48] Cmnd. No. 5705 of 1974.
[49] *ibid.*

was to effect a levelling of wealth[50]; estate duty, with all its loop-holes, had conspicuously failed to do so. Capital transfer tax was a tax on capital transfers, whether during life or on death, and was planned to tax family capital, whether or not settled, at least once a generation. The Wealth Tax would go further, and impose a tax annually on capital. The imposition of a wealth tax would take some time, and the Government appreciated that it needed to be preceded by capital transfer tax.

Capital transfer tax in its original form was a cumulative tax applying to all transfers of value made by an individual after March 26, 1974 until the final transfer on death. Rates were progressive, and those chargeable on death (or on transfers within three years of death) were double those chargeable on lifetime transfers. The tax was modified by subsequent Conservative Governments, in partic-ular by alleviating the cumulation principle. Instead of cumulating all transfers (made after March 26, 1974), only those made within the previous 10 years had to be cumulated, the figure finally being reduced to seven years.[51] The rates of tax being progressive, these amendments were beneficial to the transferor. Further substantial modifications were made by the Finance Act 1986, which renamed the tax as inheritance tax, to which we now turn.

ii. Inheritance Tax. The most significant changes brought about by the 1986 Act were the introduction of the "potentially exempt transfer" and the reintroduction of the estate duty principle of "res-ervation of benefit." These are explained in the outline of inher-itance tax which follows.

The central concept of inheritance tax is the transfer of value, which may be chargeable, exempt or potentially exempt.[52] There is a transfer of value where a person makes a disposition as a result of which the value of his estate immediately after the disposition is less than it would have been but for the transfer, and the value trans-ferred is the amount by which the estate is the less.[53] On a death, the deceased is treated as making a transfer of value of the whole of his estate immediately before the death.[54] There are special rules relat-ing to settled property,[55] which will be examined below, and a number of exemptions and reliefs. The most important exemptions relate to transfers of any amount between spouses, whether in the

---

[50] "The Government is committed to use the taxation system to promote greater social and economic equality. This requires a redistribution of wealth as well as income." Preface to Green Paper.

[51] F.A. 1986, s.101.

[52] I.H.T.A. 1984, ss.1, 2.

[53] *ibid.* s.3. It may include an omission to claim an entitlement: s.3(3).

[54] *ibid.* s.4.

[55] *ibid.* Pt. III.

lifetime or on death,[56] certain foreign property,[57] and certain personal exemptions.[58] Other reliefs and exemptions relate to situations which were familiar with estate duty, and include gifts to charities, works of art, agricultural or business property, and woodlands. They cannot be examined here.

The exemptions referred to above may be described as substantive exemptions, to distinguish them from the potentially exempt transfer, introduced by the Finance Act 1986.[59] A lifetime transfer by an individual made on or after March 18, 1986 is potentially exempt. As in the days of estate duty, it becomes chargeable if the transferor does not survive for seven years. If he dies within three years, the rates are those chargeable on a death. If he dies between three and seven years from the transfer, there is a taper relief on a sliding scale.[60] In certain exceptional cases, in particular the creation of a discretionary trust, a lifetime disposition is *immediately* chargeable,[61] although at half the rates applicable on death.[62] If the settlor dies within seven years, the rates are increased as described above.

In the case of a lifetime transfer which is either initially chargeable or which becomes so by reason of death within seven years, and in the case of a transfer on death, the rates of tax are affected by any chargeable transfers within the previous seven years, which must be cumulated.[63] No tax will, however, be payable if the transfer falls within the "nil rate band," which stands at £234,000 at the time of writing.[64] Thereafter the rate is 40 per cent if the transfer was on death or within three years of death, and 20 per cent in the case of an initially chargeable lifetime transfer. As mentioned above, there is a sliding scale applicable to a potentially exempt transfer which becomes chargeable.[65]

In the case of an initially chargeable lifetime transfer, the tax may be paid by the transferor or the transferee. If it is paid by the transferor, the value of the chargeable transfer is the amount by which his estate is reduced, therefore the amount of the transfer for

---

[56] I.H.T.A. 1984, s.18.

[57] *ibid.* s.6, not strictly an exemption; but effectively so.

[58] *ibid.* ss.19 *et seq.* These include £3,000 per donor per year; £250 per donee per year; normal expenditure out of income; gifts in consideration of marriage of various permitted amounts up to £5,000; and payments for the maintenance of dependants. (s.11). They give considerable scope for tax saving. It is obviously important for a donor to start giving early, especially since the introduction of the potentially exempt transfer.

[59] *ibid.* s.3A, introduced by F.A. 1986, s.101 and Sched. 19.

[60] *ibid.* s.7, as amended.

[61] *ibid.* s.3A. The lifetime creation of an interest in possession trust was initially chargeable under the 1986 Act, but this rule was abrogated by F.(No. 2)A. 1987, s.96 and Sched. 7.

[62] *ibid.* s.2.

[63] *ibid.* s.7.

[64] *ibid.* s.8; Inheritance Tax (Indexation) Order 2000 (S.I. 2000 No. 803). Inheritance tax is levied on four per cent of estates; Budget Speech 2000. The yield in 1998/99 was £1.8 billion (Inland Revenue statistics).

[65] I.H.T.A. 1984, s.7(4).

tax purposes must include the tax. It will be necessary to "gross up" the sum transferred. The amount of tax payable on any sum varies, not only with the size of the sum, but also with the total of prior chargeable transfers within the previous seven years. The calculations in any particular case can be formidable, and will be worked out in each case from grossing up tables. On the other hand, if the transferee pays the tax, the actual amount of the transfer is treated as the gross gift, and added to the transferor's total gifts. The amount of tax payable will be less; but the amount received by the transferee will also be less.

The last transfer which a person makes is that of the estate on death. The rates applicable are those which begin at the total value of any taxable lifetime gifts within the previous seven years, grossed up as necessary. There is no question of grossing up the estate at death. Any tax is deducted prior to distribution. The incidence of tax as between specific and residuary beneficiaries is another problem.[66]

It is thus necessary to keep a "score" of taxable lifetime gifts, pay tax on them as due, and apply the seven-year cumulation rule when calculating the tax liability on subsequent chargeable gifts, and ultimately on death. The tax planner's job is to enable the client to make the best use of available exemptions and reliefs, and of the potentially exempt transfer. The adviser's dilemma is that the calculations have to be made on a number of assumptions about future events and tax liabilities.

Before examining the special rules relating to trusts, mention must be made of the principle of reservation of benefit. Although familiar under the estate duty regime, this concept was not relevant to capital transfer tax. It was reintroduced by the Finance Act 1986 and is a fundamental feature of inheritance tax. The object of this principle is that the donor should not be permitted to take advantage of the potentially exempt transfer rule by making gifts where he effectively retains an interest. As Lord Hoffmann has put it, "Not only may you not have your cake and eat it, but if you eat more than a few *de minimis* crumbs of what was given, you are deemed for tax purposes to have eaten the lot".[67]

Where an individual makes a gift on or after March 18, 1986 the property is treated as subject to a reservation in two cases (amendments added by Finance Act 1999 are dealt with below). First, where possession and enjoyment of the property is not bona fide assumed by the donee prior to the seven-year period ending with the donor's death (or, if the donor died within seven years of the gift, at the date of the gift). Secondly, where the property is not enjoyed "to

---

[66] I.H.T.A. 1984, ss.38, 39.
[67] *Ingram v. I.R.C.* [2000] 1 A.C. 293 at 304.

the entire exclusion, or virtually to the entire exclusion, of the donor and of any benefit to him by contract or otherwise" at any time during the seven years ending with his death (or, if the donor died within seven years of the gift, at any time after the gift[68]). There are certain exceptions, for example where the donor occupies the property for full consideration in money or money's worth.[69] Nor does the principle apply where the gift falls within certain of the substantive exemptions, for example the spouse exemption.[70]

The effect of a gift with reservation of benefit is that the property is treated as remaining in the estate of the donor. Hence the making of a gift with reservation normally has no immediate inheritance tax consequence, but the property will be treated as part of the donor's estate on death (at its value at that time) and taxed accordingly.[71] If during his lifetime there is a change of circumstances so that there is no longer a reservation of benefit, for example where the donor renounces any benefit retained, a potentially exempt transfer is treated as made at that time, so that the donor must survive a further seven years if tax is to be avoided.[72] If he dies within seven years, the property is taxed on its value at the date of the release of benefit, not of the prior gift. In the rare case where the lifetime gift is initially chargeable, as in the case of the creation of a discretionary trust, the property subject to a reservation will be treated as part of the settlor's estate on his death and taxed again, but relief is given against this double charge.[73]

Cases on estate duty and comparable Commonwealth legislation afford guidance as to what is a reservation of benefit.[74] In the context of trusts, the settlor will be treated as reserving a benefit if he is among the class of objects of a discretionary trust,[75] even though he receives nothing. Similarly if the settlor is a remunerated trustee of the settlement.[76] The settlor does not, however, reserve a benefit by reason of being an unpaid trustee,[77] nor if he has a reversionary interest in the settled property, because the subject-matter of the gift does not include the reversion.[78]

---

[68] F.A. 1986, s.102.

[69] *ibid.* Sched. 20, para. 6.

[70] *ibid.* s.102(5).

[71] *ibid.* s.102(3).

[72] *ibid.* s.102(4).

[73] *ibid.* s.104; Inheritance Tax (Double Charges Relief) Regulations 1987 (S.I. 1987/1130).

[74] See *Chick v. Commissioner of Stamp Duties of New South Wales* [1958] A.C. 435; *Nichols v. I.R.C.* [1975] 1 W.L.R. 534; *Munro v. Commissioner of Stamp Duties of New South Wales* [1934] A.C. 61; *St. Aubyn v. Att.-Gen.* [1952] A.C. 11. See also (1986) 83 L.S.Gaz 3728.

[75] *Att.-Gen. v. Heywood* (1887) 19 Q.B.D. 326. It does not seem that the inclusion of his spouse would have this effect; (1986) 83 L.S.Gaz. 3728.

[76] *Oakes v. Commissioner of Stamp Duties of New South Wales* [1954] A.C. 57.

[77] *Commissioner of Stamp Duties of New South Wales v. Perpetual Trustee Co. Ltd* [1943] A.C. 425; (1986) 83 L.S.Gaz. 3728.

[78] *ibid.*

One way of attempting to reduce the value of property without losing the right to occupy it is for the owner to arrange for the grant to himself of a non-assignable lease at a low rent and to give away the freehold reversion. The value of the latter is much reduced by the lease, and the lease itself is of little value on the owner's death because it is not assignable. The efficacy of such a scheme was the issue in *Ingram v. I.R.C.*[79] Lady Ingram transferred her property to a nominee for herself who then granted her a rent-free 20-year lease which prohibited assignment and subletting (the transfer to the nominee being necessary because a freeholder cannot grant a lease to himself). The nominee then transferred the freehold reversion, subject to the lease, to trustees on certain trusts. The object was thus to "carve out" the lease before making the gift. The House of Lords held that this scheme did not amount to a gift with reservation. When Lady Ingram died, only the then-valueless lease was part of her estate.[80]

Such a scheme is no longer effective in relation to disposals by way of gift on or after March 9, 1999.[81] While the original provisions continue to operate, gifts not within them may now be caught by the new sections 102A or 102B of the Finance Act 1986. Under section 102A a lifetime gift of an interest in land is a gift with reservation in the following circumstances: during the period of seven years ending on the donor's death the donor or the donor's spouse enjoys a significant right or interest, or is party to a significant arrangement, in relation to the land, which entitles or enables the donor to occupy all or part of the land otherwise than for full consideration in money or money's worth. This would cover a case such as *Ingram*. A right, interest or arrangement is not "significant" if it does not and cannot prevent enjoyment of the land to the entire exclusion (or virtually to the entire exclusion) of the donor, or does not entitle him to occupy all or part of the land immediately after the disposal, but would do so but for the interest disposed of. Thus there is no gift with reservation where the donor gives a leasehold interest and retains the reversion.

By section 102B, a gift of an undivided share in land (an interest under a tenancy in common) is not a gift with reservation, provided: (a) the donor does not occupy (other than for full consideration) to the exclusion of the donee, or (b) the donor and donee both occupy and the donor does not receive any benefit at the expense of the

---

[79] [2000] 1 A.C. 293; (1999) 115 L.Q.R. 351 (R. Kerridge).

[80] Because Lady Ingram died within three years of the gift of the freehold reversion, it was a chargeable transfer. However, it was valued as at the date of the gift. Land values had increased sharply by the date of her death. Had the reservation rule applied, the reversion would have been treated as part of her estate at its higher value at the date of death.

[81] F.A. 1999, s.104.

donee in connection with the gift.[82] This provision reflects pre-existing Revenue practice.

Exemptions applicable to the original provisions of the 1986 Act, such as a gift to a spouse or to charity, apply also to the new provisions.[83]

3. INHERITANCE TAX AND SETTLEMENTS[84]

Family trusts have been used for many years as ways of avoiding tax. Not surprisingly, trusts in general, and discretionary trusts in particular, were treated harshly by the capital transfer and inheritance tax legislation. There are, for inheritance tax purposes, two broad categories of settlements; those in which there is an interest in possession and those in which there is not, these being primarily discretionary trusts. The rules relating to reservation of benefit, discussed above,[85] must be borne in mind in relation to both categories.

When the Finance Act 1986 introduced the potentially exempt transfer, the only type of trust to benefit from it was the accumulation and maintenance trust.[86] The lifetime creation of other settlements was initially chargeable irrespective of seven-year survival. This position was subsequently modified so that the lifetime creation of an interest in possession settlement is now potentially exempt.[87] The lifetime creation of a discretionary trust (other than an accumulation and maintenance trust) remains initially chargeable.

A. Settlements in Which There is an Interest in Possession

This category deals with the standard form situation of a fixed trust for successive beneficiaries, whose interests are specified in the trust instrument; as a trust for Mrs X for her life, and after her death for her children in equal shares. A beneficiary has an interest in possession if he is entitled to the income as it arises. He is so entitled even though the trustees have a power to revoke or to appoint elsewhere, but not if they have a power to accumulate the income, even if unexercised.[88] A person entitled to an interest in possession

---

[82] This section operates to the exclusion of ss.102 and 102A, thus a gift satisfying s.102B will not be a gift with reservation under the other sections.

[83] F.A. 1986, s.102C.

[84] I.H.T.A. 1984, Pt. III. "Settlement" is defined in s.43(2). For foreign elements, see Foster, *Inheritance Tax*, Part J.

[85] *ante*, p. 226.

[86] *post*, p. 233.

[87] F.(No. 2)A. 1987, s.96 and Sched. 7.

[88] See *Pearson v. I.R.C.* [1981] A.C. 753; (1980) 43 M.L.R. 712 (W. Murphy); (1980) 39 C.L.J. 246 (J. Tiley); (1981) 97 L.Q.R. 1; *Re Trafford's Settlement* [1985] Ch. 32; *Swales v. I.R.C.* [1984] 3 All E.R. 16; *Miller v. I.R.C.* [1987] S.T.C. 108.

under such a trust is treated for the purposes of inheritance tax as being beneficially entitled to the property in which his interest subsists.[89] Mrs X would thus be regarded, for purposes of inheritance tax, not merely as the owner of a life interest in the trust property, but as the owner of the property itself. There are special provisions to deal with cases where there is a shared entitlement to the income,[90] or where the beneficiary is entitled to a fixed amount,[91] and also for the beneficiary who is entitled to the use and enjoyment of property which does not produce income.[92]

When an interest in possession comes to an end, the person entitled to the interest is treated as having at that time made a transfer of value of his interest. His interest is regarded as coming to an end on his disposing of or surrendering his interest, or on its termination in whole or in part by an appointment being made of the property in which his interest subsisted.[93] Where the interest in possession terminates during the lifetime of the person entitled to it, the transfer is potentially exempt.[94] If the disposal is for a consideration in money or money's worth, the value of the property is treated as reduced by the amount of the consideration,[95] but in determining that amount, the value of a reversionary interest in the property (which the tenant for life may acquire on a partition) must be left out of account.[96] Additionally, depreciatory transactions between the trustees and the persons interested under the settlement (as where the value of the trust property is reduced by granting a long lease of the property at a low rent) are treated as transfers of value.[97] Where a person dies entitled to an interest in possession, he is treated as having made a transfer of value immediately before his death of the property in which the interest subsisted.[98]

As the coming to an end of an interest in possession is treated as a transfer of value by the person beneficially entitled to that interest, the *rate* of any tax chargeable is determined by his personal scorecard.[99] There is, however, no question of grossing up; for the value

---

[89] I.H.T.A. 1984, s.49. Accordingly, reversionary interests are "excluded property" (s.48); but there are exceptions (*ibid.*).

[90] *ibid.* s.50(1).

[91] *ibid.* s.50(2).

[92] *ibid.* s.50(5).

[93] *ibid.* ss.51, 52.

[94] F.(No. 2)A. 1987, s.96.

[95] Which will be less than the value of the property in which the interest subsisted. See I.H.T.A. 1984, s.49(2), dealing with the case where more than the actuarial value is paid.

[96] *ibid.* s.52(2).

[97] *ibid.* s.52(3).

[98] *ibid.*, s.4. See *I.R.C. v. Lloyds Private Banking Ltd* [1998] S.T.C. 560 (right to reside for life gave interest in possession so that capital value taxed on death).

[99] *ibid.* s.52(1). But the tax is payable out of the settled property, and the trustees are responsible for it, concurrently with the beneficiary; *ibid.* s.201.

of the transfer is not the loss to the transferor, but the value of the property in which the interest subsisted.[1]

There are certain reliefs and exemptions.[2] No tax is payable where an interest in possession comes to an end and (subject to certain qualifications) it reverts to the settlor,[3] or to the spouse, widow or widower of the settlor.[4]

There is total or partial relief where the person whose interest comes to an end becomes on the same occasion entitled either to the property or to another interest in possession in the property; there is a potentially exempt transfer only to the extent that the value of the property to which he becomes entitled is less than the value of the property in which his interest subsisted.[5] If, however, the life tenant becomes absolutely entitled by purchasing the reversion, he makes a potentially exempt transfer of the amount of the purchase price.[6] The result of these rules in the case of partition is that there is a potentially exempt transfer of that part of the fund to which the remainderman becomes absolutely entitled.

Some of the general exemptions which apply to transfers of non-settled property apply also to termination of interests in possession, for example, transfers to a spouse or to charity, the annual exemption (£3,000) and marriage consideration[7]; and also transfers for family maintenance.[8] Finally, quick succession relief reduces the rate of tax where tax is payable on the termination of an interest in possession in settled property within five years of a previous chargeable transfer.[9]

B. Settlements in Which There is No Interest in Possession

i. Discretionary Trusts. In the context of inheritance tax, a discretionary trust means a settlement in which there is no interest in possession. Such trusts were hard hit by the original provisions of the 1975 Act, but the position was somewhat rationalised and ameliorated by the modifications of the Finance Act 1982.[10] The present

---

[1] I.H.T.A. 1984, s.52(1).

[2] Terminations under protective trusts are dealt with below. (*post*, p. 235). See also I.H.T.A. 1984, s.90 (trustees' annuities).

[3] I.H.T.A. 1984, s.54(1).

[4] *ibid.* s.54(2).

[5] *ibid.* s.53(2).

[6] Otherwise the life tenant could reduce the value of his taxable estate, as his free estate is reduced by the payment, while the value of the trust property in his estate is unaffected. See I.H.T.A. 1984, ss.10, 55.

[7] *ibid.* s.57. But the small gifts exemption (£250) does not apply. Valuation reliefs on business and agricultural property are also available to settlements.

[8] *ibid.* s.11.

[9] *ibid.* s.141.

[10] It has also been mitigated by the reduction in rates; *post*, p. 233.

code applies to "relevant property,"[11] meaning settled property in which there is no interest in possession, other than certain types of settlements which are preferentially treated.[12] As explained above, the lifetime creation of a discretionary trust is initially chargeable, although at half the rate applicable on death.[13]

(a) *The "Exit" Charge.* Tax is chargeable on any part of the funds which ceases to be "relevant property."[14] This covers not only the simple case of a payment of capital to a beneficiary, including the winding-up of the trust, but also the situation where the trustees convert the trust into a settlement with an interest in possession or into an accumulation and maintenance settlement.[15] There are certain exceptions to this rule; for example, no tax is payable in respect of a payment of costs or expenses, nor where the payment is income for income tax purposes in the hands of the recipient.[16] Only a limited number of the general exemptions, such as distributions to charity, are available.[17]

(b) *The Decennial Charge.* The "exit" charge alone is not sufficient, for the capital may not be distributed until the end of the trust period, which, as has been seen, may not occur until just before the end of the perpetuity period.[18] It is provided, therefore, that tax is payable on the whole of the settled funds every 10 years, although only at 30 per cent of the "effective rate," as described below.[19] Thus the capital is fully taxed broadly once a generation, whether the capital is distributed or retained, or the trust is converted into another form.

(c) *Rates of Tax.* Different rules apply to the "exit" charge and the decennial charge, although in both cases the rates applicable to lifetime transfers are used. Only an outline can be given here.

In the case of the decennial charge, tax is charged on the value of the "relevant property" on the day before the 10-year anniversary, at 30 per cent of the "effective rate" which would have been charged

---

[11] I.H.T.A. 1984, s.58.

[12] *ibid.* The exceptions include accumulation and maintenance trusts, discussed below, and the special trusts mentioned in section C., *infra.*

[13] *ante*, p. 229.

[14] I.H.T.A. 1984, s.65(1)(*a*). Tax is also chargeable where the trustees make a disposition resulting in the reduction in the value of the property; s.65(1)(*b*). See *I.R.C. v. Macpherson* [1989] A.C. 159.

[15] *post*, p. 233; *Inglewood (Lord) v. I.R.C.* [1983] 1 W.L.R. 366.

[16] I.H.T.A. 1984, s.65(5); *Stevenson (Inspector of Taxes) v. Wishart* [1987] 1 W.L.R. 1204. See also s.65(4), (6)–(8).

[17] The annual exemption (£3,000) is not available, nor does quick succession relief apply. The valuation reliefs, however, available for business and agricultural property, do apply.

[18] *ante*, p. 204.

[19] I.H.T.A. 1984, ss.64, 66.

on a hypothetical transfer at that time, on the assumption that the hypothetical transferor's cumulative total to be taken into account includes the settlor's chargeable transfers during the seven years preceding the creation of the settlement, plus the amounts, if any, subjected to an "exit charge" in the 10 years before the 10-year anniversary in question.[20]

In the case of the "exit" charge, the rate depends on whether the charge is payable before or after the first 10-year anniversary. In both cases the amount on which tax is payable is the amount by which the value of the "relevant property" is diminished by the event in question.[21] The rate before the first 10-year anniversary is the "appropriate fraction" of the rate payable on an assumed chargeable transfer made at the time of the "exit" charge, where the amount is the value of the settled property at the date of the settlement, and the hypothetical cumulative total is the settlor's chargeable transfers during the seven years prior to the creation of the settlement. The "appropriate fraction" is $3/10 \times N/40$, where N is the number of completed quarters (*i.e.* three-month periods) between the creation of the settlement and the chargeable event.[22] Different rules apply to settlements made before March 27, 1974.[23]

Where an "exit" charge arises after a 10-year anniversary, tax is charged at the "appropriate fraction" of the rate at which it was charged on the last 10-year anniversary. The "appropriate fraction" is $N/40$, where N is the number of completed quarters between the last 10-year anniversary and the chargeable event.[24] This rule applies also to settlements made before March 27, 1974.

Although discretionary trusts are treated more harshly than other settlements, the rates outlined above are not high. Now that the maximum lifetime rate is 20 per cent,[25] the rate of the decennial charge cannot exceed 6 per cent (being 30 per cent of the rate applicable to an actual transfer, as explained above). Furthermore, a discretionary trust within the nil rate band[26] retains some attraction.

ii. Accumulation and Maintenance Settlements. An accumulation and maintenance settlement is one in which no interest in possession exists, but one or more beneficiaries will, on attaining a

---

[20] I.H.T.A. 1984, s.66.
[21] "Grossing-up" occurs, I.H.T.A. 1984, s.65(2).
[22] *ibid.* s.68.
[23] *ibid.* s.68(6).
[24] *ibid.* s.69.
[25] F.A. 1988, s.136.
[26] *ante*, p. 225. On tax planning for discretionary trusts, see Foster, *Inheritance Tax*, Part M.

specified age not exceeding 25 years, become entitled to an interest in possession.[27]

It has long been common practice to create accumulation and maintenance settlements in favour of children in the family, and to give to the trustees power to apply the income at their discretion for the maintenance and education of the children, and to accumulate any income not so applied; and power to advance some or all of the capital for the advancement or benefit of the beneficiaries. The powers are now statutory,[28] subject to the expression of a contrary intention, and are discussed in more detail in Chapter 20.

Such trusts offer some attraction to a settlor who wishes to reduce his tax liability by setting up a trust for members of the family. The income of the trust will be taxed at the rate applicable to trusts (currently 34 per cent).[29] Where income is paid to or applied for the maintenance and education of a beneficiary, the income, if the settlement is irrevocable,[30] is taxed according to the tax status of the beneficiary. But there is one important limitation. If the beneficiary is an unmarried child under 18 *of the settlor*,[31] any income paid to or applied for his maintenance or education is aggregated for tax purposes with the income of the settlor.[32] There is no aggregation, however, if such income is accumulated.

The lifetime creation of an accumulation and maintenance settlement is a potentially exempt transfer.[33] The advantage of such a trust is that it is not taxed under the principles, discussed above, which apply to settlements in which there is no interest in possession.[34] Such trusts are favourably treated because of the difficulties in the way of giving capital or income to a child absolutely. Hence the decennial charge is not payable; nor is there any charge when a payment of capital is made to a beneficiary, as on an advancement, or when his interest vests; nor on the death of a beneficiary before becoming entitled.[35] Because of these advantages, tax is payable when a discretionary trust is converted into an accumulation and maintenance settlement.[36] In any event, the advantages of such a settlement are not permanently available. The trust will cease to

---

[27] I.H.T.A. 1984, s.71. There are other conditions. See *Inglewood (Lord) v. I.R.C.* [1983] 1 W.L.R. 366.

[28] T.A. 1925, s.31; *post*, p. 586.

[29] *ante*, p. 220. The saving is not great when the top rate on unsettled income is only 40 per cent. See (1994) 110 L.Q.R. 84 (R. Kerridge).

[30] I.C.T.A. 1988, ss.663–665.

[31] *cf.* grandchildren of the settlor.

[32] I.C.T.A. 1988, s.663; *ante*, p. 220, n. 17. Similarly in the case of income retained in a bare trust for the settlor's child; F.A. 1999, s.64.

[33] I.H.T.A. 1984, s.3A.

[34] *ibid.* s.58(1)(*b*).

[35] *ibid.* s.71(4). The beneficiary's interest in the income normally vests at the age of 18; T.A. 1925, s.31(1)(ii).

[36] I.H.T.A. 1984, s.65(1)(*a*); *Inglewood (Lord) v. I.R.C., supra*.

qualify as an accumulation and maintenance settlement after 25 years have elapsed since its commencement, unless all the beneficiaries are grandchildren of a common grandparent.[37] Tax becomes chargeable when the settlement ceases to qualify.[38]

C. Protective and Other Trusts

Other forms of trusts which are entitled to special treatment are protective trusts,[39] superannuation schemes,[40] trusts for the benefit of employees[41] and for disabled persons,[42] charitable trusts,[43] newspaper trusts,[44] maintenance funds for historic buildings,[45] and various special compensation funds, such as those maintained by Lloyd's and the Law Society.[46]

A protective trust does not fit neatly into the two categories into which trusts are divided for inheritance tax purposes; for there is an interest in possession during the currency of the interest of the principal beneficiary, but a discretionary trust after the forfeiture. There is a charge to inheritance tax upon the death of the principal beneficiary; but not on the forfeiture of his interest, which, for the purpose of inheritance tax, is deemed to continue during the currency of the discretionary trusts which then arise.[47]

---

[37] I.H.T.A. 1984, s.71(2).
[38] *ibid.* s.71(3)(*a*). Also where the trustees enter into a "depreciatory transaction." Tax is charged in the same manner as under s.70 (temporary charitable trusts).
[39] *ibid.* s.88; *ante,* Chap. 7.
[40] *ibid.* ss.58(1)(*d*), 151.
[41] *ibid.* s.86.
[42] *ibid.* s.89.
[43] *ibid.* s.58(1)(*a*). As to temporary charitable trusts, see s.70.
[44] *ibid.* s.87.
[45] *ibid.* s.58(1)(*c*) and Sched. 4.
[46] *ibid.* s.58(1)(*e*).
[47] *ibid.* s.88. See *Cholmondeley v. I.R.C.* [1986] S.T.C. 384.

CHAPTER 10

RESULTING TRUSTS

1. GENERAL

A RESULTING trust is a situation in which a transferee is required by equity to hold property on trust for the transferor; or for the person who provided the purchase money for the transfer. The beneficial interest results, or comes back to the transferor or to the party who makes the payment. In effect the resulting trust is the basis of a claim to recover one's own property.[1] This situation can arise in a wide variety of circumstances, and it has been seen that resulting trusts overlap with other categories.[2]

---

[1] See *MacMillan Inc. v. Bishopsgate Investments Trust plc (No. 3)* [1995] 1 W.L.R. 978 at 989.

[2] *ante*, p. 67.

Resulting trusts are not subject to all the rules of express trusts. Their creation is not dependent on compliance with formalities[3]; and a child may be a resulting trustee.[4]

The true nature of the resulting trust has been much scrutinised in recent years. The main points for debate have been the role of intention, the question of whether the beneficial interest remains in the transferor or is returned to him, and the linked question of whether the trust comes into effect only when the conscience of the transferee is affected by notice.

It used to be said that resulting trusts fell into two categories: presumed and automatic.[5] Under this classification the presumed resulting trust, arising in the case of transfers to volunteers, depended on the presumed intent of the transferor, whereas automatic resulting trusts, arising on failure to dispose of the beneficial interest, were imposed by operation of law without regard to intention. This classification is no longer favoured.[6] The current view is that all resulting trusts are based on the absence of any intention by the transferor to pass a beneficial interest to the transferee.[7] In the case of transfers to volunteers, this absence of intention is rebuttably presumed:

> "Like a constructive trust, a resulting trust arises by operation of law, though unlike a constructive trust it gives effect to intention. But it arises whether or not the transferor intended to retain a beneficial interest—he almost always does not—since it responds to the absence of any intention on his part to pass a beneficial interest to the recipient".[8]

On one view it might be supposed that where a transferor fails to dispose of the beneficial interest, he must still have it. In other words, the effect of the resulting trust is that the beneficial interest remains in the transferor throughout. Lord Reid put it thus: "the beneficial interest must belong to or be held for somebody: so if it was not to belong to the donee or to be held by him in trust for somebody it must remain with the donor".[9] The modern analysis, however, is that the transferor's absolute beneficial interest is not to

---

[3] L.P.A. 1925, s.53(2).

[4] *Re Vinogradoff* [1936] W.N. 68.

[5] *Re Vandervell's Trust (No. 2)* [1974] Ch. 269 (Megarry J.).

[6] *Westdeutsche Landesbank Girozentrale v. Islington London Borough Council* [1996] A.C. 669 at 708 (Lord Browne-Wilkinson). See generally [1996] R.L.R. 3 (P. Birks).

[7] Chambers, *Resulting Trusts*. See also (1999) 18 N.Z.U.L.R. 305 (C. Rickett), preferring the term "presumed trusts".

[8] *Air Jamaica Ltd v. Charlton* [1999] 1 W.L.R. 1399 at 1412 (Lord Millett), giving the advice of the Privy Council.

[9] *Vandervell v. I.R.C.* [1967] 2 A.C. 291 at 308. See also 313, 329.

be regarded as comprising separate legal and equitable interests, so that only the legal interest passes to the transferee in situations where resulting trusts arise. In such cases the transferee takes the absolute title but holds on trust for the transferor, who acquires for the first time a separate equitable interest.[10] This view is crucial to the theory that resulting trusts effect restitution to the transferor and are thus part of the law of unjust enrichment.[11]

Building on this point, Lord Browne-Wilkinson has sought to establish that the resulting trust (or indeed any other trust) will take effect only when the conscience of the transferee is affected by his becoming aware that he has received property which was not intended for his benefit.[12] His Lordship regarded this theory as "uncontroversial", but it appears problematic and unsupported by authority. It has been much criticised.[13] Who would be entitled to the beneficial interest, for example dividends on shares, pending the acquisition of knowledge by the trustee? To link the creation of a resulting trust with the conscience of the trustee "would be a difficult and dangerous departure from existing law. There is little to be gained by such less move and much to be lost".[14] A preferable view is that the resulting trust arises as soon as the property is transferred, but the transferee does not become subject to fiduciary duties and liability for breach of trust until he is aware of the position.[15] Indeed, the duties of a resulting trustee have not been fully worked out.[16] Lord Browne-Wilkinson's theory is not borne out by the cases on presumed resulting trusts,[17] and is not necessary to the view that resulting trusts effect restitution.

The situations in which resulting trusts arise will now be examined. The main examples, discussed below, involve incomplete disposal of the beneficial interest and transfers of property to volunteers. There are other cases where resulting trusts have been held to arise in circumstances where the transferor intended the property to revert to him unless used for a particular purpose. Such

---

[10] *Westdeutsche Landesbank Girozentrale v. Islington London Borough Council, supra,* at 706 (Lord Browne-Wilkinson).

[11] Chambers, *Resulting Trusts*; (1998) 114 L.Q.R. 399 (Sir Peter Millett).

[12] *Westdeutsche Landesbank Girozentrale v. Islington London Borough Council, supra.*

[13] [1996] 4 R.L.R. 3 at 20 (P. Birks); (1996) 55 C.L.J. 432 (G. Jones); (1998) 114 L.Q.R. 399 and [1998] 6 R.L.R. 283 (Sir Peter Millett); (1998) 12 *Trust Law International* 228 (W. Swadling); (1997–98) 8 K.C.L.J. 147 (P. Oliver); (1998) 57 C.L.J. 33 at 35–36 (N. McBride).

[14] Chambers, *Resulting Trusts*, p. 208, highlighting problems with taxation, insurance, priorities and so forth.

[15] Chambers, *Resulting Trusts*, (1998) 114 L.Q.R. 399 at 404 (Sir Peter Millett); (1998) 57 C.L.J. 33 at 35–36, (N. McBride).

[16] Chambers, *Resulting Trusts*, Chap. 9.

[17] In particular *Re Vinogradoff* [1935] W.N. 68, *post,* p. 255, where a young child was held to be a resulting trustee.

trusts might be regarded as express. An example is *Barclays Bank Ltd v. Quistclose Investments Ltd*,[18] where the parties intended that the Bank transferee should hold the funds on trust for the transferor if they could not be used to pay the Rolls Razor dividend; but there was no formal declaration. This situation has already been considered.[19]

A. Incomplete Disposal

Where property is conveyed to a person in the capacity of a trustee, there will be a resulting trust for the grantor of any part of the beneficial interest which is not disposed of. This result arises by operation of law. As discussed above, it is based on the absence of any intention to benefit the transferee. It will be discussed in more detail in section 2.

B. Voluntary Conveyance

A conveyance to a third party will in some circumstances give rise to a resulting trust for the transferor. The trust will be raised by a presumption of a resulting trust. The presumption may of course be rebutted. In the case of a conveyance to the transferor's wife or child or to a person to whom the transferor is *in loco parentis*, the presumption is reversed by the presumption of advancement. These matters are discussed in section 3.

C. Purchase Money Resulting Trust

Closely related to the previous category are conveyances to transferees who provide none or only part of the purchase price. This category includes cases where the conveyance is made to A, but some or all of the purchase price is provided by B, or where the conveyance is to persons jointly, but the purchase price is provided unequally. The complex questions of the division of property ownership between spouses or cohabitants, where the contribution to the family may be in ways other than the payment of money, will be dealt with in outline in Chapter 11.

---

[18] [1970] A.C. 567; *ante* p. 52. See also *Carreras Rothmans Ltd v. Freeman Mathews Treasure Ltd* [1985] Ch. 207 (contractual arrangement whereby money paid into a special bank account for a specific purpose created a trust); *cf. Re Multi Guarantee Co. Ltd* [1987] B.C.L.C. 257; *Re E.V.T.R. Ltd* [1987] B.C.L.C. 647 (*Quistclose* principle applied to loan for specific purpose which partially failed).

[19] *ante*, p. 52.

2. CONVEYANCE TO TRUSTEES

A. Where a Trust Fails

A resulting trust may arise on the failure, for a variety of reasons, of an express trust. In *Morice v. Bishop of Durham*,[20] the trusts were void; so also in *Re Diplock*,[21] where a large sum of money was left to be applied for purposes which the executors thought to be charitable, and was distributed among a number of charitable institutions. The trusts were void. The next-of-kin were entitled under a resulting trust; and they were able to recover the bulk of the money from the charities. In *Essery v. Cowlard*,[22] an intending wife executed a pre-nuptial settlement in which she conveyed the trust property to trustees upon trust for herself, the intended husband and the issue of the marriage. The marriage never took place, but the parties cohabited and children were born. Six years later, the woman successfully reclaimed the property. The trusts failed as the "contract to marry had been definitely and absolutely put an end to."

In *Re Ames' Settlement*[23] property had been settled by the husband's father upon the trusts of a marriage settlement, and the marriage took place. Eighteen years later the wife obtained a decree of nullity (which then had the effect of declaring the marriage void from the outset).[24] Vaisey J. decided, after the husband's death, that the property was held on a resulting trust for the executors of the settlor.

Difficult questions arise as to the effect of void transactions. In the rare case where the vitiating factor prevents title passing,[25] there is no need for a resulting trust. Where, however, the title passes and, notwithstanding the vitiating factor, the transferor intended the transferee to become absolute owner, there is no resulting trust but merely personal restitutionary liability. Thus in *Westdeutsche Landesbank Girozentrale v. Islington London Borough Council*,[26] where

---

[20] (1804) 8 Ves. 399; (1805) 10 Ves. 522; *post*, p. 365. See also *Simpson v. Simpson* [1992] 1 F.L.R. 601 (transferee of bank deposit held on resulting trust for transferor where the latter lacked mental capacity to make a gift).

[21] [1941] Ch. 253; [1944] A.C. 341; *sub nom. Chichester Diocesan Fund and Board of Finance (Incorporated) v. Simpson*; [1948] Ch. 465; [1951] A.C. 251; *sub. nom. Ministry of Health v. Simpson*; *post*, p. 682.

[22] (1884) 26 Ch.D. 191; *Burgess v. Rawnsley* [1975] Ch. 429 (if conveyance taken jointly for a purpose which fails, resulting trust to each party of his share. Majority view that must be a common purpose).

[23] [1946] Ch. 217.

[24] A decree of nullity in respect of a voidable marriage now operates to annul the marriage only from the date of the decree absolute; Matrimonial Causes Act 1973, s.16. See also the court's power to make property adjustments under s.24.

[25] See (1998) 114 L.Q.R. 399 at 415–416 (Sir Peter Millett).

[26] [1996] A.C. 669. The judgment in *Re Ames*, *supra*, was regarded as confused; *ibid.* at 715. Title would not have passed if the transaction had been *ultra vires* the bank. It is considered in Chambers, *Resulting Trusts*, pp. 160–162, that the reasons for rejecting a resulting trust in *Westdeutsche* are unsatisfactory, and that such a trust should arise wherever vitiated consent entitles the transferor to restitution.

the bank paid money to the local authority under a transaction which was *ultra vires* the local authority, the latter was subject only to personal liability as the bank had intended the authority to become absolute owner in spite of its mistaken belief as to the validity of the transaction. Where a transaction is merely voidable, as in the case of misrepresentation or undue influence, title passes although the transferor may elect to set aside the transaction. It has been argued that a resulting trust arises on such a voidable transfer,[27] but this seems unfounded and inconsistent with the reasoning in *Westdeutsche*. The beneficial title may revest in the transferor on election to rescind, but the transferee is the absolute owner pending that event.[28]

B. Incomplete Disposal of Beneficial Interest

Unskilful draftsmanship and the failure to foresee and provide for future contingencies may leave the beneficial ownership incomplete.[29] A resulting trust will then arise, although, as will be seen, some sets of circumstances can render this result so inconvenient that other solutions are sought.

The fact that an equitable interest is not fully disposed of may not become apparent until some time has elapsed since the constitution of the trust.

> In *Re Trusts of the Abbott Fund*[30] a sum of money was collected, to be used for the maintenance of two deaf and dumb ladies. It was held by Stirling J. that the ladies had no enforceable interests in the capital sum and that on their death, the sum remaining went on resulting trust to the subscribers.

The consequent problem of distribution on resulting trust among subscribers becomes acute when the number of subscribers is great, and the gifts are mostly anonymous, as in *Re Gillingham Bus Disaster Fund*.[31]

> A number of marine cadets were injured or killed when a bus was driven into the rear of a marching column. The mayors of three towns appealed for subscriptions to a fund that would initially care for the disabled and thereafter be available for "worthy

---

[27] Chambers, *Resulting Trusts*, Chap. 7.

[28] See (1998) 114 L.Q.R. 399 at 416 and [1998] 6 R.L.R. 283 (Sir Peter Millett). However, the Court of Appeal in *Collings v. Lee, The Times*, October 26, 2000, *post*, p. 687, held that the transferor of land retained the beneficial interest where the transfer was procured by fraudulent misrepresentation, for no consideration and in breach of fiduciary duty.

[29] See *Re Cochrane* [1955] Ch. 309; *John v. George* [1995] 1 E.G.L.R. 9 (conveyance to trustees on trust for daughter at 18 gave rise to resulting trust until she reached 18).

[30] [1900] 2 Ch. 326, *post*, p. 244.

[31] [1958] Ch. 300, *post*, p. 248.

causes" in memory of those killed. More money was contributed than could be used for the object (liability at common law for the accident having been accepted) and the second object failed as it had not been confined within the limit of legal charity.[32] Harman J. held that, despite the manifest inconvenience of such a decision, a resulting trust arose. All subscribers, large or small, intended to contribute to a specific purpose; on that purpose being attained or no longer attainable, each donor had an interest by way of resulting trust. There was no evidence on which to arrive at any other conclusion. The suggestion that the money should be treated as *bona vacantia* was regarded by Harman J. as taking the line of least resistance in a manner unauthorised by law. "The resulting trust arises where [the donor's] expectation is for some unforeseen reason cheated of fruition and is an inference of law based on after-knowledge of the event."[33]

C. Methods of Disposal of Surplus Funds

A resulting trust is not, however, the most appropriate solution in many situations; and, although something of a digression, it will be convenient here to examine other solutions. The question arises particularly in two contexts: First, that of gifts to persons for stated purposes, without specifying what is to be done when the purposes are completed; and, secondly, in the context of the dissolution of unincorporated associations.

In determining the correct solution in each of these contexts, two points will be of particular significance. First, did the transferor intend to dispose of his whole interest; or did he intend to transfer for a particular purpose only? Secondly, was the transfer made to a person in a capacity of trustee? If so, a resulting trust may be expected of the surplus.

i. Transfer to Persons for Particular Purposes. If property is given for the care and maintenance of certain persons, what is to happen to the property when the period of maintenance comes to an end? Do the intended beneficiaries (or their estates) keep the property, or does it return on a resulting trust to the donor? The answer will depend on the intention of the donor, which has to be ascertained from all the surrounding circumstances. The construction of

---

[32] Charities Act 1993, s.14 (*post*, p. 457) provides the most convenient solution to this type of case, but it applies only when the gift is charitable. The fund was finally wound up in 1965, when the remainder of the money was paid into court. It was announced on April 5, 1993, that the money (£7,300) was to be paid out and used for a memorial to the victims. For a different solution, see *Re West Sussex Constabulary's Widows, Children and Benevolent Fund Trust* [1971] Ch. 1, *post*.

[33] [1958] Ch. 300 at 310.

the gift in *Re Trusts of the Abbott Fund*[34] may be regarded as unusual. It will be noted that the beneficiaries in that case had died. More commonly, the gift is regarded as absolute. The principle of construction was laid down in *Re Sanderson's Trust*[35] as follows: "If a gross sum be given, or if the whole income of the property be given, and a special purpose be assigned for that gift, the court always regards the gift as absolute, and the purpose merely as the motive of the gift, and therefore holds that the gift takes effect as to the whole sum or the whole income, as the case may be." Thus,

In *Re Andrew's Trust*,[36] a fund was subscribed for the children of a deceased clergyman. An accompanying letter showed that the contributions were made "for or towards their education; . . . as being necessary to defray the expenses of all, and that solely in the matter of education." After their formal education was completed, the question arose of the disposal of the surplus. Kekewich J. decided that the children were entitled in equal shares.

In *Re Osoba*[37] there was a gift by will of a residuary estate, consisting, for present purposes, of a freehold house in London, to the testator's widow on trust to be used "for her maintenance and for the training of my daughter up to University grade and for the maintenance of my aged mother . . . " The mother predeceased the testator; the widow died in 1970, and the daughter's education up to university grade was completed in 1975. The children under an earlier marriage claimed the residue on intestacy.

The Court of Appeal found that the testator's intention was to provide absolute gifts for the beneficiaries, the references to maintenance and to education being expressions of motive. In the absence of words of severance, the beneficiaries took as joint tenants, with the daughter becoming entitled, on her mother's death, to the whole. The result would have been the same if the daughter had not gone to university.

ii. Surplus Funds on Dissolution of Unincorporated Association.[38]

(a) *Trust or Contract.* As will be seen in Chapter 14, funds of such an association will sometimes be held by trustees on an express trust for the members and sometimes by the treasurer or committee

---

[34] [1900] 2 Ch. 326.

[35] *per* Page Wood V.-C. (1857) 3 K. & J. 497 at 503; *Barlow v. Grant* (1684) 1 Vern. 255.

[36] [1905] 2 Ch. 48.

[37] [1979] 1 W.L.R. 247.

[38] See generally Warburton, *Unincorporated Associations: Law & Practice* (2nd ed.); [1992] Conv. 41 (S. Gardner). For the meaning of "unincorporated association" see *Conservative and Unionist Central Office v. Burrell* [1982] 1 W.L.R. 522, *post*, p. 373.

on a bare trust; in either case the property rights in the assets of the society are likely to be governed by the rules of the society which operate as a contract between the members. The question whether the property is held upon the terms of any trust created by the donor, or whether it is held by the members absolutely according to their contractual rights is relevant here also. The question commonly arises on a dissolution. It will be seen in the analysis which follows that the distinction between rights governed by a trust and those governed by a contract has not always been kept clear. In the case of a failure of a trust, the most appropriate solution is by way of resulting trust. In a case of dissolution of a society where the rights of the members are governed by a contract (*i.e.* by the rules of the society) the likely solution is in accordance with the terms of the contract; and if the contract is silent; by equal division among the members. The Crown might claim the fund as *bona vacantia*. It may also have to be considered whether any third party contributors may have a claim to participate in the distribution along with the members. Whether the matter is regarded as one of trust or contract affects the question of who is entitled and the calculation of the share. All these solutions will be demonstrated here, although the analysis in the earlier cases was subject to criticism by Walton J. in *Re Bucks Constabulary Fund (No. 2).*[39]

(b) *Meaning of Dissolution.* An association may be wound up in a formal manner, but in the absence of a formal dissolution, the question arises as to the circumstances which will justify a finding that the body has ceased to exist. In *Re G.K.N. Bolts and Nuts Ltd (Automotive Division) Birmingham Works, Sports and Social Club,*[40] the trustees of a social club had purchased a sports ground for £2,200 in 1946. In 1975, membership cards ceased to be issued and the last annual general meeting was held. No further accounts were taken, the stock of drinks was sold and the steward dismissed. A special meeting was convened on December 18, 1975 to deal with an offer to buy the land. Resolutions were passed that the land be sold, but no sale then took place. In 1978, the trustees sold the land for £253,000. One question which arose was the date the club ceased to exist.[41] It was held that mere inactivity did not suffice, unless it was so prolonged or so circumstanced that the only reasonable inference was spontaneous dissolution, in which case the court must select a date. On the facts, it ceased to exist on December 18, 1975, on the basis of inactivity coupled with positive acts to wind it up.

---

[39] [1979] 1 W.L.R. 936; *post*, p. 248.
[40] [1982] 1 W.L.R. 774; [1983] Conv. 315 (R. Griffith). See also *Re William Denby & Sons Ltd Sick and Benevolent Fund* [1971] 1 W.L.R. 973; *Re Bucks Constabulary Widows' and Orphans' Fund Friendly Society (No. 2)* [1979] 1 W.L.R. 936.
[41] The question of entitlement to the money is dealt with *post*, p. 251.

This would be so even if the resolution to sell the land was invalid, as by that date the club's activities had ceased and it had become incapable of carrying out its objects.

(c) *Resulting Trust for Members.* In *Re Printers' and Transferrers' Society*,[42] a society was founded to raise funds by weekly contributions to defend and support its members in maintaining reasonable remuneration for their labour, and to provide strike and lock-out benefits for members. The scale of payments varied according to the length of time a claimant had been a member of the society, and different conditions applied to printers and transferrers respectively. No provision was made by the rules for the distribution of the funds of the society on a dissolution. At the time of its dissolution the society consisted of 201 members, and its funds amounted to £1,000. The question arose as to how the sum was to be distributed. The Attorney-General made no claim to the fund as *bona vacantia*. It was held that there was a resulting trust in favour of those who had subscribed to the fund, and that the money was divisible amongst the existing members at the time of the dissolution, in proportion to the amount contributed by each member to the funds of the society irrespective of fines, or payments made to members in accordance with the rules.

In *Re Hobourn Aero Components Air Raid Distress Fund*,[43] a fund was established during the Second World War for employees of a company who were on war service or who sustained loss in air raids. The fund was financed by voluntary subscriptions among the employees, but it was not charitable. The Crown made no claim to the fund as *bona vacantia*. After the war, the fund was found to have a surplus. It was held that each contributor, past or present, had an interest in the surplus by way of resulting trust in proportion to the amount he had contributed, but subject to adjustment in relation to any benefit he had received from the fund.

This conclusion, although logically consistent with the resulting trust analysis, is less convenient than the decision in *Re Printers' and Transferrers' Society*,[44] in that it concentrates attention on all the contributors to a society, however remote in time past, and not on those who have retained a connection with it. There is much to be said for the simpler solution of the earlier case, which, however, Cohen J. in the present case thought defensible only in cases where

---

[42] [1899] 2 Ch. 184.

[43] [1946] Ch. 86 (affirmed *ibid.* at 194), see especially 97–98; following *Re British Red Cross Balkan Fund* [1914] 2 Ch. 419, (which is doubted in Tudor, *Charities* (8th ed.), at p. 354, n. 74).

[44] [1899] 2 Ch. 184.

the ascertainment of the true entitlements would be too difficult. A more recent example is provided by *Air Jamaica Ltd v. Charlton*,[45] where, however, the surplus arose in the context of a pension trust rather than an association. That part of the surplus which derived from the members' contributions resulted to them and was divided pro rata between the members and the estates of deceased members in proportion to their contributions, irrespective of benefits received and the dates of the contributions.

(d) *Contractual Basis*. In *Cunnack v. Edwards*,[46] a society governed by the Friendly Societies Act 1829[47] had been established in 1810 to raise a fund, by the subscriptions, fines and forfeitures of its members, to provide annuities for the widows of its deceased members. By 1879 all the members had died. The last widow-annuitant died in 1892, the society then having a surplus of £1,250. A claim to the assets was made by the personal representatives of the last surviving members. It was held that there was no resulting trust in favour of the personal representatives of the members of the society. Each member had paid away his money in return for the protection given to his widow, if he left one. "Except as to this he abandoned and gave up the money for ever."[48] The assets went to the Crown as *bona vacantia*.

In *Re West Sussex Constabulary's Widows, Children and Benevolent (1930) Fund Trust*,[49] a fund had been established to provide benefits to widows and certain dependants of members who died. The income of the fund came from members' subscriptions, the proceeds of entertainments, sweepstakes, raffles and collecting boxes and various donations and legacies. On the amalgamation of the West Sussex Constabulary with other police forces in 1968, the question arose of the distribution of the fund.

Goff J. held that the surviving members had no claim because first, the members had received all that they had contracted for, and secondly, the money was paid on the basis of contract, and not of trust. The funds went as *bona vacantia* to the Crown. The possibility that living members may have a contractual claim on the basis of

---

[45] [1999] 1 W.L.R. 1399 (PC); [2000] Conv. 170 (C. Harpum); (2000) 116 L.Q.R. 15 (C. Rickett and R. Grantham). The *bona vacantia* solution of *Davis v. Richards & Wallington Industries Ltd* [1990] 1 W.L.R. 1511, *post*, p. 249, was considered wrong.

[46] [1896] 2 Ch. 679; (1966) 30 Conv.(N.S.) 117 (H. Hickling); (1980) 43 M.L.R. 626 (B. Green). The decision was distinguished in *Re Bucks Constabulary Fund (No. 2)*, *infra*, as turning upon the combined effect of the rules and the 1829 Act.

[47] For the special position of Friendly Societies, see Warburton, *Unincorporated Associations: Law & Practice* (2nd ed.), pp. 5–6.

[48] [1896] 2 Ch. 679 at 683.

[49] [1971] Ch. 1; (1971) 87 L.Q.R. 464 (M. Albery).

frustration of the contract or failure of consideration was met by the Crown giving an indemnity to the trustees.

Contributions from outside sources were divided into three categories. The first two, proceeds of entertainments, etc., and collecting boxes, could not be the subject of a resulting trust,[50] they were out-and-out payments.[51] Identifiable donations, however, and legacies were in a different position. The object of the gift had failed, and the property was held on resulting trust. On the latter point, it is difficult to see why third party contributors, even if identifiable, should have any claim in such circumstances. The validity of the initial gift is usually explained on the basis that it is an absolute gift to the members of the association.[52] If that is so, such contributions should be dealt with on the same basis as the rest of the funds. It is submitted that there is no room here for a resulting trust for third parties.

The more acceptable modern solution to the distribution of assets of an unincorporated society is among the members. The matter is regarded as one of contract between the members, express or implied. On this analysis, the resulting trust solution is no longer appropriate. This is so, even though the assets of the society may be vested in trustees; as is indeed required in the case of unincorporated Friendly Societies.[53] The trustees then hold the assets on trust for the members according to the rules of the society. The rules may provide for the distribution upon dissolution. Otherwise, the assets will be divided among the members at the time of the dissolution.

Re Bucks Constabulary Fund (No. 2)[54] was another case of the distribution of a fund established to provide benefits for the widows and orphans of deceased police officers and the provision of payments on the death of a member or during sickness. The Bucks Constabulary amalgamated with other constabularies and in 1968 the fund was wound up.

The question of the proper method of distribution came before Walton J., who held that the assets should be divided equally among members alive at the date of dissolution. If the society was moribund, as where there were no members or only one member left, the property would be ownerless. Only then would the Crown

---

[50] Not following *Re Gillingham Bus Disaster Fund* [1958] Ch. 300, *ante*, p. 242.

[51] *Re Welsh Hospital (Netley) Fund* [1921] 1 Ch. 655; *Re Hillier's Trusts* [1954] 1 W.L.R. 9; *Re Ulverston and District New Hospital Building Trust* [1956] Ch. 672.

[52] *post*, p. 377.

[53] Friendly Societies Act 1974 s.49(1). The Friendly Societies Act 1992 provides for the incorporation of Friendly Societies carrying on mutual insurance business for the members and their families.

[54] [1979] 1 W.L.R. 936; (1980) 39 C.L.J. 88 (C. Rickett); (1980) 43 M.L.R. 626 (B. Green).

be entitled. Walton J. emphasised the distinction between property held under the terms of the trust, and that governed by contract. In such a case, quoting Brightman J.[55]

"The right of the member of the fund to receive benefits is a contractual right and the member ceases to have any interest in the fund if and when he has received the totality of the benefits to which he was contractually entitled. In other words, there is no possible claim by any member founded on a resulting trust. . . . If it has been dissolved or terminated, the members entitled to participate would prima facie be those persons who were members at the date of dissolution or termination."[56]

The *West Sussex*[57] decision, although distinguishable on the ground that it did not involve a Friendly Society, was criticised by Walton J. on the basis that the principle of law applicable to the members' club cases should have governed the distribution. It made no difference whether or not the association was for the benefit of the members themselves. They controlled the assets, which were theirs all along. Thus *bona vacantia* was not an appropriate solution in that case.

Similar problems may arise in the context of surplus pension funds. As this situation involves a trust rather than an unincorporated association, it may be expected (in the absence of rules in the pension scheme to deal with it) that the surplus would be held on resulting trust for the contributors. In *Davis v. Richards & Wallington Industries Ltd*,[58] however, Scott J. considered that any resulting trust to the members would be excluded by implication, partly because of the difficulty of calculating their shares in view of the different benefits received, and partly because tax relief would be lost if the members received under a resulting trust any sums in excess of the maximum benefits permitted by the relevant legislation. Thus the *bona vacantia* solution was preferred. This analysis was considered to be wrong by the Privy Council in *Air Jamaica Ltd v. Charlton*[59] on the basis that a resulting trust cannot be avoided simply because the transferor does not intend to retain the beneficial interest: it may arise even where the transferor positively wished to part with the beneficial interest.[60] The two reasons given by Scott J.

---

[55] *Re William Denby and Sons Ltd Sick and Benevolent Fund* [1971] 1 W.L.R. 973 at 978.
[56] [1979] 1 W.L.R. 936 at 948.
[57] *supra.*
[58] [1990] 1 W.L.R. 1511; [1991] Conv. 366 (J. Martin); [1992] Conv. 41 (S. Gardner); Chambers, *Resulting Trusts*, p. 66.
[59] [1999] 1 W.L.R. 1399.
[60] As in *Vandervell v. Inland Revenue Commissioners* [1967] 2 A.C. 291, *post*, p. 253.

should not have excluded a resulting trust, which arose by operation of the general law and outside the scope of the tax legislation. The alleged difficulty of calculating the shares rested on the erroneous assumption that the benefits received by each member had to be taken into account. In the present case the proper solution was a resulting trust for the employer[61] and the members. The members' share was divided pro rata between the members and the estates of deceased members in proportion to their contributions, irrespective of benefits received and the dates of the contributions.

(e) *Methods of Distribution Among the Members.* If entitlement is on the basis of a resulting trust, the distribution will be made amongst all members, past and present, including personal representatives of deceased members, in shares proportionate to their contributions. Past members may be excluded if the calculation would prove too difficult.[62] We have seen, however, that the resulting trust analysis is not usually favoured today in cases of unincorporated associations. It is also unlikely, in view of *Re Bucks Constabulary Fund (No. 2)*,[63] that the Crown will establish a claim to the assets as *bona vacantia* in many cases, or, as submitted above,[64] that outside contributors will have any claim. Assuming that the contractual basis is adopted, only those members existing at the date of dissolution will be entitled. Unless the rules provide otherwise, the distribution will be on a *per capita* basis, prima facie in equal shares, and ignoring actual contributions.

In *Re Sick and Funeral Society of St. John's Sunday School, Golcar*,[65] a society was formed in 1866 to provide sickness and death benefits for its members. Those under 13 paid $\frac{1}{2}$d per week, and the others paid 1d. The benefits for those paying the whole subscription were twice those of the smaller subscribers. Upon the winding up of the society, the surplus funds were held distributable among the members as at that date on a *per capita* basis, but as the benefits and burdens differed among the two classes of members, the proper basis for distribution was full shares for full members and half shares for the children. The *per capita* basis did not favour new members at the expense of older ones, as each got what he paid for: the newer members had had the benefits of membership for a short

---

[61] A clause in the deed excluding any repayment to the employer was to preclude any amendment to the scheme allowing such repayment and did not rebut a resulting trust arising outside the scheme.

[62] *Re Hobourn Aero Components Air Raid Distress Fund* [1946] Ch. 86 at 97.

[63] [1979] 1 W.L.R. 936.

[64] *ante*, p. 248.

[65] [1973] Ch. 51.

time and the older members for a longer time. The latter could not complain if they did not receive more in the winding up.

In *Re Bucks Constabulary Fund (No. 2)*,[66] Walton J. held that the prima facie rule of equal division applied also to Friendly Society cases, although in the past some of those cases had favoured a distribution in proportion to contributions.[67] This approach was also adopted in *Re G.K.N. Bolts & Nuts Ltd (Automotive Division) Birmingham Works, Sports and Social Club*,[68] where those entitled to share the assets on a *per capita* basis were the full members and the ordinary members. Honorary, temporary and associate members, who neither paid subscriptions nor had voting rights, were excluded.

iii. Trust and Charge. Here also the distinction between a trust and a charge is important.[69] A distinction was drawn by Lord Eldon in *King v. Denison*[70] between devises *charged with payment* of debts, and devises *on trust to pay* debts. In the former case it is assumed that the testator intended a beneficial interest for the devisee, subject to the payment of debts; in the latter case it is assumed that he intended merely to use the devisee as a vehicle for payment of the debts, and not to confer any benefit upon him. In the latter case there will, therefore, be a resulting trust of any surplus for the residuary devisee, or those entitled on intestacy; but there will be no resulting trust in the former case. In construing the language of a gift, it must be remembered that equity will not allow trustees themselves to give evidence that what was intended was a conditional gift.[71]

D. No Declaration of Trust

Where property is conveyed to persons in circumstances in which they are intended to take as trustees, then, if no beneficial interests are declared, they will hold on resulting trust for the grantor; as where a transfer is made to a nominee.[72] We have seen this principle in operation in the case of testamentary gifts to legatees as trustees,

---

[66] *supra.*
[67] *Re Printers' and Transferrers' Society* [1899] 2 Ch. 184; *Re Lead Workmens Fund Society* [1904] 2 Ch. 196.
[68] [1982] 1 W.L.R. 774. The facts have been given, *ante*, p. 245. See also *Re St Andrew's Allotment Association* [1969] 1 W.L.R. 229.
[69] *ante*, p. 55.
[70] (1813) 1 Ves. & Bea. 260; *Smith v. Cooke* [1891] A.C. 297; *Re West* [1900] 1 Ch. 84; *Re Foord* [1922] 2 Ch. 519, distinguished in *Re Osoba* [1979] 1 W.L.R. 247, *ante*, p. 244.
[71] *Re Rees* [1950] Ch. 204; *Re Pugh* [1967] 1 W.L.R. 1262; *Re Tyler* [1967] 1 W.L.R. 1269; *ante*, p. 163, *cf. Smith v. Cooke (supra).*
[72] *Hodgson v. Marks* [1971] Ch. 892; *Vandervell v. I.R.C.* [1967] 2 A.C. 291.

without the trusts upon which they are to hold being declared prior to the testator's death.[73]

The *Vandervell* litigation serves as a warning of the crucial importance of attention to detail in tax planning. There were two visits to the House of Lords and three to the Court of Appeal. The problem was caused by the fact that Mr. Vandervell's advisers overlooked the possibility of the existence of a resulting trust; when all that Mr. Vandervell was doing was trying to give away a large sum of money to charity.

In 1958 Vandervell decided to found a Chair of Pharmacology at the Royal College of Surgeons with a gift of £250,000. This was to be effected by a scheme under which a block of shares in Vandervell Products Ltd would be transferred to the College, and the necessary dividends subsequently declared on them. Such dividends, in the hands of the College, would be free of liability to income tax and surtax.[74] The shares were to be transferred subject to an option to repurchase for £5,000 in favour of Vandervell Trustees Ltd, a private company whose only function was to act as trustee for various trusts connected with the Vandervell family and business. It was trustee of the Vandervell children's trust.

The transfer of the shares was made in 1958, and between then and 1961 the necessary dividends were paid to the College. The Revenue assessed Vandervell for surtax on the dividends on the ground that he had not entirely disposed of all his interest in the property,[75] because, in the absence of a declaration of trust of the option, it was held on resulting trust for Vandervell. The Revenue succeeded. That was *Vandervell v. I.R.C.*[76] Before discussing the reasoning, it will be best to complete the story.

On receiving the Revenue's claim in 1961, Vandervell ordered Vandervell Trustees Ltd to exercise the option, and they did so, taking £5,000 from the children's settlement to finance it. All the dividends since that date were paid to Vandervell Trustees Ltd, who applied them to the children's settlement. They so informed the Revenue.

The Revenue assessed Vandervell to surtax in respect of the years 1961–65 on the footing that the shares were held on trust for him during that period. In 1965 he at last executed a deed which transferred all or any interest which he may have in the shares in favour of the children's settlement. In 1967 he died.

---

[73] *Re Boyes* (1884) 26 Ch.D. 531; *ante*, p. 156; *Re Pugh's W.T.* [1967] 1 W.L.R. 1262.
[74] Because the College is a charity.
[75] I.T.A. 1952, s.415(2). Now I.C.T.A. 1988, s.685.
[76] [1967] 2 A.C. 291; (1966) 24 C.L.J. 19 (G. Jones); (1967) 31 Conv.(N.S.) 175 (S. Spencer); (1967) 30 M.L.R. 461 (N. Strauss).

Before this claim of the Revenue was litigated, Vandervell's estate stepped in and claimed the dividends from Vandervell Trustees Ltd. If the estate succeeded, the Revenue's claim was clearly good; and the Revenue attempted to join the litigation in support. The defendants successfully excluded them.[77] In *Re Vandervell's Trusts (No. 2)* the estate succeeded before Megarry J., but failed before the Court of Appeal.[78]

In the first case, *Vandervell v. I.R.C.*[79] the Revenue succeeded by a majority of three to two. The option was held on trust for Vandervell. He was effectively the grantor of the option, although it was in form granted by the Royal College. It was taken by Vandervell Trustees Ltd upon trust, but no effective trusts of the option were declared, "and so the defendant company held the option on an automatic trust for Mr. Vandervell."[80] In this situation, there was, as Lord Wilberforce said "no need, or room to invoke a presumption. The conclusion, on the facts found, is simply that the option was vested in the trustee company as a trustee on trusts, not defined at the time, possibly to be defined later. But the equitable, or beneficial interest, cannot remain in the air: the consequence in law must be that it remains in the settlor."[81] An indication of the parties' intention, as opposed to what they might be supposed to have desired, would of course have changed the whole situation. But the donor's mere intention not to have the beneficial interest cannot prevent a resulting trust.[82]

In *Re Vandervell's Trusts (No. 2)*,[83] the Court of Appeal, reversing Megarry J., found that the resulting trust of the option in favour of Vandervell terminated with the exercise of the option; and that a trust of the shares had been declared in favour of the children's settlements. Criticisms of the finding of a declaration of trust have already been made.[84] Another difficulty is that even if the acts of the trustees were sufficient to manifest an intention to create a new trust, how could the option and the shares be separated? Is it right to say: "Before the option was exercised, there was a gap in the beneficial ownership. So there was a resulting trust for Mr. Vandervell. But, as soon as the option was exercised and the shares registered in the trustees' name, there was created a valid trust of the shares in favour

---

[77] *Re Vandervell's Trusts (No. 1)* [1971] A.C. 912.
[78] [1974] Ch. 269.
[79] [1967] 2 A.C. 291.
[80] [1974] Ch. 269 at 296, *per* Megarry J.
[81] [1967] 2 A.C. 291 at 329.
[82] [1974] Ch. 269 at 298, *per* Megarry J.; *Air Jamaica Ltd v. Charlton* [1999] 1 W.L.R. 1399.
[83] [1974] Ch. 269; (1974) 38 Conv.(N.S.) 405 (P. Clarke); (1975) 38 M.L.R. (J. Harris); (1975) 7 D.L.R. 483 (G. Battersby).
[84] *ante*, pp. 87, 128.

of the children's settlement"?[85] Other problems relating to the formality requirements of Law of Property Act 1925, s.53(1)(c) were discussed in Chapter 4.

3. Voluntary Conveyance and the Presumptions

A. Presumption of Resulting Trust: Conveyance to a Third Party

i. Land. One of the effects of the Statute of Uses was to prevent the operation of resulting uses. Previously, a resulting use arose on a voluntary conveyance which did not declare a use; the beneficial interest reverted to the grantor. After the Statute of Uses, the use was executed, and the grantor retained the legal estate; the conveyance was thus ineffectual. When equitable interests returned under the name of trusts, the beneficial interest might again result to the grantor in cases both of realty and personalty, where the grantee was not intended to take beneficially. A number of problems remain in the ascertainment of the intention to be ascribed to the grantor.

The Law of Property Act, 1925, s.60(3), helps in solving these problems in relation to land.[86] While before 1926 it was necessary, in a voluntary conveyance, to insert a use in favour of the grantee in order to prevent a resulting trust arising, section 60(3) makes this no longer essential. Section 60(3) however, only prevents the implication of a resulting trust *merely* by reason that the conveyance is not expressed to be for the benefit of the grantee. If it is intended to take effect as a gift, it is still preferable to make this clear in the conveyance, as section 60(3) does not preclude the implication of a resulting trust on general equitable principles.[87] Where the transferor establishes that no gift was intended, section 60(3) does not prevent the finding of a resulting trust.

In *Hodgson v. Marks*,[88] Mrs. Hodgson was an old lady who was the registered owner of a house. A lodger, Evans, lived there. Mrs. Hodgson developed an affection for Evans, and trusted him to look after all her affairs. Her nephew disapproved of Evans, and tried to persuade Mrs. Hodgson to turn him out. To protect Evans,

---

[85] *per* Lord Denning M.R. at 320; Lawton L.J. made the same point: "There could not be a resulting trust of a chose in action which was no more": *ibid.* at 325.

[86] "In a voluntary conveyance a resulting trust for the grantor shall not be implied merely by reason that the property is not expressed to be conveyed for the use or benefit of the grantee." See *Lohia v. Lohia* [2001] W.T.L.R. 101; (2000) 14 *Trust Law International* 182.

[87] See Parker and Mellows, *The Modern Law of Trusts* (7th ed.), p. 255; Chambers, *Resulting Trusts*, pp. 16–19.

[88] [1971] Ch. 892.

she transferred the house to him, under an oral agreement that she would continue to be beneficial owner. Evans, as registered owner, sold it to a bona fide purchaser, Marks, and the question was whether Mrs. Hodgson was protected against Marks.

The Court of Appeal held that she remained beneficial owner in equity, and that this was an overriding interest.[89] The express oral agreement in her favour was unenforceable under the Law of Property Act 1925, s.53(1)(*b*). Evidence of her intention was however admissible, and this gave rise to a resulting trust of the beneficial interest, which was not affected by section 53(1). Section 60(3) was not discussed.

ii. Personalty. In relation to personalty, the initial presumption remains that a voluntary transfer to a third party is accompanied by the inference of a resulting trust.

In *Re Vinogradoff*,[90] the testatrix had transferred a sum of £800 War Loan, then standing in her name, into the joint names of herself and her granddaughter, then four years old. The testatrix continued to receive the dividends until her death.

Farwell J. held that, even though a child may not be appointed a trustee, the presumption of resulting trust applied, and the granddaughter held that property on resulting trust for the estate of the testatrix.

It is questionable whether such a result coincides with the real intention of the transferor. If, however, as would be one possible construction, her intention was to keep the property as her own during her lifetime and to give it to the granddaughter upon her death, such an attempted disposition would be testamentary, and void for failure to comply with the formal requirements of the Wills Act. A valid gift could be effected if intended to be held by the transferor for her life and after her death for the donee, or if a form of joint tenancy with a right of survivorship was created.[91]

It is even more doubtful whether the presumption accords with the transferor's intention in the case of a transfer to the grantee alone. The majority of such transfers must be intended as gifts. Although it seems correct to say that the presumption of a resulting trust exist in such cases,[92] it gives way to the slightest contrary

[89] Because she was in actual occupation; L.R.A. 1925, s.70(1)(*g*).
[90] [1935] W.N. 68; *Standing v. Bowring* (1885) 16 Ch.D. 282 at 287; *Fowkes v. Pascoe* (1875) L.R. 10 Ch.App. 343; *Thavorn v. Bank of Credit & Commerce International SA* [1985] 1 Lloyd's Rep. 259 (resulting trust where aunt opened bank account in name of 15 year old nephew).
[91] *Fowkes v. Pascoe* (1875) L.R. 10 Ch.App. 343; *post*, p. 265. See *Thavorn v. Bank of Credit & Commerce International SA*, *supra*, at 262.
[92] *George v. Havard* (1819) 7 Price 646 at 651, *per* Richards C.B.

evidence. The common sense of the transaction frequently prevails, and the rules of evidence do not prevent the sense of the transaction being deduced.

Lord Browne-Wilkinson has suggested that the resulting trust in such cases does not arise at the date of the transfer if the transferee was then ignorant of the facts, but arises only when the transferee's conscience becomes affected.[93] It is difficult to see how *Re Vinogradoff* supports this analysis, in view of the age of the transferee at all relevant times. This point has already been discussed.[94]

B. Presumption of Advancement

The presumption of advancement is a presumption working in the opposite direction. It arises where certain relationships exist, where the donor or purchaser is under an obligation recognised in equity, to support or provide for the transferee.[95] It arises if the person to whom a voluntary conveyance is made is the wife or child of the donor, or someone to whom he stands *in loco parentis*. It is clear from the cases, however, that adult children are within the presumption. Like the presumption of resulting trust, it is rebuttable by evidence that the donor intended to keep the beneficial interest for himself.

i. Husband and wife.

(a) *Gift by Husband.* The presumption of advancement applies where a husband makes a transfer to his wife. The strength of the presumption is diminished in modern times.[96] "It would in my view," said Lord Diplock in *Pettitt v. Pettitt,* [97] "be an abuse of the legal technique for ascertaining or imputing intention to apply to transactions between the post-war generation of married couples 'presumptions' which are based upon inferences of fact which an earlier generation of judges drew as the most likely intentions of earlier generations of spouses belonging to the propertied classes of a different social era." *Pettitt v. Pettitt* was a case of a claim to a share in the ownership of a matrimonial home, as to which special considerations apply, and will be discussed in Chapter 11.

---

[93] *Westdeutsche Landesbank Girozentrale v. Islington London Borough Council* [1996] A.C. 669 at 705–706.

[94] *ante,* p. 239.

[95] See *Cavalier v. Cavalier* (1971) 19 F.L.R. 199 (S.C.N.S.W.) at 205, where Carmichael J. considered this statement too narrow; [1974] A.S.C.L. 527 (J. Hackney).

[96] *Pettitt v. Pettitt* [1970] A.C. 777; *Gissing v. Gissing* [1971] A.C. 886; *Falconer v. Falconer* [1970] 1 W.L.R. 1333.

[97] *Supra,* at 824. See also *Simpson v. Simpson* [1992] 1 F.L.R. 601; *Harwood v. Harwood* [1991] 2 F.L.R. 274.

In *Re Eykyn's Trusts*[98] in 1877, Malins V.-C. said: "The law of this court is perfectly settled that where a husband transfers money or other property into the name of his wife only, then the presumption is, that it is intended as a gift or advancement to the wife absolutely at once ... " Transfers of chattels to a wife are within the presumption; and so is the matrimonial home which is conveyed to the wife although paid for by the husband. In *Tinker v. Tinker*,[99] the presumption was readily applied, in spite of the comments upon the presumption in *Pettitt v. Pettitt*; but there was ample evidence to show that the wife was intended to benefit.

The presumption also applies where the gift is made before marriage, but with a specific marriage (which in fact takes place) in mind.[1] There is no presumption of advancement where a man puts property into the name of his mistress,[2] nor is there such a presumption where a wife puts property into the name of her husband.[3] With a matrimonial home, at least, very little evidence will suffice to establish a sharing of the beneficial interest.[4]

(b) *Rebuttal.* The presumption can be rebutted by evidence which tends to show that no gift was intended. Thus, in *Anson v. Anson*,[5] a husband guaranteed his wife's banking account, and eventually the guarantee was called and he was obliged to pay a sum of money to the bank as a result. Pearson J. held that the husband could recover that sum from the wife, as the transaction was not in the nature of an advancement. There will be no advancement if, for example, a joint account was opened for the purposes of making it easier for the wife to draw money from an account, the husband being ill.[6] A joint

---

[98] (1877) 6 Ch.D. 115 at 118; quoted in *Pettitt v. Pettitt, supra,* at 815.

[99] [1970] P. 136.

[1] *Moate v. Moate* [1948] 2 All E.R. 486; *Ulrich v. Ulrich* [1968] 1 W.L.R. 180; (1975) 119 S.J. 108 (E. Ellis). A void marriage is not included. As to engaged couples, see Law Reform (Miscellaneous Provisions) Act 1970, s.2(1). One effect of s.2(1) is that the presumption of advancement applies to resolve disputes between couples whose engagement has ended; *Mossop v. Mossop* [1989] Fam. 77; [1988] Conv. 284 (J.E.M.); *cf. Bernard v. Josephs* [1982] Ch. 391 at 400.

[2] *Diwell v. Farnes* [1959] 1 W.L.R. 624; but the other rules for ascertaining the ownership of the home apply; *post*, p. 281.

[3] *Mercier v. Mercier* [1903] 2 Ch. 98; *Heseltine v. Heseltine* [1971] 1 W.L.R. 342. The Law Commission recommended otherwise; Law Com. No. 175 (1988), *Matrimonial Property*, para. 4.19.

[4] *per* Lord Upjohn in *Pettitt v. Pettitt* [1970] A.C. 777 at 815.

[5] [1953] 1 Q.B. 636. Similarly where the husband lacked mental capacity to make a gift; *Simpson v. Simpson* [1992] 1 F.L.R. 601.

[6] *Marshal v. Crutwell* (1875) L.R. 20 Eq. 328; *Simpson v. Simpson, supra.* Housekeeping money was dealt with by the Married Women's Property Act 1964, under which equality of ownership is presumed in the absence of other evidence; *cf. Re Figgis* [1969] Ch. 123.

account, though funded by the husband, will frequently lead to the inference of a joint tenancy in law and equity.[7]

ii. Father and Child. There is a presumption of advancement between a father and his legitimate child. The presumption here is stronger, and "should not . . . give way to slight circumstances."[8]

In *Re Roberts*,[9] a father took out an insurance policy on the life of his son and paid the premiums on it. It was contended after the father's death that the amounts paid by way of premium (by the father in his lifetime and by his estate until the son's death) were recoverable by his estate by means of a lien over the policy moneys. Evershed J. held that the presumption of advancement prevailed, and that each premium paid by the father during his lifetime was a separate advancement to the son. The premiums paid after the father's death by his estate were, however, recoverable as the relationship of father and son no longer existed.

iii. Other Relationships. But the moment one passes from this type of case to transfers from a mother to a child (whether or not the father is dead), from a father to an illegitimate child,[10] from grandparents, aunts and uncles, then the presumptions fade. Whether or not the presumption is technically in favour of a resulting trust, or technically in favour of advancement, the important consideration is whether or not there is evidence that the donor or purchaser regarded himself or herself as being *in loco parentis*, and the donee as being someone for whom an obligation to provide is felt.[11] The issue is treated as one of fact in the modern cases, and it is only in the absence of any evidence that the technical presumptions prevail.[12] Although, therefore, in cases other than that of father and legitimate child, the presumption may technically be in favour of a resulting trust, this is not, for the vast majority of cases, a decisive factor. The point is well brought out by the cases dealing with widowed mothers

---

[7] *Re Bishop* [1965] Ch. 450; *Re Figgis* [1969] Ch. 123; (1969) 85 L.Q.R. 530 (M. Cullity); *McHardy and Sons (a firm) v. Warren* (1994) 2 F.L.R. 338; *cf. Heseltine v. Heseltine* [1971] 1 W.L.R. 342 (husband had no interest where money provided by wife).

[8] *per* Viscount Simonds in *Shephard v. Cartwright, infra; cf.* Lord Upjohn in *Pettitt v. Pettitt, supra,* at 815; *McGrath v. Wallis* [1995] 2 F.L.R. 114; *post,* p. 268.

[9] [1946] Ch. 1. The policy itself was held on express trust for the son. See also *B. v. B.* (1976) 65 D.L.R. (3d) 460 (purchase of lottery ticket in name of 12-year-old daughter). A case where the presumption was rebutted is *Re Gooch* (1890) 62 L.T. 384 (father purchased shares to qualify son as director, and son handed over dividends to his father). See also *McEvoy v. Belfast Banking Co.* [1935] A.C. 24.

[10] This principle seems unaffected by the Family Law Reform Act 1987, which in general removes the property law disadvantages of children of unmarried parents.

[11] See, *per* Page-Wood V.-C. in *Tucker v. Burrow* (1865) 2 H. & M. 515 at 525–527; *Re Paradise Motor Co. Ltd* [1968] 1 W.L.R. 1125.

[12] *Re Vinogradoff* [1935] W.N. 68.

and their children.[13] In this situation, equity does not recognise in the mother, as it would have done in the father, an obligation to provide, hence there is no presumption of advancement. But the strangeness of this conclusion is wholly mitigated by the ease with which, on very little evidence, the courts will find the intent to advance.[14] In the analogous sphere of the presumption against "double portions" (whereby substantial lifetime provision for a child may be taken to adeem, or cancel, a legacy to that child), it has been held that this entirely judge-made law should move with the times. Thus the presumption should now apply to gifts made by mothers, although traditionally only a father or person *in loco parentis* could make a "portion": "both parents should nowadays be taken to be *in loco parentis* unless the contrary is proved".[15]

iv. Admissibility of Donor's Statements. In *Shephard v. Cartwright*,[16] C caused shares in companies he was promoting to be allotted to himself, his wife and his three children in 1929. The companies made considerable profits and in 1934 a public company was formed; the original shareholders received partly new shares and partly cash by way of payment for their old shares. C, in fact, controlled the whole family wealth, and the shares and money were divided between his wife and children for tax reasons. The wife and children at all times acquiesced in C's activities, and signed powers or attorney and powers to withdraw money at his wish.

By 1936, the cash had all been withdrawn by C and spent. Dividends on the shares allotted to the children were, however, treated as the income of the children, not the income of C. To a claim by the children against C's estate to recover the cash drawn by him on their bank accounts, it was argued that C's conduct showed that he had not intended the beneficial interest to vest in the children, but that they at all times held on resulting trust for C. The House of Lords rejected this contention. The onus of rebutting the presumption of advancement lay on C's executors, and there was nothing in C's conduct that was truly inconsistent with the presumption. The children had acquiesced in their father's conduct, rather than acted as trustees for him. The House of Lords also applied the rule that evidence of declarations and conduct subsequent to the original transaction is admissible only against the party making them, though

---

[13] *Bennet v. Bennet* (1879) 10 Ch.D. 474, discussing *Sayre v. Hughes* (1868) L.R. 5 Eq. 376 (where there was held to be a presumption). Commonwealth authorities favour extending the presumption of advancement to the mother/child relationship; see *Nelson v. Nelson* (1995) 132 A.L.R. 133; [1996] Conv. 274 (A. Dowling); *cf. Sekhon v. Alissa* [1989] 2 F.L.R. 94.

[14] See especially Jessel M.R. in *Bennet v. Bennet, supra.*

[15] *Re Cameron (deceased)* [1999] 3 W.L.R. 394 at 409.

[16] [1955] A.C. 431. Mellish L.J.'s judgment in *Fowkes v. Pascoe* (1875) L.R. 10 Ch.App. 343, emphasising the sense of the transaction, was expressly approved.

those made at the time of the original transaction are admissible for or against him.

v. Transfers for Unlawful Purposes. A further question is whether a transferor who has put property in the name of the transferee to achieve an unlawful purpose may rebut the presumption of advancement by proving his real intention. If the relevant presumption is that of resulting trust, the question is whether he may rely on it in spite of the illegality.

The matter was reviewed by the House of Lords in *Tinsley v. Milligan.*[17]

Two women agreed to put a house which they owned jointly into the name of one of them (the claimant) in order to facilitate fraudulent claims to housing benefit by the other (the defendant). Both were parties to the fraud, which was perpetrated over several years, but had now ceased. Eventually the claimant sought to evict the defendant.

It was held by a bare majority,[18] that the defendant could assert ownership of her equitable interest. The principle that a litigant cannot rely on his own fraud or illegality to rebut the presumption of advancement was confirmed.[19] Here, however, the operative presumption was that of a resulting trust. The defendant merely had to found her claim on that presumption and not on any illegality. Nor was she seeking to enforce executory provisions of an unlawful contract, in which the court would not assist. This result, according to the majority, promoted harmony between the approaches of equity and the common law to illegality. Policy did not require a wider application of the "clean hands" principle, which would not deter fraudulent conduct. The nineteenth century authorities supported the claimant, but, although the wide "clean hands" approach favoured by Lord Eldon[20] had never been overruled, the law on illegality had continued to develop. The reason why the property had been conveyed to the claimant was irrelevant to the defendant's claim, to which the presumption of resulting trust was crucial. The illegality only emerged because the claimant raised it; it was not necessary to the defendant's case.[21]

Lords Goff and Keith dissented on the ground that the "clean hands" principle espoused by Lord Eldon had been consistently

---

[17] [1994] 1 A.C. 340. See generally Enonchong, *Illegal Transactions.*

[18] Lords Jauncey, Lowry and Browne-Wilkinson.

[19] Discussed below. The presumption may be rebutted by evidence of illegality where the dispute is between the transferee and a third party; *R. v. London Borough of Harrow, ex p. Coker, The Times,* March 14, 1989.

[20] In *Muckleston v. Brown* (1801) 6 Ves. 52.

[21] See also *Haigh v. Kaye* (1872) 7 Ch.App. 469.

followed. Subject only to the "repentance" exception,[22] once it had come to the attention of the court that the claimant did not have clean hands, the court would refuse assistance even though the claim could be established without relying on the illegality. Both the majority and the minority agreed, however, that the "public conscience" test adopted by the Court of Appeal[23] (whereby a claim would succeed in spite of the illegality if the public conscience would not be offended) was too vague and discretionary, and not based on authority. Only Parliament could introduce such a reform.[24]

A solution which discourages illegality and also prevents the unjust enrichment of the transferee is not easy to find. It is unfortunate that the majority decision is based on the old presumptions, which are generally regarded as outmoded.[25] The result of *Tinsley v. Milligan* is that if a husband transfers to his wife or a father to his daughter for an unlawful purpose, he will be unable to assert any claim after carrying out the purpose,[26] whereas a wife who transfers to her husband, or a mother to her daughter, or a brother to his sister, will be successful. There seems little merit in this distinction, and in any event even a wife, mother or brother may be unsuccessful in the case of a voluntary conveyance of land, because section 60(3) of the Law of Property Act 1925[27] removes the presumption of a resulting trust, so that the onus of proof of entitlement is on the transferor.

The decision of the House of Lords has been much criticised.[28] Its effect has been said to be that "He who comes to equity should keep unclean hands in his pockets."[29] The decision has been subsequently applied by the Court of Appeal, although not without adverse comment. In *Silverwood (Geoffrey) (Executor of the Estate of Daisy Silverwood) v. Silverwood (Arnold)*[30] Daisy (aged 87) authorised the withdrawal from her account of over £21,000 at the request of her son, A, who put the money in another account in the names of his two children. Daisy then applied for and received income support,

---

[22] Discussed below.

[23] [1992] Ch. 310.

[24] See Illegal Contracts Act 1970 (New Zealand), ss.6, 7, permitting restitution of property at the court's discretion; *Duncan v. McDonald* [1997] 3 N.Z.L.R. 669. *Tinsley* has been rejected in Australia in favour of a more flexible public policy approach; *Nelson v. Nelson* (1995) 132 A.L.R. 133; (1997) 60 M.L.R. 102 (P. Creighton).

[25] See *Pettitt v. Pettitt* [1970] A.C. 777; *ante*, p. 256; *McGrath v. Wallis* [1995] 2 F.L.R. 114; *post*, p. 268.

[26] It is otherwise if the purpose has not been carried out; *Tribe v. Tribe* [1996] Ch. 107; *infra*.

[27] *ante*, p. 254.

[28] (1993) 52 C.L.J. 394 (R. Thornton); (1993) 7 *Trust Law International* 114 (M. Lunney); [1994] Conv. 62 (M. Halliwell); (1994) 57 M.L.R. 441 (H. Stowe); (1994) 110 L.Q.R. 3 (R. Buckley). For a different analysis, see (1995) 111 L.Q.R. 135 (N. Enonchong).

[29] (1993) 143 N.L.J. 1577 (B. Council).

[30] (1997) 74 P. & C.R. 453. The report does not state the ages of the children.

which would not have been available if she had kept the money or divested herself of it in order to qualify. It was not shown, however, that Daisy was knowingly a party to any illegal purpose. On her death her son G, the executor, claimed that the children held the money on a resulting trust for Daisy. Applying *Tinsley v. Milligan*,[31] his claim was upheld, although if the money had been put in the son's name, the estate would have been unable to rebut the presumption of advancement. Nourse L.J. criticised the *Tinsley* principle as a "straightjacket",[32] and preferred the approach of the Court of Appeal in that case, although on the present facts the outcome would have been the same. His Lordship expressed the rule as being that the claimant "is entitled to recover if he is not forced to plead or rely on the illegality. It is immaterial that he may give evidence of it. . . ".[33] The matter arose again in *Lowson v. Coombes*,[34] where elderly cohabitants both contributed to the purchase of a house, intending to share the beneficial interest. The house was put in the sole name of the woman in order to prevent the man's wife having any claim on it. This could be viewed as an illegal transaction under section 37 of the Matrimonial Causes Act 1973. When the elderly couple separated, the man sought a declaration that the woman held on resulting trust for him as to a half share. His claim was upheld, as it did not require reliance on illegality, although Robert Walker L.J. criticised the artificiality of the *Tinsley* principle.[35]

It has long been established and, as mentioned above, was confirmed by the House of Lords, that the presumption of advancement cannot be rebutted by evidence of the transferor's illegal purpose. Thus where a husband transferred property to his wife in order to evade tax[36] or to defeat his creditors[37] the property belonged to the wife even if she was a party to the scheme.[38] Similarly where a father transferred property to his son for an unlawful purpose.[39] In these cases it appears that the unlawful purpose had been carried out. The question which arose in *Tribe v. Tribe*[40] was whether the

---

[31] (1997) 74 P. & C.R. 453.

[32] *ibid.* at 458.

[33] *ibid.* at 459.

[34] Ch. 373; [1999] Conv. 242 (M. Thompson); [1999] L.M.C.L.Q. 465 (I. Cotterill). *Tinker v. Tinker* [1970] P. 136, *post*, p. 264, was distinguished.

[35] *supra* at 385.

[36] *Re Emery's Investment Trusts* [1959] Ch. 410.

[37] *Gascoigne v. Gascoigne* [1918] 1 K.B. 223.

[38] *ibid.*

[39] *Chettiar v. Chettiar* [1962] A.C. 294. It was suggested in *Muckleston v. Brown* (1801) 6 Ves. 52 at 68 that where the transferor could not recover, an innocent person claiming through him could do so, but this seems contrary to principle: *Ayerst v. Jenkins* (1873) L.R. 16 Eq. 274 at 281.

[40] [1996] Ch. 107; criticised (1996) 26 Fam.Law 30 (S. Cretney); (1996) 55 C.L.J. 23 (G. Virgo); (1996) 112 L.Q.R. 386 (F. Rose); (1996) 10 *Trust Law International* 51 (P. Pettit); [1996] R.L.R. 78 (N. Enonchong).

presumption of advancement may be rebutted by evidence of an illegal purpose where that purpose has not been carried out.

A landlord served repair notices on the tenant of two properties. The required works were substantial. If the tenant were to be held responsible, he would need to raise funds by selling his shares in his family company which occupied the premises. He transferred his shares to his son for a stated consideration which was not paid, in order to deceive the landlord as to his assets and thereby safeguard them. In fact the matter of the repairs was resolved without resort to deception, as the landlord agreed to the surrender of one lease and sold the reversion of the other to the tenant. When the son claimed to be entitled to the shares, the Court of Appeal held that the presumption of advancement was rebutted by evidence of the father's intentions, which were not consistent with a gift to the son. Although his purpose was illegal, the illegality had not been carried out.[41]

Tinsley v. Milligan did not decide that there was no exception to the rule that a claim could not be founded on an illegal act. Earlier cases established that the transferor could succeed where he "repented" and withdrew from the illegal transaction, although they were inconsistent as to whether genuine repentance was necessary. In *Sekhon v. Alissa*,[42] for example, a mother who had a house conveyed into her daughter's name was able to rebut the presumption where her alleged purpose of capital gains tax evasion had not been carried out simply because the house had not yet been sold. In *Tribe v. Tribe* there was no "repentance" because the father did not seek to recover the shares until the danger had passed. As the authorities on repentance were conflicting, it was held that a transferor could succeed if he withdrew from the transaction only because it was no longer necessary. The exception (*i.e.* that recovery is permitted where the illegal purpose has not been wholly or partly carried out) mitigates the harshness of the general rule, which could otherwise lead to injustice, and is designed to encourage withdrawal from fraud. The fact that "repentance" is not necessary does not further this policy, but it was felt that a stricter requirement could lead to bizarre results.

The Court of Appeal noted the arbitrary aspects of the principles laid down in *Tinsley v. Milligan*,[43] where so much depended on the relationship of the parties. As the presumption of advancement has fallen into disfavour, "there seems to be some perversity in its

---

[41] *Perpetual Executors and Trustees Association of Australia Ltd v. Wright* (1917) 23 C.L.R. 185 was applied.

[42] [1989] 2 F.L.R. 94.

[43] [1994] 1 A.C. 340.

elevation to a decisive status in the context of illegality."[44] Miss Milligan had recovered although she had defrauded. There would be cause for concern if a claimant who had not done so could not recover simply because the transferee was his son.

Millett L.J. sought to eliminate these arbitrary aspects by saying that the transferor would not invariably succeed where the presumption of resulting trust applied.[45] The presumption would be rebutted where the transferee led evidence that the transferor's subsequent conduct was inconsistent with any intention to retain a beneficial interest. An example would be where an uncle transferred assets to his nephew to conceal them from creditors and then settled with his creditors on the footing that he did not own the assets. He could not recover as his own conduct would be inconsistent with the retention of any interest. The problem with this is that the example is difficult to distinguish from *Tinsley v. Milligan* itself.

Of course, evidence that property was transferred to protect it from creditors does not alone rebut the presumption of advancement. Rather, it reinforces it, because the only way of protecting the property is for the transferor to divest himself of his interest. *Tinker v. Tinker*,[46] where a husband put a house in his wife's name to protect it from creditors if his new business should fail, was such a case. In fact there were no creditors and the husband in any event was not dishonest as his solicitors had advised the transfer. The evidence strengthened rather than rebutted the presumption of advancement. In order to rebut the presumption, a dishonest transferor must show that he intended to retain an interest and conceal it from his creditors. As Millett L.J. explained, compelling evidence of such an intention would be required. The court would be unlikely to reach such a conclusion where there was no imminent threat from known creditors at the transfer.

This area is currently under review by the Law Commission.[47] The illegality doctrine, which is based on deterrence, punishment, preventing profit from one's own wrongdoing, and upholding the dignity of the courts, should be retained, but the "reliance" principle of *Tinsley v. Milligan*[48] should be replaced by a statutory discretion.

---

[44] [1996] Ch. 107 at 118, *per* Nourse L.J.

[45] His Lordship considered that *Re Great Berlin Steamboat Co.* (1884) 26 Ch.Div. 616 (no recovery in resulting trust case where illegality carried out) had not been impliedly overruled.

[46] [1970] P. 136; *cf. Heseltine v. Heseltine* [1971] 1 W.L.R. 342 (presumption of resulting trust not rebutted where wife transferred assets to husband to save estate duty and qualify him as a Lloyd's "name", although these purposes would not be achieved unless the husband took beneficially).

[47] Law Com. C.P. No. 154 (1999), *Illegal Transactions: The Effect of Illegality on Contracts and Trusts*. See pp. 64–68, discussing whether the *Tinsley v. Milligan* principle assists a settlor who asserts a resulting trust where an express trust fails for illegality. On the proposals, see [2000] R.L.R. 82 (N. Enonchong); (2000) 20 L.S. 156 (R. Buckley).

[48] [1994] 1 A.C. 340.

The Commission considers that the arbitrariness of *Tinsley v. Milligan* and *Tribe v. Tribe*[49] is impossible to defend. Under the new proposals, illegality should continue to be used only as a defence. In exercising the proposed statutory discretion, the courts would consider:

   (i) the seriousness of the illegal conduct;

  (ii) the knowledge and intention of the party seeking the enforcement of the transaction or the recognition of property rights or the recovery of benefits;

 (iii) whether the refusal to assist that party would deter illegality;

 (iv) whether such refusal would further the purpose of the rule making the transaction illegal; and

  (v) whether such refusal would be proportionate to the illegality.

The discretion would not be exercisable if a statute making the conduct illegal expressly provided for the effect of the illegality.

4. Purchase Money Resulting Trusts

A. Purchase in the Name of Another

i. Presumptions in Favour of the Purchaser. Where a purchaser of realty or personalty takes a conveyance in the name of a third party, but there is nothing to indicate an intention on his part of not having the beneficial interest, then there is a presumption that he intended to obtain the beneficial interest for himself, and a resulting trust will be decreed in his favour. In the words of Eyre C.B.: "The trust of a legal estate . . . results to the man who advances the purchase-money."[50]

The presumption arises when a purchase is made in the joint names of a purchaser and a third party, and where a purchase is made in the name of third party alone; also where property purchased with the contributions of more than one person is conveyed into the name of only one of them, or where unequal contributors become joint legal owners.[51]

The classic case is *Fowkes v. Pascoe*.[52]

---

[49] [1996] Ch. 107.

[50] *Dyer v. Dyer* (1788) 2 Cox 92 at 93.

[51] See *Springette v. Defoe* (1993) 65 P. & C.R. 1; *Huntingford v. Hobbs* [1993] 1 F.L.R. 736.

[52] (1875) L.R. 10 Ch.App. 343; see also *Pettitt v. Pettitt* [1970] A.C. 777; *Hoare v. Hoare* (1983) 13 Fam.Law 142.

Mrs B purchased stock in the names of herself and the son of her widowed daughter-in-law. The son was outside the relationships where the presumption of advancement would arise, hence he would prima facie be presumed to hold on resulting trust for Mrs B. But the Court of Appeal in Chancery held that the strength of the presumption varied according to the circumstances and that, once there is some evidence to rebut it, the court must look at the facts from a common-sense point of view. In the present case, the only rational inference was that Mrs B intended the purchase as a gift, so that the presumption of resulting trust was rebutted, though the effect of the gift would not be apparent until Mrs B's death, for the court also held that any income declared on the stock during Mrs B's lifetime would belong beneficially to her. Such a gift does not infringe the Wills Act 1837, as the legal title passes by the transfer; the legal title carries with it the right of survivorship, and all that happens on the death of Mrs B is that her equitable right ceases to be outstanding.[53] There is thus no *testamentary* gift provided the lifetime transfer is complete and not revocable.[54]

It was recently held that there was nothing to rebut the presumption of a resulting trust where, in addition to paying for her own share, a wife paid £1 to a lottery syndicate in relation to a share which was in her estranged husband's name. Thus the wife was entitled to the winnings attributable to both shares.[55]

ii. Presumption of Advancement. As in the case of voluntary conveyances, a purchase in the name of a wife or child or other person to whom the purchaser stands *in loco parentis* raises a contrary presumption, as the purchase is presumed in these cases to be an advancement. As Lord Eldon said in *Marlees v. Franklin*,[56] "The general rule that on a purchase by one man in the name of another, the nominee is trustee for the purchaser is subject to exception where the purchaser is under a species of natural obligation to provide for the nominee." The presumption is weak in the case of husband and wife. It is stronger with a parent and child, at any rate

---

[53] *Young v. Sealey* [1949] Ch. 278. The argument is not an easy one, but Romer J. preferred to take this view as no previous English case had taken this point under the Wills Act, and gifts of this sort had not previously been thought to raise difficulties. See (1992) 6 *Trust Law International* 57 (J. Miller).

[54] But in the case of a joint bank account opened by a husband in the name of himself and his wife so that either can draw on it (the account being kept in credit by the husband), there is a gift to the wife of what happens to be in the account at the date of the husband's death. The difficulties of this reasoning are discussed by Megarry J. in *Re Figgis* [1969] Ch. 123, where however *Young v. Sealey, supra,* was followed. (1969) 85 L.Q.R. 530 (M. Cullity).

[55] *Abrahams v. Trustee in Bankruptcy of Abrahams, The Times,* July 26, 1999.

[56] (1818) 1 Swans. 13 at 17.

where the house is for the sole occupation of the child,[57] but may be rebutted. In *Warren v. Gurney*[58]

A father bought a house for his daughter, who was shortly to get married, to live in. The conveyance was taken in the name of the daughter, but the father retained the title deeds. On his death 15 years later, the daughter claimed to be the beneficial owner of the house. The Court of Appeal held that there was a presumption of advancement in her favour, but that it had been rebutted by the fact of the retention of the title deeds, accompanied by evidence contemporaneous with the purchase in 1929. Retention of the deeds by itself is probably insufficient evidence, however.

B. Purchase by Several in the Name of One

The general principle is that the legal title is held on trust for the purchasers in the proportions in which they contributed to the purchase price,[59] although in some circumstances the court may be able to infer an agreement (giving rise to a constructive trust) to hold in shares which are not proportionate to the contributions.[60] The purchasers thus have a concurrent interest and can claim the due proportion of the proceeds on any eventual sale of the property to include a proportion of any increase in the value of the property.[61] The resulting trust may arise where the land is purchased subject to a mortgage which is paid off by instalments.[62] No resulting trust however arose where one member of a group was tenant of a flat, and all the residents shared the payment of the rent.[63]

Cases of this kind can give rise to serious conveyancing difficulties. The true facts of the purchase may be proved by oral evidence and, not being part of the title, may not be known to a purchaser or mortgagee; who may then find himself dealing with a case of co-ownership without having appreciated this.[64] Many cases under this head are concerned with the question of the ownership of a matrimonial home, and are dealt with in Chapter 11.

---

[57] *cf. McGrath v. Wallis*; *infra*.

[58] [1944] 2 All E.R. 472; see also *Pettitt v. Pettitt* [1970] A.C. 777.

[59] *Wray v. Steele* (1814) 2 V. & B. 388. The trust is traditionally regarded as resulting, but Lord Bridge described it as constructive in *Lloyds Bank plc v. Rosset* [1991] 1 A.C. 107 at 133.

[60] *Midland Bank plc v. Cooke* [1995] 4 All E.R. 562; *Drake v. Whipp* [1996] 1 F.L.R. 826; *post*, p. 277.

[61] *Diwell v. Farnes* [1959] 1 W.L.R. 624; *cf. Hussey v. Palmer* [1972] 1 W.L.R. 1286. See further, *post*, p. 283.

[62] *Moate v. Moate* [1948] 2 All E.R. 486.

[63] *Savage v. Dunningham* [1974] Ch. 181; (1973) 37 Conv.(N.S.) 440 (F. Crane).

[64] *Cook v. Cook* [1962] P. 235; *post*, p. 289.

Where two people contribute to the purchase of a house for their joint occupation which is conveyed into the name of one, the presumption of advancement, which arises if the legal owner is the wife or child of the other party, is a last resort, and is rebuttable by comparatively slight evidence in both cases.

In *McGrath v. Wallis*[65] a house was acquired for the occupation of a family (parents, son and daughter) but was put in the adult son's name to enable a mortgage loan to be obtained (the father being unemployed). The father contributed £34,500 towards the price of £42,995, the balance being raised by the mortgage. The father's solicitors drew up a declaration of trust whereby the beneficial interest was to be held as to 80 per cent for the father and 20 per cent for the son, but, for reasons which were not established, it was never executed. After the death of the parents, the son claimed absolute entitlement, but the Court of Appeal held that the presumption of advancement was rebutted. The parties' intentions were to hold in shares proportionate to their contributions.

The decisive features were that the son alone was acceptable as mortgagor (which alone was probably enough to rebut the presumption); there was no evidence that the father had instructed the solicitors not to proceed with the declaration; and there was no reason why the father, who was only 63 at the time and not ill, should wish to give the house to the son. The observations in *Pettitt v. Pettitt*[66] and elsewhere as to the weakness of the presumption of advancement between husband and wife applied equally to father and child.

5. REFORM

The Law Commission proposed certain reforms affecting the presumptions and purchase money resulting trusts.[67] These proposals apply to spouses and engaged couples,[68] but not to cohabitants.

The main proposal was that where money is spent to buy property, or property or money is transferred by one spouse to the other, for their joint use or benefit, the property or money should be jointly owned.[69] Where money or property is transferred by one spouse to

[65] [1995] 2 F.L.R. 114; criticised in (1995) 25 Fam.Law 552 (J. Dewar).
[66] [1970] A.C. 777.
[67] Law Com. No. 175 (1988), *Family Law; Matrimonial Property.* Implementation is not in prospect.
[68] By virtue of Law Reform (Miscellaneous Provisions) Act 1970, s.2.
[69] Para. 4.1.

the other for any other purpose, it should be owned by the transferee. In both cases, this is subject to a contrary intention on the part of the paying or transferring spouse, provided it is known to the other spouse.

The proposal relating to purchases does not apply to land,[70] on the ground that most matrimonial homes are now purchased in joint names and the spouses are likely to have taken legal advice when buying the home. There is no such exclusion regarding the proposal relating to transfers of property from one spouse to the other. Such a transfer which is not for their joint use and benefit would be treated as a gift under the above proposals whether the transferor was the husband or wife. Thus the presumption of advancement would apply equally to both spouses.[71] As the presumption now applies to all kinds of property, any reform must do as well.[72]

[70] Para. 4.2. Life assurance policies are also excluded.
[71] Para. 4.19.
[72] Para. 4.10.

CHAPTER 11

TRUSTS OF THE FAMILY HOME

1. INTRODUCTION

IN the last chapter we saw the part played by the doctrine of resulting trusts in the acquisition of property interests. Most of the modern cases involve disputes between married or unmarried couples over ownership of the home. In this chapter we will examine the special considerations which apply to the matrimonial or family home. The first part of the chapter will deal with the establishment of a proprietary interest in the home, for example under the doctrines or resulting or constructive trusts. The second part will examine some of the problems of co-ownership of land. To complete the picture, reference should also be made to Chapter 27, where it will be seen that those who cannot establish an interest under a trust of the family home might nevertheless acquire rights as licensees or under the doctrine of estoppel.

2. ACQUISITION OF INTERESTS IN THE HOME

A. Background to the Problem

In the case of a married couple, one problem which arises is that the older rules of property law, which became established at a time when the wife was less likely to be earning her living than is the case

271

today, do not properly recognise her contribution to the relationship:

> "Until little more than a century ago the common law did not permit married women to own any property whatsoever. It became the property of her husband. When a measure of reform was proposed in 1856 one Member of Parliament protested, 'If a woman had not full confidence in a man, let her refrain from marrying him' ".[1]

The modern view is that marriage is a partnership between equals, in which the wife has an economic contribution to make. But she does not always insist on the matrimonial home being conveyed to the spouses jointly; or on a declaration of trust of a share of the house in favour of herself. Nor is justice done to her by the presumption of a resulting trust, based on payment of the purchase money; first, because childcare and housework are not money-producing, and secondly, because if she has a job, her earnings may be spent on household expenses and not in contributing to the purchase price of the house. "The cock can feather the nest because he does not have to spend most of his time sitting on it."[2]

Another problem stems from the fact that today a significant and increasing proportion of couples cohabit outside marriage. Should their relationship break down, the court has no statutory power to adjust their property interests. Divorcing couples, on the other hand, can invoke the court's discretionary powers to order a distribution of the property of the spouses.[3] This statutory jurisdiction will not be discussed here, but its significance must be emphasised. The following account deals only with the general law, which applies, subject to minor exceptions, equally to married and unmarried couples. A difficulty frequently encountered, as will be seen, is that the parties do not formulate their intention at the time the property is acquired, but consider the matter only when their relationship breaks down.

The question then is how to ensure that the ownership of the home is fairly shared. The possibility of giving the court, in the case of married couples, a wide discretionary power to declare what are the appropriate shares to be held by disputing spouses in any particular

---

[1] *Rooney v. Cardona* [1999] 1 F.L.R. 1236 at 1240, *per* Robert Walker L.J.

[2] *per* Sir Jocelyn Simon, extrajudicially quoted by Lord Hodson in *Pettitt v. Pettitt* [1970] A.C. 777 at 811.

[3] Matrimonial Causes Act 1973, as amended by Family Law Act 1996; *Wachtel v. Wachtel* [1973] Fam. 72; (1974) 118 S.J. 431 (S. Cretney). Property disputes between spouses are best settled under this jurisdiction; *Williams v. Williams* [1976] Ch. 278 at 286; *Suttill v. Graham* [1977] 1 W.L.R. 819 at 824. The statutory jurisdiction does not apply to engaged couples by reason of Law Reform (Miscellaneous Provisions) Act 1970, s.2(1); *Mossop v. Mossop* [1989] Fam. 77; [1988] Conv. 286 (J.E.M.).

case has been rejected[4]; likewise the concept of community of property.[5] A proposal[6] that the matrimonial home should be shared equally was not implemented. The property rights of cohabitants are currently under review.[7] Until the enactment of any reforms, the rights of the parties are determined according to the principles of property law, making whatever use is appropriate of evidence of agreement, declarations of trust (which comply with the necessary formalities applicable to trusts of land) and of inferences and presumptions.

The first question to determine is whether each party owns some share. If so, there is co-ownership, and the house is held upon trust, even though it may be vested only in one.[8] The next question is to determine what is the share of each party.[9] A number of other problems can arise, such as a decision on sale if one party wishes to sell and the other to retain; questions as to the right to possession and the payment of rent; and the protection of an occupying co-owner if the sole legal owner sells to a third party.

B. Conveyance to One Party Only

If the house is conveyed to one party only, to the man, let us assume, for that is the usual case, then he will prima facie be the owner of the whole beneficial interest as well.[10] If the documents of title expressly declare the beneficial interests, that, in the absence of fraud or mistake, is conclusive,[11] although those who were not parties to the deed cannot be prejudiced by such a declaration if they have contributed.[12] Failing that, the woman may claim a share of the beneficial interest in various ways. First, there may be an express contract in writing,[13] or a trust in her favour which is evidenced in writing.[14] Subject to estoppel arguments, an oral contract for the disposition of an interest in land is void. An oral declaration of a trust of land which is not evidenced in writing is unenforceable unless it has been acted upon so as to give rise to a constructive

---

[4] *Gissing v. Gissing* [1971] A.C. 886.

[5] Law Com. No. 52, para. 59. See also Law Com. No. 90, para. 5.20. A modified community of property scheme has been recommended; (1999) 19 L.S. 468 (A. Barlow and C. Lind).

[6] Third Report on Family Property (Law Com. No. 86). These proposals were flawed by registration requirements. Statutory co-ownership is advocated in [1998] Conv. 202 (U. Riniker).

[7] Law Com. No. 239, para. 6.7. A Consultation Paper is expected in the latter part of 2001.

[8] *post*, p. 285.

[9] *post*, p. 282.

[10] *Gissing v. Gissing* [1971] A.C. 886 at 900, 901, 910; *Burns v. Burns* [1984] Ch. 317.

[11] *Pettitt v. Pettitt* [1970] A.C. 777 at 813; *Goodman v. Gallant* [1986] Fam. 106.

[12] See *City of London Building Society v. Flegg* [1988] A.C. 54.

[13] Law of Property (Miscellaneous Provisions) Act 1989, s.2. See (1990) 10 L.S. 325 (L. Bently and P. Coughlan).

[14] L.P.A. 1925, s.53(1)(*b*).

trust.[15] This is discussed below. If there is no express agreement or declaration, direct contributions in money or money's worth have traditionally been regarded as giving rise to a resulting trust, but the House of Lords appears now to regard direct contributions as creating a constructive trust.[16] As we will see, their Lordships considered that no common intention to share (giving rise to a constructive trust) could be inferred from indirect contributions. Finally, a trust has been imposed in some cases simply in the interests of justice.[17]

i. Express Agreement or Declaration. If the declaration is contained in the documents of title, then it will be conclusive, as stated above. If it is not contained in the documents of title but is nevertheless evidenced in writing, it is enforceable under section 53(1)(*b*) of the Law of Property Act 1925. These formality requirements do not apply to resulting or constructive trusts.[18] Resulting trusts are dealt with below. In the present context, the question arises as to the circumstances necessary for the imposition of a constructive trust where there is an express oral declaration or agreement.

The first point to consider is what constitutes an express oral declaration or agreement. The question is whether prior to the acquisition, or exceptionally at some later date,[19] the parties had an agreement to share, based on evidence of express discussions, however imperfectly remembered and however imprecise the terms.[20] A common intention to renovate a house as a joint venture or to share it as a family home does not amount to a common intention to share the beneficial ownership.[21] An excuse as to why the property is in the man's name will, however, be treated as an express declaration of an intention to share the beneficial ownership.[22] An express common intention means one that is communicated between the parties.[23]

---

[15] *Midland Bank Ltd v. Dobson* [1986] 1 F.L.R. 171; *Grant v. Edwards* [1986] Ch. 638.

[16] *Lloyds Bank plc v. Rosset* [1991] 1 A.C. 107.

[17] *Cooke v. Head* [1972] 1 W.L.R. 518; (1973) C.L.P. 17 at 25 (A. Oakley); *Eves v. Eves* [1975] 1 W.L.R. 1338.

[18] L.P.A. 1925, s. 53(2); Law of Property (Miscellaneous Provisions) Act 1989, s.2(5); *Yaxley v. Gotts* [2000] Ch. 162.

[19] *Bernard v. Josephs* [1982] Ch. 391; *Burns v. Burns* [1984] Ch. 317; *Austin v. Keele* (1987) 61 A.L.J.R. 605; *Lloyds Bank plc v. Rosset* [1991] 1 A.C. 107; *Stokes v. Anderson* [1991] 1 F.L.R. 391.

[20] *Lloyds Bank plc v. Rosset, supra.* But see (1996) 16 L.S. 325 (N. Glover and P. Todd).

[21] *ibid.*

[22] *Eves v. Eves, supra* (excuse that woman under 21); *Grant v. Edwards* [1986] Ch. 638 (excuse that joint names might prejudice her divorce proceedings); criticised (1987) 50 M.L.R. 94 (B. Sufrin); *cf.* (1993) 3 Carib.L.R. 96 (R. Smith); (1995) 145 N.L.J. 423, 456 (P. Milne). See also *Rowe v. Prance* [1999] 2 F.L.R. 787 (woman entitled to half share of boat registered in man's name; "absurd" excuse that she did not possess a master's certificate); [2000] Conv. 58 (S. Baughen).

[23] *Springette v. Defoe* (1993) 65 P. & C.R. 1. See, however, *Midland Bank plc v. Cooke* [1995] 4 All E.R. 562; *post*, p. 277.

Assuming that an express common intention is established, the claimant must also show that she has acted upon it to her detriment if a constructive trust (or estoppel) is to arise.[24] An oral agreement alone cannot suffice, as this would infringe the formality rules and could prejudice the legal owner's creditors.[25] It is clear that significant contributions in money or money's worth, even though indirect, will satisfy the requirements of detrimental reliance. Thus in *Grant v. Edwards*[26] a woman was entitled to a half share where, pursuant to an express oral declaration, she had made substantial indirect contributions to the mortgage by applying her earnings to the joint household expenses in addition to keeping house and bringing up the children. The Court of Appeal considered that any detrimental act relating to the joint lives of the parties would have sufficed. Such a view, while requiring clarification, seems to provide an opportunity for a sympathetic treatment of a woman who has made no financial contribution.[27] In similar vein, the Privy Council has said that once a common intention has been established it may not be difficult to find conduct on the part of the woman which is referable to the creation of her beneficial interest.[28]

The House of Lords reviewed these principles in *Lloyds Bank plc v. Rosset*.[29] In that case there was no express common intention. If there had been, the wife's acts of decorating and supervising renovation works would not have constituted detrimental reliance, as they were acts which any wife would do.[30] Acts which have been considered sufficient include refraining from seeking repayment of a loan or interest upon it,[31] and a payment of £12,000 to the man so that he could buy out his estranged wife's share and pay the mortgage on her new house.[32] Where a constructive trust arises from an express common intention coupled with direct and indirect contributions (such as labour and contributions to household expenses) the latter may increase the share beyond that which would otherwise

---

[24] The onus is on the legal owner to prove that any detrimental act was not done in reliance upon the common intention; *Greasley v. Cooke* [1980] 1 W.L.R. 1306; *Maharaj v. Chand* [1986] A.C. 898.

[25] *Midland Bank Ltd v. Dobson* [1986] 1 F.L.R. 171; *cf. Re Densham* [1975] 1 W.L.R. 1519.

[26] *supra.* See also *Eves v. Eves, supra.*

[27] (1987) 50 M.L.R. 94 (B. Sufrin); [1987] Conv. 16 (J. Montgomery); (1996) 16 L.S. 218 (A. Lawson); *cf. Coombes v. Smith* [1986] 1 W.L.R. 808, *post,* p. 883.

[28] *Austin v. Keele* (1987) 61 A.L.J.R. 605 at 610.

[29] [1991] 1 A.C. 107; (1990) 106 L.Q.R. 539 (J. Davies); [1990] Conv. 314 (M. Thompson); All E.R.Rev. 1990, p. 138 (S. Cretney); (1991) 50 C.L.J. 38 (M. Dixon); (1991) 54 M.L.R. 126 (S. Gardner).

[30] *cf. Ungurian v. Lesnoff* [1990] Ch. 206; (1990) 49 C.L.J. 25 (M. Oldham) (common intention to create life interest sufficiently acted upon by decorating and refurbishment).

[31] *Risch v. McFee* (1991) 61 P. & C.R. 42.

[32] *Stokes v. Anderson* [1991] 1 F.L.R. 391. The woman had also spent £2,500 on decorating. The parties had drawn up a promissory note, but it was held that the £12,000 was not in fact a loan.

arise under a resulting trust.[33] In *Hammond v. Mitchell*[34] a woman was held entitled to a half share of a bungalow when, pursuant to an oral agreement, she acted as the man's unpaid business assistant and supported him in his business ventures as well as looking after the home and children. The judge also classified her act of agreeing to subordinate her rights to those of a mortgagee as one of detrimental reliance, but this seems inadequate. "Can consent to the possible loss of property one does not own make one an owner of that very property?"[35]

ii. Presumption of Resulting Trust; Direct Contributions.

There will be a purchase money resulting trust in favour of a person who has contributed to the purchase price. Beneficial ownership will normally be enjoyed in the proportion in which the purchase money has been provided.[36] If the purchase money is provided equally, the parties are beneficial joint tenants. If the contributions are unequal, they are tenants in common. Payment of, or substantial contributions to the mortgage instalments, will usually suffice[37]; however, such payments do not give rise to a resulting trust unless the payer had assumed liability to make them when the property was purchased (although they may found a constructive trust).[38] For a resulting trust to arise, any payments must be in money or money's worth.[39]

The presumption of advancement may similarly arise in a case where a husband has transferred or arranged for the transfer of the legal estate to his wife; but, as has been seen, statements in *Pettitt v. Pettitt*[40] show that the influence of the presumptions has been much reduced. There is no presumption of advancement where a wife has transferred to her husband[41]; nor in the case of an unmarried couple.[42]

---

[33] *Drake v. Whipp* [1996] 1 F.L.R. 826; *post*, p. 277.

[34] [1991] 1 W.L.R. 1127; (1992) 22 Fam. Law 523 (L. Clarke and R. Edmunds).

[35] [1992] Conv. 218 at 222 (A. Lawson); All E.R.Rev. 1992, p. 210 (P. Clarke); (1993) 56 M.L.R. 224 (P. O'Hagan).

[36] *Re Roger's Question* [1948] 1 All E.R. 328; *Bull v. Bull* [1955] 1 Q.B. 234. A strict view was taken in *Winkworth v. Edward Baron Development Co. Ltd* [1986] 1 W.L.R. 1512, where, however, the protection of creditors was a significant factor. See [1987] Conv. 217 (J. Warburton).

[37] *Springette v. Defoe* (1993) 65 P. & C.R. 1; *Huntingford v. Hobbs* [1993] 1 F.L.R. 736; [1992] Conv. 347 (H. Norman).

[38] *Re Roger's Question* [1948] 1 All E.R. 328; (1994) 8 *Trust Law International* 43 (P. Matthews). See also *Winkworth v. Edward Baron Developments Ltd* [1986] 1 W.L.R. 1512 at 1515.

[39] *Button v. Button* [1968] 1 All E.R. 1064; *Muetzel v. Muetzel* [1970] 1 W.L.R. 188; *Wachtel v. Wachtel* [1973] Fam. 72 at 92, *per* Lord Denning M.R.

[40] 1970 A.C. 777. See also *Simpson v. Simpson* [1992] 1 F.L.R. 601.

[41] *Heseltine v. Heseltine* [1971] 1 W.L.R. 342 (personalty).

[42] Unless they had agreed to marry; Law Reform (Miscellaneous Provisions) Act 1970, s.2(1); *Mossop v. Mossop* [1989] Fam. 77. As to "agreement to marry," see *Shaw v. Fitzgerald* [1992] 1 F.L.R. 357.

In the case of direct contributions, it does not seem that any actual intention to share must be proved, because the effect of the doctrine of resulting trusts is that such an intention is rebuttably presumed. Unfortunately the House of Lords has made the position uncertain by treating direct contributions as giving rise to a constructive trust.[43]

Recent cases display a broad approach to direct contributions. In *McHardy and Sons (a firm) v. Warren*[44] the Court of Appeal held that where a parent pays a deposit on a house as a wedding present, the irresistible conclusion is that all three intended the couple to have equal shares in the house and not shares measured by reference to the percentage which the deposit bore to the price. In *Midland Bank plc v. Cooke*[45] a house was bought in the husband's name with a mortgage loan of £6,450, his savings of £950 and a gift of £1,100 from his parents to the couple. The wife did not pay the mortgage directly but paid other outgoings from her earnings. Both stated that they never discussed their shares. In possession proceedings relating to a later mortgage, the Court of Appeal held that if an equitable interest has been acquired by direct contribution (the money derived from the gift) and there is no express evidence of intention, the court will assess the proportions the parties are assumed to have intended by surveying the course of dealing between them, their sharing of the burdens and benefits of the property, and all conduct throwing light on the question. The court is not bound to find that the shares are proportionate to direct contributions on a strict resulting trust basis and is free to infer an intention to share differently on general equitable principles. On that basis (which seems over generous to the wife) the parties took in equal shares, as they agreed to share everything equally: the profits of the husband's business and the risks of indebtedness if it failed, the upbringing of the children, and the home (which had been put into joint names after the date of the claimant's mortgage) which the wife had helped to maintain and improve, coupled with the added commitment of marriage. This has been described as "nothing less than the re-emergence of the doctrine of family assets."[46] Similarly in *Drake v. Whipp*,[47] where the woman made a direct contribution of about one fifth to the purchase

---

[43] *Lloyds Bank plc v. Rosset* [1991] 1 A.C. 107. See also *Birmingham Midshires Mortgage Services Ltd v. Sabherwal* (2000) 80 P. & C.R. 256.

[44] [1994] 2 F.L.R. 338, questioned in (1994) 24 Fam. Law 567 (J. Dewar). See also *Halifax Building Society v. Brown* [1996] 1 F.L.R. 103 (loan from mother-in-law for deposit).

[45] [1995] 4 All E.R. 562, applying *Gissing v. Gissing* [1971] A.C. 886. The different approaches of Dillon L.J. in *McHardy, supra*, and in *Springette v. Defoe* (1993) 65 P. & C.R. 1 were "mystifying". See All E.R.Rev. 1995, pp. 286 (S. Cretney) and 312 (P. Clarke); (1996) 112 L.Q.R. 378 (S. Gardner); (1996) 55 C.L.J. 194 (M. Oldham); (1996) 26 Fam. Law 298 (D. Wragg) and 484 (M. Pawlowski); [1996] 8 C.F.L.Q. 261 (G. Battersby); (1996) 16 L.S. 325 at 340 (N. Glover and P. Todd); [1997] Conv. 66 (M. Dixon).

[46] (1997) 60 M.L.R. 420 at 427 (P. O'Hagan).

[47] [1996] 1 F.L.R. 826; [1997] Conv. 467 (A. Dunn).

and conversion of a barn. The parties had a common intention that she should have a beneficial interest, which the Court of Appeal determined as one third, adopting a "broad brush" approach, and taking into account her work on the conversion and contribution to household expenses. The need to distinguish constructive and resulting trust principles was emphasised. Thus the finding of a common intention may enable the court to fix a fair share which differs from the proportionate resulting trust.

The next question is whether, in the absence of a direct contributions or express agreement, a common intention to share may be inferred solely from indirect contributions or other conduct.

iii. Indirect Contributions. It is important to appreciate at the outset that, since *Gissing v. Gissing*,[48] the court does not decide how the parties might have ordered their affairs; it only finds how they did. "The court cannot devise agreements which the parties never made. The court cannot ascribe intentions which the parties in fact never had".[49] In that case the House of Lords rejected the claim of a wife who had paid £220 for furnishings and for laying a lawn, plus some household expenses, because she had made no contribution to the purchase price. It was, however, accepted that a wife who contributed indirectly by relieving her husband of household expenses and thereby enabling him to pay the mortgage would be entitled to an interest.[50]

Later decisions in the Court of Appeal, primarily in Lord Denning's time, supported the view that substantial financial contributions, even though indirect, would suffice for the acquisition of a share.[51] Thus interests were acquired by the contribution of physical labour on the property,[52] or by unpaid work in the family business which enabled the husband to put the money saved towards the purchase of property.[53] Domestic duties in the home, on the other hand, have never sufficed. In *Burns v. Burns*[54] the woman's housework, childcare, decorating and the purchase of chattels for the home over a period of 17 years gave her no share. If this was unjust, it was suggested that the remedy lay with Parliament. The position is otherwise in Canada, where the view that domestic services do not

---

[48] [1971] A.C. 886.

[49] *ibid., per* Lord Morris of Borth-y-Gest at 898; *cf. Bristol and West Building Society v. Henning* [1985] 1 W.L.R. 778, *post* p. 291.

[50] [1971] A.C. 886 at 903, 907–908.

[51] *Falconer v. Falconer* [1970] 1 W.L.R. 1333; *Hargrave v. Newton* [1971] 1 W.L.R. 1611; *Wachtel v. Wachtel* [1973] Fam. 72.

[52] *Cooke v. Head* [1972] 1 W.L.R. 518. For improvements, see *post*, p. 282.

[53] *Nixon v. Nixon* [1969] 1 W.L.R. 1676.

[54] [1984] Ch. 317 (unmarried couple). See also *Richards v. Dove* [1974] 1 All E.R. 888; *Layton v. Martin* (1986) 16 Fam. Law 212; *Windeler v. Whitehall* [1990] 2 F.L.R. 505 (housework and business entertaining insufficient).

suffice is now considered untenable. Thus in *Peter v. Beblow*[55] a woman who cared for her own children and those of her partner for some years, did the housework, and contributed to the housekeeping with earnings from a part-time job was held entitled to the house under a constructive trust on the basis that her partner (who was entitled to keep a van and a houseboat acquired during the cohabitation) would otherwise be unjustly enriched by her services, which enhanced his ability to pay off the mortgage and acquire other assets. The free accommodation she had enjoyed was not sufficient compensation.

In English law it appears that, in the absence of an express common intention, indirect contributions will not suffice. In *Lloyds Bank plc v. Rosset*,[56] where the wife had made no substantial contribution, direct or indirect, Lord Bridge took the opportunity to state that direct contributions (whether initially or by payment of the mortgage) were necessary, and that "it is at least extremely doubtful whether anything less will do."[57] The earlier cases of *Eves v. Eves*[58] (extensive decorative work and heavy gardening) and *Grant v. Edwards*[59] (substantial indirect contributions to the mortgage by applying earnings to household expenses, plus running the home) were correctly decided because both involved an express common intention. In the absence of the latter, neither claimant would have succeeded, because the conduct in each case "fell far short" of conduct which would by itself have supported a claim to a share. Applying this principle, it has been held that a woman who acted as the man's unpaid business assistant, supported him in his speculative ventures and looked after the home and children, could not acquire a share in the property in the absence of an express common intention.[60] Likewise where a daughter worked full-time in her mother's public house for pocket money only, assisting her mother to make a profit which facilitated the purchase of a house. The daughter had no interest in the house as there was neither direct contribution nor express agreement.[61] We have seen, however, that where a common intention to share is inferred from a direct contribution, indirect contributions may also be taken into account in assessing the shares the parties are assumed to have intended.[62] This approach reduces

---

[55] (1993) 101 D.L.R. (4th) 621; *post*, p. 281.
[56] [1991] 1 A.C. 107. These principles were held applicable where the property was in joint names but the beneficial interest was not declared; *Rhoden v. Joseph* [1990] E.G.C.S. 115.
[57] *ibid.* at 133.
[58] [1975] 1 W.L.R. 1338.
[59] [1986] Ch. 638.
[60] *Hammond v. Mitchell* [1991] 1 W.L.R. 1127 (the Spanish house); *ante*, p. 276.
[61] *Ivin v. Blake* (1994) 67 P. & C.R. 263; criticised [1996] Conv. 462 (A. Lawson).
[62] *Midland Bank plc v. Cooke* [1995] 4 All E.R. 562.

the impact of *Lloyds Bank plc v. Rosset*,[63] but the apparent exclusion from any share of a person whose only contributions are indirect seems capable of leading to injustice, although mitigated by the ease with which an express common intention may be found to exist.

A preferable solution might be to base such claims on the doctrine of proprietary estoppel, where the act of detrimental reliance need not take the form of financial contributions, and which does not require a search for an artificial common intention,[64] although estoppel itself has elements of artificiality.[65] Recent cases have tended to assimilate the doctrines of constructive trusts and proprietary estoppel,[66] although the process is not yet complete.[67] It appears that interests under constructive trusts crystallise as soon as a sufficient act of detrimental reliance has occurred, prior to their vindication by the court, so that they can affect third parties.[68] Whether proprietary estoppel interests take effect before the court order has not yet been decisively established,[69] but the weight of authority favours the view that they do. The Court of Appeal has recently stated not only that constructive and resulting trusts in the context of the family home are "almost interchangeable" with proprietary estoppel, but also that estoppel interests of a family nature are overreachable in the same way as interests under trusts by payment to two trustees.[70] It was added that a person whose interest under a constructive or resulting trust was established had no need or room to assert a separate interest by estoppel.

Other solutions have been found in Commonwealth jurisdictions.[71] In Australia non-financial contributions have been recog-

---

[63] *supra.* See (1995) 25 Fam. Law 633 (P. Wylie).

[64] *Gillies v. Keogh* [1989] 2 N.Z.L.R. 327 (suggesting also that indirect contributions should suffice for a constructive trust); (1990) 106 L.Q.R. 213 (M. Bryan). See also [1987] Conv. 93 (J. Eekelaar); [1990] Conv. 314 (M. Thompson) and 370 (D. Hayton); *cf.* (1993) 109 L.Q.R. 114 (P. Ferguson); (1993) 109 L.Q.R. 485 (D. Hayton).

[65] *Phillips v. Phillips* [1993] 3 N.Z.L.R. 159, doubting estoppel as the way forward.

[66] *Grant v. Edwards* [1986] Ch. 638; *Austin v. Keele* (1987) 61 A.L.J.R 605; *Lloyds Bank plc v. Rosset, supra* (but see (1991) 54 M.L.R. 126 and (1993) 109 L.Q.R. 263 (S. Gardner)); *Hammond v. Mitchell* [1991] 1 W.L.R. 1127; *Lloyds Bank plc v. Carrick* [1996] 4 All E.R. 630; (1996) 112 L.Q.R. 549 (P. Ferguson); *Yaxley v. Gotts* [2000] Ch. 162 at 176–177.

[67] *Stokes v. Anderson* [1991] 1 F.L.R. 391.

[68] Implicit in *Lloyds Bank plc v. Rosset, supra.* See [1990] Conv. 370 (D. Hayton); (1991) 5 *Trust Law International* 9 (J. Warburton); [1991] Conv. 155 (P. Evans); Presidential Address to the Holdsworth Club, Birmingham University (1991) (Sir Nicolas Browne-Wilkinson), published in (1996) 10 *Trust Law International* 98.

[69] *post,* p. 902.

[70] *Birmingham Midshires Mortgage Services Ltd v. Sabherwal* (2000) 80 P. & C.R. 256; *post,* p. 903. For the distinction between trusts and estoppel concerning onus of proof, see (1993) 109 L.Q.R. 114 (P. Ferguson).

[71] See Pearce and Stevens, *The Law of Trusts and Equitable Obligations,* (2nd ed.), pp. 280–287; (1998) 18 L.S. 369 (S. Wong). For the position in Ireland, see [1993] Conv. 359 (J. Mee).

nised by legislation.[72] The principles of unjust enrichment have been utilised in Australia, New Zealand and Canada,[73] although "unconscionability is not a notion which makes hard cases easier to decide".[74] The majority of the Canadian Supreme Court in *Peter v. Beblow*[75] considered that a constructive trust should be imposed on the basis of unjust enrichment where there was a direct link between substantial indirect contributions and the acquisition or improvement of property; otherwise compensation could be available on a *quantum meruit* basis. The decision also reflects the "reasonable expectation" principle applied in New Zealand in *Lankow v. Rose*,[76] that where a claimant has contributed in more than a minor way, either directly or indirectly, to the acquisition, preservation or enhancement of the defendant's assets, a constructive trust will be imposed on the basis that the parties must reasonably have expected the claimant to have an interest. The contribution need not be financial, but must be causally related to the acquisition, preservation or enhancement. This objective test thus replaces the search for an artificial common intention, and gives effect to indirect contributions which, although giving rise to difficulties of proof and quantification, are just as real as direct contributions.[77]

Finally, it seems that the principles applicable to stable relationships between unmarried couples are the same as those applicable between husband and wife,[78] but the nature of the relationship is an important factor when considering what inferences should be drawn from the way the parties have conducted their affairs and in the ascertainment of their common intention.[79] The whole question is of reduced importance in the case of divorcing couples, as mentioned above,[80] because of the wide discretionary powers given to the court

---

[72] De Facto Relationships Act 1984 (N.S.W.); (1992) 22 Fam. Law 72 at 76 (P. Clarke). See also [1999] 11 C.F.L.Q. 43 (B. Atkin), discussing New Zealand legislation.

[73] *Baumgartner v. Baumgartner* (1988) 62 A.L.J. 29; *Gillies v. Keogh* [1989] 2 N.Z.L.R. 327; *Peter v. Beblow* (1993) 101 D.L.R. (4th) 621.

[74] (1990) 106 L.Q.R. 25 at 28 (M. Bryan); (1994) 8 *Trust Law International* 74 (M. Bryan); Halliwell, *Equity and Good Conscience in a Contemporary Context*, Chap. 4. See also (1993) 109 L.Q.R. 263 (S. Gardner), advocating the "communality" approach based on the relationship itself, with less emphasis on intention or contribution.

[75] *supra; ante*, p. 279.

[76] [1995] 1 N.Z.L.R. 277; *McMahon v. McMahon* [1996] 3 N.Z.L.R. 334. See also *The Frontiers of Liability*, Vol. 2, p. 204 (J. Eekelaar).

[77] [1995] 1 N.Z.L.R. 277 at 295.

[78] There is of course no presumption of advancement; *ante*, p. 257. See generally (1980) 96 L.Q.R. 248 (A. Zuckerman); (1976) 40 Conv. (N.S.) 351 (M. Richards).

[79] *Bernard v. Josephs* [1982] Ch. 391; (1982) 98 L.Q.R. 517 (J. Thomson); [1982] Conv. 444 (J. Warburton); All E.R.Rev. 1982, 150 (R. Deech) and 169 (P. Clarke). (1983) 42 C.L.J. 30 (K. Gray). See also *Gordon v. Douce* [1983] 1 W.L.R. 563; *Midland Bank plc v. Cooke* [1995] 4 All E.R. 562. As to engaged couples, see Law Reform (Miscellaneous Provisions) Act 1970, s.2; *Mossop v. Mossop* [1989] Fam. 77.

[80] *ante*, p. 272.

to make a distribution of property under the Matrimonial Causes Act 1973.

iv. Substantial Improvements. Some of the problems of indirect contributions arose where one of the parties had made a substantial contribution in time or money to the improvement of the property subsequent to the purchase. The Matrimonial Proceedings and Property Act 1970, s.37, which applies only to married couples,[81] provides that:

> "where a husband or wife contributes in money or money's worth to the improvement of real or personal property in which ... either or both of them has or have a beneficial interest, the husband or wife so contributing shall, if the contribution is of a substantial nature and subject to any agreement between them to the contrary express or implied, be treated as having then acquired by virtue of his or her contribution a share or an enlarged share, as the case may be, in that beneficial interest of such an extent as may have been then agreed or, in default of such agreement, as may seem in all the circumstances just ... ".[82]

Lord Denning has said that this provision was declaratory of the previous law,[83] indeed the language of the statute is declaratory. As far as unmarried couples are concerned, substantial improvements may give rise to an interest on the basis of common intention or estoppel, even though section 37 does not apply.[84]

v. Size of the Share. The size of the share of each party may be determined on resulting trust principles, or on the basis of the common intention of the parties. The time of acquisition of the property is the starting point for the ascertainment of the shares, but later events, up to and after any separation, can be taken into account.[85] Where entitlement is based on direct contributions (to the purchase price or mortgage repayments[86]), the shares will normally be pro-

---

[81] And to engaged couples by reason of Law Reform (Miscellaneous Provisions) Act 1970, s.2(1).

[82] *Griffiths v. Griffiths* [1973] 1 W.L.R. 1454; *Re Nicholson (decd.)* [1974] 1 W.L.R. 476.

[83] *Davis v. Vale* [1971] 1 W.L.R. 1021; *Jansen v. Jansen* [1965] P. 478.

[84] *Thomas v. Fuller-Brown* [1988] 1 F.L.R. 237 (where the claim failed because the inference was that the expenditure was in return for rent-free accommodation); *Cadman v. Bell* [1988] E.G.C.S. 139 (licence for life); *Passee v. Passee* [1988] 1 F.L.R. 263; [1988] Conv. 361 (J. Warburton); *Huntingford v. Hobbs* (1992) 24 H.L.R. 652 (joint names); *Drake v. Whipp* [1996] 1 F.L.R. 826. It is otherwise if the money was advanced as a loan; *Spence v. Brown* (1988) 18 Fam. Law 291; *cf. Hussey v. Palmer* [1972] 1 W.L.R. 1286; *ante*, p. 54.

[85] *Bernard v. Josephs* [1982] Ch. 391; *Gordon v. Douce* [1983] 1 W.L.R. 563; *Burns v. Burns* [1984] Ch. 317.

[86] Whether capital or interest; *Passee v. Passee, supra.* See also Insolvency Act 1986, s.338.

portionate to the contributions,[87] although an intention to hold differently may be established expressly[88] or may be inferred from additional indirect contributions and conduct.[89] If it has been agreed that one party will be liable for the mortgage, that party's share will be debited with any outstanding principal.[90] Where entitlement arises from an express common intention coupled with detrimental reliance, the share is not necessarily proportionate to the value of any indirect contributions, and may be greater.[91] Such indirect contributions are in any event difficult to evaluate. An express agreement as to the share will prevail.[92] If the parties have agreed that the woman is to acquire a specified share if she acts in a particular way, it seems that she will acquire that share by so acting, even though the value of her contribution may be less than the value of the agreed share.[93] Where there is an express common intention to share but no agreement as to the size of the share, the court will not be defeated by the element of uncertainty. An equal division based on the maxim that "equity is equality" is not the usual solution.[94] The court will determine what is a "fair share" on a broad approach, taking into account the total contributions.[95] To insist on the level of certainty required by the law of contract could lead to the unjust enrichment of the legal owner. Of course, any express declaration in the title documents as to the size of the shares is conclusive.[96]

vi. Date for Valuation of the Share. If it is established that a person is entitled to a share of the home under a trust (express, constructive or resulting), it follows that he or she is entitled to share proportionately in any increase (or decrease) in its value, although

---

[87] See *Springette v. Defoe* (1993) 65 P. & C.R. 1; *Evans v. Hayward* [1995] 2 F.L.R. 511; *Ashe v. Mumford, The Times,* November 15, 2000 (discount to council tenant exercising right to buy is normally treated as a contribution to the price, but this is not an absolute rule); [1996] 8 C.F.L.Q. 313 (C. Davis and C. Hunter); *Huntingford v. Hobbs* [1993] 1 F.L.R. 736 (cost of building conservatory included); (1993) 23 Fam. Law 176 (P. Wylie). In these cases the property was in joint names.

[88] *Drake v. Whipp, supra.*

[89] *Midland Bank plc v. Cooke* [1995] 4 All E.R. 562; *ante,* p. 277.

[90] *Savill v. Goodall* [1993] 1 F.L.R. 755; (1993) 23 Fam. Law 290 (S. Cretney).

[91] See *Eves v. Eves* [1975] 1 W.L.R. 1338; *Grant v. Edwards* [1986] Ch. 638.

[92] See *Clough v. Killey* (1996) 72 P. & C.R. Digest 22.

[93] This is the "quid pro quo" constructive trust, which distinguishes the situation from proprietary estoppel. See [1990] Conv. 370 (D. Hayton); *cf.* (1993) 109 L.Q.R. 263 at 266 (S. Gardner); *Gissing v. Gissing* [1971] A.C. 887 at 905; *Grant v. Edwards* [1986] Ch. 638 at 652; *Austin v. Keele* (1987) 61 A.L.J.R. 605 at 610.

[94] *Gissing v. Gissing, supra,* at 897, 903; *Hammond v. Mitchell* [1991] 1 W.L.R. 1127 (although equal division upheld on facts); *cf. Midland Bank plc v. Cooke* [1995] 4 All E.R. 562; *Rowe v. Prance* [1999] 2 F.L.R. 787 (boat).

[95] *Gissing v. Gissing, supra,* at 909; *Stokes v. Anderson* [1991] 1 F.L.R. 391; *Drake v. Whipp, supra.* See also *Risch v. McFee* (1991) 61 P. & C.R. 42 (loan which claimant had not sought to recover treated as contribution).

[96] *ante,* p. 273.

occurring after separation, until such time as the property is sold.[97] This principle has been firmly upheld by the Court of Appeal.[98] Credit will be given by way of "equitable accounting" for expenditure such as mortgage payments and repairs incurred by the occupying spouse after separation.[99]

C. Legal Estate in Both Parties

Where the legal title is in both parties, the beneficial interest will prima facie also be shared.[1] Any express declaration of the beneficial interests in the title documents will be conclusive.[2] A Land Registry transfer form which states that the transferees are entitled for their own benefit and that the survivor can give a valid receipt for capital money will be treated as a declaration of a beneficial joint tenancy.[3] Where, however, the words "for their own benefit" are missing, the statement that the survivor can give a valid receipt is not equivalent to a declaration of a beneficial joint tenancy.[4] The title documents should make the position clear, but if they contain no declaration, shares will be determined by any express common intention of the parties (which has been relied upon).[5] If no express common intention can be established, the parties will normally take shares proportionate to their contributions under resulting trust principles,[6] although an agreement to hold differently may be inferred from indirect contributions or conduct.[7] Where a husband purchases property and has it conveyed into the names of himself and his wife, the presumption of advancement may apply, although of limited strength today.[8] Where a wife is the purchaser, and has the property

---

[97] Or the co-ownership ends in another way, *e.g.* if one buys the other out.

[98] *Turton v. Turton* [1988] Ch. 542; [1987] Conv. 378 (J. Warburton); (1987) 103 L.Q.R. 500; (1988) 18 Fam. Law 72 (J. Montgomery); (1989) 86/31 L.S.Gaz. 31 (I. Hardcastle); *Gordon v. Douce* [1983] 1 W.L.R. 563; *Walker v. Hall* (1984) 14 Fam. Law 21; *Passee v. Passee* [1988] 1 F.L.R. 263. See also *Cousins v. Dzosens* (1984) 81 L.S.Gaz. 2855; *Bernard v. Josephs* [1982] Ch. 391.

[99] *Re Pavlou (a Bankrupt)* [1993] 1 W.L.R. 1047; [1995] Conv. 391 (E. Cooke).

[1] *Pettitt v. Petitt* [1970] A.C. 777 at 813–814; *Bernard v. Josephs* [1982] Ch. 391; *Burns v. Burns* [1984] Ch. 317.

[2] See *Goodman v. Gallant* [1986] Fam. 106; (1986) 45 C.L.J. 205 (S. Juss); [1986] Conv. 355 (J.E.M.). (Severance of beneficial joint tenancy must result in equal shares even though unequal contributions). See also *Roy v. Roy* [1996] 1 F.L.R. 541; *Hembury v. Peachey* (1996) 72 P. & C.R. Digest 46. For the position where the declaration contains inconsistent provisions, see *Martin v. Martin* (1987) 54 P. & C.R. 238.

[3] *Re Gorman* [1990] 1 W.L.R. 616 (even if the transferees have not signed the form).

[4] *Harwood v. Harwood* [1991] 2 F.L.R. 274; *Huntingford v. Hobbs* [1993] 1 F.L.R. 736; *The Mortgage Corporation v. Shaire* [2000] 1 F.L.R. 973.

[5] *Rhoden v. Jospeh* [1990] E.G.C.S. 115; *Hungtingford v. Hobbs, supra*; *Savill v. Goodall* [1993] 1 F.L.R. 755.

[6] *Dyer v. Dyer* (1788) 2 Cox Eq.Cas. 92; *Pettitt v. Pettitt* [1970] A.C. 777 at p. 814; *Springette v. Defoe* (1993) 65 P. & C.R. 1.

[7] *Midland Bank plc v. Cooke* [1995] 4 All E.R. 562; *ante*, p. 277.

[8] *ante*, p. 256.

conveyed into joint names, the presumption of a resulting trust will be easily rebutted. In modern circumstances there would seem to be no explanation other than a wish to hold equally.[9]

3. CONSEQUENCES OF CO-OWNERSHIP

A. The Trust of Land

The two forms of co-ownership existing under the modern law are the joint tenancy and the tenancy in common. Here only a brief outline will be given, as the details may be found in the land law books.[10] Under the Law of Property Act 1925 a trust for sale was imposed on both forms of co-ownership, while successive interests came within the Settled Land Act 1925. This system operated for many years, but was subject to criticism partly because the dual system was perceived as unnecessary and partly because the duty to sell which arose under the trust for sale was not readily understood by co-owners. Furthermore, this duty to sell brought into play the doctrine of conversion, often with inconvenient and artificial results. The effect of this doctrine was that the interests of the co-owners were treated as personalty, which gave rise to difficulties, particularly in the interpretation of many legislative provisions.

Following Law Commission proposals,[11] the dual system of the trust for sale and the strict settlement has been replaced by the "trust of land" under the Trusts of Land and Appointment of Trustees Act 1996, which applies to both concurrent and successive interests. While pre-existing settlements under the Settled Land Act 1925 (other than those relating to charity land) are preserved, no new settlements may be created.[12] The definition of "trust of land"[13] is "any trust of property which consists of or includes land", whether the trust is express, implied, resulting or constructive, including a trust for sale and a bare trust. With the exception of pre-existing strict settlements, the 1996 Act applies to trusts of land created before and after its commencement (January 1, 1997).

Under the trust of land, the trustees have a power of sale, but no duty to sell. (Other powers and duties will be mentioned where relevant in the following sections). The interests of the beneficiaries are overreached on sale (provided there are at least two trustees), as

---

[9] *Pettitt v. Pettitt* [1970] A.C. 777 at 815. See also *Savill v. Goodall, supra* (unmarried couple).

[10] M. & W., pp. 475 *et seq.*; Cheshire and Burn, pp. 242 *et seq.*

[11] No. 181 (1989), *Trusts of Land*. On the 1996 Act see [1996] Conv. 411 (N. Hopkins).

[12] Trusts of Land and Appointment of Trustees Act 1996, s.2. Entailed interests may no longer be created; Sched. 1, para. 5. See, however, (2000) 116 L.Q.R. 445 (E. Bennett Histed).

[13] *ibid.*, s.1.

under the previous legislation.[14] Trusts for sale may still be expressly created,[15] but, as already mentioned, fall within the definition of a "trust of land". All express trusts for sale of land, whenever created, include (despite any provision to the contrary) a power to postpone the sale, and the trustees are not liable in any way for postponing sale for an indefinite period in the exercise of their discretion.[16] Although the duty to sell remains in such a case, the doctrine of conversion is abolished in respect of all trusts for sale of land whenever created, save for those created by the will of a testator dying before the commencement of the 1996 Act.[17] Thus the interests of the beneficiaries are no longer interests in personalty, but are recognised as interests in the land itself.

As already mentioned, the 1925 legislation imposed a trust for sale on co-owned land (and in various other circumstances, such as intestacy). Under the current regime the statutory trust for sale is replaced by the trust of land. While the legal estate, if vested in more than one person, must be held jointly, the beneficial interest may be held either on a joint tenancy or on a tenancy in common. The relevant legislation is Law of Property Act 1925, section 34 (tenancies in common) and section 36 (joint tenancies), as amended by the 1996 Act to reflect the replacement of the trust for sale by the trust of land.[18] To facilitate conveyancing, the legal joint tenancy cannot be severed, but severance of any equitable joint tenancy can be effected by any of the means applicable before 1926[19]; and also by notice in writing to the other joint tenants.[20] The purpose of severance is to convert the joint tenancy into a tenancy in common and thereby prevent the application of the doctrine of survivorship (whereby the survivor of joint tenants takes the whole).

B. Occupation rights

Difficulties arose in the past concerning the occupation rights of beneficiaries under a trust for sale, whether imposed expressly or, more commonly, by statute, as in the case of co-ownership. The difficulty stemmed from the old doctrine of conversion, whereby the interests of the beneficiaries were regarded as in the proceeds of sale, not the land. Although the situation was somewhat obscure, modern decisions upheld the occupation rights of the beneficiaries,

---

[14] *ante*, p. 36.
[15] See (1997) 113 L.Q.R. 207 (P. Pettit); [1999] Conv. 84 *per* (R. Mitchell).
[16] Trusts of Land and Appointment of Trustees Act 1996, s.4.
[17] *ibid.*, s.3.
[18] Trusts of Land and Appointment of Trustees Act 1996, Sched. 2.
[19] M. & W., pp. 492 *et seq.*; Cheshire and Burn, pp. 246 *et seq.*
[20] L.P.A. 1925, s.36(2); *Re Draper's Conveyance* [1969] 1 Ch. 486; *Harris v. Goddard* [1983] 1 W.L.R. 1203.

regarding the doctrine of conversion as artificial.[21] Thus it was held in the leading case of *Bull v. Bull*[22] that a son, who held the legal estate on trust for sale for himself and his mother as equitable tenants in common, was not entitled to evict his mother.

The occupation rights of beneficiaries are now governed by the Trusts of Land and Appointment of Trustees Act 1996, whenever the trust of land arose. The Act abolished the doctrine of conversion.[23] Section 12 provides that a beneficiary beneficially entitled to an interest in possession is entitled to occupy at any time if at that time (a) the purposes of the trust include making the land available for his occupation (or for the occupation of beneficiaries of a class of which he is a member or of beneficiaries in general) or (b) the land is held by the trustees so as to be so available. The section does not confer a right to occupy land if it is either unavailable or unsuitable for occupation by him,[24] and is subject to section 13, discussed below. Thus a beneficiary will normally be entitled to occupy unless, for example, the land has been let, or it is clear that the purpose of the trust is the sale of the property and division of the proceeds among the beneficiaries.[25]

Section 13(1) of the 1996 Act provides that where two or more beneficiaries are entitled to occupy under section 12, the trustees may, provided they do not act unreasonably, exclude or restrict the entitlement of any one or more (but not all) of them. They may also impose reasonable conditions from time to time on any beneficiary in relation to his occupation.[26] The matters to which the trustees must have regard in exercising these powers include (a) the intention of the person or persons (if any) who created the trust, (b) the purposes for which the land is held, and (c) the circumstances and wishes of each of the beneficiaries who is (or apart from any previous exercise by the trustees of those powers would be) entitled to occupy the land under section 12.[27] The conditions which they may impose include the payment of outgoings or expenses in respect of the land, or the assumption of any other obligation in relation to the land or to any activity which is or is proposed to be conducted there.[28] If the entitlement of any beneficiary has been excluded or restricted under the section, conditions may be imposed on any other beneficiary requiring him to compensate the beneficiary whose

---

[21] *Williams & Glyn's Bank Ltd v. Boland* [1981] A.C. 487; *City of London Building Society v. Flegg* [1988] A.C. 54.

[22] [1955] 1 Q.B. 234; *cf. Barclay v. Barclay* [1970] 2 Q.B. 677 (express testamentary trust for sale).

[23] s.3.

[24] s.12(2). See [1997] Conv. 254 at 260 (J. Ross Martyn).

[25] As in the testamentary trust for sale in *Barclay v. Barclay, supra.*

[26] s.13(3).

[27] s.13(4).

[28] s.13(5).

rights have been excluded or restricted, or to forgo a benefit under the trust so as to benefit the other beneficiary.[29] The trustees may not exercise their powers so as to prevent any person in occupation (whether or not by reason of any entitlement under section 12) from continuing to occupy, or in a manner likely to have that result, unless he consents or the court gives approval.[30] Disputes concerning the exercise of the trustees' powers under section 13 may be resolved by an application to court under section 14, where the circumstances and wishes of each beneficiary with occupation rights will be considered.[31]

Prior to the 1996 Act occupying co-owners were in certain cases obliged to pay rent to non-occupying co-owners, as where the latter had been "ousted" by the occupier,[32] or where the occupier had presented a divorce petition against the non-occupier,[33] or as a condition of postponing a sale.[34] As a general principle, however, no rent was payable to a beneficiary who chose not to occupy.[35] The position was somewhat uncertain, but the matter now falls within section 13 which, as mentioned above, permits the imposition of conditions including the compensation of a non-occupying beneficiary by an occupier.[36]

One problem with sections 12 and 13 is that they are ill-suited to trusts arising out of co-ownership, where the trustees and beneficiaries are frequently the same persons. Indeed, it has been said that the 1996 Act has unintentionally curtailed the occupation rights of co-owners by eroding the concept of unity of possession, and that beneficiaries should be able to resort to their general law rights where these are superior to those conferred by the Act.[37]

Finally, a spouse who is not a legal owner may assert occupation rights under the Family Law Act 1996 (replacing Matrimonial Homes Act 1983) whether or not he or she has an equitable interest in the home.[38] This right is registrable, but failure to register will not affect enforcement against the other spouse, or enforcement of any rights arising independently by reason of an equitable interest in the home.

---

[29] s.13(6).

[30] s.13(7). The court will have regard to the matters set out in s.13(4).

[31] See s.15(2); *post*, p. 294.

[32] See *Dennis v. McDonald* [1982] Fam. 63.

[33] *Re Pavlou (a Bankrupt)* [1993] 1 W.L.R. 1047 (discussing also the question of set-off against mortgage interest paid by the occupier).

[34] *Harvey v. Harvey* [1982] Fam. 83.

[35] *Jones (A.E.) v. Jones (F.W.)* [1977] 1 W.L.R. 438.

[36] See also Family Law Act 1996, s.40(1)(b) (periodic payments while occupation order in force).

[37] (1998) 57 C.L.J. 123 (D. Barnsley).

[38] Former spouses, cohabitants and former cohabitants may in certain cases obtain occupation orders whether or not they have an equitable interest. These are not registrable.

C. Sale by Sole Trustee

Under the trust of land and its predecessor, the trust for sale, at least two trustees are necessary if the overreaching machinery is to operate.[39] While there are likely to be at least two trustees in the case of an expressly created trust of land, the difficulty which arises in many cases of co-ownership is that the land is vested in one person only. That person holds on trust for all those who are beneficially entitled, but the overreaching machinery will not operate. As we saw in the earlier parts of this chapter, the question whether a person other than the legal owner has acquired an interest is often difficult, so that the existence of the trust may not be appreciated, either by the parties or the purchaser (or mortgagee).

Where there are two trustees, the interests of the beneficiaries will be overreached whether or not they are occupying[40] and whether the title is registered or unregistered. Where there is a sole trustee, the principles applicable to registered and unregistered titles must be considered separately.

If the title is unregistered,[41] the question whether the transferee, typically a mortgagee, is bound by the equitable interests depends on whether the mortgagee had notice, actual or constructive, of the interest of the beneficiary. The equitable co-ownership usually arises by virtue of one party having contributed to the purchase price, or to the mortgage payments; and there will be nothing in the documents of title to indicate this. The question is whether the beneficiary's occupation gives constructive notice. It was at one time held that a bank mortgagee dealing with the husband as sole legal owner did not have constructive notice of the wife's equitable interest by contribution, even though the bank knew that the parties lived together in the house.[42] This view is now untenable.[43] So many wives today have a share in the home that a reasonable mortgagee should consider the possibility. If it makes insufficient inquiries, the fact of the wife's (or other beneficiary's) occupation will give constructive notice of her rights. The difficulty which remains is in deciding whether sufficient inquiries have been made. This arose in *Kingsnorth Finance Co. v. Tizard*[44] where a wife had a half share in a

---

[39] L.P.A. 1925, s.2.

[40] *City of London Building Society v. Flegg* [1988] A.C. 54; *cf.* Law Com. No. 188, *Transfer of Land; Overreaching; Beneficiaries in Occupation*. This Report will not be implemented; [1998] Conv. 349.

[41] *i.e.* not subject to the provisions of the Land Registration Act 1925 at the time of the transaction. Many titles remain unregistered even though the registration system applies in all areas. Sale is a transaction which triggers a duty to register. Likewise, the grant of a first legal mortgage; Land Registration Act 1997, s.1. Priority disputes, however, commonly arise some years after the mortgage and may still be governed by unregistered land principles.

[42] *Caunce v. Caunce* [1969] 1 W.L.R. 286.

[43] *Williams & Glyn's Bank Ltd v. Boland* [1981] A.C. 487.

[44] [1986] 1 W.L.R. 783.

house which was vested in her husband alone. When the marriage broke down she slept elsewhere but came to the house every day to look after the children and kept her possessions there. The husband mortgaged the property, falsely stating that he was single. The mortgagee's surveyor inspected the house at a time when the husband had arranged for the wife to be out. He saw evidence of the children's occupation and was told that the wife had left. No further inquiries were made as to her rights. The husband later emigrated, leaving the loan of £66,000 unpaid. It was held that the mortgagee had constructive notice of the wife's interest. In order for physical presence to amount to occupation, it did not need to be exclusive, continuous or uninterrupted, nor was it negatived by regular absences. The wife was accordingly in occupation for the purpose of constructive notice. When the surveyor discovered that the mortgagor was married, he was put on enquiry as to the wife's rights. The mortgagee would not have notice if a reasonable inspection had been made which did not reveal the occupier or evidence of occupation. What amounts to a reasonable inspection depends on the circumstances, but the judge considered that the pre-arranged inspection in the present case did not discharge the obligation. If this is so, there is indeed a heavy onus on the mortgagee.[45]

It should be added that where spouses occupy a matrimonial home, a spouse who has no legal title may protect his or her statutory rights of occupation under the Family Law Act 1996 (replacing Matrimonial Homes Act 1983) by registration, whether or not that spouse has any equitable interest in the home. But there is no possibility of protecting a substantive equitable interest by registration in cases of unregistered title.

In the case of registered land, notice plays no part.[46] Equitable interests are binding on a purchaser only if proper steps have been taken to protect them, as by a notice, restriction or caution; or if the interest is an "overriding interest"; which is binding regardless of notice or of any means of discovery.[47] The issue came to a head in *Williams & Glyn's Bank Ltd v. Boland.*[48]

Mr and Mrs Boland each contributed towards the purchase of, and to the mortgage payments due upon, a matrimonial home. Title was taken in the sole name of Mr Boland, and he was registered as sole proprietor.

Later, Mr Boland mortgaged the house to the Bank. On default

---

[45] See [1986] Conv. 283 (M. Thompson); (1987) 46 C.L.J. 28 (P. McHugh).

[46] [1981] A.C. 487 at p. 504, *per* Lord Wilberforce; Law Com No. 254 (1998), para. 3.50.

[47] See Law Com No. 254 (1998), para. 5.75 (occupier's rights should be overriding only if apparent on reasonable inspection).

[48] [1981] A.C. 487; [1980] Conv. 361 (J. Martin); (1980) 43 M.L.R. 692 (S. Freeman); (1980) 39 C.L.J. 243 (M. Prichard); (1981) 97 L.Q.R. 12 (R. Smith). See also [1999] Conv. 382 (D. Wilde), on the effect of L.R.A. 1925 on resulting trusts.

being made in the mortgage payments, the Bank started proceedings for possession. The wife resisted this claim on the ground that she was entitled to an equitable interest in the house which the Bank could not override. She had taken no steps to protect her interest by restriction or caution.

It was accepted that the wife had, by virtue of her financial contribution, an equitable interest in the house. The question whether this interest was valid against the Bank depended on whether it was an overriding interest under the Land Registration Act 1925, s.70(1)(g)[49]; it could not be binding as a minor interest, because the wife had taken no steps to protect it. Nor could it be overreached by the payment to a sole trustee.

The House of Lords unanimously held that the wife's interest was an overriding interest. It was a right "subsisting in reference" to registered land; and, on the plain words of sub-paragraph (g), the wife was "in actual occupation" at the execution of the mortgage.[50] Lord Scarman emphasised the importance of construing the legislation in the light of current social policy, and of protecting the "beneficial interest which English law now recognizes that a married woman has in the matrimonial home."[51] It is thus necessary to make inquiries of all persons in occupation, whether spouse, cohabitant, or other persons; for their interests are capable of being binding as overriding interests on the purchaser or mortgagee. It should be appreciated however, that a wife (or other person) with an overriding interest cannot necessarily prevent a sale by the mortgagee, although she will still have a prior claim to her share of the proceeds.[52]

The principles discussed above are subject to an important proviso. An equitable co-owner in occupation can rely neither on constructive notice (in unregistered land) nor on section 70(1)(g) (in registered land) where he or she was aware of the mortgage transaction and did not bring the equitable interest to the attention of the mortgagee.[53] This seems to be a version of the doctrine of estoppel.

---

[49] s.70(1) reads: "All registered land shall, unless . . . the contrary is expressed in the register, be deemed to be subject to such of the following overriding interests as may be for the time being subsisting in reference thereto . . .

(g) The rights of every person in actual occupation of the land or in receipt of the rents and profits thereof, save where enquiry is made of such person and the rights are not disclosed; . . . "

[50] This is the relevant date for the application of s.70(1)(g), rather than the later date of registration of the legal charge; *Abbey National B.S. v. Cann* [1991] 1 A.C. 56.

[51] [1981] A.C. 487 at p. 510.

[52] *Bank of Baroda v. Dhillon* [1998] 1 F.L.R. 524; (1998) 28 Fam. Law 208 (R. Wells); [1998] Conv. 415 (S. Pascoe); *Halifax Mortgage Services Ltd v. Muirhead* (1998) 76 P. & C.R. 418.

[53] *Bristol and West Building Society v. Henning* [1985] 1 W.L.R. 778; *Paddington Building Society v. Mendelsohn* (1985) 50 P. & C.R. 244; criticised [1985] Conv. 361 (P. Todd); [1986] Conv. 57; (1986) 49 M.L.R. 255 and (1986) 6 L.S. 140 (M. Thompson).

The principle is that in such circumstances it is impossible to infer any common intention other than that the equitable owner authorised the legal owner to raise money by mortgage which would have priority to any beneficial interest. Apparently it is not relevant that the mortgagee failed to make the inquiries which might have revealed the interest. As has been said, this seems to be a reversal of the doctrine of notice; the onus has shifted to the occupier to declare his rights to a purchaser (mortgagee) of whom he has notice, or be deemed to concede priority.[54] In the case of an acquisition mortgage, the House of Lords has taken the principle further by holding that a purchaser who depends on a mortgage in order to buy the property acquires on completion only an equity of redemption, (*i.e.* the property already subject to the mortgage). Thus a third party claiming a beneficial interest as against the purchaser can assert no rights against the mortgagee, whether or not the third party was aware of the mortgage.[55] The effect of these principles is to restrict the application of *Williams & Glyn's Bank Ltd v. Boland*[56] and *Kingsnorth Finance Co. v. Tizard*,[57] to subsequent mortgages of which the co-owner was unaware.

D. Disputes over Sale

Disputes commonly arise, primarily on the breakdown of a relationship, as to whether the property should be sold or not. The question may also arise on the death of a co-owner, if his or her share devolves on a third party.[58] Where the legal estate is vested in all the co-owners, they (being trustees) must act unanimously in the exercise of any power.[59] Since the commencement of the Trusts of Land and Appointment of Trustees Act 1996, trustees of land have a power of sale instead of the duty to sell which formerly existed under the statutory trust for sale imposed in cases of co-ownership. Thus the power of sale cannot be exercised unless all agree. In cases of dispute, as explained below, they can apply to court under section 14 of the 1996 Act, replacing section 30 of the Law of Property Act 1925.

---

[54] (1985) 44 C.L.J. 354 (M. Welstead).

[55] *Abbey National B.S. v. Cann* [1991] 1 A.C. 56; [1991] Conv. 116 (S. Baughen) and 155 (P. Evans). As to remortgages, see *Equity & Law Home Loans Ltd v. Prestidge* [1992] 1 W.L.R. 137; (1992) 108 L.Q.R. 372 (R. Smith); (1993) 56 M.L.R. 87 (M. Lunney); (1993) 23 Fam. Law 231 (J. Dewar).

[56] *supra.*

[57] [1986] 1 W.L.R. 783, *ante,* p. 289.

[58] See *Stott v. Ratcliffe* (1982) 79 L.S.Gaz. 634.

[59] *Re Mayo* [1943] Ch. 302; *post,* p. 504. The parties may have made express provisions for sale or for one to buy the other out; *Miller v. Lakefield Estates Ltd* (1989) 57 P. & C.R. 104.

It may be that the legal estate is vested in one co-owner only, as where a husband holds the legal estate on trust for himself and his wife as co-owners in equity. In the last section we saw the effect of a sale or mortgage by a sole trustee. Here we will consider the position prior to any such disposition. The question of unanimity does not arise, because there is only one trustee. In the event of a dispute, the wife (or other equitable co-owner) may apply to court under section 14 if she has the opportunity to act in time. In any event, sale will be hampered if she has registered her statutory right of occupation[60] or (in the case of registered land) has protected her equitable interest by the entry of a restriction or caution. Even if she has not done so, her interest is likely to prevail against the purchaser or mortgagee if she is in occupation.[61] She may also seek an injunction to prevent sale without the appointment of a second trustee to safeguard the proceeds of sale, or to restrain the husband from disregarding his statutory duty to consult the beneficiaries.[62] Section 11 of the Trusts of Land and Appointment of Trustees Act 1996 (replacing section 26 of the Law of Property Act 1925) provides that the trustees, in the exercise of any function relating to the land, shall (so far as practicable) consult the beneficiaries of full age and beneficially entitled to an interest in possession, and, so far as consistent with the general interest of the trust, give effect to the wishes of those beneficiaries or of the majority of them, according to the value of their combined interests.[63] Clearly this section is of limited assistance to a beneficiary with a minority interest, and will result in a stalemate if there are two disputing co-owners who are equally entitled. In certain cases, however, it will resolve the situation. A purchaser (or mortgagee) is not concerned to see that the trustees' duties to consult the beneficiaries and to have regard that their rights have been complied with, whether the title to the land is unregistered[64] or (although the position is somewhat obscure) registered.[65]

---

[60] Family Law Act 1996, re-enacting Matrimonial Homes Act 1983; *Wroth v. Tyler* [1974] Ch. 30.

[61] Under L.R.A. 1925, s.70(1)(g) (registered land) or under the doctrine of notice (unregistered land); *ante*, p. 289.

[62] *Waller v. Waller* [1967] 1 W.L.R. 451. See also *Lee v. Lee* [1952] 2 Q.B. 489n. (jurisdiction under Married Women's Property Act 1882, s.17).

[63] This duty may be excluded in an express trust. Also, the trustees must have regard to the rights of the beneficiaries when exercising the powers of an absolute owner conferred by s.6 of the 1996 Act; *ibid.*, s.6(5).

[64] Trusts of Land and Appointment of Trustees Act 1996, s.16(1).

[65] L.R.A. 1925, s.94(4) (inserted by the 1996 Act); [1996] Conv. 411 at 427–48 (N. Hopkins); *cf.* (1998) 61 M.L.R. 56 (L. Clements). It is considered in [1998] Conv. 168 (G. Ferris and G. Battersby) that a purchaser of registered land is insufficiently protected against unauthorised dealings by the trustees, but this is doubted in [2000] Conv. 267 (M. Dixon). See further T.A. 1925, s.17.

Assuming that the dispute cannot otherwise be resolved, application may be made to court under section 14 of the 1996 Act. The application may be made by a trustee or any person having an interest in the property.[66] Thus the trustee in bankruptcy of a beneficiary (whose position is discussed below) or chargee of a beneficial interest may apply, as under the previous law. The court may make such order as it thinks fit (a) relating to the exercise by the trustees of any of their functions (including an order relieving them of any obligation to obtain the consent of, or to consult, any person in connection with the exercise of any of their functions), or (b) declaring the nature or extent of a person's interest in the property[67]; but may not appoint or remove trustees under this section.[68]

The matters to which the court is to have regard include (a) the intentions of the person or persons (if any) who created the trust, (b) the purposes for which the property subject to the trust is held,[69] (c) the welfare of any child who occupies or might reasonably be expected to occupy any land subject to the trust as his home, and (d) the interests of any secured creditor of any beneficiary.[70] So far as applications relating to the exercise of the trustees' powers under section 13 to exclude or restrict occupation rights are concerned, the court will also consider the circumstances and wishes of each of the beneficiaries who is (or apart from any previous exercise by the trustees of those powers would be) entitled to occupy the land under section 12.[71] In the case of any other application, the court will also consider the circumstances and wishes of any beneficiaries of full age and entitled to an interest in possession or (in case of dispute) of the majority (according to the value of their combined interests).[72] Different considerations apply to applications by a trustee in bankruptcy, which are discussed below.

Decisions on the predecessor legislation (section 30 of the Law of Property Act 1925) may afford some guidance, bearing in mind, however, that those decisions were influenced by the primacy of the duty to sell which then arose under the statutory trust for sale in cases of co-ownership. Another distinction is that section 30, unlike section 15 of the 1996 Act, did not spell out the factors to be taken into account by the court. As under the previous law, the provision of a home for the parties' children will continue to be a significant,

---

[66] s.14(1).

[67] See *Lowson v. Coombes* [1999] Ch. 373.

[68] Trusts of Land and Appointment of Trustees Act 1996, s.14(2), (3).

[69] This appears to refer to current purposes, if different from the original.

[70] *ibid.*, s.15(1). See *The Mortgage Corporation v. Shaire* [2000] 1 F.L.R. 973, *infra*.

[71] *ibid.*, s.15(2). For ss.12 and 13, see *ante*, p. 287.

[72] *ibid.*, s.15(3). This does not apply to applications relating to s.6(2) (power to convey to adult beneficiaries absolutely entitled without request).

although not paramount, consideration in family cases.[73] The width of section 15, however, makes it unlikely that much resort will need to be made to the previous authorities, which must be treated with caution. It has recently been held that section 15 gives the court a wider discretion than under the previous law to refuse an order for sale of the family home, and that it is no longer the position that applications by chargees and trustees in bankruptcy are to be similarly treated.[74] Thus a chargee is less likely to secure an order for sale than under the previous law.

Where, however, the sale is requested by the trustee in bankruptcy of one party, different considerations arise: "Bankruptcy has, in relation to the matrimonial home, its own claim to protection".[75] The rights of the creditors are in competition with the interests of all the beneficiaries. They do not automatically defeat the interests of the family; but the reported cases indicate that it is only in exceptional circumstances that the trustee in bankruptcy will not succeed,[76] although sale may be deferred for a short time if the spouse has some prospect of buying the bankrupt's share.[77] The fact that the bankrupt's family will be unable to buy a comparable home and that his children's schooling may be disrupted are not exceptional circumstances justifying refusal of an order for sale; they are the "melancholy consequences of debt and improvidence."[78]

The law in this area was amended by the Insolvency Act 1986, following an examination by the Review Committee on Insolvency Law and Practice.[79] The 1986 provisions have in turn been amended by the Trusts of Land and Appointment of Trustees Act 1996. Where an application for sale is made under section 14 of the 1996 Act by the trustee in bankruptcy of a co-owner, the position is governed by section 335A of the Insolvency Act 1986. On such an

---

[73] See *Williams v. Williams* [1976] Ch. 278; *Re Evers' Trust* [1980] 1 W.L.R. 1327 (unmarried couple); *Harris v. Harris* (1996) 72 P. & C.R. 408 (no sale on father's death where deed of family arrangement had provided for retention as family home for father and son, who still occupied). For property other than the family home, see *Re Buchanan-Wollaston's Conveyance* [1939] Ch. 738.

[74] *The Mortgage Corporation v. Shaire* [2000] 1 F.L.R. 973; [2000] Conv. 315 (S. Pascoe) and 329 (M. Thompson).

[75] *Re Bailey* [1977] 1 W.L.R. 278 at p. 279, *per* Megarry V.-C.

[76] *Re Solomon* [1967] Ch. 573; *Re Turner* [1974] 1 W.L.R. 1556; *Re McCarthy* [1975] 1 W.L.R. 807; *Re Lowrie* [1981] 3 All E.R. 353; *Re Densham* [1975] 1 W.L.R. 1519, *cf. Re Holliday* [1981] Ch. 405 (no order until 1985, where no creditors pressing, more assets than debts, and debtor bankrupt on his own petition); (1981) 97 L.Q.R. 200 (C. Hand); [1982] Conv. 74 (A. Sydenham); [1983] Conv. 219 (C. Hand). For the equity of exoneration, see *Re Pittortou* [1985] 1 W.L.R. 58.

[77] *Re Gorman* [1990] 1 W.L.R. 616.

[78] *Re Citro* [1991] Ch. 142 at 157 (bankruptcy prior to Insolvency Act 1986). Sir George Waller dissented. See also *Barclays Bank plc v. Hendricks* [1996] 1 F.L.R. 258.

[79] 1982, Cmnd. 8558. Some jurisdictions offer greater protection by "homestead legislation." See Joint Family Homes Act 1964 (New Zealand); Gray, *Elements of Land Law* (2nd ed.), pp. 605–606. For human rights considerations, see (2000) 150 N.L.J. 1102 (H. Pines Richman).

application the court shall make such order as it thinks just and reasonable, having regard to:

(a) the interests of the bankrupt's creditors;
(b) where the application is made in respect of land which includes a dwelling-house which is or has been the home of the bankrupt or the bankrupt's spouse or former spouse,
　　(i) the conduct of the spouse or former spouse, so far as contributing to the bankruptcy,
　　(ii) the needs and financial resources of the spouse or former spouse, and
　　(iii) the needs of any children; and
(c) all the circumstances of the case other than the needs of the bankrupt.

Where, however, the application is made after a year from the vesting in the trustee in bankruptcy, the court must assume that the interests of the creditors outweigh all other considerations save in exceptional circumstances. It has been said that "exceptional circumstances" reflects the same test as has been applied in the case law prior to the 1986 Act.[80] This provision, therefore, gives some protection to the family by delaying the sale, but the trustee will normally succeed after a year. Some recent decisions, however, reveal a more "humanitarian" approach.[81] There are similar provisions relating to occupation orders under section 33 of the Family Law Act 1996 in cases of bankruptcy.[82]

---

[80] *Re Citro* [1991] Ch. 142 (in the context of s.336); (1991) 50 C.L.J. 45 (J. Hall); (1991) 107 L.Q.R. 177 (S. Cretney); [1991] Conv. 302 (A. Lawson); (1992) 55 M.L.R. 284 (D. Brown).

[81] *Judd v. Brown, Bankrupts* [1998] 2 F.L.R. 360 (no order for sale where bankrupt's wife being treated for cancer); *Re Raval (A Bankrupt)* [1998] 2 F.L.R. 718 (order suspended for a year where bankrupt's wife mentally ill); *Claughton v. Charalamabous* [1999] 1 F.L.R. 740 (order suspended until bankrupt's wife, who was chronically ill and had reduced life expectancy, vacated the house or died). See also *Re Bremner (A Bankrupt)* [1999] 1 F.L.R. 912 (where bankrupt husband terminally ill, elderly wife's need to care for him at home was an "exceptional circumstance").

[82] Insolvency Act 1986, ss.336, 337, as amended. See *Re Bremner (A Bankrupt), supra.*

CHAPTER 12

CONSTRUCTIVE TRUSTS

1. GENERAL

A CONSTRUCTIVE trust is one which arises by operation of law, and not by reason of the intention of the parties, express or implied.[1] "English law provides no clear and all-embracing definition of a constructive trust. Its boundaries have been left perhaps deliberately vague, so as not to restrict the court by technicalities in deciding what the justice of a particular case may demand".[2] It has been "a ready means of developing our property law in modern times."[3] The

---

[1] For a different view, see (1999) 18 N.Z.U.L.R. 305 (C. Rickett).
[2] *Carl Zeiss Stiftung v. Herbert Smith & Co.* [1969] 2 Ch. 276 at 300, *per* Edmund Davies L.J.
[3] *Sen v. Headley* [1991] Ch. 425 at 440 (Nourse L.J.).

principle is that where a person who holds property in circumstances in which in equity and good conscience it should be held or enjoyed by another, he will be compelled to hold the property on trust for that other.[4] Such a statement can be criticised as being too general to be helpful. It used to be said that equity had developed pragmatically in this field, relying on the precedents and paying too little attention to the general principle. Subsequently the pendulum swung the other way, and a constructive trust was used as a means of reaching a desired result over a wide variety of cases; constructive trusts of a "new model",[5] "wherever justice and good conscience require it".[6] It now seems, however, that the "new model" has lost momentum.[7] Modern developments have caused Lord Millett to say that "At present the language of constructive trust has become such a fertile source of confusion that it would be better if it were abandoned".[8] The confusion could be avoided if the term were to be confined to "a situation in which it would be unconscionable for one party to deny the other's beneficial proprietary interest in a particular and identified property".[9]

A. Overlap in Classification

We saw, in discussing the classification of trusts,[10] that there is an overlap between resulting and constructive trusts. Normally it makes little practical difference whether a trust is described as constructive or resulting. The formality rules, for example, apply to neither type.[11] But the tendency to merge the two categories makes any definition of a constructive trust even harder to formulate. "It has been suggested that nomenclature in this context is unimportant. There is, however, some risk that confusion of terminology may lead to confusion of thought".[12] Distinctions have been emphasised in the context of the conflict of laws, where it has been said that a resulting trust involves the claim of an equitable owner to assert a continuing proprietary interest in his own property, while a constructive trust may be imposed in appropriate circumstances where

---

[4] See *Beatty v. Guggenheim Exploration Co.*, 225 N.Y. 380 at 386 (1919); *Soar v. Ashwell* [1893] 2 Q.B. 390; (1913–14) 27 Harv.L.R. 125 (A. Scott); (1955) 72 L.Q.R. 39 (A. Scott); *Restatement of Restitution*, § 160; [1999] 14 *Amicus Curiae* 4 (Lord Millett); Waters, *The Constructive Trust*; Oakley, *Constructive Trusts*; Elias, *Explaining Constructive Trusts*.

[5] *Eves v. Eves* [1975] 1 W.L.R. 1338 at 1341.

[6] *Hussey v. Palmer* [1972] 1 W.L.R. 1286 at 1290, *per* Lord Denning M.R.

[7] *post*, p. 332.

[8] (1995) 9 *Trust Law International* 35 at 38.

[9] *ibid.* at 39. See also *Paragon Finance plc v. D.B. Thakerar & Co. (a firm)* [1999] 1 All E.R. 401 at 409.

[10] *ante*, p. 67.

[11] L.P.A. 1925, s.53, *ante*, p. 80.

[12] The Child & Co. Oxford Lecture (1984) "The Informal Creation of Interests in Land," at p. 4 (Sir Christopher Slade); *cf.* [1982] Conv. 424 at 431 (F. Bates).

a breach of fiduciary obligation has given rise to an equity between the parties.[13] Similarly in the context of family property, where a common intention may found a constructive trust which is quantified differently from the proportionate shares arising under a resulting trust.[14]

The constructive trust is usually regarded as a residual category; one which is called into play where the court desires to impose a trust and no other suitable category is available.[15]

B. Establishing the Existence or the Terms of the Trust

The imposition of a constructive trust is often a determination that previously declared trusts are enforceable against someone other than the original trustee, or extend to additional property.[16] Thus, a wrongful recipient of trust property, not being a bona fide purchaser without notice from a trustee, takes the property subject to the existing trusts. A trustee who makes an improper profit holds the profit on the trusts which had previously been declared of the property out of which the profit was made.[17]

It may be, however, that the constructive trust doctrine will determine the trusts on which a person, admittedly a trustee, will hold the property. Thus, in a case of mutual wills, the executor of the second party to die needs to know whether he holds on the trusts of that party's will, or under the agreement which was the basis of the mutual wills.[18] Thus the constructive trust covers situations in which either the existence of the trusteeship or the terms of the trust or both are determined by operation of law.

C. The Duties of a Constructive Trustee

The duties and liabilities of a constructive trustee are not necessarily the same as those of an express trustee. A decision that X

---

[13] *Macmillan Inc. v. Bishopsgate Investment Trust plc (No. 3)* [1995] 1 W.L.R. 978; affirmed on other grounds (to which the distinction was not relevant) at [1996] 1 W.L.R. 387. See also *Williams v. Tedcastle* [1994] 1 N.Z.L.R. 85; *Westdeutsche Landesbank Girozentrale v. Islington London Borough Council* [1996] A.C. 669 at 707.

[14] *Drake v. Whipp* [1996] 1 F.L.R. 826; *ante*, p. 277 (lax terminology a "potent source of confusion").

[15] Recent examples include *James v. Williams* [2000] Ch. 1 (intestacy beneficiary who took possession of land was constructive trustee for co-beneficiaries so that no limitation period applied); All E.R. Rev. 1999 at 232 (P. Clarke); (2000) 20 *Trusts and Estates* 19 (N. Asprey); *Ord v. Upton* [2000] Ch. 352 (cause of action vesting in claimant's trustee in bankruptcy held on constructive trust for claimant so far as it related to damages for pain and suffering as opposed to financial loss); *Banner Homes Group plc v. Luff Developments Ltd* [2000] Ch. 372 (if A and B informally agree that A shall acquire specific property for joint benefit and B in reliance thereon refrains from attempting to acquire it, A cannot retain the whole benefit and is constructive trustee of a share for B).

[16] Bowen L.J. in *Soar v. Ashwell* [1893] 2 Q.B. 390 at 396.

[17] *post*, p. 304.

[18] *post*, p. 319.

holds as constructive trustee does not necessarily subject him to the usual trustees' duties in respect of investments, etc.[19] If a person purchases property with constructive but not actual notice of a trust, the beneficiaries may enforce the trust against him; but if he is not informed of their claims for some time, it seems that he will not be subjected also to liability for failure to invest in trustee investments and to the usual standard of care which is required of express trustees in the performance of their duties. The duties of a constructive trustee have not been made clear; they probably vary with the circumstances and will be greater for a fraudulent trustee than for others.[20]

D. Distinction Between Constructive Trusts, Accountability and Proprietary Remedies

Circumstances giving rise to a constructive trust may give rise to other remedies also. Strictly speaking a person can only be a trustee, express or constructive, if there is vested in him certain property which he holds upon trust.[21] Constructive trusteeship should be distinguished from the equitable proprietary remedy of tracing, and a personal action in equity against a fiduciary for an account. They are considered in more detail below.[22]

Where a trustee (express or constructive) has had trust property vested in him but has wrongfully disposed of it, he will commonly be regarded as retaining his status as trustee.[23] Subject to what is said below concerning tracing, the absence of trust property means that the remedy against him is personal only. Where, however, no trust property has ever been vested in the defendant (as where liability arises from dishonestly assisting the trustees in a breach of trust),[24] he cannot properly be called a trustee, constructive or otherwise. As in the previous example, the remedy against him is personal only. The defendant is *accountable*; he is not a constructive trustee of any property. If he has insufficient assets, the claimant will be unable to obtain compensation in full.

There is, however, another possibility. It may be possible to show that the property, wrongly obtained and disposed of, is now represented by money or by some other property in the trustee's or a third party's hands; and, by use of the equitable proprietary remedy, to

---

[19] See *Lonrho plc v. Fayed (No. 2)* [1992] 1 W.L.R. 1 at 12.

[20] *Restatement of Restitution*, §§ 202–204.

[21] *Re Barney* [1892] 2 Ch. 265 at 272; *Westdeutsche Landesbank Girozentrale v. Islington London Borough Council* [1996] A.C. 669.

[22] *post*, Chaps. 21, 23.

[23] See Pettit, p. 61, suggesting that principle is satisfied by treating his obligation to restore the trust fund as the trust property.

[24] *post*, p. 306.

"follow" the original property into that for which it has been exchanged. This is done by the technique of "tracing".[25]

The advantages of "tracing" the money (or other property) in this way are twofold. First, if the defendant should become insolvent, the claimant takes in priority to the general creditors, for the money "traced" is trust money, and is kept out of the defendant's insolvency.[26] Secondly, if the money has been invested successfully by the defendant, the claimant is entitled to a share of the investments which is proportionate to the share which the trust money contributed to the invested fund.[27] A distinction between constructive trusteeship and liability to the "tracing" process is that the latter may be available against a person who is not liable as constructive trustee. For example, where trust property is transferred to an innocent volunteer, *i.e.* a person who is not a purchaser and who thus takes subject to the trust but who has neither actual nor constructive knowledge of it, the volunteer is apparently not liable as constructive trustee,[28] but the "tracing" remedy lies against him while he still has the property or its identifiable proceeds.[29]

There are thus three separate matters to consider: constructive trusts, proprietary remedies, and personal actions. They are all interrelated, but each is distinct. Many decisions fail to make these distinctions, and fail to make clear whether the issue is one of accountability or one of trust,[30] although the matter has been to some extent clarified by the Privy Council.[31] This chapter will examine constructive trusts properly so called and also certain cases of personal liability which have traditionally (but inappropriately) been treated as constructive trusteeship. Accountability for profits and the question of liability to proprietary remedies are considered later.[32]

E. The Remedial Constructive Trust

We saw that the duties of a constructive trustee differ from those of an ordinary trustee. If the claimant merely wishes to have the property returned, the question is whether a constructive trust need be considered as anything beyond a means of demanding the return of the property to which he is entitled in equity. This is the way in which constructive trusts are regarded in most jurisdictions in the United States of America and in the *Restatement*. "Where a person

---

[25] *post*, p. 675.
[26] *Re Hallett's Estate* (1880) 13 Ch.D. 696.
[27] *Re Tilley's W.T.* [1967] Ch. 1179.
[28] *post*, p. 311; *Restatement of Restitution*, § 203. The view that the innocent volunteer is personally liable is discussed below, p. 315.
[29] *Re Diplock* [1948] Ch. 465, *post*, p. 699.
[30] *Reading v. Att.-Gen.* [1951] A.C. 507; *Boardman v. Phipps* [1967] 2 A.C. 46.
[31] *Att.-Gen. for Hong Kong v. Reid* [1994] 1 A.C. 324; *post*, p. 625.
[32] *post*, Chaps. 21, 23.

holding title to property is subject to an equitable duty to convey it to another on the ground that he would be unjustly enriched if he were permitted to retain it, a constructive trust arises."[33] Thus the duty is to convey to those entitled; not to hold on trust for them.

Such a constructive trust is regarded as a "remedial rather than substantive" institution.[34] The constructive trust is imposed under this doctrine whenever it is needed to prevent unjust enrichment. Like other equitable remedies, it is available where the legal remedy is inadequate. Thus, in a case of unjust enrichment the claimant will sue in quasi-contract; but if the defendant still has the property, and either the claimant wants specific recovery, or the defendant is insolvent, or the property has increased in value, the claimant will be able to assert a constructive trust.[35] The English cases have however, traditionally regarded the constructive trust as a substantive institution,[36] vindicating a pre-existing proprietary right.

The existence of such a doctrine has been left open by the Privy Council.[37] Millett J., however, warned that, while equity must be flexible, "its intervention must be based on principle; there must be some relationship between the relief granted and the circumstances which give rise to it".[38] To which his Lordship has added "there is neither room nor need for the remedial constructive trust. In my view it is a counsel of despair which too readily concedes the impossibility of propounding a general rationale for the availability of proprietary remedies. We need to be more ready to categorise wrongdoers as fiduciaries and to extend the situations in which proprietary remedies are made available, but we can do all this while adhering to established principles".[39] Similarly, "the remedial constructive trust is a judicial discretion to vary property rights and, as such, an object of suspicion".[40] Lord Browne- Wilkinson, on the

---

[33] *Restatement of Restitution*, § 160; (1955) 71 L.Q.R. 71 (A. Scott); *Carl Zeiss Stiftung v. Herbert Smith & Co.* [1969] 2 Ch. 276 at 300.

[34] (1920) 33 Harv.L.R. 420 (R. Pound). See also (1983) 3 L.S. 283 at 292 (R. Goode); [1988] Conv. 259 (D. Hayton); (1991) 107 L.Q.R. 608 (C. Rickett); Elias, *Explaining Constructive Trusts*, pp. 159–163; Wright, *The Remedial Constructive Trust*.

[35] See *Lac Minerals Ltd v. International Corona Resources Ltd* (1989) 61 D.L.R. (4th) 14.

[36] See *Re Sharpe* [1980] 1 W.L.R. 219, where the notion of imposing a constructive trust as a remedy was described as a novel concept in English law.

[37] *Re Goldcorp Exchange Ltd (in receivership)* [1995] 1 A.C. 74; *cf. Metall und Rohstoff A.G. v. Donaldson Lufkin & Jenrette Inc.* [1990] 1 Q.B. 391 at 479 (overruled on another point by *Lonrho plc v. Fayed* [1992] 1 A.C. 448).

[38] *Lonrho plc v. Fayed (No. 2)* [1992] 1 W.L.R. 1 at 9 (no constructive trust where claim had no proprietary base). See also (1991) 107 L.Q.R. 71 at 85 (Sir Peter Millett).

[39] (1995) 9 *Trust Law International* 35 at 40. See also *Paragon Finance plc v. D. B. Thakerar & Co (a firm)* [1999] 1 All E.R. 401 at 413: the distinction between institutional trusts and the remedial formula is the distinction "between a trust and a catch-phrase".

[40] *The Frontiers of Liability*, Vol. 2, p. 24 (P. Birks); *cf.* at 165 (D. Waters) and 186 (S. Gardner). See also [1996] R.L.R. 3 (P. Birks); Oakley, *Constructive Trusts* (3rd ed.), p. 26; Goff and Jones (5th ed.), p. 85.

other hand, has suggested that the introduction of the remedial constructive trust may provide a satisfactory basis for developing proprietary restitutionary remedies.[41]

The question arose in *Halifax Building Society v. Thomas*,[42] where the defendant obtained a mortgage loan to buy a flat by fraudulent misrepresentation. When he fell into arrears the mortgagee sold the flat. After the repayment of the debt a surplus remained, to which the mortgagee claimed entitlement under a constructive trust in its favour, to prevent the defendant profiting from his fraud. In rejecting this claim the Court of Appeal noted that English law had not followed other jurisdictions where the constructive trust had become a remedy for unjust enrichment. There was no universal principle that there must be restitution of a benefit derived from wrongdoing. The relationship was not fiduciary but was merely one of debtor and secured creditor. The mortgagee had recovered all it was contractually entitled to, and the surplus belonged to the defendant. It was thus available for confiscation under Part VI of the Criminal Justice Act 1988, the enactment of which indicated that the profits of crime did not belong to the victim. This was also the approach of the Court of Appeal in *Re Polly Peck International plc (in administration) (No. 2)*,[43] where it was said that there was no prospect of the imposition of a remedial constructive trust[44] on the assets of an insolvent company so as to give the claimants a proprietary interest, to the detriment of creditors. To do so would confer a priority not accorded by the insolvency legislation. Although the laws moves, "it cannot be legitimately moved by judicial decision down a road signed 'No Entry' by Parliament. The insolvency road is blocked off to remedial constructive trusts, at least when judge-driven in a vehicle of discretion".[45] Nourse L.J. emphasised that his conclusions were not confined to insolvency, because property rights could only be varied by statute.[46] The decision has been said to be "the end of the remedial constructive trust"[47]; similarly, "It bangs the door shut on the 'remedial constructive trust' in this jurisdiction".[48]

---

[41] *Westdeutsche Landesbank Girozentrale v. Islington London Borough Council* [1996] A.C. 669 at 716.

[42] [1996] Ch. 217; (1996) 10 *Trust Law International* 2 (P. Birks); (1996) 112 L.Q.R. 219 (P. Watts); [1996] R.L.R. 92 (P. Jaffey).

[43] [1998] 3 All E.R. 812. See also *Fortex Group Ltd v. MacIntosh* [1998] 3 N.Z.L.R. 171.

[44] Defined by Nourse L.J. at 830 as the grant of a proprietary right, as a remedy, to someone who, beforehand, had no such right.

[45] *ibid.* at 827, *per* Mummery L.J.

[46] *ibid.* at 831.

[47] (1998) 12 *Trust Law International* 202 (P. Birks). See also (1998) 114 L.Q.R. 399 (Sir Peter Millett); (1998) 4 *Trusts & Trustees* 14 (P. Matthews); [1999] L.M.C.L.Q. 111 (C. Rickett and R. Grantham).

[48] All E.R. Rev. 1998 at 415 (P. Birks and W. Swadling); *cf.* [1999] R.L.R. 128 (D. Wright).

The remedial constructive trust has been accepted in Australia,[49] New Zealand[50] and Canada.[51] It has not replaced the traditional institutional constructive trust, but exists alongside it.[52]

One distinction between institutional and remedial constructive trusts may lie in the date from which the claimant may assert proprietary rights. This question has significance for third parties acquiring interests in the property before the court makes its order. It seems clear that the traditional institutional constructive trust vindicates a pre-existing proprietary interest which is operative before the date of the court order.[53] The effect of a remedial constructive trust, on the other hand, may be to confer a new proprietary interest on the claimant.[54] In such a case it will have prospective effect only, operating from the date of the court order which creates it.[55]

We will now examine the circumstances in which a constructive trust has been held to exist.

2. When a Constructive Trust Arises

Constructive trusts can arise over a wide variety of situations. No claim is made that those discussed in this section cover the whole field; they are merely illustrations. It will be seen that some of the selected categories lay down specific rules; others rely on general principles, which have been stated in the widest terms.

A. Unauthorised Profit by a Trustee or Fiduciary

The principle is that a fiduciary may not make use of his position to gain a benefit for himself. Trustees, personal representatives[56] and

---

[49] *Muschinski v. Dodds* (1985) 160 C.L.R. 583.

[50] *Powell v. Thompson* [1991] 1 N.Z.L.R. 579 at 615 ("a broad equitable remedy for reversing that which is inequitable or unconscionable"); *Equiticorp Industries Group Ltd v. Hawkins* [1991] 3 N.Z.L.R. 700. But caution is needed in insolvency cases; *Fortex Group Ltd v. MacIntosh, supra.*

[51] *Pettkus v. Becker* (1980) 117 D.L.R. (3d) 257; *Sorochan v. Sorochan* (1986) 29 D.L.R. (4th) 1; *Lac Minerals Ltd v. International Corona Resources Ltd* (1989) 61 D.L.R. (4th) 14; (1990) 106 L.Q.R. 207 (G. Hammond); *Rawluk v. Rawluk* (1990) 65 D.L.R. (4th) 161; [1991] Conv. 125 (C. Rickett); (1991) 11 L.S. 304 (G. Fridman); *Peter v. Beblow* (1993) 101 D.L.R. (4th) 621.

[52] *Muschinski v. Dodds, supra*, at 613–615.

[53] This is assumed in the English cases such as *Lloyds Bank plc v. Rosset* [1991] 1 A.C. 107; *ante*, p. 275. See *Westdeutsche Landesbank Girozentrale v. Islington London Borough Council, supra*, at 716.

[54] *Lac Minerals Ltd v. International Corona Resources Ltd, supra*, at 50. The term "imposed proprietary remedy" is preferred in (1999) 18 N.Z.U.L.R. 305 at 331 (C. Rickett).

[55] *Muschinski v. Dodds* (1985) 160 C.L.R. 583 at 615; *cf. Rawluk v. Rawluk, supra*. A similar question arises as to the date on which an estoppel interest takes effect, *post*, p. 902. The claim in *Polly Peck, supra*, was that the remedial constructive trust should be imposed retrospectively.

[56] *James v. Dean* (1808) 15 Ves.Jr. 236.

agents[57] are by their "position debarred from keeping a personal advantage derived directly or indirectly out of his fiduciary or quasi-fiduciary position."[58] With other fiduciaries, such as company directors[59] and partners,[60] the question is one of fact whether the benefit was obtained by reason or independently of, the fiduciary relationship. The category of fiduciaries is not closed.[61]

These matters are dealt with in Chapter 21. We will there see that a trustee must not renew in his own favour any lease held on trust; nor may he purchase the reversion on any such lease; nor may he purchase the trust property. He must not make any incidental profits out of his trusteeship. In the present context, one example must suffice.

In *Boardman v. Phipps*,[62] the trustees held a minority shareholding in a private company which was not being efficiently managed. Boardman had acted as solicitor to the trust, and was therefore a fiduciary. He decided that the beneficiaries would be in a better position if the trustees had control of the company, but no trust money was available to buy the extra shares. Boardman and one of the beneficiaries therefore bought the necessary shares themselves and reorganised the company. All this was done in good faith and with the object of enhancing the trust holding. Both the personal and the trust holdings increased in value. A majority of the House of Lords held that Boardman was constructive trustee of the profit made on his personal shareholding. The opportunity to make the profit arose out of his fiduciary relationship with the trust and certain confidential information had been used in the process. However, compensation was ordered from the trust in recognition of the work and skill involved.

B. Liability of Third Parties

Third parties may incur personal liability (in addition to the trustees' liability) in certain circumstances, in particular where they dishonestly assist the trustee (or other fiduciary)[63] in a breach of duty, or where they receive trust property transferred in breach of

---

[57] *De Bussche v. Alt* (1878) 8 Ch.D. 286 at 310; *Boardman v. Phipps* [1967] 2 A.C. 67.

[58] *Re Biss* [1903] 2 Ch. 40 at 56.

[59] *Post*, pp. 615 *et seq.*

[60] *Featherstonhaugh v. Fenwick* (1810) 17 Ves.Jr. 298; *Clegg v. Fishwick* (1849) 1 Mac. & G. 294.

[61] *English v. Dedham Vale Properties Ltd* [1978] 1 W.L.R. 93.

[62] [1967] 2 A.C. 67, *post*, p. 618.

[63] The Court of Appeal in *Brown v. Bennett* [1999] B.C.L.C. 649 considered it arguable that the principle applied where the breach was of a director's fiduciary duties.

trust. Such persons are commonly called constructive trustees,[64] although this is misleading because the liability is personal only. The two categories were until recently known as "knowing assistance" and "knowing receipt".[65] As explained below, the terminology in the first case is no longer appropriate. The terms "accessory liability" and "recipient liability" may be preferable. Whatever the heading of liability, the existence of the trust must be established.[66] Knowledge of a "doubtful equity" does not suffice; hence a solicitor was not accountable for moneys received in payment of costs and expenses paid by a client for work done in defending an action in which the claimant was asserting that the client was a trustee of the whole of its assets.[67] It would be otherwise if he knew that the claim was well-founded.

i. Dishonest Assistance

(a) *Terminology.* An agent or other third party may be liable to make good the loss to a trust without the trust property ever vesting in him and without his purporting to act as trustee; as where an agent dishonestly participates with a trustee in a breach of trust. Thus liability does not depend on unjust enrichment.

It is submitted that, as no trust property is vested in him, he should not be called a constructive, or any other kind of trustee.[68] The question at issue is one of personal liability. The matter will nevertheless be dealt with in this Chapter because the constructive trust terminology has been used in much of the caselaw,[69] although Millett L.J. recently described it as misleading and to be discarded: such third parties "are in reality neither trustees nor fiduciaries, but merely wrongdoers".[70] One explanation is that the constructive trustee label has been used to overcome the supposed difficulty in a

---

[64] Lord Millett considers the "receipt" cases to be examples of resulting trusts; (1995) 9 *Trust Law International* 35 at 39; *Macmillan Inc. v. Bishopsgate Investment Trust plc (No. 3)* [1995] 1 W.L.R. 978. Similarly Chambers, *Resulting Trusts* (Chap. 8).

[65] The categories were based on Lord Selborne's speech in *Barnes v. Addy* (1874) L.R. 9 Ch. App. 244 at 251–252.

[66] See *Box v. Barclays Bank plc* [1998] Lloyd's Rep. Bank. 185.

[67] *Carl Zeiss Stiftung v. Herbert Smith & Co. (No. 2)* [1969] 2 Ch. 276; (1969) 85 L.Q.R. 160 (P.V.B.); (1986) 102 L.Q.R. 267 at 287 (C. Harpum). See also *Williams v. Williams* (1881) 17 Ch.D. 437; *Competitive Insurance Co. Ltd v. Davies Investments Ltd* [1975] 1 W.L.R. 1240. A solicitor in doubt as to possible liability should apply to court for directions; *Finers v. Miro* [1991] 1 W.L.R. 35. See also *United Mizrahi Bank Ltd v. Doherty* [1998] 1 W.L.R. 435; *Bank of Scotland v. A Ltd* (Serious Fraud Office, interested party), *The Times*, February 6, 2001 (where bank suspects client).

[68] See McKendrick's *Commercial Aspects of Trusts and Fiduciary Obligations*, Chapter 8 (P. Birks).

[69] See *Westdeutsche Landesbank Girozentrale v. Islington London Borough Council* [1996] A.C. 669 at 705; *Ghana Commercial Bank v. C, The Times*, March 3, 1997.

[70] *Paragon Finance plc v. D.B. Thakerar & Co. (a firm)* [1999] 1 All E.R. 401 at 412. See also 414.

beneficiary being able to sue anybody but the trustee.[71] It might be added that, if it should become established that an innocent volunteer is strictly liable for receipt of trust property on a restitutionary basis,[72] although there is presently little judicial support for this view, the term "constructive trustee" could usefully be employed to indicate the more onerous personal liability which results from receipt with knowledge.[73]

(b) *Nature of Trustee's Breach.* In *Barnes v. Addy,*[74] Lord Selborne laid down the test of liability as that of as assisting "with knowledge in a dishonest and fraudulent design on the part of the trustees." This statement was *obiter,* but the principle that the third party could not be liable under this heading unless the breach of trust in which he assisted was dishonest on the part of the trustee became entrenched in the law until the recent clarification by the Privy Council in *Royal Brunei Airlines Sdn. Bhd. v. Tan.*[75]

The claimant appointed a company (BLT) to act as its travel agent and to account for the proceeds of ticket sales. It was conceded that BLT committed a breach of trust by using the money in its business. BLT fell into arrears in accounting and the contract was terminated. As BLT was insolvent, the claimant sued Tan, the principal shareholder and director. It was conceded that Tan had assisted in the breach with actual knowledge. The Brunei Court of Appeal found for Tan, holding that the breach in which he had assisted had not been shown to be fraudulent on the part of BLT. The appeal to the Privy Council centred upon the question whether accessory liability requires the breach of trust itself to be fraudulent. Tan was held personally liable for dishonestly assisting BLT's breach. There was no further requirement of dishonesty by BLT.[76]

Lord Nicholls of Birkenhead reviewed the authorities prior to *Barnes v. Addy.*[77] Those authorities did not require dishonesty on the

---

[71] (1999) 58 C.L.J. 294 at 299, 301 (L. Smith). The term "remedial constructive trust" is used in *Coulthard v. Disco Mix Club Ltd* [2000] 1 W.L.R. 707 at 731, but that term normally implies a proprietary remedy.

[72] *post,* p. 315.

[73] See [1998] Conv. 13 (J. Martin).

[74] (1874) L.R. 9 Ch.App. 255 at 251, 252.

[75] [1995] 2 A.C. 378; [1995] Conv. 339 (M. Halliwell); (1995) 111 L.Q.R. 545 (C. Harpum); (1995) 54 C.L.J. 505 (R. Nolan); (1995) 3 R.L.R. 105 (J. Stevens); (1996) 112 L.Q.R. 56 (S. Gardner); *Restitution and Banking Law* (ed. F. Rose), Chap. 9 (M. Tugendhat). For criticisms, see (1996) L.M.C.L.Q. 1 (P. Birks); (1996) 59 M.L.R. 443 (A. Berg).

[76] In fact BLT's breach was dishonest because Tan's state of mind could be imputed to it. See *El Ajou v. Dollar Land Holdings plc* [1994] 2 All E.R. 685 ("directing mind and will").

[77] *supra.*

part of the trustee whether the third party had procured the breach[78] or merely assisted in it. The law had taken a wrong turning in reliance on Lord Selborne's dictum in *Barnes v. Addy*. The trustee would be liable whether or not the breach was dishonest, but it would make no sense for a dishonest accessory, whose liability is fault-based, to escape simply because the trustee did not also act dishonestly. Although cases where the accessory is dishonest but the trustee is not will be rare, especially where the trustee is a company of which the accessories are directors,[79] this is a welcome clarification of the law.

It might be added that "assistance" requires actual participation. Thus a wife who merely accompanied her husband on holiday trips which also involved money laundering did not assist his breach.[80]

(c) *Dishonesty of Third Party.* The next question is whether the accessory must be shown to have acted dishonestly, or whether constructive knowledge of the breach (*i.e.* negligence) suffices. This is a matter of great importance, because frauds and other breaches of duty in the commercial context are complex, and can involve participants who are unaware of the wrongdoing.

Opinions have differed as to whether dishonesty is required on the part of the accessory or whether it suffices that he ought to have known of the breach. The weight of modern authority supports the view that dishonesty is required, and the matter has now been put beyond doubt by the Privy Council in *Royal Brunei Airlines Sdn. Bhd. v. Tan.*[81] Although the main issue, as we have seen, was whether the breach must be dishonest on the part of the trustee, their Lordships considered also the question whether the accessory must have acted dishonestly. In confirming that requirement, Lord Nicholls rejected the label "knowing assistance" because "knowledge" has too many shades of meaning. The five categories of knowledge elaborated by Peter Gibson J. in the *Baden* case[82] were "best forgotten". The word "dishonesty" was also to be preferred to "unconscionable conduct", a term little used save by equity lawyers. Lord Nicholls summarily rejected the view that an accessory

---

[78] See *Eaves v. Hickson* (1861) Beav. 136 (trustees innocently deceived by forgery made wrongful distrubution which the party responsible for the deceit was liable to restore). A modern authority not requiring dishonesty by the trustees is *Powell v. Thompson* [1991] 1 N.Z.L.R. 597.

[79] See n. 76, *supra.*

[80] *Brinks Ltd v. Abu-Saleh (No. 3)*, *The Times*, October 23, 1995; criticised (1996) 59 M.L.R. 443 at 447–448 (A. Berg); (1996) 10 *Trust Law International* 53 (A. Oakley); [1996] Conv. 447 (J. Stevens). See also *Brown v. Bennett* [1999] B.C.L.C. 649.

[81] [1995] 2 A.C. 378; *supra.*

[82] *Baden, Delvaux and Lecuit v. Société Générale pour Favoriser le Développement du Commerce et de l'Industrie en France SA* [1983] B.C.L.C. 325. The Court of Appeal in *Heinl v. Jyske Bank (Gibraltar) Ltd* [1999] Lloyd's Rep. Bank. 511, considered that *Baden* might still be helpful.

could never be directly liable to the beneficiaries, because they are entitled to expect that others will refrain from intentionally intruding in the trustee-beneficiary relationship. Similarly rejected was the view that even an innocent third party could be liable, as that would make commerce impossible. In rejecting the view that negligence was a sufficient basis for liability, Lord Nicholls observed that in the commercial context persons such as bankers, advisers and many other agents would be liable to the trustees if they acted negligently. There was no reason why they should also be liable to the beneficiaries.[83] Thus the conclusion was that dishonesty is the basis of accessory liability.

It remains to consider what is meant by dishonesty. Lord Nicholls explained that it combines the objective standard of not acting as an honest person would in the circumstances with a strong subjective element: the court will assess the conduct in the light of what the defendant actually knew, not what a reasonable person would have known, and will have regard to the defendant's experience, intelligence and reasons for acting as he did. The broad meaning is conscious impropriety.[84] It includes deliberately closing one's eyes or deliberately not asking questions, of which an example is *Agip (Africa) Ltd v. Jackson*:

> Payment orders from Agip to third parties were fraudulently altered by Agip's accountant, Z, who changed the name of the payees to that of B Co. and other companies. B Co. (and the other companies) had been formed by the defendants, who were two accountants in partnership (Jackson & Co.) and their employee. Two of the defendants were the sole directors and shareholders of B Co. The money was transferred to the account of B Co. and thence to Jackson's client account in the Isle of Man. It was then paid to various recipients abroad who had no connection with Agip. B Co. was then put into liquidation. Agip sought to recover from the defendants, who had throughout followed the instructions of their client, a French lawyer acting for unidentified principals.

The claim based on assistance in the breach was successful before Millett J.[85] Z had committed a fraudulent breach of his duty to Agip, which the defendants must have realised was going on. They obviously knew they were "laundering" money, and were consciously

---

[83] This would sidestep the tort principle that there is no liability for negligently causing economic loss. *cf.* (1995) 9 *Trust Law International* 102 (G. McCormack), suggesting that an accessory to fraud should be liable if negligent.

[84] See also *Heinl v. Jyske Bank (Gibraltar) Ltd, supra* (high standard of proof of dishonesty required); *Walker v. Stones* [2000] 4 All E.R. 412; *post*, p. 502.

[85] [1990] Ch. 265; (1991) 107 L.Q.R. 71 (Sir Peter Millett). See also *Finers v. Miro* [1991] 1 W.L.R. 35.

helping Z to conceal the fraud. At best, they had been indifferent to it, which amounted to dishonesty. One partner and the employee were liable for assisting the breach, and the other partner was vicariously liable for their acts.[86] The judgment of Millett J. was upheld on appeal[87]: the defendants were liable because they did not act honestly.

The issue arose again in *Lipkin Gorman v. Karpnale Ltd.*

A solicitor, C, wrongly withdrew £200,000 from his firm's client account at the bank and spent it on gambling at the Playboy Club. C's firm sued the bank and the Club. In the present context, we are concerned only with the action against the bank. The bank manager had known that C was a gambler, but made no enquiries about the withdrawals.[88]

The Court of Appeal[89] held that the bank was not liable. It was conceded that the bank could not be liable as accessory if it was not in breach of its contract with the claimant firm. There was no breach of contract because the bank had no reason to believe that there was a serious possibility that C was drawing money for his own purposes.

In the absence of a dishonest accessory, the remedy is against the trustees and against those who have received the property, whose position will now be examined.

ii. Liability for Receipt[90]

(a) *Personal and Proprietary Remedies.* A basic principle of property law is that any person who receives trust property,[91] not being a purchaser for value without notice, takes subject to the trust. This is so whether he took with actual or constructive notice. So long as he retains the property he is bound to return it, and the tracing process[92] is available to identify the property or its proceeds. However, this is different from the question whether the recipient

---

[86] *cf. Re Bell's Indenture* [1980] 1 W.L.R. 1217; *post*, p. 318.

[87] [1991] Ch. 547; [1992] Conv. 367 (S. Goulding); (1992) 12 L.S. 332 (H. Norman); (1993–94) 4 K.C.L.J. 82 (P. Oliver).

[88] Any allegation of dishonesty was insufficiently pleaded.

[89] [1989] 1 W.L.R. 1340. The House of Lords dealt only with the Club's position; [1992] A.C. 548; *post*, p. 314.

[90] Persons within this category were described in *Selangor United Rubber Estates v. Cradock (No. 3)* [1968] 1 W.L.R. 1555 as trustees *de son tort*, by analogy with executors *de son tort*. The distinction was once significant in the context of the defence of limitation, but is of no significance today; *ibid.* at 1579. As to whether the beneficiary may sue for conversion, see (1996) 55 C.L.J. 36 (A. Tettenborn).

[91] For receipt of confidential information, see *Satnam Investments Ltd v. Dunlop Heywood & Co. Ltd* [1999] 3 All E.R. 652.

[92] *post*, Chapter 23.

should be under a *personal* liability to account. The distinction is important if he no longer has the property. If he is liable to account, his liability remains. If he is not so accountable, his liability is confined to the return of the property or its proceeds while still in his possession. Not every transferee who fails to prove that he was a bona fide purchaser of the legal estate without notice is subjected to the additional personal liability. An "innocent volunteer,"[93] for example, who took without notice that the property was trust property transferred in breach of trust cannot take free of the trust, but, on the present state of the authorities, does not incur personal liability.[94] Whether the defendant has received the trust property will depend on the application of the tracing rules discussed in Chapter 23.[95]

(b) *Degree of Knowledge.* While constructive knowledge clearly suffices where the question is whether the recipient took the property subject to the trust, it does not follow that the same applies where the question is whether he has incurred the personal liability to account. Opinions have differed as to whether liability is based on actual knowledge, or constructive knowledge, or whether it is strict, so that even an innocent volunteer is liable. Formerly it appeared established that constructive notice sufficed.[96] Thus in *Belmont Finance Corporation v. Williams Furniture Ltd (No. 2)*[97] company directors who participated in an unlawful share purchase scheme were liable because they had knowledge of all the facts which established the improper use of the funds, and knew or ought to have known that the money which they received was impressed with a trust. It was immaterial that, as the judge found, the directors did not act fraudulently.

A different view was taken in *Re Montagu's S.T.*[98]

> Trustees transferred certain settled chattels to the beneficiary (the tenth Duke) absolutely, in breach of trust. The situation resulted from an "honest muddle" by all concerned. The Duke's solicitor had at an earlier stage been aware of the terms of the settlement. The Duke disposed of a number of the chattels during his lifetime. After his death, the eleventh Duke claimed that his predecessor had become a constructive trustee of them. Megarry

---

[93] *Re Diplock* [1948] Ch. 465 at 478–479; *ante*, p. 301, *post*, p. 699.

[94] For the view that liability should be strict, see *post*, p. 315. See also Law Com. No. 254, *Land Registration for the Twenty-first century*, paras. 3.48–3.49.

[95] See *El Ajou v. Dollar Land Holdings plc (No. 2)* [1995] 2 All E.R. 213; *post*, p. 691.

[96] *Karak Rubber Co. Ltd v. Burden (No. 2)* [1972] 1 W.L.R. 602.

[97] [1980] 1 All E.R. 393; see also *(No. 1)* [1979] Ch. 250; *International Sales and Agencies Ltd v. Marcus* [1982] 3 All E.R. 551 at 558. It is also assumed in *Re Diplock* [1948] Ch. 465 at 477–479 that constructive knowledge would suffice.

[98] [1987] Ch. 264 (decided 1985); (1986) 102 L.Q.R. 267 and (1987) 50 M.L.R. 217 (C. Harpum). See also *Hillsdown Holdings plc v. Pensions Ombudsman* [1997] 1 All E.R. 862.

V.-C. held that, while the tenth Duke's estate must return any remaining chattels or their traceable proceeds, the Duke was not liable as constructive trustee because he had no actual knowledge that the chattels were trust property transferred in breach of trust. Even if he had once understood the terms of the settlement, there was nothing to suggest that he remembered them so as to be aware at the date of receipt that the chattels were trust property. Nor was there any reason to impute the solicitor's knowledge to the Duke, by analogy with the doctrine of imputed notice.

The Vice-Chancellor emphasised that the relevant question was whether the recipient had *knowledge*, not whether he had *notice* according to the rules established under the doctrine of notice which dealt with the question whether an equitable interest was binding on a transferee. The question in the present context was whether a person was to have imposed on him the burdens of trusteeship. His Lordship held that liability should not be imposed unless the conscience of the recipient was affected; this required "want of probity", which includes actual knowledge, shutting one's eyes to the obvious, or wilfully and recklessly failing to make such enquiries as a reasonable and honest man would make; it does not include knowledge of circumstances which would indicate the facts to an honest and reasonable man or would put the latter on enquiry.

The question has recently been examined by the Court of Appeal in *Bank of Credit and Commerce International (Overseas) Ltd v. Akindele*,[99] where the defendant had received $6.68 million in 1988 as a return on $10 million he had paid to the bank in 1985 under an artificial loan agreement. The transaction involved a fraudulent breach of the fiduciary duties owed to the bank by certain parties, but the defendant knew nothing of the frauds within the BCCI group at that time nor of the fraudulent aspect of the particular agreement. Nourse L.J. reviewed the authorities (including Commonwealth decisions) and academic commentaries on the degree of knowledge required to found recipient liability. First, his Lordship confirmed that dishonesty had never been required. There was considerable authority supporting the view that constructive notice sufficed,[1] although in much of it the question had not been examined in depth because the defendant had actual knowledge, or the decisions were based on assistance rather than receipt. Other authorities favoured

---

[99] [2000] 3 W.L.R. 1423; (2000) 59 C.L.J. 447 (R. Nolan); (2000) 14 *Trust Law International* 229 (J. Penner). See also *Bank of America v. Arnell* [1999] Lloyd's Rep. Bank 399; *Twinsectra Ltd v. Yardley* [1999] Lloyd's Rep. Bank. 438; (2000) 59 C.L.J. 444 (D. Fox).

[1] *Belmont Finance Corporation v. Williams Furniture Ltd (No. 2)* [1980] 1 All E.R. 393; *ante*, p. 311; *Agip (Africa) Ltd v. Jackson* [1990] Ch. 265 (not dealt with on appeal at [1991] Ch. 547); *Polly Peck International plc v. Nadir (No. 2)* [1992] 4 All E.R. 769; *Houghton v. Fayers* [2000] 1 B.C.L.C. 511.

the view that constructive notice did not suffice, at any rate in the case of commercial transactions, where (in cases not involving title to land) there was no duty to investigate. In such cases purchasers have been held not liable unless they had actual knowledge of the impropriety or acted with wilful or reckless disregard,[2] although Commonwealth courts had taken a different view.[3]

Nourse L.J. regarded *Re Montagu's S.T.*,[4] where Megarry V.-C. had laid down the "want of probity" test, as the "seminal judgment". So far as the five categories of knowledge elaborated in the *Baden*[5] case were concerned, they had been formulated with "assistance" rather than "receipt" in mind. There were grave doubts as to the utility of this categorisation in receipt cases. The purpose of such a categorisation could only be to enable the court to determine whether the defendant's conscience was sufficiently affected to bind him as constructive trustee. There was, therefore, no need for the categorisation. There was a single test of dishonesty for assistance liability, and there should be a single test of knowledge for recipient liability: "The recipient's state of knowledge must be such as to make it unconscionable for him to retain the benefit of the receipt".[5a] This test should better enable the court to give common sense decisions in the commercial context. Applying the test in the present case, the defendant's knowledge was not such as to make it unconscionable for him to enter into the agreement in 1985, when the integrity of BCCI was not doubted. At the time of the receipt of $6.68 million in 1988 he had suspicions, but his state of knowledge was not such as to make it unconscionable for him to retain the money. His knowledge in 1988 concerned the general reputation of the BCCI group from late 1987 onwards, and not the particular transaction entered into in 1985. If his Lordship had thought that it was still the appropriate test, he would have held that the defendant did not have actual or constructive knowledge that his receipt was traceable to a breach of fiduciary duty.

It remains to be clarified by later cases what the distinction is between dishonesty (not required) and the degree of knowledge making it unconscionable for the defendant to retain the benefit of his receipt. As the defendant was held not even to have had constructive knowledge, the point remains unclear.

---

[2] See *Eagle Trust plc v. S.B.C. Securities Ltd* [1993] 1 W.L.R. 484; *Cowan de Groot Properties Ltd v. Eagle Trust plc* [1992] 4 All E.R. 700; *El Ajou v. Dollar Land Holdings plc* [1993] 3 All E.R. 717 (reversed on another point at [1994] 2 All E.R. 685). Banks and other financial institutions must, however, satisfy the money laundering regulations.

[3] *Powell v. Thompson* [1991] 1 N.Z.L.R. 597; *Equiticorp Industries Group Ltd v. Hawkins* [1991] 3 N.Z.L.R. 700; *Citadel General Assurance Co. v. Lloyds Bank Canada* (1997) 152 D.L.R. (4th) 411.

[4] [1987] Ch. 264; *ante*, p. 311.

[5] *ante*, p. 308.

[5a] [2000] 3 W.L.R. 1423 at 1439.

Nourse L.J. took the opportunity to comment on the debate as to whether innocent volunteers should be strictly liable to account on the ground of unjust enrichment, subject to the defence of change of position. Before examining this, the position at common law must be considered.

(c) *Common Law Remedy.* A discussion of the equitable principles alone would be misleading, because the circumstances giving rise to a receipt claim may also found the common law personal action for money had and received. It is clear that the common law personal action lies against an innocent volunteer who had no knowledge, actual or constructive, of the fact that the money belonged not to the transferor but to the claimant. The claimant must, however, show title at common law to the money which, by applying the tracing rules, the defendant can be shown to have received. It is not necessary that the money should remain identifiable in the recipient's hands (in which case a proprietary claim might be considered).[6] A recipient of the money in good faith and for value has a defence.

These issues came before the House of Lords in *Lipkin Gorman v. Karpnale Ltd*,[7] where a firm of solicitors sought to recover money paid to the Playboy Club by a member of the firm, Cass, who had withdrawn if from the firm's client account and spent it on gambling. The Club had no knowledge of the source of the money, but had not given consideration: the gaming contract was not legally enforceable, and so the Club had incurred no obligation to honour the bets. The solicitors were held entitled to recover in the common law action, subject to the defence of change of position.

The decision has been criticised on the ground that the claimant firm did not have legal title to the money after it was withdrawn from the bank, because the legal title vested in Cass.[8] Lord Goff avoided this difficulty by holding that the firm had a legal chose in action (the debt owed to them by the bank holding their client account) which they could follow into the money drawn by Cass and thence into the hands of the Club (the Club surprisingly conceded that this legal title was not defeated by reason of any mixing of the money by Cass with his own).

Of great significance was the unqualified acceptance by the House of Lords of the defence of change of position, widely recognised in the common law world, which should be left to develop on a case by

---

[6] It is not clear how far this action lies against a transferee from the recipient. See *Agip (Africa) Ltd v. Jackson* [1990] Ch. 265 at 287–288; (1990) 106 L.Q.R. 20 (A. Burrows); (1991) 107 L.Q.R. 71 (Sir Peter Millett); Goff and Jones, p. 703.

[7] [1991] 2 A.C. 548; *ante*, p. 310. The claimants were content to bring a personal action as the defendant was not insolvent.

[8] [1992] Conv. 124 (M. Halliwell); (1992) 55 M.L.R. 377 (E. McKendrick).

case basis.[9] The defence is available to an innocent defendant[10] (but not to a wrongdoer) who has so changed his position that it would be inequitable to require restitution or restitution in full. Of course, it will not be available where the recipient has applied the money to normal expenses which would have been incurred in any event. In the present case the Club could invoke the defence to the extent that it had paid out winnings to Cass. These sums could be set off against the total sums received from him.

(d) *Unjust Enrichment Theory.* A question which has been much debated, primarily by academic commentators, is whether an innocent volunteer who has received trust property transferred in breach of trust should be strictly liable to account, subject to the defence of change of position, even though he took without notice. As we have seen, this is the position with regard to the common law personal action, discussed above. It is also the position with regard to the action in equity against an innocent volunteer who has received property to which he is not entitled in the administration of an estate.[11] This view is based on the principle that restitutionary liability is receipt-based, not fault-based: the volunteer is unjustly enriched if he is not accountable.[12] Of course, there is no room for strict liability in the case of a purchaser, either at common law or in equity. Lord Browne-Wilkinson stated in *Westdeutsche Landesbank Girozentrale v. Islington London Borough Council*[13] (which involved a common law action) that an innocent volunteer is not personally liable to account as constructive trustee because he lacks the necessary knowledge. This does not preclude the strict liability argument because, as shown by *Re Diplock*[14] itself, personal liability to account in equity can arise in the absence of constructive trusteeship. It is right that an innocent volunteer should not be a constructive trustee, with consequent liability to repay with interest,[15] but it does not follow that there should be no restitutionary liability in equity in the absence of change of position, in order to prevent unjust enrichment.[16] That recipient liability is restitution-

---

[9] *post*, p. 701. The defence existed in limited form, as discussed by the House of Lords.

[10] See Goff and Jones, p. 826.

[11] *Ministry of Health v. Simpson* [1951] A.C. 251 (subject to requirement of suing personal representative first); *post*, p. 708. The volunteers were not, however, liable *as constructive trustees* because they were entitled to assume that the executors were acting properly; [1948] Ch. 465 at 477–479.

[12] Goff and Jones, pp. 745–746.

[13] [1996] A.C. 669 at 707.

[14] [1948] Ch. 465. Liability based on constructive trusteeship was rejected at 478.

[15] Liability to pay compound interest was the issue in the *Westdeutsche* case.

[16] See Goff and Jones, pp. 745–746; [1998] Conv. 13 (J. Martin); *cf. Hillsdown Holdings plc v. Pensions Ombudsman* [1997] 1 All E.R. 862 at 904 (doubting whether lower courts could give effect to a claim in restitution where no constructive trust).

based was recently emphasised by the Privy Council.[17] It has been pointed out, however, that the law does not recognise any personal unjust enrichment claim founded on equitable title, and that this is a further illustration of the principle that a beneficiary's interest does not have the same incidents as the title of a legal owner.[18]

Nourse L.J. in *Bank of Credit and Commerce International (Overseas) Ltd v. Akindele*[19] took the opportunity to discuss the issue, although it did not arise for decision because the defendant was not a volunteer. His Lordship referred to a paper in which Lord Nicholls had advocated the strict liability approach.[20] Nourse L.J. doubted whether strict liability coupled with the change of position defence would be preferable to fault-based liability in many commercial transactions. In his Lordship's view, it would appear commercially unworkable, on proof of misapplication, that the burden should shift to the recipient to defend the receipt by change of position or in some other way, and there would be obvious difficulty in saying that it would be equitable for change of position to afford a defence if the circumstances were such that it would be unconscionable to retain the benefit. It must be emphasised, however, that the advocates of the strict liability principle have never sought to apply it to commercial purchasers nor to argue that the defence of change of position, which applies only to innocent recipients,[21] should be available in circumstances where it would be unconscionable to retain the benefit.

It may be that legislation will be required to achieve coherence in this area.[22] It is indeed difficult to discern any convincing policy reason why an innocent recipient of misapplied property should be vulnerable to the claims of a legal owner (including a trustee) and of underpaid beneficiaries of estates but not to the claims of other equitable owners.[23] Although most recipient claims arise in the context of commercial fraud, it may nevertheless be said that the debate as to whether the innocent volunteer should be strictly liable in

---

[17] *Royal Brunei Airlines Sdn. Bhd. v. Tan* [1995] 2 A.C. 378 (a case of dishonest assistance). The receipt-based restitutionary claim was described by Auld L.J. as an "equitable newcomer" in *Macmillan Inc. v. Bishopgate Investment Trust plc (No. 3)* [1996] 1 W.L.R. 387 at 407.

[18] (2000) 116 L.Q.R. 412 (L. Smith).

[19] [2000] 3 W.L.R. 1423.

[20] *Knowing Receipt: the Need for a New Landmark*, published in *Restitution: Past, Present and Future-Essays in Honour of Gareth Jones* (1998). For other recent views in favour, see (1997) 50 C.L.P. 95 at 103, 112 (A. Burrows); Chambers, *Resulting Trusts*, Chap. 8. For other views, see Pearce and Stevens, *The Law of Trusts and Equitable Obligations* (2nd ed.), pp. 740–747; Halliwell, *Equity and Good Conscience in a Contemporary Context*, pp. 121, 134.

[21] *post*, p. 702.

[22] See (1995) 111 L.Q.R. 545 (C. Harpum).

[23] A beneficiary may sue a third party on behalf of the trust where the trustee unreasonably refuses to sue or has disabled himself from doing so: *Parker-Tweedale v. Dunbar Bank plc* [1991] Ch. 12.

equity has lost some of its significance now that the common law remedy has been extended to recovery of money paid by mistake of law.[24] Trustees as legal owners may now succeed on this basis against innocent volunteers.

(e) *Ministerial Receipt.* Recipient liability cannot arise where the third party has received the trust property merely in his capacity as agent and has dealt with it according to his principal's instructions. In other words, the "receipt" category is confined to third parties who have received the property for their own benefit.[25] Thus in *Agip (Africa) Ltd v. Jackson*[26] the defendants were not liable on the basis of receipt because they had merely received the money as agents and passed it on to third parties according to their principal's instructions. As we have seen, they were liable for dishonest assistance.

It has been said that banks receive merely as agents and so will not normally be liable for receipt unless they use the money to reduce an overdraft, as this amounts to receipt for their own benefit,[27] although the defence of purchaser without notice will normally be available.[28] This reasoning has been convincingly criticised.[29]

iii. Agent Assuming Trustee's Duties.[30] An agent of the trustees may, as we have seen, incur liability under the above rules if he has been dishonest or has received trust property for his own benefit. There will normally be no such liability where trust property is transferred to an agent in the ordinary process of delegation,[31] as his receipt is ministerial and there is no breach of trust. In such a case he will only be subjected to a trustee's liability if he receives the property into his hands in connection with his assumption of the trustee's office and duties. In *Williams-Ashman v. Price and Williams*,[32] Bennett J. treated *Mara v. Browne*[33] as authority for the

---

[24] *Kleinwort Benson Ltd v. Lincoln City Council* [1999] 2 A.C. 349. There is no defence of "honest receipt".

[25] Birks, *Introduction to the Law of Restitution*, p. 445; (1986) 102 L.Q.R. 114 (C. Harpum); (1989) 105 L.Q.R. 528 (P. Birks); (1991) 107 L.Q.R. 71 (Sir Peter Millett).

[26] [1990] Ch. 265, affirmed [1991] Ch. 547. The facts have been given, *ante*, p. 309.

[27] *Citadel General Insurance Co. v. Lloyds Bank Canada* (1997) 152 D.L.R. (4th) 411; [1998] 6 R.L.R. 162 (C. Rotherham).

[28] *Agip (Africa) Ltd v. Jackson, supra*, at p. 292; (1991) 107 L.Q.R. 71 at 83. See also *Polly Peck International plc. v. Nadir (No. 2)* [1992] 4 All E.R. 769 (bank receiving sterling and exchanging it for foreign currency receives the sterling for its own benefit, but could have defence of purchaser without notice); *cf. Nimmo v. Westpac Banking Corporation* [1993] 3 N.Z.L.R. 218 at 225; *Cigna Life Insurance NZ v. Westpac Securities Ltd* [1996] 1 N.Z.L.R. 80 at 86.

[29] *Laundering and Tracing* (ed. Birks, 1995), p. 126 (S. Gleeson); *Restitution and Banking Law* (ed. F. Rose), Chap. 10 (M. Bryan). Money paid to a bank becomes the property of the bank.

[30] See (1986) 102 L.Q.R. 114 at pp. 130 *et seq.* (C. Harpum).

[31] *post*, p. 576.

[32] [1942] Ch. 219 at 228.

[33] [1896] 1 Ch. 199.

proposition that "an agent in possession of money which he knows to be trust money, so long as he acts honestly, is not accountable to the beneficiaries interested in the trust money unless he intermeddles in the trust by doing acts characteristic of a trustee and outside the duties of an agent." Thus, where a solicitor received trust money through his own account, and invested it in unauthorised mortgages on the instructions of the trustees, the solicitor was held to be acting in his capacity as a solicitor, and not liable as a constructive trustee.[34] A stockbroker would not incur such liability for receiving trust money and investing it on the trustee's instructions in an unauthorised investment. The remedy is against the trustees.

If the agent does not know that the property is trust property, he is not liable if he acts honestly and within the scope of his agency, even if the facts were such as to put him on enquiry.[35]

iv. Liability of Partner of Constructive Trustee

In *Re Bell's Indenture*,[36] trustee-beneficiaries dissipated nearly £30,000 of the trust fund with the knowledge and assistance of H, a partner in a firm of solicitors acting for the trustees. The beneficiaries sought to make H's partner, who, it was conceded, had acted honestly and reasonably throughout, liable. H's liability was not disputed. Vinelott J. held that a solicitor has the implied authority of his partners to accept trust monies as agent of the trustees, but has no implied authority to accept office as trustee, nor to constitute himself as constructive trustee, and so make his partners liable for any misapplication of the trust property. The monies, which had passed through the firm's client account, had not been received by the partnership as trustees, thus H's partner was not liable as constructive trustee. Nor was he liable under the provisions of the Partnership Act 1890.[37]

The decision in *Blyth v. Fladgate*,[38] where, in similar circumstances, the solicitor's partners were held jointly liable, was treated as a case on "very special facts," where the partners became trustees because there were no trustees at the time the money was paid into

---

[34] *Mara v. Browne* [1896] 1 Ch. 199 (any negligence action would have been statute-barred); *Williams-Ashman v. Price and Williams* [1942] Ch. 219.

[35] *Williams v. Williams* (1881) 17 Ch.D. 437; *Competitive Insurance Co. Ltd v. Davies Investments Ltd* [1975] 1 W.L.R. 1240.

[36] [1980] 1 W.L.R. 1217; [1981] Conv. 310 (P. Luxton).

[37] See s.13, providing that if a partner, being a trustee, improperly employs trust property in the business or on the account of the partnership, no other partner is liable for the trust property to the beneficiaries. It is otherwise if the partner has notice of the breach of trust, and nothing in this section prevents the recovery of trust money from the firm while still in its possession or under its control. Nor was the firm liable under ss.10 or 11 of the Act, but see *Dubai Aluminium Co. Ltd v. Salaam, infra.*

[38] [1891] 1 Ch. 337.

the firm's account, and, consequently, the partners could not be considered to be merely agents of the trustees. That this was the correct explanation was clear from *Mara v. Browne*,[39] where Lord Herschell said "it is not within the scope of the implied authority of a partner in such a business that he should so act as to make himself a constructive trustee, and thereby subject his partner to the same liability."[40]

This may be contrasted with *Agip (Africa) Ltd v. Jackson*,[41] where only two of the three defendants, an accountant and an employee of his firm, had dishonestly assisted in the breach of trust. The other defendant, the accountant's partner, was held vicariously liable (with little discussion) for the acts of the other two. The issue came before the Court of Appeal in *Dubai Aluminium Co. Ltd v. Salaam*,[42] which involved a fraud of over $50 million. It was held that a partner could be vicariously liable under section 10 of the Partnership Act 1980 for dishonest assistance in a breach of trust by his partner, where the latter had acted in the ordinary course of business (which is a question of fact). In this case the dishonest partner had not been acting in the ordinary course of business when he planned, drafted and signed sham agreements giving effect to a scheme he knew to be fraudulent. His partners had not, therefore, incurred vicarious liability. It was considered that the conclusion in *Agip* could only have been on the basis that section 10 applied.

C. Mutual Wills[43]

Two persons (often husband and wife)[44] may agree that, on the death of the first to die, all their property shall be enjoyed by the survivor, and after his (her) death by nominated beneficiaries; and may make mutual wills to that effect. The survivor may be given a life interest,[45] an absolute interest[46] or no interest at all.[47] The question is whether, and to what extent, such an agreement controls the devolution of their property.

i. Agreement Necessary. Before any remedy can be obtained, an agreement to make wills and not to revoke them[48] between the

---

[39] [1896] 1 Ch. 199, *ante*, p. 317. But see [1981] Conv. 310 (P. Luxton).

[40] *Ibid.* at p. 208.

[41] [1991] Ch. 547; *ante*, p. 309. *Re Bell's Indenture* was not cited.

[42] [2000] 3 W.L.R. 910. Partners are normally insured for vicarious liability. See also *Walker v. Stones* [2000] 4 All E.R. 412.

[43] (1951) 15 Conv.(N.S.) 28 (G. Graham); (1951) 14 M.L.R. 140 (J. Mitchell); (1970) 34 Conv.(N.S.) 230 (R. Burgess); (1989) 105 L.Q.R. 534 (C. Rickett); Oakley, *Constructive Trusts* (3rd ed.), pp. 263–274.

[44] *Walpole v. Lord Orford* (1797) 3 Ves.Jr. 402.

[45] *Dufour v. Pereira* (1769) Dick. 419.

[46] *Re Green* [1951] 148.

[47] *Re Dale (deceased)* [1994] Ch. 31.

[48] *In the Goods of Heys* [1914] P. 192.

parties must be proved. The agreement must indicate that the wills are to be mutually binding, whether or not expressed in the language of revocation.[49] The standard of proof is the ordinary civil standard (*i.e.* on balance of probabilities); the evidence must be "clear and satisfactory" and may be extrinsic, as where the agreement is substantiated by family conversations.[50] The mere fact that the wills were made simultaneously and in the same form is not, of itself, proof of an agreement although it is a relevant circumstance to be taken into account.[51] The agreement must amount to a clear contract at law, not a mere common understanding.[52] But the court may infer an agreement from the conduct of the parties, the circumstances and the terms of the wills.[53] Preferably the agreement, if there was one, should be recited in the will.

In *Re Oldham*,[54] a husband and wife made mutual wills in similar form; each spouse left his (or her) property to the other absolutely with the same provisions in the event of the other predeceasing. There was no evidence of an agreement that they should be irrevocable. After the husband's death, the wife married again, and made a new will which was quite different from the earlier one. The second will was upheld; Astbury J. saying: "The fact that the two wills were made in identical terms does not necessarily connote any agreement beyond that of so making them . . . there is no evidence . . . that there was an agreement that the trust in the mutual will should in all circumstances be irrevocable by the survivor who took the benefit." The parties had left their estates to each other "absolutely." They "may have thought it quite safe to trust the other. . . . But that is a very different thing from saying that they bound themselves by a trust that should be operative in all circumstances and in all cases".[55]

In *Re Cleaver*,[56] on the other hand, the evidence of mutual wills was sufficient. An elderly couple married in 1967. The husband had three children. They made wills in each other's favour absolutely, and in default to the three children. In 1974, each of them reduced the share of one daughter, Martha, to a life interest. After the husband's death the wife made a new will consistent with the

---

[49] *Re Goodchild (deceased)* [1997] 1 W.L.R. 1216. (mistaken belief of first testator that wills mutually binding may enable intended beneficiary to claim under the Inheritance (Provision for Family and Dependants) Act 1975 on death of survivor).

[50] *Re Cleaver* [1981] 1 W.L.R. 939; *Re Newey* [1994] 2 N.Z.L.R. 590; [1996] Conv. 136 (C. Rickett).

[51] *ibid.*

[52] *Re Goodchild (deceased), supra.*

[53] *Dufour v. Pereira* (1769) Dick. 419; *Stone v. Hoskins* [1905] P. 194; *Re Hagger* [1930] 2 Ch. 190; *Re Green* [1951] Ch. 148.

[54] [1925] Ch. 75.

[55] *ibid.* at 88–89; *Gray v. Perpetual Trustee Co.* [1928] A.C. 391.

[56] *supra.*

earlier one. Thereafter she made a further will enlarging Martha's share from a life interest to an absolute interest; and by her last will she left her residue to Martha and her husband, and nothing to the other two children. It was held that the wife's executors held the estate on the trusts of the 1974 will. Sufficient evidence of an agreement to make mutual wills was shown by the simultaneity and similarity of the original wills; the pattern of successive wills made together; the fact that both parties reduced Martha's interest; the faithful terms of the first will made after the husband's death; and the fact that, in family conversations, the wife had regarded herself as under an obligation to leave her estate to the children.

ii. Remedies on the Contract. The agreement is binding between the parties. If it is broken by the first party to die, his estate will be liable in damages to the survivor.[57] If the breach is by the second party to die, as by revocation or alteration of his will, it has always been assumed that no remedy could be obtained against him or his estate under the contract. The law which has developed on the subject is based upon a trust which arises in appropriate cases in favour of the beneficiaries.

It is arguable that the principle of *Beswick v. Beswick*[58] could apply in this situation. The estate of the first to die is in a similar position to Mrs Beswick, the administratrix. It seems that an action for specific performance of the contract would lie by the estate against the survivor or his estate. An examination of the problems which have arisen in treating the interests of the beneficiaries as trusts, as will be seen, makes a contractual solution attractive.[59] The court in *Re Dale (deceased)*[60] rejected the argument that the second testator could be ordered to make a will in accordance with the contract, or restrained from revoking it. It may remain arguable that specific performance could be obtained to enforce a conveyance of the property.[61]

Until recently there could have been no question of the beneficiary suing in contract because of the privity doctrine. It may now be possible for the beneficiary to enforce the contract in his own right under the Contracts (Rights of Third Parties) Act 1999, in the case

---

[57] *Robinson v. Ommanney* (1883) 23 Ch.D. 285; but not where the revocation of the first will is by the subsequent marriage of the covenantor. See further (1991) 54 M.L.R. 581 (C. Rickett).

[58] [1968] A.C. 58.

[59] See (1979) 29 U. of Toronto L.J. 390 (T. Youdan). The executor must be willing to sue. See [1982] Conv. 228 (K. Hodkinson), suggesting that the ultimate beneficiary should be the executor; (1989) 105 L.Q.R. 534 (C. Rickett).

[60] [1994] Ch. 31; (1995) 58 M.L.R. 95 (A. Brierley). *Beswick v. Beswick* was not discussed.

[61] *post*, p. 734.

of contracts between testators made after the Act.[62] The Act does not affect rights or remedies of third parties which are otherwise available, thus the trust solution remains.[63]

iii. Trusts Created by Mutual Wills. A will is always revocable; an agreement not to revoke it does not make it irrevocable.[64] Thus, if the survivor of an agreement to make mutual wills revokes his will, he will die intestate: and if he makes a new will, that later one will be admitted to probate. But the disposition of his property on his death will be affected by the agreement. For the principle is established that the agreement between the parties, followed by the death of the first party, relying on the undertaking of the other party to observe the agreement, creates trusts in favour of the intended beneficiaries, which are enforceable against the property of the survivor.[65] Of the leading case of *Dufour v. Pereira*,[66] Clauson J. said.[67] *Dufour v. Pereira* decides that where there is a joint will . . . on the death of the first testator the position as regards that part of the property which belongs to the survivor is that the survivor will be treated . . . as holding the property on trust to apply it so as to carry out the effect of the joint will". A number of difficulties arise concerning the operation of such trusts.[68]

(a) *When Does the Trust Arise?* Mitchell says that there are three possibilities.[69] When the agreement was made; when the first testator dies; when the survivor dies. It is clear that no trust exists from the date of the agreement. For either party can revoke or alter his will[70] before either dies, on giving notice to the other[71]; and even notice is not necessary in the case of the first to die, for the survivor has notice on the first death and will not be prejudiced.[72] The survivor in such circumstances is unable to establish any trust in his favour against the estate of the first to die.[73] Nor can the death of the survivor be the correct time. For where a beneficiary died between the date of the death of the first to die and the survivor, the estate of that beneficiary was able to claim its share on the ground that the

---

[62] See s.10. The Act is outlined at p. 129, *ante.*

[63] s.7(1).

[64] *Vynior's Case* (1609) 8 Co.Rep. 81b.

[65] *In the Goods of Heys* [1914] P. 192; *Stone v. Hoskins* [1905] P. 194 (later will of first to die).

[66] (1769) Dick 419; interpreted in *Re Dale (deceased), supra,* as not requiring any benefit to pass to the survivor.

[67] *Re Hagger* [1930] 2 Ch. 190 at 195.

[68] These difficulties are discussed in (1979) 29 U. of Toronto L.J. at 411–419 (T. Youdan).

[69] (1951) 14 M.L.R. 137 (J. Mitchell).

[70] See *Re Hobley (deceased), The Times,* June 16, 1997 (effect of mutual wills destroyed where first to die had altered his will in a minor but not insignificant way).

[71] *Dufour v. Pereira* (1769) Dick. 419 at 420.

[72] *ibid.*

[73] *Stone v. Hoskins* [1905] P. 194.

interest was vested and there was no lapse.[74] Of these three possibilities, it seems therefore that the trust arises on the death of the first to die.

Until recently a fourth possibility was arguable: that the trust arises when the survivor receives a benefit under the first will. On this question there were dicta both ways. Most of the dicta favoured the view that the trust is imposed only where the survivor takes a benefit.[75] Clauson J., however, in *Re Hagger*[76] said *obiter* that the trust would arise "even though the survivor did not signify his election to give effect to the will by taking benefits under it".

It has now been held by Morritt J. in *Re Dale (deceased)*,[77] after a full review of all the authorities, that the doctrine of mutual wills applies even where the survivor does not benefit from the will of the first testator. A husband and wife agreed that each would leave his or her whole estate to their son and daughter equally. The husband died first, leaving his estate of £18,500 in this way. The wife later made a new will leaving her daughter £300 and the rest of her estate of £19,000 to her son. It was held that the son, as executor, held the estate on trust for himself and the daughter equally. Benefit by the survivor was a sufficient but not a necessary requirement for the operation of the doctrine. The survivor committed a fraud on the first testator who died in reliance upon their bargain even if he or she did not benefit from the will. That this was the true basis of the doctrine appeared from *Dufour v. Pereira*[78] "he, that dies first, does by his death carry the agreement on his part into execution. If the other then refuses, he is guilty of a fraud, can never unbind himself, and becomes a trustee of course. For no man shall deceive another to his prejudice".[79] Morritt J. considered that the imposition of the trust was consistent with all the authorities, supported by some of them and was in furtherance of equity's original jurisdiction to intervene in cases of fraud.

(b) *To what Property Does the Trust Attach?*[80] This may be clear from the express terms of the will.[81] Failing that, and subject always

---

[74] *Re Hagger* [1930] 2 Ch. 190; *cf. Re Gardner (No. 2)* [1923] Ch. 230.

[75] *Dufour v. Pereira* (1769) Dick. 419 at 421; *Stone v. Hoskins* [1905] P. 194 at 197; *Re Oldham* [1925] Ch. 75 at 87. See also *Re Cleaver* [1981] 1 W.L.R. 939.

[76] [1930] 2 Ch. 190 at p. 195. See (1970) 34 Conv.(n.s.) 230 (R. Burgess); [1982] Conv. 228 at 230 (K. Hodkinson).

[77] [1994] Ch. 31; (1993) 7 *Trust Law International* 18 (D. Brown); All E.R.Rev. 1993, 415 (C. Sherrin).

[78] As more fully reported in Hargrave's Juridical Arguments, Vol. 2, p. 304.

[79] *ibid.* at 310 (Lord Camden).

[80] See (1977) 15 Alberta L.Rev. 211 (L. Sheridan).

[81] As in *Re Green* [1951] Ch. 148, where the wills provided that if the other spouse predeceased, the residue was to be divided into halves, one half being considered as the testator's personal property and the other as the benefit received from the other spouse. It was held that the trust attached only to the latter.

to a contrary intention, there are four possibilities; that the trust attaches to the property, if any, which the survivor receives from the estate of the first to die: or to all the property that the survivor owned at that time: or to all the property which the survivor owned at *his* death: or to all property which the survivor owned at any time since the first death.

Clearly the trust must include any property received from the first to die. If the will gave only a life interest, there is no scope for the trust in respect of that property. If the gift is absolute, the imposition of a trust in favour of ultimate beneficiaries will in effect reduce the survivor's interest to a life interest.

The position is more complex in relation to the property of the survivor. *Re Hagger*,[82] suggests that the trust attaches at least to all the property which the survivor had at the time of the first death. Morritt J. held that the trust embraced the survivor's whole estate at his or her death.[83] This means that a lifetime disposition by the survivor would be a breach of trust; indeed it would make nonsense of the trust if he could so dispose of the property.[84] This raises the question of acquisitions by the survivor by his own efforts after the first death. After all, the property acquired after the date of the wills by the first to die was included in his estate; and the agreement, in the absence of a contrary provision, would apply to all property. The agreement thus acts like a covenant to settle after-acquired property, and the property becomes subject to the trust on its becoming vested in the trustee.[85] If this is correct, the effect of mutual wills is to reduce the survivor to the position of a life tenant in respect of all his property. He may use the income, but the capital is held on trust for the ultimate beneficiaries.

In *Re Cleaver*[86] Nourse J., relying on the Australian decision *Birmingham v. Renfrew*,[87] adopted the view there expressed that the survivor could enjoy the property as an absolute owner in his lifetime "subject to a fiduciary duty which, so to speak, crystallised on his death and disabled him only from voluntary dispositions *inter vivos*".[88] This meant dispositions calculated to defeat the agreement. There was no objection to ordinary gifts of small value. The difficulty however, is that any such duty not to dissipate the assets in the survivor's lifetime will be unenforceable if the beneficiary does not discover his rights until the survivor's death. Although Nourse J. affirmed the requirement of certainty of subject-matter, this is not

---

[82] [1930] 2 Ch. 190. (Interest of beneficiary vested before death of survivor).

[83] *Re Dale (deceased)* [1994] Ch. 31.

[84] See however Astbury J. in *Re Oldham* [1925] Ch. 75 at 87, 88; suggesting that the trust attaches only to property held by the survivor at death.

[85] *Paul v. Paul* (1882) 20 Ch.D. 742; *Re Ralli's W.T.* [1964] Ch. 288.

[86] [1981] 1 W.L.R. 939. Similarly in *Goodchild v. Goodchild* [1997] 1 W.L.R. 1216.

[87] (1936) 57 C.L.R. 666.

[88] (1936) 57 C.L.R. at 690. *cf. Palmer v. Bank of N.S.W.* (1975) 7 A.L.R. 671.

fully consistent with his formulation of the rights and duties of the parties.[89] If, on the other hand, the survivor's obligation is merely not to dispose of the property *by will* inconsistently with the agreement,[90] then the difficulties are all the greater; for the trust property would be indefinite until his death. These problems were not examined in *Re Dale (deceased)*.[91]

(c) *The Survivor as Trustee.* If it is correct that the survivor becomes a trustee of all the property he owns or acquires before his death, the consequences of the doctrine could be draconian for the survivor, for example if he acquires new dependants after the death of the first testator, or wins the lottery; similarly if the agreed beneficiary acquires a fortune elsewhere or is guilty of misconduct.[92] As far as the beneficiaries are concerned, there is very little opportunity to ensure that proper control over the survivor is maintained. Purchasers have no notice of the trusts, and the trust property may be lost on alienation to them.[93] Also, the survivor may have no idea that he is a trustee. If land is included in the trusts the lack of knowledge of all parties concerned may result in disputes and uncertainties as to title if it is alienated without observing the proper procedures. And, as noted above, further problems arise if the trust is treated as attaching only on the death of the survivor; and as "floating"[94] or as being "in suspense"[95] in the meantime. This is the problem, it should be noted, created in the field of secret trusts by *dicta* in *Ottaway v. Norman*.[96] The possibilities of trouble are unlimited; they have not yet been finally worked out.[97]

iv. **Conclusion.** It is clear that the imposition by law of a trust in cases of mutual wills is a clumsy and inadequate way of dealing with a complicated problem. A contractual solution under the *Beswick* principle would be much more satisfactory; but this has not been accepted.[98] The impact of the Contracts (Rights of Third Parties) Act 1999 in this area remains to be seen. A solution based on the idea of a floating charge has also been suggested.[99] For the present, persons who wish to leave property by way of mutual wills

---

[89] See [1982] Conv. 228 (K. Hodkinson).

[90] See *Palmer v. Bank of N.S.W.*, *supra*.

[91] [1994] Ch. 31; *supra*.

[92] See (1994) 144 N.L.J. 1272 (P. O'Hagan).

[93] *Pilcher v. Rawlins* (1872) L.R. 7 Ch.App. 259.

[94] *ante*, p. 324; (1972) 36 Conv.(N.S.) 129 at 132 (D. Hayton).

[95] *per* Brightman J. [1972] Ch. 698 at 713; *Re Cleaver*, *supra*.

[96] [1972] Ch. 698 at 713 ("suspended trust" where donee obliged to bequeath to X whatever remains at the donee's death), *ante*, p. 157.

[97] (1951) 14 M.L.R. 140–142 (J. Mitchell).

[98] *Re Dale (deceased)* [1994] Ch. 31.

[99] [1982] Conv. 228, at 231 (K. Hodkinson). This does not solve the problem that the "beneficiaries" are often unaware of the situation.

should be advised to consider most carefully the trusts on which they wish the property to be held; what property is to be included; the position during the survivor's lifetime; who they wish to be trustees; what administrative powers the trustees should have; and how best the scheme desired can be carried out from an inheritance tax point of view. Merely to draft mutual wills and then leave the law to sort out such a host of problems is no service to the testator. The law in this context, as in most other areas of constructive trusts, imposes a trust in an attempt to prevent one party from committing a fraud on the other. It is a kind of salvage operation; a salvage of a wreck which competent legal advice would have avoided in the first place.[1]

D. The Vendor under a Specifically Enforceable Contract for Sale

A contract for sale is specifically enforceable where the remedy of damages would be inadequate.[2] Contracts relating to personalty are rarely specifically enforceable, as the property may be purchased elsewhere. If this is not so, as in the case of shares in a private company, then the contract will be specifically enforceable.[3] In the present context, however, we are mainly concerned with contracts relating to land. The availability of specific performance means that, in equity, the purchaser is regarded as already the owner. Thus it has many times been said by high authority that a vendor of land, on the conclusion of the contract of sale, becomes a trustee of the land for the purchaser.[4] Opinions have differed as to the time at which the trusteeship arises.[5] Any changes in the nature of the property after that time, for example by fire or flooding, if they occur without the fault of the vendor, are at the purchaser's risk.[6] If the vendor sells to another, he holds the purchase money on trust for the purchaser.[7] Beyond that, however, there is little agreement.[8] It is clear at least

---

[1] For a different view, see (1988) 138 N.L.J. 351 (F. Sunnucks).

[2] *post*, Chap. 24.

[3] See *Oughtred v. I.R.C.* [1960] A.C. 206; *Neville v. Wilson* [1997] Ch. 144; *Michaels v. Harley House (Marylebone) Ltd* [2000] Ch. 104.

[4] *Lysaght v. Edwards* (1876) 2 Ch.D. 499 at 507; (1959) 23 Conv.(N.S.) 173 (V. Wellings); Waters, *The Constructive Trust*, Chap. 2; Oakley, *Constructive Trusts*, Ch. 6.

[5] It may be the date of the contract; or the date the vendor makes title. If the latter, the trust relates back to the contract date. See *Lysaght v. Edwards* (1876) 2 Ch.D. 499; *Rayner v. Preston* (1881) 18 Ch.D. 1; *Oughtred v. I.R.C.* [1960] A.C. 206.

[6] *Paine v. Meller* (1801) 6 Ves.Jr. 349. As to insurance, see L.P.A. 1925, s.47. For the view that the risk does not pass to the purchaser see [1984] Conv. 43 (M. Thompson). See further Law Com. No. 191 (1990), *Transfer of Land; Risk of Damage after Contract for Sale*, para. 2.25, suggesting that the risk should pass only on completion.

[7] *Lake v. Bayliss* [1974] 1 W.L.R. 1073; *Shaw v. Foster* (1872) 5 H.L. 321 at 327; (1974) 38 Conv.(N.S.) 357 (F. Crane).

[8] Cotton, Brett and James L.JJ. in *Rayner v. Preston* (1881) Ch.D. 1 expressed different views on the situation.

that this is not an ordinary trusteeship. Cotton L.J. said that the vendor was trustee only in a qualified sense[9]; Lord Greene M.R. called him a quasi-trustee,[10] and Stamp L.J. a "constructive trustee or a trustee *sub modo*"[11]; and Lord Cairns[12] explained that the trustee was entitled to protect his own interest in the property. Similarly, the vendor is entitled to keep for himself the rents and profits of the land (or dividends in the case of shares[13]) until the date of the completion of the sale,[14] and to retain possession against the purchaser until the purchase price has been paid; and he retains a lien on the land for the price if the land is conveyed before the price is paid,[15] and time runs under the Limitation Act 1980 against the vendor in respect of possession of the land.[16] The relationship between the parties contains a number of aspects in which they are hostile and the vendor self-interested.

Once the date for completion has arrived and the price is paid in full, the vendor must immediately convey. This is an example of a trusteeship arising because the bare legal estate is in one person, and the entire beneficial ownership in another.[17] Until that situation has arisen, it does not seem that any useful purpose is served by stating that the relationship between the parties is one of trustee and beneficiary. The position at law is that they are parties to a contract and no more. In equity additional rights arise by reason of the fact that specific performance is available as a remedy in favour of an innocent party. Equity then treats as done that which ought to be done, and considers the purchaser as being the owner in equity. Hence, where a receiver was appointed upon the vendor company's insolvency before completion, the contract remained specifically enforceable against the receiver as opposed to merely sounding in damages.[18] This is not attributable to any trust, but to the characteristics of a specifically enforceable contract for sale, whereby the equitable interest passes to the purchaser and is not destroyed by the subsequent insolvency of the vendor. The trust cannot be enforced against a purchaser if the contract, being unregistered, does not bind

[9] *Rayner v. Preston, supra,* at p. 6; *Lysaght v. Edwards* (1876) 2 Ch.D. 499 at 506; *Royal Bristol Permanent Building Society v. Bomash* (1887) 35 Ch.D. 390 at 397 ("a modified sense"); *Re Hamilton-Snowball's Conveyance* [1959] Ch. 308.

[10] *Cumberland Consolidated Holdings Ltd v. Ireland* [1946] K.B. 264 at 269.

[11] *Berkley v. Poulett* (1977) 242 E.G. 39 at 43.

[12] *Shaw v. Foster* (1872) L.R. 5 H.L. 321 at 338.

[13] *J. Sainsbury plc v. O'Connor (Inspector of Taxes)* [1991] S.T.C. 318.

[14] *Cuddon v. Tite* (1858) 1 Giff 395.

[15] *Mackreth v. Symmons* (1808) 15 Ves.Jr. 329. See further (1994) 53 C.L.J. 263 (S. Worthington).

[16] *Bridges v. Mees* [1957] Ch. 475; *cf. Hyde v. Pearce* [1982] 1 All E.R. 1029.

[17] *Lloyds Bank plc v. Carrick* [1996] 4 All E.R. 630; [1996] Conv. 295 (M. Thompson); (1997) 27 Fam. Law 95 (S. Cretney); (1998) 61 M.L.R. 486 (N. Hopkins).

[18] *Freevale Ltd v. Metrostore (Holdings) Ltd* [1984] 1 All E.R. 495 (a receiver, unlike a liquidator, has no statutory right to disclaim contracts); [1984] Conv. 446 (D. Milman and S. Coneys); *Re Coregrange Ltd* [1984] B.C.L.C. 453.

him.[19] In many other respects the contractual nature of the relationship is apparent; each party is continuing to guard his own interests against the other in a way which is quite inconsistent with the existence of the relationship of trustee and beneficiary.

A further question is whether the vendor becomes trustee for a sub-purchaser, if the purchaser has entered into a contract to sell to the sub-purchaser. In such a case, the sub-purchaser, by virtue of his contract with the purchaser, is entitled to specific performance and is treated as the owner in equity. In *Berkley v. Earl Poulett*[20] the vendor, with the concurrence of the purchaser, had allegedly allowed certain fixtures to be taken away. The sub-purchaser claimed that the vendor was in breach of the trustee's duty to take proper care of the property. A majority of the Court of Appeal considered that no fiduciary duty was owed to the sub-purchaser. It was not that the vendor was a trustee and therefore had fiduciary duties; rather that the vendor owed duties to the purchaser and was labelled a trustee. A sub-purchaser's right is to have the purchaser enforce the contract against the vendor.

No doubt it is too late now to say that the relationship between vendor and purchaser is not that of trustee and beneficiary. The terminology must, however, be received with reserve. Unlike other cases of constructive trusts, the element of improper conduct is absent and the situation must, at best, be treated as anomalous.[21]

E. Secret Trusts

It is unsettled whether secret trusts, and more particularly half-secret trusts, are to be regarded as express or constructive. The practical significance of the distinction is that, in the case of land, section 53 of the Law of Property Act 1925 requires written evidence in the case of express trusts, but not in the case of constructive trusts. The matter is examined in detail in Chapter 5.

F. Conveyance by Fraud

Where property has been obtained by the fraud of the defendant, he may be compelled to hold it as a constructive trustee. The trust is not imposed in every case.[22] While it is difficult to define the

---

[19] *Lloyds Bank plc v. Carrick, supra.*

[20] (1977) 242 E.G. 39.

[21] (1959) 23 Conv.(N.S.) 1734 (V. Wellings). We have seen that it is not treated as a constructive trust for the purpose of L.P.A. 1925, s.53(2); *Oughtred v. I.R.C.* [1960] A.C. 206, *ante*, p. 88.

[22] For example, if the claimant had acquiesced in the fraud; *Lonrho plc v. Fayed (No. 2)* [1992] 1 W.L.R. 1. See *Halifax Building Society v. Thomas* [1996] Ch. 217; *ante*, p. 303.

circumstances in which the trust will be imposed, some broad principles are in practice clear. In the case of a conveyance of land, the transferee may be prevented, by the imposition of a constructive trust, from setting up the apparently absolute nature of the conveyance in order to defeat a beneficial interest which, by oral agreement, was intended to remain in the transferor,[23] or in some third party.[24]

Similarly, situations in which a will is fraudulently revoked, or where the testator is fraudulently prevented from making a will, or fraudulently induced to leave property to a legatee or devisee, are all appropriate for the imposition of a constructive trust. These situations are discussed under the heading of secret trusts.[25]

G. Acquisition of Property by Killing[26]

Where a beneficiary kills the testator, or next of kin kills an intestate, there is good reason to prevent him from benefiting from his crime.[27] The English courts have established a rule to this effect, but they "have worked out no rational theory for their actions in depriving killers[28] . . . there has been little discussion of the theoretical basis for a deprivation . . . and generally they have considered that the killer does not gain legal title".[29] Such a result is contrary to the enactments relating to succession, testate or intestate, but clearly a rule of public policy can override statutory provisions.[30] If the killer does not acquire any title to the property in question, as in the pension and insurance cases, then there is no need for the imposition of a constructive trust. If, on the other hand, the killer acquires legal title, as is arguably the position in some of the succession cases, then he will be subjected to a constructive trust which is imposed to prevent unjust enrichment. A bona fide purchaser from the wrongdoer would then be protected.[31]

Whichever solution is reached, a number of problems remain, on which there is little authority.

---

[23] *Rochefoucauld v. Boustead* [1897] 1 Ch. 196; *Bannister v. Bannister* [1948] 2 All E.R. 133; *Hodgson v. Marks* [1972] Ch. 892; *ante*, p. 81.

[24] *Binions v. Evans* [1972] Ch. 359; *Peffer v. Rigg* [1977] 1 W.L.R. 285; *Lyus v. Prowsa Developments Ltd* [1982] 1 W.L.R. 1044; *post*, p. 336. See also [1987] Conv. 246 (J. Feltham).

[25] *supra*. For a fuller discussion, see Chap. 5.

[26] Goff and Jones, pp. 805–810; (1973) 89 L.Q.R. 235 (T. Youdan), which has been used as the basis of this account; *Restatement of Restitution*, § 187; (1969) 68 Mich. L.R. 65 (W. McGovern); [1998] 6 R.L.R. 34 at 46–61 (G. Virgo).

[27] *In the Estate of Crippen* [1911] P. 108.

[28] (1973) 89 L.Q.R. 235.

[29] *ibid.* at 251.

[30] See, for example, *R. v. Chief National Insurance Commissioner, ex p. Connor, infra*.

[31] *Re Cash* (1911) 30 N.Z.L.R. 571; *Beresford v. Royal Insurance Ltd* [1938] A.C. 586 at 600.

i. Type of Killing. Killing may be effected by any means from murder to accident. The deprivation principle only applies to criminal killing. The rule has not been applied to all cases of manslaughter.[32] However, formulations based on whether the act was deliberate or violent have not proved satisfactory. It was said in *Dunbar v. Plant*[33] that the courts should refrain from further modifications and resolve matters by exercising their powers under the Forfeiture Act 1982 (discussed below). In that case the public policy rule was applied to the survivor of a suicide pact, who had aided and abetted the other's suicide, but full relief was granted under the 1982 Act.

ii. Means of Acquisition. The principle applies when the killer benefits by testamentary gift,[34] or under the victim's intestacy,[35] and also under a life insurance policy on the victim's life[36]; and, in the days when suicide was a crime, the estate of a suicide was held to be unable to claim the benefits of an insurance policy.[37] Similarly, a woman who kills her husband cannot claim a widow's pension.[38] More complicated questions arise where one joint tenant kills another, or a remainderman kills the life tenant. In the case of a joint tenancy, the killing effects a severance, so that the joint tenant does not profit under the doctrine of survivorship. Thus he holds the legal estate on trust for himself and the victim's estate in equal shares.[39] In the case of the remainderman killing the life tenant, the best course would be to postpone the killer's enjoyment until the time at which the victim's life expectation would terminate.[40]

iii. Destination of Property. To deprive the wrongdoer does not solve all the problems. Persons claiming through the wrongdoer should not benefit from the crime. In *Re DWS (deceased)*[41] X murdered his parents, who died intestate, leaving no other children.

---

[32] *Gray v. Barr* [1971] 2 Q.B. 544; *Re K (deceased)* [1986] Ch. 180; *cf. Re Hall* [1914] P. 1; *Re Giles* [1972] Ch. 544; *Jones v. Roberts* [1995] 2 F.L.R. 422; (1995) 111 L.Q.R. 196 (R. Buckley); *Re S. (deceased)* [1996] 1 W.L.R. 235.

[33] [1998] Ch. 412; [1998] Conv. 45 (M. Thompson); (1998) 57 C.L.J. 31 (S. Bridge).

[34] *Re Pollock* [1941] Ch. 219.

[35] *Re Sigsworth* [1935] Ch. 89.

[36] *Cleaver v. Mutual Reserve Fund Life Association Ltd* [1892] 1 Q.B. 147; *Davitt v. Titcumb* [1990] Ch. 110; [1991] Conv. 50 (J. Martin) (mortgage protection policy).

[37] *Beresford v. Royal Insurance Ltd* [1938] A.C. 586.

[38] *R. v. Chief National Commissioner, ex p. Connor* [1981] 1 Q.B. 758 (manslaughter); (1981) 44 M.L.R. 718 (St J. Robilliard). See also (1972) 31 C.L.J. 144 (J. Shand). As submitted above, this is not a case of constructive trust, as the claimant acquires no title to any property.

[39] *Dunbar v. Plant* [1998] Ch. 412.

[40] (1973) 89 L.Q.R. 235 at 250.

[41] [2000] 3 W.L.R. 1910. The Crown would take as *bona vacantia* only if there were no claimants in the other classes of kin, although Sedley L.J. dissented on this point.

X's only child, Y, claimed his grandparents' estates under section 47 of the Administration of Estates Act 1925, which provides that a grandchild is entitled to the share of a child who has predeceased the intestate. Y's claim failed on the basis that the public policy rule did not require the court to treat the murderer as having predeceased the victim. Thus the property devolved on the class of next-of-kin ranking after the issue of the intestate. In other cases, the proper solution will be for the property to go to the victim's residuary legatee, or as on his intestacy,[42] or to the other members of a class of which the wrongdoer was one[43]; or, where there are special circumstances to show what the victim's intention was, as where it was shown that the killing took place in order to prevent the victim from changing his will in favour of another, then the flexibility introduced by the concept of the constructive trust should allow the property to be claimed by "the person who, in the eyes of equity, has the best right to it."[44]

iv. Statutory Relief. It is provided by the Forfeiture Act 1982[45] that the court may grant relief from the forfeiture of inheritance and other rights to persons guilty of unlawful killing[46] other than murder,[47] where the court is satisfied that the justice of the case so requires.[48] A convicted person must bring proceedings for this purpose within three months of any conviction.[49] The Act applies to benefits under a will or upon intestacy; nominations; a *donatio mortis causa*; and property held on trust before the death which would devolve on the offender as a result of the death.[50] The Court may grant relief as to all or part of the property.[51] In the case of social security benefits, such as a widow's pension, the Act confers the discretion not on the court but on the Social Security Commissioner.[52] Finally, it is provided that the forfeiture principle does not preclude an application under the Family Provision legislation.[53]

---

[42] See *Re Jones (deceased)* [1998] 1 F.L.R. 246 (court cannot rewrite contingencies attached to residuary gift).

[43] *Re Peacock* [1957] Ch. 310.

[44] (1973) 89 L.Q.R. 235 at 257.

[45] (1983) 46 M.L.R. 66 (P. Kenny); (1983) 80 L.S.Gaz. 910 (A. Mithani and A. Wilton).

[46] Including aiding, abetting, counselling or procuring the death; s.1(2). The survivor of a suicide pact will usually obtain relief; *Dunbar v. Plant* [1998] Ch. 412.

[47] s.5.

[48] s.2(2). Degree of moral blame is significant; *Re K (deceased)* [1986] Ch. 180.

[49] s.2(3). But the Act and the doctrine may apply even in the case of acquittal, because the civil standard of proof is lower; *Gray v. Barr* [1971] 2 Q.B. 544.

[50] s.2(4). See *Re S. (deceased)* [1996] 1 W.L.R. 235 (joint life insurance).

[51] s.2(1) and (5); *Re K. (deceased), supra.*

[52] s.4, as amended by Social Security Act 1986. See (1984) 81 L.S.Gaz. 288; (1988) 85 L.S.Gaz. 37 (sequel to *Re K. (deceased), supra*).

[53] s.3.

H. Constructive Trusts of a New Model: Justice and Good Conscience

Some cases indicated a wide extension of the operation of constructive trusts by the introduction of what Lord Denning M.R. called "a constructive trust of a new model."[54] The broad principle was that a constructive trust may be imposed, regardless of established legal rules, in order to reach the result required by equity, justice and good conscience. The principle was thus articulated in *Hussey v. Palmer*[55]: "It is a trust imposed by law wherever justice and good conscience require it. It is a liberal process, founded on large principles of equity. . . . It is an equitable remedy by which the court can enable an aggrieved party to obtain restitution." Such a principle, if it survived, would effect a complete swing on the pendulum so far as the principles of English law concerning constructive trusts are concerned. The law in this field was once criticised as being too restricted[56]; in that the older cases would find a constructive trust only where the facts brought the case within one of the limited and established categories of constructive trust, usually requiring a fiduciary relationship. The new model opened up the possibility of finding a constructive trust in any situation in which the established rules lead to a result which would appear to be inconsistent with equity, justice and good conscience.[57]

Not surprisingly, this doctrine has been applied in cases where satisfactory solutions under established doctrines have proved particularly difficult to find. Illustrations come from the plight of the deserted wife or cohabitant; the problem of the licensee of land whose expectations have been disappointed; and the position of a bona fide purchaser of registered land. The "new model," however, has declined since the retirement of Lord Denning M.R.

i. Family Arrangements. In Chapter 11 we saw that, in the context of claims to an interest in the family home, some decisions are difficult to reconcile with the principles of *Pettitt v. Pettitt*[58] and *Gissing v. Gissing*,[59] to the effect that the interests of the parties must be determined according to the principles of property law. In *Eves v. Eves*,[60] involving an unmarried couple, the man bought a house as a joint home. He had it conveyed into his sole name, giving as an excuse the fact that the woman was under 21 years old. She did

---

[54] *Eves v. Eves* [1975] 1 W.L.R. 1338.

[55] [1972] 1 W.L.R. 1286 at 1289. See also Cardozo J. in *Beatty v. Guggenheim Exploration Co.* (1919) 255 N.Y. 360 at 385: "A constructive trust is the formula through which the conscience of equity finds expression." (1973) 26 C.L.P. 17 at 35 (A. Oakley).

[56] Waters, *The Constructive Trust.*

[57] (1977) 28 N.I.L.Q. 123 (R. Maudsley).

[58] [1970] A.C. 777.

[59] [1971] A.C. 886.

[60] [1975] 1 W.L.R. 1338 *ante*, p. 279; *Cooke v. Head* [1972] 1 W.L.R. 518.

a great deal of heavy work in the house and garden, beyond ordinary housework. When they separated, she claimed a share of the house. "In strict law she has no claim upon him whatever. She is not his wife. He is not bound to provide a roof over her head. He can turn her into the street. . . . And a few years ago even equity would not have helped her. But things are altered now. . . . " It would be "most inequitable for him to deny her any share in the house. The law will impute or impose a constructive trust by which he was to hold it in trust for both of them."[61] Her share was one quarter. A similar principle was applied in *Heseltine v. Heseltine*[62] where a wife gave her husband £40,000 for the purpose of saving estate duty if she predeceased him; and £20,000 for the purpose of enabling him to become a member of Lloyd's. The Court of Appeal decided that the husband held the sums on constructive trust for his wife. The conclusion seems at variance with the principles of resulting trusts.[63] The presumption of a resulting trust should have been rebutted because the stated purposes could only be achieved if the husband became beneficial owner. A constructive trust appears to have been imposed in order to reach what the court regarded as a just solution.

More recent decisions, however, have turned away from this use of the constructive trust. As we have seen, the House of Lords in *Lloyds Bank plc v. Rosset*[64] restated the principles governing the acquisition of an interest in the home. Insofar as the "common intention" is, in these cases, a somewhat artificial concept, the court retains a measure of discretion. Although a "broad brush" approach has been adopted,[65] the court does not have any discretion to impose a constructive trust simply to achieve a "fair" result. So in *Burns v. Burns*[66] a woman who looked after the home for many years but who made little financial contribution failed in her claim to a share. Where the woman has made no contribution but the parties assert a common intention to share, it was held in *Midland Bank Ltd v. Dobson*[67] that an undocumented common intention cannot give rise to a constructive trust unless the woman has acted to her detriment in reliance upon it. Without such an act, section 53(1)(*b*) of the Law of Property Act 1925 is not displaced by section 53(2).[68] In *Layton*

---

[61] [1975] 1 W.L.R. 1338 at 1341.
[62] [1971] 1 W.L.R. 342; *Re Densham* [1975] 1 W.L.R. 1519 (constructive trust imposed to meet the parties' undocumented intention to hold jointly). See also (1973) 26 C.L.P. at 27. (A. Oakley).
[63] *ante* p. 264.
[64] [1991] 1 A.C. 107; *ante,* p. 275.
[65] *Drake v. Whipp* [1996] 1 F.L.R. 826; *ante,* p. 277.
[66] [1984] Ch. 317; *ante,* p. 278. A strict view was also taken by the House of Lords in *Winkworth v. Edward Baron Development Co. Ltd* [1986] 1 W.L.R. 1512.
[67] [1986] 1 F.L.R. 171. The wife was attempting to defeat the husband's creditors. *cf. Re Densham, supra.*
[68] *ante,* p. 80.

v. Martin[69] a man invited his mistress to live with him, promising to provide for her by will. When he did not, she claimed a constructive trust to give effect to his intention. Her claim failed because she had not contributed to the acquisition or preservation of any of his assets. In *Re Basham*,[70] on the other hand, the constructive trust was utilised as a means of filling what were perceived to be gaps in the proprietary estoppel doctrine. The claimant had acted to her detriment in reliance on her stepfather's assurances that she would inherit from him. There was little authority on the application of that doctrine where the belief related to a future right and to non-specific assets.[71] These problems were overcome by holding that if the belief related to a future right, a species of constructive trust arose. Hence reliance could be placed on other branches of constructive trusts such as mutual wills, where the doctrine was not confined to present rights in specific assets.[72]

ii. Licences. The new model constructive trust was once most active in the context of licences. The matter will be treated in more detail in Chapter 27. Here let it merely be said that a licensee is a person who is physically present on land whether in occupation or not, but without any proprietary interest in the land. In the simplest case, such as that of a guest invited to dinner, the licensor may revoke the licence and require the guest to leave, allowing him a reasonable time to collect his belongings. But more complex cases arise: as where the licensee has given consideration for the licence; or where the licensee has been encouraged to act to his detriment in reliance on promises by the licensor, in such a way as to raise an estoppel against the licensor. Under the doctrine of proprietary estoppel,[73] the licensee can obtain a proprietary interest in the land. In the absence of such proprietary interest, a number of problems arise concerning the protection of the licensee. He is protected against the licensor; but how is he protected against third parties? The constructive trust has been called in aid as a means of enforcing a contractual licence against a third party, thus circumventing the rule that contractual rights are not binding on third parties even if they had notice. Lord Denning M.R. pioneered this use of the constructive trust in *Binions v. Evans*,[74] where an employer agreed to allow

---

[69] [1986] 2 F.L.R. 277. Alternative claims based on contract and proprietary estoppel also failed. See further *Coombes v. Smith* [1986] 1 W.L.R. 808; *post*, p. 883.

[70] [1986] 1 W.L.R. 1498; [1987] Conv. 211 (J. Martin); (1987) 46 C.L.J. 215 (D. Hayton); All E.R.Rev. 1987 at 156 (P. Clarke) and 263 (C. Sherrin); (1988) 8 L.S. 92 at 101 *et seq.* (M. Davey); *post*, p. 900.

[71] *cf. Layton v. Martin, supra.*

[72] See *Re Cleaver* [1981] 1 W.L.R. 939; *ante*, p. 324.

[73] *post*, p. 893.

[74] [1972] Ch. 359; (1972) 88 L.Q.R. 326 (P.V.B.); (1972) 37 Conv.(N.S.) 266 (J. Martin); (1977) 36 C.L.J. 123 (R. Smith); [2000] Conv. 398 (S. Bright). The majority view was that she had a life interest.

an employee's widow to reside in a cottage rent free for life. The cottage was sold at a reduced price, expressly subject to her interest. Lord Denning M.R. regarded her interest as a licence, binding on the purchaser under a constructive trust. This principle was next applied in *D.H.N. Foods Ltd v. Tower Hamlets London Borough Council*,[75] where the constructive trust theory enabled a contractual licensee to be treated as having a sufficient interest to qualify for compensation on compulsory purchase of the land. In *Re Sharpe (a Bankrupt)*[76] the aunt of the bankrupt had lent substantial sums of money to the bankrupt to purchase a shop and maisonette. She had been told that she could remain on the premises as long as she wished. She was held to have an interest by way of constructive trust against the trustee in bankruptcy. The trustee had contracted to sell the premises to a bona fide purchaser. The purchaser was not a party to the proceedings, and no decision was made on the question of her right, if any, against him.

Thus a principle was evolving that a constructive trust could be imposed on a purchaser with notice of a contractual licence, in order to achieve what was perceived as the just result. The Court of Appeal has since clarified and restricted the use of the constructive trust in this context, while leaving it with some scope for operation. In *Ashburn Anstalt v. Arnold*[77] the question arose whether an occupier's rights were binding on a purchaser. In fact the occupier was held to have a tenancy, but the Court of Appeal nevertheless considered *obiter* what the position would have been in the case of a licence. The basic principle that a contractual licence is only a personal right was confirmed, but the constructive trust solution was justified if the facts were appropriate to support it. A purchaser of the land would not automatically be bound by a constructive trust. The test was whether he had so conducted himself that it would be inequitable to allow him to deny the licensee's rights. The mere fact that the purchaser had notice or that property was conveyed "subject to" the licence was not enough.[78] Such a term may be included merely to protect the vendor against claims by the purchaser should it turn out that he is bound by third party rights. The constructive trust solution was appropriate in *Binions v. Evans*[79] because the purchaser paid a low price and was intended to give effect to the

---

[75] [1976] 1 W.L.R. 852; (1977) 36 C.L.J. 12 (D. Hayton).

[76] [1980] 1 W.L.R. 219; [1980] Conv. 207 (J. Martin).

[77] [1989] Ch. 1; (1988) 104 L.Q.R. 175 (P. Sparkes); (1988) 47 C.L.J. 353 (A. Oakley); (1988) 51 M.L.R. 226 (J. Hill); All E.R.Rev. 1988 at 177 (P. Clarke); [1988] Conv. 201 (M. Thompson); *post*, p. 888.

[78] *Kewal Investments Ltd v. Arthur Maiden Ltd* [1990] 1 E.G.L.R. 193; *IDC Group Ltd v. Clark* [1992] 1 E.G.L.R. 187 at 190 (the point did not arise on appeal at (1993) 65 P. & C.R. 179).

[79] *supra*. Also in *Lyus v. Prowsa Developments Ltd* [1982] 1 W.L.R. 1044; *post*, p. 336.

widow's rights. In *Re Sharpe (a Bankrupt)*,[80] on the other hand, the constructive trust was not appropriate, because the aunt did not reply to the trustee's enquiries as to her interest. In the instant case the imposition of a constructive trust would not have been justified. Although the vendor had disclosed the occupier's rights, this was done to protect the vendor, rather than with the intention that the purchaser should give effect to them, and the price was not reduced. The Court of Appeal emphasised that in matters relating to title to land, certainty was of prime importance, and that constructive trusts should not be imposed in reliance on slender materials. Thus the constructive trust survives as a means of achieving justice in appropriate cases, but the wide principle that a contractual licence automatically give rise to a constructive trust binding on a purchaser with notice has gone.[81]

iii. Registered Land.

iii. Registered Land. A constructive trust was also found in *Peffer v. Rigg*,[82] where a purchaser with notice of an interest under a trust for sale was held to take subject to it, applying general equitable principles, notwithstanding that the title to the property was registered and the interest was not protected on the register, as required by the Land Registration Act 1925. It has since been affirmed by the House of Lords in *Williams & Glyn's Bank Ltd v. Boland*[83] that the concept of notice has no relevance to dealings with registered land: "The only kind of notice recognised is by entry on the register."[84] The land registration system has provided a code in which, it is submitted, the constructive trust doctrine has no part to play.[85]

Fraudulent or sham transactions would raise different considerations. There is a well known principle that a statute must not be used as an instrument of fraud. This principle was invoked in *Lyus v. Prowsa Developments Ltd*,[86] where land was brought expressly subject to the claimant's contractual rights, but the defendants sought to defeat them by relying on the Land Registration Act 1925.[87] A constructive trust was imposed on the defendants on the ground that the statute was not to be used as an instrument of fraud. It has been said, on the highest authority, that it is not fraud to rely on legal

---

[80] *supra.*
[81] See further Gardner, *An Introduction to the Law of Trusts*, pp. 242–246.
[82] [1977] 1 W.L.R. 285; (1977) 93 L.Q.R. 341 (R. Smith); [1978] Conv. 52 (J. Martin); (1977) 36 C.L.J. 227 (D. Hayton); (1977) 40 M.L.R. 602 (S. Anderson); [2000] Conv. 398 (S. Bright).
[83] [1981] A.C. 487. *Peffer v. Rigg* was not cited on this point.
[84] *ibid.* at 504 *per* Lord Wilberforce.
[85] See especially s.59(6) and s.74 of Land Registration Act 1925.
[86] [1982] 1 W.L.R. 1044.
[87] ss.29, 34(4).

rights conferred by an Act of Parliament.[88] Here, however, the defendants had gone further, by reneging on a positive stipulation in favour of the claimant. Where the agreement expressly creates a right which a third party is to have against the purchaser, a constructive trust arises if the purchaser seeks to defeat that right. The result would have been the same in unregistered land.[89] The application to these facts of the maxim that a statute cannot be used as an instrument of fraud has been much criticised.[90] The Court of Appeal, however, has approved the decision, emphasising that the parties intended the purchaser to give effect to the contract and that an assurance to that effect had been given.[91]

iv. Conclusion. The courts, in some of these cases, were "invoking the constructive trust as an equitable remedy to do justice inter partes."[92] While a liberalisation of the application of equitable remedies is generally to be welcomed, it is important to appreciate that the "new model" constructive trust left a number of problems in its wake. The concept of justice alone is too vague to be used as the basis for determining property rights, and, inevitably, the imposition of the constructive trust on this basis is impossible to forecast. Further, a trust creates equitable proprietary rights, and these can operate more widely than the dispute between the parties. The question of the rights of third parties arises: whether, in particular, a bona fide purchaser or mortgagee is bound by a licensee's right of occupation, or by a woman's claim to share in the home. It may be possible to find a just solution between the parties on the basis of a personal decree not affecting the interests or rights of third parties.[93]

It is important also to appreciate that the "new model" constructive trust went far beyond the principle of the remedial constructive trust to prevent unjust enrichment,[94] although some examples of the remedial constructive trust differ little from Lord Denning's formulation.[95] The provision of a remedy for unjust enrichment does not require an unlimited free-wheeling discretion as

---

[88] *Midland Bank Trust Co. Ltd v. Green* [1981] A.C. 513 at 531.

[89] Applying *Bannister v. Bannister* [1948] 2 All E.R. 133, and the judgment of Lord Denning M.R. in *Binions v. Evans* [1972] Ch. 359.

[90] All E.R.Rev. 1982, p. 165 (P. Clarke); (1983) 46 M.L.R. 96 (P. Kenny); [1983] Conv. 64 (P. Jackson); (1983) 42 C.L.J. 54 (C. Harpum); (1985) 44 C.L.J. 280 (M. Thompson); *cf.* (1984) 47 M.L.R. 476 (P. Bennett).

[91] *Ashburn Anstalt v. Arnold* [1989] Ch. 1, *ante*, p. 335.

[92] (1973) 26 C.L.P. 17 at 35 (A. Oakley). The trend is examined in Oakley, *Constructive Trusts* (3rd ed.), pp. 59–60, 83–84.

[93] See *Muschinski v. Dodds* (1985) C.L.R. 583 (constructive trust took effect only from date of court order); *ante*, p. 304.

[94] *ante*, p. 301.

[95] See (1994) 8 *Trust Law International* 74 at 79 (M. Bryan), discussing Australian decisions.

to the imposition of a constructive trust. There must at least be general guide-lines for the exercise of the discretion. The law of unjust enrichment lays down with reasonable clarity when an action will lie. Some of the English cases seemed to treat a constructive trust as a magic formula to reach a just result between the parties, regardless of existing proprietary rights in them, or of the interests of persons who were not parties to the dispute. Present indications, however, are that the "new model" constructive trust will not develop further. The most recent decisions, as we have seen, favour a return to more orthodox principles of property law. Similarly in the Commonwealth, where, although the remedial constructive trust is accepted, it has been said that "the legitimacy of the new model is at least suspect; at best it is a mutant from which further breeding should be discouraged."[96]

---

[96] *Allen v. Snyder* [1977] 2 N.S.W.L.R. 685 at 701. The "new model" was also rejected in *Carly v. Farrelly* [1975] 1 N.Z.L.R. 356; (1978) 94 L.Q.R. 347 (G. Samuels); *Avondale Printers & Stationers Ltd v. Haggie* [1979] 2 N.Z.L.R. 124; *Muschinski v. Dodds* (1985) 160 C.L.R. 583. The "new model" was accepted in a modified form in *Pettkus v. Becker* (1980) 17 D.L.R. (3rd) 257; (1982) 12 Fam. Law 21 (M. Bryan). See further (1978) 94 L.Q.R. 351 (W. Gummow); (1975) 53 C.B.R. 366 (D. Waters); [1982] Conv. 424 (F. Bates); [1983] Conv. 420 (K. Hodkinson) (reviewing the position also in N. Ireland). The unjust enrichment approach was favoured in *Baumgartner v. Baumgartner* (1988) 62 A.L.J. 29; [1988] Conv. 259 (D. Hayton).

CHAPTER 13

TRUSTS WHICH CONTRAVENE THE LAW

A TRUST, though otherwise valid, may fail because it contains an element of unlawfulness or immorality, or is contrary to public policy. It is impossible to categorise all the possible grounds of unlawfulness, and only some of the more important ones can be mentioned here.

1. TRUSTS CONTRARY TO THE GENERAL POLICY OF THE LAW

A. Purposes Contrary to Law, Public Policy or Morality

It will be appreciated that such trusts are likely to fail in any event, apart from any question of unlawfulness, on the ground that they are non-charitable purpose trusts.[1] There are, perhaps for this

---

[1] *post*, Chap. 14. See, for example, *Brown v. Burdett* (1882) 21 Ch.D. 667, where a "useless" trust to seal up a house for 20 years failed.

reason, few examples of cases decided on the basis of illegality, but one such is *Thrupp v. Collett*,[2] where a testator attempted to provide for paying the fines of convicted poachers. Sir John Romilly M.R. held the trust void on the ground that it was against public policy. It was held in *Bowman v. Secular Society*[3] that the denial of Christianity was not *per se* an illegal purpose, but it was suggested in *Thornton v. Howe*[4] that a trust whose purpose was adverse to all religion or subversive of morality would be void. It need hardly be added that trusts for the furtherance of illegal or immoral activities, such as, for example, terrorism or prostitution,[5] would fail. Likewise a trust for a fraudulent purpose, such as placing money with a company in order to give it the false appearance of a credit balance.[6] The Law Commission[7] regards an "illegal trust" as comprising the following: a trust which it would be legally wrongful to create or impose; a trust which is created to facilitate fraud or some other legal wrong or which arises as a result of a transaction or arrangement with that objective; a trust which is created in return for the commission of a legal wrong or the promise to commit a legal wrong; a trust which expressly or necessarily requires a trustee or beneficiary to commit a legal wrong or which tends or is intended to do so; and a trust which is otherwise contrary to public policy at common law.

It was at one time established that gifts by deed or will for future illegitimate children were void on the ground that they would tend to encourage immorality.[8] The position was changed by section 15(7) of the Family Law Reform Act 1969 (now replaced by the Family Law Reform Act 1987, section 19).[9]

B. Statutory Provisions Against Discrimination

i. Race Relations Act 1976. Discrimination, as defined by the 1976 Act, on the ground of colour, race, nationality, or ethnic or national origins is unlawful.[10] The 1976 Act applies to certain specified situations, including employment, the provision of goods and

---

[2] (1858) 26 Beav. 125.
[3] [1917] A.C. 406 (Lord Finlay L.C. dissenting).
[4] (1862) 31 Beav. 14.
[5] See Harman L.J.'s example of a "school for prostitutes or pickpockets" in *Re Pinion* [1965] Ch. 85.
[6] *Re Great Berlin Steamboat Co.* (1884) 26 Ch.D. 616.
[7] Law Com. C.P. No. 154 (1999), *Illegal Transactions: The Effect of Illegality on Contracts and Trusts*, para. 8.22; *post*, p. 348.
[8] *Occleston v. Fullalove* (1874) L.R. 9 Ch.App. 147; *cf. Re Hyde* [1932] 1 Ch. 95. The claim of an illegitimate beneficiary might have failed in any event on the ground that gifts were generally construed as confined to legitimate relatives. This is no longer the position: Family Law Reform Act 1987, s.19 (replacing F.L.R.A. 1969, s.15).
[9] This Act replaces the concept of the illegitimate child with that of the unmarried parent.
[10] s.1.

services, and the disposal of property. In these situations a person discriminates against another, for the purposes of the Act, if on any of the above-mentioned grounds he treats that other less favourably than he treats or would treat other persons. It will be noted that religion as such is not covered by the Act.[11]

Subject to what is said below about charitable trusts, the Act does not extend to discrimination in the making of a gift or trust.[12] But trustees, just as any other individuals, are bound by the provisions relating to employment, disposal of property and so on. This is especially significant in the administration of charitable trusts.

Special provisions relating to charitable trusts are contained in section 34 of the 1976 Act. The general position is that the Act does not affect a provision in a charitable instrument which provides for conferring *benefits* on persons of a class defined by reference to race, nationality, or ethnic or national origins.[13] In other words, it is lawful to discriminate in favour of such groups, but not against them.[14] But it is not permissible to discriminate even in favour of a class defined by reference to colour.[15] Any such provision is to take effect as if it provided for conferring the benefits in question on persons of the class which results if the colour qualification is disregarded.

Finally, it should be noted that even where discrimination in a charitable trust is not made unlawful by the Act, the removal of discriminatory provisions is possible under the *cy-près* doctrine.[16]

ii. Sex Discrimination Act 1975. Sex discrimination is not a ground for invalidating any provision in a private trust. As far as charitable trusts are concerned, section 43 provides that the Act does not apply to any provision in a charitable instrument for conferring benefits on persons of one sex only. Thus there is nothing unlawful in single sex charities, such as the YMCA. Of course, the trustees are bound by the Act in matters such as the employment of staff.

---

[11] The position of the Jewish religion is unclear. See the Race Relations Board First Annual Report. A condition requiring Jewish parentage was considered racial in *Clayton v. Ramsden* [1943] A.C. 320. Jews were held to be an ethnic group in *King-Ansell v. Police* [1979] 2 N.Z.L.R. 531, approved by the House of Lords in *Mandla v. Dowell Lee* [1983] 2 A.C. 548, where Sikhs were held to be a racial group. For the position of Rastafarians, see *Dawkins v. Crown Suppliers (PSA) Ltd, The Times*, February 4, 1993.

[12] For the American position on racially discriminatory trusts, see (1972) A.A.L.R. 101 (L. Sheridan).

[13] s.34(2) and (3).

[14] Thus the provisions contained in *Re Dominion Students' Hall Trust* [1947] Ch. 183 would now be unlawful. (This was also the case under the Race Relations Act 1968). See also *Re Gwyon* [1930] 1 Ch. 255.

[15] s.34(1).

[16] *post*, p. 445. See *Re Lysaght* [1966] Ch. 191; *Re Dominion Students' Hall Trust, supra; Canada Trust Company v. Ontario Human Rights Commission* (1990) 69 D.L.R. (4th) 321. The promotion of racial harmony is now considered a charitable purpose; Annual Report of the Charity Commissioners for 1983, para. 19.

Special provisions relating to educational charities enable restrictions based on sex to be removed or modified on application to the Secretary of State.[17]

C. Conditions Precedent and Subsequent; Determinable Interests

Questions involving illegality often arise in connection with the validity of conditions imposed upon otherwise valid gifts.[18] A condition precedent is one which must be satisfied before the gift can vest, whereas a condition subsequent operates to defeat an already vested gift by forfeiture. A determinable interest, on the other hand, is one which will automatically determine on the occurrence of the determining event, no question of forfeiture being involved.[19] It is not always easy, as a matter of construction, to decide whether a condition is intended to operate as a condition precedent or subsequent, or to distinguish conditional and determinable interests.[20] It seems that the latter are less susceptible to, although not immune from, attack on the ground of public policy.[21]

Apart from any question of illegality, conditions have frequently failed on the ground of uncertainty. A distinction has been drawn between conditions precedent and subsequent. A stricter test of certainty applies to a condition subsequent, which must be so framed that at the outset the beneficiary knows the exact event which will divest his interest.[22] Lord Denning M.R., has described this distinction as a "deplorable dichotomy," serving only to defeat the settlor's intention.[23] Even in the case of a condition subsequent, however, the court is reluctant to pronounce the condition void for uncertainty. So in *Re Tepper's Will Trusts*,[24] where a condition subsequent required the beneficiaries to remain within the Jewish faith and not to marry outside it, the court regarded as admissible extrinsic evidence of the

---

[17] s.78.

[18] Where several conditions are attached to one gift, the valid conditions may be severed from any which are invalid: *Re Hepplewhite Will Trusts, The Times*, January 21, 1977.

[19] *Ante*, p. 192. For a detailed account of the distinctions and their significance, see Cheshire and Burn's *Modern Law of Real Property* (16th ed.), pp. 364 *et seq.*

[20] See, for example, *Re Tuck's Settlement Trusts* [1978] Ch. 49; *Re Johnson's Will Trusts* [1967] Ch. 387; *Re Tepper's Will Trusts* [1987] Ch. 358.

[21] See *Re Johnson's Will Trusts, supra*, at p. 396; *Re Moore* (1888) 39 Ch.D. 116; Megarry and Wade, *The Law of Real Property* (6th ed.), p. 70.

[22] *Re Tepper's Will Trusts, supra.* The test applying to conditions precedent is that laid down in *Re Allen* [1953] Ch. 810: conceptual uncertainty may not defeat such conditions. A modern example is *Re Barlow's Will Trusts* [1979] 1 W.L.R. 278, *ante*, p. 115. See generally Underhill and Hayton (15th ed.), pp. 80–82; [1980] Conv. 263 (L. McKay).

[23] *Re Tuck's Settlement Trusts* [1978] Ch. 49 at p. 60. But the distinction was acknowledged by the House of Lords in *Blathwayt v. Lord Cawley* [1976] A.C. 397 at 425.

[24] *supra.* See also *Ellis v. Chief Adjudication Officer* [1998] 1 F.L.R. 184 (gift of house to daughter subject to condition subsequent that she should care for her mother in the house upheld).

Jewish faith as practised by the testator, to elucidate the meaning of his words.[25]

Assuming that the condition does not fail for uncertainty, the next question is whether it will be void as being illegal or otherwise contrary to public policy. The categories discussed below involve the types of condition which have been most frequently encountered.

i. Marriage, Separation and Divorce. Where property is given by way of a determinable gift until marriage, and then to other beneficiaries, the limitation is unobjectionable.[26] Conditions, on the other hand, will be void if they are designed to prevent marriage or to encourage divorce or separation.

As far as conditions restraining marriage are concerned, a distinction is drawn between total and partial restraints. A condition subsequent, operating to divest the property on marriage, is void if its object is to restrain marriage altogether.[27] But conditions operating only in the event of a second or subsequent marriage, or merely requiring consent to marriage,[28] are not void.[29] Nor is there any objection to a condition in restraint of marriage with certain persons, or a certain class.[30] The rules relating to partial restraints on marriage differ according to whether the gift is of realty or personalty, the reason being that the personalty rules evolved in the ecclesiastical courts, whereas the realty rules were developed by the common law. The result of this historical distinction is as follows: in the case of personalty a condition imposing a partial restraint on marriage is invalid as being merely "*in terrorem*" if there is no express gift over on the occurrence of the marriage[31] whereas in the case of realty, a partial restraint is never invalid, whether or not there is a gift over.[32]

---

[25] Relying on *Re Tuck's Settlement Trusts, supra,* where, however, the will expressly provided that the Chief Rabbi could determine the meaning of "Jewish faith" and "approved wife." *cf.* A.J.A. 1982, s.21. See All E.R. Rev. 1987 at 159 (P. Clarke) and 260 (C. Sherrin).

[26] *Re Lovell* [1920] 1 Ch. 122.

[27] *Lloyd v. Lloyd* (1852) 2 Sim.(N.S.) 255. This includes a condition which in practice amounts to a general restraint: *Re Lanyon* [1927] 2 Ch. 264. (Condition against marriage with any blood relation). It seems that similar rules would apply to a condition precedent. See *Re Wallace* [1920] Ch. 274.

[28] *Re Whiting's Settlement* [1905] 1 Ch. 96.

[29] *Allen v. Jackson* (1875) 1 Ch.D. 399.

[30] *Jenner v. Turner* (1880) 16 Ch.D. 188; *Perrin v. Lyon* (1807) 9 East. 170; condition against marrying a person born in Scotland or of Scottish parents upheld. See also the cases on religion, discussed below.

[31] *Leong v. Lim Beng Chye* [1955] A.C. 648 (A residuary gift is not a gift over).

[32] Another possible distinction is that in the case of realty, but not personalty, even a general restraint is valid if intended merely to provide for the beneficiary while unmarried, rather than to promote celibacy: *Jones v. Jones* (1876) 1 Q.B.D. 279.

Conditions designed to induce the separation or divorce of a husband and wife are void as being contrary to public policy.[33] But if the parties have already decided upon a separation, the trusts in any deed of separation are not invalid.[34] Nor is there any objection where the true object of a disposition is merely to make provision for a party during the separation.[35]

It will be seen that most of these cases were decided at a time when the sanctity of marriage was perhaps regarded more highly than it is today. A stricter view was taken of relationships outside marriage than is now the case. Thus in the past trusts or covenants to create trusts have been held void if created in consideration of a future immoral association.[36] The modern tendency might be to discover some other form of consideration from the beneficiary.[37]

A question which might arise is the effect of a condition designed to restrain the modern practice of "living in sin."[38] Such a condition might fail for uncertainty,[39] but, in any event, it might be said that while such a practice is not unlawful, "it is not yet a virtue."[40]

ii. Parental Duties. A condition calculated to bring about the separation of parent and child is void as being contrary to public policy,[41] even where the parents are divorced.[42] Similarly, a condition designed to interfere with the exercise of parental duties.[43] In *Blathwayt v. Lord Cawley*[44] a settlement provided for the forfeiture of the interest of any child who became a Roman Catholic. It was argued that the condition was void on the ground that it would hamper parental duties in religious instruction. The House of Lords rejected this argument: "To say that any condition which in any way

---

[33] *Re Johnson's Will Trusts* [1967] Ch. 387; *Re Caborne* [1943] Ch. 224. See also *Re McBride* (1980) 107 D.L.R. (3d) 233; *Re Hepplewhite Will Trusts, The Times*, January 21, 1977.

[34] *Wilson v. Wilson* (1848) 1 H.L.C. 538. It is otherwise if the provision is designed to discourage reconciliation. See also *Egerton v. Egerton* [1949] 2 All E.R. 238 at 242: "a settlement which contains provisions as to what should happen in the case of divorce is not contrary to public policy", *per* Denning L.J.

[35] *Re Lovell* [1920] 1 Ch. 122. As to the admissibility of any evidence of the settlor's motive, see *Re Johnson's Will Trusts* [1967] Ch. 387.

[36] See *Re Vallance* (1884) 26 Ch.D. 353; *Ayerst v. Jenkins* (1873) L.R. 16 Eq. 275.

[37] See, for example, *Tanner v. Tanner* [1975] 1 W.L.R. 1346 where a contract was inferred between a man and his mistress in consideration of her looking after the house and family; *cf. Coombes v. Smith* [1986] 1 W.L.R. 808.

[38] Another example might be a condition restraining a homosexual relationship.

[39] See *Re Jones* [1953] Ch. 125, where a condition prohibiting a "social or other relationship" with X failed for uncertainty.

[40] Borrowing Lord Denning's description, in a different context (tax avoidance), in *Re Weston's Settlements* [1969] 1 Ch. 223.

[41] *Re Boulter* [1922] 1 Ch. 75.

[42] *Re Piper* [1946] 2 All E.R. 503.

[43] *Re Borwick* [1933] Ch. 657; *Re Sandbrook* [1912] 2 Ch. 471. These two decisions must now be read in the light of the comments made in *Blathwayt v. Lord Cawley* [1976] A.C. 397, discussed below.

[44] [1976] A.C. 397.

might affect or influence the way in which a child is brought up, or in which parental duties are exercised, seems to me to state far too wide a rule."[45]

iii. Religion. It has already been noted that discrimination on religious grounds falls outside the Race Relations Act 1976. Conditions restricting freedom of religion have long been popular with settlors and testators. While such conditions have sometimes failed for uncertainty, especially in the case of conditions subsequent,[46] it has never been held that such provisions are contrary to public policy, even in the case of charitable trusts.[47] In *Blathwayt v. Lord Cawley*,[48] of which the facts have already been given, Lord Cross said that while it may be wrong for the government to discriminate on religion, it does not follow that it is against public policy for an adherent of one religion to distinguish in disposing of his property; any other view amounts to saying that "it is disreputable for him to be convinced of the importance of holding true religious beliefs and of the fact that his religious beliefs are the true ones."[49] It had been argued that the Race Relations Acts and the European Convention of Human Rights[50] showed that the law was now against discrimination. Lord Wilberforce said "I do not doubt that conceptions of public policy should move with the times and that widely accepted treaties and statutes may point the direction in which such conceptions, as applied by the courts, ought to move. It may well be that conditions such as this are, or at least are becoming, inconsistent with standards now widely accepted."[51] But this did not justify the introduction of a new rule, for to do so would reduce another freedom, that of testamentary disposition. "Discrimination is not the same thing as choice: it operates over a larger and less personal area, and neither by express provision nor by implication has private selection yet become a matter of public policy."[52]

---

[45] [1976] A.C. 397 at 426 (*per* Lord Wilberforce).

[46] *Clayton v. Ramsden* [1943] A.C. 320 (forfeiture on marriage to person not of Jewish parentage and faith); *Re Abraham's Will Trusts* [1969] 1 Ch. 463; *Re Tepper's Will Trusts* [1987] Ch. 358. A condition precedent is less likely to fail on this ground: see *Re Allen* [1953] Ch. 810; *Re Selby's Will Trusts* [1966] 1 W.L.R. 43; *Re Tuck's Settlement Trusts* [1978] Ch. 49 (marriage to "approved wife" of Jewish blood and faith not uncertain); (1999) 19 L.S. 339 (D. Cooper and D. Herman). See also *Re Evans* [1940] Ch. 629.

[47] See *Re Lysaght* [1966] Ch. 191. (Discrimination against Jews and Roman Catholics was merely "undesirable"); *cf. Canada Trust Company v. Ontario Human Rights Commission* (1990) 69 D.L.R. (4th) 321.

[48] [1976] A.C. 397. See also *Re Remnant's Settlement Trusts* [1970] 1 Ch. 560; *Clayton v. Ramsden, supra.* The heir to the throne may not be, or marry, a Roman Catholic: Act of Settlement 1701.

[49] [1976] A.C. 397 at 429.

[50] Art. 9. There is nothing in the Human Rights Act 1998 to affect the dispositions of settlors or testators.

[51] [1976] A.C. 397 at 426.

[52] *ibid.*

iv. Race. We have already seen that discrimination on the grounds of race or colour is made unlawful by the Race Relations Act 1976, and that, apart from special provisions relating to charities, the Act has no application to private trusts. It seems that it is not contrary to public policy for a settlor to discriminate on these grounds, although the point is not unarguable.[53] There is little authority on the point, which has arisen mainly in connection with charitable trusts.[54] Many of the comments made by the House of Lords in *Blathwayt v. Lord Cawley*[55] in the context of religion would apply equally to racial discrimination, save that the dictum of Lord Cross[56] loses all conviction if race is substituted for religious beliefs.

v. Alienation. Conditions operating as a complete restraint on the alienation of property are void as being contrary to public policy.

In *Re Brown*,[57] a testator devised realty among his four sons subject to a condition which would have produced forfeiture of his interest by any son who mortgaged or sold his interest other than among his brothers. The condition was held to be equivalent to a general restraint on alienation, and therefore void, since the class of permitted alienees was small and bound to get smaller.

A partial restraint on alienation is valid.[58] Restrictions upon alienation to groups identified by religion may be unobjectionable, but the Race Relations Act 1976 forbids racial discrimination in the disposal of property.[59]

Restraints even of a general nature may be valid if they take the form of a determinable interest.[60] Section 33 of the Trustee Act 1925 itself provides such an example.[61]

vi. Other Cases. Much difficulty has been encountered in the past with "name and arms" clauses, whereby settlors seek to ensure that the beneficiary adopts a specified name and coat of arms, usually those of the settlor. Such clauses were at one time held to be

---

[53] See Underhill and Hayton, *loc. cit.* at p. 196.

[54] See *Re Gwyn* [1930] 1 Ch. 255; *Re Dominion Students' Hall Trust* [1947] Ch. 183. In neither case was public policy discussed.

[55] [1976] A.C. 397.

[56] *ibid.* at 429; *supra.*

[57] [1954] Ch. 39; *cf. Caldy Manor Estate Ltd v. Farrell* [1974] 1 W.L.R. 1303 (covenant against alienation not unlawful).

[58] See *Re MacLeay* (1875) L.R. 20 Eq. 186. (Doubted in *Re Rosher* [1884] 25 Ch. 801). It is suggested in Cheshire and Burn's *Modern Law of Real Property* (16th ed.), at 368, that even partial restraints should be invalid as repugnant to ownership.

[59] s.21.

[60] *Re Dugdale* (1883) 38 Ch.D. 176 at 178–181, *per* Kay J.; *Re Leach* [1912] 2 Ch. 422.

[61] *ante*, p. 194 (the protective trust).

contrary to public policy, on the ground that, if the beneficiary was a married woman, the taking of another name might lead to dissension between husband and wife. It is now settled that such clauses are neither uncertain nor contrary to public policy.[62]

It was held in *Egerton v. Brownlow*[63] that a condition requiring the beneficiary to obtain a dukedom was contrary to public policy as tending to encourage corruption, but a similar provision involving a baronetcy was upheld in *Re Wallace*,[64] the distinction being that, unlike a dukedom, no legislative powers and duties would be involved, consequently the public interest could not be affected. Conditions forbidding entry into the naval or military services have also been held void.[65] The validity of conditions relating to bankruptcy has already been discussed.[66]

Finally, a condition whereby a beneficiary was to become entitled to property on becoming destitute has been held void as contrary to public policy in that it could encourage irresponsibility with money.[67]

D. The Consequence of Illegality

The general position appears to be that if an express trust fails on the ground of unlawfulness, a resulting trust to the settlor or his estate ensues.[68] This is so even if the trust was designed to encourage an offence prohibited by statute.[69] Where the trust is only partly unlawful, the whole fails if the proportion to be devoted to the unlawful purpose is unascertainable,[70] whereas if that proportion is ascertainable, only that part fails.[71] Where property has been transferred to a volunteer for an unlawful purpose, the question arises whether the court will assist the transferor to recover the property. The principle, which was discussed in Chapter 10, is that the transferor may recover if he does not have to rely on his own illegality,[72] or if the illegality has not been carried out.[73]

---

[62] *Re Neeld* [1962] Ch. 643.

[63] (1853) 4 H.L. 1.

[64] [1920] 2 Ch. 274. Since the reform of the House of Lords no legislative powers would be involved in either case.

[65] See *Re Beard* [1908] 1 Ch. 383.

[66] *ante*, p. 192.

[67] *Re Hepplewhite Will Trusts, The Times*, January 21, 1977.

[68] *Ante*, p. 241. *cf. Ayerst v. Jenkins* (1873) L.R. 16 Eq. 275 (described as a "difficult case" in Law Com. C.P. No. 154, *infra*, at 69).

[69] *Thrupp v. Collett* (1858) 26 Beav. 125.

[70] *Chapman v. Brown* (1801) 6 Ves. 404.

[71] *Mitford v. Reynolds* (1842) 1 Ph. 185. There is some authority that in such a case the whole can go to the lawful part: *Fisk v. Att.-Gen.* (1867) L.R. 4 Eq. 521.

[72] *Tinsley v. Milligan* [1994] 1 A.C. 340.

[73] *Tribe v. Tribe* [1996] Ch. 107.

This area is currently under review by the Law Commission.[74] It is considered that the law is unclear as to what happens when an express trust fails for illegality. In the case of a transfer to a volunteer, the transferor is assisted by the presumption of a resulting trust, which shifts the burden of proof to the recipient.[75] In the case of failure of an express trust for illegality, there is a sense in which the settlor who claims the return of the property under a resulting trust must "rely" on his own illegality. It is provisionally proposed that the courts should have a statutory discretion to decide the effect of illegality in this area.

Where a condition subsequent is unlawful, the gift takes effect as an absolute interest: the condition alone is void.[76] In the case of a condition precedent, a distinction is drawn between realty and personalty. As far as realty is concerned, the gift itself fails if the condition is bad.[77] Where the gift is of personalty, however, it takes effect free of the condition where the illegality is only a *malum prohibitum*.[78] But where the illegality is a *malum in se*, the gift fails. The abolition of this distinction has been proposed.[79] In the case of a determinable interest, the gift fails if the determining event is unlawful.[80]

2. PERPETUITY, DURATION AND INALIENABILITY

A. General

One of the most common causes over the years of invalidity of interests under a trust has been the failure to comply with the Rule Against Perpetuities. The hazard has been much reduced, and the law simplified by the Perpetuities and Accumulations Act 1964, which applies to dispositions coming into effect after July 15, 1964. Questions may still arise in respect of earlier instruments, as a decision on a will, for example, may be delayed until the death of a life tenant.[81] But the Act has been in operation for over 35 years, and

---

[74] Law Com. C.P. No. 154 (1999), *Illegal Transactions: The Effect of Illegality on Contracts and Trusts*, Part III.

[75] *ante*, p. 255.

[76] *Re Beard* [1908] 1 Ch. 383. This is so whether the gift is realty or personalty.

[77] *Re Elliott* [1952] Ch. 217.

[78] *i.e.* something made unlawful only by statute. See *Re Piper* [1946] 2 All E.R. 503. The distinction was apparently not discussed in *Re Hepplewhite Will Trusts*, *The Times*, January 21, 1977.

[79] Law Com. C.P. No. 154 (1999), *Illegal Transactions: The Effect of Illegality on Contracts and Trusts*, p. 170.

[80] *Re Moore* (1888) 39 Ch.D. 116. For the application of the perpetuity rule to conditional and determinable interests, see Perpetuities and Accumulations Act 1964, s.12: the interest becomes absolute if the determining event or breach of condition does not occur within the perpetuity period.

[81] See *Re Drummond* [1988] 1 W.L.R. 234, concerning a 1924 settlement.

each year which passes will reduce the likelihood of a question arising which is not governed by the Act. There is not space to deal with the subject in detail here. It is covered by books on real property,[82] a practice which can have a historical justification only; the rule grew up in connection with settlements of land, but now applies mainly to trusts of personalty. The subject is one which has caused much confusion, not least in connection with the Act; and a few general comments may be helpful.

B. Tying Up Land

The perpetuity rule is based on a policy against the tying up of lands for an undue length of time. The struggle began in the earliest years of common law. Conditions against alienation were held void. Entails were by statute inalienable, but by 1472 it was recognised that an entail could be barred, turned into a fee simple and alienated.[83] The Old Rule Against Perpetuities prevented a series of contingent life estates. Alienability was successfully being maintained. But once it was decided that executory interests were valid and indestructible,[84] it was possible to create interests limited to vest at an indefinite time in the future. The Rule Against Perpetuities was designed to restrict the extent to which future vesting could be postponed.

C. Remote Vesting. Life in Being Plus 21 Years

The permitted period was a life in being plus 21 years; permitting in effect, a grant to the first son of A to attain the age of 21 years. For A's son must attain the age of 21 years, if he ever does, within 21 years of A's death.[85] A period of gestation was also allowed in the case of posthumous children.

One could not wait and see whether the gift vested in time or not. The common law rule was that the interest was void if it *might* vest outside the period; even if in fact it vested the next day. The Rule is:

> "No interest is good unless it must vest, if at all, not later than twenty-one years after some life in being at the creation of the interest."[86]

---

[82] Cheshire and Burn, pp. 309 *et seq.*, M. & W., Chap. 7; Morris and Leach, *The Rule against Perpetuities*; Maudsley, *The Modern Law of Perpetuities*.

[83] *Taltarum's Case* Y.B. 12 Edw. 4, 19.

[84] *Pells v. Brown* (1620) Cro. Jac. 590.

[85] Scientific advances in reproduction have made this statement untrue, but if sperm or embryos are used after a man's death, he is not treated as the father; Human Fertilisation and Embryology Act 1990.

[86] Gray, *The Rule Against Perpetuities* (4th ed.), § 201.

Thus, a gift to the first son of A to attain the age of 22 years was void at common law if A was still alive; even if A had a son of $21\frac{1}{2}$ at the time. For that son might die, another son be born, and A die; and A's first son to attain the age of 22 might do so more than 21 years after the death of any persons alive at the date of the gift. A long series of bizarre situations showing the ruthless operation of the rule has often been catalogued, and need not be repeated. The one simple example makes the point.

D. Wait and See

The Act deals with this situation in three ways; first, by permitting a settlor to specify as the perpetuity period for the purpose of the disposition a period of years not exceeding 80[87]; secondly, by a number of specific reforms on individual points which had caused difficulty, and thirdly, by introducing a system of wait and see.[88] If the law was unrealistic because it made void an interest which vested in fact within the period merely because it might have vested outside it, an obvious solution would be to make its validity depend on whether or not it does in fact vest within it. That is the theory of wait and see.

There is much disagreement as to the identity of the lives in being at common law.[89] The 1964 Act, however, lays down, in section 3, its own list of statutory lives in being, which must be used where the wait and see rule is invoked. Although certain common law lives in being, such as "royal lives," are not included, the statutory class is generally wider than the class of common law lives in being.

One would have thought it obvious that, on enacting wait and see, the common law rule should be abolished. It no longer has any part to play. If a disposition must vest, if at all, within the period, then it will vest, if at all, within the period. Thus, the common law test is contained within the wait and see test. There is no advantage in knowing that an interest complies with the common law test. The interest remains contingent, and its value is dependent, not on compliance with the common law rule, but upon its likelihood of vesting. Assume that A has a son X aged 21. A gift to A's first son to attain the age of 22 is void under the common law rule, but likely to vest within the period; and would be of greater value than a gift to the first son of A to go to the moon in A's lifetime, which would be

[87] s.1.
[88] s.3.
[89] (1964) 80 L.Q.R. 486 at 495–508 (J. Morris and H. Wade); (1965) 81 L.Q.R. 106 at 108 (D. Allan); (1970) 86 L.Q.R. 357 (R. Maudsley), (1975) 60 Cornell L.R. 355 (R. Maudsley); Maudsley, *The Modern Law of Perpetuities*; (1981) 97 L.Q.R. 593 (R. Deech); (1986) 102 L.Q.R. 251 (J. Dukeminier).

valid at common law. Compliance with the common law rule is irrelevant in a system of wait and see.[90]

Nevertheless, the Act retained the common law rule. Wait and see only applies to "void" limitations.[91] So it is necessary to apply the common law rule to test validity, and to apply wait and see, if it fails to comply with the common law rule. It is tempting to ignore the common law rule. Every limitation which was valid at common law would also be valid under wait and see: unless, however, there could be some situation in which a gift was validated by a common law life who is not in the statutory list, and the interest does not in fact vest within 21 years of the death of the survivor of the statutory lives. Because the class of statutory lives does not coincide exactly with the common law lives, that is theoretically possible.[92] But it is absurd to retain all the common law learning in order to save such a rare gift. The common law rule should have been abolished.[93]

If it had been, the application of the wait and see rule would have been simple. In the case of any gift, all that would be necessary would be the writing down of the measuring lives, the recording of their deaths, and the addition of 21 years. The interests which had then vested would be valid; those which had not vested would be void.

The Law Commission[94] has proposed that the rule against remoteness of vesting should be modified by the introduction of a statutory perpetuity period of 125 years, with no lives in being, during which the "wait and see" principle will operate. Abolition of the rule was rejected on the ground that the "dead hand" rationale is still valid. The settlor or testator would not have to select the statutory period, which would override anything specified in the instrument as the perpetuity period, save only that a period shorter than 125 years may be selected. The new rules will not be retrospective, and will not apply to wills executed before the new legislation even though the testator dies after its commencement. Trustees of existing trusts will be able to "opt in" to the 125-year period if there is uncertainty as to when the currently applicable period will end (as where it is impractical to ascertain the existence or whereabouts of express lives in being). Although the proposed rule has the merit of simplicity, the drawback to the scheme is that three sets of

---

[90] (1970) 86 L.Q.R. 357 at 372 (R. Maudsley); (1975) 60 Cornell L.R. 355 (R. Maudsley); Maudsley, *The Modern Law of Perpetuities*.

[91] s.3.

[92] As in the case of dispositions governed by a royal lives clause.

[93] (1975) 60 Cornell L.R. 355 at 370 (R. Maudsley).

[94] Law Com. No. 251 (1998), *The Rules against Perpetuities and Excessive Accumulations*; (1998) 12 *Trust Law International* 148 (P. Sparkes); (2000) 59 C.L.J. 284 (T. Gallanis). The rule against excessive duration is not dealt with.

rules will be in operation, depending on the date of the instrument.

E. Duration and Inalienability

Separate from the perpetuity rule governing remoteness of vesting, but a further manifestation of the same policy, is the rule which declares void trusts which might continue for too long a period; longer, that is, than the perpetuity period.

The matter will be discussed in connection with non-charitable purpose trusts.[95] In so far as they are permitted, they must be limited to the perpetuity period. The restriction upon duration does not apply to charitable trusts, nor to most pension trusts.[96]

It should be added that this rule is not in any way inconsistent with the ownership of property in fee simple by a person or a corporation. Those owners may alienate at any time. They may of course keep the property for ever; but the property is not tied up in any way. Thus in *Bowman v. Secular Society*,[97] a gift to the "Secular Society" a society devoted to furthering anti-Christian beliefs, having survived an attack on the grounds of public policy, had nothing to fear on the score of perpetuity, as the Society was a limited company, and able to deal freely with its property.

3. ATTEMPTS TO KEEP PROPERTY FROM CREDITORS

A. General

A creditor can demand payment from his debtor out of the debtor's property. If the debtor's property is insufficient to pay his debts, he is insolvent, and it will not be possible to pay all the creditors in full. Generally speaking, before bankruptcy the debtor may choose which creditors he pays first[98]; but after bankruptcy the bankruptcy law provides for a fair sharing out of his property.

When a person foresees the danger of his own[99] future insolvency—as where he is entering upon a business venture—there is the temptation to put property out of the reach of creditors, by, for example, creating a settlement in favour of the family, in this or other jurisdictions.[1] If the business venture succeeds the profits will

---

[95] *post*, p. 380; *cf. Re Dean* (1889) 41 Ch.D. 552. For difficulties arising with unincorporated associations, see *Re Grant's Will Trusts* [1980] 1 W.L.R. 360, *post*, p. 376.

[96] *post*, pp. 396, 490.

[97] [1917] A.C. 406.

[98] *Middleton v. Pollock* (1876) 2 Ch.D. 104.

[99] Where he foresees his beneficiary's insolvency, the protective trust may be employed; *ante*, Chap. 7.

[1] For offshore asset protection trusts, see (1993) 143 N.L.J. 721 (B. Marrache and G. Davis); (1995–96) 6 K.C.L.J. 62 (P. Matthews).

flow in; if it fails, the creditors will be unpaid; but the family will be cared for.[2] It may also be that a settlement is made for other reasons, such as the reduction of tax liability,[3] but insolvency subsequently occurs. The question for consideration here is the extent to which a creditor can upset dispositions made by debtors of property which would otherwise be available for the creditors, whether or not there is a bankruptcy.

B. Insolvency Act 1986

i. Transactions Defrauding Creditors. Section 423[4] of the Insolvency Act 1986, replacing section 172 of the Law of Property Act 1925, provides that a transaction at an undervalue may be set aside if the court is satisfied that the person entering into the transaction (the debtor) did so for the purpose:

(a) of putting assets beyond the reach of a person who is making, or may at some time make, a claim against him, or

(b) of otherwise prejudicing the interests of such a person in relation to the claim which he is making or may make.

The court may make such order as it thinks fit for

(a) restoring the position to what it would have been if the transaction had not been entered into, and

(b) protecting the interests of persons who are victims of the transaction (defined as a person who is, or is capable of being, prejudiced by the transaction).

The section applies equally to transactions entered into by individuals and by corporate bodies.[5]

(a) *Transaction at an undervalue.* By section 423(1), a person enters into a transaction with another person at an undervalue if

(a) he makes a gift to the other person or he otherwise enters into a transaction with the other on terms that provide for him to receive no consideration; or

(b) he enters into a transaction with the other in consideration of marriage; or

---

[2] "If I succeed in business, I make a fortune for myself. If I fail, I leave my creditors unpaid. They will pay the loss." *per* Jessel M.R. in *Re Butterworth, ex p. Russell* (1882) 19 Ch.D. 588 at 598. See also *Midland Bank plc v. Wyatt* [1995] 1 F.L.R. 696.

[3] *ante*, p. 217.

[4] See generally [1998] Conv. 362 (G. Miller).

[5] See also I.A. 1986, s.207.

(c) he enters into a transaction with the other for a consideration the value of which, in money or money's worth, is significantly less than the value, in money or money's worth, of the consideration provided by himself.

Thus the section applies where a husband makes a gift of money to his wife, transfers his interest in the matrimonial home to her,[6] or purchases property in the joint names of himself and his wife without any contribution from her.[7] Similarly where a married couple declare a trust of the family home for the wife and children.[8]

When assessing "undervalue" the court will view the transaction as a whole. In *Agricultural Mortgage Corporation plc v. Woodward*[9] an insolvent farmer, whose land was mortgaged for £700,000, granted a tenancy at the full market rent of £37,250 to his wife, to ensure that the mortgagee could not get vacant possession. It was argued that the full rent prevented the application of section 423. The Court of Appeal set aside the tenancy on the ground that the wife received benefits beyond those granted by the tenancy agreement, namely the safeguarding of her home, the ability to carry on the family business freed from the claims of creditors, and the surrender value of the tenancy, which gave her a "ransom" position against the mortgagee. She had paid nothing for these extra benefits, which were significantly more valuable than the rent. It was argued that such benefits could not be valued in money or money's worth and so should be left out of account. However, the surrender value alone was significantly greater than the rent. It was unnecessary to decide whether a detriment to the husband which gave no corresponding benefit to the wife (*i.e.* the diminution by at least 50 per cent of the £1 million freehold value caused by the letting) could be treated as consideration provided by the husband.

(b) *Intention.* As stated above, the court must be satisfied that the person entering into the transaction did so for the purpose of putting assets beyond the reach of, or of otherwise prejudicing, an existing or potential claimant.[10] The court was so satisfied where a husband who was threatened with legal actions and who knew there was doubt as to his insurance cover made substantial gifts to his wife upon receiving a large sum from the sale of his practice.[11] Indeed,

---

[6] *Re Kumar (a Bankrupt)* [1993] 1 W.L.R. 224 (assumption of sole liability for the mortgage by the wife was worth significantly less than value of share transferred).

[7] *Moon v. Franklin, The Independent*, June 22, 1990.

[8] *Midland Bank plc v. Wyatt* [1995] 1 F.L.R. 696 (the trust was in any event a sham; *ante*, p. 97).

[9] (1995) 70 P. & C.R. 53.

[10] See, on the previous law, *Lloyds Bank Ltd v. Marcan* [1973] 1 W.L.R. 1387 (sufficient to show intent to deprive creditors of timely recourse to property otherwise applicable for their benefit).

[11] *Moon v. Franklin, The Independent*, June 22, 1990.

where a debtor transfers assets to his family at an undervalue when an action by creditors is expected, the retained assets being insufficient, there is a strong prima facie case of intention to prejudice the creditor.[12] It is not necessary, however, to establish dishonesty. Thus the section may apply where the transfer was considered proper by legal advisers.[13] Putting the assets beyond the reach of creditors must be a substantial purpose of the transaction but need not be the sole motive.[14]

As under the previous law, it is not necessary that there should be existing creditors at the time of the transaction. The section preserves the effect of *Re Butterworth, ex p. Russell*,[15] where the court set aside a settlement made by a prosperous baker immediately before purchasing a grocer's business, a trade in which he had no experience. It makes no difference whether the anticipated creditors are those of the settlor himself or of a company he plans to set up.[16] Nor is it necessary that the person seeking to set aside the transaction should be technically a "creditor."[17]

(c) *Persons who may apply to court.* Where the debtor, being an individual, is now bankrupt, or, being a body corporate, is being wound up or is the subject of an administration order under the 1986 Act, the application may only be made by the official receiver, the trustee of the bankrupt's estate or the liquidator or administrator of the body corporate. The victim of the transaction, as defined above,[18] may apply with the leave of the court, but this is in effect a class action, giving no priority to the applicant.[19] Where a voluntary arrangement has been approved under the 1986 Act, the application may be made by the supervisor of the voluntary arrangement or the victim of the transaction. In any other case, for example where there is no insolvency, the application may be made by the victim of the transaction. These provisions are found in section 424 of the 1986 Act, which further provides that any application made under the section is treated as made on behalf of every victim of the transaction.

---

[12] *Barclays Bank plc v. Eustice* [1995] 1 W.L.R. 1238.
[13] *Arbuthnot Leasing International Ltd v. Havalet Leasing (No. 2)* [1990] B.C.C. 636. It should be added that legal professional privilege will be overridden on the ground of "iniquity" if a client seeks legal advice as to how to structure a transaction to defeat creditors; *Barclays Bank plc v. Eustice, supra.*
[14] *Moon v. Franklin, The Independent*, June 22, 1990; *Midland Bank plc v. Wyatt* [1995] 1 F.L.R. 696.
[15] (1882) 19 Ch.D. 588; *Mackay v. Douglas* (1872) L.R. 14 Eq. 106.
[16] *Midland Bank plc v. Wyatt* [1995] 1 F.L.R. 696.
[17] See *Cadogan v. Cadogan* [1977] 1 W.L.R. 1041.
[18] *ante*, p. 353.
[19] *Dora v. Simper, The Times*, May 26, 1999.

(d) *Orders to be made.* Sections 423(2) and 425 of the 1986 Act set out the orders which may be made by the court.[20] These include orders

(a) requiring any property transferred by the impugned transaction to be vested in any person, either absolutely or for the benefit of all the persons on whose behalf the application is treated as made, or

(b) requiring any property representing the application of the proceeds of sale of property transferred by the impugned transaction or of money transferred by it to be so vested, or

(c) requiring any person to pay to any other person in respect of benefits received from the debtor such sums as the court may direct.

(e) *Third parties.* Section 425(2) provides that any order made may affect the property of, or impose an obligation on, any person whether or not he was a party to the transaction, but the order shall not prejudice any interest in property[21] acquired from a person other than the debtor which was acquired in good faith, for value and without notice of the circumstances making section 423 applicable, or prejudice any interest deriving from such an interest. Nor shall the order require a person who received a benefit from the transaction in good faith, for value and without notice of the circumstances to pay any sum unless he was a party to the transaction. "Value" here bears its ordinary meaning.

ii. Bankruptcy provisions. The Insolvency Act 1986 replaced section 42 of the Bankruptcy Act 1914 with provisions dealing with transactions at an undervalue and preferences by individuals or corporate bodies[22] within a certain time limit prior to insolvency.

(a) *Transaction at an undervalue.* In the case of the insolvency of an individual, section 339 permits the trustee of the bankrupt's estate to apply to court for an order where the individual entered into a transaction at an undervalue within certain time limits discussed below. The court may make such order as it thinks fit for restoring the position to what it would have been but for the transaction. "Undervalue" here bears the same meaning as under section 423.[23] Thus, as under the previous law, the trustee may obtain the wife's

---

[20] See *Moon v. Franklin, The Independent,* June 22, 1990 (order compelling return of unspent portion of gift and restraining dealing with land).

[21] See *Chohan v. Saggar* [1994] B.C.L.C. 706 (mortgage).

[22] The provisions relating to companies will not be dealt with here.

[23] *ante,* p. 353.

share in the matrimonial home to the extent that she has not contributed to its acquisition.[24] A property adjustment order on divorce may be set aside under these provisions.[25] Where the wife has compromised her claim, with the result that the order is made by consent, the compromise is capable of being consideration, but it may be difficult to assess it in money or money's worth. If so, the section is applicable.[26]

(b) *Preference of creditors.* Where an individual is adjudged bankrupt and has given a preference to any person within time limits discussed below, the trustee of the bankrupt's estate may apply to court for an order under section 340. The court may make such order as it thinks fit for restoring the position to what it would have been if that individual had not given that preference. An individual gives a preference to a person if that person is a creditor,[27] surety or guarantor, and the effect is to put that person into a better position than he would otherwise have been in in the event of the individual's bankruptcy. An order may only be made if the individual was influenced by a desire to produce the effect mentioned above, but this is presumed where the other person was an associate.[28]

(c) *Time limits.* Section 341 provides a five year time limit, ending with the day of the presentation of the bankruptcy petition, in the case of a transaction at an undervalue. In the case of a preference which is not an undervalue, the period is six months save in the case of an associate, where the period is two years.

Except in the case of a transaction at an undervalue made within two years[29] before the bankruptcy, no order may be made with respect to a transaction entered into within the above time limits unless the individual was insolvent at the time or became insolvent in consequence of the transaction or preference. In the case of a transaction at an undervalue entered into with an associate, there is a rebuttable presumption that the individual was or became insolvent at the time of the transaction. A person is insolvent for this purpose if he cannot pay his debts as they fall due, or if the value of his assets is less than his liabilities.

---

[24] *Re Densham* [1975] 1 W.L.R. 1519; *Claughton v. Charalamabous* [1999] 1 F.L.R. 740. See also *Re Windle* [1975] 1 W.L.R. 1628.

[25] I.A. 1986, Sched. 14, amending M.C.A. 1973, s.39. Similarly under s.284; *In re Flint (a bankrupt)* [1993] Ch. 319; (1993) 23 Fam. Law 211 (S. Cretney).

[26] *Re Kumar (a bankrupt)* [1993] 1 W.L.R. 224; [1993] Conv. 310 (G. Ferris); *cf. Re Abbott (a bankrupt)* [1983] Ch. 45.

[27] This result could be avoided if the apparent "creditor" was in reality a beneficiary under a trust who never became a creditor. See *Re Kayford* [1975] 1 W.L.R. 279, *ante*, p. 53.

[28] As defined by section 435. The definition includes relatives of the individual or of his spouse, partners, employers, employees and related companies.

[29] The exercise of a power of appointment within this period is not caught by the rule if the settlement was made outside the period; *Clarkson v. Clarkson* [1994] B.C.C. 921.

(d) *Orders to be made.* Section 342 sets out the orders which the court may make for the benefit of the bankrupt's estate. These are similar to the orders which may be made under section 425.[30]

(e) *Third parties.* No order may prejudice any interest in property acquired from a person other than the bankrupt and acquired in good faith and for value. A purchaser is rebuttably presumed not to be in good faith in two situations.[31] The first is where he had notice at the time he acquired his interest of the fact that the earlier transaction was at an undervalue (or was a preference) and of the fact that the earlier transferor had been adjudged bankrupt or that the petition on which he was later adjudged bankrupt had been presented. The second situation is where the purchaser was an associate of, or was connected with, the bankrupt or the person with whom the bankrupt entered into the transaction at an undervalue (or to whom preference was given). Thus mere notice of the fact that the previous transaction was at an undervalue does not suffice. Similar rules apply to a person who has received a benefit from the transaction or preference in good faith and for value. Such a person shall not be required to pay any sum to the trustee unless he was a party to the transaction or was given a preference at a time when he was a creditor of the bankrupt.

C. Protection of the Spouse and Family

The previous sections dealt with attempts by a debtor to deprive his creditors of satisfaction by transferring property by way of voluntary settlement to other persons, usually members of his family, whom the debtor wishes to protect. We now deal with what is in effect the converse of that problem; cases where the defendant is trying to deprive his spouse or family of assets which should properly be available to them. This occurs in matrimonial proceedings, and also in relation to the rights of dependants upon a death.

i. Matrimonial Causes Act 1973, s.37. Section 37 protects a spouse from activities of the other spouse which may diminish the assets available for the purposes of financial relief under the Act. If the court is satisfied that one spouse is about to make a disposition[32] or transfer with the intention of depriving the applicant of financial relief, it may make such order as it thinks fit for the purpose of

---

[30] *ante*, p. 356.

[31] s.342, as amended by the Insolvency (No. 2) Act 1994.

[32] The wide definition in s.37(6) includes a trust, but not any provision made in a will.

protecting the applicant's claim.[33] Where the defendant spouse has made a disposition of property, other than one made for valuable consideration to a bona fide purchaser without notice of any intention to defeat the applicant's claim,[34] the disposition may be set aside.[35]

The intention to defeat the applicant's claim must be affirmatively proved, except in cases where the disposition was made within three years before the date of the application, in which case there is a statutory presumption[36] that the intention is to defeat the applicant's claim for financial relief.

ii. Inheritance (Provision for Family and Dependants) Act 1975.

A similar problem arises in connection with statutory schemes which restrict a person's powers of free disposal of his property by will, in order to provide for the surviving spouse and children and other dependants. This is an old problem; originally answered by the surviving spouse's right to dower or curtesy, and now governed by a wide variety of provisions (such as "forced heirship") in various parts of the world. A common solution is to give to the surviving spouse, and sometimes to children, a fractional share of the estate. The system in England and Wales is to give to the court a discretionary power to make an award to a surviving spouse and other dependants on the ground that the disposition of the deceased's estate (whether by will or intestacy) is not such as to make reasonable financial provision for the applicant.[37] But these schemes could be thwarted if a person who wished to deprive a widow and dependants could give away all his property before death.[38]

Provisions to deal with this problem are contained in sections 10–13 of the Act. In short, the court is given power to require a donee from the deceased to provide sums of money,[39] up to, but not in excess of, the value of the gift,[40] if the gift was made within six years before the death of the donor, and was made "with the intention of defeating an application for financial provision under this

---

[33] s.37(2)(*a*).
[34] Called a "reviewable disposition" and defined in s.37(4).
[35] See also *Lowson v. Coombes* [1999] Ch. 373; *ante*, p. 262.
[36] s.37(5); rebuttable, of course.
[37] s.2.
[38] See *Schaefer v. Schuhmann* [1972] A.C. 572. It is possible that such transfers could be set aside independently of any statutory provisions in a case of fraud. See *Cadogan v. Cadogan* [1977] 1 W.L.R. 1041.
[39] s.10(2); see also s.10(6), giving the factors which the court shall take into consideration.
[40] Valued, in the case of gifts other than cash, at the date of death of the decedent, or, if the property was disposed of by the donee, the value at the date of disposal.

Act."[41] Protection is given to persons who gave full valuable consideration for a transfer. The intention is to be determined on a balance of probabilities,[42] and need not be the sole intention of the donor in making the gift. Similar provisions in section 11 deal with contracts to leave property by will; and transfers to trustees in section 13.

---

[41] s.10(2).
[42] s.12.

CHAPTER 14

NON-CHARITABLE PURPOSE TRUSTS

1. THE GENERAL PROBLEM

A. Private Trusts, Purpose Trusts, Charitable Trusts

A private trust is essentially a trust in favour of ascertainable individuals. A charitable trust is a trust for purposes which are treated in law as charitable. The question for consideration in this chapter is whether or not it is possible to establish a trust for non-charitable purposes.

We have considered in earlier chapters questions relating to the setting up of trusts for individuals. Charitable trusts are dealt with in Chapter 15. For the present purpose, it will be sufficient to state that charitable purposes are grouped into four categories: trusts for the relief of poverty, trusts for the advancement of religion, trusts for the advancement of education, and trusts for other purposes beneficial to the community. The purpose trusts at present under consideration are those which do not come within these categories. A trust, for example, to provide a cup for a yacht race,[1] to feed the testator's horses and hounds,[2] to set up a monument,[3] or to be applied for useful or benevolent purposes.[4] There is no question of any such trusts having any privilege in relation to taxation or to perpetuity, such as is allowed in the case of charitable trusts. The question is whether they are valid or void.[5]

B. Trusts for Persons and Purposes

With any particular trust, there may be a question of construction to determine whether the trust is for persons or for purposes. Most purposes affect persons, and there is no reason why a trust should not be treated as a trust for persons where the beneficiaries are to be benefited in some way other than by payment of money. Thus, a trust for the education of the children of X can be construed as a trust of which the children of X are the beneficiaries.[6] A trust for the promotion of fox-hunting would be treated as a trust for a purpose, although it might be said that the individual sportsman might benefit from it.[7]

There are various examples of trusts in which the beneficiaries enjoy only a limited proprietary interest. Where, for example, a debtor assigns an asset to trustees for the payment of his debts, his creditors do not, unless there has been an absolute assignment, take any surplus.[8] In *Re the Trusts of Abbott Fund*[9] it was accepted that a trust for the maintenance of two old ladies was valid although it seems that they did not become owners of any proprietary interest. In *Re Gillingham Bus Disaster Fund*[10] a fund collected for the benefit of injured cadets was not invalid although there was no suggestion that the cadets could ever have claimed the assets of the fund. It may be possible to support these latter decisions as examples of discretionary trusts for the benefit of individuals; but they were not so drafted, and it may be preferable to regard them as examples of trusts for persons to be benefited in a particular way.

---

[1] *Re Nottage* [1895] 2 Ch. 649.

[2] *Re Dean* (1889) 41 Ch.D. 554.

[3] *Mussett v. Bingle* [1876] W.N. 170; *Re Endacott* [1960] Ch. 232.

[4] *Morice v. Bishop of Durham* (1804) 9 Ves.Jr. 399.

[5] See generally (1953) 17 Conv.(N.S.) 46 (L. Sheridan); (1953) 6 C.L.P. 151 (O. Marshall); Morris and Leach, Chap. 12; Maudsley, *The Modern Law of Perpetuities*, pp. 166–178 (1970) 34 Conv.(N.S.) 77 (P. Lovell); (1973) 37 Conv.(N.S.) 420 (L. McKay); (1971) 87 L.Q.R. 31 (J. Harris); (1977) 40 M.L.R. 397 (N. Gravells); (1977) 41 Conv.(N.S.) 179 (K. Widdows); *Trends in Contemporary Trust Law* (ed. A. Oakley), Chap. 1 (P. Matthews).

[6] See [1968] A.S.C.L. at 439 (J. Davies). See also *Re Osoba* [1979] 1 W.L.R. 247, *ante* p. 244.

[7] *Re Thompson* [1934] Ch. 342, *post*, p. 371.

[8] *Re Rissik* [1936] Ch. 68.

[9] [1900] 2 Ch. 326, *ante*, p. 244; contrast *Re Andrew's Trust* [1905] 2 Ch. 48; *Re Foord* [1922] 2 Ch. 599; *ante*, pp. 55, 244.

[10] [1959] Ch. 62, *ante*, p. 242. The residue for "worthy causes" was void for uncertainty.

The proper analysis of trusts of this kind was little discussed until the decision of Goff J. in *Re Denley's Trust Deed* in 1969.[11]

> A plot of land was conveyed to trustees to hold, for a period determined by lives, "for the purpose of a recreation or sports ground primarily for the benefit of the employees of the company and secondarily for the benefit of such other person or persons (if any) as the trustees may allow."

Goff J. upheld the trust as one for the benefit of the employees. They were ascertainable, and the trust was one which the court could control. If it had been construed as a trust for non-charitable purposes, it would have been void. "The objection [to non-charitable purpose trusts] is not that the trust is for a purpose or an object per se, but that there is no beneficiary or cestui que trust."[12] Here, however, "the trust deed expressly states that . . . the employees of the company shall be entitled to the use and enjoyment of the land."[13] He contrasted this situation with a "purpose . . . trust, the carrying out of which would benefit an individual or individuals, where that benefit is so indirect or intangible or which is otherwise so framed as not to give those persons any *locus standi* to apply to the court to enforce the trust"[14]; in which case the trust would have been a non-charitable purpose trust, and void.

The same line of reasoning was applied in *Re Lipinski's Will Trusts*,[15] a case of a gift to an unincorporated association.

> The testator bequeathed his residuary estate to trustees in trust as to one-half for the Hull Judeans (Maccabi) Association "in memory of my late wife to be used solely in the work of constructing the new buildings for the association and/or improvements to the said buildings."

At first sight, this would appear to be a gift to an unincorporated association to be applied for its (non-charitable) purposes.[16] We will see,[17] however, that gifts to unincorporated associations are normally upheld as gifts to the members rather than invalidated as

---

[11] [1969] 1 Ch. 373. See also *Wicks v. Firth* [1983] A.C. 214 (non-charitable trust to award scholarships assumed valid).

[12] [1969] 1 Ch. 373 at 383.

[13] *ibid.* at 383.

[14] *ibid.* at 382. For discussion of *locus standi* to enforce the *Re Denley* type of trust, see [1982] Conv. 118, at 124 (A. Everton).

[15] [1976] Ch. 235; (1977) 93 L.Q.R. 167; (1977) 41 Conv.(N.S.) 179 (K. Widdows); (1977) 40 M.L.R. 231 (N. Gravells); *Re Turkington* [1937] 4 All E.R. 501.

[16] In favour of this construction, counsel relied on the reference to the testator's late wife's memory as indicating an intention to create an endowment; and on a requirement that the money was to be used "solely" for the stated purposes.

[17] *post*, p. 377.

purpose trusts. To the extent that the testator's superadded purpose hindered this construction, *Re Denley's Trust Deed*[18] came to the rescue.

The beneficiaries, the members of the association, were ascertainable; there was no problem of perpetuity,[19] because they could, according to the rules of the association, terminate the trust for their own benefit.[20] The implication of these factors will be discussed later in the chapter.

These cases show a more liberal judicial tendency in connection with the construction of gifts of this type.[21] *Re Denley*, however, could not save the trust in *R. v. District Auditor, ex p. West Yorkshire Metropolitan County Council*,[22] where a local authority, purporting to act under statutory powers, resolved to create a trust "for the benefit of any or all or some of the inhabitants of the County of West Yorkshire" in any of four ways: (i) to assist economic development in the county in order to relieve unemployment and poverty; (ii) to assist bodies concerned with youth and community problems in West Yorkshire; (iii) to assist and encourage ethnic and minority groups in West Yorkshire; (iv) to inform all interested and influential persons of the consequences of the abolition (proposed by the Government) of the Council and other metropolitan county councils and of other proposals affecting local government in the county. The capital and income were to be applied within a short period, obviating any perpetuity problems, but the trust was void as a non-charitable purpose trust. It was not within the purpose trust exceptions illustrated by *Re Denley* and *Re Lipinski* because there were no "ascertained or ascertainable beneficiaries." Even if "inhabitant" was sufficiently certain, the class of 2,500,000 potential beneficiaries was so large that the trust was unworkable. It has never been established what certainty test applies to a *Re Denley* trust,[23] but this decision suggests that the class of beneficiaries, even if conceptually certain and not capricious, must not be too wide. A private trust which fails for "administrative unworkability"[24] cannot be rescued by the *Re Denley* principle.

It is necessary now to consider the objections to non-charitable purpose trusts.

---

[18] [1969] 1 Ch. 373.

[19] *post*, p. 367. *cf. Re Grant's W.T.* [1980] 1 W.L.R. 360, *post*, p. 376.

[20] By altering the constitution of the association. The beneficiaries in *Re Denley*, on the other hand, would seem to have no right to divide up the assets under the *Saunders v. Vautier* principle (*post*, p. 629), but no perpetuity problem arose because the trust was expressly confined to the perpetuity period.

[21] (1970) 34 Conv.(N.S.) 77 (P. Lovell); (1972) 87 L.Q.R. 31 (J. Harris).

[22] [1986] R.V.R. 24; (1986) 45 C.L.J. 391 (C. Harpum). The certainty aspects are discussed in Chap. 3, *ante*, p. 111.

[23] *ante*, p. 106.

[24] *ante*, p. 109.

2. Objections to Purpose Trusts

If a disposition is construed as a trust for non-charitable purposes, there are various objections which may be made to it. The first of these objections denies the possibility of existence of non-charitable purpose trusts. It has not however been consistently applied; and purpose trusts for the building of graves and monuments and the care of specific animals, which succeeded in the nineteenth century[25] are now regarded as anomalous exceptions to the rule.[26] The other objections accept the possibility of the existence of non-charitable purpose trusts, but impose restrictions upon them.

Before examining the objections, it should be said that a case may be made out that English law does not prohibit non-charitable purpose trusts.[27] Such trusts were regularly permitted before the twentieth century, but a wrong turning was taken in cases such as *Re Endacott*,[28] where the supposed rule was "invented". Many of the cases commonly cited as supporting the invalidity of purpose trusts were in fact based on uncertainty, perpetuity or some other defect. Indeed, the trust in *Morice v. Bishop of Durham*[29] failed for uncertainty. Trusts for beneficiaries do not fail if there is no current beneficiary (for example, where they are unborn); the real point is that the trustees are accountable not to the beneficiaries but to the court. Nevertheless, the rule against non-charitable purpose trusts has become so entrenched that it is unlikely that the contrary view will prevail unless legislation intervenes.

A. The Beneficiary Principle; Enforceability

The first objection may be seen in a celebrated dictum of Sir William Grant M.R. in *Morice v. Bishop of Durham*.[30] "Every other [*i.e.* non-charitable] trust must have a definite object. There must be somebody in whose favour the court can decree performance."[31] A trust, as we have seen, is an obligation. The objection is that there cannot be an obligation upon the trustees unless there is a correlative right in someone else to enforce it. With charitable trusts, the Attorney-General is charged with the duty of enforcement.[32] With private trusts, no public official is involved. The trust is void unless there are human beneficiaries capable of enforcing the trust. In

---

[25] *post*, p. 368.
[26] *per* Roxburgh J. in *Re Astor's S.T.* [1952] Ch. 534 at 547.
[27] Baxendale-Walker, *Purpose Trusts*.
[28] [1960] Ch. 232; *post*, p. 369.
[29] *infra*.
[30] (1804) 9 Ves.Jr. 399.
[31] *ibid*. at 404.
[32] There is evidence that historically charitable trusts were enforced by individuals; Baxendale-Walker, *Purpose Trusts*.

effect the objection is that there is no beneficial owner of the property. Acceptance of this principle renders non-charitable purpose trusts totally void.

B. Uncertainty

If non-charitable purpose trusts are recognised at all by the law, they are only valid if the purposes are expressed with sufficient certainty to enable the court to control the performance of the trust. The point commonly arises in the cases where incompetent draftsmanship has failed to create a charitable trust; where, for example, the property is to be applied for charitable or benevolent purposes,[33] or, as in *Morice v. Bishop of Durham*[34] for "such objects of benevolence and liberality as the Bishop of Durham in his own discretion shall most approve of." "Benevolence" and "liberality" are wider concepts than "charity," and the trust was not therefore applicable for charitable purposes only. The purposes were uncertain and the trust void. Indeed, this reason was more clearly emphasised by Sir William Grant M.R. than was the earlier objection. Having established that the trust was not for charitable purposes, and that the Bishop did not claim any personal benefit for himself, he said[35]:

> "That it is a trust, unless it be of a charitable nature, too indefinite to be executed by this Court, has not been, and cannot be denied. There can be no trust, over the exercise of which this Court will not assume a control; for an uncontrollable power of disposition would be ownership and not trust. If there be a clear trust, but for uncertain objects, the property, that is the subject of the trust, is indisposed of; and the benefit of such trust must result to those, to whom the law gives the ownership in default of disposition by the former owner. But this doctrine does not hold good with regard to trusts for charity. Every other trust must have a definite object. There must be somebody, in whose favour the Court can decree performance."

This objection can be met by specifying in sufficient detail the purposes to which the property is to be applied. Trusts for specific purposes like feeding the testator's animals, or maintaining a tomb or monument, usually pass this test. But general projects, even carefully drafted, are likely to be held void. The point only becomes significant, of course, if the problem of the beneficiary principle has been surmounted.

---

[33] *Blair v. Duncan* [1902] A.C. 37; *Houston v. Burns* [1918] A.C. 337; *Chichester Diocesan Fund and Board of Finance v. Simpson* [1944] A.C. 341; *Re Atkinson's Will Trusts* [1978] 1 W.L.R. 586.

[34] (1804) 9 Ves.Jr. 399.

[35] *ibid.* at 404–405.

C. Excessive Delegation of Testamentary Power

There have been judicial statements to the effect that purpose trusts created by will are void because, in the absence of anyone to enforce the trust, the trustees are left to determine the application of the property; thus "the testator has imperfectly exercised his testamentary power; he has delegated it, for the disposal of his property lies with them, not with him."[36] The objection is not relevant to non-testamentary trusts. Of the trust in *Re Denley's Trust Deed*, Goff J. said[37]: "If this were a will, a question might arise whether this provision might be open to attack as a delegation of the testamentary power. I do not say that would be so, but in any case it cannot be said of a settlement inter vivos." The status of the objection was, however, not established, even with wills. Special, general and intermediate powers are permitted in wills[38]; and "an anti-delegation rule is really an anti-power rule."[39]

In *Re Beatty's Will Trusts*[40] Hoffmann J., upholding a testamentary disposition to trustees to allocate "to or among such person or persons as they think fit", rejected the supposed "anti-delegation" rule. Thus there is no objection on this basis to the validity of purpose trusts. Moreover, the acceptance of the validity of testamentary powers is significant. For one way, as will be seen,[41] of effecting a non-charitable purpose where there are willing trustees, may be to give them *power* to perform, and not attempt to require them to do so.

D. Perpetuity

A charitable trust may last for ever; a non-charitable trust is void if it is to continue beyond the perpetuity period.[42] The reason is that perpetual non-charitable purpose trusts would conflict with the *policy* of the perpetuity rule, which is the prevention of the tying up of property for too long a period.

In its more usual context the rule against perpetuities deals with the limit of time to which the vesting of future interests may be postponed. An outline of this has already been given.[43] In the present context, however, we are not concerned with future vesting. We

---

[36] *Leahy v. Att.-Gen. for New South Wales* [1959] A.C. 457 at 484; *Re Wood* [1949] Ch. 498 at 501.
[37] [1969] 1 Ch. 373 at 387.
[38] *Re Park* [1932] 1 Ch. 580; *Re Abraham's W.T.* [1969] 1 Ch. 463; *Re Gulbenkian's Settlements* [1970] A.C. 508; *Re Manisty's Settlement* [1974] Ch. 17; *Re Hay's Settlement Trusts* [1982] 1 W.L.R. 202.
[39] (1953) 69 L.Q.R. 334 at 342 (D. Gordon).
[40] [1990] 1 W.L.R. 503; [1991] Conv. 138 (J. Martin).
[41] *post*, p. 386.
[42] Most pension trusts are exempted; *post*, p. 490.
[43] *ante*, Chap. 13.

are concerned with a situation in which the property is vested in the trustees to be applied by them for certain non-charitable purposes for a period which may exceed that of perpetuity. This situation will arise if either the capital or the income of the fund is to be so applied. If the trust relates to income, then the capital must be maintained in order to produce the income. It is no answer to say that, since the trustees may sell the present investments and purchase others, the capital is not inalienable. The objection relates, not only to alienability, but to duration. Whatever happens to individual investments, an obligation to retain the capital as a fund for an excessive period violates the rule. Accordingly, a non-charitable purpose trust is valid, if at all, only if it is confined to the perpetuity period. The matter is examined below.[44]

3. Exceptional Cases Upholding Purpose Trusts[45]

Until *Re Astor's Settlement Trusts*[46] in 1952, it was arguable that it was possible to establish a trust for a non-charitable purpose for the period of perpetuity. The authorities cover a narrow field, being nearly all concerned with trusts for building or maintaining monuments or tombs, or for caring for the testator's animals. But the language of the judgments is general, and there are occasional cases outside those fields. As will be seen, *Re Astor's Settlement Trusts*[47] underlined the beneficiary principle; and it is clear now that trusts for non-charitable purposes will fail unless they are kept strictly within the narrow confines of these exceptional cases.

A. Tombs and Monuments

Reasonable provision for the building of a tomb or a gravestone for a testator may be regarded as a funeral expense, and valid independently of any doctrine relating to purpose trusts.[48] But bequests for family burial enclosures have been upheld as purpose trusts[49]; as have bequests for monuments to other people, such as the testator's wife's first husband.[50] Such a gift may be for the building of the monument which, it seems, may be assumed to be done within the

---

[44] *post*, p. 380.
[45] Morris and Leach (*op. cit.*), pp. 310–319; Maudsley, *The Modern Law of Perpetuities*, pp. 168–176.
[46] [1952] Ch. 534; *post*, p. 372.
[47] *Supra*.
[48] *Trimmer v. Danby* (1856) 25 L.J.Ch. 424. Gray thought that it was the only justification for upholding such trusts: *The Rule Against Perpetuities*, pp. 310–311.
[49] *Pirbright v. Salwey* [1896] W.N. 86; *Re Hooper* [1932] 1 Ch. 38.
[50] *Mussett v. Bingle* [1876] W.N. 170.

period of perpetuity[51]; or for the care or the maintenance of the graves for a period limited to the period of perpetuity. An example is *Re Hooper*,[52] where

> A testator gave a sum of money to trustees for the care and upkeep of certain family graves and monuments, and a tablet in a window in a church so far as the trustees could legally do so. Maugham J. upheld the gift for a period of 21 years.[53]
>
> Similarly, in *Mussett v. Bingle*,[54] Hall V.-C. held that since the executors were ready to carry out a bequest of £300 to erect a monument to the testator's wife's first husband, "it must be performed accordingly." But he held void for perpetuity a further gift for its upkeep.

Such trusts must of course comply with the requirement of certainty. In *Re Endacott*,[55] the Court of Appeal held void a residuary gift amounting to some £20,000 "to the North Tawton Devon Parish Council for the purpose of providing some useful memorial to myself." Such a trust, though specific in the sense that it indicated a purpose capable of expression, was "of far too wide and uncertain a nature to qualify within the class of cases cited."[56] No doubt was cast upon *Re Hooper*[57] and the early cases. Yet *Re Endacott*[58] may illustrate the stricter modern approach to purpose trusts; or perhaps it indicates the willingness of the court to allow reasonable sums to be spent upon these purposes, and a reluctance to uphold such grandiose schemes. This policy, as will be seen, is articulated in *Re Astor*.[59] The Parish Councils and Burial Authorities (Miscellaneous Provisions) Act 1970, s.1, now provides that a burial authority or a local authority may agree by contract to maintain a grave, or memorial or monument for a period not exceeding 99 years.

B. Animals

Gifts for the care of specific animals, though not charitable, have also been upheld. There was no argument on the point in *Pettingall v. Pettingall*[60] where an annuity of £50 to be applied in maintaining

---

[51] *post*, p. 380.
[52] [1932] 1 Ch. 38.
[53] Relying on *Pirbright v. Salwey* [1896] W.N. 86.
[54] [1876] W.N. 170. See also *Trimmer v. Danby* (1856) 25 L.J.Ch. 424.
[55] [1960] Ch. 232.
[56] *ibid.* at 247.
[57] [1932] 1 Ch. 38.
[58] [1960] Ch. 232.
[59] [1952] Ch. 534.
[60] (1842) 11 L.J.Ch. 176.

the testator's favourite black mare was held valid. In *Re Dean*,[61] the leading case, North J., relying on *Mitford v. Reynolds*[62] and the monument cases, upheld a gift of £750 per annum for the period of 50 years for the maintenance of the testator's horses and hounds if they should so long live. He met head-on the argument that the court will not recognise a trust unless it is capable of being enforced by someone, by pronouncing: "I do not assent to that view."[63] There was no objection to such a provision "provided, of course, that it is not to last for too long a period."[64] It is difficult to see how the gift could be upheld for a 50-year period; for the horses and hounds could not be the measuring lives for the period of perpetuity. This aspect of the matter is discussed below.[65] The case has been accepted as authority for the proposition that trusts for the upkeep of specific animals are valid for the perpetuity period; and it is believed that this exception to the general rule has been relied on in countless cases since *Re Dean*.[66]

A possible difficulty, it has been suggested,[67] is that the fund might be claimed by the person who now owns the animal (*e.g.* as specific or residuary legatee). A fund to maintain another's property can be claimed by that other without applying it to the purpose.[68] Another solution might be to give the fund to the person acquiring the animal on the testator's death, determinable on the death of the animal or on the trustee's decision that it is improperly maintained.[69]

C. Other Purposes

Trusts for other purposes have on occasion been upheld; and others which have failed have been refused on the ground of perpetuity, without any indication that they would not have been valid if confined to the permitted period.

Trusts for the saying of masses for the benefit of private individuals have been considered to come into this category. Until the House of Lords decision in *Bourne v. Keane*, in 1919,[70] such trusts were regarded as being trusts for superstitious uses and void. *Bourne v. Keane* held them valid. Such trusts have now been upheld as

---

[61] (1889) 41 Ch.D. 552.
[62] (1848) 16 Sim. 105.
[63] (1889) 41 Ch.D. 552 at 556.
[64] *ibid.* at 557.
[65] *post*, p. 381.
[66] (1889) 41 Ch.D. 552.
[67] (1983) 80 L.S.Gaz. 2451 (P. Matthews).
[68] *Re Bowes* [1896] 1 Ch. 507 (money directed to be laid out in planting trees on an estate belonged to the owners of the estate absolutely.) See also *Re Lipinski's Will Trusts* [1976] Ch. 235.
[69] See Matthews, *op. cit.*, discussing other possibilities.
[70] [1919] A.C. 815.

charitable in *Re Hetherington*[71] where the masses are said in public. Even where the masses are said in private, the trust is arguably charitable on the basis that public benefit can be found in the endowment of the priesthood. The acceptance of such trusts as charitable makes it unnecessary to consider them in the category of private purpose trusts.

One possible member of this category of miscellaneous purpose trusts is a trust for non-Christian private ceremonies. In *Re Khoo Cheng Teow*,[72] the Supreme Court of the Straits Settlements held valid a gift to be applied for the period of perpetuity in the performance of ceremonies called Sin Chew to perpetuate the testator's memory. The gift was not charitable; but the Court held that it was valid for a period measured by royal lives plus 21 years.

A decision which has perhaps been elevated to a position of importance which it does not merit is *Re Thompson*[73]:

> An alumnus of Trinity Hall, Cambridge, bequeathed a legacy to one Lloyd, an old friend, to be applied in such manner as he should think fit towards the promotion and furtherance of fox-hunting, and gave the residuary estate to Trinity Hall. Lloyd made no claim to any beneficial interest, but desired to carry out the testator's wishes if he should be permitted to do so. Trinity Hall also was anxious that the trust should be performed; but felt it its duty, as a charity, to submit that the trust was void for lack of a beneficiary. There was no problem of perpetuity, and Clauson J. held that the purpose was sufficiently certain. He upheld the gift by ordering the money to be paid to Lloyd upon his giving an undertaking to apply it for these stated objects, and gave to Trinity Hall liberty to apply if the money should be used for other purposes.

The case is one of very limited significance. It does not, as some have claimed,[74] provide a solution to the beneficiary problem, by holding that the party entitled in default can enforce a purpose trust. Enforcement is contrary to the interest of the party entitled in default; he is interested to restrain misapplication, which is a very different matter. In *Re Thompson*,[75] there was no contest, as all parties desired enforcement. The case was only litigated because Trinity Hall, as a charity, could not, without the court's approval, forgo its strict legal claim to the property.

---

[71] [1990] Ch. 1; [1989] Conv. 453 (N. Parry); *post*, p. 435. See also *Re Caus* [1934] Ch. 162.
[72] [1932] Straits Settlements L.R. 226.
[73] [1934] Ch. 342.
[74] See Roxburgh J. in *Re Astor's S.T.* [1952] Ch. 534 at 543.
[75] *supra*.

4. THE FAILURE OF THE ASTOR TRUST[76]

Modern decisions have made clear that this line of cases will not be extended.[77] They are regarded as "concessions to human weakness or sentiment,"[78] troublesome, anomalous and aberrant,"[79] and as "occasions when Homer has nodded."[80] Purpose trusts generally have failed under the beneficiary principle, and on the ground of uncertainty. In these circumstances, compliance with the perpetuity rule is no escape.

In *Re Astor's Settlement Trusts*,[81] a lifetime settlement was made in 1945, expressly limited to a period of lives in being plus 21 years, under which the trustees were to hold a fund upon various trusts for non-charitable purposes, including "the main-tenance of good relations between nations . . . the preservation of the independence of the newspapers," and other similar purposes in favour of independent newspapers. Roxburgh J. held the trust void; both because there was no one who could enforce the trust, and also on the ground of uncertainty.

Re Shaw[82] concerned the will of George Bernard Shaw, which provided that the residue of the estate should be applied to re-search the utility of the development of a 40-letter British alpha-bet in the place of the present one, and for the translation of his play "Androcles and the Lion" into the new alphabet. Harman J. held that the trust was not charitable, and that it failed on the beneficiary principle. The trustees were willing to carry out the testator's wishes if they were permitted to do so. But "I am not at liberty to validate this trust by treating it as a power. A valid power is not to be spelled out of an invalid trust."[83]

These cases show the current trend in situations where the gift is construed as a gift for purposes. The insistence upon an ascertained beneficiary reflects the analysis of the law of trusts before the days when discretionary trusts became common. We have seen that a beneficiary under a discretionary trust is not entitled to specific property; only to a limited right to be considered. It has been argued that *McPhail v. Doulton*[84] manifests a basic change in the conceptual

---

[76] (1953) 6 C.L.P. 151 (O. Marshall); (1953) 17 Conv.(N.S.) 46 (L. Sheridan); (1955) 18 M.L.R. 120 (L. Leigh).

[77] *Re Endacott* [1960] 2 Ch. 232 at 246.

[78] *Re Astor's S.T.* [1952] Ch. 534 at 547.

[79] *Re Endacott, supra,* at 251.

[80] *ibid.* at 250.

[81] [1952] Ch. 534.

[82] [1957] 1 W.L.R. 729.

[83] *ibid.* at 731, relying on *I.R.C. v. Broadway Cottages Trust* [1955] Ch. 20 at 36.

[84] [1971] A.C. 424; *ante,* p. 104.

development of the law of trusts. "It has broken the stranglehold imposed on the development of trusts ... by a rigid conception of a framework of fixed equitable interests and correlatively narrow obligations ... it does not take much crystal-ball gazing to see the impact this extension will have on all the old sterile purpose trust and unincorporated association debates."[85]

5. UNINCORPORATED ASSOCIATIONS

An unincorporated association exists where two or more persons are bound together for one or more common purposes by mutual undertakings, each having mutual duties and obligations, in an organisation which has rules identifying in whom control of the organisation and its funds is vested, and which can be joined or left at will.[86]

Special problems arise in connection with the holding of property by unincorporated associations.[87] An unincorporated association is not a legal person, and, with the exception of trade unions,[88] cannot be the owner of property or the subject of legal rights and duties.[89] The question we will consider here is the effect of gifts to such associations, and the various ways in which their property is held. The latter is determined by the terms of the gift or by the constitution or rules of the association. The question of entitlement to the funds on the dissolution of the association is dealt with elsewhere.[90]

A. Charitable Purposes

The assets of an unincorporated association may be held upon charitable trusts. For example, a society for the relief of the poor. A charitable trust is valid even though it is a purpose trust; the usual rules of certainty of objects do not apply; it may continue for ever; and it enjoys a number of tax privileges.

---

[85] (1974) 37 M.L.R. 643 at 655–656 (Y. Grbich); (1972) 89 L.Q.R. 31 (J. Harris); [1970] A.S.C.L. 189 (J. Davies).

[86] *Conservative and Unionist Central Office v. Burrell (Inspector of Taxes)* [1982] 1 W.L.R. 522. (The definition was for tax purposes, but seems to be of general application). See [1983] Conv. 150 (P. Creighton), doubting the last requirements; (1996) 49 C.L.P. 187 (R. Rideout).

[87] See Warburton, *Unincorporated Associations: Law and Practice* (2nd ed.), Chap. 5.

[88] Trade Union and Labour Relations (Consolidation) Act 1992, s.10.

[89] Halsbury (4th ed.), Vol. 7, p. 11. It is otherwise in the context of tax; *Worthing Rugby Football Club Trustees v. I.R.C.* [1987] 1 W.L.R. 1057.

[90] *ante*, pp. 244 *et seq.*

B. Non-Charitable Purposes

We have seen that, generally speaking, trusts for the promotion of non-charitable purposes are void. Hence gifts to non-charitable unincorporated associations will fail if construed as purpose trusts. But such a result may be avoided if it is possible to regard the gift as in favour of the members, as described below. Such a construction may be adopted even where the donor has expressly stated that his gift is for particular non-charitable purposes.[91]

C. Property Held on Trust for the Members

The property of an unincorporated association may be held on trust for the members of the association, and not for its purposes. Such a trust must comply with the usual rules for the creation of a trust. There must be an intention to create a trust, and there must be ascertainable beneficiaries. This will often be made clear by the terms of the constitution of the society; or, in the case of societies governed by statute, such as friendly societies, by the terms of the statute governing them. The Friendly Societies Act 1974, s.54(1) provides that the property of an unincorporated friendly society shall vest in the trustees for the time being of the society, for the use and benefit of the society and the members thereof.[92] It was at one time thought that there was no need to identify the beneficiaries of property held by unincorporated associations; and that a gift to persons holding the property as trustees was good so long as the trustees had power to spend the capital. A society could then dispose of any of its assets at any time; there would be no more tendency to inalienability than in the case of an individual holding property, and, it was argued, no reason for invalidating it. Thus, in *Re Drummond*,[93] a gift was made to the Old Bradfordians Club, London, to be utilised as the committee should think best in the interests of the club or school. Eve J. upheld the gift. It was not, he said, a gift to the members, but the committee was free to spend the money as it thought fit on the specified objects. It did not tend to a perpetuity, and was valid.

If the trustees could spend only the income however—if, in other words, the capital was tied up as an endowment—the trusts on which the assets were held would be perpetual and void. This view,

---

[91] *Re Lipinski's Will Trusts* [1976] Ch. 235, *ante*, p. 363.

[92] See *Re Bucks Constabulary Fund (No. 2)* [1979] 1 W.L.R. 937. The Friendly Societies Act 1992 provides for the incorporation of such societies carrying on mutual insurance business.

[93] [1914] 2 Ch. 90; *Re Price* [1943] Ch. 422 ("To the Anthroposophical Society of Great Britain to be used at the discretion of the Chairman and Executive Council of the Society for carrying out the teaching of the founder Dr. Rudolf Steiner."); (1937) 53 L.Q.R. 24 at 46 (W. Hart).

which appeared to have been approved by the House of Lords,[94] dealt, however, only with the perpetuity aspect of the problem. It ignored the necessity to analyse the property interests which were created.

In *Leahy v. Att.-Gen. for New South Wales*,[95] a testator provided that Elmslea, a sheep station of some 730 acres, should be held upon trust for "such order of nuns of the Catholic Church or the Christian Brothers as my executors and trustees shall select." The gift was not valid as a charitable trust because some of the orders were purely contemplative orders which are not charitable in law.[96]

Nor was it valid as a private trust. In view of the nature of the property and the fact that the members of the selected orders might be very numerous and spread across the world, there was no intention to create a trust in favour of the individual members of selected orders.[97] The testator's intention clearly was to establish an endowment. The gift would have failed if it had not been rescued by a statute of New South Wales which permitted partly charitable trusts to be applied wholly in favour of those parts which were charitable. The trustees' power of selection did not therefore extend to contemplative orders.

Other modern cases, however, have shown a "retreat from *Leahy*"[98] and have found a different construction, enabling the gift to be held valid as being a trust for the members of the association.[99] This has even proved possible, applying the principle of *Re Denley's Trust Deed*,[1] where the donor has stated that his gift is to be applied for specific non-charitable purposes.[2] The position was analysed in *Neville Estates v. Madden*,[3] where Cross J. held that the property interests of the members of an association would fall into one of three categories. There might be a gift to the members at the relevant date as joint tenants, giving each a right of severance of his part; or

---

[94] *Macaulay v. O'Donnell*, July 10, 1933; reported at [1943] Ch. 435n.; *Carne v. Long* (1860) 2 De G.F. & J. 75.

[95] [1959] A.C. 457.

[96] *Gilmour v. Coats* [1949] A.C. 426; *post*, p. 433.

[97] [1959] A.C. 457 at p. 486; *cf. Re Smith* [1914] 1 Ch. 937, where a bequest to the Society of Franciscan Friars of Clevedon County, Somerset was construed as a gift to the members of the community at the date of the testator's death; *Cocks v. Manners* (1871) L.R. 12 Eq. 574 (a share of residue to the "Dominican Convent of Carisbrooke payable to the Superior for the time being").

[98] (1977) 41 Conv.(N.S.) 139 (F. Crane).

[99] (1977) 41 Conv.(N.S.) 179 (K. Widdows); (1980) 39 C.L.J. 88 (C. Rickett); [1985] Conv. 318 (J. Warburton).

[1] [1969] 1 Ch. 373, *ante*, p. 363. This did not involve an unincorporated association, but the reasoning is applicable to gifts to such associations.

[2] *Re Lipinski's Will Trusts* [1976] Ch. 235, *ante*, p. 363.

[3] [1962] Ch. 832 at 849; *Re Recher's W.T.* [1972] Ch. 526 at 538, *post*, p. 378.

a gift subject to the contractual rights and liabilities of the members towards each other, which prevent severance and cause a member's interest, on his death or resignation, to accrue to the remaining members; or a gift to present and future members, in which case the gift, unless confined to the perpetuity period, would be void. A fourth possibility is that this situation creates a specialised form of co-ownership, whose rules should be worked out separately, and independently of the law of trusts.[4] All these possible solutions fail to explain how the equitable interest of a member passes on his resignation without compliance with Law of Property Act 1925, s.53(1)(*c*).[5]

Gifts to unincorporated associations can involve perpetuity problems of two distinct kinds, relating to remoteness of vesting and perpetual duration. To avoid both problems, the trust must be for the benefit of members who are both ascertainable during the perpetuity period and also able to claim a division of the funds before that period expires. If the members are not so ascertainable, the trust will fail, subject to what is said below, for remoteness of vesting. If the capital is to be retained as an endowment, the trust will be void as a perpetual trust.[6]

Cross J. in *Neville Estates v. Madden*[7] referred to the problem of remoteness of vesting in his third category (gift to present and future members). This problem has been resolved by the Perpetuities and Accumulations Act 1964, which excludes from the gift any members not ascertainable within the perpetuity period.[8] The 1964 Act does not remove the problem of perpetual duration (inalienability). The gift will fail if "there is something in its terms or circumstances or in the rules of the association which precludes the members at any time from dividing the subject of the gift between them on the footing that they are solely entitled in equity".[9] This aspect of the perpetuity rule caused the gift to fail in *Re Grant's Will Trusts*.[10] The trust was for the purposes of the Chertsey Labour Party Headquarters, which were not charitable. The members of this local association did not control the property, nor could they change the rules of the association and thereby gain control, because the rules were subject to the approval of, and capable of alteration by, an outside body (the National Executive Committee). Although it

---

[4] Ford, *Unincorporated Non-Profit Associations*, Part 1, especially at pp. 5–8, 21–23.
[5] Morris and Leach, pp. 313–318; [1971] A.S.C.L. at 379 (J. Hackney). The *Re Denley* approach (*ante*, p. 363), whereby the beneficiary has no proprietary interest, does not encounter these difficulties.
[6] *Carne v. Long* (1860) 2 De G.F. & J. 75.
[7] *supra.*
[8] s.4(4). The Act applies to dispositions made after July 15, 1964.
[9] *Re Lipinski's Will Trusts, supra,* at p. 244, quoting the summary of Cross J.'s categories in *Tudor on Charities* (6th ed., 1967), p. 150.
[10] [1980] 1 W.L.R. 360; (1980) 43 M.L.R. 459 (B. Green); [1980] Conv. 80 (G. Shindler).

seems that a way around this problem could have been found,[11] the trust was held void for perpetuity, even though the restriction on disposing of the capital was not one imposed by the testator.

D. Ownership by Members on Contractual Basis

The contractual analysis provides a method by which unincorporated associations can validly hold property without the necessity of discovering an intention to create a trust, and by which gifts to the association, in order to escape invalidity as purpose trusts, need not be regarded as taking effect as immediate distributive shares in favour of the members, which is unlikely to have been the donor's intention. Members of an association can "band themselves together as an association or society, pay subscriptions and validly devote their funds in pursuit of some lawful non-charitable purpose. An obvious example is a members' social club"[12]—where it would in most cases be difficult to find an intention to create a trust. Their assets, whether donations or members' subscriptions, are held by the trustees or by the committee or officers of the club on the terms of the constitution or rules of the club, which are themselves a contract by the members with each other. A trust is interposed simply because it is normally inconvenient (and impossible in the case of land) for the assets to be vested in all the members. This is a bare trust and does not detract from the contractual analysis.

This solution avoids some of the difficulties which arise from an analysis which regards the members as beneficiaries under a private trust. The members' rights are contractual, and of course they depend upon the rules of the association. A member will not usually be able to claim his share at any time; but the members as a whole control the committee's activities in accordance with the rules, and can usually take the decision to wind up the association and share out the proceeds. A member's rights terminate on death or resignation, and a new member obtains rights in relation to the assets during his period of membership. Questions concerning the contractual rights of members usually arise on the termination of an association, as we have seen.[13]

The fact that the assets are held by the members on a contractual basis of course does not prejudge the construction of a gift by a third

---

[11] See Heydon, Gummow and Austin, *Cases and Materials on Equity and Trusts* (4th ed.), p. 595, suggesting that control by the outside body was not as significant as the case suggests. The beneficiaries could be treated as including the members of that body also. Another possibility is that the members could disaffiliate from the national body. See also *News Group Newspapers Ltd v. SOGAT 82* [1986] I.C.R. 716, where *Re Grant* was distinguished because the members of a local branch of a trade union had control over the branch assets and could in theory secede from the union and divide the assets.

[12] *Re Recher's W.T.* [1972] Ch. 526 at 538, *per* Brightman J.

[13] *ante*, p. 247.

party to the association. But the court will lean in favour of validity, and is likely to regard such a gift as an accretion to the funds of the association. In *Re Recher's Will Trust*[14] there was a gift in trust for "The London and Provincial Anti-Vivisection Society." Brightman J. held that the assets of the society were owned by the members in accordance with the rules. "There is no private trust or trust for charitable purposes or other trust to hinder the process."[15] If it was correct that a gift to such an association must be construed as a (void) purpose trust or as distributive shares in favour of the members, then it would be difficult to make a donation in favour of the body, which would contrary to common sense. The solution was that the gift could be construed as a beneficial gift in favour of the members, not so as to entitle them to an immediate distributive share, but as an accretion to the funds of the society subject to the contract of the members as set out in the rules. Such a construction was equally available whether the society existed to promote the interest of its members ("inward-looking") or, as in the present case, to promote some outside purpose ("outward-looking"). If the society had remained in existence, the gift would have been good. In fact, however, it had been dissolved before the date of the gift.

As has been pointed out,[16] the question whether a gift to an association is subject to any restriction on its use depends on the intention of the members as expressed in their contract with each other. Thus whether the gift is one to the members in severable shares or subject to the purposes of the association normally depends not on the donor's intention but on the rules of the association. To be valid, any restrictions imposed by the donor must infringe neither the beneficiary principle nor the perpetuity rule.[17]

6. MANDATE OR AGENCY

The principles described above apply to unincorporated associations, which have already been defined.[18] It may be that an organisation (which is not incorporated) fails to satisfy the requirements of an unincorporated association. This was the case in *Conservative and Unionist Central Office v. Burrell (Inspector of Taxes)*,[19] where

---

[14] [1972] Ch. 526; (1972) 35 Conv.(N.S.) 381; (1971) 8 M.U.L.R. 1 (P. Hogg); (1973) 47 A.L.J. 305. The "accretion to funds" solution is adopted by the Queensland Succession Act 1981, s.63. See also *Artistic Upholstery Ltd v. Art Forma (Furniture) Ltd* [1999] 4 All E.R. 277.

[15] [1972] Ch. 526 at 539; *Re Bucks Constabulary Fund (No. 2)* [1979] 1 W.L.R. 937.

[16] [1995] Conv. 302 (P. Matthews). See also [1998] Conv. 8 (S. Gardner).

[17] See *Re Lipinski's .Will Trusts* [1976] Ch. 235.

[18] *ante*, p. 373.

[19] [1982] 1 W.L.R. 522. See generally [1987] Conv. 415 (P. Smart).

the Crown claimed that the Conservative Party was an unincorporated association. If this were so, Central Office would be assessable to corporation tax, as opposed to income tax, on certain income. The Court of Appeal rejected the Crown's claim. The Party was an amorphous combination of various elements, but not an unincorporated association, because the members had no mutual rights and obligations, there were no rules governing control (which lay in the party leader), and no event in history could be identified as marking the creation of the party as an association.[20]

Of interest in the present context was the analysis of the legal effect of a contribution to such a body. Where the body was not an unincorporated association, the *Re Recher*[21] analysis could not apply. The legal basis was mandate or agency. The contributor gives the recipient (*e.g.* the treasurer) a mandate to use the gift in a particular way. He can demand its return unless the mandate becomes irrevocable, as when the gift is added to a mixed fund with the authority of the contributor. There is no trust, only the fiduciary element inherent in the relationship of principal and agent. Once the mandate has become irrevocable, the contributor's rights are to an account of expenditure, and to restrain a misapplication. Difficulties might arise where there was a change of the office-holder to whom the mandate was given. More seriously, the mandate theory could not explain the validity of bequests to such organisations, as agency cannot be set up at death. No solution to this problem was offered, the Court of Appeal being content to suggest that the answer was "not difficult to find."[22]

It remains to be seen whether the mandate theory will be applied in other situations.[23] In view of its limitations, especially with regard to testamentary gifts, this is perhaps doubtful.

Another possibility, which is related to the mandate idea, is to utilise the type of trust upheld by the House of Lords in *Barclays Bank Ltd v. Quistclose Investments Ltd*[24] as a means of achieving an abstract purpose trust.[25] In that case money was lent for a specific purpose (the payment of dividends), on the basis that it would be

---

[20] Convincingly criticised in [1983] Conv. 150 (P. Creighton); "It may be as misleading to deny the organisation its status as an unincorporated association because its origins are obscure as it would be to deny the existence of a living human being on the ground that his birth certificate could not be found."

[21] *ante*, p. 378.

[22] Perhaps referring to the principle of *Re Denley's Deed Trust* [1969] 1 Ch. 373, *ante*, p. 363, or to the fact that the testator may authorise his executors to give a mandate. See also [1983] Conv. 150 (P. Creighton); [1987] Conv. 415 (P. Smart).

[23] It was referred to in connection with members' subscriptions in *Re Recher's Will Trusts* [1972] Ch. 526 at 539. The reasoning might apply to cases such as *Re Gillingham Bus Disaster Fund* [1959] Ch. 62, *ante*, p. 362, involving public donations to non-charitable purposes.

[24] [1970] A.C. 567; *ante*, p. 52.

[25] Chambers, *Resulting Trusts*, p. 90. See also (1991) 107 L.Q.R. 608 (C. Rickett).

held for the lender if not applied to the purpose. It was held that the debtor took the money on trust to apply it for the purpose. As the purpose could no longer be carried out (because of the debtor's insolvency), the money was held on trust for the lender. It seems that the same reasoning would apply if the money was not a loan. The analysis is that the transferee acquires the full beneficial interest in the money, subject to the transferor's equitable right to prevent its use for anything other than the stipulated purpose. What is created is a restriction on the use of money, enforceable by the provider. So long as the purpose is not uncertain or contrary to public policy, it is a means of achieving an abstract purpose trust.

7. PERPETUITY

A. Excessive Duration[26]
It has been said that a non-charitable purpose trust, even though otherwise valid, is void if it may last beyond the period of perpetuity; this being a rule designed to produce an effect analogous to the rule controlling remoteness of vesting, and applying the same general policy. If, therefore, a purpose trust survives an attack under the beneficiary principle, it must be restricted to the period of perpetuity: "The rule against inalienability is, in reality, just one of the devices that is employed to keep the development of such trusts in check."[27]

In applying the rule against excessive duration, the courts have been more generous than in other aspects of perpetuity law. First, they have assumed that a monument will be erected within the period.

In *Mussett v. Bingle*,[28] a testator gave £300 to be applied in the erection of a monument to his wife's first husband, and £200 the interest on which was to be applied in maintaining it. The latter gift was perpetual and void. The former was upheld. In the absence of any objection on the ground of perpetuity, the court must have assumed that the monument would be erected within the period.

Secondly a trust will be upheld if the instrument provides that it is to continue "so long as the law allows" or some similar period.

---

[26] Morris and Leach, pp. 321–327; Maudsley, *The Modern Law of Perpetuities*, pp. 166–178.
[27] Law Com No. 251 (1998), *The Rules Against Perpetuities and Excessive Accumulations*, para. 1.14.
[28] [1876] W.N. 170.

The gift is good for 21 years.[29] If no such saving phrase is included, the trust is wholly void.[30] The court will not supply the necessary words to meet the testator's obvious intention. The wait and see principle does not apply to purpose trusts.[31] If it did, it would at least have solved this problem.

Thirdly, the courts have on various occasions taken judicial notice of the fact that an animal's life span is limited to 21 years. If the animal could not live that long, the trust could not endure beyond the period. Danckwerts J. in *Re Haines*[32] took judicial notice of the fact that a cat could not live for more than 21 years. Biologists have corrected him, showing that a cat may live for 25 years.[33] It seems that, if the courts are willing to take judicial notice of longevity, it should be permissible to take evidence of the age of the cats in question; for if the youngest cat is over four, the particular trust would not last for more than 21 years.

B. Human Lives Only

Perhaps North J. in *Re Dean*[34] should be taken to have applied some such doctrine. He upheld a gift of an annual sum for the period of 50 years if any of the testator's horses and hounds should so long live. The perpetuity point was not dealt with, and it seems almost as if the learned judge assumed that the life of an animal could be used as a measuring life for the purposes of the rule. The better doctrine however was provided by Meredith J. in *Re Kelly*[35]:

> "If the lives of dogs or other animals could be taken into account in reckoning the maximum period of 'lives in being and twenty-one years afterwards' any contingent or executory interest might be properly limited, so as only to vest within the lives of specified carp, or tortoises, or other animals that might live for over a hundred years, and for twenty-one years afterwards, which, of course, is absurd. 'Lives' means human lives. It was suggested that the last of the dogs could in fact not outlive the testator by more than twenty-one years. I know nothing of that. The court does not enter into the question of a dog's expectation of life. In point of fact neighbours' dogs and cats are unpleasantly long-lived; but I have no knowledge of their precise expectation of life.

---

[29] *Pirbright v. Salwey* [1896] W.N. 86; *Re Hooper* [1932] 1 Ch. 38.

[30] *contra, Re Budge* [1942] N.Z.L.R. 356, where a trust to apply the income in keeping a grave neat and tidy was held valid for 21 years. Morris and Leach, p. 322.

[31] s.15(4); *post*, p. 382; *cf.* New Zealand Perpetuities Act 1964; Maudsley, *The Modern Law of Perpetuities*, App. D.

[32] *The Times*, November 7, 1952.

[33] Morris and Leach, p. 323; Maudsley, *op. cit.* p. 170.

[34] (1889) 41 Ch.D. 552.

[35] [1932] I.R. 255 at 260–261.

Anyway the maximum period is exceeded by the lives of specified butterflies and twenty-one years afterwards. And even, according to my decision—and, I confess, it displays this weakness on being pressed to a logical conclusion—the expiration of the life of a single butterfly, even without the twenty-one years, would be too remote, despite all the world of poetry that may be thereby destroyed ... there can be no doubt that 'lives' means lives of human beings, not of animals or trees in California."

Re Dean[36] is unsupportable on this point. All other purpose trusts which may last beyond the period of perpetuity have been held void.

C. A Fixed Number of Years

As we are dealing here with a question of duration and not one of remoteness of vesting of beneficial interests, it would be much more convenient to have a perpetuity period which was gauged by a number of years, rather than one measured by lives. It is possible to argue that a court should hold that purpose trusts can last for 21 years only; for no purpose trust, with the exception of *Re Howard*,[37] when a parrot was to be fed during the lives of the survivor of two servants, has been upheld for any other or longer period. Yet a royal lives clause was not challenged in *Re Astor's Trusts*.[38] In *Re Moore*,[39] the objection was to the excessive number of lives chosen and not to the fact that lives were chosen, and in *Re Khoo Cheng Teow*,[40] the Supreme Court of the Straits Settlements has upheld a non-charitable purpose trust for the period of royal lives plus 21 years.

It was reasonable therefore to hope that the Perpetuities and Accumulations Act 1964 would provide for a fixed period of years. A restriction to a period of 21 years would have been welcome. The 80-year period would have been an improvement.[41] In fact the Act has left the period at lives plus 21 years.

Section 15(4) provides:

"Nothing in this Act shall affect the operation of the rule of law rendering void for remoteness certain dispositions under which property is limited to be applied for purposes other than the benefit of any person or class of persons in cases where the

---

[36] (1889) 41 Ch.D. 552.

[37] *The Times*, October 30, 1908. Law Com No. 251 (1998), *The Rules Against Perpetuities and Excessive Accumulations*, para. 8.35, confirms that the period is lives (if any) plus 21 years.

[38] [1952] Ch. 534.

[39] [1901] 1 Ch. 936.

[40] [1932] Straits Settlements Report 226.

[41] See Trusts (Guernsey) Law 1989 (100 years); Belize Trusts Act 1992 (120 years).

property may be so applied after the end of the perpetuity period."

Although the contrary is not unarguable,[42] it appears that the effect of this provision is that neither the 80-year period permitted by section 1 of the Act nor the "wait and see" rule of section 3 applies to purpose trusts.[43] Recent Law Commission proposals on the reform of the perpetuity rule, the general effect of which is to recommend the replacement of the common law period with a fixed period of 125 years, do not affect the rule against exclusive duration. This has been excluded from the scope of the Report on the ground that it belongs more properly in a reivew of non-charitable purpose trusts and unincorporated associations.[44]

8. Useless or Capricious Purposes

One question which has to be faced when considering whether, as a matter of policy, purpose trusts should be enforced is that of excluding trusts which are useless, wasteful, capricious, or even harmful or illegal. This aspect of the matter was in the mind of Roxburgh J. in *Re Astor's Trusts* when he said[45]: " . . . it is not possible to contemplate with equanimity the creation of large funds directed to non-charitable purposes which no court and no department of state can control, or in the case of maladministration reform." The question ultimately is that of the extent to which one person, usually deceased, should be allowed to deprive the community or individuals within it, of the beneficial use of capital.[46] The larger the amount, and the longer the period of application, the greater the problem. No attempt has been made to draw a precise line between those which are acceptable and those which are not. We will see that the greatest difficulty has been experienced in trying to draw a line between charitable and other trusts.[47] This does not augur well for the creation of a recognisable line between acceptable and non-acceptable non-charitable purpose trusts; but it is no reason for insisting on holding all non-charitable purpose trusts void. "The answer, of

---

[42] See Maudsley, *The Modern Law of Perpetuities*, p. 177; (1965) 29 Conv.(N.S.) 165 (J. Andrews). For the view that s.15(4) does not apply to purpose trusts within the principle of *Re Denley's Trust Deed* [1969] 1 Ch. 373, see Underhill and Hayton (15th ed.), p. 94; *Trends in Contemporary Trust Law* (ed. A. Oakley), pp. 12, 18 (P. Matthews).

[43] Law Com No. 251 (1998), *The Rules against Perpetuities and Excessive Accumulations*, para. 8.35.

[44] *ibid.*, para. 1.14.

[45] [1952] Ch. at p. 542.

[46] See Gardner, *An Introduction to the Law of Trusts*, pp. 210–211.

[47] *post*, Chap. 15.

course, is that the courts will have to strike down the silly purposes and uphold the sensible ones."[48]

In *Brown v. Burdett*,[49] the testator devised a freehold house to trustees upon trust to block up almost all the rooms of the house for a period of 20 years, and, subject thereto, to a devisee. Bacon V.-C. decided that he must "unseal" this "useless, undisposed of property," and declared that there was an intestacy as to the period of 20 years.

Scottish judges have been forthright in their disapproval of the waste of money on useless projects: "I consider that, if it is not unlawful, it ought to be unlawful, to dedicate by testamentary disposition, for all time, or for a length of time, the whole income of a large estate . . . to objects of no utility, private or public, objects which benefit nobody, and which have no other purpose or use than that of perpetuating at great cost, and in an absurd manner, the idiosyncrasies of an eccentric testator."[50] "The prospect of Scotland being dotted with monuments to obscure persons cumbered with trusts for the purpose of maintaining these monuments in all time coming, appears to me to be little less than appalling. . . . "[51]

9. ALTERNATIVE SOLUTIONS

It seems therefore that non-charitable purpose trusts are void under the beneficiary principle; that there are recognised exceptions in trusts for animals and monuments, which, to be valid, must be certain, not useless or capricious, and confined to the period of perpetuity; and that a trust may be upheld if, although expressed as a purpose trust, it is directly for the benefit of ascertainable individuals. Some take the view that this is too restricted a position. We now consider in what ways the effecting of a non-charitable purpose can be achieved.

A. By the Draftsman

i. Incorporation. A society may be incorporated to advance such purposes. The matter then leaves the law of trusts, and the problem

---

[48] (1959) 4 U. of W.A.L.R. at 239 (L. Sheridan).

[49] (1882) 21 Ch.D. 667; see also *McCaig v. University of Glasgow*, 1907 S.C. 231; *McCaig's Trustees v. Kirk-Session of United Free Church of Lismore*, 1915 S.C. 426 (bronze statues at £1,000 each); *Aitken v. Aitken*, 1927 S.C. 374 (massive bronze equestrian statue); *Mackintosh's Judicial Factor v. Lord Advocate*, 1935 S.C. 406 (erection of vault); *Lindsay's Executor v. Forsyth*, 1940 S.C. 568 (£1,000 on trust to provide a weekly supply of fresh flowers on the graves of my mother and my own).

[50] *McCaig v. University of Glasgow, supra*, at 242.

[51] *McCaig's Trustees v. Kirk-Session of United Free Church of Lismore, supra*, at 434.

here discussed disappears. This is the simplest practical solution.[52]

ii. Mandate or Agency. Consideration should also be given to the possibility of utilising the mandate or agency theory expounded in *Conservative and Unionist Central Office v. Burrell (Inspector of Taxes)*,[53] discussed in section 6, above. The principle could also be invoked in the case of gifts to unincorporated associations, although it is doubtful whether it has much to offer here, not least because it cannot be the basis of a testamentary gift.[54] Where this principle can be utilised, the matter then leaves the law of trusts, as in the case of incorporation. The problem of purpose trusts disappears, but other problems, as we have seen, take its place.

iii. Gift to Members of an Association and Not for Purposes Only. In *Re Lipinski's Will Trusts*,[55] Oliver J. emphasised the distinction between "the case where a purpose is prescribed which is clearly intended for the benefit of ascertained or ascertainable beneficiaries . . . and the case where no beneficiary at all is intended . . . or where the beneficiaries are unascertainable." This distinction is crucial. A gift to provide recreational facilities may be a gift for beneficiaries if those persons are intended to be benefited[56]; and similarly a gift to an association where it is construed as a gift for the members as an accretion to their funds.[57] The problem of construction was substantial in the cases discussed; but there is no need for any difficulty to arise if the draftsman is aware of the possibilities and the difficulties and drafts the gift accordingly.

iv. Conveyancing Devices. A gift over from one charity to another may validly take place at any time in the future; the rule against perpetuities does not apply.[58] Advantage was taken of this rule in *Re Tyler*,[59] to achieve a non-charitable purpose.

A gift was made to the London Missionary Society, committing to their care the family vault, and if they failed to comply with the request the money was to go to the Bluecoat School. The gift was upheld. It could last perpetually if the value of the gift was sufficient to encourage the London Missionary Society to perform the task. If the task became unprofitable, as no doubt it would do by

---

[52] Report of the Goodman Committee on Charity Law and Voluntary Organisations, p. 24.
[53] [1982] 1 W.L.R. 522; also the *Quistclose* trust, *ante*, p. 52.
[54] *ante*, p. 379.
[55] [1976] Ch. 235, at 246.
[56] *Re Denley's Trust Deed* [1969] 1 Ch. 373.
[57] *Re Recher's W.T.* [1972] Ch. 526; *Re Lipinski's W.T.* [1976] Ch. 235.
[58] *Christ's Hospital (Governors) v. Grainger* (1849) 1 Mac & G. 460.
[59] [1891] 3 Ch. 252.

the progress of inflation, the gift over would take effect. The Bluecoat School would be under no obligation to perform the task. Indeed, if an attempt was made to impose an obligation on either donee by requiring any part of the income to be applied for the non-charitable purpose, the gift would have been void as not exclusively charitable.[60]

The Law Commission recommends no change to the exception from the perpetuity rule of gifts over from one charity to another, although noting that the exception has been employed as a means of enforcing non-charitable purpose trusts in perpetuity.[61]

v. Draft as a Power; not as a Trust. The beneficiary principle applies to trusts. There must be someone who can enforce the trust. With a power, there is no question of enforcement; although questions of certainty and perpetuity arise. Assuming however that these are overcome, could not the purpose be achieved by giving the property, not to a trustee upon trust, but to the ultimate beneficiary subject to a power in a third party to apply the property for the stated purpose for the perpetuity period?

There is little authority on the validity of such a power. Clearly, a power can be something other than a general or special power to appoint to persons.[62] It may be, then, that a power to apply the income for the improvement of land,[63] or for research into the advantages of the 40-letter alphabet,[64] could, if limited to the period of perpetuity, be valid. It seems that the same rule should apply to repairing monuments, feeding animals, or providing a cup for a yacht race. The person entitled in default could restrain misapplication.

There seems to be nothing contrary to policy in allowing the purpose to be effected in this way. Policy questions will arise, of course, where an eccentric testator provides for large sums to be applied for useless, capricious or harmful purposes for a substantial period.[65] The problem here is the same as that discussed in section 8 above.

Arguments have been put forward to the effect that an instrument which purports to create a purpose trust should be construed as a

---

[60] *Re Dalziel* [1943] Ch. 277. See further [1987] Conv. 415 (P. Smart).
[61] Law Com No. 251 (1998), *The Rules against Perpetuities and Excessive Accumulations*, paras. 7.34, 7.37.
[62] See *Re Douglas* (1887) 35 Ch.D. 472; (1902) 15 H.L.R. 67 (J. Gray); (1959) 4 U. of W.A.L.R. at 260 (L. Sheridan). See also *Re Clarke* [1923] 2 Ch. 407, where a power to appoint to *uncertain* non-charitable objects failed.
[63] *Re Aberconway's S.T.* [1953] Ch. 647.
[64] *Re Shaw* [1957] 1 W.L.R. 729.
[65] See Morris and Leach (2nd ed.), p. 320.

power so as to allow the purpose to be carried out.[66] Supporters of this view argued that this is a way of achieving the testator's or settlor's intention without conflicting with any rules of policy. In *Re Shaw*,[67] Harman J. appeared to find some attraction in the argument; but he rejected it, following what Jenkins L.J. had said in *Commissioners of Inland Revenue v. Broadway Cottages Trust*[68]; "We do not think that a valid power is to be spelt out of an invalid trust."

B. By the Legislature

If reform is to come, it will come best from the Legislature. The basic question is whether gifts for non-charitable purposes should be upheld. If so, it is necessary to find a means of overcoming the beneficiary principle, and this would most conveniently be done by enacting that trusts for non-charitable purposes (if sufficiently certain) should be construed as powers.[69] The purpose could then be carried out by the trustees if they elected to do so. If they did not, the purpose would fail and the property would go to those entitled in default. The power would be valid only if it was sufficiently certain. It may be thought best to limit such trusts to a period of 21 years,[70] or require them to be restricted to the common law perpetuity rule, or a longer specified period such as 80 years.[71] The danger of maladministration would be no greater than that already encountered in the case of the permitted purpose trusts discussed in section 3 above.

To the statutory solution, it may be objected that it does not answer the anxiety expressed by Roxburgh J. in *Re Astor's Settlement Trusts*[72] that it was not in the general interest that large sums of money should be applied for non-charitable purposes for long periods of time. The period of perpetuity can be about 100 years, and non-charitable purposes include all those which at one end are nearly charitable and those which are so useless as to be capricious. In validating gifts for purposes, it is important to ensure that funds are made available for purposes which are useful to the public rather than for the satisfaction of the private interests of a settlor or testator. Resources are scarce, and need to be put to good use. The problem

---

[66] (1949) 13 Conv.(N.S.) 418 at 424 (D. Potter); (1950) 14 Conv.(N.S.) 374 (A. Kiralfy); (1959) 4 U. of W.A.L.R. at 240–244 (L. Sheridan); (1953) 17 Conv.(N.S.) 46 at 59.

[67] [1957] 1 W.L.R. 729 at 746.

[68] [1955] Ch. 20 at 36.

[69] See Ontario Perpetuities Act 1966. Alternatively, legislation could validate a purpose trust where the trust deed requires the appointment of an "enforcer"; *Modern International Developments in Trust Law* (ed. D. Hayton), at p. 282. Indeed, a purpose trust with an "enforcer" appointed under the terms of the trust may be valid without legislation; (2001) 117 L.Q.R. 96 (D. Hayton).

[70] New Zealand Perpetuities Act 1964, s.20.

[71] Maudsley, *The Modern Law of Perpetuities*, App. D.

[72] [1952] Ch. 534.

is one which exists also in the case of gifts which are drafted in the form of powers. No doubt, the amount of money involved, and the duration of the trust will be factors which will be relevant to a decision. The line is difficult to draw. But capricious trusts are the rare ones. The fact that they exist is no reason for failing to establish a rational method of validating the useful ones.

C. Offshore Jurisdictions

Purpose trusts are now permitted by statute in many jurisdictions to facilitate estate planning and asset protection schemes, by exploiting the point that neither the settlor nor any other person is the beneficial owner of the property.[73] This has been done in the interests of attracting lucrative trusts business to the jurisdiction in question. Typically such legislation permits non-charitable purpose trusts to last for long periods such as 120 years, and provides for enforcement by the "protector" of the settlement or by an "enforcer".[74] Of particular interest is the Cayman Islands Special Trusts (Alternative Regime) Law 1997. This permits non-charitable purpose trusts (commonly known as STAR trusts) which are exempt from the perpetuity rule, which are enforceable by "enforcers" and which do not fail for uncertainty (any uncertainty may be resolved by the court settling a scheme). Such trusts may also include human beneficiaries, but they have no standing to enforce the trust. This has given rise to a debate as to whether a "STAR trust" is really a trust at all, because the fundamental obligations owed by trustees to beneficiaries are absent.[75] The danger is that a resulting trust might then arise in favour of the settlor, thus defeating his objectives. A settlor may seek to take advantage of these offshore enactments by including a provision in the trust instrument that the trust is to be governed by the law of a specified jurisdiction.[76] The attraction is that the beneficial ownership appears to be in abeyance, which is useful for confidentiality and secrecy, with possible adverse effects on dependants, creditors and tax authorities. Thus the suspicion is that "purpose trust legislation simply encourages hidden ownership

---

[73] See *Trends in Contemporary Trusts Law* (ed. A. Oakley), Chap. 1 (P. Matthews); Baxendale-Walker, *Purpose Trusts*; (1999) 5 *Trusts & Trustees*, pp. 5–92.

[74] See, for example, the Belize Trusts Act 1992; Trusts (Amendment No. 3) (Jersey) Law 1996; (1997) 1 *Jersey Law Review* 6 (P. Matthews); (1997/98) 4 *Trusts & Trustees* 17 (P. Egerton-Vernon).

[75] (1997) 11 *Trust Law International* 67 (P. Matthews); (1998) 12 *Trust Law International* 16 (A. Duckworth); *ibid.* at 98 (P. Matthews); (1999) 13 *Trust Law International* 158 (A. Duckworth).

[76] See the Hague Convention, Art. 6. Under Art. 18, effect will not be given to this if it would be manifestly incompatible with public policy. See also Art. 2, defining a trust, for the purpose of the Convention, as being "for the benefit of a beneficiary or for a specific purpose."

by putting assets into a no-man's land".[77] The purpose trust vehicle can be used for "off balance sheet" transactions, as where a company is set up to acquire an asset from another company and thus take it off the latter's balance sheet, to be held on a purpose trust. There is no plan to introduce such legislation in the United Kingdom, because "there is a feeling that pure purpose trusts may be hijacked for shady dealings involving hiding beneficial ownership".[78]

---

[77] *Modern International Developments in Trust Law* (ed. D. Hayton), p. 12.
[78] *ibid.* at 305. For a more positive view by the same author, see (2001) 117 L.Q.R. 96 (D. Hayton).

CHAPTER 15

CHARITABLE TRUSTS

I. Introduction[1]

CHARITABLE purposes are those which are considered to be of such value and importance to the community that they receive especially favourable treatment. These purposes are the relief of poverty, the advancement of education and religion, and other purposes beneficial to the community. Such a list is vague and old-fashioned. That is because the scope of charity originates in the Preamble to the Charitable Uses Act of 1601, an Act which was passed for the purpose of remedying abuses which had grown up in the administration of charitable trusts. The Preamble contained a general catalogue of the purposes then regarded as charitable. Since that time, purposes which are regarded as being within the "spirit and intendment"[2] or "within the equity"[3] of the statute have been accepted as being charitable. In 1891, Lord Macnaghten summarised these purposes into four categories given above.[4] In 1952, the Nathan Committee[5] recommended that a new statutory definition of charity

---

[1] See generally *Tudor on Charities* (8th ed., 1995); Sheridan and Keeton, *The Modern Law of Charities* (4th ed., 1992); Picarda, *The Law and Practice Relating to Charities* (3rd ed., 1999); Chesterman, *Charities, Trusts and Social Welfare* (1979). See also the Annual Reports and Decisions of the Charity Commissioners. For important reviews of the law and practice, see the Goodman Committee Report on Charity Law and Voluntary Organisations (1976); The Wolfenden Committee Report on the Future of Voluntary Organisations; The Woodfield Report, Efficiency Scrutiny of the Supervision of Charities (1987).

[2] *Morice v. Bishop of Durham* (1805) 9 Ves. 399 at 405.

[3] See *Incorporated Council of Law Reporting v. Att.-Gen.* [1972] Ch. 73 at 87–88.

[4] *Commissioners for Special Purposes of Income Tax v. Pemsel* [1891] A.C. 531.

[5] The Committee on the Law and Practice relating to Charitable Trusts (1952) Cmd. 8710.

should be enacted, based on that classification. This recommendation was not implemented.[6] In spite of further recommendations from the Expenditure Committee of the House of Commons, the Government decided not to promote a legislative definition of charity.[7] A more recent report advocating the abolition of the concept of charity and concomitant tax relief and its replacement by a state-funded voluntary sector, was rejected by the Government.[8]

The Preamble was, however, repealed by the Charities Act 1960.[9] No definition replaced it. The matter is now governed by the case law, and current developments by the decisions of the Charity Commissioners on the question of the registration of Charities under the Charities Act 1993, s.3.[10]

We will see that charitable trusts are accorded a number of concessions over other trusts in terms of enforcement, perpetuity, certainty and taxation.[11] To earn these concessions, especially in relation to taxation, a trust must be of benefit to the public, and not merely to private individuals. This is obvious in the fourth category. It exists also in connection with trusts for the advancement of religion and education, but only minimally in trusts for the relief of poverty. The policy in question behind most litigation concerning charitable trusts is an examination of whether the purposes are so useful to the public as to earn the concessions. This has to be carried out against a background of cases decided in earlier times when the condition of society was very different. In the days when the State made little or no provision for the poor and uneducated or for other general welfare purposes, and at a time when religious observance was unchallenged, trusts for these four categories were clearly for the public benefit. At the present time, however, many of the welfare and educational needs of society are provided from public sources.[12] Are these purposes so vital to present-day society that trusts for

---

[6] The Report of the Commission on the Future of the Voluntary Sector (1996) recommends a statutory definition, but there is much to be said for retaining the flexibility which the present situation provides.

[7] House of Commons Report, Vol. I, paras. 24–34; Goodman Committee, para. 32, App. 1.

[8] *Voluntary Action*, published in 1993 by the Home Office on behalf of the CENTRIS research project.

[9] s.38.

[10] Replacing Charities Act 1960. The more significant decisions are discussed in the Annual Reports of the Charity Commissioners (referred to hereafter as *Annual Reports*) and, since 1993, in the Decisions of the Charity Commissioners.

[11] *per* Lord Cross in *Dingle v. Turner* [1972] A.C. 601 at 624.

[12] The main categories of recent charitable trusts are for: (i) social welfare, *e.g.* for drug addicts, the consequences of the break-up of family life, counselling for young homosexuals, victim support schemes, care of AIDS sufferers, and the relief of youth unemployment; (ii) cultural purposes; (iii) conservation of the environment; (iv) religious cultural teachings of immigrant communities and the promotion of racial harmony. Annual Report 1978, para. 60; 1980, paras. 74–77; 1981, paras. 65–67; 1982, paras. 28–30; 1983, paras. 12–20; 1986, para. 35; 1987, para. 14; 1989, para. 29; 1991, paras. 73, 78.

them should receive special encouragement by being permitted to exist as purpose trusts, for ever, supported by the court's *cy-près* power,[13] and tax free?[14] Judicial attitudes to gifts for charitable purposes have varied. In 1908, Lord Loreburn said "now there is no better rule than that a benignant construction will be placed upon charitable bequests."[15] But since the 1940s when taxation became higher the courts have been astute to restrict the scope of charity especially by emphasising the requirement of public benefit.[16] More recently, however, Lord Hailsham of St. Marylebone said: "In construing trust deeds the intention of which is to set up a charitable trust, and in others too, where it can be claimed that there is an ambiguity, a benignant construction should be given if possible."[17] In similar vein, the intention of the legislature is to encourage charitable giving, and the development of the voluntary sector as a whole.[18] The policy changes which have been effected by changing social and economic conditions should be borne in mind when considering the cases relating to the definition of charity.

Harmonisation of non-profit making bodies in the European Union by the introduction of the "European Association", a new legal structure, has been proposed.[19] However, English charity law and the civil law of voluntary organisations are so different that progress has been slow.[20]

2. ADVANTAGES ENJOYED BY CHARITABLE TRUSTS

A. Purpose Trusts

Charitable trusts are purpose trusts. But there is no need for human beneficiaries to enforce them, as there is in the case of non-

---

[13] *post*, p. 445.

[14] (1956) 72 L.Q.R. 187 at 204 (G. Cross); (1977) 40 M.L.R. 397 (N. Gravells); (1999) 13 *Trust Law International* 21 (C. Mitchell). *Scottish Burial Reform and Cremation Society v. Glasgow Corporation* [1968] A.C. 138 at p 153; *Dingle v. Turner* [1972] A.C. 601 at 624.

[15] *Weir v. Crum-Brown* [1908] A.C. 162 at 167.

[16] The Royal Commission on the Taxation of Profits and Income (1955) Cmd. 9474, recommended (paras. 168–175) that some charitable trusts should be subject to tax liability. See also [1989] Conv. 28 (S. Bright); (1999) 62 M.L.R. 333 at 340–343 (M. Chesterman).

[17] *I.R.C. v. McMullen* [1981] A.C. 1 at 14; *Re Koeppler's W.T.* [1986] Ch. 423; *Re Hetherington (deceased)* [1990] Ch. 1; *Guild v. I.R.C.* [1992] 2 A.C. 310. The "benignant" approach applies only where a disposition would otherwise be void; *I.R.C. v. Oldham Training and Enterprise Council* [1996] S.T.C. 1218.

[18] The Goodman Committee recommended increasing the fiscal privileges of charities; Chap. 5. Some of these recommendations have been implemented; F.A. 1982, s.129; I.H.T.A. 1984, s.29(5); I.C.T.A. 1988, ss.86, 339, 577, 671. See too *Incorporated Council of Law Reporting v. Att.-Gen.* [1972] Ch. 73 at 88, *per* Russell L.J., p. 415, *post*.

[19] See Annual Report 1991, paras. 17–22; 1992, paras. 105–112; 1995, para. 108; 1996, paras. 220–222.

[20] See generally (1997) N.L.J. Charities Supplement No. 71, p. 13 (K. Lasok and D. Beard).

charitable purpose trusts.[21] Individuals who may benefit from a charitable trust have no standing to enforce them.[22] Charitable trusts are enforced by the Attorney-General in the name of the Crown,[23] although the general administration of charitable trusts is overseen by the Charity Commissioners.[24] There must of course be an obligation upon the trustees; a mere power to apply to charitable purposes cannot be a trust.[25] It should be emphasised that this Chapter deals with charitable *trusts*. The legal position differs in many ways where the charity is incorporated.[26] Indeed, a new corporate legal structure for charities has been proposed.[27]

B. Objects Need Not be Certain

There is no requirement, as with other trusts, that the objects of the trust must be certain. Thus, a trust for "charitable purposes" will be valid. The court and the Charity Commissioners[28] have jurisdiction to establish a scheme for the application of the funds for specific charitable purposes. There must, of course, be no doubt that the objects of the trust are exclusively charitable, and the purpose expressed must not be so vague and uncertain that the court could not control the application of the assets.[29] The relaxation of the certainty rule is only in respect of the particular form of charitable purpose intended.[30]

Where no trust has been created, but only a general intention expressed that the property should go to charity, the court has no jurisdiction. In such a case the Crown disposes of the gifts by sign manual.[31] But the Crown acts on principles very similar to those by which the court is governed.

---

[21] *ante*, Chap. 14.

[22] *Hauxwell v. Barton-on-Humber U.D.C.* [1974] Ch. 432; Charities Act 1993, s.33.

[23] See *Att.-Gen. v. Wright* [1988] 1 W.L.R. 164; *Att.-Gen. v. Cocke* [1988] Ch. 414. The Commissioners may exercise these powers with the consent of the Attorney-General; Charities Act 1993, s.32.

[24] Charities Act 1993, s.1.

[25] *Re Cohen* [1973] 1 W.L.R. 415, where a gift to trustees to apply to a charitable purpose "the whole or any part" of the fund "in such manner and at such time or times as my trustees shall in their absolute and uncontrolled discretion think fit," was held to create a trust.

[26] For the distinctions, see (1993–94) 2 *Charity Law and Practice Review* 133 (J. Hill). See also Charities Act 1993, s.96.

[27] See Annual Report 1996, paras. 28–29; [1997] Conv. 106 and [1999] Conv. 20 (J. Warburton).

[28] Charities Act 1993, s.16; *post*, p. 464.

[29] *Re Koeppler's Will Trusts* [1986] Ch. 423, where the formation of an informed international public opinion and the promotion of greater co-operation in Europe and the West were held too vague and uncertain to be charitable in themselves, but these aims did not destroy the charitable nature of the gift, which was to further the work of an educational project.

[30] See *Moggridge v. Thackwell* (1792) 1 Ves.Jr. 464; (1803) 7 Ves.Jr. 36; (1807) 13 Ves.Jr. 416.

[31] *Moggridge v. Thackwell, supra; Paice v. Archbishop of Canterbury* (1807) 14 Ves. 364 at 371; *Re Smith* [1932] 1 Ch. 53; *Re Bennett* [1960] Ch. 18; *Re Hetherington* [1990] Ch. 1.

C. May be Perpetual

Statements have often been made by judges to the effect that the Rule against Perpetuities does not apply to charities.[32] That is not so. With the exception of the rule in *Christ's Hospital v. Grainger*,[33] explained below, the rule governs the remoteness of vesting in the case of gifts to charities in the same way that it governs remoteness in the case of other gifts.[34]

Charitable trusts, however, may be perpetual. Indeed, the purpose of many charitable trusts could be said never to be capable of final achievement.[35] Many charitable trusts have existed for centuries. If a perpetual gift of income only is made to a charity, the charity cannot claim the capital, as an individual could do in such circumstances.[36] But where property is given absolutely to a charity with a direction to accumulate the income for a period of time, a charity may terminate the accumulation, and claim the principal forthwith.[37]

The exception to the rule regulating remoteness of vesting is that a gift over from one charity to *another charity* is not subject to the rule.[38] The gift over to the second charity is valid even if it takes effect outside the perpetuity period.[39]

The reason for the exception is that "there is no more perpetuity created by giving to two charities rather than by giving to one."[40] The explanation looks to the vesting for charitable purposes, rather than vesting in one specific charity. Once vested in charity, then, subject to express provision to the contrary, a trust will continue, even if the purposes become impossible of fulfilment; the property will be applied *cy-près*.[41] All that is done by the provision for vesting in another charity is to make expressly the selection of the charity to be benefited when the first gift terminates.

This rule therefore seems logical; and also reasonable when the gift over is to take effect upon the happening of some event related to the carrying out of the purposes of the charity, as was the case in

---

[32] *Goodman v. Mayor of Saltash* (1882) 7 App.Cas. 633 at 642; *Commissioners for Special Purposes of Income Tax v. Pemsel* [1891] A.C. 531 at 580–581; *Att.-Gen. v National Provincial and Union Bank Ltd* [1924] A.C. 262 at 266.

[33] (1849) 1 Mac. & G. 460; *Re Tyler* [1891] 3 Ch. 252; *Royal College of Surgeons v. National Provincial Bank Ltd* [1952] A.C. 631.

[34] *Re Wightwick's W.T.* [1950] Ch. 260; *Re Mander* [1950] Ch. 547; *Re Green's W.T.* [1985] 3 All E.R. 455.

[35] *Re Delius* [1957] Ch. 299.

[36] *Re Levy* [1960] Ch. 346.

[37] *Wharton v. Masterman* [1895] A.C. 186; *Re Knapp* [1929] 1 Ch. 341.

[38] A gift from non-charity to a charity is caught: *Re Bowen* [1893] 2 Ch. 291. So also a gift from a charity to a non-charity; *Re Bowen (supra)*; *Re Peel's Release* [1921] 2 Ch. 218; *Re Engels* [1943] 1 All E.R. 506.

[39] *Christ's Hospital v. Grainger* (1849) 1 Mac. & G. 460.

[40] *per* Shadwell V.-C. in the court below (1848) 16 Sim. 83 at 100. See also *Royal College of Surgeons v. National Provincial Bank Ltd* [1952] A.C. 631 at 650.

[41] *post*, p. 445.

Christ's Hospital v. Grainger,[42] and *Royal College of Surgeons v. National Provincial Bank*.[43] In the hands of conveyancers, however as has been seen,[44] it can be used to produce, in effect, a perpetual non-charitable trust by making a gift to one charity conditional upon carrying out a non-charitable purpose, and terminable in favour of another charity upon its failure to do so. This is not a satisfactory use of charity privilege: but this loophole was not questioned in the *Royal College of Surgeons* case.

The Law Commission has recently recommended that the rule against excessive accumulations of income should in general be abolished, but should still apply to charitable trusts. Otherwise income could be tied up for many years, during which there would be no public benefit. It is proposed that any power or duty to accumulate charitable income should cease after 21 years.[45] No change is recommended to the rule relating to a gift over from one charity to another, in spite of the opportunities for exploitation described above.[46]

D. Fiscal Advantages

Charities are exempt from income tax, provided that the income is applied for charitable purposes only.[47] They may recover from the Revenue income tax paid or credited prior to the payment of interest. Relief is also available with respect to "Gift Aid" donations.[48] Alternatively, donors who are employees may utilise the payroll deduction scheme.[49] Further, no income tax is chargeable in respect of profits of any trade carried on by the charity, if the profits are applied solely to the purposes of the charity and either the trade is exercised in the course of the actual carrying out of a primary purpose of the charity, or the work in connection with the trade is mainly carried out by beneficiaries of the charity.[50] Again the profits must be applied solely to the purposes of the charity. Similarly, charitable corporations are exempt from paying corporation tax.[51]

Gifts of any amount in favour of charity are exempt from inheritance tax if made by way of payment from a discretionary

---

[42] *supra.*
[43] [1952] A.C. 631.
[44] *ante*, p. 385, *Re Tyler* [1891] 3 Ch. 252.
[45] Law Com. No. 251 (1998), *The Rules against Perpetuities and Excessive Accumulations*, para. 10.21. The proposal relates only to instruments taking effect after enactment.
[46] *ibid*, para. 7.34.
[47] I.C.T.A. 1988, s.505. See *I.R.C. v. Educational Grants Association Ltd* [1967] Ch. 993; *I.R.C. v. Helen Slater Charitable Trust Ltd* [1982] Ch. 49.
[48] F.A. 1990, ss.25, 26; F.A. 2000, s.39. For company donations, see I.C.T.A. 1988, s.339; F.A. 2000, s.40.
[49] I.C.T.A. 1988, s.202, as amended; [1989] Conv. 175 (D. Morris).
[50] *ibid.* s.505(1); (1989) 3 *Trust Law & Practice* 98 (J. Hill and J. de Souza).
[51] *ibid.* ss.505(1), 506(1).

trust,[52] or by way of gift by an individual during his lifetime or on death.[53] Similarly, transfers from a charitable trust are exempt from inheritance tax.[54]

No capital gains tax arises where a gain accrues to a charity and the gain is applicable and is applied for charitable purposes.[55] Nor will a donor be under any such liability in respect of a disposal to charity.[56] Charities are also exempt from stamp duty on conveyances,[57] and from National Insurance Surcharge.[58]

Charities, however, do have to bear Value Added Tax on goods and services which they purchase.[59] This liability will be particularly burdensome for many charities in respect of the maintenance and repair of buildings. Also, VAT may be chargeable in respect of goods and services provided, on payment, by some charities.[60]

All charities are entitled to exemption in respect of 80 per cent of the non-domestic rates of the properties which they occupy,[61] wholly or mainly used for charitable purposes. This includes premises used wholly or mainly for the sale of goods donated to a charity and applied for the purposes of a charity.[62] Relief can also be granted at the discretion of the rating authority up to the whole amount of the rates.[63] Churches, church halls and similar premises used for religious purposes are entitled to relief in respect of the whole of the rates,[64] as are those providing facilities for the disabled.[65]

In view of the extent of income and other assets thus exempted, this is a formidable list of fiscal advantages. In 1997 it was estimated that the value of tax exemptions was £1.75 billion.[66] This explains the prominence of Revenue cases in charity litigation.

---

[52] Inheritance Tax Act 1984, s.76.

[53] *ibid.* s.23. See also ss.25, 26.

[54] *ibid.* s.58(1)(*a*).

[55] Taxation of Chargeable Gains Act 1992, s.256.

[56] *ibid.* s.257.

[57] F.A. 1982, s.129.

[58] F.A. 1977, s.57.

[59] For specific exemptions, see the consolidating Value Added Tax Act 1994, Sched. 9.

[60] See [1972] B.T.R. 346 at 356 (G. Glover); *Customs and Excise Commissioners v. Automobile Association* [1974] 1 W.L.R. 1447; Annual Report 1974, paras. 17–21; (1995/96) 3 *Charity Law and Practice Review* 37 (J. Warburton). However, some goods supplied to or by charities are zero-rated under Sched. 8 of the 1994 Act.

[61] Local Government Finance Act 1988, s.43(5), (6).

[62] L.G.F.A. 1988, s.64(10); Hansard, H.L., Vol. 499, col. 874, July 13, 1988.

[63] *ibid.* s.47.

[64] L.G.F.A. 1988, Sched. 5, para. 11. In *Henning v. Church of Jesus Christ of Latter-Day Saints* [1962] 1 W.L.R. 1091, the Mormon Church failed to obtain exemption in respect of premises to which only selected members of the faith were admitted. Similarly, the Exclusive Brethren in *Broxtowe Borough Council v. Birch* [1983] 1 W.L.R. 314.

[65] *ibid.* para. 16.

[66] *H.M. Treasury News Release, Charity Taxation Reviewed*, July 2, 1997. The gross income of registered charities was £24 billion in 1999/2000; Annual Report 1999/2000, para. 4.1.

Measures have been taken to prevent abuse of these tax advantages, for example by requiring charities to take reasonable steps to ensure that payments made to overseas bodies will be applied to genuine charitable purposes and requiring them to justify certain loans or investments as being for the benefit of charity and not for tax avoidance.[67] These provisions restrict tax relief where funds are applied for non-charitable purposes and prevent manipulation of charity tax advantages by individuals. The whole area of charity taxation is currently under review.[68]

3. THE DEFINITION OF CHARITY

A. The Four Categories

i. Lord Macnaghten's Classification. A claim to charitable status is determined by considering whether the purpose comes within Lord Macnaghten's classification as exemplified by the cases decided in accordance with it. Lord Macnaghten said; "Charity in its legal sense comprises four principal divisions: trusts for the relief of poverty; trusts for the advancement of education; trusts for the advancement of religion; and trusts for other purposes beneficial to the community."[69] It is obvious that the heads provide no precise definition. Lord Wilberforce had this comment to make[70]: "first, that, since it is a classification of convenience, there may well be purposes which do not fit neatly into one or other of the headings." He might also have added that there are many purposes which overlap.[71] "Secondly that the words used must not be given the force of a statute to be construed; and thirdly, that the law of charity is a moving subject which may well have evolved even since 1891." Indeed, it is continually changing, and as has been explained, the significance of tax exemption, and also the development of State agencies to provide education, relief from poverty, and other purposes needed by society have transformed the concept of charity.[72] It should be appreciated that the Charity Commissioners have a major role in the development of this concept.[73] The Commissioners are currently conducting a review of registered charities by way of public consultation, to see if there is scope for developing the

---

[67] I.C.T.A. 1988, ss.339, 427, 505, 506, 683.
[68] See H.M. Treasury Consultation Document, *Review of Charity Taxation* (1999).
[69] *Commissioners for Special Purposes of Income Tax v. Pemsel* [1891] A.C. 531 at 583.
[70] *Scottish Burial Reform and Cremation Society Ltd v. Glasgow Corporation* [1968] A.C. 138 at 154.
[71] Thus, a gift for the preparation of "poor students for the Ministry" might come under all four heads.
[72] See *Incorporated Council of Law Reporting v. Att.-Gen.* [1972] Ch. 73 at 88–89.
[73] *post*, p. 462.

boundaries of charitable status by the flexible use of their powers.[74] They have already decided to recognise the promotion of urban and rural regeneration and the relief of unemployment.[75]

ii. Public Benefit. It should also be noted at this stage that each head involves two elements; an element of benefit, such as the advancement of education, and also an element of *public* benefit, that is to say, education being advanced in a way that will benefit the whole community, or a sufficiently substantial part of it. The requirement of public benefit varies from head to head, and will be discussed in detail.[76]

iii. Exclusively Charitable. A trust will not fail to be charitable because it may in its operation incidentally benefit the rich, or other non-objects of charity.[77] But if a non-charitable purpose is an object, the trust cannot be charitable, for it is not wholly and exclusively "for charitable purposes."[78] A statement of objects which includes non-charitable purposes is not saved by adding "in so far as they are of a charitable nature."[79]

iv. Charitable Purposes Overseas. Special problems arise where the benefits arising from charitable trusts are to be enjoyed abroad. For at least 200 years there has been no rule requiring the benefits to be retained in this country.[80] But, how can the court or the (English) trustees control the application of the funds? What relationship is there between the Preamble of 1601 and the problem of a developing country suffering from drought, floods or earthquake? Should tax privileges be given by the British Revenue for the benefit of communities abroad?[81]

The Charity Commissioners have stated[82] that the relief of poverty[83] and the advancement of education and religion are presumed

---

[74] Charity Commission Consultation Paper; *Framework for the Review of the Register of Charities* (1998); criticised in *The Lawyer*, June 9, 1998 (H. Picarda).

[75] *The Times*, March 18, 1999. Several consultation documents have been issued.

[76] *post*, p. 427.

[77] *Verge v. Somerville* [1924] A.C. 496; *Re Resch's W.T.* [1969] 1 A.C. 514; *sub nom. Le Cras v. Perpetual Trustee Co.* [1967] 1 All E.R. 915. But a trust for the relief of poverty will fail if it may benefit persons who are not poor; *Re Gwyon* [1903] 1 Ch. 255.

[78] *post*, p. 439.

[79] *McGovern v. Att.-Gen.* [1982] Ch. 321.

[80] *Re Robinson* [1931] 2 Ch. 122 at 126 (gift to German Government for the benefit of its soldiers disabled in the late war held charitable).

[81] Annual Report 1963, paras. 69–76. See (1965) 29 Conv.(N.S.) 123 (D. Emrys Evans).

[82] Annual Report 1992, paras. 74, 75; Decisions, Vol. 1 (1993), 16. See *Camille and Henry Dreyfus Foundation Inc. v. I.R.C.* [1954] Ch. 672 at 684.

[83] See *Re Niyazi's Will Trusts* [1978] 1 W.L.R. 910 (trust for construction of working men's hostel in Cyprus charitable). The work overseas of organisations like Oxfam is well known.

beneficial wherever they occur, but this may be challenged by applying criteria adopted by the English courts, for example it would not be charitable to support a religion overseas if it would be considered contrary to public policy to carry it on at home. The fourth head is more difficult. The test of public benefit is the same whether the activity is at home or abroad (as is also the case with the other heads), as our courts cannot judge what is for the benefit of the public in a foreign country. This does not mean that there must be a benefit to the public in this country. The courts should first consider if the activity would be charitable if it operated at home. If so, it is charitable even though operated abroad unless it would be contrary to public policy to recognise it. For example, our courts would not consider an institution operating abroad whose object was contrary to the law of the state in question to be charitable. These views are consistent with Commonwealth authorities, which have held that fourth category purposes may be charitable even though solely of benefit to a foreign community.[84] It should be added that the jurisdiction of the court and the charity commissioners over charities may be exercised only in respect of charities established in England and Wales according to English law, and not over bodies established and administered abroad.[85]

It has been said that the court would be bound to take account of the probable results of the execution of the trust on the inhabitants of the country concerned, which would doubtless have a history and social structure quite different from that of the United Kingdom. So in *McGovern v. Att.-Gen.*,[86] a trust to procure the abolition of torture or inhuman or degrading treatment or punishment[87] in all parts of the world was not charitable, one reason being that the court would have no satisfactory means of judging the probable effects of, say, legislation to abolish the death penalty on the local community. If the purpose of a trust was to secure abolition of the death penalty for adultery in Islamic countries, the court would not be competent to deal with it because it would either have to apply English standards as to public benefit, which might not be appropriate in the local conditions, or attempt to apply local standards of which it knew little or nothing.

In *Keren Kayemeth Le Jisroel Ltd v. I.R.C.*,[88] a trust for the purchase of land in Israel and for the settlement there of Jewish

[84] *Re Levy Estate* (1989) 58 D.L.R. (4th) 375 (bequest to State of Israel for charitable purposes selected by trustee). For the Australian position, see *Re Stone* (1970) 91 W.N. (N.S.W.) 704 at 717.

[85] *Gaudiya Mission v. Brahmachary* [1998] Ch. 341.

[86] [1982] Ch. 321, *post*, p. 424.

[87] Including punishment inflicted by process of law.

[88] [1932] A.C. 650.

people was held not charitable, but the decision turned on the character of the purposes, and not on the fact that the benefit would be enjoyed abroad. In *Re Jacobs* in 1970[89] a trust for the purpose "of planting a grove of trees in Israel to perpetuate my name on the eternal soil of the Holy Land" was upheld. Soil conservation is of crucial importance in Israel. It was the benefit to the community abroad which was significant. The Commissioners have registered several organisations concerned with the preservation of the environment outside the United Kingdom.[90]

B. The Relief of Poverty

i. Meaning of Poverty. There is no definition of poverty. Its meaning can only be understood by examining the cases on the subject. "It is quite clearly established that poverty does not mean destitution; ... it may not unfairly be paraphrased as meaning persons who have to 'go short' in the ordinary acceptance of that term ... "[91] It is thus a matter of degree. Most of the cases come from a time before welfare payments were available from public funds. Such payments are intended to relieve poverty and hardship, and it could be argued that eligibility for such payments should be the test of poverty. But, if that were so, charity in this area would duplicate the work of a good welfare programme. If relief of poverty is the duty of the State, what scope is there for private charity? This is a problem which is met in many of the areas of charity today, especially in connection with trusts for the relief of poverty and for education and health. Private charity is useful to fill the gaps which the welfare state programme leaves uncovered. But in doing so, it creates some controversies. If a trust's purpose is not appealing enough to justify the expenditure of public money, should it justify the tax exemptions to which charity is entitled?

ii. Illustrations. Gifts for the benefit of the poor are clearly charitable.[92] Also "needy" persons,[93] or "indigent"[94] persons. Often a group of poor is confined to a particular location,[95] or religion,[96] or

---

[89] Annual Report 1970, para. 78.

[90] Annual Report 1989, para. 29.

[91] *Re Coulthurst* [1951] Ch. 661 at 665–666. See generally (2000) 20 L.S. 222 (A. Dunn).

[92] *Re Darling* [1896] 1 Ch. 56: "to the poor and the service of God."

[93] *Re Scarisbrick* [1951] Ch. 622; *Re Cohen* [1973] 1 W.L.R. 415.

[94] *Weir v. Crum-Brown* [1908] A.C. 162: "indigent bachelors and widowers who have shown sympathy with science."

[95] *Re Lucas* [1922] 2 Ch. 52 (oldest respectable inhabitants in Gunville).

[96] *Re Wall* (1889) 52 Ch.D. 570.

to a group which is assumed to be in need of help,[97] or victims of a disaster.[98] Persons of "limited means"[99] are included, and trusts for gentlewomen and distressed gentlefolk.[1] On the other hand, in *Re Sanders' Will Trusts*,[2] a gift for the provision of housing for the working classes was not charitable. A gift which includes persons who are not in need will be excluded. In *Re Gwyon*,[3] a fund providing for a gift of clothing to boys in Farnham and district failed on the ground that the conditions for qualification, precise though they were in many ways, failed to exclude affluent children.[4] It is no objection, however, that the scheme operates by way of bargain rather than bounty, *i.e.* that the beneficiaries are required to contribute to the cost of the benefits they receive.[5]

There is no need for the trust to be an endowment. A trust may be charitable although the trustees may distribute the capital. A trust was upheld in *Re Scarisbrick*[6] "for such relations of my . . . son and daughters as in the opinion of the survivor of my . . . son and daughters shall be in needy circumstances . . . as the survivor . . . shall by deed or will appoint." This was a trust for "poor relations," and there is no requirement, in poverty cases, for public benefit.[7] But there can be no charitable trust, even in the poverty category, where the persons to be benefited are specified individuals; and such a construction is more likely where the capital of a trust may be immediately distributed. But it is not decisive.

Nor is it an objection that the persons to be benefited are to be selected at the discretion of the trustees.[8] It is necessary, of course,

---

[97] *Att.-Gen. v. Ironmongers Co.* (1834) 2 My. & K. 526 (debtors); *Thompson v. Thompson* (1844) 1 Coll. 381 at 395 (unsuccessful literary men); *Biscoe v. Jackson* (1887) 35 Ch.D. 460 (soup kitchen for the parish of Shoreditch); *Re Coulthurst* [1951] Ch. 661 (widows and orphaned children of employees).

[98] *Re North Devon and West Somerset Relief Fund Trust* [1953] 1 W.L.R. 1260 (flood disaster).

[99] *Re Gardom* [1914] 1 Ch. 664; *Re De Carteret* [1933] Ch. 103.

[1] *Mary Clark Home Trustees v. Anderson* [1904] 2 K.B. 745; *Re Gardom (supra)*; *Re Young* [1951] Ch. 344.

[2] [1954] Ch. 265. *cf. Re Niyazi's W.T.* [1978] 1 W.L.R. 910 (gift for "the construction of a working men's hostel" in Famagusta, Cyprus held charitable by Megarry V.-C. "although it was desperately near the border-line."). But some homes for working classes have been registered as charities where there were other factors which indicated a requirement of poverty. Annual Report 1965, App. C, para. I. A.9.

[3] [1930] 1 Ch. 255.

[4] They also excluded black boys. This caused no comment at the time; but would no doubt do so today, *ante*, p. 340. See further [1981] Conv. 131 (T. Watkin); Annual Report 1983, para. 19; Annual Report 1987, para. 14.

[5] *Re Cottam's W.T.* [1955] 1 W.L.R. 1299; *Le Cras v. Perpetual Trustee Co. Ltd* [1969] 1 A.C. 514; *Joseph Rowntree Memorial Trust Housing Association Ltd v. Att.-Gen.* [1983] Ch. 159 (dwellings for sale to elderly at 70 per cent cost).

[6] [1951] Ch. 622; *Re Cohen* [1973] 1 W.L.R. 415.

[7] *Dingle v. Turner* [1972] A.C. 601; *post*, p. 428.

[8] *Gibson v. South American Stores (Gath & Chaves) Ltd* [1950] Ch. 177; *Re Scarisbrick (supra)*, *Re Cohen (supra)*.

that there should be a duty and not a mere power to select,[9] and that the discretion is exercisable only in favour of those who are poor.

C. The Advancement of Education

i. Meaning of Education. The second head has its origin in the phrases in the Preamble which speak of "the maintenance of schools of learning, free schools and scholars in universities" and "the education and preferment of orphans." The endowments, some of course very ancient, of many schools and colleges and universities are based on this provision. Education in school and university is now however accepted as being within the responsibility of the State; and it is not surprising that modern cases have substantially widened the concept of educational charity. It can now cover almost any form of worthwhile instruction or cultural advancement, except for purely professional or career courses.

The following trusts have been held charitable under this head: Education in the art of government,[10] the production of a dictionary,[11] the support of London Zoological Society,[12] the establishment and maintenance of museums,[13] the support of learned literary, scientific and cultural societies,[14] a search for the Shakespeare manuscript,[15] choral singing in London,[16] the promotion of the music of Delius,[17] classical drama and acting,[18] the publication of the Law Reports,[19] the founding of lectureships and professorships,[20] the study and dissemination of ethical principles and cultivation of a rational religious sentiment[21] and even a "sort of finishing school for the Irish people" where "self-control, oratory, deportment and the art of personal contact" were to be taught.[22]

---

[9] *Re Cohen (supra).*

[10] *Re McDougall* [1957] 1 W.L.R. 81. But not for the promotion of political causes; *post*, p. 409. The holding of conferences with a "political flavour" but not of a party political nature was upheld in *Re Koeppler's W.T.* [1986] Ch. 423.

[11] *Re Stanford* [1924] 1 Ch. 73.

[12] *Re Lopes* [1931] 2 Ch. 130.

[13] *British Museum Trustees v. White* (1826) 2 Sm. & St. 594; *Re Pinion* [1965] Ch. 85 at 105.

[14] *Royal College of Surgeons v. National Provincial Bank Ltd* [1952] A.C. 631; *Re Shakespeare Memorial Trust* [1923] 2 Ch. 398; *Re British School of Egyptian Archaeology* [1954] 1 W.L.R. 546.

[15] *Re Hopkins' W.T.* [1965] Ch. 669.

[16] *Royal Choral Society v. I.R.C.* [1943] 2 All E.R. 101.

[17] *Re Delius* [1957] Ch. 299.

[18] *Re Shakespeare Memorial Trust (supra).*

[19] *Incorporated Council of Law Reporting for England and Wales v. Att.-Gen.* [1972] Ch. 73.

[20] *Att.-Gen. v. Margaret and Regius Professors in Cambridge* (1682) 1 Vern. 55.

[21] *Re South Place Ethical Society* [1980] 1 W.L.R. 1565.

[22] *Re Shaw's W.T.* [1952] Ch. 163.

ii. Research. Education requires something more than the mere accumulation of knowledge. There must be some sharing, or teaching or dissemination, some way of showing that the public will benefit. There is no difficulty in the case of research which is likely to produce material benefit to the community, such as medical or scientific research.[23] Such purposes would in any case come under the fourth head. But, on literary, cultural and scholarly subjects, the matter is less obvious. "I think, therefore," said Wilberforce J. in *Re Hopkins*,[24] "that the word 'education' . . . must be used in a wide sense, certainly extending beyond teaching, and that the requirement is that, in order to be charitable, research must either be of educational value to the researcher or must be so directed as to lead to something which will pass into the store of educational material, or so as to improve the sum of communicable knowledge in an area which education may cover—education in this last context extending to the formation of literary taste and appreciation."

In *Re Hopkins*,[25] there was a testamentary gift to the Francis Bacon Society "to be earmarked and applied towards finding the Bacon-Shakespeare manuscripts." A "search, or research, for the original manuscripts of England's greatest dramatist (whoever he was) would be well within the law's conception of charitable purposes. The discovery would be of the highest value to history and to literature."[26] The gift was held to be a valid charitable trust under this head and the fourth head.

Re Shaw[27] was distinguished.

George Bernard Shaw, by his will, directed that his residuary estate should be devoted to researching the advantages of a proposed British alphabet of 40 letters, in which each letter would indicate a single sound; and to translate his play "Androcles and the Lion" into the new alphabet. Harman J. held that the gift was not charitable "if the object be merely the increase of knowledge, that is not in itself a charitable object unless it be combined with teaching or education."[28]

---

[23] *Royal College of Surgeons v. National Provincial Bank Ltd (supra).* See also Annual Report 1987, para. 12.
[24] [1965] Ch. 669 at 680.
[25] *ibid.* See also *McGovern v. Att.-Gen.* [1982] Ch. 321, where research into human rights and dissemination of the results would have been charitable. The trust failed for other reasons. Trusts for research into human rights have been registered; Annual Report 1987, para. 12. Likewise research into terrorism; Annual Report 1988, paras. 27–34.
[26] *ibid.* at 679.
[27] [1957] 1 W.L.R. 729.
[28] *ibid.* at 737, referring to Rigby L.J. in *Re Macduff* [1896] 2 Ch. 451.

This is thought to be too narrow a view of education. Whether the trust in this case would be held charitable under Wilberforce J.'s test depends on the usefulness of the research, and that is a matter of individual judgment. Not every type of knowledge, whether researched, disseminated or taught is capable of being education. Not schools for prostitutes or pickpockets,[29] nor the training of spiritualistic mediums.[30]

iii. Artistic and Aesthetic Education.

In *Royal Choral Society v. I.R.C.*,[31] the Court of Appeal upheld as charitable a trust to promote the practice and performance of choral works. Lord Greene said of the view that education meant a master teaching a class[32]: "I protest against that narrow conception of education when one is dealing with aesthetic education. In my opinion, a body of persons established for the purpose of raising the artistic state of the country . . . is established for educational purposes."

In *Re British School of Egyptian Archaeology*[33] a trust to excavate and discover Egyptian antiquities, to hold exhibitions and to promote the training and assistance of students in the field of Egyptian history was held educational. In *Re Delius*,[34] there was a gift to increase the general appreciation of the musical work of the composer. Roxburgh J. had no doubt that the trust was for the advancement of education. But it seems that a trust for "artistic" purposes is too vague to be charitable.[35]

iv. Subjective Evaluation.

The question whether a purpose is educational or not will depend in many cases upon the evaluation of its quality and usefulness for that purpose. Music, drama, literature, archaeology, museums; these and many more are included. But not bad music, ham acting, pornography, useless digging or collections of rubbish. In *Re Delius*,[36] Roxburgh J. recognised that there would be difficulty if a manifestly inadequate composer had been chosen. A judge may be assisted by expert evidence. But that may not be conclusive, and artistic evaluation changes with the times. It is clear that the court will require to be satisfied of the merit of artistic work.[37] The opinion of the donor that the gift is for the public benefit does not make it so.

---

[29] *per* Harman J. [1957] 1 W.L.R. 729 at 737; and in *Re Pinion* [1965] Ch. 85 at 105.

[30] *Re Hummeltenberg* [1923] 1 Ch. 237. *cf. Funnell v. Stewart* [1996] 1 W.L.R. 288 (faith healing charitable).

[31] [1943] 2 All E.R. 101.

[32] *ibid.* at 104.

[33] [1954] 1 W.L.R. 540.

[34] [1957] Ch. 299.

[35] *Associated Artists Ltd v. I.R.C.* [1956] 1 W.L.R. 752 at 758; see also *Royal Choral Society v. I.R.C.* [1943] 2 All E.R. 101 at 107.

[36] [1957] Ch. 299.

[37] The same problem arises with many situations under the fourth head.

In *Re Pinion*,[38] a testator gave his studio and its contents to trustees to enable it to be used as a museum for the display of his collection of furniture and objets d'art, and paintings, some of which were by the testator himself.

Expert opinion was unanimous that the collection had no artistic merit. One expert expressed his surprise that "so voracious a collector should not by hazard have picked up even one meritorious object."[39] The Court of Appeal held the trust void. "I can conceive," said Harman L.J., "of no useful object to be served in foisting upon the public this mass of junk. It has neither public utility nor educational value."[40]

v. Youth. Sports at School and University. Education is specially concerned with the young. In many situations a provision for the young will be held charitable although the same provision for older people would fail.

In *Re Mariette*,[41] there was a gift to provide Eton fives courts and squash rackets courts at Aldenham School. Eve J. upheld this, on the principle that learning to play games at a boarding school was as important as learning from the books.

The sporting facilities need not be limited to a particular school or institution. In *I.R.C. v. McMullen*,[42] a trust to provide facilities for pupils at schools and universities in the United Kingdom to play association football or other games or sports was held valid by the House of Lords. Lord Hailsham said[43]: "The picture of education when applied to the young ... is complex and varied ... It is the picture of a balanced and systematic process of instruction, training and practice containing both spiritual, moral, mental and physical elements ... I reject any idea which would cramp the education of the young within the school or university campus, limit it to formal instruction, or render it devoid of pleasure in the exercise of skill." But this wide definition of education is not without its limits. Lord Hailsham stated that the mere playing of games or enjoyment or amusement or competition was not *per se* charitable nor necessarily educational; and that a trust for physical education *per se* and not associated with persons of school age or just above was not necessarily a good charitable gift.[44]

---

[38] [1965] Ch. 85.

[39] *ibid.* at 107.

[40] *ibid.*

[41] [1915] 2 Ch. 284. For sport outside universities and schools, see *post*, p. 418.

[42] [1981] A.C. 1; [1980] Conv. 173, 225 (J. Warburton); (1986) 1 *Trust Law & Practice* 22 (D. Evans).

[43] [1981] A.C. 1 at 18.

[44] The Cliff Richard Tennis Development Trust was registered in 1991; Annual Report, para. 74.

Trusts for sport outside educational facilities and the services are not charitable[45] unless they come within the scope of the Recreational Charities Act 1958,[46] although this approach may now be outmoded.[47] But intelligent games like chess are educational for young people; though Vaisey J. in *Re Dupree's Deed Trusts*[48] recognised that here, as with outdoor games, the problem of distinguishing between the influence of one activity and another was very difficult. He foresaw a slippery slope from chess to draughts, to bridge and whist, and stamp collecting and acquiring birds' eggs.[49] All that can be said is that purposeful activities for the young receive favourable treatment. The Boy Scout Movement[50] and the National Association of Toy Libraries[51] are charities, and a gift for an annual treat or field day for school children at Turton has been upheld as encouraging a study of natural history.[52]

vi. Professional Bodies. Professional bodies may be charitable if their object is the advancement of education. The object of the Royal College of Surgeons[53] was stated in the royal charter of 1800 to be: "the due promotion and encouragement of the study and practice of the . . . art and science of surgery."

The fact that the College gives assistance and protection to its members is ancillary only; and the College was held to be a charity. Similarly, the Royal College of Nursing,[54] as the advance of nursing as a profession in all or any of its branches was a charitable purpose. The Construction Industry Training Board was held to be charitable,[55] and subsequently most of the Industrial Training Boards have been registered as charities.[56]

But if the object or one of the objects of the society is to promote the status of the profession or the welfare of its members, it will not be charitable. The General Nursing Council for England and Wales,

---

[45] *Re Nottage* [1895] 2 Ch. 649 (a prize for a yacht race).
[46] *post*, p. 419.
[47] Decisions, Vol. 5 (1997), p. 13.
[48] [1945] Ch. 16; (a chess contest in Portsmouth for males under 21). This is not contrary to Sex Discrimination Act 1975. Charities are excepted: s.43. Sex Discrimination Act 1975 (Amendment of Section 43) Order 1977 (S.I. 1977 No. 528). A similar trust was established for girls in Portsmouth under 18; see (1977) 41 Conv.(N.S.) 8.
[49] *ibid.* at 20.
[50] *Re Webber* [1954] 1 W.L.R. 1500.
[51] Annual Report 1973, para. 41.
[52] *Re Mellody* [1918] 1 Ch. 228.
[53] *Royal College of Surgeons v. National Provincial Bank Ltd* [1952] A.C. 631.
[54] *Royal College of Nursing v. St. Marylebone Borough Council* [1959] 1 W.L.R. 1077; *Institute of Civil Engineers v. I.R.C.* [1932] 1 K.B. 149.
[55] *Construction Industry Training Board v. Att.-Gen.* [1973] Ch. 173.
[56] Annual Report 1973, para. 39; *cf. I.R.C. v. Oldham Training and Enterprise Council* [1996] S.T.C. 1218 (not exclusively charitable because promotion of commerce conferred private benefits).

which is a statutory body, had as its main function the regulation of the nursing profession; and was not therefore charitable.[57]

vii. Political Propaganda Masquerading as Education.[58]

Political purposes are not charitable. They may be for the public benefit, but they are partisan. The court cannot determine whether any particular programme is for the public benefit.[59] Nor can such a trust be charitable even where the testator's project has subsequently been endorsed by Parliament.[60] A trust for political purposes will fail. Attempts have been made to foster the doctrines of a political party under the guise of a trust for education by providing for the advancement of adult education on the lines of the principles of that party.[61] In *Re Hopkinson*,[62] Vaisey J. explained the principle as follows: "Political propaganda masquerading ... I do not use the word in any sinister sense ... as education is not education within the statute of Elizabeth ... In other words it is not charitable."[63] But there is no doubt that the prospects of success are greater if purposes are presented in the form of education. In *Re Scowcroft*,[64] the gift was of income to be applied "for the furtherance of Conservative principles and religious and mental improvement," and this succeeded. Similarly in *Re Koeppler's Will Trusts*[65] a gift to further the work of an educational project was held charitable even though the testator's express aspirations (the formation of informed international public opinion and the promotion of greater co-operation in Europe and the West) were not regarded as charitable. The project involved conferences with a "political flavour," but did not further the interests of a particular political party, nor seek to change the law or government policies.

---

[57] *General Nursing Council for England and Wales v. St. Marylebone Borough Council* [1959] A.C. 540; *Chartered Insurance Institute v. London Corporation* [1957] 1 W.L.R. 867 (promoting the insurance profession).

[58] Annual Report 1966, para. 38 (warning the overworking of the word "education"); 1969, para. 11; 1971, paras. 7–10; 1981, para. 54.

[59] *Bowman v. Secular Society* [1917] A.C. 406 at 421.

[60] *Re Bushnell* [1975] 1 W.L.R. 1596 (national health system introduced after testator's death but before the litigation); (1975) 38 M.L.R. 471 (R. Cotterrell).

[61] *Bonar Law Memorial Trust v. I.R.C.* (1933) 49 T.L.R. 220 (Conservative); *Re Hopkinson* [1949] 1 All E.R. 346 (Socialist); *cf. McDougall* [1957] 1 W.L.R. 81. See also *Re Ogden* [1933] Ch. 678, where, however, a trust for Liberal institutions was upheld on other grounds.

[62] [1949] 1 All E.R. 346. See also *McGovern v. Att.-Gen.* [1982] Ch. 321 and *Southwood v. Att.-Gen.*, *The Times*, July 18, 2000, *post*, p. 425, where essentially political trusts were not saved by educational elements.

[63] *ibid*. at 350.

[64] [1898] 2 Ch. 638; *cf.* in the field of religion, *Re Hood* [1931] 1 Ch. 240 (spreading Christian principles by extinguishing "the drink traffic").

[65] [1986] Ch. 423; [1985] Conv. 412 (T. Watkin).

While a students' union is a charitable body, as being ancillary to the educational purposes of the college or university,[66] the donation of union funds for political, or indeed for charitable purposes which are not educational, is not permitted. So in *Baldry v. Feintuck*[67] the use of union funds to campaign for the restoration of free school milk was restrained as political, although the fact that a students' union has political clubs is not inconsistent with its charitable status.[68]

viii. Private and Independent Schools. An educational institution cannot be charitable if it is operated for profit.[69] The modern practice is to operate fee-paying schools as non-profit-making bodies which can then obtain the fiscal benefits available to educational charities.[70]

There has been no challenge in law to the charitable status of public schools. Labour Party policy, however, was at one time to deprive independent schools of the fiscal benefits of charitable status, on the ground that they exercise a divisive influence on our society, and are hostile to the public, and not beneficial.[71] Such a change could only come by legislation, for which there are no current plans.[72]

D. The Advancement of Religion[73]

i. What is Religion? In *Bowman v. Secular Society*,[74] Lord Parker of Waddington suggested that any form of monotheism will be recognised as a religion, but the restriction to monotheism is

---

[66] *London Hospital Medical College v. I.R.C.* [1976] 1 W.L.R. 613. The National Union of Students is not a charity; see *Att.-Gen. v. Ross, infra*.

[67] [1972] 1 W.L.R. 552. A donation to the charity War on Want was also restrained, as it was not an educational charity. See Annual Report 1983, paras. 95 and 96 and App. A; (1986) 1 *Trust Law & Practice* 47 (J. Warburton). In *Webb v. O'Doherty, The Times*, February 11, 1991, expenditure on a campaign to end the Gulf War was restrained.

[68] *Att.-Gen. v. Ross* [1986] 1 W.L.R. 252; All E.R. Rev. 1985 at 320 (P. Clarke). (Preliminary issue as to whether Attorney General had standing to seek injunction to restrain donation of union funds to striking miners and famine aid in Ethiopia). By similar reasoning, a charity cannot guarantee the liabilities of a non-charity; *Rosemary Simmons Memorial Housing Association Ltd v. United Dominions Trust Ltd* [1986] 1 W.L.R. 1440. See further [1988] Conv. 275 (J. Warburton).

[69] *Re Girls' Public Day School Trust* [1951] Ch. 400.

[70] *Abbey, Malvern Wells Ltd v. Minister of Local Government and Housing* [1951] Ch. 728.

[71] Recommended by the Public Schools Commission (1968); see Annual Report 1974, para. 16. See also Chesterman, *Charities, Trusts and Social Welfare*, 336–339.

[72] *The Times*, January 19, 1998.

[73] The only reference to religion in the Preamble is to the repair of churches. For the view that this head should be abolished, see (1995/6) 3 *Charity Law & Practice Review* 29 (P. Edge).

[74] [1917] A.C. 406.

probably now outmoded.[75] Religion requires a spiritual belief. It may include, but is greater than, morality, or a recommended way of life. In *Re South Place Ethical Society*,[76] one question was whether the Society's objects, which were the "study and dissemination of ethical principles and the cultivation of a rational religious sentiment," were charitable under this heading. Dillon J. held that they were not. "Religion as I see it, is concerned with man's relations with God, and ethics are concerned with man's relations with man. The two are not the same, and are not made the same by sincere enquiry into the question; what is God?"[77] Similarly, the objects of a body such as the Freemasons, whose rules demand the highest personal, social and domestic standards, do not constitute a religion, even though they insist upon a belief in a divine spirit.[78] Nor did *Keren Kayemeth Le Jisroel*, the organisation whose object was the settlement of Jews in Palestine and neighbouring lands.[79] In any event, to be charitable, a trust must be for the *advancement* of religion; and this means "the promotion of spiritual teaching in a wide sense and the maintenance of the doctrines on which this rests, and the observances that serve to promote and manifest it—not merely a foundation or cause to which it can be related."[80]

ii. Religious Toleration Within Christianity. The advent of religious toleration in the seventeenth century permitted the recognition of Christian sects other than the Established Church, and it seems now that no distinction is drawn between them.[81] Thus, trusts for Roman Catholics,[82] Quakers,[83] Baptists,[84] Methodists,[85] and the Exclusive Brethren,[86] have been upheld. So also small groups, promoting minority religions. In *Thornton v. Howe*,[87] Romilly M.R. went so far as to hold as charitable a trust for the publication of the

---

[75] *Tudor on Charities* (8th ed.), 63–64.

[76] [1980] 1 W.L.R. 1565; [1980] Conv. 150 (St. J. Robilliard).

[77] *ibid.* at 1571. The Society was charitable under the second and fourth headings; *ante*, p. 404, *post*, p. 427.

[78] *United Grand Lodge of Ancient Free and Accepted Masons of England and Wales v. Holborn B.C.* [1957] 1 W.L.R. 1080. See also *Re Macaulay's Estate* [1943] Ch. 475n; *Berry v. St. Marylebone B.C.* [1958] Ch. 406. (Theosophy held to be a philosophical or metaphysical conception, rather than the advancement of religion).

[79] *Keren Kayemeth Le Jisroel v. I.R.C.* [1931] 2 K.B. 465; *affd.* [1932] A.C. 650.

[80] *ibid.*

[81] *Dunne v. Byrne* [1912] A.C. 407; *Re Flynn* [1948] Ch. 24.

[82] *Dunn v. Byrne, supra.*

[83] *Re Manser* [1905] 1 Ch. 68.

[84] *Re Strickland's W.T.* [1936] 3 All E.R. 1027.

[85] "The Voice of Methodism" was registered in 1965; Annual Report App. C, para. 1.

[86] *Holmes v. Att.-Gen., The Times*, February 12, 1981. But their place of worship did not qualify for rating exemption in *Broxtowe Borough Council v. Birch* [1983] 1 W.L.R. 314; Annual Report 1982, App. B. See also App. C.

[87] (1862) 31 Beav. 14. As this gift was to take effect out of land, it was void as infringing the Statutes of Mortmain, now repealed. See (1997) 18 *Legal History* 1 (C. Stebbings).

sacred writings of Joanna Southcott, who claimed that she was with child by the Holy Ghost and would give birth to a new Messiah. In *Re Watson*,[88] Plowman J. upheld a trust for the continuation of the work of God . . . in propagating the truth as given in the Holy Bible" by financing the continued publication of the books and tracts of one Hobbs who, with the testator, was the leading member of a very small group of undenominational Christians. Expert evidence regarded the intrinsic value of the work as nil; but it confirmed the genuineness of the belief of the adherents of that small group.

Cases like these raise the question of the limits of such trusts. This is an area where crankish views can be held with the greatest fervour and good faith. Should any belief, however outlandish, shared perhaps by only a handful of friends, be entitled to the perpetuity and fiscal privileges given to charities? Or, should such a religion be required to show some relation to orthodox religious thought? This is not a question of public benefit, as "where the purpose in question is of a religious nature . . . the court assumes a public benefit unless the contrary is shown."[89] It seems, therefore, that, if a movement can establish that its tenets are within the scope of the Christian religion, it is no objection that those tenets are theologically unsound, or that the number of followers is minimal. Minority groups are well looked after. But "doctrines adverse to the very foundation of all religion"[90] cannot be charitable.

iii. Non-Christian Religions. "The law of charity does not now favour one religion to another."[91] The charitable status of non-Christian religions is a question of growing importance because of the increase in the numbers of members of non-Christian religions among the population. A gift for the promotion of the Jewish religion has been upheld.[92] Likewise the promotion of the faith of a Hindu sect.[93] It is believed that Sikh temples and other centres of non-Christian worship have been accorded the non-domestic rating privileges applicable to charities,[94] and there seems little doubt that all non-Christian religions will be treated equally. This situation

---

[88] [1973] 1 W.L.R. 1472. See also *Funnell v. Stewart* [1996] 1 W.L.R. 288 (faith healing upheld); (1996) 112 L.Q.R. 557 (R. Fletcher).

[89] *per* Plowman J. at 1482. See also *Holmes v. Att.-Gen., The Times*, February 12, 1981.

[90] *per* Romilly M.R. in *Thornton v. Howe* (1862) 31 Beav. 14 at 20.

[91] *Varsani v. Jesani* [1999] Ch. 219 at 235. See also *Neville Estates Ltd v. Madden* [1962] Ch. 832; *Gilmour v. Coats* [1949] A.C. 457–458. For human rights issues see (1997–99) 5 *Charity Law & Practice Review* 153 (T. Spring and F. Quint).

[92] *Neville Estates Ltd v. Madden* [1962] Ch. 832. The position of Buddhism was left open in *Re South Place Ethical Society* [1980] 1 W.L.R. 1565.

[93] *Varsani v. Jesani* [1999] Ch. 219.

[94] Local Government Finance Act 1988, Sched. 5, para. 11, as amended by L.G.F.A. 1992, Sched. 10, para. 3.

may give rise to a number of difficult questions if charitable status is claimed for some mystical oriental and other cults.[95]

iv. Related Purposes. A large number of purposes have been accepted as charitable, although indirectly connected with the advancement of religion. Again, only a few illustrations can be selected. Many of these relate to the erection of churches or the maintenance of the fabric of religious buildings; which includes a window,[96] a tomb in the church,[97] and bells.[98] A trust for a graveyard, even though restricted to one denomination, is charitable,[99] but not a trust for individual tombs in the churchyard.[1]

Similarly, a trust for the benefit of the clergy,[2] or for the church choir,[3] and also for retired missionaries.[4] Where the testator uses phrases like "for God's work,"[5] or "for his work in the parish,"[6] the court will often find circumstances to indicate that the purposes are intended to be limited to charitable religious purposes.[7]

E. Other Purposes Beneficial to the Community[8]

This is the residual head of charity; the most difficult, as Sir Samuel Romilly called it as he presented the formulation.[9] The earlier three heads are in their nature charitable. There is no need in those cases to prove that the relief of poverty or the advancement of education or religion is beneficial. The public element there, as we will see,[10] concerns the extent to which those benefits are made available to the public or a section of the public as opposed to a group of individuals. With the fourth head, however, it must be

---

[95] On "fringe" religious organisations, see Annual Report 1976, paras. 103–108; and on exorcism, paras. 65–67. The Unification Church (the "Moonies") has also been registered; Annual Report 1982, paras. 36–38, App. C. The Attorney General announced on February 3, 1988, that a High Court action to deprive the "Moonies" of charitable status was being dropped. As to Scientology, see *R. v. Registrar General, ex Segerdal* [1970] 2 Q.B. 697 (meeting place not registrable under Places of Worship Registration Act 1855). It does not have charitable status.

[96] *Re King* [1923] 1 Ch. 243; *Re Raine* [1956] Ch. 417.

[97] *Hoare v. Osborne* (1866) L.R. 1 Eq. 585.

[98] *Re Pardoe* [1906] 2 Ch. 184; an extreme case, as the purpose was to commemorate the restoration of the Monarchy.

[99] *Re Manser* [1905] 1 Ch. 68; *Re Eighmie* [1935] Ch. 524.

[1] *Lloyd v. Lloyd* (1852) 2 Sim.(N.S.) 225.

[2] *Middleton v. Clitheroe* (1798) 3 Ves. 734 (stipends); *Re Williams* [1927] 2 Ch. 283 (education of candidates for Ministry); *Re Forster* [1939] Ch. 22.

[3] *Re Royce* [1940] Ch. 514.

[4] *Re Mylne* [1941] Ch. 204; *Re Moon's W.T.* [1948] 1 All E.R. 300.

[5] *Re Barker's W.T.* (1948) 64 T.L.R. 273. See also *Re Darling* [1896] 1 Ch. 50.

[6] *Re Simson* [1946] Ch. 299; *post*, p. 439.

[7] *Re Moon's W.T.* [1948] 1 All E.R. 300.

[8] See generally (1983) 36 C.L.P. 241 (H. Cohen). Most new registrations are under this heading; Annual Report 1985, para. 8.

[9] *Morice v. The Bishop of Durham* (1805) 10 Ves. 522 at 531.

[10] *post*, pp. 427 *et seq.*

shown that the selected purposes are beneficial; beneficial, that is, in the way which the law regards as charitable.

i. The Spirit and Intendment of the Preamble. The Preamble has always constituted the general statement of charitable purposes. The purposes were:

" . . . the relief of aged, impotent and poor people; the maintenance of sick and maimed soldiers and mariners, schools of learning, free schools, and scholars in universities; the repair of bridges, ports, havens, causeways, churches, sea banks and highways; the education and preferment of orphans; the relief, stock, or maintenance of houses of correction; the marriage of poor maids; the supportation aid and help of young tradesmen, handicraftsmen and persons decayed; the relief or redemption of prisoners or captives; the aid or ease of any poor inhabitants concerning payment of fifteens, setting out of soldiers and other taxes."

Since its repeal, the cases themselves are the source of the principle. A purpose which is expressly included in the Preamble is charitable; and also one covered by case authority. But "not every object of public general utility must necessarily be a charity."[11] The purpose need not be *eiusdem generis* with those listed in the Preamble, but must be charitable in the same sense.[12] When new purposes arise, it is not sufficient to show that the purpose is beneficial. It must be shown to be beneficial within the spirit and intendment of the Preamble, or by analogy from the principles established by the cases.[13] In *Williams' Trustees v. I.R.C.*,[14] a trust for promoting the interests of the Welsh community in London failed, on the ground that the objects of the trust, though beneficial to the community, were not beneficial in the way which the law regards as charitable. Similarly, trusts for international co-operation have usually failed, either on the ground that their purposes are not within the spirit and intendment of the statute,[15] or because they are political.[16] On the other hand, in

---

[11] *per* Lindley L.J. in *Re Macduff* [1896] 2 Ch. 451 at 456; *Att.-Gen. v. National Provincial and Union Bank of England* [1924] A.C. 262 at 265.

[12] *Re Strakosch* [1949] Ch. 529.

[13] See *Williams' Trustees v. I.R.C.* [1947] A.C. 447 at 455. See also *Brisbane C.C. v. Att.-Gen. for Queensland* [1979] A.C. 411 at 422.

[14] [1947] A.C. 447. The trust was later validated under the Charitable Trusts (Validation) Act 1954, p. 443, *post*; Annual Report 1977, paras. 71–80.

[15] *Re Strakosch* [1949] Ch. 529 (the furthering of understanding between the Union of South Africa and the Mother Country); *cf.* Annual Report 1983, para. 18; *Keren Kayemeth Le Jisroel v. I.R.C.* [1932] A.C. 650 (resettlement of Jews). See Picarda, 166–167.

[16] See *McGovern v. Att-Gen.* [1982] Ch. 321, *post*, p. 424; *Re Koeppler's W.T.* [1986] Ch. 423 (formation of an informed international public opinion and promotion of greater co-operation in Europe and the West not regarded as charitable, although gift upheld as being for the furtherance of the work of a charitable educational project).

Scottish Burial Reform and Cremation Society v. Glasgow Corporation,[17] a non-profit-making cremation society was held charitable by analogy with cases holding burial grounds to be so, though neither facility receives specific mention in the Preamble. Over the years, of course, the law has been developed in a radical manner. There is no definitional boundary to the fourth class; any purpose can be argued as coming within it; and Russell L.J. went so far as to say that if a purpose is beneficial to the community, it is prima facie charitable in law, and that the analogy approach is too restrictive.[18] The treatment of the problem has been much improved by the obligation first imposed by the Charities Act 1960 to register charities with the Charity Commissioners.[19] For, as part of their jurisdiction to register or to refuse registration, the Commissioners have built up a valuable range of precedents by which they can be guided, and though this has had to be based on the existing case law, nevertheless the Commissioners feel that they can develop from it "such a concept of the field of charity as may meet the needs of the community."[20] There is an appeal from the Commissioners' decision to the court.[21]

ii. The Test is What the Law Treats as Charitable. The question whether a purpose is beneficial to the community is one that the court must decide in the light of all the evidence available. What the donor thought, or what other people think is not the issue. In a sense, the test is objective, yet the judges, as we saw in the case of artistic questions, cannot avoid making a subjective choice.

In *National Anti-Vivisection Society v. Inland Revenue Commissioners,*[22] the question was whether the Society was entitled to relief from income tax on the ground that its object, which was the total suppression of vivisection, was charitable. The protection of animals from cruelty is a charitable purpose.[23] Vivisection, on the other hand, is a necessary part of medical research and, as such, is itself beneficial to the community. The question, as Lord Simonds said "is whether the court, for the purposes of determining whether the object of the society is charitable may disregard the finding of fact that any assumed public benefit in the direction

[17] [1968] A.C. 138.
[18] *Incorporated Council of Law Reporting v. Att.-Gen.* [1972] Ch. 73 at 88. *cf. Re South Place Ethical Society* [1980] 1 W.L.R. 1565, where Dillon J. preferred the analogy approach. See Annual Report 1985, paras. 24–27 (analogy required, but strict approach to it undesirable); *Att.-Gen. of the Cayman Islands v. Wahr-Hansen* [2001] 1 A.C. 75.
[19] *post*, p. 462.
[20] Annual Report 1966, paras. 27–41.
[21] *post*, p. 463.
[22] [1948] A.C. 31. See also Decisions, Vol. 2 (1994) 1 (Animal AID, to prevent exploitation of animals by man, not charitable).
[23] *post*, p. 422.

of the advancement of morals and education was far outweighed
by the detriment to medical science and research and consequently to the public health which would result if the society
succeeded in achieving its object, and that on balance, the object
of the society, so far from being for the public benefit, was
gravely injurious thereto".[24]

The court undertook to make the value judgment, "weighing
conflicting moral and material utilities." On balance, on the evidence available to it, the suppression of vivisection was not beneficial to the public, and the claim failed.

The American Restatement takes a neutral position.[25] It sees
nothing improper in upholding trusts for both armament and disarmament and, by a parity of reasoning, vivisection and anti-
vivisection being charitable. This view greatly simplifies the task of
the court. The balancing of the merits of two different forms of
public benefit is a matter on which opinions may vary, and one on
which the court may not be the best judge.

iii. Examples of Trusts under the Fourth Head. The number of
cases decided under the fourth head is enormous, and only the main
groups can be examined.

(a) *Specific Mention in the Preamble. Age and Sickness.* The
Preamble refers to the "relief of aged, impotent and poor people."
The phrase is construed disjunctively, and there is no need to show
that the purpose of a trust includes all three. Thus, in *Re Robinson*,[26]
a gift for old people over 60 years of age was upheld; and also trusts
for the provision of housing for the aged.[27] Impotent means physically handicapped; and in *Re Lewis*,[28] a gift of £100 each to 10
blind girls and 10 blind boys in Tottenham was valid, there being no

---

[24] [1948] A.C. 31 at 60–61.

[25] *Restatement of the Law of Trusts*, § 374, comment 1; "The courts do not take sides or
attempt to decide which of two conflicting views of promoting the social interest of the
community is the better adapted for the purpose, even though the views are opposed to each
other. Thus, a trust to promote peace by disarmament, as well as a trust to promote peace
by preparedness for war, is charitable." *cf. Southwood v. Att.-Gen., The Times*, July 18,
2000; *post*, p. 425.

[26] [1951] Ch. 198; *Re Gosling* (1900) 48 W.R. 300 ("old and worn-out clerks" of the bank);
Re Wall (1889) 42 Ch.D. 510 (those "not under 50" were "aged"). This is outmoded;
Bryant (D.V.) Trust Board v. Hamilton City Council [1997] 3 N.Z.L.R. 342.

[27] *Re Cottam* [1955] 1 W.L.R. 1299; *Joseph Rowntree Memorial Trust Housing Association
Ltd v. Att.-Gen.* [1983] Ch. 159, (1983) 46 M.L.R. 782 (R. Nobles), All E.R. Rev. 1983 at
356 (P. Clarke); *Re Dunlop (deceased)* (1984) 19 *Northern Ireland Judgments Bulletin*. See
Annual Report 1967, paras. 22–29 (Homes for old people).

[28] [1955] Ch. 104.

requirement that they should also be poor. "It would be as absurd to require that the aged must be impotent or poor as it would be to require the impotent to be aged or poor, or the poor to be aged or impotent."[29]

But difficulties arise where the rich participate. What would be the effect of a gift for the relief of aged peers or impotent millionaires?[30] The answer is that "The word 'relief' implies that the persons in question have a need attributable to their condition as aged, impotent or poor persons which requires alleviating, and which those persons could not alleviate, or would find difficulty in alleviating, themselves from their own resources. The word 'relief' is not synonymous with 'benefit.' ... Thus a gift of money to the aged millionaires of Mayfair would not relieve a need of theirs as aged persons."[31]

Some of the other instances given in the preamble occasionally receive mention,[32] but there is reluctance to rely on them if the gift would not otherwise be charitable under Lord Macnaghten's classification. Their effect, now that the preamble is repealed, is obscure, but those that have been acted on by the courts will presumably continue in effect, for the preamble was never a substantive provision and hence its repeal cannot affect the authority of cases based on it.[33]

A trust for the relief of the sick is charitable,[34] and so are trusts for the support of hospitals.[35] Indeed, prior to the introduction of the National Health Service in 1946, such hospitals were probably the greatest beneficiaries of charitable gifts, and the main hospital service of the nation was dependent on charity. It is no objection in this context that the benefits will be received by the rich as well as the poor; nor that the hospital was a private hospital for paying patients.[36] Ancillary purposes consistent with the object of the hospital are included, such as benefits for the sick in hospital[37] or for nurses,[38] which improve the quality of the service, and the provision

---

[29] *Joseph Rowntree Memorial Trust Housing Association Ltd v. Att.-Gen.* [1983] Ch. 159 at 171.

[30] (1951) 67 L.Q.R. 164; (1955) 71 L.Q.R. 16 (R.E.M.). For the view that the poor cannot be excluded, see *Re Macduff* [1896] 2 Ch. 451.

[31] *Joseph Rowntree Memorial Trust Housing Association Ltd v. Att.-Gen., supra*, at 171.

[32] *e.g.* "The setting out of soldiers"; *Re Driffill* [1949] 2 All E.R. 933.

[33] See Charities Act 1960, s.38(4), unrepealed by Charities Act 1993.

[34] Including faith healing; *Funnell v. Stewart* [1996] 1 W.L.R. 288.

[35] *Re Smith's W.T.* [1962] 2 All E.R. 563. On charities engaged in fringe medicine, see Annual Report 1975, para. 70.

[36] *Re Resch's W.T.* [1969] 1 A.C. 514; [1978] Conv. 277 (T. Watkin); (1999) 62 M.L.R. 333 at 339 (M. Chesterman).

[37] *Re Roadley* [1930] 1 Ch. 524.

[38] *Re White's W.T.* [1951] 1 All E.R. 520.

of accommodation for the relatives of the critically ill.[39] A nursing home privately owned and run for profit is not however a charity.[40]

(b) *Social, Recreational and Sporting Trusts.* Great difficulty has been experienced in establishing a dividing line to determine the validity of trusts for social, recreational or sporting purposes. The uncertainty caused by a series of cases in the 1940s and 1950s created doubts as to the charitable status of a number of institutions which had always been assumed to be charitable, such as the National Playing Fields Association, the Women's Institute and a number of local activities such as village halls. The Recreational Charities Act 1958 rescued them, but made no attempt to deal with the many problems thrown up by these cases. They will provide a useful background to the Act.

A trust to provide sporting facilities was not charitable,[41] unless, as has been seen, the facilities were for pupils of schools or universities, in which case they would be regarded as being for the advancement of education,[42] or within the armed forces, when they would contribute to the safety and protection of the country,[43] or where the game was itself of an educational nature.[44]

The Charity Commissioners have recently stated that the matter might be due for reconsideration. While the promotion of sport for its own sake is not charitable, there is much to be said for the view that the promotion of sport as a means of promoting health or fitness for people of all ages is charitable.[45]

In *I.R.C. v. Glasgow Police Athletic Association*,[46] the Association, whose object was "to encourage and promote all forms of athletic sport and general pastimes" was held not to be charitable. In so far as the objects were concerned with the "encouragement of recruiting, the improvement of the efficiency of the force and the public advantage"[47] they would have been charitable. But the provision of mere recreation was not charitable; nor could it, in

---

[39] *Re Dean's W.T.* [1950] 1 All E.R. 882.
[40] *Re Resch's W.T., supra,* at 540.
[41] *Re Nottage* [1895] 2 Ch. 649 (prize for a yacht race); *Re Patten* [1929] 2 Ch. 276 (cricket); *I.R.C. v. McMullen* [1981] A.C. 1 at 15, where the point was expressly left open.
[42] *Re Mariette* [1915] 2 Ch. 284; *ante,* p. 407; *London Hospital Medical College v. I.R.C.* [1976] 1 W.L.R. 613; [1978] Conv. 92 (N. Gravells).
[43] *Re Gray* [1925] Ch. 362.
[44] *Re Dupree's Deed Trusts* [1945] Ch. 16, *ante,* p. 408.
[45] Decisions, Vol. 5 (1997), p. 13. See also (1997/98) 5 *Charity Law & Practice Review* 135 (P. Smith).
[46] [1953] A.C. 380.
[47] *per* Lord Normand, *ibid.,* at 395.

the circumstances of the case, be held to be merely incidental to the main purpose. It was therefore fatal to the claim.

Gifts for the establishment of recreation grounds for the public generally or for the inhabitants of a particular area have been held charitable,[48] likewise particular sporting facilities.[49] However, as has been seen, in *Williams' Trustees v. I.R.C.*,[50] a trust for the promotion of Welsh interests in London by various means, most of which were charitable, failed because they involved a "social" and recreational element.[51] Further problems arose in a stamp duty context in *I.R.C. v. Baddeley* in 1955.[52]

Land was conveyed to a Methodist Mission "for the promotion of the religious, social and physical well-being of persons resident in . . . West Ham and Leyton . . . by the provision of facilities for religious services and instruction; and for the social and physical training and recreation of . . . persons who . . . are in the opinion of [local Church] leaders members or likely to become members of the Methodist church . . . and of insufficient means otherwise to enjoy the advantages provided . . . By a majority of four to one (Lord Reid dissenting), the House of Lords held that the purposes were not exclusively charitable, because of the inclusion of purely "social" purposes; and three of their Lordships further held that the requirement of public benefit was not satisfied.[53]

The Recreational Charities Act 1958[54] attempted to remove the uncertainty caused by these decisions. The object[55] was to give statutory recognition to a number of trusts which had always been regarded as charitable, "without enlarging the definition of charity or encroaching on existing authorities (including *Baddeley's Case* itself), or making any institution charitable which was not ordinarily

---

[48] *Re Hadden* [1932] Ch. 133; *Re Morgan* [1955] 1 W.L.R. 738; *R. v. Doncaster Metropolitan Borough Council, ex Braim* (1989) 57 & C.R. 1; *Oldham Borough Council v. Att.-Gen.*, [1993] Ch. 210; *cf. Liverpool City Council v. Att.-Gen., The Times*, May 1, 1992 (covenant by council to use donated land as recreation ground did not create charitable trust).

[49] Annual Report 1984, paras. 18–25 (Oxford Ice Skating Association charitable under the 1958 Act and the general law). Birchfield Harriers Athletics Club was refused registration; Annual Report 1989, para. 53.

[50] [1947] A.C. 447, *ante*, p. 414.

[51] This element was deleted in 1977, when the Charity Commissioners validated the Trust under Charitable Trusts (Validation) Act 1954, *post*, p. 443; Annual Report 1971, paras. 71–80.

[52] [1955] A.C. 572.

[53] *post*, p. 436.

[54] (1959) 23 Conv.(N.S.) 15 (S. Maurice); (1958) 21 M.L.R. 534 (L. Price); [1980] Conv. 173 (J. Warburton).

[55] *Halsbury's Statutes*, Vol. 5, 806.

regarded as charitable before that decision." It validates prospectively and retrospectively certain cases of the provision of recreational or other leisure-time occupations if the facilities are provided
in the interests of social welfare.[56] Section 1 reads:

"—(1) Subject to the provisions of this Act, it shall be and be
deemed always to have been charitable to provide, or assist in the
provision of, facilities for recreation or other leisure-time occupation, if the facilities are provided in the interests of social welfare:

Provided that nothing in this section shall be taken to derogate
from the principle that a trust or institution to be charitable must
be for the public benefit.[57]

(2) The requirement of the foregoing subsection that the facilities are provided in the interests of social welfare shall not be
treated as satisfied unless—

(a) the facilities are provided with the object of improving the
conditions of life for the persons for whom the facilities
are primarily intended; and

(b) either—

(i) those persons have need for such facilities as aforesaid by reason of their youth, age, infirmity or dis-
ablement, poverty or social and economic
circumstances; or

(ii) the facilities are to be available to the members or
female members of the public at large.[58]

(3) Subject to the said requirement, subsection (1) of this section applies in particular to the provision of facilities at village
halls, community centres and women's institutes, and to the provision and maintenance of grounds and buildings to be used for
purposes of recreation or leisure-time occupation and extends to
the provision of facilities for those purposes by the organising of
any activity."

It will be seen that the Act has little effect upon the cases previously discussed. The "Welsh people" do not come within section
1(2)(b)(i)[59]; nor would the "Methodists or persons likely to become
Methodists" in *Baddeley*[60]; nor the Glasgow police, who would

---

[56] Selected as the criterion because the phrase appeared in other similar provisions, and had
been judicially interpreted; *Halsbury's Statutes*, Vol. 5, 806; House of Commons Official
Report, 322; February 11, 1958.

[57] *post*, pp. 427 *et seq.*

[58] It is no objection that the facilities may be reserved for particular groups, thereby excluding
the public at certain times; *Guild v. I.R.C.* [1992] 2 A.C. 310.

[59] *Williams v. I.R.C.* [1947] A.C. 447.

[60] *supra.*

presumably not be covered by "social and economic circumstances."[61] The Charity Commissioners, who are currently reviewing the Act,[62] have stated that it was intended to relieve the "class within a class" problem which arises where a fourth category purpose is available only to a restricted class and consequently may not satisfy the "public benefit" requirement.[63] They take the view that section 1(2)(*b*)(i) may be satisfied by groups having need of the facilities which are further restricted by reference to their race, nationality, ethnic origins or religion. Thus a community centre restricted to such a group could qualify, if the Act is otherwise satisfied.[64]

Village halls, women's institutes and so forth were included in subsection (3) to overcome any argument that their activities were not within the spirit and intendment of the Preamble. Express provision is made also for Miners' Welfare Trusts in section 2.[65]

To meet the "social welfare" qualification, the facilities must be provided with the object of improving the conditions of life for the persons for whom they are primarily intended. In *I.R.C. v. McMullen*[66] (the Football Association Youth Trust case), the majority of the Court of Appeal[67] adopted a restrictive view, considering that the words implied that only "the deprived" can benefit. On the other hand, Bridge L.J. adopted a more liberal approach. Social welfare is not limited to the deprived. "Hyde Park improves the conditions of life for residents in Mayfair as much as for those in Pimlico or the Portobello Road."[68] The approach of Bridge L.J. was adopted by the House of Lords in *Guild v. I.R.C.*,[69] where a gift for the benefit of a public sports centre was held charitable under the Act. Section 1(2) was satisfied where the object of the gift was to improve the conditions of life of the community generally. The facilities of the centre, which promoted physical well-being, would have this effect. There is no requirement under the Act for an educative element in the provision of recreational facilities.[70]

Further guidance on the construction of social welfare can be obtained from other statutes in which the phrase has been used.[71]

---

[61] *I.R.C. v. City of Glasgow Police Athletic Association* [1953] A.C. 380.
[62] *The Recreational Charities Act 1958 Discussion Document* (1999).
[63] *post*, p. 436.
[64] Decisions, Vol. 4 (1995), 17; Decisions, Vol. 5 (1997), p. 7. See *ibid.*, p. 12, suggesting that the Act is obscure and thus *Pepper v. Hart* [1993] A.C. 593 applies.
[65] *Wynn v. Skegness U.D.C.* [1966] 1 W.L.R. 52.
[66] *ante*, p. 407.
[67] [1979] 1 W.L.R. 130, especially at 138. The point was left open in the House of Lords; [1981] A.C. 1.
[68] At 143.
[69] [1992] 2 A.C. 310; [1992] Conv. 361 (H. Norman); (1992) 51 C.L.J. 429 (J. Hopkins).
[70] Decisions, Vol. 5 (1997), pp. 14–19.
[71] General Rate Act 1967, s.40. See now Local Government Finance Act 1988, s.47.

There must be something more than a group of individuals combining together, as a club or society, to benefit themselves.[72] The view of the Charity Commissioners is that social welfare has two characteristics: an ethical element (the meeting of needs which ought to be met by society, otherwise the conditions of life of the class concerned will be inadequate), and altruism (seeking to improve the conditions of life of others).[73]

(c) *Animals*. Trusts for the welfare of animals generally are charitable, though gifts for specified animals are not.[74] The charitable status of gifts to animals was originally limited to the welfare of animals which were useful to man,[75] and this rule was justified on the basis of public utility. More recently, the category has widened, although there are no words in the Preamble to support such gifts. The grounds of validity of such gifts have been differently stated in England and in Ireland. In Ireland, it is the simple and obvious good of the welfare of the animals themselves.[76] In England, the cases are justified on the ground that they "tend to promote and encourage kindness towards [animals], and to ameliorate the condition of the brute creation, and thus to stimulate humane and generous sentiments in man towards the lower animals, and by this means to promote feelings of humanity and morality generally, repress brutality, and thus elevate the human race."[77] On this basis, trusts have been upheld for a home for lost dogs,[78] cats and kittens needing care and attention,[79] the Society for the Prevention of Cruelty to Animals,[80] and for hospitals,[81] and humane slaughtering.[82] But there are limits. We have seen that a trust for the abolition of vivisection was not charitable because its purposes would, on balance, cause more harm than good to the public. The borderline in these cases is hard to draw. In *Re Grove-Grady*,[83] the Court of Appeal decided that it had been overstepped, Russell L.J. expressing the view that the

---

[72] See *Re Lipinski's W.T.* [1976] Ch. 235, *ante*, p. 363; Annual Report 1989, paras. 48–55 (Birchfield Harriers Athletics Club did not satisfy s.1(2)); Decisions, Vol. 1 (1993), 4 (rifle club not within s.1(2)); Decisions, Vol. 5 (1997), p. 7 (North Tawton Rugby Union Football Club failed public benefit and social welfare tests).

[73] Decisions, Vol. 5 (1997), p. 7.

[74] *ante*, p. 369.

[75] *London University v. Yarrow* (1857) 1 De G. & J. 72.

[76] *Armstrong v. Reeves* (1890) 25 L.R.Ir. 325.

[77] *Re Wedgwood* [1915] 1 Ch. 113, *per* Swinfen-Eday L.J. at 122. See also *Re Green's W.T.* [1985] 3 All E.R. 455.

[78] Re *Douglas* (1887) 35 Ch.D. 472.

[79] *Re Moss* [1949] 1 All E.R. 495.

[80] *Tatham v. Drummond* (1864) 4 De G.J. & Sm. 484. See Annual Report 1979, para. 20.

[81] *London University v. Yarrow* (1857) 1 De G. & J. 72.

[82] *Tatham v. Drummond (supra)*.

[83] [1929] 1 Ch. 557 (compromised on appeal; *Att.-Gen. v. Plowden* [1931] W.N. 89). *cf. Att.-Gen. (N.S.W.) v. Sawtell* [1978] 2 N.S.W.L.R. 200.

authorities had reached the furthest admissible point of benevolence in construing as charitable, gifts in favour of animals. There was a trust for the setting up of an animal refuge where the animals, birds and other creatures should be safe from molestation by man. A sanctuary which deprived mankind of all rights of involvement was not for the public benefit. This view may now be outmoded.

The decision does not cast doubt upon the charitable status of animal sanctuaries generally. Many purposes connected with animals could be made charitable by being expressed in terms of education[84] or of environmental preservation.[85]

(d) *Political Trusts.* Trusts whose object, direct or indirect, is the support of one political party are clearly not charitable.[86] The borderline between such trusts and trusts where political propaganda was "masquerading as education" has been discussed.[87]

The general principle is that political trusts are not charitable. In *Re Bushnell*,[88] the testator left money for "the advancement and propagation of the teaching of socialised medicine." The trust was neither an educational charity nor charitable under the fourth heading. The testator had died in 1941, and at that time legislation would have been required to achieve the purpose. The desirability of such legislation was a political matter. It made no difference that a national health service had subsequently been introduced, as the relevant time for judging the matter was the testator's death.

A second reason for the failure of the Anti-Vivisection trust[89] was that the objects of the Society required a change in the law. The majority treated this as necessarily being a political purpose. Lord Normand stressed that this should only be so where, as here, the change in the law was a *predominant object*,[90] while Lord Porter, who dissented, would have excluded only trusts which were purely political,[91] that is to say, where the object is to be attained *only* by

[84] *Re Lopes* [1931] 2 Ch. 130.
[85] See Annual Report 1973, para. 40.
[86] *Bonar Law Memorial Trust v. I.R.C.* (1933) 49 T.L.R. 220 (Conservative); *Re Ogden* [1933] Ch. 678 (Liberal); *Re Hopkinson* [1949] 1 All E.R. 346 (Socialist: the whole tenor of the gift was to mask political propaganda as education). It is doubtful whether *Re Scowcroft* [1898] 2 Ch. 638 would now be followed; the case itself might have been differently decided had the gift been only for the furtherance of Conservative principles. See also Annual Report 1982, paras. 45–51 (refusal to register Youth Training, whose purpose is to assist the Workers' Revolutionary Party); Annual Report 1991, para. 75 (Margaret Thatcher Foundation was political).
[87] *ante*, p. 409.
[88] [1975] 1 W.L.R. 1596.
[89] *National Anti-Vivisection Society v. I.R.C.* [1948] A.C. 31; *ante*, p. 415.
[90] *ibid.* at 77–78. See *Re Collier* [1998] 1 N.Z.L.R. 81 (promotion of euthanasia).
[91] *ibid.* at 56.

a change in the law. Ultimately "It is a question of degree of a sort well known to the courts."[92]

The treatment as political of any trust requiring a change in the law has been criticised. But whether the proposed change is for the public benefit "is not for the court to judge, and the court has no means of judging."[93] The Legislature decides on changes in the law. The judges' duty is to apply it. The judges should not be put in a position of being asked to hold that a controversial object, often a minority object, is so obviously for the public good that it should be pursued perpetually and tax-free. It is difficult, however, to answer the criticism that organisations campaigning for improvements in the law[94] cannot be registered as charities, while existing charities can and do campaign for and against change.[95]

The matter arose in *McGovern v. Att.-Gen.*,[96] where a non-charitable body, Amnesty International, sought to obtain charitable status for part of its activities by setting up the Amnesty International Trust, to which were transferred those aspects of its work which were thought to be charitable. The objects were: (i) the relief of needy persons who were, or were likely to become, prisoners of conscience, and their relatives; (ii) attempting to secure the release of prisoners of conscience; (iii) the abolition of torture or inhuman or degrading treatment or punishment; (iv) research into human rights and disseminating the results of the research.[97] These objects were to be carried out in all parts of the world. Purposes (i) and (iv), if standing alone, would have been charitable, but the inclusion of the other objects caused the trust to fail on the ground that it was political.[98] A trust could not be charitable if its direct and main object was to secure a change in the law of the United Kingdom or of foreign countries, for example by repealing legislation authorising capital or corporal punishment. The court could not judge

---

[92] *National Anti-Vivisection Society v. I.R.C.* [1948] A.C. 31 at 77.

[93] *per* Lord Simonds [1948] A.C. 31 at 62; *cf. Public Trustee v. Att.-Gen. for New South Wales* (1997) 42 N.S.W.L.R. 600.

[94] National Council for Civil Liberties; Amnesty.

[95] Lord's Day Observance Society; Temperance Societies. See [1997] 11 *Trust Law International* 35 (A. Sprince); (1999) 62 M.L.R. 333 at p. 349 (M. Chesterman).

[96] [1982] Ch. 321; [1982] Conv. 387 (T. Watkin); (1982) 45 M.L.R. 704 (R. Nobles); (1983) 46 M.L.R. 385 (F. Weiss); [1984] Conv. 263 (C. Forder); (1999) 52 C.L.P. 255 (G. Santow). See also *Re Koeppler's W.T.* [1986] Ch. 423; where the formation of an informed international public opinion and the promotion of greater co-operation in Europe and the West were not regarded as charitable, although the gift was upheld as being for the furtherance of the work of a charitable educational project.

[97] See Annual Report 1987, para. 12 (trusts for research into human rights upheld); Annual Report 1988, paras. 27–34 (Institute for the Study of Terrorism registered). See, however, *R. v. Radio Authority, ex p. Bull* [1998] Q.B. 294 (promotion of awareness of human rights with object of bringing pressure to bear on a government is political); [1997] P.L. 615 (J. Stevens and D. Feldman).

[98] It was not saved by a proviso restricting it to charitable purposes; *post*, 437.

whether this would be for the public benefit, locally or internationally. Nor could a trust be charitable if a direct and principal purpose was to procure the reversal of government policy or of governmental decisions at home or abroad.[99] Object (ii) was not simply for the "relief or redemption of prisoners or captives,"[1] but involved putting pressure on foreign governments and authorities. To ascribe charitable status to such a trust could prejudice the relations of this country with the foreign country concerned. This public policy consideration could not be ignored.

Trusts for the promotion of peace have run into difficulties. While the desirability of peace as an objective is not a matter of political controversy, the promotion of peace will be political if designed to challenge government policies. So in *Southwood v. Att.-Gen.*[2] the "advancement of the education of the public in the subject of militarism and disarmament" was not charitable as the dominant purpose was to promote pacifism and to challenge the policies of Western governments. Likewise in *Re Collier*[3] a trust to promote world peace was political and indeed unlawful where the testator was encouraging soldiers to "down arms".

A related problem arises where an existing charity is tempted to become involved in pursuing "causes" relating to the work with which it is concerned. It was suggested in *McGovern v. Att.-Gen.*[4] that if the objects had been charitable, it would not have mattered that the trustees had incidental powers to employ political means to further these objects. The Charity Commissioners have offered some revised guidelines to charity trustees, including the following points[5]:

(i) Any political activity must be in furtherance of and ancillary to the charity's stated objects and within its powers. To be ancillary, the activity must serve and be subordinate to the charity's purpose.

---

[99] The decision was distinguised in *Re Koeppler's W.T., supra,* where an educational project involving conferences with a "political flavour" was held charitable. The project was not concerned with party politics nor did it seek to change laws or government policies.

[1] Preamble to the Charitable Uses Act, 1601.

[2] *The Times,* July 18, 2000; (2000) 14 *Trust Law International* 233 (J. Garton).

[3] [1998] 1 N.Z.L.R. 81.

[4] *supra.*

[5] *Political Activities and Campaigning by Charities* (1997 revision). In 1978 the activities of three international relief charities were reviewed (War on Want; Oxfam; and the Christian Aid Division), Annual Report 1978, paras. 21–29; and in 1979 three domestic charities (Abortion, the R.S.P.C.A., and the Howard League for Penal Reform); Annual Report 1979, paras. 18–22; Annual Report 1991, paras. 111–127 (Oxfam; War on Want). Annual Report 1988, paras. 27–34 (strong political views of trustees of the Institute for the Study of Terrorism did not affect charitable status, but warned to maintain objectivity). The RSPCA has been warned not to campaign against animal experiments which benefit mankind; *The Times,* March 28, 1996. See also *The Times,* July 1, 1996 (hunting).

   (ii) Where these requirements are met, the trustees may enter into a dialogue with the Government on matters relating to their purposes, and may respond to Green and White Papers.

  (iii) The trustees may inform and educate the public on issues relevant to the charity and on solutions to its needs. They must not advocate policies nor seek to inform the public on matters having no bearing on their charity, nor indulge in propaganda.

  (iv) The trustees may engage in campaigning, by reasoned argument and not on the basis of material which is merely emotive, if the above requirements are satisfied. They may advocate a change in law or policy which they reasonably believe would help to achieve the charity's purpose, or oppose a change which would hinder it. Similarly, they may promote legislation to achieve or further its purpose.

   (v) The trustees should not seek to organise public opinion to support or oppose a political party which has a particular policy, nor may a charity participate in party political demonstrations.

  (vi) Where the charity operates overseas, it may pursue activities which would be permissible at home even if considered political elsewhere, provided they are not actually illegal in the country where they are undertaken.

   (e) *Miscellaneous.* There is no way of explaining the full width of the fourth head. But some miscellaneous examples may be helpful. Gifts for the promotion of the efficiency of the fighting services are charitable. It has been seen that the promotion of sport in the Army is included[6]; so is a gift to the officers' mess,[7] and for the protection of the Kingdom against attack by hostile aircraft.[8] On the other hand, a provision for ex-members of the services is not charitable, unless confined to the aged or poor.[9] The efficiency of the police is similarly a charitable purpose,[10] and also a gift to a voluntary fire brigade.[11] The National Trust is charitable,[12] and the Royal National Lifeboat Institution; so also are gifts for the promotion of agriculture,[13] preservation of natural amenities,[14] and for environmental

---

[6] *Re Gray* [1925] Ch. 362.
[7] *Re Good* [1905] 2 Ch. 60.
[8] *Re Driffill* [1950] Ch. 92.
[9] *Re Meyers* [1951] Ch. 534.
[10] *I.R.C. v. City of Glasgow Police Athletic Association* [1953] A.C. 380. See also Annual Report 1984, para. 17 (Police Memorial Trust to commemorate officers killed on duty).
[11] *Re Wokingham Fire Brigade Trusts* [1951] Ch. 373; Annual Report 1979, paras. 74–81.
[12] *Re Verrall* [1916] 1 Ch. 100.
[13] *I.R.C. v. Yorkshire Agricultural Society* [1928] 1 K.B. 611; *Brisbane C.C. v. Att.-Gen. for Queensland* [1979] A.C. 411.
[14] *Re Granstown* [1932] 1 Ch. 537; *Re Corelli* [1943] Ch. 332.

objects.[15] A gift for the founding of a children's home is charitable.[16] The Incorporated Council of Law Reporting has been held to be charitable under the second and fourth heads[17]; and so has the study and dissemination of ethical principles and the cultivation of a rational religious sentiment.[18] An appeal for a public memorial may be charitable, as in the case of the statue of Earl Mountbatten of Burma.[19] The Charity Commissioners concluded that "the provision of a statue might be held to have a sufficient element of public benefit where the person being commemorated was nationally, and perhaps internationally, respected and could be said to be a figure of historical importance. In such a case the provision and maintenance of a statue can be held to be charitable as likely to foster patriotism and good citizenship, and to be an incentive to heroic and noble deeds." Finally, a gift "To my country, England,"[20] was upheld, the court taking the view, based on some old "locality" cases that,[21] in the context, the property could be applied only to charitable purposes.

4. Public Benefit[22]

A. Preliminary Points

A gift can only be charitable if it is for the public benefit. A few preliminary points must be made. First, it will be seen that the requirement differs in respect of each category,[23] and that it may differ within the fourth category, dependent upon the purpose concerned. Secondly, we will see that there has been disagreement among the Law Lords on the question whether tax exemption is a factor which should be taken into consideration in deciding upon charitable status.[24] Thirdly, it may seem anomalous to speak in terms of a requirement of public benefit in the fourth category, for that category is defined in terms of trusts for the benefit of the

---

[15] Annual Report 1973, para. 40; Annual Report 1979, paras. 61–65.

[16] *Re Sahal's W.T.* [1958] 1 W.L.R. 1243; *cf. Re Cole* [1958] Ch. 877 (gift for benefit of children in home too wide); doubted in *Tudor on Charities* (8th ed.), 100.

[17] *Incorporated Council of Law Reporting for England and Wales v. Att.-Gen.* [1972] Ch. 73; (1972) 88 L.Q.R. 171.

[18] *Re South Place Ethical Society* [1980] 1 W.L.R. 1565.

[19] Annual Report 1981, paras. 68–70.

[20] *Re Smith* [1932] 1 Ch. 153.

[21] The restriction of a benefit to a specified locality may enable the judge, by applying a benevolent construction, to find that a trust was charitable; *post*, p. 438.

[22] See generally (1956) 72 L.Q.R. 187 (G. Cross); (1958) 21 M.L.R. 138 (P. Atiyah); (1974) 33 C.L.J. 63 (G. Jones); (1975) 39 Conv.(N.S.) 183 (S. Plowright); (1976) 22 N.I.L.Q. 198 (J. Brady); (1977) 40 M.L.R. 397 (N. Gravells); [1978] Conv. 277 (T. Watkin); Goodman Committee Report Chap. 2 (Benefit to the "Community"); Chap. 3 ("Benefit" to the Community).

[23] *Gilmour v. Coats* [1949] A.C. 426 at 429; *I.R.C. v. Baddeley* [1955] A.C. 572 at 615.

[24] *Dingle v. Turner* [1972] A.C. 601; *post*, p. 429.

community. To establish a trust as charitable within this category, it is necessary that the purposes are beneficial in the way which the law regards as charitable, and also that the benefits are available to a sufficient section of the public. With trusts coming under the first three heads, the matter is rather different. The beneficial aspect of trusts for the relief of poverty, or the advancement of education or religion is assumed.[25] The necessary public element needs to be shown.

B. Trusts for the Relief of Poverty

i. A Class of Poor as Opposed to Selected Individuals. Poor Relations. The requirement of public benefit has been reduced, in the field of poverty, almost to vanishing point. It is necessary to distinguish between a gift to a class or group of poor persons, and a gift to specified poor individuals. The former will be charitable, even if the group is small, and personally connected with the donor; gifts to poor relations have been upheld since the middle of the eighteenth century.[26] As Jenkins L.J. said: "I think that the true question in each case has really been whether the gift was for the relief of poverty amongst a class of persons . . . or was merely a gift to individuals, albeit with relief of poverty amongst those individuals as the motive of the gift . . . "[27] Thus, a gift to such of the testator's relatives as shall be poor or "in special need"[28] or "in needy circumstances"[29] is charitable. Similarly a gift to "poor and needy" members of a class of six named relatives of the testator and their issue, there being 26 members at the testator's death and a likelihood of a substantial increase in future.[30] It does not matter that the distribution of capital can be made so as to exhaust the principal.[31]

ii. Poor Employees. Poor relations trusts are said to constitute an anomalous exception to the requirement of public benefit,[32] and we will see that a personal nexus or relationship between the group of

---

[25] *per* Lord Simonds in *National Anti-Vivisection Society v. I.R.C.* [1948] A.C. 31.

[26] *Isaac v. Defriez* (1754) Amb. 595. They are discussed at length in *Re Compton* [1945] Ch. 123, and in *Re Scarisbrick* [1951] Ch. 622. See also *Dingle v. Turner* [1972] A.C. 601; *infra.*

[27] In *Re Scarisbrick* [1951] Ch. 622 at 655; see also at 650–651; *Re Cohen* [1973] 1 W.L.R. 415 at 426; *Dingle v. Turner* [1972] A.C. 601 at 617.

[28] *Re Cohen* [1973] 1 W.L.R. 415.

[29] *Re Scarisbrick* [1951] Ch. 622.

[30] *Re Segelman* [1996] Ch. 171; [1996] Conv. 379 (E. Histed). The inclusion of named persons as objects of charity may be an extension of the rule.

[31] *Re Scarisbrick, supra; Dingle v. Turner, supra.*

[32] *Re Compton* [1945] Ch. 123 at 139, *per* Lord Greene M.R.

persons to be benefited is fatal to gifts under the other heads.[33] This relaxation in favour of poverty trusts applies also in connection with trusts for the relief of poverty among members of a friendly society,[34] or a professional association,[35] or employees of a company.

In *Dingle v. Turner*,[36] a testator created a trust for paying pensions to "poor employees of E. Dingle and Co. Ltd who are of the age of 60 years at least or who being of the age of 45 years at least are incapacitated from earning their living by reason of some physical or mental infirmity." At the date of the testator's death, the company employed over 600 persons, and there was a substantial number of ex-employees. The House of Lords upheld the gift as a charitable trust.

The poor relations cases had been recognised for 200 years, and, even if anomalous, should not now be overruled. It would be illogical to draw a distinction between poor relations, and poor employees or poor members. All forms of trusts for the relief of poverty should be treated the same, and there was no need to introduce into the poverty cases the stricter requirements of public benefit applicable to other forms of charitable trusts. Lord Cross suggested that one reason for the different treatment of poverty trusts—a practical justification but not the historical explanation—is that there is for a settlor a "temptation to enlist the assistance of the law of charity in private endeavours"[37] in order to gain the tax benefits, though the danger is not so great in the field of relief of poverty. Three Law Lords[38] doubted whether the fiscal considerations should be given any relevance in deciding whether a gift was charitable. There seems little doubt, however, that they often have done so.[39]

C. Trusts for the Advancement of Education

i. Benefit to the Public or a Section thereof. Much of what is said in this section also applies to the next two following sections. Poverty apart, a trust will only be charitable if it is "for the benefit of the community or an appreciably important class of the community."[40] The principle appears to be that the privileges of charity, and

---

[33] *post*, p. 430.
[34] *Re Buck* [1896] 2 Ch. 727.
[35] *Spiller v. Maude* (1886) 32 Ch.D. 158n. (aged and decayed actors).
[36] [1972] A.C. 601; *Re Gosling* (1900) 48 W.R. 300 (old and worn-out clerks in a banking firm); *Gibson v. South American Stores (Gath & Chaves) Ltd* [1950] Ch. 177 ("necessitous and deserving employees, ex-employes and their dependants").
[37] At 625.
[38] Lords Dilhorne, McDermott and Hodson.
[39] *ante*, p. 394.
[40] *per* Lord Westbury in *Verge v. Somerville* [1924] A.C. 496 at 499.

the loss of public revenue, should only be accorded to trusts which
provide a benefit to the public. There is no objection to a parent
educating children expensively, nor to isolated religious communities, nor to friendly societies for the benefit of members; but there
is no reason why these activities should be supported, indirectly, by
the taxpayer. Poor relations trusts, as has been seen, are a long-
established anomaly.

ii. Personal Nexus. Not every member of the public can benefit
from every charitable trust, and it becomes necessary to determine
what is a section of the public for these purposes. Again, this will
vary with the different categories. A trust for the advancement of
education is charitable if it is for the education of the public or of a
section of the public which is not selected on the basis of a personal
nexus or connection, either with the donor or between themselves.
Thus, a trust for the education of named persons or for
descendants of named persons,[41] or the children of employees of a
company,[42] or of members of a club is not charitable. But a trust for
the education of the residents of a certain borough in 1880 and their
descendants is charitable[43]; as are trusts for the education of children
of members of a particular profession,[44] and trusts for specified
schools and colleges, and even "closed" scholarships from a specified school to a college at Oxford or Cambridge[45]; unless, of course,
the number of possible beneficiaries was derisory.

In *Oppenheim v. Tobacco Securities Trust Co.*,[46] income was to
be applied in "providing for... the education of children of
employees or former employees of the British-American Tobacco
Company Ltd ... or any of its subsidiary or allied companies"
and there was power also to apply capital. The number of employees of the company and the subsidiary and allied companies exceeded 100,000. The House of Lords held that there was a
personal nexus between the members of the class of beneficiaries
and they did not constitute a section of the public. The trust
failed.

---

[41] *Re Compton* [1945] Ch. 123. "A trust established by a father for the education of his sons
is not a charity"; *per* Lord Simonds in *Oppenheim v. Tobacco Securities Trust Ltd* [1951]
A.C. 297 at 306.
[42] *Oppenheim v. Tobacco Securities Trust Ltd* [1951] A.C. 297.
[43] *Re Tree* [1945] Ch. 325.
[44] *Hall v. Derby Sanitary Authority* (1885) 16 Q.B.D. 163, approved in *Oppenheim v. Tobacco
Securities Trust Ltd, supra.*
[45] Though it is difficult to see how some of these trusts satisfy the *Oppenheim* rule; see Lord
McDermott in *Oppenheim, ante*, at 318. See also the anomalous "founder's kin" cases;
Picarda, 68; Tudor, 61.
[46] [1951] A.C. 297.

In the leading majority speech, Lord Simonds said that to constitute a section of the community for these purposes the "possible (I emphasize the word 'possible') beneficiaries must be not numerically negligible, and, secondly, that the quality which distinguishes them from members of the community . . . must be a quality which does not depend on their relationship to a particular individual . . . A group of persons may be numerous but, if the nexus between them is their personal relationship to a single propositus or to several propositi, they are neither the community nor a section of the community for charitable purposes."[47]

Lord McDermott, dissenting, pointed out the difficulties which arise in trying to lay down a positive rule in such a situation.[48] "But can any really fundamental distinction, as respects the personal or impersonal nature of the common link, be drawn between those employed, for example, by a particular university and those whom the same university has put in a certain category as the result of individual examination and assessment? Again, if the bond between those employed by a particular railway is purely personal, why should the bond between those who are employed as railwaymen be so essentially different? Is a distinction to be drawn in this respect between those who are employed in a particular industry before it is nationalised and those who are employed therein after that process has been completed and one employer has taken the place of many? Are miners in the service of the National Coal Board now in one category and miners in a particular pit or of a particular district in another? Is the relationship between those in the service of the Crown to be distinguished from that obtaining between those in the service of some other employer? Or, if not, are the children of, say, soldiers or civil servants to be regarded as not constituting a sufficient section of the public to make a trust for their education charitable?"[49] The question, he thought, should be one of degree, depending upon the facts of each particular case. All five Law Lords, sitting in *Dingle v. Turner*,[50] supported this view. This does not necessarily mean that *Oppenheim* would be decided differently. Taking all factors into account, these educational trusts for employees are attempts to use charity's fiscal privileges for the benefit of the company by providing a tax-free fringe benefit for the employees.[51] Such trusts should fail, not on the ground that the employees,

---

[47] [1951] A.C. 297 at 306.
[48] See also Cross J. in *Re Mead's Trust Deed* [1961] 1 W.L.R. 1244 at 1249; and Lord Denning M.R. in *I.R.C. v. Educational Grants Association Ltd* [1967] Ch. 993 at 1009; "There is no logic in it."
[49] At 317–318.
[50] [1972] A.C. 601; see also Annual Report 1971, para. 21.
[51] "It is an admirable thing that the children of employees should have a higher education, but I do not see why that should be at the expense of the taxpayer" *per* Harman L.J. in *I.R.C. v. Educational Grants Association Ltd, supra*, at 1013; *cf.* Annual Report 1971, para. 21.

however numerous, can never constitute a class of the public, but because the *purpose* of the trust, being a company purpose, is not charitable.[52] A trust for the advancement of religion among employees might be different[53]; as might an "entirely altruistic educational trust . . . if the size of the company is sufficiently large."[54] It is obvious that it is easier to criticise the "personal nexus" test than it is to improve upon it; and "it may well be that Lord Cross's halfway house creates more problems than it solves."[55]

iii. Benefiting Private Individuals. The question arises as to whether a donor can effectively obtain benefits for a group of private individuals by means of a charitable trust. He cannot do so by setting up a charitable trust in favour of the public and relying on the trustees to make grants in favour of a narrow group.

In *I.R.C. v. Educational Grants Association Ltd*[56] the defendant was a charitable corporation established for the advancement of education in general terms. It was financially supported by payments under a deed of covenant by the Metal Box Co. Ltd, and by senior executives of the company. The Association claimed the repayment of tax due in respect of payment under the covenant. Between 76 per cent and 85 per cent of the income of the relevant year had been paid towards the education of children of persons connected with the Metal Box Co. Ltd, and the Court of Appeal held that the tax was not recoverable, because the money had not been applied for charitable purposes only.[57]

It is impossible to say what percentage of a trust for charity could properly be spent in favour of a private group. In *Re Koettgen's Will Trusts*,[58] there was a trust for the promotion of commercial education among members of the public unable to acquire it at their own expense; and a direction that preference be given to the families of employees of a named company in respect of a maximum of 75 per cent of the income. This was charitable. Lord Radcliffe in *Caffoor v. Income Tax Commissioner, Colombo*,[59] thought that *Re Koettgen*

---

[52] *Dingle v. Turner, supra.*
[53] (1974) 33 C.L.J. 63 at 66 (G. Jones); *Dingle v. Turner, supra.*
[54] Annual Report 1971, para. 21.
[55] (1974) 33 C.L.J. 63 (G. Jones).
[56] [1967] Ch. 993; Annual Report 1976, paras. 45–49.
[57] See I.C.T.A. 1988, s.505(1), which permits exemption for a charitable body *so far as the income is applied to charitable purposes only.* In the *Educational Grants* case the non-charitable payments were *ultra vires.* If the objects permit such payments, the body is not charitable (subject to *Re Koettgen*) and there will be no tax exemption.
[58] [1954] Ch. 252.
[59] [1961] A.C. 584.

"edged very near to being inconsistent with" *Oppenheim*.[60] If a preference in favour of a private group is desired, it is essential to make it subsidiary to the trust in favour of the public; and the 75 per cent which succeeded in *Koettgen* should be regarded as the maximum.[61] If, however, there is an absolute right in favour of a private group, and not merely a preference, then the trust cannot be charitable. It is a matter of construction into which category the gift falls.[62]

D. Trusts for the Advancement of Religion

The notion of public benefit in religious trusts is very similar to that in education. The advancement of religion among the public or a section of the public is charitable, and there is no room for the argument of the atheists that it is not beneficial. The section of the public may be a sect, whether of the Christian religion, such as the Roman Catholic[63] or the Methodist Church,[64] or of a non-Christian religion, such as the Jewish.[65] And we have seen that the law is especially generous in favour of bona fide religions, even though they have minimal following.[66] Similarly a gift to a Church will be charitable even though the congregation is small. A trust is charitable if it makes available a religious activity to the public if they should wish to take advantage of it. It may be that a sufficient benefit to the public is shown by having amongst it persons who have enjoyed the benefit of religious experience. But an enclosed, cloistered, monastic activity is excluded.

In *Gilmour v. Coats*,[67] a gift of £500 was made to a Carmelite Priory "if the purposes of [the Priory] are charitable." The Priory consisted of a community of cloistered nuns, about 20 in number, who devoted their lives to prayer, contemplation and self-sanctification, and engaged in no external work.

The House of Lords held that the purposes were not charitable because they lacked the necessary public benefit. This could not be found in the benefits conferred upon the public by the prayers

---

[60] [1961] A.C. 584 at 604.
[61] See Annual Report 1978, paras. 86–89, where the Charity Commissioners followed *Re Koettgen* in three cases; 65 per cent and 75 per cent.
[62] *Re Martin, The Times*, November 19, 1980.
[63] *Dunne v. Byrne* [1912] A.C. 407; *Re Flinn* [1948] Ch. 241.
[64] *I.R.C. v. Baddeley* [1955] A.C. 572.
[65] *Neville Estates Ltd v. Madden* [1962] Ch. 832.
[66] *Re Watson* [1973] 1 W.L.R. 1472; (1974) 90 L.Q.R. 4.
[67] [1949] A.C. 426. Likewise services in a private chapel; *Hoare v. Hoare* (1886) 56 L.T. 147. But sufficient public benefit was found in *Holmes v. Att.-Gen., The Times*, February 12, 1981 (Exclusive Brethren). See Annual Report 1982, App. C.

and intercessions of the nuns according to the doctrine of the Roman Catholic Church. Such benefit was "manifestly not susceptible of proof"[68] in a court of law, and the doctrinal belief of the Roman Catholic Church would be no substitute[69]; nor in the edification of a section of the public by the example of the spiritual life followed by the nuns, for that was too vague and intangible to constitute a proper test[70]; nor by the availability of the religious life being open to all women of the Roman Catholic faith.

The latter argument provides an interesting comparison with trusts for the advancement of education. Lord Simonds accepted that there was a "speciously logical appearance" in the argument that "just as the endowment of a scholarship open to public competition is a charity, so also is a gift to enable any woman (or, presumably, any man) to enter into a fuller religious life a charity."[71] Yet there is no conflict here. The explanation is that a public benefit is supplied in educational trusts by the presence in society of educated people. A trust for the advancement of religion among the members of Catford Synagogue was held by Cross J. in *Neville Estates Ltd v. Madden*[72] to be charitable because the court was "entitled to assume that some benefit accrues to the public from the attendance at places of worship of persons who live in this world and mix with their fellow-citizens."[73] And "if it can be imagined that it was made a condition of a gift for the advancement of education that its beneficiaries should lead a cloistered life and communicate to no one, and leave no record of the fruits of their study, I do not think that the charitable character of the gift will be sustained."[74]

This suggests that there must be some benefit to the public as a whole, however indirect, rather than the section which decides to participate. This point arises also under the fourth head. It is odd, however, that a gift to enable pious women to spend their life in religious contemplation is not charitable; while a trust to propagate

---

[68] *Gilmour v. Coats* [1949] A.C. 426 at 446. But extra-statutory tax concessions have been made; Halsbury (4th ed.), para. 1073.

[69] The Irish courts take a different view and accept the doctrine of the Church: *O'Hanlon v. Logue* [1906] 1 I.R. 247. See generally [1981] J.L.H. 207 (M. Blakeney); [1990] Conv. 35 (C. Rickett).

[70] [1949] A.C. 426 at 446. *Cf. Re Wedgwood* [1915] 1 Ch. 113, where the uplifting example of kindness to animals constituted a benefit to the public. The views expressed in *Gilmour v. Coats* seem inconsistent with the acceptance of the advancement of religion as a charitable purpose.

[71] [1949] A.C. 426 at 448.

[72] [1962] Ch. 832.

[73] *ibid.* at 853.

[74] *per* Lord Simonds in *Gilmour v. Coats* [1949] A.C. 426 at 450.

religious works of no value is.[75] The convent's problem can, however, be overcome by an extension of their activities to include external work.[76]

The decision in *Gilmour v. Coats*[77] cast doubt on the charitable status of gifts for the saying of masses. It had been held in *Bourne v. Keane*[78] that a gift for masses was not illegal as a superstitious use, and in *Re Caus*[79] that it was charitable. This was doubted in *Gilmour v. Coats*,[80] but the charitable nature of such a gift was recently upheld in *Re Hetherington (deceased)*,[81] where the testatrix left £2,000 to the Roman Catholic Bishop of Westminster for "masses for the repose of the souls of my husband and my parents and my sisters and also myself when I die." One reason was that the celebration of a religious rite in public conferred a sufficient public benefit in the edifying effect it had on those attending. Celebration of the rite in private would not suffice because the benefit conferred by prayer was incapable of proof and the edification of the private class attending was not a public benefit.[82] In the present case there was no express term that the masses should be said in public, but in practice they would be and the gift should be so construed. The second reason for upholding the gift was that it provided stipends for the priests saying the masses, and thereby assisted in the endowment of the priesthood. This reason would seem equally applicable to gifts for the saying of masses in private, but assuming such gifts are not charitable it is possible that they are valid as anomalous non-charitable purpose trusts.[83]

E. The Fourth Head

In most of the situations which have been considered under this head, the trust is for the benefit of all the public. This is so with gifts which improve the efficiency of the fighting forces, or the police, or medical research, or public parks and sea walls, or law reporting. It does not matter that it is only a limited number of people who will take advantage of the benefit provided. "A bridge which is available for all the public may undoubtedly be a charity and it is indifferent how many people use it. But confine its use to a selected number of

---

[75] *Re Watson* [1973] 1 W.L.R. 1472; *ante*, p. 412.
[76] See Annual Report 1989, paras. 56–62; Decisions, Vol. 3 (1995), 11 (Society of the Precious Blood).
[77] [1949] A.C. 426.
[78] [1919] A.C. 815.
[79] [1934] Ch. 162; *O'Hanlon v. Logue* [1906] 1 I.R. 247.
[80] *supra.*
[81] [1990] Ch. 1; [1989] Conv. 453 (N. Parry); (1989) 48 C.L.J. 373 (J. Hopkins); All E.R. Rev. 1989, 307 (C. Sherrin).
[82] *Gilmour v. Coats, supra; Hoare v. Hoare* (1886) 56 L.T. 147; *Yeap Cheah Neo v. Ong Chen Neo* (1875) L.R. 6 P.C. 381.
[83] *ante*, p. 370.

persons, however numerous and important: it is then clearly not a charity. It is not of general public utility: for it does not serve the public purpose which its nature qualifies it to serve."[84]

The problem arises where the purposes are restricted to a group of persons. We have seen that trusts for the relief of the aged and the sick are charitable. Not everyone is aged or sick. But if the benefits are generally available, there is some benefit, albeit indirect, to the public generally.[85] Clearly, a trust under the fourth head cannot be charitable if it is confined to persons bound together by a personal nexus.[86] The inhabitants of a geographical area are a section of the public in this context. But there are dicta in *Williams v. I.R.C.*[87] and in *I.R.C. v. Baddeley*[88] which suggest that trusts under the fourth head, even if otherwise charitable, are subject to a stricter rule than trusts under the other three heads in relation to the selection of persons who are to benefit.

In *Williams v. I.R.C.* Lord Simonds suggested that, even if the trust would otherwise have been charitable, the "Welsh people in London," to whom the benefit was confined, would not have constituted a section of the public.[89] He returned to this in *Baddeley*. It is necessary to distinguish between "relief extended to the whole community yet by its very nature advantageous only to the few and a form of relief accorded to a selected few out of a larger number equally willing to take advantage of it."[90] He doubted whether the test could be satisfied "if the beneficiaries are a class of persons not only confined to a particular area but selected from within it by reference to a particular creed."[91] "Who has ever heard of a bridge to be crossed only by impecunious Methodists?"[92] The persons to be benefited must be the whole community, or all the inhabitants of a particular area. Not a "class within a class." Lord Reid disagreed

---

[84] *per* Lord Simonds in *I.R.C. v. Baddeley* [1955] A.C. 572 at 592.

[85] See also *Re Dunlop (deceased)* (1984) 19 *Northern Ireland Judgments Bulletin*; [1987] Conv. 114 (N. Dawson), where a home for "Old Presbyterian Persons" was held charitable. It did not fail on the "bridge for Methodists" principle, as the public generally benefits from having some members housed.

[86] *ante*, p. 430. This problem is not encountered with learned societies, where the benefit is not confined to the members; *Re South Place Ethical Society* [1980] 1 W.L.R. 1565. *Tudor on Charities* (8th ed.), 34–35, expresses the view that a personal nexus may not defeat trusts for the sick or aged, by analogy with poverty charities.

[87] [1947] A.C. 447.

[88] [1955] A.C. 572.

[89] Similarly with the Jews in *Keren Kayemeth Le Jisroel v. I.R.C.* [1942] A.C. 650. But see Annual Report 1977, para. 79, where the Charity Commissioners, when subsequently registering the *Williams* Trust as a charity under Charitable Trusts (Validation) Act 1954, held that the beneficiary class nevertheless did comprise a sufficient section of the public; *post*, p. 444. See also Decisions, Vol. 4 (1995), 8 (preservation of law and order for benefit of Jewish members of community not charitable).

[90] [1955] A.C. 572 at 592.

[91] *ibid.* See also *Re Lipinski's Will Trusts* [1976] Ch. 235.

[92] *ibid.*

and found no justification in the suggestion that the test for determining what was a section of the community should be different under the fourth head.[93]

. The matter must be considered to be one of uncertainty. The decision shows the difficulties which arise in this area from an attempt to lay down positive rules,[94] and Lord Simonds admitted that it "was often very difficult to draw the line."[95] The only solution appears to be to accept, in all heads of charity where public benefit is required, the more general and flexible test proposed by Lord McDermott,[96] and supported by the House in *Dingle v. Turner* through Lord Cross.[97] The question whether the beneficiaries constitute a section of the public "is a question of degree and cannot be by itself decisive of the question whether the trust is a charity. Much must depend on the purpose of the trust. It may well be that, on the one hand, a trust to promote some purpose, prima facie charitable, will constitute a charity even though the class of potential beneficiaries might fairly be called a private class and that, on the other hand, a trust to promote another purpose, also prima facie charitable, will not constitute a charity even though the class of potential beneficiaries might seem to some people fairly describable as a section of the public."[98]

5. THE INTERPRETATION OF CHARITABLE GIFTS AND PURPOSES

A number of special questions arise in connection with the construction of instruments which are claimed to create charitable trusts. The problems here discussed provide a further reminder of the importance of proper draftsmanship when setting up a charitable trust. The Charity Commissioners will help with advice,[99] and they will give reasons for the refusal to register, and make it possible for the trusts to be redrafted. The Commissioners warn draftsmen not to draft object clauses in unnecessarily wide terms, for this may allow non-charitable purposes to be included.[1] In *McGovern v. Att.-Gen.*,[2] a trust included political objects, but the deed provided that the objects were "restricted to those which are charitable according to the law of the United Kingdom but subject thereto they may be carried

---

[93] See also *Re Dunlop (deceased), ante,* p. 436, n. 85, which suggests that the test for each head is different, and that the test can differ even within the same head.

[94] (1974) 33 C.L.J. 63 (G. Jones).

[95] [1955] A.C. 572 at 592.

[96] *Oppenheim v. Tobacco Securities Trust Ltd* [1951] A.C. 297; *ante,* p. 430.

[97] [1972] A.C. 601; *ante,* p. 431.

[98] *ibid.* at 624.

[99] Charities Act 1993, s.29; Annual Report 1966, para. 19.

[1] Annual Report 1971, paras. 70–71; 1966, para. 39.

[2] [1982] Ch. 321, *ante,* p. 424.

out in all parts of the world." This proviso did not have the "blue-pencil" effect of cancelling out the non-charitable parts, and hence the trust was not charitable. The restriction was merely intended to make it clear that the trustees, when operating outside the United Kingdom, should be restricted to purposes charitable by United Kingdom law. In so far as the purposes of the trust included political and thus non-charitable objects, the proviso could not save it.

A. The Motive of the Donor

The charitable motive of the donor, even if expressed, is not of major significance. The rule cuts both ways. In *Re King*,[3] a will provided for the erection of a stained-glass window in a church in memory of her parents, her sister and the testatrix herself. This was held to be a valid charitable gift. The fact that the intention was "not to beautify the church or benefit the parishioners, but to perpetuate the memory of the testatrix and her relations"[4] was immaterial. Conversely, a non-charitable gift, such as a gift for the suppression of vivisection, cannot be made charitable by the donor's charitable motive.[5] But a clear charitable intent may help to turn an ambiguity in favour of charity; especially, as has been seen, where it is possible to find an intention to benefit the poor.[6]

B. The Locality Cases

Particular difficulty has been experienced with the "locality cases." The restriction of a benefit to a precise locality seemed at one time to colour the judges' views of the nature of the benefit. By a benevolent construction, the benefits concerned were construed as being charitable. These cases[7] were discussed by Lord Simonds in *Williams' Trustees v. I.R.C.*,[8] by Lord Greene M.R. in *Re Strakosch*,[9] and by the Court of Appeal in *I.R.C. v. Baddeley*.[10] They are to be treated as anomalous and not to be extended.[11] They will, however, be followed in cases directly similar.[12] At the other end of the locality scale, a gift "unto my country England" is a valid charitable gift.[13]

---

[3] [1923] 1 Ch. 243, following *Hoare v. Osborne* (1866) L.R. 1 Eq. 585.

[4] *ibid.* at 245.

[5] *National Anti-Vivisection Society v. I.R.C.* [1948] A.C. 31.

[6] *Biscoe v. Jackson* (1887) 35 Ch.D. 460; *Re Coulthurst's W.T.* [1951] Ch. 193; *Re Cottam* [1955] 1 W.L.R. 1299; *ante*, p. 403.

[7] The leading case is *Goodman v. Saltash Corp.* (1882) 7 App. Cas. 633.

[8] [1947] A.C. 447 at 459–460.

[9] [1949] Ch. 529 at 539–540.

[10] [1955] A.C. 572.

[11] *Houston v. Burns* [1918] A.C. 337; *Att.-Gen. v. National Provincial and Union Bank of England Ltd* [1924] A.C. 262; *Re Gwyon* [1930] 1 Ch. 255.

[12] A recent example is *Peggs v. Lamb* [1994] Ch. 172.

[13] *Re Smith* [1932] 1 Ch. 153.

C. The Charitable Status of the Trustee[14]

The charitable nature of a trust is determined by the terms of the trust and not by the status of the trustee. Non-charitable trustees may hold property on charitable trusts, and charity trustees may, subject, in the case of a corporation, to the terms of their incorporation, hold property on non-charitable trusts. But the charitable status of the trustee can in some cases, where the terms of the trust are not spelled out, lead the court to construe the terms of the trust as charitable. A gift to a bishop or vicar, without the purposes being specified, may be charitable. In *Re Flinn*,[15] a gift to "His Eminence the Archbishop of Westminster Cathedral for the time being to be used by him for such purposes as he shall in his absolute discretion think fit" was upheld. So, also, gifts to such officers for their work, for this is treated as being wholly charitable. In *Re Rumball*[16] a gift "to the bishop for the time being of the diocese of the Windward Islands to be used by him as he thinks fit in his diocese" was upheld.

But there is a danger in saying too much; where the terms of the gift specify the purposes and allow any part of the fund to be used for non-charitable purposes, the gift is void. The cases turn on the finest points of construction. "Parish work," for example, includes some extra-charitable activities, and in *Farley v. Westminster Bank*[17] a gift to a vicar "for parish work" was held invalid. But in *Re Simson*,[18] a gift to a vicar "for his work in the parish" was held valid. The former phrase is held to be dispositive, thus enlarging the ambit of the gift and producing the result that a charitable trustee holds on non-charitable trusts, while the latter phrase is held to be merely descriptive of the vicar's responsibilities. The many pages in the reports dealing with these refinements bring no credit to our jurisprudence.

D. The Objects Must be Exclusively Charitable

To be charitable, the funds of a trust must be applicable for charitable purposes only.

i. Main and Subsidiary Objects. A trust may be charitable, however, even if some expenditure is permitted on non-charitable purposes, but only if those non-charitable purposes are entirely subsidiary to the main charitable purposes. The question is whether

---

[14] (1960) 25 Conv. (N.S.) 306 (V. Delaney).
[15] [1948] Ch. 241.
[16] [1956] Ch. 105.
[17] [1939] A.C. 430.
[18] [1946] Ch. 299.

"The main purpose of the body . . . is charitable and the only elements in its constitution and operation which are non-charitable are merely incidental to that purpose."[19]

Failure of a trust for this reason is fairly obvious in cases such as *Morice v. Bishop of Durham*,[20] and *I.R.C. v. Baddeley*[21] where the purposes are patently too widely expressed but it is less obvious in cases where the non-charitable element is latent. In *Ellis v. I.R.C.*,[22] land was conveyed to trustees for use "generally in such manner for the promotion and aiding of the work of the Roman Catholic Church in the district as the Trustees with the consent of the Bishop may prescribe." The Court of Appeal held that assets could be spent on subsidiary objects which were not necessarily conducive to the main (and undoubtedly charitable) object; such subsidiary objects existed in their own right and prevented the gift from being "for charitable purposes *only*."

An acute form of this problem occurs where the furtherance of a charitable purpose also benefits particular groups of persons. For instance in *I.R.C. v. City of Glasgow Police Athletic Association*,[23] the House of Lords held that a police athletic association, intended to benefit policemen in Glasgow, was not wholly ancillary to increasing the efficiency of the Glasgow police force and therefore not charitable. Again, while the benefits to the nursing profession as such loomed too large in the constitution of the General Nursing Council in proportion to the advancement of healing,[24] this was not so of surgeons, in relation to the advancement of surgery in the constitution of the Royal College of Surgeons.[25] In *Re Coxen*[26] a substantial gift to a charity included provision for an annual dinner for the trustees; and this was held charitable as being ancillary to the better administration of the charity. And in *London Hospital Medical College v. I.R.C.*,[27] a students' union was held to be a charitable trust where its predominant object was to further the purposes of the college, even though one of its objects was to confer private and personal benefits on union members.

---

[19] *per* Lord Cohen in *I.R.C. v. City of Glasgow Police Athletic Association* [1953] A.C. 380 at 405. See [1978] Conv. 92 (N. Gravells).

[20] (1804) 9 Ves.Jr. 399; (1805) 10 Ves.Jr. 522 ("objects of benevolence and liberality").

[21] [1955] A.C. 572; *ante*, p. 419.

[22] (1949) 31 T.C. 178, following *Dunne v. Byrne* [1912] A.C. 407. See also *I.R.C. v. Educational Grants Association Ltd* [1967] Ch. 993 at 1010 and 1015; *Oxford Group v. I.R.C.* [1949] 2 All E.R. 537, at 539–540; *Re Cole* [1958] Ch. 877.

[23] [1953] A.C. 380.

[24] *General Nursing Council v. St. Marylebone B.C.* [1959] A.C. 540.

[25] *Royal College of Surgeons v. National Provincial Bank Ltd* [1952] A.C. 631; see also *Incorporated Council of Law Reporting v. Att.-Gen.* [1972] Ch. 73.

[26] [1948] Ch. 747.

[27] [1976] 1 W.L.R. 613. See also *Re South Place Ethical Society* [1980] 1 W.L.R. 1565 (social activities held to be ancillary to the objects of ethical humanist society); *Funnell v. Stewart* [1996] 1 W.L.R. 288.

ii. And/Or Cases. Nowhere is the draftsman's error more obvious than in this group of cases. If a purpose is described as "charitable and benevolent"—philanthropic, useful, or any other such adjective—the purposes are wholly charitable. For the purposes, to qualify, must be, amongst other things, charitable; and that is enough. But if the draftsman says charitable *or* benevolent, there is prima facie an alternative; and the funds could be applied for purposes which are benevolent, but not charitable. But this is an oversimplification, and the question is one of construction in each case. Is the word conjunctive or disjunctive?

(a) *Cases of "or."* In *Blair v. Duncan*[28] the words were "such charitable or public purposes as my trustee thinks proper"; in *Houston v. Burns*,[29] "public, benevolent, or charitable purposes"; in *Chichester Diocesan Fund and Board of Finance v. Simpson*[30] "charitable or benevolent"; in each of these cases the gift was held not to be charitable, in that the words were wide enough to justify the trustees in disposing of the fund, or an unascertainable part of it, to non-charitable objects.

In *Re Macduff*,[31] a bequest of money "for some one or more purposes, charitable, philanthropic or—" was held to be bad, not by reason of the blank, but because there may be philanthropic purposes that are not charitable.

But in *Re Bennett*[32] the words were "for the benefit of the schools, and charitable institutions, and poor, and other objects of charity, or *any other* public objects," and Eve J. held that the addition of the word "other" entitled him to apply the *ejusdem generis* rule of interpretation and dispensed him from the necessity of reading the word "or" disjunctively; the gift was, therefore, upheld as a charitable gift of the whole.

(b) *Cases of "and."* Lord Davey in *Blair v. Duncan*[33] said that if the words had been "charitable *and* public" effect might be given to them, because they could be construed to mean charitable purposes of a public character. Some cases support this view, the word "and" being regarded as having the power to draw the other word into the

---

[28] [1902] A.C. 37. See also *Att.-Gen. of the Cayman Islands v. Wahr-Hansen* [2001] 1 A.C. 75 (trust for "religious, charitable or educational institutions or organisations or institutions operating for the public good" invalid).

[29] [1918] A.C. 337.

[30] [1944] A.C. 341; the trustees of the will paid the sums over to various charities, not anticipating the litigation by the next-of-kin which, in the event, occurred and the sequel was *Ministry of Health v. Simpson* [1951] A.C. 251.

[31] [1896] 2 Ch. 451.

[32] [1920] 1 Ch. 305. See also *Guild v. I.R.C.* [1992] 2 A.C. 310 (gift to specified recreational charitable purpose "or some similar purpose in connection with sport" upheld).

[33] [1902] A.C. 37 at 4.

orbit of the charitable. This view is borne out by *Re Sutton*[34] and *Re Best*,[35] where gifts to "charitable and deserving objects" and "charitable and benevolent" objects respectively were upheld. In *Att.-Gen. of the Bahamas v. Royal Trust Co.*,[36] on the other hand, a gift for the "education and welfare" of Bahamian children and young people was held void on a disjunctive construction. To construe the words conjunctively would result in a single purpose of educational welfare, but the word "welfare" was regarded as too wide to permit such a construction. The addition of a third word, "without any conjunction, copulative or disjunctive,"[37] was in *Williams v. Kershaw*[38] held fatal to a gift to "benevolent, charitable and religious" purposes, and in *Re Eades*[39] Sargant J. refused to uphold a gift for "such religious, charitable and philanthropic objects" as three named persons should jointly appoint.

In *Att.-Gen. v. National Provincial and Union Bank of England*[40] there was a gift "for such patriotic purposes or objects and such charitable institution or institutions or charitable object or objects in the British Empire" as the trustees should select. The House of Lords interpreted this as a gift for any or all of four categories, two of which might not be charitable, and so held the whole gift void.

So we cannot say more than that prima facie the word "or" causes the words to be read disjunctively; the word "and" causes them to be read conjunctively.

iii. Severance. Where the language permits funds to be applied partly for charitable and partly for non-charitable purposes, the court will, in some cases, apply a doctrine of severance, separating the charitable from the non-charitable, and allow the former to stand although the latter may fail.

In *Salusbury v. Denton*[41] a testator bequeathed a fund to his widow to be applied by her in her will, in part towards the foundation of a charity school, and as to the rest towards the benefit of the testator's relatives. The widow died without making any apportionment, but it was held, relying on the maxim "Equality is Equity," that the court would divide the fund into halves.

---

[34] (1885) 28 Ch.D. 464.
[35] [1904] 2 Ch. 354.
[36] [1986] 1 W.L.R. 1001, criticised as too narrow in (1987) 50 N.L.J. *Annual Charities Review* 20 (S. de Cruz).
[37] *per* Pearson J. in *Re Sutton* (1885) 28 Ch.D. 464 at 466.
[38] (1835) 5 Cl. & F. 111n.
[39] [1920] 2 Ch. 353.
[40] [1924] A.C. 262.
[41] (1857) 3 K. & J. 529.

The distinction between this and the "charitable or benevolent" cases is well brought out by Page-Wood V.-C.[42] "It is one thing to direct a trustee to give *a part* of a fund to one set of objects, and the *remainder* to another, and it is a distinct thing to direct him to give 'either' to one set of objects 'or' to another . . . This is a case of the former description. Here the trustee was bound to give a part to each." The crux of the matter is that the whole of a fund cannot be devoted to non-charity; once this is established, the court will endeavour to quantify what proportion of the capital assets is needed to support the non-charitable part,[43] and then hold the remaining part to be validly devoted to charity. In the absence of factors requiring a different division, the court will divide equally.[44] But there may be good reasons for making an unequal division.

In *Re Coxen*,[45] a testator gave the residue of his estate, amounting to more than £200,000 to the Court of Aldermen of the City of London for charitable purposes, providing however that one guinea should be paid to each of the six aldermen chosen to administer the trust on the occasion of his attending any meeting to administer the trust, and that £100 p.a. be used for an annual dinner for the Court of Aldermen when it should meet to discuss the business of the trust. On the assumption that these administrative provisions were not charitable,[46] quantification was desirable, for a division into equal parts would be absurd. Jenkins J. held that the court would find the necessary means to quantify the maximum slice of capital that would be needed to support them.

iv. Charitable Trusts (Validation) Act 1954. If the terms of a trust coming into operation before December 16, 1952,[47] are such that the property could be applied exclusively for charitable purposes, but could also be applied for non-charitable purposes (called in the Act an "imperfect trust provision") then as from July 30, 1954, the terms shall be treated as if they permitted application for charitable purposes only.[48]

The simple case covered by this provision would be a gift, prior to December 16, 1952, for "charitable or benevolent purposes." It would have saved the trusts of the *Diplock* will,[49] and was applied

---

[42] At 539; the italics are the Vice Chancellor's.

[43] In most cases this will produce *pro tanto* voidness.

[44] *Hoare v. Osborne* (1866) L.R. 1 Eq. 585.

[45] [1948] Ch. 747.

[46] Jenkins J. later decided that they were charitable; *ante*, p. 440.

[47] The date of publication of the Nathan Report; see (1954) 18 Conv.(N.S) 532; (1962) 26 Conv.(N.S.) 200 (S. Maurice).

[48] s.1(2); *Re Chitty's W.T.* [1970] Ch. 254. The Act does not apply to assets already distributed; s.2.

[49] *Chichester Diocesan Fund and Board of Finance v. Simpson* [1944] A.C. 341; *ante*, p. 441.

in the case of a trust deed some of whose purposes were charitable and others not.[50] The difficulty arises where there is no express mention of any charitable purposes, but where the purposes are capable of including charitable purposes.[51] It was said in *Re Gillingham Bus Disaster Fund*[52] that a trust for "worthy causes" was covered, and in *Re Wykes' Will Trust*,[53] a trust for welfare purposes was upheld as those purposes are akin to the relief of poverty. On the other hand, a trust for division among institutions and associations, some of which were not charitable, was not validated[54]; nor was a trust providing various benefits for employees because it was essentially a private discretionary trust and contained no indication of an intention to benefit the public.[55] The principle seems to be that where there is a clear flavour of charity present, "a quasi-charitable trust" as Cross J. has put it,[56] the donor of such a gift would not feel that his intentions were being distorted by the whole of his gift being made available to charity. It would thus cover "worthy causes," but not a case involving the mere possibility of charitable benefit.[57]

Commonwealth legislation[58] goes much further, and gives the courts a "blue pencil" power. Where non-charitable purposes are, or are deemed to be, within the ambit of a trust obviously intended to be charitable,[59] the trust is carried out as if the non-charitable elements were not present. The principle of such legislation seems acceptable and it is a pity that the Nathan Committee hesitated to recommend its adoption here.

E. Disaster Appeals

Problems can arise when public appeals for donations are made after some accident or disaster, if insufficient thought has been given to the question whether the fund is to be charitable or not. Such was the case with the loss of Penlee Lifeboat in Cornwall in 1982, when

---

[50] *Re Mead's Trust Deed* [1961] 1 W.L.R. 1244; *Re South Place Ethical Society* [1980] 1 W.L.R. 1565 ("purposes either religious or civil"). The trust in *Williams Trustees v. I.R.C.* [1947] A.C. 447, p. 419, *ante*, was eventually saved by the Act; Annual Report 1977, paras. 71–80.

[51] *Re Gillingham Bus Disaster Fund* [1959] Ch. 62; *Re Wykes* [1961] Ch. 229; *Re Mead's Trust Deed (supra)*.

[52] *supra*, at 80.

[53] *supra*. Apart from the 1954 Act, such a trust fails: *Re Atkinson's W. T.* [1978] 1 W.L.R. 586.

[54] *Re Harpur's W. T.* [1962] Ch. 78.

[55] *Re Saxone Shoe Co. Ltd's Trust Deed* [1962] 1 W.L.R. 943.

[56] *ibid.* at 957–958.

[57] cf. *Re Mead's Trust Deed*, *supra*, which goes rather far in restricting a trust to "poor" members of a union.

[58] (New South Wales) Conveyancing Act 1919–1969; s.37D; (New Zealand) Charitable Trusts Act 1957, s.61B; (Victoria) Property Law Act 1958, s.131; (Western Australia) Trustees Act 1962, s.102. See also Charities Act (Northern Ireland) 1964, s.24.

[59] *Leahy v. Att.-Gen. for New South Wales* [1959] A.C. 457.

over £2 million was donated by the public to the dependants of the lost crew, numbering eight families. If charitable, the fund would attract tax relief but, contrary to the expectations of some donors, it could not be simply divided amongst the families, as charitable funds, being essentially public in nature, cannot be used to give benefits to individuals exceeding those appropriate to their needs. Any surplus would, under the *cy-près* doctrine, be applied to related charities.[60] If, on the other hand, the fund was not charitable, it would not attract tax relief, but could be distributed entirely among the dependants if, upon construing the terms of the appeal, that was the intention of the donors. If that was not their intention, the surplus would not be applicable *cy-près*, but would result to the subscribers or perhaps devolve upon the Crown as *bona vacantia*.[61] Similar problems can arise if the appeal is on behalf of one specific person, such as a sick child. In the Penlee case[62] it was decided, after negotiations with the Attorney-General and the Charity Commissioners, to forgo tax relief and to treat the fund as private, so that the money could be divided among the families.[63]

The terms of the appeal are all-important in determining the status of the fund, and the consequences flowing from that status. The Attorney-General has issued guidelines for consideration by persons planning to launch a public appeal of this sort.[64] It appears that non-charitable status has most often been chosen.[65]

6. CY-PRÈS

A. The Cy-Près Doctrine Prior to 1960

Where property is given for charitable purposes and the purposes cannot be carried out in the precise manner intended by the donor, the question is whether the trust should fail, or whether the property

---

[60] *infra.*

[61] *Re Gillingham Bus Disaster Fund* [1959] Ch. 62; *Re West Sussex Constabulary's Widows, Children and Benevolent* (1930) *Fund Trust* [1971] Ch. 1; *ante*, p. 247.

[62] Which was not litigated. See Annual Report 1981, paras. 4–8; (1982) 132 N.L.J. 223 (H. Picarda).

[63] The Charity Commissioners have stated that the fund was not charitable; Annual Report 1981, para. 6. If it had been charitable, as being for the relief of victims of a disaster (*Re North Devon and West Somerset Relief Fund Trusts* [1953] 1 W.L.R. 1260), presumably it would not be possible to forgo that status.

[64] See Annual Report, 1981, App. A. See also Annual Report 1982, paras. 31–35 (South Atlantic Fund); Annual Report 1985, para. 19 (Bradford City Disaster Charitable Trust); Annual Report 1988, para. 25 (Armenian earthquake and Philippines Ferry); Annual Report 1989, paras. 36, 37 (Clapham Junction and Hillsborough).

[65] Annual Report 1988, para. 25; 1989, para. 36. See (1999) 19 L.S. 380 (I. McLean and M. Johnes).

should be applied for other charitable purposes. The *cy-près* doctrine, where it applies, enables the court (or the Commissioners) to
make a scheme for the application of the property for other charitable purposes as near as possible to those intended by the donor. This
is judicial *cy-près.* If a gift is to charity but not upon trust, it is
disposed of by the Crown under prerogative *cy-près.*[66] The distinction is not however always observed.

The *cy-près* jurisdiction was very narrow until the reforms of the
Charities Act 1960, and was available only where it was "impossible" or "impracticable" to carry out the purposes of the trust.[67]
Thus, trusts for the distribution of loaves of bread to the poor or of
stockings for poor maidservants continued until modern times. Their
performance was cumbersome, uneconomical, inconvenient, but not
impossible nor impracticable. But it had at least, by the turn of
the nineteenth century, become impracticable to apply money for the
advancement and propagation of the Christian religion among the
infidels of Virginia,[68] or for "the redemption of British slaves in
Turkey or Barbary."[69] *Re Dominion Students' Hall Trust*[70] showed
the furthest development of the doctrine by the courts.

> One of the objects of a charity was to promote community of
> citizenship, culture and tradition among all members of the Brit-
> ish Community of Nations; and it maintained a hostel for students
> in Bloomsbury. But the benefits of the charity were restricted to
> students of European origin. The *cy-près* power was used to re-
> move the "colour bar." It could not be said that it was "absolutely
> impracticable" to carry on the charity in its present state; but, by
> 1947, "to retain the condition, so far from furthering the charity's
> main object, might defeat it and would be liable to antagonize
> those students, both white and coloured, whose support and good-
> will it is the purpose of the charity to sustain. The case, therefore,
> can be said to fall within the broad description of impossibility
> . . . "[71]

---

[66] *ante,* p. 395 (sign manual). But even if there is no trust, the court has jurisdiction if there
is an analogous legally binding restriction; *Liverpool and District Hospital for Diseases of
the Heart v. Att.-Gen.* [1981] Ch. 193 (charitable corporation); [1984] Conv. 112 (J.
Warburton).

[67] See *Re Weir Hospital* [1910] 2 Ch. 124.

[68] *Att.-Gen. v. City of London* (1790) 3 Bro.C.C. 121. Annual Report (1971), paras. 65–69; see
also *Re Robinson* [1921] 2 Ch. 332. (The wearing of a black gown by the preacher was
impracticable because it was likely to offend the congregation and defeat the main object.).

[69] *Ironmongers' Co. v. Att.-Gen.* (1844) 10 Cl. & F. 908.

[70] [1947] Ch. 183; see Race Relations Act 1976, s.34; *ante,* p. 341; Annual Report 1976, para.
20; Annual Report 1983, para. 19; *Canada Trust Company v. Ontario Human Rights
Commission* (1990) 69 D.L.R. (4th) 321.

[71] [1947] Ch. 183 at 186, *per* Evershed J.

More recently, in *Re J. W. Laing Trust*,[72] concerning a settlement of shares worth £15,000 in 1922, the question was whether the court could delete a term imposed by the settlor that the capital and income should be distributed no later than 10 years after his death. The investment was now worth £24 million. The trust was for Christian evangelical causes, and the individuals and bodies who would be the recipients were unsuited to receive large capital sums. The deletion of this term was approved under the court's inherent jurisdiction, as it had become inexpedient in the very altered circumstances of the charity.

It is convenient also at this stage to note that a distinction is made between the initial failure of a charitable trust, and a failure after the time when the trust has been in operation. Application *cy-près* is much easier in the latter case; for, after application to charity, there is no resulting trust for the donor.[73] If the donor wants the property to pass to a third party, or to return to himself or his estate, he must expressly so provide by a gift over to take effect within the perpetuity period.[74] In the case of initial failure, the gift will lapse unless there is, on the proper construction of the instrument, a paramount intention to benefit charity. These situations will now be examined.

B. Initial Failure. Paramount Charitable Intent

i. Width of Charitable Intent. Where a charitable trust fails as being ineffective at the date of the gift, the gift will either lapse and fall into residue, or the property will be applied *cy-près*. The decision depends on the width of charitable intent shown by the donor. If the intention was that the property should be applied for a specified purpose, which cannot be carried out, or for one specific charitable institution which no longer exists, the gift will lapse. But if the court finds a wider intent, a paramount or general charitable intention, the property may be applied *cy-près*.

In *Re Rymer*,[75] there was a legacy of £5,000 "to the rector for the time being of St. Thomas's Seminary for the education of priests for the diocese of Westminster." At the time of the testator's death, the Seminary had ceased to exist, and the students had been transferred to another Seminary in Birmingham. The Court

---

[72] [1984] Ch. 143, [1984] Conv. 319 (J. Warburton); [1985] Conv. 313 (P. Luxton). Section 13 of the Charities Act 1960 (now the Act of 1993) did not apply; *post*, p. 456.
[73] *Re Wright* [1954] Ch. 347 at 362–363. But see [1983] Conv. 107 (P. Luxton).
[74] *post*, p. 454.
[75] [1895] 1 Ch. 19; *Re Spence* [1979] Ch. 483. See (1969) 32 M.L.R. 283 (J. Hutton).

of Appeal held that the gift failed. It was a gift "to a particular seminary for the purposes thereof." There was no wider intent.

This may be contrasted with *Re Lysaght*,[76] where the testatrix gave funds to the Royal College of Surgeons to found medical studentships. The gift was subject to restrictions, in that the students were to be male, the sons of qualified British-born medical men, themselves British-born, and not of the Jewish or Roman Catholic faith. The Royal College of Surgeons declined to accept the gift on these terms. As it was held that the particular trustee was essential to the gift, the refusal of the College would cause the gift to fail. Buckley J. held that there was a paramount charitable intention. The particularity of the testatrix's directions was not fatal to such a construction, as the directions were not an essential part of her true intention. A scheme was ordered whereby the money was payable to the College on the trusts of the will, but omitting the religious disqualification.

This liberal approach was followed in *Re Woodhams (deceased)*,[77] where the testator left money to two music colleges to found annual scholarships for "the complete musical education of a promising boy who is an absolute orphan and only of British Nationality and Birth from any one of Dr. Barnardo's Homes or the Church of England Children's Society Homes." The two colleges declined the gifts because it would be impractical to restrict the scholarships as required by the testator, but were prepared to accept them if available for boys of British nationality and birth generally. The gift failed for impracticability, but a paramount charitable intention to further musical education was found. The restriction to orphans from the named homes was not essential to the testator's purpose. Thus the gift was applicable *cy-près* under a scheme whereby the restriction was deleted.

ii. Has the Gift Failed? Continuation in Another Form. A gift to a defunct charity may be regarded as not having failed at all, on the basis that it is continuing in another form. It may have been amalgamated with a similar charity by scheme, or have been reconstituted under more effective trusts. In such a case the gift may take effect in favour of the body now administering the assets of the old charity. Or the court may construe the gift as being for the purposes of the named charity, so that the nomination of a defunct charity does not cause the gift to fail. Provided the purposes still exist the gift takes effect in favour of a body furthering those purposes. It will be appreciated that the significance of holding that such a gift has

---

[76] [1966] Ch. 191. See particularly at 201–202.
[77] [1981] 1 W.L.R. 493.

not failed is that it is not necessary to find a general charitable intention. A scheme will be ordered to give effect to the gift, but it will not be a *cy-près* scheme.

(a) *Gift in Augmentation of Funds of Defunct Charity*

In *Re Faraker*,[78] there was a gift to "Mrs. Bayley's Charity, Rotherhithe." A charity had been founded by a Mrs. Hannah Bayly in 1756 for the benefit of poor widows in Rotherhithe. This, with a number of other local charities, had been consolidated under a scheme by the Charity Commissioners in 1905, and the funds were held in various trusts for the benefit of the poor in Rotherhithe. The Court of Appeal held that the Bayly trusts had not been destroyed by the scheme, and that the consolidated charities were entitled to the legacy. The gift had not failed, because a perpetual charity cannot die.[79]

(b) *Gifts for Purposes. Unincorporated Associations and Charitable Corporations.*
In considering whether a gift is effectively for the purposes of the named institution, a distinction is drawn between gifts to unincorporated societies and to corporations. "Every bequest to an unincorporated charity by name without more must take effect as a gift for a charitable purpose . . . a bequest which is in terms made for a charitable purpose will not fail for lack of a trustee but will be carried into effect either under the Sign Manual or by means of a scheme"[80]; unless the testator's intention was to the contrary. On the other hand, "a bequest to a corporate body . . . takes effect simply as a gift to that body beneficially, unless there are circumstances which show that the recipient is to take the gift as a trustee. There is no need in such a case to infer a trust for any particular purpose."[81] Thus a gift to a defunct charitable corporation lapses and fails,[82] and *cy-près* application is possible only if there

---

[78] [1912] 2 Ch. 488; *Re Lucas* [1948] Ch. 424; *cf. Re Slatter's W. T.* [1964] Ch. 512; (1964) 28 Conv.(N.S.) 313 (J. Farrand).

[79] Distinguished in *Re Stemson's W.T.* [1970] Ch. 16 (involving a terminable corporate charity), and *Re Roberts* [1963] 1 W.L.R. 406, *infra*.

[80] *per* Buckley J. in *Re Vernon's W.T.* [1972] Ch. 300n; *Re Finger's W.T.* [1972] Ch. 286; (1972) 36 Conv.(N.S.) 198 (R. Cotterell); (1974) 38 Conv.(N.S.) 187 (J. Martin). See also *Liverpool and District Hospital for Diseases of the Heart v. Att.-Gen.* [1982] Ch. 193 (charitable corporation does not hold as trustee, but court has *cy-près* jurisdiction on winding-up; Companies Act 1985, s.558). See Charities Act 1993, s.64, for the position where a charitable corporation ceases to be charitable or otherwise alters its objects.

[81] *Re Vernon's W.T.* [1972] Ch. 300n. See [1984] Conv. 112 and [1990] Conv. 95 (J. Warburton). See also *Re ARMS (Multiple Sclerosis Research) Ltd* [1997] 1 W.L.R. 877 (no failure where incorporated charity existed at testator's death although insolvent, thus legacy available to its creditors).

[82] Unless the testator has indicated that the corporation was to take as trustee for its purposes.

was a general charitable intention. In *Re Finger's Will Trusts*,[83] there was a gift to the National Radium Commission (unincorporated) and to the National Council for Maternity and Child Welfare (incorporated). Both had ceased to exist by the testatrix's death. The gift to the unincorporated charity was construed as a gift to charitable purposes. As those purposes still existed there was no failure, as a trust does not fail for lack of a trustee. A scheme was ordered to settle the destination of the gift, but this was not a *cy-près* scheme and no general charitable intention was necessary.[84] In the case of the incorporated charity, on the other hand, it was a gift to a legal person which had ceased to exist, and was not a purpose trust. The gift therefore failed, but was saved from lapse by the finding of a general charitable intention, and was accordingly applied *cy-près*.

This is a technical distinction which might not be appreciated by the testator, but it has a certain logic. One difficulty which remains is that the same facts may allow either the *Re Faraker* construction or that adopted in *Re Finger's Will Trusts* in the case of the unincorporated charity, although the results are different. While both constructions avoid the finding of a failure and the need for a general charitable intention, the result of the *Re Faraker* construction is that the gift goes to the body now administering the funds of the defunct charity, even if its purposes are different. In *Re Faraker*[85] itself, the defunct charity was specifically for widows, while the new consolidated charity was for the poor generally, so that it "was not bound to give one penny to a widow,"[86] thus defeating the testator's intention to some extent. The result in *Re Finger's Will Trusts*[87] is that the gift is devoted, by means of a scheme, to the testator's purpose. It may be that the court would decline to apply *Re Faraker* where the purposes of the new body were widely different. Thus in *Re Roberts*,[88] a gift was made to the Sheffield Boys' Working Home, which had wound up and transferred most of its assets to the Sheffield Town Trust. The claim of the latter body was rejected as an undesirable extension of the *Re Faraker* principle, as it purposes were different. The money was applied, by means of an ordinary scheme, to the purposes to which the defunct Home had been dedicated.

---

[83] [1972] Ch. 286; applied by the Court of Apeal in *Re Koeppler's W.T.* [1986] Ch. 423. If the purposes had ceased to exist, the gift to the unincorporated charity would fail, but could be applied *cy-près* if there was a general charitable intention.

[84] It would be otherwise if the donor intended the particular institution and no other, as in *Re Rymer, supra.*

[85] [1912] 2 Ch. 488.

[86] *ibid.* at 496.

[87] [1972] Ch. 286.

[88] [1963] 1 W.L.R. 406. See (1974) 38 Conv.(N.S.) 187 (J. Martin).

Both constructions, however, were rejected in *Re Spence*,[89] where money was left to a specified Old Folks Home, "for the benefit of the patients." The home was no longer in use at the testatrix's death. Megarry V.-C. held that the gift failed and could not be applied *cy-près*. It was not a general gift to the old people of the district. Following *Re Harwood*,[90] it was said that if a particular institution is correctly identified, then it is that institution and no other which is intended: "It is difficult to envisage a testator as being suffused with a general glow of broad charity when he is labouring, and labouring successfully, to identify some particular specified institution or purpose as the object of his bounty."[91] This, with respect, is a very narrow view of the *cy-près* doctrine. A testator should always be careful to identify his beneficiary correctly. It is difficult to see why this should automatically negative a general charitable intention.

iii. Projects. The cases so far discussed have dealt with gifts to institutions, corporate or unincorporated. The same rules apply in principle also to cases where there is a gift for a purpose or project such as, for example, the payment of a schoolmaster at a school to be built,[92] or the establishment of a soup kitchen and cottage hospital.[93] In such cases, the question is whether the project is on the balance of probabilities capable or incapable of being implemented. If it is incapable, then, in the absence of wider intent, the gift will fail and will fall into residue. There is no "wait and see" provision.[94]

iv. Non-Existent Charity. In *Re Harwood*,[95] it was said that, where there was a gift for a non-existent charity, it was easier to find a general charitable intent in a case where the institution had never existed than it was in the case where an identifiable institution had ceased to exist.

In that case, a testatrix, who died in 1934, left £200 to the Wisbech Peace Society and £300 to the Peace Society in Belfast. The Wisbech Society had existed prior to 1934, but had ceased by that date to exist. There was no evidence that the Peace Society of Belfast had ever existed. The former failed, but in respect of the latter Farwell J. was able to find an intention to "benefit societies

---

[89] [1979] Ch. 483.
[90] [1936] Ch. 285, *infra. Re Rymer* [1895] 1 Ch. 19, *ante*, p. 447 was also relied on.
[91] [1979] Ch. 483 at 493.
[92] *Re Wilson* [1913] 1 Ch. 314.
[93] *Biscoe v. Jackson* (1887) 35 Ch.D. 460.
[94] *Re White's W.T.* [1955] Ch. 188; *Re Tacon* [1958] Ch. 447 at 453–455.
[95] [1936] Ch. 285; *cf. Re Goldschmidt* [1957] 1 W.L.R. 524, where a gift to a non-existent charity was not applied *cy-près*, but fell into residue, which was also given to charity.

whose object was the promotion of peace,"[96] and the £300 was applied *cy-près*.

Similarly, in *Re Satterthwaite's Will Trusts*,[97] where a testatrix, who hated the whole human race, left her residuary estate to a number of institutions concerned with animal welfare. Most of them were charitable, but a dispute arose over the share left to the London Animal Hospital. There was no charity of that name, but the claimant, a veterinary surgeon, carried on a practice under that trade name at a time prior to the date of the will and death. The Court of Appeal considered the gift as being to a non-existent charitable institution, and not to the claimant. A sufficiently wide charitable intent was discerned from the nature of the other shares (notwithstanding that one share was to a non-charity), and thus *cy-près* application was ordered.

v. A Group of Donees; Mostly Charitable. It may be that the testator has made a number of gifts, all of which are charitable except one. It can be argued that the intention clearly was to apply all the money for charitable purposes. On the other hand, "if you meet seven men with black hair and one with red hair, you are not entitled to say that here are eight men with black hair."[98] A gift for a non-charitable purpose is not made charitable by being included in a list of other gifts which are charitable. So held Buckley J. in *Re Jenkins' Will Trusts*[99] where a gift for the abolition of vivisection failed and could not be applied *cy-près*. This may be contrasted with *Re Satterthwaite's Will Trusts*,[1] where the gift in question was construed as charitable, and hence the *cy-près* doctrine could apply.

C. Subsequent Failure

Once assets are effectively dedicated to charity, there can be no question of a lapse or a resulting trust save where the gift effectively provides for it. Width of charitable intent is irrelevant. All that is necessary is that the property has been given "out and out" to charity, in the sense that the donor did not envisage its return in any circumstances.

---

[96] [1936] Ch. 285 at 288. But the decision was doubted by the High Court in *Re Koeppler's Will Trusts* [1984] Ch. 243, on the basis that the purpose was political and not charitable. It was not cited in the Court of Appeal [1986] Ch. 423.

[97] [1966] 1 W.L.R. 277.

[98] *per* Buckley J. in *Re Jenkins' W.T.* [1966] Ch. 249.

[99] *supra.*

[1] *supra.*

In *Re Wright*,[2] a testatrix who died in 1933 provided for the foundation, on the death of a tenant for life, of a convalescent home for impecunious gentlewomen. The scheme was practicable in 1933, but not in 1942 when the tenant for life died. The Court of Appeal held that 1933 was the crucial date; at that date the scheme was practicable, dedication to charity occurred, and the possibility of a lapse or resulting trust was excluded. *Cy-près* was available in 1942 irrespective of width of charitable intent.

This rule is now firmly established,[3] but it was not always so, and it is not possible to reconcile some earlier cases on the subject, in particular the "surplus" cases.

In *Re King*,[4] £1,500 was bequeathed for one stained-glass window in a church. The cost of the window could not exceed £800. Romer J. held that the whole of £1,500 had been dedicated to charity with the necessary consequences that any surplus would be applied *cy-près* (in fact for a second window) irrespective of width of intent.

But in *Re Stanford*,[5] where £5,000 was bequeathed for the purpose of completing and publishing an etymological dictionary and over £1,500 remained unspent when the task was complete, Eve J. held that the surplus fell into residue.

Such a result is only justifiable if the surplus can be regarded as a case of initial impossibility *pro tanto*.[6] Similar confusion can be seen in the cases where the surplus has arisen in the circumstances of a public appeal. In *Re Welsh Hospital (Netley) Fund*[7] and *Re North Devon and West Somerset Relief Fund Trusts*[8] money was collected for purposes which were fulfilled, leaving surplus. The surplus was held applicable *cy-près* on the basis that there was a general charitable intention. If these cases are to be regarded as involving subsequent failure, it is difficult to see why such an intention is necessary. All that is required is an "out and out" gift to

---

[2] [1954] Ch. 347; *Re Slevin* [1891] 2 Ch. 236, where an orphanage was in existence at the testator's death, but came to an end before the money was paid over. *Cy-près* application was ordered; *Re Moon's W.T.* [1948] 1 All E.R. 300.

[3] *Re Tacon* [1958] Ch. 447, a case of a contingent gift; *cf. Re J. W. Laing Trust* [1984] Ch. 143, [1984] Conv. 319 (J. Warburton).

[4] [1923] 1 Ch. 243.

[5] [1924] 1 Ch. 73.

[6] See Picarda, p. 345; *Tudor on Charities* (8th ed.), 434–436.

[7] [1921] 1 Ch. 655; *cf. Re British Red Cross Balkan Fund* [1914] 2 Ch. 419. The latter case is doubted in *Tudor on Charities* (8th ed.), 354, n. 74.

[8] [1953] 1 W.L.R. 1260.

charity. Thus in *Re Wokingham Fire Brigade Trusts*[9] a surplus was applicable *cy-près* without the need to discover a general charitable intention. It is submitted that this approach, which was approved *obiter* by the Court of Appeal in *Re Ulverston and District New Hospital Building Trusts*[10] (involving initial failure as insufficient funds were collected) is to be preferred.

D. Termination in Favour of Non-Charity

It was seen that a donor could, if he wished, make express provision for a gift over to a third party or to himself or to his estate upon the failure of a charitable gift within the period of perpetuity.[11] Before the Perpetuities and Accumulations Act 1964, a resulting trust after a determinable interest was immune from the perpetuity rule, although any express gift over was subject to it. Thus a determinable charitable gift could terminate at a remote time and result to the settlor. It could not be applied *cy-près* because, although a subsequent failure, there was no "out and out" gift to charity.[12] However, in the case of a charitable gift subject to a condition subsequent, the gift took effect as absolute if the gift over was void for perpetuity. The *cy-près* doctrine would then apply in the usual way on any subsequent failure, to the exclusion of a resulting trust.[13]

Under section 12 of the 1964 Act, the perpetuity rule became applicable to resulting trusts, but the Act also introduced the "wait and see" rule.[14] Thus in the case of a determinable charitable gift, a gift over or resulting trust will operate to the exclusion of the *cy-près* doctrine if the determining event occurs within the perpetuity period. If it does not, the gift becomes absolute, so that *cy-près* will apply on any subsequent failure. Likewise if the charitable gift is subject to a condition subsequent. On breach of condition within the perpetuity period, the gift over (or resulting trust in default) will take effect. If, however, the condition is not broken within that period, the charitable gift becomes absolute. Thus the *cy-près* doctrine is available because, whatever the donor's intention, the gift is by statute an "out and out" gift to charity.

---

[9] [1951] Ch. 373.

[10] [1956] Ch. 622. The case illustrates the difficulties now resolved by Charities Act 1993, s.14, *post*, p. 457. s.14 does not apply to the surplus cases unless it becomes established that a general charitable intention is necessary, contrary to the view expressed in the text.

[11] *ante*, p. 447.

[12] *Re Randell* (1888) 39 Ch.D. 213.

[13] *Re Peel's Release* [1921] 2 Ch. 218; *Bath and Wells Diocesan Board of Finance v. Jenkinson, The Times*, September 6, 2000.

[14] s.3(1).

E. The Widening of Cy-Près Jurisdiction. Charities Act 1993, s.13

i. General. As part of the policy of modernising charitable trusts, the Charities Act 1960 introduced far-reaching reforms (now found in the consolidating Act of 1993) in the application of the *cy-près* doctrine. Before examining these reforms it must be emphasised that it is the trustees' duty, where some or all of the property may be applied *cy-près*, to take steps to have the property so applied.[15] This situation will arise where there is an existing trust for outdated objects; for purposes which were once useful, but are now unnecessary, or overtaken by statutory services; or where the income of the trust has during the years become inadequate for the purpose, or, perhaps so large that there is a surplus. In short, the policy is to enable the trustees, with the help of the Charity Commissioners, to make the best use, in modern conditions, of funds dedicated to charity.

ii. Section 13. Section 13 provides for application *cy-près* in five situations:

(1) Subject to subsection (2) below, the circumstances in which the original purposes of a charitable gift can be altered to allow the property given or part of it to be applied *cy-près* shall be as follows:
  (*a*) where the original purposes, in whole or in part,—
      (i) have been as far as may be fulfilled; or
      (ii) cannot be carried out, or not according to the directions given and to the spirit of the gift; or
  (*b*) where the original purposes provide a use for part only of the property available by virtue of the gift; or
  (*c*) where the property available by virtue of the gift and other property applicable for similar purposes can be more effectively used in conjunction, and to that end can suitably, regard being had to the spirit of the gift, be made applicable to common purposes; or
  (*d*) where the original purposes were laid down by reference to an area which then was but has since ceased to be a unit for some other purpose, or by reference to a class of persons or to an area which has for any reason since ceased to be suitable, regard being had to the spirit of the gift, or to be practical in administering the gift; or
  (*e*) where the original purposes, in whole or in part, have, since they were laid down,—

---

[15] s.13(5).

    (i) been adequately provided by other means; or

    (ii) ceased, as being useless or harmful to the community or for other reasons, to be in law charitable; or

    (iii) ceased in any other way to provide a suitable and effective method of using the property available by virtue of the gift, regard being had to the spirit of the gift.

(2) Subsection (1) above shall not affect the conditions which must be satisfied in order that property given for charitable purposes may be applied *cy-près*, except in so far as those conditions require a failure of the original purposes.

In the case of subsequent failure, width of charitable intent is of no significance, but the Commissioners endeavour to follow the spirit of the original gift, so far as this is consistent with proper application of the funds. "The paramount principle that the donor's intent must be followed as closely as possibly has been preserved, but his intention is now interpreted in the light of modern conditions and having regard to the spirit of the gift."[16] Nothing in section 13 requires a *cy-près* scheme where such a scheme was not required before the 1960 Act.[17]

Many schemes have been made by the Commissioners under this section and its predecessor.[18] The first occasion on which the section was litigated was *Re Lepton's Charity*.[19]

A will dating from 1715 instructed trustees to pay £3 per annum to the Minister, and the "overplus of the profits" to the poor. At that time, the income was £5 per annum, and in 1970 the income from the proceeds of sale of the land was nearly £800. Pennycuick V.-C. raised the payment to £100 per annum. This was consistent with the spirit of the gift. Subsection (1)(*a*) applied because "the original purposes" covered the purposes as a whole; it was not necessary to consider separately the gift of the annuity and that of the surplus. In any case (1)(*e*)(iii) would have applied.

In *Re J. W. Laing Trust*,[20] the question which arose was whether section 13 could be utilised in order to dispense with the donor's requirement that the capital and income be distributed no later than 10 years after his death. It was held that the provision could not be deleted under section 13(1), as the "original purposes"[21] which the court could there review meant the objects of the trust, whereas the

---

[16] Annual Report 1970, para. 41; see also 1973, para. 11. See (1995/6) 3 *Charity Law & Practice Review* 1 (J. Warburton).

[17] *Oldham Borough Council v. Att.-Gen.* [1993] Ch. 210.

[18] Annual Report 1970, para. 43.

[19] [1972] Ch. 276.

[20] [1984] Ch. 143. The facts were given at p. 447, *ante*.

[21] See further *Oldham Borough Council v. Att.-Gen* [1993] Ch. 210.

settlor's direction was merely administrative. The provision was, however, deleted under the court's inherent jurisdiction. In *Peggs v. Lamb*[22] a trust was created in the Middle Ages for the freemen of Huntingdon and their widows. It was charitable on the basis of the anomalous "locality" cases.[23] In the past the freemen were a substantial section of the public and a suitable class of charitable objects. At present there were only fifteen members, and they claimed equal division of the annual income, irrespective of need, which would give them over £30,000 each. A *cy-près* scheme was ordered to enable the money to be distributed amongst the inhabitants of the borough as a whole, in accordance with the spirit of the gift. The case fell within section 13(1)(d), on the basis that the class had ceased to be suitable recipients of charitable funds. It was not necessary to decide whether section 13(1)(*e*)(ii) also applied, on the basis that they were no longer a section of the public. Section 13(1)(*e*)(iii) was satisfied in *Varsani v. Jesani*,[24] where a Hindu sect split into two groups. The groups could not resolve their differences, as each thought that it alone professed the faith. To give the sect's assets to one group would have been contrary to the spirit of the gift, which was the desire to provide facilities for followers of the sect. The solution was to divide the assets between the two groups.

Subsection (1)(*e*)(ii) may give rise to difficulty at some future time. Clearly, it will apply to the endowments of independent schools if charitable status should be withdrawn.[25] Perhaps also the section would, if then available, have applied to anti-vivisection trusts, for these had been held charitable in *Re Foveaux*,[26] but non-charitable in *National Anti-Vivisection Society v. I.R.C.*[27] in 1948. The same would seem to apply to charities which have been removed from the Register on the ground that they have ceased to be charitable.

iii. Section 14.[28] **Charity Collections.** Finally, it is necessary to refer to section 14. This provides that property given for specific charitable purposes which fail shall be applicable *cy-près* as if given for charitable purposes generally, where it belongs—

[22] [1994] Ch. 172.
[23] *ante*, p. 438.
[24] [1999] Ch. 219.
[25] See [1996] Conv. 24 (J. Jaconelli).
[26] [1895] 2 Ch. 501.
[27] [1948] A.C. 31. Lord Simonds suggested at 64–65 that application *cy-près* would have been possible before the 1960 Act.
[28] Re-enacting s.14 of the 1960 Act, as amended by Charities Act 1992, s.15.

(*a*) to a donor who after—
    (i) the prescribed[29] advertisements and inquiries have been published and made, and
    (ii) the prescribed period beginning with the publication of those advertisements has expired,[30]
    cannot be identified or cannot be found,[31] or
(*b*) to a donor who has executed a disclaimer in the prescribed form of his right to have the property returned.

In the case of the proceeds of cash collections by means of collecting boxes or other means not adapted for distinguishing one gift from another, or the proceeds of lotteries and similar money-raising activities, the property is conclusively presumed to belong to unidentifiable donors, without any advertisement or inquiry. In other cases the court may direct the property to be treated as belonging to unidentifiable donors, without any advertisement or inquiry, if it appears that it would not be reasonable, having regard to the amounts or the lapse of time since the gifts, to return it.

Section 14 applies only to cases of initial failure, subsection (7) providing that charitable purposes are deemed to fail, for the purposes of the section, where any difficulty in applying the property to those purposes makes it available for return to the donors.[32] In the case of subsequent failure, the property is not so available.

This solution is much more sensible than any attempt to solve the problem by applying the usual *cy-près* doctrine, involving either the imputation of an artificial general charitable intent, or, failing that, a search for the many donors of tiny gifts, with the possibility of a claim by the Crown to the property as *bona vacantia*.

F. Small Charities

The Charities Act 1985 introduced a principle enabling trustees of certain small charities in effect to determine their own *cy-près* application with the concurrence of the Charity Commissioners. The response from trustees was disappointing,[33] and so the Act was

---

[29] The Charities (Cy-près Advertisements, Inquiries and Disclaimer) Regulations 1993.

[30] The trustees are not liable to any person in respect of the property if no claim is received before expiry of this period; s.14(2).

[31] Such donors may claim from the *cy-près* recipient within six months of the scheme; s.14(5). For an example of the operation of s.14 see *Re Henry Wood Memorial Trust* [1966] 1 W.L.R. 1601 (failure of Mile End Memorial Hall Fund through lack of financial support); Annual Report 1965, paras. 19–21.

[32] See [1983] Conv. 40 (D. Wilson), arguing that this is never the case where the gift is anonymous and indistinguishable, because the property either goes *cy-près* by the imputation of a general charitable intent (see *Re Hillier* [1954] 1 W.L.R. 700) or to the Crown as *bona vacantia*.

[33] For statistics, see Annual Report 1986, para. 14; 1987, para. 49; 1988, para. 95; 1989, para. 105; 1990, para. 91; 1991, para. 30.

repealed and replaced by provisions now found in the 1993 Act which both extend and simplify the principle.

Under section 74 of the 1993 Act, powers are given to trustees of small charities, meaning those having a gross income not exceeding £5,000 in the last financial year and which do not hold land on trusts stipulating that it must be used for the purposes of the charity. If at least two-thirds of the trustees agree, they may resolve to transfer the property to one or more specified charities. They must be satisfied that their charity's resources are no longer being effectively applied and the purposes of the recipient are as similar as is reasonably practicable. Alternatively, they may modify the trusts by replacing all or any of the purposes with other specified charitable purposes which are as similar in character as is practical, if satisfied that the existing purposes have ceased to be conducive to an effective application of their resources.

Section 75 applies to a charity having a permanent endowment which does not include land and a gross income not exceeding £1,000 in the last financial year. If at least two-thirds of the trustees agree, they may resolve to remove the restrictions on spending capital if of the opinion that the property is too small, in relation to the charity's purposes, to achieve a useful purpose by spending income. They must first consider a transfer under section 74.

Under both sections, the trustees must give public notice of their resolution, of which a copy must be sent to the Commissioners. The Commissioners may require further information and must consider any representations from persons interested in the charity. They will then notify the trustees whether or not they concur, and, if they do, the trustees may proceed accordingly. Neither section applies to an exempt or corporate charity. Much use has been made of these provisions.[34]

7. The Administration of Charities

A. Reform

Reform of the law of charities was long overdue when the Charities Act was passed in 1960. The major problems were: the narrow limits of the *cy-près* doctrine; the gap and the competition which existed between the established charities and the statutory services of the welfare state; the haphazard state of existing charities and the lack of information about them. The Charities Act 1960 contained reforms on these matters.

Reform has subsequently been directed towards increasing the supervision of charities by the Charity Commissioners in order to

---

[34] Annual Report 1995, para. 16.

minimise abuse and maladministration by charity trustees. To this end the powers of the Commissioners were increased by the Charities Act 1992, following the Woodfield Report.[35] The reforms were mainly directed to increasing the duty of trustees to prepare annual accounts, to disqualifying certain persons from trusteeship, to controlling fundraising and public charitable collections, and to providing effective means of enforcement. The provisions are now found in the consolidating Charities Act 1993.[36]

B. The Authorities

i. The Charity Commissioners. There is a minimum of three Commissioners, and two at least must be solicitors or barristers.[37] They are charged with "the general function of promoting the effective use of charitable resources by encouraging the development of better methods of administration, by giving charity trustees information and advice on any matter affecting the charity and by investigating and checking abuses."[38] Their purpose is to give the public confidence in the integrity of charity, and their objectives are:

(i) to deliver an effective legal, accounting and governance framework for charities,

(ii) to improve the accountability, efficiency and effectiveness of charities, and

(iii) to identify and deal with abuse and poor practice.[39]

The Commissioners are under a duty to submit an Annual Report to the Secretary of State,[40] and their reports give an excellent picture of the administration of the law of charities, and of the problems of the day. The reports emphasise continually the duty and the desire of the Commissioners to be helpful to trustees.[41] Provision is made for the payment of fees to the Commissioners in certain cases.[42]

---

[35] Efficiency Scrutiny of the Supervision of Charities, 1987; National Audit Office Report, House of Commons Paper 380, 1986–87; Annual Report 1987; (1993) 7 *Trust Law International* 9 (J. Hill).

[36] For the territorial limits of the Act, see *Gaudiya Mission v. Brahmachary* [1998] Ch. 341 (no jurisdiction over charity established in India, operating in India and London).

[37] Charities Act 1993, s.1; First Sched. para. 1(1), (2).

[38] s.1(3).

[39] Annual Report 1997, paras. 11–12.

[40] s.1(5).

[41] Leaflets for the guidance of charity trustees are regularly published by the Commissioners.

[42] s.85.

ii. The Official Custodian for Charities. The Commissioners are required to appoint an Official Custodian for Charities,[43] a corporation sole. The object was that charity trustees could vest trust property in the custodian and thereby avoid "the necessity for periodical transfers of land and securities upon the appointment of new trustees,"[44] and the necessity to reclaim income tax on investments, as dividends are remitted without deduction. One effect of the recent reforms is to reduce the role of the Official Custodian, in order to increase the responsibility of the trustees. The Official Custodian is being divested of property other than land,[45] and may transfer investments to the trustees or persons nominated by them.

iii. The Visitor.[46] Ecclesiastical[47] and eleemosynary[48] corporations are subject to the jurisdiction of the visitor in relation to their internal affairs. Modern decisions illustrate that the visitor has an important role to play in the universities.[49] Ecclesiastical corporations are visitable by the ordinary. In the case of eleemosynary corporations, the founder may appoint a visitor. If none is appointed, the founder (or his heirs) is the visitor by operation of law.[50] A similar principle applies where the Crown is the founder. Where visitatorial powers are exercisable by the Crown, they are in practice exercised by the Lord Chancellor.

The visitor's jurisdiction stems from the power recognised by the common law in the founder of an eleemosynary corporation to provide the law under which it was to be governed and to be sole judge of the interpretation and application of those laws, either himself or via the person appointed as visitor. Thus the visitor has exclusive jurisdiction over matters of internal management, including the admission and removal of students,[51] and the award of prizes

---

[43] s.2. See Annual Report 1974, para. 107. The Custodian has no management powers; *Muman v. Nagasena* [2000] 1 W.L.R. 299.

[44] Annual Report 1970, para. 75.

[45] Charities Act 1992, s.29 (unrepealed). For the provisions as to land, see Charities Act 1993, ss.21–23.

[46] See generally (1970) 86 L.Q.R. 531 (J. Bridge); Picarda, Chap. 42; *Tudor on Charities* (8th ed.), 369–388; (1981) 97 L.Q.R. 610 (P. Smith); (1986) 136 N.L.J. 484, 519, 567 and 665 (P. Smith), adopted in *Thomas v. University of Bradford, infra.*

[47] Corporations existing for the furtherance of religion and the perpetuation of the rites of the Church.

[48] The original meaning was corporations whose object was the distribution of free alms, or the relief of individual distress; *Re Armitage's W. T.* [1972] Ch. 438. But for the purpose of visitatorial powers, corporate schools and most universities are included. Similarly the Inns of Court; see *R. v. Visitors to the Inns of Court, ex Calder* [1994] Q.B. 1.

[49] The "new" universities make no provision for a visitor; *Clark v. University of Lincolnshire and Humberside* [2000] 1 W.L.R. 1988.

[50] *Phillips v. Bury* (1694) Skinn. 447. If the heirs die out or cannot act, the Crown is the visitor.

[51] *Patel v. University of Bradford Senate* [1979] 1 W.L.R. 1066; *c.f. Herring v. Templeman* [1973] 3 All E.R. 569.

and degrees,[52] but not disputes between the foundation and out-
siders.[53] The jurisdiction of the visitor in these matters is sole and
exclusive.[54] No appeal lies from his decisions unless the statutes of
the corporation so provide,[55] but he is subject to prerogative remedies such as a quashing order[56]; although only if he has acted outside
his jurisdiction, abused his powers, or acted in breach of the rules of
natural justice.[57] The Education Reform Act 1988 abolished the
visitor's jurisdiction in relation to appointment, employment and
dismissal of university staff.[58]

C. The Register

Section 3 of the 1993 Act requires the Commissioners to maintain
a public register on which all charities are to be included except for
(*a*) exempt charities,[59] (*b*) any charity excepted by order or regulation,[60] (*c*) any charity having no permanent endowment, nor the use
and occupation of land, and whose income does not exceed £1,000
a year, and (*d*) in respect of a registered place of worship. The
purpose of the register, now computerised and on the Internet, is to
obtain information about charities. Those which are excepted are
those which are national institutions (exempt charities), small ones
not occupying land, and others such as ecclesiastical charities where
provision for obtaining the necessary information already exists.

D. Decisions on Registration

It is the duty of trustees of charities to register,[61] enforceable by
order of the Commissioners.[62] Registration is much to the advantage
of the trustees, for it raises a conclusive presumption of being a

[52] *R. v. Her Majesty the Queen in Council, ex Vijaytunga* [1990] Q.B. 444; *Oakes v. Sidney
Sussex College, Cambridge* [1988] 1 W.L.R. 431.
[53] *Casson v. University of Aston in Birmingham* [1983] 1 All E.R. 88 (dispute over contract
entered into with student before he was a member). In *Thomas v. University of Bradford*
[1987] A.C. 795 this decision was upheld as correct on the facts but criticised as taking too
narrow a view of the visitor's jurisdiction.
[54] *Thomas v. University of Bradford, supra.*
[55] *Thorne v. University of London* [1966] 2 Q.B. 237; *Patel v. University of Bradford Senate,
supra*; (1974) 37 M.L.R. 324 (D. Christie); (1974) 33 C.L.J. 23 (S. de Smith).
[56] *Thomas v. University of Bradford, supra.* (This remedy was then called *certiorari*).
[57] *R. v. Hull University Visitor, ex Page* [1993] A.C. 682; (1993) 109 L.Q.R. 155 (H.
Wade).
[58] s.206. See (1991) 54 M.L.R. 137 (P. Pettit). The Act applies to publicly funded universities
and similar institutions; s.202.
[59] Sched. 2.
[60] S.I. 1963 No. 2074; S.I. 1964 No. 1825 (Regligious Charities); S.I. 1961 No. 1044 (Boy
Scouts and Girl Guides); S.I 1965 No. 1056 (Armed Forces); S.I. 1966 No. 965 (Non-
exempt Universities).
[61] Charities Act 1993, s.3(7).
[62] *ibid.*, s.87.

charity,[63] and of being entitled therefore to the privileges accorded to charity. Non-entry gives rise to no presumption either way.

The decision to register a claimant is that of the Charity Commissioners, and an account of recent decisions is given in the Annual Reports and Decisions. In this way, the development of charity law is greatly influenced by the Commissioners. Any person who may be affected by registration, such as a residuary legatee in the case of a will charity, may object to registration, or apply for removal.[64] Nearly all these matters are finally disposed of by the Commissioners but there is provision for an appeal to the High Court.[65] In making their decision, the Commissioners are aware of the need for flexibility, and for keeping the law of charities in tune with changing circumstances. They have not always been able to satisfy the critics, who assume that charitable purposes should include all useful projects of reform. The Commissioners are currently conducting a review of the Register.[66] By the end of March 2000, over 185,000 charities had been registered, and during 1999/2000 10,500 charities were removed from the Register,[67] mainly because they had ceased to operate. On the matter of removal, the Commissioners are not bound by the view of the Attorney-General.[68]

E. Advice

The Commissioners may also give to any charity trustee an opinion or advice on any matter affecting the performance of his duties, and a trustee acting upon it is deemed to have acted in accordance with the trust.[69] The Commissioners' advice is also available where an application is made to register a new charity. If the application is refused, the reason will be given so that the language may be amended. It is not of course possible to alter the terms of established trusts which fail to be registered.

---

[63] *ibid.*, s.4(1); *Re Murawski's W.T.* [1971] 1 W.L.R. 707.

[64] *ibid.* s.4(2). Annual Report 1978, para. 84.

[65] *ibid.* s.4(3); *Incorporated Council of Law Reporting for England and Wales v. Att.-Gen.* [1972] Ch. 73; *Re Construction Industry Training Board* [1973] Ch. 173; *I.R.C. v. McMullen* [1981] A.C. 1, where H.L. upheld the decision of the Commissioners to register; *McGovern v. Att.-Gen.* [1982] Ch. 321, where Slade J. upheld the Commissioners' refusal to register; *Joseph Rowntree Memorial Trust Housing Association Ltd v. Att.-Gen.* [1983] Ch. 159, where refusal was reversed.

[66] *ante*, p. 399.

[67] Annual Report 1999/2000, para. 4.5. In that year 5,409 were registered; *ibid.*, para. 3.2.

[68] See Annual Report 1982, paras. 36–38, App. C, for the Commissioners' refusal to accede to the request of the Attorney-General to remove the Church of Unification (the "Moonies") from the register. (The Attorney-General's action was subsequently dropped).

[69] Charities Act 1993, s.29. The Commissioners owe no duty of care to potential objects of a charity; *Mills v. Winchester Diocesan Board of Finance* [1989] Ch. 428; (1989) 3 *Trust Law & Practice* 114 (N. Reville).

F. Powers of the Charity Commissioners

i. Schemes. The Charity Commissioners have concurrent juris-diction with the High Court in establishing schemes for the admini-stration of a charity.[70] This helps the trustees of charities to administer them more efficiently and to make better use of their funds and property. Schemes may cover the appointment of new bodies of trustees, the vesting of property in new trustees, the provi-sion of new *cy-près* objects in place of objects which have become impracticable, the extension of the trustees' investment powers, and the grouping or amalgamation of charities. Schemes are usually made by the Commissioners on the application of a charity, or where the court, on directing a scheme, orders that the Commissioners shall settle the scheme.[71] It is the duty of charity trustees to secure the effective use of charity property.[72] If they unreasonably refuse or neglect to apply for a scheme in circumstances in which they ought, in the interest of the charity, to do so, the Commissioners may proceed as if an application for a scheme had been made in the case of a charity at least 40 years old.[73]

ii. Consent to Proceedings. By section 33 of the Charities Act 1993, no court proceedings relating to the administration of a charity (other than an exempt charity) shall be entertained unless authorised by the Commissioners.[74] This is to prevent the dissipation of chari-table funds in legal proceedings over matters which the Commis-sioners could resolve.

iii. Dealings with Charity Property. Charity trustees are sub-ject to various statutory restrictions on dealings in charity property. Of particular importance is section 36 of the Charities Act 1993,[75] restricting the trustees' powers[76] to sell, lease or otherwise dispose of charity land.[77] The trustees require an order of the court or of the

---

[70] Charities Act 1993, s.16(1).

[71] *ibid.* s.16(2). As to the right of appeal, see *Childs v. Att.-Gen.* [1973] 1 W.L.R. 497.

[72] *ibid*, s.13(5).

[73] *ibid.* s.16(6). The restriction to charities 40 years old was introduced in order to protect donors against official intervention to alter the terms of trusts wihtin the donor's life-time.

[74] See *Haslemere Estates Ltd v. Baker* [1982] 1 W.L.R. 1109; *Re Hampton Fuel Allotment Charity* [1989] Ch. 484; *Richmond upon Thames London Borough Council v. Rogers* [1988] 2 All E.R. 761; *Mills v. Winchester Diocesan Board of Finance* [1989] Ch. 428; *Gunning v. Buckfast Abbey Trustees Registered, The Times,* June 9, 1994; *Scott v. National Trust for Places of Historic Interest or Natural Beauty* [1998] 2 All E.R. 705; *Muman v. Nagasena* [2000] 1 W.L.R. 299.

[75] See also s.38 (mortgages).

[76] Which derive from the Trusts of Land and Appointment of Trustees Act 1996, s.6 (which cannot be excluded by the settlor; s.8(3)), or under the founding instrument or statute.

[77] Such land is no longer settled land but is held on a trust of land; Trusts of Land and Appointment of Trustees Act 1996, s.2(5).

Commissioners unless the following conditions are satisfied: (*a*) the trustees have obtained and considered a written report on the proposed disposition from a qualified surveyor; (*b*) they have advertised the proposed disposition as advised by the surveyor; and (*c*) they are satisfied that the terms are the best reasonably obtainable.[78] The requirements are less stringent in the case of a lease not exceeding seven years.[79] Where the trustees hold land on trusts which stipulate that it is to be used for the purposes (or any particular purpose) of the charity, they must also give public notice and invite and consider representations.[80] Such land could be sold in certain circumstances under the previous law.[81]

Under section 26 of the Act of 1993 the Commissioners have a general power to authorise dealings with charity property which the trustees would otherwise have no power to do.

iv. Accounts; Inquiries. The Commissioners oversee the trustees' duty to provide accounts,[82] and, if dissatisfied in any way, may institute inquiries.[83] Ultimately, they may remove trustees from office.[84] The Commissioners may be alerted by the Inland Revenue to the possible misapplication of charity funds.[85]

It is in the area of accounts and audit that much disquiet was felt over the possibility of abuse and maladministration by charity trustees. The Charities Act 1993 imposes more rigorous duties on trustees of unincorporated charities[86] to keep accounting records and to prepare annual accounts, which must be audited.[87] The trustees must send annual reports to the Commissioners of their activities, with a statement of accounts and the auditor's report.[88] The Commissioners may grant a unifying order enabling two or more charities with

---

[78] s.36(2), (3). For exceptions, see s.36(9). Neither s.36 nor s.38 (mortgages) applies to exempt charities. A disposition not complying with s.36 is valid in favour of a purchaser in good faith; s.37(4); *cf. London Borough of Hounslow v. Hare* (1992) 24 H.L.R. 9 (on Charities Act 1960, s.29). See further Decisions, Vol. 5 (1997), p. 21.

[79] s.36(5).

[80] s.36(6). This does not apply if they are acquiring replacement property, or in the case of a lease not exceeding two years; s.36(7).

[81] See *Oldham Borough Council v. Att.-Gen.* [1993] Ch. 210.

[82] Charities Act 1993, ss.41–49; Charities (Accounts and Reports) Regulations (S.I. 1995 No. 2724), as amended by Charities (Accounts and Reports) Regulations 2000 (S.I. 2000 No. 2868).

[83] *ibid.*, s.8. See Annual Report 1998, p. 20. Examples may be found in most of the Annual Reports.

[84] *ibid.* s.18, *post*, p. 467. See also *Att-Gen. v. Schonfeld* [1980] 1 W.L.R. 1182.

[85] *ibid.*, s.10.

[86] Companies Act 1985, Part VII, applies to corporate charities. Those with a gross income of up to £90,000 are exempted by s.249A. The new rules do not apply to exempt charities, but s.46 of the 1993 Act imposes a duty to keep accounts on them.

[87] ss.42–44.

[88] s.45; Charities (Accounts and Reports) Regulations 2000 (S.I. 2000 No. 2868). The reports are subject to public inspection; s.47. The trustees must also send annual returns in prescribed form to the Commissioners; s.48. Persistent default in these duties is an offence; s.49. See also s.87.

the same trustees to file consolidated accounts.[89] More work needs to be done, however, to achieve the effective supervision of charities.[90]

G. Investment

i. Investment Powers.[91] The wide powers of investment conferred by the Trustee Act 2000 (discussed in Chapter 18) apply to charity trustees. As mentioned below, the new legislation also permits them to delegate their investment powers.

ii. Pooling. C.O.I.F. Common Deposit Scheme. Without statutory authority, different bodies of trustees could not pool their funds for investment purposes, for this would involve a delegation of the trustees' investment powers, which was not permitted prior to the Trustee Act 2000. Section 24 of the 1993 Act (re-enacting earlier provisions) gives power to the court or the Commissioners to create common investment schemes under which the investment of property transferred to the fund is invested by trustees appointed to manage the fund, and the participating charities are entitled to shares related to their contributions.[92] Under the predecessor legislation, the Commissioners established the Charities Official Investment Fund, which is open to all charities.

The Charities Act 1993 also authorises the creation of common deposit schemes,[93] whereby money can be deposited at interest.

H. Delegation

The Trustee Act 2000 widened trustees' delegation powers, as discussed in Chapter 20. Special rules, however, apply to delegation by charity trustees. They may delegate:

(a) any function consisting of carrying out a decision that the trustees have taken;

---

[89] s.96(6), inserted by the Charities (Amendment) Act 1995. The order may apply to all or any of the purposes of the 1993 Act.

[90] See Select Committee on Public Accounts, 28th Report (1998); *Charity Commission— Regulation and Support of Charities*; (1998) 148 N.L.J. 752 (H. Wilkinson). See now Annual Report 1999/2000, para. 5.4, indicating improvements.

[91] As to ethical investment by charity trustees, see *Harries v. Church Commissioners for England* [1992] 1 W.L.R. 1241; *post*, p. 545.

[92] Annual Report 1970, paras. 68–74; 1971, para. 90; *Re London University's Charitable Trust* [1964] Ch. 284. For ethical investment opportunities, see Annual Report 1996, paras. 54–55.

[93] s.25. See also Trustee Act 2000, s.38.

(b) any function relating to the investment of trust assets (including the management of land held as an investment); and

(c) any function relating to the raising of funds otherwise than by means of profits of a trade which is an integral part of carrying out the trust's charitable purpose.[94]

Charity trustees may exercise the new statutory powers of appointing nominees and custodians,[95] save in relation to assets vested in the official custodian for charities.[96]

I. Trustees

i. Capacity. One of the means by which the Charities Act 1993 seeks to prevent fraud and maladministration is by the disqualification of certain persons from holding the office of trustee of a charity.[97] Those disqualified include persons convicted of an offence involving dishonesty or deception, undischarged bankrupts and persons previously removed from charity trusteeship on the grounds of misconduct or mismanagement.[98] Also a Local Authority may not be trustee of an eleemosynary charity.[99] We have seen that the appointment of a charity as trustee may colour the construction which a court will place upon the language of the trust, but does not ensure that a trust is charitable.[1]

ii. Number. Majority Vote. There is no limit upon the number of persons who may be trustees of a charity.[2] Too great a number of trustees is an obvious inconvenience. But decisions of trustees of a charity may be taken by majority vote and need not be unanimous.[3]

iii. Retirement, Removal and Suspension. Charity trustees may retire in the same way as trustees of private trusts.[4] The Commissioners may suspend a trustee on being satisfied as a result of inquiries[5] that (*a*) there has been misconduct or mismanagement or (*b*) that it is necessary or desirable for the purpose of protecting the

---

[94] Trustee Act 2000, s.11(3). Other functions may be added by statutory instrument.
[95] *ibid.*, ss.16, 17.
[96] *ante*, p. 461.
[97] s.72. By s.73, it is an offence to act while disqualified.
[98] The Commissioners are to keep a public register of persons so removed.
[99] *Re Armitage* [1972] Ch. 438.
[1] *ante*, p. 439.
[2] T.A. 1925, s. 34.
[3] *Re Whiteley* [1910] 1 Ch. 600 at 608.
[4] *post*, p. 521.
[5] Under Charities Act 1993, s.8.; *Jones v. Att.-Gen.* [1974] Ch. 148.

property if the charity,[6] or they may appoint additional trustees or make orders for the protection of the property, such as the appointment of a receiver and manager. Where they are satisfied that both conditions (*a*) and (*b*) are fulfilled, they may order the removal of a trustee or other officer who has been responsible for or privy to the misconduct or mismanagement or has contributed to or facilitated it.[7] They may also (or instead) order a scheme for the administration of the charity. The Commissioners may also, by order made of their own motion, remove a charity trustee who has been discharged from bankruptcy within the last five years, who is a corporation in liquidation, is mentally incapable, has failed to act, or is abroad or cannot be found.[8] In such cases they may appoint a replacement or additional trustee. These provisions do not apply to exempt charities.

iv. Remuneration. The Trustee Act 2000 extends trustees' powers to charge for their services, as discussed in Chapter 21. The Law Commission recommended that charity trustees should be excluded, on the ground that public confidence in the sector might otherwise be undermined.[9] The new provisions whereby trust corporations may receive remuneration although the trust instrument confers no such entitlement do not apply to charity trustees, but the Secretary of State may by regulations make provision for the remuneration of charity trustees who are trust corporations or who act in a professional capacity.[10]

A related question is whether charity trustees should be prohibited from supplying goods and services to a charity on the ground that this might create a conflict of interest and duty.[11] This is permitted in certain circumstances.[12]

v. Misapplication. An application by the trustee for purposes not covered by the terms of the trust is a misapplication of charity funds, which may give rise to personal liability on the trustee, and may be restrained by injunction,[13] or may be the subject of an inquiry by the Charity Commissioners.[14]

---

[6] s.18.

[7] See *Weth v. Att.-Gen.* [1999] 1 W.L.R. 686.

[8] Charities Act 1993, s.18(4).

[9] Law Com. No. 260 (1999); *Trustees' Powers and Duties*, para. 7.22. See also Charity Com. leaflet CC11, September 2000

[10] Trustee Act 2000, ss.29, 30.

[11] *post*, Chap. 21.

[12] Annual Report 1971, para. 93.

[13] *Baldry v. Feintuck* [1972] 1 W.L.R. 552. (Resolution to apply Students' Union funds for political purposes). See Annual Report 1983, paras. 95 and 96 and App. A.

[14] *ante*, p. 465.

J. Ex Gratia Payments

Difficulty and distress has been caused by the fact that a charity was thought to be unable to make *ex gratia* payments for non-charitable purposes, however compelling the moral obligation to do so. Thus, if a testator gave to his family his shares in certain companies, and left his residuary estate to charity, and at the time of the testator's death all the shares had been sold and the proceeds of sale fell into the residuary estate, the charity would be obtaining much more than the testator intended. Cross J. decided that, in appropriate circumstances, the court and the Attorney-General had power to give authority to make *ex gratia* payments from charitable funds; but only in case of strong moral obligation.[15] Trustees wishing to make such a payment should apply to the Charity Commissioners, who can authorise such payments under the supervision of the Attorney-General.[16]

K. Co-operation Between Charities and Statutory Services[17]

If the best value is to be obtained from the resources available to charity trustees and local authorities, it is essential that they work in harmony. The social services of the Welfare State have taken over most of the ground of charity work, as it has been understood. This raises the question of the role of charity, which has certainly changed in the last 100 years. If it is argued that all the important needs of the community are now the responsibility of the State, one conclusion is that the State should take over all funds held in charitable trusts. On the other hand, a giant bureaucratic system has its gaps and limitations. One of the most striking developments of recent years has been the advent of the "contract culture", which describes the system whereby the State increasingly engages the voluntary sector under contract to deliver services previously provided by government agencies.[18] Charities should remain independent, however, and "co-operation between them and the statutory services should be on the basis of partnership not subordination."[19] These are principles on which sections 76–78 of the 1993 Act, re-enacting provisions of the 1960 Act, are based.

[15] *Re Snowden* [1970] Ch. 700; *Re Henderson* [1960] Ch. 700; Annual Report 1969, paras. 26–31; Annual Report 1977, paras. 154–156.

[16] Charities Act 1993, s. 27.

[17] See Annual Report 1970, paras. 28–36; 1971, paras. 101 *et seq.*; 1972, para. 49; 1976, paras. 76–84; 1977, paras. 51–56 (Motability: charity in partnership with State); paras. 58–62 (care of disabled); 1978, paras. 61–63, Apps. A and B suggesting ways in which the income of charities for the relief of poverty and sickness may be spent without overlapping the statutory services; 1987, para. 4. See also *Charity and the National Health, The Times,* December 6, 1989.

[18] See [1991] Conv. 419 (J. Warburton and D. Morris); (1999) 62 M.L.R. 333 at 335 (M. Chesterman); (2000) 20 L.S. 409 (D. Morris).

[19] Annual Report 1970 para. 29; 1971, paras. 80, 84.

Section 76 authorises a local authority to maintain a public index of local charities. Under section 77, the authority may initiate a review of local charities, and report to the Commissioners and make recommendations. Section 78 permits any local council to make arrangements for the co-ordination of the work of the council and of the charities in the interests of persons who may benefit from the service of either.

Although many schemes arising out of local reviews have been made,[20] few local authorities can now afford to initiate a review.[21] The ineffectiveness of many local authority reviews of charities to achieve modernisation and use of resources in co-operation with the welfare services led to the passing of the Charities Act 1985. This Act and the provisions of the Charities Act 1993 which replace it[22] were designed to promote greater accountability to the community by trustees of local charities and to facilitate the modernisation of these and other small charities and the disposal of funds which can no longer be effectively used.

---

[20] H.C. Expenditure Committee Report, Vol. II, 20–21; Goodman Committee Report, paras. 184–185; Annual Report 1979, para. 123.
[21] Annual Report 1980, para. 154.
[22] *ante*, 458.

CHAPTER 16

TRUSTS OF PENSION FUNDS

1. INTRODUCTION

PENSION fund trusts have received much public scrutiny in recent years, primarily as a result of the misappropriation of about £453 million from the pension funds of the employees of Mirror Group Newspapers and the Maxwell Communications Corporation by the late Robert Maxwell.[1] The focus of the ensuing debate was the question whether pension schemes should continue to be governed by the law of trusts, and how the scheme members (the beneficiaries) could be better safeguarded against fraud, mismanagement and insolvency. The matter was referred to the Pension Law Review Committee, chaired by Professor Roy Goode. The Goode Report[2] favoured retaining the law of trusts as the most suitable mechanism for dealing with pension funds, primarily because of the well-established principles concerning the fiduciary responsibilities of

---

[1] Most of the money was recovered; *The Times*, February 20, 1996.
[2] *Pension Law Reform: Pension Law Review Committee Report* (1993), Cmnd. 2342; (1993) 7 *Trust Law International* 91 (D. Chatterton). See also [1993] Conv. 283 (D. Hayton).

trustees and the proprietary rights of beneficiaries, conferring protection from the employer's insolvency. Of course, no legal mechanism can prevent deliberate wrongdoing.

The Committee recommended various ways in which the rights of pension beneficiaries might be enhanced and safeguarded by the enactment of special rules going beyond the protection afforded to beneficiaries of traditional trusts under the general law. In particular, they recommended the introduction of a regulatory body, a compensation scheme to apply in cases of misappropriation, a minimum funding requirement to prevent a shortfall of funds in the case of funded schemes, restrictions on employers' rights to surplus funds, and reforms relating to the appointment, removal and disqualification of trustees. Most of their recommendations, some in modified form, were implemented by the Pensions Act 1995.[3] The special treatment of pension fund beneficiaries reflects the fact that their entitlements arise from their contracts of employment. Unlike traditional beneficiaries, they are not volunteers. In many ways, however, pension trusts are subject to the same principles as any other trusts, and the pension trust caselaw has contributed much to the development of the general law of trusts.[4]

A long-term European goal is cross-border membership of pension schemes through the establishment of European pension funds covering workers in several member states, to reflect the principle of free movement of workers.

The purpose of this chapter is to examine pension funds as an important modern illustration of the law of trusts in operation (about £800 billion is currently invested in pensions[5]), and to consider the ways in which pension fund trusts are treated differently from traditional trusts. Before doing so it is necessary to appreciate the different types of pension schemes available and to understand the terminology.

A. Types of Pension Scheme

Pension provision falls into three broad categories: the state pension, a personal pension (a form of investment made by an individual with an insurance company, to which the employer may contribute) and an occupational pension scheme, which is organised by an employer to provide pensions and other benefits for employees (and usually for their dependants) on leaving employment (by

---

[3] See (1996) 59 M.L.R. 241 (R. Nobles).
[4] See (1993) 56 M.L.R. 471 (G. Moffat), examining whether a separate pensions law is developing, or whether the developments in recent pensions cases are applicable generally. See also (1994) 8 *Trust Law International* 35 (Vinelott J.); [1997] Conv. 89 (M. Milner). For the "property" rights of pension beneficiaries, see (1994) 14 L.S. 345 (R. Nobles).
[5] *The Times*, July 2, 1999.

retirement or otherwise) or on death.[6] The latter category is the subject of this chapter. Occupational pension schemes themselves take various forms, but in essence trust law will apply where assets are segregated and invested to provide pension benefits. In 1991 10.7 million employees were members of occupational pension schemes.[7] Fewer than 40 per cent of private sector employees were scheme members in contrast with over 70 per cent of public sector employees. Many public sector schemes (such as those for teachers and the civil service) are established by legislation and are unfunded in the sense that there is no trust fund set aside to provide benefits. The employees' security is founded on the statute rather than on the segregation of assets. State pensions are also unfunded, benefits being paid from current contributions. A non-statutory scheme is unfunded where the employer does not set aside and accumulate assets in a separate trust fund in advance of the benefits commencing to be paid. Most private schemes, however, are funded. (There is no obligation on an employer, other than by contract, to provide a funded scheme, or indeed any pension scheme at all). We are concerned with funded schemes, where a fund is held on trust to make provision in advance for future liabilities to members by accumulating assets. The assets are invested and the investments held by the trustees. This may be contrasted with an insured scheme, where the trustees have effected an insurance contract for each member which guarantees benefits corresponding to those promised under the scheme rules. In other words, this is an investment through the medium of an insurance company, the trustees using the contributions to pay the premiums. The insurance is the only significant asset of the scheme. If the sums payable by the insurer are sufficient at all times to cover all benefits, the scheme is said to be fully insured. Most small schemes are run through insurers.

The benefits to which an employee is entitled depend on whether the scheme is earnings-related (a defined *benefit* scheme) or whether it is a "money purchase" scheme (a defined *contribution* scheme). An earnings-related scheme (sometimes called a final salary scheme) is where the benefit is calculated by reference to the member's pensionable earnings for a period of pensionable service ending at or before normal pension date or leaving service. There is normally a restriction on the number of years (*e.g.* 40) which qualify as pensionable service, and not all earnings (*e.g.* a bonus or allowance) are pensionable. The scheme may require contributions from employees (a contributory scheme) or may not (non-contributory). The benefits are usually based on a fraction of the final salary for

[6] Another, less common, variant is the "executive pension plan", in which a scheme is established by a private company (the employer) for one employee (the director). Such a scheme was involved in *Brooks v. Brooks* [1996] 1 A.C. 375, *post*, p. 493.
[7] *Pension Law Review Committee Report*, para. 2.2.4.

each year of pensionable service. The cost of providing these defined benefits cannot be accurately predicted, so the employer in a contributory scheme undertakes to pay whatever sum is needed to top up employee contributions. If the fund is in surplus, the employer may be able to take a "contributions holiday", by temporarily suspending its contributions.[8] It follows that the risk of poor investment performance falls on the employer in an earnings-related scheme.

A "money purchase" scheme is where the benefits of an individual member are determined by reference to the contributions paid into the scheme by or on behalf of that member, usually increased by an amount based on the investment return of those contributions. The contributions are fixed (normally a percentage of salary) by the scheme, and the benefits vary according to investment performance. Thus the employee takes the risk of poor investments, but also takes the benefit of a good performance.[9] The fund is either used to purchase an annuity to provide the pension, or a pension may be paid from the fund according to the size of the member's account in the fund. The majority of older schemes are earnings-related, but "money purchase" is more popular for new schemes. As explained below, one attraction to employers is that a money purchase scheme is not subject to the minimum funding requirements introduced by the Pensions Act 1995.

When a funded scheme is being set up, the trust deeds are lengthy and take time to prepare. It is, therefore, usual to have an interim trust deed with outline rules, which appoints the first trustees. This enables the scheme to be started without delay, and provisional tax relief to be secured.[10] In due course this is replaced by the final (or definitive) trust deed, and the Inland Revenue normally gives approval (necessary for tax relief) backdated to the execution of the interim deed. The construction of the scheme by the court should be practical and purposive.[11]

Much of the caselaw deals with entitlement to surplus funds, the contest normally involving beneficiaries, employers, creditors of an insolvent employer, or companies which have taken over the employer company and wish to syphon off the surplus ("takeover raiders" or "predators"). Of course, a surplus cannot arise in the case of a money purchase scheme or an unfunded scheme. In the

---

[8] This is one of the permitted methods of reducing an excessive surplus under the pension trust tax regime; *post*, p. 492. A thirty year "holiday" was a breach of trust by the trustees of the British Airways pension fund; (1996) 10 *Trust Law International* 26. See also *Jefferies v. Mayes* [1999] P.L.R. 37 (*sub nom. National Grid Co. plc v. Mayes* [2000] I.C.R. 174).

[9] The trustees are subject to the usual standard of prudence with regard to the investments; see (1999) 13 *Trust Law International* 2 (N. Moore).

[10] For the fiscal benefits, see *post*, p. 490.

[11] *Jefferies v. Mayes, supra.*

case of a funded earnings-related scheme, any surplus is notional if the scheme is ongoing. A surplus is said to exist whenever, according to actuarial calculations, the value of the assets exceeds the estimated liabilities. There will be an actual surplus only if the scheme is wound up, leaving an excess after discharge of liabilities. Where a pension scheme is terminated by winding-up, the assets will usually be applied to the purchase of annuities to provide pensions for members, or the assets and liabilities may be transferred to another pension scheme.

B. Beneficiaries Not Volunteers

The fact that pension trust beneficiaries are not volunteers puts them in certain respects in a different position from the beneficiaries of traditional family trusts. The consideration arises from the fact that the pension benefits are a form of deferred remuneration for their services[12] and from their contributions (if any) to the fund. In *Mettoy Pension Trustees Ltd v. Evans*[13] the scheme contained a power of appointment in favour of the members, any surplus not so appointed going to the employer, which was in liquidation. The fact that the members were not volunteers was influential in classifying the power as fiduciary rather than personal. Had it been only personal (*i.e.* a bare power), the unpalatable conclusion would have been that the entire surplus would have gone to the creditors, the power proving to be of illusory benefit to the members. The classification of the power as fiduciary meant that it could not be released[14] (in the interests of the creditors), and, further, that the court could intervene to secure the exercise of the power.[15]

In *Davis v. Richards & Wallington Industries Ltd*[16] there were doubts whether the definitive (final) trust deed had been validly executed. This deed provided that any surplus should belong to the employers after increasing the pension benefits to the statutory maximum. If the deed was invalid the trust would be incompletely constituted. However, as the beneficiaries were not volunteers they could compel the execution of a valid deed and their rights (by

---

[12] See *Brooks v. Brooks* [1996] 1 A.C. 375. This meant that the husband (the employee) and not the employer was regarded as settlor of the marriage settlement constituted by the pension scheme.

[13] [1990] 1 W.L.R. 1587; *ante*, p. 176. See also *Thrells Ltd v. Lomas* [1993] 1 W.L.R. 456; *In re Makin (William) & Sons Ltd* [1993] B.C.C. 453; *British Coal Corp. v. British Coal Staff Superannuation Scheme Trustees Ltd* [1995] 1 All E.R. 912 at 925; *Air Jamaica Ltd v. Charlton* [1999] 1 W.L.R. 1399 at 1407.

[14] See also *Re Courage Group's Pension Schemes* [1987] 1 W.L.R. 495; *ante*, p. 188.

[15] This controversial aspect of the decision was discussed at 176, *ante*. See now Pensions Act 1995, s.25 (fiduciary powers exercisable by independent trustee on insolvency); *post*, p. 480.

[16] [1990] 1 W.L.R. 1511; *ante*, p. 249. The decision was disapproved on another point in *Air Jamaica Ltd v. Charlton, supra.*

applying the maxim that equity regards as done that which ought to be done) were as if such a deed had already been executed. In fact the deed was held valid.

In a pension trust the trustee/beneficiary relationship exists in parallel with the contractual employer/employee relationship and the pension scheme must be interpreted against this background. In *Imperial Group Pension Trust Ltd v. Imperial Tobacco Ltd*[17] the company had power under the scheme to consent to an increase in benefits. The issue was whether it was under a duty to consider the interests of the members and not just its own interests when granting or withholding consent. It was held that the implied contractual obligation of good faith between employer and employee (meaning that the employer would not act in a manner calculated or likely to destroy or damage the relationship of confidence and trust between employer and employee) applied to the exercise of the employer's rights and powers under the pension scheme just as it applied to its other rights and powers. The power to give or withhold consent was accordingly subject to a restriction that it could not be validly exercised in breach of the obligation of good faith. Although the employer is not a fiduciary when exercising its powers under a pension scheme, its obligation of good faith means that in any dealings with a surplus it must pay fair regard to the interests of the members, for whose benefit the scheme exists.[18] Thus the pension trust "lies at the interface between trust and employment law."[19]

The fact that pension trust beneficiaries are not volunteers may allow them to be more favourably treated than other beneficiaries in the matter of costs. In *McDonald v. Horn*[20] it was held that, contrary to the usual rule, pension beneficiaries may obtain a "pre-emptive costs order" where there are serious allegations of impropriety and breach of trust against the employers and trustees. Thus the beneficiaries would obtain their costs, and any costs which they might be ordered to pay to the defendants, out of the fund whether or not their action ultimately proved successful. The fact that the beneficiaries had given consideration made the action analogous to an action by a minority shareholder on behalf of a company, where such an order could be made.

As a general proposition, however, the ordinary principles of trust law apply to pension trusts as to other trusts. This was emphasised in *Wilson v. Law Debenture Trust Corp plc*,[21] where it was held that

---

[17] [1991] 1 W.L.R. 589.

[18] *Jefferies v. Mayes* [1999] P.L.R. 37; *sub nom. National Grid Co. plc v. Mayes* [2000] I.C.R. 174.

[19] (1994) 8 *Trust Law International* 35 (Vinelott J.).

[20] [1995] 1 All E.R. 961.

[21] [1995] 2 All E.R. 337; (1995) 145 N.L.J. 1414 (P. O'Hagan). Member trustees will have access to reasons.

the principle of *Re Londonderry's Settlement*,[22] whereby trustees are not obliged to give reasons for the exercise of their discretions to the beneficiaries, applied equally to pension fund trusts.[23] Although the court must have regard to the fact that the beneficiaries are not volunteers when construing the trust deed, effect must be given to settled principles of trust law in determining the effect of the deed on its true construction.

2. Special Rules Applicable to Pension Trusts

In view of the special nature of pension fund trusts in terms of the size of the funds, their quasi-public nature, the opportunities for misappropriation by the employer, the non-volunteer status of the beneficiaries, and the public interest in the encouragement of such trusts, there are many statutory provisions which apply special rules to pension trusts. Most of these are contained in the Pensions Act 1995, but others, relating in particular to taxation and the application of the perpetuity rule, are found elsewhere.

A. Pensions Act 1995[24]

As discussed at the beginning of this chapter, the main objective of the Act is to protect the beneficiaries from the effects of maladministration, fraud and insolvency. Illustrations of this objective include the provision that the trustees must keep proper books and records and must keep any money received by them in a separate account at an institution authorised under the Banking Act 1987,[25] and that an employer who fails to pay over any contributions deducted from members within a certain period commits an offence.[26] The 1995 Act seeks also to strike a fair balance between the interests of current employees, pensioners and employers. To the extent that any of the statutory provisions discussed below conflict with the terms of a pension scheme, such terms are overridden by the Act.[27] Provision is also made for modifying pension schemes in order to implement the requirements of the Act.[28]

---

[22] [1965] Ch. 198; *post*, p. 525.

[23] A contrary view is taken in (1992) 6 *Trust Law International* 119 at 125 (Lord Browne-Wilkinson), (1994) 8 *Trust Law International* 27 and 118 (D. Schaffer) and [1996] P.L.R. 107 (Sir Robert Walker). Pension scheme trustees must record their decisions but not the reasons for them; Occupational Pensions Schemes (Scheme Administration) Regulations (S.I. 1996 No. 1715). See (1997) 11 *Trust Law International* 11 and 42 (D. Pollard).

[24] See generally Arthur, *Pensions and Trusteeship*.

[25] Pensions Act 1995, s.49.

[26] s.49(8).

[27] s.117.

[28] ss.68, 69. Schemes often contain express modification powers, the exercise of which is restricted by s.67.

i. Regulatory Authority. Following the recommendations of the Goode Report, the 1995 Act set up the Occupational Pensions Regulatory Authority[29] (replacing the Occupational Pensions Board) to supervise pension trusts and thereby reduce the likelihood of maladministration and fraud. The Authority may, by an order under section 3 of the Act, prohibit a person from being a trustee of a particular pension trust in various circumstances, as where it is satisfied that the person has been in serious or persistent breach of his duties under the Act while a trustee of the pension trust. Such an order, which is revocable, operates to remove the trustee. Section 4 enables the Authority to make an order suspending a trustee in various circumstances, as where a bankruptcy petition has been presented against him or proceedings commenced for an offence involving dishonesty or deception, and such proceedings have not been concluded. While the order is in force, the person is prohibited from exercising any functions as trustee.[30] A person who purports to act as trustee while prohibited or suspended is guilty of an offence, but things done by him while purporting to act are not invalid merely because of the prohibition or suspension.[31] The power of the Authority to disqualify certain persons from acting as trustee of any occupational pension scheme is dealt with below.[32] Section 7 permits the Authority to appoint a new trustee in place of one who has been removed or disqualified, or where the appointment is necessary to secure that the number of trustees is sufficient or that the trustees as a whole have the necessary skills. Such a trustee may be paid fees out of the trust assets.

In addition to the powers discussed above, the Authority has jurisdiction under section 10 to impose financial penalties on trustees and other persons, such as the director of a corporate trustee, in respect of various breaches of their duties under the 1995 Act. It may also seek injunctions to restrain misuse or misappropriation of assets, apply to court for the restitution of assets transferred to the employer or invested in the employer's business in breach of the Act, and give directions to trustees.[33] Trustees must not be indemnified out of the trust assets for any fine imposed for an offence under the Act nor for any civil penalty imposed by the Authority.[34] Nor may the premiums of an insurance policy be paid out of trust assets where the risk is or includes the imposition of such a fine or penalty.

---

[29] s.1 and Sched. 1.
[30] The procedure for making orders under ss.3 and 4 is found in s.5.
[31] s.6.
[32] *post*, p. 480.
[33] ss.13–15. For information gathering by the Authority, see s.98–102.
[34] s.31.

Finally, the Authority may order an occupational pension scheme to be wound up in order to protect the interests of the members or, on the application of the trustees or employer, if the scheme is no longer required or should be replaced by a different scheme.[35]

In addition to the Authority, the Pensions Ombudsman has jurisdiction over occupational and personal pension schemes. He may investigate and determine various complaints and disputes relating primarily to maladministration.[36] A breach of trust does not automatically constitute maladministration.[37] The Ombudsman may not direct steps to be taken (such as the repayment of money to the fund or the setting aside of a deed) unless the court could do so.[38] It appears that he may direct the payment of damages for distress,[39] although this remains to be confirmed by the higher courts.

ii. Trustees. The supervisory powers of the regulatory authority over trustees, including the power of removal, suspension and appointment, were noted above. The 1995 Act contains further important provisions concerning trustees, which are designed primarily to ensure good administration and to dilute the influence of the employer.

(a) *Constitution.* The constitution of the trustee body requires that representatives of the scheme members must be included, and that a trustee who is independent of the employer must be appointed on the employer's insolvency.

The trustees must normally make arrangements for the selection of "member-nominated trustees".[40] There must be at least two (or at least one if the scheme comprises less than 100 members) and they must constitute at least one third of the total number of trustees. A greater number cannot be appointed without the employer's approval. Where the trustee is a company connected with the employer, the requirement is for "member-nominated directors".[41] A person who is not a scheme member cannot be selected as a member-nominated trustee (or director) without the employer's approval, if the employer so requires.[42]

---

[35] s.11.
[36] Pension Schemes Act 1993, ss.146–151, as amended by Pensions Act 1995, s.157. On the resolution of pension disputes, see (1998) 12 *Trust Law International* 26 (J. Clifford).
[37] *Law Debenture Trust Corp plc v. Pensions Ombudsman* [1998] 1 W.L.R. 1329.
[38] *Hillsdown Holdings plc v. Pensions Ombudsman* [1997] 1 All E.R. 862; *Edge v. Pensions Ombudsman* [2000] Ch. 602.
[39] *City and County of Swansea v. Johnson* [1999] Ch 189.
[40] Pensions Act 1995, s.16, subject to significant exceptions in s.17. See Occupational Pension Schemes (Member-nominated Trustees and Directors) Regulations (S.I. 1996 No. 1216). The failure to make member trustees mandatory is criticised in (1996) 59 M.L.R. 241 at 259 (R. Nobles).
[41] s.18.
[42] s.19(5).

Where a person is both a trustee and a beneficiary, as in the case of member-nominated trustees, difficult problems of conflict of interest and duty might arise. Where, for example, trustees have a discretion to use a surplus to augment the benefits of the members, any balance going to the employer, the question arises whether they can validly exercise their discretion in such a way as to benefit themselves in their capacity as members.[43] This is now resolved by section 39 of the 1995 Act, which provides that "no rule of law that a trustee may not exercise the powers vested in him so as to give rise to a conflict between his personal interest and his duties to the beneficiaries shall apply to a trustee of a trust scheme, who is also a member of the scheme, exercising the powers vested in him in any manner, merely because their exercise in that manner benefits, or may benefit, him as a member of the scheme."

At least one independent trustee must be appointed in circumstances connected with the insolvency of the employer, namely when an insolvency practitioner begins to act in relation to the employer or if the official receiver becomes the liquidator of the employer company or the receiver and manager or trustee in bankruptcy of an individual employer.[44] The appointment is the responsibility of the insolvency practitioner or official receiver.[45] Once appointed, and so long as the circumstances requiring the appointment continue, only the independent trustee may exercise any discretionary powers of the trustees under the scheme and any fiduciary powers of the employer.[46]

(b) *Disqualification.* Certain categories of persons are disqualified by section 29 from being trustee of any occupational pension scheme. Broadly, the disqualification applies to a person convicted of any offence involving dishonesty or deception; an undischarged bankrupt; a company of which any director is disqualified under the section; a person who has made a composition with creditors and has not been discharged; and a person disqualified from acting as a company director. There are other circumstances in which the regulatory authority may disqualify a person from acting as trustee of any occupational pension scheme. A person who has been removed

---

[43] See *In re Makin (William) & Sons Ltd* [1993] B.C.C. 453; (1996) 10 *Trust Law International* 15 (M. Milner); *British Coal Corp. v. British Coal Staff Superannuation Scheme Trustees Ltd* [1995] 1 All E.R. 912; *Re Drexel Burnham Lambert UK Pension Plan* [1995] 1 W.L.R. 32; *Edge v. Pensions Ombudsman* [2000] Ch. 602.

[44] s.22; Occupational Pension Schemes (Independent Trustees) Regulations (S.I. 1997 No. 252). "Independent" is defined in s.23(3). He may be paid fees from the trust fund; s.25(6). An independent trustee was already required in such circumstances under previous legislation.

[45] s.23. Scheme members may apply to court to enforce this duty under s.24.

[46] s.25. The employer, if previously sole trustee, ceases to be trustee on the appointment of the independent trustee.

by the Authority under section 3 of the Act or by court order on the ground of misconduct or mismanagement may be disqualified if the Authority considers that it is not desirable for him to be a trustee of any occupational pension scheme.[47] The Authority may also disqualify a company which has gone into liquidation or a person it considers incapable of acting as such a trustee by reason of mental disorder.[48]

A trustee who becomes disqualified ceases to be a trustee and commits an offence if he purports to act while disqualified,[49] although things done by him while purporting to act as trustee are not invalid merely because of the disqualification.[50] The Authority must keep a register of persons disqualified by its order.[51]

(c) *Majority Decisions.* Under the general law, trustees (other than charity trustees) must act unanimously, unless the trust instrument provides otherwise.[52] Section 32 of the 1995 Act provides an exception for trustees of an occupational pension scheme, who may, unless the trust scheme provides otherwise, make decisions by majority. As a safeguard, the trustees must give notice of occasions at which decisions may be taken to each trustee, so far as reasonably practicable.[53]

iii. **Professional Advisers.** The trustees or managers of every occupational pension scheme must appoint an individual or a firm as auditor and an individual as actuary.[54] Where the trust assets include investments, an individual or firm must be appointed as fund manager.[55] If the auditor or actuary has reasonable cause to believe that any duty imposed on the trustees or managers, employer or professional adviser relating to the administration of the pension scheme has not been or is not being complied with, he must give a written report to the regulatory authority.[56] If he fails to do so, he may be subjected to a financial penalty under section 10 and may be disqualified by the regulatory authority from being the auditor or actuary of the pension scheme or of any other specified scheme.

---

[47] s.29(3).
[48] s.29(4). Orders under subsections (3) and (4) are revocable. Any disqualification under the section may be waived by the Authority.
[49] s.30(3).
[50] s.30(5).
[51] s.30(7).
[52] *post*, p. 504.
[53] s.32(2)(b).
[54] s.47. The duty to obtain audited accounts is imposed by regulations, the present source of which is s.41.
[55] *ibid.* For delegation of investment powers to the fund manager, see below.
[56] s.48 ("blowing the whistle"). Other persons, such as the trustees or professional advisers other than the auditor or actuary, may also report such matters to the regulatory authority.

The trustees of the pension scheme (and any connected persons and associates) are ineligible to act as auditor or actuary of the scheme.[57]

iv. Investment. Under the general law, pension trusts have been governed by the same investment principles as traditional trusts,[58] although the courts, recognising the need for the trustees of large pension funds to have wide investment powers, have been ready to exercise their jurisdiction to vary trusts by extending these powers.[59] It is now recognised, in the 1995 Act, that the special nature of pension trusts requires special treatment.

(a) *General Principles.* The trustees of an occupational pension scheme have, subject to any restriction in the scheme, the same power to make an investment of any kind as if they were absolutely entitled to the assets.[60] They must ensure that a written statement of the principles governing investment decisions is prepared, maintained and revised from time to time.[61] This statement must include the trustees' policy for securing compliance with the minimum funding requirement (discussed below) and on various other matters such as the kind of investments to be held, the balance between them, risk, expected return and realisation. It is now expressly required that the statement must cover the extent (if at all) to which social, environmental or ethical considerations are to be taken into account in investment decision-making.[62] The trustees must obtain and consider the advice of a person they reasonably believe to be qualified in investment matters and consult the employer before making or revising this statement, but neither the trust scheme nor the statement may restrict the investment power by reference to the employer's consent.

In choosing investments the trustees (or any fund manager to whom investment powers have been delegated, as discussed below) must have regard to the need to diversify investments so far as appropriate to the scheme, and to the suitability to the scheme of investments of the description of investment proposed and of the investment proposed as an investment of that description.[63] Before investing and at suitable intervals thereafter, the trustees must obtain

---

[57] s.27. Contravention is an offence under s.28.

[58] See *Cowan v. Scargill* [1985] Ch. 270; *post*, p. 543.

[59] See *Mason v. Farbrother* [1983] 2 All E.R. 1078; *post*, p. 548.

[60] Pensions Act 1995, s.34(1). "Investment" is not defined. The wide investment powers conferred by the Trustee Act 2000 do not apply as there is no need for them; T.A. 2000, s.36.

[61] s.35.

[62] Occupational Pension Schemes (Investment, and Assignment, Forfeiture, Bankruptcy etc.) Amendment Regulations (S.I. 1999 No. 1849).

[63] s.36(2), modelled on Trustee Investment Act 1961, s.6(1).

and consider proper advice[64] on the question whether the investment is satisfactory having regard to the factors just mentioned and the principles contained in their policy statement.[65] The trustees or fund manager must exercise their powers with a view to giving effect to the principles of their policy statement, so far as reasonably practicable.[66] Failure to comply with these investment duties may result in removal under section 3 and the imposition of a financial penalty under section 10, but the statutory duty of care under the Trustee Act 2000 does not apply to investment powers under occupational pension schemes.[67]

(b) *Delegation to Fund Manager.* Under the general law a trustee may not delegate the exercise of his discretions without authority, and this led to inconvenient problems over the delegation of investment decisions to fund managers prior to the Trustee Act 2000.[68] The Pensions Act 1995 already provided that trustees of occupational pension funds could delegate investment decisions to a fund manager authorised to conduct investment business under the financial services legislation (now the Financial Services and Markets Act 2000).[69] The trustees are not responsible for the act or default of such a fund manager if they have taken all reasonable steps to satisfy themselves that the manager has appropriate knowledge and experience and is carrying out his work competently and in accordance with statutory duties.[70] Alternatively, the trustees may delegate investment decisions by power of attorney under section 25 of the Trustee Act 1925,[71] or to a fund manager not authorised to conduct investment business under the Financial Services and Markets Act 2000, or, subject to any restriction in the trust scheme, may authorise two or more of their number to make investment decisions on their behalf.[72] In these three cases, however, the trustees as a whole remain liable for any breaches resulting from any acts or defaults in the exercise of the discretion.[73]

As the Pensions Act 1995 provides for delegation of investment decisions by trustees of occupational pension schemes, the power to delegate such decisions under the Trustee Act 2000 is inapplicable, as is the power under that Act to appoint nominees and custodians.[74] Other powers of delegation under the Trustee Act 2000 do apply to

---

[64] Defined in s.36(6).
[65] s.36(3), (4).
[66] s.36(5).
[67] T.A. 2000, s.36.
[68] *post*, p. 540.
[69] Pensions Act 1995, s.34(2).
[70] s.34(4).
[71] *post*, p. 582.
[72] s.34(5)(a).
[73] s.34(5); Trustee Act 1925, s.25(5).
[74] T.A. 2000, s.36.

pension scheme trustees, although subject to certain restrictions.[75] The statutory duty of care under the new legislation does not apply to pension scheme trustees when delegating investment decisions or appointing nominees or custodians pursuant to their powers under the 1995 Act or under the pension scheme provisions.[76]

(c) *Exclusion of Liability.* Liability for failure to take care or to exercise skill in the performance of investment functions exercisable by the trustees or the fund manager cannot be excluded or restricted by an instrument or agreement.[77] On the question whether the trustees may be exempted from responsibility for the acts and defaults of fund managers, we have seen that the trustees are not liable for the acts of fund managers who are authorised to conduct investment business under the Financial Services and Markets Act 2000, and so the point does not arise in such a case. In the case of delegation to fund managers who are not authorised to conduct investment business, where such delegation is permitted by section 34(5)(b) of the 1995 Act, the trustees are normally liable for the acts and defaults of such a person, as mentioned above. In this case, however, the liability may be validly excluded or restricted provided the trustees have taken all reasonable steps to satisfy themselves that the fund manager has appropriate knowledge and experience and is carrying out his work competently and in accordance with statutory duties.[78]

(d) *Employer-Related Investments.* Investments of pension fund assets in the employer's business, such as the purchase of shares in the employer company or loans to the employer, are subject to restrictions[79] because of the danger they present on the employer's insolvency. If a substantial proportion of the fund could be invested in the employer company, the losses would be great if the employer went into liquidation. Section 40 of the Pensions Act 1995 obliges the trustees or managers of an occupational pension scheme to ensure that current restrictions on employer-related investments are complied with. Failure to do so may result in removal under section 3 and the imposition of a financial penalty under section 10, and a trustee or manager who agrees to invest in contravention of the restrictions commits an offence.

v. Minimum Funding.[80] The minimum funding requirement is designed to ensure that any inadequacies of funding will be revealed

---

[75] *ibid.*

[76] *ibid.*

[77] Pensions Act 1995, s.33. On trustee exemption clauses generally, see p. 501, *post.*

[78] s.34(6).

[79] Currently 5 per cent of the assets by regulations under Pension Schemes Act 1993, s.112. See (1994) 8 *Trust Law International* 56 (I. Greenstreet).

[80] For further details see Arthur, *Pensions and Trusteeship*, Chap. 5.

by a regular monitoring process and remedied by an increase in contributions or, in the case of serious underfunding, by a payment by the employer. The requirement is that the value of the assets is not less than the amount of the scheme's liabilities.[81] The provisions apply to occupational pension schemes other than money purchase schemes.

The trustees (or managers) must obtain a valuation by the scheme actuary at intervals (normally a three-year cycle) prescribed by regulations.[82] The actuary must prepare a certificate stating whether or not the contributions are adequate to secure minimum funding. If they are considered inadequate, the trustees must obtain a further valuation within six months unless the assets were certified to be not less than 90 per cent of the liabilities and the contributions have since been increased to eradicate the shortfall.

The trustees must maintain a schedule of contributions showing the rates payable by the employer and members.[83] This must be revised after each actuarial valuation. The rates of contribution must be certified by the scheme actuary as being adequate to secure that the minimum funding requirement will be or will continue to be met.

If the amounts payable under the schedule of contributions are not paid by the due date, the trustees must give notice to the regulatory authority and the scheme members.[84]

If the actuarial valuation shows that the assets are less than 90 per cent of the liabilities, the employer must restore the scheme to 90 per cent solvency within one year by making a payment to the trustees.[85] If the employer fails to do so, the trustees must inform the regulatory authority and the scheme members. Trustees who fail to take all reasonable steps to secure compliance with the minimum funding requirement may be removed under section 3 or subjected to a financial penalty under section 10.

So far as the valuation of liabilities is concerned, it must be borne in mind that the 1995 Act requires pension rates to be increased annually.[86]

vi. Surplus. Much of the pension trust litigation has involved entitlement to surplus funds. Surpluses arose primarily in the 1980s because of the huge growth in the value of investments at that time. Where the scheme is ongoing, the surplus is notional, and means that the actuarial estimation of the assets at a given time exceeds the

---

[81] Pensions Act 1995, s.56.
[82] s.57; Occupational Pension Schemes (Minimum Funding Requirement and Actuarial Valuations) Regulations 1996 (S.I. 1996/1536).
[83] s.58.
[84] s.59.
[85] s.60; S.I. 1996/1536, *supra*.
[86] s.51.

actuarial estimation of the liabilities. Such a calculation involves many projections and assumptions. There will be an actual surplus only if the scheme is wound up and all liabilities discharged. Surplus on a winding up is dealt with in the following section. Where the scheme is ongoing, the question is one of rights and duties in the application of the surplus rather than ownership as such. Although the members have no right to an actuarial surplus, they have a reasonable expectation that the employer in dealing with it will pay fair regard to their interests, in accordance with the duty of good faith owed to employees.[87]

The application of a surplus (actual or notional) will be crucial where the employer is insolvent,[88] or where the employer company is taken over by a company which proposes to "raid" the surplus,[89] or where, on a partial sale of the employer company, the employees are transferred to the purchaser's pension scheme and dispute the decision of the trustees of the original scheme not to transfer any of the substantial surplus to the purchaser's scheme.[90]

As explained below, the tax regime requires the elimination of excessive surpluses in an ongoing scheme and the taxation of any payments to the employer, to avoid exploitation of pension fund tax reliefs.[91]

The Pensions Act 1995 imposes further restrictions on payments of surplus to the employer from an approved scheme which is on-going. Where the scheme confers power on any person (including the employer) other than the trustees to make payments to the employer, it can be exercised only by the trustees.[92] The power can be exercised only pursuant to Revenue-approved proposals to reduce an excessive surplus and is subject to further conditions, such as that the trustees are satisfied that it is in the interest of members to exercise it in the manner proposed, and that the pension rates have been increased annually.[93] In certain circumstances the regulatory authority must confirm that these requirements have been satisfied.[94]

vii. Winding Up. On this event, which may occur on the employer's insolvency and in other circumstances specified in the scheme

---

[87] *Jefferies v. Mayes* [1999] P.L.R. 37; *sub nom. National Grid Co. plc v. Mayes* [2000] I.C.R. 174 (1999) 13 *Trust Law International* 155 (M. Doherty and N. Ryder). See also (2000) 14 *Trust Law International* 66 (Lord Millett).

[88] See *Mettoy Pension Trustees Ltd v. Evans* [1990] 1 W.L.R. 1587; *ante*, p. 475; *Thrells Ltd v. Lomas* [1993] 1 W.L.R. 456.

[89] See *Re Courage Group's Pension Scheme* [1987] 1 W.L.R. 495.

[90] *Wilson v. Law Debenture Trust Corp plc* [1995] 2 All E.R. 337; *ante*, p. 476; *post*, p. 525.

[91] *post*, p. 491.

[92] s.37(2).

[93] s.37(4).

[94] s.37(5).

rules,[95] the members' rights crystallise. Liabilities to them must be discharged and any surplus assets distributed.[96] It has already been noted that a pension scheme may be wound up by the order of the regulatory authority in certain circumstances.[97] The 1995 Act contains other provisions dealing with the discharge of liabilities and distribution of surplus on the winding up of an earnings-related scheme. (The question of insufficient or excess assets will not arise with a money purchase scheme, where the level of benefits is not defined and depends on the performance of the investments). The assets must be applied to discharge liabilities to members in a specified order, for example liability for pension increases ranks last.[98] Liabilities may be discharged in various ways, such as by transferring credits to another scheme, by transfer to certain personal pension schemes, or by the purchase of annuities.[99] If the assets are insufficient to discharge the liabilities, the deficit is treated as a debt from the employer to the trustees, without prejudice to any other right or remedy of the trustees.[1]

Where there are surplus assets, the scheme will normally provide for their allocation, often by requiring payment to the employer after augmenting benefits. In the rare case where the scheme makes no effective provision for surplus, the general law applies. Such a case came before the Privy Council in *Air Jamaica Ltd v. Charlton*,[2] where the pension scheme had been discontinued. An amendment to the scheme purporting to permit the payment of surplus to the employer was invalid because the power to amend was void for perpetuity. The surplus was held on a resulting trust as to half for the employer and half for the members (including the estates of deceased members) in proportion to their contributions. The decision of Scott J. in *Davis v. Richards & Wallington Industries Ltd*,[3] to the effect that any share of the members would go to the Crown as *bona vacantia* on the basis (primarily for tax reasons) that the members must have intended to exclude a resulting trust, was wrong, having been based on an incorrect analysis of the role of intention. The fact that the extra benefits under a resulting trust would exceed the limits for tax relief was not a proper ground for rejecting a resulting trust for members.

---

[95] For example, a solvent employer may wish to wind up an earnings-related scheme in order to replace it with a money-purchase scheme.

[96] See (1995) 9 *Trust Law International* 127 (P. Docking), considering unknown beneficiaries.

[97] s.11; *ante*, p. 479.

[98] s.73. Any power in the scheme to apply assets to pensions and benefits may be exercised only by the trustees or managers.

[99] s.74. See *Polly Peck International plc (in Administration) v. Henry* [1999] 1 B.C.L.C. 407.

[1] s.75. Such a debt is not a preferential debt on insolvency.

[2] [1999] 1 W.L.R. 1399; *ante*, p. 247.

[3] [1990] 1 W.L.R. 1511.

As stated above, on insolvency of the employer any fiduciary powers, including powers relating to the allocation of surplus, are exercisable only by the independent trustee.[4] The 1995 Act makes further provisions for the allocation of surplus assets on the winding up of an approved scheme, of which the rules either permit or prohibit distribution to the employer. If the scheme confers power on the employer or trustees to distribute assets to the employer, the power can only be exercised where all liabilities have been fully discharged and the pension rates increased. In certain circumstances the regulatory authority must confirm that these requirements have been satisfied.[5]

Where a surplus remains after the discharge of all liabilities and the scheme prohibits distribution to the employer, the pension rates must be increased and additional benefits provided, after which the trustees may distribute any surplus to the employer.[6] Sanctions for failure to comply with these provisions include removal of trustees under section 3 and the imposition of a financial penalty under section 10.

viii. Information to Members. As explained in Chapter 19, trustees are under a general law duty to provide information and accounts to the beneficiaries. In addition, section 41 of the 1995 Act provides for regulations requiring the trustees to make copies of various documents available to the members and prospective members and their spouses (and to certain other persons).[7] The documents in question include audited accounts, actuarial valuations of assets and liabilities of the scheme, certificates relating to the minimum funding requirement and reports (required by the Act) concerning any failure to meet that requirement.

ix. Compensation. Although the aim of the 1995 Act is to prevent the misappropriation of pension funds, no statutory mechanism can provide totally effective safeguards. The Act, therefore, provides a compensation scheme to diminish hardships such as those suffered by the victims of Robert Maxwell's fraud. Application may be made to the Pensions Compensation Board[8] in respect of an occupational pension scheme where the value of the assets has been reduced[9] (and, in the case of a salary related scheme, is less than 90

---

[4] Pensions Act 1995, s.25(2); *ante*, p. 480.

[5] s.76.

[6] s.77.

[7] Occupational Pension Schemes (Disclosure of Information) Regulations 1996 (S.I. 1996/1655); Occupational Pension Schemes (Requirement to Obtain Audited Accounts and a Statement from the Auditor) Regulations 1996 (S.I. 1996/1975).

[8] Set up under s.78 and Sched. 2 of the Pensions Act 1995.

[9] For money-purchase schemes the reduction must be to below 90 per cent of the pre-offence value of the assets.

per cent of the liabilities) and there are reasonable grounds for believing that the reduction was attributable to a prescribed offence (*i.e.* misappropriation). The compensation provisions apply only where the employer is insolvent.[10] To this extent the scheme is narrower than that recommended in the Goode Report, and would not have helped the Maxwell pensioners had the Act been in force at that time, as the employer companies did not go into liquidation.

The application must be made within the period of twelve months beginning with the insolvency or, if later, the time when the scheme's auditor or actuary or the trustees knew or ought to have known that a reduction of assets had occurred.[11] The compensation must not exceed the shortfall and, in the case of a salary related scheme, must not exceed the amount required to ensure that the assets are not less than 90 per cent of the scheme's liabilities.[12] Payments may be made subject to conditions or terms requiring repayment, for example if the misappropriated money is recovered.[13] No compensation will be paid, however, until the Board considers that further recoveries of the lost funds are unlikely.[14] Thus the trustees must take all reasonable steps to recover the lost assets, for example by tracing, before compensation will be paid.[15] The Board may vary or revoke an award if satisfied that there has been a change of circumstances or that the award was made in ignorance of a material fact or based on a mistake of fact or law.[16]

x. Alienability; Bankruptcy. Other provisions of the Pensions Act 1995 deal with the alienability of pension rights and the position on the bankruptcy of a scheme member. The object of a pension scheme is not to provide members with a disposable asset but to ensure an income on retirement. Accrued rights under an occupational pension scheme cannot be assigned, surrendered, charged or subjected to any right of set-off.[17] This general prohibition, which reflects the provisions normally found in pension schemes,[18] does not apply to assignments to or surrenders for the benefit of the

---

[10] s.81.
[11] s.82. These dates must have occurred after s.81 came into operation.
[12] s.83, as amended by the Welfare Reform and Pensions Act 1999. Interim payments may be made under s.84.
[13] s.78(4).
[14] ss.81(3)(d), 83(1).
[15] s.81(5).
[16] s.80.
[17] s.91. Forfeiture, meaning any manner of deprivation or suspension (*e.g.* for misconduct), is prohibited, subject to certain exceptions, by s.92. There is no forfeiture on bankruptcy as the pension rights are protected from creditors.
[18] See *Re Scientific Investment Pension Plan Trusts* [1999] Ch. 53, *ante*, p. 192.

member's widow, widower or dependant, and there are limited exceptions permitting a charge or set-off by the employer.

Where a member of an occupational or personal pension scheme is made bankrupt, his pension rights are excluded from his estate for the purposes of the Insolvency Act 1986 and are thus unavailable to creditors.[19] The provisions of the 1986 Act relating to the setting aside of certain dispositions made prior to bankruptcy[20] are extended so that contributions to an occupational or personal pension scheme may be ordered by the court to be recovered by the trustee in bankruptcy to the extent that the contributions were excessive and have unfairly prejudiced the creditors.[21] The court will consider in particular whether the contributions were made for the purpose of putting assets beyond the reach of creditors.

B. Other Statutory Provisions

i. Rule Against Perpetuities. As explained in Chapter 14, the perpetuity rule prevents the vesting of property at a remote date beyond the perpetuity period (lives in being plus 21 years or a specified period not exceeding 80 years under the Perpetuities and Accumulations Act 1964) and also invalidates non-charitable purpose trusts which are not confined in duration to the perpetuity period. It will be appreciated that the perpetuity rule could prove troublesome if applied to occupational pension schemes.[22] The perpetuity rule is based on public policy, namely that it is undesirable for economic and other reasons to have property tied up for long periods of time save for charitable purposes (to which the rule does not apply). In the case of pension funds there is a countervailing public interest in encouraging the provision of retirement pensions. The Pension Schemes Act 1993[23] provides, therefore, that qualifying occupational pension schemes (primarily those approved by the Inland Revenue for tax relief purposes) are exempted from the perpetuity rule.[24] It seems, however, that the rule applies to nominations of benefits by scheme members.[25]

ii. Tax Relief. The public interest in the provision of retirement benefits beyond the state pension results in significant tax relief for

[19] Welfare Reform and Pensions Act 1999, s.11.

[20] *ante*, p. 353.

[21] ss.342 A, B and C of the Insolvency Act 1986, inserted by Pensions Act 1995, and amended by Welfare Reform and Pensions Act 1999, s.15.

[22] See *Air Jamaica Ltd v. Charlton* [1999] 1 W.L.R. 1399 (no exemption in Jamaica).

[23] s.163, replacing earlier legislation; Personal and Occupational Pension Schemes (Perpetuities) Regulations 1990 (S.I. 1990/1143), as amended.

[24] A wider exemption is proposed in Law Com. No. 251 (1998), *The Rules against Perpetuities and Excessive Accumulations*, para. 7.36.

[25] *ibid.*, para. 3.59.

"exempt approved schemes". To secure this status, pension schemes must satisfy certain conditions,[26] for example the sole purpose of the scheme must be to provide benefits in respect of service as an employee, the normal retirement age must be at least 60, and the pension must not exceed two thirds of the final salary. A scheme may be approved whether it is earnings-related or money purchase, and whether the investments are held by the trustees or through the medium of an insurer. The benefits are such that an unapproved scheme would not be entertained unless it is inherently impossible for it to satisfy the conditions for exemption. The court will not vary a pension trust in a manner which could put at risk its tax exempt status.[27] The effect of loss of exempt status is severe, but this does not justify the exclusion of a resulting trust of surplus funds in favour of the members which would put their benefits above the statutory limits for exemption.[28]

(a) *Tax Relief for Contributions.* Provided the scheme is an exempt approved scheme, tax relief is given to both employer and employee contributions. Contributions by the employer are treated as trading expenses and thus deductible from income and corporation tax liability.[29] Contributions by the employee are deductible from taxable income, but must not exceed 15 per cent of annual remuneration.[30] A further benefit is that the employer's contributions are not taxable as remuneration of the employee. Ultimately the pension itself will be subject to income tax whether or not the scheme is approved,[31] although lump sums payable on retirement are tax free.[32]

(b) *Tax Relief for the Pension Fund.* Provided the scheme is an exempt approved scheme, the fund itself attracts significant relief. Neither income tax[33] nor capital gains tax[34] is payable on the investments. Equivalent benefits are available for insured schemes.

(c) *Overfunding.* In view of the above reliefs there might be a temptation to put more money than is required into the pension fund, which could either be used to pay excessive benefits or retrieved by

---

[26] I.C.T.A. 1988, s.590(2), (3).

[27] *Brooks v. Brooks* [1996] 1 A.C. 375; *post*, p. 493.

[28] *Air Jamaica Ltd v. Charlton* [1999] 1 W.L.R. 1399, disapproving *Davis v. Richards & Wallington Industries Ltd* [1990] 1 W.L.R. 1511; *ante*, p. 249.

[29] I.C.T.A. 1988, s.592(4).

[30] *ibid.*, s.592(7), (8).

[31] *ibid.*, s.19(1).

[32] *ibid.*, s.189.

[33] *ibid.*, s.592(2).

[34] *ibid.*, Sched. 29, para. 26. For inheritance tax relief, see I.H.T.A. 1984, s.86 (employee trusts).

the employer as surplus. The exploitation of tax relief is prevented in various ways. It has already been noted that there is a restriction (15 per cent) on the amount of earnings which an employee may contribute. A minimum of 20 years' service is required to generate the maximum pension of two thirds of final salary. Further, there is an inflation-linked earnings cap[35] on the final salary which can be reflected in a pension, to limit the extent to which highly paid employees can secure large pensions and tax free lump sums from a tax exempt scheme. The other way in which pension funds are prevented from being used as tax shelters is by the rule that any surplus funds in an exempt scheme must be reduced so as not to exceed 5 per cent of assets over liabilities.[36] Failure to do so will result in loss of tax exemptions for the investments. The fund must be regularly valued, and any prohibited surplus eliminated in various ways. The first call on the surplus is the increase of benefits, after which contributions may be reduced or suspended. Any payment to the employer (which must be authorised by the scheme or any amendments to it) is taxed at 40 per cent.[37]

3. EQUAL TREATMENT

Article 119 of the Treaty of Rome embodies the principle that men and women should receive equal pay for equal work. Clearly this has no scope for application to traditional trusts conferring benefits by way of bounty, but it does apply to occupational pension schemes because, as we have seen, pension entitlements are a form of deferred remuneration for services. Thus it was held by the European Court of Justice in *Barber v. Guardian Royal Exchange Assurance Group*[38] that pension rights fell within Article 119, with the result that the common practice of conferring pension entitlements on women employees at an earlier age than their male counterparts was no longer permissible. There were doubts as to the precise scope of the *Barber* decision, and so the matter was tested again in the European Court of Justice in *Coloroll Pension Trustees Ltd v. Russell*.[39] It was there held that trustees are bound to do everything within the scope of their powers to ensure compliance with the equal pay principle. Thus the trustees are bound, in the exercise of the

---

[35] £91,800 for 2000/01; I.C.T.A. 1988, s.640A (index-linked). This restricts the maximum pension (two thirds of final salary) to £61,200.
[36] I.C.T.A. 1988, ss.601–603, Sched. 22.
[37] *ibid.*, s.601. See also Pensions Act 1995, s.37, *supra* (restrictions on exercise of power to make payments to employer).
[38] [1991] 1 Q.B. 344.
[39] [1995] I.C.R. 179.

powers and the performance of the duties laid down in the trust deed, to observe the principle of equal pay and treatment.

The Pensions Act 1995 now provides that an occupational pension scheme which does not contain an equal treatment rule shall be treated as including one.[40]

4. Pensions on Divorce

Another matter of current concern, which will be dealt with only in outline here, is the extent to which the pension entitlement of one spouse (usually the husband) must be shared with the other spouse on divorce. A wife who has brought up a family instead of working may have no pension provision of her own and may be reduced to penury in old age if her former husband's pension (often the most valuable family asset after the matrimonial home) is not available to her. The question whether and how pension benefits should be shared is a matter of government policy. One way it to take the husband's pension into account by giving a greater share of other assets to the wife on divorce. Alternatively, the pension itself may be split or earmarked as a source of payments to the spouse, either on divorce or later, when it comes to be paid. Pension sharing on divorce may now be ordered under the Matrimonial Causes Act 1973, as amended by Part III of the Welfare Reform and Pensions Act 1999. An alternative possibility is "earmarking", whereby an order made on divorce takes effect when the pension benefits under an occupational or personal pension scheme become payable to the scheme member. At that stage all or part of the benefits may be diverted to the former spouse.[41] The details of pension sharing and earmarking are outside the scope of this book. Finally, the House of Lords in *Brooks v. Brooks*[42] held that a pension trust which constituted a marriage settlement within section 24(1)(c) of the Matrimonial Causes Act 1973 could be varied by the court in the wife's favour, but this decision is of limited application because few pension schemes will fall within the 1973 Act.

---

[40] s.62. See also s.65 (power to alter schemes to secure conformity).
[41] M.C.A. 1973, ss.25B, C and D, inserted by Pensions Act 1995, s.166 and amended by Welfare Reform and Pensions Act 1999, s.21.
[42] [1996] 1 A.C. 375; *post*, p. 636. See (1995) 25 Fam. Law 504 (R. Ellison).

PART III

TRUSTEES

CHAPTER 17

GENERAL PRINCIPLES: CAPACITY; APPOINTMENT; REMOVAL; RETIREMENT; CONTROL

1. ONEROUS NATURE OF OFFICE

THE office of trustee is an onerous one. We will discuss in some detail a trustee's duties, powers and liability; there is little to be said as to his rights. In the performance of his office a trustee must act exclusively in the interest of the trust. He stands to gain nothing from his work in the absence of a clause authorising remuneration, although professional trustees now have charging powers under the Trustee Act 2000.[1] He is required to observe the highest standards of integrity,[2] and a reasonable standard of care and skill in the management of the affairs of the trust; and he is subjected to onerous personal liability if he fails to reach the standards set. Nor may he compete in business with the trust; or be in a position in which his personal interests conflict with those of the trust. He may thus be forced to forgo opportunities which would be available to him if he were not a trustee.[3]

It may well be asked why people consent to become trustees. To this there are two answers. First, professional trustees undertake the work only where they are entitled to be paid. Solicitors, banks (Executor and Trustee Departments) and insurance companies come into this category. The Public Trustee is entitled to charge.[4] Most trusts of any size will have a professional trustee. There may be non-professional trustees also; but in any case the bulk of the work of administration—investment, distribution, accounting, tax payments, etc. —will in fact be done by professionals, either the trustees or others employed by them. Secondly, members of the family of the settlor or testator will often consent to be trustees out of feelings of duty to the settlor or testator. Where there is no professional trustee, the non-professionals will, as will be seen,[5] usually employ professional agents such as a solicitor, investment manager and accountant to perform the technical duties of the trust. It may well be better to have such experts appointed as trustees in the first place, so that technical matters will not be overlooked.[6] It is usual and common to appoint a mixture of professional trustees and non-professional. There is much to be said for appointing a corporation such as a bank which has unrivalled facilities, dependability and permanence.

The settlor (typically in the case of an offshore trust) may also provide for the appointment of a "protector", an independent fiduciary to oversee the exercise of the trustees' powers.[7]

---

[1] *post*, p. 603.

[2] *post*, p. 499.

[3] *Phipps v. Boardman* [1967] 2 A.C. 46; *post*, pp. 618 *et seq.*

[4] Public Trustee Act 1906, s.9; as amended by the Public Trustee (Fees) Act 1957.

[5] *post*, p. 576.

[6] For the dangers inherent in appointing no professional trustees, see *Turner v. Turner* [1984] Ch. 100, *ante*, p. 176. See generally (1988) 2 *Trust Law & Practice* 86 (C. Bell).

[7] See [1995] 4 J.Int.P. 31 (A. Penney); (1995) 9 *Trust Law International* 108 (P. Matthews); (1996) 2 *Trusts & Trustees* 6 (P. Hobson); (1997) 3 *Trusts & Trustees* 5 (A. Duckworth); *Trends in Contemporary Trust Law* (ed. A. Oakley), p. 63 (D. Waters); Underhill and Hayton (15th ed.), pp. 23–25.

2. STANDARDS APPLICABLE TO TRUSTEES

A. Duties and Discretions

A distinction must be made between a trustee's duties and his powers or discretions. A duty is an obligation which *must* be carried out. The rules of equity require strict and diligent performance of a trustee's duties. On the other hand, a power is discretionary; it may be exercised, or it may not. This is so whether the power is one given to trustees by statute, or is a power or discretion contained in the instrument creating the trust, or relates to the general management of the affairs of the trust.

Trustees must act honestly; and must take, in managing trust affairs, "all those precautions which an ordinary prudent man of business would take in managing similar affairs of his own."[8] This formula has now been largely overtaken by the statutory duty of care discussed in the next section. If the trustee properly performs his duties, powers and discretions, he is not liable for loss[9] to or depreciation[10] of the trust property arising from factors beyond his control.

We will see that many of the rules relating to trustees' duties are more strict in their terms than in their practical application. The past 100 years have brought a great alleviation in the lot of the honest trustee. We saw that much of the work of administration of a trust is necessarily done by professionals. This development has led to great relaxation, first by the courts[11] and then by statute,[12] of the requirement that the trustee should act personally. Further, exemption clauses (discussed below) which exclude the trustees' personal liability in certain circumstances have become widespread; and Trustee Act 1925, s.61, gives the court a discretion to excuse a trustee who has acted honestly and reasonably and ought fairly to be excused.[13]

B. The Statutory Duty of Care

The standard of conduct required of trustees has been put on a statutory basis by the Trustee Act 2000. It was previously laid down in *Speight v. Gaunt*[14] that in the management of trust affairs the

---

[8] *per* Lord Blackburn in *Speight v. Gaunt* (1883) 9 App.Cas. 1 at 19; in similar terms, Lord Watson in *Learoyd v. Whiteley* (1887) 12 App.Cas. 727 at 733.

[9] *Morley v. Morley* (1678) 2 Ch.Cas. 2.

[10] *Re Chapman* [1896] 2 Ch. 763.

[11] *Speight v. Gaunt* (1883) 9 App.Cas. 1: *post*, p. 576; *Learoyd v. Whiteley, supra*; *Shaw v. Cates* [1909] 1 Ch. 389.

[12] T.A. 2000, Part IV, replacing the more limited provisions of T.A. 1925; *post*, pp. 578 *et seq.*

[13] *post*, p. 667.

[14] (1883) 9 App.Cas. 1.

trustee must act as an ordinary prudent business person would act in managing similar affairs of his own. It had been established by the courts prior to the Trustee Act 2000 that a higher standard was expected of paid trustees.

In *Re Waterman's Will Trusts*[15] Harman J. said "I do not forget that a paid trustee is expected to exercise a higher standard of diligence and knowledge than an unpaid trustee and that a bank which advertises itself largely in the public press as taking charge of administrations is under a special duty." More recently, in *Bartlett v. Barclays Bank Trust Co. Ltd (No. 1)*[16] Brightman J. said:

> "I am of opinion that a higher duty of care is plainly due from someone like a trust corporation which carries on a specialised business of trust management. A trust corporation holds itself out in its advertising literature as being above ordinary mortals. With a specialist staff of trained trust officers and managers ... the trust corporation holds itself out, and rightly, as capable of providing an expertise which it would be unrealistic to expect and unjust to demand from the ordinary prudent man or woman who accepts, probably unpaid and sometimes reluctantly from a sense of family duty, the burdens of a trusteeship ... so I think that a professional corporate trustee is liable for breach of trust if loss is caused to the trust fund because it neglects to exercise the special care and skill which it professes to have."

The distinction between lay and professional trustees is maintained in section 1 of the Trustee Act 2000, which provides that a trustee:

> "must exercise such care and skill as is reasonable in the circumstances, having regard in particular (a) to any special knowledge or experience that he has or holds himself out as having, and (b) if he acts as trustee in the course of a business or profession, to any special knowledge or experience that it is reasonable to expect of a person acting in the course of that kind of business or profession."

The duty of care, which may be excluded by the trust instrument,[17] applies to various functions of trustees listed in Schedule 1 of the Act, whether arising by statute or by corresponding express provision in the trust instrument. The relevant functions are as follows: investment[18]; the acquisition of land[19]; the appointment of

---

[15] [1952] 2 All E.R. 1054 at 1055; *cf. Jobson v. Palmer* [1893] 1 Ch. 71; (1969) 33 Conv.(N.S.) 179 (M. Davies); (1973) 37 Conv.(N.S.) 48 (D. Paling).

[16] [1980] Ch. 515 at 534. See also *Re Rosenthal* [1972] 1 W.L.R. 1373.

[17] T.A. 2000, Sched. 1, para. 7.

[18] *post*, pp. 532 *et seq.*

[19] *post*, p. 532.

agents, nominees and custodians[20]; compounding liabilities[21]; insurance[22]; and powers relating to reversionary interests, valuations and audit.[23] It does not apply to dispositive powers of trustees, such as the power to select from a class of beneficiaries. Nor does it apply to the powers of maintenance and advancement which (as will be seen in Chapter 20) are in essence dispositive. The duty of care is primarily concerned with powers, and applies to the manner of their exercise, not to the trustee's decision whether to exercise them or not. So far as duties are concerned, the question is simply whether the duty has been performed or not. If it has not, as where a distribution has been made to the wrong beneficiary, a breach has been committed however careful the trustee was, although he may be relieved under section 61 of the Trustee Act 1925 if he acted honestly and reasonably.

A further distinction between paid and unpaid trustees is maintained through the application of section 61, under which an unpaid family trustee is more likely to be relieved from liability than a professional trustee.[24] Further, a paid trustee will be expected to do more of the work himself and to delegate less; and a paid trustee will be given less opportunity to rely upon the fact that he acted upon legal advice.[25]

C. Trustee Exemption Clauses

A question which has attracted much attention in recent years is whether and how far the settlor may effectively exempt a trustee from liability. Before considering the construction of express clauses, it should be noted that the Trustee Act 2000 does not deal specifically with trustee exemption clauses, but, as noted above, it does provide that the statutory duty of care is inapplicable "if or in so far as it appears from the trust instrument that the duty is not meant to apply".[26] Further, as will be seen below, an exemption clause may be more strictly construed against a solicitor trustee than against a lay trustee.[26a]

---

[20] *post*, pp. 579 *et seq.*
[21] *post*, p. 575.
[22] *post*, p. 574.
[23] *post*, p. 576.
[24] *National Trustee Co. of Australasia Ltd v. General Finance Co. of Australasia* [1905] A.C. 373; *Re Pauling's S.T.* [1964] Ch. 303 at 338, 339.
[25] *Re Windsor Steam Co. (1901) Ltd* [1929] 1 Ch. 151. See also *Steel v. Wellcome Custodian Trustees Ltd* [1988] 1 W.L.R. 167, at 174.
[26] T.A. 2000, Sched. 1, para. 7.
[26a] *Walker v. Stones* [2001] 2 W.L.R. 623; *post*, p. 502 (test of honesty depended on role and calling of trustee).

Nineteenth-century English[27] and Scottish[28] authorities indicated that exemption clauses, which are strictly construed against trustees,[29] would not protect them in cases of bad faith, recklessness or deliberate breach of duty.[29a] To allow protection in cases of fraud would be contrary to public policy. It is, however, possible to confer protection against liability for gross negligence if the clause is unambiguous. In *Armitage v. Nurse*[30] the clause provided that the trustees should not be liable for loss or damage unless "caused by his own actual fraud". This, it was held, would protect the trustees so long as they did not act dishonestly, no matter how indolent, imprudent or negligent they were. As Millett L.J. explained, the "irreducible core of obligations" owed by trustees included the duty to act honestly and in good faith but did not include any duty of skill or care, thus it was not repugnant to their duties, nor contrary to public policy, to allow exemption from liability for gross negligence, which differed only in degree from ordinary negligence.[31] The expression "actual fraud" excluded notions of constructive or equitable fraud, arising for example under the doctrine of "fraud on a power".[32] Older cases appearing to suggest that it was not possible to exclude liability for gross negligence turned on the wording of particular clauses. Reference was made, however, to the prevailing view that exemption clauses had gone too far, and to the possibility of intervention by Parliament.[33] It has since been held that an exemption clause covering defaults other than dishonesty could not be relied on, at least in the case of a solicitor trustee, where he had committed a deliberate breach of trust which no reasonable solicitor trustee could have thought was for the benefit of the beneficiaries, even if he genuinely believed that it was.[33a]

A further question which arises in relation to exemption clauses concerns the application of the Unfair Contract Terms Act 1977 to

---

[27] *Wilkins v. Hogg* (1861) 31 L.J. Ch. 41; *Pass v. Dundas* (1880) 43 L.T. 665. See also *Rehden v. Wesley* (1861) 29 Beav. 213.

[28] *Knox v. Mackinnon* (1888) 13 App.Cas. 753; *Rae v. Meek* (1889) 14 App.Cas. 558. See generally [1989] Conv. 42 (P. Matthews).

[29] This principle does not prevent a solicitor trustee who drafted the clause from relying on it; *Bogg v. Raper, The Times*, April 22, 1998. See also *Wight v. Olswang, The Times*, May 18, 1999.

[29a] See *Walker v. Stones* [2001] 2 W.L.R. 623, *infra*.

[30] [1998] Ch. 241; [1998] Conv. 100 (G. McCormack); (1998) 57 C.L.J. 33 (N. McBride). Leave to appeal to the House of Lords was refused; [1998] 1 W.L.R. 270. See also (1997) 11 *Trust Law International* 93 (D. Pollard).

[31] His Lordship, writing extra-judicially, doubted the *propriety* of exemption clauses covering gross negligence; (1998) 114 L.Q.R. 214.

[32] *ante*, p. 182.

[33] See the Trust Law Committee Consultation Paper (1999), *Trustee Exemption Clauses*, seeking views as to whether paid trustees should be able to be exempted from negligence liability. Legislation in Jersey precludes exemption in the case of "fraud, wilful misconduct or gross negligence".

[33a] *Walker v. Stones* [2001] 2 W.L.R. 623.

professional trustees appointed by the settlor. Provided the appointment may be regarded as contractual, which is doubtful, the validity of the clause would depend upon its reasonableness, under section 2(3) of the Act.[34]

There is a distinction between clauses which exempt from breach and those which prevent the duty from arising. Such a clause as the latter may be effective where there was no pre-existing fiduciary relationship between the parties, especially in the context of a commercial agreement between parties of equal status.[35]

Finally, special rules apply to pension trusts,[36] unit trusts[37] and debenture trusts.[38]

3. LIABILITY TO THIRD PARTIES

Persons entering into a contractual relationship with trustees, for example by supplying goods or by lending money, can enforce their rights against the trustees personally, but have no direct right to payment out of the trust assets. From the point of view of the trustees, they are entitled to an indemnity out of the trust fund for liabilities properly incurred, but this leaves them exposed to personal risk if the trust fund is insufficient,[39] unless they have limited their liability to the amount of the trust assets when dealing with the third party. From the point of view of third parties, although they may be subrogated to the trustees' right to an indemnity out of the trust fund, the difficulty is that the creditor cannot make any claim against the trust fund which the trustees could not have made.[40] If the trustees have committed a breach of trust, then of course they are not entitled to an indemnity,[41] and the creditor can be in no better position.

The absence of direct rights against the trust assets may cause difficulties with large commercial trusts, such as pension funds,

---

[34] See (1996) 10 *Trust Law International* 38 at 42 (W. Goodhart). The Unfair Terms in Consumer Contract Regulations (S.I. 1999 No. 2083) apply only to terms in consumer contracts which have not been individually negotiated.

[35] Law Com. No. 236 (1995), *Fiduciary Duties and Regulatory Rules*. See also *Kelly v. Cooper* [1993] A.C. 205.

[36] Pensions Act 1995, ss.33, 34(6) (investment functions); *ante*, p. 484.

[37] Financial Services and Markets Act 2000, s.253 (exemption for negligence not permitted for manager or trustee).

[38] Companies Act 1985, s.192 (exemption for negligence not permitted for trustee of debenture deed).

[39] See *Perring v. Draper* [1997] E.G.C.S. 109 (trustees personally liable for £96,000 rent arrears on termination of lease vested in them as trustees). For the liability of directors of trustee companies, see (1999) 5 *Trust & Trustees* 14 (P. O'Hagan).

[40] See *Re Johnson* (1880) 15 Ch.D. 548; *Re Oxley* [1914] 1 Ch. 604.

[41] See *Holding & Management Ltd v. Property Holding & Investment Trust plc* [1989] 1 W.L.R. 1313.

wishing to borrow money on a large scale. Reform has been proposed by the Trust Law Committee,[42] to protect creditors by giving them a primary right of action against the trust assets.

4. UNANIMITY[43]

Each trustee should be active in the administration of the trust. Equity does not recognise a "sleeping" trustee. A trustee who concurs with his co-trustees has, in so agreeing, as much "acted" as those others, and thus will be equally liable with them to beneficiaries who suffer loss if a breach results.[44] Nor will the concurring trustee necessarily escape liability when his co-trustee was a solicitor, unless he reasonably deferred to what could legitimately be regarded as superior knowledge.[45] But blind trust cannot safely be placed in a co-trustee. For although there is no rule that trustees are vicariously liable for the acts of co-trustees, a non-active trustee may himself be liable for neglecting to take the steps necessary to have prevented the breach.[46]

Trustees (other than trustees of charities and pension trusts[47]) cannot act by a majority, unless expressly authorised in the trust instrument.[48] A majority binds neither a dissenting minority nor the trust estate.[49] The consequences of this rule need to be appreciated.

In *Re Mayo*,[50] for instance, one trustee of a trust for sale wished to sell, two to postpone. The trustees were by virtue of the trust to sell, under a *duty* to sell, but possessed *power* to postpone. Simonds J. held that their duty to sell prevailed unless they were unanimous in exercising their power to postpone. They were not unanimous on this point; the view of the single trustee who

---

[42] *Rights of Creditors Against Trustees and Trust Funds* (1999); (1997) 11 *Trust Law International* 58 (D. Hayton). For earlier proposals of the Law Reform Committee, see 23rd Report, *The Powers and Duties of Trustees* (1982, Cmnd. 8733), paras. 2.17–2.24.

[43] See [1991] Conv. 30 (J. Jaconelli).

[44] *Bahin v. Hughes* (1886) 31 Ch.D. 390; *Re Turner* [1897] 1 Ch. 536; *Wynne v. Tempest* (1897) 13 T.L.R. 360. But the co-trustee who concurs may be able to obtain an indemnity from the active trustee; *post*, p. 661.

[45] See *Head v. Gould* [1898] 2 Ch. 250; *Bahin v. Hughes, supra.*

[46] *Bahin v. Hughes, supra.*

[47] *ante*, pp. 467, 481.

[48] *Re Butlin's W.T.* [1976] Ch. 251. *Re Whiteley* [1910] 1 Ch. 600 at 608. See also T.A. 1925, s.63(3).

[49] *Luke v. South Kensington Hotel Ltd* (1879) 11 Ch.D. 121.

[50] [1943] Ch. 302; *cf. Tempest v. Lord Camoys* (1882) 21 Ch.D. 571; but the unanimity rule did not affect the validity of a notice to quit served by only one of two joint tenants holding on trust for sale, because the characteristic of a periodic tenancy is that all parties must concur in its continuance; *Hammersmith and Fulham L.B.C. v. Monk* [1992] 1 A.C. 478.

wished to sell prevailed, and the other two were directed to join in the sale.

5. Who may be a Trustee

In principle, any person who is able to hold property may be a trustee. Special rules apply to charity and pension trustees,[51] and other categories need special consideration.

i. Children. A child cannot hold a legal estate in land[52]; and Law of Property Act 1925, s.20, provides that the appointment of a child to be a trustee in relation to any trust shall be void. A child of four years old was, however, held to be able to hold personalty on resulting trust.[53] As will be seen,[54] if a child is a trustee of personalty, he may be replaced, whether or not he consents.

ii. The Crown. It is usually said that the Crown may be a trustee[55] "if it chooses deliberately to do so,"[56] but attempts to claim funds in the hands of the Crown on the ground that the Crown should be treated as a trustee have not been successful.[57] The circumstances in which the Crown will accept a trusteeship must be rare indeed, and there would be substantial difficulties in enforcing the trust if it did.[58]

iii. Judicial Trustees. The High Court may, on the application of a person creating or intending to create a trust, or by or on behalf of a trustee or beneficiary, appoint a person to be a judicial trustee of that trust.[59] The court may appoint any fit and proper person,[60] and, in the absence of the nomination of such person, may appoint an official of the court.[61] Remuneration may be paid,[62] and

---

[51] *ante*, pp. 467, 480.
[52] L.P.A. 1925, s.1(6).
[53] *Re Vinogradoff* [1935] W.N. 68; *ante*, p. 255.
[54] *post*, p. 511.
[55] *Penn v. Lord Baltimore* (1750) 1 Ves.Sen. 444, *per* Lord Hardwicke at 453; *Burgess v. Wheate* (1757–59) 1 Eden 177.
[56] *Civilian War Claimants Association Ltd v. R.* [1932] A.C. 14, *per* Lord Atkin at 27 (a claim by the Association for payment by the Crown of reparations money received from Germany: "There is nothing so far as I know, to prevent the Crown acting as agent or trustee if it chooses deliberately to do so.")
[57] *Re Mason* [1929] 1 Ch. 1; *Civilian War Claimants Association Ltd v. R., supra*; *Tito v. Waddell (No. 2)* [1977] Ch. 106; *ante*, p. 72.
[58] Hanbury, *Essays in Equity*, pp. 87–89; Holdsworth H.E.L., Vol. IX, pp. 30–32.
[59] Judicial Trustees Act 1896, s.1(1); Judicial Trustee Rules 1983 (S.I. 1983 No. 370). The procedure has not been much used in practice.
[60] *ibid.* subs. (3); Public Trustee Act 1906, s.2(i)(*d*).
[61] *ibid.* subs. (3); usually the Official Solicitor of the court; Judicial Trustees Act 1896, s.5.
[62] Judicial Trustees Act 1896, s.1(5).

the court may direct an inquiry into the administration of the trust by a judicial trustee.[63] The court may give a judicial trustee any general or special directions in regard to the trust or to the administration thereof,[64] not, however, so as to "reduce the administration of an estate by a judicial trustee to very much the same position as where an estate is being administered by the court and every step has to be taken in pursuance of the court's directions. ... The object of the Judicial Trustees Act 1896 ... was to provide a middle course in cases where the administration of the estate by the ordinary trustees had broken down, and it was not desired to put the estate to the expense of a full administration ... a solution was found in the appointment of a judicial trustee, who acts in close concert with the court and under conditions enabling the court to supervise his transactions."[65]

A judicial trustee may also be appointed in respect of the administration of an estate.[66] At the time when there was no machinery whereby a personal representative could retire, this provided a method of replacing one who could no longer act. Now, however, the court may appoint a substitute executor or administrator under section 50 of the Administration of Justice Act 1985. In an application under the 1896 Act for the appointment of a judicial trustee, the court may proceed as if it was an application under the 1985 Act, and vice versa.[67]

iv. The Public Trustee

(a) *Functions.* The Public Trustee, established by the Public Trustee Act 1906,[68] may be appointed as trustee alone or jointly with another or others, and may act as a custodian trustee[69] or an ordinary trustee or as a judicial trustee. He may be appointed as sole trustee although there were originally two or more trustees, and although the trust deed stipulates at least two trustees.[70] The Public Trustee is a corporation sole,[71] covered in respect of liability for breach of trust by the State,[72] and entitled to charge fees on a scale fixed by the

---

[63] Judicial Trustees Act 1896, subs. (6), as amended by A.J.A. 1982, s.57(1). On the auditing of accounts, see Judicial Trustees Act 1896, s.4(1), as amended by A.J.A. 1982, s.57(2). See also Judicial Trustee Rules 1983, rr. 2, 13.

[64] *ibid. subs.* (4); Judicial Trustee Rules 1983, r. 8.

[65] *Re Ridsdel* [1947] Ch. 597 at 605.

[66] Judicial Trustees Act 1896, s.1(2).

[67] A.J.A. 1985, s.50(4); Judicial Trustees Act 1896, s.1(7), added by the 1985 Act.

[68] He is appointed by the Lord Chancellor, and may be the same person as the Accountant General of the Supreme Court; Public Trustee Act 1906, s.8(1); Public Trustee and Administration of Funds Act 1986, s.1 and Sched.

[69] s.4, *post.*

[70] s.5(1); *In re Duxbury's S.T.* [1995] 1 W.L.R. 425; [1996] Conv. 50 (J. Snape).

[71] Public Trustee Act 1906, s.1.

[72] *ibid.* s.7.

Lord Chancellor.[73] One special function is the administration of small estates and, although he may decline to accept any trust, he may not do so on the ground "only of the small value of the trust property."[74] Once appointed, the Public Trustee has the same powers and duties and liabilities, and is entitled to the same rights and immunities as a private trustee.[75] The functions of the Public Trustee were extended by the Public Trustee and Administration of Funds Act 1986,[76] which conferred on him all the functions conferred on the judge of the Court of Protection by Part VII of the Mental Health Act 1983 with respect to the property and affairs of mental patients. However, the Lord Chancellor announced in April 2000 that the Public Trustee would cease to exercise this function as from April 2001.[77] Another role of the Public Trustee is the holding of the property of a person who has died intestate, pending the appointment of an administrator.[78]

(b) *Restrictions.* There are certain trusts that the Public Trustee may not accept; such as a trust exclusively for religious or charitable purposes,[79] or any trust under a deed of arrangement for the benefit of creditors, or the administration of an estate known by him to be insolvent,[80] and he may only accept a trust involving the management of a business under special restrictions limiting him to a short period of operation and requiring the Treasury's consent.[81]

v. Custodian Trustees.[82] The Public Trustee,[83] the Official Custodian for Charities[84] and a large number of other corporations[85] are authorised by statute to act as custodian trustees, and they may all charge fees not exceeding those chargeable by the Public Trustee.[86] Others may act under the terms of the trust instrument, outside the

---

[73] Public Trustee Act 1906, s.9; Public Trustee (Fees) Act 1957. See also Public Trustee and Administration of Funds Act 1986, s.3(6).
[74] *ibid.* s.2(3).
[75] *ibid.* s.2(2).
[76] s.3.
[77] *Making Changes: The Future of the Public Trust Office* (Lord Chancellor's Department).
[78] Law of Property (Miscellaneous Provisions) Act 1994, s.14, amending A.E.A. 1925, s.9.
[79] Public Trustee Act 1906, s.2(5).
[80] *ibid.* s.2(4).
[81] Public Trustee Rules 1912, r. 7.
[82] (1960) 24 Conv.(N.S.) 196 (S. Maurice).
[83] Public Trustee Act 1906, s.4(3).
[84] *ante,* p. 461.
[85] Public Trustee Rules 1912, r. 30, as substituted by the Public Trustee (Custodian Trustee) Rules 1975 (S.I. 1975 No. 1189), r. 2. See also Public Trustee (Custodian Trustee) Rules 1976 (S.I. 1976 No. 836), 1981 (S.I. 1981 No. 358) and 1994 (S.I. 1994 No. 2519). Qualifying corporations include those of EU States which comply with the requirements and have a place of business in the U.K. carrying on trust business.
[86] Public Trustee Act 1906, s.4(3).

statutory schemes The custodian trustee holds property and the documents relating thereto while leaving to the managing trustee the day-to-day administration of the trust.[87] It is doubtful whether the Public Trustee can act in both capacities in relation to the same trust.[88]

The advantage of the scheme of custodian trusteeship is that new managing trustees can be appointed without the necessity of undergoing the trouble and expense—which can be considerable in the case of a large trust—of vesting all the trust investments in new trustees whenever there is a death, retirement or new appointment. It should be noted that this advantage cannot be gained by appointing the holder of an office as trustee, as the investments must be transferred to the names of the new holders of the office when a change is made. This can be avoided if the trustee is a corporation sole.[89]

In determining a number of trustees for the purpose of the Trustee Act 1925, the custodian trustee is not included.[90]

vi. Trust Corporations. Trust corporations play a large part in the administration of trusts. Their size, stability, dependability and expertise give them advantages over individual trustees.[91]

They enjoy a special status in that they can often act alone in circumstances in which at least two trustees would otherwise be necessary.[92] A trust corporation can give a valid receipt for capital money arising from the sale of land[93]; and a trust of land has greater overreaching powers if a trust corporation is trustee.[94] Further, trustees may retire and leave a sole trustee only if that trustee is a trust corporation.[95]

In most private trusts, a trust corporation is typically a bank. The legal definition is: "Trust corporation means the Public Trustee or a corporation either appointed by the court in a particular case to be a trustee, or entitled by rules made under subsection (3) of section four of the Public Trustee Act 1906, to act as custodian trustee."[96] The qualifications are contained in the Public Trustee (Custodian

---

[87] For the relationship between custodian trustees and managing trustees, see Public Trustee Act 1906, s.4(2); *Forster v. Williams Deacon's Bank Ltd* [1935] Ch. 359; *Re Brooke Bond and Co. Ltd's Trust Deed* [1963] Ch. 357.

[88] *Forster v. Williams Deacon's Bank Ltd, supra,* at 369–371.

[89] *Bankes v. Salisbury Diocesan Council of Education* [1960] Ch. 631 at 647–649.

[90] Public Trustee Act 1906, s.4(2)(g).

[91] See, however, (1997/98) 4 *Trusts & Trustees* 6 (N. Johnson), as to the advantages of a private company as trustee.

[92] See *In re Duxbury's S.T.* [1995] 1 W.L.R. 425; *ante*, p. 506 (Public Trustee).

[93] T.A. 1925, s.14; L.P.A. 1925, s.27(2).

[94] L.P.A. 1925, s.2(2).

[95] T.A. 1925, s.39; *post*, p. 521.

[96] T.A. 1925, s.68(18); see also L.P.A. 1925, s.205(1)(xxviii); A.E.A. 1925, s.55(1)(xxvi); Supreme Court Act 1981, s.128.

Trustee) Rules 1975.[97] The Law of Property (Amendment) Act 1926, s.3 added, amongst others, a trustee in bankruptcy, the Treasury Solicitor, and the Official Solicitor. A trust corporation now has power to charge remuneration under the Trustee Act 2000, but express powers will normally be given for a fee to be charged for the service.

6. DISCLAIMER

Nobody can be compelled to accept the office of trustee against his will.[98] A person appointed as trustee who wishes to disclaim should do so by deed,[99] as this provides clear evidence of the disclaimer. However, a disclaimer may be implied; apathy will be evidence of an intention to disclaim, provided the apathy is consistent.[1] But if the trustee meddles with the estate, his conduct will be construed as an acceptance. Once he has disclaimed, he can no longer accept. Once he has accepted he can no longer disclaim[2] but as we will see, he may retire.[3]

7. NUMBER OF TRUSTEES

There is no restriction upon the number of trustees of personalty. It is inconvenient to have too many; and rare to have more than four, save in the case of charity and pension trustees, who can act by majority.[4] Where additional trustees are appointed under the statutory power, appointments may only be made up to a total of four.[5] A sole trustee is most unsatisfactory because of the opportunities for maladministration and fraud which then arise.

In trusts of land, the Trustee Act 1925, s.34, restricts the number of trustees to four. There are exceptions, the most important of

---

[97] S.I. 1975 No. 1189. They include any corporation which (i) is constituted under the law of the U.K. or of any other Member State of the E.U.; and (ii) is empowered by its constitution to undertake trust business in England and Wales; (iii) has one or more places of business in the U.K.; and (iv) being a registered company has a capital (in stock or shares) for the time being issued of not less than £250,000 (or its equivalent in the currency of the state where the company is registered), of which not less than £100,000 (or its equivalent) has been paid up in cash. See also the Public Trustee (Custodian Trustee) Rules 1976 (S.I. 1976 No. 836) and 1981 (S.I. 1981 No. 358).

[98] A person can, of course, become a constructive or resulting trustee against his will.

[99] *Re Schär* [1951] Ch. 280; *Holder v. Holder* [1968] Ch. 353 (an executor).

[1] *Re Clout and Frewer's Contract* [1924] 2 Ch. 230.

[2] *Re Sharman's W.T.* [1942] Ch. 311; *Holder v. Holder, supra.*

[3] *post*, p. 521.

[4] *ante*, p. 467. The special rules for the constitution of the trustees of pension funds are explained in Chapter 16.

[5] T.A. 1925, s.36(6), *post*, p. 514.

which is that of land vested in trustees for charitable, ecclesiastical or public purposes.[6]

While a sole trustee of land is not forbidden,[7] the Trustee Act 1925, s.14(2), makes it impossible for a sole trustee (not being a trust corporation) to give a valid receipt for the proceeds of sale or other capital money arising under a trust of land, or capital money arising under the Settled Land Act 1925.[8]

8. APPOINTMENT OF TRUSTEES

A. The First Trustees

The first trustees will ordinarily be appointed by the settlor or testator in the deed or will creating the trust. In the case of a trust created by a settlor, the trustees will ordinarily be parties to the deed, and the trust is constituted upon the conveyance of the trust property to them. In a will, the same persons may be appointed executors and trustees. Where they are different persons, the trust is constituted upon the testator's death, for the title of the executors relates back to the death, and they hold on trust pending transfer to the persons appointed trustees in the will.

Trustees hold as joint tenants, and if one of several trustees dies, the survivors are the trustees, and they, and their successors, retain the same powers and duties as the original trustees.[9] On the death of a sole trustee, his personal representatives become trustees.[10] If he dies intestate, the trust estate will vest, pending the grant of administration, in the Public Trustee.[11] A trust does not normally fail for lack of a trustee; hence if the trustees disclaim, the trust still subsists, save in the rare cases where the settlor or testator has himself made the validity of the trust dependent upon the acceptance of office by particular trustees.[12] If all the nominated trustees predecease the testator in the case of a testamentary trust, the personal representatives of the testator will hold until such time as trustees are appointed.[13]

---

[6] T.A. 1925, s.34(3)(*a*).

[7] *Re Myhill* [1928] Ch. 100.

[8] Also L.P.A. 1925, s.27(2); L.P.(A.)A. 1926, Sched.

[9] T.A. 1925, s.18; *contra*, a bare power given to two persons in their individual capacity: *Re Smith* [1904] 1 Ch. 139; *Re de Sommery* [1912] 2 Ch. 622; *Re Harding* [1923] 1 Ch. 182; *ante*, p. 172.

[10] A.E.A. 1925, ss.1–3; T.A. 1925, s.18(2).

[11] Law of Property (Miscellaneous Provisions) Act 1994, s.14. Previously such property vested in the President of the Family Division.

[12] *Re Lysaght* [1966] Ch. 191; *Re Woodhams (deceased)* [1981] 1 W.L.R. 493.

[13] *Re Smirthwaite's Trust* (1871) L.R. 11 Eq. 251.

B. Who May Appoint New Trustees

i. Express Power. The trust instrument may include an express power to appoint new trustees, although it is normally sufficient to rely on the statutory power. Where an express power is given, it is often reserved to the settlor. The statutory power will be available in addition, unless a contrary intention appears in the instrument.[14]

ii. The Statutory Power: Trustee Act 1925, s.36(1) (2).[15]

"(1) Where a trustee, either original or substituted, and whether appointed by the court or otherwise, is dead,[16] or remains out of the United Kingdom for more than 12 months,[17] or desires to be discharged from all or any of the trusts or powers reposed in or conferred on him,[18] or refuses[19] or is unfit to act therein, or is incapable of acting therein,[20] or is an infant,[21] then, subject to the restrictions imposed by this Act on the number of trustees,—

> (a) the person or persons nominated for the purpose of appointing new trustees by the instrument, if any, creating the trust; or
>
> (b) if there is no such person, or no such person able and willing to act, then the surviving or continuing trustees or trustee for the time being, or the personal representatives of the last surviving or continuing trustee;

---

[14] T.A. 1925, s.69(2). See *Re Wheeler and De Rochow* [1896] 1 Ch. 315; *Re Sichel's Settlements* [1916] 1 Ch. 358.

[15] The statutory power does not apply to personal representatives; *Re King's W.T.* [1964] Ch. 542; *ante*, p. 59. The court, however, may appoint a substitute personal representative under Administration of Justice Act 1985, s.50. Special rules for the appointment of pension trustees are dealt with in Chapter 16.

[16] Which includes the case of a person nominated trustee in a will but dying before the testator: T.A. 1925, s.36(8), and *ante*, p. 510.

[17] The period must be continuous: *Re Walker* [1901] 1 Ch. 259; see also *Re Stoneham S.T.* [1953] Ch. 59. T.A. 1925, s.25, permits a trustee in such a case to delegate his duties by power of attorney for a period not exceeding 12 months; *post*, p. 582.

[18] For retirement of a trustee, see *post*, p. 521.

[19] This includes disclaimer.

[20] "Unfit" has a wider meaning than "incapable." "Incapable" refers to personal incapacity, such as illness or mental disorder; see T.A. 1925, s.36(9). "Unfit" is more general and an absconding bankrupt has been held to be "unfit" but not "incapable": *Re Roche* (1842) 2 Dr. & War. 287. See s.36(3), providing that a corporation is "incapable" from the date of dissolution, and Mental Health Act 1983, s.148 and Sched. 4. L.P.A. s.22(2) requires a mentally incapacitated trustee of land to be discharged before the legal estate is dealt with. This is not required where a donee of an enduring power of attorney is entitled to act for the incapable trustee; s.22(3), inserted by the Trustee Delegation Act 1999. See also Trusts of Land and Appointment of Trustees Act 1996, s.20; *post*, p. 515.

[21] L.P.A. 1925, ss.1(6), 20; *Re Parsons* [1940] Ch. 764.

may, by writing,[22] appoint one or more other persons (whether or not being the persons exercising the power) to be a trustee or trustees in the place of the trustee so deceased remaining out of the United Kingdom, desiring to be discharged, refusing, or being unfit or being incapable, or being an infant, as aforesaid.

(2) Where a trustee has been removed under a power contained in the instrument creating the trust, a new trustee or new trustees may be appointed in the place of the trustee who is removed, as if he were dead, or, in the case of a corporation, as if the corporation desired to be discharged from the trust, and the provisions of this section shall apply accordingly, but subject to the restrictions imposed by this Act on the number of trustees."

In favour of a purchaser of a legal estate in land, a statement in an instrument appointing a new trustee to the effect that a trustee is unfit, incapable or refuses to act, or has remained out of the United Kingdom for more than 12 months, is conclusive evidence of the matter. Similarly, any appointment of a new trustee depending on that statement, and the consequent vesting of the trust property in the new trustee, is valid in favour of such a purchaser.[23]

iii. Exercise of the Statutory Power. It is usual to appoint someone to exercise the statutory power.

(a) *By Persons Appointed under section* 36(1)(*a*). If two or more persons are given power to exercise it jointly, the power is not, in the absence of a contrary intention, exercisable by the survivor. This is consistent with the usual rule relating to bare powers given to individuals.[24]

Complications can arise if the power is subjected to conditions and limitations.

In *Re Wheeler and De Rochow*,[25] the settlor gave power to donees to appoint a new trustee if one of the existing trustees should be "incapable." One of the trustees was bankrupt, and absconded. This made him "unfit" but not "incapable."[26] The question was whether a new trustee should be appointed by the donees under section 36(1)(*a*) or by the continuing trustees under section 36(1)(*b*). It was held that the situation was not within the

[22] See *post*, p. 517, and T.A. 1925, s.40.

[23] T.A. 1925, s.38.

[24] *Re Harding* [1923] 1 Ch. 182; *Bersel Manufacturing Co. Ltd v. Berry* [1968] 2 All E.R. 552; *ante*, p. 172; *contra* where the power is given to persons as trustees: T.A. 1925, s.18(1).

[25] [1896] 1 Ch. 315; followed reluctantly in *Re Sichel's Settlements* [1916] 1 Ch. 358; *cf. Re Brockbank* [1948] Ch. 206.

[26] *Re Roche* (1842) Dr. & War. 287, *ante*, p. 511.

terms of the power given to the donees and that section 36(1)(*b*) applied.

(b) *By the Surviving or Continuing Trustees under section* 36(1)(*b*). In the case of continuing trustees it is expressly provided by section 36(8) that the provisions of section 36 "relative to a continuing trustee include a refusing or retiring trustee, if willing to act in the execution of the provisions of this section." This provision enables a retiring sole trustee or a retiring group of trustees to appoint their successors.[27] It raises the question, however, whether their participation is essential; whether an appointment in which they did not participate would be void. Such an objection failed in *Re Coates to Parsons*[28]; the retiring trustee is only included if it is shown that he is competent and willing to act. The concurrence of a trustee who is removed on the ground that he remained outside the United Kingdom for more than 12 months[29] is not required.[30] It is advisable, in order to avoid these difficulties, that refusing or retiring trustees should participate in the appointment of new trustees if possible, and this is the usual practice.

Section 37(1)(*c*) requires the replacement of trustees who are being discharged unless there will be either a trust corporation or at least two persons[31] to act if the vacancy is not filled. The exception is where only one trustee was originally appointed and a sole trustee will be able to give a good receipt for capital money. It appears that the settlor may override this provision.[32]

The statutory power to appoint a new trustee can be exercised by the executor of a sole trustee appointed by will,[33] but not by the personal representative of the survivor of a body of trustees named in a will, who has died in the testator's lifetime, as the Act does not contemplate the case of all the trustees named in the will predeceasing the testator.[34] Nor can the sole surviving trustee exercise the power by his will, so as thereby to appoint new trustees in succession to himself.[35] The aim of the Act of 1925 is to ensure the making

---

[27] But two retiring trustees cannot be replaced by one, not being a trust corporation; *Adam and Company International Trustees Ltd v. Theodore Goddard (a Firm)*, *The Times*, March 17, 2000.

[28] (1886) 34 Ch.D. 370.

[29] *ante*, p. 511.

[30] *Re Stoneham S.T.* [1953] Ch. 59.

[31] As amended by Trusts of Land and Appointment of Trustees Act 1996, Sched. 3, para. 3(12), substituting "persons" for "individuals". A corporate trustee (whether or not it is a "trust corporation") is a "person" but not an "individual".

[32] *LRT Pensions Fund Trustee Company Ltd v. Hatt* [1993] O.P.L.R. 225 at p. 260; *Adam and Company International Trustees Ltd v. Theodore Goddard (a Firm)*, *The Times*, March 17, 2000.

[33] *Re Shafto's Trusts* (1885) 29 Ch.D. 247.

[34] *Nicholson v. Field* (1893) 2 Ch. 511.

[35] *Re Parker's Trusts* [1894] 1 Ch. 707.

of an appointment in all events. The executors who have proved the will need not have the concurrence of those who have not proved or intend to renounce probate.[36] A sole or last surviving executor who intends to renounce probate can nevertheless fulfil this one function without thereby accepting the office of executor,[37] but the title of an executor to exercise the statutory power can only be proved by a proper grant of administration.[38]

(c) *Additional Trustees.* A broad power is given by section 36(6),[39] restricted only by the limitation to a total number of four trustees, and by the fact that the power is to appoint "another person or other persons" and that consequently (and unlike appointments under subsection (1)) the appointor may not appoint himself.[40] Section 36(6) reads:

> "Where, in the case of any trust, there are not more than three trustees—
>
> (a) the person or persons nominated for the purpose of appointing new trustees by the instrument, if any, creating the trust; or
> (b) if there is no such person, or no such person able and willing to act, then the trustee or trustees for the time being;
>
> may, by writing, appoint another person or other persons to be an additional trustee or additional trustees, but it shall not be obligatory to appoint any additional trustee, unless the instrument, if any, creating the trust, or any statutory enactment provides to the contrary, nor shall the number of trustees be increased beyond four by virtue of any such appointment."

Section 36(6) has been amended by the Trustee Delegation Act 1999 in order to give a limited power of appointing additional trustees to the donee of an enduring power of attorney, to whom trustee functions relating to land or its proceeds of sale have been delegated under the 1999 Act or under section 25 of the Trustee Act 1925.[41] This is to ensure that there are at least two trustees to act, as required for the purpose of giving a good receipt for capital money.

---

[36] T.A. 1925, s.36(4).

[37] *ibid.*, s.36(5).

[38] *Re Crowhurst Park* [1974] 1 W.L.R. 583.

[39] As amended by Trusts of Land and Appointment of Trustees Act 1996, Sched. 3, para. 3(11).

[40] *Re Power's S.T.* [1951] Ch. 1074.

[41] Trustee Delegation Act 1999, s.8, inserting s.36(6A)–(6D) into the 1925 Act. For enduring powers of attorney, see *post*, p. 584. The new provisions applies only to powers of attorney created after the commencement of the 1999 Act.

The new power is primarily designed to deal with the situation where one co-owner of land has, prior to losing capacity, delegated his trustee functions to the other co-owner by enduring power of attorney.

iv. By Direction of the Beneficiaries. A new power was given to beneficiaries by section 19[42] of the Trusts of Land and Appointment of Trustees Act 1996, which applies to trusts of land and personalty, whenever created, unless excluded by the settlor.[43] Provided the beneficiaries are of full age and capacity and together absolutely entitled, and there is no person with an express power to appoint, the beneficiaries may direct the trustees in matters of retirement[44] and appointment. They may give directions of either or both of the following kinds:

(a) a written direction to a trustee or trustees to retire from the trust; and

(b) a written direction to the trustees or trustee for the time being (or, if there are none, to the personal representative of the last person who was a trustee) to appoint by writing to be a trustee or trustees the person or persons specified in the direction.

The beneficiaries may give joint or separate directions, but they must specify the same person for appointment or retirement.[45] Section 19 has effect subject to the restrictions imposed by the 1925 Act on the number of trustees. In the absence of the exercise of the new power by the beneficiaries, the trustees' power of appointment is exercisable in the usual way.

C. Appointment by the Court

i. Trustee Act 1925, s.41.[46] Subsection (1) provides:

"The court[47] may, whenever it is expedient to appoint a new trustee or new trustees, and it is found inexpedient difficult or

---

[42] This in effect reverses *Re Brockbank* [1948] Ch. 206. See also s.20 (replacement by direction of beneficiaries where trustee mentally incapacitated and no person entitled, willing and able to act under T.A. 1925, s.36(1)). S. 20 (unlike s.19) contains no provisions on vesting or indemnity. See (1996) 146 N.L.J. 1779 (M. Keppel-Palmer); [1996] Conv. 411 at pp. 428–430 (N. Hopkins).

[43] s.21(5). Living settlors of trusts created before the 1996 Act may exclude the power by deed under s.21(6). The same applies to the power under s.20.

[44] *post*, p. 522.

[45] s.21(1), (2).

[46] The section does not apply to the appointment of personal representatives (s. 41(4)).

[47] *i.e.* the High Court; or where the estate or trust fund does not exceed its financial jurisdiction, the county court.

impracticable so to do without the assistance of the court, make an order appointing a new trustee or new trustees either in substitution for or in addition to any existing trustee or trustees, or although there is no existing trustee.

In particular and without prejudice to the generality of the foregoing provision, the court may make an order appointing a new trustee in substitution for a trustee who is [incapable, by reason of mental disorder within the meaning of the Mental Health Act 1983, of exercising his functions as trustee] or is a bankrupt, or is a corporation which is in liquidation or has been dissolved."

ii. Circumstances in which the Jurisdiction will be Exercised. The section gives the court a discretion. Cases arise in a variety of circumstances, *e.g.* where a sole surviving trustee has died intestate, or where all the trustees of a testamentary trust predeceased the testator,[48] and difficulty is experienced in obtaining administration of his estate,[49] or where the donee is incapable of making an effective appointment by reason of being under age.[50] The court has power to replace a trustee against his will[51]; and also where the trustees were the life tenant and remainderman and there was friction between them; or where a trustee has, through age or infirmity,[52] become incapable of acting, or who permanently resides abroad.[53] The statutory power of beneficiaries to direct appointments reduces the need to apply to court.[54]

It was held not to be "expedient" to appoint a new trustee of a pension fund on terms that it would be paid out of the fund in circumstances where the administrator of the employer company had sufficient expertise to administer the pension fund and could be paid only out of the company's free assets.[55]

The court should not be asked to exercise its jurisdiction where a statutory power can be exercised.[56] It has no jurisdiction to appoint a new trustee against the wishes of the persons who have a statutory power to appoint, even in a case where an application has been made to it by a majority of the beneficiaries.[57] Where the beneficiaries are

---

[48] *Re Smirthwaite's Trust* (1871) L.R. 11 Eq. 251.
[49] *Re Matthews* (1859) 26 Beav. 463.
[50] *Re Parsons* [1940] Ch. 973; (1941) 57 L.Q.R. 25 (R.E.M.).
[51] *Re Henderson* [1940] Ch. 764.
[52] *Re Lemann's Trust* (1883) 22 Ch.D. 633.
[53] *Re Bignold's S.T.* (1872) L.R. 7 Ch.App. 223.
[54] Trusts of Land and Appointment of Trustees Act 1996, ss.19, 20; *ante*, p. 515.
[55] *Polly Peck International plc (in administration) v. Henry* [1999] 1 B.C.L.C. 407.
[56] *Re Gibbon's Trusts* (1882) 30 W.R. 287 (where, however, such an appointment was made); *cf. Re May's W.T.* [1941] Ch. 109.
[57] *Re Higginbottom* [1892] 3 Ch. 132.

of full capacity, absolutely entitled and unanimous, they may exercise the statutory power referred to above.

9. Vesting of the Trust Property in Trustees

A. Requirement of Vesting

The trust property must be vested in the trustees to enable them to deal with outside parties. Before and after the vesting, however, a trustee, whether appointed under section 36 or by the court under section 41, or by direction of the beneficiaries under sections 19 or 20 of the Trusts of Land and Appointment of Trustees Act 1996,[58] has "the same powers, authorities, and discretions, and may in all respects act as if he had been originally appointed a trustee by the instrument, if any, creating the trust."[59]

B. Vesting Declaration under Section 40

i. Subsection (1). In order to avoid the necessity of a formal transfer of the trust property from the old trustees to the new, section 40 provides that the vesting may, with important exceptions, be effected automatically if the appointment of the trustees has been made by *deed*.[60] It does not apply, however, where the property is held by personal representatives and not by a trustee.[61]

Subsection (1) of section 40 provides that the deed of appointment shall operate to vest any land, chattel or chose in action subject to the trust in the new trustee, unless the deed expressly provides to the contrary.

ii. Exceptions under subsection (4). These in outline are:

(a) a mortgage of land to secure a loan of trust money;
(b) land held under a lease which contains a covenant against assignment without consent, and the consent has not been obtained prior to the execution of the deed;
(c) stocks and shares.[62]

These exceptions are necessary. Where trust money is lent on mortgage, no mention is made in the mortgage deed of the existence

---

[58] s.21(3).
[59] T.A. 1925, ss.36(7), 43.
[60] *ante*, p. 512.
[61] *Re Cockburn's W.T.* [1957] Ch. 438; *Re King's W.T.* [1964] Ch. 542; *ante*, p. 59.
[62] "Any share, stock, annuity or property which is only transferable in books kept by a company or other body, or in manner directed by or under an Act of Parliament." This includes money in a bank account, for example, but not bearer bonds.

of the trust, nor upon a transfer of the mortgage, such as would occur on the appointment of a new trustee. If section 40(1) applied, the mortgagor on redeeming would have to investigate the appointments of new trustees to make sure he was paying the right persons. The second exception is included in order to avoid an unintended breach of covenant, such as could occur in the appointment of a new trustee. The most serious exception in practice is the third; for this is the most important and valuable form of property in modern settlements. The provision, however, was necessary, because title to stocks and shares depends on the registration of the owners in the register of shareholders, and it is essential that the current trustees should be registered.[63]

It will be seen that vesting orders relating to registered land are not expressly excepted; however, the legal title cannot pass until registration. By the Land Registration Act 1925, s.47, the registrar is required to give effect on the register to any vesting order or vesting declaration made on the appointment or discharge of a trustee. The provisions of the Trustee Act 1925 relating to the appointment and discharge of trustees and the vesting of trust property apply to registered land subject to proper entry being made on the register.[64]

C. Vesting Orders under Sections 44 to 56

Sections 44 to 56 contain the rules as to vesting orders by the court. These overlap section 40, for vesting orders as to all kinds of property can be made not only where the appointment has been made by the court, but also where it has been made out of court under an express or statutory power. The court is given wide powers to make such orders in a variety of eventualities.

10. SELECTION OF TRUSTEES

A. On Appointment by the Court under Section 41

The factors which a court will take into account when exercising its jurisdiction to appoint a trustee were discussed by Turner L.J. in *Re Tempest*.[65] The court should always have regard to three prime requirements: the wishes of the person by whom the trust was created; the interests, which may be conflicting, of *all* the beneficiaries; the efficient administration of the trust. It is important that the trustees act harmoniously together; but Turner L.J. thought it would be going too far to say that the court should refuse to appoint a particular trustee on the ground that the continuing trustee refused to act

---

[63] See (1992) 142 N.L.J. 541 (M. Russell). For electronic transfer, see *ante*, p. 121.
[64] See further [1998] Conv. 380 (R. Towns).
[65] (1866) L.R. 1 Ch.App. 485.

with him. That would give the continuing trustee a veto; rather, the reasons for the refusal should be examined to see whether the objection is well founded.

The court is reluctant to appoint a person who, though not himself interested, is related to, or connected with, someone who is. Thus a relative of one of the beneficiaries is not a desirable appointment,[66] nor is one nominated by a relative of the testator with whom the testator was on bad terms.[67] Again, the solicitor to the trust,[68] or to one of the beneficiaries[69] or trustees, should not be appointed, as there might be a conflict of duties; unless, of course, no other person can be found to undertake the position. If the solicitor to the trust is a continuing trustee, his partner should not be appointed.[70] Persons out of the jurisdiction will not be appointed[71] except in a case where circumstances require it, or where the beneficiaries are resident outside the jurisdiction also.[72] Even where the trust can be more conveniently administered by trustees resident abroad, the court may exact an undertaking from them that they will consult the court before proceeding to the appointment of new trustees out of the jurisdiction.[73] Trusts administered abroad have enjoyed a number of fiscal advantages, and this has encouraged the movement of many trusts to other jurisdictions.

B. On Appointment under Express Power or under Section 36

i. Choice by Donee of Power. It is said that the above principles should guide persons exercising their power to appoint under section 36. In practice, however, it is common for beneficiaries and other members of the beneficiaries' families, and for solicitors to the beneficiaries, to be appointed. A conflict of interest and duty or of two duties should of course be avoided. However, even if the trustee appointed is one whom the court itself would not have selected, it seems that the court will not rectify it.[74]

---

[66] *Re Coode* (1913) 108 L.T. 94; *Re Parsons* [1940] Ch. 973 (where a child purported to appoint his mother).

[67] *Re Tempest* (1866) L.R. 1 Ch. 485.

[68] *Wheelwright v. Walker* (1883) 23 Ch.D. 752; *Re Orde* (1883) 24 Ch.D. 271.

[69] *Re Kemp's S.E.* (1883) 24 Ch.D. 485; *Re Earl of Stamford* [1896] 1 Ch. 288; *Re Spencer's S.E.* [1903] 1 Ch. 75; *Re Cotter* [1915] 1 Ch. 307.

[70] *Re Norris* (1884) 27 Ch.D. 333.

[71] *Re Weston's Settlements* [1969] 1 Ch. 223.

[72] *Re Liddiard* (1880) 14 Ch.D. 310; *Re Simpson* [1897] 1 Ch. 256; *Re Seale's Marriage S.T.* [1961] Ch. 574; *Re Windeatt's W.T.* [1969] 1 W.L.R. 692; *Re Whitehead's W.T.* [1971] 1 W.L.R. 833.

[73] *Re Freeman's S.T.* (1888) 37 Ch.D. 148.

[74] In *Re Norris* (1884) 27 Ch.D. 333, the funds were being administered by the court; *Re Higginbottom* [1892] 3 Ch. 132; in *Re Coode* (1913) 108 L.T. 94, an appointment of a child was held void; *Re Parsons* [1940] Ch. 973; (1941) 57 L.Q.R. 25 (R.E.M.).

ii. Foreign Trusts. Problems have arisen in relation to the appointment of foreign trustees with the intention of enjoying the tax advantages of offshore trusts. The tax advantages are now minimal unless there are beneficiaries who are resident abroad, or the settlor was domiciled[75] abroad at the date of the creation of the settlement. We have seen that the court was unwilling to appoint trustees resident abroad unless the beneficiaries have made their homes in the country in question.[76] It was said in *Re Whitehead's Will Trusts*[77] that trustees or persons with an express power should only appoint foreign resident trustees in similar circumstances (although an appointment inconsistent with this rule would be a valid appointment[78]). More recently, however, Millett J. held that the *Whitehead* approach is outdated.[79] Where the trustees are exercising their own discretion and are merely seeking the authorisation of the court for their own protection, the test is simply whether the proposed transaction is not so inappropriate that no reasonable trustee could entertain it. Thus Bermudan trustees were sanctioned although the trust had no Bermuda connection. Where it is clear that this test is satisfied, there is no need to apply to court. It is might be added that many settlements now expressly authorise the appointment of non-resident trustees.

iii. Direction by Beneficiaries. We saw that in certain circumstances, beneficiaries may give directions as to the exercise of the statutory power of appointment.[80] It appears that the beneficiaries are under no restrictions in the choice of person they direct to be appointed.

C. On Appointment by the Settlor

The settlor is under no restrictions in the selection of the original trustees whether English or foreign. The question is not merely one of selecting efficient, businesslike and fair-minded trustees who will carry out their duties according to law. They are commonly given wide discretions. They therefore should be people who will be relied on to respect the wishes of the settlor on matters on which they are

---

[75] Inheritance Tax Act 1984, s.267.

[76] *Re Weston's Settlements* [1969] 1 Ch. 223; *cf. Re Seale's Marriage S.T.* [1961] Ch. 574; *Re Windeatt's W.T.* [1969] 1 W.L.R. 692; *Re Whitehead's W.T.* [1971] 1 W.L.R. 833; (1976) 40 Conv.(N.S.) 295 (T. Watkin). See generally Parker and Mellows, *The Modern Law of Trusts* (7th ed.), Chap. 26.

[77] [1971] 1 W.L.R. 833 at 838.

[78] *Meinertzhagen v. Davis* (1844) 1 Coll. 353; (1969) 85 L.Q.R. 15 (P.V.B.); *Re Whitehead's W.T.*, *supra*, at 837.

[79] *Richard v. The Hon. A.B. Mackay* (1997) 11 *Trust Law International* 22 (decided 1987); The Offshore Tax Planning Review (1990/91), Vol. 1, p. 1 (R. Bramwell). See also *Re Beatty's W.T. (No. 2)* (1997) 11 *Trust Law International* 77.

[80] Trusts of Land and Appointment of Trustees Act 1996, ss.19–22; *ante*, p. 515.

in law virtually uncontrolled; and in circumstances which may have greatly changed since the trust was created.

11. RETIREMENT

A trustee may retire from a subsisting trust in any one of the ways explained below.[81] Retirement means a discharge from further responsibility and liability under the trust. A trustee should not retire when faced with disputes among beneficiaries and leave them to settle their differences among themselves. If he retires in order to facilitate a breach of trust by his successors, he will remain liable.[82]

A. Under an Express Power in the Trust Instrument

This is rare, since (the predecessors of) sections 36 and 39 made express powers unnecessary.

B. Under Section 39

We saw that a trustee desiring to be discharged could be replaced by a newly appointed trustee.[83] He may retire, without being replaced, if he complies with section 39 of the Trustee Act 1925.

> "(1) Where a trustee is desirous of being discharged from the trust, and after his discharge there will be either a trust corporation or at least two persons[84] to act as trustees to perform the trust, then, if such trustee as aforesaid by deed declares that he is desirous of being discharged from the trust, and if his co-trustees and such other person, if any, as is empowered to appoint trustees, by deed consent to the discharge of the trustee, and to the vesting in the co-trustees alone of the trust property, the trustee desirous of being discharged shall be deemed to have retired from the trust, and shall, by the deed, be discharged therefrom under this Act, without any new trustee being appointed in his place."

---

[81] A personal representative may be discharged by the court; Administration of Justice Act 1985, s.50.

[82] *Head v. Gould* [1898] 2 Ch. 250.

[83] T.A. 1925, s.36(1); *ante*, p. 511. *cf.* (1989) 9 L.S. 323 (Y. Tan), suggesting that s.36 permits retirement without replacement.

[84] A sole trustee other than a trust corporation does not suffice even if he has power to give a valid receipt for capital money, in contrast with the position under T.A. 1925, s.37(1)(*c*). The word "persons" in s.39(1) was inserted by Trusts of Land and Appointment of Trustees Act 1996, Sched. 3, para. 3(13), in place of "individuals." A corporate trustee (whether or not a "trust corporation") is a "person" but not an "individual."

A retirement not complying with the statutory provisions is invalid, hence the trustee remains in office.[85]

C. Under an Order of the Court

The court will only discharge a trustee under its statutory jurisdiction where it replaces him by a new appointment under section 41. It has however an inherent power to discharge him without replacement in the case of an action to administer the trust. While it will not, in the exercise of this jurisdiction, encourage capricious retirement,[86] it will allow a trustee to retire where it is entirely proper for him to do so.[87]

D. By Direction of the Beneficiaries

We saw that section 19 of the Trusts of Land and Appointment of Trustees Act 1996 gives beneficiaries of full age and capacity and together absolutely entitled the power to give directions to the trustees in matters of appointment and retirement.[88] Where a trustee has been given a direction to retire under section 19 and reasonable arrangements have been made for the protection of any rights of his in connection with the trust, he must execute a deed declaring his retirement, provided that after his retirement there will be either a trust corporation or at least two persons to act, and either another person is to be appointed in his place (by direction of the beneficiaries or otherwise) or the continuing trustees by deed consent to his retirement.[89]

12. REMOVAL

We have seen that the court[90] may, on the appointment of a new trustee, remove an existing trustee and that some appointments by a donee of a power will have this effect.[91] The power of beneficiaries to direct a trustee to retire was discussed above. The court has also an inherent jurisdiction in actions for the administration of trusts to

---

[85] *Mettoy Pension Trustees Ltd v. Evans* [1990] 1 W.L.R. 1587.

[86] *Courtenay v. Courtenay* (1846) 3 Jo. & La.T. 519, 533.

[87] *Re Chetwynd's Settlement* [1902] 1 Ch. 692.

[88] *ante*, p. 515. The power may be excluded by the settlor under s.21(5), (6). For potential problems, see (1998) 61 M.L.R. 56 at 67 (L. Clements).

[89] s.19(3). For vesting and divesting of the trust property, see s.19(4) of the 1996 Act and T.A. 1925, s.40(2), as amended.

[90] Normally the Chancery Division, but the Family Division has such jurisdiction; *E. v. E.* [1990] 2 F.L.R. 233 (post-nuptial settlement).

[91] T.A. 1925, ss.36, 41, *ante*, pp. 511, 515; *Re Stoneham S.T.* [1953] Ch. 59; as to removal of a charitable trustee, see Charities Act 1993, s.18; *ante*, p. 467.

remove a trustee compulsorily; but the principles on which this power is exercised are somewhat vague.[92]

Actual misconduct on the part of a trustee need not be shown, but the court must be satisfied that his continuance in office would be prejudicial to the due performance of the trust, and so to the interests of the beneficiaries.[93] The court has a clear ground for removal in cases where a trustee is ignoring one of his duties. Thus, though it will not necessarily constitute a breach of trust for a trustee of a will carrying on the business of his testator to set up a rival business, yet it will be a ground for his removal,[94] as he has put himself in a position wherein his duty and interest are bound to be in conflict. Similarly if trustees were to persist in an investment policy based on considerations other than the best interests of the beneficiaries.[95] Harman J. has suggested that a member of a discretionary class could procure the removal of a trustee who "deliberately refused to consider any question" relating to the qualification of members to receive payments.[96]

In the case of a foreign settlement, the court has inherent jurisdiction to make *in personam* orders removing and replacing foreign trustees, whether or not the assets are in England, provided that the individual trustee is subject to the jurisdiction of the English courts.[97] However, where the applicable law of the trust is not English law, matters such as the appointment, resignation and removal of trustees are governed by the law of the relevant jurisdiction.[98]

In administration actions the powers of the court are very elastic.[99] The court can, at any time during such proceedings, remove the trustees, if it considers such removal necessary for the preservation of the trust estate or the welfare of the beneficiaries, notwithstanding that such removal has not been expressly asked for in the statement of case. But each case must be weighed carefully on its merits; and the court will sometimes find it necessary to place in one

---

[92] *Letterstedt v. Broers* (1884) 9 App.Cas. 371; *Re Wrightson* [1908] 1 Ch. 789; *Re Pauling's S.T. (No. 2)* [1963] Ch. 576; *Jones v. Att.-Gen.* [1974] Ch. 148 (trustee of charitable trust); *Re Edwards' W.T.* [1982] Ch. 30.

[93] See *E. v. E., supra.*

[94] *Moore v. M'Glynn* [1894] 1 Ir.R. 74.

[95] *Cowan v. Scargill* [1985] Ch. 270, *post*, p. 543.

[96] *Re Gestetner Settlement* [1953] Ch. 672 at 688; see also *per* Lord Wilberforce in *McPhail v. Doulton* [1971] A.C. 424 at 456; *ante*, p. 105.

[97] By reason of service of the claim form in England, or because the trustee has submitted to the jurisdiction, or because the court has assumed jurisdiction under R.S.C. Ord. 11, C.P.R. 1998, Sched. 1.

[98] Recognition of Trusts Act 1987, Sched., Art. 8. For the applicable law, see Arts. 6, 7; *ante*, p. 45.

[99] *Re Harrison's Settlement Trusts* [1965] 1 W.L.R. 1492. On the removal of an executor, see *I.R.C. v. Stype Investments (Jersey) Ltd* [1982] Ch. 456.

scale a minor breach of trust, and in the other the certain expense to the trust estate of a change of trustees.[1]

Special rules relating to the suspension, removal, disqualification and replacement of pension trustees are discussed in Chapter 16.

13. CONTROL OF TRUSTEES

The basic principle governing trustees is that, while duties must be discharged, the exercise of discretions needs only to be considered. The trustee is not obliged to exercise them in any particular manner, or indeed at all. Thus in *Tempest v. Lord Camoys*,[2] one trustee wished to take advantage of a power in a trust instrument to purchase land but his co-trustee would not agree. It could not be shown that he had failed to consider the matter, and the court refused to issue any directive to him.

Nor is there a general principle that trustees should consult beneficiaries, though they should inform them that they have certain rights.[3] Frequently consultation takes place as a matter of practice, but only occasionally does statute[4] impose an obligation on them to do so, and even then their wishes are not mandatory but must be related to the overall welfare of the trust.

But what is the position if trustees exercise a discretion in a manner that appears wholly unreasonable? Is it a satisfactory answer to state simply that the matter has been fully considered? The law on this subject is neither wholly clear not wholly satisfactory.

A. Giving of Reasons

There is a basic rule that trustees cannot be compelled to explain their reasons for exercising or not exercising a discretionary power.

> In *Re Beloved Wilkes' Charity*,[5] trustees were directed to select a boy to be educated for Orders in the Church of England. Their freedom of choice was limited by a preference for certain parishes, if a fit and proper candidate therefrom could be found.
>
> The trustees selected Charles Joyce, a boy who did not come from one of these parishes. It appeared that Charles' brother was a minister who had sought assistance on his behalf from one of

---

[1] *Re Wrightson* [1908] 1 Ch. 789.

[2] (1882) 21 Ch.D. 571. The statutory duty of care under Trustee Act 2000, s.1 (*ante*, p. 499) does not apply to the discretion whether or not to exercise a power.

[3] *Hawkesley v. May* [1956] 1 Q.B. 304; *X v. A* [2000] 1 All E.R. 490.

[4] *e.g.* Trusts of Land and Appointment of Trustees Act 1996, s.11; *ante*, p. 293.

[5] (1851) 3 Mac. & G. 440.

the trustees. The trustees gave no reasons for their choice, but asserted that they had considered the candidates impartially.

Lord Truro refused to set aside the trustees' selection, or to require the trustees to explain how they had arrived at their conclusion.[6]

No distinction exists in this context between oral and documentary evidence, which is a matter of some importance in view of the large amount of trust business which is conducted by correspondence or at meetings with written agenda and minutes. In *Re Londonderry's Settlement*,[7] the court drew a sharp distinction between written material of this nature which related to management of the trust property (which should be disclosed to requesting beneficiaries) and material which related to the exercise of discretions (which need not be disclosed). But if trustees do give reasons, then the courts will look into their adequacy.[8]

The principle that trustees need not give reasons for their decisions is based on the fact that trustees have a confidential role which, it is said, they cannot properly exercise if they are to be subjected to an investigation to see whether they have exercised it in the best possible manner.[9] Documents relating to the trust may contain confidential information, the disclosure of which could cause trouble in the family, out of all proportion to the benefit gained from inspecting them. Thus the principle is designed not to encourage secrecy but to avoid litigation and family disputes.[10]

Whether the principle is appropriate to pension trusts may be doubted,[11] but it was held to apply in *Wilson v. Law Debenture Trust Corporation plc*,[12] even though pension trusts are in many ways treated differently from traditional trusts because the beneficiaries are not volunteers.[13] There the employees failed to obtain disclosure of the trustees' reasons for not transferring a surplus to another scheme to which the employees had been transferred. Any change, it was said, would require legislation.[14] The significance of member

---

[6] For a discussion on policy grounds, see (1965) 28 M.L.R. 220 (A. Samuels); (1965) S.J. 239 (A. Hawkins and F. Taylor).

[7] [1965] 1 Ch. 918; the facts are given *post*, p. 566; *Butt v. Kelson* [1952] Ch. 197.

[8] *Klug v. Klug* [1918] 2 Ch. 67.

[9] *Re Londonderry's Settlement* [1965] Ch. 918 at 935–936.

[10] *Hartigan Nominees Pty Ltd v. Rydge* (1992) 29 N.S.W.L.R. 405, holding that *Londonderry* accorded with principle and common sense; [1994] 3 J.I.P. 60 (J. Lehane).

[11] (1992) 6 *Trust Law International* 119 at 125 (Lord Browne-Wilkinson); (1994) 8 *Trust Law International* 27 (D. Schaffer); [1996] P.L.R. 107 (Sir Robert Walker); (1997) 11 *Trust Law International* 11 and 42 (D. Pollard).

[12] [1995] 2 All E.R. 337; criticised (1994) 8 *Trust Law International* 118 (D. Schaffer); All E.R. Rev. 1995 at 321 (P. Clarke).

[13] *ante*, p. 475.

[14] Regulations under the Pensions Act 1995 require the decisions of the trustees to be recorded, but do not impose any general duty to give reasons. For the implications of the Data Protection Act 1998, see The TACT Review, April 2000, p. 3 (M. Shillingford).

trustees (required by the Pensions Act 1995) in this context should not, however, be overlooked.[15]

It is otherwise where there is evidence of bad faith or other impropriety. The difficulty is that it may not be possible to establish impropriety without seeing the documents which the trustees are not obliged to disclose. The beneficiaries may obtain disclosure of documents to support their case, but may not use that process to ascertain if a case exists.[16] Indeed the order made in the *Londonderry* case was without prejudice to the beneficiary's right to disclosure in separate proceedings against the trustees.[17]

B. Intervention by the Court

The cases are not clear, however, on whether the courts will look into the exercise of a discretion that *appears* to be wholly unreasonable. The duty of care under section 1 of the Trustee Act 2000 does not apply to the exercise of dispositive powers. If there is an allegation of fraud or misconduct, the courts must investigate it; but the complainant is in a difficulty in that the evidence which he requires is the personal motivation of the trustees. If fraud is proved, or if the exercise of the discretion is shown to be "capricious,"[18] or if the trustees have blindly followed the settlor's wishes,[19] the court will declare the trustees' decision void. Likewise if the trustees have improperly exercised a power for a collateral purpose, by analogy with the doctrine of "fraud on a power",[20] which can occur even though the trustees acted honestly in the sense that they thought their action was in the interests of the beneficiaries.[21] There is some authority that the court will not intervene in the absence of bad faith if the instrument provides that the trustees' discretion is "uncontrollable."[22] It is not clear how far the court has greater powers in the absence of such a statement.[23] Although some nineteenth century decisions[24] asserted a wide jurisdiction, it seems that the court will not intervene simply on the ground that the trustees have exercised their discretion in good faith but unreasonably. The House of

---

[15] (1995) 145 N.L.J. 1414 (P. O'Hagan).

[16] *Hartigan Nominees Pty Ltd v. Rydge* (1992) 29 N.S.W.L.R. 405.

[17] [1965] Ch. 918 at 939. See also *Scott v. National Trust for Places of Historic Interest or Natural Beauty* [1998] 2 All E.R. 705; All E.R. Rev. 1998 at 276–277 (P. Clarke).

[18] *Re Manisty's Settlement* [1974] Ch. 17; *ante*, p. 111.

[19] *Turner v. Turner* [1984] Ch. 100.

[20] *ante*, p. 182.

[21] *Hillsdown Holdings plc v. Pensions Ombudsman* [1997] 1 All E.R. 862 (transfer of surplus funds to employer).

[22] *Gisborne v. Gisborne* (1877) 2 App.Cas. 300.

[23] See [1989] Conv. 244 (N. Parry).

[24] *Re Hodges* (1878) 7 Ch.D. 754; *Re Roper's Trust* (1879) 11 Ch.D. 272.

Lords in a Scottish appeal[25] (which has been said to reflect also the law of England[26]) indicated that the court could intervene, whether or not the trustees had given their reasons, if it was clear that they had not applied their minds to the right question or had perversely shut their eyes to the facts. This reflects the rule in *Re Hastings-Bass*,[27] applying where trustees exercise a discretion in good faith but their disposition does not have the full effect which they intended (due to some rule of law or other cause). The court will set aside the disposition (wholly or partly) if it was outside the terms of the power or if it is clear that the trustees would not have acted as they did had they not taken into account considerations which they should not have taken into account or failed to take into account considerations which they ought to have taken into account. It is not enough to show that the trustees did not fully understand the effect of their act. It must also be clear that, if they had fully understood, they would not have acted as they did. Where, however, the trustees' power of appointment had expired at the time they purported to exercise it, the court had no jurisdiction to treat it as properly exercised in equity on the basis that the trustees had failed to appreciate the time limit.[27a] Although these principles have yet to be fully worked out, it has been emphasised that to impose too stringent a test could put intolerable burdens on trustees and lead to damaging uncertainty as to the validity of their decisions.[28]

Where the court does intervene, the result is normally negative: the decision of the trustees may be declared void, or a future course of action restrained. Usually the court makes no positive direction that a discretion must be exercised in a particular way. However, this can be done in an appropriate case, as in *Klug v. Klug*,[29] where a trustee refused to exercise a power of advancement for an extraneous reason (because the beneficiary, her daughter, had married without her consent). The court directed the trustee to agree to the

---

[25] *Dundee General Hospitals v. Walker* [1952] 1 All E.R. 896. The trustees accepted that unreasonableness was the test, but this was doubted.

[26] *Scott v. National Trust for Places of Historic Interest or Natural Beauty, supra.*

[27] [1975] Ch. 25, *post*, p. 598; *Re Vestey's Settlement* [1951] Ch. 209; *Mettoy Pension Trustees Ltd v. Evans* [1990] 1 W.L.R. 1587; [1991] Conv. 364. (J. Martin); *Stannard v. Fisons Pension Trust Ltd* [1992] I.R.L.R. 27; *Edge v. Pensions Ombudsman* [2000] Ch. 602; *Green v. Cobham* [2000] W.T.L.R. 1101.
See also *Wild v. Pensions Ombudsman* [1996] P.L.R. 275 (jurisdiction of ombudsman to deal with maladministration).

[27a] *Breadner v. Granville-Grossman* [2001] 2 W.L.R. 593.

[28] *Scott v. National Trust for Places of Historic Interest or Natural Beauty* [1998] 2 All E.R. 705.

[29] [1918] 2 Ch. 67. See also *Re Hodges* (1878) 7 Ch.D. 754; *Re Roper's Trust* (1879) 11 Ch.D. 272. The appointment of new trustees is considered preferable to positive intervention (*i.e.* the judicial exercise of fiduciary discretions) in (1990) 107 L.Q.R. 214 at 219–220 (S. Gardner), discussing *Mettoy Pension Trustees Ltd v. Evans, supra.*

advancement. Alternatively, a trustee may be persuaded by the prospect of removal.

C. Power of Decision

A trust deed may give the trustees or a third party power to decide a particular matter. We saw in Chapter 3 that this may be a means of curing conceptual uncertainty,[30] in which case the question arises whether the court may intervene if the decision appears unreasonable or wrong. Lord Denning in *Re Tuck's Settlement Trusts* would only have accepted the decision of the Chief Rabbi "so long as he does not misconduct himself or come to a decision which is wholly unreasonable."[31]

The trustees cannot be given power to decide legal issues in such manner as to oust the jurisdiction of the court, as this would be contrary to public policy.[32] They may be given power to decide limited issues, such as where the beneficiaries reside, or what is their ancestry or faith. The House of Lords in *Dundee General Hospitals v. Walker*[33] thought it possible, as mentioned above, that the decisions of trustees in such cases could be attacked on the grounds of perversity or failure to appreciate the issue, as well as on grounds of bad faith. Where a clause in a trust of a pension fund provided that the determination of matters such as eligibility and the construction of the instrument adopted by the trustees in good faith should be binding on all parties and beneficiaries, the Canadian court held that its jurisdiction was not excluded where the trustees acted in breach of their duty of impartiality, although in good faith.[34]

The general principle that beneficiaries cannot control trustees in the manner in which they exercise their powers applies even though all the beneficiaries are ascertained and of full capacity and desirous of the power being exercised in a particular way.[35] But in such a case the trust can of course be brought to an end.

---

[30] *ante*, p. 107.

[31] [1978] Ch. 49 at 62.

[32] *Re Wynn*, [1952] Ch. 271. See also *Re Raven* [1915] 1 Ch. 673 (trustees cannot be given conclusive power to resolve doubts as to identity of beneficiary).

[33] [1952] 1 All E.R. 896 at p. 905. This was a Scottish appeal, but "of the highest persuasive value": *per* Lord Denning M.R. in *Re Tuck's S.T., supra*, at 61.

[34] *Boe v. Alexander* (1988) 41 D.L.R. (4th) 520. See also *Jones v. Shipping Federation of British Columbia* (1963) 37 D.L.R. (2d) 273.

[35] *Re Brockbank* [1948] Ch. 206; *cf. Re George Whichelow Ltd* [1954] 1 W.L.R. 5 at 8. See, however, s.19 of the Trusts of Land and Appointment of Trustees Act 1996; *ante*, p. 515.

CHAPTER 18

DUTIES OF TRUSTEES IN RELATION TO THE TRUST PROPERTY

1. DUTY TO COLLECT IN THE ASSETS

A. Duty on Accepting Office

Trustees must, on their appointment, make themselves acquainted with the terms of the trust and the state and the details of the trust property, check that the trust fund is invested in accordance with the provisions of the trust deed, and that the securities and any chattels are in proper custody.[1] They should not wait until the trust property is formally vested in them. The discharge of their duties will obviously depend upon circumstances. The trustees of a trust newly constituted, and with suitable assets, are in an easier situation than personal representatives who find, as part of the estate, assets which are highly speculative or precarious. In the latter case the duty is to consider the best method of protecting the value of the assets, and

---

[1] *Re Miller's Deed Trust* (1978) 75 L.S.Gaz. 454.

this may involve delaying a decision to dispose of them. Liability for loss will not be imposed on them if their decision to delay was reasonable, even though subsequent events show it to have been the less wise course.[2]

A replacement trustee must make all reasonable inquiries[3] to satisfy himself that nothing has been done by his predecessor and the continuing trustees which amounts to a breach of trust; and the continuing trustees must provide this information from trust documents.[4] Omission to inquire may render the new trustee liable, but he is not to be fixed with notice of matters that do not appear on any of the trust documents, though the matter may be known to the retiring trustee.[5] On a similar principle, if he is ignorant of the existence of some right forming part of the trust, he is not liable for loss of that right through non-enforcement unless he could have discovered its existence from materials at his disposal.[6]

B. Extent of Duty

The duty to safeguard trust assets is a stringent one; indeed, it has sometimes been almost too strictly applied.

In *Re Brogden*,[7] the trustees of a marriage settlement took what they considered to be all reasonable steps to ensure that a covenant to pay £10,000 to them at the end of a stated period of five years was carried out. They did not sue because the covenantor's estate was the basis of the family partnership, the stability of which might have been imperilled by an action at a time of trade depression. The trustees were held liable. They should have taken every possible step to insist on payment, irrespective of the claims of sentiment within a family.

In *Buttle v. Saunders*,[8] trustees had orally agreed to sell a freehold reversion to the leaseholder. Then a beneficiary made a higher offer. The trustees declined to consider it, feeling themselves bound by commercial morality to complete the agreement.

---

[2] *Buxton v. Buxton* (1835) 1 My. & Cr. 80.

[3] *Harvey v. Oliver* (1887) 57 L.T. 239; *Re Lucking's W.T.* [1968] 1 W.L.R. 866.

[4] *Tiger v. Barclays Bank* [1951] 2 K.B. 556.

[5] *Hallows v. Lloyd* (1888) 39 Ch.D. 686.

[6] *Youde v. Cloud* (1874) L.R. 18 Eq. 634. A similarly reasonable rule governs the inquiries trustees should make in relation to covenants to settle after-acquired property: *Re Strahan* (1856) 8 De. G.M. & G. 291.

[7] (1888) 38 Ch.D. 546. An extreme case, when litigation would have ruined a beneficiary, is *Ward v. Ward* (1843) 2 H.L.C. 777n. See also *Harris v. Black* (1983) 46 P. & C.R. 366 (duty to preserve assets did not require court to compel a trustee-beneficiary to seek the renewal of a business tenancy which he did not want, the partnership with the other trustee-beneficiary having been dissolved).

[8] [1950] 2 All E.R. 193; (1950) 14 Conv.(N.S.) 228 (E. Bodkin); (1975) 30 Conv.(N.S.) 177 (A. Samuels). See also *Sergeant v. National Westminster Bank* (1991) 61 P. & C.R. 518.

Wynn-Parry J. held that, although there may be cases where a trustee should accept a lower offer—as where that offer may be lost if not honoured—and although the honourable course was to stand by the earlier offer, the trustees had an overriding duty to obtain the best price for their beneficiaries.

C. Litigation

In *Re Brogden*,[9] the Court of Appeal laid down that the only excuse for not taking action to enforce payment was a well-founded belief on the part of the trustees that such action would be fruitless; and the burden of proof was on the trustees. Now trustees have extensive powers of compounding liabilities, allowing time for the payment of debts, and compromising doubtful actions, etc., given by the Trustee Act 1925, s.15.[10] Trustees are not liable for loss caused by any acts done by them in good faith in exercise of these powers, provided they have directed their minds to the problem and not just let the matter slide.[11] A trustee will be allowed the costs of litigation from the trust assets if properly incurred,[12] but not where the litigation results from an unreasonable withholding of property from those entitled to it,[13] nor where the litigation is speculative and turns out to be unsuccessful,[14] nor where the trustee has acted in a manner hostile to the beneficiaries.[15] A beneficiary may sue a third party on behalf of the trust where the trustee unreasonably refuses to sue or has disabled himself from doing so.[16] (Where, however, the trustees are able and willing to sue, the beneficiary will be penalised in costs.[17]) Trustees who discontinue litigation against third parties because the trust fund could be exhausted in indemnifying them for costs do not act unreasonably, and the beneficiaries may not take over the action.[18]

D. A Continuing Duty

Trustees must regard their duty of safeguarding trust assets as a continuing one. In regard to investment in securities, the point is

---

[9] (1888) 38 Ch.D. 546.

[10] *post*, p. 575.

[11] *Re Greenwood* (1911) 105 L.T. 509. *cf. Re Ezekiel's Settlements* [1942] Ch. 230.

[12] See generally *Alsop Wilkinson v. Neary* [1996] 1 W.L.R. 1220; *post*, p. 602; *Singh v. Basin, The Times*, August 21, 1998.

[13] *Re Chapman* (1895) 72 L.T. 66.

[14] *Re Beddoe* [1893] 1 Ch. 547; *Re England's S.T.* [1918] 1 Ch. 24.

[15] *Holding and Management Ltd v. Property Holding and Investment Trust plc.* [1989] 1 W.L.R. 1313.

[16] *Parker-Tweedale v. Dunbar Bank plc* [1991] Ch. 12; (1997) 11 *Trust Law International* 60 (G. McCormack).

[17] *D'Abo v. Paget (No. 2), The Times*, August 10, 2000. There is more flexibility as to costs under the Civil Procedure Rules 1998.

[18] *Bradstock Trustee Services Ltd v. Nabarro Nathanson (a firm)* [1995] 1 W.L.R. 1405.

dealt with below. In regard to land, there is a duty to consider the maintenance and general welfare of the property, and in regard to deeds and chattels, a duty to see that they are kept securely.[19] There is no duty to insure unless required by the trust deed, but trustees have a power to insure.[20]

2. DUTY TO INVEST[21]

A. Meaning of Investment

A trustee is under a duty to invest trust money in his hands. To invest means "to employ money in the purchase of anything from which interest or profit is expected".[22] From the point of view of an individual investing his own money, he may not mind whether the profit comes from income earned by the investment or from capital appreciation. But trustees often have to consider the interests of a life tenant, who is entitled to the income, and also of the remainder-men who are interested in the capital.[23] The trustees' duty is to act fairly between them. The investments should produce income, and maintain the capital. Thus premium bonds and chattels, such as antiques or silver, are not investments for this purpose. For this reason a purchase of a house for occupation by a beneficiary, and which therefore produces no income, was held not to be an investment,[24] but this has been remedied by statute.[25] It remains the case that investments which yield a high rate of income because the capital is wasting away, or an unsecured loan,[26] should be avoided.

Part II of the Trustee Act 2000, which confers wide investment powers on trustees, retains the traditional terminology of "investment" without elaboration. The Law Commission preferred to avoid any definition of "investment", which was said to be an evolving concept, and had little doubt that "profit" could be capital appreciation rather than income yield.[27] The Explanatory Notes (which accompany, but are not part of, the Act) state that the general power of investment permits the trustees to invest in a way which is expected

---

[19] *Jobson v. Palmer* [1893] 1 Ch. 71.

[20] *post*, p. 574.

[21] Trustees conducting investment business are required by Financial Services and Markets Act 2000, s.19, to be authorised under the Act or exempted.

[22] *Shorter Oxford English Dictionary; Re Wragg* [1919] 2 Ch. 58 at 64, *per* P.O. Lawrence J. who added: "and which property is purchased in order to be held for the sake of the income which it will yield."

[23] Compare "percentage trusts," *post*, p. 561.

[24] *Re Power* [1947] Ch. 572.

[25] Trusts of Land and Appointment of Trustees Act 1996, s.6(3); Trustee Act 2000, s.8; *post*, p. 535.

[26] *Khoo Tek Keong v. Ch'ng Joo Tuan Neoh* [1934] A.C. 529.

[27] No. 260 (1999), *Trustees' Powers and Duties*, p. 22.

to produce an income or capital return. The point remains somewhat uncertain, and it is to be expected that express clauses permitting the application of trust funds in a manner which may not strictly be an "investment" will continue to be used.

B. Types of Investment

In most general terms, there are basically two types of investment. The first is a loan at a rate of interest. The second is a participation in a profit-making activity; such as the purchase of ordinary shares in a company ("equities"). Ordinary shares were first included in the list of permitted investments for trustees by the Trustee Investments Act 1961. Mention should also be made of "derivatives", such as futures and options. A "future" obliges the holder to buy or sell (shares, currency, commodities etc.) at a set price at a future date. An option gives the holder the right, but not the obligation, to buy or sell at a set price at a set date. Pension fund trustees and others with sufficiently wide powers may make use of derivatives in appropriate circumstances, but they are not within the traditional meaning of "investments." Dealing in derivatives can be risky, as illustrated in extreme form by the collapse of Barings Bank in 1995.

i. Loans at a Rate of Interest. In the case of an investment such as a deposit account at a bank or a building society, the capital sum does not alter (save by additions or withdrawals). Interest is earned at a rate which is normally variable.

Most fixed interest securities issued by the Government and local authorities are in the form of stock and pay a fixed rate of interest. The purchaser may sell the stock to other purchasers. The value of the stock is whatever a purchaser will give for it. That depends on many factors; essentially the current rate of interest chargeable on loans. Where interest rates have increased since the stock was issued, the value of the stock declines. A three per cent stock, paying £3 per annum on an investment of £100, needs to pay the current rate of interest in order to be saleable, but the interest is fixed at a lower rate. Assuming a current market rate of return of 10 per cent, a three per cent stock would be worth £30. £3 per annum on an outlay of £30 is a 10 per cent return.

Some stocks however are "dated"; that is, they will be repaid at "par" (100) at a stated date in the future. The nearer the date, the higher the price. Thus in March 2001, Treasury seven per cent 2002 was priced at 102. Capital gains on certain government stocks are free of capital gains tax.[28] This and other factors contribute to the price.

---

[28] Taxation of Chargeable Gains Act 1992, s.115; *ante*, p. 221.

A debenture is an acknowledgement of indebtedness by a company, supported in practice by a charge upon the undertaking and assets of a company. This is a floating, as opposed to a fixed, charge. The company is free to deal with any of its specific assets unaffected by the charge. The charge crystallises when the debenture holders take the necessary steps to enforce their security. The value of a debenture is dependent partly upon the ability of the assets and undertaking of the company to provide sufficient security for the loan, and it is therefore to some extent dependent upon the commercial stability of the company.

Preference shares are shares in a company which have a preference in relation to the payment of a fixed rate of dividend, and may have other preferential rights as well. Being dependent upon the earning by the company of sufficient profits to pay the dividends, they are less secure than government securities (gilts) or debentures, and consequently they normally carry a higher return. That does not mean that the rate of dividend rises. It is the price at which the shares can be purchased on the market which varies. If 5 per cent preference shares, paying £5 per annum on their par value were priced at 50, the dividend of £5 per annum on an outlay of £50 would put the shares on a return of 10 per cent.

ii. Equities.

(a) *Ordinary shares.* The capital of a company is laid down in its Memorandum[29] and its division into classes of shares usually contained in the Articles, and it normally includes ordinary shares. Ownership of an ordinary share entitles the purchaser to vote at the general meeting, to participate in dividends when declared on the ordinary shares, and to participate in a winding up.

The Annual General Meeting will declare the dividend payable for the year, if any. The value of ordinary shares varies with the fortunes of the company. They necessarily contain an element of speculation, and it is for this reason that ordinary shares were not authorised investments for trustees until 1961.

(b) *Unit Trusts and Investment Trusts.*[30] The selection of ordinary shares for investment is a highly specialised matter. Further, it is important that the investment of a trust should be spread over a wide range of companies. But a small trust cannot provide a satisfactory spread. This can be achieved by participating in an investment fund which is managed by investment experts. There are basically two types. First the unit trust, in which the managers receive money from

---

[29] Companies Act 1985, s.2.
[30] See (1995) 92/09 L.S.Gaz. p. 18 (A. Harris).

investors, and form a single fund, divided up into units which are owned by the investors. The management is paid expenses and salary. The investors have the advantage of investment expertise, and of the spread of investments. Units in a trust can be bought and sold. Secondly, the misleadingly named investment trust. This is a limited company in which shares can be bought and sold like other shares. The company buys shares in other companies, and the investors receive their return in the form of dividends from the investment trust.

C. Express Powers of Investment

A trustee may be given wide power by the trust instrument to select investments; or his selection may be left to investments authorised by the general law. Express clauses at one time were strictly construed, reflecting the court's fear of investment in ordinary shares in the nineteenth century. Thus it seemed to be established that words such as a "power to invest in such securities as they might think fit"[31] gave power merely to select among securities then authorised for trustee investment. This had changed by the time of *Re Harari's Settlement Trusts*,[32] where the words "in or upon such investments as to them may seem fit" permitted the trustees to invest in equities.

It is likely to remain the usual practice to include a clause giving trustees wide powers of investment even after the extension of investment powers by the Trustee Act 2000; and the trustees, or other persons, may be given authority to amend the power.[33]

D. The Purchase of Land

Until recently trustees could not purchase land unless the trust instrument so provided. Even where the instrument did authorise investment in land, we saw that the purchase of a house for the occupation of a beneficiary was not an "investment."[34] Statutory power to purchase land was first given to trustees of land by the Trusts of Land and Appointment of Trustees Act 1996.[35] The power has now been widened and extended to trustees in general by the Trustee Act 2000. Subject to any restriction or exclusion in the trust instrument, trustees may acquire freehold or leasehold land in the United Kingdom:

---

[31] *Re Braithwaite* (1882) 21 Ch.D. 121; *Re Maryon-Wilson's Estate* [1912] 1 Ch. 55.
[32] [1949] 1 All E.R. 430.
[33] *Re Harari's S.T., supra,* at 434.
[34] *Re Power* [1947] Ch. 572, *ante,* p. 532.
[35] s.6(3).

(a) as an investment, or

(b) for occupation by a beneficiary, or

(c) for any other reason.[36]

There is no restriction as to the length of any lease which may be acquired. Trustees who acquire land under this provision have all the powers of an absolute owner in relation to the land for the purpose of exercising their functions as trustees.[37] The statutory duty of care applies to trustees in the exercise of their powers under the Act in relation to land and also to the exercise of express powers relating to land.[38] Land outside the United Kingdom is excluded from the statutory power because such a purchase could create problems in a jurisdiction which does not recognise trusts. Trustees may, however, be given express power to purchase such land.

Trustees' power to invest in a mortgage of land is dealt with below.[39]

E. Authorised Investments

i. Traditional Rule. The rules on investment by trustees have been governed by the principles, first that trustees must avoid all risk to the capital of the fund, and secondly, that the value of the £ will remain stable. Throughout the nineteenth century, the system worked well enough. At first, trustees were restricted to consols,[40] and were subsequently permitted to choose among a narrow range of fixed interest investments, known as trustee securities. Investment was not yet a technical or specialised matter. The income beneficiaries were assured of an income, and the capital was secure. But progressive inflation changed all that.

Much of the problem of the decline of the value of the currency should be solved by investment in equities. A purchaser of a share in a company owns a share of the operation. If the business prospers, its actual value may increase. Assume, however, that the actual value of the business remains the same; if the value of money is reduced to one-third, the value of the shares will treble, providing "a hedge against inflation".

But in times of recession, the prices of ordinary shares fall even faster than those of gilts. Prices on investment exchanges are established by buyers and sellers, and a number of irrational factors play

---

[36] T.A. 2000, s.8. Only the acquisition of a legal estate in the land is permitted. The provision does not apply to settled land; s.10.

[37] *ibid.*, s.8(3).

[38] *ibid.*, Sched. 1, para. 2.

[39] *post*, p. 538.

[40] Fixed interest Government securities without redemption date.

their part in establishing and undermining confidence. The overall prices of shares are gauged by an index called the *Financial Times Index*.[41] The fluctuations in prices underline the dangers involved in investment in ordinary shares, and emphasise the need for expertise in selecting investments; and the avoidance of speculation.

ii. Trustee Investments Act 1961. Authorised investments were extended by the Trustee Investments Act 1961. The object of the Act was to permit trustees to invest a proportion of trust funds in equities. The original permitted proportion was one-half, but the Treasury increased this to three-quarters, pending a more fundamental reform of trustee investments.[42]

The Act of 1961 had long been criticised as outdated, and it was invariably side-stepped in any well-drawn trust by the provision of wider powers. Nevertheless, the Act remained an obstacle in cases such as trusts arising on intestacy or under home-made wills. The criticisms were broadly twofold. First, the Act had not kept pace with the developments in the world of investments and thus did not permit trustees to utilise many advantageous investments. Secondly, its machinery was cumbersome as a result of the requirement of division of the fund before any investment in equities could be made.

iii. Trustee Act 2000. The expansion of investment powers was one of the major purposes of the Trustee Act 2000. The new legislation substantially widens investment powers so that trust income may be maximised without eroding the capital. The beneficiaries remain protected by the requirement of professional advice, the financial services legislation and the general law on investment duties.

Before examining the investment provisions of the new Act in detail, mention should be made of the modern "portfolio theory", whereby trustees' investment decisions must be evaluated not in relation to individual assets in isolation but in the context of the trust portfolio as a whole and as part of an overall investment strategy.[43] This theory has been approved by the Law Commission[44] and also adopted in a Treasury consultation paper.[45] Although not expressly dealt with in the new legislation, it may now be regarded as part of the general law.

---

[41] This is now the FT30-share index. Since 1984 there is also the broader-based FT-SE 100 Index.

[42] Trustee Investments (Division of Trust Fund) Order (S.I. 1996 No. 845).

[43] See (1995) *Trust Law International* 71 (Lord Nicholls); (1996) 10 *Trust Law International* 102 (E. Ford); (2000) 14 *Trust Law International* 75 (I. Legair).

[44] No. 260 (1999), *Trustees' Powers and Duties*, p. 23.

[45] *Investment Powers of Trustees* (May 1996), paras. 35(ii), 40(iii).

Section 3 of the Trustees Act 2000 provides that, subject to the other provisions of Part II of the Act, "a trustee may make any kind of investment that he could make if he were absolutely entitled to the assets of the trust". This is called "the general power of investment", and it applies to trusts whenever created.[46] The general power is additional to any express powers, but may be restricted or excluded by the trust instrument or by other legislation.[47] For example, a settlor may wish to exclude investments he does not consider ethical.[48] The general power does not apply to trustees of pension funds or authorised unit trusts, nor to trustees managing common investment or common deposit schemes under the Charities Act 1993.[49] Trustees in these categories are subject to their own statutory regimes.

Trustees' powers to acquire land have already been dealt with.[50] So far as mortgages are concerned, the limited powers contained in the Trustee Act 1925 and the Trustee Investments Act 1961 have been replaced by a power to invest by way of a loan secured on land.[51] It appears from the general power to acquire land contained in section 8, which is confined to legal estates, that any secured loan must take effect by way of a legal mortgage, as under the previous law, although the point is unclear. While the power to acquire land is restricted to land in the United Kingdom, there is no geographical limit on other investments.

F. The Standard Investment Criteria

Section 4 of the Trustee Act 2000 provides that trustees must have regard to the standard investment criteria when exercising any statutory or express power of investment. They must "from time to time review the investments of the trust and consider whether, having regard to the standard investment criteria, they should be varied". The standard investment criteria are:

"(a) the suitability to the trust of investments of the same kind as any particular investment proposed to be made or retained and of that particular investment as an investment of that kind, and (b) the need for diversification of investments of the trust, in so far as is appropriate to the circumstances of the trust".

---

[46] T.A. 2000, s.7. The Act of 1961 is substantially, although not entirely, repealed.
[47] *ibid.*, s.6. No provision in a trust instrument made before August 3, 1961 is to be treated as a restriction or exclusion; s.7(2).
[48] *post*, p. 545.
[49] T.A. 2000, ss.36–38.
[50] *ante*, p. 535.
[51] T.A. 2000, s.3(3), (4).

These criteria are based on similar provisions in the Trustee Investments Act 1961 and, in conjunction with the duty to review, are consistent with the "portfolio theory" discussed above.[52] Diversification is particularly important with large funds.[53] A small fund may achieve it by investing in unit trusts or shares in an investment trust company.[54]

G. Advice

Section 5 of the Trustee Act 2000, following similar provisions in the previous legislation, requires trustees to obtain and consider proper advice about the way in which, having regard to the standard investment criteria, the power of investment (whether express or statutory) should be exercised. Similarly, when reviewing the investments, the trustees must obtain and consider proper advice as to whether the investments should be varied. "Proper advice" is the advice of a person who is reasonably believed by the trustees to be qualified to give it by his ability in and practical experience of financial and other matters relating to the proposed investment.[55] The advice need not be written. By way of exception, trustees need not obtain such advice if they reasonably conclude that, in all the circumstances, it is unnecessary or inappropriate to do so.[56] An example may be when they propose to make a small and secure investment.

The trustees must, of course, consider the advice and then make their own decision.[57] They must not repose blind faith in the adviser. They may, however, delegate investment decisions, as discussed below. In the case of a trust corporation, there seems no reason why the advice should not be that of a competent officer, as under the previous law.

H. Duty of Care

Prior to the Trustee Act 2000, the standard of conduct required of a trustee was that of the "prudent man of business".[58] This has been reformulated by section 1 of the Trustee Act 2000, which provides that a trustee must exercise such care and skill as is reasonable in all circumstances. What is reasonable will vary according to whether

---

[52] *ante*, p. 537.

[53] *Cowan v. Scargill* [1985] Ch. 270; *Nestlé v. National Westminster Bank plc* [1993] 1 W.L.R. 1260.

[54] *ante*, p. 534.

[55] Persons acting as investment advisers must be authorised under Financial Services and Markets Act 2000, s.19.

[56] T.A. 2000, s.5(3).

[57] *Shaw v. Cates* [1909] 1 Ch. 389; *Martin v. City of Edinburgh District Council* [1988] S.L.T. 329; *Jones v. AMP Perpetual Trustee Company NZ Ltd* [1994] 1 N.Z.L.R. 690.

[58] *Speight v. Gaunt* (1883) 9 App. Cas. 1.

the trustee is a layman or a professional.[59] The duty of care applies to trustees in the exercise of statutory or express powers of investment, including their duty to have regard to the standard investment criteria and to obtain and consider proper advice.[60] It applies also in relation to their power to acquire land.[61] So, for example, trustees may be in breach of duty if they invest by way of a secured loan which equals the value of the property, leaving no margin for depreciation, even though the former restrictions on the amount of the loan have gone. As will be seen in the following section, trustees may delegate investment decisions and may appoint nominees and custodians to hold the trust investments. The duty of care applies also to the exercise of these powers.[62]

I. Delegation of Investment Powers

We have seen that investment normally needs expert advice. Trustees may wish to go further and delegate their investment powers to a professional such as an investment manager authorised under the financial services legislation. As this involves the delegation of a discretion, it could not be done prior to the Trustee Act 2000 unless permitted by the trust instrument. An exception existed in the case of pension trustees,[63] but other trustees (in the absence of an express power) needed to apply to court for an extension of investment powers.[64] Alternatively, they could delegate by power of attorney under section 25 of the Trustees Act 1925.

Reform of this area was one of the major purposes of the Trustee Act 2000. Section 11 achieves this by listing functions which may *not* be delegated, investment powers being omitted from the list. Where investment powers are delegated, the agent must satisfy the requirements relating to the standard investment criteria and the duty to review the investments from time to time.[65] He does not, however, need to obtain advice if he is the kind of person from whom the trustees could properly have obtained advice.[66] The delegation of asset management functions[67] must be done by an agreement in writing or evidenced in writing.[68] Further, the trustees must

---

[59] *ante*, p. 500.

[60] T.A. 2000, Sched. 1, para. 1.

[61] *ibid.*, para. 2.

[62] *ibid.*, para. 3.

[63] Pensions Act 1995, s.34. Thus the new powers in the Trustee Act 2000 do not apply to pension trusts.

[64] See *Anker-Petersen v. Anker-Petersen* (1998) 12 *Trust Law International* 166 (decided 1991).

[65] T.A. 2000, s.13(1).

[66] *ibid.*, s.13(2).

[67] These are investment, the acquisition of property, the management of trust property and disposing of the property or of interests in it; s.15(5).

[68] T.A. 2000, s.15.

prepare a "policy statement" giving guidance as to how these functions should be exercised in the best interests of the trust, and the agent must agree to comply with it.[69]

Section 16 of the Trustee Act 2000 confers on trustees the power to appoint a nominee (save in regard to settled land) and to vest the trust property in question in the nominee. Section 17 permits the appointment of a custodian, to undertake safe custody of the assets in question or of any documents or records concerning them. Neither power applies to a trust which has a custodian trustee.[70] There are various restrictions as to who may be appointed as a nominee or custodian.[71] Normally the agent will be a person who carries on a business including acting as a nominee or custodian. The trustees may appoint one of their number if that one is a trust corporation, or may appoint two (or more) of their number if they are to act as joint nominees or joint custodians.[72] Charity trustees must act in accordance with any guidance given by the Charity Commissioners concerning the selection of a nominee or custodian.

The trustees may pay the nominee or custodian from the trust fund, and, if reasonably necessary, may appoint him on terms which permit him to appoint a substitute, restricting his liability, or permitting him to act in circumstances capable of giving rise to a conflict of interest.[73] This reflects the fact that persons acting as nominees or custodians may in practice insist on the inclusion of such terms.

Unless the trust instrument provides otherwise, trustees who delegate to investment managers, nominees or custodians must keep the arrangements under review, including the review of any policy statement.[74] Trustees are not liable for the default of such agents unless they have failed to comply with the statutory duty of care when making the appointment or reviewing the arrangements.[75] The duty of care applies to the exercise of statutory or express powers to appoint agents, nominees or custodians. It applies in particular to the selection of the person who is to act, the terms upon which he is to act, and the preparation of a policy statement where asset management functions are delegated.[76] If, however, the trustees fail to act within their statutory powers of delegation, the appointment of the agent, nominee or custodian is not thereby invalidated.[77]

---

[69] T.A. 2000, s.15. This may refer to liquidity, the balance between capital and income, or ethical considerations.

[70] *ibid.* ss.16(3), 17(4). Nor do they apply to assets vested in the official custodian for charities. For bearer securities, see s.18.

[71] *ibid.*, s.19.

[72] The trustee(s) so appointed must satisfy the conditions laid down in s.19, *e.g.* that he or they carry on a business including acting as a nominee or custodian.

[73] T.A. 2000, s.20.

[74] *ibid.*, ss.21, 22.

[75] *ibid.*, s.23. See s.23(2) for liability for substitute agents.

[76] *ibid.*, Sched. 1, para. 3.

[77] *ibid.*, s.24.

As in the case of other powers conferred by the Trustee Act 2000, the power to delegate to investment managers, nominees and custodians applies to trusts whenever created, but is subject to any restriction or exclusion in the trust instrument or other legislation.[78] Further details of the general power of delegation will be found in Chapter 20.

J. General Duty in Choosing Investments; Ethical Investments

We have seen that the Trustees Act 2000 provides a framework for the exercise of trustee investment powers. The traditional standard of the "prudent man of business"[79] has been reformulated by section 1 of the Act as a duty to exercise such care and skill as is reasonable in the circumstances. No doubt it remains true that trustees must avoid investments "which are attended with hazard".[80] Although a trustee now has statutory power to "make any kind of investment that he could make if he were absolutely entitled to the assets of the trust",[81] the fact that he is not absolutely entitled places him in a different position from an absolute owner, who may speculate as he pleases. He must also consider the competing interests of the life tenant and the remainderman, investing so as to provide a reasonable income, and to keep secure the capital.[82] We have seen that the modern "portfolio theory"[83] requires the investment decisions of trustees to be made and evaluated in the context of the portfolio as a whole rather than in relation to individual assets.

These general investment duties were reviewed in *Nestlé v. National Westminster Bank plc*,[84] where the remainder beneficiary complained that the fund of £270,000 would have been worth over £1m if properly invested. The claim failed because, although the trustees had failed to appreciate the scope of their investment power and to conduct regular reviews, the beneficiary had not proved that these failures had resulted in wrong investment decisions and loss. Although the investments fell "woefully short" of maintaining the real value of the fund, failure to maintain the value was not in itself a breach of trust, as to do so would require extraordinary skill and

---

[78] T.A. 2000, ss.26, 27.
[79] *Speight v. Gaunt* (1883) 9 App.Cas. 1; *cf. Nestlé v. National Westminster Bank plc* [1993] 1 W.L.R. 1260 (standard of prudence regarded as "undemanding" and likely to result in complacency and inactivity). See generally [1983] Conv. 127 (P. Pearce and A. Samuels).
[80] *Learoyd v. Whiteley* (1887) 12 App.Cas. 727 at 733.
[81] Trustee Act 2000, s.3.
[82] *post*, Chap. 19.
[83] *ante*, p. 537. This is reflected in Pensions Act 1995, s.35; *ante*, p. 482.
[84] [1993] 1 W.L.R. 1260; (1992) 142 N.L.J. 1279 (J. Martin); [1993] Conv. 63 (A. Kenny); [1998] Conv. 352 (G. Watt and M. Stauch).

luck, and would at times be impossible.[85] Further, the trustees were entitled and bound to consider tax implications, which justified investment in government stock rather than equities where the life tenant was non-resident. In the absence of such special factors, however, it was accepted that trustees should invest at least half of the fund in equities. If the case had arisen after the Trustee Act 2000, no doubt the trustees would have been held to be in breach of the statutory duty of care, but the issue of establishing loss would remain. A trustee who commits a mere error of judgment is unlikely to be held in breach of the duty of care.[86] Further, it has been held that a beneficiary could not successfully claim against the trustee over an investment decision unless no reasonable trustee could have made it.[87]

The question whether trustees may adopt non-financial investment criteria arose in *Cowan v. Scargill.*[88]

A mineworkers' pension fund with large assets and very wide powers of investment was managed by ten trustees, of whom five, including the defendant, were appointed by the National Union of Mineworkers. They were assisted in investment decisions by an advisory panel of experts. An investment plan was submitted, which the union trustees, on the basis of union policy, refused to accept unless it was amended so that there should be no increase in overseas investments; those already made should be withdrawn; and there should be no investment in energies in competition with coal. It was held that the trustees would be in breach of duty if they refused to adopt the investment strategy. They must exercise their powers in the best interests of present and future beneficiaries. If the purpose of the trust was the provision of financial benefit, the best interests of the beneficiaries normally meant their best *financial* interests. This duty to the beneficiaries was paramount. The trustees must exercise their investment powers so as to yield the best return, putting aside personal interests and social and political views. If investments in, for example, armaments, tobacco or South African companies, were beneficial, they must not refrain because of their own views, however sincere. But financial benefit was not *inevitably* paramount. If all the

---

[85] See *Jones v. AMP Perpetual Trustee Company NZ Ltd* [1994] 1 N.Z.L.R. 690 (trustee is neither insurer nor guarantor of fund).

[86] See *Jones v. AMP Perpetual Trustee Company NZ Ltd, supra* (not liable for mere error of judgment in retaining shares in a falling market).

[87] *Wight v. Olswang (No. 2)* [2000] Lloyd's Rep. P.N. 662 (claim concerning retention of shares which trustee had discretion to retain).

[88] [1985] Ch. 270; (1984) 81 L.S.Gaz. 2291 (S. Butler); All E.R.Rev. 1984, 306 (P. Clarke). See also Uniform Prudent Investor Act 1994, s.5 (U.S.A.), requiring investment solely in the interest of the beneficiaries; *Modern International Developments in Trust Law* (ed. D. Hayton), Chap. 11 (J. Langbein).

beneficiaries were adults with strict views on, say, tobacco, it might not "benefit" them to make such investments. Here, however, there was no justification for reducing the benefit because the trustees had an investment policy intended to assist the union or the industry. The trustees were pursuing union policy, and the ultimate sanction was removal.[89]

It is difficult to see, however, why the trustees would be failing in their duties if they confined themselves to the investments proposed by the union trustees. In the case of a pension fund, maintenance of the prosperity of the industry must be in the financial interests of the beneficiaries, and to invest in a competing industry may be harmful.[90] Overseas investments may be risky, and there is an ample range of authorised investments at home: "no trust fund is so big as to exhaust the home market."[91] Perhaps the outcome would have been different if the union trustees had not argued their case on ideology rather than law.[92]

Presumably there would be no breach if trustees were to pursue an ethical investment policy only after satisfying themselves that their selected investments were at least as financially sound as those rejected on ethical grounds (a "socially sensitive" policy).[93] The point is that they must not fetter their discretion by adopting a policy which excludes any consideration of the financial merits of a particular class of investments (a "socially dictated" policy). Thus in *Martin v. City of Edinburgh District Council*[94] the Scottish court granted a declaration that a policy to oppose apartheid by disinvesting in companies which had South African interests was a breach of duty, even though no loss was incurred. The trustees (the local authority) had failed to consider whether their policy was in the best financial interests of the beneficiaries. These principles should be adhered to whether the trustees have a negative investment policy (to avoid certain types of investments) or, less commonly, a positive investment policy (to make only certain types of investments). They

---

[89] Damages would not be recoverable unless the policy was implemented and caused loss, which is unlikely.

[90] This argument was rejected by Megarry V.-C. on the facts. The miners' pension fund is fully funded and is unusual in that its value far exceeds that of the declining coal industry, and there are many more pensioners than miners.

[91] [1985] Conv. 52 at 53 (P. Pearce and A. Samuels). Overseas investments are permitted by the Trustee Act 2000.

[92] (1986) 102 L.Q.R. 32 (J. Farrar and J. Maxton). See also (1980) 79 Mich. L.Rev. 72 (J. Langbein and R. Posner).

[93] See generally (1990) 4 *Trust Law & Practice* 25 (P. Docking and I. Pittaway); (1990) 87/23 L.S.Gaz. 17 (N. Convey); (1991) 5 *Trust Law International* 157 (R. Ellison); (1994) 8 *Trust Law International* 10 (L. Irish and A. Kent); (1995) 9 *Trust Law International* 71 (Lord Nicholls).

[94] [1988] S.L.T. 329.

must remember that their duty is the provision of financial benefits, "not the reform of the world."[95]

In the case of a charity, an additional factor is that the trust is pursuing an aim, so that the question arises whether the trustees can invest in undertakings which are incompatible with their objective. For example, can trustees of a cancer charity invest in the tobacco industry?[96] As we have seen, trustees (including charity trustees) must have regard to "the suitability to the trust of investments of the same kind as any particular investment proposed to be made or retained".[97] In *Harries v. Church Commissioners for England*[98] the plaintiff claimed that the Commissioners, whose purpose was to promote the Christian faith through the Church of England, should not invest in a manner incompatible with that purposes even if this involved a risk of significant financial detriment. It was held that they could take non-financial ethical considerations into account only in so far as they could do so without jeopardising the profitability of investments. Their charitable purpose would be best served by seeking the maximum financial return. There might be rare cases where certain investments would directly conflict with the objects of the charity (as in the cancer/tobacco example). In these cases the trustees should not make such investments even if this results in financial detriment, but this was unlikely to arise because of the width of other investments. There might also be rare cases where a particular investment might alienate potential donors or recipients. The Commissioners already had a policy which excluded investment in armaments, gambling, tobacco, newspapers and South Africa, considering that there was an adequate width of alternative investments, and the propriety of this was not doubted.[99]

A settlor may secure ethical investments by providing in the instrument that the trustees must or must not make certain kinds of investments.[1] Where the trustees have delegated their investment powers, any such direction by the settlor will be reflected in the policy statement which they must prepare for the agent.[2] Where the trust instrument is silent on the matter, trustees may include ethical

---

[95] (1991) 5 *Trust Law International* 157 at 165–166; *Harries v. Church Commissioners for England, infra* (trustees must not make moral statements at the expense of the trust).

[96] See B.M.A. Report on Investment in the U.K. Tobacco Industry; (1982) 45 M.L.R. 268 (H. Beynon); (1987) 1 *Trust Law & Practice* 162 (J. Thurston); Annual Report of the Charity Commissioners, 1987, paras. 41–45; Annual Report 1996, paras. 54–55 (pooled funds set up to exclude incompatible investments).

[97] Trustee Act 2000, s.4(3)(a).

[98] [1992] 1 W.L.R. 1241; [1992] Conv. 115 (R. Nobles); (1992) 55 M.L.R. 587 (P. Luxton); (1992) 6 *Trust Law International* 119 at 123 (Lord Browne-Wilkinson).

[99] The Commissioners appeared to have fettered their discretion, but this seems permissible where the excluded investments conflict with the charity's purpose, even if not directly incompatible.

[1] Trustee Act 2000, s.6(1)(b); *Harries v. Church Commissioners for England, supra.*

[2] Trustee Act 2000, s.15(2).

considerations in the policy statement, subject to their general law duties discussed above. The guidance in the policy statement must be formulated "with a view to ensuring that the functions will be exercised in the best interests of the trust",[3] and the statutory duty of care applies to its preparation.[4]

The investment policy of pension trustees must now be explicit as to the extent (if any) of ethical considerations.[5]

K. Trustees Holding Controlling Interest in a Company

Difficult questions arise in relation to the trustees' duties where the trust owns a controlling interest in a company. The first question is whether the shareholding is a proper investment at all. If the company is a private company, as is the usual case in this situation, express authorisation was needed prior to the Trustee Act 2000 to purchase such shares. Now the issue is whether such a purchase satisfies the standard investment criteria laid down in section 4 of the new Act.[6] Usually the question is one of retention. A provision expressly authorising retention is desirable (whether the holding is a majority or a minority), but the right to retain will be implied where the trust deed or will specifically refers to the property, as in the case of a specific bequest on trust.[7] A right to retain does not impliedly authorise a right to purchase more of the shares.[8]

But that is not the end of the matter. It is not sufficient for the trustees to determine that the investment is suitable, and leave it at that. For the company or its directors may engage in practices which are wholly unsuitable for a trust investment, such as speculative activities. Can the trustees shelter behind the directors, whose acts they are in a position to control?

In *Bartlett v. Barclays Bank Trust Co. Ltd*,[9] the bank was trustee of the Bartlett trust. The sole asset of the trust was a shareholding amounting to virtually all the shares in a family property company, which held some £500,000 worth of rent-producing properties.

Tax would need to be paid on the death of the life tenants, and a suggestion was made that cash would be more easily raised if the company went public; and merchant bankers advised that a

---

[3] Trustee Act 2000, s.15(3).

[4] *ibid.* Sched, 1, para. 3.

[5] Pensions Act 1995, s.35; Occupational Pension Schemes (Investment, and Assignment, Forfeiture, Bankruptcy etc) Amendment Regulations (S.I. 1999 No. 1849).

[6] *ante.*, p. 538.

[7] *Re Pugh* [1887] W.N. 143; *Re Van Straubenzee* [1902] 2 Ch. 779.

[8] *Re Pugh, supra.*

[9] [1980] Ch. 515; *Walker v. Stones* [2000] 4 All E.R. 412. See (1995) 9 *Trust Law International* 71 at 76 (Lord Nicholls).

public issue would be more successful if the company were not only a manager of existing property, but a developer of new properties also. The bank agreed to a policy of active development, so long as the income available to the income beneficiaries was not prejudiced.

The board then embarked upon speculative developments, one of which was a disaster, because planning permission for the intended office development could not be obtained. This resulted in a large loss to the trust shareholding.

The Bank was held liable. It was not sufficient that they believed the directors to be competent and capable of running a profitable business. Their duty was "to conduct the business of the trust with the same care as an ordinary prudent man of business would extend to his own affairs."[10] To do that it was necessary, especially as the bank was aware that the company was moving into speculative development, to get the fullest information on the conduct of the business; and not merely to be content with the supply of information which they received as shareholders. Cross J. in *Re Lucking's Will Trusts*[11] held that a controlling shareholder should insist on being represented on the board; but Brightman J. treated this as one convenient way of ensuring that all the necessary information was available.[12]

So the controlling shareholder must obtain the necessary information, as a means of "enabling the trustee to safeguard the interests of the beneficiaries."[13] How do the trustees do that? Ultimately, of course, the majority shareholder will get its way; as by adopting "the draconian course of threatening to remove, or actually removing, the board in favour of compliant directors,"[14] which is asking a lot of the trust department of a bank. Brightman J. was able to avoid the practical difficulties of such a course by finding that the members of the board were "reasonable persons, and would (as I find) have followed any reasonable policy desired by the bank had the bank's wishes been indicated to the board."[15]

---

[10] [1980] Ch. 515 at 531, quoting *Speight v. Gaunt* (1883) 9 App.Cas. 1. Now the question would be whether the trustees had complied with the duty of care under Trustee Act 2000, s.1.

[11] [1968] 1 W.L.R. 866 at 874.

[12] [1980] Ch. 515 at 533. "Other methods may be equally satisfactory and convenient depending upon the circumstances of the individual case. Alternatives which spring to mind are the receipt of copies of the agenda and minutes of board meetings if regularly held, the receipt of monthly management accounts in the case of a trading concern . . . the possibilities are endless. . . . " See *Re Miller's Trust Deed* (1978) 75 L.S.Gaz. 454, where one of the trustees was a member of a firm of accountants which acted as auditors for the company.

[13] *ibid.* at 534.

[14] *ibid.* at 530.

[15] *ibid.*

L. Extension of Investment Powers by the Court

Trustees may apply to court under section 57 of the Trustee Act 1925[16] or under the Variation of Trusts Act 1958[17] to widen investment powers. An application under section 57 is more convenient provided the beneficial interests are not affected.[18] Applications have been rare since the passing of the Trustee Investment Act 1961, the court taking the view (here described as the *Re Kolb* principle[19]), that special circumstances have to be shown to justify an extension beyond the powers conferred by a modern statute. The question arose in *Mason v. Farbrother*,[20] concerning a pension fund which had limited investment powers. By 1982, as a result of inflation, the fund had vastly increased, and the trustees wished to have wider powers. They applied to court under section 57 of the Trustee Act 1925.[21] It was held that there was no absolute rule that the court should not widen investment powers after the 1961 Act. The court approved a wide modern clause, as there were special circumstances, which included the effect of inflation and the fact that it was in the nature of a public fund.

A different approach was subsequently taken by Megarry V.-C. in *Trustees of the British Museum v. Att.-Gen.*,[22] where the trustees were granted a relaxation of their existing scheme, made in 1960, as they needed a wider choice and a power to invest abroad. The trustees were eminent and responsible, and had highly skilled advice. The size of the fund (£5 million–£6 million) made it unlike a private trust and more like a pension fund or large institutional investor. Referring to *Mason v. Farbrother*,[23] where, as we have seen, the court treated the *Re Kolb*[24] principle as still binding in the absence of special circumstances, Megarry V.-C. disagreed that inflation could be called a special circumstance, and preferred to say that the *Re Kolb* principle had gone, although if the statutory powers were increased, the principle could apply again. Now, as we have seen, the Trustee Act 2000 has revolutionised investment powers,

---

[16] *post*, p. 634.

[17] *post*, p. 637.

[18] *Anker-Petersen v. Anker-Petersen*; (1998) 12 *Trust Law International* 166 (decided 1991).

[19] *Re Kolb's Will Trusts* [1962] Ch. 531; *Re Cooper's Settlement* [1962] Ch. 826; *Re Clarke's Will Trusts* [1961] 1 W.L.R. 1471.

[20] [1983] 2 All E.R. 1078; [1984] Conv. 373 (H. Norman).

[21] The application under the 1958 Act did not proceed because of difficulties with the representative parties. The aspect concerning the court's inherent jurisdiction to approve a compromise is dealt with *post*, p. 633.

[22] [1984] 1 W.L.R. 418. See also *Steel v. Wellcome Custodian Trustees Ltd* [1988] 1 W.L.R. 167; [1988] Conv. 380 (B. Dale). (Trustees of large charity with funds of £3,200 million including share capital in W. Ltd which could not be sold sought wider powers of beneficial owner. Variation approved, having regard to size of fund, eminence of trustees and provisions requiring advice).

[23] *supra*.

[24] [1962] Ch. 531, *supra*.

making it unlikely that trustees will have much need to apply to court for extended powers. Should they do so, for example if they should wish to purchase land abroad (which the new Act does not permit), the *Re Kolb* principle would again be relevant. It is more likely that applications to court after the commencement of the new Act will involve attempts to lift specific restrictions and exclusions imposed by the settlor. In such cases the *Re Kolb* principle would not apply, as the trustees would not be seeking powers beyond those contained in the Trustee Act 2000. The issue for the court would be whether it would be justified in overturning the wishes of the settlor.

3. Duty to Distribute. Satisfaction of Claims

A. Liability for Wrongful Payments

A trustee is obliged to make payments of income and capital as they become due, and to make them to the persons properly entitled. Failure to do so is a breach of trust, which the trustee must normally make good, such as for example, a payment based on a forged document,[25] or upon an erroneous construction of a document,[26] even if legal advice was taken,[27] or without regard to the entitlement of illegitimate beneficiaries.[28]

Where a trustee makes an overpayment of income or of instalments of capital, the error may be adjusted in later payments.[29] If the payment is to a person who is not entitled, the trustee's right of recovery is a quasi-contractual one, and the money will be recoverable if the mistake is one of fact or law.[30] An unpaid or underpaid beneficiary may, in addition to his right to sue the trustee, proceed against the property in the hands of the wrongly paid recipient not being a bona fide purchaser for value without notice.[31] A trustee-beneficiary who fails to pay himself in full has been held to have no remedy,[32] but this rule appears too extreme.[33]

---

[25] *Eaves v. Hickson* (1861) 30 Beav. 136.

[26] *Hilliard v. Fulford* (1876) 4 Ch.D. 389.

[27] *National Trustees Company of Australasia Ltd v. General Finance Company of Australasia Ltd* [1905] A.C. 373.

[28] Family Law Reform Act 1987, s.20, reversing the previous position under F.L.R.A. 1969, s.17.

[29] *Dibbs v. Goren* (1849) 11 Beav. 483 (administration by the court); *Re Musgrave* [1916] 2 Ch. 417; [1994] 2 R.L.R. 44 (P. Matthews).

[30] *Kleinwort Benson Ltd v. Lincoln City Council* [1999] 2 A.C. 349.

[31] *Re Diplock* [1948] Ch. 465.

[32] *Re Horne* [1905] 1 Ch. 76.

[33] It may have been overtaken by developments in the law of restitution.

B. Doubtful Claims

i. Application to Court for Directions. Where the trustees are in any doubt in relation to the claims of the beneficiaries, they may make an application to the court for directions; and will be protected if they obey the directions of the court.[34] This course can now be taken with a minimum of complication.[35] In this way problems of construction of the trust instrument and difficulties in administering the trust can be brought before the court, so that the trustees are not forced to take the risk of making decisions upon a false premise.[36] An application to the court can also be helpful in cases where the trustees are in difficulty in connection with the exercise of a discretion, for instance a discretionary power to make advancements. In such a case the trustees surrender their discretion to the court, and must put all relevant information before it to enable the discretion to be exercised.[37] Trustees cannot, however, surrender the future exercise of discretions to the court.[38] Trustees or beneficiaries may, in suitable cases, apply for the trust to be administered by the court,[39] but an unsuccessful applicant may be liable for costs.

ii. Payment into Court. Where beneficiaries cannot be ascertained, or where for some exceptional reason trustees cannot obtain a good discharge from the trust, there is a residual power in trustees to pay the trust moneys into court.[40] The residue of the fund in *Re Gillingham Bus Disaster Fund*,[41] for instance, was eventually paid into court.

But this will not be tolerated by the court as a means of trustees evading their obligations when difficulties arise.[42] It is a last resort when all other methods of dealing with the problem have proved unsuccessful. Trustees who pay trust funds into court when a different course was preferable, may be liable for costs.[43]

iii. "Benjamin" Order. The court has a power to authorise distribution of the whole of the assets of an estate, although not all the

---

[34] *Re Londonderry's Settlement* [1965] Ch. 918; *Finers v. Miro* [1991] 1 W.L.R. 35.

[35] R.S.C., Ord. 85, r. 2; C.P.R. 1998, Sched. 1; C.P.R. 1998, Part 8.

[36] See also A.J.A. 1985, s.48, giving the court power to authorise action to be taken in reliance on counsel's opinion respecting the contruction of a will or trust.

[37] *Marley v. Mutual Security Merchant Bank and Trust Co. Ltd* [1991] 3 All E.R. 198. For the position in Scotland, see *Harding v. Joy Manufacturing Holdings Ltd, The Times*, April 21, 1999.

[38] *Re Allen-Meyrick's W.T.* [1966] 1 W.L.R. 499.

[39] See (1968) 84 L.Q.R. 68 (A. Hawkins).

[40] Payment into court furnishes an exception to the rule that a majority of trustees cannot defeat a dissentient minority, for T.A. 1925, s. 63, provides that the payment may in certain circumstances be made by a majority of the trustees.

[41] [1959] Ch. 62; *ante*, p. 242.

[42] See *Re Knight's Trust* (1859) 27 Beav. 45.

[43] *Re Cull's Trusts* (1875) L.R. 20 Eq. 561; (1968) 84 L.Q.R. 64 at 65–67 (A. Hawkins).

beneficiaries or creditors have made themselves known so as to be able to receive their share. A typical situation is where the whereabouts or continued existence of a certain beneficiary is not known. The procedure is sometimes known as a "Benjamin" order, and its purpose is to protect those distributing the assets.[44] If those entitled who have received nothing under the distribution eventually come forward to establish their claim, they may still be able to proceed, within the period of limitation, against the person wrongly paid,[45] or against the property itself. Such an order will of course only be made after all practicable inquiries have been instituted. A modern example as *Re Green's Will Trusts*,[46] where the testatrix left her property to her son, providing that it should go to charity if he did not claim it by the year 2020. The son had disappeared on a bombing raid in 1943, and all but his mother were satisfied that he was dead. A "Benjamin" order was made, allowing distribution to the charity, it being no bar to such an order that it was contrary to the intention of the testatrix.[47] "Missing beneficiary" insurance may be a preferable course, especially in the case of a small estate.[48]

iv. Distribution after Advertisement. Under the Trustee Act 1925, s.27, trustees have themselves the power to advertise for claimants[49] and, after compliance with certain formalities, the power to distribute the whole of their trust assets to claimants who have made themselves known. Those who subsequently demonstrate an entitlement are enabled to proceed against the property distributed, save when it is in the hands of a purchaser.[50]

v. Setting Aside a Fund. The Trustee Act 1925, s.26,[51] provides a procedure whereby trustees can set aside out of trust assets a sum to meet any potential liabilities under a lease or rentcharge, and then to distribute the remainder of the trust assets to those entitled. Again, should the sum set aside prove insufficient, those entitled to the extra sums may still follow the distributed property. In the case of contingent liabilities outside section 26, the trustees can either

---

[44] *Re Benjamin* [1902] 1 Ch. 723; *Re Gess* [1942] Ch. 37; *Re Taylor* [1969] 2 Ch. 245.

[45] *Ministry of Health v. Simpson* [1951] A.C. 251; *Re Lowe's W.T.* [1973] 1 W.L.R. 882 at 887. The overpaid beneficiary may be protected from this risk by "missing beneficiary" insurance; *Re Evans* [1999] 2 All E.R. 777.

[46] [1985] 3 All E.R. 455.

[47] Criticised on this point in [1986] Conv. 138 (P. Luxton).

[48] *Re Evans* [1999] 2 All E.R. 777.

[49] Normally creditors, but also beneficiaries, for example claimants under an intestacy. Advertising is not sufficient protection against contingent debts; *Re Yorke* [1997] 4 All E.R. 907. For the application of s.27 to pension funds, see (1995) 9 *Trust Law International* 127 (P. Docking).

[50] s.27(2)(*a*); and see *Re Aldhous* [1955] 1 W.L.R. 459.

[51] As amended by Landlord and Tenant (Covenants) Act 1995, Sched. 1.

retain a fund, distribute under a court order, or obtain an indemnity from the beneficiaries and then distribute.[52]

C. Relief under Section 61

A trustee who makes an erroneous distribution may be relieved from liability if he acted honestly and reasonably and ought fairly to be excused.[53]

D. Discharge

On the termination of the trust, the trustees should present their final accounts and obtain a discharge from the beneficiaries. The best protection is provided by a release by deed, for that places on a complaining beneficiary the burden of proving fraud, concealment, mistake or undue influence.[54] But a trustee is not entitled to a release by deed.[55] If the beneficiaries are unwilling to give one, the trustees may apply to the court for the accounts to be taken and approved.[56]

---

[52] See Mellows, *The Law of Succession* (5th ed.), p. 379; *Re Yorke* [1997] 4 All E.R. 907 (contingent liabilities of Lloyd's underwriter).
[53] *post*, p. 667; *Re Evans, supra.*
[54] *Fowler v. Wyatt* (1857) 24 Beav. 232.
[55] *King v. Mullins* (1852) 1 Drew. at 311, *per* Kindersley V.-C.
[56] Underhill and Hayton (15th ed.) p. 803.

Chapter 19

DUTIES OF TRUSTEES IN RELATION TO THE BENEFICIARIES

1. DUTY TO MAINTAIN EQUALITY BETWEEN THE BENEFICIARIES

A trustee is under a general duty to maintain equality between the beneficiaries. This duty forms the basis of the specific rules of conversion and apportionment, discussed below, which apply as between life tenant and remainderman. It is not, however, confined to such cases. A modern example of the wider general duty is *Lloyds Bank plc v. Duker*,[1] where a testator's residuary estate included 999 company shares. He left 46/80 to his wife, and the rest to other beneficiaries. In spite of the general rule that a beneficiary is entitled *in specie* to his share of divisible personalty held on trust for sale, it was held that the wife could not claim 574 shares, as such a majority holding would be worth more than 46/80. The only fair solution was for the trustees to sell the shares and divide the proceeds in the

---

[1] [1987] 1 W.L.R. 1324. See also *Nestlé v. National Westminster Bank plc* [1993] 1 W.L.R. 1261; *X v. A* [2000] 1 All E.R. 490.

specified proportions. Of course, where the trustees have a discretionary power to choose between various classes of beneficiaries, the duty to act impartially has no application. In such a case the trustees are entitled to prefer some beneficiaries over others, provided they do not take irrelevant matters into account.[2]

A. Rule in Howe v. Earl of Dartmouth[3]

i. Life Tenant and Remainderman. A trustee must act impartially between life tenant and remainderman. This duty applies to the selection of investments[4]; and the rules governing investment by trustees are an attempt to strike a balance between the provision of income for the life tenant and the preservation of the capital for the remainderman.[5] So long as those rules are observed, a trustee is usually under no duty to rearrange the investments so as to balance equally the interests of the life tenant and remainderman.[6] Nor, if there are investments in the fund which have ceased to be authorised, are the trustees under any immediate duty to convert them into authorised investments.[7] However the fund is invested, the normal rule is that the tenant for life takes all the income; the remainderman's interest is in the capital. The capital is not of course available until the life tenant's death; but he may, if he wishes, deal with or dispose of his reversionary interest in the fund.

There are, as we will see, some situations in which there is a duty to convert into authorised investments; and this duty carries with it a duty to apportion the income earned before the conversion is effected.

ii. The Duty to Convert. A duty to convert (*i.e.* sell) and reinvest in authorised investments may arise by reason of the existence of an express trust to sell or to convert, or, in the case of a

---

[2] *Edge v. Pensions Ombudsman* [2000] Ch. 602.

[3] (1943) 7 Conv.(N.S.) 128 and 191 (S. Bailey); (1952) 16 Conv.(N.S.) 347 (L. Sheridan).

[4] *Raby v. Ridehalgh* (1855) 7 De G. M. & G. 104 at 109; *Re Dick* [1891] 1 Ch. 423 at 431.

[5] *ante*, p. 532. There is no duty to preserve the real value of the capital; *Nestlé v. National Westminster Bank plc* [1993] 1 W.L.R. 1261 (suggesting also that trustees entitled to incline towards high income investments if rich remainderman and poor life tenant).

[6] "It is perhaps surprising that equity has not cast upon trustees, in every such case, a duty to convert the trust property as soon as practicable into something more likely to produce an equitable result" (1943) 7 Conv.(N.S.) 128 at 129 (S. Bailey); *Re Searle* [1900] 2 Ch. 829 at 834; *cf. Re Smith* (1971) 18 D.L.R. (3d) 405, (1972) 50 Can.B.R.116 (M. Cullity) (duty to reinvest where authorised shares producing low return because of company policy to pursue capital growth).

[7] The point is less likely to arise after the extension of investment powers by the Trustee Act 2000.

bequest of residuary personalty, under the rule in *Howe v. Earl of Dartmouth*.[8]

(a) *Express Trust for Sale of Personalty.* The trustees' duties under an express trust, of course, depend on the terms of the trust. It is important to note that an express trust to convert involves, as does a duty to convert under the rule in *Howe v. Earl of Dartmouth*,[9] an apportionment of the income pending conversion.[10] A mere power to sell is not sufficient to create a trust to convert.[11] In the case of an express trust for sale of land, the duty to sell is counter-balanced by a power to postpone sale for an indefinite period, notwithstanding any provision to the contrary in the instrument, and the trustees are not liable in any way for postponing sale in the exercise of their discretion.[12]

(b) *Rule in Howe v. Earl of Dartmouth.* *Howe v. Earl of Dartmouth* establishes that, subject to a contrary provision in the will, there is a duty to convert where residuary personalty is settled by will in favour of persons in succession. The trustees should convert all such parts of it as are of a wasting[13] or future or reversionary[14] nature or consist of unauthorised securities,[15] into authorised investments.

Thus property such as royalties and copyrights[16] should be converted in the interest of the remainderman. For these may be of reduced or of no value at the life tenant's death. On the other hand, "future" property such as a remainder or reversionary interest, or other property which at present produces no income, is of no immediate benefit to the tenant for life. In his interest therefore it should be converted into income-bearing properties. And, as we shall see, provision is made for apportionment between the life tenant and remainderman of the value of such property when it falls into possession.[17]

---

[8] (1802) 7 Ves.Jr. 137. The duty to sell the assets of an intestate has been replaced by a power of sale; A.E.A. 1925, s.33, as amended by Trusts of Land and Appointment of Trustees Act 1996, Sched. 2.

[9] *supra.*

[10] *Gibson v. Bott* (1802) 7 Ves.Jr. 89.

[11] *Re Pitcairn* [1896] 2 Ch. 199.

[12] Trusts of Land and Appointment of Trustees Act 1996, s.4. One effect of this Act is to abolish the statutory trust for sale.

[13] Such as mines or ships which will eventually become worthless; or patents or copyrights which expire.

[14] *i.e.* property which will only come into possession after the death of the life tenant.

[15] *i.e.* not authorised by the terms of the will, nor by Trustee Act 2000. *cf. Re Smith* (1971) 18 D.L.R. (3d) 405, *ante*, p. 554 (authorised securities). See further [1999] Conv. 84 at 101–102 (R. Mitchell) for the view that there is no clear authority that the rule cannot apply to authorised investments.

[16] *Re Evans' W.T.* [1921] 2 Ch. 309; *Re Sullivan* [1930] 1 Ch. 84.

[17] *Re Earl of Chesterfield's Trust* (1883) 24 Ch.D. 643; *post*, p. 557.

It will be seen that, on its terms, the rule is of limited application. It does not apply to life-time settlements[18]; nor to specific as opposed to residuary bequests[19] (for the settlor's or testator's intention in such cases is for the specific property settled to be enjoyed successively). Nor does it apply to leaseholds.[20]

iii. Apportionment. Where there is a duty to convert, whether under an express trust for sale of personalty or under the rule in *Howe v. Earl of Dartmouth*,[21] there is, in the absence of an intention that the life tenant shall enjoy the income until sale, a duty also to apportion fairly between the life tenant and the remainderman the original property pending conversion. The detailed rules appear complicated at first sight; but they are simple if their purpose is understood.

(a) *Wasting, Hazardous or Unauthorised Investments.* It is assumed that wasting, hazardous and unauthorised securities produce income in excess of that which the life tenant should reasonably receive; and do so at the expense of the security of the capital. With such property therefore the object of the apportionment rule is to provide that the life tenant receives an income which represents the current yield on authorised investments,[22] and that the excess is added to capital.[23] If the interest received is less than 4 per cent, the balance should be made up out of subsequent income or from the proceeds of the unauthorised investments when sold.[24]

The question arises of the time at which the capital should be valued for the purpose of calculating the 4 per cent income. A distinction must be made between cases where the trustees are given power to postpone conversion and those where they are not.

First: where there is no power to postpone. In this situation the trustees should convert within the "executor's year"[25] the period during which the administration of the deceased's estate is expected to be completed. If the investments are sold within the year, the net

[18] *Re Van Straubenzee* [1901] 2 Ch. 779.
[19] *ibid.* at 782.
[20] *post*, p. 559.
[21] (1802) 7 Ves.Jr. 137.
[22] The life tenant's income was fixed at 4 per cent in *Re Baker* [1924] 2 Ch. 271, and applied at that figure in *Re Berry* [1962] Ch. 97 at 113. However, this became out of line with the return from gilt-edged investments, although interest rates are low at the time of writing. Trustees who have to decide what income to pay may be well advised to take instructions from the court. Interest rates in other contexts have been increased, for example judgment debts, legacies and overdue taxes. See also *Wallersteiner v. Moir (No. 2)* [1975] Q.B. 373; *Bartlett v. Barclays Bank Trust Co. Ltd (No. 2)* [1980] Ch. 515.
[23] The life tenant will of course receive the income from the capital as thus increased.
[24] *Re Fawcett* [1940] Ch. 402.
[25] A.E.A. 1925, s.44.

proceeds of sale are taken as their value[26]; if not, these investments are valued *en bloc* as at the end of one year from the death.[27] In either case the life tenant is entitled, as from the date of the death of the testator, to four per cent on that sum.

Secondly: where the trustees postpone sale in the exercise of a power to postpone.[28] The executor's year here has no relevance. There is a duty to convert, but no time within which the conversion should be effected. The date of the valuation is the date of the testator's death.

In *Brown v. Gellatly*,[29] the estate consisted of (i) some ships (wasting assets) which the testator directed his executors to continue to use until they could be conveniently sold, and (ii) unauthorised securities. Both were retained for more than a year from the death. The question was whether, for the purpose of apportionment, the assets should be valued at the date of death or at a year from the death.

Lord Cairns held that the ships, being subject to a power to postpone sale, should be valued at the death; the unauthorised investments, on the other hand, a year from the death.

(b) *Future, Reversionary or other Non-Income Producing Property.* Where personalty which is subject to a duty to convert includes reversionary property, it is necessary, in the interest of the life tenant, to provide for apportionment[30]; otherwise the life tenant would obtain no benefit from the property until it fell into possession. The reversion should be sold and the proceeds re-invested; until that is done there is no way of producing income for the life tenant. When it has been sold, there is still the problem of determining how much of the proceeds of sale should be apportioned to capital and how much to the life tenant. This is done by[31] ascertaining the sum "which, put out at 4 per cent per annum . . . and accumulating at compound interest at that rate with yearly rests,[32] and deducting income tax at the standard rate, would, with the accumulation of interest, have produced, at the respective dates of receipt, the amounts actually received; and that the aggregate of the sums so

---

[26] *Re Fawcett, supra.*

[27] *Dimes v. Scott* (1828) 4 Russ. 195.

[28] We are here concerned with an administrative power to postpone which is not sufficient to exclude the rule; see *post*, p. 559.

[29] (1867) L.R. 2 Ch. App. 751; *Re Owen* [1912] 1 Ch. 519; *Re Parry* [1947] Ch. 23; *Re Berry* [1962] Ch. 97.

[30] The interest may be contingent: *Re Hobson* (1855) 55 L.J.Ch. 422. The rule also applies where the sum in question is itself a mixture of capital and income; *Re Chance's W.T.* [1962] Ch. 593. A reversionary interest in land is not within the rule (*Re Woodhouse* [1941] Ch. 336).

[31] *Re Earl of Chesterfield's Trusts* (1883) 24 Ch.D. 643.

[32] *i.e.* the income is transferred to capital at the end of each year.

ascertained ought to be treated as principal and be applied accordingly, and the residue should be treated as income." In other words, the proceeds of sale of the reversion are part principal, part interest. The principal is the sum which, if invested at four per cent at the date of the testator's death, would have produced the sum now received. The balance goes to the tenant for life.[33]

iv. Contrary Intention. All the rules above discussed are subject to a contrary intention by the testator.[34] A number of very fine points of construction arise; but the matter can only be discussed in outline here. The onus is on the person alleging that the equitable rules are excluded.[35]

(a) *Express Trust to Convert.* An express trust to convert personalty normally carries with it the duty to apportion the income received pending conversion.[36] There is no question in this situation of a contrary intention with regard to conversion; but there may be a contrary intention with regard to apportionment. This will arise where there is an indication of intention that, although the property should be converted, the life tenant is to enjoy the whole income produced by it pending conversion.

Such an intention is commonly indicated by the inclusion of a provision to the effect that "the income of so much of the residue as for the time being shall remain unsold, shall be applied as if the same were income arising from investments of the proceeds of sale thereof."[37]

It may of course be indicated in other ways. The question depends upon the construction of the particular instrument. A power in the trustees to postpone a sale in their discretion is not a sufficient indication. Such a provision does not entitle the life tenant to the income produced by unauthorised investments.[38]

---

[33] The calculation can be made by taking the value of the reversion on sale or on falling in (£x), and working backwards year by year until the date of the testator's death. If the standard rate of income tax is 25 per cent, the net income earned at 4 per cent on £100 of capital is £3.00. The sum needed to produce £x after *one* year of investment can be found by applying the formula:

$$\frac{£x \times 100}{103}$$

The application of this formula *to the sum* so calculated will produce the sums needed to produce £x after *two* years of investment. The calculation then needs to be continued back to the date of the testator's death. See Parker and Mellows, *Modern Law of Trusts* (7th ed.), pp. 580–581.

[34] See [1999] Conv. 84 at 98–103 (R. Mitchell).

[35] *MacDonald v. Irvine* (1878) 8 Ch.D. 101 at 124; *Re Wareham* [1912] 2 Ch. 312 at 315.

[36] *Gibson v. Bott* (1802) 7 Ves.Jr. 89.

[37] Key & Elphinstone, *Precedents in Conveyancing* (15th ed.), Vol. 2, pp. 926–928; (1943) 7 Conv.(N.S.) 128 (S. Bailey).

[38] *Re Chaytor* [1905] 1 Ch. 233; *Re Berry* [1962] Ch. 97.

(b) *No Express Trust to Convert.* Here it is necessary to examine whether the will indicates an intention to retain the asset; or to permit the life tenant to retain the whole income. Either such intent will exclude apportionment. In *Gray v. Siggers*[39] the trustees were given power to retain any portion of the testator's property in the same state in which it should be at his decease, or to sell and convert the same *as they should in their absolute discretion think fit.* Such a power excluded the duty to convert.

An indication that the life tenant is to enjoy the whole income of the property also prevents apportionment and has the effect of excluding the duty to convert.[40] It may also have the effect of authorising the investments. A power to retain investments or to postpone conversion is thus more likely to exclude the duty to convert and to apportion in cases where there is no express trust to convert. But it may be so framed that it is intended to do no more than allow a suitable time to be selected for the sale.[41] Such a power, being merely administrative, will neither prevent conversion nor apportionment.

(c) *Reversionary Interests.* Similarly the rule in *Re Earl of Chesterfield's Trusts*[42] may be excluded.[43] A clause expressly excluding the rule in *Howe v. Earl of Dartmouth*[44] usually operates to exclude the rule in *Re Earl of Chesterfield's Trusts* also[45]; but it is the general practice to add a special clause for this purpose.

v. Leaseholds. The rule in *Howe v. Earl of Dartmouth*[46] applied before 1926 to leaseholds. After 1925 leases with 60 years or more to run were authorised investments for trustees of land,[47] so the rule could not apply to leases of that length. In the case of shorter leases, it was held in *Re Brooker*,[48] which involved an *express* trust for sale of leaseholds, that there was no duty to apportion because the effect of the Law of Property Act 1925[49] was to entitle the tenant for life to all of the rents and profits until sale. It was unclear whether the rule in *Howe v. Earl of Dartmouth* still applied to residuary short

---

[39] (1880) 15 Ch.D. 74; *Alcock v. Sloper* (1833) 2 Myl. & K. 699; *Re Pitcairn* [1896] 2 Ch. 199.
[40] *Alcock v. Sloper, supra; cf. Re Evans' W.T.* [1921] 2 Ch. 309; *Re Gough* [1957] Ch. 323.
[41] As with the ships in *Brown v. Gellatly* (1867) L.R. 2 Ch.App. 751, *ante,* p. 557.
[42] (1883) 24 Ch.D. 643; *ante,* p. 557.
[43] *Re Pitcairn* [1896] 2 Ch. 199.
[44] (1802) 7 Ves.Jr. 137.
[45] See *Rowlls v. Bebb* [1900] 2 Ch. 107.
[46] (1802) 7 Ves.Jr. 137; *ante,* p. 555.
[47] S.L.A. 1925, s.73; L.P.A. 1925, s.28(1) (now repealed).
[48] [1926] W.N. 93.
[49] s.28(2) (now repealed).

leaseholds where there was no express trust for sale, but the better view was that the rule had gone.[50]

As trustees now have power to acquire freehold or leasehold land, without any restrictions as to the length of any lease,[51] it appears that even if the rule in *Howe v. Earl of Dartmouth* in relation to leases survived the 1925 legislation, it can no longer apply. Thus the tenant for life is entitled to all the income from a short leasehold included in a trust of a residuary estate.

vi. Howe v. Earl of Dartmouth Today. The rules relating to conversion and apportionment demonstrate basic principles of equity. But they should be understood in their proper perspective.

(a) *Exclusion of Duty to Apportion.* The duty to apportion is in practice nearly always excluded, both in respect of income from unauthorised securities and in respect of reversionary interests. The duty to convert, where it exists, thus appears in the context of a duty to change the investments.

(b) *Effect of Current Investment Situation.* The utility of the rules of conversion and apportionment varies according to the current investment situation:

"The dividend yield on the shares in the most regarded index of 100 leading equities has for years been far less than the interest yield obtainable on medium-dated fixed-interest government stock. In present-day circumstances, retaining unauthorised equities therefore tends to depress the life tenant's income, whereas when *Howe v. Dartmouth* was decided the effect was the opposite. It no longer makes sense to say that the income of a life tenant from a fund of unauthorised equities ought to be limited to the yield of government stocks, since that would usually be higher, not lower".[52]

Thus the life tenant wants fixed interest investments when they provide a high income; the remainderman wants unauthorised securities for the preservation of the real value of the capital. It is the life tenant who will be pressing the trustees to convert urgently into gilt-edged securities at times when they can bring an income in excess of the mere four per cent allowed to the life tenant by the rule of apportionment.

---

[50] *Re Trollope* [1927] 1 Ch. 596 at 601.
[51] Trusts of Land and Appointment of Trustees Act 1996, s.6(3); Trustee Act 2000, s.8; *ante*, p. 535.
[52] Trust Law Committee Consultation Paper, *Capital and Income of Trusts* (1998).

(c) *Reform.* The apportionment rules were reviewed by the Law Reform Committee,[53] whose conclusion was that, rather than complete abolition, the rules in *Howe v. Earl of Dartmouth* and *Re Earl of Chesterfield's Trusts* should be subsumed into a statutory duty to hold a fair balance between the beneficiaries. The trustees should have express power to convert income to capital and vice versa. They should have regard to the whole investment policy of the trust, and should convert and apportion to the extent necessary to maintain an even hand. Reform of the various apportionment rules has been more recently recommended by the Trust Law Committee, and models may be found in the legislation of other jurisdictions.[54] It might be added that the widening of investment powers by the Trustee Act 2000 should enable the trustees to obtain higher income for the tenant for life without eroding the capital.

Another way of resolving some of the problems discussed in this chapter might be the use of the "percentage trust",[55] under which all receipts (capital and income) are paid into the trust fund and all outgoings (capital and income) are paid out. The fund is valued annually and a percentage of it (fixed or variable) as specified by the settlor is given to the life tenant each year. The balance goes to the remainderman on termination of the life tenant's interest. Thus equality between the beneficiaries is maintained.

B. Other Methods of Apportionment

Apportionment is necessary in other situations, and these will be mentioned in outline only.

i. Apportionment Act 1870. When a testator or a life tenant dies, the question arises of the entitlement to periodical income, such as rents, interest and dividends, earned in whole or in part, but not paid, at the time of the death. That which is treated as being earned before the death will be added to the estate, and that earned afterwards is payable as income to the income beneficiary under the will or, in the case of the death of a life tenant, to the next life tenant, or to the capital.

The division is governed by the Apportionment Act, section 2, which provides that "all rents, annuities, dividends, and other periodical payments in the nature of income . . . shall . . . be considered

---

[53] 23rd Report, *supra*, para. 3.31 (1982).
[54] Consultation Paper, *Capital and Income of Trusts* (1998), citing (amongst others) the Uniform Principal and Income Act 1977 of the United States.
[55] See (1990) 106 L.Q.R. 87 at 94 (D. Hayton).

as accruing from day to day, and shall be apportionable in respect of time accordingly." It is necessary therefore to ascertain the proportion of the earning period which expired prior to the death, and to divide the payment, when received, in the same proportion.[56] When rent is due, or a dividend earned, but not paid prior to the death, the whole income is paid to the testator's estate or to that of the life tenant. The Act may be excluded by an expression of an intention to do so. This is now common in order to avoid the complications which are introduced into the administration of an estate. Reform has been proposed.[57]

ii. The Rule in Allhusen v. Whittell.

This rule attempts to strike a fair balance between life tenant and remainderman in respect of the payment of the debts of an estate. The life tenant under a will is entitled to income earned after the testator's death. The debts of the testator must also be paid; and it may take some time to do so. In the meantime the assets of the estate are earning income for the life tenant. He should, in fairness, only have the income from the net estate. The rule in *Allhusen v. Whittell*[58] provides that the life tenant shall make a contribution.

Romer L.J. in *Corbett v. Commissioners of Inland Revenue*[59] explained the rule as follows:

"For the purposes of adjusting rights as between the tenant for life and the remainderman of a residuary estate, debts, legacies, estate duties, probate duties and so forth, are to be deemed to have been paid out of such capital of the testator's estate as will be sufficient for that purpose, when to that capital is added interest on that capital from the date of the testator's death to the date of the payment of the legacy or debt, or whatever it may have been, interest being calculated at the average rate of interest[60] earned by the testator's estate during the relevant period."[61]

---

[56] For class gifts, see *Re Joel* [1967] Ch. 14.

[57] Law Reform Committee, 23rd report, *supra*. See paras. 3.40, 3.41.

[58] (1867) L.R. 4 Eq. 295.

[59] [1938] 1 K.B. 567.

[60] *Re Wills* [1915] 1 Ch. 769.

[61] Assuming a debt of £50, an average rate of income of 10 per cent, income tax at 25 per cent, and payment of the debt one year from the death, the apportionment will be:

From Capital: 46.47 (being $\dfrac{100}{107.16} \times 50$)

From Income: 3.53 (being $\dfrac{7.6}{107.6} \times 50$)

The rule may be excluded by an expression of contrary intent, or where its application would in the circumstances be inappropriate.[62]

Witnesses to the Law Reform Committee described the rule as "complex, fiddlesome and resulting in a disproportionate amount of work and expense," adding that where the rule was not excluded it was often simply ignored.[63] The committee accordingly recommended that, as in the case of the rules in *Howe v. Earl of Dartmouth* and *Re Earl of Chesterfield's Trusts*,[64] it should be subsumed into a new statutory duty to hold a fair balance between the beneficiaries, as described above.[65]

iii. The Rule in Re Atkinson. Where an authorised mortgage security is sold by the trustee mortgagees and the proceeds are insufficient to satisfy the principal and interest in full, it is necessary to determine the way in which the loss is to be shared between life tenant and remainderman. The sum realised must be apportioned between the life tenant and the remainderman in the proportion which the amount due for the arrears of interest bears to the amount due in respect of the principal.[66]

iv. Interest on Damages. Where loss of the trust fund results in an award of compensation, interest will be payable on the sum awarded from the date of the claim form until judgment. The interest should be apportioned between life tenant and remainderman. In *Jaffray v. Marshall*,[67] a fair apportionment was considered to be half and half, taking a broad view.

v. Purchase or Sale of Shares Cum Dividend. One of the factors which affects the price of shares is the date of payment of the next dividend. A share whose dividend will be paid tomorrow is worth more than it would be if the dividend has been paid yesterday. It would seem reasonable to require an apportionment when shares are bought or sold cum dividend, but the general rule is that there is none.[68] In this respect, the beneficiaries take "the rough with the

---

[62] *Re McEuen* [1913] 2 Ch. 704; *Re Darby* [1939] Ch. 905.

[63] 23rd Report, *supra*. See para 3.31.

[64] *supra*.

[65] 23rd Report, *supra*, para. 3.36. See *ante*, p. 561.

[66] *Re Atkinson* [1904] 2 Ch. 160.

[67] [1993] 1 W.L.R. 1285 (overruled as to the assessment of damages in *Target Holdings Ltd v. Redferns (a firm)* [1996] 1 A.C. 421).

[68] *Bulkeley v. Stephens* [1896] 2 Ch. 241; *Re Ellerman's S.T.* (1984) 81 L.S.Gaz. 430, where the decision to the contrary in *Re Winterstoke's W.T.* [1938] Ch. 158 was regarded as wrong; (1986) 1 *Trust Law & Practice* 62 (I. Pittaway). See also Law Reform Committee, 23rd Report, *supra*.

smooth."[69] This is probably more convenient overall than an insistence on an apportionment in every case. But an apportionment will be required if there would otherwise be "a glaring injustice."[70]

vi. Company Distributions. Questions can also arise as to the entitlements of life tenant and remainderman to certain distributions by companies. The question of entitlement and that of the liability of the distribution to income tax are related questions, but are not identical.[71] The tax aspect is the reason for the attraction to shareholders generally of distributions as capital. The question whether the life tenant or remainderman is entitled (or whether an apportionment must be made) will arise, for example, where the company has taken steps to capitalise profits,[72] or where shareholders are given the right to choose between a cash dividend and an allotment of shares. The modern context in which the question arises is the company demerger, where a company in effect splits into two, and shares in the new company are given to shareholders in the original company. The demerger may be "direct", where the original company allocates to its shareholders the shares in the new company, or "indirect", where the new company allocates its own shares to shareholders of the original company. Whether these shares are to be treated as income or capital is relevant to beneficial entitlement and, as mentioned above, to taxation. When ICI transferred its bioscience business to a new company, Zeneca, and shares in the latter were given to ICI shareholders (the ICI shares being reduced in value by the demerger) in satisfaction of a dividend, it was held in *Sinclair v. Lee*[73] that the new shares were capital assets, and hence did not pass under a gift by will of income from the ICI shares. The effect of the reconstruction was that two capital assets replaced one. Investment philosophy had greatly changed since the older cases,[74] and any other result would not reflect reality. *Sinclair* involved an "indirect" demerger. The Revenue view, however, is that shares distributed under a "direct" demerger are treated as income. This view has been described as absurd, and reform has been called for.[75]

---

[69] *Re Maclaren's S.T.* [1951] 2 All E.R. 414 at 420.
[70] *ibid.*
[71] *Re Bates* [1928] Ch. 682; *Re Doughty* [1947] Ch. 263; *Re Sechiari* [1950] 1 All E.R. 417; I.C.T.A. 1988, ss.209–211, 234, 254.
[72] *Bouch v. Sproule* (1887) 12 App.Cas. 385.
[73] [1993] Ch. 497. See *Modern International Developments in Trust Law*, pp. 288–291 (D. Hayton).
[74] Such as *Hill v. Permanent Trustee Co. of N.S.W.* [1930] A.C. 720.
[75] (1995) 9 *Trust Law International* 55 (P. Duffield). See also Parker and Mellows, *The Modern Law of Trusts* (7th ed.), pp. 591–592. The issue is to be considered by the Law Commission.

2. DUTY TO PROVIDE ACCOUNTS AND INFORMATION

A. Accounts

i. Extent of Duty. A trustee must keep accounts and be constantly ready to produce them for the beneficiaries.[76] It seems that a beneficiary is entitled only to see and inspect the accounts; if he wants a copy himself, he must pay for it; but it is common practice to provide a copy for each of the beneficiaries.[77] An income beneficiary is entitled to full accounts, but a remainderman is entitled only to such information as relates to capital transactions.[78] A member of a class of discretionary beneficiaries is entitled to accounts,[79] but a person who is merely a potential object of a discretionary trust has no such right, at any rate where there is a large number of possible beneficiaries.[80]

ii. Audit. Apart from the case of pension trusts and charitable trusts,[81] it is neither necessary nor, except in large and complicated trusts or where trouble with a beneficiary is foreseen, usual to have trust accounts audited. However, trustees may, in their absolute discretion, have the trust accounts examined and audited by an independent accountant, and may pay the costs out of income or capital. Audit should not be effected more than once in every three years, except in special cases.[82]

Any trustee or beneficiary may apply for the accounts of any trust to be investigated and audited by such solicitor or public accountant as may be agreed upon, or in default of agreement by the Public Trustee or by some person appointed by him.[83] The costs are usually

---

[76] *Pearse v. Green* (1819) 1 Jac. & W. 135, *per* Plumer M.R. at 140.

[77] *Ottley v. Gilby* (1845) 8 Beav. 602; *Kemp v. Burn* (1863) 4 Giff. 348.

[78] Mellows, *The Trustee's Handbook* (3rd ed.), p. 52.

[79] *Chaine-Nickson v. Bank of Ireland* [1976] I.R. 393; *Re Murphy's Settlements* [1999] 1 W.L.R. 282.

[80] *Hartigan Nominees Pty Ltd v. Rydge* (1992) 29 N.S.W.L.R. 405. It has been held in the Cayman Islands that the right to see accounts is not absolute: *Lemos v. Coutts & Co.* [1992–93] Cayman I. L.R. 400 at 518–519.

[81] Pensions Act 1995, s.41 and regulations thereunder; *ante*, p. 481; Charities Act 1993, ss.42–44; *ante*, p. 465.

[82] T.A. 1925, s.22(4). For the audit by the court of the accounts of a judicial trustee, see Administration of Justice Act 1982, s.57; Judicial Trustee Rules 1983 (S.I. 1983 No. 370). By r. 2 there is to be no automatic audit by the court of the accounts of a "corporate trust," meaning the Official Solicitor, Public Trustee or a corporation appointed by the court to be a trustee, or which is entitled to be a custodian trustee by the Public Trustee Act 1906, s.4(3).

[83] Public Trustee Act 1906, s.13. The Law Reform Committee recommended the repeal of s.13, which is rarely used and is ineffective because there are no powers to enforce the findings of the Public Trustee. (23rd report, 1982, Cmnd. 8733, para. 4.48).

borne by the trust, but the Public Trustee may order that the appellant or the trustees must pay them or share them.[84]

B. Information. Trust Documents

The beneficiaries are entitled to be informed about matters currently affecting the trust.[85] Beneficiaries of pension trusts have a statutory right to information.[86] A large trust will keep many documents, such as the minutes of trustees' meetings. Documents connected with the trust are trust documents, and prima facie the property of the beneficiaries, and as such open to their inspection.[87]

We saw, however, in Chapter 17, that trustees are not bound to give reasons for the exercise of their discretions. The policy of that principle has already been discussed.[88] In the present context, the problem is to reconcile that principle with the principle that beneficiaries are entitled to see the trust documents. If reasons for the exercise of discretionary powers are recorded in documents relating to the trust, are the beneficiaries entitled to see the documents?

In *Re Londonderry's Settlement*,[89] the donees of a power under a discretionary trust decided to distribute the capital. One member of the discretionary class was dissatisfied with the sum which they intended to give her. She asked for copies of the minutes of trustees' meetings, documents prepared for the meetings, and correspondence between various interested persons. The trustees were willing only to show her documents giving the intended distributions and the annual trust accounts. They declined, in the general interest of the family, to disclose further documents, and brought a summons to determine the nature and extent of their duties in relation to disclosures.

The Court of Appeal found great difficulty in defining in general terms what were the "trust documents" which a beneficiary

---

[84] See *Re Oddy* [1911] 1 Ch. 532.

[85] But this does not go so far as to put the trustees "under any duty to proffer information to their beneficiary, or to see that he has proper advice merely because they are trustees for him and know that he is entering into a transaction with his beneficial interest with some person or body connected in some way with the trustees, such as a company in which the trustees own some shares beneficially.": *Tito v. Waddell (No. 2)* [1977] Ch. 106 at 243, *per* Megarry V.-C.; questioned at (1977) 41 Conv.(N.S.) 438 (F. Crane).

[86] Pensions Act 1995, s.41 and regulations thereunder; *ante*, p. 488.

[87] *O'Rourke v. Darbishire* [1920] A.C. 581 at 619, 626.

[88] *ante*, pp. 524–526.

[89] [1965] Ch. 918; (1965) 81 L.Q.R. 192 (R.E.M.). See further *Trends in Contemporary Trust Law* (ed. A. Oakley) at 49 *et seq.* (D. Hayton); *Modern International Developments in Trust Law*, pp. 13–16, 325–327 (D. Hayton).

prima facie had a right to see. Salmon L.J. said that the category of trust documents could not be defined. They have however:

" . . . these characteristics in common: (1) they are documents in the possession of the trustees as trustees; (2) they contain information about the trust, which the beneficiaries are entitled to know; (3) the beneficiaries have a proprietary interest[90] in the documents and, accordingly, are entitled to see them. If any parts of a document contain information which the beneficiaries are not entitled to know, I doubt whether such parts can be truly said to be integral parts of a trust document."[91]

Applying this reasoning, it was held in *Hartigan Nominees Pty Ltd v. Rydge*[92] that the beneficiaries were not entitled to see the settlor's confidential memorandum of wishes, a document of no legal force setting out how he wished the trustees to exercise their discretions. It was also doubted whether a potential beneficiary of a discretionary trust had any right to information, at any rate if one of a large number of such persons. The question of a discretionary beneficiary's right to information arose again in *Re Murphy's Settlements*,[93] where a member of a class of beneficiaries of a discretionary trust sought to compel the settlor to disclose the names and addresses of the trustees. It was held that the court could make such an order, as a discretionary beneficiary was entitled to enquire as to the nature and value of the trust property, its income and how the fund had been invested and distributed. The court would be unlikely, however, to exercise its discretion in favour of a "remote" potential beneficiary, as it would be undesirable for the trustees to be "badgered" with claims by numerous beneficiaries for information. Each case was to be judged on its merits.

Subject to the above, a trustee's duty is not merely one of answering questions; but also to provide beneficiaries with information concerning their interests under the trust; or, in the case of a child beneficiary, to inform him of his entitlement on coming of age.[94]

---

[90] The right to information does not, however, depend on the beneficiary having a proprietary right. It extends to beneficiaries of an unadministered estate; *Att-Gen. for Ontario v. Stavro* (1994) 119 D.L.R. (4th) 750. Likewise a discretionary beneficiary, as in *Londonderry* itself.

[91] [1965] Ch. 918 at 938.

[92] (1992) 29 N.S.W.L.R. 405; [1994] 3 J.Int.P. 60 (J. Lehane). On "letters of wishes", see (1995) 5 O.T.P.R. 176, 181, 184 (P. Matthews); (1999) 32 Vanderbilt Journal of Transnational Law 555 at 573–578 (D. Hayton).

[93] [1999] 1 W.L.R. 282; (1999) 115 L.Q.R. 206 (C. Mitchell).

[94] *Hawkesley v. May* [1956] 1 Q.B. 304; including, it seems, his rights under the rule in *Saunders v. Vautier* (1841) Cr. & Ph. 240; *post*, p. 629; (1970) 34 Conv.(N.S.) 29 (A. Samuels).

There is, however, no duty to search out possible objects of a discretionary trust and inform them of their position.[95] Executors are under no positive duty, as a will is a public document.[96]

---

[95] *Hartigan Nominees Pty Ltd v. Rydge* (1992) 29 N.S.W.L.R. 405.
[96] *Re Lewis* [1904] 2 Ch. 656; *Re Mackay* [1906] 1 Ch. 25; *Cancer Research Campaign v. Ernest Brown & Co (a firm)* [1997] S.T.C. 1425 (resulting in loss of opportunity to vary estate for inheritance tax purposes within statutory time limit).

CHAPTER 20

POWERS OF TRUSTEES

TRUSTEES may exercise such powers as are given to them by the trust instrument or by statute. A power, as has been seen,[1] is to be distinguished from a duty, in that its exercise is not compulsory. In the absence of bad faith, the court will not interfere with the exercise

---

[1] *ante*, p. 62.

of discretions. At most, the holder of a fiduciary power is under a duty to consider its exercise.[2]

Originally, it was necessary to spell out a trustee's powers in detail in the trust instrument. The Trustee Act 1925 (as amended) provided the basic powers needed by trustees. They may unless otherwise stated be excluded or amended as desired.[3] The 1925 Act became outdated in many respects, in particular with regard to delegation, insurance, remuneration, investment and the power to employ nominees and custodians. The powers have now been substantially modernised by the Trustee Act 2000, as will be explained in the relevant sections of this Chapter. The new Act came into force on February 1, 2001. No doubt practitioners will continue to insert detailed provisions into the trust instrument. It should be added that many modern trust instruments give the trustees a power to amend the trust.[4]

1. TRUSTEES OF LAND

Section 6(1) of the Trusts of Land and Appointment of Trustees Act 1996 provides that "For the purpose of exercising their functions as trustees, the trustees of land have in relation to the land subject to the trust all the powers of an absolute owner." Where the trust includes land and personalty, these powers are thus confined to the land. The width of the statutory powers is reduced by an important proviso: the powers conferred by section 6 "shall not be exercised in contravention of, or of any order made in pursuance of, any other enactment or any rule of law or equity."[5] The trustees, in exercising their powers under section 6, must also have regard to the rights of the beneficiaries,[6] and they have a general duty to consult adult beneficiaries with an interest in possession.[7] Thus trustees of land remain subject to the general duties imposed by equity on trustees and to restrictions on the statutory powers of trustees contained in other legislation or in other sections of the 1996 Act.[8] They are also

---

[2] As to whether trustees can fetter their powers by deciding in advance how to exercise them, see (1993) 7 *Trust Law International* p. 69 (H. Arthur).

[3] T.A 1925, s.69(2).

[4] See *Society of Lloyd's v. Robinson* [1999] 1 W.L.R. 756; *post*, p. 631.

[5] s.6(6). See also s.6(7).

[6] s.6(5). A purchaser of unregistered land is not concerned to see that this duty has been complied with; s.16(1). For registered land, see L.R.A. 1925, s.94(4), inserted by the 1996 Act, *ante*, p. 293.

[7] s.11(1). This duty may be excluded by the settlor.

[8] See s.6(8). If a conveyance of unregistered land by the trustees (other than charity trustees) contravenes s.6(6) or (8), it is not invalid if the purchaser had no actual notice of the contravention; s.16(2). For registered land, see L.R.A. 1925, s.94(4), *supra*.

subject to the statutory duty of care under section 1 of the Trustee Act 2000.[9]

Section 6 applies whether the trust of land is express, implied, resulting or constructive, and whether arising before or after the commencement of the 1996 Act; trusts for sale and bare trusts are also included.[10] In the case of an expressly created trust of land, however, section 6 may be excluded by the settlor or the powers made exercisable subject to consent.[11] In such a case the trustees must take all reasonable steps to bring the limitation to the notice of any purchaser of the land from them, but the conveyance is not invalid if the purchaser had no actual notice of the limitation.[12]

In addition to the general powers described above, the 1996 Act confers certain specific powers on trustees of land. Under the general law, beneficiaries who are of full age and capacity and together absolutely entitled may call for a transfer of the trust property.[13] In the case of land, section 6(2) gives the trustees power to convey to such beneficiaries provided each is absolutely entitled,[14] even though they have not required the trustees to do so. If the beneficiaries do not co-operate, the court may order them to do whatever is necessary to secure that the land vests in them. Where the trustees convey unregistered land to persons they believe to be such beneficiaries, they must execute a deed declaring that they are discharged from the trust of that land, and a purchaser of it is entitled to assume that the land is no longer subject to the trust unless he has actual notice that the trustees were mistaken in their belief.[15]

Where beneficiaries of full age are absolutely entitled as tenants in common, the trustees may partition the land or any part of it, obtaining the consent of each beneficiary and providing (by mortgage or otherwise) for the payment of any equality money.[16] This power may be excluded or made subject to other consents in an expressly created trust of land.[17] The delegation powers of trustees of land are dealt with later in this Chapter.

---

[9] s.6(9), introduced by T.A. 2000.

[10] s.1. The Act came into force on January 1, 1997. For the application of the Act to personal representatives; see s.18.

[11] s.8. The settlor of a charitable trust may not exclude s.6. See [1997] Conv. 263 (G. Watt), discussing whether the power of sale may be excluded.

[12] s.16(3). This is confined to unregistered land. For registered land, see L.R.A. 1925, s.94(4), *supra*.

[13] *Saunders v. Vautier* (1841) Cr. & Ph. 240; *post*, p. 629.

[14] *i.e.* they are equitable co-owners. That their interests together add up to the whole does not otherwise suffice.

[15] Trusts of Land and Appointment of Trustees Act 1996, s.16(4), (5). For registered land, see L.R.A. 1925, s.94(5), inserted by the 1996 Act.

[16] *ibid.*, s.7. A purchaser of unregistered land is not concerned to see that the beneficiaries have consented; s.16(1). For registered land, see L.R.A. 1925, s.94(4).

[17] *ibid.*, s.8.

2. POWER OF SALE[18]

A. Land

Land is held either by an owner absolutely entitled or under a trust of land or, in the case of a settlement created before the commencement of the Trusts of Land and Appointment of Trustees Act 1996, under a strict settlement. In the latter case the tenant for life has the legal estate and a power of sale.[19] In the case of a trust of land, the legal estate is vested in the trustees, and they have a power of sale.[20] Where an express trust for sale is created, the trustees have power to postpone the sale indefinitely in the exercise of their discretion, despite any provision to the contrary in the trust instrument.[21] The receipt of at least two trustees or of a trust corporation is required for all capital money arising under a trust of land or strict settlement,[22] and the same rule applies to the overreaching of the beneficial interests.[23]

B. Chattels

Where chattels or other personalty are held upon trust for sale, the position is the same as with land except that the receipt of a sole trustee is sufficient discharge to a purchaser.[24] The trust for sale may arise expressly or be implied, as we have seen, under the rule in *Howe v. Earl of Dartmouth*.[25] Personal representatives have power to sell chattels (and other property) on intestacy.[26]

C. Other Property

In the case of many other forms of property, a power of sale, if not given expressly, will usually be implied. Unauthorised investments, investments which the trustees think are not suitable for the trust, and trust property which is not in a state of investment at all, should be sold and invested in accordance with the express terms of the relevant investment power, or with the provisions of the Trustee Act 2000.[27]

---

[18] See generally [1999] Conv. 84 (R. Mitchell).

[19] S.L.A. 1925, s.38(1).

[20] Trusts of Land and Appointment of Trustees Act 1996, s.6(1); *supra*. This includes bare trusts; s.1(2). See [1997] Conv. 263 (G. Watt), as to whether the power of sale may be excluded. Personal representatives on intestacy have a power to sell land; A.E.A. 1925, s.33, as amended by the 1996 Act.

[21] *ibid.*, s.4.

[22] T.A. 1925, s.14; L.P.A. 1925, s.27(2); S.L.A. 1925, s.94(1).

[23] L.P.A. 1925, s.2.

[24] T.A. 1925, s.14; *post*, p. 573.

[25] (1802) 7 Ves.Jr. 137; *ante*, p. 555.

[26] A.E.A. 1925, s.33, as amended by Trusts of Land and Appointment of Trustees Act 1996, Sched. 2.

[27] *ante*, pp. 537 *et seq.*

Whenever trustees are authorised to pay or apply capital money for any purpose or in any manner, they have power to raise such money by sale, mortgage, etc., of the trust property then in possession.[28] But this does not authorise trustees to raise money by charging existing investments in order to purchase others.[29]

D. Sales by Trustees

The detailed provisions relating to sales by trustees are contained in the Trustee Act 1925, s.12.[30] Trustees may sell all or any part of the property, by public auction or by private contract, subject to any such conditions respecting title or other matter as the trustee thinks fit.

As we have seen, trustees are under an overriding duty to obtain the best price for the beneficiaries.[31] If they fail to do so, the beneficiaries may seek an injunction restraining the sale.[32] But if the sale has taken place, it may not be impeached by a beneficiary on the ground that any of the conditions of the sale were unduly depreciatory, unless it also appears that the consideration for the sale was thereby rendered inadequate.[33] A purchaser will not be affected unless he was acting in collusion with the trustees.[34]

3. POWER TO GIVE RECEIPTS: SECTION 14

By the Trustee Act 1925, s.14, the written receipt by a trustee for money, securities, investments etc., is a sufficient discharge to the person paying, and effectually exonerates him from being answerable for any loss or misapplication of the money. The section applies notwithstanding anything to the contrary in the trust instrument,[35] and applies to sole trustees, except in the case of proceeds of sale or other capital money arising under a trust of land or under the Settled Land Act where, unless the trustee is a trust corporation, the receipt of at least two trustees is necessary.[36] Where there is more than one

---

[28] T.A. 1925, s.16(1).

[29] *Re Suenson-Taylor* [1974] 1 W.L.R. 1280 (land).

[30] As amended by Trusts of Land and Appointment of Trustees Act 1996, Sched. 3.

[31] *Buttle v. Saunders* [1950] 2 All E.R. 193; *ante*, p. 530. See also *Sergeant v. National Westminster Bank* (1991) 61 P. & C.R. 518. As to whether trustees can sell at a valuation to be determined by a third party, see [1985] Conv. 44 (G. Lightman).

[32] *Wheelwright v. Walker* (1883) 23 Ch.D. 752.

[33] T.A. 1925, s.13(1); *Dance v. Goldingham* (1873) L.R. 8 Ch.App. 902. The trustee may, of course, be liable.

[34] T.A. 1925, s.13(2).

[35] *ibid.*, s.14(3).

[36] *ibid.* s.14(2) as amended by Trusts of Land and Appointment of Trustees Act 1996, Sched. 3.

trustee, all must sign, in accordance with the rule that they must act together.[37]

4. POWER TO INSURE: SECTION 19

A. Insurance

At common law trustees have a power to insure the trust property, and possibly a duty to do so (of uncertain scope) in accordance with their general duty of acting in the best interests of the trust.[38] As a general rule, however, they are not liable if the property is destroyed; and if the trustees differ on the question whether the property should be insured, it seems that nothing can be done to compel them.[39]

Section 19 of the Trustee Act 1925 provided a power to insure, but it was limited and unsatisfactory. A new section 19 has been substituted by the Trustee Act 2000.[40] This provides that a trustee may insure any trust property against risks of loss or damage due to any event and pay the premiums out of income or capital. In the case of property held on a bare trust (*i.e.* where the beneficiary is of full age and capacity and absolutely entitled or, where there is more than one beneficiary, each of them is of full age and capacity and they are together absolutely entitled), the power is subject to their directions.[41] The statutory duty of care[42] applies to the exercise of the power to insure, whether under section 19 or under an express power.[43]

The policy moneys must be treated as capital and applied in accordance with the terms of the trust.[44]

B. Reinstatement

Trustees may apply the policy money relating to land or other property in reinstatement, subject to the consent of any person whose consent is required by the trust instrument,[45] and without prejudice to the statutory or other right of any person to require the money to be spent in reinstatement.[46] Persons interested under the trust can, therefore, insist on having the premises rebuilt if they

---

[37] *ante*, p. 504; charitable and pension trustees may act by a majority.
[38] Law Com No. 260 (1999), *Trustees' Powers and Duties*, paras. 6.7–6.8.
[39] *Re McEacharn* (1911) 103 L.T. 900.
[40] s.34. The new provision applies to trusts whenever created.
[41] T.A. 1925, s.19(2), (3).
[42] T.A. 2000, s.1; *ante*, Chap. 17.
[43] *ibid.*, Sched. 1, para. 5.
[44] T.A. 1925, s.20.
[45] *ibid.*, s.20(4).
[46] *ibid.* s.20(5).

wish; or, if they do not wish it, can prevent the trustees from using the money for that purpose, but in any case the money is capital money.

5. POWER TO COMPOUND LIABILITIES: SECTION 15

Trustees are given a wide discretion in settling claims which may be made by third persons against the trust estate,[47] or by the trust estate against third persons. Adult beneficiaries who are under no disability may, of course, make any arrangement that they wish among themselves. Until the Variation of Trusts Act 1958[48] was passed, the court had no general power to approve adjustments in the beneficial interests. But the dividing line is difficult to draw. The Court has inherent power to compromise a genuine dispute between beneficiaries[49] and section 15 has been held to authorise the settlement of a dispute with a person claiming to be a beneficiary,[50] and also litigation between the trustees and beneficiaries on the question whether certain property was subject to the trust or not.[51] It was no objection to the jurisdiction under section 15 that the proposed compromise involved an adjustment of interests among the beneficiaries.[52]

Personal representatives and trustees may accept compositions for debts; allow time for payment of debts; compromise, abandon, submit to arbitration or otherwise settle any claim; and may enter into such agreements and execute such instruments as may be necessary for the efficient performance of these duties.[53] A wide power of this nature is of great practical importance in enabling the trustee to make a reasonable compromise instead of being obliged to litigate in respect of every possible claim, or risk liability for breach of trust if he fails to do so.[54] Trustees are not liable for loss caused by any act done by them in the exercise of the powers conferred by this section as long as they have discharged the statutory duty of care under the Trustee Act 2000,[55] and they have reached their decision by exercising their discretion and not by failing to consider the matter.[56] They may apply to the court to sanction a compromise. The court must

---

[47] The section confers no power to make reasonable provision for satisfying contingent claims. See *Re Yorke (deceased)* [1997] 4 All E.R. 907.

[48] *post*, Chap. 22.

[49] *Re Barbour's Settlement* [1974] 1 W.L.R. 1198; *Re Downshire S.E.* [1953] Ch. 218.

[50] *Eaton v. Buchanan* [1911] A.C. 253; *cf. Abdallah v. Rickards* (1888) 4 T.L.R. 622.

[51] *Re Earl of Strafford* [1980] Ch. 28.

[52] *ibid.*

[53] See *Re Shenton* [1935] Ch. 651.

[54] *Re Brogden* [1948] Ch. 206; *ante*, p. 530.

[55] s.15(1), as amended by T.A. 2000. For the duty of care, see Chap. 17.

[56] *Re Greenwood* (1911) 105 L.T. 509.

consider what is the best from the point of view of everybody concerned, paying especial attention to the interests of child beneficiaries.[57]

6. Power in Regard to Reversionary Interests: Section 22[58]

Where part of the trust property consists of choses in action or reversionary interests the trustees may, on such interests falling into possession, "agree or ascertain the amount or value thereof in such manner as they think fit," without being responsible for any loss, if they have discharged the statutory duty of care under the Trustee Act 2000. But nothing in the section is to be construed as relieving trustees from the duty of getting in such interests as soon as possible after their falling into possession, for this is one of their primary duties.[59]

7. Power to Delegate

A. The Early Rule in Equity

The basic rule is that a person entrusted with a fiduciary duty does not fulfil it if he delegates it to someone else; he remains liable for the other person's default.[60] But this rule was never, even in the times when the most rigorous views were being taken of the standard of conduct required from a trustee, inflexible. Indeed, there are certain things which a business person would always delegate to a skilled agent. Thus, the employment of solicitors for legal, and brokers and bankers for financial, business was sanctioned by the ordinary business practice. This was recognised as early as 1754, by Lord Hardwicke in *Ex p. Belchier*,[61] and the trend of judicial decision, fortified by occasional statutory provisions, grew more and more tolerant of delegation in cases of commercial necessity. Following the two famous decisions of the House of Lords in *Speight v. Gaunt*[62] and *Learoyd v. Whiteley*,[63] it could be said that delegation was permissible if the trustees could show that it was reasonably necessary in the circumstances or was in accordance with ordinary business practice. The trustees had to exercise proper care in the selection of the agent, employ him in his proper field,[64] and exercise

---

[57] *Re Ezekiel's S.T.* [1942] Ch. 230; *Re Earl of Strafford (supra)*.
[58] As amended by T.A. 2000.
[59] See *ante*, p. 529.
[60] *Turner v. Corney* (1841) 5 Beav. 515 at 517, *per* Lord Langdale.
[61] (1754) Amb. 218.
[62] (1884) 9 App.Cas. 1.
[63] (1887) 12 App.Cas. 727.
[64] *Fry v. Tapson* (1884) 28 Ch.D. 268.

general supervision.[65] Trustees who delegated without authority remained vicariously liable for any resulting loss.[66] They were not vicariously liable for the acts of authorised agents, but incurred personal liability for failing to act prudently in matters of supervision and so forth. A trustee's discretions could not, however, be delegated.[67] Further, exemption clauses expressly limiting his liability to cases of "wilful default" did not relieve him from the responsibility of acting as a prudent man of business.[68] Nor did the statutes of 1859 and 1893, the predecessors of the Trustee Act 1925, s.30(1) (now repealed), which restricted the liability of trustees to cases of wilful default, do more than change the onus of proof; these statutes placed the onus on "those who seek to charge an executor or trustee with a loss arising from the default of an agent, when the propriety of employing the agent has been established."[69]

The kind of delegation referred to above is sometimes termed "collective delegation", meaning that all the trustees acting together appoint an agent to carry out some function. This may be contrasted with "individual delegation", where one trustee delegates all his functions to another person, which may now be done by power of attorney.[70]

B. Trustee Act 1925

Under the Trustee Act 1925 trustees were no longer required to show a need to delegate. Delegation as such was accepted as a normal method of performing the duties incidental to trusteeship; but the overall duties of trusteeship remained of course in the trustees. Section 23(1) of the 1925 Act provided that a trustee could delegate acts (of an administrative nature) to agents, and that he would not be responsible for the default of the agent "if employed in good faith". Section 30(1) provided that a trustee was responsible for his own acts and defaults but not for those of any co-trustee or agent, nor for any other loss unless occasioned by "his own wilful default". The proper interpretation of, and the relationship between, these provisions remained a matter of doubt until their repeal by the Trustee Act 2000. In *Re Vickery*[71] an executor employed a solicitor to wind up the estate. He was unaware that the solicitor had twice been suspended from practice. Eventually the solicitor absconded

---

[65] *Rowland v. Witherden* (1851) 3 Mac. & G. 568.
[66] *Clough v. Bond* (1838) 3 My. & Cr. 490 at 496–497; *Speight v. Gaunt, supra; Target Holdings Ltd v. Redferns (a firm)* [1996] 1 A.C. 421 at 434.
[67] *Speight v. Gaunt, supra; post,* p. 582.
[68] *Re Chapman* [1896] 2 Ch. 763; *Re Brier* (1884) 26 Ch.D. 238; *cf. Armitage v. Nurse* [1998] Ch. 241 at 252; *post,* p. 578. Exemption clauses are discussed at p. 501, *ante.*
[69] *per* Lord Selborne in *Re Brier, supra,* at 243; *Re Chapman, supra,* at 776.
[70] *post,* p. 582.
[71] [1931] 1 Ch. 572.

with money belonging to the estate. Maugham J. considered that section 23(1) had not removed the need to exercise care in the selection of the agent. There was no suggestion that the executor had not done so. He was not liable, because he was not guilty of "wilful default" within section 30(1), which meant intentional or reckless breach of duty. This interpretation was inconsistent with the settled construction of the expression in trustee exemption clauses, where it included imprudence.[72] Maugham J.'s interpretation of section 30(1) was long criticised, although Millett L.J. in *Armitage v. Nurse*[73] rejected the criticisms. It was confirmed, however, in *Re Lucking's Will Trusts*[74] that the 1925 Act had not removed the duty to supervise the agent adequately. In that case the trustee was liable for a loss of £16,000 caused by his signing blank cheques in favour of the agent, an old and trusted friend, and failing to supervise his drawings on the funds after the time at which there was reason to suspect his honesty.

It was mentioned above that section 23(1) permitted the delegation of administrative acts. It did not permit the delegation of the exercise of discretions. That may be done by power of attorney under section 25 of the Trustee Act 1925,[75] but the trustee remains liable for the defaults of the attorney. The Law Commission concluded that "Far from promoting the more conscientious discharge of the obligations of trusteeship, the prohibition on the delegation of fiduciary discretions may force trustees to commit breaches of trust in order to achieve the most effective administration of the trust".[76]

A major purpose of the Trustee Act 2000 was to reform trustees' powers of delegation. First, it has repealed the problematic sections 23 and 30 of the Act of 1925 and provided in their place a clearer framework for delegation. Secondly, it has extended the circumstances in which discretionary functions may be delegated. This is particularly important in the context of investment, but is not confined to that. We will now consider the delegation provisions of the Trustee Act 2000. Other statutory provisions permitting the delegation of discretions are dealt with separately below.[77]

C. Trustee Act 2000

The new wide powers of delegation apply to trusts whenever created, but are subject to any restrictions or exclusions in the trust

---

[72] *ante*, p. 577.
[73] [1998] Ch. 241 at 252.
[74] [1968] 1 W.L.R. 866.
[75] *post*, p. 582.
[76] Law Com. No. 260 (1999), *Trustees' Powers and Duties*, para. 4.6.
[77] *post*, Sections D, E.

instrument or other legislation.[78] The powers apply to pension trusts, save that the trustees may not delegate investment functions nor appoint nominees and custodians under the new Act, as these matters should be dealt with under the pensions legislation.[79] The scope and effect of the power to delegate will now be considered.

i. General Power to Delegate. The approach taken in the new Act is that trustees may delegate any or all of their "delegable functions". Section 11 does not (save in the case of charitable trusts) provide a list of such functions, but instead lists those which may *not* be delegated. The delegable functions are those *other than*:

(a) any function relating to whether or in what way any assets of the trust should be distributed,
(b) any power to decide whether any fees or other payment due to be made out of the trust funds should be made out of income or capital,
(c) any power to appoint a person to be a trustee of the trust, or
(d) any power conferred by any other enactment or the trust instrument which permits the trustees to delegate any of their functions or to appoint a person to act as nominee or custodian.

Thus the trustees cannot delegate their power of selection amongst the beneficiaries of a discretionary trust. They may, however, delegate investment decision-making, and thereby obtain the benefit of the skilled professional service of an investment manager authorised under the financial services legislation. The detailed provisions of the Act in relation to the delegation of investment and other asset management functions were considered in Chapter 18.[80] The new powers are additional to a trustee's power of individual delegation by power of attorney.[81] In the case of a charitable trust, section 11 lists the functions which may be delegated. Broadly, these are matters relating to income generation, including investment, but are otherwise administrative acts. These have already been mentioned.[82]

---

[78] T.A. 2000, ss.26, 27. For transitional provisions, see Sched. 3.
[79] *ibid.*, s.36. The delegation provisions do not apply to trustees of unit trusts or those managing a fund under a common investment or common deposit scheme for charities; ss.37, 38.
[80] *ante*, p. 540.
[81] *post*, Sections D, E.
[82] *ante*, p. 466.

The trustees may delegate to one or more of their number, but not to a beneficiary, even if he is also a trustee.[83] If the same function is delegated to two or more persons, they must act jointly.

If it is reasonably necessary to do so, the trustees may delegate on terms permitting sub-delegation, restricting the liability of the agent, or permitting him to act in circumstances capable of giving rise to a conflict of interest.[84] It was doubtful under the previous law whether this could be done, thus the reform was needed in order to permit delegation to fund managers on their standard terms of business.

Whether the delegation is under the new Act or otherwise, the trustees may pay the agent from the trust funds if the terms of his appointment so provide, but the amount must not exceed what is reasonable for the services in question.[85] They may also reimburse him from the trust funds for expenses properly incurred.

Where the trustees have appointed an agent under the new Act or under the trust instrument or other legislation, they must keep the arrangement under review and must consider whether there is a need to revoke the appointment or to exercise any power they may have to give directions to the agent.[86]

ii. Nominees and Custodians. Prior to the new legislation it was doubtful whether trustees could appoint nominees or custodians in the absence of an express power. This is a convenient practice which reduces delays in completing share transactions. As trust property (such as shares) would be vested in the nominee, the practice appeared contrary to the rule (mentioned below) that trustees must have the trust property under their control.

In order to allow trustees to benefit from modern investment practices, section 16 of the Trustee Act 2000 permits trustees to appoint nominees and vest trust assets in them, while section 17 permits the appointment of a custodian to undertake safe custody of the assets or of any documents or records concerning them. Further details may be found in Chapter 18.[87] The provisions already discussed concerning the terms of appointment of agents, remuneration and the duty to keep the arrangement under review apply also to nominees and custodians.

As mentioned above, a trustee may not vest trust assets in a third party unless authorised by the trust instrument or legislation. Thus under the general law investments must be in the joint names of the trustees. If two trustees divide investments or invest separately, and

---

[83] T.A. 2000, s.12.

[84] *ibid.*, s.14.

[85] *ibid.*, ss.14, 32. See also s.29(6) (remuneration of co-trustee appointed as agent).

[86] *ibid.*, ss.21, 22. This is subject to any contrary intention in the trust instrument or other legislation.

[87] *ante*, p. 541.

one commits a breach of trust, the other will be equally liable for any loss.[88]

It is convenient also to mention here the related rule that trust capital should be received by all the trustees unless the trust instrument or legislation provides otherwise.[89] However, it has always been possible to delegate the receipt of income to one of several trustees,[90] although the co-trustees may be liable if they permit the payee to retain the money for longer than necessary.[91] In the case of company shares, the articles provide that trusts shall not be recognised.[92] In the case of joint ownership, the dividend is paid to the first named who can give a valid receipt.[93]

iii. Duty of Care. Prior to the new legislation, the standard of conduct applicable to trustees was that expected of a "prudent man of business". However, as a result of the "good faith" terminology of section 23(1) of the Trustee Act 1925, there remained uncertainty as to exactly what standard applied in the context of delegation. The matter has now been put beyond doubt by the application of the statutory duty of care laid down in section 1 of the Trustee Act 2000. This duty applies to a trustee when exercising the power of delegation under the Act of 2000 or under any other power of delegation.[94] He is subject to the duty of care when appointing an agent, nominee or custodian and when carrying out the obligation to keep the arrangement under review. In particular, he must comply with the duty when selecting the person to act, determining the terms on which he is to act, and, where asset management functions are delegated, when preparing the policy statement under section 15 of the new Act.[95] It appears that the duty of care applies to the selection of a person to act under a power of attorney, even though the delegating trustee in any event remains liable for any defaults of the person appointed.[96]

iv. Liability of Trustee. We saw that the provisions of the Trustee Act 1925 left room for doubt as to the circumstances in which a trustee would be liable for the defaults of an agent. The uncertainty has been removed by section 23 of the Trustee Act 2000, which provides that a trustee is not liable for any act or default of the agent, nominee or custodian unless he has failed to comply with the duty

---

[88] *Lewis v. Nobbs* (1878) 8 Ch. D. 591.

[89] See *Lee v. Sankey* (1873) L.R. 15 Eq. 204; T.A. 1925, s.14; *ante*, p. 573.

[90] *Townley v. Sherborne* (1634) J. Bridg. 35.

[91] *Carruthers v. Carruthers* [1896] A.C. 659.

[92] Companies Act 1985, s.360.

[93] Companies (Tables A–F) Regulations 1985, Table A, reg. 106 (S.I. 1985 No. 805).

[94] T.A. 2000, Sched. 1, para. 2.

[95] *ante*, p. 541.

[96] See Section D, *infra*.

of care when entering into the arrangement or when keeping it under review. Where the arrangement permitted the agent to appoint a substitute, the trustee is not liable for the acts of the substitute unless he failed to comply with the duty of care when agreeing the term permitting substitution or when reviewing the arrangement. Section 23 applies whether the delegation was in the exercise of the power under the Act of 2000 or under an express power or pursuant to other legislation, unless it would be inconsistent with the trust instrument or other legislation. So, for example, section 23 will not apply to the question whether a trustee is liable for the acts of a person to whom he has granted a power of attorney, because section 25(5) of the Trustee Act 1925 provides that the trustee remains liable (irrespective of fault) for the acts and defaults of the donee of the power.

D. Other Statutory Provisions Permitting Delegation of Discretions

We have seen that trustees cannot as a general rule delegate their discretions, for example the distribution of funds to beneficiaries of a discretionary trust. The delegation of discretions is permitted by Part IV of the Trustee Act 2000, section 25 of the 1925 Act, section 9 of the Trusts of Land and Appointment of Trustees Act 1996, and under section 1 of the Trustee Delegation Act 1999.

Section 25[97] enables a trustee to delegate by deed[98] to any person[99] by power of attorney for 12 months or any shorter specified period "all or any of the trusts, powers and discretions vested in him as trustee either alone or jointly with any other person or persons." Written notice must be given within seven days to each of the other trustees and to each person who has the power to appoint new trustees.[1] It was previously doubted whether a trustee who was not himself entitled to remuneration could pay the delegate out of the trust fund. This has now been alleviated by the provisions of the Trustee Act 2000 enabling professional trustees to charge even though the trust instrument does not so provide.[2] Delegation to a sole trustee is permitted, but this cannot circumvent the rule requiring payment of capital money to at least two trustees.[3] Following the Trustee Delegation Act 1999, a power of attorney under section 25

---

[97] As amended by Trustee Delegation Act 1999, s.5.
[98] In the case of delegation by a single donor, a prescribed form must be used; s.25(5), (6).
[99] Including a trust corporation; subs. (3).
[1] Subs. (4). But failure to give notice does not, in favour of a person dealing with the donee of the power, invalidate any act done by the donee.
[2] T.A. 2000, s.29.
[3] Trustee Delegation Act 1999, ss.7, 8. Previously delegation to a sole co-trustee was not permitted.

of the 1925 Act may be an enduring power, meaning one which survives the incapacity of the trustee.[4]

These provisions should only be used when such delegation is essential, for the donor of the power of attorney remains liable for the acts and defaults of the donee.[5]

The position relating to trusts of land is now found in section 9 of the Trusts of Land and Appointment of Trustees Act 1996, which permits the trustees to delegate any of their functions as trustees relating to the land, including sale, to any beneficiary (or beneficiaries) of full age and beneficially entitled to an interest in possession.[6] The delegation may be for any period or indefinite,[7] and must be by power of attorney[8] given by all the trustees jointly. It is revocable by any one or more of them, and will also be revoked if another person is appointed trustee.[9] Where a beneficiary ceases to be beneficially entitled, the delegation is revoked so far as it relates to him, but the functions remain exercisable by the remaining beneficiaries in the case of joint delegation.[10]

Beneficiaries to whom functions have been delegated under section 9 are in the same position as the trustees in relation to the exercise of the functions, but are not regarded as trustees for any other purpose. In particular, they cannot sub-delegate or give a valid receipt for capital money.[11] The provisions of the 1996 Act dealing with the trustees' liability for any defaults of the beneficiary to whom they have delegated have been changed by the Trustee Act 2000. The duty of care under section 1 of the new Act applies to trustees of land in deciding whether to delegate their functions under section 9 of the 1996 Act. If the delegation is not irrevocable, they must keep the arrangement under review, including the need to exercise any power they have to revoke the delegation or to give directions to the beneficiary. The trustees are not liable for the acts or defaults of the beneficiary unless they have failed to comply with their duty of care in deciding to delegate or in reviewing the arrangement.[12]

A more general power of delegation applying to trustees of land who are also beneficiaries, in other words co-owners, is provided by section 1 of the Trustee Delegation Act 1999. Such a trustee may

---

[4] Trustee Delegation Act 1999, s.6, repealing s.2(8) of the Enduring Powers of Attorney Act 1985. For enduring powers, see section E, below.

[5] T.A. 1925, s.25(7).

[6] Where the trustees purport to delegate to a person who is not such a beneficiary, third parties dealing with that person in good faith are protected by s.9(2).

[7] s.9(5).

[8] s.9(6) provides that this cannot be an enduring power within the Enduring Powers of Attorney Act 1985; *post*, p. 584.

[9] s.9(3). It is not revoked if any grantor ceases to be a trustee.

[10] s.9(4).

[11] s.9(7).

[12] See s.9A of the 1996 Act, inserted by T.A. 2000, Sched. 2.

delegate all trustee functions, including discretions, relating to the land or to income arising from it or to its proceeds of sale by power of attorney, which may be an enduring power.[13] Trustees who are not also beneficiaries do not fall within the scope of this provision. If they wish to delegate their discretions, they must do so under section 25 of the Trustee Act 1925, discussed above.

E. Delegation by Enduring Power of Attorney

We have seen that section 25 of the Trustee Act 1925 permits a trustee to delegate all of his functions by power of attorney for a maximum of 12 months, subject to various procedural requirements.[14] This could be done, for example, if he was going abroad.

Until 1985 there was no possibility of a power of attorney which would continue in force after the donor had become mentally incapable, as such incapacity automatically revoked the power. The Enduring Powers of Attorney Act 1985 permits the creation of a power of attorney which will survive the donor's subsequent incapacity. Unfortunately the 1985 Act inadvertently produced inconsistent but overlapping regimes for delegation by power of attorney by individual trustees under section 3(3) of the 1985 Act and under section 25 of the 1925 Act. Following recommendations of the Law Commission,[15] the problems have now been resolved by the Trustee Delegation Act 1999.

The 1999 Act draws a distinction between trustees who have a beneficial interest and those who do not. Its broad effect is first, to permit the delegation by power of attorney of all the functions of a trustee who also has a beneficial interest in the property. This is primarily directed to co-owners of land, who are normally both trustees and beneficiaries. Secondly, it ensures that a trustee who has no beneficial interest may only delegate trustee functions by power of attorney subject to the safeguards imposed by section 25 of the Trustee Act 1925. Thirdly, it ensures that the rule requiring capital money to be paid to at last two trustees cannot be circumvented by using a power of attorney.

In the case of a trustee who has a beneficial interest, section 1 of the 1999 Act permits the delegation by power of attorney of the trustee's powers and duties in relation to land, income from the land or its proceeds of sale. This may take the form of an enduring power

---

[13] See section E, *infra*, where the 1999 Act is more fully discussed.
[14] *ante*, p. 582.
[15] Law Com. No. 222 (1994), *Delegation by Individual Trustees*.

of attorney.[16] The donor (the trustee) is liable for the acts and defaults of the donee, although not for the act of delegation itself. Section 1 applies only to powers of attorney created after the Act, although, by way of exception, it applies to enduring powers of attorney created before the commencement of the Act at the end of a transitional period during which section 3(3) of the 1985 Act (which subsection is otherwise repealed) may continue to apply to such a power.[17] Thus there is no need for the donor of an enduring power to execute a fresh power under the new Act, which indeed he may be unable to do by reason of loss of capacity. In favour of a purchaser dealing with the donee of a power of attorney, a signed statement by the donee at the time of the transaction or within the following three months to the effect that the donor trustee had a beneficial interest in the property is conclusive evidence of that fact.[18]

A co-owner may, therefore, delegate his trustee functions by power of attorney without being subject to the restrictions contained in section 25 of the Trustee Act 1925, for example the 12-month time limit. An enduring power of attorney may be utilised to provide for the onset of mental incapacity. Where, however, one of two co-owners creates the power in favour of the co-trustee, the latter cannot give a good receipt for capital money.[19] In such a case another trustee must be appointed for the purpose,[20] but there is no need for the incapacitated trustee to be discharged.[21]

Prior to the 1999 Act it was not possible to delegate by way of enduring power of attorney under section 25 of the Trustee Act 1925.[22] That restriction has now been removed by section 6 of the 1999 Act in relation to powers created after its commencement. A trustee who has no beneficial interest may now delegate his trustee functions by way of an enduring power, but this may be done only by complying with section 25 of the 1925 Act, which is subject to more restrictions and safeguards than a co-owner's power of delegation under section 1 of the 1999 Act. As in the case of delegation by a trustee who is a co-owner, delegation under section 25 to a co-trustee cannot circumvent the rule requiring payment of capital money to at least two trustees.[23]

---

[16] Such a power may not be created by trustees of land under s.9(1) of the Trusts of Land and Appointment of Trustees Act 1996; *ibid.*, s.9(6).

[17] Trustee Delegation Act 1999, s.4.

[18] *ibid.*, s.2.

[19] *ibid.*, s.7.

[20] Such an appointment may be made by the donee of the power under s.36 of the Trustee Act 1925 (*ante*, p. 514), as amended by s.8 of the 1999 Act.

[21] L.P.A. 1925, s.22, as amended by s.9 of the 1999 Act.

[22] Enduring Powers of Attorney Act 1985, s.2(8).

[23] Trustee Delegation Act 1999, ss.7, 8.

8. POWERS OF MAINTENANCE AND ADVANCEMENT

Where any person has a contingent interest in property the question arises as to the use which should be made of the income until the gift vests. Otherwise the income would not be put to any use during the period. The policy is to allow the gift to "carry the intermediate income" unless there are good reasons to the contrary. Generally speaking, all testamentary gifts except contingent pecuniary legacies carry the intermediate income unless it is otherwise disposed of.[24]

One of the most common contingencies is that of attaining the age of 21 or more. It is important to make provision for the use of the income for the maintenance and education of the beneficiary before the interest vests.

A similar question arises in the opposite case of children who have a vested interest in property; for it may then be desirable that they should not be entitled to draw the whole of the income. It is better that they should receive what is reasonably necessary for their maintenance and education, and that the balance should be invested for them. Again, it may be that capital sums may be needed to establish them in a profession or in business or on marriage.

These matters may be expressly provided for in the trust instrument. If not, the court has an inherent power to approve the use of income, or even of capital for the maintenance of children.[25] But the statutory powers of maintenance[26] and advancement[27] about to be discussed are sufficient to meet the needs of most situations, and they can be amended as required to meet the needs of a particular trust. Such powers have commonly been used, not only, or mainly, for their original purposes, but rather for the fiscal advantages which they have been able to offer.[28] The duty of care under section 1 of the Trustee Act 2000 does not apply to these powers.

A. Maintenance.[29] Trustee Act 1925, s.31

i. Subsection (1).

"Where any property is held by trustees in trust for any person for any interest whatsoever, whether vested or contingent, then, subject to any prior interests or charges affecting that property—

---

[24] *post*, p. 590.
[25] *post*, p. 599.
[26] T.A. 1925, s.31.
[27] *ibid.*, s.32.
[28] *Pilkington v. I.R.C.* [1964] A.C. 612. See (1994) 8 *Trust Law International* 49 (J. Brown).
[29] See (1953) 17 Conv.(N.S.) 273 (B. Ker) for a most helpful discussion of s.31.

(i) during the infancy of any such person, if his interest so long continues, the trustees may, at their sole discretion, pay to his parent or guardian, if any, or otherwise apply for or towards his maintenance, education, or benefit,[30] the whole or such part, if any, of the income of that property as may, in all the circumstances, be reasonable, whether or not there is—

  (*a*) any other fund applicable to the same purpose; or

  (*b*) any person bound by law to provide for his maintenance or education[31]; and

(ii) if such person attaining the age of [18][32] years has not a vested interest in such income, the trustees shall thenceforth pay the income of that property and of any accretion thereto under subsection (2) of this section to him, until he either attains a vested interest therein or dies, or until failure of his interest: . . . "

(a) *Prior Interests.* The power of maintenance can only arise where a person is entitled to the income, whether by virtue of a vested interest, or by virtue of a contingent interest which carries the intermediate income.[33] If the income is applicable in favour of a prior interest, no question of its use for maintenance can arise. Similarly, a member of a discretionary class is not entitled to any income and the section does not therefore apply to payments made by the trustees in the exercise of their discretion.[34]

(b) *Child Beneficiary.* The question of application of income for the child's maintenance, education or benefit, whether his interest is vested or contingent, is a matter for the trustees' discretion. The decision to apply income for such maintenance must be taken as a result of a conscious exercise of their discretion, and not automatically.[35] So long as the trustees have regard only to the interests of the children, it is no objection that the exercise of their discretion may incidentally benefit a parent.[36] The trustees should, so far as practicable, arrange for maintenance payments to be shared proportionately among various funds available for the purpose.[37] The payments are usually made to the parent or guardian whose receipt is a sufficient discharge for the trustees.

---

[30] See *Re Heyworth's Contingent Reversionary Interest* [1956] Ch. 364; *Pilkington v. I.R.C. supra; Re Pauling's S.T.* [1964] Ch. 303; (1959) 23 Conv.(N.S.) 27 (D. Waters).

[31] See *Fuller v. Evans* [2000] 1 All E.R. 636.

[32] Reduced from 21 by Family Law Reform Act 1969. See *Begg-McBrearty (Inspector of Taxes) v. Stilwell* [1996] 1 W.L.R. 951.

[33] T.A. 1925, s.31(3); *post,* pp. 590, 591.

[34] *Re Vestey's Settlement* [1951] Ch. 209.

[35] *Wilson v. Turner* (1883) 22 Ch.D. 521.

[36] *Fuller v. Evans, supra.*

[37] T.A. 1925, s.31(1), proviso.

(c) *Adult Contingently Entitled.* A beneficiary contingently entitled to the principal becomes entitled under paragraph (ii) of subsection (1) to the income at majority.[38] His entitlement to the capital must, of course, await the happening of the contingency. The entitlement to income at majority is subject to a contrary intention; and this has been found to exist where there is a direction to accumulate.

In *Re Turner's Will Trusts*,[39] a testator provided interests in favour of his grandchildren contingently on their attaining the age of 28, and expressly gave the trustees power to apply the income for their maintenance, education and benefit until that time, and instructed the trustees to accumulate the surplus.

One grandchild, Geoffrey, was 21 when the testator died; and himself died three years later aged 24. No income had been paid to him, and some £3,000 had been accumulated since the testator's death. The question was whether section 31(1) applied. If it did, Geoffrey's estate would have become entitled to the income. The Court of Appeal held that, in spite of the imperative terms of section 31, it gave way to an expression of a contrary intention in accordance with the Trustee Act 1925, s.69(2).

ii. Subsection (2).[40]

(a) *Surplus Income to be Accumulated for Child Beneficiaries.* Subsection (2) provides that the residue of the income, not applied for maintenance, shall be accumulated by investment until the person contingently entitled reaches majority. Income from such investments becomes available for future maintenance; and the accumulations themselves may be applied, before the beneficiary reaches majority, as if they were income arising in the then current year.

(b) *Entitlement to Accumulations.* On the majority (or earlier marriage) of a child, the question arises whether or not any accumulations should be given to him. As would be expected, he is entitled to the accumulations if he had a vested interest before reaching full

---

[38] *Re Jones' W.T.* [1947] Ch. 48.
[39] [1937] Ch. 15; *Re Ransome* [1957] Ch. 348; [1979] Conv. 243 (J. Riddall); *Brotherton v. I.R.C.* [1978] 1 W.L.R. 610; *I.R.C. v. Bernstein* [1961] Ch. 399; *Re McGeorge* [1963] Ch. 544, where the contrary intention was shown by deferring the gift to a daughter until after the death of a widow; *Re Erskine's S.T.* [1971] 1 W.L.R. 162.
[40] T.A. 2000, Sched. 2, para. 25, has made minor amendments.

age (for he was entitled all along to the income)[41]; or if, on attaining his majority, he "becomes entitled to the property from which the income arose in fee simple, absolute or determinable, or absolutely or for an entailed interest." In short, he is entitled to the accumulations on his majority (or earlier marriage) if he is then entitled to the capital.[42]

The question arose in *Re Sharp's Settlement Trusts*[43] whether the provision covered the case where the children of the settlor became entitled, subject to an overriding power of appointment, to the capital on attaining the age of 21. Were they then entitled absolutely? Pennycuick V.-C. held that they were not: the fact that their interests could be defeated by the exercise of the power prevented their becoming entitled absolutely. It is anomalous that "a person having a determinable interest in realty should qualify to take accumulations at 21,"[44] but "a person having a like interest in personalty should not equally so qualify."[45] This is just another one of those curious instances where the 1925 legislation just did not go far enough in its expressed intention so far as possible to assimilate the rules relating to realty and personalty."[46] In all other cases, as for example the case of a contingent beneficiary whose interest never vests, or where the beneficiary, although having a vested interest, fails to reach majority, the accumulations are added to capital for all purposes.[47]

The provisions relating to the destination of accumulations in section 31(2) are also subject to a contrary intention in the trust instrument.[48] In *Re Delamere's Settlement Trusts*,[49] the trustees appointed income to beneficiaries "absolutely" in 1971. All the beneficiaries were then children. By 1981, £122,000 had been accumulated. The question arose whether section 31(2) applied, so that the share of any beneficiary dying before majority would devolve with the capital, or whether there was a contrary intention, so that the accumulations were held indefeasibly for the appointees. It

---

[41] For income tax liability, see *Stanley v. I.R.C.* [1944] K.B. 255.

[42] T.A. 1925, s.31(2)(i).

[43] [1973] Ch. 331; (1972) 36 Conv.(N.S.) 436 (D. Hayton). See also *Re Delamere's Settlement Trusts, infra.*

[44] The words "fee simple, absolute or determinable," applying only to realty.

[45] [1973] Ch. 331 at 346.

[46] (1972) 36 Conv.(N.S.) 436 at 438. The accumulations of income were added to the share of each child, subject to the exercise of the power: *Re King* [1928] Ch. 330; *Re Joel's W.T.* [1967] Ch. 14; *post*, p. 592.

[47] T.A. 1925, s.31(2)(ii). On the distinction between contingent interests and interests subject to defeasance, see *Phipps v. Ackers* (1842) 9 Cl. & F. 583; *Brotherton v. I.R.C.* [1978] 1 W.L.R. 610.

[48] T.A. 1925, s.69(2).

[49] [1984] 1 W.L.R. 813; [1985] Conv. 153 (R. Griffith).

was held that the word "absolutely" in the 1971 appointment indicated indefeasibility, thus excluding section 31(2). Clearly the mere fact that the interest is vested is not sufficient to achieve this result.[50]

iii. Gifts Carrying Intermediate Income.

iii. Gifts Carrying Intermediate Income. Section 31 only applies to contingent interests which carry the intermediate income; that is to say, to gifts which entitle the donee to claim the income earned by, or interest upon, the subject matter of the gift between the date of the gift and the date of payment. Whether or not a gift should do so is not self-evident, and there are some complex and technical rules which do not provide any conceptual unity. Some rules are based on case law, and some on statute. It is unfortunate that there is not a single comprehensive code.

Vested gifts carry the intermediate income unless a contrary intention appears, as where the income is given to someone other than the donee for a period. A direction to accumulate the surplus income until majority, on the other hand, does not indicate that the gift does not carry the income, but merely that the power of maintenance is excluded.

With contingent gifts, the rules, subject always to an expression of contrary intention, are as follows.[51]

(a) *Contingent Residuary Bequest.* A contingent bequest of residuary personalty carries all income earned from the testator's death.[52] The undisposed of income "becomes part of the residue."[53] But it seems that, if a residuary bequest of personalty (whether vested or contingent) is postponed "to a future date which must come sooner or later,"[54] the intermediate income is undisposed of and therefore not carried by the gift.[55]

(b) *Contingent or Future Specific Gifts of Personalty or Realty and Contingent Residuary Devises of Freehold Land.* The Law of Property Act 1925, s.175 provides that a contingent specific bequest of personalty or devise of realty and a contingent residuary devise of freehold land, and a devise of freehold land to trustees on trust for persons whose interests are contingent or executory shall carry the intermediate income. It will be noticed that the section does not

---

[50] See T.A. 1925, s.31(2)(i)(*a*).

[51] (1953) 17 Conv.(N.S.) 273 (B. Ker); (1963) 79 L.Q.R. 184 (P.V.B.).

[52] *Re Adams* [1893] 1 Ch. 329.

[53] *ibid.* at 334.

[54] *per* Cross J. in *Re McGeorge* [1963] Ch. 544 at 551; such as the death of an annuitant.

[55] *Re Oliver* [1947] 2 All E.R. 161; *Re Gillett's W.T.* [1950] Ch. 102; *Re Geering* [1964] Ch. 136.

affect a residuary gift of a leasehold interest, which ranks as personalty.[56]

(c) *Contingent Pecuniary Legacy.* A contingent pecuniary legacy does not carry the intermediate income.[57] To this rule there are three exceptions, in which cases the contingent pecuniary legacy will carry interest, and it will be available for the maintenance of a child.

First: Where the legacy was given by the father of the child legatee, or by some person *in loco parentis*, so long as no other fund is provided for his maintenance,[58] and the contingency is the attainment of majority.[59]

Secondly: Where the testator shows an intention to maintain.[60]

Thirdly: Where the testator has set aside the legacy as a separate fund for the benefit of the legatee.[61]

Section 31, having laid down that the section applies only to a gift which carries the intermediate income, refers expressly to the first of these exceptions, and provides that the rate of interest shall (if the income available is sufficient, and subject to any rules of court to the contrary) be 5 per cent.[62] Thus, the subsection refers only to the first of the recognised exceptions, and the question arises whether that is an indication that the other two are not intended to apply. The better view is that they are unaffected by subsection (3), and that "the specific mention of the rule in [the first exception] is only for the purpose of establishing a suitable rate of interest".[63] The statute widens the exception by making it applicable in the case of either parent, and not only in the case of a father.

iv. Aggregation of Income of Children with that of their Parents. It has been seen that an accumulation and maintenance settlement[64] giving contingent gifts to children with power to use the income for maintenance, and to accumulate that not so used, offers tax advantages, both in the context of income tax and of inheritance tax, but that income so accumulated carries the income tax disadvantage of liability to the rate applicable to trusts (currently 34 per cent).[65] Where income is paid to the unmarried child of the settlor,

---

[56] *Re Woodin* [1895] 2 Ch. 349.
[57] *Re Raine* [1929] 1 Ch. 716; *Re George* (1877) 5 Ch.D. 837.
[58] *Re George* (1877) 5 Ch.D. 837 at 843.
[59] *Re Abrahams* [1911] 1 Ch. 108.
[60] *Re Churchill* [1909] 2 Ch. 431.
[61] *Re Medlock* (1886) 54 L.T. 828.
[62] *cf.* R.S.C. Ord. 44, r. 10, C.P.R. 1998, Sched. 1 (6 per cent where legacy ordered to be paid by the court).
[63] See (1953) 17 Conv.(N.S.) 273 at 279.
[64] *ante*, p. 233.
[65] I.C.T.A. 1988, s.686, as amended.

the income is treated as that of his parent.[66] In other cases, the income is treated as part of the child's total income.

v. Gifts to Classes. Where there is a gift to a class contingently on attaining the age of 21, the trustees may treat separately, for these purposes, each person's presumptive share. That is to say, that when one member of the class attains 21 and becomes entitled to his share, the trustees may continue to exercise their powers of maintenance in respect of the other members.[67] Similarly, income may only be used for the maintenance of any member of the class if that income was earned during the lifetime of that member,[68] but if a member of a class dies without obtaining a vested interest, the accumulation of income representing his contingent share is added to the capital under section 31(2)(ii), although this means that future born members will thus benefit from it.[69]

B. Advancement

i. The Meaning of Advancement. We saw that maintenance was concerned with the payment of income for the benefit of child beneficiaries. Advancement is concerned with the payment or application of capital sums to the beneficiary's advantage before the time comes when he is entitled to demand the fund. The scope of the power depends upon the terms of the instrument giving it,[70] and upon Trustee Act 1925, s.32.[71] Payments under such power have been made not only for the purpose of providing capital sums when needed, but also for the purpose of tax saving.

Thus, suppose a fund is held on trust for A, the capital being payable to him on attaining 25. If A marries, or sets up in business or in a profession before that time, a power of advancement makes possible the payment to him of some or all of the capital of the fund to help with such a project. There is a similar but more complicated question if A's interest is subject to a prior life interest in X; for X's income will be affected by any payments out of the capital fund which produces it. Likewise if A's interest is contingent on his attaining 25; for if payments are made to A and A never attains 25 the capital payments will have been made to the wrong person.

---

[66] I.C.T.A. 1988, ss.660, 663, 664; F.A. 1990, s.82. Similarly where income is retained in a bare trust for the settlor's child; F.A. 1999, s.64.

[67] *Re King* [1928] Ch. 330.

[68] *Re Joel's W.T.* [1967] Ch. 14.

[69] *ibid.*; not following *Re King, supra*, on this point. The Law Reform Committee, 23rd Report, *The Powers and Duties of Trustees* (1982 Cmnd. 8733), para. 3.41, recommended the abrogation of the rule in *Re Joel*. See also Trust Law Committee Consultation Paper, *Capital and Income of Trusts* (1999), para. 7.6.

[70] See *Re Collard's W.T.* [1901] Ch. 293.

[71] *infra.*

The tax-saving question arises where trustees hold a large sum on trust for A for life and then to A's children equally at 21. Independently of the fund A is rich enough to provide the children with all they need. It may be advantageous to make transfers of capital from the trust for the children. Inheritance tax will be avoided if the advancement was made more than seven years before A's death.[72] Such a payment is certainly not an "advancement" within the usual meaning of the word, but no one could deny that the saving of tax on the trust is a benefit to the children. A further question arises, whether such sums must be held in trust for the children absolutely, or whether they may themselves be settled by the creation of sub-trusts for the benefit of themselves and also for other persons such as future dependants. These questions are dealt with below.

ii. Original Meaning of Advancement. "The word 'advancement' itself meant in this context the establishment in life of the beneficiary who was the object of the power or at any rate some step that would contribute to the furtherance of his establishment.[73] ... Typical instances of expenditure for such purposes under the social conditions of the nineteenth century were an apprenticeship or the purchase of a commission in the Army or of an interest in business. In the case of a girl there could be advancement on marriage."[74]

iii. Express Powers. Until 1925 there was no statutory power of advancement. Express powers of advancement were given narrow scope consistent with the established meaning of the word.[75] So, "to prevent uncertainties about the permitted range of objects for which moneys could be raised and made available, such words as 'or otherwise for his or her benefit' were often added to the word 'advancement.' It was always recognised that these added words were 'large words'[76] and indeed in another case[77] the same judge spoke of preferment and advancement of being 'both large words' but of 'benefit' as being the 'largest of all.' "[78] The combined phrase "advancement or benefit" is read disjunctively,[79] it now means "any use of the money which will improve the material situation of the

---

[72] F.A. (No. 2) 1987, s.96.

[73] See *per* Jessel M.R. in *Taylor v. Taylor* (1875) L.R. 20 Eq. 155; *Lowther v. Bentinck* (1874) L.R. 19 Eq. 166 (payment of debts); *Roper-Curzon v. Roper-Curzon* (1871) L.R. 11 Eq. 452 (starting a career at the Bar); *Re Long's Settlement* (1868) 38 L.J.Ch. 125 (passage money to go to a colony); *Re Williams' W.T.* [1953] Ch. 138 (purchase of a house as a surgery); *Hardy v. Shaw* [1976] Ch. 82 (shares in family company), (1976) 126 N.L.J. 117 (F. Glover).

[74] *per* Lord Radcliffe in *Pilkington v. I.R.C.* [1964] A.C. 612 at 634.

[75] *per* Kennedy L.J. in *Molyneux v. Fletcher* [1898] 1 Q.B. 648 at 653.

[76] See Jessel M.R. in *Re Breed's Will* (1875) 1 Ch.D. 226 at 228.

[77] *Lowther v. Bentinck* (1874) L.R. 19 Eq. 166 at 169.

[78] *per* Lord Radcliffe in *Pilkington v. I.R.C.* [1964] A.C. 612 at 634; *Re Halsted's W.T.* [1937] 2 All E.R. 570 at 571; *Re Moxon's W.T.* [1958] 1 W.L.R. 165 at 168.

[79] *Lowther v. Bentinck* (1874) L.R. 19 Eq. 166; *Re Halsted's W.T., supra,* at 571.

beneficiary."[80] The scope of an express power depends of course upon its own language. The standard form of express power was incorporated in the Trustee Act 1925, s.32; and express provisions on the question of advancement are now usually confined to extensions of the statutory power by making the power applicable to the whole of the beneficiary's presumptive share,[81] or by giving express powers to the trustees to create sub-trusts.[82]

iv. The Statutory Power. Trustee Act 1925, s.32.

Section 32—"(1) Trustees may at any time or times pay or apply any capital money subject to a trust, for the advancement or benefit, in such manner as they may, in their absolute discretion, think fit, of any person entitled to the capital of the trust property or of any share thereof, whether absolutely or contingently on his attaining any specified age or on the occurrence of any other event, or subject to a gift over on his death under any specified age or on the occurrence of any other event, and whether in possession or in remainder or reversion, and such payment or application may be made notwithstanding that the interest of such person is liable to be defeated by the exercise of a power of appointment or revocation, or to be diminished by the increase of the class to which he belongs:

Provided that—

(*a*) the money so paid or applied for the advancement or benefit of any person shall not exceed altogether in amount one-half of the presumptive or vested share or interest of that person in the trust property[83]; and

(*b*) if that person is or becomes absolutely and indefeasibly entitled to a share in the trust property the money so paid or applied shall be brought into account as part of such share; and

(*c*) no such payment or application shall be made so as to prejudice any person entitled to any prior life or other interest, whether vested or contingent, in the money paid or applied unless such person is in existence and of full age and consents in writing to such payment or application."

The section does not apply to capital money arising under the Settled Land Act 1925.[84] Its application is always subject to the

---

[80] *per* Lord Radcliffe in *Pilkington v. I.R.C.* [1964] A.C. 612 at 635.

[81] By proviso (a) to T.A. 1925, s.32, the statutory power extends only to one-half of the beneficiary's presumptive share; *infra.*

[82] *post*, p. 596; (1959) 23 Conv.(N.S.) 27 (D. Waters).

[83] The possible advancement of one half must be taken into account as resources for supplementary benefit purposes; *Peters v. Chief Adjudication Officer* (1989) 19 Fam. Law 318.

[84] T.A. 1925, s.32(2), as substituted by Trusts of Land and Appointment of Trustees Act 1996, Sched. 3, para. 3(8).

expression of a contrary intention[85] and it has been held to be excluded by provision for accumulation.[86]

v. Problems in the Application of section 32. Pilkington v. I.R.C.[87] The wide construction of the phrase "advancement" or "benefit" must have been carried into the statutory power created by section 32, since it adopts without qualification the accustomed wording "for the advancement or benefit in such manner as they may in their absolute discretion think fit."[88] But this leaves open a number of questions; can payments be made for the "benefit" of a person who is not in any way in need? To what extent can an advancement re-settle the money advanced, the re-settlement changing the original trust? Can trustees, exercising the statutory power of advancement, delegate their discretion by giving a dispositive discretion to the trustees of the re-settlement; *i.e.* can they make an advancement on protective or discretionary trusts? These questions were discussed and largely settled in the long litigation over the will of William Pilkington.

> The testator left a share of his residuary estate on trust for his nephew Richard upon protective trusts during his life and after Richard's death upon trust for such of his children or remoter issue as he should by deed or will appoint and in default of appointment in trust for such of Richard's children as attained 21 (or, if female, married under that age) in equal shares. Richard had three children all born after the death of the testator of whom a two-year-old daughter Penelope was one. Richard's father (brother of the testator and grandfather of Penelope) proposed to make a settlement in favour of Penelope, providing that the trustees hold the property on trust to pay the income to Penelope at 21, and the capital for her absolutely at 30 and if Penelope died under 30 leaving children, on trust for such children at 21 with further family trusts in default. The trustees had power to apply the income for Penelope's maintenance until she reached the age of 21, and were to accumulate the surplus income.
>
> The trustees proposed to advance, with the consent of Richard, one-half of Penelope's expectant share under the testator's will, and pay it to the trustees of Richard's father's settlement.

---

[85] *Re Evans' Settlement* [1967] 1 W.L.R. 1294.
[86] *I.R.C. v. Bernstein* [1961] Ch. 399. This is so even if the direction for accumulation contravenes L.P.A. 1925, ss.164–166; *Re Ransome* [1957] Ch. 348; *Brotherton v. I.R.C.* [1978] 1 W.L.R. 610.
[87] [1964] A.C. 612.
[88] *per* Lord Radcliffe in *Pilkington v. I.R.C., supra*, at 635; *Re Pauling's S.T.* [1964] Ch. 303.

The House of Lords held that this proposal was within the trustees' power under section 32. They held also that the exercise of the power of advancement was analogous to the exercise of a special power of appointment and that in the circumstances the advancement would be void for perpetuity.

(a) *Benefit.* On the question of the benefit to Penelope, Lord Radcliffe held that it was immaterial that other persons, such as her future dependants, would benefit also. " . . . if the disposition itself, by which I mean the whole provision made, is for her benefit, it is no objection to the exercise of the power that other persons benefit incidentally as a result of the exercise."[89] The relief from anxiety about the future maintenance of a wife and a family has been held to be a sufficient benefit[90]; as has the performance of the obligation felt by a rich man to contribute to a charitable trust where it would be a great burden to do so out of taxed income[91]; and also the payment from a wife's fund to her husband to enable him to set up in business in England and prevent a separation of the family.[92] Similarly, there was no need to show that the benefit was "related to his or her own real or personal needs."[93] The estate duty saving was a sufficient benefit.[94]

(b) *Settlement of Funds Advanced. Sub-Trusts.* Nor was it any objection that the funds were being subjected to a settlement, and not paid for the sole benefit of Penelope; nor that her enjoyment was deferred. The settlement of advanced funds had many times been approved[95] and this inevitably meant that the trusts on which the funds would be held under the advancement were different from those laid down by the original settlor.

(c) *Delegation.* Closely connected with the question of resettlement is that of the extent to which trustees, in making an advancement on new trusts, can give discretionary powers to the trustees of the new settlement. In general, *delegatus non potest delegare.*[96]

---

[89] *per* Lord Radcliffe in *Pilkington v. I.R.C.* [1964] A.C. 612 at 636; *Re Halsted's W.T.* [1937] 2 All E.R. 570.

[90] *Re Halsted's W.T., supra.*

[91] *Re Clore's Settlement Trust* [1966] 1 W.L.R. 955.

[92] *Re Kershaw's Trusts* (1868) L.R. 6 Eq. 322.

[93] *per* Lord Evershed in *Re Pilkington's W.T.* [1961] Ch. 466 at 481.

[94] " . . . if the advantage of preserving the funds of a beneficiary from the incidence of death duty is not an advantage personal to that beneficiary, I do not see what is"; *per* Lord Radcliffe in *Pilkington v. I.R.C., supra,* at 640; see also Upjohn J. in *Re Wills W.T.* [1959] Ch. 1, 11–12; *Re Clore's S.T.* [1966] 1 W.L.R. 955.

[95] *Re Halsted's W.T.* [1937] 2 All E.R. 570; *Re Moxon's W.T.* [1958] 1 W.L.R. 165; *Re Wills' W.T.* [1959] Ch. 1; *Re Abrahams' W.T.* [1969] 1 Ch. 463; *Re Hastings-Bass* [1975] Ch. 25; (1974) 38 Conv.(N.S.) 293 (F. Crane).

[96] *Re May* [1926] 1 Ch. 136; *Re Mewburn* [1934] Ch. 112; *Re Wills' W.T., supra.*

However, "the law is not that trustees cannot delegate: it is that trustees cannot delegate unless they have authority to do so. If the power of advancement which they possess is so read as to allow them to raise money for the purpose of having it settled, then they do have the necessary authority to let the money pass out of the old settlement into the new trusts. No question of delegation of their powers or trusts arises. If, on the other hand, their power of advancement is read so as to exclude settled advances, cadit quaestio."[97]

This does not, however, solve all the problems. The statutory power allows trustees to advance money by paying it to other trustees to hold on new trusts. Such trusts may include a power of advancement[98]; and presumably section 32 applies to the new trustees. Further, acting on the analogy of cases on special powers of appointment, it seems that the new trusts may include a protective and forfeitable life interest[99]; but that the discretionary trusts which come into effect upon the determination of the life interest may be invalid, because the duties of trustees of a discretionary trust involve dispositive (as opposed to administrative) discretions,[1] and these cannot be delegated without express authority.[2] This latter point is unaffected by the Trustee Act 2000.[3]

If that is correct, section 32 appears to give trustees no power to make an advancement upon a new settlement which takes the form of discretionary trusts. Such a situation appears necessarily to raise questions of delegation; and not to be covered by Lord Radcliffe's dictum quoted above.[4] Whether a settlement on discretionary trusts would satisfy the test of "benefit" is another matter; for under such a trust no interest of course is technically given to the advanced beneficiary.[5] The delegation problem can be met by expressly empowering the trustees of the original settlement to delegate their powers in that manner.[6]

(d) *Perpetuity.* For the purposes of the perpetuity rule, the exercise of a power of advancement is treated, as has been seen,[7] on the analogy of a special power of appointment. Where a sub-trust is

---

[97] *per* Lord Radcliffe in *Pilkington v. I.R.C.* [1964] A.C. 612 at 639.

[98] *Re Mewburn* [1934] Ch. 112; *Re Morris* [1951] 2 All E.R. 528; *Re Hunter's W.T.* [1963] Ch. 372.

[99] *Re Boulton's S.T.* [1928] Ch. 703; *Re Hunter, supra; Re Morris, supra.*

[1] See (1953) 17 Conv.(N.S.) 285 at 289 (A. Kiralfy).

[2] *per* Eve J. in *Re Boulton's S.T. ante*, at 709.

[3] See T.A. 2000, s.11(2)(a); *ante*, p. 579.

[4] *supra.*

[5] *Gartside v. I.R.C.* [1968] A.C. 553. This is not *per se* an objection; *Re Clore's Settlement Trust, supra.*

[6] For the view that *Pilkington v. I.R.C.* ([1964] A.C. 612) does authorise the creation of discretionary trusts under the statutory power of advancement, see (1963) 27 Conv.(N.S.) 65; Parker and Mellows, *The Modern Law of Trusts* (7th ed.), pp. 626–627.

[7] *Pilkington v. I.R.C.* [1964] A.C. 612; *ante*, p. 596.

created by an advancement, the limitation in the sub-trust is tested for validity by being read back into the original instrument under which the power was exercised.[8] The advancements made in *Re Abrahams' Will Trusts*[9] and *Re Hastings-Bass*[10] failed, in part, to comply; as the intended advancement would have done in *Pilkington v. I.R.C.*[11] In *Re Abrahams' Will Trusts*, the failure of the void parts of the sub-trust wholly changed the character of the benefit being conferred on the beneficiary, and the advancement was held void. In *Re Hastings-Bass*, however, the trustees' prime consideration was to create a life interest in the life tenant of the sub-trust in order to save estate duty on the death of his father, the life tenant of the original settlement. The fact that the interests in remainder in the sub-trust were void for perpetuity did not make the advancement itself void.

In the case of advancements made under powers coming into existence after July 15, 1964 the interests under the sub-trust would be treated as valid until it became known that they would in fact vest outside the perpetuity period.[12]

vi. The Provisos.[13] (*a*) Only half the presumptive share of each beneficiary may be advanced under the statutory power.[14] No doubt this is a wise limitation as a general rule; for if the contingent interest of the advanced beneficiary never vests, the fund in the hands of the person next entitled is reduced by the amount advanced. However, it may be advantageous to be able to advance the whole; and it is common to extend the statutory power so as to give the trustees power to advance the whole if they see fit.

(*b*) This attempts to effect an equality between the members of a class of beneficiaries, by requiring those who have received benefits in advance of other members of a class of beneficiaries to count the advancement against their ultimate share.[15] Of course it is otherwise if the share never vests.[16]

(*c*) By advancing some or all of the capital, the fund which provides the income of the tenant for life is reduced. The consent of

[8] *Re Paul* [1921] 2 Ch. 1.
[9] [1969] 1 Ch. 463.
[10] [1975] Ch. 25; *ante*, p. 527.
[11] [1964] A.C. 612.
[12] Perpetuities and Accumulations Act 1964, s.3.
[13] Set out *ante*, p. 594.
[14] See *Re Marquess of Abergavenny's Estate Act Trusts* [1981] 1 W.L.R. 843; [1982] Conv. 158 (J. Price); (express power to pay life tenant any part or parts not exceeding one-half in value of the settled fund was exhausted by the advance of one-half, even though the remainder subsequently increased in value).
[15] The advance is brought into account at its value at the date of advancement. In times of inflation this can have capricious results. A form of indexation was therefore recommended by the Law Reform Committee, 23rd Report, *The Powers and Duties of Trustees* (1982 Cmnd. 8733), paras. 4.43–4.47.
[16] *Re Fox* [1904] 1 Ch. 480 (express power).

the tenant for life is therefore requisite to the exercise of the power. The court has no power to dispense with this consent.[17] A member of a discretionary class is not, however, a person whose consent is required.[18]

C. The Court's Inherent Power to Provide Maintenance and Advancement

The court has inherent power to order provision to be made for a child out of his property. This power is usually applied in respect of income,[19] but occasionally capital is used.[20] Also, the court has statutory power to make an order authorising a person to make use of a child's property with a view to the application of the capital or income for the child's maintenance, education or benefit.[21]

D. Responsibility of the Trustees to See to the Application of the Money Advanced

We have seen that the trustees must be satisfied that the proposed advancement is for the benefit of the beneficiary. The next question is whether the trustees, in making an advancement, are under an obligation to see that the money is applied towards the purposes for which the payment was made. In *Re Pauling's Settlement Trusts*[22] the Court of Appeal, dealing with an express power to advance one-half of an expected or presumptive share for the "absolute use" of a beneficiary, held that the power was fiduciary; the trustees could hand over a sum of capital quite generally to a beneficiary if they thought that he was the type of person who could be trusted with the money. Or, if the trustees made the advance for a particular purpose, which they stated, they could quite properly pay it over if they reasonably thought that he could be trusted to carry it out. "What they cannot do is prescribe a particular purpose, and then raise and pay the money over to the advancee leaving him or her entirely free, legally and morally, to apply it for that purpose or to spend it in any way he or she chooses without any responsibility on the trustees even to inquire as to its application."[23]

---

[17] *Re Forster's Settlement* [1942] Ch. 199. See also *Henley v. Wardell, The Times,* January 29, 1988. (Power in will giving trustees "absolute and uncontrolled discretion" to advance whole capital did not give them power to dispense with the consent of the prior income beneficiary. The purpose of the clause was merely to enlarge the power as to the amount advanced).

[18] *Re Beckett's Settlement* [1940] Ch. 279.

[19] *Wellesley v. Wellesley* (1828) 2 Bli.(N.S.) 124.

[20] *Barlow v. Grant* (1684) 1 Vern. 255.

[21] *post,* p. 635; T.A. 1925, s. 53.

[22] [1964] Ch. 303; *post,* p. 663.

[23] [1964] Ch. 303 at 334.

CHAPTER 21

THE FIDUCIARY NATURE OF TRUSTEESHIP

1. REMUNERATION AND REIMBURSEMENT

THE basic principle of equity is that a trustee acts voluntarily and is not paid for his services.[1] It does not matter whether his services are of a professional nature, as where he is a solicitor, or whether they are personal. It follows, therefore, that a trustee can only claim remuneration if he can show a specific entitlement to it. The discussion that follows is essentially an account of how that entitlement can arise.

It is also a basic principle that a trustee may recover, by means of a lien over the trust property, for his legitimate out-of-pocket expenses, which include the payment of agents' fees wherever their

---

[1] *Robinson v. Pett* (1734) 3 P. Wms. 249; *Re Barber* (1886) 34 Ch.D. 77; *Dale v. I.R.C.* [1954] A.C. 11 at 27. This rule is to the contrary in many of the American States. English executors were held to be entitled to retain a fee earned by taking out a grant of probate in New York in respect of American assets; *Re Northcote's W.T.* [1949] 1 All E.R. 442.

employment is permitted,[2] and the proper costs of litigation,[3] including the costs of successfully (but not unsuccessfully) defending themselves from liability for breach of trust.[4] Trustees should seek the court's authorisation before suing or defending, to avoid the risk that their costs are found to have been improperly incurred.[5] Where there is hostile litigation between rival claimants to the trust fund, the trustee should not become involved but should offer to submit to the court's direction; where the trustee is sued successfully by the beneficiaries, his costs will not come out of the trust fund; but where the dispute is with a third party, the trustee's duty is to protect the trust and he will be indemnified so long as the proceedings are properly brought or defended for the benefit of the trust, whether or not successfully.[6] Trustees do not fail in their duty where they discontinue litigation against a third party because the trust fund is likely to be exhausted in indemnifying them, leaving them personally exposed as to any insufficiency.[7] The trustee's lien over the fund extends to an indemnity against contingent liabilities.[8]

The right to reimbursement is statutory,[9] and prevails against trust property generally, both capital and income, and in some cases against the beneficiaries personally,[10] as in the case of a bare trust.[11]

A. Remuneration Authorised by the Trust Instrument

Express remuneration clauses are extremely common, and are frequently very widely drafted. Otherwise, prior to the reforms of the Trustee Act 2000 discussed in Section B below, it would have been difficult to persuade professional people to act as trustees. While the principle of equity is that clauses authorising remuneration are to be strictly construed,[12] this has been relieved by section 28 of the Act of 2000. This provides that where there is an express clause permitting the trustee to be paid for his services, and the

---

[2] This must be borne in mind when considering the principle that the trustee's office is gratuitous. His burden is alleviated to the extent that he can properly delegate the work to agents; *ante*, p. 576.

[3] *ante*, p. 531. See *Re Spurling's Will Trusts* [1966] 1 W.L.R. 920; *Holding and Management Ltd v. Property Holding and Investment Trust plc* [1989] 1 W.L.R. 1313 (costs not recoverable where trustees had acted in a manner hostile to the beneficiaries).

[4] *Armitage v. Nurse* [1998] Ch. 241 at 262.

[5] See *Singh v. Basin, The Times*, August 21, 1998.

[6] *Alsop Wilkinson v. Neary* [1996] 1 W.L.R. 1220. See also *McDonald v. Horn* [1995] 1 All E.R. 961.

[7] *Bradstock Trustee Services Ltd v. Nabarro Nathanson (a firm)* [1995] 1 W.L.R. 1405.

[8] *X v. A* [2000] 1 All E.R. 490; [2000] Conv. 560 (A. Kenny).

[9] Trustee Act 2000, s.31, replacing previous legislation. Interest is not payable; *Foster v. Spencer* [1996] 2 All E.R. 672.

[10] See generally *Stott v. Milne* (1884) 25 Ch.D. 710; *Re Grimthorpe* [1958] Ch. 615.

[11] *Hurst v. Bryk* [1999] Ch. 1 (partners holding lease on trust for partnership).

[12] *Re Chalinder & Herington* [1907] 1 Ch. 58; *Re Gee* [1948] Ch. 284.

trustee is a trust corporation or is acting in a professional capacity, the trustee is entitled to be paid even if the services are capable of being provided by a lay trustee. The remuneration may take the form of the income from a part of the estate[13] or capital under a power of appointment,[14] or the trustee may be given power to make use of trust money in other ways.[15] A clause in a will authorising remuneration is no longer treated as a legacy.[16]

B. Trustee Act 2000

Part V of the Trustee Act 2000 facilitates the remuneration of professional trustees in cases where neither the trust instrument nor any other legislation provides for it. Section 29 (which applies whenever the trust was created) provides that a trust corporation[17] is entitled to receive reasonable remuneration out of the trust fund for services provided. A professional trustee who is neither a trust corporation nor a sole trustee is similarly entitled if each other trustee has agreed in writing that he may be remunerated. A sole trustee is excluded because the safeguard of collective scrutiny would be absent. Section 29 extends to personal representatives acting professionally,[18] but does not apply to trustees of charitable trusts. The Secretary of State, however, may make provision by regulations for the remuneration of charity trustees.[19]

C. Other Statutory Provisions

Other statutory provisions enable fees to be charged by the Public Trustee,[20] by persons appointed to be Judicial Trustees,[21] and by corporations appointed as custodian trustees.[22] In this last case, the corporation concerned cannot also be a managing trustee.[23] But where a corporation is appointed to be a trustee by the court, the

---

[13] *Public Trustee v. I.R.C.* [1960] A.C. 398. See (1988) 2 *Trust Law & Practice* 93 (J. Thurston).

[14] *Re Beatty's W.T.* [1990] 1 W.L.R. 1503.

[15] See *Space Investments Ltd v. Canadian Imperial Bank of Commerce Trust Co. (Bahamas) Ltd* [1986] 1 W.L.R. 1072 (settlement provided that bank trustee could deposit trust money with itself and use for own purposes, subject to normal obligation to repay).

[16] Trustee Act 2000, s.28.

[17] As defined in the Trustee Act 1925.

[18] Trustee Act 2000, s.35.

[19] *ibid.*, s.30. It was considered that to apply the general provision to charity trustees might undermine public confidence in the sector; Law Com. No. 260 (1999), para. 7.22. See also s.32 (remuneration and reimbursement of agents, nominees and custodians).

[20] Public Trustee Act 1906, s.9; Public Trustee (Fees) Act 1957. He is paid such salary as the Lord Chancellor determines; Public Trustee Act 1906, s.8(1A).

[21] Judicial Trustees Act 1896, s.1.

[22] Public Trustee Act 1906, s.4.

[23] *Forster v. Williams Deacon's Bank Ltd* [1935] Ch. 359; *Arning v. James* [1936] Ch. 158.

court has full discretion as to its fees, and is not restricted by this distinction.[24]

D. Remuneration Authorised by the Court

The court has an inherent jurisdiction, which is exercisable retro-spectively[25] and prospectively, but in exceptional cases only, to authorise remuneration for trustees and other fiduciaries. The power has even been exercised in favour of a fiduciary who was guilty of undue influence. In *O'Sullivan v. Management Agency and Music Ltd*[26] a contract between a performer and his agent was set aside for undue influence and breach of fiduciary duty, but the agent was awarded remuneration (including a reasonable profit element) as he had contributed significantly to the claimant's success. The argument that the jurisdiction was exercisable only in favour of the morally blameless was rejected.

The jurisdiction extends to increasing the rate of remuneration authorised by the settlor.[27] The court in such a case would have regard to the nature of the trust, the experience and skill of the trustee, and the sums claimed in comparison with the charges of other trustees.

Factors in favour of the exercise of the court's discretion include the fact that the fiduciary's work has been of substantial benefit to the trust, as in *Boardman v. Phipps*,[28] and that if the work had not been done by the fiduciary it would have had to be done by someone else at the expense of the trust.[29] A recent example is where trustees (a surveyor and a building contractor) used special skills over many years to bring about a sale of trust land at a profit. They had not appreciated the extent of the task when appointed, otherwise they would have declined to act gratuitously. Remuneration was awarded for the work done, but not for remaining tasks, which required no

---

[24] Trustee Act 1925, s.42.

[25] *Re Worthington* [1954] 1 W.L.R. 526; *Re Jarvis* [1958] 1 W.L.R. 815; *Phipps v. Boardman* [1967] 2 A.C. 46; *Foster v. Spencer* [1996] 2 All E.R. 672.

[26] [1985] Q.B. 428; (1986) 49 M.L.R. 118 (W. Bishop and D. Prentice). See also *Warman International Ltd v. Dwyer* (1995) 69 A.L.J.R. 362 (share of profits of business); (1996) 55 C.L.J. 201 (R. Nolan).

[27] *Re Duke of Norfolk's S.T.* [1982] Ch. 61; (1982) 45 M.L.R. 211 (B. Green); (1982) 98 L.Q.R. 181 (P.V.B.); [1982] Conv. 231 (K. Hodkinson). See also *Re Barbour's Settlement* [1974] 1 W.L.R. 1198 (application for increase should be made directly and not included as a term of a compromise of an unconnected dispute); *cf. Re Codd's W.T.* [1975] 1 W.L.R. 1139. The court will not appoint a paid trustee unless in the best interests of the beneficiaries; *Polly Peck International plc (in Administration) v. Henry* [1999] 1 B.C.L.C. 407.

[28] [1967] 2 A.C. 46, *post*, p. 618.

[29] *Re Berkeley Applegate (Investment Consultants) Ltd* [1989] Ch. 32 at 50–51.

special expertise.[30] The House of Lords in *Guinness v. Saunders*[31] refused a claim to remuneration by a company director who, it was assumed, had acted bona fide but in circumstances involving a clear conflict of interest and duty. It was doubted whether the jurisdiction would ever be exercised in favour of a director, as this would constitute interference by the court in the administration of the company's affairs. The company's articles gave the power to remunerate to the board of directors, to whom the claim should be addressed. Lord Goff considered that the jurisdiction could only be reconciled with the fundamental rule that a trustee is not entitled to remuneration to the extent that its exercise did not conflict with the policy underlying that rule. Such a conflict would only be avoided if the exercise of the jurisdiction was restricted to cases where it could not have the effect of encouraging trustees to put themselves in a position of conflict of interest and duty.[32] *Boardman v. Phipps*[33] was such a case. There the merits of the claim were overwhelming, but the present case was very different: the director had put himself in a position where his interests were in stark conflict with his duty. Also, he had received money which belonged to the company.

E. Remuneration for Litigious Work by Solicitor-Trustees

Under the rule in *Cradock v. Piper*,[34] a solicitor-trustee may charge costs if he has acted for a *co-trustee as well as himself*[35] in respect of business done in an action or matter *in court*, provided that his activities have not increased the expenses. It is not necessary that the court action should be hostile in character, but it must be some form of litigious matter.[36] The rule will not be extended by analogies.

It may also be noted here that a solicitor-trustee may employ his *partner* in cases where it would be proper to employ an outside solicitor, provided that he himself will derive no benefit, direct *or* indirect, from such an employment.[37] There must be complete separation of the trust work from the firm's general work, so as to make it clear that the solicitor-trustee is not involved in the former.

---

[30] *Foster v. Spencer, supra.*

[31] [1990] 2 A.C. 663; (1990) 106 L.Q.R. 365 (J. Beatson and D. Prentice); (1990) 49 C.L.J. 220 (J. Hopkins); Law Com. C.P. No. 146 (1997), p. 155. The facts are given at p. 616, *post.*

[32] *ibid.* at 701; *cf. O'Sullivan v. Management Agency and Music Ltd* [1985] Q.B. 428, *ante*, p. 604, which was not referred to.

[33] *supra.*

[34] (1850) 1 Mac. & G. 664. See (1983) 46 M.L.R. 289 at 306 (W. Bishop and D. Prentice); (1998) 19 Legal History 189 (C. Stebbings).

[35] *Lyon v. Baker* (1852) 5 De G. & Sm. 622.

[36] *Re Corsellis* (1887) 34 Ch.D. 675.

[37] *Clack v. Carlon* (1861) 30 L.J.Ch. 639.

This power is not restricted to matters in court, but it does not enable a solicitor-trustee to employ his own *firm*.[38]

F. Authorisation by Contract

Trustees may contract for remuneration with those beneficiaries who are *sui juris*.[39] But such agreements may somewhat easily be brought under the head of undue influence,[40] and are not encouraged. Nor, in fact, are they at all common.

2. TRUSTEES MUST NOT BE PURCHASERS

A. Purchase of the Trust Property

This rule and those which follow are based on the principle that a trustee may not place himself in a position where his duty and his interest may conflict.[41] This means that trustees are not to become the owners or lessees of trust property. This rule is independent of any question of inadequacy of price, or unfairness, or undue advantage; the sale may have been at auction and the trustee may have taken the bidding well above the reserve price, but he is still caught by the rule, which derives from his status and position and not from his conduct in the particular case.[42] Nor does it matter that he left the decision to sell and the manner of sale wholly to his co-trustee; nor that he retired from the trust before making an offer.[43] His responsibility as trustee is such that he must not contemplate the purchase at all.

The rule was somewhat relaxed in *Holder v. Holder*,[44] involving an executor who had purported to renounce the executorship, but invalidly, as he had already done some minor acts in the administration of the estate. After his purported renunciation, the executor took no further part in the administration. He later purchased at auction for a fair price some farmland belonging to the estate, of which he

---

[38] *Christophers v. White* (1847) 10 Beav. 523; *Re Gates* [1933] Ch. 913; *Re Hill* [1934] Ch. 623.

[39] No remuneration may be paid out of the trust property by agreement with the beneficiaries if they are not all *sui juris*. In such a case, application must be made to court, as in *Re Duke of Norfolk's S.T., supra,* (living beneficiaries did not object, but some unborn).

[40] *Ayliffe v. Murray* (1740) 2 Atk. 58; *post,* pp. 854 *et seq.*

[41] *Boardman v. Phipps* [1967] 2 A.C. 46 at 123. This principle does not apply if it is the settlor who has placed the trustees in such a position; *Sargeant v. National Westminster Bank plc* (1991) 61 P. & C.R. 518.

[42] *Campbell v. Walker* (1800) 5 Ves.Jr. 678; *ex p. Lacey* (1802) 6 Ves.Jr. 625; *Movitex Ltd v. Bulfield* [1988] B.C.L.C. 104.

[43] *Wright v. Morgan* [1926] A.C. 788; *Re Boles and British Land Co.'s Contract* [1902] 1 Ch. 244.

[44] [1968] Ch. 353. *cf. Re Mulholland's W.T.* [1949] 1 All E.R. 460 (option to purchase acquired before trusteeship).

had previously been tenant. The Court of Appeal declined to set aside the purchase. The circumstances were special, because the executor had not interfered in the administration of the estate; nor had he taken part in organising the auction; nor was there any conflict of interest and duty, as the beneficiaries were not looking to him to protect their interests; and finally, any special knowledge he had about the property was acquired as tenant and not as executor. In any event, the claimant beneficiary had acquiesced in the sale. As a general rule, however, a trustee or executor who has once involved himself in his office is affected by the rule for a considerable period after retirement.

The effect of the rule is that the purchase is voidable at the option of a beneficiary, who is allowed a generous time to discover the position.[45] The right to avoid the sale is effective against a purchaser with notice of the circumstances. The rule cannot be got around by sales to nominees,[46] for a repurchase by the trustee will be regarded as on behalf of the trust (unless the original sale was bona fide).[47] A sale to the trustee's spouse is looked upon with suspicion,[48] and likewise a sale to a company in which the trustee has a substantial interest.[49] The rule was applied by analogy in *Kane v. Radley-Kane*,[50] where a widow who was sole administratrix appropriated unquoted shares worth £50,000 to herself in satisfaction of the statutory legacy to which she was entitled on her husband's intestacy. This was done without the consent of her stepsons, who were entitled on the intestacy subject to her rights. The estate at that time was worth only £93,000, thus it appeared that the widow was entitled to it all. She sold the shares two years later for over £1 million. It was held that the appropriation of the shares breached the self-dealing rule and was equivalent to a purchase of trust property by a trustee. Thus the widow held the shares and their proceeds for the estate.

The court may in certain circumstances prefer to order a re-sale, and, if the price is higher than the previous sale price, the trustee

[45] For an illustration see *Re Sherman* [1954] Ch. 653.

[46] *Silkstone & Haigh Moor Coal Co. v. Edey* [1900] 1 Ch. 167.

[47] *Re Postlethwaite* (1888) 60 L.T. 514.

[48] See *Burrell v. Burrell's Trustees* 1915 S.C. 33, where the sale was upheld; *Tito v. Waddell (No. 2)* [1977] Ch. 106.

[49] See *Re Thompson's Settlement* [1986] Ch. 99; (1986) 1 *Trust Law & Practice* 66 (C. Sherrin), where the contract for sale to a company of which the trustee was managing director and majority shareholder was held unenforceable; *Movitex Ltd v. Bulfield* [1988] B.C.L.C. 104. A mortgagee is also debarred from selling the property to himself, but it has been held that he can sell to a company in which he has an interest if he acts in good faith and gets the best price reasonably obtainable; *Tse Kwong Lam v. Wong Chit Sen* [1983] 1 W.L.R. 1349. See also *Farrar v. Farrar's Ltd* (1889) 40 Ch.Div. 395.

[50] [1999] Ch. 274; All E.R. Rev. 1998 at 463 (C. Sherrin); (1998) 28 Fam.Law 526 (S. Cretney).

must convey; otherwise he is held to his purchase. The trustee will not be allowed to bid at the new sale if this is objected to.[51]

The rule discussed above is subject to certain exceptions. The trust instrument may expressly permit the purchase by a trustee.[52] Secondly, the court has a discretion to allow such a purchase in a proper case,[53] or to permit the trustee to bid at an auction.[54] Finally, a tenant for life of settled land, which he holds on trust, is permitted by statute to purchase the property.[55]

B. Purchase of the Beneficial Interest

Equity's view is less stringent when dealing with a purchase by a trustee of the beneficial interest of a beneficiary.[56] This is a type of transaction which is carefully watched; the onus is on the trustee to show that he gave full value, and that all information was laid before the beneficiary when it was sold.[57] The principles of undue influence apply; but it is open to a trustee in this type of case to show that the whole transaction was conducted at arm's length. This must how-ever be very distinctly proved.[58]

3. INCIDENTAL PROFITS

A. Trustees

The rules discussed below apply in full force to trustees. Many of them apply also to other fiduciaries. Although we are mainly con-cerned here with trustees, it will be convenient to mention also, where relevant, the application of the rules to persons who are not strictly trustees.

i. Rule in Keech v. Sandford.[59] This rule prevents a trustee from keeping for his own benefit a renewal of a lease which he was able to obtain for himself by reason of his being the trustee of the original lease; and even though the trustee had tried unsuccessfully

---

[51] See Cross J. in *Holder v. Holder* [1968] Ch. 353 at 371.

[52] See *Sargeant v. National Westminster Bank plc* (1991) 61 P. & C.R. 518.

[53] *Farmer v. Dean* (1863) 32 Beav. 327. Or the beneficiaries, all being *sui juris*, may agree to it.

[54] *Holder v. Holder, supra*, at 398, 402.

[55] S.L.A. 1925, s.68.

[56] *Tito v. Waddell (No. 2) supra*, at 241; *Re Thompson's Settlement* [1986] Ch. 99.

[57] *Thomson v. Eastwood* (1877) 2 App.Cas. 215 at 236; *Hill v. Langley, The Times*, January 28, 1988.

[58] See generally *Coles v. Trecothick* (1804) 9 Ves.Jr. 234; *Morse v. Royal* (1806) 12 Ves.Jr. 355; *cf. Williams v. Scott* [1900] A.C. 499.

[59] (1726) Sel. Cas. t. King 61; (1969) 33 Conv.(N.S.) 161 (S. Cretney); *Re Edwards' W.T.* [1982] Ch. 30; *Chan v. Zacharia* (1984) 154 C.L.R. 178; *cf. Harris v. Black* (1983) 127 S.J. 224.

to obtain a renewal for the benefit of his beneficiary. In the leading case, from which the rule takes its name, the defendant held a lease of the profits of a market on trust for a child. Before the expiration of the lease, the defendant asked the lessor to renew the lease in favour of the child. The lessor refused to grant a lease to the child on the grounds that, as the lease was of the profits of the market, he would be unable to distrain, and would be unable to enforce the covenant against the child. The trustee then took a lease for his own benefit.

Lord Chancellor King held that the trustee must hold the lease on trust for the child. "This may seem hard," he said,[60] "that the trustee is the only person of all mankind who might not have the lease; but it is very proper that the rule should be strictly pursued, and not in the least relaxed; for it is very obvious what would be the consequences of letting trustees have the lease, on refusal to renew to *cestui que use*." A similar principle applies to the renewal of contracts.[61]

It is otherwise, however, where there is no fiduciary relationship.

In *Re Biss*,[62] a lessor had refused to renew a seven-year lease of premises, and the lessee remained in possession as tenant from year to year. He died, leaving a widow and three children. The widow, who was his administratrix, and two of the children continued the business under the existing lease. The lessor terminated the lease, and then granted a three-year lease to one of the children. The Court of Appeal allowed him to keep the lease for his own benefit. Romer L.J. said that[63] "where the person renewing the lease does not clearly occupy a fiduciary position" he "is only held to be a constructive trustee of the renewed lease if, in respect of the old lease, he occupied some special position and owed, by virtue of that position, a duty towards the other persons interested."

ii. Purchase of the Reversion. Where the trustee acquires the freehold reversion, the position is unclear.[64] The trustee is liable if he has in any way made use of his position to get a personal benefit: thus if the lessor makes an offer to all his lessees giving them the right to enfranchisement on favourable terms, or if the lessee had

---

[60] (1726) Sel. Cas. t. King 61 at 62.

[61] *Don King Productions Inc. v. Warren* [2000] Ch. 291.

[62] [1903] 2. Ch. 40; *Brenner v. Rose* [1973] 1 W.L.R. 443. See also *Savage v. Dunningham* [1974] Ch. 181.

[63] [1903] 2 Ch. 40 at 61.

[64] The converse situation where a trustee of the reversion purchases the lease was left open in *Re Thompson's Settlement* [1986] Ch. 99.

any statutory right of enfranchisement, there could be no doubt that the trustee who sought to take the reversion for his own benefit would be liable. The courts have, however, vacillated in deciding whether there is any *absolute* liability in the absence of such abuse.[65] In *Protheroe v. Protheroe*[66] the Court of Appeal, without referring to the relevant authorities, held that the rule was applicable, without qualification, to purchases of the freehold. A husband held the lease of the matrimonial home on trust for his wife and himself in equal shares. After the wife had petitioned for divorce, he purchased the freehold reversion. When he sold, the wife was held to be entitled to a share of the proceeds.[67] In earlier cases the courts had limited the rule to cases where the lease, the reversion on which was being purchased, was renewable by law or custom.[68] The rationale of that limitation was that if the lease were normally renewed in practice,[69] the lessee would suffer if the lease passed to a third party who might not follow the custom (particularly if the lease, as was commonly the case with church leases, was generally renewed at less than the market rent). Thus it was wrong to allow the trustee, who ought to be protecting his beneficiary's interests, to damage them. Today, by statute, many lessees are given valuable rights of renewal or enfranchisement. It is submitted that the proper question in each case is: has the trustee taken advantage of his position to get a personal benefit? If so, he is liable, otherwise he is not. "It seems to me," said Pennycuick V.-C. in *Thompson's Trustee in Bankruptcy v. Heaton*,[70] "that apart from the fact that it binds me, this decision [*Protheroe v. Protheroe*], like the rule in *Keech v. Sandford*, is really in modern terms an application of the broad principle that the trustee must not make a profit out of the trust estate." The onus would be on the trustee to satisfy the court, and it can be a very difficult one to discharge.

iii. Trustees as Company Directors. The question has arisen several times in connection with the remuneration of directorships

---

[65] *Norris v. Le Neve* (1743) 3 Atk. 26; *Randall v. Russell* (1817) 3 Mer. 190; *cf. Phillips v. Phillips* (1885) 29 Ch.D. 673.

[66] [1968] 1 W.L.R. 519; (1968) 31 M.L.R. 707 (P. Jackson); (1968) 32 Conv.(N.S.) 220 (F. Crane); *Thompson's Trustee v. Heaton* [1974] 1 W.L.R. 605; (1974) 38 Conv.(N.S.) 288; (1975) 38 M.L.R. 226 (P. Jackson); *Popat v. Shonchhatra* [1997] 1 W.L.R. 1367.

[67] "It may be that there were facts in the case which indicated that the husband obtained the freehold by virtue of his position as leaseholder, but they are not apparent from the report"; (1968) 84 L.Q.R. 309 (L. Megarry).

[68] *Bevan v. Webb* [1905] 1 Ch. 620; *cf. Griffith v. Owen* [1907] 1 Ch. 195; *per* Wilberforce J. in *Phipps v. Boardman* [1964] 1 W.L.R. 993 at 1009.

[69] See generally (1969) 33 Conv.(N.S.) 161 (S. Cretney), where the history of the doctrine is traced.

[70] [1974] W.L.R. 605 at 606. See also *Don King Productions Inc. v. Warren* [2000] Ch. 291, favouring the *Protheroe* approach. Textbook criticisms of *Protheroe* were rejected.

which trustees have obtained by virtue of their position as trustees.

In *Re Macadam*,[71] trustees had power under the articles by virtue of their office to appoint two directors of a company. They appointed themselves, and were held liable to account for the remuneration which they received because they had acquired it by the use of their powers as trustees.

On the other hand, the remuneration may be retained if the trustees were directors before they became trustees,[72] or if the trustees were appointed directors independently of the votes of the shares of the trust,[73] or if the trustee did not obtain the remuneration by the use of his position as a trustee, but by an independent bargain with the firm employing him.[74] Indeed, as Cohen J. said in *Re Macadam*.[75] " . . . the root of the matter really is: Did [the trustee] acquire the position in respect of which he drew the remuneration by virtue of his position as trustee?" Trustees will not be liable even within that test if the terms of the trust authorised them to appoint themselves and receive remuneration.[76]

iv. Other Profits by Trustees. Incidental profits come to trustees in a variety of ways and must always be disgorged. "Whenever it can be shewn that the trustee has so arranged matters as to obtain an advantage, whether in money or money's worth, to himself personally through the execution of his trust, he will not be permitted to retain, but will be compelled to make it over to his constituent."[77]

A few examples must suffice. A trustee who introduced to a firm, of which he was a member, business of the trust, was compelled to account for the profit[78]; similarly, a trustee who received a sum of £75 to induce him to retire[79] and a trustee who used trust funds in

---

[71] [1946] Ch. 73; *Re Francis* (1905) 92 L.T. 77; *Williams v. Barton* [1927] 2 Ch. 9.
[72] *Re Dover Coalfield Extension Ltd* [1908] 1 Ch. 65. See also *Re Orwell's W.T.* [1982] 1 W.L.R. 1337.
[73] *Re Gee* [1948] Ch. 284.
[74] *Re Lewis* (1910) 103 L.T. 495, as explained in *Re Gee, supra.*
[75] [1946] Ch. 73 at 82. Harman J. accepted this test in *Re Gee, supra.*
[76] *Re Llewellin's W.T.* [1949] Ch. 225. The court may sanction the retention of the fees; *Re Keeler's S.T.* [1981] Ch. 156.
[77] *Huntingdon Copper Co. v. Henderson* (1872) 4 R. (Court of Session) 294 at 308; *cf. Patel v. Patel* [1981] 1 W.L.R. 1342 (no breach where trustees sought to live in the trust property where the beneficiaries were young children adopted by the trustees on the death of their parents).
[78] *Williams v. Barton* [1927] 2 Ch. 9; *cf. Jones v. AMP Perpetual Trustee Company NZ Ltd* [1994] 1 N.Z.L.R. 690 (no breach where subsidiary placed trust business with parent company).
[79] *Sugden v. Crossland* (1856) 3 Sm. & G. 192; *Re Smith* [1896[1 Ch. 71.

his own business was required to account for the profits he received[80]; and a trustee may be liable for profits which he ought reasonably to have received.[81] It has been suggested that trustees of pension funds who are also beneficiaries are excluded from benefit where they exercise a power to apply funds among a class of which they are members.[82] This over-strict interpretation of the principle, which has not been applied to trustee-beneficiaries of other trusts, has now been overturned by statute.[83]

v. Trustee must not be in Competition with the Trust. One possible area of conflict of interest and duty is where the trustee operates in business in competition with the trust. Such competition was inevitable in *Re Thompson*[84] where executors of a will were directed to carry on the business of the testator who had been a yacht broker. One of the executors was intending to set up on his own account as a yacht broker in competition. It was held that he must not set up in a competing business.

This rule applies to other fiduciaries who are not trustees. A partner is required by statute to "account for and pay over to the firm all profits made" by carrying on a business "of the same nature as and competing with that of the firm"[85] unless he has the consent of the other partners. It is a question of fact in each case whether or not the activity is in conflict with the fiduciary duty.[86]

B. Other Fiduciaries[87]

i. The Principle. A similar rule applies to profits made by other persons in breach of a fiduciary relation; indeed such persons are grouped with trustees in many formulations of the rule although there is no rule that they must act gratuitously. "It is an inflexible rule of a Court of Equity that a person in a fiduciary position, . . . is

---

[80] *Brown v. I.R.C.* [1965] A.C. 244 (a Scottish solicitor compelled to account for interest earned by deposits of clients' moneys).

[81] *Re Waterman's W.T.* [1952] 2 All E.R. 1054.

[82] *British Coal Corp. v. British Coal Staff Superannuation Scheme Trustees Ltd* [1995] 1 All E.R. 912 at 925; *cf. In re Drexel Burnham Lambert U.K. Pension Plan* [1995] 1 W.L.R. 32; (1996) 10 *Trust Law International* 49 (J. Mowbray).

[83] Pensions Act 1995, s.39; *ante*, p. 480. See *Edge v. Pensions Ombudsman* [2000] Ch. 602.

[84] [1930] 1 Ch. 203; *Aberdeen Railway Co. v. Blaikie Bros.* (1854) 1 Macq. 461; *Warman International Ltd v. Dwyer* (1995) 69 A.L.J.R. 362.

[85] Partnership Act 1890, s.30.

[86] *Moore v. M'Glynn* [1894] 1 Ir.R. 74.

[87] Goff and Jones, Chap. 33; (1968) 84 L.Q.R. 472 (G. Jones); (1976) 92 L.Q.R. 360 at 372 (R. Goode); Oakley, *Constructive Trusts* (3rd ed.), Chap. 3; (1981) 97 L.Q.R. 51 (J. Shepherd); Shepherd, *The Law of Fiduciaries* (1981); Snell, pp. 284–287. See Law Com. No. 236 (1995), *Fiduciary Duties and Regulatory Rules*, examining the mismatch between general law obligations and regulatory rules.

not, unless otherwise expressly provided, entitled to make a profit; he is not allowed to put himself in a position where his interest and duty conflict."[88] But it is not safe to make the attractive over-simplification of saying that a fiduciary must always account for all gains which come to him by reason of his fiduciary position. Indeed, Lord Herschell in the paragraph containing the above quotation "plainly recognised its limitations."[89] But I am satisfied that it might be departed from in many cases, without any breach of morality, without any wrong being inflicted, and without any consciousness of wrong-doing. Indeed, it is obvious that it might sometimes be to the advantage of the beneficiaries that their trustee should act for them professionally rather than a stranger, even though the trustee were paid for his services."[90]

It is not always easy, however, to determine whether a particular relationship should be classified as fiduciary. While some examples are well established, the boundaries of the category of fiduciary relationships are not clear, and the category is not closed.[91] It includes certain agents,[92] (including "self-appointed" agents[93]), solicitors,[94] company directors,[95] partners,[96] confidential employees,[97] a

---

[88] Lord Herschell in *Bray v. Ford* [1896] A.C.44 at 51; see also Lord Cranworth in *Aberdeen Railway Co. v. Blaikie Bros.* (1854) 1 Macq. 461 at 471; *Regal (Hastings) Ltd v. Gulliver* [1942] 1 All E.R. 378; [1967] 2 A.C. 134n.

[89] Lord Upjohn in *Boardman v. Phipps* [1967] 2 A.C. 46 at 123.

[90] *Bray v. Ford* [1896] A.C. 44 at 52.

[91] *English v. Dedham Vale Properties Ltd* [1978] 1 W.L.R. 93; (1997) 113 L.Q.R. 601 at 619–626 (A. Duggan); (1997–98) 8 K.C.L.J. 1 at 6 *et seq.* (Sir Anthony Mason); (1998) 114 L.Q.R. 214 (Sir Peter Millett); (1999) 58 C.L.J. 500 (S. Worthington); *Privacy and Loyalty* (Birks ed.), Chaps. 10, 11.

[92] *De Bussche v. Alt* (1878) 8 Ch.D. 286; *N.Z. Netherlands Society v. Kuys* [1973] 1 W.L.R. 1126 at 1129. Not all agents are fiduciaries, although there may be a presumption that they are; *Aluminium Industrie Vaasen B.V. v. Romalpa Aluminium Ltd* [1976] 1 W.L.R. 676; *post*, p. 704. See Goff and Jones, p. 105, n. 8, suggesting that "much depends on whether the agent is under a duty to keep separate his own money from his principal's money."; *cf. Re Air Canada and M. & L. Travel Ltd* (1994) 108 D.L.R. (4th) 592.

[93] *English v. Dedham Vale Properties Ltd, supra.* (where the intending purchaser obtained planning permission in the vendor's name); (1978) 41 M.L.R. 474 (A. Nicol); (1978) 94 L.Q.R. 347 (G. Samuel).

[94] *Brown v. I.R.C.* [1965] A.C. 244; (1964) 80 L.Q.R. 480; *Islamic Republic of Iran Shipping Lines v. Denby* [1987] 1 Lloyd's Rep. 367. See also *Hanson v. Lorenz* [1987] 1 F.T.L.R. 23 (no liability to account to client for his profits from a joint venture where client had understood the agreement). As to whether a head of chambers is in a fiduciary position to the members, see *Appleby v. Cowley, The Times*, April 14, 1982.

[95] *Regal (Hastings) Ltd v. Gulliver, supra*; *Industrial Development Consultants Ltd v. Cooley* [1972] 1 W.L.R. 443; *post*, p. 616. See also *Horcal Ltd v. Gatland* [1984] B.C.L.C. 549.

[96] *Featherstonhaugh v. Fenwick* (1810) 17 Ves.Jr. 298; *Clegg v. Fishwick* (1849) 1 Mac. & G. 294.

[97] *Att.-Gen. v. Guardian Newspapers Ltd (No. 2)* [1990] 1 A.C. 109 (The "Spycatcher" case; duty to account for profits). A former member of the security service does not owe a continuing fiduciary duty to the Crown in relation to information which is not confidential; *Att.-Gen. v. Blake* [2000] 3 W.L.R. 625; [2000] R.L.R. 578 (P. Jaffey). See also *Nottingham University v. Fishel, The Times*, March 31, 2000.

pawnbroker,[98] and certain bailees,[99] but not a vendor of goods to which title has not yet passed to the purchaser.[1]

Indeed, it may sometimes appear that the defendant may be classified as a fiduciary, or not, in order to achieve the desired result.

> In *Reading v. Attorney-General*,[2] a staff-sergeant in the British Army stationed in Cairo was bribed by Egyptians to ride in their civilian lorries carrying contraband goods, enabling the lorries to pass check posts without difficulty. The British authorities seized £20,000 from Reading; later he petitioned to recover it. He had obtained the money wrongfully, but he argued that this fact did not mean that the British Government was entitled to claim it. Reading failed, however, and one of the grounds for the decision in the House of Lords was that he, as a non-commissioned officer, was in a fiduciary relation to the Crown, and was therefore under a duty to account for the profit wrongfully made.

Illegal or secret commissions or bribes obtained by a confidential servant or agent are recoverable by the principal or employer regardless of any quantifiable loss by him.[3] If the fiduciary relationship in this case is accepted, the result merely follows the earlier cases on agents. The application of the rule to a policeman[4] and a staff-sergeant may be an extension; indeed it has been said that the speeches in the House of Lords in *Reading v. Attorney-General*[5] "confirm that the status of a fiduciary may . . . be easily acquired."[6]

In *Swain v. The Law Society*,[7] on the other hand, the House of Lords declined to find such a relationship.

> The Society negotiated a compulsory insurance scheme on behalf of all solicitors. It kept the commission on the policy, which it applied for the purposes of the profession. The claimant, a

---

[98] *Mathew v. T.M. Sutton Ltd* [1994] 1 W.L.R. 1455; All E.R. Rev. 1994 p. 26 (N. Palmer). (Surplus proceeds of sale held on trust for pawnor and interest payable).

[99] *Aluminium Industrie Vaasen B.V. v. Romalpa Aluminium Ltd, supra; Re Andrabell Ltd (in liq.)* [1984] 3 All E.R. 407.

[1] *Re Goldcorp Exchange Ltd (in receivership)* [1995] 1 A.C. 74.

[2] [1951] A.C. 507.

[3] *Att.-Gen. for Hong Kong v. Reid* [1994] 1 A.C.; *post*, p. 625. See also *Brown v. I.R.C.* [1965] A.C. 244; *Mahesan v. Malaysia Government Officers Cooperative Housing Society Ltd* [1979] A.C. 374; (1979) 95 L.Q.R. 68 (A Tettenborn); *Logicrose Ltd v. Southend United Football Club Ltd* [1988] 1 W.L.R. 1256 (principal can recover from agent whether he affirms or repudiates the transaction between the agent and the third party); (1989) 48 C.L.J. 22 (G. Jones); *Swindle v. Harrison* [1997] 4 All E.R. 705 (undisclosed profit by solicitor from loan transaction arranged for client).

[4] *Att.-Gen. v. Goddard* (1929) 98 L.J.K.B. 743 (bribes received when on duty).

[5] *supra.*

[6] Goff and Jones, p. 739.

[7] [1983] A.C. 598; [1982] Conv. 447 (A. Kenny).

solicitor, objected to the scheme and claimed that the Society must account for the commission as a profit made out of a fiduciary position. The alleged conflict of interest and duty lay in the fact that it was in the interest of the Society to negotiate a high premium (resulting in a higher commission) while its duty to the solicitors was to obtain a low one. The House of Lords found in favour of the Society. It had not acted unconscionably, and there was no fiduciary relationship. The scheme was entered into with statutory authority.[8] The Society was acting in its public capacity. Private law concepts such as accountability and breach of trust did not apply.

ii. Company Directors.[9] Company directors are treated as fiduciaries[10] in so far as they are prohibited from making a profit out of their office[11] unless the articles permit it or the shareholders consent.[12] The leading case is the House of Lords decision in *Regal (Hastings) Ltd v. Gulliver.*[13]

> R. Ltd set up a subsidiary, A. Ltd, to acquire the leases of two cinemas. A. Ltd had a share capital of 5,000 £1 shares. The owner of the cinemas was only willing to lease them if the share capital of A. Ltd was completely subscribed for. However, R. Ltd had resources to subscribe for only 2,000 of the 5,000 shares and it was therefore agreed that the directors of R. Ltd should subscribe for the rest. When the business of R. Ltd was transferred to new controllers the directors made a profit from their holdings in A. Ltd. The new controllers of R. Ltd caused the company to sue the ex-directors of R. Ltd for an account of the profit. The directors were held liable. They had made the profit out of their position as directors and, in the absence of shareholder approval,[14] they were obliged to account.

---

[8] Solicitors Act 1974, s.37.

[9] See also, on insider dealing, Criminal Justice Act 1993, ss.52, 53; Parker and Mellows, *The Modern Law of Trusts* (7th ed.), pp. 573–574.

[10] The duty is traditionally regarded as owed to the company, not to the shareholders; *Percival v. Wright* [1902] 2 Ch. 421. But see (1975) 28 C.L.P. 83 (D. Prentice).

[11] The office of director should not, however, be equated with that of trustee. The assets of the company, unlike trust property, are not vested in the director but in the company which is a separate legal entity and, more importantly, directors "are . . . commercial men managing a trading concern for the benefit of themselves and of all other shareholders in it . . . ": *per* Jessell M.R. in *Re Forest of Dean Coal Mining Co. Ltd* (1878) 10 Ch.D. 450, at 451–452.

[12] See *Neptune (Vehicle Washing Equipment) Ltd v. Fitzgerald* [1996] Ch. 274.

[13] [1967] 2 A.C. 134n.

[14] Lord Russell of Killowen considered that the shareholders could have ratified the director's breach of duty: [1967] 2 A.C. 134n. at 150. On this controversial aspect of the case, see (1958) 16 C.L.J. 93 at 102–106; (K. Wedderburn); *Prudential Assurance Co. Ltd v. Newman Industries Ltd (No. 2)* [1981] Ch.'257; (1981) 44 M.L.R. 202.

There are a number of noteworthy features of *Regal*. First, the directors were found by the court to have acted bona fide, but the liability of a fiduciary to account for a profit made from his office "in no way depends on fraud, or absence of bona fides."[15] Secondly, the new controllers obtained a windfall.[16] Thirdly, it was arguable that the directors by purchasing the shares in A. Ltd had enabled R. Ltd to enter into a transaction which it was otherwise commercially impossible for the company to enter into. While there is some truth in this, the decision that R. Ltd did not have the necessary financial resources to enter into the transaction was made by the directors who were the very persons who benefited from this decision. Because of this a compelling argument can be made that a "reasonable man looking at the relevant facts and circumstances of the particular case would think that there was a real sensible possibility of conflict."[17]

A clear case of conflict of interest and duty arose in *Guinness plc v. Saunders*,[18] where a director (Ward) agreed to provide his services in connection with a proposed take-over of another company (Distillers), on terms that he would be paid a fee the size of which depended on the amount of the take-over bid if successful. The bid was successful, and the fee paid to Ward was £5.2 million. The claim by Guinness for summary judgment for the repayment of this sum was upheld in the House of Lords. Ward's interest in obtaining a fee calculated on the above basis conflicted with his duty as director, which was to give impartial advice concerning the take-over. The agreement for the fee, made with two other directors, but not the board of directors, was void for want of authority. Ward had no arguable defence to Guinness's claim that he had received the money, paid under a void contract, as a constructive trustee.

The courts have imposed liability on directors to account where the directors have made the profit out of an economic opportunity, or information, even though they acquired it in a personal capacity, if it was information which could have been exploited by their company.[19]

In *Industrial Development Consultants Ltd v. Cooley*,[20] the defendant was a director and general manager of the claimant company, which provided construction consultancy services. He

[15] [1967] 2 A.C. 134n. at 144.

[16] See (1979) 42 M.L.R. 215 (D. Prentice).

[17] *Boardman v. Phipps* [1967] 2 A.C. 46 at 124, *per* Lord Upjohn.

[18] [1990] 2 A.C. 663; (1990) 106 L.Q.R. 365 (J. Beatson and D. Prentice); (1990) 49 C.L.J. 220 (J. Hopkins); [1990] Conv. 296 (S. Goulding).

[19] See *Canadian Aero Service Ltd v. O'Malley* (1973) 40 D.L.R. (3d) 371 (S.C.C.).

[20] [1972] 1 W.L.R. 443; [1972] 2 All E.R. 162 (the reports on the case are not identical); (1973) 89 L.Q.R. 187 (A. Yoran); (1972A) 30 C.L.J. 222 (J. Collier); (1972) 35 M.L.R. 655 (H. Rajak); (1972) 50 C.B.R. 623 (D. Prentice).

attempted to interest a public Gas Board in a project, but was unsuccessful because the Gas Board's policy was not to employ development companies. The defendant was a distinguished architect who had worked in the gas industry for many years. For this reason the Gas Board decided to offer the contract to him personally, which he accepted, obtaining a release from the claimant by falsely representing that he was ill. He was held to be liable to account to the claimant for the profits of the contract.

The significance of the case is twofold. First, the court rejected Cooley's defence that the information concerning the Gas Board's contract came to him in his private capacity, and not as director of the claimant company; this "is the first case in which it was decided that the prohibition on exploiting a corporate opportunity applies also to an opportunity which was presented to the director personally and not in his capacity with the company."[21] Secondly, the decision whether or not the contract went to the company lay not with the fiduciary, Cooley, but with a third party, the Gas Board.[22] In *Cooley's* case there were special circumstances; this was exactly the type of opportunity which the company relied on Cooley to obtain; furthermore, the absence of bona fides was clear. Also, the imposition of liability will provide directors with an incentive to channel opportunities to their companies and not exploit them for their personal advantage.

There are other decisions which suggest a more benign attitude towards directors.

In *Queensland Mines Ltd v. Hudson*[23] the claimant company had been interested in developing a mining operation and the defendant, the managing director, was successful in obtaining for the company the licences necessary to enable it to do so. However, because of financial problems it could not proceed. Hudson resigned as managing director and, with the knowledge of the company's board, successfully developed the mines. The Privy Council held that Hudson was not liable to account, for either of two reasons: (a) the rejection of the opportunity by the company because of cash difficulties took the venture outside the scope of

---

[21] (1973) 89 L.Q.R. 187 at 189.

[22] Roskill J. found that there was only a 10 per cent chance that the Gas Board would have awarded the contract to the company. Thus the company only benefited because Cooley had breached his duty.

[23] (1978) 18 A.L.R. 1; [1980] Conv. 200 (W. Braithwaite); applied in *Jones v. AMP Perpetual Trustee Company NZ Ltd* [1994] 1 N.Z.L.R. 690. See also *Island Export Finance Ltd v. Umunna* [1986] B.C.L.C. 460 (defendant not liable for developing a business opportunity after resigning as managing director because company was not actively pursuing the venture when he resigned, and his resignation was influenced not by any wish to acquire the business opportunity but by dissatisfaction with the company).

Hudson's fiduciary duties or (b) because Hudson had acted with the full knowledge of the company's board, they should be taken to have consented to his activities.[24]

This decision causes difficulties.[25] First, to argue that a board's rejection to the opportunity immunises a director against liability is difficult to reconcile with *Regal (Hastings) Ltd v. Gulliver*. Although in that case Lord Reid deliberately left open the question of the effect of board rejection,[26] it is difficult to see how there would still not be a serious conflict of interest if directors were permitted to acquire for themselves opportunities which they had rejected on behalf of the company. Secondly, only the shareholders could condone Hudson's breach, not the board.

iii. Boardman v. Phipps. Many of the difficulties relating to the application of the rule came to the fore in *Boardman v. Phipps*.[27]

The Phipps trust owned a substantial minority holding of shares in a private company. John Phipps, the claimant, was one of the beneficiaries under the trust, and the defendants were Boardman, a solicitor, and Tom Phipps, also a beneficiary. The trustees were an elderly widow who died in 1958, her daughter and an accountant. Boardman acted as solicitor to the trust.

In 1956 the defendants were dissatisfied with the way in which the company was managed. They made various inquiries on behalf of the trust, and in that capacity obtained confidential information about the company. They realised that it would be advantageous to sell some of the non-profit-making assets. They obtained control of the company by purchasing the remainder of the company's shares, and carried out the desired sales and reorganisation. The transaction was highly profitable. The trust gained in respect of its holding and the defendants gained in respect of the shares which they had purchased for the purpose of obtaining control.

Boardman had informed the beneficiaries and the two active trustees (the widow being senile and taking no part in the affairs

---

[24] (1978) 18 A.L.R. 1 at 10. Lord Upjohn's reasoning in *Boardman v. Phipps* [1967] 2 A.C. 46 was adopted on the basis that he had "dissented on the facts, but not on the law." (at 3).

[25] (1979) 42 M.L.R. 711 (G. Sullivan).

[26] [1967] 2 A.C. 137n. at 152–153. In *Peso Silver Mines Ltd v. Cropper* (1966) 58 D.L.R. (2d.) 1, it was held that board rejection did immunise a director against any action to account; criticised in (1967) 30 M.L.R. 450 (D. Prentice); (1971) 49 C.B.R. 80 (S. Beck).

[27] [1967] 2 A.C. 46; (1968) 84 L.Q.R. 472 (G. Jones); [1978] Conv. 114 (B. Rider). The case was distinguished in *Satnam Investments Ltd v. Dunlop Heywood & Co. Ltd* [1999] 3 All E.R. 652, where the defendant, who took advantage of an opportunity arising from another's breach of fiduciary duty, was not himself a fiduciary.

of the trust) giving them an outline of the negotiations and asking them whether they had any objection to his taking a personal interest, bearing in mind that his initial inquiry had been on behalf of the trust. Boardman acted bona fide throughout and thought that he had made a full disclosure and had the beneficiaries' consent. Wilberforce J. however found that the claimant was justified in thinking that he had only been told half the truth. The trustees had been invited to consider whether the trust should find the money for the purchase of the shares; but the trustees were unable and unwilling to do so.

John Phipps then called upon the defendants to account for the profits which they had made. The House of Lords (3–2) held that they must do so; but having acted bona fide, they were entitled to payment on a liberal scale for their work and skill.[28]

A number of points of importance arise from the case. First, Boardman was not a trustee. The fiduciary relation arose from his employment as solicitor by the trustees. He was not, however, employed to act for the trust in the dealings in question and he claimed, as he stated at the time, to have been acting in a private capacity. The members of the House of Lords took different views on this issue. In the early negotiations with the company, the defendants, who were not shareholders in their own right, purported to represent the trust, although strictly they did not do so. Lord Cohen, in the majority, said[29] "that information and that opportunity they owed to their representing themselves as agents for the holders of the 8,000 shares held by the trustees." Lord Upjohn, dissenting[30]: "though they portrayed themselves as representing the Phipps Trust, it is quite clear the offer was made by these two personally."

Secondly, the liability of the defendants was unaffected by the fact that the trust had lost nothing; nor that the trust had greatly benefited; nor did it matter that the Phipps Trust could not have found the money; nor that the trustees would not have wished to use the money for that purpose even if they had it; nor that such user would have been in breach of trust, unless they had applied to the court and obtained consent to the investment.[31]

It is extremely difficult to determine the limits of this inflexible rule. Part of the difficulty stems from the lack of agreement as to whether the confidential information acquired by the appellants was

---

[28] *ante*, p. 604.

[29] [1967] 2 A.C. 46 at 103.

[30] *ibid* at 120; see also Viscount Dilhorne at 91; and *N.Z. Netherlands Society v. Kuys* [1973] 1 W.L.R. 1126, (1973) 37 Conv.(N.S.) 362.

[31] Lord Denning M.R. in the Court of Appeal mentioned this as a source of a potential conflict of interest and duty; [1965] Ch. 992, at 1020. The suggestion, however, seems unrealistic. See [1967] 2 A.C. 46 at 92, 124; *cf.* Lord Cohen at 103–104.

trust property, although this debate is less important since *Att.-Gen. for Hong Kong v. Reid*,[32] discussed below. The dissenting judges considered that it was not property. Of the majority, Lords Hodson and Guest considered that it was,[33] while Lord Cohen merely held that it was not property "in the strict sense of that word", so that liability to account for profits from its use depended on the facts of the case.[34] In *Aas v. Benham*,[35] Lindley L.J. laid down that information obtained in the course of a partnership business must not be used by the partners for their own benefit within the scope of the partnership business; but that they may make use of it for "purposes which are wholly without the scope of the firm's business . . . It is not the source of the information, but the use to which it is applied, which is important in such matters."[36] This was not disapproved in *Boardman v. Phipps*,[37] but it seems that a stricter view there prevailed; the defendants were held accountable because they had obtained the information by purporting to represent the trust; and although they were acting independently when they made the purchase. It is submitted that it is difficult to answer Lord Upjohn's argument in dissent[38]:

"I think, again, that some of the trouble that has arisen in this case, it being assumed rightly that throughout he was in such a [fiduciary] capacity, is that it has been assumed that it has necessarily followed that any profit made by him renders him accountable to the trustees. That is not so. . . . It is perfectly clear that a solicitor can if he so desires act against his clients in any matter in which he has not been retained by them provided, of course, that in acting for them generally he has not learnt information or placed himself in a position which would make it improper for him to act against them. This is an obvious application of the rule that he must not place himself in a position where his duty and his interest conflict. So, in general, a solicitor can deal in shares in a company in which the client is a shareholder, subject always to the general rule that the solicitor must never place himself in a position where his interest and his duty conflict; and in this connection it may be pointed out that the interest and duty may refer (and frequently do) to a conflict of interest and duty on behalf of different clients and have nothing to do with any conflict between

---

[32] [1994] 1 A.C. 324.
[33] Criticised (1968) 84 L.Q.R. 472 (G. Jones); Oakley, *Constructive Trusts* (3rd ed.), p. 170; (1998) 114 L.Q.R. 214 at 222 (Sir Peter Millett).
[34] [1967] 2 A.C. 46 at 102.
[35] [1891] 2 Ch. 244.
[36] *ibid.* at 256.
[37] [1967] 2 A.C. 46.
[38] *ibid.* at 126.

the personal interest and duty of the solicitor, beyond his interest in earning his fees."

His Lordship concluded "To extend the doctrines of equity to make the [defendants] accountable in such circumstances, is, in my judgment, to make unreasonable and inequitable applications of such doctrines."[39]

If this rule applies, the only escape of the fiduciary is that he made full disclosure, and obtained the consent of the other parties. It is not, however, clear whether the "other parties" are the trustees or the beneficiaries. In the straightforward case of a profit made by a trustee, the relevant consent must be that of the beneficiaries, to whom the duty is owed. Difficulties will arise if any of the beneficiaries are children or unborn. *Boardman v. Phipps*,[40] however, was not such a case. Boardman was a fiduciary agent, the principals being the trustees. To whom did he owe his fiduciary duties? Presumably consent must be obtained from those persons. If the trustees had not consented, they would, as principals, have a right of recovery against their agent, any money thus recovered being held by them on trust for the beneficiaries. If the trustees had consented, the agent would nevertheless be liable to the beneficiaries if he owed fiduciary duties to *them*.[41] The result of *Boardman v. Phipps*[42] was that the beneficiary successfully sued the agent, but the basis of this is not clear. Their Lordships spoke, rather ambiguously, of his being a fiduciary "to the trust".[43] Lord Guest spoke of the "knowledge and assent of the trustees."[44] Lord Hodson held that the relevant consent was that of the beneficiary; Boardman "was in a fiduciary position *vis-à-vis* the trustees, and through them *vis-à-vis* the beneficiaries."[45] Viscount Dilhorne regarded the consent of the principals as necessary, but also referred to the fact that the beneficiary was not fully informed.[46] Lord Upjohn said that Boardman was "in a fiduciary capacity at least to the trustees. Whether he was ever in

---

[39] [1967] 2 A.C. 46 at 133–134, quoting Lord Selborne L.C. in *Barnes v. Addy* (1874) 9 Ch.App. 244, at 251. See also *Chan v. Zacharia* (1984) 154 C.L.R. 178 at 204, suggesting that there should be no liability if it would be unconscientious to assert it, or if there was no possible conflict of interest and duty and it was plainly in the interest of the beneficiary that the fiduciary obtain the rights for himself that he was absolutely precluded from seeking or obtaining for the beneficiary.

[40] *supra.*

[41] Presumably the beneficiaries could sue the trustees in such circumstances even if they could not sue the agent.

[42] *supra.*

[43] [1967] 2 A.C. 46 at 100, 104, 110.

[44] *ibid.* at 117.

[45] *ibid.* at 112. Lord Cohen also regarded the consent of the beneficiary as necessary; *ibid.* at 104. See further Law Com. C.P. No. 146 (1997), *Trustees' Powers and Duties*, paras. 3.29, 3.32, describing *Boardman v. Phipps* as a "particularly difficult case in this regard".

[46] *ibid.* at 93.

a fiduciary capacity to the [claimant] was not debated before your Lordships and I do not think that it matters."[47]

This raises the question whether trustees can, if acting unanimously, give consent to dealings by their agent which would otherwise be a breach of his fiduciary obligations.[48] In the present case Boardman had obtained the consent of the two active trustees, but did not inform the third because she was senile. Russell L.J. in the Court of Appeal[49] held that this was insufficient because two out of the three trustees "had no authority to turn this aspect of the trust property [the exploitation of the shares] over to the defendants, unless to be used exclusively for the benefit of the trust", and that the fiduciary could not "rid himself of the disqualification inherent in that position save with the informed consent of all three." It is submitted that the better view is that of Lord Upjohn, who replied that "not all the trustees acting together could do it for they cannot give away trust property."[50] On this view it is only the beneficiaries or the settlor (by express provision in the trust instrument) who can authorise such dealings. The Law Commission has doubted whether trustees can authorise others to do what they themselves have no power to do.[51] However, it is now provided by section 14 of the Trustee Act 2000 that trustees may authorise their agent to act in circumstances capable of giving rise to a conflict of interest, provided it is reasonably necessary for the trustees to do so. This provision is primarily applicable to investment management functions.

Finally, it is important to determine what remedy was decreed in *Boardman v. Phipps.*[52] This is discussed below.

iv. The Extent of the Fiduciary Principle. Essentially the problem is one of determining the limits of the rule. "Rules of equity have to be applied to such a great diversity of circumstances that they may be stated only in the most general terms and applied with particular attention to the exact circumstances of each case."[53] If a fiduciary obtains a benefit for himself at the expense of his beneficiary, there is no difficulty. The case is one of unjust enrichment. The position is more difficult where the beneficiary loses nothing; where he did not wish to make the profitable purchase

---

[47] [1967] 2 A.C. 46 at 125–126.

[48] See (1990) 106 L.Q.R. 87 at 91–92 (D. Hayton), taking the view that prior specific (but not general) authority may be given if there is full disclosure by the agent and provided the "prudent businessman" test is satisfied.

[49] [1965] Ch. 992 at 1031.

[50] [1967] 2 A.C. 46 at 128.

[51] Law Com. C.P. No. 146 (1997), *Trustees' Powers and Duties*, paras 3.26–3.33; Law Com. No. 260 (1999), para. 4.27.

[52] [1967] 2 A.C. 46.

[53] *Boardman v. Phipps* [1967] 2 A.C. 46 at 123.

which the trustee makes; where the fiduciary acted honestly; or even where the fiduciary conferred by his activities every possible benefit on the beneficiary, but received an additional benefit for himself. A windfall has been received through the exertions of the fiduciary; the beneficiary has risked nothing, and lost nothing; should he be entitled to the profits?[54] *Boardman v. Phipps* answers this question in the affirmative.

Such a principle might be criticised on the ground that it fails to draw any distinction between the honest and the dishonest fiduciary. Both are liable. However, it should be borne in mind that the honest fiduciary may be remunerated by order of the court, as in *Boardman v. Phipps*.[55] A dishonest fiduciary, on the other hand, may be made to pay a higher rate of interest.[56]

But this still leaves open the question, to be determined on the facts of each case, whether the opportunity for profit arose by reason of the fiduciary position.[57] For example, a merchant banker, insurance broker, solicitor or company director learns through the proper course of his business information from a confidential source which may be of advantage to other clients in companies with which he is associated. Having satisfied the requirements of a particular client, is he precluded from making use of this information in respect of other trusts with which he is concerned or for himself? Similarly with the directors of several (non-competing) companies? Or, does his fiduciary duty to the second client place him under a duty to provide that client with the confidential information?[58] There is the danger that the rule, if applied inflexibly, may impose an impossible burden: As Lord Cohen said in *Boardman v. Phipps*[59]:

" . . . it does not necessarily follow that because an agent acquired information and opportunity while acting in a fiduciary capacity he is accountable to his principals for any profit that comes his way as the result of the use he makes of that information and opportunity. His liability to account must depend on the facts of the case."

---

[54] See generally (1968) 84 L.Q.R. 472 (G. Jones); Oakley, *Constructive Trusts* (3rd ed.), pp. 168–179. A rigid application of the rule may lead to the unjust enrichment of the claimant; *Warman International Ltd v. Dwyer* (1995) 69 A.L.J.R. 362 at 369.

[55] *supra*. A fiduciary guilty of undue influence has, however, been remunerated by the court; *O'Sullivan v. Management Agency and Music Ltd* [1985] Q.B. 428, *ante*, p. 604.

[56] *post*, p. 657.

[57] (1970) 86 L.Q.R. 463 (G. Jones).

[58] See [1978] Conv. 114 (B. Rider); *North and South Trust Co. v. Berkeley* [1971] 1 W.L.R. 470; (1972) 35 M.L.R. 78 (M. Kay and D. Yates); *Movitex Ltd v. Bulfield* [1988] B.C.L.C. 104 (fiduciary must not place himself in a position where his duty to X conflicts with his duty to Y).

[59] [1967] 2 A.C. 46 at 102–103; see also Lord Upjohn at 126.

Viscount Dilhorne[60] quoted Lindley L.J. as saying "to hold that a partner can never derive any personal benefit from information which he obtains from a partner would be manifestly absurd."[61]

It is difficult to formulate any single test which may be applied to determine whether a fiduciary has incurred liability. It is submitted that liability will arise if any of the following factors is present:

(a) The fiduciary has used trust property;

(b) The profit has been made by use of or by reason of the fiduciary position or of an opportunity or knowledge resulting from it, even though no trust property was used;

(c) There was a conflict (or a significant possibility of a conflict) of interest and duty, even if no trust property was used, and the opportunity did not arise from the fiduciary relationship.[62]

C. Personal and Proprietary Remedies

It is often said that a fiduciary who is required to account for profits becomes a constructive trustee. But a duty to account is a personal liability; a constructive trust is a proprietary remedy; the significance of the distinction appears where the fiduciary is bankrupt, or where the assets in question have been profitably invested. A related question is whether tracing is available, which is discussed in Chapter 23. Liability to account is not synonymous with constructive trusteeship, but the cases do not always maintain the distinction. Indeed, Lord Lane C.J. has said "We find it impossible to reconcile much of the language used in these decisions."[63]

In *Boardman v. Phipps*, Wilberforce J. had held that the shares were held on constructive trust[64] for the beneficiaries; and that Boardman was accountable for profits he made, less a sum for his skill and effort. The House of Lords did not distinguish between accountability and constructive trust. Lord Guest concluded that the defendants held the shares as constructive trustees, and were bound to account to the claimant.[65] The other members spoke of accountability only.

As submitted above, there is a difference between a duty to hold specific property on trust and a duty to account. Could Boardman

---

[60] [1967] 2 A.C. 46 at 90.

[61] *Aas v. Benham* [1891] 2 Ch. 244 at 255–256.

[62] *Industrial Development Consultants Ltd v. Cooley* [1972] 1 W.L.R. 443. See also Stephenson L.J. in *Swain v. Law Society* [1982] 1 W.L.R. 17 at 31: there must be a possibility of a conflict of interest and duty, and a nexus between the fiduciary position and the profit made.

[63] *Re Att.-Gen.'s Reference (No. 1 of 1985)* [1986] Q.B. 491 at 503.

[64] [1964] 2 All E.R. 187; *cf.* [1964] 1 W.L.R. 993.

[65] [1967] 2 A.C. 46 at 117. See (1990) 106 L.Q.R. 87 at 102 (D. Hayton), suggesting that the liability was personal only.

have satisfied the judgment by payment of the value of the shares at that time, keeping any subsequent increase? Would a purchaser (with notice) have taken the shares subject to the same obligation? What would have been the position if Boardman had been bankrupt? None of these matters arose, and it was not necessary to discuss them.

If the fiduciary has used or received trust property, then any profits made are held on constructive trust for the beneficiaries.[66] Whether the remedy in other cases was personal or proprietary was not always clear, but until recently a special rule applied to bribes and secret commissions. It was laid down by the Court of Appeal in *Lister & Co. v. Stubbs*[67] that where an agent or other fiduciary took a bribe, the principal's remedy was personal. The fiduciary had to account for the bribe, but did not hold it on constructive trust. The result in that case was that the fiduciary could keep any profit made from investing the bribe money. This decision was long criticised[68] as contravening the principles of unjust enrichment and treating a dishonest fiduciary more leniently than an honest fiduciary such as Boardman in *Boardman v. Phipps*.[69] It was, however, affirmed by the Court of Appeal in *Re Att.-Gen.'s Reference (No. 1 of 1985)*,[70] although in a criminal law context, with the result that an employee who made a secret profit was not guilty of theft of his employer's property.

Lister & Co. v. Stubbs has now been disapproved by the Privy Council in a decision which concerned bribes but which is very significant in the wider area of profits made by fiduciaries.

In *Att.-Gen. for Hong Kong v. Reid*[71] the defendant, a public prosecutor, took bribes of over $HK12 million to obstruct prosecutions, in breach of his fiduciary duty as a Crown servant. He failed to comply with an order to repay and was imprisoned. He had purchased three freehold properties with the money, which had since increased in value. The Privy Council decided that these properties were held on trust for the Crown.

Lord Templeman pointed out that bribes cause loss and damage to the principal, although it may not be quantifiable, as in the present case, where unquantifiable harm to the administration of justice had

---

[66] *Guinness plc v. Saunders* [1990] 2 A.C. 663, *ante*, p. 616; *Neptune (Vehicle Washing Equipment) Ltd v. Fitzgerald* [1996] Ch. 274.

[67] (1890) 45 Ch.D. 1.

[68] Although supported in (1987) 103 L.Q.R. 433 (R. Goode); *Law at the Centre* (B. Rider ed.), p. 185 (R. Goode).

[69] [1967] 2 A.C. 46.

[70] [1986] Q.B. 491.

[71] [1994] 1 A.C. 324. The person who bribed the agent is accountable to the principal for any resulting profit; *Fyffes Group Ltd v. Templeman, The Times*, June 14, 2000.

been done. A constructive trust of the bribe money arose because the fiduciary was under an immediate duty to pay it over to the principal. Applying the maxim "equity regards as done that which ought to be done", the money was the property of the principal in equity. The fiduciary's creditors should be in no better position than the fiduciary. If the bribe money was profitably invested, the profits belonged to the principal. If it decreased in value, the fiduciary was personally liable for the deficit. The constructive trust arose whether the fiduciary took property from the trust or from a third party in breach of duty. Any other result, it was said, would be inconsistent with the principle that a fiduciary must not profit from his office. There was no logic in treating a dishonest fiduciary more favourably than an honest fiduciary who had become liable as constructive trustee.

The decision has been welcomed so far as it prevents the unjust enrichment of a dishonest fiduciary, but certain difficulties remain. Instead of dealing with the policy issue of when proprietary remedies should be available, the Privy Council based its decision more narrowly on the equitable maxim, the application of which is controversial in that it is founded on the availability of specific performance, but an obligation to pay money is not normally specifically enforceable.[72] It might also be doubted whether the claimant deserves priority over the defendant's unsecured creditors, who have not necessarily taken the risk of insolvency. So far as the bribe has increased in value, the increase is a windfall to the claimant. To balance the interests of creditors and the prevention of unjust enrichment, a compromise solution might be mere personal liability for any increase in value.[73] By allowing the claimant to assert ownership of the bribe money and any profits made from it, the decision amounts to "proprietary overkill".[74] As leading commentators have said, "By the light of nature it is not easy to see why bribery should trigger a proprietary response if other wrongs do not."[75]

The Privy Council in *Reid*[76] answered some of the points discussed above in relation to *Boardman v. Phipps*.[77] Lord Templeman clearly regarded Boardman as a constructive trustee and not merely subject to a personal liability to account. He became such not by

---

[72] *post*, p. 725; (1994) 53 C.L.J. 31 (A. Oakley); [1994] 2 R.L.R. 57 (D. Crilley); All E.R. Rev. 1994, at 252 (P. Clarke); (1995) 54 C.L.J. 60 (S. Gardner); *cf.* (1998) 114 L.Q.R. 399 at 407 (Sir Peter Millett).

[73] Birks, *An Introduction to the Law of Restitution*, p. 389; (1994) 110 L.Q.R. 178 (P. Watts); All E.R. Rev. 1994, 365 (W. Swadling); [1994] Conv. 156 (A. Jones); (1995) 58 M.L.R. 87 (T. Allen).

[74] [1994] 2 R.L.R. 57 (D. Crilley).

[75] All E.R. Rev. 1998 at 415 (P. Birks and W. Swadling); (1998) 12 *Trust Law International* 228 (W. Swadling).

[76] [1994] 1 A.C. 324.

[77] [1967] 2 A.C. 46.

reason of any classification of confidential information as trust property but because he obtained the information by virtue of his office. The effect of the decision in the criminal law context remains to be seen.[78] Where the fiduciary retains neither the bribe nor any property deriving from it, then of course his personal liability to account remains.

Finally, a claimant cannot have an account of profits and also damages for what he would have received had he been able to use the property for the period in question. These remedies are alternative, not cumulative, and the claimant must elect between them at the time of judgment in his favour, by which time it will be clear which remedy is the more advantageous.[79]

---

[78] *Re Att.-Gen.'s Reference (No. 1 of 1985)* [1986] Q.B. 491; (1994) 110 L.Q.R. 180 (J. Smith).
[79] *Tang Man Sit (Personal Representatives) v. Capacious Investments Ltd* [1996] 1 A.C. 514 (secret profits from wrongful lettings of houses in breach of trust); (1996) 112 L.Q.R. 375 (P. Birks); [1996] R.L.R. 117 (J. Stevens).

CHAPTER 22

VARIATION OF TRUSTS

1. THE BACKGROUND

A TRUSTEE must administer the trust according to its terms. Any deviation is a breach of trust for which the trustee will be personally liable.[1] However, any adult beneficiary *sui juris* may deal with his equitable interest under the trust in any way he wishes; and may consent to the trustee dealing with the trust funds in a way which affects his interest. Further, adult beneficiaries who together are absolutely entitled to the trust property may terminate the trust and demand that the fund be handed over to them[2]; but not if any interests are outstanding,[3] nor if the trustees have no power to transfer the property.[4]

---

[1] *ante*, p. 497; *post*, Chap. 23.

[2] *Love v. L'Estrange* (1727) 2 E.R. 532; *Saunders v. Vautier* (1841) Cr. & Ph. 240; *Re Smith* [1928] Ch. 915; *Re Nelson* [1928] Ch. 920n; *Re Becket's Settlement* [1940] Ch. 279. See also Trusts of Land and Appointment of Trustees Act 1996, s.6(2); *ante*, p. 000.

[3] *Berry v. Green* [1938] A.C. 575; *Re Robb* [1953] Ch. 459; *Re Wragg* [1959] 1 W.L.R. 922.

[4] *Don King Productions Inc v. Warren* [2000] Ch. 291 (trust of benefit of non-assignable contracts). The point was not discussed on appeal.

They may wish to do this for various reasons. In *Saunders v. Vautier*,[5] the beneficiary wished to terminate an accumulation which was to continue until he reached 25; he was able to claim the fund at 21 (then the age of majority). If property is given to A for life and then to B, and both A and B are adult, they may each wish to have capital immediately available, and may agree to partition the fund. The main reason is the possibility of reducing tax liability and especially liability for inheritance tax on the death of A. Inheritance tax, an outline of which was given in Chapter 9, is chargeable on transfers on or within seven years before death. It is also chargeable on certain lifetime transfers even if the transferor survives for seven years, for example the creation of a discretionary trust, although in such a case the rate is lower.[6] In the case of a non-discretionary trust, the advantage of partitioning the fund between life tenant and remainderman is that, provided the life tenant survives for seven years (which may be covered by insurance), no tax will be payable on the partition, whereas the whole capital is taxable if the life interest terminates on death.[7]

It may be advantageous in terms of income tax liability to share out the entitlement to income. Whether or not a variation is a disposal for capital gains tax purposes has never been decided.[8] As far as inheritance tax is concerned, trustees of a discretionary trust may wish to improve the tax position of the settlement by converting it to a trust where there is an interest in possession or to an accumulation and maintenance settlement.[9] Such a conversion will itself be taxable.[10] The tax saving aspect of the matter is emphasised here because it has been the motive force in the passing of the Variation of Trusts Act 1958, and the variations which have been made under it. "Nearly every variation" said Lord Denning M.R. "that has come before the court has tax-avoidance for its principal object."[11] Variations have, of course, been made for other purposes, as will be seen.

One particular tax exemption should be noted. Where, not more than two years after a death of a person, testate or intestate, the disposition of his property taking effect upon his death is varied by an instrument in writing, such a variation is not a transfer of value

---

[5] (1841) Cr. & Ph. 240. For the meaning of "absolutely entitled" in a tax context, see *Figg v. Clarke (Inspector of Taxes)*, [1997] 1 W.L.R. 603 (class consisting of children of X not absolutely entitled for capital gains tax purposes until death of X, although X incapable of fathering more children).

[6] Inheritance Tax Act 1984, s.7.

[7] F.A. (No. 2) 1987, s.96. See *Gibbon v. Mitchell* [1990] 1 W.L.R. 1304.

[8] Harris, *Variation of Trusts*, pp. 97 *et seq.* There would be a disposal if the effect of the variation is to revoke the original settlement and to create a new one, but not if the original settlement continues as varied.

[9] *ante*, p. 233.

[10] *ante*, p. 232.

[11] In *Re Weston's Settlements* [1969] 1 Ch. 234 at 245.

for inheritance tax purposes,[12] nor a disposal for capital gains tax purposes,[13] and the variation takes effect as if made by the deceased. These provisions may be of great help where, for example, a wealthy testator has created a disadvantageous discretionary trust by will.[14] They clearly apply to an agreed variation by adult beneficiaries and to a variation under the Variation of Trusts Act 1958. A similar principle applies to an order under the Family Provision legislation.[15]

It should be added that the trust instrument may give the trustees a power to amend the trust. Such a power must be exercised for the purpose for which it was granted.[16] It has been recently said (in the context of a commercial trust) that, although the power must not be exercised beyond the reasonable contemplation of the parties, it would be going too far to say that such a power may never be exercised to alter rights or to bring a new class of property within the scope of the trust.[17]

2. VARIATIONS WHICH NEED THE APPROVAL OF THE COURT[18]

We have seen that children and persons not *sui juris* are not able to deal irrevocably with their property. If a situation arose where variations needed to be made to a trust in the interests of such persons, nothing could be done which involved any negotiation with or compromise by the persons under disability, without the approval of the court. The person under disability could be benefited at the expense of the adult parties. The life tenant may be willing to agree to an advancement by the trustees,[19] or to surrender his life interest. But if the life tenant wanted something in return, there was no way in which he could negotiate it.

Yet, especially in the tax context, it was in the interest of the remaindermen that the variation should be made. Adult remaindermen could agree to a variation; it was hard for children, persons under a disability and unborn persons to be denied advantages which competent adults could obtain for themselves. The court, however, has no inherent jurisdiction to vary a trust in favour of children and unborn persons.[20] But there are cases where the court can intervene, and these have been substantially increased by several statutes.

[12] Inheritance Tax Act 1984, ss.17, 142.
[13] Taxation of Chargeable Gains Act 1992, s.62(6).
[14] Inheritance Tax Act 1984, Part III, Chap. III, *ante*, p. 231.
[15] *ibid.* s.146.
[16] *Hole v. Garnsey* [1930] A.C. 472.
[17] *Society of Lloyd's v. Robinson* [1999] 1 W.L.R. 756. See also Pensions Act 1995, ss.67–71.
[18] (1954) 17 M.L.R. 420 (O. Marshall); Harris, *Variation of Trusts*.
[19] *Pilkington v. I.R.C.* [1964] A.C. 612, *ante*, p. 595.
[20] *Chapman v. Chapman* [1954] A.C. 429.

A. Inherent Jurisdiction

i. Salvage and Emergency. A court has inherent power in the case of absolute necessity to sanction the mortgage of a child's property in order to protect the property which he retains. The jurisdiction is very narrow and is usual where expenditure is necessary to save buildings from collapse.[21] An extension of this jurisdiction allows the court in an emergency, not foreseen or anticipated by the settlor, to authorise the trustees to perform certain acts which are beyond the powers given to them in the trust instrument, where this is in the best interests of the trust estate and where the consent of all the beneficiaries cannot be obtained because they are not in existence or are under a disability.

In *Re New*,[22] the court approved a scheme of capital reconstruction of a company, splitting the shares into different and smaller denominations, and authorised the trustees to take the new shares, subject to an undertaking to apply for further authorisation to retain the shares after one year. This decision was said in *Re Tollemache*[23] to be the "high water-mark" of the emergency jurisdiction. Kekewich J. and the Court of Appeal refused to sanction a widening of the trustees' investment powers merely because this would be for the advantage of the beneficiaries. There was no emergency. It is clear that the jurisdiction applies to administrative matters only, and does not cover schemes for the variation of beneficial interests.

ii. Compromise.[24] Until the decision of the House of Lords in *Chapman v. Chapman*[25] in 1954, the courts had accepted a wide definition of the word "compromise" as the basis of a useful jurisdiction to approve a variation from the terms of a trust although there was no dispute between the parties in any real sense of the term. The cases were more akin to bargains or exchanges approved by the court as being fair to children or remaindermen, than to compromised litigation. There was a question whether the jurisdiction effected a variation of beneficial interests as distinct from varying the property subject to the trusts,[26] and the jurisdiction did not extend to the redrafting of a settlement as such—there had to be some element of composition of rights.[27] But this distinction was of course paper-thin. Denning L.J., the minority judge in the Court of Appeal in the *Chapman* case, would have got round the difficulty by

[21] *Re Jackson* (1882) 21 Ch.D. 786; *Conway v. Fenton* (1888) 40 Ch.D. 512; *Re Montagu* [1897] 2 Ch. 8 at 11, *per* Lopes L.J.
[22] [1901] 2 Ch. 534.
[23] [1903] 1 Ch. 457, affirmed, *ibid*, at 955.
[24] (1954) 17 M.L.R. 427 (O. Marshall).
[25] [1954] A.C. 429.
[26] *Re Downshire Settled Estates* [1953] Ch. 218.
[27] *Re Chapman's S.T.* [1953] Ch. 218.

accepting for the courts a general jurisdiction to vary trusts on behalf of those unascertained or not *sui juris*, but the House of Lords preferred the other solution—that of limiting the jurisdiction to sanction compromises to cases where there was a genuine dispute. Nor could matters that did not genuinely contain an element of dispute be made to look as if they did.[28] Where there is a genuine dispute, the court of course has power to sanction a compromise, even if the compromise solution contains tax-saving advantages for the beneficiaries.

In *Allen v. Distillers Co. (Biochemicals) Ltd*[29] the question was whether the court, in approving a settlement of the action of the child victims of the thalidomide drug, had jurisdiction to postpone the vesting of the capital in the children to an age greater than 18. Eveleigh J. held that the court had no inherent jurisdiction to order a postponement; a beneficiary with a vested interest under a trust was entitled to demand possession on majority.[30] Nor was there a trust to which the Variation of Trusts Act 1958 applied; the payment out to trustees of sums paid into court did not give rise to the kind of trust contemplated by that Act. However, it was found that the terms of the settlement of the action were wide enough to authorise a postponement of payment.

An attempt to invoke the court's compromise jurisdiction occurred in *Mason v. Farbrother*,[31] where trustees of a pension fund set up in 1929 for Co-operative Society employees had power to invest principally in the society itself and otherwise in authorised trustee securities. By 1982, as a result of inflation, the fund had increased to £127 million, and the trustees, who were anxious to have the wide powers of investment appropriate for modern pension funds, applied to the court for approval of an investment clause giving wider powers than those of the Trustee Investments Act 1961, which at that time governed trustee investments. The trustees were uncertain as to the proper construction of the original investment clause, one view being that the whole fund should be invested in the society, and the other that the whole should be invested under the 1961 Act. This was sufficient to give the court jurisdiction, as genuine points of difference existed. It was not necessary that there should be a contested dispute. While a compromise need not be something between the two views, it was doubtful whether the court could substitute an entirely new investment clause. Thus the variation was not permitted under the court's jurisdiction to approve a

---

[28] *Re Powell-Cotton's Resettlement* [1956] 1 W.L.R. 23. Nor should the trustees, in their application to court for the exercise of the compromise jurisdiction, insert an unrelated claim for increased remuneration; *Re Barbour's Settlement Trusts* [1974] 1 W.L.R. 1198.
[29] [1974] Q.B. 384.
[30] *Saunders v. Vautier* (1841) 4 Beav. 115; *ante*, p. 630.
[31] [1983] 2 All E.R. 1078; All E.R. Rev. 1984 at 308 (P. Clarke).

compromise. (It was, however, authorised by section 57 of the Trustee Act 1925).[32]

B. Statutory Provisions (other than Variation of Trusts Act 1958)

i. Trustee Act 1925, s.57(1). "Where in the management or administration of any property vested in trustees, any sale, lease, mortgage, surrender, release, or other disposition, or any purchase, investment, acquisition, expenditure, or other transaction, is in the opinion of the court expedient, but the same cannot be effected by reason of the absence of any power for that purpose vested in the trustees by the trust instrument, if any, or by law, the court may by order confer upon the trustees . . . the necessary power . . . on such terms . . . as the court may think fit . . . "

This subsection overlaps the "emergency" jurisdiction discussed above, and widens it by making the statutory jurisdiction available in cases of expediency rather than emergency. It operates as if its provisions were read into every settlement.[33] It is clear from the opening words of the section that it is only available in questions arising in the *management* or *administration* of property; it is not therefore available for the purpose of remoulding beneficial interests or for tax saving generally.[34]

Applications are usually heard in private, and it is not possible to learn from reported cases the full scope of the operation of the subsection. It has however been effectively used to authorise the sale of land where necessary consents had been refused[35]; to authorise partition[36]; and to authorise the purchase of a residence for the tenant for life,[37] the sale of a reversionary interest which under the terms of the trust instrument was not to be sold until it fell into possession,[38] and wider investment powers.[39] It has been held that section 57 should be used in preference to the Variation of Trusts Act 1958 where wider investment powers are sought, provided the beneficial interests are not affected.[40]

---

[32] *infra.*

[33] *Re Mair* [1935] Ch. 562; see also *Re Salting* [1932] 2 Ch. 57.

[34] *Re Downshire S.E.* [1953] Ch. 218; *cf. Re Forster's Settlement* [1954] 3 All E.R. 714.

[35] *Re Beale's S.T.* [1932] 2 Ch. 15.

[36] *Re Thomas* [1930] 1 Ch. 194.

[37] *Re Power* [1947] Ch. 572; (1947) 91 S.J. 541.

[38] *Re Cockerell's S.T.* [1956] Ch. 372.

[39] *Re Shipwrecked Fishermen and Mariners' Royal Benevolent Society* [1959] Ch. 220; *cf. Re Powell-Cotton's Resettlement* [1956] 1 W.L.R. 23; *Mason v. Farbrother* [1983] 2 All E.R. 1078.

[40] *Anker-Petersen v. Anker-Petersen* (1998) 12 *Trust Law International* 166 (decided 1991).

ii. Settled Land Act 1925, s.64(1). "Any transaction affecting or concerning the settled land, or any part thereof, or any other land . . . which in the opinion of the court would be for the benefit of the settled land, or any part thereof, or the persons interested under the settlement, may, under an order of the court, be effected by a tenant for life, if it is one which could have been validly effected by an absolute owner."[41]

It will be seen that this subsection is wider than Trustee Act, s.57(1). "Transaction" is widely defined[42]; and there is no limitation restricting the court's powers to cases of management and administration.[43] The subsection enables the court to alter beneficial interests in such a way as to reduce tax liability[44] and was the most effective vehicle for this purpose before 1958. It applies however only to cases of settled land, and not to the ordinary case of a personalty settlement. In *Hambro v. Duke of Marlborough*[45] the Duke and the trustees considered that the second defendant, the Marquess of Blandford, who was tenant in tail in remainder, would be incapable of managing the Blenheim estate on the death of the Duke because of his "unbusinesslike habits" and lack of responsibility. They proposed a scheme whereby the estate would be conveyed to trustees of a new trust, to pay the income to the Duke for life, and then to hold on protective trusts for the second defendant for life, thereafter on the trusts of the existing settlement. This was held to be a "transaction" within section 64, which could vary the beneficial interests even where an ascertained adult beneficiary did not consent.[46]

iii. Trustee Act 1925, s.53.[47] Under section 53 the court is given power to authorise certain dealings with a child's property "with a view to the application of the capital or income thereof for the maintenance, education, or benefit of the infant." As with section 57, the section overlaps and extends the inherent power to make provision for the maintenance of children. The word "benefit" has been widely construed, and the court has authorised transactions

---

[41] See also Settled Land and Trustee Acts (Court's General Powers) Act 1943. Settlements of land cannot be created after the Trusts of Land and Appointment of Trustees Act 1996.

[42] S.L.A. 1925, s.64(2). See *Raikes v. Lygon* [1988] 1 W.L.R. 281; *Hambro v. Duke of Marlborough* [1994] Ch. 158.

[43] It is used for such purposes. *Re White-Popham's S.E.* [1936] Ch. 725; *Re Scarisbrick's Re-Settlement Estates* [1944] Ch. 229.

[44] *Re Downshire S.E.* [1953] Ch. 218; *Raikes v. Lygon* [1988] 1 W.L.R. 281.

[45] *supra*; [1994] Conv. 492 (E. Cooke).

[46] This was a preliminary issue. The scheme was subsequently approved; *The Times*, July 23, 1994.

[47] (1957) 21 Conv.(N.S.) 448 (O. Marshall).

whose object was the reduction of estate duty for the child's bene-fit.[48] Thus, entails have been barred in order to exclude the interests of large numbers of remote beneficiaries with a view to raising money for the child's benefit[49] or to simplifying an application to the court under the Variation of Trusts Act 1958[50]; and reversionary interests have been sold to the tenant for life.[51] However, the pro-ceeds of sale should be resettled; this will be an "application" for the child's benefit[52]; while an outright payment to him of the pro-ceeds of sale will not be.[53]

iv. Matrimonial Causes Act 1973. The court has wide power to make orders affecting the property of parties to matrimonial pro-ceedings. It may order capital provision to be made, by cash pay-ment, or property transfer, or by the making of a settlement for the benefit of the other spouse and the children of the family.[54] It may also effect the variation of ante-nuptial or post-nuptial settlements,[55] and the variation of orders for settlements made under the Act.[56]

The jurisdiction to vary a "post-nuptial settlement" under section 24 of the 1973 Act enabled the provision of a pension for a wife on divorce in *Brooks v. Brooks*.[57] A company pension scheme of which the husband was the sole member provided that on retirement he could direct that part of his benefit should be used to make provision for his wife after his death, and that a lump sum would be payable at the discretion of the trustee to a class including the wife if he were to die prematurely. These factors made it a "marriage settlement", which had a wide meaning. The scheme could be varied so far as it constituted a settlement made by the husband. Under the scheme the surplus belonged to the employer company, and was thus not part of the settled property. The trust was varied by directing that an im-mediate annuity and a deferred pension were to be provided in priority to and, if necessary, in diminution of the husband's pension. Had there been any other scheme members, the court would not have ordered a variation to their detriment, nor would it sanction a variation with adverse tax consequences.[58]

---

[48] *Re Meux* [1958] Ch. 154.
[49] *Re Gower's Settlement* [1934] Ch. 365.
[50] *Re Bristol's S.E.* [1964] 3 All E.R. 939; *Re Lansdowne's W.T.* [1967] Ch. 603.
[51] *Re Meux, supra, cf. Re Heyworth's Contingent Reversionary Interest* [1956] Ch. 364.
[52] *Re Meux, supra.*
[53] *Re Heyworth's Contingent Reversionary Interest, supra*; criticised (1957) 21 Conv.(N.S.) 448 at 450–454 (O. Marshall).
[54] Matrimonial Causes Act 1973, ss.23 and 24. See also s.25, laying down the principles to be observed by the court in exercising its jurisdiction under ss.23, 24.
[55] s.24(1)(c), (d). See *E. v. E.* [1990] 2 F.L.R. 233.
[56] s.31(2)(e). Further details must be obtained from the Family Law books.
[57] [1996] 1 A.C. 375; (1995) 145 N.L.J. 1009 (M.Rae); [1997] Conv. 52 (M. Thomas).
[58] It was significant that the wife had once been employed by the company, otherwise the variation might have forfeited Inland Revenue approval (necessary for tax relief) by reason of an immediate payment to a non-employee.

This decision is of limited application and does not solve the problem of pension-splitting on divorce, which is dealt with by other legislation.[59]

v. Mental Health Act 1983. Mental Health Act 1983, s.96(1)(*d*) gives to the Court of Protection a power to make a settlement of the property of the patient; and also, if any material fact was not disclosed when the settlement was made, or where there has been any substantial change in circumstances, to vary the settlement in such manner as the judge thinks fit.[60]

C. Variation of Trusts Act 1958[61]

The Variation of Trusts Act 1958 gives to the court a "very wide and, indeed, revolutionary discretion"[62] to approve on behalf of four groups of persons[63] "any arrangement . . . varying or revoking all or any of the trusts, or enlarging the powers of the trustees of managing or administering any of the property subject to the trusts."[64] On its terms, this provision covers not only administrative matters, but also variations in the beneficial interests; but the court may only approve such an arrangement if it would be for the benefit of the person on whose behalf the approval is given.[65]

The courts have approved a wide variety of variations, and, in addition to approving changes in the beneficial interests, have inserted a power of advancement,[66] terminated an accumulation,[67] inserted an accumulation period[68] and have widened the investment powers of trustees.[69] Investment clauses are rarely the subject of an application, for it became established that only in exceptional circumstances should a court give its approval to wider investment powers than those given to trustees in the Trustee Investments Act

---

[59] Welfare Reform and Pensions Act 1999. See also Pensions Act 1995, *ante*, p. 493 (earmarking).

[60] M.H.A. 1983, s.96(3).

[61] Harris: *Variation of Trusts*, Chaps. 3 *et seq.*; (1958) 22 Conv.(N.S.) 373 (M. Mowbray); (1963) 27 Conv.(N.S.) 6 (D. Evans); (1965) 43 Can.B.R. 181 (A. Maclean). The jurisdiction given by the Act is independent of T.A. 1925, s.57, and S.L.A. 1925, s.64, *ante*. There may be technical reasons, *e.g.* difficulties as to representative parties, why it is not possible to invoke the 1958 Act. See *Mason v. Farbrother* [1983] 2 All E.R. 1078.

[62] *per* Evershed M.R. in *Re Steed's W.T.* [1960] Ch. 407 at 420–421.

[63] *infra.*

[64] V.T.A. 1958, s.1(1). But see *Allen v. Distillers Co. (Biochemicals) Ltd* [1974] Q.B. 384, *ante*, p. 633.

[65] Except for persons in para. (*d*), *infra.*

[66] *Re Lister's W.T.* [1962] 1 W.L.R. 1441.

[67] *Re Tinker's Settlement* [1960] 1 W.L.R. 1011.

[68] *Re Lansdowne's W.T.* [1967] Ch. 603; *Re Holt's Settlement* [1961] Ch. 100.

[69] *Re Coates' Trusts* [1959] 1 W.L.R. 375; *Re Burney's S.T.* [1961] 1 W.L.R. 545.

1961.[70] The Act of 1961, however, became outdated, and the courts were prepared to sanction an extension of investment powers.[71] It was held that section 57 of the Trustee Act 1925 was more appropriate than the 1958 Act where wider investment powers were sought, provided the beneficial interests were not affected.[72] Under section 57 the court would consider the interests of the beneficiaries collectively in income and capital but would not need to consent on behalf of the various categories of beneficiaries as required by the 1958 Act, nor would it require the consent of adult beneficiaries. Such applications are less likely to be made now that investment powers have been widened by the Trustee Act 2000.

It is of course in connection with schemes which vary beneficial interests for tax saving purposes that the 1958 Act has been mainly applied.

i. Persons on whose Behalf Approval may be Given. The principle is that the court is not asked to approve on behalf of ascertainable adults who can consent for themselves. The classes (as set out in Variation of Trusts Act 1958, s.1) are:

"(*a*) any person having, directly or indirectly, an interest, whether vested or contingent, under the trusts who by reason of infancy or other incapacity is incapable of assenting, or

(*b*) any person (whether ascertained or not) who may become entitled, directly or indirectly, to an interest under the trusts as being at a future date or on the happening of a future event a person of any specified description or a member of any specified class of persons, so however that this paragraph shall not include any person[73] who would be of that description, or a member of that class, as the case may be, if the said date had fallen or the said event had happened at the date of the application to the court, or

(*c*) any person unborn, or

---

[70] *Re Kolb's W.T.* [1962] Ch. 531; *Re Cooper's Settlement* [1962] Ch. 826; *Re Clarke's W.T.* [1961] 1 W.L.R. 1471. See also *Re Rank's S.T.* [1979] 1 W.L.R. 1242, where an arrangement included a power of appointment in terms wide enough to permit the donee to give wider powers of investment to the trustees for the benefit of the appointees.

[71] In *Mason v. Farbrother* [1983] 2 All E.R. 1078, *ante*, p. 548, concerning T.A. 1925, s.57, the effect of inflation and the fact that the trust was in the nature of a public fund were regarded as special circumstances; *cf. Trustees of the British Museum v. Att.-Gen.* [1984] 1 W.L.R. 418, [1984] Conv. 373 (H. Norman), where Megarry V.-C. preferred the view that the *Re Kolb* principle, *supra*, had gone. This was discussed in Chap. 18. See also *Steel v. Wellcome Custodian Trustees Ltd* [1988] 1 W.L.R. 167; [1988] Conv. 380 (B. Dale).

[72] *Anker-Petersen v. Anker-Petersen* (1998) 12 *Trust Law International* 166 (decided 1991).

[73] This presumably means any ascertained person; Harris, *op. cit.* pp. 39–40.

(*d*) any person in respect of any discretionary interest of his under protective trusts where the interest of the principal beneficiary has not failed or determined."[74]

Paragraph (*b*) may well of course include adults; but because the class is ascertainable only at a future time, its members cannot yet be known. Under the proviso, however, those who would qualify if the future event happened at the date of the application to the court must themselves consent. If however they are children, they come within paragraph (*a*).

In *Re Suffert*,[75] income was given under protective trusts to an unmarried woman for life, and, in the event of her having no issue, and subject to a general testamentary power, in trust for those who would become entitled under her intestacy. She had three adult cousins, who would be entitled in equal shares to her estate if she had died at the date of the application to the court. One cousin was made a party, and consented, but the others were not. In asking the court to approve the arrangement, it was argued that the court should approve on behalf of those who would be entitled on intestacy, as they came within paragraph (*b*). Buckley J. however held that the proviso applied and that he could not approve on behalf of the two cousins. Otherwise he approved the arrangement.

The meaning of the words "may become entitled" in paragraph (*b*) were examined in *Knocker v. Youle*.[76]

Property was held on trust for the settlor's daughter for life under a settlement in which her cousins had very remote contingent interests. It was not practicable to get the approval of the cousins to the proposed variation because they were very numerous, and some were in Australia.[77] Approval was therefore sought on their behalf under section (1)(1)(*b*). The question was whether paragraph (*b*) included persons with an existing contingent interest, however remote. Warner J. held that it did not. A person having a contingent interest was not a person who "may become entitled" to an interest. Paragraph (*b*) covered the case of a person who had a mere *spes* (an expectation) such as the prospective next

---

[74] See *Gibbon v. Mitchell* [1990] 1 W.L.R. 1304.

[75] [1961] Ch. 1.

[76] [1986] 1 W.L.R. 934; criticised [1987] Conv. 144 (J. Riddall), also discussing persons who are objects of mere powers and discretionary trusts.

[77] The Act does not deal with the problem of the beneficiary who must consent on his own behalf but who is untraceable. In such a case a *Benjamin* order (*ante*, p. 550) could be used. See (1986) 136 N.L.J. 1057 (P. Luxton).

of kin of a living person in *Re Suffert*,[78] or a potential future spouse.[79] The adult cousins were in any event excluded by the proviso to paragraph (*b*).

ii. Parties. In general, the settlor, if living,[80] and all beneficaries under the trusts, both adults and children, should be made parties. The children, unless their interests coincide with those of adult beneficiaries who consent, should be separately represented,[81] and a litigation friend must give full consideration to the way in which the proposed variation will affect the children's interests.[82] In the case of a class, those who are members of the class at the date of the application should be included[83]; but it is not necessary to join persons who may become members later[84]; nor persons who may become interested under discretionary trusts[85]; nor those who are possible objects of a power.[86] Persons unborn cannot of course be made parties, but their interests must be represented.[87] Where a mental patient is involved the Court of Protection should be informed and proceedings then taken in the Court of Protection to look after the interests of the patient.[88]

iii. Applicants. The application should be made by a beneficiary, usually the person currently receiving the income. But the settlor may do so.[89] It is not usually satisfactory for the trustees to make the application because there might be an undesirable conflict of interest between their interest as an applicant, and as guardian of some of the beneficial interests for which they are responsible.[90] They may apply if no-one else will do so, and the variation is in the interests of the beneficiaries.[91]

---

[78] *supra*; *Re Moncrieff's S.T.* [1962] 1 W.L.R. 1344. But see [1987] Conv. 144 at p. 146 (J. Riddall) for the view that such persons do have a contingent interest in the *settlement*, although not, of course, in the estate of their living relative.

[79] See *Re Clitheroe's S.T.* [1959] 1 W.L.R. 1159; *Re Lister's W.T.* [1962] 1 W.L.R. 1441.

[80] R.S.C., Ord. 93, r. 6(2) (C.P.R. 1998, Sched. 1).

[81] *Re Whigham's S.T.* [1971] 1 W.L.R. 831.

[82] *Re Whittall* [1973] 1 W.L.R. 1027. See C.P.R. 1998, Part 21.

[83] *Re Suffert's Settlement* [1961] Ch. 1.

[84] *Re Moncrieff's S.T.* [1962] 1 W.L.R. 1344.

[85] *Re Munro's S.T.* [1963] 1 W.L.R. 145.

[86] *Re Christie-Miller's Marriage Settlement* [1961] 1 W.L.R. 462; *Practice Direction* [1976] 1 W.L.R. 884.

[87] The court must consider the position of any individual who may be born and become a beneficiary, not merely the class of unborn beneficiaries as a whole; *Re Cohen's S.T.* [1965] 1 W.L.R. 1229.

[88] *Practice Direction* [1960] 1 W.L.R. 17; *Re Sanderson's W.T.* [1961] 1 W.L.R. 36; Mental Health Act 1983, s.96.

[89] *Re Clitheroe's S.T.* [1959] 1 W.L.R. 1159.

[90] *Re Druce's S.T.* [1962] 1 W.L.R. 363.

[91] *ibid.* at 370.

iv. Foreign Trusts. The court will not approve an agreement which provides for a settlement under the law of a foreign jurisdiction if the beneficiaries remain resident and domiciled in England; nor, as in *Re Weston's Settlement*,[92] where the connection with Jersey, the foreign jurisdiction, was recent and tenuous, and where the court doubted whether the living beneficiaries really intended to make Jersey their permanent home. Trusts have, however, been "exported" in favour of a settlement with foreign trustees and governed by foreign law where the beneficiaries have emigrated permanently to the foreign country[93]; and approval has been given for the transfer of funds from a trust governed by English law to one governed by the law of Guernsey where the primary beneficiaries were resident and domiciled in France and the remainderman in Indonesia.[94] The advantages of trust exporting have been much reduced since the introduction of capital transfer and inheritance tax.[95]

It should be added that the appointment of a foreign trustee may be made in a proper case without the intervention of the court.[96]

Where the question is not one of exporting a trust to another jurisdiction but of varying a foreign trust, such a variation is governed by the applicable law of the trust.[97]

v. Effect of Approval by the Court. It appears that the arrangement is effective from the time of the approval by the court. The reasons why this is so are not clear; and the result may be due to the practice established by *Re Viscount Hambledon's Will Trusts*.[98] Several, and in some cases conflicting, accounts have been given of the effect of approval by the court.

In *Re Joseph's Will Trusts*[99] Vaisey J. included in his order approving the variation a direction that the variation should be carried into effect. In *Re Viscount Hambleden's Will Trusts*,[1] Wynn-Parry J. thought that he had no jurisdiction to make such a direction. Nor was it required. "I hold that the effect of my approval is effective for

---

[92] [1969] 1 Ch. 223.
[93] *Re Seal's Marriage Settlement* [1961] Ch. 574 (Canada); *Re Windeatt's W.T.* [1969] 1 W.L.R. 692 (Jersey); see also *Re Whitehead's W.T.* [1971] 1 W.L.R. 833.
[94] *Re Chamberlain* (unreported) discussed in (1976) 126 N.L.J. 1034 (J. Morcom); (1976) 40 Conv.(N.S.) 295 (T. Watkin).
[95] See I.H.T.A. 1984, ss.48(3), 201(1)(*d*), 267.
[96] *Re Whitehead's W.T.*, *supra*. But application will often be made to the court, and a variation will be necessary if the form of the trust needs to be altered in order to comply with the foreign law, if there is no power in the trust instrument to do this. See Parker and Mellows, *The Modern Law of Trusts* (7th ed.), Chap. 26; (1990/91) 1 The Offshore Tax Planning Review, p. 1 (R. Bramwell), discussing *Richard v. The Hon, A.B. Mackay* (1987, unreported), *ante*, p. 520.
[97] Recognition of Trusts Act 1987, Sched., Art. 8. The applicable law is determined by Arts. 6, 7; *ante*, p. 45.
[98] [1960] 1 W.L.R. 82; *Re Holt's Settlement* [1969] 1 Ch. 100 at 113.
[99] [1959] 1 W.L.R. 1019.
[1] [1960] 1 W.L.R. 82.

all purposes to vary the trusts."[2] In *Re Holt's Settlement*,[3] Megarry
J. was unconvinced. Before him it was argued that the Act gives the
court power to approve only on behalf of the persons mentioned in
section 1(1); and the consent of the adults to a change in their
beneficial interests was a "disposition," and ineffective unless in
writing, as required by section 53(1)(*c*) of the Law of Property Act
1925.[4] Megarry J. was reluctant to disturb what had become a very
convenient practice based on *Re Viscount Hambleden*,[5] and searched
for a theory to justify it. The suggestion that there was no "disposition" of the interests of the consenting adults, but a "species of
estoppel"[6] operating against them was "unattractive." He was satisfied however that it could be explained on the ground that section
53(1)(*c*) was by necessary implication excluded; or that, where the
variation was made for consideration, the consenting adults could be
compelled to perform their contract and they held their original
interests on constructive trusts, these being unaffected by section
53(1)(*c*).[7] The view that the variation obtains its effect by reason of
the consent of the beneficiaries is supported by dicta in *I.R.C. v.
Holmden*,[8] where however the question of section 53(1)(*c*) did not
arise.

The arrangement coupled with the court's order is an "instrument" for the purposes of the Perpetuities and Accumulations Act
1964, s.15(5), and future interests or accumulations permitted by the
Act may be provided for in an arrangement.[9] Because the variation
does not owe its authority to the settlor, its provisions need not be
such that the settlor could have created them.[10] In contrast with
powers of appointment and advancement,[11] the perpetuity period
does not relate back to the original settlement. A variation which is
inconsistent with the continuous existence of a power operates as a
release of a power.[12]

vi. Variation or Resettlement. The jurisdiction, as we have
seen, is very wide. It is however a jurisdiction to "vary" and not to

---

[2] [1960] 1 W.L.R. 82 at 86.
[3] [1969] 1 Ch. 100; (1968) 84 L.Q.R. 162 (P.V.B.).
[4] *ante*, p. 82; *Grey v. I.R.C.* [1960] A.C. 1.
[5] [1960] 1 W.L.R. 82.
[6] [1969] 1 Ch. 100 at 114; *Spens v. I.R.C.* [1970] 1 W.L.R. 1173.
[7] L.P.A. 1925, s.53(2); *Oughtred v. I.R.C.* [1960] A.C. 206; *Re Holt's Settlement* [1969] 1 Ch. 100 at 115–116.
[8] [1968] A.C. 685; *cf.* T.A. 1925, s.57; *Re Mair* [1935] Ch. 562.
[9] *Re Lansdowne's W.T.* [1967] Ch. 603; *Re Holt's Settlement, supra.*
[10] *Re Holt's Settlement, supra.*
[11] *Pilkington v. I.R.C.* [1964] A.C. 612, *ante*, p. 596.
[12] *Re Christie-Miller's Marriage Settlement* [1961] 1 W.L.R. 462; *Re Courtauld's Settlement* [1965] 1 W.L.R. 1385; *Re Ball's S.T.* [1968] 1 W.L.R. 899; *ante*, p. 189.

"resettle."[13] This is a difficult dividing line. In *Re Ball's Settlement*, Megarry J. laid down the general test as follows[14]:

> "If an arrangement changes the whole substratum of the trust, then it may well be that it cannot be regarded merely as varying the trust. But if an arrangement, while leaving the substratum, effectuates the purpose of the trust by other means, it may still be possible to regard that arrangement as merely varying the original trusts, even though the means employed are wholly different and even though the form is completely changed."

vii. Fraud on a Power. Nor will the court approve a variation which involves a fraud on a power, as for example where property is held on trust for A for life and to such of A's children as he shall appoint, and A, in order to avoid tax liability on his death, appoints in favour of his living children, and does so with a view to partitioning the fund, with the court's approval, between his children and himself. Such an appointment has been held to be fraudulent and void on the ground that it was made so that the appointor may obtain a benefit for himself under the variation.[15]

viii. The Settlor's Intention. In giving approval, the court must be satisfied about the arrangement as a whole.[16] One relevant factor is whether or not the arrangement is consistent with the general plan of the settlor or testator.

In *Re Steed's Will Trusts*[17] a testator had left property to a faithful housekeeper for her life on protective trusts and after her death as she should appoint, the trustee having power to pay capital moneys to her as they should think fit. The property included a farm which was let to the housekeeper's brother. The terms of the will were designed to give the maximum benefit in the property to the housekeeper, without giving her an absolute interest, because of the danger which the testator "thought was real, of being, to use a common phrase, sponged upon by one of her brothers."[18]

The trustees decided to sell the farm. The housekeeper started proceedings to stop them, exercised the power of appointment in

---

[13] *Re T.'s S.T.* [1964] Ch. 158; *Re Ball's S.T.* [1968] 1 W.L.R. 899; criticised (1968) 84 L.Q.R. 458 (P.V.B.); *Re Holt's Settlement* [1969] 1 Ch. 100 at 117; *Allen v. Distillers Co. (Biochemicals) Ltd* [1974] Q.B. 384.

[14] [1968] 1 W.L.R. 899 at 905.

[15] *Re Robertson's W.T.* [1960] 1 W.L.R. 1050; *Re Brook's Settlement* [1968] 1 W.L.R. 1661; *cf. Re Wallace's Settlement* [1968] 1 W.L.R. 711.

[16] *Re Burney's S.T.* [1961] 1 All E.R. 856.

[17] [1960] Ch. 407; *Re Michelham's W.T.* [1964] Ch. 550.

[18] [1960] Ch. 407 at 415.

favour of herself, and applied under the Variation of Trusts Act, s.1, for the elimination of the protective element in her life interest. The result would be that she would become absolutely entitled to the property, because she would then be the life tenant, having appointed to herself the reversion. The only persons who might be prejudiced by such a variation would be those who might benefit under the discretionary trusts which would arise if the protective life interests were forfeited[19]; and under paragraph (d), the court is not concerned to see that they benefit from a variation. Was there any reason why approval should not be given?

The Court of Appeal refused:

> "It is the *arrangement* which has to be approved not just the limited interest of the person on whose behalf the court's duty is to consider it . . . the court must regard the proposal as a whole, and so regarding it, then ask itself whether in the exercise of its jurisdiction it should approve that proposal on behalf of the person who cannot give a consent . . . it was part of the testator's scheme . . . that this trust should be available for the [claimant] so that she should have proper provision made for her throughout her life, and would not be exposed to the risk that she might, if she had been handed the money, part with it in favour of another individual about whom the testator felt apprehension, which apprehension is plainly shared by the trustees."[20]

The question also arose in *Re Remnant's Settlement Trusts*,[21] where the proposed variation was the deletion of a forfeiture clause whereby beneficiaries who practised Roman Catholicism or married a Roman Catholic would lose their entitlement. The fact that the variation would defeat the settlor's intention was regarded as a serious matter, but not conclusive. As the forfeiture clause was undesirable in the circumstances of the family (unlike the disputed provision in *Re Steed's Will Trusts*,[22] which was not cited), it was fair and proper to delete it, notwithstanding the settlor's intention.

In *Goulding v. James*[23] the clear intention of the testatrix was that her daughter should have only a life interest and that her grandson should not have capital until aged 40 (because she mistrusted her son-in-law and her grandson had not "settled down"). A variation

---

[19] *ante*, p. 195; assuming that she would not now have children, this was only a prospective husband, described in the case of the "spectral spouse."

[20] [1960] Ch. 407 at 421–422.

[21] [1970] Ch. 560; *post*, p. 647.

[22] *supra*.

[23] [1997] 2 All E.R. 239; criticised (1997) 60 M.L.R. 719 (P. Luxton).

was sought whereby the daughter would have capital and the grandson would become entitled before the age of 40. As the proposed terms substantially increased the financial benefit to unborn beneficiaries, approval was given by the Court of Appeal, even though the proposal was contrary to the intention of the testatrix. Her wishes related only to the adult beneficiaries, and so carried little weight. *Re Steed's Will Trusts*,[24] which laid down no general rule, was distinguishable because there the testator's purpose was evidenced in the will itself, and no benefit needed to be established for the class of beneficiaries on whose behalf consent was sought. In the present case extrinsic evidence of the wishes of the testatrix could not be allowed to outweigh considerations of benefit to the class of unborns, to whom this evidence had no relevance. The role of the court is not to stand in for the settlor but to consent on behalf of the beneficiaries who are unable to consent.

ix. Benefit. It is necessary that the variation should be for the benefit of the persons in categories (*a*) or (*c*) on whose behalf approval is sought. There is no such requirement of benefit in respect of persons under category (*d*).[25]

(a) *Financial Benefit.* There is usually no difficulty in showing financial benefit. But evidence must be presented to show that there is an advantage to each person required to be benefited.[26] Variations have commonly been made to save estate duty or inheritance tax,[27] capital gainst tax,[28] and income tax.[29] Any saving provides a larger sum for distribution, and remaindermen may also be benefited by the termination of an interest in possession as their interests will be accelerated. As stated above,[30] a partition of the settled fund between tenant for life and remainderman has inheritance tax advantages. Provided the tenant for life survives for seven years, no tax will be payable, whereas the whole capital is taxable if a life interest terminates on death. It is usual for the life tenant to pay the costs of the application.

(b) *Moral and Social Benefit.* But benefit is not only financial. The court must also consider the general welfare of the persons on whose behalf approval is sought; this does not necessarily coincide with their financial interest.

[24] *supra.*
[25] V.T.A. 1958, s.1, proviso. See *Re Van Gruisen's W.T.* [1964] 1 W.L.R. 449.
[26] *Re Clitheroe's S.T.* [1959] 1 W.L.R. 1159 at 1163.
[27] *Re Druce's S.T.* [1962] 1 W.L.R. 363; *Gibbon v. Mitchell* [1990] 1 W.L.R. 1304.
[28] *Re Sainsbury's Settlement* [1967] 1 W.L.R. 476.
[29] *Re Clitheroe's S.T.* [1959] 1 W.L.R. 1159.
[30] *ante*, p. 630.

In *Re Weston's Settlements*,[31] two settlements had been made in 1964, one in favour of each of the settlor's sons (both young men and one still under age) and their children. The settlor moved to Jersey in 1967, and the sons followed him. The application was for the appointment of new trustees under Trustee Act 1925, s.41,[32] and for the insertion into the settlement of a power for the trustees to discharge the trust of the settlements and to create almost identical Jersey settlements. The object was to take advantage of the favourable fiscal situation in Jersey. The Court of Appeal refused. The variation would make the beneficiaries richer but would not be for their benefit:

"The court should not consider merely the financial benefit to the infant and unborn children, but also their educational and social benefit. There are many things in life more worthwhile than money. One of these things is to be brought up in this our England, which is still 'the envy of less happier lands.' I do not believe that it is for the benefit of the children to be uprooted from England and transported to another country simply to avoid tax . . . many a child has been ruined by being given too much.[33] The avoidance of tax may be lawful, but it is not yet a virtue. The Court of Chancery should not encourage or support it—it should not give its approval to it—if by so doing it would imperil the true welfare of the children, already born or yet to be born."[34]

Similarly, as has been seen, with the housekeeper who wished to become the absolute owner of a farm which would then have been at the mercy of her brother.[35] In *Re C.L.*[36] it was held to be for the benefit of a mental patient to consent to the surrender of a protected life interest and a contingent remainder interest in favour of her daughter. It was what the patient would have done if she had been of sound mind. Mental patients should not be denied the opportunity of taking proper steps to preserve the family fortune.

(c) *Postponing Vesting.* It may be for the benefit of a child that the date of vesting of an interest in the capital should be postponed.

---

[31] [1969] 1 Ch. 233.
[32] *ante*, p. 518.
[33] A further objection concerned the absence of trusts legislation in Jersey. For the present position, see Matthews, *Jersey Law of Trusts* (3rd ed.), 1993.
[34] [1969] 1 Ch. 233 at 245.
[35] *Re Steed's W.T.* [1960] Ch. 407; *ante*, p. 643.
[36] [1969] 1 Ch. 587.

In *Re T.'s Settlement Trusts*,[37] a beneficiary who was irresponsible and immature was entitled to a vested interest on attaining her majority, which she would do a few months after the application. The proposal was that her interest should be varied to become a protected life interest. Wilberforce J. could not regard such protection as a "benefit in its own right"; but he made an order postponing the vesting of the capital until a specified age and providing that the property should be held on protective trusts in the meantime.

(d) *Trouble in the Family.* Where a trust treats members of the family unequally, it may be for everyone's benefit, even for those who surrender a claim to property as a result, to vary the trust so as to treat each of them equally. Russell J. thought not in *Re Tinker's Settlement*,[38] where, owing to the draftsman's oversight, the settlement provided that the share of the settlor's son should accrue to his sister's share if he died under the age of 30 years, even if he left children. It was not for the benefit of the sister's children to surrender their contingent interest.

A broader view was taken in *Re Remnant's Settlement Trusts*.[39]

A trust fund gave contingent interests to the children of two sisters Dawn and Merrial, and contained a forfeiture provision in respect of any of the children who practised Roman Catholicism or was married to a Roman Catholic at the time of vesting, with an accruer provision in favour of the children of the other. Dawn's children were Protestant, but Merrial's were Roman Catholic.

Pennycuick J. approved the deletion of the forfeiture provision. This was clearly not for the financial benefit of Dawn's children, for they surrendered a very good chance of gaining by it. But it was overall for their benefit. "Obviously, a forfeiture provision of this kind might well cause very serious dissension between the families of the two sisters."[40] The forfeiture clause could also operate as a deterrent in the selection of a spouse. Freedom from such problems would be more important to the lives of the children than some more money.

(e) *Taking a Chance.* A difficulty arises where the proposed variation will almost certainly confer a benefit, but there may possibly

---

[37] [1964] Ch. 158; *Re Holt's Settlement* [1969] 1 Ch. 100. See also *Allen v. Distillers Co. (Biochemicals) Ltd* [1974] Q.B. 384; *ante*, p. 633. It was reported in *The Times*, February 16, 1999, that a trust had been varied so that the son of the Duke of Northumberland would receive £250,000 a year from the age of 25 instead of 18.

[38] [1960] 1 W.L.R. 1011.

[39] [1970] Ch. 560; (1971) 34 M.L.R. 98 (R. Cotterrell).

[40] [1970] Ch. 560 at 566. Another benefit, of less weight, was to be freed from having to choose between one's religion and the entitlement under the will.

be circumstances in which it will not. Thus, in *Re Cohen's Settlement Trust*,[41] an application was made to vary a settlement so as to make the interest of the grandchildren vest on a specified date, and not upon the death of a life tenant, in order to reduce estate duty. Although it was most unlikely (but not impossible) that the life tenant would live until the specified date, any children born after that date but before his death would lose their interests. Thus approval could not be given on behalf of unborn children. Where trustees wish to distribute on the footing that a middle-aged woman will not have further children, this may be sanctioned by court order (made in the exercise of its jurisdiction to secure the proper administration of a trust) without recourse to the 1958 Act.[42] Indeed, no application to court is needed where the woman is elderly.[43]

The question is one of degree. The court will not give its approval where the benefit is a matter of chance, but it will not require absolute certainty of benefit,[44] if the risk is one which a "prudent and well advised adult would be prepared to take."[45] Most risks can be covered by insurance.

[41] [1965] 1 W.L.R. 1229.

[42] *Re Westminster Bank Limited's Declaration of Trust* [1963] 1 W.L.R. 820 (over 50). The order did not extinguish the rights of any future child.

[43] *Re Pettifor's S.T.* [1966] Ch. 257 (over 70); *cf. Figg v. Clarke (Inspector of Taxes)* [1997] 1 W.L.R. 603 (presumption of fertility until death in context of capital gains tax, where a deemed disposal occurs when beneficiaries become absolutely entitled to the trust property).

[44] *Re Holt's Settlement* [1969] 1 Ch. 100; *Re Robinson's S.T.* [1976] 1 W.L.R. 806.

[45] (1960) 76 L.Q.R. 22 (R.E.M.).

CHAPTER 23

BREACH OF TRUST

1. Personal Liability to Beneficiaries

A. General[1]

i. Liability is Compensatory. A trustee who fails to comply with his duties is liable to make good the loss to the trust estate. Even if there is no loss, the trustee is accountable for any profit made in breach of trust.[2] The object of the rule is not to punish the trustee, but to compensate the beneficiaries. However, the court will, on suitable occasions, authorise acts which are technical breaches of trust; a trustee will not be liable for a technical breach which the court would have authorised[3]; but there is no need to take the risk; he should obtain the directions of the court before acting.[4] The effect of exemption clauses was considered in Chapter 17.[5]

ii. Liability is Personal, not Vicarious. The rule has always been that a trustee is liable for his own breaches and not for those of his co-trustees.[6] The dividing line however is extremely difficult to draw; for if there is a breach by a co-trustee, the trustee may himself be at fault by leaving the matter in the hands of a co-trustee without inquiry, or for standing by while a breach of trust is being committed,[7] or for allowing trust funds to remain in the sole control of a co-trustee, or for failing to take steps to obtain redress on becoming aware of a breach of trust.

iii. Breaches before Appointment. A trustee is not liable for breaches of trust committed before his appointment in the absence of evidence indicating a breach of trust.[8] On appointment, however, he should examine the books and documents relating to the trust, and should ensure that the trust property is vested in him. If in the course of his inquiries he discovers a breach of trust, he should take steps against the former trustees; unless for some reason he can show that such proceedings would have been useless.[9]

iv. Breaches after Retirement. A trustee remains liable after retirement for breaches committed by him during office; and similarly his estate remains liable after his death. He may on the other

---

[1] See the definitions of breach of trust discussed by Megarry J. in *Tito v. Waddell (No. 2)* [1977] Ch. 106 at 247. As to costs, see *McDonald v. Horn* [1995] 1 All E.R. 961; *ante*, p. 602. For the liability of a director for breach by a corporate trustee, see (1997) 11 *Trust Law International* 48 (D. Pollard).

[2] See Chap. 21.

[3] *Brown v. Smith* (1878) 10 Ch.D. 377.

[4] *ante*, p. 550.

[5] *ante*, p. 501.

[6] *Townley v. Sherborne* (1643) J. Bridg. 35 at 37, 38.

[7] *Bahin v. Hughes* (1886) 31 Ch.D. 390; *post*, p. 660.

[8] *Re Strahan* (1856) 8 De G.M. & G. 291.

[9] *Re Forest of Dean Coal Co* (1878) 10 Ch.D. 450 at 452.

hand have been released by the other trustees, or by the beneficiaries being of full capacity and in possession of all the facts. He will not usually be liable in respect of breaches committed after his retirement; but he may be if he retired in order to facilitate a breach of trust.[10]

v. Trustee-Beneficiary. Where the trustee in breach is also a beneficiary, his beneficial interest bears the loss against the other beneficiaries,[11] and, as we will see,[12] against the trustees[13]; and this liability applies although the beneficial interest was acquired by him derivatively, even by purchase.[14]

B. Measure of Liability

i. General Principles. In the case of an unlawful profit, the trustee must account for the profit, which will normally be held on constructive trust. Thus any increase in value belongs to the trust, while the trustee remains personally liable for the deficit if there is a decrease in value.[15] Indeed, he may be liable to account for the highest value between the date of breach and the date of judgment.[16] Thus the principle that liability is measured as at the date of judgment, applicable to other breaches, does not apply to profits.[17] Where a profit has been made from the wrongful use of property, the claimant must elect at judgment between an account of profits and compensation for loss sustained by the deprivation of the use of the property.[18]

With other breaches of trust or fiduciary duty, the measure of liability is the loss caused to the trust estate, directly or indirectly,[19]

---

[10] *Head v. Gould* [1898] 2 Ch. 250 at 272. This question came into prominence in the context of pressure upon English resident trustees to retire in favour of foreign resident trustees in order to allow a trust fund to escape liability for capital gains tax: *Re Whitehead's W.T.* [1971] 1 W.L.R. 833; *ante*, p. 520.

[11] *Re Dacre* [1915] 2 Ch. 480; [1916] 1 Ch. 344. Assignees are also bound, unless they took for value and without notice.

[12] *post*, p. 662.

[13] *Chillingworth v. Chambers* [1896] 1 Ch. 685.

[14] *Re Dacre, supra.*

[15] *Att.-Gen. for Hong Kong v. Reid* [1994] 1 A.C. 324; *ante*, p. 625.

[16] *Nant-y-glo and Blaina Ironworks Co. v. Grave* (1879) 12 Ch.D. 738 (liable to account for shares at previous value of £80 each although since fallen to £1 each).

[17] *Target Holdings Ltd v. Redferns (a firm)* [1996] 1 A.C. 421, *infra*.

[18] *Tang Man Sit (Personal Representatives) v. Capacious Investments Ltd* [1996] 1 A.C. 514; *ante*, p. 627.

[19] *Knott v. Cottee* (1852) 16 Beav. 77; *Bartlett v. Barclays Bank Trust Co. Ltd (No. 2)* [1980] Ch. 515.

and the onus is on the claimant to prove that there is a loss and that it would not have occurred but for the breach.[20]

The principles of equitable compensation have not yet been fully worked out.[21] Liability is restitutionary, and the principles are not identical to the common law rules for the assessment of damages.[22] Thus the rules of remoteness and foreseeability applicable in contract and tort are not relevant, but causal connection must be established. In *Canson Enterprises Ltd v. Boughton & Co.*[23] a solicitor committed a breach of fiduciary duty in a sale transaction in which he knew that the vendor made a secret profit. The purchaser (who would not have completed if aware of the facts) then built a warehouse which, due to the negligence of the builders, was defective. The purchaser's claim for compensation against the solicitor for the defective building was unanimously dismissed by the Canadian Supreme Court because there was insufficient causal connection between the breach and the loss, but different views were taken as to whether the common law rules of remoteness applied by analogy in equity.

The principles were reviewed in *Target Holdings Ltd v. Redferns (a firm)*[24]

> Target agreed to advance £1,525,000 to C Ltd, to purchase property valued (allegedly negligently) at £2m, to be secured by a mortgage. The arrangement, unknown to Target, was that the vendor would sell to P Ltd for £775,000, which would sell to K Ltd for £1.25m, which in turn would sell to C Ltd for £2m. This appeared to be a mortgage fraud by the three related companies. The defendant solicitors acted for the three companies and for Target. Target transferred £1,525,000 to the solicitors, who held it on a bare trust for Target. In breach of trust the solicitors paid away the money to P Ltd and K Ltd before completion of the purchase and the mortgage. The mortgage was in fact completed a few days later. On the insolvency of C Ltd the property was sold

---

[20] *Re Miller's Trust Deed* (1978) L.S.Gaz. 454; *Nestlé v. National Westminster Bank plc* [1993] 1 W.L.R. 1260 (holding also that "loss" includes a gain which is less than the profit a prudent trustee would have made); *Target Holdings Ltd v. Redferns (a firm)* [1996] 1 A.C. 421 at 440.

[21] See (1994) 14 L.S. 313 (D. Capper). This is discussed in the context of "fusion"; *ante* p. 25. See also *Medforth v. Blake* [2000] Ch. 86; (2000) 59 C.L.J. 31 (L. Sealy).

[22] See *Re Bell's Indenture* [1980] 1 W.L.R. 1217 (trustee must restore trust property without deducting tax which would have been payable if it had not been misappropriated, in contrast with principles of assessing loss of earnings).

[23] (1991) 85 D.L.R. (4th) 129. See also *Mahoney v. Purnell* [1996] 3 All E.R. 61; (1997) L.Q.R. 8 (J. Heydon).

[24] [1996] 1 A.C. 421; (1995) 9 *Trust Law International* 86 (J. Ulph); (1996) 112 L.Q.R. 27 (C. Rickett); [1996] L.M.C.L.Q. 161 (R. Nolan); [1997] Conv. 14 (D. Capper); (1997–98) 8 K.C.L.J. 1 (Sir Anthony Mason) and 86 (R. Davern). The proceedings were interlocutory, as a result of which the defendants obtained leave to defend. See also *Bank of New Zealand v. New Zealand Guardian Trust Co. Ltd* [1999] 1 N.Z.L.R. 664 at 687–688.

by Target as mortgagee, but, because of the property slump, raised only £500,000. Target sued the solicitors for breach of trust in paying away the £1,525,000 and claimed that sum less the proceeds of sale. The House of Lords found for the solicitors. Target was in the same position as it would have been if the money had not been transferred until the security was in place and had thus failed to establish that the loss would not have occurred but for the breach.

Lord Browne-Wilkinson considered that it was wrong to apply rules developed in the context of traditional trusts to trusts arising in commercial dealings. In the case of a traditional trust for A for life then for B, each beneficiary was entitled to a restoration of the fund.[25] The present case involved a bare trust of a commercial kind. Before the transaction had been completed the solicitors could have been required to restore the money wrongly paid away. But "the clock did not stop" when the money was paid away. Once the transaction had been completed, equity required a trustee to make good a loss suffered which, using hindsight and common sense, could be seen to have been caused by the breach. The quantum of liability was to be assessed not at the date of the breach but at the date of judgment.[26] Although the principles underlying the common law and equitable rules were similar, the detailed rules were different. If it could be shown that the loss would not have occurred but for the breach,[27] the trustee would be liable even if the immediate cause of the loss was the dishonesty or negligence of a third party, as the common law rules of remoteness and causation would not apply.

It is important, however, to distinguish a breach of trust or fiduciary duty from other breaches of duty by a fiduciary. The special restitutionary principles of assessment of equitable compensation discussed above apply only where there is a breach of trust or fiduciary duty. A breach of fiduciary duty means a breach of those proscriptive, *i.e.* negative, duties which are special to fiduciaries, whose core obligation is loyalty.[28] Where a fiduciary (such as a

---

[25] See *Clough v. Bond* (1838) 3 My. & Cr. 490; *Hillsdown Holdings plc v. Pensions Ombudsman* [1997] 1 All E.R. 862.

[26] *Jaffray v. Marshall* [1993] 1 W.L.R. 1285, which measured the loss as the highest value of the property between breach and judgment, was overruled. See also *Re Dawson* [1966] 2 N.S.W.L.R. 211 (date of judgment equally applicable where this operates to the detriment of the trustees).

[27] Target would be able to prove this at trial if it could show that P Ltd could not have purchased from the vendor (and then sold on) without the funds advanced in breach of trust. Thus leave to defend was conditional upon paying £1m into court.

[28] See (1997) 113 L.Q.R. 220 and (1997) 56 C.L.J. 39 (R. Nolan); (1999) 13 *Trust Law International* 74 (S. Elliott); *Bristol and West Building Society v. Fancy & Jackson (a firm)* [1997] 4 All E.R. 582.

solicitor) commits some other breach, as where he acts incompetently, there is no reason why compensation in equity should be assessed differently from common law damages.[29]

The principle that equity does not require a trustee to compensate for a loss which would have occurred had there been no breach is surely correct. However, it is not clear exactly how the rules applicable to traditional trusts and commercial trusts differ. Sir Peter Millett said of the supposed distinction: "It is difficult to know what to make of this".[30] Would the result in *Target Holdings* have been any different if the trustees of a family trust investing on mortgage had committed a similar breach? Indeed, it has been said that *Target Holdings* "has not done a great deal to clarify the rules of causation employed in equity."[31] The distinction between traditional and commercial trusts in this context may prove illusory. A more useful distinction is that between breaches of fiduciary duty and other breaches by fiduciaries, as mentioned above.

Different considerations apply where the fiduciary has misrepresented or failed to disclose a material fact.[32] Thus a solicitor who misled his mortgagee client could not challenge the client's claim that it would not have proceeded with the loan but for the misrepresentation.[33] The Court of Appeal in *Swindle v. Harrison*[34] emphasised that this special principle applies only where the fiduciary's breach was the equivalent of fraud. In that case a client of the solicitor claimants mortgaged her house in order to purchase an hotel, anticipating a loan from a brewery to provide the balance. When, after exchange of contracts, the brewery refused to lend, the solicitors lent the money, secured on the hotel. They failed to disclose that the firm was (by arrangement with the bank) making a hidden profit on the loan and that they had known that the brewery would not lend. The hotel business failed, so that the client defaulted on both mortgages and her house was repossessed. When the solicitors sought to enforce the charge over the hotel, the client claimed the value of the lost equity in her house as compensation for breach of fiduciary duty. Her claim failed because she could not prove that,

---

[29] *Bristol & West Building Society v. Mothew* [1998] Ch. 1; *cf. Bristol & West Building Society v. May May & Merrimans*, *supra*, where the breach was considered to be of fiduciary duty, and *Target Holdings* itself, where breach of trust was conceded. The concession is criticised in *Privacy and Loyalty* (P. Birks ed.), p. 288 (D. Hayton).

[30] (1998) 114 L.Q.R. 214 at 224.

[31] [1996] L.M.C.L.Q. 161 at 164 (R. Nolan).

[32] The principle derives from *Brickenden v. London Loan and Savings Co.* [1934] 3 D.L.R. 465. See (1997) 3 *Trusts & Trustees* 6 (P. Matthews).

[33] *Bristol and West Building Society v. May May & Merrimans* [1998] 1 W.L.R. 336. As in *Target Holdings*, the solicitor held the money on trust for the lender before paying it to a purchaser, the security later proving inadequate.

[34] [1997] 4 All E.R. 705; (1997) 11 *Trust Law International* 72 and (1998) 12 *Trust Law International* 66 (L. Ho); [1998] 6 R.L.R. 135 (S. Elliott); (1998) 114 L.Q.R. 181 (H. Tjio and T. Yeo). See also *Gilbert v. Shanahan* [1998] 3 N.Z.L.R. 528.

but for the breach, she would not have accepted the loan and completed the purchase. Thus she would have lost her house in any event. In the absence of proof of fraud, *Target Holdings* applied, not the special principle relating to misrepresentation and non-disclosure. The remedy for the latter would have been rescission of the loan agreement.[35] It has subsequently been held that breaches involving dishonesty or bad faith attract the special principle,[36] but further clarification is needed as to the kind of fraudulent breach to which it applies.

Subsidiary rules applicable to particular situations will now be considered.

ii. Purchase of Unauthorised Investments. When trustees make an unauthorised investment, they will be liable for any loss incurred on the sale. This is so even if the sale is at a time chosen by the court, and if the investments would have shown a profit if they had been retained until the decision of the court holding them to be improper.[37] The beneficiaries may, if they are of full capacity and so wish, adopt the unauthorised investment[38]; if they do so, there is dispute whether that is the limit of their remedy,[39] or whether they may claim the difference between the value of the investment and the purchase price.[40]

iii. Improper Retention of Investments.

(a) *Unauthorised Investments.* A trustee who improperly retains an unauthorised investment is liable for the difference between the present value (or selling price) and the price which it would have raised if it had been sold at the proper time. How hard this can be on a trustee holding property in a falling market is shown by *Fry v. Fry*[41] where trustees were liable for the difference between the price offered for a hotel in 1837 which they refused as inadequate, and the much lower price prevailing in 1859, the fall being largely due to the diversion of road traffic by the building of a railway.

(b) *Authorised Investments.* We have seen that the Trustee Act 2000, section 5, following the pattern of earlier legislation, requires

---

[35] See further (1998) 114 L.Q.R. 9 (S. Moriarty).
[36] *Nationwide Building Society v. Various Solicitors (No.3), The Times,* March 1, 1999; *cf. Collins v. Brebner* [2000] Lloyd's Rep. P.N. 587 (*Target* applies to fraudulent breaches of trust).
[37] *Knott v. Cottee, supra.*
[38] *Re Jenkin's and Randall's Contract* [1903] 2 Ch. 362; *Wright v. Morgan* [1926] A.C. 788 at 799.
[39] *Thornton v. Stokill* (1855) 1 Jur.(N.S.) 751.
[40] *Re Lake* [1903] 1 K.B. 439.
[41] *Fry v. Fry* (1859) 27 Beav. 144.

advice to be taken on the question of retaining investments.[42] Failure to do so will constitute a breach of the statutory duty of care.[43]

iv. Improper Sale of Authorised Investments. When an authorised investment is improperly sold, the beneficiaries may require the trustees either to account for the proceeds of sale or to replace the investment, valued as at the date of judgment.[44] Thus where trustees sold Consols and invested in an unauthorised investment, the whole matter was treated as a single transaction and the trustees were held liable to replace the Consols at the higher price then prevailing.[45] This is so even though the improper investment was realised without loss.[46]

v. Failure to Invest. Trustees should invest within a reasonable time. Failure to do so will constitute a breach of the statutory duty of care.[47]

If a trustee is required to make a specific investment and fails to make any investment, and the price of the specific investment has risen, he will be liable to purchase as much of that investment as would have been purchased at the proper time.[48] Similarly if he chooses an investment other than that specified,[49] profit in the unauthorised investment being surrendered, of course, to the trust.[50] Where, as is nearly always the case in practice, the trustees may select investments at their discretion, it is not practicable to base recovery upon the price of a particular investment. The beneficiary will be entitled to the difference between the actual value of the trust fund and the value which a prudent trustee is likely to have achieved (by considering the average performance of ordinary shares during the period in question).[51]

vi. Employment of Trust Fund in Trade. A trustee who employs trust funds in his trade or business is liable to account for the profits he makes,[52] or for the sums involved with interest, whichever

---

[42] *ante*, p. 539.
[43] Trustee Act 2000, s.1; Sched. 1, para. 1.
[44] *Re Bell's Indenture* [1980] 1 W.L.R. 1217. But where the asset sold in breach of trust would have been properly sold at a later date, the trustee is liable to replace it at its value on that date, and not as at the date of judgment.
[45] *Phillipson v. Gatty* (1848) 7 Hare 516.
[46] *Re Massingberd's Settlement* (1890) 63 L.T. 296.
[47] Trustee Act 2000, s.1; Sched. 1, para. 1.
[48] *Byrchall v. Bradford* (1822) 6 Madd. 235.
[49] *Pride v. Fooks* (1840) 2 Beav. 430.
[50] *post*, p. 658.
[51] *Nestlé v. National Westminster Bank plc* [1993] 1 W.L.R. 1260; *cf. Shepherd v. Moulis* (1845) 4 Hare 500 (trust fund plus interest).
[52] *Re Davis* [1902] 2 Ch. 314; *Re Jarvis* [1958] 1 W.L.R. 815.

is the greater. Difficult questions arise when he employs a mixed fund, being partly his own and partly trust money. Here the rule is that the beneficiaries may claim a proportionate share of the profits[53] or demand the return of the trust money with interest.[54]

vii. Interest. "It is well established in equity that a trustee who in breach of trust misapplies trust funds will be liable not only to replace the misapplied principal fund but to do so with interest from the date of the misapplication. This is on the notional ground that the money so applied was in fact the trustee's own money and that he has retained the misapplied trust money in his own hands and used it for his own purposes. Where a trustee has retained trust money in his own hands, he will be accountable for the profit which he has made or which he is assumed to have made with the use of the money. . . . The defaulting trustee is normally charged with simple interest only,[55] but if it is established that he has used the money in trade he may be charged compound interest. . . . Precisely similar equitable principles apply to an agent who has retained monies of his principal in his hands and used them for his own purposes.[56]"[57] If the trustee or agent has received a sum in excess of what the court would impose, he is accountable for what he has actually received, or the beneficiaries may adopt the investment.[58]

The rate of interest, and the choice between simple and compound,[59] is in the discretion of the court. The nineteenth century cases laid down 4 per cent[60] as the general rule, with an increase to 5 per cent where the trustee or other fiduciary was guilty of fraud[61] or active misconduct,[62] or where he ought to have received more than 4 per cent.[63] These rates are out of line with current commercial

---

[53] *post*, p. 688.

[54] *Heathcote v. Hulme* (1819) 1 Jac. & W. 122.

[55] *Belmont Finance Corporation Ltd v. Williams Furniture Ltd (No. 2)* [1980] 1 All E.R. 393.

[56] *Burdick v. Garrick* (1870) 5 Ch.App. 233.

[57] *Wallersteiner v. Moir (No. 2)* [1975] Q.B. 373 at 397; *Guardian Ocean Cargoes Ltd v. Banco do Brasil (No. 3)* [1992] 2 Lloyd's Rep. 193 (presumed used in investment business); *Mathew v. T. M. Sutton Ltd* [1994] 1 W.L.R. 1455; *cf. O'Sullivan v. Management Agency and Music Ltd* [1985] Q.B. 428, (1986) 49 M.L.R. 118 (W. Bishop and D. Prentice), *ante*, p. 604 (simple interest where profits used in trade, but trade benefited claimant, being in the nature of a joint venture).

[58] *Re Jenkins' and Randalls' Contract* [1903] 2 Ch. 362; *Wright v. Morgan* [1926] A.C. 788 at 799; *ante*, p. 655.

[59] With yearly rests (*Jones v. Foxall* (1852) 15 Beav. 388 at 393; *Guardian Ocean Cargoes Ltd v. Banco do Brasil (No. 3)*, *supra*; *El Ajou v. Dollar Land Holdings plc (No. 2)* [1995] 2 All E.R. 213); and sometimes half-yearly rests (*Re Emmet's Estate* (1881) 17 Ch.D. 142).

[60] *Att-Gen. v. Alford* (1855) 4 De G.M. & G. 843; *El Ajou v. Dollar Land Holdings plc (No. 2) supra*; *Fletcher v. Green* (864) 33 Beav. 426 at 430.

[61] *Att.-Gen. v. Alford*, *supra*, at 852.

[62] *Jones v. Foxall* (1852) 15 Beav. 388 at 393; *Gordon v. Gonda* [1955] 1 W.L.R. 885.

[63] *Jones v. Foxall*, *supra*, at 388 (calling in a mortgage which was returning 5 per cent); see *Re Waterman's W.T.* [1952] 2 All E.R. 1054.

interest rates, and more recent decisions have charged 1 per cent above the London clearing banks' base rate in force at the time[64]; or that allowed from time to time on the court's short-term investment account (now called the court special account), established under section 6(1) of the Administration of Justice Act 1965.[65] Compound interest is charged where that fairly represents what the trustee may reasonably be treated as having received,[66] or where there is a duty to accumulate,[67] and sometimes in cases of fraud or misconduct.[68]

The question which arose in *Westdeutsche Landesbank Girozentrale v. Islington London Borough Council*[69] was whether the equitable jurisdiction to award compound interest could be invoked in a common law personal action. The House of Lords, by a majority, held that it could not. Lords Goff and Woolf, dissenting, held that equity should supplement the common law remedies to achieve full restitution, but the majority considered that this was a matter for Parliament.

viii. Profit in One Transaction: Loss in Another. Any gains made out of the trust property belong to the beneficiaries while a loss incurred by reason of a breach of trust must be made good by the trustee. A trustee cannot set off a gain in one transaction against a loss made in another unauthorised transaction.

In *Dimes v. Scott*[70] trustees retained an unauthorised mortgage returning 10 per cent all of which was paid to the tenant for life. When the mortgage was paid off, trustees were able to purchase more Consols than they would have done if the reinvestment had taken place at the end of a year from the testator's death. Lord Lyndhurst held the trustees liable for the excess interest paid to the tenant for life[71] over that which would have been payable if the capital of the unauthorised investment had been invested in Consols at the end of a year from the testator's death, and the

---

[64] *Wallersteiner v. Moir (No. 2)* [1975] Q.B. 373; [1982] Conv. 93 (J.T.F.); *Belmont Finance Corporation v. Williams Furniture Ltd (No. 2)* [1980] 1 All E.R. 393; *O'Sullivan v. Management Agency and Music Ltd* [1985] Q.B. 428; *Guardian Ocean Cargoes Ltd v. Banco do Brasil (No. 3)* [1992] 2 Lloyd's Rep. 193 (1 per cent above New York prime rate); *Rama v. Millar* [1996] 1 N.Z.L.R. 257.

[65] *Bartlett v. Barclays Bank Trust Co. Ltd (No. 2)* [1980] Ch. 515; *cf. Re Evans* [1999] 2 All E.R. 777 (lower rate of 8 per cent against non-professional administrator in times of "more gentle" inflation).

[66] *Wallersteiner v. Moir (No. 2), supra.*

[67] *Re Emmet's Estate* (1881) 17 Ch.D. 142.

[68] *Jones v. Foxall, supra; Gordon v. Gonda, supra; cf. O'Sullivan v. Management Agency and Music Ltd, supra.* As to costs, see Snell, p. 326.

[69] [1996] A.C. 669.

[70] (1828) 4 Russ. 195.

[71] The tenant for life was entitled only to 4 per cent under the rule in *Howe v. Earl of Dartmouth* (1802) 7 Ves.Jr. 137; *ante*, p. 554.

trustees were unable to set off against this the gain arising from the fall in the price of Consols.

The rule is harsh though logical. It has not been applied where the court finds that the gain and loss were part of the same transaction. There is often difficulty in determining whether the matter should or should not be regarded as a single transaction.

In *Fletcher v. Green*[72] trust money was lent on mortgage to a firm of which one trustee was a partner. The trustees reclaimed the money; the security was sold at a loss and the proceeds paid into court and invested in Consols. The question was whether the trustees' accounts should credit them with the amount of the proceeds of sale or with the value of the Consols, which had risen in price. They were held entitled to take advantage of the rise. No reasons were given. The case is usually explained on the ground that the whole matter was treated as one transaction. If that is so, they should logically have been at risk in relation to a possible fall in the price of Consols; the trustees can hardly be allowed to take advantage of a rise but not the burden of a fall; but it would be hard on the trustees if they have to run the risk of loss on an investment made by the court.

The difficulty of laying down a clear rule was recognised in *Bartlett v. Barclays Bank Trust Co. Ltd (No. 1)*[73] where the defendant bank was held liable as trustee for failing to exercise proper supervision of the board of directors of a private company whose shares were almost wholly owned by the trust. The board embarked on speculative ventures in property development: the Old Bailey project was a disaster; the Guildford project was a success. In finding the bank liable, Brightman J. allowed the gain on the Guildford project to be set off against the Old Bailey. Without considering the case in detail, he said,[74] after recognising the general rule: "The relevant cases are, however, not altogether easy to reconcile. All are centenarians and none is quite like the present. . . . I think it would be unjust to deprive the bank of the element of salvage in the course of assessing the cost of the shipwreck." Thus a gain can be set off against a loss if, even though not arising from the same transaction, they resulted from the same wrongful course of conduct; in the present case a policy of speculative investment.

---

[72] (1864) 33 Beav. 426.
[73] [1980] Ch. 515; [1980] Conv. 155 (G. Shindler); *ante*, p. 546.
[74] *ibid*, at 538.

2. Liability Inter Se: Contribution and Indemnity

A. Joint and Several Liability

Where two or more trustees are liable for a breach of trust, their liability is joint and several. Thus a beneficiary may claim the whole loss by suing all or some or any one of those who are liable; and may levy execution for the whole sum against any one.[75]

B. Contribution

The rule used to be that the joint liability of trustees required an equal sharing of the liability, regardless of fault, and therefore that one trustee who had paid more than his share of the liability for a breach of trust was entitled to equal contribution from the other trustees who were also liable[76]; or from their estates after death.[77] The effect of this rule was shown dramatically in *Bahin v. Hughes*,[78] where the Court of Appeal held that a passive trustee was liable with the active trustee. Cotton L.J. said[79]:

> "Miss Hughes was the active trustee and Mr Edwards did nothing, and in my opinion it would be laying down a wrong rule to hold that where one trustee acts honestly, though erroneously, the other trustee is to be held entitled to indemnity who by doing nothing neglects his duty more than the acting trustee."

The Civil Liability (Contribution) Act 1978 gives the court a discretion in relation to the amount to be recovered against two or more defendants who are liable in respect of the damage. The amount recoverable against any defendant shall be "such as may be found by the court to be just and equitable having regard to the extent of that person's responsibility for the damage in question"[80]; and includes breach of trust as one of the forms of liability to which the Act applies.[81] It will be interesting to see how the passive trustee will fare under this provision. The Act appears not to apply to situations in which one trustee is entitled to an indemnity.[82]

---

[75] *Fletcher v. Green* (1864) 33 Beav. 426 at 430.

[76] *Fletcher v. Green, supra; Ramskill v. Edwards* (1885) 31 Ch.D. 100; *Robinson v. Harkin* [1896] 2 Ch. 415.

[77] *Jackson v. Dickinson* [1903] 1 Ch. 947.

[78] (1886) 31 Ch.D. 390; *Bishopsgate Investment Management Ltd v. Maxwell (No. 2)* [1994] 1 All E.R. 261 (no defence that blindly followed co-director's lead). See Goff and Jones, *The Law of Restitution* (5th ed.), p. 422.

[79] *ibid.* at 396.

[80] s.2(1). This may extend to a complete indemnity; s.2(2). See generally [1997] 5 R.L.R. 27 (C. Mitchell).

[81] s.6(1). See *Friends' Provident Life Office v. Hillier Parker May & Rowden (a firm)* [1997] Q.B. 85; *Dubai Aluminium Co. Ltd v. Salaam* [2000] 3 W.L.R. 910.

[82] s7(3); Law Commission Report on Contribution, No. 79 (1977), para. 26; *cf.* Snell, p. 334; Parker and Mellows, *The Modern Law of Trusts* (7th ed.), p. 693.

C. Indemnity

There are a few cases where one trustee is not liable to contribute; where, that is, he is entitled to an indemnity from his co-trustee against his own liability. Such cases are rare; for such relief "would act as an opiate upon the consciences of the trustees; so that instead of the *cestui que trust* having the benefit of several acting trustees, each trustee would be looking to the other or others for a right of indemnity, and so neglect the performance of his duties."[83] The situations are:

i. Fraud. In some cases where one trustee alone is fraudulent, the other will not be liable at all, and so no question of contribution or indemnity will arise.[84] If both are in breach but one alone has made personal use of trust money, the latter must indemnify his co-trustee.[85] If all are fraudulent the rule used to be that the one who has paid the damages could not claim contribution from the others,[86] because a claimant should not base his claim upon his wrong. No specific exception, however, is made under the modern legislation authorising the court to determine how liability will be shared, and the Civil Liability (Contribution) Act 1978 is applicable.[87]

ii. Solicitor and Trustee. Many of the cases of indemnity are cases where one trustee is a solicitor and has exercised such a controlling influence that the other trustee has been unable to exercise an independent judgment.[88] There is no rule, however, that:

"a man is bound to indemnify his co-trustee against loss merely because he was a solicitor, when that co-trustee was an active participator in the breach of trust complained of, and is not proved to have participated merely in consequence of the advice and control of the solicitor."[89]

iii. Beneficiary-Trustee. When a person who is a trustee and beneficiary participates in a breach of trust, he may not claim any share of the trust estate until he has made good his liability as

---

[83] *per* Fry L.J. in *Bahin v. Hughes, supra*, at 398.

[84] *Re Smith* [1896] 1 Ch. 71 was an exceptional case of two trustees who acted together, but only one of whom was liable to the beneficiaries for the consequences. One trustee had chosen an investment honestly but the other had received a bribe in order to induce him to make it.

[85] *Bahin v. Hughes* (1886) 31 Ch.D. 390 at 395; *Thompson v. Finch* (1856) 25 L.J.Ch. 681 (where trustee also a solicitor).

[86] *Att.-Gen. v. Wilson* (1840) Cr. & Ph. 1 at 28.

[87] See *K. v. P.* [1993] Ch. 140 (not a case on trustees).

[88] *Re Partington* (1887) 57 L.T. 654.

[89] *Head v. Gould* [1898] 2 Ch. 250 at 265, *per* Kekewich J.; *ante*, p. 504; *Lockhart v. Reilly* (1856) 25 L.J. Ch. 697; *Re Turner* [1897] 1 Ch. 536.

trustee.[90] He will be required to indemnify his co-trustee to the extent of his beneficial interest; but this does not take away his right to contribution from his co-trustee. The rule in *Chillingworth v. Chambers*[91] effects a compromise between these rules. A beneficiary trustee must indemnify his co-trustee to the extent of his beneficial interest. That property is taken first to meet the claims; after that, their liability is shared equally. The non-beneficiary trustee is thus given a partial indemnity; partial in that it extends only to the value of the beneficiary-trustee's interest.

3. CRIMINAL LIABILITY[92]

Breach of trust was not, at common law, a crime at all. The trustee was regarded as the owner of the trust property by the common law, which disregarded the rights of the beneficiary. But in 1857 breach of trust was made a statutory crime, and the law on the subject was incorporated in the Larceny Arts 1861 and 1916.

These Acts were repealed and replaced by the Theft Act 1968, which defines "theft" as the dishonest appropriation of property "belonging to another" with the intention of depriving the other of it permanently. By section 5(2) of the Act, "any person having a right to enforce the trust" is regarded as a person to whom the subject-matter of the trust "belongs." so that the criminal liability of trustees is in this way brought within the general law.[93] The objects of a discretionary trust can presumably be regarded as having a sufficient right of enforcement to bring section 5(2) into operation for such trusts. Section 4(2)(*a*) also brings within the definition of "theft" an appropriation by a trustee of "land or anything forming part of it," and section 2(1)(*c*) makes a trustee guilty of theft if he appropriates property though he believes that the equitable owners cannot be discovered. A trustee cannot be convicted of theft on any evidence which has first been elicited from him in the course of civil proceedings instituted against him by the person aggrieved, but trustees have no privilege of refusing to incriminate themselves in civil proceedings.[94]

---

[90] *Re Rhodesia Goldfields Ltd* [1910] 1 Ch. 239; *Selangor United Rubber Estates Ltd v. Cradock (No. 4)* [1969] 3 All E.R. 965.

[91] [1896] 1 Ch. 685; similarly if he becomes a beneficiary after the date of the breach, (1887) 37 Ch.D. 329, at 344.

[92] (1975) 39 Conv.(N.S.) 29 (R. Brazier). For guidelines on sentencing in trustee cases, see *R. v. Barrick* (1985) 81 Cr.App.R. 78.

[93] See *Re Att.-Gen.'s Reference (No. 1 of 1985)* [1986] Q.B. 491; *R. v. Clowes (No. 2)* [1994] 2 All E.R. 316 (misappropriation of money held on trust for investors was theft).

[94] Theft Act 1968, s.31(1).

Finally, a trustee who is ordered to pay by a court of equity any sum in his possession or under his control, may be imprisoned in default of payment for a period not exceeding one year.[95]

4. PROTECTION OF TRUSTEES

A trustee who has committed a breach of trust may be able to escape personal liability by bringing the case within one of the categories discussed below. Many of the relevant points arose in *Re Pauling's Settlement Trusts*.[96]

> The children of the Younghusband family sued to recover from the trustees of their mother's marriage settlement various payments which were alleged to have been made in breach of trust. The Younghusbands were often in financial difficulties. Their main source of money was Mrs. Younghusband's marriage settlement under which she was tenant for life. The trustees had power, with her consent, to advance up to one-half of the presumptive share of each child in the trust fund. Several advances were made under this power to the children when they had attained ages varying from 27 (Francis) to 21 (Ann and Anthony). In most cases the advances were, to the knowledge of everyone concerned, applied for family purposes and usually towards the reduction of Mrs. Younghusband's overdraft. On several occasions, but not on all, independent legal advice was obtained. The trustees relied on the consent and acquiescence of the advanced beneficiaries, and claimed an indemnity under Trustee Act 1925, s.62, and asked for relief under section 61. Several of the payments were held to be in breach of trust and the defences set up by the trustees are considered in the following sections.

A. Participation in, or Consent to, a Breach of Trust

A beneficiary who has participated in, or consented to, a breach of trust may not sue. "It is clear to us," said Willmer L.J. in *Re Pauling's Settlement Trusts*,[97]

> "that if the [trustee] can establish a valid request or consent by the advanced beneficiary to the advance in question, that is a good defence on the part of the [trustee] to the beneficiary's claim, even

---

[95] Debtors Act 1869, s.4.
[96] [1964] Ch. 303.
[97] *ibid.* at 335; *Re Bucks Constabulary Widow's and Orphans' Fund Friendly Society (No. 2)* [1979] 1 W.L.R. 936 at 955.

though it be plain that the advance was made in breach of trust."

A reversioner is not "less capable of giving . . . assent when his interest is in reversion than when it is in possession,"[98] but he will not be treated as having given consent wherever he fails to take steps to remedy a breach of trust of which he has knowledge.[99]

i. Knowledge. Consent is not a mere formality. It is a judgment upon the propriety of the proposed transaction.[1] For, if mere knowledge and a passive assent constituted consent, then a trustee could always escape liability by informing a beneficiary of what he proposed to do. The consent must be given by an adult of full capacity in circumstances in which he had a free choice. However, a child beneficiary may exceptionally be taken to have assented to a breach, for instance where he fraudulently misstated his age[2]:

> "The court has to consider all the circumstances in which the concurrence of the *cestui que trust* was given with a view to seeing whether it is fair and equitable that, having given his concurrence, he should afterwards turn around and sue the trustees: that, subject to this, it is not necessary that he should know what he is concurring in is a breach of trust, provided that he fully understands what he is concurring in, and that it is not necessary that he should himself have directly benefited by the breach of trust."[3]

Thus a beneficiary, who otherwise had a right to set aside a sale, was unable to do so when he had affirmed the sale, accepted part of the purchase money, and caused the purchaser to embark upon further liabilities which he could not repay.[4]

ii. Benefit. It is not necessary that the beneficiary should have been motivated to derive a personal benefit from the breach, nor that he actually received one.[5] Where a beneficiary may recover even though he has received a benefit he must give credit for any benefit which he has received from the breach.[6]

---

[98] *Life Association of Scotland v. Siddal* (1861) 3 De G.F. & J. 58 at 73.
[99] *ibid.*
[1] *Re Massingberd's Settlement* (1890) 63 L.T. 296 at 299.
[2] See *Overton v. Bannister* (1884) 3 Hare 503.
[3] *per* Wilberforce J. in *Re Pauling's S.T.* [1962] 1 W.L.R. 86 at 108, accepted by counsel in the Court of Appeal but not commented on by the Court [1964] Ch. 303, at 339; approved in *Holder v. Holder* [1968] Ch. 353 at 394, 399, 406.
[4] *Holder v. Holder, supra.*
[5] *Fletcher v. Collis* [1905] 2 Ch. 24.
[6] *Re Pauling's S.T.* [1964] Ch. 303. (The £300 received by Ann; and the policies received by Francis and George). See 354 for the reasons why Anthony was not required to account for benefits received indirectly through his mother.

iii. Freedom of Decision. The decision must be freely taken by a person not under disability. Even where the beneficiary is an adult of full capacity, it may be possible to show that the consent was due to undue influence. Thus, in *Re Pauling*,[7] the advancements were in each case delayed until the child had become 21; but several of the payments which had been made to, or indirectly for, the benefit of the parents were presumed to have been the result of undue influence exercised by them over the children. Indeed it was clear that the advances were all made to meet the financial needs of the father. The Court of Appeal refused to accept the trustees' argument that undue influence was only relevant as between the children and their parents where the parents had acquired the benefit; they suggested that:

> "a trustee carrying out a transaction in breach of trust may be liable if he knew, or ought to have known, that the beneficiary was acting under the undue influence of another, or may be presumed to have done so, but will not be liable if it cannot be established that he so knew, or ought to have known."[8] It is impossible to say how long after the attainment of majority the presumption continues; this depends upon the circumstances of each case.[9]

B. Release and Acquiescence

These defences relate to the conduct of the beneficiary after the breach has taken place; where they apply, they become equivalent to consent *ex post facto*. A release may be, but need not be, formal; it may be inferred from conduct, as where a beneficiary accepted benefits under his mother's will which prohibited him from setting up any claim in respect of the administration of his father's estate.[10] Length of time in making a claim will not of itself be fatal, but will assist the trustee by requiring less evidence to establish a release.[11] Many of the points raised in connection with consent apply also here: "I . . . agree that either concurrence in the act, or acquiescence without original concurrence, will release the trustees; but that is only a general rule, and the Court must inquire into the circumstances which induced concurrence or acquiescence."[12] There will

---

[7] [1964] Ch. 303.

[8] *ibid.* at 338.

[9] *Huguenin v. Baseley* (1807) 14 Ves.Jr. 273; *Allcard v. Skinner* (1887) 36 Ch.D. 145 at 171.

[10] *Egg v. Devey* (1847) 10 Beav. 444.

[11] *Stackhouse v. Barnston* (1805) 10 Ves.Jr. 453; *Life Association of Scotland v. Siddall* (1861) 3 De G.F. & J. 58 at 77.

[12] *Walker v. Symonds* (1818) 3 Swans. 1 at 64, *per* Lord Eldon; *Stackhouse v. Barnston, supra.*

be no release for the trustees where the beneficiary acquiesced without knowledge of the facts; but, as with consent, it is not necessary that the beneficiary should have been aware of his legal rights.[13]

C. Impounding the Beneficiary's Interest: Trustee Act 1925, s.62

i. Inherent Power. Independently of the Trustee Act 1925, s.62, the court has power to impound the interest of a beneficiary who has instigated or requested a breach of trust. The impounding of the beneficiary's interest means that it will be applied so far as it will go towards providing an indemnity to the trustee. The trustee must show that the beneficiary acted with knowledge of the facts, although he may not have known that these amounted to a breach of trust.[14] If the beneficiary instigated or requested the breach, it is not necessary to show that the beneficiary received a benefit[15]; but where a beneficiary merely concurred in or consented to a breach of trust, it seems necessary that a benefit be shown.[16] The trustee, as has been seen, is protected against an action from the consenting beneficiary in respect of the breach.

ii. Trustee Act 1925, s.62. Section 62 extends this jurisdiction,[17] permitting the court to make an impounding order regardless of any question of benefit. As will be seen, consent, if it is to be effective, must be in writing.[18] Section 62(1) reads as follows:

> "Where a trustee commits a breach of trust at the instigation or request or with the consent in writing of a beneficiary, the court may, if it thinks fit, . . . make such order as to the court seems just, for impounding all or any part of the interest of the beneficiary in the trust estate by way of indemnity to the trustee or persons claiming through him."

The effect of an impounding order is not only that the beneficiary is unable to sue the trustee, but also that the liability to make up losses suffered by other beneficiaries will fall on him, rather than on the trustee. The liability cannot, however, be for a greater sum than

---

[13] *Holder v. Holder* [1968] Ch. 353.

[14] See *Hillsdown Holdins plc v. Pensions Ombudsman* [1997] 1 All E.R. 862.

[15] *Fuller v. Knight* (1843) 6 Beav. 205; *Chillingworth v. Chambers* [1896] 1 Ch. 685 (a trustee beneficiary).

[16] *Chillingworth v. Chambers, supra.* It has, however, been said that, even in the case of a beneficiary who requests a breach, the indemnity is limited to the benefit received by the beneficiary: *Raby v. Ridehalgh* (1855) 7 De G.M. & G. 104.

[17] See Romer J. in *Bolton v. Curre* [1895] 1 Ch. 544 at 549.

[18] The requirement of writing applies only to consent; *per* Lindley M.R. in *Re Somerset* [1894] 1 Ch. 231 at 265–266.

the subsisting value of his own interest in the trust, and it is subject to the discretion of the court. The discretion is exercised in the light of the earlier cases on which section 62 is founded,[19] and generally speaking an indemnity will be given to a trustee against a beneficiary who has been at all active in inducing a breach. Again, however, the knowledge of the beneficiary must amount to a definite appreciation of what is being done. In *Re Somerset*,[20] an impounding order was refused to trustees who had invested trust funds on a mortgage of a particular property at the instigation of a beneficiary, since the beneficiary had no intention of being a party to a breach, which occurred only because the loan exceeded the authorised limit. He had left it entirely to the trustees to determine how much money to lend on the security.

The principle applies to a beneficiary who, only subsequently to the breach, became entitled to a beneficial interest.[21] The right to indemnity by impounding is available to former trustees after their resignation or replacement. The trustees in *Re Pauling's Settlement Trusts (No. 2)*[22] claimed an indemnity out of the life interest of the parents of the claimants, and Wilberforce J. held that they were entitled to it, and would remain so entitled, although, as was intended, they would at a future time be replaced by new trustees.

D. Statutory Relief: Trustee Act 1925, s.61[23]

Under this section the court may excuse trustees from the consequences of a breach of trust. It reads:

> "If it appears to the court that a trustee, . . . is or may be personally liable for any breach of trust . . . but has acted honestly and reasonably, and ought fairly to be excused for the breach of trust and for omitting to obtain the directions of the court in the matter in which he committed such breach, then the court may relieve him either wholly or partly[24] from personal liability for the same."

The courts have preferred not to lay down formal rules for the application of the section. "It would be impossible," said Byrne J., "to lay down any general rules or principles to be acted on in carrying out the provisions of the section, and I think that each case

---

[19] See Romer J. in *Bolton v. Curre* [1895] 1 Ch. 544 at 549.
[20] [1894] 1 Ch. 231; *Mara v. Browne* [1895] 2 Ch. 69; *cf. Raby v. Ridehalgh, supra.*
[21] *Evans v. Benyon* (1888) 37 Ch.D. 329.
[22] [1963] Ch. 576; *Re Bucks Constabulary Widow's and Orphans' Fund Friendly Society (No. 2)* [1979] 1 W.L.R. 936 at 955.
[23] (1955) 19 Conv.(N.S.) 420 (L. Sheridan); [1977] *Estates and Trusts Quarterly* 12 (D. Waters). The section also applies to executors; T.A. 1925, s.68(17).
[24] See *Re Evans* [1999] 2 All E.R. 777; *post*, p. 669.

must depend upon its own circumstances."[25] The only way to show how the discretion has been exercised is to catalogue the cases; but there is inadequate space here. A few general rules, however, can be extracted.

The jurisdiction is available where a trustee "is or may be personally liable" for a breach of trust. There is thus no need to establish the liability; indeed it would put a trustee in a strange position if he had to prove his own liability in order to obtain relief. Several cases allowing relief have done so without reaching a conclusion on the question of liability.[26] However, " 'may be' has . . . been interpreted as indicating doubt, not futurity";[27] the court will not commit itself in advance to giving relief in the case of a future breach of trust.[28]

In exercising the discretion three factors must be considered[29] the trustee's honesty, reasonableness, and the question whether he ought "fairly" to be excused. There is little authority on honesty; dishonest trustees do not apply. But Kekewich J. once characterised as dishonest "a trustee who does nothing, swallows wholesale what is said by his co-trustee, never asks for explanation, and accepts flimsy explanations."[30]

There is some uncertainty as to the standard to be applied in determining reasonableness, but the usual standard is that of a prudent man of business managing his own affairs.[31] (Compliance with this standard may mean that there is no breach, but it is otherwise where, for example, payment has been made to the wrong person).[32] The amount of money involved will be a relevant factor.[33] In *Re Stuart*[34] it was said that, in connection with lending trust money on mortgage, the statutory procedure for valuations and reports[35] "constitute a standard by which reasonable conduct will be judged"; but failure to follow this is "not necessarily a fatal objection to the application of the section."

---

[25] *Re Turner* [1897] 1 Ch. 536 at 542; *Re Kay* [1897] 2 Ch. 518 at 524 (referring to the predecessor section).

[26] *e.g. Re Grindey* [1898] 2 Ch. 593.

[27] (1955) 19 Conv. (N.S.) 425.

[28] *Re Tollemache* [1903] 1 Ch. 457 at 465–466; affirmed at 953; *Re Rosenthal* [1972] 1 W.L.R. 1273. The court may, however, authorise an act so as to prevent it being a breach.

[29] *Marsden v. Regan* [1954] 1 W.L.R. 423 at 434.

[30] *Re Second East Dulwich, etc., Building Society* (1899) 79 L.T. 726 at 727.

[31] See Chitty L.J. in *Re Grindey, supra,* at 601; *Re Turner* [1897] 1 Ch. 536 at 542; *Re Lord de Clifford's Estate* [1900] 2 Ch. 707 at 716; *Re Stuart* [1897] 2 Ch. 583 at 590; *Re Rosenthal, supra.* The trustees in *Bartlett v. Barclays Bank Trust Co. Ltd (No. 1)* [1980] Ch. 515, *ante,* p. 659, were unable to rely on the section because they had not acted reasonably.

[32] See *Eaves v. Hickson* (1861) Beav. 136.

[33] *Re Grindey* [1898] 2 Ch. 593; *Marsden v. Regan, supra*

[34] [1897] 2 Ch. 583.

[35] *Re Stuart, supra,* at 591–592; *Shaw v. Cates* [1909] 1 Ch. 389; *Palmer v. Emerson* [1911] 1 Ch. 758.

The distinction between conduct that is reasonable and that for which a trustee ought fairly to be excused is a fine one. In *Davis v. Hutchings*[36] trustees, on the distribution of the trust fund, paid the share of one beneficiary to the solicitor to the trust (employed by them) in reliance upon the solicitor's statement that he was the assignee of the share. The share had in fact been mortgaged and assigned to him subject to the mortgage. Kekewich J. held that the trustees were liable to the mortgagee. They had acted honestly and reasonably in relying on the solicitor, but they should not be excused.[37] Fairness should be considered in relation to all the parties, the trustees, the beneficiaries and the creditors, and is "essentially a matter within the discretion of the judge."[38] In *Re Evans*[39] the administratrix took out insurance to cover the share of a missing beneficiary and then distributed the estate. The beneficiary appeared and claimed his share, but the insurance covered only the capital sum to which he was entitled. The administratrix relied on section 61 as a defence to his claim for interest. It was held that she had acted reasonably, but ought fairly to be excused only to the extent that the claim could not be satisfied by assets retained by her which derived from the estate.

Little seems to be added to this section by the reference to omission to obtain the directions of the court: "I do not see how the trustee can be excused for the breach of trust without being also excused for the omission referred to, or how he can be excused for the omission without also being excused for the breach of trust."[40]

The onus of showing that he acted honestly and reasonably is on the trustee.[41] Applications for relief have most commonly arisen in connection with unauthorised investments.[42] A trustee will not usually be excused if he has:

"relied on a co-trustee, or on the testator's solicitor, or on some other adviser of the testator's, or on the testator's own course of conduct. . . . The honest taking of what is conceived to be reliable advice will be no ground for excuse if the court believe a prudent man of business would have acted differently in ordering his own affairs."[43]

---

[36] [1907] 1 Ch. 356.
[37] Some of the dicta of Kekewich J. were disapproved in *Re Allsop* [1914] 1 Ch. 1 at 11, 12; see also *Marsden v. Regan* [1954] 1 W.L.R. 423, at 434–435.
[38] *Marsden v. Regan, supra*, at 435.
[39] [1999] 2 All E.R. 777.
[40] *Perrins v. Bellamy* [1898] 2 Ch. 521 at 528.
[41] *Re Stuart* [1897] 2 Ch. 583.
[42] *Re Turner, supra; Re Stuart, supra; Re Dive* [1909] 1 Ch. 328; *Bartlett v. Barclays Bank Trust Co. Ltd (No. 1)* [1980] Ch. 515.
[43] (1955) 29 Conv. (N.S.) 420 at 427.

Another and common situation is that of payment of the funds to the wrong beneficiary,[44] or the payment of void claims by creditors.[45] The taking of legal advice is a relevant factor, but does not automatically entitle a trustee to relief.[46]

The section extends to professional trustees who are being paid for their services, but the court is less ready to grant relief in such cases.[47]

E. Limitation and Laches[48]

i. Six-Year Period under Limitation Act 1980, s.21(3).[49] Subject to exceptions discussed below, the Limitation Act 1980, s.21(3), provides a six-year limitation for the protection of trustees. The subsection reads:

"Subject to the preceding provisions of this section, an action by a beneficiary[50] to recover trust property or in respect of any breach of trust,[51] not being an action for which a period of limitation is prescribed by any other provision of this Act, shall not be brought after the expiration of six years from the date on which the right of action accrued.

For the purposes of this subsection, the right of action shall not be treated as having accrued to any beneficiary entitled to a future interest in the trust property, until the interest fell into possession."

---

[44] *Re Allsop* [1914] 1 Ch. 1; *Re Pawson's Settlement* [1917] 1 Ch. 541; *National Trustees Co. of Australasia v. General Finance Co. of Australasia* [1905] A.C. 373; *Re Wightwick's W.T.* [1950] Ch. 260.

[45] *Re Lord de Clifford's Estate* [1900] 2 Ch. 707; *Re Mackay* [1911] 1 Ch. 300; *cf. Re Windsor Steam Coal Co. Ltd* [1929] 1 Ch. 151.

[46] *National Trustees Co. of Australasia v. General Finance Co. of Australasia* [1905] A.C. 373; *Marsden v. Regan* [1954] 1 W.L.R. 423 at 434–435; *Re Evans* [1999] 2 All E.R. 777.

[47] *National Trustees Co. of Australasia v. General Finance Co. of Australasia* [1905] A.C. 373; *Re Windsor Steam Coal Co.* [1929] 1 Ch. 151; *Re Waterman's W.T.* [1952] 2 All E.R. 1054; *Re Pauling's S.T.* [1964] Ch. 303 at 356–359.

[48] See Preston and Newsom's *Limitation of Actions* (4th ed.), Chap. 7; Franks, *Limitation of Actions*, pp. 62–80; (1989) 48 C.L.J. 472 (H. McLean).

[49] See Law Com. C.P. 151 (1998), *Limitation of Actions*, para. 13.102, suggesting a three-year period from the date the breach was discoverable, applicable to all breaches of trust, with a long-stop of 10 years from the breach.

[50] The section does not apply to a claim by the Attorney General against the trustee of a charitable trust, which has no 'beneficiary"; *Att.-Gen. v. Cocke* [1988] Ch. 414; [1988] Conv. 292 (J. Warburton).

[51] In *Tito v. Waddell (No. 2)* [1977] Ch. 106 at 249, Megarry V.-C. concluded that this provision did not apply to situations governed by the self-dealing and fair dealing rules applicable to trustees. Those cases are covered by the doctrine of laches.

In this subsection, "trustee" includes personal representatives[52] and also certain fiduciary agents,[53] company directors[54] and a mortgagee in respect of the proceeds of sale,[55] but not a trustee in bankruptcy,[56] nor the liquidator of a company in voluntary liquidation.[57] It will also be noted that there is no distinction between the protection given to an express trustee and that given to an implied or constructive trustee; until Trustee Act 1888, s.8, no protection based upon passage of time had been available to an express trustee.[58] It will be seen that the subsection only applies to cases where an action is brought by a beneficiary in respect of the trust property.[59] Under the proviso, time only begins to run against remaindermen or reversioners when their interest falls into possession; and it has been held that this does not occur when improper advancements are made in favour of remaindermen.[60] If a beneficiary is entitled to two interests in the property, one in possession and one in remainder, he does not lose a claim in respect of the latter where time has run against him in respect of the former.[61]

ii. Exceptions to the Six-Year Rule. There are some exceptions to the six-year rule.

(a) *Limitation Act 1980, s.21(1).*[62]

"(1) No period of limitation prescribed by this Act shall apply to an action by a beneficiary under a trust, being an action—
(*a*) in respect of any fraud or fraudulent breach of trust to which the trustee was a party or privy; or
(*b*) to recover from the trustee trust property or the proceeds of trust property in the possession of the trustee, or previously received by the trustee and converted to his use."[63]

This subsection reproduces in the situations to which it applies the rule of permanent liability which was applicable in equity to the case of express trustees.

---

[52] Limitation Act 1980, s.38(1); T.A. 1925, s.68(17).
[53] *Burdick v. Garrick* (1870) L.R. 5 Ch.App. 233.
[54] *Belmont Finance Corporation v. Williams Furniture Ltd (No. 2)* [1980] 1 All E.R. 393.
[55] *Thorne v. Heard* [1895] A.C. 495.
[56] *Re Cornish* [1896] 1 Q.B. 99.
[57] *Re Windsor Steam Coal Co.* [1928] Ch. 609; affirmed on other grounds [1929] 1 Ch. 151.
[58] Franks, *loc. cit.* p. 64.
[59] *Re Bowden* (1890) 45 Ch.D 444 at 451.
[60] *Re Pauling's S.T.* [1964] Ch. 303.
[61] *Mara v. Browne* [1895] 2 Ch. 69, reversed on another point [1896] 1 Ch. 199.
[62] See (1989) 48 C.L.J. 472 at 495 (H. McLean).
[63] But where a trustee is also a beneficiary and has received his share on a distribution of the trust property, paragraph (b) shall only apply in respect of the excess over his share, so long as the trustee acted honestly and reasonably in making the distribution; s.21(2).

In *North American Land Co. v. Watkins*,[64] an agent had been sent to America to buy land for his company. He bought it, and it was duly conveyed to the company, but the agent made and retained a profit for himself. After the expiration of the period applicable for the recovery of money had and received, the company successfully recovered the money on two grounds, first that the agent was in the position of a trustee and had retained trust money, and secondly that this conduct had been fraudulent.

It seems that the fraud must be that of the trustee himself.

In *Thorne v. Heard*[65] a trustee was protected where he had negligently left funds in the hands of a solicitor who had embezzled them; for the trustee to come within section 21(1) he must be "party or privy" to the fraud.

Dishonesty is not relevant where a trustee is in posseession of the trust property.

In *James v. Williams*[66] X, who was entitled to a one third share of a house on the intestacy of Y, treated the house as his own and purported to leave it by will to Z. It was held that X had been in the position of a constructive trustee, so that an action brought against Z by one of the other intestacy beneficiaries more than 12 years after the death of Y was not barred.

In *Re Howlett*[67] a trustee, who was income beneficiary until remarriage, continued in possession of a wharf until he died, and the remainderman was held able to sue the life tenant's representatives after his death for an occupation rent for the premises.

Conversion to the trustee's own use requires some wrongful application in his own favour. A trustee was held to escape from the subsection where he applied the trust funds for the maintenance of a child beneficiary,[68] or where the funds were dissipated by a co-trustee.[69]

It must be emphasised that section 21(1) cannot be relied upon where there is no trustee/beneficiary relationship beween the parties. Thus a personal action against a third party who has dishonestly assisted in a breach of trust does not fall within section 21(1)(a).

---

[64] [1904] 1 Ch. 242; [1904] 2 Ch. 233.
[65] [1894] 1 Ch. 599; [1895] A.C. 495; *Re Fountaine* [1909] 2 Ch. 382.
[66] [2000] Ch. 1.
[67] [1949] Ch. 767. See also *Re Sharp* [1906] 1 Ch. 793.
[68] *Re Page* [1893] 1 Ch. 304; *Re Timmis* [1902] 1 Ch. 176.
[69] *Re Fountaine* [1909] 2 Ch. 382.

Although such a third party is often (misleadingly) called a con-structive trustee,[70] he is not a true trustee and has no trust property. Thus the action must be brought within the six-year period applic-able to an action for damages for fraud.[71]

(b) *Claim to the Personal Estate of a Deceased Person.* Under section 22, which is subject to section 21(1), an action in respect of any claim to the personal estate of a deceased person must be brought within the period of 12 years.[72] Difficult questions on the inter-relation of this section and section 21(3) can arise where the personal representatives administering an estate would normally be treated as having become trustees. In that case the question is whether the 12-year or six-year rule is applicable.[73] The better view, it is submitted, is that the 12-year rule applies even though the personal representatives would for other purposes be treated as hav-ing become trustees.[74]

(c) *Sections 28 and 32.* Section 28 allows an extension of the period of limitation in cases in which the claimant has been under disability. Section 32 provides that where any action is based upon fraud or where the right of action is concealed by fraud or where the action is for relief from the consequences of a mistake, "the period of limitation shall not begin to run until the [claimant] has dis-covered the fraud, concealment or mistake . . . or could with reason-able diligence have discovered it."[75] This section applies to actions against trustees.[76]

iii. Assignees. A transferee from the trustee is in the same posi-tion as the trustee was[77] unless he is bona fide purchaser for value without notice in which case he will presumably be treated as if he had purchased from someone who was not a trustee.

iv. Where No Period is Applicable. It has been seen that the Limitation Act 1980 deals comprehensively with the running of

---

[70] *ante,* p. 306.

[71] *Paragon Finance plc v. D.B. Thakerar & Co. (a firm)* [1999] 1 All E.R. 401.

[72] See Law Com. C.P. 151 (1998), *Limitation of Actions,* para. 13.105, suggesting that the 12-year period is too long.

[73] *Re Timmis* [1902] 2 Ch. 176; *Re Richardson* [1920] 1 Ch. 423; *Re Oliver* [1927] 2 Ch. 323; *Re Diplock* [1948] Ch. 465; [1951] A.C. 251.

[74] See Pettit, *Equity and The Law of Trusts,* p. 499; Franks, *Limitation of Actions,* pp. 49–50; Preston and Newsom, p. 51; *Re Diplock* [1948] Ch. 465, *sub nom. Minister of Health v. Simpson* [1951] A.C. 251.

[75] For limitation problems where the mistake was of law, see *Kleinwort Benson Ltd v. Lincoln City Council* [1999] 2 A.C. 349.

[76] See *Kitchen v. R.A.F. Association,* [1958] 1 W.L.R. 563; *Bartlett v. Barclays Bank Trust Co. Ltd* [1980] Ch. 515 at 537.

[77] See *Baker v. Medway Building and Supplies Ltd* [1958] 1 W.L.R. 1216; *Eddis v. Chichester Constable* [1969] 2 Ch. 345.

time in actions against trustees. In situations not covered, it is necessary to return to the law as it existed before the statutory protection was given. No provision is made, for example, either for claims for equitable relief by way of specific performance, rescission or rectification, or injunction,[78] or in cases of redemption of a mortgage of pure personalty,[79] or the setting aside of a purchase of trust property by a trustee.[80] The rule of equity is that either no period is applicable, or that the relevant common law period is applied by analogy.[81] In any situation for which no period of limitation is expressly applicable to an equitable claim, the defendant may rely on the doctrine of laches.[82] Delay by a claimant in pursuing his rights "may furnish a defence in equity to an equitable claim."[83] Whether such a defence is available in a particular case is a matter for the discretion of the court, and will depend to a large extent upon the hardship caused to the defendant by the delay, and the effect upon third parties; and generally upon the balance of justice in granting or refusing relief.[84] There is no maximum period beyond which the equitable relief cannot be sought but a period of 20 years may be taken as a convenient guide.[85] The defendant will be more likely to succeed if he can show not merely delay, but acquiescence. Both defences appear to have been retained by the Limitation Act 1980 which provides in section 36(2): "Nothing in this Act shall affect any equitable jurisdiction to refuse relief on the ground of acquiescence or otherwise."

These defences are therefore relevant to cases to which no period is applicable, including those within section 21(1). Prior to the Limitation Act 1939 the doctrine of laches applied differently in regard to express and other trustees; but it seems that there should no longer be a distinction,[86] and that the position of express trustees alone need be considered. The rule "seems to be that while the doctrine of laches applies to claims by beneficiaries, relief will only be refused in plain cases."[87]

---

[78] See Limitation Act 1980, s.36(1); Law Com. C.P. 151 (1998), *Limitation of Actions*, para. 13.103. For criticisms of the present law, see *Cia de Seguros Imperio v. Heath (REBX) Ltd* [2001] 1 W.L.R. 112 at 124.

[79] *Weld v. Petre* [1929] 1 Ch. 33.

[80] *Baker v. Read* (1854) 18 Beav. 398; *Morse v. Royal* (1806) 12 Ves.Jr. 355; Snell, pp. 35–36.

[81] Limitation Act 1980, s.36(1). See *Knox v. Gye* (1872) 5 App. Cas. 656 at 674.

[82] *Re Pauling's S.T.* [1964] Ch. 303. See also *Alec Lobb (Garages) Ltd v. Total Oil G.B. Ltd* [1985] 1 W.L.R. 173.

[83] *Re Sharpe* [1892] 1 Ch. 154 at 168; Franks, *loc. cit.*, pp. 233 *et seq.*

[84] *Lindsay Petroleum Co. v. Hurd* (1874) L.R. 5 P.C. 221 at pp. 239–241; *Weld v. Petre* [1929] 1 Ch. 33 at 51, 52.

[85] *Weld v. Petre, supra*, at 54, 55; *Kershaw v. Whelan (No. 2), The Times*, February 10, 1997.

[86] Franks, *loc. cit.* p. 260; *cf. Re Jarvis* [1958] 1 W.L.R. 815.

[87] Franks, *loc. cit.* p. 261. As to whether laches applies to a claim to an express trust, see *Orr v. Ford* (1988–89) 167 C.L.R. 316.

A question which has recently arisen is whether any limitation period applies to an action for an account. Section 23 of the 1980 Act provides that "an action for an account shall not be brought after the expiration of any time limit under this Act which is applicable to the claim which is the basis of the duty to account." This confirms that the period applicable to a particular cause of action (*e.g.* copyright infringement) applies equally to the relief by way of account which flows from it. In *Coulthard v. Disco Mix Club Ltd*[88] an action for an account arising out of a contractual fiduciary relationship was brought more than six years after the alleged breaches. The claimant sought to overcome this by arguing that no period of limitation applied to a dishonest breach by a fiduciary of his duty to account. It was held that there was no distinction in the limitation period applicable to a common law fraud action for damages and an action in equity for dishonest breach of fiduciary duty, unless the defendant had misappropriated trust property, in which case no period applied.[89] The present case involved no trust property, as the defendant was not obliged to keep the money in question separate from his own. The duty to account was contractual, even if owed by a fiduciary. It would have been "a blot on our jurisprudence" if the same facts gave rise to a time bar at common law but not in equity. The alleged dishonest breaches of fiduciary duty were simply the equitable counterparts of the common law claims, and so the common law period applied by analogy.

5. PROPRIETARY REMEDIES

A. Personal and Proprietary Actions

Most actions at law and in equity are personal. We now have to consider the occasions on which a claimant has the right to proceed against a particular asset in the defendant's hands. Such proprietary claims exist to a very limited extent at law; and these, for convenience and for the sake of comparison, will be described here.[90] In equity the right to follow or trace property is more extensive. We will see that proprietary rights may be asserted where the claimant is making a claim at law or in equity to a specific piece of property, and also where he is making a claim in equity against a mixed fund to which property of his (in equity) has contributed. The tracing rules are also involved in personal actions based on receipt of property.[91] On a point of terminology, "tracing" is an identification

---

[88] [2000] 1 W.L.R. 707. See also *Paragon Finance plc v. D.B. Thakerar & Co. (a firm)* [1999] 1 All E.R. 400; *ante*, p. 23; *Raja v. Lloyds TSB Bank plc, The Times*, May 16, 2000; *Cia de Seguros Imperio v. Heath (REBX) Ltd* [2001] 1 W.L.R. 112.

[89] Limitation Act 1980, s.21(1); *ante*, p. 671.

[90] *post*, p. 677.

[91] *ante*, Chap. 12.

process involved where one asset has been substituted for another; "following" is the process of establishing that a particular asset has passed from one person to another; while "claiming" will ensue once either process has been completed.[92]

There are two main advantages of a proprietary over a personal claim. First and foremost, satisfaction of the claimant's demand does not depend on the solvency of the defendant. If the property traced is the claimant's in equity, it escapes the defendant's bankruptcy.[93] Secondly, in some cases, the claimant will be able to take advantage of increases in the value of the property. This is obvious where specific property is treated as being the claimant's in equity, and was more recently established where a mixed fund is in question.[94]

Although the English and American rules on these matters are not identical, anyone who is faced with a question on tracing should be acquainted with paragraphs 160–162 and 202–215 of the *Restatement of Restitution*, whose authors have foreseen and provided solutions for most if not all the problems which have arisen in the English cases.[95]

B. Unjust Enrichment; Restitution[96]

Proprietary remedies cannot be fully understood without some appreciation of the doctrine of unjust enrichment. This is a doctrine which appears in nearly every system of law. It lays down as a general principle that where the defendant is unjustly enriched at the claimant's expense, the defendant must make restitution.[97] Such a principle has its greatest scope in the area of quasi-contract, but it overlaps into many areas of equity. Even though there is no right to restitution in every case of unjust enrichment, all restitutionary claims are unified by the principle.[98]

Assume that A has a right to sue B on the ground that A has paid money to B by mistake, or under compulsion, or under a contract that was void, or in any other situation in which B is enriched at the expense of A. If B is solvent, a personal action will satisfy A's claim. What should be the effect on this situation if, (a) B is bankrupt, or (b) B invests the money and it doubles in value? In case (a)

---

[92] Smith, *The Law of Tracing*, p. 4; *Foskett v. McKeown* [2000] 2 W.L.R. 1299 at 1322.
[93] Insolvency Act 1986, s.283.
[94] *Re Tilley's W.T.* [1967] Ch. 1179; *Foskett v. McKeown, supra; post*, p. 688.
[95] Including that of the personal claim in *Re Diplock* [1948] Ch. 465; see *Restatement of Restitution*, para. 126, comment (c), and *Restatement of Trusts*, para. 199.
[96] Goff and Jones, *The Law of Restitution* (5th ed.); Birks, *An Introduction to the Law of Restitution; Restatement of Restitution*.
[97] *Restatement of Restitution*, para. 1.
[98] Goff and Jones (5th ed.), p. 15; *Woolwich Equitable Building Society v. I.R.C.* [1993] A.C. 70 at 196.

it is arguable that since B should never have had the money, nor should his creditors. In case (b) it can be argued that neither B nor his creditors should reap the full measure of the profit which B has made out of money which he should never have had. Should A have it? Would it make any difference if the invested funds were part A's and part B's? We might here pose a further case (c). If B uses the money to pay off a mortgage on his property and is insolvent, should A be placed in the position, by subrogation, of the mortgagee? These are all interesting and difficult questions, to most of which the English cases provide answers. But the principles which govern the availability of a proprietary remedy have not been fully worked out. Indeed, it has been said with some justification that the law in this area lacks all coherence.[99] What is clear is that the defendant's unjust enrichment is not of itself sufficient to give the claimant a proprietary remedy. Equally clearly, a claimant who can establish his proprietary rights by the tracing process may vindicate them without any need to rely on unjust enrichment.[1] The account which follows shows that different rules currently operate at law and in equity, although Lord Millett took the opportunity in *Foskett v. McKeown*[2] to say that there is no sense in this, although it was not the occasion to explore the matter further. A single set of rules suffices to identify the claimant's property, although the distinction between law and equity may be relevant to his claim. It seems likely, therefore, that a unified tracing process may eventually evolve.

C. Tracing at Common Law[3]

A proprietary remedy is one which entitles a claimant to treat specific property, or a portion thereof, as his own. If the common law had developed a real action for chattels which entitled a claimant to specific recovery, he would be able to demand the return of the chattel. But although the court recognised the claimant as being the owner, there was no such action at common law. The defendant had the choice of paying damages or returning the chattel. A discretion to award specific recovery in an action in detinue was given to the court in 1854.[4]

---

[99] (1997) 50 C.L.P. 95 at 114 (A. Burrows). See also Goff and Jones (5th ed.), pp. 84–91; (1999) 115 L.Q.R. 469 (S. Evans); *Law at the Centre* (B. Rider ed.), p. 185 (R. Goode).

[1] *Foskett v. McKeown* [2000] 2 W.L.R. 1299.

[2] *supra*, at 1324. See his Lordship's extra-judicial views in (1998) 114 L.Q.R. 399 at 409 and [1999] 14 *Amicus Curiae* 4. See also Smith, *The Law of Tracing*, pp. 278–279.

[3] (1966) 7 W.A.L.R. 463 (M. Scott); (1976) 40 Conv.(N.S.) 277 (R. Pearce); (1979) 95 L.Q.R. 78 (S. Khurshid and P. Matthews); (1976) 92 L.Q.R. 360 at 364 *et seq.* (R. Goode); *Laundering and Tracing* (Birks ed., 1995), p. 23 (P. Matthews). See Birks, *An Introduction to the Law of Restitution*, pp. 358 *et seq.*; Goff and Jones (5th ed.), pp. 93–103.

[4] Common Law Procedure Act 1854, s.78. Detinue has been abolished: Torts (Interference with Goods) Act 1977, s.2; but the discretionary power of the court to order specific recovery is retained by s.3.

The claimant's ownership was relevant however in that his entitlement was to the chattel or to its value—its full value that is, even if the defendant was insolvent, and not merely to a dividend in the insolvency. In the case of a loan, the claim for the money lent to an insolvent defendant would abate; it was something owed. The position is different with the chattel; that was something owned.

The question then arises whether this right is limited to the case of a specific chattel. Should this right not continue if the defendant had exchanged one chattel for another; or the chattel for a sum of money; or had spent that money on another chattel? The answer was given by Lord Ellenborough in *Taylor v. Plumer*[5]:

> "It makes no difference in reason or law into what other form, different from the original, the change may have been made, whether it be into that of promissory notes for the security of the money which was produced by the sale of the goods of the principal, as in *Scott v. Surman*,[6] or into other merchandise, as in *Whitecomb v. Jacob*,[7] for the product of or substitute for the original thing still follows the nature of the thing itself, as long as it can be ascertained to be such, and the right only ceases when the means of ascertainment fail, which is the case when the subject is turned into money, and mixed and confounded in a general mass of the same description. The difficulty which arises in such a case is a difficulty of fact and not of law, and the dictum that money has no ear-mark must be understood in the same way; *i.e.* as predicated only of an undivided and undistinguishable mass of current money. But money in a bag or otherwise kept apart from other money, guineas, or other coin marked (if the fact were so) for the purpose of being distinguished, are so far ear-marked as to fall within the rule on this subject, which applies to every other description of personal property whilst it remains (as the property in question did) in the hands of the factor [the bankrupt] or his general legal representatives."

In *Taylor v. Plumer*,[8] the defendant handed money to a stockbroker, Walsh, to purchase bonds. Walsh instead purchased American investments and bullion and hurried off to Falmouth to sail to America. He was apprehended, and the investments and bullion were seized by the defendant. On Walsh's bankruptcy, his assignees in bankruptcy sought to recover them from the defendant. They failed. The investments were the ascertainable product of the defendant's money and owned by him. If the parties had been reversed, and the

---

[5] (1815) 3 M. & S. 562 at 575.
[6] (1742) Willes 400.
[7] (1710) Salk. 160.
[8] (1815) 3 M. & S. 562; *Re J. Leslie Engineers Co. Ltd* [1976] 1 W.L.R. 292 at 297.

defendant had been suing for the recovery of the securities and bullion, his action would have succeeded, but the assignees would have had the choice of returning them or of paying their full value in damages; just as if Walsh had taken the defendant's coach and horses and had them in his possession on his bankruptcy.

It is important to appreciate that the common law action of conversion and the action for money had and received are personal actions as was detinue, though, as has been seen,[9] the court may exercise a discretionary power to order the specific recovery of a chattel. Personal actions as a general rule abate in a bankruptcy, which is the normal situation in which tracing is attempted. In the conversion cases, however, full damages without abatement may be obtained against the trustee in bankruptcy if the chattel is not returned.[10] The claimant's proprietary rights are thus preserved to this extent.[11] A claimant who can establish by tracing that the defendant has received his money will be able to bring a personal action for money had and received, but, if he cannot identify his money or its product in the defendant's hands after receipt, he will not recover in full if the defendant is bankrupt. If he can still identify his money or its product, then he may assert a proprietary claim at common law against the defendant's trustee in bankruptcy on the basis of legal ownership.[12]

The crucial question at common law was whether there was identifiable property, the title to which did not pass to the defendant.[13] In *Banque Belge pour L'Etranger v. Hambrouck*[14] money passing through substantially unmixed bank accounts was treated by the majority of the Court of Appeal as still identifiable. In *Lipkin Gorman v. Karpnale Ltd*[15] the House of Lords considered that the claimant firm could have traced at common law where money was drawn out of its client account by a partner, Cass, and paid to the Playboy Club. Although the claimant had no proprietary interest in the money in the account, the bank's debt was a chose in action which

---

[9] *ante*, p. 677.

[10] (1979) 95 L.Q.R. 78 (S. Khurshid and P. Matthews); (1966) 7 W.A.L.R. 463 (M. Scott). See *Giles v. Perkins* (1807) 9 East. 12; *Scott v. Surman* (1742) Willes 400.

[11] (1976) 40 Conv.(N.S) 277 (R. Pearce); Goff and Jones (5th ed.), p. 97, n. 54.

[12] *Jones (F.C.) & Sons (Trustee) v. Jones* [1997] Ch. 159; *infra*.

[13] See (1966) 7 W.A.L.R. 463 at 481 *et seq.*

[14] [1921] 1 K.B. 321.

[15] [1991] 2 A.C. 548 (a personal action); (1991) 107 L.Q.R. 521 (P. Watts); [1992] Conv. 124 (M. Halliwell); (1992) 5 M.L.R. 377 (E. McKendrick); All E.R.Rev 1992, p. 262 (W. Swadling). It was conceded (p. 572) that the claimant's legal title to the money was not defeated by any mixing by Cass with his own money before payment to the club (*cf. Bank of America v. Arnell* [1999] Lloyd's Rep. Bank. 399). Presumably mixing by the club would defeat a common law tracing claim. The claimant could have traced in equity, as Cass held the withdrawn money on trust for the firm.

was the legal property of the claimant. This could be traced into its product, the money withdrawn (apparently even though Cass had legal title to that), and followed into the hands of the volunteer recipient. In *Jones (F.C.) & Sons (Trustee) v. Jones*[16] a partner withdrew £11,700 from a partnership account by cheques in favour of his wife after an act of bankruptcy on the part of the firm and the wife opened an account with a broker, into which the money was paid. The money was profitably invested and the wife received cheques from the broker for £50,760 which she paid into another account she had opened with R. Bank. The wife conceded that the trustee in bankruptcy was entitled to £11,700 but claimed to keep the profit. Her claim was rejected by the Court of Appeal. She had taken possession of money (£11,700) the legal title to which was vested in the trustee in bankruptcy under the insolvency legislation. He was entitled at common law not only to trace his property into its exchange product but also to trace any profit made from it.

It had been persuasively argued that *Taylor v. Plumer*[17] was in fact a decision on tracing in equity and thus not authority for the proposition that tracing into an "exchange product" is possible at common law.[18] It is clear, however, that *Taylor v. Plumer* has been accepted in the subsequent caselaw as authority for that proposition.[19] In the *Jones* case Millett L.J. acknowledged that *Taylor v. Plumer* was concerned with the rules of equity but held that this did not mean that the common law did not recognise claims to substitute assets or their products. Thus the trustee in bankruptcy could follow the chose in action constituted by the partnership account into the cheques drawn on it, and could follow those cheques into the account with the broker, the cheques from the broker, and ultimately the chose in action constituted by the account with R. Bank. He was entitled at law to the balance in that account, whether greater or less than the original amount withdrawn from the partnership account.

What the common law could not do was to provide full protection to the claimant in the most important type of case in which these questions arise: where the defendant has received the claimant's money, mixed it with other money in a bank account, and has gone

---

[16] [1997] Ch. 159; All E.R. Rev. 1996, p. 366 (P. Birks and W. Swadling); (1997) 113 L.Q.R. 21 (N. Andrews and J. Beatson); (1997) 11 *Trust Law International* 2 (P. Birks); (1997) 56 C.L.J. 30 (D. Fox); [1997] 5 R.L.R. 92 (R. Davern); (1997–98) 8 K.C.L.J. 123 (C. Mitchell); [1999] 7 R.L.R. 55 (D. Fox); Smith, *The Law of Tracing*, pp. 320–340.

[17] (1815) 3 M. & S. 562; *supra*.

[18] (1979) 95 L.Q.R. 78 (S. Kurshid and P. Matthews); [1995] L.M.C.L.Q. 240 (L. Smith); *Laundering and Tracing* (Birks ed., 1995), pp. 49–51 (P. Matthews) and 297–298 (P. Birks).

[19] *Banque Belge pour L'Etranger v. Hambrouck, supra; Lipkin Gorman v. Karpnale Ltd, supra; Agip (Africa) Ltd v. Jackson* [1991] Ch. 547, *infra*.

bankrupt.[20] In *Agip (Africa) Ltd v. Jackson* the claimant sought to trace money transferred to the defendants as a result of the fraud of the claimant's accountant, who had changed the names on payment orders. The money had been paid out (to B Co. and thence to the defendants) by a London bank on the telexed instructions of a Tunis bank (where the claimant maintained an account), which then instructed a New York bank to reimburse the London bank. The defendants had paid most of the money away, but part of it remained and was paid into court. Millett J.[21] rejected the common law tracing claim on the ground that no physical asset of the claimant (such as a cheque or its proceeds) could be identified in the defendant's hands. Nothing but a stream of electrons passed between the banks as a result of the telegraphic transfers. The London bank paid with its own money, subject to reimbursement, and not with anything identifiable as the product of the claimant's property. It was not possible to show the source from which the London bank was reimbursed without tracing the money through the New York clearing system. There it was mixed, which defeated the common law claim. The decision was upheld on appeal on the basis that mixing defeated the claim, although Fox L.J. (giving the only reasoned judgment) thought it did not matter that no cheque was involved.[22] Lord Millett has restated the view that the common law cannot trace money transferred electronically both judicially and extra-judicially,[23] and it has found support elsewhere.[24] It may be, however, that such money remains traceable at common law if it has not been mixed by passing through an inter-bank clearing system.[25]

---

[20] (1992) 45 C.L.P. 69 (P. Birks). For the view that mixing does not prevent common law tracing, see Smith, *The Law of Tracing*, pp. 162 *et seq.* For the position at common law in respect of mixed or improved goods, see (1981) 34 C.L.P. 159 (P. Matthews).

[21] [1990] Ch. 265 at 286; (1989) 105 L.Q.R. 528 (P. Birks); (1991) 107 L.Q.R. 71 (Sir Peter Millett). See also *Bank of America v. Arnell* [1999] Lloyd's Rep. Bank. 399; (2000) 59 C.L.J. 28 (D. Fox).

[22] [1991] Ch. 547 at 565; (1991) 50 C.L.J. 409 (C. Harpum); [1992] Conv. 367 (S. Goulding); All E.R. Rev. 1992, 259 (W. Swadling). Tracing in equity was allowed; *post*, p. 683. In *Jones (F.C.) & Sons (Trustee) v. Jones, supra,* it was not necessary to trace the passage of the money through a clearing system.

[23] *El Ajou v. Dollar Land Holdings plc* [1993] 3 All E.R. 717 at 733 (not discussed on appeal at [1994] 2 All E.R. 685); (1991) 107 L.Q.R. 71 at 74; (1995) 9 *Trust Law International* 35 at 39; [1999] 14 *Amicus Curiae* 4.

[24] *Nimmo v. Westpac Banking Corporation* [1993] 3 N.Z.L.R. 218; *Bank Tejarat v. Hong Kong and Shanghai Banking Corporation (CI) Ltd* [1995] 1 Lloyd's Rep. 239; criticised (1995) 9 *Trust Law International* 91 (P. Birks). Where a payment is made between two bank accounts telegraphically, electronically or by cheque, one chose in action is reduced or extinguished and another created, thus no property of the payer is obtained by the payee within the Theft Act 1968; *R. v. Preddy* [1996] A.C. 815 (see now Theft (Amendment) Act 1996).

[25] (1995) 54 C.L.J. 377 (A. Oakley). See also Smith, *The Law of Tracing*, pp. 253–258; *Restitution and Banking Law* (F. Rose ed.), Chap. 8 (L. Smith); (1997–98) 8 K.C.L.J. 123 (C. Mitchell).

As we will see, mixing does not prevent tracing in equity, although other limitations upon the availability of the equitable remedy leave scope for tracing at common law. In practical terms, however, most of the situations in which a claim to trace arises are cases of money in mixed bank accounts, in which the common law remedy is not available. It has therefore limited practical importance at the present day.

D. Tracing in Equity

Equity has developed more sophisticated methods of tracing. The rules have developed, and are usually applied, in the context of property in the hands of trustees or other fiduciaries, and often on the bankruptcy of the fiduciary. But the rules apply also in a commercial context; as where a vendor, in order to protect himself in a customer's bankruptcy, provides expressly that property shall not pass in goods supplied until payment. Equity will assist in the location and preservation of traceable property by disclosure and injunctions.[26]

i. Who is Entitled to Trace. The remedy in equity is not confined to claims between trustee and beneficiary. *Re Hallett*[27] decided that the remedy was not restricted to such a case but was available against other fiduciaries.[28]

(a) *Requirement of Fiduciary Relationship.* The courts have insisted that the existence of a fiduciary relationship is a prerequisite to tracing in equity, although this relationship need not exist between the parties to the action. In *Re Diplock*[29] the action was not against the executors, but against the innocent volunteers (the charities) to whom they handed the money.

> By his will Diplock gave the residue of his property on trust for such "charitable or benevolent . . . objects in England as my . . . executors . . . may in their . . . absolute discretion select." He and the executors thought that this was a valid charitable gift, but it was not.[30] The executors distributed £203,000 among a considerable number of charitable institutions; and when the validity of

---

[26] *Bankers Trust Co. v. Shapira* [1980] 1 W.L.R. 1274; *A. v. C.* [1981] Q.B. 956; *In re D.P.R. Futures Ltd* [1989] 1 W.L.R. 778. For cross-border tracing, see [1998] 6 R.L.R. 73 (G. Panagopoulos).

[27] (1880) 13 Ch.D. 696 at 709.

[28] See Goff and Jones (5th ed.), p. 105, n. 8, where they point out how difficult it is to define precisely who is a fiduciary. They refer to the analogy of decisions on the Statutes of Limitation, which suggest that "much depends on whether the agent is under a duty to keep separate his own money from his principal's money."

[29] [1948] Ch. 465.

[30] *ante*, p. 441, *Chichester Diocesan Fund v. Simpson* [1944] A.C. 341.

the charitable gift was discovered, the next-of-kin claimed to recover the money from the charities. They succeeded in a personal claim[31] and were also entitled to trace, the Court of Appeal laying down as the test that[32]: "equity may operate on the conscience not merely of those who acquire a legal title in breach of some trust, express or constructive, or of some other fiduciary obligation, but of volunteers provided that as a result of what has gone before some equitable proprietary interest has been created and attaches to the property in the hands of the volunteer."

Although a beneficiary is not normally regarded as the equitable owner of assets in an unadministered estate,[33] the "equitable proprietary interest" was established for present purposes by the equitable claim by the claimants as next-of-kin against the executors; and this gave the claimants the right to trace against the charities.

The requirement of a fiduciary relationship has been much criticised,[34] but has been accepted in modern decisions of the Court of Appeal[35] and (although somewhat ambiguously) by the House of Lords in *Westdeutsche Landesbank Girozentrale v. Islington London Borough Council*,[36] where the principles established in *Re Diplock* were approved.[37] In *Foskett v. McKeown*,[38] on the other hand, Lord Millett said that there was no logical justification for insisting on a fiduciary relationship as a precondition in equity, although such a relationship could be relevant to the claim. The issue, however, did not arise in that case. So long as the traditional approach prevails, the position may be relieved by the apparent ease with which a fiduciary relationship may be recognised, as in most cases of commercial fraud.[39]

(b) *Requirement of an Equitable Proprietary Interest.* In the days before the fusion of the jurisdiction of law and equity, it was only possible to obtain equitable remedies if the litigation were "in equity." It is not therefore surprising that the test which has been laid

---

[31] [1951] A.C. 251. The appeal to the House of Lords concerned only the personal action; post, p. 708.

[32] [1948] Ch. 465 at 530.

[33] *Commissioner of Stamp Duties v. Livingston* [1965] A.C. 694; *ante*, p. 60.

[34] (1995) 9 *Trust Law International* 124 at 126 (P. Birks); Goff and Jones, p. 104; *Bristol and West Building Society v. Mothew* [1998] Ch.1 at 23; Smith, *The Law of Tracing*, pp. 123–130, 340–347.

[35] *Aluminium Industrie Vaassen B.V. v. Romalpa Aluminium Ltd* [1976] 1 W.L.R. 676; *Agip (Africa) Ltd v. Jackson* [1991] Ch. 547; *Boscawen v. Bajwa* [1996] 1 W.L.R. 328 at 335; *Jones (F.C.) & Sons (Trustee) v. Jones* [1997] Ch. 159.

[36] [1996] A.C. 669. See (1996) 55 C.L.J. 432 (G. Jones), pointing out inconsistencies.

[37] *ibid.* at 714. But see All E.R. Rev. 1996, p. 373 (P. Birks and W. Swadling); [1997] Conv. 1 at 4 (A. Oakley).

[38] [2000] 2 W.L.R. 1299 at 1324. See also [1999] 14 *Amicus Curiae* 4 (Lord Millett).

[39] *Agip (Africa) Ltd v. Jackson, supra* (senior accountant and employer).

down historically for the availability of equitable tracing is that the claimant should be entitled to an *equitable* proprietary interest; and this requirement of an equitable proprietary interest is distinct from absolute ownership at law.

There seems to be no reason at all on the merits why the equitable tracing process should not be available also to the beneficial legal owner. All that should be required is a proprietary base. Indeed, it was arguable, before *Re Diplock*[40] was decided, that this situation had been recognised by *Banque Belge v. Hambrouck*.[41] Atkin L.J. treated equitable tracing as a means of overcoming the common law's difficulty in identifying the claimant's money in a mixed fund[42]:

> "The question always was, Had the means of ascertainment failed? But if in 1815 the common law halted outside the bankers' door, by 1879 equity had had the courage to lift the latch, walk in and examine the books: *Re Hallett's Estate*.[43] I see no reason why the means of ascertainment so provided should not now be available both for common law and equity proceedings."

It has been doubtful, since *Re Diplock*, whether equitable tracing will be available in the absence of some situation creating equitable as opposed to legal ownership.[44] In *Aluminium Industrie Vaassen B.V. v. Romalpa Aluminium Ltd*[45] however, the Court of Appeal permitted tracing by a legal owner to whom a fiduciary duty was owed, although this point was not discussed.

Consider this case; B owes £1,000 to his creditors and has only £100. He steals £1,000 from A and mixes that money in his account which now has £1,100. He now "owes" £2,000. Should the available money be shared rateably between A and the creditors, or should A get back first his £1,000, which B should never have had? Common law tracing is not available because the funds are mixed; nor equitable tracing if there is no fiduciary relation between a thief and

---

[40] [1948] Ch. 465; (1971) 34 M.L.R. 12 (F. Babafemi).

[41] [1921] 1 K.B. 321.

[42] *ibid.* at 335; criticised in *Agip (Africa) Ltd v. Jackson, supra,* for treating common law and equitable remedies as the same. See also *Chief Constable of Kent v. V.* [1983] Q.B. 34 at 41, *per* Lord Denning M.R.: "It may be that 150 year ago the common law halted outside the banker's door, but for the last 100 years, since the fusion of law and equity, it has had the courage to lift the latch, walk in and examine the books: see *Banque Belge pour l'Etranger v. Hambrouck* [1912] 1 K.B. 321 at p. 335, *per* Atkin L.J. and *Re Diplock's Estate, Diplock v. Wintle* [1948] Ch. 465, *per* Lord Greene M.R."

[43] (1880) 13 Ch.D. 696.

[44] For arguments to the effect that legal, as opposed to equitable, ownership is a sufficient basis for a right to trace, see (1975) 28 C.L.P. 64 (A. Oakley); (1976) 40 Conv.(N.S.) 227 (R. Pearce); Goff and Jones (5th ed.), p. 105.

[45] [1976] 1 W.L.R. 676, *post*, p. 704; *cf. Re Andrabell Ltd* [1984] 3 All E.R. 407. See Heydon, Gummow and Austin, *Cases and Materials on Equity and Trusts* (4th ed.), pp. 898, 906.

his victim. Fortunately Lord Templeman in *Lipkin Gorman v. Karpnale Ltd*[46] has approved Australian authority[47] to the effect that a thief holds stolen money on trust for his victim, who can accordingly trace it. Similarly, Lord Browne-Wilkinson has confirmed that the money is traceable on the ground that equity imposes a constructive trust on a fraudulent recipient.[48]

One question which came before the House of Lords in *Westdeutsche Landesbank Girozentrale v. Islington London Borough Council*[49] was whether the claimant bank retained an equitable proprietary interest in money paid to the defendant under a transaction (an "interest rate swap") which was *ultra vires* (so far as the defendant was concerned) and void. Tracing would in any event have been impossible because the money had been mixed with other money in an account and used for general expenditure, the account having been subsequently overdrawn several times.[50] The defendant now conceded personal liability to repay, the issue being whether compound interest could be awarded to the bank. Their Lordships unanimously agreed that the bank retained no equitable proprietary interest in the money, which, according to the majority, meant that there was no jurisdiction to award compound interest.[51] *Sinclair v. Brougham*,[52] where the House of Lords had permitted tracing by creditors (depositors) of a bank whose business was *ultra vires*, was overruled. Although in the present case the bank's belief in the validity of the transaction was mistaken, it intended the money to become the absolute property of the defendant and had been prepared to take the risk of insolvency. As a general rule, property in money passes even though a contract is void, although there may be limited exceptions in the case of "fundamental mistake" in the orthodox sense.[53] Thus there was considered to be no moral or legal reason why, had there been an insolvency, the claimant should have

[46] [1991] 2 A.C. 548.
[47] *Black v. S. Freedman & Co.* (1910) 12 C.L.R. 105. See also *Lennox Industries (Canada) Ltd v. The Queen* (1987) 34 D.L.R. 297; *Bishopsgate Investment Management Ltd v. Maxwell* [1993] Ch. 1 at 70; *Ghana Commercial Bank v. C, The Times*, March 3, 1997.
[48] *Westdeutsche Landesbank Girozentrale v. Islington London Borough Council* [1996] A.C. 669 at pp. 715–716; *cf. Jones (F.C.) & Sons (Trustee) v. Jones* [1997] Ch. 159 (No constructive trust nor fiduciary relationship where wife obtained possession of, but not title to, funds of bankrupt partnership. Thus only the common law tracing rules applied). See also Chambers, *Resulting Trusts*, p. 117, preferring a resulting trust analysis; Smith, *The Law of Tracing*, pp. 343–347.
[49] [1996] A.C. 669; (1996) 112 L.Q.R. 521 (M. Cope); [1996] R.L.R. 3 (P. Birks); (1996) 55 C.L.J. 432 (G. Jones); (1996) 10 *Trust Law International* 84 (C. Mitchell).
[50] See *post*, p. 691.
[51] *ante*, p. 658.
[52] [1914] A.C. 398. Lord Goff would have allowed it to stand in the confined area of *ultra vires* loans. The present case did not involve loans. See (1997) 50 C.L.P. 95 (A. Burrows).
[53] [1996] A.C. 669 at 690 (Lord Goff); [1996] 55 C.L.J. 547 and [1996] R.L.R. 60 (D. Fox).

had priority over general creditors. The defendant received the money neither as resulting trustee (because the property had passed, as intended) nor as constructive trustee (because it was unaware of the invalidity until after the money had been spent and its conscience was thus unaffected) but was merely subject to personal liability at common law to repay.

Grave doubt was cast on the correctness of *Chase Manhattan Bank NA v. Israel-British Bank (London) Ltd*,[54] where the claim to trace money paid by mistake of fact[55] to the defendant (now insolvent) was upheld on the basis that the claimant retained an equitable proprietary interest in the money. Lord Goff found it unnecessary to review that decision. Lord Browne-Wilkinson disagreed with the reasoning but considered that the result could be justified on the basis that the defendant bank became aware of the mistake within two days and retained the money in traceable form. Thus its conscience was sufficiently affected to found a constructive trust.[56] His Lordship could not have meant, however, that notice was sufficient to trigger a proprietary interest which the claimant could not otherwise have asserted.[57]

There has been some support for the view that in the case of a voidable transaction (for example, one induced by misrepresentation or undue influence) a claimant who elects to rescind can trace on the basis that the property, having initially passed to the defendant, revests in the claimant on rescission.[58] This argument may need reconsidering in the light of *Westdeutsche Landesbank Girozentrale v. Islington London Borough Council*.[59] If a claimant who has paid under a void transaction cannot trace, it is difficult to see why one whose transaction was merely voidable should be able to do so. Another view is that the proprietary remedy should be available in the case of a voidable transaction only where a money judgment would be inadequate, as in the case of land or unique chattels, by analogy with specific performance.[60] On the other hand, a payment

[54] [1981] Ch. 105; (1996) 16 L.S. 110 (W. Swadling); [1996] Conv. 86 (G. McCormack).

[55] The personal action (subject to solvency) would now lie in cases of payment by mistake of law; *Kleinwort Benson Ltd v. Lincoln City Council* [1999] 2 A.C. 349.

[56] [1996] A.C. 669 at 715. The correctness of *Chase Manhattan* had been left open by the Privy Council in *Re Goldcorp Exchange Ltd* [1995] 1 A.C. 74.

[57] See [1966] R.L.R. 3 at 21 (P. Birks); (1996) 55 C.L.J. 432 (G. Jones); All E.R. Rev. 1996 at 373 (P. Birks and W. Swadling); (1998) 12 *Trust Law International* 288 (W. Swadling); (1998) 114 L.Q.R. 399 (Sir Peter Millett); *Privacy and Loyalty* (P. Birks ed.), pp. 301–304 (D. Hayton).

[58] *Daly v. Sydney Stock Exchange* (1986) 160 C.L.R. 371; *Lonrho plc v. Fayed* (No. 2) [1992] 1 W.L.R. 1; *El Ajou v. Dollar Land Holdings plc* [1993] 3 All E.R. 717 (not discussed on appeal at [1994] 2 All E.R. 685); *Halifax Building Society v. Thomas* [1996] Ch. 217; *Twinsectra Ltd v. Yardley* [1999] Lloyd's Rep. Bank. 438 at 461–462; *Privacy and Loyalty* (P. Birks ed.), p. 304 (D. Hayton).

[59] *supra*. It was also doubted by the Privy Council in *re Goldcorp Exchange Ltd* [1995] 1 A.C. 74. See also (1997–98) 8 K.C.L.J. 147 at 152 (P. Oliver).

[60] [1999] 14 *Amicus Curiae* 4 (Lord Millett).

induced by forgery may be traced on the basis that equity imposes a constructive trust on a fraudulent recipient.[61] Further, it has been held by the Court of Appeal that the transferor of land retains the equitable interest where the transfer was procured by fraudulent misrepresentation, for no consideration and in breach of fiduciary duty.[61a]

As we have seen, the requirement of an equitable proprietary interest for tracing in equity is now satisfied in the case of bribes, on the basis that the defendant holds the bribe on constructive trust for his principal.[62] An equitable proprietary interest normally goes hand in hand with a fiduciary relationship, assuming the latter is still required. A fiduciary relationship alone, however, is not a sufficient basis for tracing. Thus, assuming it is correct to call a person who dishonestly assists in a breach of trust a constructive trustee, no proprietary rights may be asserted against him if he has received no trust property.[63]

ii. Unmixed Funds. The easy case is that in which there has been no mixing of the trust funds with the trustee's own money. If the trustee has sold the trust property, the beneficiary may take the proceeds if he can identify them. (If the purchaser had notice, the beneficiary may elect to take either the property or the proceeds.[64]) If the proceeds of sale have been used to purchaser other property the beneficiary may "follow" them and may "elect either to take the property purchased, or to hold it as a security for the amount of trust money laid out in the purchase; or, as we generally express it, he is entitled at his election either to take the property, or to have a charge on the property for the amount of the trust money."[65] The beneficiary is entitled to any profit even though the trustee could have made the purchase with his own money.[66] Claims in equity will never, of course, be valid against a bona fide purchaser for value.[67] If, however, the property has come into the hands of an innocent volunteer, the tracing remedy lies against him while he retains it.[68]

---

[61] *Bankers Trust Co. v. Shapira* [1980] 1 W.L.R. 1274, as explained by Lord Brown-Wilkinson in the *Westdeutsche* case, at 716.

[61a] *Collings v. Lee, The Times,* October 26, 2000. The decision may necessitate a review of the principle that the right to set aside a voidable transaction constitutes a "mere equity".

[62] *Att.-Gen. for Hong Kong v. Reid* [1994] 1 A.C. 324; *ante*, p. 625.

[63] *ante*, p. 306; (1995) 54 C.L.J. 377 at 383 (A. Oakley).

[64] See (1992) 45 C.L.P. 69 at 95 (P. Birks); Smith, *The Law of Tracing*, pp. 377–383; *Jones (F.C.) & Sons (Trustee) v. Jones* [1997] Ch. 159 (common law).

[65] *per* Jessel M.R. in *Re Hallett's Estate* (1880) 13 Ch.D. 696 at 709.

[66] See the example of the winning lottery ticket in *Foskett v. McKeown* [2000] 2 W.L.R. 1299 at 1329.

[67] *post*, p. 701.

[68] *post*, p. 699. As to whether he has any personal liability, see *ante*, p. 315.

iii. Mixed Funds. The position is more complicated where the trustee has mixed the trust funds with other money, and possibly converted the mixed funds into other property. The position differs according to whether the claim is against the trustee (or his successors), or whether the ownership of the mixed fund must be apportioned between two trusts or a trust and an innocent volunteer. Also, there are special rules applicable to cases of mixed funds in bank accounts.

(a) *Position as Against the Trustee.* The rule here is that the beneficiaries have a first claim over the mixed fund or any property purchased with it. The onus is on the trustee to prove that part of the mixed fund is his own. " . . . if a trustee amalgamated [trust property] with his own, his beneficiary will be entitled to every portion of the blended property which the trustee cannot prove to be his own."[69] Assuming the trustee can prove his contribution, the beneficiaries share any property purchased from the mixed fund with the trustee (or his successors), the shares being proportionate to the contributions. In *Foskett v. McKeown*[70] the trustee used his own money to pay the first three premiums on a life assurance policy and trust money to pay the fourth and fifth, after which he died. It was held by a majority of the House of Lords that the beneficiaries were entitled to a 40 per cent share in the policy proceeds. The trustee had settled the policy on his children but they, being volunteer successors, could be in no better position than the trustee. Lord Millett expressed the rule as follows:

"Where a trustee wrongfully uses trust money to provide part of the cost of acquiring an asset, the beneficiary is entitled *at his option* either to claim a proportionate share of the asset or to enforce a lien upon it to secure his personal claim against the trustee for the amount of the misapplied money. It does not matter whether the trustee mixed the trust money with his own in a

---

[69] *Lewin on Trusts* (16th ed.), p. 223, quoted in *Re Tilley's W.T.* [1967] Ch. 1179 at 1182; *Lupton v. White* (1808) 15 Ves.Jr. 432; *Indian Oil Corp. Ltd v. Greenstone Shipping S.A.* [1987] 2 Lloyd's Rep. 286; (1987) 46 C.L.J. 369 (P. Stein); *Coleman v. Harvey* [1989] 1 N.Z.L.R. 723; *Brinks Ltd v. Abu-Saleh* [1995] 1 W.L.R. 1478. Contrary views expressed in *Re Att.-Gen.'s Reference (No. 1 of 1985)* [1986] Q.B. 491 cannot stand in the light of *Att.-Gen. for Hong Kong v. Reid* [1994] 1 A.C. 324; *ante*, p. 625.

[70] [2000] 2 W.L.R. 1299; (2000) 63 M.L.R. 905 (R. Grantham and C. Rickett); (2000) 59 C.L.J. 440 (C. Rotherham); (2000) 14 *Trust Law International* 194 (P. Jaffey); [2000] R.L.R. 573 (Sir Robert Walker); [2001] Conv. 94 (J. Stevens). The dissenting judgments proceeded on the basis that, on the particular facts, the premiums paid with trust money did not add to the value of the policy, so that the beneficiaries were entitled only to the return of the sums paid with their money.

single fund before using it to acquire the asset, or made separate payments (whether simultaneously or sequentially) out of the differently owned funds to acquire a single asset . . . As against the wrongdoer and his successors, the beneficiary is entitled to locate his contribution in any part of the mixture and to subordinate their claims to share in the mixture until his own contribution has been satisfied. This has the effect of giving the beneficiary a lien for his contribution if the mixture is deficient."[71]

It has been held that the trustee is not to be treated as having made any contribution where he uses trust money in part payment for a property and provides the balance by borrowing on mortgage on the security of the property. Thus the beneficiaries take the whole of any profit.[72] Even where the trustee has contributed his own money, the trust should take all the profit if the asset (such as a house) could not have been bought without the trust contribution, in contrast with the case where a trustee buys shares and could have bought fewer with his funds alone.[73]

An extremely wide view of tracing into mixed funds emerged from *dicta* of the Privy Council in *Space Investments Ltd v. Canadian Imperial Bank of Commerce Trust Co. (Bahamas) Ltd.*[74] A bank trustee deposited trust money with itself under an express power to do so, and was then wound up. It was held that if a bank trustee misappropriated trust money for its own benefit, tracing would be possible. But where the mixing was done lawfully, as here, the trust money became the bank's, subject only to a personal obligation to pay. Hence the beneficiaries had no interest in the bank's assets and were unsecured creditors. The settlor had accepted the risk of insolvency by allowing the deposit. Lord Templeman went on to discuss the position if tracing had been available, saying that if the beneficiaries could not trace their money into any particular asset belonging to the trustee bank, equity would allow them "to trace the trust money to all the assets of the bank and to recover the trust money by the exercise of an equitable charge over all the assets of the bank."[75] The difficulty with this is that it suggests that if a commingled fund has been lost, the beneficiaries still have a proprietary claim to the trustee's remaining assets, which are impressed

---

[71] [2000] 2 W.L.R. 1299 at 1327.

[72] *Davies (Paul A.) (Australia) Pty. Ltd v. Davies* [1983] 1 N.S.W.L.R. 440.

[73] See *Australian Postal Corporation v. Lutak* (1991) 21 N.S.W.L.R. 584; (1993) 13 L.S. 371 (L. Aitken).

[74] [1986] 1 W.L.R. 1072. See also *Ross v. Lord Advocate* [1986] 1 W.L.R. 1077.

[75] [1986] 1 W.L.R. 1072 at 1074.

with a charge. Such a view would be unfair to the general creditors, and is supported neither by principle nor by policy.[76]

The point was discussed again by the Privy Council in *Re Goldcorp Exchange Ltd*,[77] where customers who had paid for bullion but had not taken delivery sought to trace into the assets of the now insolvent company. Save for one class of customers whose bullion had been segregated, the claim failed because the customers never had any proprietary rights in any bullion,[78] nor in the money paid over, which had never been impressed with any trust.[79] Thus they were simply unsecured creditors. As the customers had no proprietary rights in the purchase money, it was unnecessary to consider whether they could have traced into the company's assets. It was doubted, however, whether Lord Templeman's *dicta* in *Space Investments*[80] could overcome the difficulty that the money had been paid into an overdrawn account. The *dicta*, it was said, were concerned with tracing into a mixed fund, not a non-existent fund.

In the case of the customers whose bullion had been segregated, only a small amount could be traced because it had been mixed with other bullion, depleted by withdrawals, and not replaced by the addition of other bullion.[81] They could not improve their position by asserting an equitable lien over all the assets of the company in reliance on the *dicta* in *Space Investments*. It was accepted, however, that where a bank uses all borrowed money as a mixed fund for lending or investing, any trust money unlawfully borrowed by a bank trustee could be said to be latent in property subsequently acquired by the bank so that an equitable lien could be imposed on that property.[82] In the present case there was no evidence that the bullion of these customers continued to exist as a fund latent in property vested in the company's receivers and no reason to favour them above other customers by the grant of a lien. Thus it was not appropriate to consider the scope of *Space Investments* nor its application to trustees other than bank trustees.

Although the Privy Council did not expressly reject Lord Templeman's observations (and it should be noted that his Lordship sat also in *Re Goldcorp Exchange Ltd*),[83] it has been said that after *Re*

---

[76] See the cogent criticisms in (1987) 103 L.Q.R. 433 (R. Goode).
[77] [1995] 1 A.C. 74 (on appeal from New Zealand); (1994) 110 L.Q.R. 509 (E. McKendrick); (1994) 8 *Trust Law International* 91 (N. Richardson); (1994) 53 C.L.J. 443 (L. Sealy); All E.R. Rev. 1994 at 40 (N. Palmer); *ante*, p. 99.
[78] See now Sale of Goods (Amendment) Act 1995; (1996) 59 M.L.R. 260 (T. Burns); *ante*, p. 99 (co-ownership solution).
[79] In contrast with *Re Kayford Ltd* [1975] 1 W.L.R. 279; *ante*, p. 53.
[80] *supra*.
[81] Applying *Roscoe v. Winder* [1915] 1 Ch. 62; *post*, p. 693.
[82] Criticised (1994–95) 5 K.C.L.J. 143 (D. Hayton).
[83] *supra*.

Goldcorp the *dicta* are "now as good as dead."[84] This is reinforced by *Bishopsgate Investment Management Ltd v. Homan*,[85] where Maxwell pension funds were wrongly paid into the overdrawn account of a company now found to be insolvent. The Court of Appeal confirmed that there could be no tracing into an overdrawn bank account (whether overdrawn at the payment or later) and that no equitable charge could be imposed on the company's assets in reliance on the *dicta* in *Space Investments*. The Privy Council in *Re Goldcorp Exchange Ltd*[86] had rejected a wide interpretation of those *dicta*, which related specifically to tracing into a bank's credit balances where a bank trustee had wrongfully deposited trust money with itself.[87]

(b) *Position as Between Two Trusts, or Trust and Third Party.* It may be, however, that the trustee has mixed the funds of two trusts, whether or not with his own,[88] or has transferred the funds to an innocent volunteer, who has mixed them with his own. The rule here is that the two trusts, or the trust and the volunteer, share *pari passu* (*i.e.* rateably) in the mixed funds or any property purchased out of them.[89] The position of the innocent volunteer is further dealt with below.

Where there have been several victims but there is no realistic possibility that other claimants will seek to assert a charge ranking rateably with the claimant's, the claimant may be permitted to trace an amount in excess of that which he would obtain on a rateable division. Whether the rights of third parties may be raised as a partial defence to a tracing claim depends on the circumstances of each case.[90]

(c) *Bank Accounts.* The mixing is likely, however, to occur in the context of a banking account, to which special rules apply. Again, it is necessary to distinguish the position as between trustee and beneficiary and as between two trusts or trust and innocent volunteer. These rules govern the allocation of payments out of the mixed

---

[84] (1995) 9 *Trust Law International* 43 at 45 (P. Birks). See also *ibid.*, p. 78 (P. Oliver); *Laundering and Tracing* (Birks ed., 1995), pp. 82–88 (S. Moriarty) and 294 (P. Birks).

[85] [1995] Ch. 211; [1996] Conv. 129 (A. Jones); *infra*, p. 694. See also *Fortex Group Ltd v. MacIntosh* [1998] 3 N.Z.L.R. 171; *Box v. Barclays Bank plc* [1998] Lloyd's Rep. Bank. 185.

[86] *supra*.

[87] [1995] Ch. 211 at 221–222.

[88] Any claim to ownership by the trustee will be governed by the principle discussed in paragraph (a) above.

[89] *Re Diplock* [1948] Ch. 465. The principle was affirmed in *Foskett v. McKeown* [2000] 2 W.L.R. 1299.

[90] *El Ajou v. Dollar Land Holdings plc (No. 2)* [1995] 2 All E.R. 213.

fund.[91] The principle as between trustee and beneficiary is that the trustee is presumed to spend his own money first.

In *Re Hallett's Estate*,[92] Hallett, a solicitor, mixed with his own money certain funds from two trusts, one his own marriage settlement of which he was trustee, and the other a trust of which a client, Mrs Cotterill, was beneficiary. At his death there were insufficient funds to pay his personal debts and to meet these claims.

Three questions arose; (i) whether Mrs Cotterill, not being a beneficiary of a trust of which Hallett was a trustee, was entitled to trace on the ground of the fiduciary relationship; (ii) (assuming that she was) how to allocate the payments from the fund as between Hallett and the claimants; and (iii) as between the claimants themselves.

The Court of Appeal held that Mrs Cotterill was entitled to trace, and that the payments out must be treated as payments of Hallett's own money. This left sufficient to satisfy the claims of Mrs Cotterill and of the beneficiaries under the marriage settlement, so the third question did not arise.[93]

We are at present concerned with (ii). The other matters are discussed elsewhere.[94] The reason given by Jessel M.R. for allocating payments to Hallett's money and not to the trust is that wherever an act "can be done rightfully, [a man] is not allowed to say, against the person entitled to the property or the right, that he has done it wrongfully."[95]

It should be appreciated, however, that this principle operates in the context of a claim against a balance in the account, and does not derogate from the general principle, described above, that the beneficiaries have a first claim on any property bought out of a mixed fund.[96]

In *Re Oatway*,[97] the trustee withdrew money from the mixed fund and invested it. Later he withdrew the balance of the fund

---

[91] In the case of insuperable accounting difficulties, these rules will not be applied. See *Cunningham v. Brown*, 265 U.S. 1, 44 Sup.Ct. 424; 68 L.Ed. 873 (1923), where a tracing remedy was refused in respect of a mass of claims arising out of a fraud. Taft C.J. said "It would be running the fiction of *Knatchbull v. Hallett* into the ground to apply it here." The claimants shared equally.

[92] (1880) 13 Ch.D. 696; see (1975) 28 C.L.P. 64 (A. Oakley).

[93] In the court below, where, on the view taken by Fry J., the third question did arise, it was solved by applying the rule in *Clayton's Case* (1817) 1 Mer. 572.

[94] *ante*, p. 682; *post*, p. 695.

[95] (1880) 13 Ch.D. 696 at 727.

[96] Thus it cannot be relied on in a criminal case to show that the accused was withdrawing his own money; *R. v. Clowes (No. 2)* [1994] 2 All E.R. 316.

[97] [1903] 2 Ch. 356; *Re Tilley's W.T.* [1967] Ch. 1179 at 1185.

and dissipated it. Joyce J. rejected the argument that the money drawn out first must be treated as his own, holding that the beneficiaries' claim must be satisfied from any identifiable part of the mixed fund before the trustee could set up his own claim. Thus the beneficiaries were entitled to the investments in priority to the creditors of the trustee.

It is arguable that *Re Oatway* merely gives the beneficiaries a charge over the property rather than a right to assert that it has been purchased with their money. On this approach, any increase in the value of the property will remain available for the claims of any other beneficiaries whose money may have been subsequently mixed in the account.[98] If the trustee is insolvent, this approach may also allow any increase in value to be available to the creditors, as there is little merit in permitting the beneficiaries to retrieve more than they have lost where the real contest is with the creditors.[99] This factor must always be borne in mind when considering whether, theoretically, the tracing remedy ought to be available. The question is essentially one of competition between the beneficiary and the creditors. The House of Lords in *Foskett v. McKeown*[1] did not deal with the special rules relating to funds mixed in a current account, nor was the contest with creditors. The tenor of the majority judgments, however, lends support to the view that the beneficiaries may assert their property rights without regard to policy factors of this kind.

So far as claims against a bank balance are concerned, the rule is that tracing can succeed against a mixed fund in the bank account to the extent that the trust funds can still be shown to be there. If the account falls below that sum, that part of the trust money must have been spent.[2] Later payments in are not treated as repayments of the trust fund unless the trustee shows an intention to do so.[3] It is essential therefore to ascertain from the accounts the lowest balance in the fund; to that extent the tracing remedy is available against that balance. Of course the personal claim remains as to any shortfall, in cases where the trust money withdrawn cannot be followed into other property. Where the money has been withdrawn from the

---

[98] Such beneficiaries could not assert that the property was bought with their money because of *Clayton's Case, post*, p. 695.

[99] (1988) 37 King's Counsel 15 at 16 (G. Jones). The beneficiaries will be entitled to any profits if they can establish that the property was bought with their money; *post* p. 698.

[1] [2000] 2 W.L.R. 1299.

[2] In *Roscoe v. Winder* [1915] 1 Ch. 62, 69 Sargant J. said that the tracing remedy applied to "such an amount of the balance ultimately standing to the credit of the trustee as did not exceed the lowest balance of the account during the intervening period." It may be otherwise if "backwards tracing", *infra*, becomes accepted; Smith, *The Law of Tracing*, p. 354; (1999) 115 L.Q.R. 469 (S. Evans).

[3] *Roscoe v. Winder, supra.*

account and paid into various different accounts, the beneficiaries can claim a charge over all such accounts and, as against the wrong-doer, are not bound to identify one.[4] This is because the payments derive from a fund which was subject to a charge in their favour.

We saw that the Privy Council in *Re Goldcorp Exchange Ltd*[5] held that there could be no tracing of money paid into an overdrawn account, confirming the principle that later payments in are not normally treated as repayments to the trust.[6] A related question is whether "backwards tracing" is possible, as where a trustee borrows money to buy a car and then repays the loan with trust money.[7] May the trust trace the car? In *Bishopsgate Investment Management Ltd v. Homan*[8] Leggatt L.J. firmly rejected the concept of tracing into an asset acquired by the trustee before the trust money was misappropriated and thus without its aid.[9] Dillon L.J., however, regarded it as arguable that the beneficiary could assert a charge over an asset if there was a connection between the misappropriated money and the acquisition of the particular asset, as where the asset was bought with borrowed money and at the time of the borrowing it could be inferred that the trustee intended to repay with trust money.[10] In this limited situation "backwards tracing" may be supportable, but to permit it on a wider basis would be contrary to the principles of tracing.[11]

There is little English authority on the question whether the bene-ficiaries may claim property purchased out of a mixed account when a sufficient balance remains to satisfy their claim. The point will be significant where the property purchased has increased in value, or it may be that the balance has been spent on a property which has made a smaller profit. Under *Re Hallett*[12] the first expenditure is presumed to have been the trustee's money. *Re Oatway*[13] is dis-tinguishable because the balance has not been dissipated. *Re Tilley's Will Trusts*[14] suggests that the beneficiaries must be content with a

---

[4] *El Ajou v. Dollar Land Holdings plc* [1993] 3 All E.R. 717 at 735 (not discussed on appeal at [1994] 2 All E.R. 685); (1995) 9 *Trust Law International* 78 (P. Oliver).

[5] [1995] 1 A.C. 74; *ante*, p. 690.

[6] *Roscoe v. Winder, supra* (applied also in *Bishopsgate Investment Management Ltd v. Ho-man, infra*).

[7] If the loan was secured, subrogation to the security may assist; *post*, p. 696.

[8] [1995] Ch. 211; *ante*, p. 691. Henry J., agreed with both judgments.

[9] *ibid.* at 221–222.

[10] This view was favoured in *Foskett v. McKeown* [1998] Ch. 265 at 283–284 (C.A.), but was not discussed on appeal. See also (1995) 111 L.Q.R. 517 (Sir Peter Millett); *Laundering and Tracing* (Birks ed., 1995), p. 18 (D. Hayton).

[11] (1995) 54 C.L.J. 377 at 414 (A. Oakley); (1998) 57 C.L.J. 218 at 219 (A. Tettenborn); *cf*, Smith, *The Law of Tracing*, pp. 146–152, 354–356; Goff and Jones (5th ed.), p. 113; (1999) 115 L.Q.R. 469 at 488 (S. Evans).

[12] (1880) 13 Ch. D. 696.

[13] [1903] 2 Ch. 356.

[14] [1967] Ch. 1179, *post*, p. 698.

claim to the balance (or the second property, as the case may be).[15] If the trustee is insolvent, the claims of the creditors must also be considered, as discussed above. In *Foskett v. McKeown*,[16] where the point did not arise, Lord Millett said "It is not necessary to consider whether there are any circumstances in which the beneficiary is confined to a lien in cases where the fund is more than sufficient to repay the contributions of all parties."

It remains to consider the position where the mixed funds in the bank account represent the funds of two trusts,[17] or of a trust and an innocent volunteer. Here the rule in *Clayton's* case[18] applies, which lays down that in the case of a current bank account, the first payment in is appropriated to the earliest debt which is not statute-barred; in other words, first in, first out. This is a rule which has some relevance and convenience in commercial matters. We have seen that it does not apply to accounts between trustee and beneficiary. Nor, it is submitted, should it appear in any aspect of the present subject,[19] but it has been applied as a means of determining entitlement in a mixed banking account between rival persons with a right to trace,[20] and also between a person with a right to trace and an innocent volunteer.[21] It never appears in any context other than that of a current bank account.[22] Although the rule has been much criticised, the Court of Appeal has confirmed it as settled law, although subject to a contrary intention, express or presumed, and subject to exceptions as established in the case law.[23]

---

[15] See Pettit, pp. 514–515; Birks, *An Introduction to the Law of Restitution*, p. 370; (1995) 54 C.L.J. 377 at 416 (A. Oakley); *cf. Laundering and Tracing* (Birks ed., 1995), pp. 6 *et seq.* (D. Hayton).

[16] [2000] 2 W.L.R. 1299 at 1327.

[17] If the trustee's own money is also mixed, the principle of *Re Hallett's Estate, supra*, will apply to determine withdrawals to be allocated to the trustee; *i.e.* he is presumed to spend his own money before that of either trust.

[18] (1817) 1 Mer. 572; (1963) 79 L.Q.R. 388 (D. McConville); (1965) 6 W.A.L.R. 428, at 437 (P. Higgins). *cf. Re British Red Cross Balkan Fund* [1914] 2 Ch. 419 (where later subscribers to a fund could not claim surplus to the exclusion of earlier subscribers).

[19] (1963) 79 L.Q.R. 401–402 (D. McConville); *Laundering and Tracing* (Birks ed., 1995), p. 14 (D. Hayton); Smith, *The Law of Tracing*, p. 189. See the Report of the Review Committee on Insolvency Law and Practice (1982, Cmnd. 8558) paras. 1076–1080, preferring a rateable distribution.

[20] *Re Hallett's Estate* (1879) 13 Ch.D. 696 (Fry J.); *Re Stenning* [1895] 2 Ch. 433; *Re Diplock* [1948] Ch. 465 (the National Institute for the Deaf). It was not applied in *Re Ontario Securities Commission* (1986) 30 D.L.R. (4th) 1, *Re Registered Securities* [1991] 1 N.Z.L.R. 545 or *Keefe v. Law Society N.S.W.* (1998) 44 N.S.W.L.R. 45.

[21] *Re Stenning* [1895] 2 Ch. 433; *Mutton v. Peat* [1899] 2 Ch. 556 at 560, *per* Bryne J.; *Re Diplock, supra.*

[22] *Re Diplock* [1948] Ch. 465 at 554 (The Royal Sailors Orphan Girls' School and Home (Action 111C)).

[23] *Barlow Clowes International Ltd v. Vaughan* [1992] 4 All E.R. 22 (rule displaced by contrary intention where investors knew their money would be pooled); All E.R.Rev. 1992, at 207 (P. Clarke); [1993] Conv. 372 (J. Martin); (1993–94) 4 K.C.L.J. 86 (A. Jones).

As has been said, the presumptions discussed above only work if the withdrawals and deposits are modest in number and amount.[24] If millions of pounds flow daily into and out of a bank, equity's rules and presumptions cannot identify the claimant's money.

iv. Subrogation. This is a doctrine with common law and equitable origins whereby one person is entitled to stand in the shoes of another and assert that other's rights.[25] The most common examples are insurance and suretyship. An insurer who pays the loss is entitled to stand in the shoes of the insured and assert his rights against the wrongdoer. The House of Lords in *Napier and Ettrick (Lord) v. Hunter*[26] held that an insurer's subrogation rights should have proprietary protection in the form of a lien (rather than a more onerous constructive trust) over damages paid to the insured by the wrongdoer. Thus unsecured creditors would not benefit from the double payment at the expense of the insurer on the bankruptcy of the insured.

In the insurance cases the payer is subrogated to the rights of the payee against third parties. In other cases the payer is subrogated to the rights of third parties against the payee, as where the payee has used the money to pay off creditors. Subrogation may assist where, because of the *ultra vires* doctrine, no direct action lies against the payee.[27] In such a case the payer cannot be subrogated to any securities of the repaid creditors, otherwise he would be in a better position than an *intra vires* creditor.[28]

In the context of tracing, the question is whether the claimant may be subrogated to the position of a secured creditor paid off by the defendant with the claimant's money. (If the creditor was unsecured, subrogation will not improve the claimant's position). In *Re Diplock*[29] the next-of-kin's money had been wrongly paid to hospital charities, two of which used it (innocently) to pay off secured and unsecured debts. It was held that there was no right of subrogation, because that would require reviving debts and securities which had

---

[24] See Goff and Jones (5th ed.), p. 114. The rule was not applied in *Re Eastern Capital Futures Ltd* [1989] B.C.L.C. 371, where it was impossible to attribute particular sums to particular claimants.

[25] See Mitchell, *The Law of Subrogation*; Goff and Jones (5th ed.), Chap. 3; (1995) 54 C.L.J. 290 (L. Smith).

[26] [1993] A.C. 713; [1993] Conv. 391 (A. Jones); (1993) 143 N.L.J. 1061 (J. Martin); (1993) 109 L.Q.R. 159 (W. Gummow); (1998) 114 L.Q.R. 399 at 406 (Sir Peter Millett). See also *Lonrho Exports Ltd v. Export Credits Guarantee Department* [1999] Ch. 158 (if insurer recovers from the third party a sum greater than its entitlement by subrogation, it holds the surplus on trust for the insured).

[27] See *Wenlock (Baroness) v. River Dee Company* (1887) 19 Q.B.D. 155.

[28] See Goff and Jones (5th ed.), p. 157; Birks, *Introduction to the Law of Restitution*, pp. 390–393. A surety, on the other hand, is entitled to be subrogated to any securities on paying the creditor.

[29] [1948] Ch. 465.

been extinguished. This has long been criticised as allowing the unjust enrichment of the charities at the expense of the next-of-kin. The position was reviewed by the Court of Appeal in *Boscawen v. Bajwa*,[30] which has been described as "the most important case on tracing in recent years."[31] A building society advanced money for the purchase of property and the discharge of a legal charge on that property. The society intended to have a first legal charge on completion. It sent the money to the solicitor[32] acting for itself and the purchaser, intending to retain the beneficial interest in the money until the security was in place, but its instructions were not carried out. The purchase was not completed, but the society's money was used to redeem the existing charge. It was held that the society was entitled to be subrogated to the position of the legal chargee. It would be unconscionable to assert that the charge had been redeemed for the landowner's benefit.

The application of the doctrine to a loan which is valid, intended to be secured, and which is used to pay off a secured loan, is not surprising.[33] However, the Court of Appeal took the opportunity to state that the doctrine applied in circumstances such as those of *Re Diplock*.[34] The passage in that case which denied the remedy was considered difficult and in need of review in the light of later developments in the law of restitution. It could not be objected that the creditor's security had been extinguished: that was not a bar to subrogation but a precondition. What had motivated the Court of Appeal to deny the remedy in *Re Diplock* was a desire to avoid injustice to a charity which had redeemed a mortgage which the bank was content to leave outstanding indefinitely. "It may be doubted whether in its anxiety to avoid injustice to the hospital the court may not have done an even greater injustice to the next of kin, who were denied even the interest on their money."[35] Instead of denying a remedy, the solution should have been to delay enforcement of the revived security until the charity had had a reasonable opportunity to obtain a fresh loan on suitable terms, which would now be possible as an application of the defence of change of position.[36]

---

[30] [1996] 1 W.L.R. 328. See also *Castle Phillips Finance v. Piddington* [1995] 1 F.L.R. 783.

[31] (1995) 9 *Trust Law International* 124 (P. Birks). See also (1996) 55 C.L.J. 199 (N. Andrews); [1997] Conv. 1 (A. Oakley); (1997) 3 *Trusts & Trustees* 18 (P. Matthews).

[32] The sole partner was subsequently bankrupt.

[33] See Goff and Jones (5th ed.), p. 152.

[34] *supra*.

[35] [1996] 1 W.L.R. 328 at 341 (Millett L.J.).

[36] *post*, p. 701.

The House of Lords has recently examined the role of intention in subrogation.[37] It was considered that in cases where the doctrine rested upon a contractual basis, as in the insurance cases, it was based on the common intention of the parties. However, no such intention was required where the claim was founded on the law of restitution (as in *Boscawen v. Bajwa*[38]), where the aim was to reverse or prevent unjust enrichment. Where the claimant's money had been used to pay off a first chargee, the availability of subrogation did not depend on any common intention between the claimant and the second chargee or between the claimant and the payee that the claimant should be subrogated to the security of the first chargee. This issue was whether the second chargee would be unjustly enriched at the claimant's expense in the absence of such subrogation. Intention was, however, relevant to the question whether the enrichment would be unjust: it would not be if the transaction had been intended to create merely an unsecured loan.

v. Increase in Value. We saw that Jessel M.R. said in *Re Hallett's Estate*[39] that where trust funds, unmixed, could be traced, the claimant could choose to take the property purchased with them, or to have a charge upon it for the amount; but that if property had been mixed with the trustee's own, and property purchased with the mixed fund, the claimant's remedy was that of a charge. Such a rule would mean, however, that the beneficiary would be able only to claim the original money taken (with interest, and in priority to the creditors) and that the trustee would keep all the profits. This would be a startling result; all the more so in view of the extreme strictness with which the courts deal with cases of profits made by trustees.[40]

It is now confirmed that the appropriate remedy in such a situation is to allow the beneficiary to claim a share of the fund in the proportion which the original trust funds bore to the mixed fund at the time of the mixing. If the fund increased in value, it would be in his interest to do so. If the fund decreased in value, it would be to his interest to have a charge. The principle of proportionate entitlement was conceded in *Re Tilley's Will Trusts*.[41] In that case an executrix had paid small sums from an estate (in which she had a life interest) into her account, from which, with the aid of an overdraft

[37] *Banque Financière de la Cité v. Parc (Battersea) Ltd* [1999] 1 A.C. 221. Subrogation was held to apply only as between the claimant and the second chargee. See (1998) 114 L.Q.R. 341 (P. Watts); [1998] 6 R.L.R. 144 (C. Mitchell); [1998] J.B.L. 323 (M. Bridge); (1999) 115 L.Q.R. 195 (D. Friedmann); [1999] Conv. 113 (D. Wright); [1999] L.M.C.L.Q. 233 (T. Villiers).
[38] *supra.*
[39] (1880) 13 Ch.D. 696; *ante*, p. 692.
[40] *Boardman v. Phipps* [1967] 2 A.C. 46; *ante*, pp. 618 *et seq.*
[41] [1967] Ch. 1179 at 1189; (1968) 26 C.L.J. 28 (G. Jones).

facility, she purchased properties which increased in value. On her death the remaindermen claimed a share of the profits. Although the principle of proportionate entitlement was conceded, it was surprisingly held that the trust money had not been used in the purchase of the properties, but merely went in reduction of the overdraft. On that basis the beneficiaries were entitled only to the return of the money with interest. The matter has now been put beyond doubt by the House of Lords in *Foskett v. McKeown.*[42]

A trustee used £20,440 of trust money to pay for two of the five premiums on a life assurance policy which were paid prior to his death. On his death the proceeds of the policy were just over £1 million. It was held that the beneficiaries were entitled to 40 per cent of this sum. The windfall was attributable to their property rights. *Re Hallett's Estate*[43] was not authority for any proposition that the beneficiaries should be confined to a charge, as the fund in that case had diminished and only a charge was claimed.

vi. The Innocent Volunteer. The tracing remedy is never available against a bona fide purchaser for value. A volunteer of course is in a different position. The usual rule is that they take the property subject to any equitable interest affecting it. In the tracing situation, however, it appears from *Re Diplock*[44] that a person who receives a mixed fund bona fide[45] but without payment (the innocent volunteer) is raised to a position equal to that of the equitable owner who is entitled to trace:

"But this burden on the conscience of the volunteer is not such as to compel him to treat the claim of the equitable owner as paramount. That would be to treat the volunteer as strictly as if he himself stood in a fiduciary relationship to the equitable owner which *ex hypothesi* he does not. The volunteer is under no greater duty of conscience to recognise the interest of the equitable owner than that which lies upon a person having an equitable interest in one of two trust funds of 'money' which have become mixed towards the equitable owner of the other. Such a person is not in conscience bound to give precedence to the equitable owner of the other of the two funds."[46]

Thus the charities in *Re Diplock* were allowed to take rateably with the claimants; in other words, they were treated in the same

---

[42] [2000] 2 W.L.R. 1299.
[43] *supra.*
[44] [1948] Ch. 465.
[45] A recipient who, although not dishonest, ought to have known that the money was not his is not an innocent volunteer; *Boscawen v. Bajwa* [1996] 1 W.L.R. 328 at 337.
[46] *ibid.* at 524.

way as they would have been if they had themselves been entitled to trace. This principle of rateable sharing applies whether the mixed property has increased or deceased in value.[47]

We will see that, as far as the personal action in *Re Diplock* was concerned, the action against the volunteer could be brought only after the remedies against the personal representatives had been exhausted.[48] Any money recovered from them reduced the sum recoverable from the volunteer. It is not clear whether the proprietary action against a third party is similarly limited. Without suggesting that there was any obligation to sue the executors before proceeding to trace against the volunteer, the Court of Appeal in *Re Diplock* took the preliminary view that "prima facie and subject to discussion"[49] the next-of-kin's proprietary claim should be reduced by any amounts recovered from the executors. It is difficult to see why this should be so. Of course, the beneficiary should not recover twice over, but:

> "it should be no defence to the volunteer that the next-of-kin have recovered *in personam* against the executors. The executors should then be subrogated . . . to that part of the next-of-kin's fund which represents the difference between the total of the sums recovered from the executors and the volunteer and the loss suffered by the next-of-kin."[50]

Another solution is to require the claimant to sue the volunteer before suing the executors, who are liable only for that which cannot be recovered from the volunteer.[51]

vii. Loss of Right to Trace. There are some situations in which the right to trace will be lost. Some of these have already been mentioned, but they will be included here for the sake of completeness.[52]

(a) *The Property Ceases to be Identifiable.* It is clear from the preceding discussion that tracing is not available to a claimant who cannot identify his property, for example where the trust funds or the

---

[47] *Foskett v. McKeown* [2000] 2 W.L.R. 1299 at 1327. Their Lordships distinguished innocent volunteers who were contributors from those who were merely successors in title to the wrongdoer and in no better position.

[48] *post*, p. 709.

[49] [1948] Ch. 465 at 556. The dictum may be confined to claims arising out of the administration of estates.

[50] Goff and Jones (5th ed.), p. 114.

[51] This is the rule adopted by the New Zealand Administration Act 1952, s.30B(5) and the Western Australia Trustee Act 1962, s.65(7); *cf.* Trusts Act (Queensland), s.109, whereby the trustee must be sued before the third party.

[52] See also Goff and Jones (5th ed.), pp. 113–114, on the question how far the right to trace against an innocent volunteer is reduced by the amount recoverable from the trustee; *Re Diplock* [1948] Ch. 465 at 556.

proceeds of sale of trust assets have been dissipated.[53] Of course, the personal action remains.

(b) *Bona Fide Purchaser.*[54] Where trust property has been transferred to a bona fide purchaser for value without notice, the latter must take free of the claims of the beneficiaries, which must be pursued against the proceeds of sale or against the trustee personally.[55] A purchaser in an arm's length transaction not involving investigation of title to land will not normally have constructive notice.[56] This is not a species of the change of position defence because the consideration does not need to be adequate.[57]

(c) *Change of Position.*[58] The doctrine of change of position lays down that "the right of a person to restitution from another because of a benefit received is terminated or diminished if, after the receipt of the benefit, circumstances have so changed that it would be inequitable to require the other to make full restitution."[59] It is the mechanism by which the tension between the right to restitution and the general interest in the protection of security of receipts is reconciled.[60] This doctrine, essential to any satisfactory system of restitutionary remedies, was accepted by the House of Lords in *Lipkin Gorman v. Karpnale Ltd.*[61] That case involved a personal action, but it is clear that the defence will be generally available. Indeed, their Lordships envisaged that it would encourage a more consistent approach to tracing at law and in equity. An earlier version of this defence can be seen in *Re Diplock*,[62] where innocent volunteers (charities) had spent the claimant's money on improvements and alterations to their own land. It was held that no charge should be imposed, because a charge is enforceable by sale and it would be harsh to make the volunteers sell their land. This has now been subsumed into the wider defence of change of position. Similarly

---

[53] *cf. Space Investments Ltd v. Canadian Imperial Bank of Commerce Trust Co. (Bahamas) Ltd* [1986] 1 W.L.R. 1072, *ante*, p. 689.

[54] See Smith, *The Law of Tracing*, pp. 386–396; [1999] 14 *Amicus Curiae* at 4 (Lord Millett).

[55] *Thorndike v. Hunt* (1859) 3 De G. & J. 563; *Thomson v. Clydesdale Bank* [1893] A.C. 282.

[56] The position is the same as in the case of personal liability for receipt of trust property; *ante*, p. 313.

[57] *Lipkin Gorman v. Karpnale Ltd* [1991] 2 A.C. 548; [1999] 7 R.L.R. 75 (K. Barker).

[58] See Smith, *The Law of Tracing*, pp. 34–38. For comparative studies, see [1999] 7 R.L.R. 92 (P. Hellwege) and [2000] 8 R.L.R. 1 (M. Jewell). For the differences between change of position and estoppel, see (2001) 117 L.Q.R. 14 (E. Fung and L. Ho).

[59] *Restatement of Restitution*, para. 142. It is no defence to the personal restitutionary claim that, because of transactions with third parties, the claimant has suffered no overall loss; *Kleinwort Benson Ltd v. Birmingham City Council* [1997] Q.B. 380.

[60] *National Bank of New Zealand Ltd v. Waitaki International Processing (NI) Ltd* [1999] 2 N.Z.L.R. 211.

[61] [1991] 2 A.C. 548; (1993–94) 4 K.C.L.J. 93 (G. Jones); *ante*, p. 314.

[62] [1948] Ch. 465 at 546–548.

where an innocent volunteer has spent his own money improving the claimant's property.[63] It must be emphasised that there is no defence of "honest receipt".[64]

The defence is available to an innocent defendant but not to a wrongdoer.[65] A defendant who, although honest, ought to have known that the property was not his may not be "innocent" for this purpose.[66] It will operate to eliminate or reduce the claim where the defendant has disposed of money or other property in an exceptional and irretrievable manner in reliance upon the validity of his receipt of the claimant's property.[67] The defence is not available where a lender, at the direction of the defendant, pays money directly to a third party who then fails to repay the defendant, as in such a case the defendant has taken the risk of loss.[68]

Where it is the claimant's property that has been disposed of, tracing will fail if neither the property nor anything representing it can be identified. The defence may then operate in the context of a personal claim against the defendant.[69] Where the defendant still has the proceeds of the claimant's property[70] but has disposed of his own in reliance upon ownership of the claimant's property, the defence may operate in the context of tracing. The payment of debts cannot normally be relied on as a change of position, as the defendant was obliged to pay them in any event and there is no hardship sufficient to deny the claim.[71] Where the defendant has used the claimant's money to pay off a secured debt, we have seen that the claimant may recover by being subrogated to the position of the repaid creditor.[72] The defence of change of position is not available in the usual sense of eliminating or reducing the claim,[73] but any

---

[63] *Restatement of Restitution*, para. 178.

[64] *Kleinwort Benson Ltd v. Lincoln Council* [1999] 2 A.C. 349.

[65] *Lipkin Gorman v. Karpnale Ltd, supra.*

[66] Law Com. No. 227 (1994), para. 2.23; *South Tyneside Metropolitan Council v. Svenska International plc* [1995] 1 All E.R. 545 at 569; *Laundering and Tracing* (Birks ed., 1995), p. 158 (R. Nolan) and 325 (P. Birks); [2000] R.L.R. 1 at 16 *et seq.* (M. Jewell); *cf.* Goff and Jones (5th ed.), p. 826; [1996] R.L.R. 103 (R. Chambers); (2000) 14 *Trust Law International* 217 at 223–227 (P. Birks).

[67] See *Philip Collins Ltd v. Davis* [2000] 3 All E.R. 808 (overpaid royalties: partial defence where defendants had geared their outgoings to income over an extended period); *cf. Hillsdown Holdings plc v. Pensions Ombudsman* [1997] 1 All E.R. 862 at 904 (no defence where money used to pay tax which was recoverable).

[68] *Goss v. Chilcott* [1996] A.C. 788. The case involved a restitutionary claim for money advanced under a mortgage instrument which had become unenforceable.

[69] *ante*, p. 314.

[70] The defence would not apply where the defendant retains the claimant's actual property, such as a chattel. See Smith, *The Law of Tracing*, pp. 35, 383–385.

[71] *cf.* (1995) 54 C.L.J. 377 at 426 (A. Oakley); Oakley, Constructive Trusts (3rd ed.), p. 15.

[72] *Boscawen v. Bajwa* [1996] 1 W.L.R. 328; *ante*, p. 697.

[73] See *Scottish Equitable plc. v. Derby* [2000] 3 All E.R. 793 (no defence where money used to pay off two-thirds of mortgage); (2000) 14 *Trust Law International* 201 (A. Simmonds); [2000] Conv. 548 (M. Thompson); (2001) 117 L.Q.R. 14 (E. Fung and L. Ho).

hardship may be avoided by delaying enforcement by the claimant until the defendant has had a reasonable opportunity to obtain a fresh loan on suitable terms.[74] The defence is not confined to cases of disposal of money or other property. It could apply where the defendant has performed services in reliance on entitlement to payment, although solicitors paid for services under the terms of an invalid will were not entitled to the defence when sued for recovery of the payment: they took the risk of invalidity in view of their knowledge of the law.[75]

The question which arose in *South Tyneside Metropolitan Borough Council v. Svenska International plc*[76] was whether the defence was available where the defendant had relied on the validity of certain *ultra vires* transactions (interest-rate "swaps") when entering into other irrevocable transactions ("hedges") *prior* to receipt of the claimant's money. It was held that the defence was not available, as, save in exceptional circumstances,[77] it required reliance on *actual receipt* and not merely on events before the receipt. Thus an employee who spent money on a holiday in reliance on the promise of a forthcoming bonus would have no defence if the bonus turned out to be *ultra vires* after payment, whereas an employee who spent an *ultra vires* bonus on a holiday would have.[78] To deny pre-enrichment reliance, although in accordance with the *Restatement of Restitution*,[79] places an unwarranted restriction on the flexibility of the defence. Indeed, reliance may not be necessary at all, as in the case where the claimant's property is lost or stolen after receipt by the defendant.[80]

viii. Retention of Title Clauses. In recent years the rules of equity have been utilised in the context of the supply of goods to manufacturers. By means of a retention of title clause, the supplier stipulates that the property in the goods shall not pass until payment.[81] He may also seek to reserve ownership where his goods have been mixed with others in a manufacturing process, or of the

---

[74] *Boscawen v. Bajwa* [1996] 1 W.L.R. 328 at 341; (1995) 9 *Trust Law International* 124 (P. Birks).

[75] *Gray v. Richards Butler (a Firm)*, The Times, July 23, 1996.

[76] *supra*; criticised [1995] Conv. 490 (A. Jones); [1995] 3 R.L.R. 15 at 21 (A. Burrows); *Laundering and Tracing* (Birks ed., 1995), p. 168 (R. Nolan) and p. 329 (P. Birks); All E.R. Rev. 1995, at 455 (W. Swadling); Goff and Jones (5th ed.), p. 823; [2000] 8 R.L.R. 1 at 7–16 (M. Jewell).

[77] See *Lipkin Gorman v. Karpnale Ltd* [1991] 2 A.C. 548 (total receipts reduced by winnings paid to Cass regardless of order).

[78] [1995] 1 All E.R. 545 at 564–565.

[79] para. 142, *supra*.

[80] (1995) 58 M.L.R. 505 (P. Key); *Laundering and Tracing* (Birks ed., 1995), p. 147 (R. Nolan) and p. 330 (P. Birks); *National Bank of New Zealand Ltd v. Waitaki International Processing (NI) Ltd* [1999] 2 N.Z.L.R. 211.

[81] See Sale of Goods Act 1979, s.19.

proceeds of sale by the manufacturer on a sub-sale. He may further, by means of an "all-monies" clause, stipulate that the property shall not pass until all the buyer's obligations to him have been satisfied, not merely as to the particular consignment.[82] Retention of title clauses are often called "*Romalpa* clauses," and take their name from the leading case, *Aluminium Industrie Vaassen B.V. v. Romalpa Aluminium Ltd.*[83]

> The claimant vendor sold aluminium foil to the defendant, a manufacturing company. One clause in the contract provided that legal ownership in the foil was not to pass to the defendant until payment. Until that time, the defendant could be required to store the foil in such a way that it was clearly the property of the claimant. Other clauses dealt with the position where the foil was mixed with other materials. The defendant company got into financial difficulties and a receiver was appointed at a time when over £122,000 was owing to the claimant. The receiver certified that £35,152 in his hands represented the proceeds of sale of unmixed foil sold by the defendant to third parties. The claimant claimed priority in respect of that sum over the secured and unsecured creditors. The Court of Appeal, applying *Re Hallett's Estate*,[84] upheld the claim. Although the third parties acquired title to the foil sold to them,[85] the position as between the claimant and defendant was that the foil was the claimant's property, which the defendant was selling as agent. The defendant's position as agent and bailee gave rise to a fiduciary relationship,[86] which entitled the claimant to trace the proceeds of the unmixed foil and recover in priority to the secured and unsecured creditors.

---

[82] For the effect of such a clause in Scotland, see *Armour v. Thyssen Edelstahlwerke A.G.* [1991] 2 A.C. 339; (1991) 141 N.L.J. 537 (B. Avery); (1991) 54 M.L.R. 726 (R. Bradgate). The Review Committee on Insolvency Law and Practice (1982, Cmnd, 8558), para. 1645, proposed that such clauses should be regarded as creating a charge (and hence be registrable).

[83] [1976] 1 W.L.R. 676; (1976) 92 L.Q.R. 360, 528 (R. Goode); (1976) 39 M.L.R. 585 (R. Prior); (1977) 93 L.Q.R. 324 (D. Donaldson) and 487 (R. Goode); (1977) 36 C.L.J. 27 (J. Farrow and N. Furey); [1978] Conv. 37 (O. Wylie); (1980) 39 C.L.J. 48 (J. Thornley); (1980) 43 M.L.R. 489 (W. Goodhart and G. Jones); [1994] Conv. 129 (G. McCormack). See Smith, *Property Problems in Sale*; Goode, *Proprietary Rights and Insolvency in Sales Transactions;* McCormack, *Reservation of Title*; Worthington, *Proprietary Interests in Commercial Transactions.*

[84] (1880) 13 Ch.D. 696.

[85] See also *Four Point Garage Ltd v. Carter* [1985] 3 All E.R. 12 (purchaser in good faith from buyer where resale in the ordinary course of business gets legal title even though, as between buyer and supplier, buyer did not get title); Sale of Goods Act 1979, ss.24, 25.

[86] Such relationships are not always fiduciary; *Hendy Lennox (Industrial Engines) Ltd v. Grahame Puttick Ltd* [1984] 1 W.L.R. 485; *Re Andrabell Ltd* [1984] 3 All E.R. 407; *Napier and Ettrick (Lord) v. Hunter* [1993] A.C. 713 at 744.

It was conceded in *Romalpa* that the defendant held the goods as bailee.[87] Normally, however, the relationship of the parties under a title retention clause hardly fits the concept of bailment or agency. It has been held that if sub-sales are permitted, the normal implication is that the buyer will sell on his own account and not as fiduciary agent for the seller.[88] But where the sub-purchaser's contract also contains a reservation of title clause, the unpaid vendor may assert title against the sub-purchaser until the latter has paid the purchaser.[89]

(a) *Unmixed Goods.* Retention of title clauses have proved effective where, as in *Romalpa*, the property has retained its identity. In *Clough Mill Ltd v. Martin*[90] the Court of Appeal held that a clause reserving legal title to yarn until payment entitled the seller, on the buyer's insolvency, to recover unused yarn which had not been paid for. As no title passed to the buyer, the buyer could not be regarded as having created a (registrable) charge over the yarn in favour of the seller. Similarly in *Hendy Lennox (Industrial Engines) Ltd v. Grahame Puttick Ltd*,[91] where the seller reserved title to a diesel engine which had been used by the buyer as a major component of a diesel generating set. The seller's claim to ownership of the engine succeeded as the engine remained readily identifiable and could be disconnected quite easily from the generator. In *Re Peachdart Ltd*[92] on the other hand, where leather was supplied for the manufacture of handbags, it was not regarded as retaining its identity even though it remained recognisable in the product. Thus the claim fell to be considered under the following heading.

(b) *Incorporation into Manufacturing Process.* Vendors have been unsuccessful, however, where the property has been incorporated into a manufacturing process. In *Re Bond Worth Ltd*[93] the

---

[87] See *Re Bond Worth Ltd*, *infra*.

[88] *E. Pfeiffer Weinkellerei-Weineinkauf GmbH & Co. v. Arbuthnot Factors Ltd* [1988] 1 W.L.R. 150; *Compaq Computer Ltd v. Abercorn Group Ltd* [1991] B.C.C. 484.

[89] *Re Highway Foods International Ltd* [1995] 1 B.C.L.C. 209; (1996) 55 C.L.J. 26 (A. Tettenborn).

[90] [1985] 1 W.L.R. 111, distinguishing *Re Bond Worth Ltd*, *infra*, as to unused material. See All E.R. Rev. 1984 at 31 (N. Palmer); (1985) 135 N.L.J. 224, 271 (S. Jones); (1985) 36 N.I.L.Q. 165 (McKee); (1985) 44 C.L.J. 33 (J. Thornely); [1987] Conv. 434 (J. Bradgate).

[91] [1984] 1 W.L.R. 485. The seller's proprietary claim to the engine was transferred to the proceeds of sale as the property in the engine had not passed to the defendant's customers at the time of receivership. As to other engines where the property had passed, see *infra*.

[92] [1984] Ch. 131; All E.R. Rev. 1983, p. 48 (N. Palmer); (1984) 100 L.Q.R. 35 (S. Whittaker); (1984) 43 C.L.J. 35 (J. Thornely); [1984] Conv. 139 (D. Milman). The contract expressly provided for a fiduciary relationship.

[93] [1980] Ch. 228. See also *Tatung (U.K.) Ltd v. Galex Telesure Ltd* [1989] B.C.C. 325. For the Australian position, see [1993] Conv. 375 (J. de Lacy).

vendor supplied fibre to the purchaser, which was spun into yarn
with other fibre and used in the manufacture of carpets, becoming an
inseparable component of the yarn and the carpets. The contract
provided that "equitable and beneficial ownership" should remain
with the vendor until payment. If resold, the vendor's rights should
attach to the proceeds. If converted to other products, the vendor's
rights should extend to those products. Upon the purchaser's insolvency £587,397 was owing to the vendor. The receiver held little
raw fibre but much yarn and carpets. Slade J. rejected the vendor's
claim to priority. The contract was primarily a contract of sale,
whereby the legal title and the risk passed to the purchaser, who was
at liberty to resell or use the fibre in the manufacturing process. The
purchaser was neither an agent nor a bailee. The retention of title
clause, upon its true construction, did not reserve full equitable
ownership to the vendor, but gave the vendor an equitable charge
over the fibre or its products. This charge, which was created by the
purchaser company,[94] was void for non-registration under the Companies Act.[95] *Romalpa*[96] was distinguishable, primarily because
there the clause reserved *legal* ownership to the vendor.[97]

The result was similar in *Borden U.K. Ltd v. Scottish Timber
Products Ltd*,[98] where the vendor supplied resin to the purchaser, to
be used in the manufacture of chipboard, of which it became an
inseparable component. The contract reserved legal ownership in
the resin to the vendor until payment, but did not purport to give the
vendor rights over the chipboard. Upon the purchaser's insolvency,
£318,321 was owing to the vendor. The Court of Appeal held that
the clause merely reserved rights over the resin, which had disappeared, leaving nothing to trace. There was no fiduciary relationship, as the contract was a contract of sale, giving the purchaser
liberty to use the resin in the manufacturing process, destroying its
very existence. It was doubted whether the tracing remedy could
ever apply when heterogeneous goods were mixed in a manufacturing process wherein the original goods lost their character.[99] If there
was such a remedy, how could the value of the original goods be
quantified? There had been no mixing in issue in *Romalpa*, where it
was conceded that the defendant was a bailee of the foil. In the
present case, even if the vendor had acquired rights over the chipboard, the claim would have failed for non-registration under the
Companies Act. The vendor was similarly unsuccessful in *Re*

---

[94] See *Stroud Architectural Systems Ltd v. John Laing Construction Ltd* [1994] B.C.C. 18.
[95] s.95(1) of the Act of 1948. Companies Act 1985, ss.395–404, as substituted by Companies
Act 1989, have not been brought into operation.
[96] *supra.*
[97] Might the claimant in *Romalpa* have succeeded at common law?
[98] [1981] Ch. 25; doubted in (1992) 45 C.L.P. 69 at 98 (P. Birks).
[99] This view is not inconsistent with the retention of proprietary rights prior to such mixing;
Clough Mill Ltd v. Martin, supra.

Peachdart Ltd,[1] where leather was supplied for the manufacture of handbags. The retention of title clause was held to create a charge over the handbags or their proceeds, which was void for non-registration. In *Chaigley Farms Ltd v. Crawford, Kaye & Grayshire Ltd (T/A Leylands)*[2] the claimant supplied live animals for slaughter and processing. The retention of title clause was held to cover live animals only, as the claimant's title was extinguished on slaughter. The question of mixing was not in issue in *Clough Mill Ltd v. Martin*,[3] but the Court of Appeal there expressed the view that if the material is incorporated into other goods, it is assumed that they are owned by the buyer subject to a charge in favour of the seller, unless they are still in a separate and identifiable state.

(c) *Proceeds of Sale.* Even where the seller's goods have not been amalgamated with others, claims to proprietary rights in the proceeds of sale have been unsuccessful.

First, the claimant may fail because he cannot establish a fiduciary relationship, which is necessary for tracing into a mixed fund.[4] Such was the case in *Re Andrabell Ltd*,[5] where a claim to the proceeds of sale of travel bags supplied by the claimant failed. The rights and duties of the parties were inconsistent with a fiduciary relationship and were merely those of debtor and creditor. Similarly in *Hendy Lennox (Industrial Engines) Ltd v. Grahame Puttick Ltd*,[6] where the claimant supplied engines for incorporation into generators. Where the property in the engines had passed to the defendant's customers, the supplier's claim to the proceeds failed, because the terms of the contract (in particular the granting of credit) were inconsistent with a fiduciary relationship.

Secondly, even if a fiduciary relationship can be established, the true analysis of the position is that the claimant has a charge over the proceeds,[7] which will fail unless registered under the Companies Act.

The reform of this area of the law, which has been called "a maze if not a minefield,"[8] was considered by the Review Committee on

---

[1] *supra.*

[2] [1996] B.C.C. 957; (1997) 56 C.L.J. 28 (L. Sealy); [1998] Conv. 52 (J. de Lacy).

[3] *Supra.* See also *Specialist Plant Services Ltd v. Braithwaite Ltd* [1987] B.C.L.C. 1 (retention of title clause concerning parts incorporated into machines, and expressed to be as surety for debt, created charge which was void for non-registration).

[4] *ante*, p. 682. The terms used in the documents are not conclusive; *Compaq Computer Ltd v. Abercorn Group Ltd* [1991] B.C.C. 484.

[5] [1984] 3 All E.R. 407.

[6] [1984] 1 W.L.R. 485; *ante*, p. 705.

[7] *Re Peachdart Ltd* [1984] Ch. 131; *Re Weldtech Equipment Ltd* [1991] B.C.C. 16, (1991) 54 M.L.R. 736 (J. de Lacy); *Compaq Computer Ltd v. Abercorn Group Ltd*, *supra*; (1992) 51 C.L.J. 19 (L. Sealy).

[8] *Hendy Lennox (Industrial Engines) Ltd v. Grahame Puttick Ltd* [1984] 1 W.L.R. 485 at 493.

Insolvency Law and Practice.[9] Some of the Committee's proposals were enacted by the Insolvency Act 1986 in the case of corporate insolvency. The Act provides that an administrator may be appointed to manage the affairs of a company which is in financial difficulties.[10] After the presentation of a petition for an administration order, no steps may be taken to enforce any security or to repossess goods under a retention of title agreement[11] without leave of the court.[12] Nor may any such steps be taken while an administration order is in force without the consent of the administrator or the leave of the court.[13] Where any property of the company is subject to a security or goods are subject to a retention of title agreement, the administrator may dispose of the property or goods as if they were not subject to the security or the agreement, if the court is satisfied that the disposal would be likely to promote the purposes specified in the administration order.[14] The net proceeds of the disposal must be applied towards discharging the sums secured by the security or payable under the retention of title agreement.[15] The object of these provisions is to enable the business to be kept as a going concern, for the benefit of all creditors.

The real question, however, is whether retention of title clauses are desirable as a matter of policy. Save where construed as creating charges and hence registrable, they effectively create a hidden security, enabling the seller to "leapfrog" other creditors.[16] This objection could be overcome if *all* retention of title clauses were registrable, but this is not yet the case.[17]

6. THE PERSONAL ACTION IN DIPLOCK

It will be recalled that in *Re Diplock*[18] executors distributed large sums of money to numerous charities under the terms of a residuary bequest which was subsequently held to be invalid. The misapplied money belonged, therefore, to the testator's next-of-kin, whose proprietary claim to the money has already been considered.[19] The next-of-kin claimed alternatively that a direct personal action lay

---

[9] (1982 Cmnd. 8558), paras. 1587–1651.
[10] Insolvency Act 1986, s.8.
[11] Defined in s.251 as an agreement which does not constitute a charge but which gives the seller priority over other creditors.
[12] Insolvency Act 1986, s.10.
[13] *ibid.* s.11.
[14] *ibid.* s.15. See also s.43.
[15] s.15(5).
[16] See [1987] Conv. 434 (J. Bradgate).
[17] See (1995) 54 C.L.J. 43 (S. Cowan, A. Clark and G. Goldberg).
[18] [1948] Ch. 465, [1951] A.C. 251. (Where the earlier authorities are extensively reviewed). For a historical survey, see (1983) 4 *Journal of Legal History* 3 (S. Whittaker).
[19] *ante*, p. 682.

against the innocent recipients in equity. This claim succeeded in the Court of Appeal, whose judgment was unanimously affirmed by the House of Lords.[20] Such an action may be brought by an unpaid or underpaid creditor, legatee or next-of-kin against the recipient, whether the latter is an overpaid creditor or beneficiary or a "stranger" having no claim to any part of the estate.[21] While the common law action for money had and received was then confined to mistakes of fact,[22] it was held that the action in equity lay whether the mistake was of fact or, as in the present case, of law. The mistake in such a case is not that of the claimant, but that of the personal representative, who is not a party to the action. The claimant has no way of finding out whether the mistake was of fact or law, nor whether it was a mistaken or deliberate misapplication,[23] hence "it would be a strange thing if the Court of Chancery, having taken upon itself to see that the assets of a deceased person were duly administered, was deterred from doing justice to a creditor, legatee or next-of-kin because the executor had done him wrong under a mistake of law."[24]

The action will not lie against a bona fide purchaser without notice, but, as far as a volunteer is concerned, it is no defence that he was unaware of the mistake,[25] "it is prima facie at least a sufficient circumstance that the defendant, as events have proved, has received some share of the estate to which he was not entitled."[26] But the claim will fail if the claimant has acquiesced in the wrongful payment,[27] or has failed to bring his action within the time permitted by the Limitation Act 1980.[28] It is not settled whether the action lies against the recipient's successor in title.[29]

The personal action in equity lies for the principal sum only, without interest,[30] and is subject to two further important qualifications. First, the direct claim against the recipient is limited to the amount which cannot be recovered from the personal representative,

---

[20] [1951] A.C. 251 (*sub nom. Ministry of Health v. Simpson*).

[21] [1948] Ch. 465 at 502; [1951] A.C. 251 at 269.

[22] The action now lies for recovery of money paid by mistake of law; *Kleinwort Benson Ltd v. Lincoln City Council* [1999] 2 A.C. 349.

[23] It seems that the action will lie where the wrongful payment was deliberate: [1951] A.C. 251 at 270.

[24] [1951] A.C. 251 at 270, *per* Lord Simonds. The personal representative can now himself recover from the recipient whether the mistake was of fact or law; *ante*, n. 22.

[25] This was, however, a defence to an alternative claim based on constructive trusteeship; [1948] 1 Ch. 465 at 478.

[26] [1948] Ch. 465 at 503, *per* Lord Greene M.R.

[27] [1951] A.C. 251 at 276.

[28] By s.22, the period is 12 years. (For creditors the period is six years). See [1948] Ch. 465 at 514.

[29] Goff and Jones (5th ed.), p. 703. This may depend on whether it becomes accepted that liability for receipt is not fault-based; *ante*, p. 315.

[30] *Re Diplock, supra.* This is described as "curious" by Goff and Jones, *loc. cit.* at p. 702.

who is primarily liable.[31] Thus the recipient will only be liable in respect of the whole sum if nothing can be recovered from the personal representative, for example because he is insolvent, or acted under a court order,[32] or is protected by section 27 of the Trustee Act 1925.[33] This limitation has been criticised.[34] Why should the recipient's liability depend on the personal representative's solvency? The solution adopted in *Re Diplock*[35] benefits the recipient at the expense of the personal representative, who, on paying the claimant, should be subrogated to the claimant's right to sue the recipient. Another solution might be to require the claimant to exhaust his remedies against the recipient before suing the personal representative.[36]

The second qualification is that the action appears to be limited to claims arising out of the administration of estates.[37] The action originated at a time when the Court of Chancery was attempting to acquire the jurisdiction then exercised by the ecclesiastical courts over the administration of assets,[38] and is not necessarily available to beneficiaries of lifetime trusts.[39] But more recent cases indicate that the court is not unwilling to extend the action beyond the administration of estates. This approach is consistent with the doctrine of unjust enrichment.[40] In *Butler v. Broadhead*[41] it was suggested that the liquidator of a company had a sufficiently analogous position to that of an executor to allow a creditor of the company to recover from overpaid contributories in a winding-up, at any rate where the liquidator had not advertised for claims. But the action was held to be barred by the Companies Act 1948.[42] In *Re J. Leslie Engineers Co. Ltd*[43] Oliver J. was prepared to allow a personal action where a liquidator claimed recovery of money paid to X after

---

[31] [1948] Ch. 465 at p. 503. Here the executors paid £15,000 under a compromise approved by the court. For the position concerning the proprietary action, see *ante*, p. 682.

[32] For example, a Benjamin order (*Re Benjamin* [1902] 1 Ch. 723), giving him liberty to distribute on the footing that a particular person is dead.

[33] *ante*, p. 551.

[34] See (1949) 65 L.Q.R. 37 at 44 (A. Denning); Goff and Jones, *loc. cit.* at p. 702; (1983) 4 *Journal of Legal History* 3 (S. Whittaker).

[35] [1948] Ch. 465, [1951] A.C. 251.

[36] See New Zealand Administration Act 1952; Western Australia Trustee Act 1962.

[37] See [1951] A.C. 251 at 265–266, *per* Lord Simonds.

[38] See (1990) 49 C.L.J. 217 at 219 (C. Harpum).

[39] Although if a trustee pays trust money under a mistake of fact (or now, by mistake of law) he may recover it, and may be compelled by the beneficiaries to do so: *Re Robinson* [1911] 1 Ch. 502.

[40] See (1989) 105 L.Q.R. 352 (P. Birks); (1991) 107 L.Q.R. 71 (Sir Peter Millett), suggesting strict liability, subject to change of position, for innocent receipt of another's property; *ante*, p. 315.

[41] [1975] Ch. 97. See also *G.L. Baker Ltd v. Medway Building and Supplies Ltd* [1958] 1 W.L.R. 1216; *Nelson v. Larholt* [1948] 1 K.B. 339; *Eddis v. Chichester Constable* [1969] 1 All E.R. 566 (affirmed, without discussing this point, [1969] 2 Ch. 345).

[42] Now Companies Act 1985, s.557.

[43] [1976] 1 W.L.R. 292.

the commencement of a winding-up (the transaction being void
under the Companies Act). But the claim failed because the liquidator had not exhausted his remedies against the person primarily
responsible, and, in any event, it appeared that X had given consideration for the payment.

Much criticism has centred around the apparent refusal of the
House of Lords in *Re Diplock*[44] to recognise the defence of change
of position. Where the volunteer has received the money in good
faith, his liability to repay it could cause hardship if he has acted to
his detriment by spending the money in an exceptional and irretrievable manner. It will be recalled that in *Re Diplock* money had been
paid to a hospital charity, and used in the erection of new buildings.
This, it was considered, made it inequitable to allow tracing,[45] but
was no defence to the personal action.[46] Now that the House of
Lords in *Lipkin Gorman v. Karpnale Ltd*[47] has accepted the defence
of change of position, the *Diplock* personal action can develop on a
fairer and more rational basis.

Finally, it seems that the action does not lie if there was a suffi-
ciency of assets at the date of the payment to the defendant. Where
the deficiency has arisen subsequently, the personal representative
alone is liable.[48]

[44] [1951] A.C. 251.
[45] *ante.*
[46] The Court of Appeal rejected the claim that the volunteers were personally liable *as
constructive trustees*, holding that they were not under any duty to investigate the validity
of the gift and were entitled to assume that the executors were acting properly; *Re Diplock*
[1948] Ch. 465 at 477–479. A finding of constructive trusteeship would have resulted in
liability to pay interest. See *Westdeutsche Landesbank Girozentrale v. Islington London
Borough Council* [1996] A.C. 669.
[47] [1991] 2 A.C. 548; (1991) 50 C.L.J. 407 (W. Cornish); *ante*, p. 701.
[48] See *Peterson v. Peterson* (1866) L.R. 3 Eq. 111.

PART IV

**MISCELLANEOUS EQUITABLE REMEDIES
AND DOCTRINES**

CHAPTER 24

SPECIFIC PERFORMANCE

1. GENERAL PRINCIPLES[1]

AN outline of the nature of equitable remedies has already been given.[2] Their characteristics, in relation to specific performance in particular, must now be examined.

---

[1] See Fry, *Specific Performance*; Spry, *Equitable Remedies*; Jones and Goodhart, *Specific Performance*; Sharpe, *Injunctions and Specific Performance*.
[2] *ante*, p. 31.

A. Discretionary

Specific performance, like other equitable remedies, is only given as a matter of discretion, although the discretion is exercised in accordance with settled principles.[3] Thus there are some cases, notably contracts for the sale of land,[4] where the claimant may expect to obtain specific performance as a matter of course, and other cases, such as contracts for personal services,[5] where he may expect not to. The discretionary nature of the remedy is well illustrated by a consideration of the matters, such as the conduct of the claimant, which the court may regard as a bar to specific performance.[6]

B. Common Law Remedies Inadequate

Equitable remedies are only available where common law remedies are inadequate[7]; for example where the obligation is a continuing one, necessitating a series of actions at law for damages,[8] or where the loss would be difficult to quantify.[9] But specific performance will not be available if, on the true construction of the contract, the parties have agreed that a specific sum of money is to be paid as an alternative to performing the contract.[10]

C. Specific Performance is a Remedy in Personam[11]

An order of specific performance issues against the individual defendant. If the defendant is within the jurisdiction of the court and can be compelled personally to carry out his obligation, the court may order him to do so even though the subject-matter of the contract is outside the jurisdiction of the court.

> In *Penn v. Lord Baltimore*[12] the parties had entered into a written agreement fixing the boundaries of Pennsylvania and Maryland, the former of which belonged to the claimants and the

---

[3] *Lamare v. Dixon* (1873) L.R. 6 H.L. 414; *Haywood v. Cope* (1858) 25 Beav. 140 at 151 (Romilly M.R.).

[4] *post*, p. 721.

[5] *post*, p. 730.

[6] *post*, p. 738.

[7] *Beswick v. Beswick* [1968] A.C. 58, *post*, p. 752; *Tito v. Waddell (No. 2)* [1977] Ch. 106 at 327.

[8] *ibid*. But see *post*, p. 753.

[9] See, however, *Co-operative Insurance Society Ltd v. Argyll Stores (Holdings) Ltd* [1998] A.C. 1.

[10] *Legh v. Lillie* (1860) 6 H. & N. 165; Pettit, p. 612.

[11] *ante*, pp. 7, 18.

[12] (1750) 1 Ves.Sen. 444; *Richard West and Partners (Inverness) Ltd v. Dick* [1969] Ch. 424.

latter to the defendant. The claimants sued the defendant in England to have the agreement specifically performed, and one of the objections taken by the defendant was to the jurisdiction of the court. This objection was overruled by Lord Hardwicke on the ground that "the conscience of the party was bound by this agreement; and being within the jurisdiction of this court, which acts *in personam*, the court may properly order it as an agreement."[13] Although the land was not within the jurisdiction, the defendant was, and the court would hold him in contempt unless he complied.

But this jurisdiction is not, perhaps so wide as might at first appear. The land in question was subject at that time to the Crown. The court was invited in *Re Hawthorne*[14] to apply it to land in Saxony (not subject to the Crown) but refused to do so. It appears that the tendency of modern decisions is to restrict the limits within which this jurisdiction will be exercised.[15]

D. Ensuring Observance

Equitable remedies will never issue unless the court can ensure that they will be observed. As equity does not act in vain, specific performance will be ordered only where the defendant is in a position to comply.

In *Jones v. Lipman*[16] the defendant entered into a contract to sell some land to the claimant, then sought to avoid specific performance by selling the land to a company acquired by him solely for this purpose and controlled by him. While specific performance would not normally be ordered against a vendor who no longer owned the property, here the defendant was still in a position to complete the contract, because the company was "the creature of the vendor, a device and a sham, a mask which he holds before his face in an attempt to avoid recognition by the eye of Equity."[17] This specific performance was ordered against the vendor and the company.

---

[13] (1750) 1 Ves. Sen. 444 at 447.

[14] (1883) 23 Ch.D. 743.

[15] See *per* Parker J. in *Deschamps v. Miller* [1908] 1 Ch. 856, at 863; Dicey and Morris, *The Conflict of Laws* (13th ed.), pp. 952 *et seq.* See also Civil Jurisdiction and Judgments Act 1982, s.30.

[16] [1962] 1 W.L.R. 832. And see *Elliott v. Pierson* [1948] Ch. 452.

[17] *ibid.*, at 836, *per* Russell J.

E. The Enforcement of Positive Contractual Obligations

Unlike injunctions, the remedy of specific performance is confined to the enforcement of positive contractual obligations. These obligations must be binding on the defendant.[18] A prohibitory injunction is appropriate to restrain the breach of a negative contract, while a mandatory injunction is used to force the defendant to take positive steps to undo an act already done in breach of contract. But this classification is not inflexible. Even where the claimant wishes to enforce a positive contractual obligation, he may ask for an injunction instead of specific performance. The advantage of such a course is that an injunction can be obtained on an interlocutory basis, while specific performance cannot.[19] It should also be added that specific performance does not lie against the Crown.[20]

F. Time for Performance

While specific performance is a remedy for breach of contract, it may in some circumstances be obtained before the time for performance has arrived. In *Marks v. Lilley*[21] the claimant commenced an action for specific performance of a contract for the sale of land after the contractual completion date but without first having served a notice making time of the essence of the contract. It was held that this action was not premature, as the equitable right to specific performance, based on the defendant's equitable duty to perform his contract, had already accrued. But the court would not normally interfere before the time for performance had arrived, and a premature claimant may be penalised in costs. In *Hasham v. Zenab*[22] specific performance of a contract for the sale of land was granted even before the contractual completion date where the defendant had been guilty of anticipatory breach of contract.[23] The order would not, of course, take effect before the fixed date.

---

[18] For specific performance against a party estopped from denying the existence of a contract, see *Spiro v. Lintern* [1973] 1 W.L.R. 1002; *Worboys v. Carter* [1987] 2 E.G.L.R. 1.

[19] See *Sky Petroleum Ltd v. V.I.P. Petroleum Ltd* [1974] 1 W.L.R. 576; *Astro Exito Navegacion S.A. v. Southland Enterprise Co Ltd (No. 2)* [1983] 2 A.C. 787; *Peninsular Maritime Ltd v. Padseal Ltd* (1981) 259 E.G. 860; *Parker v. Camden London Borough Council* [1986] Ch. 162.

[20] Crown Proceedings Act 1947, s.21(1)(a). The proper remedy is a declaration.

[21] [1959] 1 W.L.R. 749. There is a breach of contract at law and in equity if completion does not occur on the contractual date, even though time has not become of the essence: *Raineri v. Miles* [1981] A.C. 1050, *post*, p. 741.

[22] [1960] A.C. 316; (1960) 76 L.Q.R. 200 (R.E.M.). This is similar to the position at law, where an immediate right to damages accrues upon an anticipatory breach of contract: *Hochster v. De la Tour* (1853) 2 E. & B. 678.

[23] Anticipatory breach is not essential, but there must be a sufficient likelihood of breach; Spry, *Equitable Remedies*, p. 77. See further *Oakacre Ltd v. Claire Cleaners (Holdings) Ltd* [1982] Ch. 197.

G. Specific Performance and Damages or Compensation

Damages may be awarded either in addition to or in substitution for specific performance.[24] Similarly, there are some cases, involving misdescription in contracts for the sale of land, where the court may grant specific performance with compensation in the form of an abatement of the purchase price.[25]

2. THE EFFECT OF AN ORDER OF SPECIFIC PERFORMANCE ON OTHER REMEDIES

If specific performance is granted, but enforcement subsequently becomes impossible, what remedies are available to the claimant?

A. Common Law Remedy not Excluded

In *Johnson v. Agnew*[26] the claimant, having contracted to sell mortgaged properties to the defendant, obtained an order of specific performance. Subsequently, owing to the defendant's delay, the properties were sold by the mortgagees so that it became impossible to comply with the order. The price obtained by the mortgagees was lower than the contract price, so the claimant sought damages from the defendant at common law for breach of contract.[27] The defendant claimed that the claimant's election to seek specific performance was irrevocable, so that he could not claim damages at common law. The House of Lords found in favour of the claimant. Lord Wilberforce explained the vendor's position as follows:

If a purchaser fails to complete, the vendor can treat this as a repudiation and claim damages for breach of contract, or he may seek specific performance. If he proceeds for these remedies in the alternative, he must elect at trial.[28] If an order for specific performance is made, the contract still exists and is not merged in the

---

[24] Lord Cairns' Act 1858; Judicature Act 1873; *post*, p. 747.

[25] *post*, p. 747 (damages), and p. 744 (compensation). See also *Seven Seas Properties Ltd v. Al-Essa* [1988] 1 W.L.R. 1272 (specific performance and damages combined with asset-freezing injunction).

[26] [1980] A.C. 367; (1979) 95 L.Q.R. 321 (P. Baker); [1979] Conv. 293 (F. Crane); (1979) 42 M.L.R. 696 (G. Woodman); (1980) 96 L.Q.R. 403 (M. Hetherington); (1980) 39 C.L.J. 58 (A. Oakley); (1981) 97 L.Q.R. 26 (D. Jackson).

[27] Or, alternatively, damages under Lord Cairns' Act, *supra*.

[28] See *Meng Leong Development Pte. Ltd v. Jip Hong Trading Co. Pte. Ltd* [1985] A.C. 511 (P.C.): P claimed in the alternative and was awarded damages. V appealed against the amount. P insisted that the damages be placed with a stakeholder, otherwise he would levy execution. It was held that P was estopped from later seeking specific performance. He was not bound to make an election at that stage, and could have retained the right to elect until after the appeal. Here, however, he had elected to take the benefit of the damages award, and thereby relinquished the right to seek specific performance. The reasoning is criticised at (1985) 101 L.Q.R. 309 on the ground that the damages had not come under P's control.

judgment. If the defendant then fails to comply with the order, the claimant may apply either to enforce or to dissolve the contract. It follows from the fact that the contract still exists that the claimant can recover damages at common law. The argument based on irrevocable election is unsound: "A vendor who seeks (and gets) specific performance is merely electing for a course which may or may not lead to implementation of the contract; what he elects for is not eternal and unconditional affirmation, but a continuance of the contract under control of the court, which control involves the power, in certain events, to terminate it. If he makes an election at all, he does so when he decides not to proceed under the order for specific performance; but to ask the court to terminate the contract."[29] If the claimant accepts a repudiation, he cannot afterwards seek specific performance, because the defendant has been discharged from further performance by the claimant's acceptance of the repudiation. But if the claimant obtains an order of specific performance, and enforcement becomes impossible, there is no reason why the claimant should be precluded from seeking a remedy at common law.[30]

B. The Court's Discretion

The control of the court is exercised according to equitable principles: the relief sought by the claimant will be refused if it would be unjust to the other party to grant it. In *Johnson v. Agnew*[31] it was the purchaser's fault that it had become impossible to enforce the order, therefore the vendor was entitled not only to its discharge and the termination of the contract, but to damages at common law for breach of contract.

C. Subsequent Performance Regulated by Terms of Order

Although the contract still exists after specific performance is granted and does not merge into the order until the legal title has been conveyed, the rights under the contract may be affected by the order. By applying for specific performance, the claimant puts into the hands of the court how the contract is to be carried out: the performance of the contract is regulated by the provisions of the order and not those of the contract. In *Singh v. Nazeer*[32] a purchaser was granted specific performance of a contract for the sale of land.

---

[29] [1980] A.C. 367 at 398 (*per* Lord Wilberforce). See also *Hillel v. Christoforides* (1992) 63 P. & C.R. 301; *Homsy v. Murphy* (1997) 73 P. & C.R. 26.

[30] Damages are also available in lieu of specific performance under Lord Cairns' Act (*post*, p. 747); *Biggin v. Minton* [1977] 1 W.L.R. 701.

[31] *supra*.

[32] [1979] Ch. 474; criticised in (1980) 96 L.Q.R. 403 (M. Hetherington). *cf.* (1981) 97 L.Q.R. 26 (D. Jackson).

The purchaser then delayed, so the vendor served a completion notice and claimed damages and forfeiture of the deposit. Megarry J. held that the completion notice was invalid. The machinery provisions of the contract, for example as to mode and date of completion, were intended to apply to performance out of court. Once specific performance was granted, they must yield to any directions in the order. Unless the parties agree, the working out, variation or cancellation of an order for specific performance is a matter for the court. Applying these principles, a vendor who obtains specific performance is not free to sell to a third party if the purchaser fails to comply with the order. Unless the purchaser agrees to the resale, the vendor's remedy in such a case is to apply to court either for enforcement of the order or for an order terminating the contract.[33]

3. Specific Performance in Particular Situations

It is a fundamental rule that specific performance will not be granted where the claimant would be adequately compensated by the common law remedy of damages.[34] There are some situations, few in number, in which it is settled that the claimant may expect to obtain specific performance.[35] There are also numerous situations in which it can firmly be said that the claimant will *not* be awarded specific performance. It may be that many of the arguments for restricting specific performance are no longer wholly convincing, and that the trend is towards expansion of the remedy.[36]

A. Contracts for the Sale of Land

A claimant seeking specific performance of a contract for the sale (or other disposition) of land must first satisfy the requirements of section 2 of the Law of Property (Miscellaneous Provisions) Act 1989. These requirements apply also to a claim for damages. Section 2 provides that a contract for the sale or other disposition of an interest in land can only be made in writing incorporating all the

---

[33] *GKN Distributors Ltd v. Tyne Tees Fabrication Ltd* [1985] 2 E.G.L.R. 181. (Vendor's claim against purchaser for declaration, forfeiture of deposit and damages dismissed).

[34] *Hutton v. Watling* [1948] Ch. 26 at 36, affirmed [1948] Ch. 398. On the effect on the defendant's insolvency, see *Freevale Ltd v. Metrostore (Holdings) Ltd* [1984] Ch. 199; [1984] Conv. 446 (D. Milman and S. Coneys); *Amec Properties Ltd v. Planning Research & Systems plc* [1992] 1 E.G.L.R. 70 (insolvency of defendant before completion is no bar to specific performance).

[35] See *Haywood v. Cope* (1858) 25 Beav. 140, *per* Romilly M.R. at 151; *Lamare v. Dixon* (1873) L.R. 6 H.L. 414.

[36] Treitel, *The Law of Contract* (10th ed.), p. 949. See generally (1984) 4 L. S. 102 (A. Burrows). See, however, *Co-operative Insurance Society Ltd v. Argyll Stores (Holdings) Ltd* [1998] A.C. 1; *post*, p. 728.

terms which the parties have agreed. The document must be signed by or on behalf of each party. Under the previous law the contract needed only to be *evidenced in* writing, and an oral contract could be enforced under the doctrine of part performance. The present rule leaves no scope for part performance, which can only cure *evidential* defects.[37] Estoppel could apply in situations previously covered by part performance, although specific performance would not necessarily be the remedy.[38]

Assuming section 2 is satisfied, specific performance is readily granted to enforce a contract to create or convey a legal estate in land (for example, to sell land[39] or to grant a lease) unless some special consideration arises to prevent it. It cannot however be said that the claimant is *entitled* to specific performance, as the order is always subject to the discretion of the court.

Each piece of land is unique, and it is accepted as a general rule that an award of damages is not adequate compensation for the purchaser or lessee.[40] If the purchaser does not acquire the land he will not have to pay the price, thus "the damages for loss of such a bargain would be negligible and, as in most cases of breach of contract for the sale of land at a market price by refusal to convey it, would constitute a wholly inadequate and unjust remedy for the breach. That is why the normal remedy is by a order for specific performance by the vendor of his primary obligation to convey, on the purchaser's performing or being willing to perform his own primary obligations under the contract."[41] The court, treating each party equally, will also give specific performance to the vendor or lessor,[42] although a monetary payment might be adequate compensation.

If a vendor fails to comply with the order, the purchaser may apply to the court for an order nominating some person to execute the conveyance in the vendor's name.[43]

---

[37] *cf. Singh v. Beggs* (1996) 71 P. & C.R. 120 at 122, where this point is not taken.

[38] See *Yaxley v. Gotts* [2000] Ch. 162. Remedies in estoppel cases are flexible, but specific performance could be granted; *Spiro v. Lintern* [1973] 1 W.L.R. 1002. See (1990) 10 L.S. 325 (L. Bentley and P. Coughlan).

[39] On specific performance of options and rights of pre-emption, see *Pritchard v. Briggs* [1980] Ch. 338; *Sudbrook Trading Estate Ltd v. Eggleton* [1983] 1 A.C. 444. See also *Berkley v. Poulett* (1976) 120 S.J. 836, *ante*, p. 328 (sub-purchaser).

[40] *cf.* Heydon, Gummow and Austin, *Cases and Materials on Equity and Trusts* (4th ed.), p. 946, preferring the explanation that "the process of looking for, negotiating for and completing the purchase of land is a lengthy and irritating one; ... so that it is better to get specific performance ... rather than get damages and use them to buy something similar." See also Law Com. No. 238 (1996), para. 9.3, n. 5.

[41] *Sudbrook Trading Estate Ltd v. Eggleton, supra*, at 478.

[42] *Cogent v. Gibson* (1864) 33 Beav. 557.

[43] Supreme Court Act 1981, s.39; Trustee Act 1925, ss.44(vi), 50; A.E.A. 1925, s.43(2). For other remedies, see *ante*, p. 719.

B. Contractual Licences

It was at one time thought that specific performance would not be granted of a contractual licence to occupy land, on the ground that the licence created no estate in the land.[44] This view has now been seen to be inconsistent with the court's power to grant an injunction to restrain the wrongful revocation of a contractual licence.[45] Thus in *Verrall v. Great Yarmouth Borough Council*[46] the Court of Appeal affirmed the grant of specific performance to enforce a contractual licence whereby the National Front was to occupy the defendant's premises for the purpose of its annual conference. The remedy of damages would be inadequate as the claimant could not find any other premises. Roskill L.J. held it to be the duty of the court "to protect, where it is appropriate to do so, any interest, whether it be an estate in land or a licence, by injunction or specific performance as the case may be."[47]

C. Contracts for the Sale of Personal Property

Chattels and stocks and shares do not usually possess such individual character as land. Most commercial contracts for the purchase of goods,[48] or for a loan of money,[49] or contracts for the purchase of government stock, will not be specifically performed.[50] But if stocks or shares cannot always be bought in the market, the court may order specific performance[51]; or where a chattel has especial value by reason of its individuality, beauty or rarity.[52] Indeed, in such situations, there is an ancient jurisdiction to order the specific recovery of such a chattel if wrongly detained.[53] Where specific performance of a contract to sell a house is granted, the remedy is also available in respect of a related contract to sell the chattels in it.[54]

---

[44] *Booker v. Palmer* [1942] 2 All E.R. 674 at 677, *per* Lord Greene M.R.

[45] *Winter Garden Theatre (London) Ltd v. Millennium Productions Ltd* [1948] A.C. 173.

[46] [1981] Q.B. 202; [1981] Conv. 212 (A. Briggs). See also *Tanner v. Tanner* [1975] 1 W.L.R. 1346 at 1350.

[47] [1981] Q.B. 202 at 220.

[48] *Dominion Coal Co. Ltd v. Dominion Iron and Steel Co. Ltd* [1909] A.C. 293; *Cohen v. Roche* [1927] 1 K.B. 169; *Société Des Industries Metallurgiques S.A. v. The Bronx Engineering Co. Ltd* [1975] 1 Lloyd's Rep. 465. See the examples given by Goff L.J. in *Price v. Strange* [1978] Ch. 337 at 359.

[49] *South African Territories Ltd v. Wallington* [1898] A.C. 309.

[50] *Cud (or Cuddee) v. Rutter* (1720) 1 P.Wms. 570 (South Sea Bubble Stock); *Mason v. Armitage* (1806) 13 Ves.Jr. 25. For other reasons against the grant of specific performance, see Treitel, *The Law of Contract* (10th ed.), pp. 950, 953.

[51] *Duncuft v. Albrecht* (1841) 12 Sim. 189; (1953) 51 Mich.L.R. 408 (A. Neef).

[52] *Falcke v. Gray* (1859) 4 Dr. 651; *Philips v. Lamdin* [1949] 2 K.B. 33.

[53] *Pusey v. Pusey* (1684) 1 Vern. 273 (an antique horn, supposedly given by King Canute); *Duke of Somerset v. Cookson* (1735) 3 P.Wms. 390 (an altar piece); *Fells v. Reed* (1796) 3 Ves.Jr. 70; (the tobacco box of a club).

[54] *Record v. Bell* [1991] 1 W.L.R. 853.

Further, the Sale of Goods Act 1979, s.52 (replacing earlier legislation) enables the court to order specific performance of a contract for the sale of specific or ascertained goods, either unconditionally, or upon such terms as to damages, payment of the price or otherwise as to the court may seem just. The power is discretionary, and it must still be shown that the remedy of damages is inadequate.[55] It was intended to broaden the scope of the remedy of specific performance in connection with the purchase of chattels, but less use has been made of it than might have been expected.[56] In *Cohen v. Roche*,[57] the claimant agreed to purchase from the defendants a set of eight Hepplewhite chairs. This was a contract for the sale of specific goods; but McCardie J., finding that the chairs were "ordinary articles of commerce and of no special value or interest," refused to order specific performance and awarded damages. In *Behnke v. Bede Shipping Co.*,[58] Wright J. made an order for specific performance of a contract for the sale of a ship, being satisfied that the ship was of peculiar and practically unique value to the claimant.

The boldest exercise of jurisdiction was in *Sky Petroleum Ltd v. V.I.P. Petroleum Ltd.*[59]

A contract had been entered into whereby the claimant company would buy all the petrol needed for its garages from the defendant company, which would supply the claimant with all its requirements. The defendant, alleging breach, purported to terminate the contract in November 1973, at a time when petrol supplies were limited, so that the claimant would have little prospect of finding an alternative source. An interlocutory injunction was granted to restrain the withholding of supplies.

Goulding J. acknowledged that it amounted to specific performance, the matter being one of substance, and not of form; but held that the court had jurisdiction to order specific performance of a contract to sell chattels, although they were not specific or ascertained, where the remedy of damages was inadequate. The usual rule that specific performance was not available to enforce contracts for the sale of chattels was well established and salutary; but it was based on the adequacy of damages, and was therefore not applicable

---

[55] *C.N. Marine Inc. v. Stena Line A/B., The Times*, June 12, 1982.

[56] [1969] J.B.L. 211; *Société Des Industries Metallurgiques S.A. v. The Bronx Engineering Co. Ltd, supra.*

[57] [1927] 1 K.B. 169.

[58] [1927] 1 K.B. 649 at 661; *cf. Hart v. Herwig* (1873) L.R. 8 Ch.App. 680.

[59] [1974] 1 W.L.R. 576. See also *Howard E. Perry & Co. Ltd v. British Railways Board* [1980] 1 W.L.R. 1375; (1980) 39 C.L.J. 269 (J. Thornely).

to the present case, where the company might be forced out of business if the remedy was not granted.

D. Contracts to Pay Money

Contracts to pay money are normally not specifically enforceable, because damages will usually be an adequate remedy. So, for example, specific performance of a contract of loan will not be awarded against the borrower, because the remedy of damages is adequate.[60] Exceptionally, however, specific performance may be obtainable in the following situations:

i. Where the contract is to pay money to a third party, so that any damages awarded would probably be nominal[61];

ii. Where the contract is for the payment of an annuity[62] or other periodical sums. This exception is based on two grounds: first that specific performance avoids the inconvenience of a series of actions for damages every time payment is not made; and, secondly, even if substantial damages were available, it has been suggested that the common law remedy would still be inadequate as the amount in the case of an annuity would be conjectural.[63]

iii. A contract with a company to take up and pay for debentures.[64]

iv. A contract of indemnity, if, on its true construction, the obligation is to relieve a debtor by preventing him from having to pay his debt. Instead of compelling the debtor first to pay the debt and perhaps to ruin himself in doing so, equity will order the indemnifier to pay the debt. It will be otherwise if the obligation is merely to repay the debtor a sum of money after he has paid it. Damages will then be an adequate remedy.[65]

v. As has been seen, in the case of a contract for the sale of land, the vendor will be granted specific performance of the purchaser's obligation to make a money payment. Although the remedy of damages may be adequate, specific performance is allowed because of the mutuality principle.

---

[60] See *Locabail International Finance Ltd v. Agroexport* [1986] 1 W.L.R. 657 (no mandatory injunction).

[61] *Beswick v. Beswick* [1968] A.C. 58; *post*, p. 752. The third party may now be able to enforce the contract under the Contracts (Rights of Third Parties) Act 1999.

[62] *Beswick v. Beswick, supra.*

[63] *Adderly v. Dixon* (1824) 1 Sim. & St. 607 at 611. But see *post*, p. 753.

[64] Companies Act 1985, s.195.

[65] *McIntosh v. Dalwood (No. 4)* (1930) 30 S.R.(N.S.W.) 415 at 418.

vi. A contract to pay a debt out of specific property segregated by the debtor for that purpose is specifically enforceable, and creates an equitable interest in the specific property, unless there is evidence of a contrary intention.[66]

E. Volunteers

Specific performance will not be awarded to a volunteer. Indeed, unless the contract is by deed, consideration is necessary for the validity of the contract itself. Parties to a deed of covenant may sue at law, even though there is no consideration, but they will not be able to obtain specific performance.[67] Problems commonly arise in this connection in relation to covenants to make family settlements.[68] Inadequacy of consideration is not a bar to specific performance, but may be relevant to the exercise of the court's discretion.[69]

The Contracts (Rights of Third Parties) Act 1999 now permits a third party in certain circumstances to enforce a term of a contract which is for his benefit.[70] Section 1(5) provides that "there shall be available to the third party any remedy that would have been available to him in an action for breach of contract if he had been a party to the contract (and the rules relating to damages, injunctions, specific performance and other relief shall apply accordingly)". This provision arguably enables the third party to obtain specific performance in a case where the remedy of damages would be inadequate. However, the volunteer principle, which is one of the "rules relating to . . . specific performance", may mean that the third party should be confined to damages, as in the case of a volunteer who is a party to a covenant.[71]

It is no objection, provided that the party seeking specific performance is not a volunteer, that the order will have the direct consequence of benefiting a volunteer[72]; nor, in the case of the due exercise of an option to purchase land, that the option was granted for a token payment or for no payment at all.[73]

---

[66] *Swiss Bank Corporation v. Lloyds Bank Ltd* [1982] A.C. 584 at 613 (*per* Lord Wilberforce); *Napier and Ettrick (Lord) v. Hunter* [1993] A.C. 713.

[67] See *Cannon v. Hartley* [1949] Ch. 213.

[68] *ante*, p. 130.

[69] Spry, *Equitable Remedies*, p. 59, See *post*, p. 743.

[70] The Act is not retrospective. For transitional provisions, see s.10.

[71] *Cannon v. Hartley, supra.*

[72] See *Beswick v. Beswick* [1968] A.C. 58, *post*, p. 752.

[73] *Mountford v. Scott* [1975] Ch. 258, affirming on different grounds the decision of Brightman J., *ibid.*; (1975) 39 Conv.(N.S.) 270 (F. Crane); *Midland Bank Trust Co. Ltd v. Green* [1980] Ch. 590 C.A.; [1979] Conv. 441 (F. Crane).

F. Contracts Requiring Supervision

i. The Principle. It is settled law that a court will not grant specific performance where the order would require constant supervision by the court.[74] The reason is that supervision would be impracticable. Equity does nothing in vain; and will not issue orders which it cannot be certain to enforce. Of course, the threat of imprisonment would be effective in many cases; but imprisonment of the defendant for contempt, if he proves recalcitrant, is a "heavy-handed" mechanism which will not get the duty performed.[75]

Orders for the specific performance of contracts to create or convey a legal estate in land do not meet with this difficulty. All that the defendant needs to do to perform such a contract is to execute the document; and, as has been seen, if he refuses, he may be threatened with imprisonment for contempt; and if he still refuses, the court may nominate any person to effect the conveyance.[76]

One important question is whether there is a sufficient definition of what has to be done in order to comply with the order of the court.[77]

In *Posner v. Scott-Lewis*[78] a lease contained a landlord's covenant to employ a resident porter, whose duties were to clean the common parts, to look after the heating and to carry rubbish to the dustbins. Specific performance of this covenant was granted, to procure the appointment of a porter. The earlier decision to the contrary in *Ryan v. Mutual Tontine Westminster Chambers Association*,[79] was difficult to distinguish, but the authority of that case had been weakened by later decisions.[80] The relevant questions were: (a) was there a sufficient definition of what had to be done? (b) would an unacceptable degree of superintendence be involved? (c) what would be the respective hardship to the parties if the order was made or refused? The answer to these questions supported a grant of specific performance; the remedy of damages was clearly inadequate.

---

[74] *Ryan v. Mutual Tontine Westminster Chambers Association* [1893] 1 Ch. 116; *Blackett v. Bates* (1865) L.R. 1 Ch. App. 117 (maintenance of railway); *Joseph v. National Magazine Co.* [1959] Ch. 14; *Re C (A Minor)* [1991] 2 F.L.R. 168 (schooling).

[75] *Co-operative Insurance Society Ltd v. Argyll Stores (Holdings) Ltd* [1998] A.C. 1.

[76] *ante*, p. 722.

[77] *Tito v. Waddell (No. 2)* [1977] Ch. 106 at 322, *per* Megarry V-C; (1977) 41 Conv.(N.S.) 432 at 436 (F. Crane).

[78] [1987] Ch. 25; (1987) 46 C.L.J. 21 (G. Jones).

[79] [1893] 1 Ch. 116.

[80] *Giles (C.H.) & Co. Ltd v. Morris* [1972] 1 W.L.R. 307 at 318; *Shiloh Spinners Ltd v. Harding* [1973] A.C. 691 at 724; *Tito v. Waddell (No. 2)* [1977] Ch. 106 at 321. The House of Lords in *Co-operative Insurance Society Ltd v. Argyll Stores (Holdings) Ltd* [1998] A.C. 1, however, considered that the dicta in *Shiloh Spinners* had been too widely interpreted.

Other modern illustrations include *Beswick v. Beswick*[81] where specific performance was ordered of a contract to make a regular payment to the claimant for life. In *Sky Petroleum Ltd v. V.I.P. Petroleum Ltd*[82] an interlocutory injunction, which was regarded as tantamount to specific performance, was granted to enforce the defendant's obligation to supply petrol regularly to the claimant. In the related area of mandatory injunctions the requirement of supervision has not been regarded as an unsurmountable obstacle.[83] Specific performance is more likely to be granted, in spite of supervision difficulties, against a defendant who has had some or all of the benefit to which he was entitled under the contract.[84]

The principle was recently reviewed by the House of Lords in *Co-operative Insurance Society Ltd v. Argyll Stores (Holdings) Ltd.*[85] The question was whether specific performance should be granted of a covenant in a lease of a supermarket (which was the focal point of a shopping centre) to keep open during the usual hours of business. The supermarket had been trading at a loss and the lease had 19 years to run. The House of Lords, reversing the Court of Appeal, rejected the landlord's claim for specific performance, even though any damages would be difficult to quantify. Although the breach was deliberate, specific performance would be oppressive to the tenant, whose loss in complying might be far greater than the loss to the landlord should the covenant be broken. As in the analogous sphere of mandatory injunctions, it was not in the public interest to require the carrying on of a business at a loss if there was some other plausible means of compensation. In any event, the covenant was not sufficiently certain for an order of specific performance. The supervision principle remained important, although there were fewer objections where an order simply required the defendant to achieve a specified result[86] (as in the repairs cases, discussed below) than where an order was sought to require the defendant to carry on an activity. The decision has been broadly welcomed in view of the undoubted difficulties of supervision,[87] but another view is that the House of Lords failed to liberalise the principles of specific performance and to grant an effective remedy to a landlord who was likely to be "shortchanged" by any award of damages.[88]

---

[81] [1968] A.C. 58; *post.*
[82] [1974] 1 W.L.R. 576.
[83] *Redland Bricks Ltd v. Morris* [1970] A.C. 652; *Gravesham Borough Council v. British Railways Board* [1978] Ch. 379, *post*, p. 772.
[84] *Tito v. Waddell (No. 2), supra* at 322.
[85] [1998] A.C. 1.
[86] This was the context of Lord Wilberforce's rejection of supervision difficulties in *Shiloh Spinners Ltd v. Harding* [1973] A.C. 691 at 724, which had been too widely interpreted in other cases.
[87] See (1997) 56 C.L.J. 488 (G. Jones); (1998) 61 M.L.R. 421 (A. Phang); [1998] Conv. 396 (P. Luxton).
[88] [1998] Conv. 23 (A. Tettenborn).

ii. The Construction Cases. The court does not, as a rule, order specific performance of a contract to build or repair[89]; but there are certain exceptional cases. "The first [requirement] is that the building work, of which he seeks to enforce the performance, is defined by the contract; that is to say, that the particulars of the work are so far definitely ascertained that the court can sufficiently see what is the exact nature of the work of which it is asked to order the performance. The second is that the claimant has a substantial interest in having the contract performed, which is of such a nature that he cannot adequately be compensated for breach of the contract by damages. The third is that the defendant has by the contract obtained possession of land on which the work is contracted to be done."[90]

In *Wolverhampton Corporation v. Emmons*[91] a plot of land had been sold by an urban sanitary authority, in pursuance of a scheme of street improvement, to the defendant, who agreed to erect buildings thereon, and went into possession. A later agreement provided for the erection of the buildings in accordance with detailed plans. The Court of Appeal ordered specific performance.

This exception is said to be based on a "balance of convenience." Historically it originates in a series of cases relating to the early days of railways.[92] Where a railway was built through a farmer's land and the railway company undertook to provide a bridge or tunnel to connect the separated parts of the farmer's land, it would have been most unjust to leave the farmer to a remedy in damages. These specialised cases have been given more general application, and the formulation in *Wolverhampton Corporation v. Emmons*[93] was further extended in *Carpenters Estates v. Davies*,[94] where Farwell J. held that it was sufficient that the defendant was in possession of the land, whether he came in by the contract or not. After all, the defendant's possession is the material factor; for the claimant cannot then enter to perform the construction or repair work himself.

iii. Enforcement of Leasehold Covenants. The "construction contracts" exception was extended to cover a landlord's repairing

---

[89] *Wheatley v. Westminster Brymbo Coal Co.* (1869), L.R. 9 Eq. 538; *Haywood v. Brunswick Building Society* (1881) 8 Q.B.D. 403.
[90] *Wolverhampton Corporation v. Emmons* [1901] 1 K.B. 515 at 525, *per* Romer L.J.; *Hounslow L.B.C. v. Twickenham Developments Ltd* [1971] Ch. 233.
[91] [1901] 1 K.B. 515. See also *Price v. Strange* [1978] Ch. 337 at 359.
[92] *Ryan v. Mutual Tontine Westminster Chambers Association* [1893] 1 Ch. 116 at 128.
[93] [1901] 1 K.B. 515.
[94] [1940] Ch. 160.

covenant in *Jeune v. Queens Cross Properties Ltd*,[95] where a balcony which was not part of the demised premises fell into disrepair. The three conditions laid down in *Wolverhampton Corporation v. Emmons*[96] were satisfied, as the landlord was in possession of the balcony, and the work involved was specific. There was a clear breach, and no doubt as to what was required to be done to remedy it. A mandatory order was much more convenient than an award of damages, leaving it to the tenant to do the work. The decision was extended by statute, now Landlord and Tenant Act 1985, s.17, which provides that the court may order specific performance of a landlord's repairing covenant relating to any part of the premises in which the tenant's dwelling is comprised, notwithstanding any equitable rule restricting this remedy.

It has recently been established that, contrary to the previous understanding, specific performance of a tenant's repair covenant may be granted in rare cases where there is no other adequate remedy. *Rainbow Estates Ltd v. Tokenhold Ltd*[97] was such a rare case, as the property (a listed building) was in serious disrepair and deteriorating but the lease contained no right of forfeiture nor any right for the landlord to have access to do the repairs at the tenant's expense. The schedule of works was sufficiently certain to be enforceable, and objections based on mutuality[98] or difficulties of supervision were of little force. The order simply required the tenant to achieve a result rather than carry on an activity.[99]

G. Contracts for Personal Services

It is well established that contracts which are personal in nature or which involve the performance of personal services will not be specifically enforced.[1] In this respect, it is necessary to distinguish contracts of employment from other contracts for personal services. The former are governed by a firm prohibition against specific enforcement by Trade Union and Labour Relations (Consolidation) Act 1992, s.236, which provides that "no court shall . . . by way of

---

[95] [1974] Ch. 97; *Francis v. Cowcliff Ltd* (1977) 33 P. & C.R. 368; *Gordon v. Selico Ltd* [1985] 2 E.G.L.R. 79; *Hammond v. Allen* [1994] 1 All E.R. 307. If the matter is urgent, a mandatory interlocutory injunction may be granted; *Parker v. Camden London Borough Council* [1986] Ch. 162 (boiler strike threatened tenants' health).

[96] [1901] 1 K.B. 515.

[97] [1999] Ch. 64; [1998] Conv. 495 (M. Pawlowski and J. Brown); (1999) 58 C.L.J. 283 (S. Bridge).

[98] *post*, p. 736.

[99] See *Co-operative Insurance Society Ltd v. Argyll Stores (Holdings) Ltd* [1998] A.C. 1; *ante*, p. 728.

[1] Fry, *Specific Performance*, pp. 50–51; *Lumley v. Wagner* (1852) 1 De G.M. & G. 604, *post*, p. 813; *Thomas Marshall (Exports) Ltd v. Guinle* [1979] Ch. 227; *Provident Financial Group plc. v. Haywood* [1989] 3 All E.R. 298 at 302. See (1984) 4 L. S. 102 at 112–114 (A. Burrows).

an order for specific performance . . . compel an employee to do any work or to attend at any place for the doing of any work." A contract of employment is defined in section 295(1).[2] Not every contract for personal services constitutes a contract of employment; for it may be a contract between an employer and an independent contractor.

In cases of contracts not covered by the Act, or where enforcement is sought against an employer,[3] the equitable principle applies. The reasons traditionally given for the rule are first, that such contracts would require constant supervision, and would in practice be impossible to enforce; and secondly, that it is contrary to public policy to compel one person to submit to the orders of another. "The courts," said Fry L.J., "are bound to be jealous, lest they should turn contracts of service into contracts of slavery."[4] Nor, as we will see, can the rule be avoided by seeking an injunction instead of specific performance, where the injunction would in effect compel performance.[5] Megarry J. hoped that the court might look again at this "so-called rule." It was not based on these difficulties alone; but was rather a question of human nature. "If a singer contracts to sing, there could no doubt be proceedings for committal if, ordered to sing, the singer remained obstinately dumb. But if instead the singer sang flat, or sharp, or too fast, or too slowly, or too loudly, to too quietly, or resorted to a dozen of the manifestations of temperament traditionally associated with some singers, the threat of committal would reveal itself as a most unsatisfactory weapon, for who could say whether the imperfections of performance were natural or self induced? To make an order with such possibilities of evasion would be vain, and so the order will not be made . . . the matter is one of balance and advantage and disadvantage in relation to the particular obligations in question, and the fact that the balance will usually lie on one side does not turn this probability into a rule."[6]

In *Giles (C.H.) & Co. Ltd v. Morris*,[7] a distinction was drawn between the performance of a contract of service and the execution of such a contract which provided for the claimant to be appointed managing director of a company for a period of five years. As we

---

[2] "Contract of employment" means "a contract of service or of apprenticeship."

[3] If an employee is unfairly dismissed the Employment Rights Act 1996, ss.114, 115 empower an industrial tribunal to order reinstatement or re-engagement. But if the order is not complied with the sanction is an award of compensation; s.117.

[4] *De Francesco v. Barnum* (1890) 45 Ch.D. 430; *post*, p. 813.

[5] *post*, p. 813.

[6] [1972] 1 W.L.R. 307 at 318. This passage was approved by Goff L.J. in *Price v. Strange* [1978] Ch. 337 at 359; *cf.* Buckley L.J., *ibid.* at 369. But the House of Lords in *Scandinavian Trading Tanker Co. A/B v. Flota Petrolera Ecuatoriana* [1983] 2 A.C. 694, concerning a time charter, took the view that there was no jurisdiction to grant specific performance of a service contract.

[7] [1972] 1 W.L.R. 307.

have seen, this approach was also adopted in *Posner v. Scott-Lewis*,[8] where specific performance was granted of a covenant in a lease to appoint a resident porter. Nor should it be assumed that as soon as any element of personal service or continuous services can be discerned in a contract, the court will always refuse an order. In *Beswick v. Beswick*,[9] Lord Upjohn said that a small element of personal services in a contract did not warrant the refusal of specific performance on the ground of want of mutuality.

In *Hill v. C.A. Parsons & Co. Ltd*[10] the claimant was a senior engineer in the employment of the defendant. In May 1970 a trade union successfully introduced a closed shop, under which it became a term of employment that all the defendant's employees were to be members of the union. The claimant refused, and received a month's notice of dismissal. He obtained an interlocutory injunction restraining the termination. The circumstances were special, in that the notice was short; a reasonable notice would probably have given him protection under the Industrial Relations Act 1971; and the employee and employer retained their mutual confidence.

Lord Denning M.R. said[11]: "It may be said that, by granting an injunction in such a case, the court is indirectly enforcing specifically a contract for personal services. So be it. Lord St. Leonards L.C. did something like it in *Lumley v. Wagner*.[12] And I see no reason why we should not do it here." But Stamp L.J., dissenting, felt that the rule against specific performance of service contracts, while not without exceptions, was deeply embedded in the law. The rule, he said, was a salutary one, which benefited the employer and employee equally.[13]

H. Contracts for the Creation of Transient or Terminable Interests

As equity does not act in vain, specific performance will not be granted of an agreement for a lease which has already expired by the

---

[8] [1987] Ch. 25; (1987) 46 C.L.J. 21 (G. Jones); *ante*, p. 727.

[9] [1968] A.C. 58 at 97.

[10] [1972] Ch. 305; *cf. Chappell v. Times Newspaper Ltd* [1975] 1 W.L.R. 482, where the employer "had every reason to suspect the plaintiff's loyalty"; *Wishart v. National Association of Citizens Advice Bureaux Ltd* [1990] I.C.R. 794. It seems that injunctions of the kind granted in *Hill v. Parsons* are no longer rare; see *Powell v. London Borough of Brent* [1987] I.R.L.R. 466, *Hughes v. London Borough of Southwark* [1988] I.R.L.R. 55, *post*, p. 816.

[11] *ibid.* at 315.

[12] (1852) 1 De G.M. & G. 604; *post*, p. 813.

[13] [1972] Ch. 305 at 324.

date of the hearing,[14] nor of an agreement for a tenancy at will or a partnership at will.[15]

An agreement for a tenancy from year to year is specifically enforceable,[16] but in *Lavery v. Pursell*[17] specific performance of an agreement for a lease for one year was refused, one ground being that, although rights should not be prejudiced by delays in litigation, it was normally impossible to get the action heard and the order made within the year.

But the nineteenth century authorities on transient interests must now be treated with caution.

In *Verrall v. Great Yarmouth Borough Council*[18] the defendant council had granted a contractual licence to the National Front to occupy its premises for two days (on a date which had not yet occurred) for an annual conference. The defendant wrongfully repudiated the contract, but sought to avoid specific performance, partly on the ground that the licence was a transient interest. This argument was rejected by the Court of Appeal. It was held that there was no reason why the court could not order specific performance of a contractual licence of short duration. Authorities to the contrary were inconsistent with the decision of the House of Lords in *Winter Garden Theatre (London) Ltd v. Millennium Productions Ltd*,[19] whereby an injunction could be granted to restrain the wrongful revocation of the licence. "In my judgment the old view, such as it was, that courts of equity would not protect a so-called transient interest can no longer be supported, at any rate to its full extent."[20]

Thus while specific performance remains inappropriate in respect of an interest which has already expired or which is revocable at the will of the defendant, the mere fact that the interest is of short

---

[14] *Turner v. Clowes* (1869) 20 L.T. 214. But the doctrine of *Walsh v. Lonsdale* (1882) 21 Ch.D. 9, *ante*, p. 15, will govern the rights and obligations of the parties if specific performance of a contract for a lease would have been available during its currency, even though it has terminated by the date of the hearing: *Industrial Properties (Barton Hill) Ltd v. Associated Electrical Industries Ltd* [1977] Q.B. 580; *cf.* (1977) 40 M.L.R. 718 at 720 (P. Jackson). See also *Tottenham Hotspur Football and Athletic Co. v. Princegrove Publishers* [1974] 1 W.L.R. 113; (1974) 90 L.Q.R. 149 (M. Albery).

[15] *Hercy v. Birch* (1804) 9 Ves. 357. Even if not merely at will, a partnership agreement involves the difficulty of supervision; *ante*, p. 727.

[16] *Manchester Brewery Co. Ltd v. Coombs* [1901] 2 Ch. 608.

[17] (1888) 39 Ch.D. 508 at 519. See also *Gilbey v. Cossey* [1911–13] All E.R. 644 at 645.

[18] [1981] Q.B. 202, *ante*, p. 723.

[19] [1948] A.C. 173.

[20] [1981] Q.B. 202 at 220, *per* Roskill L.J. See also the comments of Lord Denning M.R. at 215.

duration is no longer a bar to specific performance, which may be granted at the discretion of the court in an appropriate case.

I. Contracts to Leave Property by Will[21]

The remedy for breach of such a contract is normally damages, for any other result would amount to interference with testamentary freedom.[22] But specific performance might be orderd, as was indicated *obiter* by the Court of Appeal in *Synge v. Synge*,[23] where the contract is in consideration of marriage, and the marriage takes place on the faith of it. The court has power to order a conveyance of a defined piece of real property after the death of the contracting party, against those who have acquired it as volunteers. While the court could not order the defendant to make a will in any particular terms,[24] it could order the executor or devisee to convey to the claimant.

In *Schaefer v. Schuhmann*[25] Lord Cross treated it as established that where there is a contract to leave specific property by will, the claimant "can obtain a declaration of his right to have it left to him by will and an injunction to restrain the testator from disposing of it in breach of contract: *Synge v. Synge*.[26] No doubt if the property is land he could also register the contract or a caution against the title."[27] If the testator retains the property until his death, but dies insolvent, the promisee can only rank as a creditor for value in competition with other such creditors.[28]

Finally, it seems that specific performance will not be granted of a contract by the donee of a testamentary power of appointment to exercise the power in favour of the claimant.[29]

J. Contracts to Transfer Goodwill

A contract to sell the goodwill of a business alone is not specifically enforceable, because the subject-matter of the contract is too

---

[21] See (1971) 87 L.Q.R. 358 (W. Lee); A.R. Mellows, *The Law of Succession* (5th ed.); Chap. 3.

[22] *ante*, p. 321.

[23] [1894] 1 Q.B. 466. See also *Wakeham v. Mackenzie* [1968] 1 W.L.R. 1175.

[24] *Re Dale (deceased)* [1994] Ch. 31 (mutual wills); *ante*, p. 321.

[25] [1972] A.C. 572 (P.C.): see also Inheritance (Provision for Family and Dependants) Act 1975, s.11; Law Com. No. 61 (1974), paras. 222–242.

[26] [1894] 1 Q.B. 466.

[27] [1972] A.C. 572 at 586. If the contract relates to land, it must be writing, in order to satisfy s.2 of the Law of Property (Miscellaneous Provisions) Act 1989; *Taylor v. Dickens* [1998] 1 F.L.R. 806.

[28] [1972] A.C. 572. See also *Beyfus v. Lawley* [1903] A.C. 411.

[29] *Re Parkin* [1892] 3 Ch. 510. The proper remedy is damages. See also *Robinson v. Ommanney* (1883) 23 Ch.D. 285.

uncertain.[30] But specific performance will be granted of a contract to transfer the goodwill together with the premises or other assets of a business.[31]

K. Contracts to Refer to Arbitration

Such a contract is not specifically enforceable.[32] But if the claimant sues on a contract which includes an arbitration provision, the defendant may ask for a stay of proceedings under Arbitration Act 1996, s.9 so that the claimant must proceed with the arbitration or be left with no remedy.[33] The court will, however enforce the arbitrator's award.[34]

L. No Specific Performance of Part of a Contract[35]

A court will not usually order specific performance of any part of a contract unless it can order performance of the whole. In *Ogden v. Fossick*,[36] an agreement between the parties provided that the defendant would grant to the claimant a lease of a coal wharf, and that the defendant should be appointed manager of the wharf. In an action for specific performance of the agreement to grant the lease, specific performance was denied on the ground that the part of the agreement which the court could enforce was inseparably connected with the contract of employment which it would not.

But the rule is not absolute.[37] It may be possible to construe a contract which contains several parts as being in effect several separate and distinct contracts, so that the enforcement of one part is independent of the others.[38] This question often arises where several lots of land are sold and the question is whether there is one sale of several lots,[39] or several sales of individual lots.[40]

---

[30] *Darbey v. Whitaker* (1857) 4 Drew. 134.

[31] *ibid.* at p. 140. And see *Beswick v. Beswick* [1968] A.C. 58; *post*, p. 753.

[32] *Doleman & Sons v. Ossett Corporation* [1912] 3 K.B. 257 at 268.

[33] See also s.86. As to the court's jurisdiction to intervene by way of injunction, see *post*, p. 000.

[34] *Wood v. Griffith* (1818) 1 Swans. 43. See also *Sudbrook Trading Estate Ltd v. Eggleton* [1983] 1 A.C. 444, as to the possibility of specific performance of a contract to appoint a valuer or arbitrator to fix the price in an option to renew a lease.

[35] Fry, *op. cit.*, Chap. 16. Compare the doctrine of partial performance; *Thames Guaranty Ltd v. Campbell* [1985] Q.B. 210.

[36] (1862) 4 De G.F. & J. 426.

[37] *Beswick v. Beswick* [1968] A.C. 58; *C.H. Giles & Co. Ltd v. Morris* [1972] 1 W.L.R. 307 at 317–318; *Astro Exito Navegacion S.A. v. Southland Enterprise Co. Ltd (No. 2)* [1983] 2 A.C. 787.

[38] *Wilkinson v. Clements* (1872) L.R. 8 Ch. App. 96, *post*, p. 737. But specific performance of the one contract will not be granted if the claimant is in breach of his obligations in the other contract which are material to the transaction as a whole; *National & Provincial Building Society v. British Waterways Board* [1992] E.G.C.S. 149.

[39] *Roffey v. Shallcross* (1819) 4 Madd. 227.

[40] *Lewin v. Guest* (1826) 1 Russ. 325.

4. MUTUALITY

A. Refusal of Specific Performance for Lack of Mutuality[41]

It has been seen that where specific performance may be ordered in favour of a purchaser or lessee, the remedy will be available also in favour of the vendor or lessor.[42] Such a person can compel the other party to take the property even though in many cases an award of damages would be adequate compensation for his loss. He can obtain specific performance under a principle of mutuality.

A similar principle applies to deny specific performance, on grounds of lack of mutuality, where the situation is one in which that remedy could not be available to the other party.[43] "It is not disputed," said Leach M.R., "that it is a general principle of courts of equity to interpose only where the remedy is mutual."[44] Thus one party is not compelled specifically to perform his obligation if he would himself be left with only a remedy in damages. In *Flight v. Bolland*,[45] the claimant failed to obtain specific performance because, as he was below the age of majority, it could not be obtained against him.[46] Nor can a person whose own obligation is to perform personal services obtain specific performance, as it could not be obtained against him.[47]

There is, however, a statutory exception to the mutuality principle in the Landlord and Tenant Act 1985, s.17, which allows a court to order specific performance of a landlord's repairing covenant, notwithstanding any equitable rule restricting this remedy, "whether based on mutuality or otherwise."[48] Now that it has been held that specific performance may be ordered against a tenant (although in rare cases), mutuality has been restored.[49] It might be added that the claimant may be able to overcome the absence of mutuality by waiving the benefit of a term,[50] or submitting to perform an obligation, which could not be specifically enforced against him.[51]

Finally, the mutuality principle goes only to discretion, not to jurisdiction. Thus the absence of mutuality does not deprive the

---

[41] See Spry, *Equitable Remedies*, pp. 7–12, 89–101.

[42] *ante*, p. 722.

[43] This defence based on lack of mutuality may be waived by the conduct of the defendant: *Price v. Strange* [1978] Ch. 337.

[44] (1828) 4 Russ. 298 at 301.

[45] *ibid.*

[46] *Lumley v. Ravenscroft* [1895] 1 Q.B. 683.

[47] *Pickering v. Bishop of Ely* (1843) 2 Y. & C. Ch. 249; *Ogden v. Fossick* (1862) 4 De G.F. & J. 426; *ante*, p. 735.

[48] *ante*, p. 730.

[49] *Rainbow Estates Ltd v. Tokenhold Ltd* [1999] Ch. 64.

[50] *Heron Garage Properties Ltd v. Moss* [1974] 1 W.L.R. 148.

[51] *Scott v. Bradley* [1971] Ch. 850; (1951) 67 L.Q.R. 300 (R.E.M.)

court of jurisdiction to award damages in lieu of specific performance under Lord Cairns' Act 1858.[52]

B. The Time at which the Remedy must be Mutual

Must the requirement of mutuality be satisfied at the date of the
contract, or will it suffice that the remedy has become mutually
available by some later date, such as the date of the hearing? This
question has been the source of much academic disagreement. Fry's
proposition was that, subject to certain exceptions, the contract must
be mutual when entered into.[53] Ames, on the other hand, considered
that "Equity will not compel specific performance by a defendant if,
after performance, the common law remedy of damages would be
his sole security for the performance of the [claimant's] side of the
contract."[54]

The courts, it must be said, had never applied a principle as rigid
as that propounded by Fry. It was laid down in *Hoggart v. Scott*[55]
that a vendor may obtain specific performance if he can show a good
title at the time of the hearing, even though he had none when the
contract was made. We saw that there could be no specific performance of a contract where the obligation of one party was the performance of services. It was held, however, in *Wilkinson v.
Clements*[56] that if the claimant has already performed the services,
he may enforce the contract.

The formulation of Ames was adopted by the Court of Appeal in
preference to Fry's rule.

In *Price v. Strange*[57] D contracted to grant an underlease of a
flat to P, and the agreement contained an undertaking by P to
execute internal and external repairs. P did the internal repairs,
and was ready and willing to complete the external; but D repudiated the contract, and did the external repairs herself. P sued
for specific performance of the contract to grant the underlease.
D claimed that P was not entitled to specific performance

---

[52] *Price v. Strange* [1978] Ch. 337. For Lord Cairns' Act, see *post*, p. 747.
[53] Fry, *Specific Performance*, p. 219.
[54] Ames, *Lectures in Legal History*, p. 370.
[55] (1830) 1 Russ. & M. 293; *Joseph v. National Magazine Co. Ltd* [1959] Ch. 14 (a case of
personal property); *Price v. Strange* [1978] Ch. 337 at 355 and 364. See (1977) 41
Conv.(N.S.) 18 (C. Emery).
[56] (1872) L.R. 8 Ch.App. 96. If the claimant has not performed all the obligations, justice can
be done by granting specific performance on terms of a monetary readjustment. See also
Wakeham v. Mackenzie [1968] 1 W.L.R. 1175.
[57] [1978] Ch. 337; (1978) 128 N.L.J. 569 (F. Glover); applied in *Sutton v. Sutton* [1984] Ch.
184 (wife agreed to consent to divorce and not to seek maintenance in return for a transfer
of the home. Husband could not have enforced her promises, but once she had performed
an appreciable part by giving formal consent to the petition, he could not rely on absence
of mutuality).

because, relying on Fry's rule, there was no mutuality at the date of the contract: P's repair obligations were not specifically enforceable. It was held that Fry's rule was wrong; the time for considering mutuality was the date of the judgment. If by that time those obligations which were not specifically enforceable had been performed, P could obtain specific performance.

The principle is that the court will not compel a defendant to perform his obligations specifically if it cannot at the same time ensure that any unperformed obligations of the claimant will be specifically performed, unless, perhaps, damages would be an adequate remedy to the defendant for any default on the claimant's part.[58] Specific performance was, accordingly, granted on terms that P should pay compensation to D for the cost of the repairs done by D.

5. DEFENCES TO SPECIFIC PERFORMANCE[59]

The situations discussed below are those in which the discretion of the court is unlikely to be exercised in favour of specific performance, although the contract is of a type to which the remedy is appropriate. Most of the illustrations relate to land, for, as we have seen, few contracts outside this area are specifically enforceable. It will be noted that, in some of the circumstances discussed below, such as hardship or delay, the contract is unaffected, and the defendant remains liable in damages; the claimant is merely denied specific performance. In others, as in some cases of mistake and misrepresentation, the contract may be rescinded in equity, which is of course a defence to specific performance, and which may or may not affect the parties' rights at law.[60] In cases of substantial misdescription or lack of good title, the vendor may be in breach; not only is the vendor unable in such circumstances to obtain specific performance; he may be liable in damages to the purchaser.

A. Mistake and Misrepresentation

There are situations in which equity, although refusing to rescind a contract or cancel a deed for mistake or misrepresentation, will not give the other party positive equitable help in enforcing it. The

---

[58] [1978] Ch. 337 at 367–378.
[59] See also *BICC v. Burndy Corp.* [1985] Ch. 232; (1985) 101 L.Q.R. 145; (1985) 44 C.L.J. 204 (C. Harpum); All E.R.Rev. 1985, at 36 (N. Palmer); discussing set-off as a defence to specific performance.
[60] *ante*, p. 33.

claimant will be left to his remedy in damages.[61] The court is not bound to order specific performance in every case in which it will not set aside the contract, nor to set aside every contract that it will not specifically enforce.[62]

A defendant cannot usually resist specific performance by alleging merely his own fault and mistake,[63] nor on the ground that he was mistaken as to the legal effect of the agreement,[64] although "unilateral mistake may, in some circumstances, afford an answer to a claim for specific performance."[65] Generally, equity will hold the defendant to enforcement of his bargain unless it can be shown that this would involve real hardship amounting to injustice.[66]

> In *Webster v. Cecil*[67] A, by letter, offered to sell some property to B. He intended to offer it at £2,250 but by mistake wrote £1,250. B agreed to buy at £1,250. A immediately gave notice of the error and was not compelled to carry out the sale.

> In *Tamplin v. James*[68] an inn was offered for sale, and was correctly described with reference to plans. At the rear of the inn was a piece of land, not belonging to the vendors, and so not included in the sale, which had commonly been occupied with the inn. The defendant knew the premises, but did not consult the plans, and he agreed to purchase in the belief that he was buying both the inn and the land at the rear. Specific performance was ordered against him.

> A case that goes further, and perhaps too far, is *Malins v. Freeman*,[69] where an estate was purchased at an auction and the defendant bid under a mistake as to the lot put up for sale. Specific performance was refused although the mistake was due entirely to the defendant's fault and not in any way caused by the

---

[61] See *per* Lord Eldon in *Mortlock v. Buller* (1804) 10 Ves.Jr. 292.

[62] *e.g. Wood v. Scarth* (1855) 2 K. & J. 33 (in equity); 1 F. & F. 293 (at law).

[63] *Duke of Beaufort v. Neeld* (1845) 12 Cl. & F. 248 at 286.

[64] *Powell v. Smith* (1872) L.R. 14 Eq. 85; *Hart v. Hart* (1881) 18 Ch.D. 670.

[65] *per* Brightman J. in *Mountford v. Scott* [1975] Ch. 258 at 261; *Malins v. Freeman* (1837) 2 Keen 25; *Riverlate Properties Ltd v. Paul* [1975] Ch. 133, *per* Russell L.J. at 140; *Watkin v. Watson-Smith, The Times*, July 3, 1986.

[66] *Van Praagh v. Everidge* [1902] 2 Ch. 266; reversed on another ground [1903] 1 Ch. 434. The type of mistake that renders a contract liable to be set aside in equity though not at law would also be a defence to specific performance. See *Solle v. Butcher* [1950] 1 K.B. 671; *Grist v. Bailey* [1967] Ch. 532; *post*, p. 846; *Laurence v. Lexcourt Holdings* [1978] 1 W.L.R. 1128; [1978] Conv. 380 (F. Crane); *post*, p. 850.

[67] (1861) 30 Beav. 62; *Day v. Wells* (1861) 30 Beav. 220; *cf. Hartog v. Colin and Shields* [1939] 3 All E.R. 566. See also *Watkin v. Watson-Smith, The Times*, July 13, 1986, *post*, p. 863 (no specific performance where elderly vendor offered bungalow for sale at £2,950 by mistake, intending £29,500. There was no contract).

[68] (1880) 15 Ch.D. 215; *cf. Denny v. Hancock* (1870) L.R. 6 Ch.App. 1, where specific performance was refused because the mistake was induced unintentionally by the claimant.

[69] (1837) 2 Keen 25.

Specific Performance

vendor; and the defendant waited until the auction was over before declaring the mistake.

Where the mistake is in the written record of the contract, the claimant may obtain rectification and specific performance in the same action.[70]

B. Conduct of the Claimant

The claimant must come to equity with clean hands.[71] Before specific performance can be orderd in his favour, he must show that he has performed all his own obligations under the contract,[72] or has tendered performance, or is ready and willing to perform them.[73] Thus a person holding under an agreement for a lease is not entitled to specific performance of the lease if he is himself in breach of one of its covenants.[74] Nor could a purchaser obtain specific performance if he had taken advantage of the illiteracy of a defendant who was not separately advised.[75] The conduct in question must be connected to the contract of which specific performance is sought.[76]

If both parties have "unclean hands," there is no question of balancing the misconduct of the one against that of the other. The "clean hands" defence is concerned with the conduct of the claimant alone, although all the circumstances, including the conduct of the defendant, are relevant to the exercise of the discretion.[77]

Where the contract, although not void, is affected by some element of illegality, it has been proposed by the Law Commission that legislation should be enacted to give the courts a discretion as to enforcement. Matters relevant to the exercise of the discretion will include the conduct and knowledge of the claimant. So far as equitable remedies such as specific performance (and injunctions) are

---

[70] *Craddock Bros. v. Hunt* [1923] 2 Ch. 136.

[71] This doctrine cannot be ousted by the terms of the contract; *Quadrant Visual Communications Ltd v. Hutchison Telephone (UK) Ltd, The Times,* December 4, 1991.

[72] Except the most trivial ones; *Dyster v. Randall* [1926] Ch. 932 at 942–943. See also *Sport International Bussum B.V. v. Inter-Footwear Ltd* [1984] 1 W.L.R. 776; *National & Provincial Building Society v. British Waterways Board* [1992] E.G.C.S. 149.

[73] *Lamare v. Dixon* (1873) L.R. 6 H.L. 414; *Australian Hardwoods Pty. Ltd v. Railways Commissioner* [1961] 1 W.L.R. 425; *Cornish v. Brook Green Laundry* [1959] 1 Q.B. 391; *National & Provincial Building Society v. British Waterways Board, supra.* See also *Ailion v. Spiekermann* [1976] Ch. 158.

[74] *Walsh v. Lonsdale* (1882) 21 Ch.D. 9; *Coatsworth v. Johnson* (1886) 55 L.J.Q.B. 220.

[75] *Mountford v. Scott* [1975] Ch. 258.

[76] *van Gestel v. Cann, The Times,* August 7, 1987 (no defence where alleged fraudulent expenses claims not connected to contract).

[77] *Sang Lee Investment Co. Ltd v. Wing Kwai Investment Co. Ltd, The Times,* April 14, 1983. See also *Wilton Group plc v. Abrams, The Times,* February 23, 1990 (no specific performance of "commercially disreputable" agreement).

concerned, it is proposed that this statutory discretion will replace the "clean hands" doctrine.[78]

C. Laches or Delay

Generally, in equity, time is not held to be of the essence of a contract,[79] thus specific performance may be orderd although the contractual date for performance has passed. Failure to complete on the contractual date may, however, render the delaying party liable to damages for breach of contract. The fact that time is not of the essence in equity does not negative a breach of contract in such a case. It means that the breach does not amount to a repudiation of the contract. Thus the delaying party, although liable to damages, does not lose the right to seek specific performance, nor will he forfeit his deposit, provided he is ready to complete within a reasonable time.[80]

There is no statutory period of limitation barring claims to specific performance or to the refusal of relief on the ground of acquiescence,[81] but a claimant who delays unreasonably in bringing an action for specific performance may lose his claim.[82] There is no rule to lay down what is meant by unreasonable delay. One relevant factor is the subject-matter of the contract. If it has a speculative or fluctuating value, the principle of laches will be especially applicable.[83] It was once thought that the claimant must normally seek specific performance well within one year,[84] but it now seems that this approach may be too strict.

In *Lazard Bros. & Co. Ltd v. Fairfield Property Co. (Mayfair) Ltd*[85] a contract was entered into on March 12, 1975. The claimants commenced an action for specific performance on May 14, 1977. In ordering specific performance, Megarry V.-C. said that if specific performance was to be regarded as a prize, to be awarded

---

[78] Law Com. C.P. No. 154 (1999), *Illegal Transactions: The Effect of Illegality on Contracts and Trusts*, p. 96.

[79] This rule now applies also at law; LPA. 1925, s.41. (Time may be made of the essence in a contract for the sale of land by the service of a notice to complete.)

[80] *Raineri v. Miles* [1981] A.C. 1050; *Oakacre Ltd v. Claire Cleaners (Holdings) Ltd* [1982] Ch. 197; *cf. United Scientific Holdings Ltd v. Burnley Borough Council* [1978] A.C. 904 (as to rent review clauses). See (1980) 96 L.Q.R. 481; (1981) 44 M.L.R. 100 (A. Samuels).

[81] Limitation Act 1980, s.36(1), (2). For criticisms of the present law, see *Cia de Seguros Imperio v. Heath (REBX) Ltd* [2001] 1 W.L.R. 112 at 124.

[82] *Southcomb v. Bishop of Exeter* (1847) 6 H. 213; *Eads v. Williams* (1854) 4 De G.M. & G. 674; *M.E.P.C. Ltd v. Christian-Edwards* [1981] A.C. 205. Even a delay for which neither party is to blame may be a reason for leaving the purchaser to damages; *Patel v. Ali* [1984] Ch. 283, *post*, p. 743.

[83] *Mills v. Haywood* (1877) 6 Ch.D. 196.

[84] *Huxham v. Llewellyn* (1873) 21 W.R. 570 (delay of five months in the case of commercial premises prevented specific performance); *cf. Wroth v. Tyler* [1974] Ch. 30, Farrand, *Contract and Conveyance* (4th ed.), p. 216.

[85] (1977) 121 S.J. 793; [1978] Conv. 184.

by equity to the zealous and denied to the indolent, then the claimants should fail. But whatever might have been the position over a century ago that was the wrong approach today. If between the parties it was just that the claimant should obtain the remedy, the court ought not to withhold it merely because he had been guilty of delay. There was no ground here on which delay could properly be said to be a bar to a order of specific performance.

Thus the modern approach is not to look at the principles of previous cases to see if the circumstances fitted into them, but to ask whether, broadly considered, the claimant's actions were such as to render it unconscionable for him to assert his rights.[86] An exceptional case where delay will not be a bar is where the claimant has taken possession under the contract,[87] so that the purpose of specific performance is merely to vest the legal estate in him. In *Williams v. Greatrex*[88] a delay of 10 years in such circumstances did not bar specific performance. But a significant factor there was that the transaction creating the proprietary interest was not in issue. It is otherwise where the contract itself is disputed. In such a case the doctrine of laches does apply.[89]

Where the claimant has delayed, but specific performance is refused for another reason, the effect of his delay may be that the date for assessing damages in lieu of specific performance under Lord Cairns' Act is moved back from the date of judgment to the date upon which the matter might have been disposed of.[90]

The situation discussed above is where the delay has occurred before the claimant has sought specific performance. Where the claimant commences the action for specific performance promptly but then delays in bringing the matter to trial, he may, in a clear case, be disentitled to the remedy.[91] Where he obtains an order for specific performance but then delays in enforcing it for a long period, leave to enforce it will be refused only if there is an insufficient explanation and detriment to the defendant. Thus, in *Easton v. Brown*,[92] a

---

[86] *Frawley v. Neill, The Times*, April 5, 1999.

[87] It is otherwise if possession has been taken other than pursuant to the contract: *Mills v. Haywood, supra*. The principle applies, however, where the claimant remains in possession after buying the co-owner's share, but the legal title has not been conveyed into his sole name; *Frawley v. Neill, supra*, (rights under 1975 contract not barred by laches).

[88] [1957] 1 W.L.R. 31.

[89] *Joyce v. Joyce* [1979] 1 W.L.R. 1170.

[90] *Malhotra v. Choudhury* [1980] Ch. 52.

[91] *Du Sautoy v. Symes* [1967] Ch. 1146 at 1168. *Towli v. Fourth River Property Co. Ltd, The Times*, November 24, 1976 (delay of nine years between writ and hearing) was such a clear case. See also *Lamshed v. Lamshed* (1963) 109 C.L.R. 440 (specific performance refused where delay of over five years between commencement of action and setting down for trial).

[92] [1981] 3 All E.R. 278. The claimant also obtained an order for inquiry as to damages arising from the defendant's failure to complete.

delay of eight years in seeking to enforce the order was no bar where the defendant's former wife and children had remained in occupation and the claimant had been legally advised that it would be difficult to remove them. The claimant had an explanation for the delay and had acted reasonably; detriment to the defendant was not on its own a ground for refusing leave to enforce the order.

Finally, in cases where time is of the essence, specific performance is not normally available after the stipulated date. It has been held in Australia, however, that the court may, in the exercise of its equitable jurisdiction to relieve against forfeiture, grant specific performance to prevent the "forfeiture" of the purchaser's equitable interest under the contract.[93] The Privy Council has rejected the Australian approach, although leaving open the possibility of relief based on restitution or estoppel if injustice would otherwise result.[94]

D. Hardship

In general, specific performance may be refused in the discretion of the court where it would cause unnecessary hardship to either of the parties,[95] or to a third party.[96] Inadequacy of price is not, standing by itself, a ground for refusing specific performance; but it may be evidence of other factors, such as fraud[97] or undue influence,[98] which would render enforcement inequitable.

These matters arose in *Patel v. Ali*,[99] where the vendor and her husband were co-owners of a house which they contracted to sell in 1979. The husband's bankruptcy caused a long delay in completion,

---

[93] *Legione v. Hateley* (1983) 57 A.L.J.R. 292; (1983) 99 L.Q.R. 490.

[94] *Union Eagle Ltd v. Golden Achievements Ltd* [1997] A.C. 514; (1997) 113 L.Q.R. 385 (J. Heydon); [1997] Conv. 382 (M. Thompson); (1998) 61 M.L.R. 255 (J. Stevens).

[95] *Denne v. Light* (1857) 8 De G.M. & G. 774; *Warmington v. Miller* [1973] Q.B. 877 (no specific performance of contract to sublet if result would be to expose tenant to liability for breach of covenant against subletting); *Mountford v. Scott* [1975] Ch. 258; *Francis v. Cowcliff Ltd* (1977) 33 P. & C.R. 368; *Shell U.K. Ltd v. Lostock Garage Ltd* [1976] 1 W.L.R. 1187 at 1202. For further details, see Fry, *Specific Performance*, Chap. 16; Spry, *Equitable Remedies*, pp. 196 *et seq.*

[96] *Earl of Sefton v. Tophams Ltd* [1966] Ch. 1140; *Sullivan v. Henderson* [1973] 1 W.L.R. 333; *Watts v. Spence* [1976] Ch. 165; *Cedar Holdings Ltd v. Green* [1981] Ch. 129 at 147; [1979] Conv. 372 (F. Crane); (1979) 38 C.L.J. 215 (M. Prichard). This case was disapproved on another point in *Williams and Glyn's Bank Ltd v. Boland* [1981] A.C. 487 at 507. See also *Thames Guaranty Ltd v. Campbell* [1985] Q.B. 210; *cf. Patel v. Ali* [1984] Ch. 283, *infra*, (interests of vendor's children in their own right not material, but relevant to hardship of vendor).

[97] *Coles v. Trecothick* (1804) 9 Ves.Jr. 234 at 246; *Callaghan v. Callaghan* (1841) 8 Cl. & F. 374.

[98] *Fry v. Lane* (1888) 40 Ch.D. 312 (sale set aside).

[99] [1984] Ch. 283; (1984) 100 L.Q.R. 337. There was evidence that the Muslim community would pay the damages.

for which neither the vendor nor the purchaser was to blame. After the contract the vendor had a leg amputated. She later gave birth to her second and third children. The purchaser obtained an order for specific performance, against which the vendor appealed on the ground of hardship. She spoke little English, and relied on help from nearby friends and relatives, hence it would be a hardship to leave the house and move away. Goulding J. held that the court in a proper case could refuse specific performance on the ground of hardship subsequent to the contract, even if not caused by the claimant and not related to the subject-matter. On the facts, there would be hardship amounting to injustice, therefore the appropriate remedy was damages.

E. Misdescription of Subject-Matter

i. Specific Performance Subject to Compensation.[1] If the property agreed to be sold is incorrectly described in the contract, the vendor cannot fulfil his promise to transfer property which corresponds exactly with that which he contracted to convey. A frequent instance is an inaccurate measurement in the plan.[2] A misdescription is a term of the contract; the vendor is therefore in breach. To deny him specific performance on that account would introduce a rigid rule capable of producing injustice. Equity adopts a more flexible approach; the circumstances may be such that justice will be done by compelling completion, notwithstanding the error, compensating the purchaser by allowing him a reduction in the price he had agreed to pay ("abatement").[3] This course will not be followed if it would prejudice the rights of a third party interested in the estate.[4] On the other hand the misdescription may be so serious that to order specific performance would be in effect to force the purchaser to take something wholly different from what he intended.[5] If so, the only way of achieving justice may be to permit the purchaser to rescind; or to refuse to grant specific performance to the vendor.

---

[1] See (1981) 40 C.L.J. 47 (C. Harpum), taking the view that this should not be distinguished from specific performance with damages under Lord Cairns' Act, *post*, p. 747.

[2] See, *e.g. Watson v. Burton* [1957] 1 W.L.R. 19; *Topfell Ltd v. Galley Properties Ltd* [1979] 1 W.L.R. 446 (inability to give vacant possession); [1979] Conv. 375 (F. Crane).

[3] If the misdescription goes against the vendor, he cannot increase the price: *Re Lindsay and Forder's Contract* (1895) 72 L.T. 832. (But specific performance might be refused on the ground of hardship, *ante*, p. 743). See also *Seven Seas Properties Ltd v. Al-Essa* [1988] 1 W.L.R. 1272.

[4] *Cedar Holdings Ltd v. Green* [1981] Ch. 129.

[5] See *Cedar Holdings Ltd v. Green, supra*. (Specific performance with abatement not appropriate where vendor's interest merely a co-ownership share).

ii. Refusal of Specific Performance. The rule is thus that a purchaser will not be forced to take something which is *different in substance* from that which he agreed to buy.[6] Differences of quality or quantity will not *by themselves* suffice as a defence to an action for specific performance (although of course they will give rise to a claim for compensation) unless they can fairly be said to make the property, as it in fact is, different in substance from that contracted to be sold.[7] A misdescription is substantial for this purpose if it so far affects "the subject-matter of the contract that it may be reasonably supposed, that, but for such misdescription, the purchaser might never have entered into the contract at all."[8] This will always be a question of fact in each case: obviously A, who has contracted to sell Blackacre to B, cannot force him to take Whiteacre, even if Whiteacre is larger, more valuable, and better suited to B's purposes. It is often difficult to say whether a misdescription of the area of land involves a difference of substance or of quantity; the rule is "easy to be understood, though often difficult of application."[9] However, although the vendor cannot compel a purchaser to take something different from that contracted to be sold, it is only just to give the purchaser the option of insisting on completion, and being paid compensation[10] for what he has lost. If it were not so, a person in default could in effect take advantage of his own wrong. Thus the purchaser has a choice: he may elect to take the property,[11] notwithstanding that it may be substantially different from the contract description.

iii. Conditions of Sale. The above is true of "open" contracts, but the parties are free to make their own conditions to regulate what is to happen if there is a misdescription. In the case of contracts for the sale of land, most contracts prepared by a solicitor will now be made subject to the Standard Conditions of Sale or the Standard Commercial Property Conditions. In every case, therefore, the first question must be: what does the contract provide? But even then caution is necessary, since the courts have been reluctant to permit

---

[6] *Flight v. Booth* (1834) 1 Bing.N.C. 370; *Watson v. Burton* [1957] 1 W.L.R. 19.

[7] If a vendor contracts to sell a lease of Blackacre, a purchaser cannor be compelled to take an underlease; *Madeley v. Booth* (1845) 2 De G & Sm. 718; nor if he contracts to sell a "registered freehold property," can he compel the purchaser to take a possessory (as distinct from *absolute*) freehold title; *Re Brine and Davies' Contract* [1935] Ch. 388.

[8] *per* Tindal C.J. in *Flight v. Booth* (1834) 1 Bing.N.C. 370 at 377.

[9] *per* Lord Esher M.R. in *Re Fawcett and Holmes' Contract* (1889) 42 Ch.D. 150 at 156; *cf. Watson v. Burton* [1957] 1 W.L.R. 19.

[10] *Mortlock v. Buller* (1804) 10 Ves.Jr. 292 at 316. The compensation must generally be claimed before completion; *Joliffe v. Baker* (1883) 11 Q.B.D. 255.

[11] In the absence of special circumstances, *e.g.* if he was himself aware of the misdescription at the date of the contract; *Castle v. Wilkinson* (1870) L.R. 5 Ch. 534. See [1978] Conv. 338 at 340 (C. Emery).

either party to contract out of the rights conferred on him by equity.[12]

iv. Want of Good Title. The court will not force a doubtful title on a purchaser. The phrase "defect in title" is loosely used in some of the cases to indicate that the vendor, through some material error in description, fails in effect to convey to the purchaser the property he intended to buy. In other cases the expression may be used in a more literal sense; where, for example, the vendor's land is burdened with restrictive covenants.[13] Yet there are other cases where there is not merely a defect in the vendor's title, but no title at all. Clearly the purchaser cannot be compelled to take a bad title, nor be allowed to refuse a good one. Between the good and the bad is an infinite variety of doubtful titles, and the question inevitably arises of drawing a line between those titles which a purchaser will, and those which he will not, be compelled to accept. The test is whether there is likely to be litigation. If the doubt is one of law, the court will normally resolve it.[14] If the doubt is one of fact, it is the court's duty, unless there are exceptional circumstances, to decide the question of title as between the vendor and purchaser. If the court concludes that the purchaser will not be at risk of a successful assertion against him of an incumbrance, then the court should declare in favour of a good title, and should not be deterred by the mere possibility of future litigation by a claimant to an incumbrance who is not bound by the declaration.[15] But if good title is not shown, the purchaser will be entitled to rescind, unless the vendor removes the doubt. The court will not compel a party to purchase a law suit.[16]

F. Public Policy

The court will not order specific performance of a contract where the result would be contrary to public policy.

---

[12] See *Topfell Ltd v. Galley Properties Ltd* [1979] 1 W.L.R. 446; [1979] Conv. 375 (F. Crane); *Rignall Developments Ltd v. Halil* [1988] Ch. 190. Conditions of sale are subject to the Unfair Contract Terms Act 1977; *Walker v. Boyle* [1982] 1 W.L.R. 495.

[13] *Re Nisbet and Potts' Contract* [1906] 1 Ch. 386; *Faruqui v. English Real Estates Ltd* [1979] 1 W.L.R. 963; [1979] Conv. 444 (F. Crane). See generally [1978] Conv. 338 (C. Emery).

[14] *Wilson v. Thomas* [1958] 1 W.L.R. 422.

[15] *M.E.P.C. Ltd v. Christian-Edwards* [1981] A.C. 205 (doubt as to abandonment of 1912 contract: good title established). See also *Re Handman and Wilcox's Contract* [1902] 1 Ch. 599; *Selkirk v. Romar Investments Ltd* [1963] 1 W.L.R. 1415.

[16] *Re Nichols and Von Joel's Contract* [1910] 1 Ch. 43 at 46. See also *Pips (Leisure Productions) Ltd v. Walton* (1981) 260 E.G. 601 (purchaser entitled to rescind contract for sale of lease which was already forfeited).

In *Wroth v. Tyler*,[17] a husband, the owner of the matrimonial home, entered into a contract to sell with vacant possession. Before completion, his wife registered a charge under the Matrimonial Homes Act 1967.[18] The purchasers sued for specific performance, and failed on two grounds:

i. The husband could only carry out his obligation by obtaining a court order terminating the wife's right of occupation, and this would depend on the discretion of the court. To grant specific performance would compel the husband to embark on difficult and uncertain litigation. He had attempted to obtain the wife's consent by all reasonable means short of litigation, and it would be most undesirable to require a husband to take proceedings against his wife, especially where they were still living together.

ii. Nor could the purchasers get specific performance subject to the wife's right of occupation. The husband and daughter would remain liable to eviction by the purchasers, and the family would be split up. The court would be slow to order specific performance in such circumstances.

6. DAMAGES IN SUBSTITUTION FOR, OR IN ADDITION TO, SPECIFIC PERFORMANCE

A. Chancery Amendment Act 1858. Lord Cairns' Act[19]

Section 2 of Lord Cairns' Act gave to the Court of Chancery discretionary power to award damages either in addition to or in substitution for specific performance, the damages to be assessed in such manner as the court shall direct.

Before this Act, it was only in the common law courts that damages were awarded.[20] The Act gave power to award damages where none would be available at law.[21] But it did not give the Court of

---

[17] [1974] Ch. 30. See also *Malhotra v. Choudhury* [1980] Ch. 52 at 71; *Verrall v. Great Yarmouth Borough Council* [1981] Q.B. 202, *ante*, p. 723 (specific performance of contract to hire conference hall to National Front), where this defence failed: the risk of public disorder was outweighed by the freedom of speech and assembly and the sanctity of contract.

[18] Now Family Law Act 1996.

[19] See generally (1975) 34 C.L.J. 224 (J. Jolowicz); [1981] Conv. 286 (T. Ingman and J. Wakefield); [1994] Conv. 110 (T. Ingman); McDermott, *Equitable Damages* (1994).

[20] It appears that the Court of Chancery had inherent power to award damages in equity, but this was rarely exercised. See Spry, *Equitable Remedies*, p. 623; (1992) 108 L.Q.R. 652 (P. McDermott); *cf. Surrey v. Bredero Homes Ltd* [1993] 1 W.L.R. 1361 at 1368, where Dillon L.J. said that the Court of Chancery had "no power to award damages" before the 1858 Act. For the Court of Chancery's ancient statutory jurisdiction to award damages, see McDermott, *Equitable Damages*, p. 8.

[21] See *Johnson v. Agnew* [1980] A.C. 367 (Lord Wilberforce); *Price v. Strange* [1978] Ch. 337; *Oakacre Ltd v. Claire Cleaners (Holdings) Ltd* [1982] Ch. 197 (cause of action for damages at law not accrued when action commenced).

Chancery power to award common law damages.[22] It applied only to cases where the court had jurisdiction to award specific performance. Thus Lord Cairns' Act does not apply where the contract is of a type which is not specifically enforceable[23]; but it does apply where the contract is of a type which is, even though specific performance is refused on some discretionary ground, such as the absence of mutuality.[24] There is no jurisdiction under Lord Cairns' Act if specific performance is no longer possible, as where the land has been sold to a third party.[25] However, the jurisdiction exists if, when the proceedings were begun, the court could have granted specific performance, notwithstanding that thereafter, but before judgment, specific performance has become impossible.[26] But it has been held that the court has no jurisdiction to award damages in lieu of specific performance under Lord Cairns' Act where specific performance is not sought by the claimant.[27]

It was not until the Judicature Act 1873 that common law damages were available in the Chancery Division. Today it is only necessary to rely on Lord Cairns' Act if no damages would be available at law.[28] It was at one time thought that it could be advantageous to the claimant to rely on Lord Cairns' Act even where common law damages were available, as the measure of damages might be different.[29] This is now discredited.[30]

Lord Cairns' Act was repealed in 1883 by the Statute Law Revision Act, but section 5 of that Act preserved its general effect,[31]

---

[22] But see *Price v. Strange* [1978] Ch. 337 at 358, where Goff L.J. said "One purpose and a very important purpose of that Act was, of course, to avoid circuity of action by enabling the old Court of Chancery to award damages at law. . . . "

[23] *Lavery v. Pursell* (1888) 39 Ch.D. 508 (tenancy for one year; *ante* p. 733). As to whether contracts for personal services come into this category, see the different views expressed in *Price v. Strange* [1978] Ch. 337 at 359 (Goff L.J.) and at 369 (Buckley L.J.). The House of Lords in *Scandinavian Trading Tanker Co. A.B. v. Flota Petrolera Ecuatoriana* [1983] 2 A.C. 694 took the view that there was no jurisdiction to grant specific performance of a contract for services.

[24] *Price v. Strange* [1978] Ch. 337. Even where the contract concerns building or repair works, the court has jurisdiction under the 1858 Act: *ibid.* at 359. See also *Wroth v. Tyler* [1974] Ch. 30; *Malhotra v. Choudhury* [1980] Ch. 52, (1979) 38 C.L.J. 35 (D. Hayton); and the cases on injunctions, *post*, pp. 000, *et seq.*

[25] *Surrey County Council v. Bredero Homes Ltd* [1993] 1 W.L.R. 1361.

[26] *Johnson v. Agnew* [1978] Ch. 176, C.A.

[27] *Horsler v. Zorro* [1975] Ch. 302. But see (1975) 91 L.Q.R. 337 (M. Albery) at 352–353; *Jaggard v. Sawyer* [1995] 1 W.L.R. 269 (injunction); [1995] Conv. 141 (T. Ingman). See also *Malhotra v. Choudhury* [1980] Ch. 52. *Horsler v. Zorro* was overruled in part on a different point in *Johnson v. Agnew* [1980] A.C. 367. Damages may be awarded under Lord Cairns' Act, although not expressly claimed; (1985) 34 I.C.L.Q. 317 (A. Burgess); *Jaggard v. Sawyer, supra.*

[28] See *Oakacre Ltd v. Claire Cleaners (Holdings) Ltd* [1982] Ch. 197 (cause of action for damages not yet accrued).

[29] *Wroth v. Tyler* [1974] Ch. 30, *infra.*

[30] *Johnson v. Agnew, infra.*

[31] See *Leeds Industrial Co-operative Society Ltd v. Slack* [1924] A.C. 851.

although that section was unnecessary because section 16 of the Judicature Act 1873 had transferred all Chancery jurisdiction to the High Court.[32] Its provisions are now found in section 50 of the Supreme Court Act 1981.

B. Measure of Damages under Lord Cairns' Act

Where a purchaser claims damages for breach of a contract for the purchase of land, he is normally entitled to damages for any loss of bargain. In *Wroth v. Tyler*[33] the purchasers contracted to buy a bungalow for £6,000. Contracts were exchanged on May 27, 1971, but on May 28 the vendor's wife registered a charge under the Matrimonial Homes Act 1967,[34] and refused to remove it. The vendor was thus unable to pass a clear title. At the date at which completion was due, the property was worth £7,500, but at the date of the judgment in January 1973, its value had risen to £11,500.

Megarry J. refused specific performance for reasons mentioned above.[35] Therefore the main issue was the measure of damages. It was "common ground" that the normal rule is that damages for breach of a contract for the sale of land are measured by the difference (if any) between the contract price and the market price at the date of the breach, which is normally the completion date (with interest from that date until judgment). Applying that rule, damages would be £1,500. Although Fry had said that "the measure would be the same under Lord Cairns' Act"[36] Megarry J. held that damages under the Act may be assessed on a basis which is not identical with that of the common law[37]: they should be a true substitute for specific performance, and must put the claimants in as good a position as if the contract had been performed. Damages could be measured as at the date of judgment, and the purchasers were awarded £5,500.

It has since been doubted by the House of Lords[38] whether Lord Cairns' Act permits a departure from the common law rule on the quantum of damages, and, indeed, whether the damages awarded in *Wroth v. Tyler*[39] could not have been equally available at common law. There is no inflexible rule at common law that damages must be

---

[32] McDermott, *Equitable Damages*, pp. 41–44.
[33] [1974] Ch. 30; applied in *Grant v. Dawkins* [1973] 1 W.L.R. 1406. See also *Oakacre Ltd v. Claire Cleaners (Holdings) Ltd* [1982] Ch. 197 (damages awarded in addition to specific performance not limited to those accrued when action commenced).
[34] Now Family Law Act 1996.
[35] *ante*, p. 747.
[36] *op. cit.* p. 602.
[37] [1974] Ch. 30 at 58–60.
[38] In *Johnson v. Agnew, infra.* The reasoning in *Wroth v. Tyler* is preferred in McDermott, *Equitable Damages*, p. 108; *cf.* [1994] Conv. 110 (T. Ingman).
[39] *supra.*

assessed as at the date of the breach of contract.[40] The principle is
that the claimant should be put in the same position as if the contract
had been duly performed. The rule that damages are to be assessed
as at the date of the breach evolved in times of financial stability
when the subject-matter was unlikely to have increased in value
between the breach and the judgment. The position at common law
will be more readily appreciated by considering the doctrine of
mitigation of damages. The principle that the claimant is to be put
in the same position as if the contract had been performed is subject
to the principle of mitigation.[41] Thus in the case of chattels, damages
will usually be assessed at the breach, because at that date the
claimant could have acquired an equivalent chattel elsewhere. But in
the case of a specifically enforceable contract, such as a contract to
buy land, the purchaser cannot reasonably be expected to mitigate
the damages by seeking an equivalent property elsewhere as soon as
the breach occurs, because he will normally wish to wait and see if
specific performance is obtainable. In such a case, the common law
principle of putting the claimant in the same position as if the
contract had been performed is only adhered to in times of rising
property prices by assessing the damages at a date subsequent to the
breach.[42]

In *Johnson v. Agnew*[43] Lord Wilberforce rejected the view that
damages under Lord Cairns' Act could be assessed on a different
basis from that of the common law. Subject to the point that in some
cases damages would be available under the Act where none at all
would be available at common law, the quantum is the same. The
words in section 2 that damages "may be assessed in such manner
as the court shall direct" relate only to procedure.[44] *Wroth v. Tyler*[45]
could not be supported in so far as it suggested that damages under
the Act may be assessed on a different basis than at common law.
Where, after the breach, the innocent party has reasonably continued
to try for completion, the damages, however awarded should be

---

[40] *Wroth v. Tyler* [1974] Ch. 30 at 57; *Radford v. De Froberville* [1977] 1 W.L.R. 1262, (1978)
94 L.Q.R. 327 (A. Zuckerman), [1978] Conv. 163 (F. Crane); *Malhotra v. Choudhury*
[1980] Ch. 52, (1979) 38 C.L.J. 35 (D. Hayton); *Johnson v. Agnew* [1980] A.C. 367;
Suleman v. Shahsavari [1988] 1 W.L.R. 1181.

[41] *Wroth v. Tyler* [1974] Ch. 30 at 57; *Radford v. De Froberville* [1977] 1 W.L.R. 1262;
Malhotra v. Choudhury, supra; cf. Kaunas v. Smyth (1977) 75 D.L.R. 368.

[42] See generally (1979) 95 L.Q.R. 270 (D. Feldman and D. Libling); (1981) 97 L.Q.R. 445 (S.
Waddams); (1982) 98 L.Q.R. 406 (I. Duncan Wallace); (1985) 34 I.C.L.Q. 317 (A. Bur-
gess). If the market is falling, damages will be assessed at the date of breach; *Woodford
Estates Ltd v. Pollack* (1979) 93 D.L.R. (3d) 350.

[43] [1980] A.C. 367. The facts have been given, *ante*, p. 750. See also *William Sindall plc v.
Cambridgeshire County Council* [1994] 1 W.L.R. 1016 at 1037.

[44] This phrase does not appear in Supreme Court Act 1981, s.50.

[45] [1974] Ch. 30.

assessed as at the date the contract was lost.[46] This will normally be the date of the hearing, provided the proceedings have been conducted with due expedition: an earlier date will be substituted if the claimant has delayed.[47]

The assessment of damages under Lord Cairns' Act has been recently reviewed in the context of injunctions,[48] and is further considered in Chapter 25.

7. SPECIFIC PERFORMANCE AND THIRD PARTIES

Claims for specific performance are usually made between the parties to the contract.[49] In such a case, all the parties to the contract must be parties to the action.[50] Other difficulties arise where the issue is between assignees, or where the person to be benefited was not a party to the contract.

Difficulties have arisen as to whether the right to (or liability to) specific performance passes to an assignee of the agreement. These problems mainly arose in the context of agreements for leases, where the question was whether the assignee of either party could sue or be sued on the obligations of the agreed lease. These matters are now dealt with by the Landlord and Tenant (Covenants) Act 1995,[51] and will not be further discussed here. As far as contracts for the sale of land are concerned, such a contract confers an equitable interest on the purchaser. Whether specific performance is available against an assignee of the vendor will depend on the registration rules.[52]

A different question is whether specific performance may be obtained for the benefit of a third party, as where A has contracted with B to confer a benefit on C. As discussed below, C may now be able to enforce the contract in his own right under the Contracts (Rights of Third Parties) Act 1999. If, however, because the contract was entered into before the application of the 1999 Act, C cannot enforce

---

[46] This was the date on which the vendor's mortgagees contracted to sell the property; *ante*, p. 719. See also *Domb v. Isoz* [1980] Ch. 548; *Suleman v. Shahsavari* [1988] 1 W.L.R. 1181 (£29,500 awarded where property worth £76,000 at hearing but contract price £46,500); *Johnson & Co. (Barbados) Ltd v. N.S.R. Ltd* [1997] A.C. 400.

[47] *Radford v. De Froberville* [1977] 1 W.L.R. 1262 (assuming a rising market); *Malhotra v. Choudhury* [1980] Ch. 52.

[48] *post*, p. 808.

[49] Land Charges Act 1925; Land Registration Act 1925. For the rights of a sub-purchaser to obtain specific performance of the head contract, see *Berkley v. Poulett* (1976) 120 S.J. 836, *ante* p. 328.

[50] See *Tito v. Waddell (No. 2)* [1977] Ch. 106 at 324 (Megarry V.-C.).

[51] The Act extends to agreements for leases and equitable assignments of leases; s.28(1).

[52] Land Charges Act 1972, s.2(4); Land Registration Act 1925, ss.49, 70(1)(g) (estate contracts).

the contract himself, the question is whether B may obtain specific performance, compelling A to confer the benefit on C.

In *Beswick v. Beswick*,[53] one Peter Beswick, a coal merchant who wished to retire, made an arrangement with his nephew under which the business was transferred to the nephew, and the nephew promised to employ Peter as consultant for a weekly wage, and after his death to pay to Peter's widow £5 per week for her life. Payments were made to Peter during his lifetime, but soon after his death ceased to be paid to his widow. The widow took out letters of administration of Peter's estate and sued both as administratrix and in her own right under the contract.

The House of Lords held that she was entitled as administratrix to specific performance of the promise to make the weekly payments to her as Peter's widow. She was unable to sue in her own right because of the rule of privity.

The difficulties which faced the widow in her action as administratrix were essentially threefold: (a) Peter's estate, which she represented, had lost nothing by the breach; (b) the widow, in her own capacity, had suffered the loss but had no right of action; (c) the agreement was for the payment of money and was not the type of agreement where breach is usually remedied by an order of specific performance.[54]

The widow, as administratrix, overcame them all. Lord Upjohn thought that (a) was an argument in favour of specific performance; " . . . the court ought to grant a specific performance order all the more because damages *are* nominal."[55] She had no other effective remedy; "justice demands that [the promisor] pay the price and this can only be done in the circumstances by equitable relief."[56] This disregards the principle that equitable remedies are available where the legal remedy is inadequate to compensate for the loss. It is not that equitable remedies are available where the claimant has suffered no loss,[57] nor where an independent person has suffered a loss for which there is no cause of action.

---

[53] [1968] A.C. 58; (1988) 8 L.S. 14 (N. Andrews).

[54] *ante*, p. 725.

[55] [1968] A.C. 58 at 102; *cf. Re Cook's S.T.* [1965] Ch. 902; *ante*, p. 138. On damages for loss suffered by third parties, see also *Jackson v. Horizon Holidays Ltd* [1975] 1 W.L.R. 1468; *ante*, p. 133, *Woodar Investment Development Ltd v. Wimpey Construction U.K. Ltd* [1980] 1 W.L.R. 277.

[56] *ibid.*

[57] *cf. Marco Productions Ltd v. Pagola* [1945] 1 K.B. 111; injunction available to restrain breach of negative covenant even though the breach causes no loss to claimant; or if only nominal damages would be available at law; *Rochdale Canal Co. v. King* (1851) 2 Sim.(N.S.) 78.

Their Lordships found no difficulty in treating the case as a suitable one for specific performance. "Had [the promisor] repudiated the contract in the lifetime of [the promisee] the latter would have had a cast-iron case for specific performance."[58] The orthodox view has been that specific performance will not be ordered in cases where the promise is to pay money unless the claimant is a vendor or lessor against whom the purchaser or lessee could have demanded specific performance. *Beswick v. Beswick*[59] may have been regarded as such a case, for the nephew "could on his part clearly have obtained specific performance of it if Beswick senior or his administratrix had defaulted."[60] That, it is submitted, is questionable; for the contract was essentially for the sale of the goodwill of the business; such a contract is not normally specifically enforceable, in contrast to a contract to sell premises along with the goodwill.[61]

It is said also that a contract to pay an annuity is specifically enforceable. In *Adderly v. Dixon*,[62] Leach M.R. gave the reason that the amount of damages would be conjectural. While such a proposition may have been sound in 1824, the development of life assurance and of actuarial valuation of life interests has made an annuity and a capital sum in effect interchangeable. Annuities are freely purchased from insurance companies in exchange for capital payments and can similarly be freely sold for a capital sum. Thus the conjectural element is less marked than it was over a century ago. If the claimant was awarded damages, and desired the annuity, all he has to do is to buy one.

The cases on which their Lordships relied to support the view that the contract to pay was specifically enforceable, at the instance of a personal representative, were all cases either of a contract to transfer land or contracts to pay an annuity. It is possible to treat *Beswick v. Beswick*[63] as consistent with authority by saying that there was mutuality, that the contract (being to pay an annuity) was capable of specific performance, and that the common law remedy of damages (assuming them to be nominal) was inadequate. The claimant barely succeeds on the first two; and only on the third by relying on cases which uphold it without explaining the logical dilemma of holding an award of nominal damages inadequate where no loss was suffered by the party able to sue.

In spite of these criticisms, the House of Lords should be applauded for taking a broad equitable view of the situation. There was "an unconscionable breach of faith [and] the equitable remedy

---

[58] [1968] A.C. 58 at 98.
[59] *ibid.*
[60] *ibid.* at 89, *per* Lord Pearce.
[61] *Darbey v. Whitaker* (1857) 4 Drew. 134 at 139, 140; *ante*, p. 735.
[62] (1824) 1 Sim. & St. 607 at 611; (1966) 29 M.L.R. 657 at 663 (G. Treitel).
[63] [1968] A.C. 58.

sought is apt."[64] Lord Pearce and Lord Upjohn both approved the dictum of Windeyer J. in *Coulls v. Bagot's Executor and Trustee Co. Ltd* in which he said[65]:

"It seems to me that contracts to pay money or transfer property to a third person are always, or at all events very often, contracts for breach of which damages would be an inadequate remedy—all the more so if it be right (I do not think it is) that damages recoverable by the promisee are only nominal . . . I see no reason why specific performance should not be had in such cases . . . There is no reason today for limiting by particular categories, rather than by general principle, the cases in which orders for specific performance will be made."

There were no technical or practical difficulties preventing an award of specific performance and "justice demands that [the promisor] pay the price and this can only be done in the circumstances by equitable relief."[66] Perhaps the correct explanation is that damages must be considered from the point of view of both claimant and defendant. Thus the remedy of damages is inadequate if it would lead to the unjust enrichment of the wrongdoer. Substantial damages have been awarded under Lord Cairns' Act for this reason.[67]

Now the widow Beswick would be able to enforce the contract in her own right if it were entered into after the Contracts (Rights of Third Parties) Act 1999. Whether she would be able to obtain specific performance by virtue of section 1(5) is less clear.[68] This depends on whether the subsection must be taken to override the principle that specific performance is not available to a volunteer. The Law Commission simply stated that the widow would have "the right of enforcement", without reference to specific performance.[69] Even if specific performance would not be available, at least the widow would be able to obtain substantial damages, being a person with a cause of action who has suffered a loss by the breach. To that extent, the remedy of damages is adequate.

This chapter began by indicating how narrow was the scope of the remedy of specific performance in practice. Other systems of law tend to be much more free in their use of this type of remedy. *Beswick v. Beswick*[70] indicates a willingness in the House of Lords to make freer use of the remedy in the interests of justice. The case

---

[64] [1968] A.C. 58, *per* Lord Hodson at 83.
[65] (1967) 40 A.L.J.R. at 487; (1978) 37 C.L.J. 301 (B. Coote).
[66] *Beswick v. Beswick* at 102, *per* Lord Upjohn.
[67] *Wrotham Park Estate Co. v. Parkside Homes Ltd* [1974] 1 W.L.R. 798. For further developments in the context of injunctions, see p. 805, *post*.
[68] Discussed *ante*, p. 726.
[69] Law Com. No. 242, para. 7.46.
[70] [1968] A.C. 58.

is however concerned with its own particular problem, now resolved by legislation, of the contract to pay to a third party. We have seen that their Lordships were recently more orthodox in the context of the supervision principle, refusing to extend the remedy of specific performance to a landlord seeking to enforce a "keep open" covenant in a lease.[71]

8. JURISDICTION

Both the High Court and the county court have jurisdiction to grant specific performance, but the jurisdiction of the county court, in cases of specific performance of contracts to sell or to let land, is limited to cases where the purchase money, or the value of the property in the case of a lease, does not exceed the county court limit.[72]

The county court must give effect to every defence or counterclaim to which effect would be given in the High Court.[73] Thus, in *Kingswood Estate Co. Ltd v. Anderson*,[74] where the landlord brought an action for possession based on the termination of a common law periodic tenancy, the county court gave effect to the tenant's defence that she held the property under a specifically enforceable agreement for a lease for life, even though it had no jurisdiction to grant specific performance of that agreement. Similarly, in *Rushton v. Smith*,[75] the county court had no jurisdiction to grant specific performance of an agreement for a business tenancy where the value of the property exceeded the county court limit, but it nevertheless had jurisdiction to decide whether or not the tenant would be entitled to such an order.

---

[71] *Co-operative Insurance Society Ltd v. Argyll Stores (Holdings) Ltd* [1998] A.C. 1; *ante*, p. 728.

[72] County Courts Act 1984, s.23. The current limit is £30,000. See also *Joyce v. Liverpool City Council* [1996] Q.B. 252 (small claims).

[73] County Courts Act 1984, s.38.

[74] [1963] 2 Q.B. 169. See also *Cornish v. Brook Green Laundry Ltd* [1959] 1 Q.B. 394.

[75] [1976] Q.B. 480.

CHAPTER 25

INJUNCTIONS

1. JURISDICTION

AN injunction is an order by the court to a party to do or refrain from doing a particular act. Originally the Court of Chancery alone[1] had jurisdiction to grant an injunction. This inevitably led to much duplication of proceedings; as where a claimant required an injunction as a remedy for a legal right. The Common Law Procedure Act 1854 gave to common law courts a power to grant injunctions in certain cases. The present jurisdiction is governed by the Supreme Court Act 1981, replacing the Judicature Acts, which vested the jurisdiction of the Court of Chancery and of the common law courts in the High Court.

A. The High Court

Section 37(1) of the Supreme Court Act 1981 provides that "The High Court may by order (whether interlocutory or final) grant an injunction . . . in all cases in which it appears to the court to be just and convenient to do so."[2] The jurisdiction is however not so wide as would appear from a first reading of the section. It is exercised, not on the individual preference of the judge, but "according to sufficient legal reasons or on settled legal principles."[3] There have been differences of opinion as to whether section 25(8) of the Judicature Act 1873, which introduced the provision similar to that now contained in the Act of 1981, gave the court power to grant injunctions in cases where they had not previously been granted.[4] It has been said that the Act of 1873 "has not revolutionised" but "has to some extent enlarged" the jurisdiction.[5] The restrictive approach, namely that the court's jurisdiction has not been extended, was affirmed by the House of Lords in *Gouriet v. Union of Post Office Workers*.[6] Lord Edmund-Davies said that section 25(8) of the Act of

---

[1] Or the Court of Exchequer in its equity jurisdiction, *ante*, p. 4. See generally Sharpe, *Injunctions and Specific Performance*.

[2] This consolidates the previous legislation. Compare the wording of s.25(8) of the Supreme Court of Judicature Act 1873 and s.45 of the Act of 1925: "just *or* convenient"; *Day v. Brownrigg* (1878) 10 Ch.D. 294; *L. v. L.* [1969] P. 25.

[3] *per* Jessel M.R. in *Beddow v. Beddow* (1878) 9 Ch.D. 89 at 93. Thus a claimant with no "rights" cannot obtain an injunction, however "just and convenient" it may be: *Gouriet v. Union of Post Office Workers* [1978] A.C. 435; *Paton v. Trustees of British Pregnancy Advisory Service* [1979] Q.B. 76, *post*, p. 768.

[4] See the different views of Lord Esher M.R. and Cotton L.J. in *North London Ry. v. Great Northern Ry.* (1883) 11 Q.B.D. 30. See also *The Siskina* [1979] A.C. 210; *Maclaine Watson & Co. Ltd v. International Tin Council (No. 2)* [1989] Ch. 286; *Channel Tunnel Group Ltd v. Balfour Beatty Construction Ltd* [1993] A.C. 334.

[5] *Cummins v. Perkins* [1899] 1 Ch. 16 at 20.

[6] [1978] A.C. 435. See also *Bremer Vulkan Schiffbau und Maschinenfabrik v. South India Shipping Corp.* [1981] A.C. 909.

1873 "dealt only with procedure and had nothing to do with juris-diction."[7] But former rules of practice no longer hamper the exercise of discretion; thus enabling the merits of new situations to be dealt with as they arise.[8] A similar question is whether the Act of 1981 enlarged the previous jurisdiction, but the better view is that it did not.[9] A claimant with no cause of action cannot invoke section 37(1).[10]

B. The County Court

The jurisdiction of the county court, which is wholly statutory, has been enlarged by the Courts and Legal Services Act 1990.[11] Under section 38 of the County Courts Act 1984 the court could only grant an injunction if it was ancillary to a claim for some other specific relief, such as damages, within its jurisdiction. The amended section 38 provides that (subject to exceptions) the court may make an order which could be made by the High Court. It appears, therefore, that no other relief need be claimed. The county court has no jurisdiction, however, to grant a search order[12] or a freezing injunction[13] (other than in family proceedings or in aid of execution of a county court judgment).[14]

2. TYPES OF INJUNCTIONS

A. Prohibitory and Mandatory Injunctions

The most common form of an injunction, as the name implies, is one which is prohibitory or restrictive. However, if the unlawful act has been committed and an order restraining its commission is there-fore meaningless, justice can sometimes be done by issuing a man-datory injunction ordering the act to be undone. At one time the negative character of an injunction used to be insisted upon; if the court intended to order a party to pull down a building, the order would be that he should refrain from permitting the building to

---

[7] [1978] A.C. 435 at 516. *cf.* the wider views of Lord Denning M.R. in *Rasu Maritima S.A. v. Perusahaan* [1978] Q.B. 644 at 659–660.

[8] *Argyll v. Argyll* [1967] Ch. 302 at 345; *Rasu Maritima S.A. v. Perusahaan, supra.* See generally search orders and freezing injunctions, *post*, pp. 831, 834.

[9] Contrast the views of Lord Denning M.R. with those of Donaldson and Slade L.JJ. in *Chief Constable of Kent v. V.* [1983] Q.B. 34; (1983) 99 L.Q.R. 1; (1983) 42 C.L.J. 51 (A. Tettenborn); All E.R. Rev. 1982, at 205 (G. Zellick); *Richards v. Richards* [1984] A.C. 174. The wording of the 1981 Act and its predecessors is not identical.

[10] *Ainsbury v. Millington* [1986] 1 All E.R. 73.

[11] s.3. In the case of land, its value must be within the county court limits (currently £30,000). See also *Joyce v. Liverpool City Council* [1996] Q.B. 252 (small claims).

[12] *post*, p. 831.

[13] *post*, p. 834.

[14] County Courts Remedies Regulations 1991 (S.I. 1991 No. 1222).

remain on his land. Such an injunction may have a positive effect, as in *Sky Petroleum Ltd v. V.I.P. Petroleum Ltd*,[15] where an injunction restraining the defendant from withholding supplies of petrol was equivalent to specific performance of the contract. But a mandatory injunction is now couched in positive form,[16] but just for this reason it may be harder to obtain. For example, it has been held that it ought not to issue to compel a ferry owner to run a ferry when it could only be run at a loss.[17] But the fact that a local authority may have to borrow money, or get a building licence to comply with a mandatory injunction is a ground, not for refusing the remedy, but for granting it subject to a suspension.[18]

B. Perpetual and Interlocutory (or Interim) Injunctions

Prohibitory or mandatory injunctions may be perpetual or interlocutory. "Perpetual" does not mean necessarily that the effect of the order must endure for ever; it means that the order will finally settle the present dispute between the parties, being made as the result of an ordinary action, the court having heard in the ordinary way the arguments on both sides. But a claimant may not always be able to wait for the action to come on in the normal course; it may be that irreparable damage will be done if the defendant is not immediately restrained. If such is the case, the claimant will serve on him a notice that an application is being made to the court for an interlocutory injunction. The service of this notice will enable the defendant also to be heard, if he wishes, but the hearing will not be a final decision on the merits of the case. If the claimant's affidavit has made out a sufficient case, the judge will grant an interlocutory injunction, which is effective only until the trial of the action or some earlier specified date.

C. Injunctions Without Notice[19]

If the urgency of the case is such that the claimant cannot even follow the procedure described above, he is still not without a remedy, for he can apply for an injunction without notice, which will take effect immediately. Notice will then be served on the defendant,

---

[15] [1974] 1 W.L.R. 576.

[16] *Jackson v. Normanby Brick Co.* [1899] 1 Ch. 438.

[17] *Att.-Gen. v. Colchester Corporation* [1955] 2 Q.B. 207; *Gravesham Borough Council v. British Railways Board* [1978] Ch. 379; *Morris v. Redland Bricks Ltd* [1970] A.C. 652; *Co-operative Insurance Society Ltd v. Argyll Stores (Holdings) Ltd* [1998] A.C. 1, *ante*, p. 728.

[18] *Pride of Derby Angling Association v. British Celanese Co.* [1953] Ch. 149.

[19] Called *ex parte* injunctions before the C.P.R. 1998 came into operation.

who will then have a chance of having the order set aside or varied.[20]

D. *Quia Timet* Injunctions

A *quia timet* injunction is one which issues to prevent an infringement of the claimant's rights where the infringement is threatened, but has not yet occurred. The jurisdiction is one of long standing, and exists in relation to both perpetual and interlocutory injunctions, and to both prohibitory and mandatory injunctions. The claimant must show a very strong probability of a future infringement, and that the ensuing damage will be of a most serious nature.[21]

3. PRINCIPLES APPLICABLE TO THE ISSUE OF INJUNCTIONS

A. General

i. Discretionary Remedy. While the injunction is a much wider remedy than specific performance, the characteristics of the two remedies are similar. Thus, the injunction is a discretionary remedy,[22] based on the inadequacy of common law remedies. As will be seen, similar principles apply to the exercise of the discretion of the court. As in the case of specific performance, the court may award damages under Lord Cairns' Act, either in lieu of, or in addition to, an injunction.[23] In a rare case the court will grant a declaration that a person who has yet to seek an injunction has no entitlement to it.[24]

ii. Remedy in personam.[25] Like specific performance, the injunction is a remedy *in personam*. It is possible to enjoin a defendant who is not personally within the jurisdiction, provided service out of the jurisdiction can properly be done under the civil procedure rules.[26] But, as a general rule, no injunction will be granted in connection with the title to land outside the jurisdiction, even if the

---

[20] C.P.R. 23.9, 23.10, 25.3.

[21] *Fletcher v. Bealey* (1885) 28 Ch.D. 688; *Att.-Gen. v. Nottingham Corporation* [1904] 1 Ch. 673; *Redland Bricks Ltd v. Morris* [1970] A.C. 652; *post*, p. 795.

[22] Unless it is a statutory remedy to enforce a right for which there is no common law remedy; *Bristol City Council v. Lovell* [1998] 1 W.L.R. 446 at 453 (right to buy). Similarly, a claimant who has been totally dispossessed by trespass is entitled to an injunction as of right; *Harrow London Borough Council v. Donohue* [1995] 1 E.G.L.R. 257; *post*, p. 818.

[23] *post*, p. 801, Spry, pp. 625 *et seq.*

[24] *Greenwich Healthcare N.H.S. Trust v. London Quadrant Housing Trust* [1998] 1 W.L.R. 1749.

[25] *ante*, p. 716.

[26] R.S.C., Ord. 11 (C.P.R. 1998, Sched. 1). See *Re Liddell's S.T.* [1936] Ch. 365.

defendant is within the jurisdiction.[27] It is otherwise in the case of chattels, and, even in the case of land, the rule is subject to exceptions.[28] Finally, an injunction may be granted against all the members of a class or organisation to restrain the unlawful acts of unidentified members.[29]

iii. The Public Interest. Divergent views have been expressed in the Court of Appeal on the question whether the court, in considering an application for an injunction to protect a private right, has a duty to take into account the interests of the general public. In *Miller v. Jackson*[30] a cricket club committed the torts of nuisance and negligence in allowing cricket balls to land on the claimants' property. An injunction was refused by the Court of Appeal. The public interest in enabling the inhabitants to enjoy the benefits of outdoor recreation prevailed over the claimants' private right to quiet enjoyment of their house and garden. But in *Kennaway v. Thompson*,[31] where the claimant sought an injunction to restrain a motor boat racing club from committing nuisance by excessive noise, the Court of Appeal granted the injunction, holding that the rights of the claimant should not be overridden by the interests of the club or of the general public. In considering whether to grant an injunction or damages in lieu under Lord Cairns' Act,[32] the public interest does not prevail over private rights. The views expressed in *Miller v. Jackson* ran counter to the well-established principles laid down in *Shelfer v. City of London Electric Lighting Co.*,[33] which was binding on the Court of Appeal.

iv. Contempt. Non-compliance with an injunction (or an undertaking given in lieu[34]) is a contempt of court,[35] punishable by imprisonment, sequestration of property (in the case of a corporation)

---

[27] *Deschamps v. Miller* [1908] 1 Ch. 856; *Re Hawthorne* (1883) 23 Ch.D. 743. See Dicey and Morris, *The Conflict of Laws* (13th ed.), pp. 945 *et seq.*, discussing also the effect of Civil Jurisdiction and Judgments Act 1982, s.30. This principle applies also to foreign intellectual property; *Tyburn Productions Ltd v. Conan Doyle* [1991] Ch. 75.

[28] See *Penn v. Lord Baltimore* (1750) 1 Ves.Sen. 444, *ante*, p. 716; *Hamlin v. Hamlin* [1986] Fam. 11.

[29] *M. Michaels (Furriers) Ltd v. Askew, The Times*, June 25, 1983 (nuisance by members of "Animal Aid"); *E.M.I. Records Ltd v. Kudhail, The Times*, June 28, 1983; *cf. United Kingdom Nirex Ltd v. Barton, The Times*, October 14, 1986.

[30] [1977] Q.B. 966. For interlocutory injunctions, see *post*, p. 783. See also the cases on libel and breach of confidence, *post*, pp. 718, 720.

[31] [1981] Q.B. 88; (1981) 97 L.Q.R. 3; (1981) 44 M.L.R. 212 (R. Buckley); *Sevenoaks District Council v. Pattullo & Vinson Ltd* [1984] Ch. 211; *Elliott v. Islington London Borough Council* [1991] 1 E.G.L.R. 167.

[32] *post*, p. 801.

[33] [1895] 1 Ch. 287, *post*, p. 802. See (1982) 41 C.L.J. 87 (S. Tromans).

[34] *Hussain v. Hussain* [1986] Fam. 134; *Roberts v. Roberts* [1990] 2 F.L.R. 111.

[35] Contempt of Court Act 1981. See also *Parker v. Camden London Borough Council* [1986] Ch. 162. As to children and mental patients, see *Wookey v. Wookey* [1991] Fam. 121.

or a fine.[36] Acts done in breach of an injunction may be void for illegality.[37] As disobedience may lead to imprisonment, the injunction must be expressed in exact terms, so that the defendant knows precisely what to do, or refrain from doing.[38] As committal proceedings are equivalent to a criminal charge, the breach of injunction must be established beyond reasonable doubt.[39]

In matrimonial cases, committal orders should be made very reluctantly. As Ormrod L.J. said in *Ansah v. Ansah*,[40] "Committal orders are remedies of last resort; in family cases they should be the very last resort." It should be added that a power of arrest may be attached to occupation or non-molestation orders granted under the Family Law Act 1996.

A question which has recently been prominent is whether third parties commit contempt if they knowingly act contrary to an injunction. A third party who aids and abets a breach of injunction is guilty of contempt.[41] An agent of the party enjoined is also bound by the injunction.[42] The court has jurisdiction in wardship and other special cases to make an injunction against the world at large,[42a] although a person who contravened the order in good faith and without notice of its terms would not commit contempt.[43] In *Att.-Gen. v. Times Newspapers Ltd*[44] newspapers which published confidential material which other newspapers had been enjoined from publishing were guilty of contempt. The House of Lords held that strangers who knowingly took action to damage or destroy confidentiality before the trial committed contempt by nullifying the purpose

---

[36] As to a company's liability for employee's breach, see *Re Supply of Ready Mixed Concrete (No. 2)* [1995] 1 A.C. 456. For liability of directors, see *Director General of Fair Trading v. Buckland* [1990] 1 W.L.R. 920; *Att.-Gen. for Tuvalu v. Philatelic Distribution Corporation Ltd* [1990] 1 W.L.R. 926. Non-compliance with an injunction may be an element in a subsequent award of exemplary damages: *Drane v. Evangelou* [1978] 1 W.L.R. 455.

[37] *Clarke v. Chadburn* [1985] 1 W.L.R. 78 (union rules); All E.R. Rev. 1985 at 76 (C. Miller); *cf. Harrow London Borough Council v. Johnstone* [1997] 1 W.L.R. 459 (notice to quit). Compliance with a statute affords a defence; *A. v. B. Bank (Governor and Company of the Bank of England intervening)* [1993] Q.B. 311.

[38] *Redland Bricks Ltd v. Morris* [1970] A.C. 652; *Co-operative Insurance Society Ltd v. Argyll Stores (Holdings) Ltd* [1998] A.C. 1.

[39] *Re Bramblevale Ltd* [1970] Ch. 128; *Kent County Council v. Batchelor* (1977) 33 P. & C.R. 185.

[40] [1977] Fam. 138 at 144. See also (1977) 40 M.L.R. 220 (P. Pettit); *Brewer v. Brewer* [1989] 2 F.L.R. 251; *Hale v. Tanner, (Practice Note)* [2000] 1 W.L.R. 2377.

[41] *Acro (Automation) Ltd v. Rex Chainbelt Inc.* [1971] 1 W.L.R. 1676.

[42] *Cretanor Maritime Co. Ltd v. Irish Marine Management Ltd* [1978] 1 W.L.R. 966. See the asset-freezing cases, *post*, p. 834, particularly the "world-wide assets" cases.

[42a] *post*, p. 821.

[43] *Re X. (a minor)* [1984] 1 W.L.R. 1422; *Att.-Gen. v. Times Newspapers Ltd* [1992] 1 A.C. 191 at 224; *Re Z (a minor) (Identification: Restrictions on Publication)* [1997] Fam. 1; *Kelly v. B.B.C.* [2001] 2 W.L.R. 253.

[44] [1992] 1 A.C. 191 (the *Spycatcher* case). See also *Bank Mellat v. Kazmi* [1989] Q.B. 541; *Derby & Co. Ltd v. Weldon (Nos. 3 and 4)* [1990] Ch. 65; *Re C (Adult: Refusal of Treatment)* [1994] 1 W.L.R. 290; *Harrow London Borough Council v. Johnstone* [1997] 1 W.L.R. 459.

of the trial. The question was not whether third parties were bound by the injunction, but whether they could commit contempt even though they were not bound. As they were not parties to the order, the basis of the contempt would not be a breach of the order (unless they had aided and abetted a breach) but knowing interference with the administration of justice.

v. Crown Proceedings. An injunction will not normally lie against the Crown.[45] The proper remedy in such a case is the declaration. A former disadvantage that an interim declaration could not be granted has now gone.[46] An interlocutory injunction may, exceptionally, be granted against the Crown to protect rights enforceable under European Community law.[47] Further, an injunction, final or interlocutory, may be granted against ministers and other officers of the Crown, and a minister can be liable for contempt.[48]

B. Protection of Rights

i. Locus Standi. "It is a fundamental rule that the court will only grant an injunction at the suit of a private individual to support a legal right."[49] The type of right which may be protected by injunction in the field of private law is dealt with below, but the question also arises as to who may seek an injunction to protect a public right. This requires a consideration of the extent to which the civil courts may restrain a breach of the criminal law by injunction. The general rule is that public rights are protected by the Attorney-General, acting either on his own initiative or on the relation of a member of the public. He may obtain an injunction to restrain breaches of the criminal law even if there is a statutory remedy, where that remedy is inadequate,[50] and the view of the court is that injunctions should be granted at his request to prevent clear breaches of the law irrespective of the weighing of benefits and detriments which characterises most other injunctions.[51]

---

[45] Crown Proceedings Act 1947, s.21; *R. v. Secretary of State for Transport, ex p. Factortame Ltd* [1990] 2 A.C. 85.

[46] C.P.R. 25.1. See *R. v. R. (Interim Declaration: Adult's Residence)* [2000] 1 F.L.R. 451; *Bank of Scotland v. A Ltd (Serious Fraud Office, interested party), The Times,* February 6, 2001.

[47] *R. v. Secretary of State for Transport, ex p. Factortame Ltd (No. 2)* [1991] 1 A.C. 603; (1991) 107 L.Q.R. 4 (H. Wade).

[48] *M. v. Home Office* [1994] 1 A.C. 377; (1994) 57 M.L.R. 620 (C. Harlow); (1994) 53 C.L.J. 1 (T. Allen).

[49] *per* Lord Denning M.R. in *Thorne v. British Broadcasting Corporation* [1957] 1 W.L.R. 1104 at 1109. But compare the different views expressed in *Chief Constable of Kent v. V.* [1983] Q.B. 34.

[50] *Att.-Gen. v. Sharp* [1931] 1 Ch. 121; *Att.-Gen. v. Chaudry* [1971] 1 W.L.R. 1623.

[51] *Att.-Gen. v. Bastow* [1957] 1 Q.B. 514; *Att.-Gen. v. Harris* [1961] 1 Q.B. 74; *post,* p. 824.

By way of exception to this general rule, an individual may seek an injunction if interference with a public right, created by statute or existing at common law, would also infringe some private right of his or would inflict special damage on him,[52] save where statute has, for instance by providing an exclusive remedy, excluded it.[53] But an individual who does not come within the established exceptions has no remedy, for it is no part of English law that a person who suffers damage by reason of another person's breach of statute has a civil action against that person.[54] Thus a record company could not get an injunction against a defendant who traded in "bootleg" records in breach of statute, as there is no principle that a person can restrain a crime affecting his property rights by injunction where the statute was not designed for the protection of the class of which he is a member.[55]

Another important question is whether a private individual may obtain an injunction to restrain a threatened criminal offence which would interfere with a public right when the Attorney-General has refused his consent to a relator action, the case not being one where private rights or special damage to the claimant are involved.[56]

In *Gouriet v. Union of Post Office Workers*[57] the claimant, a member of the public, sought an injunction to restrain a threatened boycott of postal communications between Britain and South Africa, in breach of statute. The Attorney-General had refused consent to a relator action, without giving reasons. It was unanimously held in the House of Lords that the court had no jurisdiction to grant such an injunction, nor to control the exercise of the Attorney-General's discretion in any way.

It was a fundamental principle that private rights could be asserted by the individual and public rights by the Attorney-General,

---

[52] *Gouriet v. Union of Post Office Workers* [1978] A.C. 435; *Lonrho Ltd v. Shell Petroleum Co. Ltd* [1982] A.C. 173; *R.C.A. Corpn. v. Pollard* [1983] Ch. 135. An action also lies if the claimant can show that he is a member of the class for whose benefit the statute was passed and upon whom Parliament intended to confer a cause of action; *R. v. Deputy Governor of Parkhurst Prison, ex p. Hague* [1992] 1 A.C. 58. See also *Francome v. Mirror Group Newspapers* [1984] 1 W.L.R. 892; *Barrs v. Bethell* [1982] Ch. 294.

[53] *Stevens v. Chown* [1901] 1 Ch. 894; *cf. Meade v. London Borough of Haringey* [1979] 1 W.L.R. 637; Spry, pp. 364 *et seq.*

[54] *Lonrho Ltd v. Shell Petroleum Co. Ltd, supra*; *CBS Songs Ltd v. Amstrad Consumer Electronics plc* [1988] A.C. 1013; *P. v. Liverpool Daily Post and Echo Newspapers plc* [1991] 2 A.C. 370.

[55] *R.C.A. Corpn. v. Pollard* [1983] Ch. 135; *Rickless v. United Artists Corp.* [1988] Q.B. 40. See now Copyright, Designs and Patents Act 1988, s.194.

[56] The right to bring a private prosecution, once the offence is committed, is a different matter, but the Attorney-General has power to veto such proceedings.

[57] [1978] A.C. 435; (1977) 36 C.L.J. 201 (D. Williams); (1978) 94 L.Q.R. 4 (H.W.R.W.); (1978) 41 M.L.R. 58 (T. Hartley); (1978) 41 M.L.R. 63 (R. Simpson); (1979) 42 M.L.R. 369 (D. Feldman). See also Lord Denning's observations in *The Discipline of Law*, pp. 137 *et seq.*

and that "the criminal law is enforced in the criminal courts by the conviction and punishment of offenders, not in the civil courts."[58] Any interference by the civil courts exposes the defendant to "double jeopardy"; the penalty of imprisonment for contempt of court, if the offence is committed, is added to the criminal penalties fixed by Parliament.[59] Not only are the punishments different, but the contempt proceedings will be decided by a judge alone while the defendant may be entitled to a jury in the criminal proceedings.[60] These considerations are, of course, also present in cases where injunctions may be granted to enforce the criminal law. No doubt for this reason the House of Lords expressed the view that the cases where the Attorney-General can seek an injunction to restrain the commission of an offence are narrow and not to be extended. The jurisdiction is "of great delicacy and is one to be used with caution." The Attorney-General's power is "not without its difficulties and these may call for consideration in the future."[61]

The House of Lords affirmed that the Attorney-General is responsible to Parliament, not to the court. Any error he might make would be of political judgment, not law, and would not be appropriate for decision in the courts. Others have doubted whether responsibility to Parliament is a sufficient control to compensate for the exclusion of the court's jurisdiction.[62]

But the effect of the decision may not be so great as first appears. The prerogative remedies, with their broader concept of standing,[63] may be available where the defendant is a public authority.[64] Here the court feels able to judge on matters of public interest, even where there are political implications,[65] but the House of Lords has doubted the analogy.[66]

In the case of a crime which has already been committed, it has been held that the police have *locus standi* to seek an injunction to

---

[58] [1978] A.C. 435 at 490 (*per* Viscount Dilhorne). Although the case concerned criminal law enforcement, many statements in the House of Lords were wide enough to cover all public law actions. See also *Ashby v. Ebdon* [1985] Ch. 394; (1985) 44 C.L.J. 6 (J. Jolowicz).

[59] [1978] A.C. 435 at 498, *per* Lord Diplock. See *Kent County Council v. Batchelor* [1979] 1 W.L.R. 213. But in other areas the civil court adds to the criminal penalty; see p. 329, *ante*, (forfeiture of property acquired by killing).

[60] But the standard of proof will be the same; see (1979) 42 M.L.R. 369 (D. Feldman).

[61] See also *Stoke-on-Trent City Council v. B. & Q. (Retail) Ltd* [1984] A.C. 754; *Waverley Borough Council v. Hilden* [1988] 1 W.L.R. 246; *Kirklees Borough Council v. Wickes Building Supplies Ltd* [1993] A.C. 227; *post*, p. 825.

[62] [1977] Q.B. 729 at 758–759 (*per* Lord Denning M.R.); (1977) 36 C.L.J. 201 (D. Williams); (1978) 41 M.L.R. 58 (T. Hartley); (1979) 42 M.L.R. 369 (D. Feldman); *cf.* (1978) 41 M.L.R. 63 (R. Simpson).

[63] *post*, pp. 826–827.

[64] See *R. v. Commissioner of Police of the Metropolis* [1968] 2 Q.B. 118; *R. v. I.R.C., ex p. National Federation of Self-Employed and Small Businesses Ltd* [1982] A.C. 617 at 640, *post*, p. 826; *R. v. Her Majesty's Treasury, ex p. Smedley* [1985] Q.B. 657.

[65] See, for example, *Secretary of State for Education and Science v. Tameside Metropolitan Borough Council* [1977] A.C. 1014.

[66] *Gouriet v. Union of Post Office Workers* [1978] A.C. 435 at 483.

"freeze" money in a bank account which is reasonably believed to be the proceeds of a crime.[67] This principle is not without difficulty, and is confined to an asset which can be identified as the stolen item or as property representing it.[68] No such injunction is available in respect of moneys not themselves obtained by fraud but which were profits made by means of a loan obtained by fraud.[69] The House of Lords in *Att.-Gen. v. Blake*[70] considered that the Attorney-General had no entitlement to an injunction which effectively froze the proceeds of crime (royalties from a book written by a former KGB spy), because this would amount to confiscation outside the statutory provisions permitting confiscation orders. Their Lordships decided that the private law remedy of an account of profits was available,[71] and thus the point did not arise. No view was expressed as to the correctness of the police cases, which were distinguishable.

Finally, the rule that only the Attorney-General may enforce public rights is subject to certain limited statutory exceptions, enabling a local authority to seek an injunction in its own name to protect public rights in the locality or to enforce planning control.[72]

ii. Legal and Equitable Rights. A right that is to be protected by an injunction must be one that is known to law or equity.[73] Thus it must not be one of which cognisance will be taken only in ecclesiastical law.[74] The point was firmly made in *Day v. Brownrigg*.[75]

> The claimant lived in a house that had been called "Ashford Lodge" for 60 years. The defendant lived in a smaller neighbouring house called "Ashford Villa." The defendant started to call his house "Ashford Lodge" and the claimant sought an injunction to restrain him from doing so. The Court of Appeal took the view that there was no violation of a legal or equitable right of the claimant so that no injunction would be granted.[76]

---

[67] *Chief Constable of Kent v. V.* [1983] Q.B. 34; *West Mercia Constabulary v. Wagener* [1982] 1 W.L.R. 127; (1982) 98 L.Q.R. 190 (D. Feldman); All E.R. Rev. 1982 at 205 (G. Zellick); (1983) 99 L.Q.R. 1; (1983) 42 C.L.J. 51 (A Tettenborn).

[68] *Chief Constable of Hampshire v. A. Ltd* [1985] Q.B. 132; (1984) 100 L.Q.R. 537 (G. Samuel). See also *Malone v. Metropolitan Police Commissioner* [1980] Q.B. 49.

[69] *Chief Constable of Leicestershire v. M.* [1989] 1 W.L.R. 20; *cf. Securities and Investments Board v. Pantell S.A.* [1990] Ch. 426.

[70] [2000] 3 W.L.R. 625.

[71] *ante*, p. 24.

[72] Local Government Act 1972, s.222; Town and Country Planning Act 1990, s.187B; *post*, p. 825.

[73] In *Chief Constable of Kent v. V.* [1983] Q.B. 34, Lord Denning M.R. considered that this was no longer the case after the Supreme Court Act 1981, but this was firmly rejected by the House of Lords in *P. v. Liverpool Daily Post and Echo Newspapers plc* [1991] 2 A.C. 370. A broad approach is favoured in *Broadmoor Hospital Authority v. Robinson* [2000] 1 W.L.R. 1590.

[74] *Att.-Gen. v. Dean and Chapter of Ripon Cathedral* [1945] Ch. 239.

[75] (1878) 10 Ch.D. 294; *Beddow v. Beddow* (1878) 9 Ch.D. 89 at 93.

[76] See also *Montgomery v. Montgomery* [1965] P. 46.

Similarly, in *Paton v. Trustees of British Pregnancy Advisory Service*[77] it was held that a husband could not obtain an injunction to prevent his wife from having, or a registered medical practitioner from performing, a legal abortion: the husband had "no legal right enforceable at law or in equity."

Injunctions have proved valuable in protecting confidential material.[78] Before 1875, it was accepted that equity would, in suitable cases, restrain a defendant from revealing or distributing information or other material obtained in confidence,[79] regarding the breach of confidence as an equitable wrong needing protection by injunction. It has now been accepted[80] that the jurisdiction in this type of case does not depend on any notion of property or contract, but that an obligation of confidence can exist by virtue of the circumstances, and independently of any actual agreement to that effect. Confidential commercial information will be restrained from publication along similar lines.

Other rights which may be protected by injunction include the right (contractual or otherwise) not to be subjected to arbitration proceedings which could not lead to a fair trial[81]; the right (contractual or otherwise) not to be sued in a foreign court[82]; the right of the police to "freeze" money in a bank account which is reasonably believed to be the identifiable proceeds of crime[83]; the right to restrain a breach of European Community law[84]; the right to restrain the export of works of art by means of forged documents[85]; the right to refuse surgery[86]; the right not to be harassed[87]; the right of a public body to prevent interference with the performance of its statutory responsibilities[88]; and the right to ensure the effectiveness of a court order.[89] The latter right is the basis of the novel use of the

---

[77] [1979] Q.B. 276; (1979) 95 L.Q.R. 332 (J. Phillips); (1979) 30 C.L.P. 217 (C. Lyon and G. Benett). For a discussion of the position if the proposed abortion would be illegal, see (1979) 42 M.L.R. 324 (I. Kennedy); *C. v. S.* [1988] Q.B. 135; (1987) 103 L.Q.R. 340 (A. Grubb and D. Pearl).

[78] *post*, p. 820.

[79] *Prince Albert v. Strange* (1849) 1 H. & T. 1 (copies of etchings made by the Prince and Queen Victoria: distribution restrained).

[80] See particularly *Argyll v. Argyll* [1967] Ch. 302 at 322; *Fraser v. Evans* [1969] 1 Q.B. 349 at 361; (1972) J.S.P.T.L. 149 (P. North).

[81] *Bremer Vulkan Schiffbau und Maschinenfabrik v. South India Shipping Corpn.* [1981] A.C. 909.

[82] *British Airways Board v. Laker Airways Ltd* [1985] A.C. 58; *South Carolina Insurance Co. v. Assurantie Maatschappij "De Zeven Provincien" N.V.* [1987] A.C. 24.

[83] *ante*, p. 766.

[84] *Cutsforth v. Mansfield Inns Ltd* [1986] 1 W.L.R. 558; *Taittinger v. Allbev Ltd* [1994] 4 All E.R. 75.

[85] *Kingdom of Spain v. Christie, Manson & Woods Ltd* [1986] 1 W.L.R. 1120.

[86] *Re C (Adult: Refusal of Treatment)* [1994] 1 W.L.R. 290.

[87] Protection from Harassment Act 1997, s.3.

[88] *Broadmoor Hospital Authority v. Robinson* [2000] 1 W.L.R. 1590.

[89] *Maclaine Watson & Co. Ltd v. International Tin Council (No. 2)* [1989] Ch. 286 (unpaid judgment debt).

injunction to prevent the defendant from leaving the country,[90] although this has been described as draconian and requiring careful examination.[91] Such an injunction may be granted even though there is no pre-existing cause of action.[92] The jurisdiction, which arises under section 37(1) of the Supreme Court Act 1981, is in aid of the court's procedures leading to the disposal of proceedings, and is available after judgment to aid enforcement. The injunction is ancillary to other powers of the court and is not a free-standing enforcement procedure in its own right.[93]

C. Perpetual Injunctions

It is axiomatic that the jurisdiction to grant injunctions is purely discretionary. But, as with specific performance, the court, in exercising its discretion, pays attention to certain factors established by the precedents as being of particular relevance.

i. Prohibitory Injunctions. If a claimant has established the existence of a right, infringement of that right should be restrained, but injunctions will not be granted where an award of damages[94] would be sufficient. Damages will not be an adequate remedy if they are not quantifiable, or if money could not properly compensate the claimant, as in the case of nuisance and other continuous or repeated injuries requiring a series of actions for damages, or even where the remedy would be ineffective because the defendant is a pauper.[95]

The extent of the damage is not the crucial point. An injunction may be granted even if only nominal damages would be recoverable at law.[96] The smallness of the damage and the fact that a monetary sum could easily be assessed to compensate for it, is no reason for withholding an injunction if the consequence is that the defendant is

---

[90] *Bayer A.G. v. Winter* [1986] 1 W.L.R. 497 *post*, p. 836; *Arab Monetary Fund v. Hashim* [1989] 1 W.L.R. 565; *cf. Al Nahkel for Contracting and Trading Ltd v. Lowe* [1986] Q.B. 235 and *Allied Arab Bank Ltd v. Hajjar* [1988] Q.B. 787; (1988) 47 C.L.J. 364 (N. Andrews) *(ne exeat regno)*. See also *Re I. (a minor), The Times*, May 22, 1987.

[91] *Bayer A.G. v. Winter (No. 2)* [1986] 1 W.L.R. 540; (1990) 20 U.W.A.L.R. 143 (J. Martin).

[92] *Re Oriental Credit Ltd* [1988] Ch. 204 (to prevent director leaving the country prior to examination under Companies Act 1985, s.561); criticised in (1988) 47 C.L.J. 177 (C. Forsyth); *Morris v. Murjani* [1996] 1 W.L.R. 848 (to prevent bankrupt leaving the country without complying with Insolvency Act 1986, s.333).

[93] *B. v. B. (Injunction: Jurisdiction)* [1998] 1 W.L.R. 329 (judgment debtor).

[94] The jurisdiction to award damages under Lord Cairns' Act is considered below, *post*, p. 801.

[95] *Hodgson v. Duce* (1856) 28 L.T.(o.s.) 155.

[96] *Rochdale Canal Co. v. King* (1851) 2 Sim.(n.s.) 78; *Woollerton and Wilson Ltd v. Richard Costain Ltd* [1970] 1 W.L.R. 411.

in effect compulsorily "buying" a right which is the claimant's to sell only if he wants to.[97] This principle was applied in *Express Newspapers Ltd v. Keys*.[98]

Certain trade unions had issued instructions to their members to support a "Day of Action" in protest against Government policies. The claimants sought an injunction to restrain the unions from inducing a breach of contract between the members and their employers. Griffiths J., in granting the injunction, held that damages would be inadequate. The employers did not want money; they wanted their newspapers to be published. To refuse the injunction would be giving a licence to the unions to commit an unlawful act merely because they could afford to pay the damages. It would not be fair to leave the employers to their remedy in damages, as there would be real difficulty in attributing any particular breach of contract to incitement by the unions as opposed to the voluntary act of the employees. "It is one thing to suffer damage and it is another to prove it."[99]

Similarly in cases in which the defendant has trespassed on the claimant's property: actual loss does not need to be shown before an injunction is granted.[1] But there may be cases in which injunctions will be refused, for example if the infringement is occasional or temporary, or if it is a trivial matter. One such case was *Armstrong v. Sheppard and Short*,[2] where the claimant had misled the court and had suffered no real damage. Lord Evershed M.R. said "A proprietor who establishes a proprietary right is ex debito justitiae entitled to an injunction unless it can be said against him that he has raised such an equity that it is no longer open to him to assert his legal or proprietary rights."[3] Similarly, in *Behrens v. Richards*[4] an injunction was not granted to restrain the public from using tracks on the claimant's land on an unfrequented part of the coast, causing no

---

[97] *Wood v. Sutcliffe* (1851) 2 Sim.(N.S.) 163. In *Express Newspapers Ltd v. Keys* [1980] I.R.L.R. 247, and *Patel v. W.H. Smith (Eziot) Ltd* [1987] 1 W.L.R. 853, it was held that this principle applied equally to interlocutory injunctions, and was not affected by *American Cyanamid Co. v. Ethicon Ltd* [1975] A.C. 396, *post*, p. 777.

[98] [1980] I.R.L.R. 247. The injunction in this case was interlocutory but the judgment on this aspect is of general application.

[99] *ibid.* at 250.

[1] *Goodson v. Richardson* (1874) L.R. 9 Ch.App. 221; *Trenberth (John) Ltd v. National Westminster Bank Ltd* (1979) 39 P. & C.R. 104. See also *Marco Productions Ltd v. Pagola* [1945] K.B. 111 on breach of contract.

[2] [1959] 2 Q.B. 384.

[3] *ibid.* at 394. See *Harrow London Borough Council v. Donohue* [1995] 1 E.G.L.R. 257.

[4] [1905] 2 Ch. 614.

damage to him. Such cases are, however, to be regarded as exceptional.[5]

It is obvious that these various factors are not to be considered in isolation and no complete list can be given of instances where an injunction will be refused. The principle applied by the courts is the protection of existing rights which are recognised by the law. But an injunction will not issue in every such case; it may be refused where damages are an adequate remedy, or where the claimant has by his conduct disentitled himself from injunctive relief,[6] or where the defendant gives to the court an undertaking not to do the act complained of[7]; or where, even if there is no other suitable remedy, the court considers that the claimant has suffered no injustice.[8]

ii. Mandatory Injunctions. These are governed by the same general principles as prohibitory injunctions, save that the problems of enforcement, supervision and hardship may be more acute. Mandatory injunctions are less frequently granted than prohibitory injunctions, and, as Lord Upjohn stated in *Redland Bricks Ltd v. Morris*,[9] are entirely discretionary, although it has been held that the court has no real discretion in cases involving trespass by total dispossession.[10]

There are two broad categories of mandatory injunctions: the "restorative" injunction, requiring the defendant to undo a wrongful act in situations where a prohibitory injunction might have been obtained to prevent the commission of the act[11]; and the mandatory injunction to compel the defendant to carry out some positive obligation. If the matter is one of contract, specific performance is more usual in the latter situation, but an injunction may be granted.[12] We have already seen that the terms of an injunction must be certain. It

---

[5] *Patel v. W.H. Smith (Eziot) Ltd* [1987] 1 W.L.R. 853; *Anchor Brewhouse Developments Ltd v. Berkley House (Docklands Developments) Ltd* [1987] 2 E.G.L.R. 173; (1988) 138 N.L.J. 23 (E. McKendrick) and 385 (H. Wilkinson).

[6] Discretionary bars are considered below, *post*, p. 796.

[7] *Halsey v. Esso Petroleum Co. Ltd* [1961] 1 W.L.R. 683; *Att.-Gen. v. Times Newspapers Ltd, The Times*, June 27, 1975 (interlocutory injunction refused where defendant undertook not to publish Crossman diaries before trial); *British Broadcasting Corporation v. Hearn* [1977] 1 W.L.R. 1004.

[8] See *Glynn v. Keele University* [1971] 1 W.L.R. 487.

[9] [1970] A.C. 652 at 655. See also *Leakey v. National Trust for Places of Historic Interest or Natural Beauty* [1980] Q.B. 485; *Re C. (a minor)* [1991] 2 F.L.R. 168.

[10] *Harrow London Borough Council v. Donohue* [1995] 1 E.G.L.R. 257.

[11] *Charrington v. Simons & Co. Ltd* [1971] 1 W.L.R. 598; *Pugh v. Howells* (1984) 48 P. & C.R. 29; *Jones v. Stones* [1999] 1 W.L.R. 1739. Failure to obtain a prohibitory injunction does not preclude the issue subsequently of a mandatory injunction: see *Wrotham Park Estate v. Parkside Homes Ltd* [1974] 1 W.L.R. 798, *infra*. It is, however, an important consideration; *Gafford v. Graham* (1999) 77 P. & C.R. 73.

[12] See *Evans v. B.B.C. and I.B.A., The Times*, February 26, 1974 (interlocutory).

follows from this that a duty which is itself uncertain cannot be enforced by injunction.[13]

Problems of supervision may arise with mandatory injunctions as with specific performance.[14] This will not normally prevent the grant of a "restorative" mandatory injunction, which merely requires an act of restoration, but a mandatory injunction is unlikely to be granted in cases involving the continuous performance of a positive obligation.

> In *Gravesham Borough Council v. British Railways Board*,[15] the defendant planned to curtail the services of its ferry. As this would cause inconvenience to some local workers, a mandatory injunction was sought to compel the defendant to maintain existing timetables, even though this would cause the ferry to be run at a loss. It was held that in fact there was no breach of the defendant's common law duty to operate the ferry, but even if there had been, a mandatory injunction would not be appropriate, because of enforcement difficulties and financial hardship to the defendant. Slade J. said that there was no absolute and inflexible rule that the court will never grant an injunction requiring a series of acts involving the continuous employment of people over a number of years. But the jurisdiction to grant such an injunction would be exercised only in exceptional circumstances.

As in the case of prohibitory injunctions, it is not necessary for the claimant to show grave damage or inconvenience. In *Kelsen v. Imperial Tobacco Co. Ltd*[16] a mandatory injunction was granted to enforce the removal of a sign which trespassed in the airspace above the claimant's premises, causing no real damage to him, save in so far as he could have charged for the use of the space.

While the extent of the damage is not crucial, the question of hardship to the defendant is more significant.[17] In *Charrington v. Simons & Co. Ltd*,[18] Buckley J. thought that the criterion for the grant of a mandatory injunction was a fair result, taking into consideration the benefit which the order would confer on the claimant

---

[13] *Bower v. Bantam Investments Ltd* [1972] 1 W.L.R. 1120 (interlocutory); *cf. Acrow (Automation) Ltd v. Rex Chainbelt Inc.* [1971] 1 W.L.R. 1676; *Peninsular Maritime Ltd v. Padseal Ltd* (1981) 259 E.G. 860.

[14] *ante*, p. 727.

[15] [1978] Ch. 379. See also *Dowty Boulton Paul Ltd v. Wolverhampton Corporation* [1971] 1 W.L.R. 204 (no injunction to enforce a covenant to maintain land as an airfield); *cf. Co-operative Insurance Society Ltd v. Argyll Stores (Holdings) Ltd* [1998] A.C. 1 (no specific performance of covenant in lease to keep open in trading hours as a retail shop); *ante*, p. 728.

[16] [1957] 2 Q.B. 334.

[17] *Gravesham Borough Council v. British Railways Board, supra; Jordan v. Norfolk County Council* [1994] 1 W.L.R. 1353 (disproportionate cost). See also *Colls v. Home and Colonial Stores Ltd* [1904] A.C. 179, and other cases on Lord Cairns' Act, *post*, p. 802.

[18] [1970] 1 W.L.R. 725 at 730. See also *Shepherd Homes Ltd v. Sandham* [1971] Ch. 340.

and the detriment which it would cause the defendant. But the Court of Appeal doubted the usefulness of the "fair result" test.[19]

In *Wrotham Park Estate v. Parkside Homes Ltd*,[20] the defendant had erected houses in breach of a restrictive covenant which it had thought was unenforceable. Although purchasers were now in occupation, the claimants sought a mandatory injunction for the demolition of the houses. For various reasons, they had not sought interlocutory relief to prevent the erection of the houses, but this was not fatal to the grant of a mandatory injunction.[21] The fact that the action was commenced before much building had been done was a relevant but not a conclusive factor. The injunction was refused, as it would result in the unpardonable waste of needed houses. Instead, damages were awarded under Lord Cairns' Act.

Finally, it has been held that the court should be reluctant to intervene in industrial disputes by the grant of a mandatory injunction.

In *Harold Stephen and Co. Ltd v. Post Office*,[22] an industrial dispute had arisen whereby postal workers were suspended for unlawfully "blacking" the mail of a certain company (Grunwick). This resulted in the claimant company's mail being held up and its business seriously disrupted. The company sought a mandatory injunction against the Post Office to release its mail. The Court of Appeal refused the injunction, which would require the Post Office to take back the suspended workers, who would be likely to continue the unlawful action. The injunction would, therefore, have the effect of revoking the Post Office's disciplinary measures and making it appear that the court endorsed the continuance of the unlawful action. Geoffrey Lane L.J. said that "It can only be in very rare circumstances and in the most extreme circumstances that this court should interfere by way of mandatory injunction in the delicate mechanism of industrial disputes and industrial negotiations."[23]

Such an extreme case was *Parker v. Camden London Borough Council*,[24] where a strike of boilermen employed by the landlord

[19] [1971] 1 W.L.R. 598, *post*, p. 810.
[20] [1974] 1 W.L.R. 798; (1974) 39 Conv.(N.S.) 289 (F. Crane); (1975) 34 C.L.J. 224 (J. Jolowicz); distinguished in *Wakeham v. Wood* (1982) 43 P. & C.R. 40, where the building was in flagrant disregard of the covenant.
[21] See also *Shaw v. Applegate* [1977] 1 W.L.R. 970 at 978.
[22] [1977] 1 W.L.R. 1172.
[23] *ibid.* at 1180. See also *Meade v. London Borough of Haringey* [1979] 1 W.L.R. 637.
[24] [1986] Ch. 162 (interlocutory).

council meant that the tenants, many of whom were elderly or had young children, had no heating or hot water. In these exceptional circumstances, involving risk to life and health, the court was prepared to grant a mandatory injunction to turn on the boiler even though industrial action was involved.

The principles applicable to the grant of mandatory interlocutory injunctions and mandatory *quia timet* injunctions are discussed below.[25]

iii. Suspension of Injunctions. If it would be very difficult for the defendant to comply immediately with the injunction, he will not be made to do the impossible. The injunction may be granted but suspended for a reasonable period, particularly if such a course will not result in financial damage to the claimant. The defendant may be required to undertake to pay damages to the claimant for any loss. Suspension is not unusual where the defendant is a local authority, which must make alternative arrangements for the performance of its duties. Thus, in *Pride of Derby Angling Association v. British Celanese and Others*[26] an injunction was granted against a local authority to restrain the pollution of a river, but was suspended for a reasonable time, with the possibility of further suspension should the circumstances require it.

The courts have sometimes suspended injunctions not in order to give the defendant time to comply, but rather to enable him to continue his wrongful activity in cases involving no substantial injury to the claimant. Thus, in *Woollerton and Wilson Ltd v. Richard Costain Ltd*[27] an injunction to restrain aerial trespass (causing no danger or damage) by a crane during building works was granted but suspended until a date when the crane would no longer be needed. This was doubted by the Court of Appeal in *Charrington v. Simons & Co. Ltd*,[28] where a three-year suspension of an injunction to reinstate a track (which had been resurfaced in breach of covenant) was held improper.

D. Interlocutory (or Interim) Injunctions

i. General. Interlocutory injunctions raise somewhat different considerations. The jurisdiction is related not to the most just

---

[25] *post*, pp. 790, 795.

[26] [1953] Ch. 149. See also *Halsey v. Esso Petroleum Co. Ltd* [1961] 1 W.L.R. 683 (suspension for six weeks in nuisance case); *Miller v. Jackson* [1977] Q.B. 966; *Waverley Borough Council v. Hilden* [1988] 1 W.L.R. 246.

[27] [1970] 1 W.L.R. 411; (1970) 33 M.L.R. 552 (G. Dworkin).

[28] [1971] 1 W.L.R. 598; and in *Jaggard v. Sawyer* [1995] 1 W.L.R. 269. See also *Trenberth (John) Ltd v. National Westminster Bank Ltd* (1979) 39 P. & C.R. 104; [1980] Conv. 308 (H. Street). A better solution might have been an award of damages under Lord Cairns' Act: see (1975) 34 C.L.J. 224 at 247 (J. Jolowicz).

method of protecting established rights, but to the most convenient method of preserving the status quo while rights are established. The object of an interlocutory injunction is "to prevent a litigant, who must necessarily suffer the law's delay, from losing by that delay the fruit of his litigation."[29]

Interlocutory injunctions may be prohibitory, mandatory, or *quia timet*. Normally such an injunction remains in force until the trial of the action, but it may be granted for some shorter specified period. If the parties consent, the interlocutory hearing may be treated as a final trial if the dispute is of law. But this will not be possible if the dispute is of fact, as affidavit evidence is unsuitable for such issues.

As we have seen, failure to seek an interlocutory injunction to restrain the commission of a wrongful act will not necessarily preclude the claimant from later obtaining a final mandatory injunction to compel the defendant to undo the act.[30]

(a) *Without Notice Procedure.* The claimant should give at least three clear days' notice, so that, when the application is heard, the defendant can oppose it. But exceptionally an injunction may be granted without serving notice on the defendant, if the matter is one of such urgency that irreparable damage would be caused if the claimant had to go through the normal procedure.[31] The "without notice" injunction may be subsequently set aside or varied on the defendant's application.[32] Such an injunction may be granted even before the proceedings have started. In *Re N. (No. 2)*,[33] an injunction was granted without notice by a High Court judge at his residence on a Sunday, to prevent the applicant's husband from taking their children to Australia.

In family matters injunctions should not be granted without notice unless there is real immediate danger of serious injury or irreparable damage.[34] Only in the most exceptional circumstances will an injunction be granted without notice requiring a spouse to leave the matrimonial home.[35]

---

[29] *Hoffman-La Roche (F.) & Co. v. Secretary of State for Trade and Industry* [1975] A.C. 295 at 355 (Lord Wilberforce).

[30] *Wrotham Park Estate v. Parkside Homes Ltd* [1974] 1 W.L.R. 798. But such an omission may be relevant to the defence of acquiescence: *Shaw v. Applegate* [1977] 1 W.L.R 970, *post*, p. 798.

[31] C.P.R. 25.3. It is otherwise if the claimant had the opportunity to give notice; *Bates v. Lord Hailsham of St. Marylebone* [1972] 1 W.L.R. 1373. Where a trade dispute is involved, see the Trade Union and Labour Relations (Consolidation) Act 1992, s.221(2), *post*, p. 784.

[32] C.P.R. 23.9, 23.10.

[33] [1967] Ch. 512.

[34] *Ansah v. Ansah* [1977] Fam. 138; *G. v. G.* [1990] 1 F.L.R. 395.

[35] *Masich v. Masich* (1977) 121 S.J. 645; (1977) 7 Fam. Law 245.

In the commercial sphere, injunctions should not normally be granted without notice where they would prevent banks from honouring contractual obligations, such as payouts under letters of credit.[36]

The "without notice" procedure has been found most useful in the search order and asset-freezing cases, where there is a danger that the defendant, if aware of the application, would destroy or remove vital evidence, or move assets out of the jurisdiction. These developments are discussed below.[37]

(b) *Discharge of Interlocutory Injunctions.* The court has inherent jurisdiction to discharge an interlocutory injunction, even when the defendant has not applied for its discharge.[38] Furthermore, where an injunction has been granted which affects someone who was not a party to the action, he can apply to court for the variation or discharge of the injunction.[39]

(c) *Injunctions Pending Appeal.* Where a claim for an interlocutory injunction is dismissed, the judge has jurisdiction to grant a limited injunction pending an appeal, on the claimant's without notice application.[40] Such an injunction may be granted in order that the appeal, if successful, is not nugatory.

(d) *Complete Relief.* It is no objection that the grant of an interlocutory injunction gives complete relief to the claimant without requiring him to prove his case, so that he need bring no final action.[41] In *Woodford v. Smith*,[42] Megarry J. granted an interlocutory injunction to restrain a residents' association from breaking its contract by holding a meeting without the claimant members. There was nothing to prevent the court in a proper case from granting on an interim application all the relief claimed in the action. It may be a more serious objection in the case of mandatory interlocutory injunctions,[43] where positive action is required, but in *Evans v. B.B.C. and*

---

[36] *Bolivinter Oil S.A. v. Chase Manhattan Bank* [1984] 1 W.L.R. 392n.

[37] *post*, pp. 831, 834.

[38] *R.D. Harbottle (Mercantile) Ltd v. National Westminster Bank Ltd* [1978] Q.B. 146.

[39] *Cretanor Maritime Co. Ltd v. Irish Marine Management Ltd* [1978] 1 W.L.R. 966; *Iraqi Ministry of Defence v. Arcepey Shipping Co. S.A.* [1981] Q.B. 65, *post*, p. 841 (asset-freezing injunctions).

[40] *Erinford Properties Ltd v. Cheshire County Council* [1974] Ch. 261; *Chartered Bank v. Daklouche* [1976] 1 W.L.R. 107. See also *Ketchum International plc v. Group Public Relations Holdings Ltd* [1997] 1 W.L.R. 4 (jurisdiction to restrain disposal of assets pending appeal if good arguable appeal).

[41] As to whether the principle of *American Cyanamid Co. v. Ethicon Ltd, infra*, applies in such cases, see *post*, p. 786.

[42] [1970] 1 W.L.R. 806; see also *Manchester Corporation v. Connolly* [1970] Ch. 420, where there was plainly no defence.

[43] *Locabail International Finance Ltd v. Agroexport* [1986] 1 W.L.R. 657.

I.B.A.[44] a mandatory interlocutory injunction was granted to enforce the Welsh Nationalist Party's alleged contractual right to a Party Political Broadcast on television just before an election. The interlocutory injunction was thus a complete remedy, making it unnecessary to continue to trial and prove the case.

(e) *Injunction Ineffective.* As equity does not act in vain, an interlocutory injunction will not be granted where it would be of no effect.[45] In *Bentley-Stevens v. Jones*[46] a director was removed by irregular proceedings. This was not a case for an interlocutory injunction, as the irregularities could be cured by going through the proper processes; the result therefore would be the same.

ii. Principles Applicable to the Issue of Interlocutory Injunctions.

As in the case of mandatory injunctions, the interlocutory injunction is discretionary and is never granted as of course. Prior to the decision of the House of Lords in *American Cyanamid Co. v. Ethicon Ltd*,[47] discussed below, it was well established that the claimant had to show a strong prima facie case that his rights had been infringed.[48] He was then required to show that damages would not be an adequate remedy if he succeeded at the trial, and that the balance of convenience favoured the grant. In other words, an interlocutory injunction would not be granted unless the claimant could show that it was more likely than not that he would succeed in obtaining a final injunction at the trial.

(a) *American Cyanamid Co. v. Ethicon Ltd.*[49] The principles mentioned above were replaced by the rules laid down by Lord Diplock in *American Cyanamid*, which were designed to circumvent the necessity of deciding disputed facts or determining points of law without hearing sufficient argument.[50] The case concerned an application for a *quia timet* interlocutory injunction to restrain the infringement of a patent. It was unanimously held that there was no

---

[44] *The Times*, February 26, 1974. See also *Shepherd Homes Ltd v. Sandham* [1971] Ch. 340 at 347, and *Acrow (Automation) Ltd v. Rex Chainbelt Inc.* [1971] 1 W.L.R. 1676 at 1683.

[45] Similarly with final injunctions; *Att-Gen. v. Guardian Newspapers Ltd (No. 2)* [1990] 1 A.C. 109. A declaration may be appropriate; *Love v. Herrity* (1991) 23 H.L.R. 217.

[46] [1974] 1 W.L.R. 638.

[47] [1975] A.C. 396; (1975) 38 M.L.R. 672 (A. Gore); (1976) 35 C.L.J. 82 (P. Wallington); (1975) 91 L.Q.R. 168 (P. Prescott); (1981) 40 C.L.J. 307 (C. Gray).

[48] See *J. T. Stratford & Son Ltd v. Lindley* [1965] A.C. 269, especially at 338 (Lord Upjohn). The contrary was not there argued. The decision was not cited in *American Cyanamid*.

[49] [1975] A.C. 396.

[50] *Smith v. Inner London Education Authority* [1978] 1 All E.R. 411, at 426.

rule requiring the claimant to establish a prima facie case.[51] The rule is that the court must be satisfied that the claimant's case is not frivolous or vexatious and that there is a serious question to be tried. Once that is established, the governing consideration is the balance of convenience. The court should not embark on anything resembling a trial of the action. At the interlocutory stage it is no part of the court's function to resolve conflicts of evidence on affidavit nor to resolve difficult questions of law.[52] These are matters for the trial. At the interlocutory stage the facts may be disputed and the evidence incomplete and there is no cross-examination; the court's discretion would be stultified if, on untested and incomplete evidence, it could only grant the injunction if the claimant had shown that he was more than 50 per cent likely to succeed at trial.

While the balance of convenience is the governing consideration, a significant factor in assessing it is the inadequacy of damages to each party. If that does not provide an answer, then other aspects of the balance of convenience will arise. If the balance of convenience does not clearly favour either party, then the preservation of the status quo will be decisive. Only as a last resort is it proper to consider the relative strength of the cases of both parties, and only then if it appears from the facts set out in the affidavit evidence, as to which there is no credible dispute, that the strength of one party's case is disproportionate to that of the other.[53] Finally, other special factors may have to be considered in individual cases.

Thus it will be seen that there is a series of rules, most of which will apply only if the previous one has not afforded a solution. But, as Browne L.J. stated in *Fellowes & Son v. Fisher*,[54] the remedy is discretionary and the principles enunciated by Lord Diplock contain some elements of flexibility. The House of Lords cannot have intended to lay down rigid rules.[55] They are best described as guidelines,[56] which "must never be used as a rule of thumb, let alone as a strait-jacket."[57]

---

[51] But Lord Diplock himself had said that an applicant for an interlocutory injunction had to show a "strong prima facie case" that he would succeed at trial: *Hoffman-LaRoche (F.) & Co. v. Secretary of State for Trade and Industry* [1975] A.C. 295 at 360. For an explanation, see *Series 5 Software Ltd v. Clarke* [1996] 1 All E.R. 853; All E.R. Rev. 1996, p. 327 (A. Zuckerman).

[52] *Derby & Co. Ltd v. Weldon* [1990] Ch. 48.

[53] See *Cambridge Nutrition Ltd v. British Broadcasting Corporation* [1990] 3 All E.R. 523; cf. *Series 5 Software Ltd v. Clarke, supra.*

[54] [1976] Q.B. 122 at 139.

[55] See *Hubbard v. Vosper* [1972] 2 Q.B. 84, advocating the flexibility of the remedy, and referred to with apparent approval by Lord Diplock in *American Cyanamid* [1975] A.C. 396 at 407; *Kirklees Borough Council v. Wickes Building Supplies Ltd* [1993] A.C. 227.

[56] *Cayne v. Global Natural Resources plc* [1984] 1 All E.R. 225.

[57] *Cambridge Nutrition Ltd v. British Broadcasting Corporation, supra,* at 535.

But the *American Cyanamid* principles have not satisfied everybody. Lord Denning M.R. in *Fellowes & Son v. Fisher*[58] expressed a preference for the "prima facie case" approach, which had been required for a century, because most cases never went to trial,[59] as the parties usually accepted the court's prima facie view, which was a sensible and convenient practice. The other members of the Court of Appeal expressed the need for further guidance, as the new rules were a complete departure from previous practice. But the majority of the Court of Appeal in *Hubbard v. Pitt*[60] considered that the *American Cyanamid* principles were convenient and had often been adopted.

The principles laid down by Lord Diplock in *American Cyanamid* were these:

(i) Claimant's Case not Frivolous or Vexatious. This requirement was designed to remove "any attempt by [claimants] to harass defendants, any case which was futile and any case which was misconceived or an abuse of the process of the court."[61] Such claims fail at the threshold. The claimant must also show that there is a serious question to be tried, which means that he must have a good arguable case,[62] or, in other words, a real prospect of success at the trial.[63]

(ii) The Balance of Convenience. This concept was well known before the decision in *American Cyanamid*,[64] thus the earlier cases remain useful illustrations, but it must be borne in mind that this is now the governing consideration, assuming that the preliminary requirement outlined above is satisfied.

We have seen that the inadequacy of damages is a significant factor in assessing the balance of convenience. The court must first of all consider the adequacy of damages to each party, namely whether damages would adequately compensate the claimant for any loss caused by the acts of the defendant prior to the trial[65] and whether, should the claimant fail at the trial, any loss caused to the

---

[58] [1976] Q.B. 122.
[59] See *British Broadcasting Corporation v. Hearn* [1977] 1 W.L.R. 1004; *Dunford & Elliott Ltd v. Johnson & Firth Brown Ltd* [1977] 1 Lloyd's Rep. 505 at 513; *Cayne v. Global Natural Resources plc.* [1984] 1 All E.R. 225.
[60] [1976] Q.B. 142. Lord Denning M.R. dissented.
[61] *Honeywell Information Systems Ltd v. Anglian Water Authority, The Times*, June 29, 1976 (Geoffrey Lane L.J.).
[62] *Morning Star Cooperative Society Ltd v. Express Newspapers Ltd, The Times*, October 18, 1978; *cf. Derby & Co. Ltd v. Weldon* [1990] Ch. 48; *post*, p. 840.
[63] *Re Lord Cable* [1977] 1 W.L.R. 7 at 20; *Smith v. Inner London Education Authority* [1978] 1 All E.R. 411; *Cayne v. Global Natural Resources plc, supra*.
[64] [1975] A.C. 396. The "balance of justice" was preferred in *Att.-Gen. v. Barker* [1990] 3 All E.R. 257 at 260.
[65] See *Lion Laboratories Ltd v. Evans* [1985] Q.B. 526.

defendant by the grant of the injunction could be adequately compensated by the claimant's undertaking in damages.[66]

An example of irreparable loss is the distribution of a dividend to shareholders on the basis of supposedly erroneous calculations.[67] Another is the loss of trade when members of the public "picketed" the claimant's business premises,[68] or when a trade union proposed unlawfully to induce the claimant's employees to break their contracts by supporting a political strike[69]; the loss cannot be measured, but it may be great. Similarly, the publication of confidential material,[70] or the loss of a job with good prospects.[71] Damages will also be inadequate if the defendant is a foreign company whose government's exchange control may not permit the payment, or is a foreign company of unknown financial status so that the chances of any substantial damages being paid are questionable.[72] Likewise if an individual defendant does not have the means to pay any appreciable damages,[73] or if the damages would be unquantifiable,[74] as in the case of injury to goodwill[75] or reputation.[76]

While the adequacy of damages is a most significant factor, other considerations may be taken into account in assessing the balance of convenience. Where the dispute between the parties is a political one, the damage to both parties may not be calculable in monetary terms.[77] All the circumstances must be considered, including difficulties of compliance or enforcement, and the principle that the

---

[66] *Chancellor, Masters and Scholars of the University of Oxford v. Pergamon Press Ltd* (1977) 121 S.J. 758. See also *Laws v. Florinpace Ltd* [1981] 1 All E.R. 659 (injunction to restrain nuisance by running "sex shop" in residential area).

[67] *Bloxham v. Metropolitan Ry.* (1868) L.R. 3 Ch.App. 337.

[68] *Hubbard v. Pitt* [1976] Q.B. 142, *post*, p. 782. See also *Cutsforth v. Mansfield Inns Ltd* [1986] 1 W.L.R. 558.

[69] *Express Newspapers Ltd v. Keys* [1980] I.R.L.R. 247.

[70] *Att.-Gen. v. Times Newspapers Ltd, The Times*, June 27, 1975 (The Crossman Diaries); *Att.-Gen. v. Guardian Newspapers Ltd* [1987] 1 W.L.R. 1248 (*Spycatcher*). But the perpetual injunctions were refused: *Att.-Gen. v. Jonathan Cape Ltd* [1976] Q.B. 752; *Att.-Gen. v. Guardian Newspapers (No. 2)* [1990] 1 A.C. 109.

[71] *Fellowes & Son v. Fisher* [1976] Q.B. 122, *post*, p. 782; *Powell v. London Borough of Brent* [1987] I.R.L.R. 466.

[72] *Evans Marshall & Co. Ltd v. Bertola S.A.* [1973] 1 W.L.R. 349.

[73] *Morning Star Cooperative Society Ltd v. Express Newspapers Ltd, The Times*, October 18, 1978; *De Falco v. Crawley Borough Council* [1980] Q.B. 460 (no injunction where claimant could not give worthwhile undertaking in damages); *cf. Bunn v. British Broadcasting Corporation* [1998] 3 All E.R. 552 at 558. See also *Thomas Marshall (Exports) Ltd v. Guinle* [1979] Ch. 227.

[74] *Morning Star Cooperative Society Ltd v. Express Newspapers Ltd, supra.* See also *Express Newspapers Ltd v. Keys, supra.*

[75] *Chancellor, Masters and Scholars of the University of Oxford v. Pergamon Press Ltd* (1977) 121 S.J. 758.

[76] *British Broadcasting Corporation v. Hearn* [1977] 1 W.L.R. 1004. (Injunction to restrain interference with claimant's broadcast of the Cup Final to South Africa); *Schering Chemicals Ltd v. Falkman Ltd* [1982] Q.B. 1.

[77] See *Lewis v. Heffer* [1978] 1 W.L.R. 1061. Geoffrey Lane L.J., at 1078, found great difficulty in applying *American Cyanamid* in such a case.

court should be reluctant to interfere in industrial disputes or political decisions by injunction.[78] In *Smith v. Inner London Education Authority*,[79] where an interlocutory injunction was sought to restrain an alleged breach of statutory duty, it was said that where the defendant is a public body, the balance of convenience must be looked at more widely; the court must consider the interests of the general public to whom the duty is owed. The public interest was also a relevant consideration in *Express Newspapers Ltd v. Keys*,[80] where an interlocutory injunction was granted to restrain a trade union from unlawfully inducing a breach of contract by the claimant's employees, by persuading them to support the "Day of Action," a political strike. Where it was clear that the defendant was acting unlawfully,[81] "it would require wholly exceptional circumstances to justify a proper exercise of the discretion to allow such conduct to continue." If the injunction was refused, the employer would suffer unquantifiable damage, whereas if it was granted, the union would suffer no harm save political embarrassment. It was in the interest of the members of the union and of the public that the injunction be granted.

If the balance of convenience does not clearly favour either party, then, as we have seen, the deciding factor will be the preservation of the status quo,[82] which means the circumstances prevailing when the defendant began the activity which the claimant seeks to restrain.[83]

We have also seen that the relative strength of each party's case is a factor to be considered as a last resort, and only then if the strength of one party's case is disproportionate to that of the other.[84] Prior to the decision in *American Cyanamid*,[85] however, this was a vital consideration: the claimant had to show a strong prima facie

---

[78] *Meade v. London Borough of Haringey* [1979] 1 W.L.R. 637, *ante*, p. 773; *Jakeman v. South West Thames Regional Health Authority and London Ambulance Service* [1990] I.R.L.R. 62.

[79] [1978] 1 All E.R. 411. (Injunction to restrain phasing out of grammar schools refused.) See also *R. v. Ministry of Agriculture Fisheries and Food, ex p. Monsanto plc* [1999] 2 W.L.R. 599.

[80] [1980] I.R.L.R. 247, *ante*, p. 770.

[81] See also *Thanet District Council v. Ninedrive Ltd* [1978] 1 All E.R. 703; interlocutory injunction granted to restrain plain breach of statute where defendant making profits by flouting the statute (Sunday trading).

[82] See *Lewis v. Heffer* [1978] 1 W.L.R. 1061; *Chancellor, Masters and Scholars of the University of Oxford v. Pergamon Press Ltd* (1977) 121 S.J. 758.

[83] *Fellowes & Son v. Fisher* [1976] Q.B. 122 at 141; *Garden Cottage Foods Ltd v. Milk Marketing Board* [1984] A.C. 130. But delay by the claimant will be taken into account in considering this principle: *Shepherd Homes Ltd v. Sandham* [1971] Ch. 340, *post*, p. 796.

[84] Relative strength was decisive in *Cambridge Nutrition Ltd v. British Broadcasting Corporation* [1990] 3 All E.R. 523, where the timing of a broadcast was vital and a contract to restrain it was doubtful.

[85] [1975] A.C. 396.

case.[86] This departure from the previous practice was regarded as a source of difficulty by the Court of Appeal in *Fellowes & Son v. Fisher*,[87] where it was felt that the relative strength of the parties must be a factor in assessing the balance of convenience, and that sometimes the court could not do justice without considering the merits. The view was expressed that perhaps the House of Lords had not had all types of cases in mind.[88]

(iii) OTHER SPECIAL FACTORS. Lord Diplock in *American Cyanamid* concluded his exposition of the guiding principles by saying that "other special factors" may have to be considered in individual cases. A question which arises is whether these special factors are merely an aspect of the balance of convenience, or whether they justify a departure from the principles laid down in *American Cyanamid* and a return to the previous practice of requiring a prima facie case.

In *Fellowes & Son v. Fisher*,[89] the claimants, a firm of solicitors, sought to restrain the breach of a restrictive covenant in the contract of a former employee. The covenant was of doubtful validity, but there was a serious question to be tried. As there was no evidence as to the adequacy of damages to either party, the decisive factor, according to the majority of the Court of Appeal, was the balance of convenience, which favoured refusal of the injunction.

Lord Denning M.R., refusing the injunction on different grounds, did not feel bound by *American Cyanamid*.[90] There were two escape routes from it. First, Lord Diplock had indicated that other special factors could be considered in individual cases. These "individual cases" were numerous and important, and included the present case. Secondly, the relative strength of the parties could be looked at where the court found that there was little difference in the uncompensatable disadvantages to both sides. Thus the injunction should be refused because there was no prima facie case.

The question next arose in *Hubbard v. Pitt*.[91]

---

[86] Relative strength is still a governing consideration in Scotland, where *American Cyanamid* does not apply. See (1980) 43 M.L.R. 327 (R. Simpson).

[87] [1976] Q.B. 122, *infra*. See further *Series 5 Software Ltd v. Clarke* [1996] 1 All E.R. 853; *Intelsec Systems Ltd v. Grech-Cini* [2000] 1 W.L.R. 1190.

[88] Possible special cases are dealt with below.

[89] [1976] Q.B. 122.

[90] [1975] A.C. 396.

[91] [1976] Q.B. 142; (1976) 35 C.L.J. 82 (P. Wallington).

Certain members of the public disapproved of the extensive development which had taken place in Islington, and they picketed a leading firm of estate agents which had acted in connection with many developments in the area. The pickets held placards and distributed leaflets to passers-by, thus impeding access to the premises, and deterring potential clients. The estate agents obtained an injunction to restrain them and this was upheld by the majority of the Court of Appeal.

There was a serious question to be tried, and the balance of convenience favoured the grant. Damages could not compensate the claimants for loss of business, even if the defendants could pay, whereas the injunction would not prevent a legitimate campaign. The majority held that there were no circumstances in which "special factors" would take a case out of the general rule that no prima facie case was required. "It appears to me clear beyond peradventure that Lord Diplock was there referring to special factors affecting the balance of convenience and not to special factors enabling the court to ignore the general principles laid down or, more particularly, to ignore ... the admonition not to require of a party seeking an interlocutory injunction that he should have made out a prima facie case."[92] But Lord Denning M.R. again held that "special factors" took the case out of the *American Cyanamid* rules. In his view a prima facie case was required. The appeal should be allowed because the injunction would interfere with free speech and the right to demonstrate and protest.

The better view, it is submitted, is that "special factors" are merely an aspect of the balance of convenience. In *Smith v. Inner London Education Authority*[93] it was held, as we have seen, that where the defendant is a public body, the balance of convenience must be looked at more widely, and the interests of the general public, to whom the defendant's duties are owed, must be considered. This was treated as a "special factor." Similarly where an injunction is sought to prevent a public authority from enforcing a law which is claimed to be invalid (as being incompatible with European Community law). In such an exceptional case an injunction should not be granted unless there is firm ground for the challenge, and the public interest must be considered when assessing the balance of convenience.[94]

---

[92] *ibid.* at 185, *per* Stamp L.J.
[93] [1978] 1 All E.R. 411. See also *Lewis v. Heffer* [1978] 1 W.L.R. 1061, *supra; Bryanston Finance Ltd v. de Vries (No. 2)* [1976] Ch. 63, *infra.*
[94] *R. v. Secretary of State for Transport, ex p. Factortame (No. 2)* [1991] 1 A.C. 603; (1991) 107 L.Q.R. 196 (A. Zuckerman).

It has long been established that interlocutory injunctions will rarely be granted in libel cases where the defendant intends to justify.[95] It has been held that *American Cyanamid* has not affected this principle,[96] which might, therefore, be regarded as a "special factor." Similarly the rule that a bank will not be enjoined from paying under a letter of credit unless there is a clear prima facie case of fraud by the beneficiary.[97] Special considerations affecting the grant of search orders and asset-freezing interlocutory injunctions are discussed elsewhere.[98]

(b) *Exceptional cases.* The following are cases where the *American Cyanamid* principles do not apply, or apply in modified form. Other exceptional cases may arise outside these categories.[99] Thus it has been held that *American Cyanamid* is inapplicable to an order to give life-sustaining treatment to a child.[1] Nor does it apply where there is a clear statutory power to grant an injunction.[2] Indeed, the growing number of exceptions may indicate that the principles are flawed.[3]

(i) TRADE DISPUTES. After the decision in *American Cyanamid*, provisions now found in s.221(2) of the Trade Union and Labour Relations (Consolidation) Act 1992[4] were enacted, providing that where, in an application for an interlocutory injunction, the defendant claims that he acted in contemplation or furtherance of a trade dispute, the court in exercising its discretion is to have regard to the likelihood of the defendant's establishing at the trial any of the matters which, under the Act, confer immunity from tortious liability.[5] Thus *American Cyanamid* is modified in trade dispute cases by

---

[95] *Bonnard v. Perryman* [1891] 2 Ch. 269, *post*, p. 819. See also *Hubbard v. Vosper* [1972] 2 Q.B. 84 (similarly in copyright actions where reasonable defence of fair dealing). See further section (iv), *infra*, on human rights considerations.

[96] *J. Trevor & Sons v. P. R. Solomon* (1978) 248 E.G. 779 (*per* Lord Denning M.R.); *Bestobell Paints Ltd v. Bigg* (1975) 119 S.J. 678; *Herbage v. Pressdram Ltd* [1984] 1 W.L.R. 1160; *Att.-Gen. v. British Broadcasting Corporation* [1981] A.C. 303 at 342 (expressing a similar principle as to contempt in civil actions); *Gulf Oil (Great Britain) Ltd v. Page* [1987] Ch. 327; *Holley v. Smyth* [1998] Q.B. 726.

[97] See *Group Josi Re v. Walbrook Insurance Co. Ltd* [1996] 1 W.L.R. 1152.

[98] *post*, pp. 831, 834.

[99] *R. v. Secretary of State for Health, ex p. Generics (UK) Ltd, The Times*, February 25, 1997. See also *R. v. Secretary of State for Health, ex p. Imperial Tobacco Ltd* [2001] 1 All E.R. 850 (left open whether community law on interim relief, not *American Cyanamid*, applies where interlocutory injunction sought against Crown pending outcome of reference to the European Court of Justice to determine validity of E.C. Directive).

[1] *Re J (a minor) (medical treatment)* [1993] Fam. 15.

[2] *Runnymede Borough Council v. Harwood* (1994) 68 P. & C.R. 300 (Town and Country Planning Act 1990, s.187B).

[3] See (1993) 3 Carib. L.R. 76 and (1993–94) 4 K.C.L.J. 52 (J. Martin); (1993) 56 M.L.R. 325 at 328 (A. Zuckerman).

[4] The amendments have been said to have made little impact; (1987) 50 M.L.R. 506 (B. Simpson). See also s.221(1) (orders without notice).

[5] See s.219 of the 1992 Act.

the opportunity for the defendant to prove a prima facie defence under the labour relations legislation.

The reason for this amendment was that applications for injunctions in industrial disputes rarely went beyond the interlocutory stage, and if *American Cyanamid* was applied without modification, the balance of convenience would invariably favour the claimant (*i.e.* the employer),[6] thus denying the trade unions their power to pressurise employers. Industrial action is unlikely to be effective if it has to be postponed, thus the unions' bargaining counter would disappear. In view of the immunity from liability in tort mentioned above, this might be thought to be unfair.[7] But trade dispute cases should not be approached on the basis that they will not go to trial.[8] Since the Employment Act 1982 the injunction may be sought against the union itself, as opposed to an office-holder personally, which increases the likelihood of a trial.[9]

A question which arises is whether the predecessor to section 221(2) restored the previous law, requiring a prima facie case, to interlocutory injunctions concerning trade disputes,[10] or whether it merely added an extra element to the *American Cyanamid*[11] principles. It is submitted that the latter is the correct approach.[12] Sometimes the likelihood of the defendant's establishing the defence of statutory immunity has been regarded simply as an aspect of the balance of convenience.[13] Perhaps the better view[14] is that it adds a third stage to the enquiry. Thus the court must consider first whether there is a serious question to be tried, secondly the balance of convenience, and thirdly the likelihood of the establishment of the defence of statutory immunity.[15]

Section 221(2) requires the court to "have regard" to the likelihood of the defence of statutory immunity succeeding at the trial.

---

[6] Especially in public service disputes, where public interest is relevant to the balance of convenience; see *Beaverbrook Newspapers Ltd v. Keys* [1978] I.R.L.R. 34.

[7] See *N.W.L. Ltd v. Woods* [1979] 1 W.L.R. 1294; (1980) 43 M.L.R. 327 (R. Simpson); (1980) 96 L.Q.R. 189 (A. Clarke and J. Bowers). *Woods* was regarded as of general application and not confined to trade disputes in *Cayne v. Global Natural Resources plc* [1984] 1 All E.R. 225; *post*, p. 786.

[8] *Hadmor Productions Ltd v. Hamilton* [1983] 1 A.C. 191; *Dimbleby & Sons Ltd v. National Union of Journalists* [1984] 1 W.L.R. 427; (1984) 100 L.Q.R. 342 (H. Carty).

[9] *post*, p. 787.

[10] See *The Camilla M* [1979] 1 Lloyd's Rep. 26; (1979) 42 M.L.R. 458 (B. Doyle).

[11] [1975] A.C. 396.

[12] See *N.W.L. Ltd v. Woods* [1979] 1 W.L.R. 1294; *British Broadcasting Corporation v. Hearn* [1977] 1 W.L.R. 1004; (1978) 41 M.L.R. 80 (Lord Wedderburn); (1977) 127 N.L.J. 654 (R. Kidner); *Hadmor Productions Ltd v. Hamilton, supra.*

[13] *N.W.L. Ltd v. Woods, supra* (Lords Diplock and Fraser).

[14] So considered by Lord Wedderburn in (1978) 41 M.L.R. 80 and (1980) 43 M.L.R. 319. See also (1980) 43 M.L.R. 372 (R. Simpson).

[15] *British Broadcasting Corporation v. Hearn* [1977] 1 W.L.R. 1004 at 1016 (Scarman L.J.); *N.W.L. Ltd v. Woods, supra*, at 1315 (Lord Scarman).

Thus the injunction will not normally be granted where the likelihood is that this defence would succeed.[16] But even in such a case the court retains a residual discretion which it may exercise in favour of granting the injunction, for example if the industrial action "endangers the nation or puts at risk such fundamental rights as the right of the public to be informed and the freedom of the Press,"[17] or "would probably have an immediate and devastating effect on the applicant's person or property" or would "cause immediate serious danger to public safety or health."[18] But such cases would be "altogether exceptional", because "When disaster threatens, it is ordinarily for the government, not the courts, to act to avert it."[19] Where it is unlikely that the defence of statutory immunity will be established, it does not always follow that an injunction is appropriate, for example if it would be of no practical use.[20]

(ii) WHERE TRIAL OF THE ACTION UNLIKELY OR DELAYED. We have seen that Lord Denning M.R. in *Fellowes & Son v. Fisher*[21] preferred the "prima facie case" approach to the principles laid down in *American Cyanamid* because most cases never went to trial; and also that amendment was required in the area of trade disputes for the same reason.[22] It has since been held by the Court of Appeal in *Cayne v. Global Natural Resources plc*[23] that the *American Cyanamid* principles do not apply to cases where no trial is likely to take place. Likewise in a restraint of trade case if the trial is unlikely to come on before the end of the period of the restraint.[24] Where the question is whether information can be published in spite of its confidentiality, delay in coming to trial could result in the stifling of legitimate comment until it is no longer important if only an arguable case is required.[25] In these cases it is best to decide on the basis of relative strength, otherwise the defendant might be effectively precluded at the interlocutory stage from disputing the claim at trial.

---

[16] As to the degree of likelihood necessary to produce this result, see *Duport Steels Ltd v. Sirs* [1980] 1 W.L.R. 142; *Hadmor Productions Ltd v. Hamilton* [1983] 1 A.C. 191.

[17] *Express Newspapers Ltd v. MacShane* [1980] A.C. 672 at 695 (Lord Scarman). See also the views of Lords Diplock and Scarman in *N.W.L. Ltd v. Woods* [1979] 1 W.L.R. 1294.

[18] *Duport Steels Ltd v. Sirs* [1980] 1 W.L.R. 142 at 166 (Lord Fraser).

[19] *ibid.* at 171. The existence of this residual discretion has been challenged; (1980) 43 M.L.R. 319 at 326 (Lord Wedderburn), and at 327 (R. Simpson).

[20] *Hadmor Productions Ltd v. Hamilton, supra*; (1982) 45 M.L.R. 447 (R. Simpson).

[21] [1976] Q.B. 122; *ante*, p. 782.

[22] *ante*, p. 784.

[23] [1984] 1 All E.R. 225, applying *N.W.L. Ltd v. Woods* [1979] 1 W.L.R. 1294; *Thomas v. National Union of Mineworkers (South Wales Area)* [1986] Ch. 20; (1985) 44 C.L.J. 374 (K. Ewing); *Cambridge Nutrition Ltd v. British Broadcasting Corporation* [1990] 3 All E.R. 523.

[24] *David (Lawrence) Ltd v. Ashton* [1991] 1 All E.R. 385; *Lansing Linde Ltd v. Kerr* [1991] 1 W.L.R. 251 (treated as a "wider view of the balance of convenience").

[25] *Att.-Gen. v. Times Newspapers Ltd* [1992] 1 A.C. 191 at 226.

In the area of trade disputes, however, it is possible to obtain an injunction and damages against the union itself as opposed to an office-holder personally, and to obtain substantial damages.[26] This means that there is no reason for a judge to exercise his discretion on the assumption that the case will not proceed to trial in cases where the union itself is the defendant.[27]

(iii) WHERE NO ARGUABLE DEFENCE. It has been held that the *American Cyanamid*[28] rules do not apply where the defendant has no arguable defence.[29] In such a case it is not necessary to consider the balance of convenience. Thus the claimant may obtain an interlocutory injunction to restrain a clear trespass even where it causes no damage[30]; or to restrain a clear misapplication of union funds.[31] It is probable that the principle that the claimant is entitled almost as of right to an injunction to restrain a plain breach of a negative contract provides another example.[32]

(iv) HUMAN RIGHTS ACT 1998: FREEDOM OF EXPRESSION. Article 10 of the European Convention on Human Rights protects the right to freedom of expression, subject to certain qualifications. Section 12 of the Human Rights Act 1998 applies where a court is considering whether to grant any relief which, if granted, might affect the exercise of the Convention right to freedom of expression. Section 12(3) provides that no such relief is to be granted so as to restrain publication before trial unless the court is "satisfied that the applicant is likely to establish that publication should not be allowed". Under section 12(4) the court must have particular regard to the importance of the Convention right to freedom of expression and, where the proceedings relate to material which appears to be journalistic, literary or artistic, to the extent to which the material has or is about to become available to the public, or to which publication is or would be in the public interest, and to any relevant privacy code.

---

[26] Trade Union and Labour Relations (Consolidation) Act 1992, ss.20–23 (replacing 1982 legislation).

[27] *Dimbleby & Sons Ltd v. National Union of Journalists* [1984] 1 W.L.R. 427; (1984) 100 L.Q.R. 342 (H. Carty); (1984) 47 M.L.R. 577 (B. Simpson); *Hadmor Productions Ltd v. Hamilton* [1983] 1 A.C. 191.

[28] [1975] A.C. 396.

[29] *Official Custodian for Charities v. Mackey* [1985] Ch. 168; *Love v. Herrity* (1991) 23 H.L.R. 217.

[30] *Patel v. W.H. Smith (Eziot) Ltd* [1987] 1 W.L.R. 853; *Anchor Brewhouse Developments Ltd v. Berkley House (Docklands Developments) Ltd* [1987] 2 E.G.L.R. 173; *London & Manchester Assurance Co. Ltd v. O. & H. Construction Ltd* [1989] 2 E.G.L.R. 185.

[31] *Taylor v. National Union of Mineworkers (Derbyshire Area)*, The Times, December 29, 1984.

[32] *Doherty v. Allman* (1878) 3 App.Cas. 709; *post*, p. 809, applied to interlocutory injunctions in *Hampstead & Suburban Properties Ltd v. Diomedous* [1969] 1 Ch. 248; *Att.-Gen. v. Barker* [1990] 3 All E.R. 257.

Thus where interlocutory injunctions are sought to restrain publication before trial in cases involving breach of confidence, privacy or libel,[32a] the court must look at the strength of the case and not merely apply *American Cyanamid*, although the difference between the two tests has been said to be very small.[32b] In any event, even if the claimant is likely to establish at trial that publication should not be allowed (see section 12(3), above), it does not follow that the injunction must be granted, as factors such as the balance of convenience must still be considered. So in *Douglas v. Hello! Ltd*,[32c] where a celebrity couple sought to restrain publication of wedding photographs by the defendant magazine in breach of exclusive rights agreed with a rival magazine, they were left to their remedy in damages because, although the test in section 12(3) was satisfied, the balance of convenience favoured the defendant.

(v) INJUNCTIONS TO RESTRAIN THE PRESENTATION OF A WINDING-UP PETITION. It has been held that a prima facie case (of abuse of process) is still required where a company seeks to restrain a creditor from presenting a winding-up petition.[33] If a prospective petitioner intends to petition on the basis of a debt alleged to be presently due, and there is a bona fide dispute as to whether it is presently due, it has been held by the Court of Appeal that the company is entitled as of right to an interlocutory injunction restraining the presentation of the petition, other than on the basis of a contingent or future debt.[34]

Difficulty was also experienced in applying the *American Cyanamid* rules where a company sought an interlocutory injunction to restrain a takeover bid.[35]

(vi) MANDATORY INTERLOCUTORY INJUNCTIONS. *American Cyanamid* itself involved a prohibitory injunction, but the principles there expressed were not in terms confined to such applications. But it may still be said that mandatory interlocutory injunctions, which

---

[32a] For special factors relating to interlocutory injunctions in libel cases, see p. 784, *ante*.

[32b] *Imutran Ltd v. Uncaged Campaigns Ltd, The Times*, January 30, 2001.

[32c] *The Times*, January 16, 2001.

[33] *Bryanston Finance Ltd v. De Vries (No. 2)* [1976] Ch. 63. But Buckley L.J., at 78, regarded this as a "special factor." The other members of the Court of Appeal said that *American Cyanamid* did not apply. See (1976) 35 C.L.J. 82 at 86 (P. Wallington). *American Cyanamid* was applied, albeit with difficulty, in *Re Euro Hotel (Belgravia) Ltd* [1975] 3 All E.R. 1075.

[34] *Stonegate Securities Ltd v. Gregory* [1980] Ch. 576 (*American Cyanamid* was not cited).

[35] *Dunford & Elliott Ltd v. Johnson & Firth Brown Ltd* [1977] 1 Lloyd's Rep. 505. Lord Denning M.R. held that the *American Cyanamid* principles did not apply, but Lawton and Roskill L.JJ. preferred to apply those principles, notwithstanding the difficulties.

are discussed below,[36] will be granted less readily than the prohibitory, as was the case before *American Cyanamid*,[37] because the balance of convenience is likely to favour the refusal more often than the grant.[38]

The *American Cyanamid* principles have been applied to mandatory injunctions,[39] but a strong prima facie case was required in *De Falco v. Crawley Borough Council*,[40] where the claimant sought a mandatory interlocutory injunction to secure the provision of housing by the defendant. The Court of Appeal, refusing the injunction, held that the claimant had to show a strong prima facie case that the defendant's decision was invalid. Lord Denning M.R. held *American Cyanamid* to be inapplicable because the claimant could not give a worthwhile undertaking in damages.[41] Bridge L.J. held that *American Cyanamid*, which governed the grant of prohibitory interlocutory injunctions, did not apply to the present case, which exhibited "sufficiently unusual features to make a comparison even with other types of litigation where a mandatory injunction may be granted on an interim application difficult and possibly misleading."[42] If the defendant was wrong, the claimant would suffer homelessness which was not compensatable in damages. But if the claimant was wrong, a heavy financial burden, with no prospect of recovery, would fall on the ratepayers, and there would also be a detriment to others on the housing list.[43] Therefore such an injunction should be granted only if the claimant had a strong prima facie case. *De Falco* could be regarded as a special case because of the public law element. The Court of Appeal has stated, however, that the "high degree of assurance", required in *Shepherd Homes Ltd v. Sandham*[44] for the grant of mandatory interlocutory injunctions, was not affected by the *American Cyanamid* principles.[45]

Finally, the search order, formerly known as an *Anton Piller* injunction,[46] which is partly mandatory, has been held to require an

---

[36] *post*, p. 790.

[37] [1975] A.C. 396.

[38] See *Shotton v. Hammond* (1976) 120 S.J. 780.

[39] *Meade v. London Borough of Haringey* [1979] 1 W.L.R. 637.

[40] [1980] Q.B. 460; overruled in *Cocks v. Thanet District Council* [1983] 2 A.C. 286, on another point. The requirement of a strong prima facie case was upheld in *R. v. Kensington and Chelsea Royal London Borough Council, ex p. Hammell* [1989] Q.B. 518 and *R. v. Westminster City Council, ex p. Augustin* [1993] 1 W.L.R. 730, regarding *De Falco* as still good law on the point.

[41] [1980] Q.B. 460 at 478. This, it is submitted, might more properly be regarded as a factor in assessing the balance of convenience.

[42] *ibid.* at 481.

[43] This, again, might be regarded simply as an aspect of the balance of convenience, without departing from *American Cyanamid*.

[44] [1971] Ch. 340; *post*, p. 791.

[45] *Locabail International Finance Ltd v. Agroexport* [1986] 1 W.L.R. 657; *post*, p. 791.

[46] *Anton Piller K.G. v. Manufacturing Processes Ltd* [1976] Ch. 55.

extremely strong prima facie case.[47] This, it is submitted, is an exceptional case because such applications are usually without notice, and because of the "draconian" nature of the injunction.[48]

iii. Mandatory Interlocutory Injunctions. These are less readily granted than prohibitory interlocutory injunctions,[49] especially on an application without notice, because the mandatory order may be more drastic in effect. If the defendant has been required to do some positive act, it may not be easy to restore the parties to their previous position if the claimant turns out to be wrong at the trial.[50]

Mandatory interlocutory injunctions will be granted in a suitable case, for example, to compel the demolition of a building where the defendant has deliberately hurried on with the building,[51] to reinstate a wrongfully evicted occupier to possession[52]; to enforce the return of passports wrongfully detained by the police[53]; to compel performance of a landlord's obligations[54]; to enforce the planning legislation[55]; to compel surrender of an unlawful sublease[56]; or in the search order cases,[57] to compel the defendant to submit articles for inspection.

The court will be reluctant to grant such an injunction where the case involves an industrial dispute,[58] but will do so in exceptional circumstances if the balance of convenience so requires. Such a case was *Parker v. Camden London Borough Council*,[59] where a strike of boilermen was endangering the life and health of council tenants. The court was prepared to grant a mandatory interlocutory injunction to resume the supply of heating and hot water.

---

[47] *post*, p. 833. See also (1987) 103 L.Q.R. 246 (L. Anderson), suggesting likewise in the case of an injunction against leaving the country.

[48] See *Yousif v. Salama* [1980] 1 W.L.R. 1540 at 1544; *post*, p. 832; *Derby & Co. Ltd v. Weldon (No. 7)* [1990] 1 W.L.R. 1156 at 1173.

[49] *Daniel v. Ferguson* [1891] 2 Ch. 27; *Shotton v. Hammond* (1976) 120 S.J. 780.

[50] See *Shepherd Homes Ltd v. Sandham* [1971] Ch. 340 at 349.

[51] *Von Joel v. Hornsey* [1895] 2 Ch. 774; *London & Manchester Assurance Co. Ltd v. O. & H. Construction Ltd* [1989] 2 E.G.L.R. 185.

[52] *Luganda v. Service Hotels* [1969] 2 Ch. 209; *Parsons v. Nasar* (1991) 23 H.L.R. 1.

[53] *Ghani v. Jones* [1970] 1 Q.B. 693; *cf. Malone v. Metropolitan Police Commissioner* [1980] Q.B. 49.

[54] *Hart v. Emelkirk Ltd* [1983] 1 W.L.R. 1289; *Peninsular Maritime Ltd v. Padseal Ltd* (1981) 259 E.G. 860. See also *Cork v. Cork* [1997] 1 E.G.L.R. 5.

[55] *Croydon London Borough Council v. Gladden* (1994) 68 P. & C.R. 300 (removal of replica spitfire from roof).

[56] *Hemingway Securities Ltd v. Dunraven Ltd* [1995] 1 E.G.L.R. 61.

[57] *post*, p. 831.

[58] *Meade v. London Borough of Haringey* [1979] 1 W.L.R. 637; (1979) 38 C.L.J. 228 (J. Griffiths). (No injunction to reopen schools closed by a strike.) See also *Harold Stephen and Co. Ltd v. Post Office* [1977] 1 W.L.R. 1172, *ante*, p. 773. *cf. Express Newspapers Ltd v. Keys* [1980] I.R.L.R. 247, where the dispute was political.

[59] [1986] Ch. 162; *ante*, p. 773.

It has been held, in a case concerning trespass by building operations, that if the claimant could have got a prohibitory *quia timet* injunction to restrain the commission of the wrongful act, had he known about it in time, then the defendant should be in no better position if he in fact commits the act: a mandatory interlocutory injunction should be granted to enforce the removal of the building works.[60]

Modern decisions illustrate an increasing readiness to grant mandatory interlocutory injunctions. The principles were reviewed in *Shepherd Homes Ltd v. Sandham,*[61] where the defendant erected a fence in breach of covenant, which the claimant sought to have removed. Megarry J. said that the case has to be unusually strong and clear before a mandatory interlocutory injunction will be granted. The court must feel "a high degree of assurance" that at the trial it will appear that the injunction was rightly granted, and this is a higher standard than is required for a prohibitory injunction. In view of the claimant's delay, the injunction was refused.

The "high degree of assurance" test has been approved by the Court of Appeal,[62] holding that although the test was formulated before *American Cyanamid Co. v. Ethicon Ltd,*[63] it was unaffected by that case. It was added that the application should be approached with caution where the relief sought on the interim application would amount to a major part of the relief claimed at the trial. Hoffmann J. has since held that in exceptional cases, where the refusal of the injunction carried a greater risk of injustice than the grant, then the injunction should be granted even though the "high degree of assurance" test was not satisfied. That test is a guideline which applies in "normal" cases.[64]

The following are cases where a mandatory interlocutory injunction was clearly required:

In *Esso Petroleum Co. Ltd v. Kingswood Motors,*[65] the defendant agreed with the claimant not to sell a garage without first procuring that the purchaser would enter a solus agreement with the claimant. The land was sold to a purchaser who conspired with the defendant to effect a breach. A mandatory interlocutory injunction was granted to compel a retransfer of the land to the

---

[60] *Trenberth (John) Ltd v. National Westminster Bank Ltd* (1979) 39 P. & C.R. 104.
[61] [1971] Ch. 340. See also *Astro Exito Navegacion S.A. v. Southland Enterprise Co. (No. 2)* [1982] Q.B. 1248, C.A.; *Minja Properties Ltd v. Cussins* [1998] 2 E.G.L.R. 52.
[62] *Locabail International Finance Ltd v. Agroexport* [1986] 1 W.L.R. 657.
[63] [1975] A.C. 396; *ante,* p. 777.
[64] *Films Rover International Ltd v. Cannon Film Sales Ltd* [1987] 1 W.L.R. 670; (1988) 47 C.L.J. 34 (N. Andrews). See also *Channel Tunnel Group Ltd v. Balfour Beatty Construction Ltd* [1992] 1 Q.B. 656 at 678, C.A.
[65] [1974] Q.B. 142; *Hemingway Securities Ltd v. Dunraven Ltd* [1995] 1 E.G.L.R. 61.

defendant. There could be no clearer case of inducing breach of contract, and damages would be wholly inadequate.

In *Sky Petroleum v. V.I.P. Petroleum Ltd*,[66] such an injunction was granted to enforce a contract to supply petrol to the claimant. As there was no alternative supply, damages would be inadequate, and the claimant might be forced out of business unless the court intervened.

In *Evans v. B.B.C. and I.B.A.*,[67] an order was made to compel the television authorities to show a party political broadcast. On the balance of probabilities[68] there was a contract with the Welsh Nationalist Party to broadcast it. Damages would be manifestly useless, as the election was about to take place. In such a case the court should take the risk of it turning out that there was no contract.

iv. Conditions and Undertakings. On the grant of an interlocutory injunction, the claimant is normally required to give an undertaking in damages[69] in the event that the injunction is discharged at the trial as having been granted without good cause[70]; but a defendant may also be put on similar terms as a condition of an injunction not being granted.[71] One reason for the practice of undertakings is that it aids the court in achieving its object of abstaining from expressing any opinion on the merits until the hearing.[72] While an undertaking by the claimant is exacted for the benefit of the defendant, it is not a contract with the defendant. The undertaking is given to the court, so that non-performance is a contempt of court and not a breach of contract.[73] Enforcement is at the court's discretion.[74] Damages will normally become payable if the claimant is unsuccessful at the trial, either because he cannot establish his case or because the judge who granted the interlocutory injunction took a wrong view of the law. The claimant may be required to give security or to pay the money into court. Any damages will be assessed

---

[66] [1974] 1 W.L.R. 576. (The injunction was negative in form, but mandatory in substance.)

[67] *The Times*, February 26, 1974.

[68] *cf.* Megarry J.'s requirement of a "high degree of assurance," *ante*, p. 791.

[69] Or to do some other act; *P.S. Refson & Co. Ltd v. Saggers* [1984] 1 W.L.R. 1025. See generally (1994) 53 C.L.J. 546 (A. Zuckerman).

[70] Search orders and asset-freezing injunctions, *post*, pp. 831, 834, provide good examples of the need for undertakings. See *Digital Equipment Corporation v. Darkcrest Ltd* [1984] Ch. 512.

[71] *Elwes v. Payne* (1879) 12 Ch.D. 468.

[72] *American Cyanamid Co. v. Ethicon Ltd* [1975] A.C. 396 at 407.

[73] See *Hussain v. Hussain* [1986] Fam. 134. But the undertaking may include a contractual obligation to the other party; *Midland Marts Ltd v. Hobday* [1989] 1 W.L.R. 1143.

[74] *Cheltenham and Gloucester Building Society v. Ricketts* [1993] 1 W.L.R. 1545.

on the same basis as damages for breach of contract.[75] A claimant's refusal to seek an interlocutory injunction, in order to avoid the need to give an undertaking, is not a ground for striking out his application for a final injunction,[76] but is a factor to be taken into account.[77]

Where interlocutory injunctions are sought in matrimonial and children's matters, undertakings may be required if the claim concerns the protection of property rights, but will not be required in respect of matters concerning personal conduct.[78]

In *Hoffman-La Roche (F.) & Co. v. Secretary of State for Trade and Industry*[79] the question arose whether the Crown should be required to give an undertaking as a condition of the grant of an interlocutory injunction to restrain the company from charging prices for drugs in excess of those specified in an order (which the company claimed was *ultra vires*). The House of Lords held that the undertaking should not be required.

A distinction had to be drawn between two cases: first, where the Crown was asserting a proprietary or contractual right,[80] the ordinary rule applied and the Crown should give an undertaking; but, secondly, where an injunction was sought to enforce the law, the defendant must show special reason why justice required that it should not be granted, or should only be granted on terms. The present case was within the second category. The reason for this distinction is that where a person is prosecuted and acquitted, he may suffer loss but cannot normally recover from the prosecutor. There is therefore no reason why the Crown should incur liability when an injunction is sought to enforce the law.

This principle applies also to a local authority seeking a law-enforcement injunction[81]; likewise where the Attorney-General acts *ex officio* to enforce the law by injunction. But where the Attorney-General brings the action under the relator procedure, the relator

---

[75] *Hoffman-La Roche (F.) & Co. v. Secretary of State for Trade and Industry* [1975] A.C. 295 at 361, *per* Lord Diplock.

[76] *Oxy Electric Ltd v. Zainuddin* [1991] 1 W.L.R. 115, doubting *Blue Town Investments Ltd v. Higgs & Hill plc* [1990] 1 W.L.R. 696; All E.R. Rev. 1990, p. 201 (A. Zuckerman); (1991) 141 N.L.J. 243 (R. Chaplin). The final injunction in *Oxy Electric* was later refused; [1990] E.G.C.S. 128.

[77] *Snell & Prideaux Ltd v. Dutton Mirrors Ltd* [1995] 1 E.G.L.R. 259.

[78] *Practice Direction* [1974] 1 W.L.R. 576.

[79] [1975] A.C. 295. The statute in question expressly provided for the grant to the Crown of an injunction as the only means of enforcing the statute.

[80] Including the case where the Crown is asserting proprietary rights on behalf of a charity; *Att-Gen. v. Wright* [1988] 1 W.L.R. 164; All E.R.Rev. 1987 at 190 (A. Zuckerman).

[81] *Kirklees Borough Council v. Wickes Building Supplies Ltd* [1993] A.C. 227 (Sunday trading); criticised All E.R.Rev. 1992 at 319 (A. Zuckerman); *Director General of Fair Trading v. Tobyward Ltd* [1989] 1 W.L.R. 517. See also *Securities and Investments Board v. Lloyd-Wright* [1993] 4 All E.R. 210; *Customs and Excise Commissioners v. Anchor Foods Ltd* [1999] 1 W.L.R. 1139. Company liquidators are not within this principle; *Re D.P.R. Futures Ltd* [1989] 1 W.L.R. 778.

must give the usual undertaking,[82] as must a local authority acting as a relator.[83]

E. Quia Timet Injunctions

A *quia timet* injunction may be available where the injury to the claimant's rights has not yet occurred, but is feared or threatened.[84] The injunction may be perpetual or interlocutory, prohibitory or mandatory. It may further be subdivided into two broad categories: "first, where the defendant[85] has as yet done no hurt to the [claimant] but is threatening and intending (so the [claimant] alleges) to do works which will render irreparable harm to him or his property if carried to completion . . . those cases are normally, though not exclusively, concerned with negative injunctions. Secondly, the type of case where the [claimant] has been fully recompensed both at law and in equity for the damage he has suffered but where he alleges that the earlier actions of the defendant may lead to future causes of action . . . It is in this field that the undoubted jurisdiction of equity to grant a mandatory injunction . . . finds its main expression."[86]

How serious must the fears of the claimant be, and how grave the suspected damage? As Lord Dunedin has said, it is not sufficient to say "timeo."[87] The requirements have been described in the following terms: a strong case of probability[88]; proof of imminent danger, and there must also be proof that the apprehended damage will, if it comes, be very substantial.[89] Thus in *Att.-Gen. v. Nottingham Corporation*[90] a *quia timet* injunction was not granted to restrain the corporation from building a smallpox hospital, as there was no proof of genuine danger to nearby residents.

---

[82] *Hoffman-La Roche (F.) & Co. v. Secretary of State for Trade and Industry, supra*, at 363.

[83] *Kirklees Borough Council v. Wickes Building Supplies Ltd, supra.*

[84] For different views on the meaning of *quia timet*, see (1975) 34 C.L.J. 224 (J. Jolowicz); *cf.* (1977) 36 C.L.J. 369, (1978) 37 C.L.J. 51 (P. Pettit); Spry, p. 377.

[85] The defendant must himself have threatened the act in question. See *Celsteel Ltd v. Alton House Holdings Ltd* [1986] 1 W.L.R. 512 (no injunction against freeholder where act threatened by tenant).

[86] *Redland Bricks Ltd v. Morris* [1970] A.C. 652 at 665, *per* Lord Upjohn. See also *Hooper v. Rogers* [1975] Ch. 43; *Allen v. Greenhi Builders Ltd* [1979] 1 W.L.R. 136 (registration as "pending land action").

[87] *Att.-Gen. for the Dominion of Canada v. Ritchie Contracting and Supply Co. Ltd* [1919] A.C. 999 at 1005.

[88] *Att.-Gen. v. Manchester Corporation* [1893] 2 Ch. 87 at 92.

[89] *Fletcher v. Bealey* (1885) 27 Ch.D. 688 at 698. *cf. Trenberth (John) Ltd v. National Westminster Bank Ltd* (1979) 39 P. & C.R. 104.

[90] [1904] 1 Ch. 673; *Att.-Gen. v. Guardian Newspapers (No. 2)* [1990] 1 A.C. 109 (no general injunction against publication of any material the media might obtain from Crown servants in breach of confidence). See also *British Data Management plc v. Boxer Commercial Removals plc* [1996] 3 All E.R. 707 (libel); *Re Q's Estate* [1997] 1 Lloyd's Rep. 931 (asset freezing).

The principles applicable to the grant of a mandatory *quia timet* injunction were laid down by the House of Lords in *Redland Bricks Ltd v. Morris*.[91]

> The defendant company's digging activities caused landslips on the claimants' adjoining property, which they used as a market garden. The claimants' land, of which about one-tenth of an acre was affected, was worth about £12,000, but the cost of remedying the landslips would be about £30,000. The claimants were awarded damages, a prohibitory injunction to restrain further withdrawal of support, and a mandatory injunction that the defendants "take all necessary steps to restore support within six months." But the House of Lords allowed the defendant's appeal against the grant of the mandatory injunction on the ground that it did not specify exactly what it had to do. Lord Upjohn set out the following four principles applicable to the grant of a mandatory *quia timet* injunction:
>
> i. The claimant must show a very strong probability that grave damage will accrue to him in the future. It is a jurisdiction to be exercised sparingly and with caution, but, in the proper case, unhesitatingly.
>
> ii. Damages will not be an adequate remedy if such damage does happen, applying the general principle of equity.
>
> iii. Unlike the case where a negative injunction is granted to prevent the continuance or recurrence of a wrongful act, the cost to the defendant to do works to prevent or lessen the likelihood of a future apprehended wrong must be taken into account:
>
> > (*a*) where the defendant has acted wantonly and quite unreasonably, he may be ordered to do positive work even if the expense to him is out of all proportion to the advantage thereby accruing to the claimant;
> >
> > (*b*) but where the defendant has acted reasonably, although wrongly, the cost of remedying his earlier activities is most important. If it seems unreasonable to inflict such expenditure on one who is no more than a potential wrongdoer the court must exercise its jurisdiction accordingly. The court may order works which may not remedy the wrong but may lessen the likelihood of further injury. It must be borne in mind that the injury may never in fact occur, and that, if it does, the claimant may then seek the appropriate legal or equitable remedy.

---

[91] [1970] A.C. 652. See critical commentary in Heydon, Gummow and Austin, *Cases and Materials on Equity and Trusts* (4th ed.), p. 1050.

iv. If a mandatory injunction is granted, the court must see that the defendant knows exactly in fact what he has to do.[92] A more recent statement is that, in the issue of mandatory *quia timet* injunctions, "what is aimed at is justice between the parties, having regard to all the relevant circumstances."[93]

4. DEFENCES TO PERPETUAL AND INTERLOCUTORY INJUNCTIONS

A. Delay

As in the case of specific performance, laches may be a defence even though the claimant's rights have not yet become statute-barred.[94] But a smaller degree of delay will defeat a claim for an interlocutory injunction than is necessary in the case of a perpetual injunction.[95] This is because, if an interlocutory claim is dismissed, the claimant is not unduly prejudiced, as he can still seek a perpetual injunction. But the refusal of a perpetual injunction amounts to a final dismissal.

As we have seen, the claimant must act promptly in the case of an injunction without notice, as any delay illustrates that his case is not urgent.[96] Where the claimant has delayed his application for an interlocutory injunction, he is unlikely to establish that it would be unreasonable to make him wait until trial. An unexplained delay of five months prevented the grant of an interlocutory injunction in *Shepherd Homes Ltd v. Sandham,*[97] where Megarry J. explained that if the injunction is also mandatory, any delay by the claimant will mean that the injunction, if granted, would disturb rather than preserve the status quo.[98] It may be otherwise, however, if there is no arguable defence.[99]

The authorities are not reconcilable on the question of delay in perpetual injunctions. It is sometimes said that laches is no defence,[1] or, to go to the other extreme, that mere lapse of time is a bar.[2] In

---

[92] See also *Harold Stephen & Co. Ltd v. Post Office* [1977] 1 W.L.R. 1172; *Parsons v. Nasar* (1991) 23 H.L.R. 1; *Co-operative Insurance Society Ltd v. Argyll Stores (Holdings) Ltd* [1998] A.C. 1.

[93] *Hooper v. Rogers* [1975] Ch. 43 at 50, *per* Russell L.J.

[94] See Limitation Act 1980, s.36.

[95] *Johnson v. Wyatt* (1863) 2 De G.J. & S. 18.

[96] *Bates v. Lord Hailsham of St. Marylebone* [1972] 1 W.L.R. 1373.

[97] [1971] Ch. 340; *ante,* p. 791; *cf Texaco Ltd v. Mulberry Filling Station Ltd* [1972] 1 W.L.R. 814; *Express Newspapers plc v. Liverpool Daily Post and Echo plc* [1985] 1 W.L.R. 1089; *Newport Association Football Club Ltd v. Football Association of Wales Ltd* [1995] 2 All E.R. 87 (explanation for delay).

[98] See *Shotton v. Hammond* (1976) 120 S.J. 780: mandatory interlocutory injunction granted in spite of delay of six weeks by the claimant, who was not legally aided.

[99] See *Patel v. W.H. Smith (Eziot) Ltd* [1987] 1 W.L.R. 853.

[1] *Archbold v. Scully* (1861) 9 H.L.C. 360 at 383.

[2] *Brooks v. Muckleston* [1909] 2 Ch. 519.

Kelsen v. Imperial Tobacco Co. Ltd[3] a mandatory injunction was granted to restrain a trespass even though it appeared that the state of affairs had existed for seven years. In *Fullwood v. Fullwood*,[4] Fry J. held that a delay of two to three years was no defence, on the ground that mere lapse of time unaccompanied by acquiescence was no bar unless the legal right itself was barred.

In *H.P. Bulmer Ltd & Showerings Ltd v. Bollinger S.A.*[5] the appellants had described their products as "champagne perry" and "champagne cider" since 1950 and 1906 respectively. The latter usage had been known to the respondents since about 1930. Injunctions were granted in the High Court to restrain both descriptions. The defence of delay failed. This was a continuing wrong, and the right in question was legal. Whitford J. held that in such a case the delay must be "inordinate" if it is to prevent the grant of an injunction. Here it was not, because advice had to be sought, and interests consulted. There was no appeal against one injunction, but the other was discharged by the Court of Appeal because passing-off was not established, but their Lordships considered that the injunction would not have been refused on account of delay. Goff L.J. thought that "inordinate" delay would be a ground for refusing an injunction, even in the case of a legal right, but that delay in the present case was not of that order.

Laches may be regarded more strictly if third parties would be affected. It is possible that a claimant who has delayed will be awarded damages in lieu of an injunction under Lord Cairns' Act.[6]

It has been suggested that a longer delay is required before a claimant will be refused an injunction where the right is legal than where it is equitable[7]; or alternatively that a less strict view of laches might be taken as to matters within equity's exclusive jurisdiction, such as a breach of trust, where there is no alternative remedy at law.[8] But the Court of Appeal has described the distinction between legal and equitable rights in this context as archaic and arcane.[9]

---

[3] [1957] 2 Q.B. 334.

[4] (1878) 9 Ch.D. 176.

[5] [1977] 2 C.M.L.R. 625, C.A. *cf. Vine Products Ltd v. McKenzie & Co. Ltd* (1969) R.P.C. 1 (no injunction to restrain description as "sherry," the usage having been common knowledge for 100 years). See also *Erlanger v. New Sombrero Phosphate Co.* (1873) 3 App.Cas. 1218 at 1279–1280.

[6] *Shelfer v. City of London Electric Lighting Co.* [1895] 1 Ch. 287 at 322; see also *Bracewell v. Appleby* [1975] Ch. 408; *Ketley v. Gooden* (1997) 73 P. & C.R. 305.

[7] *Cluett Peabody & Co. Inc. v. McIntyre Hogg Marsh and Co. Ltd* [1958] R.P.C. 335 at 354, *per* Upjohn J.; *H.P. Bulmer and Showerings Ltd v. J. Bollinger S.A., supra.*

[8] See Spry, *Equitable Remedies*, p. 437; *Knight v. Bowyer* (1858) 2 De G. & J. 421; *cf. Oxy Electric Ltd v. Zainuddin* [1990] E.G.C.S. 128 (final injunction to enforce restrictive covenant refused because of seven month delay).

[9] *Habib Bank Ltd v. Habib Bank A.G. Zurich* [1981] 1 W.L.R. 1265 at 1285 and 1287; *cf.* Spry, p. 437.

Finally, where an injunction is sought in a claim for judicial review,[10] it is provided that, in the case of "undue delay," the injunction may be refused if the granting of relief "would be likely to cause substantial hardship to, or substantially prejudice the rights of, any person or would be detrimental to good administration."[11]

B. Acquiescence[12]

Lapse of time will be taken into account in that it may indicate acquiescence. It is, of course, possible to find acquiescence without delay and delay without acquiescence but there is normally some overlap. As in the case of laches, a greater degree of acquiescence is needed to defeat a claim for a final injunction than an interlocutory injunction. It has also been suggested that acquiescence is easier to establish where the right in question is equitable only,[13] but this is now discredited.[14] In *Richards v. Revitt*[15] it was said that the fact that the claimant has previously overlooked trivial breaches of covenant does not debar him, on the ground of acquiescence, from acting on a serious breach. A leading authority is *Sayers v. Collyer*,[16] where a house was being used as a beershop in breach of covenant. The claimant could not get an injunction, as he had known of the breach for three years, and, furthermore, had bought beer there. This was sufficient to bar any remedy. But a lesser degree of acquiescence, while not sufficient to bar the action completely, might be a reason for giving damages in lieu of an injunction under Lord Cairns' Act.

In *Shaw v. Applegate*[17] the claimant sought to enforce a covenant entered into by the defendant in 1967 not to use his land as an "amusement arcade." Breaches of covenant occurred from about 1971. The claimant was aware of the facts but was unsure whether they constituted a breach of covenant. He began proceedings for an injunction in 1973, but did not seek interlocutory relief, so that the defendant continued to carry on his business, investing money and building up goodwill, until the trial in 1976. It was held that the claimant was not guilty of such a degree of

---

[10] *post*, p. 826.
[11] Supreme Court Act 1981, s.31(6); C.P.R. 1998, Part 54.5, replacing R.S.C., Ord. 53, r. 4.
[12] See Limitation Act 1980, s.36(2). The Act does not affect this defence.
[13] *Shaw v. Applegate* [1977] 1 W.L.R. 970 at 979 (the right in this case was legal).
[14] *Habib Bank Ltd v. Habib Bank A.G. Zurich, supra*; *Gafford v. Graham* (1999) 77 P. & C.R. 73 at 80–81.
[15] (1877) 7 Ch.D. 224 at 226.
[16] (1885) 28 Ch.D. 103.
[17] [1977] 1 W.L.R. 970; (1977) 41 Conv.(n.s.) 355 (F. Crane). See also on this point *Sayers v. Collyer* (1885) 28 Ch.D. 103 at 110.

acquiescence as to bar all remedies, the real test being whether, on the facts of the particular case, it would be dishonest or unconscionable for him to seek to enforce his rights.[18] This was not the case, because of the claimant's doubts as to his legal rights. But there was sufficient acquiescence to bar the remedy of an injunction because the defendant had been lulled into a false sense of security by the claimant's inactivity and failure to seek interlocutory relief. Thus the appropriate remedy was damages in lieu of an injunction under Lord Cairns' Act.

Similarly in *Gafford v. Graham*,[19] where the claimant sought mandatory and prohibitory injunctions to demolish a building erected in breach of covenant and to restrain an unlawful use of the land. In the case of one breach where, knowing of his rights, he had failed to complain for three years, all relief was barred by acquiescence. In the case of another breach, the claimant had acted promptly but had not sought interlocutory relief. This was an important factor which made a final injunction inappropriate, thus damages were awarded. The modern approach to acquiescence is to enquire;

(a) whether the defendant was encouraged to believe he was entitled to act as he did; and
(b) if so, whether the encouragement caused detriment; and
(c) if so, whether it was unconscionable in all the circumstances for the claimant to assert his legal rights.[20]

C. Hardship

Hardship to the defendant is a relevant consideration in injunctions as in specific performance.[21] It is perhaps of more weight in the case of an interlocutory injunction[22] than in the case of a final injunction, where the infringement of the claimant's rights has been established. Hardship may also carry more weight in the case of mandatory injunctions,[23] where it has been said that the benefit to the claimant in granting the injunction must be balanced against the detriment to the defendant.[24] As we shall see, damages may be

---

[18] *ibid.* at 978. See also *H.P. Bulmer & Showerings Ltd v. J. Bollinger S.A.* [1977] 2 C.M.L.R. 625 at 682; *Blue Town Investments Ltd v. Higgs and Hill plc* [1990] 1 W.L.R. 696.

[19] (1999) 77 P.& C.R. 73; (1998) 114 L.Q.R. 555 (P. Milne), *post*, p. 803.

[20] *Jones v. Stones* [1999] 1 W.L.R. 1739.

[21] See *Shell U.K. Ltd v. Lostock Garages Ltd* [1976] 1 W.L.R. 1187. As to difficulty in compliance, see generally *Att.-Gen. v. Colney Hatch Lunatic Asylum* (1868) L.R. 4 Ch.App. 146.

[22] See the "balance of convenience" requirement, *ante*, p. 779.

[23] *Att.-Gen. v. Colchester Corporation* [1955] 2 Q.B. 207; *Gravesham Borough Council v. British Railways Board* [1978] Ch. 379 (A mandatory injunction would not be granted to compel the running of a ferry at a heavy loss, which would benefit few passengers).

[24] *Shepherd Homes Ltd v. Sandham* [1971] Ch. 340; *Charrington v. Simons & Co. Ltd* [1970] 1 W.L.R. 725.

awarded in lieu of an injunction under Lord Cairns' Act if the injunction would be oppressive to the defendant.[25]

The element of hardship to the defendant might be overcome in appropriate cases by granting an injunction but suspending its operation.[26] Even if there is no hardship to the defendant, an injunction may be refused if it would prejudice an innocent third party.[27]

It has previously been noted that the disproportionate cost of complying with a mandatory *quia timet* injunction may be a ground for refusing the grant if the defendant has acted reasonably.[28] Lord Upjohn, however, thought that such considerations would not be taken into account in the case of a negative injunction to prevent the continuance or recurrence of a wrongful act; any argument by the wrongdoer that the injunction would be very costly to him, perhaps by preventing him from carrying out a contract with a third party, would carry little weight.

D. Conduct of the Claimant

The claimant must come to equity with clean hands.[29] If, therefore, he is in breach of his own obligations, or otherwise guilty of unfair conduct,[30] he will not be granted an injunction, although trifling breaches may not disentitle him.[31] Similarly, he who comes to equity must do equity, therefore the claimant will not succeed if he is unable or unwilling to carry out his own future obligations.[32]

But the defence of "clean hands" must be related to the subject-matter of the dispute, and does not embrace the claimant's general conduct. Thus in *Argyll v. Argyll*,[33] the fact that the wife's conduct had caused the divorce was no answer to her claim to an injunction to restrain a breach of confidence by her husband. In *Hubbard v. Vosper*,[34] one reason for refusing the interlocutory injunction was that the claimant had not come with clean hands, in that he had

---

[25] There are other conditions: see *Shelfer v. City of London Electric Lighting Co.* [1895] 1 Ch. 287. See also *Shaw v. Applegate, supra*, at 978–979.

[26] *ante*, p. 774.

[27] *Maythorn v. Palmer* (1864) 11 L.T. 261; cf. *PSM International plc v. Whitehouse and Willenhall Automation Ltd* [1992] I.R.L.R. 279.

[28] *Redland Bricks Ltd v. Morris* [1970] A.C. 652 at 666.

[29] See *Malone v. Metropolitan Police Commissioner* [1980] Q.B. 49 at p. 71. In cases of illegality it has been proposed that the principle be replaced by a statutory discretion; Law Com. C.P. No. 154 (1999), *Illegal Transactions: The Effect of Illegality on Contracts and Trusts*.

[30] *Shell U.K. Ltd v. Lostock Garages Ltd* [1976] 1 W.L.R. 1187.

[31] *Besant v. Wood* (1879) 12 Ch.D. 605.

[32] *Measures v. Measures* [1910] 2 Ch. 248; *Chappell v. Times Newspapers Ltd* [1975] 1 W.L.R. 482 (employees failed to obtain injunction to restrain their dismissal where they refused to give an undertaking not to strike).

[33] [1967] Ch. 302.

[34] [1972] 2 Q.B. 84.

protected his secrets by deplorable means, namely by a private criminal code for dealing with the "enemies" of scientology.

Similarly, the injunction may be refused if the court is not impressed with the claimant on the merits.[35]

5. The Jurisdiction under Lord Cairns' Act

The Chancery Amendment Act 1858[36] allowed damages to be awarded in lieu of, or in addition to, an injunction or specific performance. The Chancery Division has, of course, been able, since the Judicature Act 1873, to award damages in any case where the common law courts could have done so, but these are common law damages. It will still be necessary to rely on Lord Cairns' Act where no damages would be available at law, for example in lieu of a *quia timet* injunction where no legal injury has yet occurred[37]; or if some damage has occurred but may continue in the future, and damages are awarded to cover future loss[38]; or where the claimant's right is exclusively equitable, as in the case of a restrictive covenant.[39] In other cases, it will not be necessary to invoke Lord Cairns' Act, and damages may be awarded at common law; but there is no need to distinguish the ground of jurisdiction. The discretion exercisable under Lord Cairns' Act is similar to the discretion which the court has had since the Judicature Act to grant injunctions or damages at common law, in cases where they are available. The principle is the same; the court will not give damages instead of an injunction if damages will not be adequate to protect the claimant's rights. It seems that the court will consider the principles set out in *Shelfer v. City of London Electric Lighting Co.*[40] governing the award of damages under Lord Cairns' Act even where the claimant has a cause of action at law, and there is jurisdiction to award damages at law.[41]

---

[35] See *Glynn v. Keele University* [1971] 1 W.L.R. 487; *Shelfer v. City of London Electric Lighting Co.* [1895] 1 Ch. 287 at 317.

[36] *ante*, p. 747; repealed and replaced by Statute Law Revision Act 1883 and Judicature Act 1873. The jurisdiction now derives from Supreme Court Act 1981, s.50. In *Leeds Industrial Co-operative Society v. Slack* [1924] A.C. 851 Viscount Finlay suggested that the repeal may have been a mistake, made under the false impression that it dealt only with common law damages, and was therefore redundant after the Judicature Act 1873. The better view is that s.16 of the 1873 Act, which transferred all Chancery jurisdiction to the High Court, made the 1858 Act redundant. See McDermott, *Equitable Damages* (1994), pp. 44–45.

[37] *Leeds Industrial Co-operative Society v. Slack, supra*; establishing the point after some doubt; *Hooper v. Rogers* [1975] Ch. 43; *Johnson v. Agnew* [1980] A.C. 367 at 400.

[38] See *Kennaway v. Thompson* [1981] Q.B. 88.

[39] *Baxter v. Four Oaks Properties Ltd* [1965] Ch. 816; *Wrotham Park Estate Ltd v. Parkside Homes Ltd* [1974] 1 W.L.R. 798.

[40] [1895] 1 Ch. 287; *infra*.

[41] See *Kelsen v. Imperial Tobacco Co. Ltd* [1957] 2 Q.B. 334; *Woollerton and Wilson Ltd v. Richard Costain Ltd* [1970] 1 W.L.R. 411.

Lord Cairns' Act enables the award of damages in lieu of a final (not interlocutory) injunction only if there is *jurisdiction* to grant one,[42] in the sense that the claimant has established a prima facie case for equitable relief. It does not matter that the injunction is refused on some discretionary ground, such as, for example, delay or acquiescence.[43] If, on the other hand, the claimant has no case at all for an injunction, then damages cannot be awarded under Lord Cairns' Act, but, as we have seen, such a claimant can be awarded common law damages, provided he has a cause of action at law. Lord Cairns' Act applies even though the claimant does not seek an injunction, but the statement of case should make it clear whether he seeks damages at common law for past injury or under the Act in lieu of an injunction.[44]

A. Award of Damages under Lord Cairns' Act

If the claimant can establish that his rights have been infringed, he is prima facie entitled to an injunction. Damages will only be awarded in lieu in special circumstances; otherwise the defendant would be allowed to "buy" the right to continue the wrongful act.[45] Thus an injunction is appropriate where the defendant threatens to continue a breach of copyright.[46]

The leading case is *Shelfer v. City of London Lighting Co.*,[47] a case of nuisance. A.L. Smith L.J. laid down a "good working rule," that damages should only be awarded in lieu if all the following requirements were satisfied:

    (i) the injury to the claimant is small; and
    (ii) the injury is capable of being estimated in monetary terms; and

---

[42] *Hooper v. Rogers* [1975] Ch. 43; *Wrotham Park Estate Ltd v. Parkside Homes Ltd, supra.*

[43] *Shaw v. Applegate* [1977] 1 W.L.R. 970; *Gafford v. Graham* (1999) 77 P. & C.R. 73. Distinguish a case of *jurisdiction* being lost through the passage of time. See generally *Lavery v. Pursell* (1883) 39 Ch.D. 508 at 519. The position is the same for specific performance, *ante*, p. 748.

[44] *Jaggard v. Sawyer* [1995] 1 W.L.R. 269; criticised [1995] Conv. 141 (T. Ingman).

[45] See *Wakeham v. Wood* (1982) 43 P. & C.R. 40; *Sampson v. Hodson-Pressinger* [1981] 3 All E.R. 710; *Oxy Electric Ltd v. Zainuddin* [1991] 1 W.L.R. 115; *Elliott v. Islington London Borough Council* [1991] 1 E.G.L.R. 167; *Harrow London Borough Council v. Donohue* [1995] 1 E.G.L.R. 257.

[46] *Phonographic Performance Ltd v. Maitra* [1998] 1 W.L.R. 870.

[47] [1895] 1 Ch. 287. See Viscount Finlay's valuable account of the Act in *Leeds Industrial Co-operative Society v. Slack* [1924] A.C. 851 at 856–863. Damages are not appropriate where the nuisance is actionable without proof of damage; *Sevenoaks District Council v. Pattullo & Vinson Ltd* [1984] Ch. 211 (right to hold market).

(iii) the injury would be adequately compensated by a small payment[48]; and

(iv) it would be oppressive to grant an injunction.[49]

Lindley L.J. said[50] that the injunction should not be refused merely because it would not greatly benefit the claimant, as the court is not a tribunal for legalising wrongful acts where the wrongdoer is able and willing to pay. Damages will not normally be substituted in a case of nuisance, as they cannot be easily estimated, but it was suggested that damages would be appropriate if it was a trivial or occasional nuisance, or if it is a vexatious case, or if the claimant has shown that he only wants money.[51] If damages are awarded in a case where the wrong is continuing, they must include a sum for the future as well as the past.

Even if the above four principles are satisfied, an injunction may still be awarded if the defendant has acted in reckless disregard of the claimant's rights,[52] or has acted in a high-handed manner, or tried to steal a march on the claimant, or to evade the jurisdiction of the court.[53]

The Court of Appeal in *Redland Bricks Ltd v. Morris*,[54] while accepting the principles of *Shelfer's* case, disagreed on the question whether the injury could be regarded as small, or could be adequately compensated in money. The defendant's excavations caused damage by subsidence to the value of £1,500, but the correction of the situation, if an injunction was issued, would require expenditure of some £30,000. An injunction was granted, but the House of Lords reversed on a different ground, and Lord Upjohn rejected the applicability of Lord Cairns' Act to the case. But the reasons for his Lordship's rejection of the Act are unclear and, it is submitted, unconvincing.[55]

---

[48] The jurisdiction to grant injunctions is based on the inadequacy of common law damages. It might be argued that compliance with the third requirement should alone be sufficient to prevent the grant of an injunction. But common law damages may not be available, and cannot be awarded for the future; *Jaggard v. Sawyer* [1995] 1 W.L.R. 269. See (1975) 34 C.L.J. 224 (J. Jolowicz).

[49] See *Jaggard v. Sawyer, supra* (injunction would prevent access to defendants' house).

[50] [1895] 1 Ch. 287 at 315–316.

[51] See *Gafford v. Graham* (1999) 77 P. & C.R. 73.

[52] *Shelfer v. City of London Electric Lighting Co.* [1895] 1 Ch. 287; *Pugh v. Howells* (1984) 48 P. & C.R. 298; *cf. Ketley v. Gooden* (1997) 73 P. & C.R. 305; *Gafford v. Graham* (1999) 77 P. & C.R. 73.

[53] *Colls v. Home and Colonial Stores Ltd* [1904] A.C. 179 at 193, a case on an easement of light, where it was suggested that the court should incline to damages if there is any doubt, and the defendant has not acted in an unneighbourly spirit. See also *Pugh v. Howells, supra* (injunction to remove extension interfering with easement of light, where built quickly over a bank holiday, although warning given); *Daniells v. Mendonca* (1999) 78 P. & C.R. 401.

[54] [1967] 1 W.L.R. 967; *ante*, p. 795.

[55] See (1975) 34 C.L.J. 224 (J. Jolowicz); (1977) 36 C.L.J. 369; (1978) 37 C.L.J. 51 (P. Pettit). See also *Hooper v. Rogers* [1975] Ch. 43.

It has recently been emphasised that *Shelfer's* case provides only a "working rule", and that the principles must be adaptable to the facts of individual cases. Thus damages could be awarded in lieu of an injunction to demolish a building put up in breach of covenant and to restrain a prohibited use of the land, even though the injury was not "small", nor could it be remedied by a "small payment".[56] Thus damages of £25,000 were awarded, as the essential pre-requisite that it would be oppressive to grant an injunction was satisfied. The claimant had previously shown that he was willing to settle for money, and this tipped the balance in favour of damages.

The four principles of *Shelfer's* case have not always met with approval, notably in cases concerning rights to light and trespass, where the burden of remedying the situation will often be out of all proportion to the injury to the claimant. In *Fishenden v. Higgs and Hill Ltd*[57] the defendant erected a building which obstructed the claimant's light in a manner that justified substantial damages, but not, by reason of the very high property values involved and the conduct of the defendant, an injunction. The Court of Appeal said that the principles of *Shelfer's* case were a useful guide, but not intended to be exhaustive or rigidly applied, and not a universal or even a sound rule in the case of rights to light.

Similarly in the case of trespass, the injury to the claimant may bear no relationship to that imposed on the defendant by the grant of an injunction. It was assumed in *Kelsen v. Imperial Tobacco Co. Ltd*[58] that *Shelfer's* case applied to trespass. The question was whether the defendant should be required to remove an advertisement which trespassed upon the claimant's airspace. The injury was minimal, but an injunction was granted. In *Woollerton and Wilson Ltd v. Richard Costain Ltd*[59] Stamp L.J. doubted whether *Shelfer's* case could apply to trespass involving nominal damage, as the award of damages would amount to a licence to continue the trespass. An injunction was granted although the four principles were satisfied, but the injunction was suspended.[60] That decision was considered wrong in *Jaggard v. Sawyer*,[61] where *Shelfer's* case was

---

[56] *Gafford v. Graham, supra*; (1998) 114 L.Q.R. 555 (P. Milne).

[57] (1935) 153 L.T. 128; *Colls v. Home and Colonial Stores Ltd, supra; Lyme Valley Squash Club Ltd v. Newcastle under Lyme Borough Council* [1985] 2 All E.R. 405.

[58] [1957] 2 Q.B. 334.

[59] [1970] 1 W.L.R. 411.

[60] *ante*, p. 774; criticised in (1975) 34 C.L.J. 224 (J. Jolowicz). Trespass is an exception to the rule that damages require proof of loss; *Stoke-on-Trent City Council v. W. & J. Wass Ltd* [1988] 1 W.L.R. 1406.

[61] [1995] 1 W.L.R. 269; *post*, p. 807; *Ketley v. Gooden* (1997) 73 P. & C.R. 305 (no injunction if injury small, even if reckless disregard by defendant).

applied to a trespass which caused little injury and the other conditions were satisfied. The damages could reflect the amount the defendants should have been prepared to pay for a right of way. Thus *Shelfer's* case remains good law in relation to trespass, and continues applicable to nuisance.

In *Kennaway v. Thompson*[62] the claimant sought an injunction to restrain a nuisance by excessive noise against a motor boat racing club. The High Court had awarded damages in lieu under Lord Cairns' Act. The Court of Appeal, in granting the injunction, held that the jurisdiction to award damages in lieu of an injunction should be exercised only in very exceptional circumstances in cases of continuing nuisance. *Shelfer's* case had been applied countless times over the last 85 years, and was binding on the Court of Appeal. In the present case the injury to the claimant was not small, nor was it capable of estimation in monetary terms, nor could the sum awarded in the High Court (£16,000) be called a "small payment." In considering whether to award damages in lieu of an injunction, the public interest does not prevail over the private rights of the claimant. Any statements to the contrary in *Miller v. Jackson*[63] ran counter to the principles of *Shelfer's* case and were based on old authorities decided before *Shelfer's* case and now subject to it.

But there is much to be said for the view which regrets an attempt to reduce the court's function to "a series of inelastic rules."[64] "The general rule is . . . that . . . this substitution [of damages for specific relief] ordinarily occurs only when the hardship caused to the defendant through specific enforcement would so far outweigh the hardship caused to the [claimant] if specific enforcement were denied that it would be unjust in all the circumstances to do more than to award damages."[65]

B. The Measure of Damages under Lord Cairns' Act

In *Leeds Industrial Co-operative Society v. Slack*,[66] Lord Sumner said[67]: "No money awarded in substitution can be justly awarded, unless it is at any rate designed to be a preferable equivalent to an

---

[62] [1981] Q.B. 88; (1981) 97 L.Q.R. 3; (1981) 44 M.L.R. 212 (R. Buckley); *Elliott v. Islington London Borough Council* [1991] 1 E.G.L.R. 167.

[63] [1977] Q.B. 966; *ante*, p. 762. The principle of *Miller v. Jackson* was also rejected in *Webster v. Lord Advocate* (1984) S.L.T. 13. See also *Sevenoaks District Council v. Pattullo & Vinson Ltd* [1984] Ch. 211.

[64] Spry, *Equitable Remedies*, p. 639.

[65] *ibid.* p. 640.

[66] [1924] A.C. 851.

[67] *ibid.* at 870.

injunction and therefore an adequate substitution for it." This principle was re-echoed in *Wroth v. Tyler*[68] in respect of specific performance. This decision was once regarded as authority for the proposition that greater damages may be awarded under Lord Cairns' Act than would be available at law. But in *Johnson v. Agnew*[69] the House of Lords held, in a case concerning specific performance, that there is no difference in the measure of damages obtainable under Lord Cairns' Act and at common law. Of course, damages may be recoverable under Lord Cairns' Act where none at all would be obtainable at law,[70] but in general equity follows the law, and it may generally be expected that if only nominal damages would be available at law, then no more will be awarded in equity.[71] A different view had been taken in *Wrotham Park Estate Ltd v. Parkside Homes Ltd*,[72] a case where no damages were available at law.

> The defendant had erected houses in breach of covenant. There was jurisdiction to grant a mandatory injunction against the defendant and the purchasers, who had aided and abetted the breach; but the injunction was refused, in order to avoid the demolition of valuable houses. As a restrictive covenant was involved, damages were available only under Lord Cairns' Act. The value of the claimant's estate was not diminished by the breach, but it did not follow that only nominal damages were available. It would not be right to leave the defendants in possession of the fruits of their wrongdoing. Brightman J. held that a just substitute would be such sum as the claimant could reasonably have demanded to relax the covenant, assessed at £2,500.

The question whether substantial damages may be awarded under Lord Cairns' Act (or at common law) in the absence of loss cannot be answered without distinguishing various causes of action. Clearly damages cannot be awarded on the *Wrotham Park* basis in all cases, because to do so would be inconsistent with the principle expressed in *Johnson v. Agnew*[73] that the measure of damages under Lord Cairns' Act is the same as at common law. The basic principle at common law is that damages are to compensate for loss suffered. One exception is trespass, where substantial damages may be

---

[68] [1974] Ch. 30.
[69] [1980] A.C. 367, *ante*, p. 719.
[70] As in *Hooper v. Rogers* [1975] Ch. 43 (*quia timet*).
[71] *Johnson v. Agnew* [1980] A.C. 367.
[72] [1974] 1 W.L.R. 798; not cited in *Johnson v. Agnew, supra.*
[73] [1980] A.C. 367.

awarded without proof of loss.[74] Thus an award of substantial damages (including such sum as the claimant might reasonably have charged to permit the otherwise tortious act) may be awarded in lieu of an injunction under Lord Cairns' Act.[75]

In cases of nuisance it is essential to prove damage, but once that is established, any damages awarded in lieu of an injunction may properly include such sum as the claimant could reasonably have charged to permit the nuisance.[76] Indeed, tort damages at common law may include this element.[77]

So far as contract actions are concerned, a claimant who cannot establish loss is not normally entitled to damages at common law to reflect the sum he might have charged to release the defendant from the contract. However, the House of Lords has recently held that, in exceptional cases, the remedy of an account of profits is available for breach of contract.[78]

The *Wrotham Park* principle was reviewed by the Court of Appeal in *Surrey County Council v. Bredero Homes Ltd*,[79] where the defendant, a property developer, increased its profits by building five extra houses in breach of covenant. The claimant sued for damages, and did not seek an injunction because the defendant had sold all the houses. For that reason it was considered that Lord Cairns' Act did not apply.[80] The claimant could not establish that the breach of covenant caused it any loss, but sought such part of the profits made from the breach as would reflect a reasonable payment for release of the covenant, relying on *Wrotham Park*. It was held that only nominal damages could be awarded, under the ordinary contract principle. *Wrotham Park* was distinguished as a decision on Lord Cairns' Act.

The matter arose again in *Jaggard v. Sawyer*,[81] where the defendant built a house in breach of covenant and trespassed upon a private road to gain access to it. The claimant sought an injunction to restrain the trespass (which caused little injury) or damages in

---

[74] See *Inverugie Investments Ltd v. Hackett* [1995] 1 W.L.R. 713 (claimant entitled to reasonable rent for wrongful use whether or not he would have let the property to a third party or used it himself).

[75] *Bracewell v. Appleby* [1975] Ch. 408; *Jaggard v. Sawyer* [1995] 1 W.L.R. 269; *infra*. Doubts expressed in *Anchor Brewhouse Developments Ltd v. Berkley House (Docklands Developments) Ltd* [1987] 2 E.G.L.R. 173 were considered misplaced in *Jaggard v. Sawyer*. See also *Bosomworth v. Faber* (1995) 69 P. & C.R. 288.

[76] *Carr-Saunders v. Dick McNeill Associates Ltd* [1986] 1 W.L.R. 922; *Stoke-on-Trent City Council v. W. & J. Wass Ltd* [1988] 1 W.L.R. 1406.

[77] So considered in *Surrey County Council v. Bredero Homes Ltd* [1993] 1 W.L.R. 1361 and *Jaggard v. Sawyer* [1995] 1 W.L.R. 269, *infra*.

[78] *Att.-Gen. v. Blake* [2000] 3 W.L.R. 625.

[79] [1993] 1 W.L.R. 1361.

[80] See the discussion of this aspect in *Jaggard v. Sawyer* [1995] 1 W.L.R. 269.

[81] [1995] 1 W.L.R. 269; [1995] 3 R.L.R. 3 (W. Goodhart); All E.R.Rev. 1995, p. 453 (W. Swadling). The decision was applied in *Gafford v. Graham* (1999) 77 P. & C.R. 73; *ante*, p. 803.

lieu. The judge below refused the injunction, which would have rendered the property landlocked, and awarded a sum reflecting what the defendant should have paid for a right of way and a release of the covenant. This was upheld by the Court of Appeal, applying *Wrotham Park.*

The matter has now been resolved by the House of Lords in favour of the *Wrotham Park* principle. In *Att.-Gen. v. Blake*[82] the issue was whether the remedy of an account of profits was available for breach of contract. In that case the Attorney-General sought to recover the royalties from the publication of a book in breach of contract by the defendant, a former KGB spy. The House of Lords held that this remedy was available in exceptional circumstances, where the remedy of damages was inadequate. Although the case did not concern Lord Cairns' Act, their Lordships reviewed the modern decisions on the Act and confirmed that in cases such as *Wrotham Park* and *Jaggard v. Sawyer*[83] the correct analysis was that the claimant was compensated for the loss of a bargaining opportunity, or, to put it another way, for the compulsory acquisition of his rights. *Surrey County Council v. Bredero Homes Ltd*[84] was a "difficult decision". If the defendant could escape with impunity, that would be a sorry reflection on the law. To the extent that it conflicted with *Wrotham Park*, the latter was to be preferred. In the words of Lord Nicholls:

> "The *Wrotham Park*, case, therefore, still shines, rather as a solitary beacon, showing that in contract as well as tort damages are not always narrowly confined to recoupment of financial loss. In a suitable case damages for breach of contract may be measured by the benefit gained by the wrongdoer from the breach."[85]

Thus a claimant may, in an appropriate case, obtain a remedy for breach of contract or covenant without establishing loss, whether the case is decided under the Lord Cairns' Act jurisdiction or the general law.

6. Injunctions in Particular Situations

A. To Restrain a Breach of Contract

An injunction is the appropriate remedy to restrain the breach of a negative undertaking in a contract. In some measure it corresponds

---

[82] [2000] 3 W.L.R. 625; [2000] R.L.R. 578 (P. Jaffey).
[83] *supra.*
[84] [1993] 1 W.L.R. 1361.
[85] [2000] 3 W.L.R. 625 at 637.

to specific performance in the area of positive undertakings.[86] But, as will be seen,[87] the jurisdiction to grant an injunction is wider.

i. Contract Wholly Negative

(a) *Perpetual Injunctions.* Where the essence of the contractual undertaking is negative, the court will grant an injunction to restrain a breach almost as a matter of course. As Lord Cairns L.C. explained in *Doherty v. Allman and Dowden*,[88] if the parties "contract that a particular thing shall not be done, all that a Court of Equity has to do is to say, by way of injunction, that which the parties have already said by way of covenant, that the thing shall not be done . . . ".

It is not necessary even to prove damage,[89] except where the action is by a reversioner.[90]

But the *Doherty v. Allman* principle must be applied "in the light of the surrounding circumstances in each case,"[91] and it does not prevent the court from considering the effect of delay or other supervening circumstances.[92]

Thus an injunction was refused in *Baxter v. Four Oaks Properties Ltd*,[93] where the defendants, innocently, but in breach of the covenant, intended to use a new building as flats. "The effect of granting such an order would . . . be to put the [claimants] in a very strong bargaining position, for unless the defendants were prepared to leave the building unused, they would be forced to buy a release of the injunction . . . what the [claimants] would get in the end would be damages—though, no doubt, more damages than they would get if no injunction were granted."[94]

(b) *Interlocutory Injunctions.* Interlocutory injunctions are not granted as a matter of course, but it was said in *Hampstead and Suburban Properties Ltd v. Diomedous*[95] that the *Doherty v.*

---

[86] *ante*, pp. 718 *et seq*. Mandatory injunctions may also be available.

[87] *post*, p. 810; *Donnell v. Bennett* (1883) 22 Ch.D. 835.

[88] (1878) 3 App.Cas. 709 at 720; *Sefton v. Tophams Ltd* [1967] A.C. 50; *Sutton Housing Trust v. Lawrence* (1988) 55 P. & C.R. 320 (granted to prevent tenant keeping dog in breach of covenant).

[89] *Grimston v. Cuningham* [1894] 1 Q.B. 125; *Marco Productions Ltd v. Pagola* [1945] K.B. 111, where dancers agreed not to perform for another producer; injunction granted although the claimants could not show that they would suffer greater damage if the dancers performed elsewhere than if they remained idle; *cf. Provident Financial Group plc v. Hayward* [1989] I.C.R. 160.

[90] *Johnstone v. Hall* (1856) 2 K. & J. 414; *Martin v. Nutkin* (1724) 2 P.Wms. 266 (injunction to restrain ringing of church bells at 5 a.m.).

[91] *Shaw v. Applegate* [1977] 1 W.L.R. 970 at 975, *per* Buckley L.J.

[92] *ibid*. at 980, *per* Goff L.J.

[93] [1965] Ch. 816.

[94] *ibid*. at 829, *per* Cross J.

[95] [1969] 1 Ch. 248 (excessive noise made in breach of covenant by restaurant).

Allman[96] principle applied where there was a plain breach of a clear negative covenant. In such a case, there was no reason why the defendant "should have a holiday from the enforcement of his obligation until the trial."[97] But where the validity of the covenant is in dispute, *Doherty v. Allman* cannot apply to interlocutory injunctions.[98]

(c) *Mandatory Injunctions.* Mandatory injunctions are entirely discretionary, and can never be granted automatically, even if a negative covenant is involved.[99] It is not possible to give precise guidance as to the way in which the discretion will be exercised. In *Shepherd Homes Ltd v. Sandham*,[1] Megarry J. said of *Doherty v. Allman*[2] that "a court of equity which says by way of injunction 'that which the parties have already said by way of covenant that the thing shall not be done,' is not thereby in the same breath adding 'and what is more, if it has been done, it shall be undone.' "[3] The application of the principle of *Doherty v. Allman* is tempered by a judicial discretion which withholds a mandatory injunction more readily than a prohibitory injunction, even where the claimant is blameless. Benefit to the claimant must be balanced against detriment to the defendant. But the search is not merely for "a fair result."[4]

ii. Positive and Negative Terms. Where a contract contains both positive and negative stipulations, and the positive ones are not susceptible to specific performance, the question arises whether the claimant can restrain the breach of the negative stipulation by injunction. In suitable cases, this can be done. The jurisdiction to grant an injunction is wider than that to order specific performance.[5]

The principle is that an injunction will not be granted if that would amount to indirect specific performance of the positive terms. Thus, it used to be said with confidence that no injunction would lie to restrain the termination of employment in breach of contract, for this would indirectly enforce the contract.[6] It has been seen, however, that in the special circumstances of *Hill v. C.A. Parsons & Co.*

---

[96] (1878) 3 App.Cas. 709.
[97] [1969] 1 Ch. 248 at 259; *Att.-Gen. v. Barker* [1990] 3 All E.R. 257 (proposed publication, in breach of contract, of book about royal family).
[98] *Texaco Ltd v. Mulberry Filling Station Ltd* [1972] 1 W.L.R. 814 at 831.
[99] See *Wrotham Park Estate Ltd v. Parkside Homes Ltd* [1974] 1 W.L.R. 798. But the claimant may obtain summary judgment in a flagrant case; *Chelsea (Viscount) v. Muscatt* [1990] 2 E.G.L.R. 48.
[1] [1971] Ch. 340; *Sharp v. Harrison* [1922] 1 Ch. 502 at 512.
[2] (1878) 3 App.Cas. 709.
[3] [1971] Ch. 340 at 346.
[4] *Charrington v. Simons & Co. Ltd* [1971] 1 W.L.R. 598 at 603, *per* Russell L.J.
[5] See *Thomas Marshall (Exports) Ltd v. Guinle* [1979] Ch. 227 at 243.
[6] *Davis v. Foreman* [1894] 3 Ch. 654.

Ltd,[7] where an employer was reluctantly obliged to terminate the employment of a senior engineer who refused to join a trade union operating a closed shop principle, an interim injunction was issued to restrain the termination.

iii. No Express Negative Stipulation. Where a contract, drafted in positive form, contains no express negative stipulation, it may be possible to discover in the contract, on its proper construction, an implied negative undertaking which can be remedied by injunction.[8] This is especially important where the positive obligation is not specifically enforceable. It is not possible to lay down a rule to determine the circumstances in which an injunction may be obtained. The question in each case depends upon the construction which the court places upon the particular contract.

The principle was laid down by Lord Selborne in *Wolverhampton and Walsall Railway Co. Ltd v. L.N.W. Ry. Ltd*[9] as being that the court should "look in all such cases to the substance and not to the form. If the substance of the agreement is such that it would be violated by doing the thing sought to be prevented, then the question will arise, whether this is the court to come to for a remedy. If it is, I cannot think that ought to depend on the use of a negative rather than an affirmative form of expression."

A negative stipulation is rarely implied in contracts of personal service, for to do so might allow the indirect enforcement of a contract which is not specifically enforceable.[10] Thus, it will not be implied although the servant has contracted to devote the whole of his time to his employer,[11] nor where there was a contract to sell to a purchaser all the "get" of a colliery for five years[12]; nor where a boxer agreed that his manager should have the "sole arrangements" for his boxing and other engagements.[13] However, in *Metropolitan Electric Supply Co. v. Ginder*,[14] the defendant applied for a supply of electricity on terms which provided that the defendant agreed to

---

[7] [1972] 1 Ch. 305; *C.H. Giles & Co. Ltd v. Morris* [1972] 1 W.L.R. 307; (1975) 34 C.L.J. 36 (B. Napier).

[8] *Tulk v. Moxhay* (1848) 2 Ph. 774; *Catt v. Tourle* (1869) L.R. 4 Ch.App. 654; *Clegg v. Hands* (1890) 44 Ch.D. 503; *Jones & Sons Ltd v. Tankerville* [1909] 2 Ch. 440. Breach of an obligation imposed by law can be restrained by injunction even though the contract contains no express negative term: *Hivac v. Park Royal Scientific Instruments* [1946] Ch. 169; *Provident Financial Group plc v. Hayward* [1989] I.C.R. 160 (confidential information).

[9] (1873) L.R. 16 Eq. 433 at 440; *Whitwood Chemical Co. Ltd v. Hardman* [1891] 2 Ch. 416 at 441, *per* Lindley L.J.; *Bower v. Bantam Investments Ltd* [1972] 1 W.L.R. 1120.

[10] *ante*, p. 730.

[11] *Whitwood Chemical Co. Ltd v. Hardman* [1891] 2 Ch. 416; *Bower v. Bantam Investments Ltd* [1972] 1 W.L.R. 1120.

[12] *Fothergill v. Rowland* (1873) L.R. 17 Eq. 132.

[13] *Mortimer v. Beckett* [1920] 1 Ch. 571. See also *Fraser v. Thames Television Ltd* [1984] Q.B. 44.

[14] [1901] 2 Ch. 799. See also *Sky Petroleum Ltd v. V.I.P. Petroleum Ltd* [1974] 1 W.L.R. 576.

take all the electricity required by his premises from the claimant for a stated period. The claimant was not bound to supply, nor the defendant to take, any electricity. The contract was construed as an undertaking not to take electricity from any other persons, and the defendant was restrained by injunction from doing so. In *Manchester Ship Canal v. Manchester Racecourse Co.*[15] the grant of a "first refusal" was construed as an undertaking enforceable by injunction, not to sell to anyone else in contravention of the undertaking.

It is established that a negative term may be implied in the following types of case:

(a) *Contracts Affecting the Use of Land.* A covenant which touches and concerns the land so as to be binding in equity upon successors in title under the doctrine of *Tulk v. Moxhay*[16] will be construed as negative and subjected to an injunction if it is negative in substance although positive in form. Indeed, in *Tulk v. Moxhay* itself, the covenant was to "keep and maintain the said piece of ground in its then form, and in sufficient and proper repair . . . in an open state, uncovered with any buildings in neat and ornamental order."[17] The fact that a court was powerless to interfere against third parties except by the use of an injunction no doubt encouraged the courts to extend its use of the concept.

(b) *Contractual Licences.* After a long search for the proper solution to the problem of the revocation by a licensor of a contractual licence in breach of contract, the courts found it in the issue of an injunction to restrain the breach of contract.[18] Where the wrongful revocation occurs before the licensee has entered, the court may, in an appropriate case, grant specific performance or a mandatory injunction to compel performance of the licensor's obligations.[19] A contractual licence is commonly in positive form—permitting the licensee to occupy premises. But where the licence on its proper construction gives no right to the licensor to revoke in the way in which he has purported to do, the court will treat the matter as one in which the licensor has contracted not to revoke inconsistently with the terms of the licence, and will restrain him from doing so.[20]

---

[15] [1901] 2 Ch. 37. See also *Gardner v. Coutts & Co.* [1968] 1 W.L.R. 173 (implied term in right of pre-emption that property will not be given to another); *cf. Pritchard v. Briggs* [1980] Ch. 338.

[16] (1848) 2 Ph. 774.

[17] *ibid.* at 775.

[18] *post*, p. 878.

[19] *Verrall v. Great Yarmouth Borough Council* [1981] Q.B. 202, *ante*, p. 723.

[20] See *Jones (James) and Sons Ltd v. Earl of Tankerville* [1909] 2 Ch. 440.

iv. Contracts for Personal Services. It has been seen that contracts for personal services would not be specifically enforced either by specific performance or by an injunction.[21] In the case of contracts of employment, the Trade Union and Labour Relations (Consolidation) Act 1992, s.236 provides that "no court shall . . . by way of . . . injunction . . . restraining a breach or threatened breach of [a contract of employment] compel an employee to do any work or to attend at any place for the doing of any work." This provision, as with the corresponding provision relating to specific performance, applies only to contracts of employment[22] and only to enforcement against an employee. The equitable principle which denies specific enforcement of contracts of service has in appropriate circumstances permitted the issue of an injunction to restrain a negative undertaking in a contract for personal services, and this may have the effect indirectly of causing a contract to be performed. It remains to be determined whether and how far the provision now found in section 236 affects the operation of this principle. Two aspects of the question of the issue of an injunction in this circumstance need to be examined.

(a) *Restraining Breach by Employee or Independent Contractor.*

In *Lumley v. Wagner*,[23] Miss Wagner, an opera star, had agreed with Lumley that she would sing at Her Majesty's Theatre during a certain period, and would not sing anywhere else without his written permission. She made another engagement with Gye to sing at Covent Garden and abandoned her previous commitment to Lumley, who sought an injunction to restrain her from singing for Gye. Lord St. Leonards held that an injunction should be granted to restrain the breach of the negative stipulation; it would not of course have been possible to obtain specific performance of the promise to sing.

The principle of *Lumley v. Wagner* has been much criticised.[24] It is said that the issue of an injunction in this situation is the equivalent of specific performance; and that a number of principles are

---

[21] *ante*, p. 730.

[22] *cf.* independent contractors.

[23] (1852) 1 De G.M. & G. 604. The injunction may be granted even though it interferes with the contractual rights of innocent third parties; *PSM International plc v. Whitehouse and Willenhall Automation Ltd* [1992] I.R.L.R. 279; *cf. Maythorn v. Palmer* (1864) 11 L.T. 261. See also *Thomas Marshall (Exports) Ltd v. Guinle* [1979] Ch. 227 at 240–242.

[24] Ames, *Lectures on Legal History*, p. 370; *per* Lindley L.J. in *Whitwood Chemical Co. v. Hardman* [1891] 2 Ch. 416 at 428; "I think that the court . . . will generally do much more harm by attempting to decree specific performance in cases of personal service than by leaving them alone; and whether it is attempted to enforce these contracts directly by a decree of specific performance, or indirectly by an injunction, appears to me to be immaterial."

thereby disregarded, especially the rule that the court will not supervise the performance of contracts; and the principle that the contracting parties must not become tied together in a relationship involving a status of servitude. On the other hand, the carrying out of agreements must be encouraged by the courts, whatever remedy is used.[25]

It is submitted that the correct approach in these situations, as in other cases of injunctions, is that the injunction should issue to restrain the breach of a negative undertaking, unless the defendant can show that the court should in its discretion refuse on the ground that undesirable consequences may follow. Each case, in other words, should be treated on its merits.

Thus an employee should not be put into a position in which he must either perform the contract or do nothing.

In *Rely-a-Bell Burglar and Fire Alarm Co. v. Eisler*[26] the employee had contracted to serve the employer and to take no other employment for the period of the contract of service. An injunction was refused, and damages awarded.

In *Warner Bros. v. Nelson*,[27] a well-known actress, Bette Davis, contracted to work for the claimants and not to work as a film actress for any other film company for the period of her contract, "or to be engaged in any other occupation." The term was not void under the restraint of trade doctrine,[28] and the question was whether an injunction was an appropriate remedy. "[I]t would, of course, be impossible to grant an injunction covering all the negative covenants in the contract. That would, indeed, force the defendant to perform her contract or remain idle; but this objection is removed by the restricted form in which the injunction is sought. It is confined to forbidding the defendant, without the consent of the [claimants], to render any services for or in any motion picture or stage production for any one other than the [claimants]."[29] An injunction was given on these terms.[30] Miss Davis was still free to earn a living in other ways, even if they were less lucrative.

---

[25] *Lane v. Newdigate* (1804) 10 Ves.Jr. 192.

[26] [1926] Ch. 609.

[27] [1937] 1 K.B. 209.

[28] *per* Russell L.J. in *Instone v. A. Schroeder Music Publishing Co. Ltd* [1974] 1 All E.R. 171 at 178, C.A. He also criticised Branson J. who suggested in *Warner Bros. v. Nelson* [1937] 1 K.B. 209 at 214 that the doctrine of restraint of trade could not apply during the continuance of the contract; see also *Clifford Davis Management Ltd v. W.E.A. Records Ltd* [1975] 1 W.L.R. 61.

[29] [1937] 1 K.B. 209 at 219, *per* Branson J.

[30] *Robinson & Co. Ltd v. Heuer* [1898] 2 Ch. 451.

In *Evening Standard Co. Ltd v. Henderson*[31] an employee had failed to give the required notice. The Court of Appeal was prepared to grant an interlocutory injunction to prevent him from working for a rival paper during the notice period. As the employer had undertaken to pay his salary for that period even if he did not work ("garden leave"), the injunction did not compel him to perform the contract or starve, but was rather a means of enforcing the notice requirement. It may be otherwise if the "garden leave" is so long that the employee may lose his skills.[32]

(b) *Compelling Employer to Employ.*

In *Page One Records v. Britton*,[33] a group of musicians appointed the claimant as their manager for five years, contracting not to engage anyone else as manager. They wished to change, and the claimant sought an injunction to prevent the employment of another manager, arguing, on the lines of *Warner Bros. v. Nelson*[34] that the defendants could retain him or continue without a manager. The injunction was refused, as it would *persuade* them to retain the claimant, which would be undesirable in a personal and fiduciary relationship in which the defendants had lost confidence in him.

Although the group could have earned their living in another way, just as Bette Davis could have done, it would be unrealistic to expect any of them to do so. Unless the period of the injunction is short, it puts economic pressure on the defendant to perform an obligation which is not specifically enforceable. The Court of Appeal has now held in *Warren v. Mendy*[35] that *Page One Records* is preferable to *Warner*. The claimant was refused an injunction which in effect would have compelled a boxer to retain him as manager for at least two years. In relationships involving skill or talent and a high degree of mutual confidence,[36] the court should not enforce negative terms of a contract if this would in effect compel performance of the positive terms.

---

[31] [1987] I.R.L.R. 64; (1989) 139 N.L.J. 1716 (J. Hand and P. Smith).

[32] *Provident Financial Group plc v. Hayward* [1989] I.C.R. 160; *William Hill Organisation Ltd v. Tucker* [1999] I.C.R. 291.

[33] [1968] 1 W.L.R. 157.

[34] [1937] 1 K.B. 209.

[35] [1989] 1 W.L.R. 853; (1990) 49 C.L.J. 28 (H. McLean); (1990) 140 N.L.J. 1007 (A. Burrows); (1997) 17 L.S. 65 (J. McCutcheon).

[36] The obligation of the claimants in *Warner Bros. v. Nelson, supra*, and *Lumley v. Wagner, ante*, p. 813, was merely to pay money.

In *Hill v. C.A. Parsons & Co. Ltd*,[37] we saw that the Court of
Appeal granted an injunction restraining an employer from acting on
a wrongful dismissal. This amounted to indirect specific performance of a service contract; but the circumstances were special. Personal confidence still existed between the parties; a proper length of
notice would have safeguarded the claimant's right under the Industrial Relations Act 1971; and the claimant was due to retire in
two years, and his pension depended on his average salary during
the last three years of employment. Stamp L.J. dissented, and would
have allowed the pension claim to be included in an award of
damages. The question arose again in *Chappell v. Times Newspapers
Ltd*,[38] where employees sought an injunction to restrain their dismissal during an industrial dispute. As mutual confidence no longer
existed between the parties, the case was not within the *Hill v.
Parsons* exception. The fact that unfair dismissal was unlawful did
not mean that a service contract was enforceable by injunction. That
would be a "plain recipe for disaster."[39]

It appears that the grant of an injunction within the *Hill v. Parsons*
exception is no longer a rarity. Although the claimant must normally
show that mutual confidence still exists,[40] this is not inevitably
precluded by the fact that the employer opposes the claim. It suffices
to establish that the employer has no rational ground to lack confidence, as where there has been no friction at the workplace.[41]

B. To Restrain a Breach of Trust

There are many examples of the issue of an injunction to restrain
a breach of an equitable obligation, and a few must suffice here.

---

[37] [1972] Ch. 305; *ante*, p. 732. See also *Jones v. Lee* [1980] I.R.L.R. 67. For the position
where the employment is protected beyond the common law by procedural requirements
relating to dismissal, see *R. v. British Broadcasting Corporation, ex p. Lavelle* [1983] 1
W.L.R. 23.

[38] [1975] 1 W.L.R. 482; see also *G.K.N. (Cwmbran) Ltd v. Lloyd* [1972] I.C.R. 214; *Sanders
v. Ernest A. Neale Ltd* [1974] I.C.R. 565; *Ali v. London Borough of Southwark* [1988]
I.R.L.R. 100; *Wishart v. National Association of Citizens Advice Bureaux Ltd* [1990] I.C.R.
794.

[39] *ibid.* at 506. See also the Employment Rights Act 1996, s.117: an industrial tribunal may
order reinstatement, but the sanction in the event of non-compliance is an award of
compensation.

[40] *cf. Robb v. London Borough of Hammersmith and Fulham* [1991] I.R.L.R. 72 (no dismissal
prior to disciplinary procedure even though loss of confidence); *Jones v. Gwent County
Council* [1992] I.R.L.R. 521.

[41] *Powell v. London Borough of Brent* [1987] I.R.L.R. 466; *Hughes v. London Borough of
Southwark* [1988] I.R.L.R. 55; (1988) 85/5 L.S.Gaz. 28 (J. Hendy and J. McMullen);
(1989) 48 C.L.J. 28 and (1993) 52 C.L.J. 405 (K. Ewing); (1989) 52 M.L.R. 449 (H.
Carty).

Trustees have been restrained from distributing an estate inconsistently with the terms of the instrument,[42] or from selling under
depreciatory conditions of sale[43]; or for a price below that offered
firmly by a prospective purchaser[44]; or selling land without appointing a second trustee and without consulting the beneficiary.[45] Where
the claimant has a claim to trace property in equity,[46] an injunction
may be granted to restrain the defendant from disposing of the
property.[47]

C. To Restrain the Commission or Continuance of a Tort

In each of the many cases in which an injunction issues to restrain
the commission of a tort, equity is exercising its "concurrent" jurisdiction. Equity plays no part in determining whether a wrong has
been committed; that is a matter solely of law. It is the remedy alone
that is equitable. Thus the claimant must first establish the commission or threat of something which constitutes a tort at law. If it is, the
court may, in its discretion, grant an injunction. The rules and practice vary with the tort in question.

i. Nuisance.[48] The act complained of must constitute a nuisance
at law. "There is no such thing as an equitable nuisance."[49] The
interference must cause or threaten damage.[50] No injunction will
issue to deal with a trifling interference[51]; and even if damage is
proved, equity will not grant an injunction in every case in which the
common law would award damages. The remedy is discretionary,
and is particularly appropriate in cases of nuisance.[52] Damages may
be awarded in lieu under Lord Cairns' Act.[53]

---

[42] *Fox v. Fox* (1870) L.R. 11 Eq. 142.
[43] *Dance v. Goldingham* (1873) L.R. 8 Ch.App. 902.
[44] *Buttle v. Saunders* [1950] 2 All E.R. 193 (*ante*, p. 530) where the trustee had promised (but not in binding form) to sell land to another purchaser.
[45] *Waller v. Waller* [1967] 1 W.L.R. 451.
[46] *ante*, p. 682.
[47] *A. v. C.* [1981] Q.B. 956n.; *Polly Peck International plc v. Nadir (No. 2)* [1992] 4 All E.R 769.
[48] See generally (1982) 41 C.L.J. 87 (S. Tromans).
[49] *per* Kindersley V.-C. in *Soltau v. de Held* (1851) 2 Sim.(N.S.) 133 at 151.
[50] It is otherwise where the nuisance is actionable without proof of damage; *Sevenoaks District Council v. Pattullo & Vinson Ltd* [1984] Ch. 211; *Halton Borough Council v. Cawley* [1985] 1 W.L.R. 15 (right to hold market).
[51] *Ankerson v. Connelly* [1907] 1 Ch. 678.
[52] *Halsey v. Esso Petroleum Co. Ltd* [1961] 1 W.L.R. 683; *Leakey v. National Trust for Places of Historic Interest or Natural Beauty* [1980] Q.B. 485; *Laws v. Florinpace* [1981] 1 All E.R. 659; *Pugh v. Howells* (1984) 48 P. & C.R. 298.
[53] *ante*, p. 801.

It was held in *Miller v. Jackson*,[54] by a majority of the Court of Appeal, that the court should weigh the interests of the public against those of the individual, and should refuse the injunction if, on balance, it was felt that the interest of the public should prevail. This proposition was doubted in *Kennaway v. Thompson*[55] by the Court of Appeal. It was there held that, when considering whether to award damages in lieu of an injunction under Lord Cairns' Act in a nuisance case, the public interest does not prevail over the private interest of the claimant.[56]

ii. Trespass. An injunction will issue to restrain a threatened or existing trespass. In minor cases, the court will leave the claimant to such remedy as he has at law; as where a clergyman of the Church of England held services on the seashore between high and low water mark which was leased by the Crown to the Corporation[57]; or where collectors chased a butterfly on to the claimant's land.[58] Where, however, the defendant entered the claimant's wood, cut down trees and clearly intended to cut more, he was restrained.[59] Indeed, there is no real discretion to refuse in cases of total dispossession.[60]

Where the defendant has no arguable defence, the claimant may be granted an interlocutory injunction even where the trespass has caused no damage.[61]

A mandatory injunction will be granted where necessary, for example requiring the removal of an advertising sign which projected into the airspace above the claimant's single-storey shop.[62]

iii. Libel. The granting of injunctions to restrain the publication of a libel has caused particular difficulty, partly because of the

---

[54] [1977] Q.B. 966, *ante*, p. 762; *Tetley v. Chitty* [1986] 1 All E.R. 663.
[55] [1981] Q.B. 88. It was also rejected in *Webster v. Lord Advocate* (1984) S.L.T. 13. See also *Sevenoaks District Council v. Pattullo & Vinson Ltd*, *supra*; *Rosling v. Pinnegar* (1987) 54 P. & C.R. 124.
[56] Authorities supporting the contrary proposition were decided before *Shelfer v. City of London Electric Lighting Co.* [1895] 1 Ch. 287, *ante*, p. 802.
[57] *Llandudno Urban District Council v. Woods* [1899] 2 Ch. 705. Refusal terminates self-help remedies; *Burton v. Winters* [1993] 1 W.L.R. 1077.
[58] *Fielden v. Cox* (1906) 22 T.L.R. 411; *Behrens v. Richards* [1905] 2 Ch. 614.
[59] *Stanford v. Hurlstone* (1873) L.R. 9 Ch.App. 116. See also *League Against Cruel Sports Ltd v. Scott* [1986] Q.B. 240 (persistent trespass by hunt).
[60] *Harrow London Borough Council v. Donohue* [1995] 1 E.G.L.R. 257.
[61] *Patel v. W.H. Smith (Eziot) Ltd* [1987] 1 W.L.R. 853; *Anchor Brewhouse Developments Ltd v. Berkley House (Docklands Developments) Ltd* [1987] 2 E.G.L.R. 173.
[62] *Kelsen v. Imperial Tobacco Co. Ltd* [1957] 2 Q.B. 334. See also *Trenberth (John) Ltd v. National Westminster Bank Ltd* (1979) 39 P. & C.R. 104; *London & Manchester Assurance Company Ltd v. O. & H. Construction Ltd* [1989] 2 E.G.L.R. 185 (interlocutory).

complexity of proof of the tort, but largely because of the importance of allowing to be said things that ought to be said.[63] It was not until *Quartz Hill Consolidated Gold Mining Co. v. Beall* in 1882[64] that the courts positively asserted a jurisdiction to restrain publication. The matter is usually one of urgency, requiring an interlocutory injunction, and Jessel M.R. was careful to point out the need for great caution in its exercise.

The claimant must satisfy the court of the falsity of the statements and, where they are privileged, the presence of malice. "The court will not restrain the publication of an article, even though it is defamatory, when the defendant says that he intends to justify it or to make fair comment on a matter of public interest. . . . The reason sometimes given is that the defences of justification and fair comment are for the jury, which is the constitutional tribunal, and not for a judge; but a better reason is the importance in the public interest that the truth should out."[65] The interest of the public in knowing the truth outweighs the interest of a claimant in maintaining his reputation.[66] Thus, it was laid down in *Bonnard v. Perryman*[67] as a working rule that an interlocutory injunction ought never to be granted except in the clearest cases, in which, if a jury did not find the matter complained of to be libellous, the court would set aside the verdict as unreasonable. Lord Denning M.R. stated that all requests for "gagging injunctions" which seek to prevent true and fair comment on matters of public interest should fail.[68] But in *Hubbard v. Pitt*[69] the Court of Appeal upheld the grant of an interlocutory injunction to restrain, amongst other things, the display of allegedly libellous placards and leaflets outside the claimants' business premises. The necessity of preserving the freedoms of speech, assembly and demonstration should "not constrain the court to refuse a [claimant] an injunction to prevent defendants exercising these liberties in his front garden."[70] The injunction may also be granted if there is a clear case that publication is part of a concerted plan to inflict

---

[63] For the implications of the Human Rights Act 1998, see (1999) 58 C.L.J. 509 at 531–536 (I. Leigh and L. Lustgarten).

[64] (1882) 20 Ch.D. 501.

[65] *Fraser v. Evans* [1969] 1 Q.B. 349 at 360, *per* Lord Denning M.R.; *Bryanston Finance Ltd v. de Vries* [1975] Q.B. 703 (privileged occasions); *Crest Homes Ltd v. Ascott, The Times*, February 4, 1975 (no injunction when defendant chose "flamboyant and vulgar method of airing his complaints"); *Khashoggi v. I.P.C. Magazines Ltd* [1986] 1 W.L.R. 1412; *Att.-Gen. v. News Group Newspapers Ltd* [1987] Q.B. 1; *Holley v. Smyth* [1998] Q.B. 726.

[66] *Woodward v. Hutchins* [1977] 1 W.L.R. 760, at 764 (*per* Lord Denning M.R.).

[67] [1891] 2 Ch. 269. See also *Hermann Loog v. Bean* (1884) 26 Ch.D. 306; *Harakas v. Baltic Mercantile & Shipping Exchange Ltd* [1982] 1 W.L.R. 958.

[68] *Att-Gen. v. British Broadcasting Corporation* [1981] A.C. 303 at 311, C.A.

[69] [1976] Q.B. 142; (Lord Denning M.R. dissenting). See (1976) 35 C.L.J. 82 (P. Wallington).

[70] *ibid.* at 187, *per* Stamp L.J.

deliberate damage without just cause.[71] In *Monson v. Tussaud's*,[72] an injunction was refused because it appeared that there might be a question at the trial whether the claimant had agreed to the publication. The court will only intervene where the issue is clear and certain. It "will not prejudice the issue by granting an injunction in advance of publication."[73] It has been held that the principles laid down in *American Cyanamid Co. v. Ethicon Ltd*[74] governing the grant of an interlocutory injunction have no application to libel injunctions, thus preserving the rule in *Bonnard v. Perryman*.[75] Regard must also be had to section 12(3) of the Human Rights Act 1998, which has already been considered.[75a]

Once libel has been proved at the trial, the claimant may obtain an injunction to restrain its repetition.

D. Breach of Confidence

An injunction will be available to restrain a breach of confidence, whether arising out of a personal, commercial or other relationship.[76] Many of the questions which arise are similar to those discussed in connection with the cases on libel, but the principle of freedom of speech plays a less dominant part here. Unlike libel, the truth of the statement is no defence to a breach of confidence. As will be seen, the search order[77] has evolved to protect the victims of commercial malpractice and espionage. Also in the commercial context, an injunction may be granted to restrain a firm of solicitors or accountants from acting for one client against a former client in respect of whom confidential information is retained, unless a clearly effective "Chinese wall" is in place.[78]

An obligation of confidence exists in respect of communications between husband and wife. "It is the policy of the law

---

[71] *Gulf Oil (Great Britain) Ltd v. Page* [1987] Ch. 327 (airborne sign over Cheltenham racecourse); *Femis-Bank (Anguilla) Ltd v. Lazar* [1991] Ch. 391.

[72] [1894] 1 Q.B. 671. The claimant, who had been tried in Scotland for murder, where the jury had returned a verdict of "not proven," complained of the exhibition of a figure of himself in a room next to the "Chamber of Horrors."

[73] *Fraser v. Evans, supra,* at 361, *per* Lord Denning M.R.

[74] [1975] A.C. 396, *ante,* p. 777.

[75] *Bestobell Paints Ltd v. Bigg* (1975) 119 S.J. 678; *J. Trevor & Sons v. P. R. Solomon* (1978) 248 E.G. 779 (*per* Lord Denning M.R.); *Herbage v. Pressdram Ltd* [1984] 1 W.L.R. 1160; *Gulf Oil (Great Britain) Ltd v. Page* [1987] Ch. 327.

[75a] *ante,* p. 787.

[76] See generally (1977) 30 C.L.P. 191 and (1976) 92 L.Q.R. 180 (M. Bryan); Goff and Jones, *The Law of Restitution* (5th ed.), Chap. 34.

[77] *post,* p. 831. See *Lock International plc v. Beswick* [1989] 1 W.L.R. 1268.

[78] *Bolkiah (Prince Jefri) v. KPMG* [1999] 2 W.L.R. 215; *Young v. Robson Rhodes (a firm)* [1999] 3 All E.R. 524; (2000) 59 C.L.J. 370 (H. McVea).

(which is the basis of the court's jurisdiction) to preserve the close confidence and mutual trust between husband and wife."[79] Other kinds of confidential information will be restrained from publication along similar lines,[80] and even, in some cases, where the information is available from other public sources,[81] but not if it has already been disseminated worldwide, for in such a case the injunction would be futile.[82] It is necessary that the claimant should himself have an interest in preventing the disclosure,[83] although he need not show that the use of the information would cause him detriment.[84] Even where the injunction is granted, it may be that the defendant is enjoined from making use of the confidential information only for a limited period rather than for all time.[85] However, in exceptional cases an injunction may be granted against the whole world restraining publication of confidential information indefinitely, to protect adults who would be seriously at risk of injury or death if their identity or whereabouts were to become public knowledge, if there is no other way to ensure protection of their rights to life under the European Convention on Human Rights as given effect by the Human Rights Act 1998.[85a]

It has now been established that English law recognises the right of personal privacy, which is grounded in the equitable doctrine of breach of confidence.[85b] This is partly a development of the general law and partly a result of the European Convention on Human Rights and the Human Rights Act 1998. Article 8 of the Convention protects the right to respect for private and family life, while Article 10 protects the right to freedom of expression, in both cases subject to qualifications. Thus the courts now recognise privacy as a legal principle drawn from the fundamental

---

[79] *Argyll v. Argyll* [1967] Ch. 302 at 332.

[80] *Saltman Engineering Co. Ltd v. Campbell Engineering Co. Ltd* [1963] 3 All E.R. 413n; *Peter Pan Manufacturing Corporation v. Corsets Silhouette Ltd* [1964] 1 W.L.R. 96; *Seager v. Copydex* [1967] 1 W.L.R. 923; *Thomas Marshall (Exports) Ltd v. Guinle* [1979] Ch. 227; *Fraser v. Thames Television Ltd* [1984] Q.B. 44; (1983) 42 C.L.J. 209 (A. Tettenborn). See generally (1977) 9 Patent L.Rev. 271 (J. Berryhill); (1979) 95 L.Q.R. 323 (W. Braithwaite).

[81] *Schering Chemicals Ltd v. Falkman Ltd* [1982] Q.B. 1; *Att.-Gen. v. Guardian Newspapers Ltd* [1987] 1 W.L.R. 1248 (*Spycatcher* at the interlocutory stage).

[82] *Att.-Gen. v. Guardian Newspapers Ltd (No. 2)* [1990] 1 A.C. 109 (*Spycatcher* final injunction refused). The European Court of Human Rights held that the Government had violated Article 10 of the Convention in maintaining the injunctions after publication abroad.

[83] *Fraser v. Evans* [1969] 1 Q.B. 349; *Hubbard v. Vosper* [1972] 2 Q.B. 84.

[84] *X. v. Y.* [1988] 2 All E.R. 648. See the varying views in *Att.-Gen. v. Guardian Newspapers Ltd (No. 2)*, *supra*.

[85] This is the "springboard" doctrine. See (1979) 42 M.L.R. 94 (W. Braithwaite); (1976) 92 L.Q.R. 180 (M. Bryan).

[85a] *Venables v. Newsgroup Newspapers, The Times*, January 16, 2001.

[85b] *Douglas v. Hello! Ltd, The Times*, January 16, 2001.

value of personal autonomy, there being no need to construct an artificial relationship of confidentiality. The provisions of the Human Rights Act 1998 affecting the grant of interlocutory injunctions in the area of breach of confidence and privacy have already been noted.[85c]

As the right to the preservation of confidence is an equitable interest, third parties with notice may be bound by the duty of confidence.[86] Injunctions may, therefore, be granted against third parties, such as the press, who seek to publish confidential information knowing it to be such.[87] The third party, however, is not necessarily in the same position as the original confidant, as their respective duties may be different.[88] Worldwide publication releases third parties[89] (but probably not the original confidant[90]) from any duty of confidence, although in exceptional cases publication on the Internet after the injunction has been issued may not bring this principle into play, as the injunction could prevent wider circulation of the information.[90a]

The injunction will be refused if the public interest in the preservation of confidence is overridden by some other public interest. While the precise scope of the "public interest" defence remains uncertain,[91] it is clear that matters such as confidentiality or national security[92] must be balanced against the public interest in freedom of speech and the press and the right to receive information. More particularly, there is no confidence as to the disclosure of "iniquity." This principle was discussed by the House of Lords in *Att.-Gen. v. Guardian Newspapers Ltd (No. 2)*,[93] where the question was whether newspapers should be enjoined from publishing *Spycatcher* (the Peter Wright memoirs). It was said that the "iniquity" defence was subject to two limitations. First, the disclosure of confidential

---

[85c] *ante*, p. 787.

[86] *Att.-Gen. v. Guardian Newspapers Ltd (No. 2)*, *supra* (*Sunday Times* liable to account for profits of publication). See also *Printers and Finishers Ltd v. Holloway* [1965] 1 W.L.R. 1; *Goddard v. Nationwide Building Society* [1987] Q.B. 670.

[87] *Att.-Gen. v. Guardian Newspapers Ltd* [1987] 1 W.L.R. 1248, and (*No. 2*) [1990] 1 A.C. 109 (*Spycatcher*); (1989) 52 M.L.R. 389 (J. Michael); (1989) C.L.P. 49 (G. Jones).

[88] *Att.-Gen. v. Guardian Newspapers Ltd (No. 2)*, *supra*.

[89] *ibid.* (*Spycatcher* final injunction refused). See also *Lord Advocate v. The Scotsman Publications Ltd* [1990] 1 A.C. 812.

[90] *ibid.*; the reasoning being that he must not profit from his own wrong.

[90a] *Venables v. Newsgroup Newspapers, The Times*, January 16, 2001, *supra*.

[91] Goff and Jones, *op. cit.*, pp. 764–770. See also *Att.-Gen. v. Jonathan Cape Ltd* [1976] Q.B. 752; *Schering Chemicals Ltd v. Falkman Ltd* [1982] Q.B. 1; (1982) 41 C.L.J. 40 (G. Jones); (1982) 98 L.Q.R. 5 (A. Tettenborn).

[92] *Att.-Gen. v. Guardian Newspapers Ltd* [1987] 1 W.L.R. 1248, and (*No. 2*) [1990] 1 A.C. 109 (*Spycatcher*). The latter decision, however, is not based on the balancing of public interests but on the fact that no further damage could be caused by publication. See generally *X. Ltd v. Morgan Grampian (Publishers) Ltd* [1991] 1 A.C. 1.

[93] *supra*. The "iniquity" involved alleged plots to overthrow the Wilson government and to kill President Nasser. See also *Finers v. Miro* [1991] 1 W.L.R. 35 (fraud).

information revealing wrong-doing should in some cases be to interested parties such as the police rather than to the public at large.[94] Secondly, the duty of confidence was not overridden by mere allegations of wrong-doing. While the wrong-doing need not be proved, there must be at least a prima facie case. Further, it was not the case that *any* breach of the law was within the "iniquity" defence. In the present case, the publication of the entire book or substantial extracts could not be within this defence when the allegations of "iniquity" covered only a few pages. The final injunction was, however, refused because the information was by this time within the public domain.

Where there is no wrong-doing by the claimant the public interest defence will succeed only in exceptional cases. Such a case was *Lion Laboratories Ltd v. Evans*,[95] where the claimant failed to restrain the publication of confidential documents concerning the accuracy of a "breathalyser" device manufactured by the claimant. The public interest in confidentiality had to be weighed against its interest in the accuracy of a device upon which depended liability to criminal penalties. There might be circumstances where it was right to publish confidential material even if unlawfully obtained in flagrant breach of confidence, and irrespective of the motive of the informer. But, it was added, what is interesting to the public should not be confused with the public interest.

Other cases where the public interest defence has succeeded include *Woodward v. Hutchins*,[96] where "publicity seeking" pop singers failed to restrain the publication of newspaper articles revealing "discreditable incidents" about them, and *W. v. Egdell*[97] where a prisoner in a secure hospital failed to enjoin the disclosure by a doctor to the authorities having power to discharge him of a confidential report on his mental state. In *X. v. Y.*,[98] on the other hand,

---

[94] See *Francome v. Mirror Group Newspapers* [1984] 1 W.L.R. 892 (injunction to restrain publication of illegally taped telephone conversations revealing possible criminal offences and breaches of Jockey Club regulations. Public interest could be served by making tapes available to police or Jockey Club); *cf. Cork v. McVicar, The Times*, October 31, 1984 (Exposure of corrupt practices in the administration of justice not to be restrained by injunction, although clear breach of contract and confidence. Argument that disclosure should only be to the appropriate authorities rejected). See also *Re a Company's Application* [1989] Ch. 477; (1990) 106 L.Q.R. 42 (E. Lomnicka); (no injunction to restrain disclosure to tax and regulatory authorities); *Woolgar v. Chief Constable of Sussex Police* [2000] 1 W.L.R. 25 (no injunction to restrain disclosure to nursing regulatory body).

[95] [1985] Q.B. 526 (interlocutory); (1984) 100 L.Q.R. 517; (1985) 44 C.L.J. 35 (Y. Cripps); (1985) 48 M.L.R. 592 (N. Lowe and C. Willmore).

[96] [1977] 1 W.L.R. 760 (interlocutory); criticised in Goff and Jones, *op. cit.*, p. 770. See also *Stephens v. Avery* [1988] Ch. 449; (1989) 105 L.Q.R. 37 (P. Sparkes); (1990) 53 M.L.R. 43 (W. Wilson); *Hellewell v. Chief Constable of Derbyshire* [1995] 1 W.L.R. 804.

[97] [1990] Ch. 395.

[98] [1988] 2 All E.R. 648; All E.R. Rev. 1988 at 214 (A. Grubb).

the defence failed when a health authority sought to restrain publication of the identity of two doctors suffering from AIDS, disclosed by its employee in breach of contract and confidence.

In the sphere of judicial proceedings, the public interest requiring the truth to be disclosed in the administration of justice does not override the confidentiality of matters disclosed in other proceedings, which may be protected by injunction.[99]

E. Public Wrongs

Although an injunction normally issues to prevent a breach of the claimant's own rights, it is available, at the suit of the Attorney-General, to restrain an act which is illegal or detrimental to the public. Thus the Attorney-General may obtain an injunction to restrain a public nuisance, either on his own initiative, or on the relation of some other person.[1] A private individual may only sue in respect of public wrongs where a private right of his own is interfered with,[2] or where he suffers special damage from the interference with the public right.[3] We have seen that, subject to this exception, the individual cannot sue in his own name to enforce a public right. He must bring a relator action, with the consent of the Attorney-General.[4]

An injunction may issue in circumstances where it is the only effective way of protecting the interests of the public, or where the criminal penalty has proved inadequate to prevent continuous breaches of the law. It should be added that where the Attorney-General brings such an action, the injunction is almost always granted. Thus injunctions were issued where the defendant ran buses in Manchester without licence and in defiance of the corporation's objections, the profits being greater than the fines,[5] and where the defendant operated a hotel without a fire certificate, causing danger

---

[99] *Medway v. Doublelock Ltd* [1978] 1 W.L.R. 710. See also *Distillers Co. (Biochemicals) Ltd v. Times Newspapers Ltd* [1975] Q.B. 613; *Goddard v. Nationwide Building Society* [1987] Q.B. 670. But the Banking Act 1987 overrides the duty of confidence; *A. v. B. Bank (Governor and Company of the Bank of England intervening)* [1993] Q.B. 311.

[1] *Att.-Gen. v. P.Y.A. Quarries* [1975] 2 Q.B. 169.

[2] *Lyon v. Fishmongers Co.* (1876) 1 App.Cas. 662.

[3] *Meade v. London Borough of Haringey* [1979] 1 W.L.R. 637; *Gravesham Borough Council v. British Railways Board* [1978] Ch. 379; *Barrs v. Bethell* [1982] Ch. 294; *Lonrho Ltd v. Shell Petroleum Co. Ltd* [1982] A.C. 173; *Ashby v. Ebdon* [1985] Ch. 394; *Rickless v. United Artists Corp.* [1988] Q.B. 40; *CBS Songs Ltd v. Amstrad Consumer Electronics plc* [1988] A.C. 1013; *P. v. Liverpool Daily Post and Echo Newspapers plc* [1991] 2 A.C. 370; *R. v Deputy Governor of Parkhurst Prison, ex p. Hague* [1992] 1 A.C. 58.

[4] *Gouriet v. Union of Post Office Workers* [1978] A.C. 435, *ante*, p. 765.

[5] *Att.-Gen. v. Sharp* [1931] 1 Ch. 121; *Att.-Gen. v. Harris* [1961] 1 Q.B. 74 (selling flowers illegally from stalls); *Att.-Gen. v. Bastow* [1957] 1 Q.B. 514; *Att.-Gen. v. Smith* [1958] 2 Q.B. 173. Such cases could now be dealt with by an action by the local authority under the Local Government Act 1972, s.222, *infra*.

to the public.[6] The Attorney-General may not, however, obtain an injunction to "freeze" the proceeds of crime, as that would amount to confiscation outside the statutory provisions permitting confiscation orders.[7]

We have already seen that the view of the House of Lords is that the cases where the Attorney-General can invoke the aid of the civil courts to restrain the commission of a criminal offence are narrow and not to be extended, and may require reconsideration.[8]

Some statutory provisions enable local authorities to seek injunctions in their own name to enforce public rights, without the concurrence of the Attorney-General. For example, the Local Government Act 1972, s.222[9] enables the local authority to act where it is "expedient for the promotion or protection of the interests of the inhabitants of their area." Applications under section 222 are usually successful. Although the Attorney-General's power to seek injunctions to restrain criminal offences is limited to cases of emergency or inadequate criminal penalty, it has been held that the local authority's power under section 222 is not limited in this way: the only limitation is that the action must promote or protect the interests of the inhabitants.[10] But the court will be reluctant to grant an injunction if the sanctions for disobeying it would be more onerous than the criminal penalty.[11] Where the defendant is flouting a statute, an injunction may be sought before the statutory remedies have been exhausted.[12] In exceptional cases, involving a plain breach and a clear intention to continue with it, the injunction may be granted before proceedings for the statutory remedy have even been commenced.[13]

Although injunctions under section 222 are typically granted in cases of deliberate flouting or where the criminal penalty is inadequate, the jurisdiction is not confined to these circumstances.[14] Flagrant breaches of the criminal law need not be shown where there

---

[6] *Att.-Gen. v. Chaudry* [1971] 1 W.L.R. 1623.

[7] *Att.-Gen. v. Blake* [2000] 3 W.L.R. 625 (no injunction to prevent receipt of royalties by KGB spy for his autobiography, but private law action for account of profits available).

[8] *Gouriet v. Union of Post Office Workers* [1978] A.C. 435.

[9] This exception was described as "limited" in *Gouriet v. Union of Post Office Workers, supra*. See also the wider provisions of Town and Country Planning Act 1990, s.187B; *Runnymede Borough Council v. Harwood* (1994) 68 P. & C.R. 300.

[10] *Kent County Council v. Batchelor* [1979] 1 W.L.R. 213 (breach of tree preservation order); (1979) 95 L.Q.R. 174 (D. Feldman). See also *Thanet District Council v. Ninedrive Ltd* [1978] 1 All E.R. 703 (Sunday trading); *Solihull Metropolitan Borough Council v. Maxfern Ltd* [1977] 1 W.L.R. 127 (Sunday trading); *Hammersmith Borough Council v. Magnum Automated Forecourts Ltd* [1978] 1 W.L.R. 50 (nuisance).

[11] *Stoke-on-Trent City Council v. B. & Q. (Retail) Ltd* [1984] A.C. 754.

[12] *Runnymede Borough Council v. Ball* [1986] 1 W.L.R. 353.

[13] *Stafford Borough Council v. Elkenford Ltd* [1977] 1 W.L.R. 324; *Stoke-on-Trent City Council v. B. & Q. (Retail) Ltd, supra,* (Sunday trading).

[14] *Runnymede Borough Council v. Ball* [1986] 1 W.L.R. 353; *Kirklees Borough Council v. Wickes Building Supplies Ltd* [1993] A.C. 227.

is clear evidence of persistent and serious conduct.[15] However, an injunction in aid of the criminal law is a remedy of last resort and should not be granted if a less draconian means of securing obedience is available.[16]

In the sphere of public law an injunction, declaration or prerogative order may be sought, with the permission of the court, in a "claim for judicial review".[17] This was until recently governed by Order 53 of the Rules of the Supreme Court, but Order 53 has been replaced by Part 54 of the Civil Procedure Rules.[18] The court may grant the injunction or declaration if, in all the circumstances, it is "just and convenient" to do so.[19] On the question of *locus standi*, the claimant must have a sufficient interest in the matter.[20] In a case concerning a declaration and a mandatory order, then called mandamus, it was held that one taxpayer had no sufficient interest to ask the court to investigate the tax affairs of another taxpayer or to complain that the latter had been under or over-assessed.[21]

The question arose whether, in the field of administrative law, the claim for judicial review was an exclusive remedy, so that the claimant could not seek an injunction in the ordinary way. In *O'Reilly v. Mackman*[22] the House of Lords held that, as a general rule, it would be contrary to public policy and an abuse of process for a claimant complaining of a public authority's infringement of his public law rights to seek redress by an ordinary action and thus avoid the protection afforded to statutory tribunals.[23] It is otherwise where the claimant's private law rights have been infringed.[24] The Civil Procedure Rules 1998 now provide more flexibility where the claimant has used the wrong procedure.[25–26]

An ordinary injunction is appropriate where the defendant is a domestic body with no public role. Where the defendant is a public body, a distinction is drawn between its public and private law

---

[15] *City of London Corporation v. Bovis Construction Ltd* [1992] 3 All E.R. 697.

[16] *Waverley Borough Council v. Hilden* [1988] 1 W.L.R. 246; *Newport Borough Council v. Khan* [1990] 1 W.L.R. 1185.

[17] C.P.R. 1998, Part 54.

[18] There are alterations in terminology but the substance is little changed.

[19] Supreme Court Act 1981, s.31(2).

[20] See the comments of Lord Denning in *The Discipline of Law*, p. 133.

[21] *R. v. I.R.C., ex p. National Federation of Self-Employed and Small Businesses Ltd* [1982] A.C. 617; (1982) 45 M.L.R. 92 (D. Feldman); (1982) 41 C.L.J. 6 (J. Griffiths). *cf. R. v. Her Majesty's Treasury, ex p. Smedley* [1985] Q.B. 657.

[22] [1983] 2 A.C. 237; (1983) 99 L.Q.R. 166 (H.W.R.W.); (1983) 42 C.L.J. 15 (J. Jolowicz); (1983) 46 M.L.R. 645 (M. Sunkin); (1987) 103 L.Q.R. 34 (J. Beatson).

[23] Which includes the requirement of the permission of the court, and a three-month time limit.

[24] No private right was involved in a decision as to remission of a prison sentence. There may be other exceptions, such as where none of the parties objects.

[25–26] C.P.R. Part 54.20. See also Part 30, as to transfers to and from the Administrative Court.

functions. Thus a local authority's decision as to whether it has a duty to house a homeless person is a public law function, while its functions as landlord or licensor once it has implemented its duty are matters of private law.[27]

Even before the Civil Procedure Rules 1998, the House of Lords favoured a broader approach, namely that a litigant could seek to enforce a private law right by ordinary action, notwithstanding that the proceedings involved a challenge to a public law act or decision, judicial review being necessary only when private law rights were not at stake.[28] It was concluded that, unless the procedure was ill suited to dispose of the question at issue, "there is much to be said in favour of the proposition that a court having jurisdiction ought to let a case be heard rather than entertain a debate concerning the form of the proceedings."[29] This flexible approach was developed by the Court of Appeal in *Clark v. University of Lincolnshire and Humberside*,[30] which involved a dispute as to whether an action for breach of contract brought by a student against the university should properly have been commenced as judicial review. It was held that, in cases where judicial review would have been more appropriate, the court would not strike out the action merely because of the procedure adopted. Under the Civil Procedure Rules 1998 the court could prevent unfair exploitation of the longer limitation period applicable to private law actions without resorting to a rigid exclusionary rule capable of doing equal injustice: "The intention of the Civil Procedure Rules is to harmonise procedures as far as possible and to avoid barren procedural disputes which generate satellite litigation."[31] Thus the emphasis has changed since *O'Reilly v. Mackman*.[32]

F. Family Matters

The court has a statutory jurisdiction to grant injunctions to restrain a husband from dealing with property so as to defeat his wife's claim to maintenance.[33] Injunctions are commonly granted in relation to occupation of the home under the provisions of the matrimonial homes legislation.[34] Thus injunctions have been granted to

---

[27] *O'Rourke v. Camden London Borough Council* [1998] A.C. 188. See the review by the House of Lords in *X (Minors) v. Bedfordshire County Council* [1995] 2 A.C. 633.

[28] *Roy v. Kensington and Chelsea and Westminster Family Practitioner Committee* [1992] 1 A.C. 624; (1992) 108 L.Q.R. 353 (S. Fredman and G. Morris); (1992) 51 C.L.J. 201 (I. Hare); *Mohram Ali v. Tower Hamlets London Borough Council* [1993] Q.B. 407.

[29] *ibid.* at 655.

[30] [2000] 1 W.L.R. 1988 (decided before the introduction of C.P.R. Part 54).

[31] *ibid.* at 1998, *per* Lord Woolf M.R.

[32] [1983] 2 A.C. 237, *supra*.

[33] Matrimonial Causes Act 1973, s.37; Matrimonial and Family Proceedings Act 1984, s.24.

[34] Now the Family Law Act 1996.

restrain a husband from installing his lover in the matrimonial home,[35] or to exclude the husband from the home,[36] or to restrain a man from living near his former wife,[37] or, in a grave case, to exclude an adult child from his parents' home.[38] But the jurisdiction is sparingly exercised; it must be necessary to protect the applicant or a relevant child and should never be regarded as routine.[39]

Orders may be made under the Family Law Act 1996 (replacing and extending earlier legislation) to regulate the occupation of the family home.[40] The jurisdiction extends to spouses, former spouses, cohabitants and former cohabitants, but the details are outside the scope of this book. Non-molestation orders may be granted under the 1996 Act,[41] and under the court's general jurisdiction. They should not be granted against mental patients, nor against children where there is no effective means of enforcement.[42] It should be added that injunctions of this kind should not be granted without notice unless there is real danger of serious injury or damage.[43]

The remedy of injunction is also employed in the protection of children[44]; for example, to restrain persons who had enticed a girl of 16 away from her father, from continuing to harbour her[45]; in support of a custody order[46]; to protect a child from publicity (although press freedom should not be restricted any more than is essential[47]); or to restrain the mother of a ward from leaving the jurisdiction before submitting to a test to establish its paternity.[48] It is in connection with equity's special care concerning children that most risks are taken with regard to the issue of injunctions against persons outside the jurisdiction.[49]

---

[35] *Pinckney v. Pinckney* [1966] 1 All E.R. 121.

[36] *Hall v. Hall* [1971] 1 W.L.R. 404; *Phillips v. Phillips* [1973] 1 W.L.R. 615.

[37] *M v. M* (1983) 13 Fam.Law 110; *Burris v. Azadani* [1995] 1 W.L.R. 1372.

[38] *Egan v. Egan* [1975] Ch. 218 (a clear history of assaults, and threats of more).

[39] *Des Salles d'Epinoix v. Des Salles d'Epinoix* [1967] 1 W.L.R. 553; *Wiseman v. Simpson* [1988] 1 W.L.R. 35; Family Law Act 1996, ss.33, 35, 36.

[40] See ss.33, 35, 36.

[41] See ss.42, 45 (orders without notice), 47 (power of arrest).

[42] *Wookey v. Wookey* [1991] Fam. 121.

[43] *Ansah v. Ansah* [1977] Fam. 138. See Family Law Act 1996, s.45 (risk of significant harm).

[44] For the practical limitations on the exercise of the jurisdiction, see *Re C. (a minor)* [1991] 2 F.L.R. 168.

[45] *Lough v. Ward* [1945] 2 All E.R. 338.

[46] *Re W. (a minor)* [1981] 3 All E.R. 401; doubted (1982) 45 M.L.R. 468 (G. Douglas). As to adoption orders, see *Re D. (a minor)* [1991] Fam. 137.

[47] The authorities are reviewed in *Re Z (a minor) (Identification: Restrictions on Publication)* [1997] Fam. 1. See also *Nottingham City Council v. October Films Ltd* [1999] 2 F.L.R. 347.

[48] *Re I. (a minor), The Times*, May 22, 1987.

[49] *Re Liddell's S.T.* [1936] Ch. 365; *Harben v. Harben* [1957] 1 W.L.R. 261; *Re O.* [1962] 1 W.L.R. 724. See also *Practice Direction* [1983] 1 W.L.R. 558 (injunctions to restrain removal of child from jurisdiction).

As we have seen, a husband cannot obtain an injunction to prevent his wife from having an abortion.[50]

Finally, the use of search orders and asset-freezing injunctions in family matters is dealt with below.[51]

G. Trade Unions, Clubs and Colleges

Some use of the injunction has been made as a remedy against trade unions.[52] Perhaps the most important use of the injunction in this field has been to restrain the expulsion of a member by his union where such expulsion is contrary to the rules of the union,[53] or the rules of natural justice.[54]

The right of a member of an association to invoke the assistance of the courts in resisting expulsion is essentially a contractual right.[55] Modern decisions have established that the right to an injunction is not confined to cases where the claimant has some proprietary right. A member may seek an injunction, for example, to protect his "right to work,"[56] or where matters of public importance are concerned.[57] But the mere fact of membership is not, in the absence of these special considerations, sufficient to found a claim to an injunction.[58] Equity will not compel persons to remain in continual and personal relations with one another.[59]

Injunctions have also been granted to professional people who have been dismissed contrary to the rules of their profession, though usually only where improper motive or bad faith can be shown,[60] and to members expelled by social clubs, either in breach of the rules of the club, or where the club has acted in breach of natural

---

[50] *Paton v. Trustees of British Pregnancy Advisory Service* [1979] Q.B. 276; *ante*, p. 768; *C. v. S.* [1988] Q.B. 135.

[51] *post*, p. 831.

[52] See also Trade Union and Labour Relations (Consolidation) Act 1992, s.176, providing additional remedies against unreasonable exclusion or expulsion.

[53] See *Osborne v. Amalgamated Society of Railway Servants* [1911] 1 Ch. 540; *Lee v. Showmen's Guild* [1952] 2 Q.B. 329. The claimant should normally, however, first exhaust other remedies available under the rules: *White v. Kuzych* [1951] A.C. 585; but *cf. Lawlor v. Union of Post Office Workers* [1965] Ch. 712.

[54] *Edwards v. SOGAT* [1971] Ch. 354; *Breen v. A.E.U.* [1971] 2 Q.B. 175; *Shotton v. Hammond* (1976) 120 S.J. 780.

[55] *White v. Kuzych, supra*; *Bonsor v. Musicians' Union* [1956] A.C. 104.

[56] *Edwards v. SOGAT, supra*; *cf. Gaiman v. National Association for Mental Health* [1971] Ch. 317 (no injunction as membership involved no question of property, livelihood or reputation).

[57] *Woodford v. Smith* [1970] 1 W.L.R. 806, concerning membership of a ratepayers' association, where an injunction was granted to restrain the holding of a meeting without permitting the claimant members to attend and vote.

[58] *Baird v. Wells* (1890) 44 Ch.D. 661.

[59] *Lumley v. Wagner* (1852) 1 De G.M. & G. 604.

[60] *Hayman v. Governors of Rugby School* (1874) L.R. 18 Eq. 28; *Cassel v. Inglis* [1916] 2 Ch. 211; *Weinberger v. Inglis* [1919] A.C. 606.

justice. Thus, in *Labouchere v. Earl of Wharncliffe*,[61] the general meeting of a club, summoned without proper notice, expelled the claimant without full inquiry, without giving him notice of any definite charge, and by a resolution carried by an insufficient majority. The court granted an injunction against such purported expulsion.

Injunctions are sometimes sought by students or teachers dismissed from a university without a fair hearing, in breach of the rules of natural justice, to restrain the university authorities from acting on the dismissal.[62] This raises the question of the visitor's jurisdiction which was discussed in Chapter 15.[63]

H. Judicial Proceedings

In proper cases, judicial proceedings in inferior courts,[64] administrative tribunals,[65] and private prosecutions[66] may be restrained. So also the initiation of proceedings in the High Court,[67] but once commenced, proceedings in the High Court are not subject to injunction; indeed interference with such proceedings may itself be restrained by injunction as a contempt of court.[68] It might be added that arbitration proceedings may, in certain cases, be restrained by injunction.[69]

Judicial proceedings in foreign courts may be restrained by injunction, where this is appropriate to avoid an injustice, but this is a jurisdiction to be exercised with great caution. Such an injunction will only be issued against a party who is amenable to the jurisdiction of the English court. It is directed not to the foreign court, but

---

[61] (1879) 13 Ch.D. 346; and see *Harington v. Sendall* [1903] 1 Ch. 921; *cf. Dawkins v. Antrobus* (1881) 17 Ch.D. 615.

[62] *Glynn v. Keele University* [1971] 1 W.L.R. 487; *Herring v. Templeman* [1973] 3 All E.R. 569; *cf. R. v. Senate of the University of Aston, ex p. Roffey* [1969] 2 Q.B. 538 (where certiorari, now called a quashing order, was thought appropriate).

[63] *ante*, p. 461.

[64] *Re Connolly Bros. Ltd* [1911] 1 Ch. 731 (Lancaster Palatine Court); *Thames Launches v. Trinity House Corporation (Deptford Strond)* [1966] Ch. 197 (magistrates' court); *Murcutt v. Murcutt* [1952] P. 266 (county court).

[65] de Smith, *Judicial Review of Administrative Action* (5th ed.), pp. 730–731.

[66] *Thames Launches v. Trinity House Corporation (Deptford Strond)* [1966] Ch. 197.

[67] *McHenry v. Lewis* (1882) 22 Ch.D. 397; *Ellerman Lines v. Read* [1928] 2 K.B. 144; *Orr-Lewis v. Orr-Lewis* [1949] P. 347; *Settlement Corporation v. Hochschild* [1966] Ch. 10. See also *Bryanston Finance Ltd v. de Vries (No. 2)* [1976] Ch. 63 (winding-up petition).

[68] *Att.-Gen. v. Times Newspapers Ltd* [1974] A.C. 273. But this decision was held by the European Court (April 26, 1979) to infringe Art. 10 of the European Convention on Human Rights, which guarantees freedom of expression. See (1979) 95 L.Q.R. 348 (F. Mann); (1979) 38 C.L.J. 242 (C. Gray); Lord Denning, *The Due Process of Law*, pp. 45–49. See also *Att.-Gen. v. London Weekend Television Ltd* [1973] 1 W.L.R. 202.

[69] Mustill and Boyd, *The Law and Practice of Commercial Arbitration in England* (2nd ed.), pp. 518 *et seq*.

to the parties.[70] Generally comity requires that the English court should have a sufficient interest in, or connection with, the matter to justify indirect interference.[71]

I. Legislative Proceedings

It is very doubtful whether an injunction will lie to restrain the introduction or enactment of a Bill,[72] or to restrain the making of a subordinate legislative instrument.[73] It is, however, possible that an injunction may be granted to restrain the breach of contractual obligations not to promote or to petition against a private Bill,[74] or to restrain unauthorised expenditure of public funds in promoting or opposing a private Bill.[75] But no injunction will lie to restrain any procedure concerning a public Bill.[76]

J. To Prevent Removal or Destruction of Evidence: Search Orders

This type of injunction is designed to secure that pending trial[77] the defendant does not dispose of any articles in his possession which could be prejudicial at the trial. It is "an illustration of the adaptability of equitable remedies to new situations."[78] It is particularly useful to the victims of commercial malpractice, such as breach of confidence, breach of copyright and passing off. It has also been used in the family context, as in *Emanuel v. Emanuel*,[79] where a husband had been ordered in matrimonial proceedings to transfer properties to his wife. He failed to comply, and had sold a property and spent the proceeds. An order was granted to allow the wife's solicitors to enter his home to inspect documents relating to his finances. It is essential that such an order be available without notice, so that the defendant is not forewarned: "If the stable door cannot be bolted, the horse must be secured. . . . If the horse is liable

---

[70] See Dicey and Morris, *The Conflict of Laws* (13th ed.), pp. 414–422; *Société Nationale Industrielle Aerospatiale v. Lee Kui Jak* [1987] A.C. 871. See also Civil Jurisdiction and Judgments Act 1982, s.49.

[71] *Airbus Industrie GIE v. Patel* [1999] 1 A.C. 119.

[72] Bill of Rights 1688, s.1, Art. 9; see de Smith, *op. cit.* pp. 722 *et seq.*

[73] *Harper v. Secretary of State for Home Affairs* [1955] Ch. 238; see also *Bates v. Lord Hailsham of St. Marylebone* [1972] 1 W.L.R. 1373.

[74] *Bilston Corporation v. Wolverhampton Corporation* [1942] Ch. 391.

[75] *Att.-Gen. v. London and Home Counties Joint Electricity Authority* [1929] 1 Ch. 513.

[76] *Att.-Gen. for New South Wales v. Trethowan* [1932] A.C. 526; doubted in *Hughes and Vale Pty. Ltd* (1954) 90 C.L.R. 203 at 204.

[77] Or after judgment, in aid of execution; C.P.R. 25.2.

[78] *Rank Film Distributors Ltd v. Video Information Centre* [1982] A.C. 380 at 439 (*per* Lord Wilberforce).

[79] [1982] 1 W.L.R. 669. It remains a rare weapon in family cases; *Burgess v. Burgess* [1996] 2 F.L.R. 34.

to be spirited away, notice of an intention to secure the horse will defeat the intention."[80]

Search orders were formerly known as *Anton Piller* orders, taking their name from the case (discussed below) in which the Court of Appeal confirmed the practice over 20 years ago. They were put on a statutory footing by section 7 of the Civil Procedure Act 1997, and are governed also by the Civil Procedure Rules 1998.[81] They are now called "search orders", although of course they are referred to as *Anton Piller* orders or injunctions in the case law preceding these developments.

The search order has been variously described as "a draconian power which should be used only in very exceptional cases",[82] and as "an innovation which has proved its worth time and time again."[83] The first reported decision was *EMI Ltd v. Pandit*,[84] where an order was made without notice in a breach of copyright action to enable the claimant to enter the defendant's premises to inspect, photograph and remove infringing articles. The jurisdiction to make such an order was confirmed by the Court of Appeal in *Anton Piller KG v. Manufacturing Processes Ltd.*[85]

> The defendants had received confidential information and plans concerning the claimant's electrical equipment in their capacity as the claimant's selling agents in England. The claimant had reason to believe that the defendants were selling the information to competitors, but were unable to prove this without access to documents situated on the defendants' premises.
>
> The Court of Appeal made an order without prior notice to the defendants, requiring them to permit the claimant to enter their premises and inspect documents relating to the equipment. Such an order would only be made in exceptional circumstances, where it was essential that the claimant should inspect the documents to enable justice to be done between the parties, and there was a danger that vital evidence would otherwise be destroyed.

Unlike a search warrant, the order does not authorise the claimant to enter against the defendant's will. But it does order him to permit the claimant to enter, so that, if the defendant does not comply, not only does he commit a contempt of court, but adverse inferences

---

[80] *Rank Film Distributors Ltd v. Video Information Centre* [1982] A.C. 380 at 418.

[81] Part 25 (Interim Remedies). See also Supreme Court Act 1981, s.33(1).

[82] *Yousif v. Salama* [1980] 1 W.L.R. 1540 at 1544, *per* Donaldson L.J. His Lordship, dissenting, regarded the order granted by the majority as a power to "take" disclosure.

[83] *Rank Film Distributors Ltd v. Video Information Centre* [1982] A.C. 380 at 406 (Lord Denning M.R.).

[84] [1975] 1 W.L.R. 302.

[85] [1976] Ch. 55; Lord Denning, *The Due Process of Law*, pp. 123 *et seq.*

will be drawn against him at the trial. Ormrod L.J. laid down three conditions for the grant of the order.[86] The claimant must:

   (i) have an extremely strong prima facie case;
   (ii) show actual or potential damage of a very serious nature;
   (iii) have clear evidence that the defendant has incriminating documents or things and a real possibility of their destruction before an application with notice can be made.[87]

It might be added that the order should not be sought as a "fishing expedition."[88]

In the enforcement of the order, the claimant must act with circumspection. He should be attended by his solicitor, and must undertake in damages (giving security in appropriate cases), so as to safeguard the defendant's rights. Because of the draconian nature of the order, the applicant is under a strict duty to make full and frank disclosure of all relevant matters to the court.[89] Strict requirements have been developed to avoid oppression.[90] For example, the order must be executed in office hours so that legal advice is available; a woman must be present at a search of a private house where a woman may be alone; and a list of items must be prepared before they are removed, which the defendant may check. Where the claimant or his solicitor has acted improperly the court may set aside the order. Even if it is not set aside, the defendant may be entitled to exemplary damages.[91]

As the practice became established, grave disquiet was expressed that it had gone too far in favour of claimants,[92] and was "inherently oppressive."[93] An example of its abuse is *Lock International plc v. Beswick*,[94] where the claimant's solicitors searched the business premises and homes of the defendants and removed not only documents containing confidential information but nearly all their commercial papers, computer records and prototypes. The search order,

---

[86] In *Anton Piller KG v. Manufacturing Processes Ltd, supra.* For further guidelines, see *CBS United Kingdom Ltd v. Lambert* [1983] Ch. 37; *Digital Equipment Corporation v. Darkcrest Ltd* [1984] Ch. 512.

[87] See *Yousif v. Salama, supra.*

[88] *i.e.* as a means of finding out what charges can be made.

[89] *Behbehani v. Salem* [1989] 1 W.L.R. 723; *Lock International plc v. Beswick* [1989] 1 W.L.R. 1268; *Tate Access Floors Inc. v. Boswell* [1991] Ch. 512.

[90] *Universal Thermosensors Ltd v. Hibben* [1992] 1 W.L.R. 840; C.P.R. 25 *Practice Direction*, para. 7.

[91] *Columbia Picture Industries Inc. v. Robinson.* [1987] Ch. 38.

[92] *Columbia Picture Industries Inc. v. Robinson* [1987] Ch. 38; All E.R. Rev. 1986, p. 225 (A. Zuckerman); (1987) 46 C.L.J. 50 (N. Andrews); (1987) 1 *Trust Law & Practice* 146 (C. Bell).

[93] *Bhimji v. Chatwani* [1991] 1 W.L.R. 989 at 1002; All E.R. Rev. 1991, p. 263 (A. Zuckerman). It was held in *Chappell v. U.K.* [1989] F.S.R. 617 that the order did not breach Art. 8 of the European Convention on Human Rights.

[94] [1989] 1 W.L.R. 1268; All E.R. Rev. 1989, p. 221 (A. Zuckerman).

which should never have been granted, was discharged. Commentators said that "an exceptional device intended to avoid injustice has become almost a routine method of creating it."[95] It seems that these warnings have been heeded.[96]

The utility of the serach order suffered a set-back when the House of Lords held in *Rank Film Distributors Ltd v. Video Information Centre*,[97] a copyright case, that the defendant could invoke the privilege against self-incrimination. But the privilege was subsequently withdrawn by section 72 of the Supreme Court Act 1981, in the case of proceedings to obtain disclosure of information relating to the infringement of rights pertaining to any intellectual property[98] or passing-off. Matters disclosed as a result of such proceedings are not admissible in evidence against the defendant in proceedings against him for a related offence.[99] The defendant may still invoke the privilege against self-incrimination in a case where the possible offence is not included in section 72.[1] The House of Lords has suggested further reforms, but none have been enacted.[2]

K. To Prevent Removal of Assets: Freezing Injunctions

i. General Principles. This injunction was for many years known as a *Mareva* injunction, taking its name from *Mareva Compania Naviera S.A. v. International Bulkcarriers S.A.*,[3] although the first reported exercise of this novel jurisdiction occurred in *Nippon Yusen Kaisha v. Karageorgis*.[4] It is now called a freezing injunction.[5] It was described by Lord Denning M.R. as "the greatest piece of judicial law reform in my time."[6]

---

[95] (1990) 106 L.Q.R. 601 at 620 (M. Dockray and H. Laddie); (1990) 20 U.W.A.L.R. 143 (J. Martin).

[96] See C.P.R. 25 *Practice Direction*, para. 7.

[97] [1982] A.C. 380. Templeman L.J. in the Court of Appeal, at 423, thought the court would award high damages where the defendant sought to rely on the privilege.

[98] Defined by s.72(5). See *Cobra Golf Inc v. Rata* [1998] Ch. 109.

[99] s.72(3). It is otherwise in the case of proceedings for contempt or perjury, s.72(4).

[1] *Emanuel v. Emanuel* [1982] 1 W.L.R. 669 (Revenue offences); *Tate Access Floors Inc. v. Boswell* [1991] Ch. 512; *IBM United Kingdom Ltd v. Prima Data International Ltd* [1994] 1 W.L.R. 719 (conspiracy).

[2] *Istel (A.T. & T.) Ltd v. Tully* [1993] A.C. 45. The position is not changed by the Civil Procedure Act 1997; s.7(7).

[3] [1975] 2 Lloyd's Rep. 509; (1978) J.B.L. 11 (D. Powles); (1980) 2 W.I.L.J. 60 (A. Bland); [1982] Conv. 265 (R. Horsfall); (1982) 99 L.Q.R. 7 (C. Hodgekiss); (1993) 56 M.L.R. 325 and (1993) 109 L.Q.R. 432 (A. Zuckerman). There is no such jurisdiction in the U.S.A.: (1999) 115 L.Q.R. 601 (L. Collins).

[4] [1975] 1 W.L.R. 1093. See *The Siskina* [1979] A.C. 210 at 229, where Lord Denning M.R. described this injunction as a "rediscovery" of the procedure known as foreign attachment; *Z Ltd v. A–Z and AA–LL* [1982] Q.B. 558.

[5] C.P.R. 25.1(1)(f).

[6] *The Due Process of Law*, p. 134; *The Closing Chapter*, p. 225. See also Donaldson L.J. in *Bank Mellat v. Nikpour* [1985] F.S.R. 87 at 91–92, describing the freezing injunction, along with the search order, as "one of the law's two 'nuclear' weapons."

"A *Mareva* injunction is interlocutory, not final; it is ancillary to a substantive pecuniary claim for debt or damages; it is designed to prevent the judgment . . . for a sum of money being a mere 'brutum fulmen.' "[7] The usual purpose of a freezing injunction is to prevent the dissipation or removal of assets before trial, so that if the claimant succeeds in the action, there will be property of the defendant available to satisfy the judgment. It may also be granted after final judgment if the claimant can show grounds for believing that the defendant will dispose of his assets to avoid execution.[8] In such a case the injunction may even be granted against the defendant's wife.[9] In view of the advent of electronic banking, the significance of the injunction will be readily appreciated. Its effectiveness is assisted by ancillary orders to enable the claimant to obtain disclosure of documents and information as to assets,[10] and by the availability of contempt proceedings against third parties.

The freezing injunction is always interlocutory, and usually without notice: speed is of the essence.[11] It is frequently sought in conjunction with a search order. The basis of the jurisdiction is now the Supreme Court Act 1981, s.37: the injunction may be granted whenever it is "just and convenient" to do so,[12] but with "great circumspection."[13] It is unlimited as to its subject-matter and the nature of the proceedings.[14] As in the case of interlocutory injunctions generally, the claimant must satisfy the conditions laid down by the House of Lords in *American Cyanamid Co. v. Ethicon Ltd*[15]: he must have a good arguable case and the balance of convenience must favour the grant.[16] The claimant must give an undertaking in damages in case he should be unsuccessful at the trial, and the defendant may apply within seven days of service of the order on him for it to be discharged.[17] The defendant may be able to rely on the privilege against self-incrimination to avoid compliance with the

---

[7] *The Siskina* [1979] A.C. 210 at 253 (Lord Diplock). Compare the French "saisie conservatoire."

[8] *Babanaft International Co. SA v. Bassatne* [1990] Ch. 13; C.P.R. 25.2.

[9] *Mercantile Group (Europe) A.G. v. Aiyela* [1994] Q.B. 366.

[10] *Bekhor (A.J.) & Co. Ltd v. Bilton* [1981] Q.B. 923; *Bankers Trust Co. v. Shapira* [1980] 1 W.L.R. 1274; C.P.R. 25.1(1)(g).

[11] *Third Chandris Shipping Corp. v. Unimarine S.A.* [1979] Q.B. 645.

[12] *Mareva Compania Naviera S.A. v. International Bulkcarriers S.A., supra; Nippon Yusen Kaisha v. Karageorgis* [1975] 1 W.L.R. 1093; *Third Chandris Shipping Corp. v. Unimarine S.A., supra; Rasu Maritima S.A. v. Perusahaan Pertambangan Minyak Dan Gas Bumi Negara (Pertamina)* [1978] Q.B. 644.

[13] *Mercedes-Benz AG v. Leiduck* [1996] 1 A.C. 284 at 297 (Lord Mustill).

[14] *Z Ltd v. A–Z and AA–LL* [1982] Q.B. 558. It may be combined with specific performance; *Seven Seas Properties Ltd v. Al-Essa* [1988] 1 W.L.R. 1272.

[15] [1975] A.C. 396; *cf. Polly Peck International plc v. Nadir (No. 2)* [1992] 4 All E.R. 769 at 786.

[16] *Rasu Maritima S.A. v. Perusahaan, etc. supra; Third Chandris Shipping Corp. v. Unimarine S.A., supra; Allen v. Jambo Holdings Ltd* [1980] 1 W.L.R. 1252; *Derby & Co. Ltd v. Weldon* [1990] Ch. 48. See (1978) 41 M.L.R. 1 (M. Kerr) and n. 25, *infra*.

[17] *Mareva Compania Naviera S.A. v. International Bulkcarriers S.A., supra*; C.P.R. 23.10.

injunction or a disclosure order, unless he is adequately protected by a term of the order preventing the use of the disclosures in a prosecution. The House of Lords has said that the privilege should be abolished or modified by Parliament,[18] but this has not been done and the position remains unsatisfactory.[19]

It has been held that the old writ *ne exeat regno*[20] may be granted in support of a freezing injunction,[21] or, if its requirements are not satisfied, an interlocutory injunction under section 37(1) of the Supreme Court Act 1981 to restrain the defendant from leaving the country.[22] While this development increases the efficacy of the freezing injunction, it has been criticised as an unjustified restriction on individual liberty.[23]

ii. Guidelines for the Grant of the Injunction. While the discretion of the court is not fettered by rigid rules, Lord Denning M.R. suggested the following guidelines[24]:

(a) The claimant must have a good arguable case[25];

(b) Where the injunction applies to goods, caution is required to avoid bringing the defendant's business to a standstill[26];

(c) The court should favour the grant if it would be likely to compel the defendant to provide security;

(d) The claimant must make full and frank disclosure of all material matters[27];

(e) He should give particulars of his claim and its amount, and (in an application without notice) he should fairly state the points made against it by the defendant;

---

[18] *Istel (A. T. & T.) Ltd v. Tully* [1993] A.C. 45 (where S.C.A. 1981, s.72, and Theft Act 1968, s.31, inapplicable). As to the incrimination of third parties, see *Arab Monetary Fund v. Hashim (No. 2)* [1990] 1 All E.R. 673.

[19] *Den Norske Bank A.S.A. v. Antonatos* [1999] Q.B. 271; All E.R. Rev. 1998, p. 341 (A. Zuckerman). See also *Memory Corporation plc v. Sidhu* [2000] 2 W.L.R. 1106.

[20] *ante*, p. 32. "Writ" has now been replaced by "claim form"; C.P.R. 7.

[21] *Al Nahkel for Contracting and Trading Ltd v. Lowe* [1986] Q.B. 235; *cf. Allied Arab Bank Ltd v. Hajjar* [1988] Q.B. 787. This is doubtful, as *ne exeat regno* is to assist prosecution of an action, not execution of a judgment.

[22] *ante*, p. 769.

[23] (1986) 45 C.L.J. 189 (C. Harpum); All E.R. Rev. 1986 at 225 (A. Zuckerman); (1987) 104 L.Q.R. 246 (L. Anderson); (1990) 20 U.W.A.L.R. 143 (J. Martin).

[24] *Rasu Maritima S.A. v. Perusahaan, etc.* [1978] Q.B. 644; *Third Chandris Shipping Corp. v. Unimarine S.A.* [1979] Q.B. 645. See also *Barclay-Johnson v. Yuill* [1980] 1 W.L.R. 1259; (1981) 97 L.Q.R. 4; *Z Ltd v. A–Z and AA–LL* [1982] Q.B. 558; *Derby & Co. Ltd v. Weldon, supra.* See *Practice Direction* [1996] 1 W.L.R. 1552.

[25] See *Etablissement Esefka International Anstalt v. Central Bank of Nigeria* [1979] 1 Lloyd's Rep. 445; *Barclay-Johnson v. Yuill, supra.*

[26] As to chattels, see *CBS United Kingdom Ltd v. Lambert* [1983] Ch. 37.

[27] Failure to make full disclosure may result in discharge. See *Columbia Picture Industries Inc. v. Robinson* [1987] Ch. 38; *Lloyds Bowmaker Ltd v. Britannia Arrow Holdings plc* [1988] 1 W.L.R. 1337; *Brink's-MAT Ltd v. Elcombe* [1988] 1 W.L.R. 1350; *Behbehani v. Salem* [1989] 1 W.L.R. 723n; *Memory Corporation plc v. Sidhu (No. 2)* [2000] 1 W.L.R. 1443.

(f) He must undertake in damages, giving security in suitable cases, in case he is unsuccessful in the action.

Lord Denning added that the claimant had to give grounds for believing that the defendant had assets in the jurisdiction, that there was a risk of their removal, and a danger of default if so removed. It is no longer necessary for the claimant to establish in all cases that there is a risk of removal of the assets from the jurisdiction, as section 37(3) of the Supreme Court Act 1981 provides that the injunction may be granted to prevent the defendant from removing from the jurisdiction "or otherwise dealing with" the assets. Thus a risk of dissipation within the jurisdiction[28] (or, in an extreme case, damage or destruction[29]) is sufficient. The developments as to foreign assets are discussed below.

Exceptionally, the injunction may be made against all the defendant's assets; but usually a limit will be specified.[30] In rare cases it may be made in respect of a joint account,[31] but not assets of the defendant's wife or another third party,[32] save in aid of enforcement of a judgment.[33] An order made in relation to "his assets" does not include those of which the defendant is legal owner, but which he holds on trust for a third party.[34] The injunction may be granted to restrain a sale of assets at an independently assessed price, although this will rarely be done in the case of a transaction in good faith in the ordinary course of business.[35] The injunction should rarely be granted where the defendant is a bank, otherwise its business could be irreparably harmed.[36]

iii. The Jurisdiction of the Court. The House of Lords in *The Siskina*[37] emphasised that the injunction had to be ancillary to substantive relief which the High Court had jurisdiction to grant; and that there was no power to grant the injunction save in protection or

---

[28] See *Z Ltd v. A–Z and AA–LL* [1982] Q.B. 558.

[29] *Standard Chartered Bank v. Walker* [1992] 1 W.L.R. 561.

[30] *Z Ltd v. A–Z and AA–LL*, *supra*; See also *Oceanica Castelana Armadora S.A. of Panama v. Mineralimportexport* [1983] 1 W.L.R. 1294. After-acquired assets may be included; *TDK Tape Distributors (U.K.) Ltd v. Videochoice Ltd* [1986] 1 W.L.R. 141.

[31] *ibid.*

[32] *S.C.F. Finance Co. Ltd v. Masri* [1985] 1 W.L.R. 876; *Allied Arab Bank Ltd v. Hajjar* (1989) 19 Fam.Law 68; *cf. T.S.B. Private Bank International S.A. v. Chabra* [1992] 1 W.L.R. 231.

[33] *Mercantile Group (Europe) A.G. v. Aiyela* [1994] Q.B. 66.

[34] *Federal Bank of the Middle East v. Hadkinson* [2000] 1 W.L.R. 1695. The order could be worded differently, so as to cover all assets in his name, although it would be varied if it later became clear that certain assets were held on trust.

[35] *Customs and Excise Commissioners v. Anchor Foods Ltd* [1999] 1 W.L.R. 1139; All E.R. Rev. 1999 at 283 (A. Zuckerman).

[36] *Polly Peck International plc v. Nadir (No. 2)* [1992] 4 All E.R. 769; (1992) 108 L.Q.R. 559 (A. Zuckerman). See also *Themehelp Ltd v. West* [1996] Q.B. 84 (guarantee).

[37] [1979] A.C. 210.

assertion of some legal or equitable right which the High Court had jurisdiction to enforce by final judgment. *The Siskina* was reversed for cases within section 25 of the Civil Jurisdiction and Judgments Act 1982,[38] which was originally confined to proceedings in countries which were parties to the Brussels and Lugano Conventions. Section 25 was extended in 1997[39] to proceedings in countries which are party to neither Convention, with the result that *The Siskina* has no further application. However, in cases where the court has no independent jurisdiction as to the subject-matter of the proceedings, it may refuse to grant the injunction on the basis of inexpedience.[40]

It has been held that a freezing injunction may not be granted unless the cause of action has accrued,[41] but this was influenced by *The Siskina*, and the current view is that equity will "lend a hand" in advance of the appropriate time at law, to prevent injustice.[42]

iv. The English-based Defendant. The freezing injunction evolved as a remedy against a foreign-based defendant having assets within the jurisdiction. It was assumed in the earlier decisions that there was no power to grant such an injunction against an English-based defendant, although the merit of such a distinction was questioned.[43]

The difficulty in the way of extending the freezing injunction to English-based defendants was the clear line of authority to the effect that there is "no statutory or other power in the Court to restrain a person from dealing with his property at a time when no order against him has been made."[44] It must be said, however, that this principle had already been eroded by the development of the injunction against foreign-based defendants.

Eventually the jurisdiction to enjoin an English-based defendant became established.[45] It was confirmed by section 37(3) of the Supreme Court Act 1981, providing that the court's power to grant an interlocutory injunction restraining a party to any proceedings from

---

[38] See *Haiti (Republic of) v. Duvalier* [1990] 1 Q.B. 202.
[39] Civil Jurisdiction and Judgments Act 1982 (Interim Relief) Order 1997 (S.I. 1997 No. 302). See also R.S.C. Ord. 11, Rule 8A (C.P.R. 1998, Sched. 1).
[40] Civil Jurisdiction and Judgments Act 1982, s.25(2); *Crédit Suisse Fides Trust S.A. v. Cuoghi* [1998] Q.B. 818 at 829, 831; (1997) 147 N.L.J. 1234 (A. Lenon). See also *Refco Inc. v. Eastern Trading Co.* [1999] 1 Lloyd's Rep. 159.
[41] *Veracruz Transportation Inc. v. V.C. Shipping Co. Inc.* [1992] 1 Lloyd's Rep. 353, criticised (1992) 108 L.Q.R. 175 (L. Collins).
[42] *Re Q's Estate* [1999] 1 Lloyd's Rep. 931.
[43] See *The Siskina* [1979] A.C. 210.
[44] *Jagger v. Jagger* [1926] P. 93 at 102, *per* Scrutton L.J. See also *Lister & Co. v. Stubbs* (1890) 45 Ch.D. 1 (disapproved on another point in *Att.-Gen. for Hong Kong v. Reid* [1994] 1 A.C. 324).
[45] See *A.J. Bekhor & Co. Ltd v. Bilton* [1981] Q.B. 923; *The Due Process of Law*, pp. 147 *et seq.*

removing from the jurisdiction, or otherwise dealing with, assets located within the jurisdiction shall be exercisable whether or not that party is domiciled, resident or present within the jurisdiction.

v. Assets outside the Jurisdiction. The freezing injunction was originally confined to assets within the jurisdiction. It is now established that the injunction (and ancillary disclosure order) may be granted against a defendant who is amenable to the jurisdiction[46] of the court in respect of assets outside the jurisdiction, even on a world-wide basis. The objections to extending the injunction to foreign assets were that the order would be oppressive and unenforceable, and that the territorial limitations were confirmed by section 37(3) of the Supreme Court Act 1981.[47] But the Court of Appeal held in *Babanaft International Co. S.A. v. Bassatne*[48] that section 37(3) did not restrict the scope, geographical or otherwise, of section 37(1). This case involved a post-judgment freezing injunction. Such an order would more readily be made against assets abroad than in a pre-judgment case, but would nevertheless be rare. A personal order binding the defendant alone was made. It is now provided in the Civil Procedure Rules that the injunction may be granted in relation to assets "whether located within the jurisdiction or not",[49] but the decisions on "world-wide assets" remain important.

The issue next arose in the Court of Appeal in *Haiti (Republic of) v. Duvalier*,[50] which concerned the alleged embezzlement of $120m. from the Republic during the presidency of Jean-Claude Duvalier. No substantive relief in England was sought. The court granted a pre-judgment freezing injunction in respect of world-wide assets, although recognising that this was a most unusual measure which should very rarely be granted. While the court would be more willing in a post-judgment case, or where the claimant had a tracing or other proprietary claim, the injunction could be granted in respect of a pre-judgment money claim such as the present case, where international co-operation was demanded. Previous limitations arose from practice rather than from any restriction on the court's power. The injunction was granted subject to a *"Babanaft* proviso"[51] in respect of the foreign assets, to protect third parties outside the jurisdiction save to the extent that the order might be enforced by the local court. Even stricter safeguards were required by the Court of

---

[46] See (1989) 105 L.Q.R. 262 (L. Collins); (1994) 144 N.L.J. 932 (P. Friedman).
[47] *supra.*
[48] [1990] Ch. 13.
[49] C.P.R. 25.1(1)(f).
[50] [1990] 1 Q.B. 202. It has been said that *Duvalier* "goes to the very edge of what is permissible"; (1989) 105 L.Q.R. 262 at 281 (L. Collins). This comment was noted by Millett L.J. in *Crédit Suisse Fides Trust S.A. v. Cuoghi* [1998] Q.B. 818.
[51] For the current form of the proviso, see C.P.R. 25 *Practice Direction.*

Appeal in *Derby & Co. Ltd v. Weldon*,[52] where a pre-judgment
world-wide freezing injunction was granted. It was emphasised that,
in addition to a good arguable case, the claimant must show that any
English assets are insufficient, that there are foreign assets, and that
there is a real risk of disposal of the latter. The injunction will not
be granted if it would be oppressive. The court must be satisfied, by
means of undertaking or proviso, that (a) the defendant will not be
oppressed by exposure to a multiplicity of proceedings[53]; (b) the
defendant will be protected against misuse of information gained
from the order for disclosure of assets; and (c) third parties are
protected. The present case was sufficiently exceptional because a
very large sum was involved (£15m.), the English assets were totally
inadequate, and there was a high risk of dissipation of the foreign
assets through inaccessible overseas companies. In *Derby & Co. Ltd
v. Weldon (No. 3 and No. 4)*[54] a similar injunction was granted
against companies in Luxembourg and Panama which had no assets
within the jurisdiction. The Luxembourg company was subject to
the jurisdiction of a court which would enforce the orders of the
English court under the Civil Jurisdiction and Judgments Act 1982.
Concerning the Panama company, the fact that the order could not
be specifically enforced was no bar. The order would not be made if
there was no effective sanction, but the sanction of being debarred
from defending in the event of disobedience normally sufficed.[55]
More recently it has been emphasised that, where an injunction is
sought in aid of foreign proceedings, the focus is on whether it is
expedient to grant it, in view of the court's lack of jurisdiction over
the subject-matter of the proceedings, and not whether the circumstances are exceptional.[56] However, a world-wide order should not
be granted routinely or without very careful consideration. Finally,
the court may, in exceptional cases, order the transfer of assets from
one foreign jurisdiction to another to prevent their dissipation.[57]

vi. Operation in Personam. The usual subject-matter of a freezing injunction is a sum of money, often in a bank account. But there
is no reason why other assets, such as a ship,[58] or an aeroplane,[59]
should not be "frozen" by this method. It is important to note,

---

[52] [1990] Ch. 48.
[53] See *Re Bank of Credit and Commerce International S.A.* [1994] 1 W.L.R. 708; All E.R. Rev.
1994 at 305 (A. Zuckerman).
[54] [1990] Ch. 65.
[55] See (1989) 105 L.Q.R. 262 at 296 (L. Collins).
[56] *Crédit Suisse Fides Trust S.A. v. Cuoghi* [1998] Q.B. 818; Civil Jurisdiction and Judgments
Act 1982, s.25(2).
[57] *Derby & Co. Ltd v. Weldon (No. 6)* [1990] 1 W.L.R. 1139.
[58] *The Rena K* [1979] Q.B. 377. There is no conflict here with the jurisdiction to arrest ships.
See [1982] Conv. 265 at 270 (R. Horsfall).
[59] *Allen v. Jambo (Holdings) Ltd* [1980] 1 W.L.R. 1252 (A fatal accident case).

however, that such an injunction, even if related to a specified asset, operates only *in personam*.[60] It is not a form of pre-trial attachment. It does not effect seizure of the asset, nor is it analogous to a lien. It merely prohibits the defendant personally from removing or transferring the asset. It gives no proprietary right in the asset, nor priority over other creditors.[61] The claimant's right is merely to have the asset preserved so that, if he succeeds in his action, judgment may be executed against it, but the rights of a third-party with an interest in the asset will not be prejudiced.[62] The injunction may (initially or by variation) permit the assets to be used for living expenses or to make payments in good faith in the ordinary course of business.[63] Such a term does not protect the recipient of the payments in a case where the claimant establishes proprietary rights over the assets.[64]

vii. Position of Third Parties.[65] As far as the liabilities of a third party are concerned, we have seen that a third party who aids and abets the breach of an injunction by the defendant is guilty of contempt.[66] So in the case of a freezing injunction against a sum of money in a bank account, the bank, once it has notice, must not facilitate the disposal of the money without a court order.[67] It is clear that any expenses incurred by a bank or other third party in complying with the injunction must be met by the claimant.[68] Furthermore, a bank can exercise any right of set-off it had before notification of the injunction.[69]

Similarly, the injunction must not interfere with the convenience or freedom of action of a third party. So in *Galaxia Maritime S.A. v.*

---

[60] *cf. Z Ltd v. A–Z and AA–LL* [1982] Q.B. 558 at 573, "it operates *in rem* just as the arrest of a ship does.", *per* Lord Denning M.R. This was *per incuriam; Att.-Gen. v. Times Newspapers Ltd* [1992] 1 A.C. 191 at 215.

[61] See *Sanders Lead Co. Inc. v. Entores Metal Brokers Ltd* [1984] 1 W.L.R. 452; *Bank Mellat v. Kazmi* [1989] Q.B. 541. Assets subject to a tracing claim may be protected by an ordinary interlocutory injunction; *Polly Peck International plc v. Nadir (No. 2)* [1992] 4 All E.R. 769; (1999) 62 M.L.R. 539 (P. Devonshire).

[62] *Cretanor Maritime Co. Ltd v. Irish Marine Management Ltd* [1978] 1 W.L.R. 966.

[63] *Iraqi Ministry of Defence v. Arcepey Shipping Co. S.A.* [1981] Q.B. 65; *Z Ltd v. A–Z and AA–LL* [1982] Q.B. 558; *TDK Tape Distributors (U.K.) Ltd v. Videochoice Ltd* [1986] 1 W.L.R. 141; *Law Society v. Shanks* [1988] 1 F.L.R. 504; *Atlas Maritime Co. S.A. v. Avalon Maritime Ltd* [1991] 4 All E.R. 769 and *(No. 3)* [1991] 1 W.L.R. 917.

[64] *United Mizrahi Bank Ltd v. Doherty* [1998] 1 W.L.R. 435; All E.R. Rev. 1998 at 341 (A. Zuckerman).

[65] See (1999) 62 M.L.R. 539 (P. Devonshire).

[66] *ante*, p. 763. See *Bank Mellat v. Kazmi* [1989] Q.B. 541. A post-judgment freezing injunction may be granted against the defendant's wife; *Mercantile Group (Europe) A.G. v. Aiyela* [1994] Q.B. 366; *ante*, p. 837.

[67] *Z Ltd v. A–Z and AA–LL* [1982] Q.B. 558; *cf. Law Society v. Shanks, supra.* The injunction should not be granted against a bank as defendant; *ante*, p. 837.

[68] *Rahman (Prince Abdul) Bin Turki Al Sudairy v. Abu-Taha* [1980] 1 W.L.R. 1268; *Searose Ltd v. Seatrain (U.K.) Ltd* [1981] 1 W.L.R. 894. Undertakings will normally be given in this respect; *Z Ltd v. A–Z and AA–LL, supra.*

[69] *Oceanica Castelana Armadora S.A. of Panama v. Mineralimportexport* [1983] 1 W.L.R. 1294; All E.R. Rev. 1983 at 262 (A. Zuckerman).

Mineralimportexport,[70] where a freezing injunction had been obtained as to a ship's cargo, the shipowner obtained its discharge, as it would interfere with the crew's arrangements for Christmas.

The protection of third parties where a world-wide freezing injunction is granted has already been considered.[71]

---

[70] [1982] 1 W.L.R. 539. See also *Clipper Maritime Co. Ltd of Monrovia v. Mineralimportexport* [1981] 1 W.L.R. 262; *Arab Monetary Fund v. Hashim (No. 2)* [1990] 1 All E.R. 673 (where compliance with disclosure order might incriminate third parties abroad).
[71] *ante*, p. 839.

CHAPTER 26

RESCISSION AND RECTIFICATION

1. RESCISSION

A. General

The right to rescind is the right of a party to a contract[1] to have it set aside and to be restored to his former position. The contract remains valid unless and until rescinded, so that, as we shall see, third parties may acquire interests under it in the meantime. This is rescission in the strict sense, and must be distinguished on the one hand from contracts void *ab initio*, for example on the ground of illegality, and on the other hand from contracts with no inherent invalidity which are subsequently discharged by breach.[2] Rescission is not a judicial remedy as such, for it may be achieved by act of the parties, nevertheless the assistance of the court is often invoked, for example to secure restitution of any property. The role of equity is, first, that equity might set aside a contract in circumstances where the common law would not; secondly, that equity is more flexible in its view of *restitutio in integrum*, and can effect what is necessary,

---

[1] Or voluntary deed; *Gibbon v. Mitchell* [1990] 1 W.L.R. 1304; *Dent v. Dent* [1996] 1 W.L.R. 683.

[2] See *Johnson v. Agnew* [1980] A.C. 367. On the right to rescind for fraud, see *Logicrose Ltd v. Southend United Football Club Ltd* [1988] 1 W.L.R. 1256.

for example by ordering accounts and inquiries[3] or an allowance for services rendered[4]; and thirdly, that equity can grant relief on terms, by applying the maxim "he who comes to equity must do equity."[5]

The party rescinding is entitled to be restored to the position he would have been in had the contract not been entered into. He cannot recover damages, as that would put him in the position he would have been in had the contract been performed.[6]

B. Grounds for Rescission

i. Mistake. While mistake alone may justify refusal of an order for specific performance,[7] mistake alone is not an automatic ground for rescission, although a mistake induced by fraud, or by misrepresentation, or deliberately not corrected in a situation that called for full disclosure[8] is a more compelling case than a mistake arising without the responsibility of the other party. If two parties enter into a contract and one makes a mistake concerning it, the general principle is that behind the maxim *caveat emptor*; a party who knows he is making a better bargain than the other is under no duty to divulge the fact. A party who wishes to secure a form of guarantee as to any aspect of the transaction must raise the matter at the time and have it dealt with on the basis of representation or a term of the contract. All this is inherent in freedom of contract; but it is subject to some limits even at common law. For instance, a party cannot remain silent when he knows the other party is mistaken as to what the actual terms of the contract are[9]; or in certain cases of mistake as to the identity of the person contracted with.[10]

Equity does not disturb these long-established principles. It is true that equity has limited their effect when it has granted rescission on a ground not recognised at law, but it does not grant rescission

---

[3] *Erlanger v. New Sombrero Phosphate Co.* (1878) 3 App.Cas. 1218. If all that was required was a return of money or other property without any adjustments, this could be achieved by the common law action for money had and received.

[4] *Guinness plc v. Saunders* [1990] 2 A.C. 663 at 698.

[5] See *Solle v. Butcher* [1950] 1 K.B. 671, *post*, p. 846; *cf. TSB Bank plc v. Camfield* [1995] 1 W.L.R. 430, *post*, p. 861. For "partial rescission", see *Vadasz v. Pioneer Concrete (S.A.) Pty Ltd* (1995) 184 C.L.R. 102; (1997) 113 L.Q.R. 16 (D. O'Sullivan); (2000) 59 C.L.J. 509 (J. O'Sullivan).

[6] *Redgrave v. Hurd* (1881) 20 Ch.D. 1.

[7] *e.g. Wood v. Scarth* (1855) 2 K. & J. 33, *ante*, p. 739.

[8] *e.g. Gordon v. Gordon* (1816) 3 Swan. 400, *post*, p. 852.

[9] *Smith v. Hughes* (1871) L.R. 6 Q.B. 597; *Hartog v. Colin & Shields* [1939] 3 All E.R. 566.

[10] *Cundy v. Lindsay* (1878) 3 App.Cas. 459; *Ingram v. Little* [1961] 1 Q.B. 31; *Lewis v. Averay* [1972] 1 Q.B. 198.

except on a recognised ground. Generally speaking, the mistake of the claimant is no ground as such for rescission,[11] but only when coupled with, for example, a misrepresentation that induced it. Thus there is no separate set of rules in equity relating to rescission for mistakes as to the person or mistakes as to the extent of the terms of a contract.[12] Of course, if the contract is void at law, no question of mistake in equity arises.

In the absence of misrepresentation, the general principle is that, in order to justify rescission, the mistake must be common to both parties.[13] The law concerning a mistake made in common by both parties is difficult to state due to common law's own ambivalent attitude to it.[14] It has been said at various times that such a mistake may be so fundamental as to render an apparent contract based on it necessarily void,[15] and at the other extreme that, if there is an apparent agreement on all points, then the contract can be avoided only be reference to the further intention of the parties or by equity.[16] This is a larger problem than can be solved here, but the cases in equity can be considered to a substantial degree apart from it.

In *Cooper v. Phibbs*,[17] A was the legal owner and trustee of land which, unknown to either party, belonged in equity to B. A improved the land and agreed to let it to B. On discovering the facts B sought to rescind the letting agreement. The House of Lords held that, subject to a lien for A's expenditure, it should be set aside: "If parties contract under a mutual mistake and misapprehension as to their relative and respective rights, the result is, that that agreement is liable to be set aside as having proceeded upon a common mistake."[18]

---

[11] See *Clarion Ltd v. National Provident Institution* [2000] 1 W.L.R. 1888 (equity does not relieve from mistake as to commercial consequences).

[12] The judgment of Denning L.J. in *Solle v. Butcher* [1950] 1 K.B. 671, at 692–693 contains propositions asserting a wider equitable jurisdiction than is usually accepted. See (1961) 24 M.L.R. 421 (P. Atiyah and F. Bennion); Goff and Jones (5th ed.), p. 292; (1989) 9 L.S. 291 (A. Phang); *Grist v. Bailey* [1967] Ch. 532; *Magee v. Pennine Insurance Co. Ltd* [1969] 2 Q.B. 507; *post*, p. 848.

[13] See *Riverlate Properties Ltd v. Paul* [1975] Ch. 133; *post*, p. 869.

[14] See Heydon, Gummow and Austin, *Cases and Materials on Equity and Trusts* (4th ed.), p. 271: "In this field no case is certain, none hopeless, no advice given with assurance sufficient to foreclose a journey through the courts."

[15] *Bell v. Lever Bros.* [1932] A.C. 161; *Scott v. Coulson* [1903] 2 Ch. 249; *Associated Japanese Bank International Ltd v. Credit du Nord SA* [1989] 1 W.L.R. 255 (sale of machines which did not exist); (1989) 48 C.L.J. 173 (G. Marston).

[16] *McRae v. Commonwealth Disposals Commission* (1951) 84 C.L.R. 377; *Solle v. Butcher* [1950] 1 K.B. 671; (1954) 70 L.Q.R. 385 (C. Slade); (1957) 73 L.Q.R. 340 (P. Atiyah); *Magee v. Pennine Insurance Co.* [1969] Q.B. 507.

[17] (1867) L.R. 2 H.L. 149; (reversing (1865) 17 Ir.Ch.Rep. 73).

[18] (1867) L.R. 2 H.L. 149 at 170. See (1989) 105 L.Q.R. 599 (P. Matthews), explaining that the agreement was not void *ab initio* because B was not the legal owner.

Equity's jurisdiction has been reaffirmed in subsequent cases, and in the widest language.[19] The jurisdiction has not been confined to mistakes of fact in any technical sense; it has been said that it should not be exercised in respect of mistakes as to public law such as the construction of a statute[20] and that it should not be exercised in cases where parties have finally settled their difference but on an assumption which has since turned out to be false in point of law.[21] Attempts to formulate the jurisdiction more precisely in terms of "mistakes as to private rights" have not proved successful.

In *Solle v. Butcher*,[22] a flat was leased for seven years on an erroneous assumption (made by both parties) that structural alterations had taken the premises out of the provisions of the Rent Restriction Acts imposing rent control. The lessee sued to recover rent paid in excess of the amount permitted by the Act. He failed. The landlord obtained rescission of the lease on "just and equitable" terms on the ground of mistake.

The judgments in the Court of Appeal reveal a variety of possible views on the nature of the mistake. It can be viewed as one of fact, of private rights, of misconstruction of a statute, of misapprehension of the legal consequences of an agreement; and this variety is not surprising, as it is not feasible to distinguish the causes, natures and effects of mistakes in this way. There are elements of each in the mistake as it is eventually made, so that the only question for the courts can be whether it is right in a general sense to remedy by rescission the particular mistake in question, and this jurisdiction cannot be limited by reference to the kind or type of mistake made.

ii. Policy Considerations. The question of the availability of rescission should therefore be answered only after considering the issues involved. For instance, would remedying a common mistake by rescinding a contract lead to insecurity of a certain type of contract, as in *Rogers v. Ingham*?[23] Further, the effect of the common law view of the question should be considered as a matter of

---

[19] *e.g.* Lord Chelmsford in *Earl Beauchamp v. Winn* (1873) L.R. 6 H.L. 223 at 233–234. See Goff and Jones, pp. 288–298.

[20] Lord Westbury and Lord Chelmsford both appear mindful of the need to make this reservation.

[21] *Rogers v. Ingham* (1876) 3 Ch.D. 351; contrast the facts in *Gordon v. Gordon* (1816) 3 Swan. 400, *post*, p. 852.

[22] [1950] 1 K.B. 671, followed in *Grist v. Bailey* [1967] Ch. 532, and *Magee v. Pennine Insurance Co. Ltd* [1969] 2 Q.B. 507, *post*, p. 848. See Jackson, *Principles of Property Law*, pp. 334, 358–364; (1987) 103 L.Q.R. 594 (J. Cartwright); (1994) 110 L.Q.R. 400 (J. Smith).

[23] (1876) 3 Ch.D. 451; (estate divided among family in accordance with counsel's advice cannot be reopened even if division incorrect).

policy before deciding whether equity should intervene by rescission.[24] These wide aspects are in fact implicit in some cases in which rescission has been refused, for instance *Bell v. Lever Bros. Ltd*[25] and the contemporaneous case of *Munro v. Meyer*.[26] In the former case, the company gave Bell a "golden handshake" to compensate him for the early termination of his contract of service. The company then discovered that the contract of service was voidable by reason of Bell's breach of fiduciary duty, so that he could have been dismissed without compensation. There was no fraudulent concealment, as Bell's mind was not directed to his breach of duty at the time of the compensation agreement. The House of Lords declined to rescind the latter agreement.

It can be seen that this wide doctrine of rescission has less scope in ordinary commercial transactions. The common law is more disposed to examine such cases on their merits, and in many cases it will be best to let the loss lie where it falls. In such circumstances there is no need for the application of a doctrine like rescission which will readjust the loss. This can be perceived particularly well on the facts of *Oscar Chess v. Williams*.[27]

A car was disposed of to a garage without any warranty as to its age. Both parties had in fact relied on the log-book, on which the date of manufacture had been altered from 1939 to 1948, by some person unknown. Not only was there no term of the contract as to the car's age, but the garage had not been misled by anything said by the owner. The result was that the loss due to mistake fell on the garage; no ground of action was available against the former owner. But in a dictum,[28] Denning L.J. canvassed the possibility of rescission for common mistake. This seems an unsuitable case for rescission, which would make the former owner

---

[24] Thus the considerations discussed in *McRae v. Commonwealth Disposals Commission* (1951) 84 C.L.R. 377, based on the intentions and responsibilities of the parties, would seem to be a matter for determination prior to consideration of the question of rescission in equity. Yet the common law aspects are not fully discussed in cases such as *Solle v. Butcher*, *supra*, or *Grist v. Bailey* [1967] Ch. 532, *post*, p. 848. But see Winn L.J. (dissenting) in *Magee v. Pennine Insurance Co.* [1969] 2 Q.B. 507 at 515–517.

[25] [1932] A.C. 161. "It is perhaps not fanciful to suggest that in *Bell v. Lever Bros. Ltd* a narrow doctrine of mistake corrected an injustice that would have flowed from the rule of law under which a relatively trivial breach, which caused the innocent party no loss, nevertheless gave that party a ground for rescinding the contract." (1988) 104 L.Q.R. 501 at 505 (G. Treitel). The position may be otherwise in the case of fraudulent concealment; *Sybron Corp. v. Rochem Ltd* [1984] Ch. 112; All E.R.Rev. 1983 at 65 (D. Prentice), 115 (M. Furmston) and 176 (P. Elias); (1983) 42 C.L.J. 218 (S. Honeyball). See also *Horcal Ltd v. Gatland* [1984] B.C.L.C. 549; (1985) 44 C.L.J. 215 (M. Owen); *van Gestel v. Cann, The Times*, August 7, 1987.

[26] [1930] 2 K.B. 312 (Wright J., who tried *Bell v. Lever Bros.* a few days later).

[27] [1957] 1 W.L.R. 370.

[28] *ibid.*, at 374; he did not proceed with this possibility as in his view too long a period of time had elapsed.

pay a sum of money to the garage which was in excess of the
value of the car which he would get back in exchange. This is not
different in effect from an award of damages, for which the court
held there was no justification.

Despite, therefore, the very wide statement of the remedy to be
found in some cases and the impossibility of limiting its width by
reference to types or kinds of mistake, its exercise is to be associated
with a comparatively narrow range of cases. These cases concern
land more than commerce in the wider sense, and tend to involve
mistakes as to private rights more than mistakes as to facts or to
qualities. To be more exact than that, however regrettable, is not
possible.

iii. Modern Formulations of the Remedy

In *Grist v. Bailey*[29] a freehold house was sold for £850 in a
belief shared by both parties that it was subject to a protected
tenancy; in fact no protected tenancy existed, in which event a fair
price would have been £2,500. The vendor refused to complete
the purchase and successfully claimed rescission of the contract
for sale; but rescission was made subject to an undertaking that he
would sell to the purchaser at a proper price. Goff J. treated *Solle
v. Butcher*[30] as authority for the exercise on such facts of the
remedy of rescission, subject to (1) the mistake being common
and (2) sufficiently fundamental, and (3) the vendor not being at
fault.

In *Magee v. Pennine Insurance Co. Ltd*,[31] the claimant obtained
insurance cover for a car, having signed an application form, the
details of which had been filled in by a third party. The form
incorrectly stated that he had a provisional licence, and that the
car would be driven by himself, his eldest son who was an experienced driver, and a younger son aged 18. In truth, Magee had no
licence, and the car was for the younger son, who alone drove
it.

The car was destroyed in an accident. The claim was compromised by an agreement to pay £385, the claimant not being fraudulent in that he was not aware that the policy was voidable for

---

[29] [1967] Ch. 532; Jackson, *Principles of Property Law*, p. 361. The formulation of Goff J. in
this case was applied in *Laurence v. Lexcourt Holdings Ltd* [1978] 1 W.L.R. 1128, *post*,
p. 850, where a common mistake as to the availability of planning permission was sufficiently fundamental to allow rescission.

[30] [1950] 1 K.B. 671.

[31] [1969] 2 Q.B. 507; (1969) 85 L.Q.R. 454; (1969) 32 M.L.R. 688 (J. Harris). If, however,
the company had paid out under the policy without entering into any contractual compromise, the money would have been recoverable in quasi-contract as having been paid
under a mistake of fact; *Kelly v. Solari* (1841) 9 M. & W. 54 (where the insurance company
made a payment under a policy, forgetting the policy had lapsed).

non-disclosure. The insurer refused to pay, arguing that the compromise could not be enforced. The Court of Appeal, Winn L.J. dissenting, held that the action for the money failed.

The difficulty lies in reconciling this decision with that of the House of Lords in *Bell v. Lever Bros. Ltd.*[32] The compromise was an agreement whose basis was the validity of the insurance contract. The contract was voidable for misrepresentation, but not void. The compromise was therefore not void for mistake. But, said Lord Denning M.R.[33]:

> "A common mistake, even on a most fundamental matter, does not make a contract void at law[34]; but it makes it voidable in equity ... it is clear that, when the insurance company and Mr Magee made the agreement to pay £385, they were both under a common mistake which was fundamental to the whole agreement."

This view, if correct, would greatly increase the scope of equitable jurisdiction, but it appears inconsistent with many decisions on the effect of mistake.[35] It is doubtful whether *Bell v. Lever Bros. Ltd*[36] can be regarded as dealing only with the position at common law.[37] It is submitted, therefore, that there is much force in the dissenting judgment of Winn L.J.[38]

It is clear that the mistake must be one common to both parties; and that both parties must have acted on the common incorrect assumption; the mistake must result in something being contracted for where, but for the mistake, no such contract would have been made. A similar emphasis on the causative nature of the mistake appears in actions for the restitution of money paid by mistake.[39]

---

[32] [1932] A.C. 161; *Bank of Credit and Commerce International S.A. (in liquidation) v. Ali* [1999] 2 All E.R. 1005. See Goff and Jones, p. 292.

[33] [1969] 2 Q.B. 507 at 514. Fenton Atkinson L.J. agreed with Lord Denning's decision, but it is not clear whether he did so on the basis that the contract was voidable in equity or void at law.

[34] Steyn J. in *Associated Japanese Bank International Ltd v. Credit du Nord SA* [1989] 1 W.L.R. 255 at 267 considered that Lord Denning's interpretation of *Bell v. Lever Bros.* did not do justice to the speeches of the majority. For a valuable commentary on this case, see (1988) 104 L.Q.R. 501 (G. Treitel).

[35] Treitel (10th ed.), p. 293.

[36] [1932] A.C. 161.

[37] Steyn J. in *Associated Japanese Bank International Ltd v. Credit du Nord SA, supra*, at 266 considered that it should be so regarded.

[38] See Heydon, Gummow and Austin, *Cases and Materials on Equity and Trusts* (4th ed.), p. 286, describing the decision as "indicative of the confusion which swathes the subject of common mistake in contract."

[39] *Barclay's Bank Ltd v. W.J. Simms Son and Cooke (Southern) Ltd* [1980] Q.B. 677; Robert Goff J. said, at 692, that money paid under mistake of fact was prima facie recoverable "provided the [claimant's] mistake is 'vital' or 'material,' which I understand to mean that the mistake caused the [claimant] to pay the money."

It was said in *Grist v. Bailey*[40] that the claimant should not be "at fault." This concept is more enigmatic; it appears to reflect the discretionary nature of the remedy, and permits all the factors leading to the creation of the contract to be taken into account. This was done in *Magee v. Pennine Insurance Co. Ltd*[41] for Magee had no claim under the policy, and "it is not equitable that he should have a good claim on the agreement to pay the £385. . . . "[42] If the vendor in *Grist v. Bailey*[43] had been at fault in any material way in not appreciating the circumstances of the tenancy, the loss might have remained on him, as common law would have ordained.[44] In *Laurence v. Lexcourt Holdings Ltd*,[45] where the parties had entered into a tenancy agreement under a common and fundamental mistake of fact as to the availability of planning permission, the tenants' claim to rescission succeeded even though they had made no enquiries or searches. They acted imprudently, but were not "at fault" within the formulation of Goff J. in *Grist v. Bailey*,[46] because they owed no duty of care to the landlord to make the searches, nor were they responsible for the landlord's mistake. However, both *Grist v. Bailey* and *Laurence v. Lexcourt Holdings Ltd* might have been decided differently if the court had considered the question of the contractual allocation of risk. The general principle is *caveat emptor* in the absence of an express warranty. Thus where the risk of the existence of an incumbrance is expressly allocated to the purchaser by the contract, there is no room to rescind for mistake.[47]

The discretionary character of the remedy is also emphasised by the rescission being granted in appropriate cases on the terms which appear to the court to be just and equitable,[48] the term in *Grist v. Bailey*[49] being the sale of the house at a fair price. A more precise account of the scope of the equitable jurisdiction to rescind on the ground of common mistake cannot be given; "In the present confused state of the authorities one can only conclude that the courts recognise the existence of the equitable jurisdiction; but no clear answer can be given to the question just when a contract which is

---

[40] [1967] Ch. 532.
[41] *supra.*
[42] *ibid.* at 515, *per* Lord Denning M.R.
[43] [1967] Ch. 532.
[44] In *Associated Japanese Bank International Ltd v. Credit du Nord SA* [1989] 1 W.L.R. 255 at 269 Steyn J. regarded the lack of fault requirement of equity as consistent with the principle that a party cannot rescind at law for common mistake if he had no reasonable grounds for his mistaken belief.
[45] [1978] 1 W.L.R. 1128.
[46] [1967] Ch. 532.
[47] *William Sindall plc v. Cambridgeshire County Council* [1994] 1 W.L.R. 1016 at 1035.
[48] *cf.* the much more complicated terms in the rescission decree in *Solle v. Butcher* [1950] 1 K.B. 671 at 697, *ante*, p. 846.
[49] [1967] Ch. 532. *cf. Magee v. Pennine Insurance Co. Ltd, supra,* where no terms were imposed, for example as to repayment of the insurance premiums by the company.

valid at common law will be rescinded in equity."[50] Evans L.J. has stated that there is a category of mistake which is "fundamental", so as to permit the equitable remedy of rescission, which is wider than the "serious and radical" mistake which makes a contract void at law. "The difference may be that the common law rule is limited to mistakes with regard to the subject matter of the contract, whilst equity can have regard to a wider and perhaps unlimited category of 'fundamental' mistake."[51] It seems, however, that the latter statement may be too wide.[51a] As Treitel has said, the differing results in the cases illustrate a conflict of policies, "respect for the sanctity of contract" and "the need to give effect to the reasonable expectations of honest men." "The fact that each policy has its own validity accounts for the interest of this branch of the law and for the impossibility of explaining the authorities by reference to any single set of sharp distinctions."[52]

iv. Other Grounds. In addition to mistake in the sense discussed above, the right to rescind may arise where the mistake results from a misrepresentation; similarly in a case of constructive fraud, which embraces the doctrines of undue influence and unconscionable bargains. These will be discussed below. The right to rescind may also be granted expressly by the terms of the contract, which will then govern its exercise.[53] The right to rescind where there has been a substantial misdescription in a contract for the sale of land has already been discussed.[54]

(a) *Misrepresentation.*[55] Where the misrepresentation was fraudulent, the contract could be set aside both at common law and in equity. "Fraudulent" here means that the misrepresentation was made knowingly or recklessly.[56] It must have been intended to be acted upon, and actually have had this result. Equity alone, however, gave relief where the misrepresentation was not fraudulent. Such an

---

[50] Treitel (10th ed.), pp. 294–295. See also Goff and Jones, pp. 292–297. Steyn J. in *Associated Japanese Bank International Ltd v. Credit du Nord SA* [1989] 1 W.L.R. 255 at 267–268 was more optimistic: "No one could fairly suggest that in this difficult area of the law there is only one correct approach or solution. But a narrow doctrine of common law mistake (as enunciated in *Bell v. Lever Bros. Ltd*), supplemented by the more flexible doctrine of mistake in equity (as developed in *Solle v. Butcher* and later cases), seems to me to be an entirely sensible and satisfactory state of the law."

[51] *William Sindall plc v. Cambridgeshire County Council, supra,* at 1042.

[51a] *Clarion Ltd v. National Provident Institution* [2000] 1 W.L.R. 1888 at 1904.

[52] (1988) 104 L.Q.R. 501 at 507, comparing *Bell v. Lever Bros. Ltd* [1932] A.C. 161 with *Associated Japanese Bank International Ltd v. Credit du Nord SA, supra.* See also (1998) 114 L.Q.R. 399 at 416 (Sir Peter Millett).

[53] See Snell, pp. 686–687.

[54] *ante,* p. 744.

[55] Only an outline can be given here, and reference should be made to the standard works on contract.

[56] *Derry v. Peek* (1889) 14 App.Cas. 337. Damages for deceit are also available: *Archer v. Brown* [1985] Q.B. 401; *Saunders v. Edwards* [1987] 1 W.L.R. 1116.

"innocent misrepresentation" was not recognised at common law unless it had become a term of the contract.[57]

It should be noted that mere silence does not constitute a misrepresentation unless it creates a false impression by distorting the meaning of any positive statement.[58] Further, there is a duty of disclosure in the case of a contract *uberrimae fidei*,[59] such as contracts of insurance of all kinds,[60] and contracts for family settlements. Breach of such a duty of disclosure is not a misrepresentation within the Misrepresentation Act 1967,[61] nor does it sound in damages,[62] the proper remedy being rescission. Thus in *Gordon v. Gordon*[63] a deed of settlement of property within a family was entered into by an eldest son in the belief that he was illegitimate, though a younger son knew of a secret marriage of his parents by virtue of which the eldest son was legitimate. Lord Eldon held that a duty of candour recognised in equity had been breached so that the settlement should be set aside.

Similar duties may be owed to the court. In *Jenkins v. Livesey (formerly Jenkins)*,[64] a divorcing couple agreed that the husband would transfer his half-share of the home to the wife, who would give up all claims to financial provision. Shortly after this agreement, the wife became engaged to marry a man she had met before the agreement. This was not disclosed to the husband nor to her own solicitor. The agreement was then embodied in a consent order under section 25(1) of the Matrimonial Causes Act 1973. Two days after the husband conveyed his share of the home, the wife remarried. The House of Lords set aside the consent order. The remarriage ended the wife's right to financial provision, thus the husband would not have entered into the agreement had it been disclosed. Under section 25(1) the court must have regard to all the circumstances, and therefore a duty is owed to the court to make full and frank disclosure of material facts to the other party and to the court. But not every failure to disclose would result in the setting

---

[57] See *Heilbut Symons & Co. v. Buckleton* [1913] A.C. 30.

[58] *Oakes v. Turquand* (1867) L.R. 2 H.L. 325.

[59] Or where a fiduciary or other similar special relationship exists between the contracting parties; *van Gestel v. Cann, The Times*, August 7, 1987; *Guinness plc v. Saunders* [1990] 2 A.C. 663.

[60] Also company prospectuses. See *London Assurance Co. v. Mansel* (1879) 11 Ch.D. 363, and Kindersley V.-C.'s well-known judgment in *The New Brunswick and Canada Railway and Land Company v. Muggeridge* (1860) 1 Dr. & Sm. 363 at 381.

[61] *Banque Keyser Ullman S.A. v. Skandia (U.K.) Insurance Co. Ltd* [1990] 1 Q.B. 665 at 789–790; affirmed [1991] 2 A.C. 249.

[62] *ibid.*; *Bank of Nova Scotia v. Hellenic Mutual War Risks Association (Bermuda) Ltd* [1990] 1 Q.B. 818.

[63] (1816) 3 Swan 400.

[64] [1985] A.C. 424. See (1985) 44 C.L.J. 202 (R. Ingleby); All E.R.Rev. 1985 at 175 (S. Cretney). The decision is based on the requirements of s.25, rather than the concept of *uberrima fides* in the agreement for a consent order.

aside of the order. The test was whether the order was substantially different from that which would have been made upon full disclosure.

As far as innocent misrepresentation was concerned, equity's jurisdiction depended on the force of the misrepresentation on the claimant's mind rather than the mental state of the defendant when he made it, or on the relative importance of the fact misrepresented to the contract as a whole. Thus a claimant seeking rescission on this ground did not have to prove negligence or any other degree of fault in the defendant but only the fact of his own reliance on the statement, and its untruth.

Until the Misrepresentation Act 1967 the claimant could rescind,[65] or possibly resist specific performance, but he could not recover damages on the basis of an innocent misrepresentation. Since that Act, however, the claimant may recover damages under section 2(1) for an innocent misrepresentation unless the defendant had reasonable grounds to believe and did believe that the statement was true.[66] The measure of damages is the same as that which applies to a fraudulent misrepresentation.[67] By section 2(2),[68] damages may be awarded in lieu of rescission wherever the court thinks it would be equitable to do so, having regard to the nature of the misrepresentation and the loss that would be caused by it if the contract were upheld, as well as the loss that rescission would cause to the defendant. Damages may be awarded under section 2(2) although the misrepresentation was wholly innocent, (*i.e.* non-negligent). The measure is as in contract, and is thus different from the measure of damages under subsection (1).[69] The result intended would seem to be that damages are the most suitable remedy in cases of misrepresentations inducing a contract, save where the facts reveal a real justification for there being rescission of the contract as well. A term in the contract purporting to restrict or exclude liability for misrepresentation is of no effect except insofar as it satisfies the

---

[65] See generally *Redgrave v. Hurd* (1881) 20 Ch.D. 1.

[66] See *Laurence v. Lexcourt Holdings Ltd* [1978] 1 W.L.R. 1128 (negligent misrepresentation as to permitted user); *Walker v. Boyle* [1982] 1 W.L.R. 495 (negligent statement by vendor that no boundary disputes); *Resolute Maritime Inc. v. Merchant Investors Assurance Co. Ltd* [1983] 1 W.L.R. 857; *Government of Zanzibar v. British Aerospace (Lancaster House) Ltd* [2000] 1 W.L.R. 2333.

[67] *Royscot Trust Ltd v. Rogerson* [1991] 2 Q.B. 297; (1991) 107 L.Q.R. 547 (R. Hooley). But the correctness of *Royscot* was left open in *Smith New Court Securities Ltd v. Scrimgeour Vickers (Asset Management) Ltd* [1997] A.C. 254; (1997) 56 C.L.J. 17 (J. Payne). See also *East v. Maurer* [1991] 1 W.L.R. 461 (loss of profits); (1992) 108 L.Q.R. 386 (J. Marks); (1994) 110 L.Q.R. 35 (P. Chandler); *Clef Aquitaine SARL v. Laporte Materials (Barrow) Ltd* [2000] 3 W.L.R. 1760 (reduced profits).

[68] (1967) 30 M.L.R. 369 (G. Treitel and P. Atiyah).

[69] *William Sindall plc v. Cambridgeshire County Council* [1994] 1 W.L.R. 1016; (1995) 111 L.Q.R. 60 (H. Beale); (1995) 54 C.L.J. 17 (A. Oakley).

requirement of reasonableness as stated in section 11(1) of the Unfair Contract Terms Act 1977.[70]

Equity's remedy of rescission now forms part of a hierarchy of remedies for misrepresentation that are available generally to a claimant, instead of being the only and not always very apposite remedy available in the absence of fraud. It is thus now more important as a supplementary than as a basic remedy. The history and rationale of the remedy are, however, of interest in considering rescission for mistakes not induced by misrepresentation, discussed in the earlier part of this section.

(b) *Undue Influence*.[71] Under the head of constructive fraud,[72] equity recognises a wide variety of situations in which intervention is justified by reason of a defendant's influence or dominance over the claimant in procuring his execution of a document (such as a settlement) or his entering into an obligation; equity's intervention here is independent of any question of the accuracy of information supplied to the claimant. Equity intervenes in such cases, not because, as is the case with misrepresentations, the defendant has positively (albeit innocently) misled the claimant on a particular and relevant point of fact, but because the defendant had caused the claimant's judgment to be clouded, with the result that he has failed to consider the matter as he ought.

Actual threats, or physical duress, are remedied both at law and in equity, but equity's view is the wider. Where threats have made it impossible for the claimant either to consider the relevant matter normally or to feel a free agent, as when a son was threatened with disclosure to his sick father of the forging of the father's signature by his brother, equity will intervene.[73] But influence by means other than threats is the more usual type of case. It is possible for a defendant to have obtained almost complete domination over the mind of another,[74] but in most cases the undue influence is exerted only to secure a specific objective.[75] The varieties of methods are infinite also; they may range from developing a sense of complete confidence[76] over many years to quick seizure of an opportunity

---

[70] s.3, as amended by the 1977 Act. See *Walker v. Boyle* [1982] 1 W.L.R. 495.

[71] See generally Keeton and Sheridan's *Equity* (3rd ed.), pp. 255 *et seq.*; [1985] Conv. 387 (C. Barton and P. Rank); (1988) 2 *Trust Law & Practice* 98 (S. Foster); Halliwell, *Equity and Good Conscience in a Contemporary Context*, Chap. 3.

[72] See Snell, pp. 610 *et seq*; *O'Sullivan v. Management Agency and Music Ltd* [1985] Q.B. 428, at 455.

[73] *Mutual Finance Co. v. Wetton* [1937] 2 K.B. 389; *Barton v. Armstrong* [1976] A.C. 104. See (1939) 3 M.L.R. 97 (W. Winder).

[74] *Smith v. Kay* (1875) 7 H.L.Cas. 750; *Morley v. Loughnan* [1893] 1 Ch. 736.

[75] *Lyon v. Home* (1868) L.R. 6 Eq. 655.

[76] *Tate v. Williamson* (1866) L.R. 2 Ch.App. 55.

presented by a defendant's weakness. In *Tufton v. Sperni*,[77] the claimant was prevailed upon to buy a house from the defendant at an over-value and at the same time to make it available to the defendant on a lease on absurdly favourable terms. The Court of Appeal, in rescinding the transaction, emphasised that these cases cannot be categorised, but are all variations on the one theme of undue[78] use of a mental domination possessed or gained over another. Undue influence may be exercised by a corporation, although there may be no special personal relationship with any individual representative.[79] The novel point as to whether undue influence could be exercised by an unincorporated association arose in *Roche v. Sherrington*,[80] where the claimant had been a member of Opus Dei (an international Roman Catholic association) for some years. After leaving, he sought repayment of gifts to the association on the basis of undue influence. Slade J. held it to be arguable that a transaction between an individual and an unincorporated association might give rise to a presumption of undue influence on the part of the members. But the action was dismissed as it had been brought against the defendant as representative of all present members, including many persons who were not members at the time of the gifts.

There are two categories of cases; first, those in which equity presumes undue influence. While the presumption does not apply to every relationship of trust and confidence,[81] it does arise in certain well defined cases such as parent and child, guardian and ward, doctor and patient, religious adviser and pupil,[82] and other situations where it is shown that a similar relationship of confidence existed.[83] Here equity requires positive evidence that no undue influence was

---

[77] [1952] 2 T.L.R. 516. See also *Langton v. Langton* [1995] 2 F.L.R. 890 (father pressured to make gift of house).

[78] It may be undue without being for personal gain, as where a parent's influence leads to an improvident settlement by a child that is only of marginal benefit to the parent: *Bullock v. Lloyds Bank* [1955] Ch. 317.

[79] See *Lloyds Bank Ltd v. Bundy* [1975] Q.B. 326.

[80] [1982] 1 W.L.R. 599.

[81] *National Westminster Bank plc v. Morgan* [1985] A.C. 686; *Goldsworthy v. Brickell* [1987] Ch. 378.

[82] *Allcard v. Skinner* (1887) 36 Ch.D. 145 (nun and mother superior); *Huguenin v. Baseley* (1807) 14 Ves. 273.

[83] *Re Craig* [1971] Ch. 95 (aged widower and secretary); *Lloyd's Bank Ltd v. Bundy (supra)*, (banker and aged customer); *O'Sullivan v. Management Agency and Music Ltd* [1985] Q.B. 428 (manager and entertainer); *Re Brocklehurst* [1978] Ch. 14 at 42; *Simpson v. Simpson* [1992] 1 F.L.R. 601 (incapacitated elderly husband and younger wife); *Goldsworthy v. Brickell* [1987] Ch. 378 (elderly farmer and manager); *Cheese v. Thomas* [1994] 1 W.L.R. 129 (elderly uncle and great nephew); *Langton v. Langton* [1995] 2 F.L.R. 890 (vulnerable ex-convict and son); *Mahoney v. Purnell* [1996] 3 All E.R. 61 (elderly father-in-law and son-in-law). See also *Mathew v. Bobbins* (1980) 41 P. & C.R. 1 (there is no presumption of undue influence arising from the relationship of master and servant or landlord and tenant, or a combination of the two).

in fact exerted. In cases outside this category equity requires positive proof of influence having actually been exerted.[84] But in all cases the question is whether a defendant has taken advantage of his position, or has been assiduous not to do so. Many cases turn on whether a defendant discouraged independent legal advice or proceeded in such a way as to make it unlikely that the claimant would think of taking it.[85] For, as with many of the flexible remedies of equity, a defendant is not placed under an absolute bar by virtue of this equitable obligation, but has to adopt proper steps, in view of the obligation, if he wishes to proceed in certain ways. So a genuine insistence on independent legal advice from a fully informed adviser is a natural means of repudiating a charge of having exerted undue influence, even in a case where the possibility of influence was strong[86] and especially where there is a conflict of interest and duty.[87] But the presumption of undue influence is not rebuttable only by establishing insistence on independent legal advice (which, however, does not always suffice to rebut the presumption[88]); it may also be rebutted by showing that a gift was a "spontaneous and independent act".[89] In any event, the presumption will not operate unless the gift is so large or the transaction so improvident that it cannot reasonably be accounted for on grounds of friendship, relationship, charity or other motives.[90]

Most of the illustrations relate to situations of special relationship existing between particular people, and often involve settlements of property. The principle is less often seen in operation in commercial matters, where it has had little impact in derogating from the more widely applicable principle that lies behind the maxim *caveat emptor*.[91] Mere inequality of bargaining power, which is a relative concept, does not justify interference with a commercial transaction.

---

[84] As in the case of gifts by will, where no presumption of undue influence arises by reason of the relationship of the parties. See Mellows, *The Law of Succession* (5th ed.), pp. 53 *et seq*. There is no presumption of undue influence between husband and wife, although a transaction may be set aside if a relationship of confidence is shown to have existed, or failing that, on proof of undue influence; *Bank of Montreal v. Stuart* [1911] A.C. 120; *Kingsnorth Trust Ltd v. Bell* [1986] 1 W.L.R. 119; *Simpson v. Simpson, supra; Midland Bank plc v. Shephard* [1988] 3 All E.R. 17; [1989] Conv. 63 (B. Dale).

[85] *Baker v. Monk* (1864) 4 De G.J. & S. 388; *Backhouse v. Backhouse* [1978] 1 W.L.R. 243; *Cresswell v. Potter* (1968); [1978] 1 W.L.R. 255n.

[86] See *Zamet v. Hyman* [1961] 1 W.L.R. 1442 at 1445–1446; *Banco Exterior Internacional SA v. Thomas* [1997] 1 W.L.R. 221.

[87] *Lloyds Bank Ltd v. Bundy* [1975] Q.B. 326.

[88] *Credit Lyonnais Bank Nederland NV v. Burch* [1997] 1 All E.R. 144 (because the influence may cause the advice to be disregarded); *Claughton v. Price* (1998) 30 H.L.R. 396; *cf. Banco Exterior Internacional SA v. Thomas, supra*, at 230.

[89] *Re Brocklehurst* [1978] Ch. 14. See also *Simpson v. Simpson* [1992] 1 F.L.R. 601; *Goldsworthy v. Brickell* [1987] Ch. 378.

[90] *Goldsworthy v. Brickell* [1987] Ch. 378; (1987) 104 L.Q.R. 160; All E.R.Rev. 1987, p. 311 (M. Furmston).

[91] "Extravagant liberality and immoderate folly do not provide a passport to equitable relief," *per* Evershed M.R. in *Tufton v. Sperni* [1952] 2 T.L.R. 516 at 519.

There is rarely absolute equality, and the court only interferes in exceptional cases as a matter of common fairness.[92] The principles of undue influence have generally been discussed in the types of transaction which attracted equity's particular attention in the nineteenth century, such as the cases on bargains with expectant heirs, and the modern form of such cases. These include cases where a beneficiary under a trust, who, although past the age of majority, is still subject to parental influence, and is persuaded to use his fortune to support the family finances[93]; or where a secretary companion takes advantage of her dominance of a vulnerable old man[94]; or where an elderly farmer grants a tenancy on terms disadvantageous to himself to the manager upon whom he relies.[95] Bridge L.J. summarised these cases as those in which there is a "duty on the donee to advise the donor, or a position of actual or potential dominance of the donee over the donor."[96] But there was no such position of dominance in *Re Brocklehurst*,[97] where an "autocratic and eccentric old gentleman" made a valuable gift of shooting rights to the defendant, a "subservient garage proprietor." The relationship was not one of confidence and trust such as to give rise to a presumption of undue influence.

The House of Lords reviewed the doctrine in *National Westminster Bank v. Morgan*,[98] where a husband and wife mortgaged their home to the bank to secure a loan to the husband, who was in difficulties with his business. The wife claimed that the bank manager had exercised undue influence in obtaining her signature during a visit to the home. Although the wife had not received independent legal advice before signing, her claim failed because the relationship never went beyond the normal business relationship of banker and customer, nor was the transaction disadvantageous to the wife. The principle which justifies setting a transaction aside for undue influence is the victimisation of one party by the other. The party alleging undue influence must show, it was said, that the transaction was manifestly disadvantageous to him (which will, of course, be easier to establish in cases of gifts). While there are no precisely defined

---

[92] *Alec Lobb (Garages) Ltd v. Total Oil G.B. Ltd* [1985] 1 W.L.R. 173; (1985) 101 L.Q.R. 306. The cases where a commercial transaction such as a mortgage may be set aside because the mortgagee has constructive notice of undue influence exerted by a third party are discussed below; *post*, p. 858.
[93] *Re Coomber* [1911] 1 Ch. 732 at 726, 727; *Bullock v. Lloyds Bank Ltd* [1955] Ch. 317; *Re Pauling's S.T.* [1964] Ch. 303.
[94] *Re Craig* [1971] Ch. 95.
[95] *Goldsworthy v. Brickell* [1987] Ch. 378.
[96] *Re Brocklehurst* [1978] Ch. 14 at 41.
[97] [1978] Ch. 14 (Lord Denning M.R. dissented).
[98] [1985] A.C. 686; (1985) 101 L.Q.R. 305 and (1985) 44 C.L.J. 192 (N. Andrews); (1985) 48 M.L.R. 579 (D. Tiplady); All E.R. Rev. 1985 at 20 (N. Palmer) and at 89 (M. Furmston).

limits to the equitable jurisdiction to relieve against undue influence, the doctrine is sufficiently developed not to need the support of a principle of inequality of bargaining power. This decision, in rejecting the broad approach of inequality of bargaining power, restricted the scope of the doctrine of undue influence.

The requirement of manifest disadvantage proved troublesome, especially where a wife was seeking to set aside (on the basis of undue influence) a charge over the matrimonial home to secure a loan made to assist the husband's business. If the loan was the only way to keep the business afloat, the wife had difficulty in showing that it was to her manifest disadvantage even though the business ultimately failed.[98a] "Manifest" means "clear and obvious", on an objective view as at the date of the transaction. It may be small, so long as it is more than *de minimis*.[99] The House of Lords has held that manifest disadvantage need not be shown in cases of actual, as opposed to presumed, undue influence.[1] It was considered that *National Westminster Bank v. Morgan*[2] did not intend to lay it down as a universal requirement, and that there was no logic in requiring it in a case of actual undue influence, which is a species of fraud. The requirement of manifest disadvantage remains in cases of presumed undue influence,[3] but is open to review in the House of Lords.

An important question which has arisen in the context of mortgages and guarantees is whether the creditor should be prejudiced by any misrepresentation or undue influence exercised by the debtor over a third party who executes the mortgage or guarantee in favour of the creditor, or agrees to give priority to the mortgagee. As a general rule, a creditor owes no duty to the debtor's surety or guarantor to ensure that the third party understands the transaction and has given a free and informed consent. The transaction will, however, be set aside if the creditor had actual or constructive notice at the time of the execution of the security that the third party's consent was procured by the undue influence or misrepresentation of the debtor. Likewise in the very rare case where the creditor has made the debtor its agent in procuring the execution of the security by the third party (agency not being established merely by reason that the creditor has left it to the debtor to procure the execution), and the debtor has been guilty of undue influence or misrepresentation.

[98a] See *National Westminster Bank plc v. Leggatt, The Times*, November 16, 2000.
[99] *Barclays Bank plc v. Coleman* [2001] 1 Q.B. 20; [2000] Conv. 444 (M. Thompson).
[1] *CIBC Mortgages plc v. Pitt* [1994] 1 A.C. 200.
[2] [1985] A.C. 686.
[3] See *Cheese v. Thomas* [1994] 1 W.L.R. 129, *post*, p. 866 (transaction set aside where elderly man aged 86 spent £43,000 to buy an insecure right to reside in a particular house for life); *Mahoney v. Purnell* [1996] 3 All E.R. 61; *Dunbar Bank plc v. Nadeem* [1998] 3 All E.R. 876; (1999) 115 L.Q.R. 213 (A. Chandler); *Barclays Bank plc v. Coleman, supra*.

These propositions were confirmed by the House of Lords in *Barclays Bank plc v. O'Brien*,[4] where the principles were fully reviewed. In that case a wife (who was neither uneducated nor vulnerable) executed a charge securing her husband's unlimited guarantee of a company's liability to the bank. Owing to her husband's misrepresentation, she thought it was a temporary security for the sum of £60,000. The wife did not read the documents before signing. It was held that the bank could not enforce the charge because it had constructive notice of the wife's right to set aside the transaction. Such cases involved a consideration of two questions: was the creditor put on inquiry as to the existence of undue influence, misrepresentation or other legal wrong and, if so, had the creditor taken reasonable steps to ensure that the third party entered into the transaction freely and knowing the true facts? If reasonable steps had not been taken, the creditor would have constructive notice of the third party's right to set aside the transaction, which would be accordingly unenforceable by the creditor. Where a wife charged her property or stood surety for her husband's debt, the creditor would be put on inquiry by a combination of two factors: first, the transaction on its face was not to the wife's financial advantage; secondly, although there was no presumption of undue influence between husband and wife, there was a substantial risk that the husband had committed a legal or equitable wrong entitling the wife to set aside the transaction. The principle was not confined to wives, but extended to cohabitants[5] (including homosexual couples), provided the creditor was aware of the cohabitation, and other relationships may be included.[6] It was emphasised, however, that the principle did not apply to a third party who merely misunderstood the transaction, without wrongdoing by the debtor. It has since been confirmed that the doctrine may be invoked by husbands also, although as a matter of evidence a husband may find it harder to persuade the court that he left his affairs to his wife.[7]

Where the creditor is put on inquiry,[8] the next question, as mentioned above, is whether it can prove that it has taken reasonable steps to ensure that the third party has entered into the transaction

---

[4] [1994] 1 A.C. 180. The bank had recovered £60,000, and the appeal did not deal with that. See generally *Restitution and Banking Law* (F. Rose ed.), Chaps 3, 4; [1999] R.L.R. 1 (J. Cartwright); [1999] Conv. 176 (M. Draper); Fehlberg, *Sexually Transmitted Debt*.

[5] See also *Massey v. Midland Bank plc* [1995] 1 All E.R. 929 (couple not cohabiting but longstanding relationship); *Allied Irish Bank plc v. Byrne* [1995] 2 F.L.R. 325 (divorced but partly reconciled). This reflects the Code of Banking Practice.

[6] The House of Lords approved *Avon Finance Ltd v. Bridger* [1985] 2 All E.R. 281 (vulnerable elderly parents and adult son). See also *Credit Lyonnais Bank Nederland NV v. Burch* [1997] 1 All E.R. 144 and *Steeples v. Lea* (1998) 76 P. & C.R. 157 (employer and employee whose relationship gave rise to a presumption of undue influence).

[7] *Barclays Bank plc v. Rivett* [1999] 1 F.L.R. 730.

[8] The burden of proving constructive notice is on the wife; *Barclays Bank v. Boulter* [1999] 1 W.L.R. 1919; [2000] Conv. 43 (M. Thompson); [2000] R.L.R. 114 (K. Barker).

freely. For transactions after *O'Brien* this means that, unless the circumstances are exceptional, the creditor must warn the third party, at a meeting not attended by the debtor, of the potential liability and risks, and must advise the third party to take independent legal advice.[9] Cases involving transactions entered into before the House of Lords gave these guidelines are dealt with on their merits, as explained below.

Some older authorities had treated the wife as having a "special equity" deserving of extra protection. Lord Browne-Wilkinson in *Barclays Bank plc v. O'Brien*,[10] rejecting this theory, considered the true basis to be the doctrine of notice, which "lies at the heart of equity."[11] Although his Lordship spoke in terms of earlier rights prevailing against later rights, it must be emphasised that it is not the traditional doctrine of notice which is at work here, because there is only one transaction, and not a contest between a prior interest and a later one. The real issue is the validity of the transaction. The doctrine of notice is applied in its wider sense, and for that reason is equally applicable to cases of registered title.[12]

Lord Browne-Wilkinson was concerned to hold a fair balance between the vulnerability of wives (and others) and the practical problems of lenders. This factor was particularly significant in the contemporaneous decision of the House of Lords in *CIBC Mortgages plc v. Pitt*,[13] where a husband exercised undue influence in relation to a mortgage to secure a joint loan of £150,000 to himself and his wife. The loan application stated that the money was required to pay off an existing mortgage and to buy a holiday home. After paying off the prior mortgage the husband used the surplus in unsuccessful speculation on the stock market. The wife, who had not read the documents nor received separate advice, failed to set aside the mortgage. The bank was not put on inquiry because it was a joint loan and, in contrast with the surety cases, there was nothing to indicate that it was not for their joint benefit. To have decided

---

[9] Instead of a personal interview, creditors normally insist that the third party obtain independent advice; *Royal Bank of Scotland v. Etridge (No. 2)* [1998] All E.R. 705.

[10] *supra*. The "special equity" approach has been preferred in Australia; *Garcia v. National Australia Bank Ltd* (1998) 72 A.L.J.R. 1243; (1999) 115 L.Q.R. 1 (S. Gardner); (1999) 62 M.L.R. 604 (E. Stone); [1999] L.M.C.L.Q. 327 (M. Bryan); [2000] R.L.R. 152 (M. Brown).

[11] [1994] 1 A.C. 180 at 195.

[12] *ante*, p. 40. See All E.R. Rev. 1993, 367 (W. Swadling); (1994) 144 N.L.J. 765 (P. O'Hagan); [1994] Conv. 421 (M. Dixon and C. Harpum); [1995] Conv. 250. (P. Sparkes); (1995) 54 C.L.J. 280 (A. Lawson) and 536 (J. Mee); (1995) 15 L.S. 35 (G. Battersby); [1996] Conv. 34 (J. Howell). For the position where the debtor was not a party to the transaction in question, see *Banco Exterior Internacional SA v. Thomas* [1997] 1 W.L.R. 221.

[13] [1994] 1 A.C. 200; (1994) 57 M.L.R. 467 (B. Fehlberg); [1994] 2 R.L.R. 3 (S. Cretney). See also *Britannia Building Society v. Pugh* [1997] 2 F.L.R. 7; *Scotlife Home Loans (No. 2) Ltd v. Hedworth* (1996) 28 H.L.R. 771 (not set aside where in fact used for joint benefit, contrary to stated purpose).

otherwise would have had the detrimental result in practice of restricting the availability of joint mortgage loans for the purchase of homes. The mere fact that the loan is joint will not, however, automatically disapply the principle of *Barclays Bank plc v. O'Brien*,[14] if in substance the situation is one of suretyship,[15] or if the stated purpose is for the couple's joint benefit but the creditor knows that the money will be used for the husband's sole benefit,[16] or knows that the benefit to the wife is disproportionately small in comparison with her potential liability.[17]

It was held by the Court of Appeal in *TSB Bank plc v. Camfield*[18] that where a third party has established the right to set aside a transaction against the creditor, the right is absolute. The court will not impose terms which make the security or guarantee partially enforceable. Thus where the husband misrepresented that the security was limited to £15,000, but in fact it was unlimited, the wife had no liability even as to the £15,000. Although the court recognised the "abstract justice" of partial enforcement, the position was the same as any other case where a person was affected by notice of another's rights. The right to rescind is that of the third party, who does not need to ask the court for equitable relief, to which terms may be attached. In *Camfield*, however, the wife received no benefit from the transaction and thus had nothing to restore under the *restitutio in integrum* principle.[19] The Court of Appeal subsequently confirmed in *Dunbar Bank plc v. Nadeem*[20] that the *restitutio* principle applies in these cases where the wife has received a benefit, although on the facts it did not arise because the wife failed to set aside the mortgage. Where, however, a joint mortgage on the home is set aside by the wife, it may take effect as a charge on the

---

[14] [1994] 1 A.C. 180.

[15] *Allied Irish Bank plc v. Byrne* [1995] 2 F.L.R. 325 (joint loan but bank aware that for benefit of husband). See also [1994] Conv. 140 (M. Thompson); (1994) 53 C.L.J. 21 (M. Dixon).

[16] *Halifax Mortgage Services Ltd v. Stepsky* [1996] Ch. 207 (not set aside because knowledge of borrowers' solicitor acquired before instructed by lender not imputed to lender).

[17] *Goode Durrant Administration v. Biddulph* (1994) 26 H.L.R. 625 (joint loan to spouses and company but wife entitled only to 2.5 per cent shareholding); (1994) 24 Fam. Law 675 (S. Cretney). See also *Bank of Cyprus (London) Ltd v. Markou* [1999] 2 All E.R. 707.

[18] [1995] 1 W.L.R. 430; [1995] Conv. 325 (A. Dunn); (1995) 111 L.Q.R. 555 (P. Ferguson); All E.R. Rev. 1995, 450 (W. Swadling); [1996] R.L.R. 71 (L. Proksch); *Castle Phillips Finance v. Piddington* (1995) 70 P. & C.R. 592. The point did not arise in *Barclays Bank plc v. O'Brien* [1994] 1 A.C. 180; *ante*, p. 859, n. 4. *Camfield* has been rejected in Australia; *Vadasz v. Pioneer Concrete (S.A.) Pty Ltd* (1995) 184 C.L.R. 102; (1997) 113 L.Q.R. 16 (D. O'Sullivan); (2000) 59 C.L.J. 509 (J. O'Sullivan).

[19] *post*, p. 865.

[20] [1998] 3 All E.R. 876 (loan for purpose of acquiring lease in joint names); criticised in All E.R. Rev. 1998, p. 407–8 (P. Birks and W. Swadling), where the result is said to be "barely intelligible". See also *Barclays Bank plc v. Caplan* (1999) 78 P. & C.R. 153, where a mortgage not vitiated by undue influence could be severed from later extensions of the liability which were so vitiated.

husband's equitable interest, and in any event the creditor may bring about a sale of the home by making the husband bankrupt.[21]

As stated above, the requirements laid down in *Barclays Bank plc v. O'Brien*, which a creditor with constructive notice must satisfy in order to establish that reasonable steps have been taken to ensure that the third party entered into the transaction freely, apply in their full rigour only to post-*O'Brien* transactions. Subsequent decisions have treated creditors somewhat leniently in this regard.[22] Further guidelines on the requirement of independent legal advice have been given by the Court of Appeal in *Royal Bank of Scotland v. Etridge (No. 2)*.[23] The duty of the solicitor[24] is to satisfy himself that the client is free from improper influence and to ensure that she understands the full implications of the transaction. Even where the solicitor is instructed by the creditor or by the husband, he acts as the wife's solicitor when advising her and his duty when doing so is to her alone. The creditor is normally entitled to assume that the solicitor who has been instructed to advise the wife (or other third party) has discharged his duties properly. If he has not done so, the wife's remedy is against the solicitor. Thus the emerging principle is that a wife who has received independent legal advice will rarely succeed in setting aside the security. On the other hand, the terms of the transaction may be so manifestly disadvantageous (as where a junior employee mortgaged her home to the bank to secure an unlimited guarantee of her employer's overdraft) that the creditor cannot be said to have taken reasonable steps unless it ensures that the third party actually receives independent legal advice, and even then the creditor will have no defence if it must have known that no competent solicitor could have advised the third party to enter into the transaction.[25]

After previous doubts it has been held by the House of Lords in *Smith v. Governor and Company of Bank of Scotland*[26] that these principles apply also in Scotland, although Lord Jauncey distinguished undue influence and misrepresentation, doubting whether it

---

[21] *Zandfarid v. Bank of Credit and Commerce International S.A. (in liquidation)* [1996] 1 W.L.R. 1420; *Alliance & Leceister plc v. Slayford, The Times*, December 19, 2000. See also *Albany Home Loans Ltd v. Massey, The Times*, February 14, 1997 (possession proceedings against H to be adjourned where W has arguable *O'Brien* defence).

[22] (1994) 24 Fam. Law 563 (S. Cretney); (1995) 111 L.Q.R. 51 (A. Chandler); [1995] Conv. 148 (J. Mee); [1995] 7 C.F.L.Q. 104 (M. Oldham); (1995–96) 6 K.C.L.J. 108 (P. Giliker); (1996) 59 M.L.R. 675 (B. Fehlberg).

[23] [1998] 4 All E.R. 705; (1998) 28 Fam. Law 666 (S. Cretney); (1999) 115 L.Q.R. 8 (N. Price); [1999] Conv. 126 (M. Thompson); (1999) 58 C.L.J. 28 (S. Bridge); (1999) 62 M.L.R. 609 (P. Giliker).

[24] Or legal executive; *Barclays Bank plc v. Coleman* [2001] 1 Q.B. 20.

[25] *Credit Lyonnais Bank Nederland NV v. Burch* [1997] 1 All E.R. 144; (1997) 113 L.Q.R. 10 (H. Tjio); (1997) 147 N.L.J. 726, 767 (A. Pugh-Thomas); (1997–98) 8 K.C.L.J. 139 (J. Phillips); (1997) 56 C.L.J. 60 (M. Chen-Wishart); (1997) 9 C.F.L.Q. 173 (M. Haley).

[26] [1997] 2 F.L.R. 862.

can be said in Scots law that one class of persons is more likely than any other to make a misrepresentation.[27] It was suggested that the doctrine rests on the principle of good faith rather than notice: good faith requires a creditor to give advice where it should reasonably suspect that the intimate relationship might undermine the validity of the transaction. Another view is that the courts are simply laying down a code of practice for a species of transaction which is regarded as unsafe to leave to the normal bargaining process.[28]

The review of this area by the House of Lords in *Barclays Bank plc v. O'Brien*[29] leaves some matters still uncertain, in particular the relationship between cases of presumed undue influence, where "manifest disadvantage" is still required, and cases of breach of fiduciary duty, where transactions can be set aside without proof of disadvantage. Likewise the distinction between cases of actual undue influence and "unconscionable bargains", discussed below, needs to be clarified.[30]

(c) *Unconscionable Bargains.*[31] Equity intervenes to set aside unfair transactions made with "poor and ignorant" persons. The doctrine does not apply to gifts.[32] It is not enough to show that the transaction was hard and unreasonable.[33] Three elements must be established.[34] First, that one party was at a serious disadvantage to the other by reason of poverty, ignorance or otherwise,[35] so that circumstances existed of which unfair advantage could be taken[36];

---

[27] *ibid.*, at 866. See also (1998) 114 L.Q.R. 17 (C. Rickett), suggesting that the doctrine could be based on the creditor's equitable duty of care to safeguard the interests of persons with whom it deals who come from a particular class at risk.

[28] All E.R. Rev. 1997, p. 390–397 (P. Birks and W. Swadling).

[29] [1994] 1 A.C. 180.

[30] (1994) 110 L.Q.R. 167 (J. Lehane), considering Lord Browne-Wilkinson's comments in *CIBC Mortgages plc v. Pitt* [1994] 1 A.C. 200; (1994) 110 L.Q.R. 238 at 249 (Sir Anthony Mason); *cf.* (1995) 9 *Trust Law International* 35 at 37 (Sir Peter Millett). See also (1998) 114 L.Q.R. 479 (D. Capper), advocating merger of the two doctrines.

[31] See Keeton and Sheridan's *Equity* (3rd ed.), pp. 255 *et seq.* and 280–282.

[32] *Langton v. Langton* [1995] 2 F.L.R. 890 (set aside only if undue influence or equitable fraud); (1996) 26 Fam. Law 87 (S. Cretney); [1996] Conv. 308 and (1998) 114 L.Q.R. 479 (D. Capper).

[33] *Alec Lobb (Garages) Ltd v. Total Oil G.B. Ltd* [1985] 1 W.L.R. 173; *Boustany v. Piggott* (1995) 69 P. & C.R. 298; (1993) 109 L.Q.R. 530 (J. Cartwright); [1996] Conv. 454 (M. Pawlowski)

[34] *Fry v. Lane* (1888) 40 Ch.D. 312. The list is not exhaustive; *Cresswell v. Potter* [1978] 1 W.L.R. 255.

[35] See *Watkin v. Watson-Smith, The Times*, July 3, 1986 (old age with diminution of capacity and judgment, together with a desire for a quick sale, satisfied the requirement). See also *Mountford v. Scott* [1975] Ch. 259. The modern equivalent of "poor and ignorant" is a member of the lower income group or a "less highly educated" person; *Cresswell v. Potter, supra*, at 257; *Credit Lyonnais Bank Nederland NV v. Burch* [1997] 1 All E.R. 144.

[36] This requirement is not satisfied where, unknown to the purchaser, the vendor is of unsound mind; *Hart v. O'Connor* [1985] A.C. 1000; [1986] Conv. 178 (A. Hudson).

secondly, that the transaction was at an undervalue; and thirdly, that there was a lack of independent legal advice.[37] A similar principle applies in the case of unconscionable bargains with reversioners or "expectant heirs."[38] The Court of Appeal has recently stated that the doctrine needs careful confinement if it is not itself to become an instrument of oppression.[39] It was held that a bank guarantee could not be set aside on the basis of illiteracy or unfamiliarity with English in the absence of substantial unfairness in the transaction itself, otherwise banks would not lend to those in a weak bargaining position. An example of substantial unfairness readily justifying the setting aside of a transaction was where a junior employee mortgaged her home to secure an unlimited guarantee of her employer's debts to a bank without receiving independent legal advice.[40] It seems that the unconscionable bargain cases should now be treated as cases where a presumption of undue influence arises from the facts.[41]

There are also at the present time other types of situation which call for relief. Oppressive hire purchase contracts and other credit arrangements are controlled by legislation,[42] and statutory protection is now given to unfair contractual terms, especially in the field of exemption clauses, by the Unfair Contract Terms Act 1977.[43] Relief has long been given against oppressive provisions in mortgages,[44] and a similar general principle is evident in the protection of the weak against the strong in the context of relief against forfeiture, in the development of the principles of restraint of trade, and in certain other contexts.[45] The view of the House of Lords is that there is no need to erect a general principle of relief against inequality of bargaining power. Parliament has undertaken this essentially legislative task, and the courts should not formulate further restrictions.[46]

---

[37] See *Butlin-Sanders v. Butlin* (1985) 15 Fam. Law 126, where the claim was in any event barred by laches and acquiescence.

[38] Mere undervalue is not sufficient. See L.P.A. 1925, s.174(1).

[39] *Barclays Bank plc v. Schwartz, The Times*, August 2, 1995. See also *Portman Building Society v. Dusangh* [2001] W.T.L.R. 117; [2000] Conv. 573 (L. McMurtry); where a mortgage by an elderly, illiterate man for the benefit of his son was not set aside, as there was no unconscionable conduct by the son or the lender.

[40] *Credit Lyonnais Bank Nederland NV v. Burch* [1997] 1 All E.R. 144 (decided on the basis of undue influence, however).

[41] *Langton v. Langton, supra.*

[42] Consumer Credit Act 1974.

[43] See also Unfair Terms in Consumer Contracts Regulations 1999 (S.I. 1999 No. 2083).

[44] See *Cityland and Property (Holdings) Ltd v. Dabrah* [1968] Ch. 166; *cf. Multiservice Bookbinding Ltd v. Marden* [1979] Ch. 84.

[45] *e.g.* salvage agreements; *The Port Caledonia and The Anna* [1903] P. 184.

[46] *National Westminster Bank plc v. Morgan* [1985] A.C. 686, disapproving wider statements in *Lloyds Bank Ltd v. Bundy* [1975] Q.B. 326.

C. Loss of the Right to Rescind

Formerly a contract entered into in reliance upon an innocent misrepresentation could not be rescinded after execution of the contract by the transfer of property under it. This rule was abrogated by the Misrepresentation Act 1967, s.1. However, the court has a discretion under section 2(2) to award damages in lieu of rescission in any case of innocent misrepresentation if it would be equitable to do so.[47] This discretion is more likely to be exercised where the contract has been executed than where it remains executory.

More generally, the right to rescind may be lost in any of three ways:

i. Affirmation. Where the party entitled to rescind affirms the contract, for example by taking a benefit under it, with knowledge of the facts giving rise to the right to rescind and of his legal rights,[48] he will be taken to have waived that right.[49] Affirmation may be shown by words or acts, or may be indicated by lapse of time, the remedy being subject to the doctrine of laches.[50]

ii. *Restitutio in Integrum* not Possible. A contract will cease to be capable of rescission if the parties can no longer be restored to their original position.[51] Any money paid or other property transferred under the contract must be restored. But a precise restoration is not required, particularly in cases involving fraud. Equity is concerned to restore the parties, and especially the defendant, to their former positions so far as practically possible.[52] This might be achieved by, for example, ordering an account of profits and making

---

[47] (1967) 30 M.L.R. 369 (G. Treitel and P. Atiyah).

[48] *Peyman v. Lanjani* [1985] Ch. 457; [1985] Conv. 408 (L. Anderson). (Mere knowledge of facts not enough. Claimant can rely on ignorance of law unless estopped from denying affirmation by unequivocal act showing intention to proceed with the contract coupled with detriment to defendant; or unless claimant's solicitor aware of right to rescind); *Stevens & Cutting Ltd v. Anderson* [1990] 1 E.G.L.R. 95; *cf. Goldsworthy v. Brickell* [1987] Ch. 378.

[49] *Clough v. London and North Western Rail Co.* (1871) L.R. 7 Ex.Ch. 26.

[50] *Life Association of Scotland v. Siddal* (1861) 3 De G.F. & J. 58; *Alec Lobb (Garages) Ltd v. Total Oil G.B. Ltd, supra.* In the case of company shares it seems that delay is viewed more strictly; *Re Scottish Petroleum Co.* (1883) 23 Ch.D. 434. See also *Leaf v. International Galleries* [1950] 2 K.B. 86. For the application of the Limitation Act 1980, s.32(1)(c), see *Peco Arts Inc. v. Hazlitt Gallery Ltd* [1983] 1 W.L.R. 1315.

[51] *Thorpe v. Fasey* [1949] Ch. 649; *Erlanger v. New Sombrero Phosphate Co.* (1873) 3 App.Cas. 1218.

[52] *Spence v. Crawford* [1939] 3 All E.R. 271; *Newbigging v. Adam* (1886) 34 Ch.D. 582. Where a principal rescinds a contract with a third party, there is no obligation to return a bribe paid by the third party to the agent and recovered by the principal, as it is not money paid under the contract; *Logicrose Ltd v. Southend United Football Club Ltd* [1988] 1 W.L.R. 1256.

allowances for deterioration of the property,[53] or by ordering fair compensation in equity where it is not possible to restore the property nor (because its value has since been lost) to account for profits.[54]

In *Cheese v. Thomas*[55] the claimant, aged 86, and the defendant, his great nephew, agreed to buy a house for £83,000 in the defendant's name, where the claimant would reside for life, after which it would belong to the defendant. The claimant contributed £43,000 and the defendant raised the balance on mortgage. When the mortgage payments fell into arrears, the claimant sought to set aside the transaction and to recover £43,000. The relationship of the parties was one of confidence, giving rise to a presumption of undue influence, but there was no evidence of impropriety. The lower court ordered a sale and division of the proceeds in the proportions of 43:40. Owing to the property slump, the sale realised only £55,000. The Court of Appeal held that the claimant was entitled only to a proportionate share, and not £43,000. Justice required each party to be restored to his original position so far as possible; it would be harsh to make the defendant stand all the loss.

iii. Third Party Acquiring Rights. The right to rescind is lost if an innocent third party acquires an interest under the contract for value before the claimant seeks to set it aside.[56] There is no bar to rescission if the third party is a volunteer, such as the defendant's trustee in bankruptcy.[57]

2. RECTIFICATION

A. Nature of the Remedy[58]

Rectification is a discretionary equitable remedy whereby an instrument[59] which does not accord with the intentions of the parties to it may be corrected. It operates as an exception to the "parol

---

[53] *Erlanger v. New Sombrero Phosphate Co.*, *supra*. See also *O'Sullivan v. Management Agency and Music Ltd* [1985] Q.B. 428 (contracts between manager and entertainer rescinded for undue influence; *restitutio* principle not applied with full rigour in cases of breach of fiduciary relationship; practical justice achieved by ordering account of profits, giving credit for defendant's labour and skill).

[54] *Mahoney v. Purnell* [1996] 3 All E.R. 61 (sale of shares in company now in liquidation); (1997) 113 L.Q.R. 8 (J. Heydon); [1997] 5 R.L.R. 72 (P. Birks).

[55] [1994] 1 W.L.R. 129; (1994) 144 N.L.J. 264 (J. Martin); (1994) 53 C.L.J. 232 (M. Dixon); (1994) 110 L.Q.R. 173 (M. Chen-Wishart), considering change of position a preferable basis.

[56] *Oakes v. Turquand* (1867) L.R. 2 H.L. 325.

[57] *Re Eastgate* [1905] 1 K.B. 465.

[58] See Goff and Jones, pp. 298–305.

[59] Distinguish cancellation of an instrument that is void or voidable on some ground, *e.g.* forgery: *Peake v. Highfield* (1826) 1 Russ. 559. For the effect of an unexecuted alteration to a deed, see *Co-operative Bank plc v. Tipper* [1996] 4 All E.R. 366.

evidence rule," whereby oral evidence is not admissible to alter a written instrument. It must be emphasised that the court does not rectify a mistake in the contract itself, but only a mistake in the instrument recording the contract. It must be very clearly shown that the parties had come to a genuine agreement and that the instrument had failed to record it. Thus where both a written agreement to sell land and the ensuing conveyance incorrectly described the land which it had been agreed to sell, it was possible to obtain rectification on proof of the real oral agreement.[60] Rectification may also occur where there are grounds for rescission and the court grants rescission on terms which include an option to the defendant to submit to rescission or rectification.[61]

It is no objection that the rectification may have the effect of saving tax[62]; nor that the mistake arose through the negligence of the claimant or his legal advisers[63]; nor that one of the parties has since died.[64]

When rectification is ordered, a copy of the order may be indorsed on the instrument. There is no need to execute a new document.[65] Rectification is retrospective, and affects steps taken by the parties in the meantime.[66] But the instrument remains binding in its uncorrected form until rectification is actually ordered. The claimant may obtain rectification and specific performance in the same action.[67]

Rectification must be distinguished from the court's power to correct an obvious error as a matter of construction. If an instrument contains a manifest mistake in its drafting, neither common law nor equity is prevented from discerning the fact and substituting the words that were intended to be there. But this is a limited jurisdiction for it applies only when the mistake is obvious from the instrument itself and what should have been written is obvious too.[68] Extrinsic evidence is not admissible. This jurisdiction is one based

---

[60] *Craddock Bros. v. Hunt* [1923] 2 Ch. 136.

[61] See the terms imposed in *Solle v. Butcher* [1950] 1 K.B. 671 and *Grist v. Bailey* [1967] Ch. 532. But where the mistake is unilateral, see *post*, p. 869.

[62] *Re Colebrook's Conveyance* [1972] 1 W.L.R. 1397; *Re Slocock's W.T.* [1979] 1 All E.R. 358; *Lake v. Lake* [1989] S.T.C. 865; *Seymour v. Seymour, The Times*, February 16, 1989.

[63] *Weeds v. Blaney* (1977) 247 E.G. 211 (discussing also the position as to costs); *Central & Metropolitan Estates Ltd v. Compusave* (1983) 266 E.G. 900 (rectification ordered on terms in such a case); *Boots The Chemist Ltd v. Street* (1983) 268 E.G. 817.

[64] *Johnson v. Bragge* [1901] 1 Ch. 28.

[65] *White v. White* (1872) L.R. 15 Eq. 247.

[66] *Malmesbury v. Malmesbury* (1862) 31 Beav. 407. See also *Freer v. Unwins Ltd* [1976] Ch. 288, contrasting rectification under the Land Registration Act 1925.

[67] *Craddock Bros. v. Hunt* [1923] 2 Ch. 136.

[68] *Re Bacharach's W.T.* [1959] Ch. 245; *Re Doland* [1970] Ch. 267; *Schnieder v. Mills* [1993] 3 All E.R. 377.

on the duty of the court to construe documents correctly and is not a jurisdiction to rectify as such.

B. The Nature of the Mistake

i. Common Mistake. The general rule is that rectification requires a mistake common to both parties, whereby the instrument records the agreement in a manner contrary to the intention of both.[69] It must be shown that there was some prior agreement, although not necessarily an enforceable contract, whereby the parties expressed a common intention regarding the provisions in question.[70] It must also be shown that the common intention continued until the execution of the instrument. Rectification is not possible where the instrument departs from the prior agreement because the parties had agreed to vary the terms.[71] Next, it must be established that the instrument is not in accordance with the true agreement of the parties, and that, if rectified in the manner claimed, it will represent the agreement. But only the actual agreement of the parties is relevant, not what they would have agreed if they had not been under a misapprehension. Thus in *Frederick E. Rose (London) Ltd v. William H. Pim Jnr. & Co. Ltd*,[72] rectification was not possible where the parties agreed to buy and sell horsebeans, and the written contract referred to horsebeans, but the parties mistakenly believed that horsebeans were the same as feveroles. The mistake was made when entering into the contract in the first place. The crux of the remedy is proof of what the parties actually had decided at the time of reaching their agreement and not what they, or one of them, had thought at a later date, or what they might have thought if they had considered the matter in greater detail or in the light of more information than that available to them. In other words, the remedy exists to correct, but not to improve, an instrument.

The mistake is usually one of fact, but relief may be possible where the mistake is of law. In *Re Butlin's Settlement Trust*,[73] rectification was ordered where the settlor and his solicitor were mistaken

---

[69] *Murray v. Parker* (1854) 19 Beav. 305. See also *Fowler v. Fowler* (1859) 4 De G. & J. 250.

[70] *Joscelyne v. Nissen* [1970] 2 Q.B. 86, (1970) 86 L.Q.R. 303 (P.V.B.), (1971) 87 L.Q.R. 532 (L. Bromley), arguing that an outward expression of accord is not *per se* a requirement. See also *Shipley U.D.C. v. Bradford Corpn.* [1936] Ch. 375; *Crane v. Hegeman-Harris Co. Inc.* [1939] 1 All E.R. 662, [1939] 3 All E.R. 68, [1971] 1 W.L.R. 1390n.; *C.H. Pearce & Sons Ltd v. Stonechester Ltd, The Times*, November 17, 1983 (a claimant who pleads two claims for rectification in the alternative based on inconsistent assertions of the parties' common intentions demonstrates at the outset that there was no certain intention which would found such a claim).

[71] *Breadalbane v. Chandos* (1837) 2 My. & Cr. 711.

[72] [1953] 2 Q.B. 450, described as a "hard case" in Goff and Jones, p. 300. See also *London Regional Transport v. Wimpey Group Services Ltd* (1987) 53 P. & C.R. 356.

[73] [1976] Ch. 251.

as to the effect of a clause giving power to the trustees to decide by a majority. Rectification has been granted where the parties used the then ineffective phrase "free of tax" to carry out their agreement to pay such sum as after deduction of tax would leave the sum in question.[74] It is no bar to rectification that the parties are in agreement and there is thus no dispute, but there must be an issue capable of being contested between the parties.[75] The remedy was accordingly refused in *Whiteside v. Whiteside*[76] as the parties had already corrected the error by executing a supplemental deed.

ii. Unilateral Mistake. Where one party incorrectly records a term of the agreement, but it is bona fide accepted as it is written by the other party, the mistake is unilateral and there is no ground for rectification. Thus, the rent may be incorrectly stated, or the lessor's obligations, or the land or buildings incorrectly described. The party making the mistake can only obtain rectification if he can show that the mistake is due to the fraud[77] of the other party, or that the other party was aware of the mistake.

In *Riverlate Properties Ltd v. Paul*,[78] the claimant, who was the landlord of property in London, intended to provide in the lease that the defendant should be liable to contribute one half of the landlord's expenditure on matters contained in clauses 6*(a)*, *(b)*, *(c)*. By mistake, the lease referred to 6*(b)*, *(c)*, *(d)*. The defendant and her solicitors were unaware of the mistake. The lease stood, as signed.

On the other hand, in *A. Roberts and Co. Ltd v. Leicestershire County Council*,[79] the claimant had undertaken to build a school for the defendants. The agreement provided that the school should be completed within 18 months, but the officers of the Council altered the period to 30 months in the draft contract, not drawing the company's attention to the alteration. The company signed the contract without noticing the change, and one of the defendant's officials was aware of the mistake. Rectification was ordered.

---

[74] *Burroughes v. Abbott* [1922] 1 Ch. 86; *Seymour v. Seymour, The Times*, February 16, 1989; *Lake v. Lake* [1989] S.T.C. 865.

[75] *Seymour v. Seymour, supra; Lake v. Lake, supra*; All E.R.Rev. 1989, p. 320 (J. Tiley); *Racal Group Services Ltd v. Ashmore* [1995] S.T.C. 1151.

[76] [1950] Ch. 65. The claimant's purpose in seeking the order was to improve his tax position. Such a motive is immaterial if the requirements of rectification are satisfied.

[77] Constructive fraud suffices. See *Lovesy v. Smith* (1880) 15 Ch.D. 655.

[78] [1975] Ch. 133; (1974) 90 L.Q.R. 439; (1975) 53 Can.Bar.Rev. 339 (S. Waddams); *Agip S.p.A. v. Navigazione Alta Italia S.p.A.* [1984] 1 Lloyd's Rep. 353.

[79] [1961] Ch. 555. See Goff and Jones, p. 301, expressing the view that the principle is akin to estoppel.

The Court of Appeal has held[80] that, in order for the *Roberts* doctrine to apply, it must be shown first that one party, A, erroneously believed[81] that the document sought to be rectified contained a particular provision; secondly, that the other party, B, was aware of the mistake and that it was due to an error on the part of A; thirdly, that B had omitted to draw the mistake to the notice of A; fourthly, that the mistake must be one calculated to benefit B.[82] Although it need not amount to sharp practice, the conduct of B must be such as to make it inequitable that he should be allowed to object to rectification. The graver the character of the conduct involved, the heavier the burden of proof, but the conduct must be such as to affect the conscience of the party who had suppressed the fact that he had recognised the presence of a mistake. Thus, rectification was ordered where a rent review clause in a lease failed to provide machinery for determining the rent in default of agreement. The landlord realised the omission only when the time for review arrived, whereas the tenant had been aware of the mistake at all times. An arbitration clause was ordered to be inserted into the lease, according to the original mutual intention of the parties. Similarly where the defendant "put up a smokescreen" during negotiations to divert the claimant from discovering its mistake.[83] In such a case it suffices that the defendant merely suspected the claimant's mistake, without proof of actual knowledge of it.

It was at one time thought that the court could give the defendant a choice of submitting to rescission or rectification, even though the mistake was unilateral and the court was unable to satisfy itself that the defendant was aware of the mistake. A practice developed of imposing such an option,[84] but this was firmly disapproved by the Court of Appeal in *Riverlate Properties Ltd v. Paul*.[85] Unilateral mistake can only give rise to rectification in cases of fraud or upon the principle of *A. Roberts and Co. Ltd v. Leicestershire County*

---

[80] *Bates (Thomas) & Son Ltd v. Wyndham's (Lingerie) Ltd* [1981] 1 W.L.R. 505; *Kemp v. Neptune Concrete Ltd* (1989) 57 P. & C.R. 369. See also *Central & Metropolitan Estates Ltd v. Compusave* (1983) 266 E.G. 900 (20 year lease rectified to include rent review clause. Negotiations contemplated such a provision, but mistakenly omitted from lease. Tenant aware of landlord's mistake. Rectification on terms that tenant should have opportunity to surrender lease after first review).

[81] The belief need not have been induced by any misrepresentation by the other party; *Commission for the New Towns v. Cooper (Great Britain) Ltd* [1995] Ch. 259.

[82] Or, *per* Eveleigh L.J., be detrimental to A.

[83] *Commission for the New Towns v. Cooper (Great Britain) Ltd, supra.*

[84] See *Paget v. Marshall* (1882) 28 Ch.D. 255.

[85] [1975] Ch. 133 at 145; in the absence of fraud or sharp practice, mere unilateral mistake was not a ground for rescission "either with or without the option to the [defendant] to accept rectification to cure the [claimant's] mistake." *Solle v. Butcher* [1950] 1 K.B. 671, *ante*, p. 846, was there distinguished as being a case of common mistake. Rectification may, however, be ordered on terms. See *Central & Metropolitan Estates Ltd v. Compusave, supra*, n. 80.

Council,[86] where rectification was particularly appropriate, for the school had been built at the time of the action; and if the contract had been rescinded or held void at law, the claimant would have been forced to bring a restitutionary claim.

Where the transaction is unilateral, a unilateral mistake is sufficient. This is discussed below.

C. Proof of the Mistake

The burden of proof on the party seeking rectification is a heavy one. According to older authority, the claimant must establish the mistake with a "high degree of conviction."[87] A more recent description is "convincing proof."[88] Oral evidence is admissible to prove the agreement, and there is no need to show anything in the nature of error on the face of the instrument. It is no objection that the transaction is one required by statute to be evidenced in writing; it suffices that the rectified instrument will comply with the statute.[89]

In the case of a settlement, the settlor's evidence alone,[90] or even a mere perusal of the document[91] may suffice to establish the mistake, but the court is slow to act without the support of other evidence such as any written instructions given by the settlor prior to the execution of the settlement. In the case of a will (discussed below) extrinsic evidence of the testator's intentions is admissible but, although the standard of proof is the balance of probabilities, convincing proof is needed to rectify a formally executed will.[92]

D. Instruments which may be Rectified

The remedy is widely available, being applicable to leases and other conveyances of land,[93] insurance policies,[94] bills of exchange[95] and many other instruments; but not the articles of a company.[96]

Rectification can also be obtained of a voluntary deed, such as a settlement, if the court is satisfied on the evidence that the donor's

---

[86] [1961] Ch. 555.
[87] *Crane v. Hegeman-Harris Co. Inc.* [1939] 4 All E.R. 68 at 71.
[88] *Joscelyne v. Nissen* [1970] 2 Q.B. 86 at 98. See also *Bates (Thomas) and Son Ltd v. Wyndham's (Lingerie) Ltd* [1981] 1 W.L.R. 505 at 514; *Racal Group Services Ltd v. Ashmore* [1995] S.T.C. 1151.
[89] *Craddock Bros. v. Hunt* [1923] 2 Ch. 136.
[90] *Hanley v. Pearson* (1870) 13 Ch.D. 545.
[91] *Banks v. Ripley* [1940] Ch. 719.
[92] *Re Segelman* [1996] Ch. 171; [1996] Conv. 379 (E. Histed).
[93] *Bates (Thomas) and Son Ltd v. Wyndhams (Lingerie) Ltd* [1981] 1 W.L.R. 505.
[94] *Collett v. Morrison* (1851) 9 Hare 162.
[95] *Druiff v. Lord Parker* (1868) L.R. 5 Eq. 131.
[96] *Scott v. Frank F. Scott (London) Ltd* [1940] Ch. 794.

real intent at the time of entering into it was not accurately reflected in the instrument.[97] It is not necessary to show that the intent of the trustees was inaccurately reflected.[98] Clearly the requirement of a common mistake has no application to unilateral transactions.[99] Rectification of a settlement may be ordered not only at the instance of the settlor but also at the instance of a volunteer beneficiary, although this will not be done during the settlor's lifetime without his agreement.[1] A unilateral document may not be rectified so as to make it into a document effecting something other than was intended at the time.[2] If an omitted term invalidates the document, rectification requires clear and convincing evidence of the missing term.[3]

Formerly it was not possible to rectify a will except in the case of fraud,[4] although the court could, as a matter of construction, correct a manifest error in drafting.[5] It is now provided by section 20 of the Administration of Justice Act 1982[6] that a will may be rectified if the court is satisfied that it fails to carry out the testator's intentions in consequence of a clerical error or a failure to understand his instructions,[7] as where a solicitor failed to delete a clause for which the testator had not given instructions and which restricted the class of beneficiaries intended by the testator.[8] There is no rule that rectification must be sought before suing the solicitor for negligence.[9] The statutory power does not permit rectification where the testator himself has misunderstood the legal effect of the wording used.[10]

E. Defences

The remedy of rectification, which, like other equitable remedies, is discretionary, will not be granted where a bona fide purchaser for

---

[97] *Lackersteen v. Lackersteen* (1864) 30 L.J. Ch. 5; *Bonhote v. Henderson* [1895] 1 Ch. 742; [1895] 2 Ch. 202 (where rectification was refused); *Tankel v. Tankel* [1999] 1 F.L.R. 676. Such a deed may be set aside for mistake if rectification would not be appropriate; *Gibbon v. Mitchell* [1990] 1 W.L.R. 1304.

[98] *Re Butlin's Settlement* [1976] Ch. 251 at 262.

[99] *Wright v. Goff* (1856) 22 Beav. 207.

[1] *Thompson v. Whitmore* (1860) 1 J. & H. 268; *Lister v. Hodgson* (1867) L.R. 4 Eq. 30.

[2] *Collins v. Jones, The Times*, February 3, 2000 (ineffective nomination under pension scheme).

[3] *Pappadakis v. Pappadakis, The Times*, January 19, 2000 (no rectification of purported assignment of policy to unidentified trustees).

[4] *Collins v. Elstone* [1893] P. 1.

[5] *Re Bacharach's W.T.* [1959] Ch. 245; *Re Doland* [1970] Ch. 267; *ante*, p. 867.

[6] For time limits and the position of the personal representatives, see s.20(2), (3). See generally (1983) 46 M.L.R. 191 at 201 (A. Borkowski and K. Stanton).

[7] See *Wordingham v. Royal Exchange Trust Co. Ltd* [1992] Ch. 412.

[8] *Re Segelman* [1996] Ch. 171.

[9] *Horsfall v. Haywards (a Firm)* [1999] 1 F.L.R. 1182, distinguishing *Walker v. G.H. Medlicott & Son (a Firm)* [1999] 1 W.L.R. 727.

[10] See *Collins v. Elstone* [1893] P. 1.

value without notice has acquired an interest under the instrument.[11] Laches or acquiescence will bar the claim[12]; similarly if the contract is no longer capable of performance,[13] or has been fully performed under a judgment of the court.[14] In the case of a voluntary settlement, it has been held that the court may decline to rectify if a trustee, having taken office in ignorance of the mistake, has a reasonable objection to the rectification.[15]

[11] *Smith v. Jones* [1954] 1 W.L.R. 1089; *Lyme Valley Squash Club Ltd v. Newcastle under Lyme Borough Council* [1985] 2 All E.R. 405. In the case of registered land, the right to rectify may be asserted against the purchaser as an overriding interest under s.70(1)(g) of the Land Registration Act 1925: *Blacklocks v. J.B. Developments (Godalming) Ltd* [1982] Ch. 183; *Ramsden (D.B.) & Co. Ltd v. Nurdin & Peacock plc, The Times,* September 14, 1998. The benefit of the right to rectify in cases concerning land will pass with the land; *Boots The Chemist Ltd v. Street* (1983) 268 E.G. 817; L.P.A. 1925, s.63.

[12] *Beale v. Kyte* [1907] 1 Ch. 564.

[13] *Borrowman v. Rossell* (1864) 16 C.B.(N.S.) 58.

[14] *Caird v. Moss* (1886) 33 Ch.D. 22.

[15] *Re Butlin's S.T.* [1976] Ch. 251 (where rectification was granted).

CHAPTER 27

LICENCES AND ESTOPPEL

1. GENERAL

A LICENCE is a permission. We are here concerned with licences to enter land.[1] The licence makes lawful what would otherwise be a trespass.[2] The licence may be express; or it may be implied; as in the case of a shopkeeper's invitation[3] to enter the premises to do business.

Express licences arise in a myriad of factual situations, as where the owner invites guests to dinner; or to stay in a room in his hotel. Some of these situations will be expected to give minimal rights to a licensee. He has no interest in the land. The licence prevents him from being a trespasser, and no more. In other situations there will be a contract which gives certain rights to the licensee; and some

---

[1] A licence, however, may be a permission to a neighbour to do on his own land something which would otherwise be a wrong to the licensor; *Hopgood v. Brown* [1955] 1 W.L.R. 213; *Ward v. Kirkland* [1967] Ch. 194.

[2] *Winter Garden Theatre (London) Ltd v. Millennium Productions Ltd* [1946] 1 All E.R. 678 at 680.

[3] *Davis v. Lyle* [1936] 2 K.B. 434 at 440, *per* Goddard L.J.

situations create difficulties in determining whether a person is a contractual licensee or a lessee.[4] Different situations create different types of licences; and different levels of protection to the licensee.

The main question for discussion in this chapter is the protection of the licensee; as where the licensor purports to revoke the licence. The common law cases prior to the Judicature Acts will demonstrate what difficulties the common law met in dealing with this question; largely through the inadequacy of the remedies available at common law. If the licence was coupled with a proprietary interest, the licensor clearly could not revoke; but, as a licence was not a proprietary interest, it was difficult to see how the licensee could be protected. The common law judges found themselves saying that if a licence were granted by deed, it would not be revocable; which still leaves open the question of finding a proper remedy available to the licensee.

Equity provided the remedies. If the licensor could not lawfully revoke the licence, equity could grant an injunction to restrain him. The licence may be irrevocable for various reasons; most commonly because the terms of the contractual licence make it irrevocable; or because an estoppel has worked in favour of the licensee. Thus, the licensee would enjoy the licence for the period covered by the injunction.

The protection of the licensee against the licensor soon raised the question of whether the licensee should be protected against a third party; not being a bona fide purchaser of the legal estate for value without notice. Where the licensee is protected against third parties, the question arises whether the licence has, by this roundabout route, become an interest in land.

Another question is whether the licensee can only properly be satisfied by a permanent right, and not merely by an injunction. The doctrine known as "proprietary estoppel" has developed, allowing the courts to exercise a wide range of remedies in favour of the licensee, including the award to him of a proprietary interest in the land, with or without monetary compensation; and intended to provide the solution which is the most just and proper in all the circumstances.

2. The Situation at Common Law

The common law never reached a satisfactory solution to the problem of the protection of the licensee. Essentially, this was because the inquiry was to see what it was that the licensor had *granted* to

---

[4] *Street v. Mountford* [1985] A.C. 809.

the licensee; and a licence *grants* nothing. The true issue is the extent of the protection which should be given against the licensor or against a third party; and, without the remedy of an injunction to restrain interference, the common law had no adequate means of protection. A number of propositions were, however, established prior to 1875.

A. Bare or Gratuitous Licence

A simple permission to enter the licensor's land gives no contractual or proprietary right to the licensee. The permission may be withdrawn at any time by the licensor. On revocation, the licensee becomes a trespasser, but is allowed a reasonable time to leave the land.[5]

B. Licence Coupled with a Grant (or an Interest)

It has long been established that a licence coupled with a grant of a proprietary interest is irrevocable[6]; where for example an occupier sells some cut timber,[7] and expressly or by implication gives the purchaser permission to enter the land to collect it. Such a licence is irrevocable. Similarly where there is a grant of a right to take away part of the realty, as with a *profit à prendre*. The grant carries with it an irrevocable licence to enter. We do not speak of a licence coupled with a grant where the proprietary interest is one which itself includes a presence on the land; with a lease or an easement, the grantee enters by force of the grant and not under any licence.

C. Contractual Licences

Most of the difficulties which arose at common law were concerned with contractual licences. If the licensor (A) contracted to allow the licensee (B) to enter his land for a particular purpose or for a particular period of time, and A, in breach of contract, ordered B to leave, and perhaps forcibly ejected him, the common law held that B had become a trespasser and could be ejected.

In *Wood v. Leadbitter*,[8] the claimant purchased a ticket for the grandstand at Doncaster Racecourse. The defendant, on the orders

---

[5] *Winter Garden Theatre (London) Ltd v. Millennium Productions Ltd* [1948] A.C. 173 at p. 199.

[6] *Webb v. Paternoster* (1619) Palm 71; *James Jones & Son Ltd v. Tankerville* [1909] 2 Ch. 440.

[7] *James Jones & Son Ltd v. Tankerville, supra.*

[8] (1845) 13 M. & W. 838. See (1954) 12 C.L.J. 201 and (1955) 13 C.L.J. 47 (H. Hanbury).

of the steward, required him to leave. He refused to go, and was physically removed, no more force being used than was reasonably necessary. He sued for assault and false imprisonment, and failed. The Court of Exchequer distinguished between a mere licence, such as this, which was revocable; and a licence coupled with an interest, which was not.

In the circumstances, nothing had been *granted*. As Latham C.J. said in *Cowell v. Rosehill Racecourse Co.*[9]: "50,000 people who pay to see a football match do not obtain 50,000 interests in the football ground." An action for breach of contract no doubt lay,[10] but that was not the issue. Whether or not the defendant had the *right*, under the terms of the contract, to eject the claimant, he had a *power* to do so.[11]

The conclusion must be that the common law provided no adequate doctrine nor any adequate remedies to deal with the problem of protection of licensees.

3. CONTRACTUAL LICENCES AFTER THE JUDICATURE ACTS

The treatment of contractual licences at common law was clearly unsatisfactory. This situation, and that of licences generally, has been transformed by the application of equitable remedies, not available to common law courts; by the recognition of the part that estoppel has to play; and finally by the willingness of modern courts to seek the most appropriate remedy for the particular situation. "It is for the court in each case to decide in what way the equity can be satisfied."[12]

A. Injunction to Restrain a Licensor from Breaking a Contractual Licence

The reasoning of the common law, established in *Wood v. Leadbitter*,[13] was that a licence was revocable unless it validly granted a proprietary interest. In the absence of such a grant, it was said, even as late as 1944,[14] that, though the licensor had no *right* to revoke, he had a *power* to revoke, and could then turn the licensee into a trespasser. The opposite conclusion had been reached in 1915 in

---

[9] (1937) 56 C.L.R. 605 at 616.

[10] *per* Viscount Simon L.C. in *Winter Garden Theatre (London) Ltd v. Millennium Productions Ltd* [1948] A.C. 173 at 190.

[11] *per* Goddard L.J. in *Thompson v. Park* [1944] K.B. 408 at 410; later disapproved in *Verrall v. Great Yarmouth Borough Council* [1981] Q.B. 202.

[12] Lord Denning M.R. in *Ives (E.R.) Investments Ltd v. High* [1967] 2 Q.B. 379 at 395.

[13] (1845) 13 M. & W. 838.

[14] *Thompson v. Park* [1944] K.B. 408 at 412.

Hurst v. Picture Theatres Ltd,[15] but on grounds that show that the courts still thought that it was the grant of a proprietary interest which made the licence irrevocable. In that case the claimant paid to watch a cinema show in the defendants' theatre. The defendants mistakenly thought that he had entered without paying. On being requested to leave, he refused and was ejected. He sued for assault and false imprisonment and succeeded.

Buckley L.J. gave two grounds for distinguishing the case from *Wood v. Leadbitter*,[16] both based upon the availability of equitable doctrine, the first reason being, it is submitted, clearly wrong, and the second being the basis of the modern doctrine protecting contractual licensees. The first ground was that the claimant had a licence coupled with an interest—"the right to see"—and that the interest could now be granted in equity by a contract, whereas before 1875 a deed was required. The fallacy in this reasoning is that there was no identifiable proprietary interest to be granted.[17]

As a second ground for the decision, Buckley L.J. treated the matter as one of construing the parties' rights under the contract. Here "there was included in that contract a contract not to revoke the licence until the play had run to its termination".[18] This is the germ of the later development; and the significance of the Judicature Act in this context is that it makes available the equitable remedy of an injunction to restrain the breach of contract by the licensor. This precludes the argument that he has no right to revoke, but has a power to do so; he has no power if an injunction is available to restrain him.

Winter Garden Theatre (London) Ltd v. Millennium Productions Ltd[19] finally established that the rights of the parties must be determined upon the proper construction of the contract. In that case, as the licence was held to have been revoked in accordance with its terms, the problem in *Hurst's* case[20] did not arise. In the Court of Appeal, however, the contract had been construed as irrevocable by the licensor. In that situation, they held, the licensee would be protected by the issue of an injunction to restrain a breach of contract by the licensor. Lord Greene M.R., in words referred to with approval in the House of Lords, explained that the revocation of the licence was a breach[21]:

---

[15] [1915] 1 K.B. 1.

[16] (1845) 13 M. & W. 838.

[17] These matters are demonstrated by Phillimore L.J. in his dissenting judgment; see *Hounslow L.B.C. v. Twickenham Garden Developments Ltd* [1971] Ch. 233 at 244; *cf. Cowell v. Rosehill Racecourse* (1937) 56 C.L.R. 605.

[18] *Hurst v. Picture Theatres Ltd* [1915] 1 K.B. 1 at 10; see also Kennedy L.J. at 14.

[19] [1948] A.C. 173.

[20] [1915] 1 K.B. 1.

[21] [1946] 1 All E.R. 678 at 648 *et seq.*

"It may well be that, in the old days, that would only have given rise to a right to sue for damages. The licence would have stood revoked, but after the expiration of what was the appropriate period of grace the licensees would have been trespassers and could have been expelled, and their right would have been to sue for damages for breach of contract . . . But the matter requires to be considered further, because the power of equity to grant an injunction to restrain a breach of contract is, of course, a power exercisable in any court. The general rule is that, before equity will grant such an injunction, there must be, on the construction of the contract, a negative clause express or implied. In the present case it seems to me that the grant of an option which, if I am right, is an irrevocable option, must imply a negative undertaking by the licensor not to revoke it. That being so, in my opinion, such a contract could be enforced in equity by an injunction."

B. The Licensee's Remedy for the Breach

i. Damages. The normal remedy for breach of contract is, of course, damages; and there is little doubt that this was recognised even in the old common law cases which held that the licensee could be evicted. The question did not arise in *Wood v. Leadbitter*,[22] because the form of action was for assault and not for breach of contract.

In *Tanner v. Tanner*,[23] the defendant was the mistress of the claimant. She lived in a rent-controlled flat, which she left in 1970, when the claimant purchased a house for her and for their children. The relationship ended, and in 1973 the claimant offered her £4,000 to vacate. She refused, claiming that she could stay in the house until the children left school. The Court of Appeal would have permitted her to stay, but she had been rehoused by the local authority before the appeal. The defendant's remedy was compensation for the loss of the licence, which was quantified at £2,000.

ii. Injunction. The normal way of protecting a contractual licensee against improper revocation is by issuing an injunction to restrain the breach by the licensor. A number of questions arise:

(a) *The Judge at your Elbow.* It was said in 1915[24] in connection with *Hurst's* case, that an injunction would be a useless remedy unless a Chancery judge was sitting at your elbow, because the

[22] (1845) 13 M. & W. 838.
[23] [1975] 1 W.L.R. 1346.
[24] See (1915) 31 L.Q.R. 217 at 221 (Sir John Miles); and Lord Greene M.R. in *Millennium Productions Ltd v. Winter Garden Theatre (London) Ltd* [1946] 1 All E.R. 678 at 685.

breach and ejection would take place before the injunction could issue. But the court will treat the licence as not revoked in circumstances in which an injunction would issue, and this will prevent the licensee from being a trespasser. As has been seen, monetary compensation was awarded in *Tanner v. Tanner*[25] where it was no longer practicable to issue an injunction. Moreover, a mandatory injunction may be obtained, in a suitable case, to enable the licensee to re-enter.[26]

(b) *Discretionary Nature of the Remedy.* An injunction, like all equitable remedies, is discretionary. An injunction will not therefore be available to a licensee who is himself in breach of the terms of the licence. A licensee who himself misbehaves will not be protected.[27] Further, an injunction will not be granted where it will have the effect of compelling persons to live together in circumstances which are intolerable. If this situation arises in the case of a licence, an injunction may be refused, and the parties may be left to their rights at common law to sue for breach of contract.[28]

iii. Specific Performance. The Court of Appeal had no hesitation in holding in *Verrall v. Great Yarmouth Borough Council*[29] that a contractual licence was enforceable by specific performance.

The National Front entered into a contract in April 1979 with the Council to hire a hall for a conference. In May 1979, after local authority elections, the new Labour controlled Council purported to revoke the licence; on the ground that the Front's extremist political stance would create unrest in the borough. Specific performance of the contract was granted.

The old argument that a licence can be revoked by the licensor on payment of damages was firmly and finally disposed of. The Front was entitled to the benefits of the contractual licence.

The issue of an order for specific performance raised a number of questions of principle. It used to be said that specific performance would not issue in relation to a transient matter; because the issue

---

[25] [1975] 1 W.L.R. 1346.

[26] As in *Luganda v. Services Hotels Ltd* [1969] 2 Ch. 209.

[27] *Thompson v. Park* [1944] K.B. 408. For a consideration of the question of the circumstances in which misbehaviour by a licensee by estoppel will allow his licence to be terminated, see *Williams v. Staite* [1979] Ch. 291, [1986] Conv. 406 (M. Thompson), suggesting that termination is only possible where the previous court order was not the grant of an estate in the land. A smaller degree of misconduct will prevent an estoppel licence arising, under the "clean hands" principle, than will cause it to terminate; *J. Willis & Son v. Willis* [1986] 1 E.G.L.R. 62.

[28] *Thompson v. Park* [1944] K.B. 408 at 409.

[29] [1981] Q.B. 202; [1981] Conv. 212 (A. Briggs).

may not come to the court in time.[30] That view was held to be out of date. Presumably, however, it would have been a defence if the date of the conference had passed before the issue was tried. Another possible difficulty might be the question of the continued supervision by the court, although, as we have seen,[31] inroads have already been made into the supervision principle. A further question is whether specific performance is available to enforce a contract which does not create a proprietary interest. The older view was that the order would not be made in such a case.[32] But more recent authorities indicate that specific performance is a remedy based on the inadequacy of damages rather than on the vindication of some proprietary interest.[33] This, it is submitted, is the correct approach today; "it is the duty of the court to protect, where it is appropriate to do so, any interest, whether it be an estate in land or a licence, by injunction or specific performance as the case may be."[34] Such an approach is consistent with the court's power to grant a prohibitory injunction to restrain the wrongful revocation of a contractual licence, or to grant a mandatory injunction to re-instate a licensee whose licence has been revoked in breach of contract.[35]

C. Express or Implied Contracts

The contract may be express or implied. In the older cases, which dealt mainly with commercial transactions, it was not difficult to recognise the existence of a contract, though its terms may have been difficult to construe. Many of the recent cases concern arrangements within the family. These are situations in which the terms of an agreement are usually not spelled out; and a contract may in any case fail because of a lack of intention to create legal relations.

In these circumstances, it is not surprising that it is difficult to distinguish clearly between cases in which a contract has been found and those where it has not. As has been seen, a contractual licence was implied in *Tanner v. Tanner*.[36] That indeed was the only way to find an adequate remedy; and Lord Denning M.R., conscious of the difficulty of finding a contract in the circumstances, went so far as to say that the court should "imply a contract by him—or if need be

---

[30] *ante*, p. 732.

[31] *ante*, p. 727.

[32] *Booker v. Palmer* [1942] 2 All E.R. 674 at 677, *per* Lord Greene M.R. This was the view that prevailed at the time of *Hurst's* case.

[33] *Beswick v. Beswick* [1968] A.C. 58; *Tanner v. Tanner* [1975] 1 W.L.R. 1346 at 1350; *Hutton v. Watling* [1948] Ch. 26 at 36 (affirmed, *ibid.* at 398); (1980) 96 L.Q.R. 483.

[34] [1981] Q.B. 202 at 220, *per* Roskill L.J.

[35] *Winter Garden Theatre (London) Ltd v. Millennium Productions Ltd* [1948] A.C. 173 (prohibitory); *Luganda v. Service Hotels Ltd* [1969] 2 Ch. 209 (mandatory).

[36] [1975] 1 W.L.R. 1346; (1976) 92 L.Q.R. 168 (J. Barton).

impose the equivalent of a contract by him."[37] In *Coombes v. Smith*,[38] the court failed to find a contract in circumstances which were basically similar. There the defendant bought a house into which the claimant, his lover, moved. As she was pregnant, she gave up her job, the defendant assuring her that he would always provide for her. The defendant paid the outgoings, but the claimant did some decorating and gardening. When the couple separated 10 years later, the defendant offered her £10,000 to move out, but she claimed a contractual licence for life. Her claim failed, as she had provided no consideration, and it was impossible to infer a contract. *Tanner v. Tanner*[39] was distinguished as the claimant there had provided consideration in giving up her rent-controlled flat and was not claiming a licence for life. The defendant, however, conceded that the claimant could remain until the child was 17. It is indeed easier to see why there was not a contract in *Coombes v. Smith*,[40] than it is to see how one could be implied in *Tanner v. Tanner*.[41]

In other cases the occupier has received protection by the court's finding that there was a contractual licence which was irrevocable for a period of time.

> In *Hardwick v. Johnson*,[42] a mother purchased a house, on her son's marriage, for occupation by him and his bride. The young couple were to pay £7 a week as rent to the mother. But this soon ceased to be paid, and the mother did not demand it because the couple had little money.
>
> The son left his bride, now pregnant, for another woman. The mother sued for possession. The wife claimed to be entitled to remain in possession on payment of £7 per week.

The Court of Appeal found a contractual licence. The daughter-in-law was held entitled, subject to resuming the weekly payments, to protection by injunction for an indefinite period of time. Lord Denning M.R. thought, however, that no enforceable contract could arise in a family situation of this kind,[43] preferring to find a licence by estoppel. On the face of it, it would seem to be unlikely that the parties would intend to bind themselves contractually in a situation of this type.

---

[37] [1975] 1 W.L.R. 1346 at 1350.
[38] [1986] 1 W.L.R. 808; (1986) 45 C.L.J. 394 (D. Hayton); *post*, p. 894. See also *Horrocks v. Forray* [1976] 1 W.L.R. 230; (1976) 40 Conv.(N.S.) 362 (M. Richards).
[39] *supra*.
[40] *supra*.
[41] [1975] 1 W.L.R. 1340.
[42] [1978] 1 W.L.R. 683. See also *Chandler v. Kerley* [1978] 1 W.L.R. 693 ("mistress" entitled to remain for a period determinable upon 12 months' notice).
[43] *ibid*. at 688.

D. Contractual Licences and Third Parties

Protection of the licensee against the licensor inevitably gives rise to the question whether a licensee will be protected also against an assignee of the licensor. On the one hand, protection given to a licensee is in many cases of little use if the licensor can transfer the land and leave the licensee helpless. On the other hand, if a licensee is protected against third parties, the licence begins to look like some sort of proprietary interest.[44]

The extent to which a licence is binding on a third party will vary with the type of licence. Bare licences are obviously not binding. The question whether a contractual licence can bind a purchaser under a constructive trust is considered later[45]; likewise whether an estoppel licence can bind third parties.[46] First the position as to contractual licences outside these situations will be examined.

It is important to appreciate that there is no principle which requires that the availability of an injunction against one contracting party will make it available against third parties coming to the land. The jurisdiction to apply an injunction against a third party was demonstrated by the development of the law of restrictive covenants from *Tulk v. Moxhay.*[47] The policy decision to refuse an injunction against third parties was shown by the unsuccessful attempts to make covenants run with chattels.[48]

As far as contractual obligations are concerned, the estate of a deceased party to the contract is not properly a third party. The devisee of the licensor is a third party, but takes as a volunteer. One of the landmark cases on the enforcement of licences against third parties, *Errington v. Errington and Woods,*[49] is such a case; the report fails to say whether the licensor's widow, who was the devisee, was also his executrix; but both Lord Denning M.R. and Hodson L.J. refer to her as successor in title. Such a person is in a different position from a purchaser.

Authority leads to the conclusion that contractual licences are not ordinarily binding on third parties.

In *King v. David Allen & Sons, Billposting Ltd,*[50] the licensor agreed that the licensees should have the exclusive right of affixing advertisements upon a building. Later the licensor leased the building to a cinema company, no provision being made to protect

---

[44] See, however, (1986) 49 M.L.R. 741 (J. Dewar), suggesting that it is wrong to attempt to fit licences into traditional academic land law.

[45] *post*, p. 886.

[46] *post*, p. 903.

[47] (1848) 2 Ph. 774.

[48] *Port Line v. Ben Line Steamers* [1958] 2 Q.B. 146; *Lord Strathcona S.S. Co. v. Dominion Coal Co.* [1926] A.C. 108.

[49] [1952] 1 K.B. 290.

[50] [1916] 2 A.C. 54.

the rights of the licensees. The licensees sued the licensor for breach of contract. The licensor was liable if the lease to the company deprived the licensees of their contractual right. The House of Lords held that it did.

In *Clore v. Theatrical Properties Ltd*,[51] a deed which was drafted in the form of a lease purported to grant the lessee the "front of the house" rights in a theatre; that is, the right to use refreshment rooms etc. to provide for the needs of patrons. The instrument provided that the terms "lessor" and "lessee" should include their executors, administrators and assigns.

It was held to be a licence and not a lease. The "lessor" and "lessee" both assigned; and the question was whether the "lessee's" assignee could enforce the right under the agreement. He failed; because the licence was a personal contract and enforceable only between the parties to it.

As has now been reaffirmed,[52] these cases lay down a correct doctrine relating to contractual licences. Licences were indeed treated as binding on third parties in a number of cases decided in the days when a deserted wife was treated as a licensee protected by injunction[53]; and these provided a very compelling case for applying the injunction also against the party to whom the deserting husband sold the house. But these cases were incorrect; because the House of Lords decided that a deserted wife was not a licensee of her husband, and had no interest capable of binding the land.[54] Legislation followed.[55] There are some cases in which a contractual arrangement, outside the context of a deserted wife, was held to bind a third party, but they are best explained as being decided on other grounds.

In *Errington v. Errington and Woods*[56] the father, A, of a young man who was about to be married purchased a house through a building society, made a down-payment and told the young couple that the house would be theirs when they paid all the instalments due under the mortgage. They went into possession and paid all the instalments which fell due. Nothing was stated concerning the rights of the young couple during the currency of the mortgage payments. A died, leaving all his property to Mrs A. The son returned to his mother, who took steps to evict

---

[51] [1936] 3 All E.R. 483.
[52] *Ashburn Anstalt v. Arnold* [1989] Ch. 1, *post*, p. 888.
[53] *Bendall v. McWhirter* [1952] 2 Q.B. 466; *Lee v. Lee* [1952] 2 Q.B. 489n; *Ferris v. Weaven* [1952] 2 All E.R. 233.
[54] *National Provincial Bank Ltd v. Ainsworth* [1965] A.C. 1175.
[55] Matrimonial Homes Act 1967 (now Family Law Act 1996).
[56] [1952] 1 K.B. 290; *Duke of Beaufort v. Patrick* (1853) 17 Beav. 60.

the daughter-in-law. She failed. The daughter-in-law was held to be a licensee who was entitled to protection not only against A in his lifetime, but also against Mrs A, taking as a volunteer.

There was clearly a flavour of contract in the licence, and the case is usually treated as one of contractual licence. But the wide views expressed in the case as to the enforceability of such licences were disapproved, *obiter*, by the House of Lords in *National Provincial Bank Ltd v. Ainsworth*,[57] and have since been said by the Court of Appeal in *Ashburn Anstalt v. Arnold*[58] to be neither practically necessary nor theoretically convincing. They could not be reconciled with *King*[59] and *Clore*,[60] but the decision was, however, correct on the facts. It could be justified on any of three grounds:

   (i) there was a contract to convey on completion of the payments, giving rise to an equitable interest in the form of an estate contract which would bind the widow as a volunteer;

  (ii) the daughter-in-law had changed her position in reliance upon a representation by the deceased, the estoppel binding the widow;

 (iii) the payment of instalments gave rise to a direct proprietary interest by way of a constructive trust under the principle later formulated in *Gissing v. Gissing*.[61]

Thus the result could have been achieved without accepting Lord Denning's broad principles, which were unnecessary and *per incuriam*. The correct principle is that a contractual licence cannot bind a third party unless the circumstances are such that a constructive trust has arisen. Further examination of this principle will be deferred until the development of the constructive trust solution has been outlined.

4. CONSTRUCTIVE TRUSTS

A few cases in this field have been decided on the basis of a constructive trust. Lord Denning has described a constructive trust as one:

"imposed by law whenever justice and good conscience require it. It is a liberal process, founded upon large principles of equity,

---

[57] [1965] A.C. 1175.
[58] [1989] Ch. 1, *infra*.
[59] *supra*.
[60] *supra*.
[61] [1971] A.C. 886, *ante*, p. 278.

to be applied in cases where the legal owner cannot conscientiously keep the property for himself alone, but ought to allow another to have the property or the benefit of it or a share of it."[62]

In those terms, the constructive trust solution is at once too vague and too far-reaching. Too vague in that such broad statements provide no way of determining when such a trust will be held to exist.[63] It may be unobjectionable in cases such as *D.H.N. Food Distributors Ltd v. Tower Hamlets London Borough Council*,[64] where the issue was whether a contractual licensee could claim compensation for disturbance upon compulsory purchase. But it is not appropriate where title to land is at stake.

Lord Denning M.R. pioneered this solution in *Binions v. Evans*.[65]

> Mrs Evans was the widow of an employee of the Tredegar Estate. The trustees made an agreement with her, under which she would be allowed to reside in a cottage, free of rent and rates, for life. She undertook to keep the cottage in repair.
>
> Two years later, the trustees sold the cottage to Mr and Mrs Binions, expressly subject to the agreement, the purchase price being reduced accordingly. The purchasers claimed possession of the cottage. Lord Denning M.R. held that the purchasers were bound by Mrs Evans' contractual licence and also by a constructive trust in her favour, whereas Megaw and Stephenson L.JJ. relied upon the agreement as creating a life interest.[66]

Clearly, the case provides no support for the view that contractual licences generally are binding on third parties. Nevertheless, it was cited subsequently as authority for the proposition that a contractual licence is capable of binding a third party.

> In *Re Sharpe*[67] an elderly aunt lent money to her nephew towards the purchase of a house on the understanding that she would live there with the nephew and his wife for the rest of her life. The nephew subsequently went bankrupt, and his trustee in bankruptcy contracted to sell the house to a purchaser. The trustee

---

[62] *Hussey v. Palmer* [1972] 1 W.L.R. 1286, at 1290.

[63] (1973) 32 C.L.J. 123 at 142 (R. Smith).

[64] [1976] 1 W.L.R. 852. See also *Pennine Raceway Ltd v. Kirklees Metropolitan Council* [1983] Q.B. 382 (Licensee a "person interested in the land" within Town and Country Planning Act 1971, s.164).

[65] [1972] Ch. 359; (1972) 88 L.Q.R. 336 (P.V.B.); (1972) 36 Conv.(N.S.) 266 (J. Martin); (1973) 32 C.L.J. 123 (R. Smith).

[66] Applying *Bannister v. Bannister* [1948] 2 All E.R. 133. See also *Costello v. Costello* (1995) 70 P. & C.R. 297.

[67] [1980] 1 W.L.R. 219; [1980] Conv. 207 (J. Martin).

failed in his claim to recover possession of the house from the aunt. Her rights were held to be more than merely contractual, and gave rise to a constructive trust binding upon the trustee in bankruptcy. The purchaser was not a party to the action, and it was left open whether he would also be bound. However, as the aunt had sold her home and paid for improvements to the nephew's house, a preferable basis for the decision might have been proprietary estoppel.

The position has now been clarified by the Court of Appeal in *Ashburn Anstalt v. Arnold*,[68] which has "put the *quietus* to the heresy that a mere licence creates an interest in land."[69] The claimant purchaser sought possession against the defendant, who was in occupation under an agreement with the purchaser's predecessor in title. The claimant had been aware of the agreement and had purchased expressly subject to its provisions "so far as the same are enforceable against the Vendor." In fact it was held that the defendant had a tenancy which was binding on the purchaser under the Land Registration Act 1925.[70] However, the Court of Appeal proceeded to consider the position if the defendant had been a contractual licensee. On the clear authority of *King v. David Allen & Sons, Billposting Ltd*,[71] the correct principle was that a contractual licence could not normally bind a third party. However, the law must be free to develop, and the finding of a constructive trust was considered a beneficial adaptation of old rules to new situations in appropriate circumstances. But there could be no bare assertion that a licence gives rise to a constructive trust. It would arise only if the conscience of the third party was affected. Mere notice would not be sufficient,[72] nor the fact that the property was conveyed "subject to" the interest. Such a term does not mean that the grantee is necessarily intended to be under an obligation to give effect to the interest, but may be merely to protect the grantor against claims by the grantee (for example as in the case of an old restrictive covenant which may or may not be enforceable). The question is whether the grantee has acted in such a way that, as a matter of justice, a trust must be imposed on him. In the present case there would be no constructive trust because the transfer "subject to" the defendant's rights was done to protect the vendor, and the purchaser had not paid

---

[68] [1989] Ch. 1; (1988) 51 M.L.R. 226 (J. Hill); (1988) 104 L.Q.R. 175 (P. Sparkes); [1988] Conv. 201 (M. Thompson); (1988) 47 C.L.J. 353 (A. Oakley); All E.R. Rev. 1988 at 177 (P. Clarke).

[69] *IDC Group Ltd v. Clarke* [1992] 1 E.G.L.R. 187 at 189, upheld (1993) 65 P. & C.R. 172 (where the issue was not discussed).

[70] As an overriding interest under s.70(1)(g).

[71] [1916] 2 A.C. 54, *ante*, p. 884.

[72] See *IDC Group Ltd v. Clark* [1992] 1 E.G.L.R. 187 at 190 (in the High Court); *Chattey v. Farndale Holdings Inc.* (1998) 75 P. & C.R. 299.

a reduced price. As far as the previous cases were concerned, *Binions v. Evans*[73] was a legitimate application of the constructive trust doctrine because the parties intended the purchaser to give effect to the interest and the price was reduced accordingly. Also approved was *Lyus v. Prowsa Ltd*,[74] where the intention had been similar and the purchaser had given assurances. The doctrine was not, however, appropriate in *Re Sharpe*,[75] where the aunt had not replied to the trustee in bankruptcy's enquiries as to her interest.

The Court of Appeal added that certainty was of prime importance as far as title to land was concerned, and it was not desirable to impose a constructive trust on slender materials.[76] One difficulty is that the imposition of a constructive trust, in the case of a fee simple, creates an equitable interest which is not registrable (in unregistered land).[77] If the interest protected by a constructive trust is for life only, problems once arose with the Settled Land Act, but settlements cannot now be created.[78] Similar points arise with the doctrine of proprietary estoppel, as discussed below.[79] In that context also the constructive trust has been invoked in order to achieve a just result.[80]

The new formulation, it is submitted, provides welcome guidelines as to the circumstances in which a constructive trust will be imposed, and thereby achieves a compromise between the sometimes divergent goals of certainty and justice.

5. Licences by Estoppel

The doctrine of estoppel has played a significant part in the modern development of the law of licences.[81] A situation in which a licensee has acted to his detriment in reliance upon a representation or promise by the licensor presents a compelling case for the intervention of equity in order to protect the licensee; more compelling, in a sense, than the case of a contractual licence, because the licensee by estoppel has no alternative remedy in damages.[82] The doctrine of

---

[73] [1972] Ch. 359, *supra*.

[74] [1982] 1 W.L.R. 1044, *ante*, p. 336.

[75] [1980] 1 W.L.R. 219, *supra*.

[76] Reiterated in *IDC Group Ltd v. Clark*, *supra* (in the High Court).

[77] Formerly the interest of a beneficiary absolutely entitled under a constructive trust was not overreachable, but this has been changed by the Trusts of Land and Appointment of Trustees Act 1996; *ante*, p. 285. Overreaching, however, requires two trustees.

[78] Life interests now give rise to the less complex trust of land under the 1996 Act, *supra*.

[79] *post*, p. 893.

[80] *Re Basham* [1986] 1 W.L.R. 1498, *post*, p. 900.

[81] It seems that a licence by estoppel was first so referred to judicially in *Inwards v. Baker* [1965] 2 Q.B. 29, *per* Danckwerts L.J. at 38, *post*, p. 896.

[82] As to how far a contractual licence may also be a licence by estoppel, see [1983] Conv. 50 (M. Thompson) and 285 (A. Briggs).

estoppel by encouragement or acquiescence has found a fruitful area of operation in the field of licences, under the name of proprietary estoppel; its success in this area has been largely due to the fact that, unlike estoppel by representation or promissory estoppel, it can found a cause of action and, in the licence context, enables the court to award a proprietary interest to the licensee. In the enthusiasm for the application of this doctrine, it has become confused with other estoppels, and has been credited with the solution to many cases in which it is quite clear that the judges reached their decision on other grounds. The utility of the doctrine stems from the fact that the court will "look at all the circumstances in each case to decide in what way the equity can be satisfied"[83]; and the most suitable solution is often an award to the licensee of a proprietary interest, rather than merely an injunction. A sword and not a shield is sometimes required.

A. Types of Estoppel

There are many different types of estoppel at law and in equity. We are concerned with three of these, each having a separate origin and history.[84] The Australian courts have asserted that distinctions should not be drawn between the various categories of estoppel, nor between their common law or equitable origin.[85] The courts in this country have not yet reached this conclusion, although there have been *dicta* to the effect that it is undesirable to distinguish between types of estoppel.[86] If this view prevails, the existing differences (such as whether the type of estoppel operates as a sword or a shield) will have to be modified in order to achieve a coherent unified

---

[83] *Plimmer v. Wellington Corporation* (1884) 9 App.Cas. 699 at 714; *Greasley v. Cooke* [1980] 1 W.L.R. 1306 at 1312. It may be held that the claimant has already had sufficient satisfaction for his expenditure; *Appleby v. Cowley, The Times*, April 14, 1982; *Sledmore v. Dalby* (1996) 72 P. & C.R. 196.

[84] For estoppel by convention, *i.e.* by a course of dealing, see *Amalgamated Investment and Property Co. (in liquidation) v. Texas Commerce International Bank Ltd* [1982] Q.B. 84; *Pacol Ltd v. Trade Lines Ltd* [1982] 1 Lloyd's Rep. 456; *Troop v. Gibson* [1986] 1 E.G.L.R. 1; (1982) 79 L.S.Gaz. 662 (P. Matthews). See generally Wilken and Villiers, *Waiver, Variation and Estoppel*; Cooke, *The Modern Law of Estoppel*.

[85] *Waltons Stores (Interstate) Ltd v. Maher* (1988) 62 A.L.J.R. 110 at 123; (1988) 104 L.Q.R. 362 (A. Duthie); *Commonwealth of Australia v. Verwayen* (1990) 65 A.L.J.R. 540 at 546; (1991) 107 L.Q.R. 221 (M. Spence); [1992] Conv. 239 (M. Lunney). Likewise in New Zealand: *Gillies v. Keogh* [1989] 2 N.Z.L.R. 327 at 331. See Halliwell, *Equity and Good Conscience in a Contemporary Context*, Chap. 2.

[86] *Crabb v. Arun District Council* [1976] Ch. 179 at 193; *Amalgamated Investment and Property Co. Ltd (in liquidation) v. Texas Commerce International Bank Ltd* [1982] Q.B. 84 at 103; *Troop v. Gibson* [1986] 1 E.G.L.R. 1 at 5 (distinguishing, however, estoppel by representation and by convention); *cf.* (1981) 97 L.Q.R. 513; [1988] Conv. 46 (P. Evans); *J.T. Developments Ltd v. Quinn* (1991) 62 P. & C.R. 33 at 45; *First National Bank plc v. Thompson* [1996] Ch. 231.

doctrine.[87] The most recent pronouncements, however, are against the idea of "an overarching principle" which would blur the distinctions.[88]

i. Estoppel by Representation. Estoppel by representation operates over a wide field of common law and equity. The basic principle is that a person who makes an unambiguous[89] representation, by words,[90] or conduct,[91] or by silence,[92] of an existing fact, and causes another party to act to his detriment in reliance on the representation will not be permitted subsequently to act inconsistently with that representation. The doctrine was originally applied only where there was a representation of existing fact,[93] and not where the representation was one of law or of intention. The representor could not subsequently allege, in dealing with the representee, that the facts were different from those represented. Apart from a few long-established exceptions,[94] such an estoppel works negatively. It is not capable of creating a cause of action. It works like a rule of evidence, a rule which excludes a particular defence or line of argument.

This is not to say that estoppel is available only to a defendant. A claimant may take advantage of the doctrine if he has an independent cause of action, and can show that the defence is inconsistent with a representation of the defendant on which he relies.[95]

A well-known example is *Roberston v. Minister of Pensions*,[96] where an officer claimed a pension, relying upon a statement by the War Office that his disability had been accepted as due to military service, and forbore to obtain an independent medical opinion. It was held that the Crown, through the Minister of Pensions, could

---

[87] See (1994) 14 L.S. 15 (M. Halliwell), suggesting the remedying of unconscionable conduct as the unifying factor. See generally Pawlowski, *The Doctrine of Proprietary Estoppel* (1996).

[88] *Republic of India v. India Steamship Co. Ltd (No. 2)* [1998] A.C. 878 at 914; [1999] L.M.C.L.Q. 256 (R. Halson); *Dun & Bradstreet Software Services (England) Ltd v. Provident Mutual Life Assurance Association* [1998] 2 E.G.L.R. 175.

[89] *Low v. Bouverie* [1891] 3 Ch. 82.

[90] *Hunt v. Carew* (1649) Nels. 46; or through an agent; *Moorgate Mercantile Ltd v. Twitchings* [1977] A.C. 890.

[91] *Waldron v. Sloper* (1852) 1 Drew. 193.

[92] *Fung Kai Sun v. Chan Fui Hing* [1951] A.C. 489; *Pacol Ltd v. Trade Lines Ltd* [1982] 1 Lloyd's Rep. 456.

[93] *Jorden v. Money* (1845) 5 H.L.C. 185; not followed in Australia; *Legione v. Hateley* (1983) 57 A.L.J.R. 292; *Foran v. Wight* (1989) 168 C.L.R. 385.

[94] *e.g.* a tenancy by estoppel, M. & W., pp. 799 *et seq.*; see also *Ramsden v. Dyson* (1866) L.R. 1 H.L. 129; *post*, p. 898.

[95] Similarly with promissory estoppel; *Amalgamated Investment and Property Co. (in liquidation) v. Texas Commerce International Bank Ltd* [1982] Q.B. 84; *Pacol Ltd v. Trade Lines Ltd* [1982] 1 Lloyd's Rep. 456.

[96] [1949] 1 K.B. 227; *Combe v. Combe* [1951] 2 K.B. 215 at 219, *per* Denning L.J. See also *Western Fish Products Ltd v. Penwith District Council* [1981] 2 All E.R. 204; *Rootkin v. Kent County Council* [1981] 1 W.L.R. 1186.

not go back on the statement previously made. The officer was no longer in a position to supply the necessary evidence; but the Minister was estopped from denying that he qualified.

ii. Promissory Estoppel. The doctrine is expanded in equity, so as to include not only representations of fact, but also representations of intention; or promises. The doctrine came into prominence with the decision of Denning J. in *Central London Property Trust Ltd v. High Trees House Ltd* in 1947,[97] and became firmly established in later cases.[98]

Where, by words or conduct, a person makes an unambiguous representation as to his future conduct, intending the representation to be relied on, and to affect the legal relations between the parties, and the representee alters his position in reliance on it, the representor will be unable to act inconsistently with the representation if by so doing the representee would be prejudiced.[99]

The doctrine emerged in *Loffus v. Maw*[1] and *Hughes v. Metropolitan Railway Co.*,[2] and developed through a line of cases which was little known until 1947. Denning J. then applied it in *Central London Property Trust Ltd v. High Trees House Ltd.*[3]

The landlord company in 1937 leased to the defendant a block of flats for 99 years at a rent of £2,500 a year. Early in 1940, because of the war, the defendants were unable to find sub-tenants for the flats, and unable in consequence to pay the rent. The landlord agreed to reduce the rent to £1,250 from the beginning of the term. By the beginning of 1945 all the flats were let, and the landlord was held entitled to the full rent as from the middle of that year. Denning J., however, stated that the landlord would have been estopped from claiming the full rent for the period from 1940 to 1945, on the ground that though not technically bound because of the lack of consideration, the landlord had intended the defendants to rely on the promise and the defendants had acted on the faith of it.

Promissory estoppel contains a number of features which distinguish it from estoppel by representation of fact.[4] First, in that the representation may be one of intention and not one of fact; which

---

[97] [1947] K.B. 130.
[98] *Combe v. Combe* [1951] 2 K.B. 215; *Ajayi v. R.T. Briscoe (Nigeria) Ltd* [1964] 1 W.L.R. 1326; *W.J. Alan & Co. Ltd v. El Nasr Export and Import Co.* [1972] 2 Q.B. 189.
[99] See *Combe v. Combe* [1951] 2 K.B. 215 at 220.
[1] (1862) 3 Giff. 592.
[2] (1877) 2 App.Cas. 439.
[3] [1947] K.B. 130.
[4] See generally (1947) 63 L.Q.R. 283 (G. Cheshire and C. Fifoot); (1951) 67 L.Q.R. 330 (J. Wilson); (1952) 15 M.L.R. 1 (Denning L.J.); (1952) 15 M.L.R. 325 (L. Sheridan).

raises the question whether it is inconsistent with the House of Lords decision in *Jorden v. Money*.[5] But the doctrine is now well established.[6] Secondly, the requirement of detriment to the representee is less stringent in the case of promissory estoppel. Financial loss or other detriment is of course sufficient; but it seems that it is not necessary to show more than that the representee committed himself to a particular course of action as a result of the representation.[7] Thirdly, the effect of the estoppel may not be permanent. The representor may escape from the burden of the equity if he can ensure that the representee will not be prejudiced.[8] But, consistently with estoppel by representation, promissory estoppel does not create a cause of action. It is a shield and not a sword.[9]

iii. Proprietary Estoppel.

(a) *General Principles.* This doctrine is applicable where one party knowingly encourages another to act, or acquiesces in the other's actions, to his detriment and in infringement of the first party's rights. He will be unable to complain later about the infringement, and may indeed be required to make good the expectation which he encouraged in the other party. Unlike other estoppels, therefore, this doctrine may, in some circumstances, create a claim, and an entitlement to positive proprietary rights; in others, it can operate negatively, or can produce a compromise situation appropriate to the particular circumstances. It can overcome statutory requirements, such as the rule contained in section 2 of the Law of Property (Miscellaneous Provisions) Act 1989 requiring contracts relating to land to be made in writing.[10] As far as interests in the home are concerned, the modern tendency is to assimilate proprietary estoppel and common intention constructive trusts.[11]

One question which arises is whether the courts should award a remedy which fufils the expectations of the claimant[12] or one which

---

[5] (1854) 5 H.L.Cas. 185. See *Foran v. Wight* (1989) 168 C.L.R. 385 at 411.
[6] But it "may need to be reviewed and reduced to a coherent body of doctrine by the Courts": *Woodhouse A.C. Israel Cocoa Ltd v. Nigerian Produce Marketing Co. Ltd* [1972] A.C. 741 at p. 758 (*per* Lord Hailsham).
[7] *Central London Property Ltd v. High Trees House Ltd* [1947] K.B. 130; *W.J. Alan & Co. Ltd v. El Nasr Export and Import Co.* [1972] 2 Q.B. 189; *Ajayi v. R.T. Briscoe (Nigeria) Ltd* [1964] 1 W.L.R. 1326.
[8] *Tool Metal Manufacturing Co. Ltd v. Tungsten Electric Co. Ltd* [1955] 1 W.L.R. 766.
[9] *Combe v. Combe* [1951] 2 K.B. 215 at 224. See generally (1983) 42 C.L.J. 257 (M. Thompson); *cf. Waltons Stores (Interstate) v. Maher* (1988) 62 A.L.J.R. 110.
[10] *Yaxley v. Gotts* [2000] Ch. 162; (2000) 116 L.Q.R. 11 (R. Smith); (2000) 59. C.L.J. 23 (L. Tee); [2000] Conv. 245 (M. Thompson); (2000) 63 M.L.R. 912 (I. Moore).
[11] *ante*, p. 280.
[12] *Pascoe v. Turner* [1979] 1 W.L.R. 431, *post*, p. 897; (1984) 100 L.Q.R. 376 (S. Moriarty); [1986] Conv. 406 (M. Thompson); *Re Basham* [1986] 1 W.L.R. 1498, *post*, p. 900; *Wayling v. Jones* (1995) 69 P. & C.R. 170; *Yaxley v. Gotts, supra*. For the view that this approach is correct, see (1997) 17 L.S. 258 (E. Cooke); *cf.* (1998) 18 L.S. 360 (A. Robertson).

merely reverses the detriment. The latter is all that is required to avoid unjust enrichment, whereas the former might be said to give a promise unsupported by consideration the effect of a contract. The better view is that the aim should be the reversal of detriment, as it would normally be inequitable to insist on a remedy which is disproportionate to the detriment.[13] There may, however, be special reasons for going further in some cases.[14]

Detrimental reliance need not involve the expenditure of money on the land.[15] In *Greasley v. Cooke*,[16] the claimant served notice to quit on the defendant, who had moved into the property as a servant, but had cohabited with the owner's son, K, and had stayed on after the owner's death, continuing to care for the family, which included a mentally-ill daughter. She had remained without payment since 1948, encouraged by K, now deceased, and his brother (the claimant) to believe that it was her home for life. The Court of Appeal held that she was entitled to remain as long as she wished. Lord Denning M.R. appeared to suggest that it was not necessary that the claimant should have acted to her detriment[17]:

> "it is sufficient if the party, to whom the assurance is given, acts on the faith of it—in such circumstances that it would be unjust and inequitable for the party making the assurance to go back on it. . . . There is no need for her to prove that she acted to her detriment or to her prejudice."[18]

Subsequent cases, however, have made it clear that these comments related only to the burden of proving reliance. In *Coombes v. Smith*[19] (the facts of which have already been given[20]) Lord Denning's statement was interpreted as meaning merely that where the claimant has adopted a detrimental course of conduct after the defendant's assurances, there is a rebuttable presumption that this was

---

[13] *Waltons Stores (Interstate) Ltd v. Maher* (1988) 62 A.L.J.R. 110 at 126; *Commonwealth of Australia v. Verwayen* (1990) 64 A.L.J.R. 540 at 546; *cf. Giumelli v. Giumelli* (1999) 161 A.L.R. 473; (1999) 58 C.L.J. (D. Wright). See also *Crabb v. Arun District Council* [1976] Ch. 179 at 198; *Baker v. Baker* [1993] 2 F.L.R. 247 (an unusual case where the detriment exceeded the value of the expected interest); *Sledmore v. Dalby* (1996) 72 P. & C.R. 196 (proportionality required); *Gillett v. Holt* [2000] 3 W.L.R. 815.

[14] *Pascoe v. Turner, supra* (interest less than fee simple considered insecure against future purchasers). See generally (1999) 115 L.Q.R. 438 (S. Gardner).

[15] For the application of the doctrine to property other than land, see *Western Fish Products Ltd v. Penwith District Council* [1981] 2 All E.R. 204 at 218; *Moorgate Mercantile Co. Ltd v. Twitchings* [1976] Q.B. 225 at 242; (1981) 40 C.L.J. 340 (P. Matthews).

[16] [1980] 1 W.L.R. 1306; (1981) 44 M.L.R. 461 (G. Woodman).

[17] Here in any event the claimant had foregone wages and perhaps lost job opportunities.

[18] *ibid.* at 1311–1312. This resembles the requirements of promissory estoppel (*supra*, note 7).

[19] [1986] 1 W.L.R. 808; (1986) 45 C.L.J. 394 (D. Hayton); *Wayling v. Jones* (1995) 69 P. & C.R. 170. See also *Stevens & Cutting Ltd v. Anderson* [1990] 1 E.G.L.R. 95, suggesting that the headnote in *Greasley* is wrong: the decision was on the burden of proof of reliance, not of detriment.

[20] *ante*, p. 883 (the contract claim).

done in reliance upon the assurances. Here the claim based on proprietary estoppel failed. The claimant had no mistaken belief that she had a right to remain indefinitely, and in any event there was no detrimental act. Her acts in leaving her husband, becoming pregnant and looking after the house were not done in reliance on any expectation of an interest and were not detrimental.[21] Other decisions have shown more lenience on "reliance". In *Matharu v. Matharu*[22] a married couple had improved property owned by the husband's father, who had encouraged the wife to believe that it belonged to her husband. She was granted a licence to occupy for life even though some of the improvements were done after she discovered the truth. In *Wayling v. Jones*[23] the claimant helped the deceased, with whom he cohabited, to run a café merely for pocket money, and acted as his chauffeur and companion. The deceased promised to leave him a house and business, but all he received by will was a car and furniture. The café had been sold and at his death the deceased owned a hotel. The claimant was awarded the proceeds of sale of the hotel (over £72,000), even though his evidence was that he would have stayed with the deceased if no promise had been made. It was held that the promise did not need to be the sole inducement for the claimant's conduct.

(b) *Remedies.* Early illustrations of the doctrine dealt with the protection of a lessee; as where a life tenant granted a 30 year lease, to the knowledge of remainderman who "stood by and encouraged" the tenant to take the lease and incur expenditure. Lord Hardwick confirmed the tenant in the balance of his lease after the life tenant's death.[24]

Other cases deal with activities on a party's own land which require facilities from a neighbour; allowing that party to acquire a right in the nature of an easement; as where a millowner erects a mill on the understanding, to the knowledge of a canal owner, that he could use canal water to generate steam[25]; or where the defendants constructed a sewer over a strip of the claimant's land, and the claimant failed to complain until the construction of the sewer was complete,[26] or where a landowner subdivides his land in reliance on a right of way being granted by a neighbour (the local authority)

---

[21] cf. *Grant v. Edwards* [1986] Ch. 638, *ante*, p. 275.

[22] (1994) 68 P. & C.R. 93; (1994) 24 Fam. Law. 625 (J. Dewar); [1995] Conv. 61 (M. Welstead); (1995) 58 M.L.R. 411 (P. Milne); [1995] 7 C.F.L.Q. 59 (G. Battersby).

[23] *Supra*; (1995) 111 L.Q.R. 389 (E. Cooke); [1995] Conv. 409 (C. Davis); (1996) 16 L.S. 218 (A. Lawson).

[24] *Huning v. Ferrers* (1711) Gilb.Eq. 85; *Jackson v. Cator* (1800) 5 Ves. 688 (tenant making alterations to landlord's knowledge).

[25] *Rochdale Canal Co. v. King* (1853) 16 Beav. 630.

[26] *Armstrong v. Sheppard & Short Ltd* [1959] 2 Q.B. 384.

through a specified outlet[27]; or where one party with the knowledge and consent of his neighbour, builds so as to encroach on the neighbour's land.[28] The doctrine does not, however, apply where the claimant does acts on his own land which are not done in the expectation of acquiring rights over the land of another.[29]

The most extreme cases are those where a non-owner, in reliance upon a gratuitous promise of a gift of the land, has built on or improved the land. Clearly some remedy is required. In some cases the licensee has been protected from eviction without obtaining a proprietary interest in the land.

In *Inwards v. Baker*,[30] Mr Baker's son, Jack, decided to build a bungalow upon land which he hoped to purchase, but the project proved to be too expensive. Mr Baker suggested that Jack should put the bungalow on land already owned by him; that would save some expense, and Jack could build a bigger bungalow. This was done. Jack lived there some 40 years before the proceedings began in 1963. The father died in 1951, leaving a will dated 1922, under which the land was left to others.

The Court of Appeal held that the son should not be disturbed as long as he wished to stay. This is the first case, as far as is known, in which a licence is expressly referred to as one "created by estoppel."[31] Negative protection only was considered, because "proprietary estoppel" had not yet been introduced into the licence cases.

On other occasions, the non-owner has been given a lien on the land for his expenditure[32]; or compensation for the value of the improvements[33]; or awarded the improved land on payment of a reasonable price for the site[34]; or a right to occupy until expenditure

---

[27] *Crabb v. Arun D.C.* [1976] Ch. 179.

[28] *Hopgood v. Brown* [1955] 1 W.L.R. 213; *Ives (E.R.) Investments Co. v. High* [1967] 2 Q.B. 379.

[29] *Western Fish Products Ltd v. Penwith District Council* [1981] 2 All E.R. 204 (no estoppel where claimant spent money on own land relying on planning officer's assurance that planning permission would be granted; doctrine in any event not available against statutory body exercising statutory discretion or performing statutory duty; *Rootkin v. Kent County Council* [1981] 1 W.L.R. 1186); *Lloyds Bank plc v. Carrick* [1996] 4 All E.R. 630; [1996] Conv. 295 (M. Thompson); All E.R. Rev. 1996 at 257 (P. Clarke); (1997) 56 M.L.R. 32 (M. Oldham); (1998) 61 M.L.R. 486 (N. Hopkins). *cf. Lim Teng Huan v. Ang Swee Chuan* [1992] 1 W.L.R. 113 (co-owned land).

[30] [1965] 2 Q.B. 29; *Jones v. Jones* [1977] 1 W.L.R. 438; *Matharu v. Matharu* (1994) 68 P. & C.R. 93.

[31] By Danckwerts L.J. at 38.

[32] *Unity Joint Stock Mutual Banking Association v. King* (1858) 25 Beav. 72.

[33] *Raffaele v. Raffaele* [1962] W.A.R. 29. See also *Plimmer v. Wellington Corporation* (1884) 9 App.Cas. 699.

[34] *Duke of Beaufort v. Patrick* (1853) 17 Beav. 60; *Lim Teng Huan v. Ang Swee Chuan* [1992] 1 W.L.R. 113 (house built on land co-owned by parties, but contract to build house void for uncertainty).

on improvements has been reimbursed[35]; or a non-assignable lease at a nominal rent, determinable on death.[36] A monetary award may be given where a right to occupy would be oppressive or unworkable,[37] or where the land in question has been sold.[38] In some cases, however, the minimum equity to do justice may have expired, so that it is no longer inequitable to enforce legal rights.[39] In other cases a conveyance of the freehold has been ordered.

In *Dillwyn v. Llewelyn*[40] a father encouraged his son to build a house on the father's land, and signed a memorandum purporting to convey the land to the son; but it was not by deed. The father's will left all his land upon certain trusts in favour of others. The son spent some £14,000 in building a house on the land, with his father's knowledge and approval. On the father's death, it was held that the son was entitled to a conveyance of the land.

On its face, the decision is inconsistent with two basic rules, namely that a gratuitous promise is not enforceable, and that an incomplete gift will not be completed in favour of a volunteer.[41] Detrimental reliance is not consideration under English law. Further, the solution is not just and equitable. There was no reason why the son should have a transfer of the land at the expense of the father's estate. Too much has been read into this case. It has been regarded as the origin of the doctrine of proprietary estoppel[42]; though that phrase would have meant nothing to Lord Westbury.[43]

Perhaps the most extreme of the cases on proprietary estoppel, resulting in an extraordinary windfall for the licensee, is *Pascoe v. Turner*.[44]

The claimant and defendant lived together in the claimant's home. Later the claimant purchased another house and the couple moved in. When the relationship ended he told the defendant that the house was hers and everything in it. In reliance on this gratuitous promise, she expended, to the claimant's knowledge, her own money on repairs, improvements and redecoration, and also

[35] *Dodsworth v. Dodsworth* (1973) 228 E.G. 1115.
[36] *Griffiths v. Williams* (1977) 288 E.G. 947.
[37] *Baker v. Baker* [1993] 2 F.L.R. 247.
[38] *Wayling v. Jones* (1995) 69 P. & C.R. 170.
[39] *Sledmore v. Dalby* (1996) 72 P. & C.R. 196 (rent-free occupation for past 18 years sufficient recompense for improvements); [1997] Conv. 458 (J. Adams); (1997) 113 L.Q.R. 232 (M. Pawlowski).
[40] (1862) 4 De G.F. & J. 517; *Chalmers v. Pardoe* [1963] 1 W.L.R. 677; *Raffaele v. Raffaele, supra*; (1963) 79 L.Q.R. 238 (D. Allen).
[41] See (1980) 96 L.Q.R. 534 at 539–542 (S. Naresh).
[42] See *Sen v. Headley* [1991] Ch. 425 at 439.
[43] Dawson & Pearce, p. 34.
[44] [1979] 1 W.L.R. 431; *Voyce v. Voyce* (1991) 62 P. & C.R. 290.

on furniture. Later the claimant gave the defendant two month's notice to determine the licence. Even though the defendant never sought to establish that she had spent more money on the house than she would have done had she believed that she only had a licence to live there for her lifetime, the Court of Appeal felt that protection for her lifetime was insecure, and awarded a conveyance of the house.

Finally, the court will not make an order which would be unworkable in view of family discord. In such a case a clean break may be the best solution, involving an award of compensation rather than a proprietary interest.[45] Thus the equity may be satisfied in a different way from that which the parties intended when on good terms.

(c) *Judicial Formulations.* Two early judicial formulations of the doctrine come from statements of Lord Kingsdown and Fry J. Lord Kingsdown, with the old cases of disappointed lessees in mind, explained the doctrine as follows[46]:

"If a man, under a verbal agreement with a landlord for a certain interest in land, or, what amounts to the same thing, under an expectation, created or encouraged by the landlord, that he shall have a certain interest, takes possession of such land, with the consent of the landlord, and upon the face of such promise or expectation, with the knowledge of the landlord, and without objection by him, laid out money on the land, a Court of Equity will compel the landlord to give effect to such promise or expectation."

Fry J. in *Willmott v. Barber*[47] laid down the principle in more specific detail, in what have been called the "five probanda." He said:

"In the first place the [claimant] must have made a mistake as to his legal rights.[48] Secondly, the [claimant] must have expended some money or must have done some act (not necessarily upon the defendant's land) on the faith of his mistaken belief. Thirdly, the defendant, the possessor of the legal right, must know of the existence of his own right which is inconsistent with the right claimed by the [claimant]. If he does not know of it he is in the

---

[45] *Burrows v. Sharp* (1991) 23 H.L.R. 82; [1992] Conv. 54 (J. Martin); *Baker v. Baker* [1993] 2 F.L.R. 247; (1994) 144 N.L.J. 264 (J. Martin).

[46] *Ramsden v. Dyson* (1866) L.R. 1 H.L. 129 at 170. It would be otherwise if the expectation was not created nor encouraged by the landlord; *ibid.*, at 171.

[47] (1880) 15 Ch.D. 96 at 105–106.

[48] The claim failed on this ground in *Att.-Gen. of Hong Kong v. Humphreys Estate (Queen's Gardens) Ltd* [1987] A.C. 114 (expenditure in reliance upon "subject to contract" agreement which was never finalised).

same position as the [claimant], and the doctrine of acquiescence is founded upon conduct with a knowledge of your legal rights. Fourthly, the defendant, the possessor of the legal right, must know of the [claimant's] mistaken belief to his rights. If he does not, there is nothing which calls upon him to assert his own rights. Lastly, the defendant, the possessor of the legal right, must have encouraged the [claimant] in his expenditure of money or in the other acts which he has done, either directly or by abstaining from asserting his legal right."[49]

Modern judicial formulations of the doctrine have moved away from the inflexibility of the "five probanda." In *Taylors Fashions Ltd v. Liverpool Victoria Trustees Co. Ltd*,[50] Oliver J. held that estoppel by acquiescence was not restricted to cases where the defendant knew his rights. There were many circumstances of estoppel, and it was not possible to lay down strict and inflexible rules. The application of the *Ramsden v. Dyson*[51] principle:

"requires a very much broader approach which is directed to ascertaining whether, in particular individual circumstances, it would be unconscionable for a party to be permitted to deny that which, knowingly or unknowingly, he has allowed or encouraged another to assume to his detriment rather than to inquiring whether the circumstances can be fitted within the confines of some preconceived formula serving as a universal yardstick for every form of unconscionable behaviour[52] . . . The inquiry which I have to make therefore . . . is simply whether, in all the circumstances of the case, it was unconscionable for the defendants to seek to take advantage of the mistake, which, at the material time, everybody shared. . . . "[53]

This broad approach was adopted in *Amalgamated Investment and Property Co. Ltd (in liquidation) v. Texas Commerce International Bank Ltd*,[54] where Robert Goff J. said that "Of all doctrines, equitable estoppel is surely one of the most flexible . . . it

---

[49] See *Brinnand v. Ewens* (1987) 19 H.L.R. 415 (tenant had no claim for voluntary improvements where no reliance on any interest and no encouragement or acquiescence by landlord).

[50] [1981] 2 W.L.R. 576; [1982] Q.B. 133n.; [1982] Conv. 450 (P. Jackson).

[51] *supra*.

[52] [1981] 2 W.L.R. 576 at 593. See also *Ives (E.R.) Investments Co. v. High* [1967] 2 Q.B. 379; *Shaw v. Applegate* [1977] 1 W.L.R. 970 at 977–978, 980; *Jones v. Stones* [1999] 1 W.L.R. 1739 at 1743.

[53] [1981] 2 W.L.R. 576 at 596. It was suggested that the "five probanda" might be necessary in a case of "standing by," where the defendant has done no positive act. The "five probanda" were, however, applied in *Coombes v. Smith* [1986] 1 W.L.R. 808 and *Matharu v. Matharu* (1994) 68 P. & C.R. 93.

[54] [1982] Q.B. 84; *Pacol Ltd v. Trade Lines Ltd* [1982] 1 Lloyd's Rep. 456; *Lloyds Bank plc v. Carrick* [1996] 4 All E.R. 630.

cannot be right to restrict [it] to certain defined categories."[55] Similarly, Lord Denning M.R., in the Court of Appeal, considered that:

"The doctrine of estoppel is one of the most flexible and useful in the armoury of the law. But it has become overloaded with cases. . . . It has evolved during the last 150 years in a sequence of separate developments: proprietary estoppel, estoppel by representation of fact, estoppel by acquiescence, and promissory estoppel. At the same time it has been sought to be limited by a series of maxims: estoppel is only a rule of evidence; estoppel cannot give rise to a cause of action; estoppel cannot do away with the need for consideration; and so forth. All these can now be seen to merge into one general principle shorn of limitations. When the parties to a transaction proceed on the basis of an underlying assumption—either of fact or of law—whether due to misrepresentation or mistake makes no difference—on which they have conducted the dealings between them—neither of them will be allowed to go back on that assumption when it would be unfair or unjust to allow him to do so. If one of them does seek to go back on it, the courts will give the other such remedy as the equity of the case demands."[56]

It seems that we have moved away from the basic rule that an estoppel is a shield and not a sword. If an injunction suffices as the remedy, the estoppel operates in the traditional way as a shield and not a sword. But if something more is needed, like the grant to the licensee of a proprietary interest, then we call it a case of proprietary estoppel, and make use of the additional remedies. The constructive trust has even been called upon to fill in possible gaps in the estoppel doctrine.

In *Re Basham*[57] the claimant's mother married her stepfather in 1936 when the claimant was aged 15. The claimant lived with them until her marriage in 1941, helping to run the business without pay on the understanding that she would inherit from her stepfather. He dissuaded her husband from taking a job with a tied cottage, saying he would help them to get a house. After the mother's death in 1976, the claimant and her husband helped her stepfather in his house and garden, prepared his meals, bought

---

[55] [1982] Q.B. 84 at 103.
[56] *ibid.* at 122. See also *Att.-Gen. of Hong Kong v. Humphreys Estate (Queen's Gardens) Ltd* [1987] A.C. 114; *Lim Teng Huan v. Ang Swee Chuan* [1992] 1 W.L.R. 113 (where both parties wrongly assumed they had a contract); [1993] Conv. 173 (S. Goo); *John v. George* (1996) 71 P. & C.R. 375.
[57] [1986] 1 W.L.R. 1498; *Wayling v. Jones* (1995) 69 P. & C.R. 170.

carpets for the house, and paid solicitors for advice over a boundary dispute. The stepfather constantly assured her that the house would be hers, but he died intestate. The claimant, who did not benefit under the intestacy, succeeded in her claim to the whole estate under the doctrine of proprietary estoppel. It was held that the doctrine was not confined to a case where the claimant's belief related to an existing right and to specific assets.[58] Where the belief related to a future right, a species of constructive trust arose. The doctrines of estoppel, mutual wills[59] and secret trusts[60] had a common theme, and thus reliance could be placed on cases such as *Re Cleaver*,[61] where an expectation of inheritance of non-specific assets gave rise to a constructive trust under the mutual wills doctrine. The proper remedy was an award of the entire estate, to satisfy the expectations encouraged by the deceased.

Clearly the claimant should have some remedy, however it is doubtful whether the introduction of the constructive trust is either necessary or desirable.[62] Under the modern flexible approach to proprietary estoppel,[63] the claimant may succeed without a constructive trust. If that is not so, the claimant should not succeed under estoppel but should look to other remedies.[64]

More recently a restrictive approach was taken in relation to promises to leave property by will, on the basis that it is well known that a testator is free to change his testamentary intentions. In *Taylor v. Dickens*[65] the testatrix told her gardener that she planned to leave him her house by will, whereupon he said that he would no longer accept wages for his work. In her last will the testatrix left the property elsewhere but did not tell the gardener of her change of mind. His claim under the proprietary estoppel doctrine (and also in contract) failed on the ground that an unconscionable broken promise was insufficient. It was held that in the case of a promised legacy, it must be shown that the promisor created or encouraged a belief that he would not exercise his right to change his mind and that the

---

[58] *cf. Layton v. Martin* (1986) 16 Fam. Law. 212, where the deceased's assurances that he would provide for the claimant by will could not found a claim to proprietary estoppel, which arose only in connection with specific assets. See [1996] Conv. 193 (C. Davis).

[59] *ante*, p. 319.

[60] *ante*, Chap. 5.

[61] [1981] 1 W.L.R. 939, *ante*, p. 320. If the analogy with the surviving testator in *Re Cleaver* is taken too far, a finding that the estopped party holds his estate on constructive trust seems to restrict the choice of discretionary remedies open to the court.

[62] See [1987] Conv. 211 (J. Martin); (1987) 46 C.L.J. 215 (D. Hayton); All E.R.Rev. 1987 at 156 (P. Clarke) and 263 (C. Sherrin); (1988) 8 L.S. 92 at 101 *et seq.* (M. Davey). See, however, *Sen v. Headley* [1991] Ch. 425 at 440.

[63] *supra*.

[64] For example, under the Inheritance (Provision for Family and Dependants) Act 1975.

[65] [1998] 1 F.L.R. 806, distinguishing *Re Basham*, *supra*, and *Wayling v. Jones* (1995) 69 P. & C.R. 170, *ante*, p. 895. An appeal in *Taylor* was settled.

promisee relied on that belief. This was rightly criticised as too rigid a view of proprietary estoppel.[66] The criticisms were held to be well founded by the Court of Appeal in *Gillett v. Holt,*[67] where the defendant over many years had indicated that he would leave his farm to the claimant, who had worked there since the age of 16 in 1956, depriving himself of the opportunity of trying to better himself in other ways. In 1995 the friendship broke down and the defendant made a new will in favour of another. The proprietary estoppel claim against the defendant (who was still living) was upheld. In a case where assurances had been given over many years, the court should look at the matter in the round. If the assurances were intended to be relied on and had been relied on, it was not necessary to look for an *irrevocable* promise, as it was the other party's detrimental reliance which made it irrevocable. The inherent revocability of testamentary dispositions was irrelevant to an assurance that "all this will be yours". The question of detriment should be approached as part of a broad inquiry as to whether repudiation of an assurance was unconscionable. A quantifiable financial detriment was not required, so long as the detriment was substantial. In this case the equity was satisfied by a transfer to the claimant of one of the three farms and £100,000 to compensate him for exclusion from the rest of the farming business.

B. Conveyancing Problems Caused by Licences by Estoppel[68]

The question to be considered in this section is whether a licence by estoppel has the status of a proprietary interest prior to the litigation, and, if so, how it may be protected against successors in title of the estopped party. If it is incapable of binding successors, then the licensee (unless the licence is contractual[69]) has no remedy.

i. Status Prior to Court Order. Clearly a recognised proprietary interest may be conferred by the court, such as the conveyance of the fee simple or the grant of a life interest. More difficult is the

---

[66] (1998) 28 Fam.Law 192 (G. Douglas); [1998] Conv. 210 (M. Thompson); (1998) 114 L.Q.R. 351 (M. Pawlowski).

[67] [2000] 3 W.L.R. 815; (2000) 59 C.L.J. 453 (M. Dixon); [2001] Conv. 13 (R. Wells) and 78 (M. Thompson). For the position in New Zealand, see (2000) 20 L.S. 85 (S. Nield).

[68] See generally (1984) 100 L.Q.R. 376 (S. Moriarty); [1981] Conv. 212 (A. Briggs) and 347 (P. Todd); [1983] Conv. 50 (M. Thompson) and 285 (A. Briggs); (1988) 51 M.L.R. 226 (J. Hill).

[69] In which case he may sue the licensor. He cannot sue a third party unless a constructive trust has arisen; *Ashburn Anstalt v. Arnold* [1989] Ch. 1; *ante,* p. 888.

question whether the estoppel licensee has an interest capable of binding a third party prior to the order of the court. What would have happened, for example, if the legal owner in *Pascoe v. Turner*[70] had conveyed the house to a purchaser before the matter came to court? One view is that the estoppel interest is too uncertain and unstable to qualify as a proprietary interest, even a "mere equity", before the court's decision.[71] Another view is that the interest is a "mere equity" capable of binding third parties, at any rate volunteers and purchasers with actual notice.[72] Another is that it can bind third parties under the ordinary rules of priorities, even though the interest is inchoate and does not "crystallise" until the court order.[73]

There is growing support for the view that the question of whether a third party is bound depends on whether his conscience is affected.[74] The Law Commission has stated that "there are good reasons for regarding the inchoate equity as a property right", and that an estoppel interest should be treated as an interest in land from the time it arises. In most cases this will be when the other party has acted to his detriment. At the latest, it will be when the circumstances make it unconscionable for the owner to go back on the expectation.[75] The consquence of this view is that the interest can be a minor or overriding interest in registered land, capable of binding a third party.[76] Indeed, the view of the Court of Appeal that a "family" estoppel interest may be overreached by a disposition by two trustees supports its proprietary status, as a purchaser or chargee paying capital money to a sole trustee would presumably have been bound by the interest.[77]

Estoppel interests have been held binding on volunteers[78] and (prior to the establishment of the application of overreaching) on

---

[70] [1979] 1 W.L.R. 431; *ante*, p. 897.

[71] (1990) 106 L.Q.R. 87 at 97 and [1990] Conv. 370 at 380–384 (D. Hayton); [1991] Conv. 155 (P. Evans); (1992) 22 Fam. Law. 72 (P. Clarke); (1993) 109 L.Q.R. 114 (P. Ferguson); (1996) 16 L.S. 325 at 342 (N. Glover and P. Todd).

[72] Warburton, *Sharing Residential Property*, pp. 156–157; (1991) 5 *Trust Law International* 9 (J. Warburton).

[73] [1991] Conv. 36 and (1995) 58 M.L.R. 637 at 640–643 (G. Battersby); (1993) 3 Carib.L.R. 96 at 109 (R. Smith); (1994) 14 L.S. 147 (S. Baughen); [1996] Conv. 34 (J. Howell) and 193 (C. Davis).

[74] *United Bank of Kuwait plc v. Sahib* [1997] Ch. 107; [1998] Conv. 502 (P. Critchley). This test does not apply to a personal representative, who steps into the shoes of the estopped party and is not an independent third party.

[75] Law Com. (Consultative Document) No. 254 (1998), *Land Registration for the Twenty-first Century* paras. 3.35, 3.36.

[76] *post*, p. 904.

[77] *Birmingham Midshires Mortgage Services Ltd v. Sabherwal* (2000) 80 P. & C.R. 256; (2000) 116 L.Q.R. 341 (C. Harpum).

[78] *Dillwyn v. Llewelyn* (1862) 4 De G.F. & J. 517 and *Inwards v. Baker* [1965] 2 Q.B. 29 (trustees of will); *Voyce v. Voyce* (1991) 62 P. & C.R. 290, *infra*.

purchasers with actual notice.[79] In *Voyce v. Voyce*[80] the Court of Appeal held that the estoppel was binding on a donee taking with notice from the estopped party, and ordered the donee to convey the fee simple to the claimant. Dillon L.J. held that the claimant was the equitable owner before the conveyance (in the context of a dispute between the parties concerning a right to light), because his equitable right (an "equity") had accrued long before the conveyance.[81] Similarly Nourse L.J. in *Sen v. Headley*[82] said that in estoppel cases where the promisee had a right to a conveyance, an implied or constructive trust arose once all the requirements of the estoppel doctrine were satisfied. All this suggests that a proprietary interest capable of binding a third party does arise before the court order, although presumably this cannot be so where the expectation did not relate to specific property.[83]

ii. Registered and Unregistered Land. Assuming that estoppel interests are capable of binding successors in title, the difficulty is that they do not readily fit into the conveyancing system. As mentioned above, the Court of Appeal has stated that estoppel interests of a "family" nature are overreachable by a disposition by two trustees.[84] In cases where capital money is paid to a sole trustee, so that overreaching cannot occur, the interest will depend on the doctrine of notice in unregistered land. In the case of registered land, again assuming a transaction by a sole trustee, an estoppel interest coupled with occupation will constitute an overriding interest under section 70(1)(g) of the Land Registration Act 1925.[85] Estoppel interests of a commercial nature are not overreachable.[86] In unregistered land such interests are not registrable under the Land Charges Act 1972[87] and, therefore, depend on the doctrine of notice. In registered land they would be overriding interests if coupled with occupation, and could be protected by registration of a caution.

Thus conveyancing complications may arise if an estoppel interest is capable of binding a successor prior to the order of the court

---

[79] *Ives (E.R.) Investments Ltd v. High* [1967] 2 Q.B. 379; *Duke of Beaufort v. Patrick* (1853) 17 Beav. 60. A purchaser was bound in *J.T. Developments Ltd v. Quinn* (1991) 62 P. & C.R. 33, but the point was not argued. See also *Hopgood v. Brown* [1955] 1 W.L.R. 213 (estoppel by representation); *Lloyds Bank plc v. Carrick* [1996] 4 All E.R. 630 at 642.

[80] (1991) 62 P. & C.R. 290; [1992] Conv. 56 (J. Martin). See also *Sledmore v. Dalby* (1996) 72 P. & C.R. 196 at 201; (1997) 56 C.L.J. 34 (P. Milne).

[81] (1991) 62 P. & C.R. 290 at 294.

[82] [1991] Ch. 425 at 440; *Re Basham* [1986] 1 W.L.R. 1498.

[83] *Re Basham, supra; ante,* p. 897.

[84] *Birmingham Midshires Mortgage Services Ltd v. Sabherwal* (2000) 80 P. & C.R. 256.

[85] *ibid.* See also Law Com. (Consultative Document) No. 254 (1998), *Land Registration for the Twenty-first Century,* paras 3.35, 3.36.

[86] *ibid.*

[87] s.2 (easement, right or privilege, being merely equitable) has been narrowly construed; *Shiloh Spinners Ltd v. Harding* [1973] A.C. 691.

which crystallises the interest. However, the difficulties seem no greater than those which arise in respect of other informally created interests, such as shares in the family home under constructive trusts.[88]

iii. Other Problems Arising Under the Doctrine of Proprietary Estoppel.

(a) *Necessity for Litigation.* The problems here are the same as those met in the context of licences giving rise to a constructive trust. No one knows, without the court's decision, whether or not the licensee is entitled to have an interest in the land transferred to him, nor what the interest will be. If the court orders the transfer of any interest, the documentation will be completed. Until then, a third party's position is as discussed above.

(b) *Effect of Life Interest.* Where the expectation of the licensee was to occupy the licensor's property for life, as is not uncommon in the family context, the award of a life interest to the licensee caused problems until recently. The difficulty was that such a life interest brought the complex provisions of the Settled Land Act 1925 into play, under which the life tenant acquired the legal estate and extensive powers of sale and leasing. Thus in *Ungurian v. Lesnoff*[89] a life interest under the Settled Land Act arose (either on the basis of estoppel or a common intention constructive trust[90]) in favour of the defendant, who had given up her flat, nationality and career to live with the claimant. He bought a house for them to live in, which the defendant improved, but they separated after four years. An irrevocable licence was considered inadequate, but an outright conveyance would have gone beyond what the parties intended.

Most modern cases, however, have avoided a solution involving the Settled Land Act. In *Dodsworth v. Dodsworth*[91] the defendants had spent over £700 on improvements in the belief that they would have a right to occupy for life. They were held entitled to occupy until the expenditure had been reimbursed. Similarly in *Griffiths v. Williams*,[92] where a daughter looked after her mother and spent money on repairs and improvements to the house in the belief that she had a home there for life, but the house was left to another

---

[88] *ante*, Chap. 11. The tendency to assimilate the doctrines of estoppel and constructive trusts has been mentioned, *ante*, p. 893.

[89] [1990] Ch. 206. The 1925 Act was also applied in *Costello v. Costello* (1995) 70 P. & C.R. 297, where a deed provided that parents could occupy rent free for life.

[90] *ante*, p. 275.

[91] (1973) 228 E.G. 1115.

[92] (1977) 248 E.G. 947.

relative. In order to avoid the complications of the Settled Land Act, she was awarded a non-assignable lease at a nominal rent, determinable on death.

Since the Trusts of Land and Appointment of Trustees Act 1996 came into operation it is no longer possible to create a settlement under the 1925 Act. The problem discussed above has diminished because the award of a life interest will now bring into play the less complex "trust of land", which was explained in Chapter 11.

INDEX